1993 BASEBALL ALMANAC

Contributing Writers:
Dan Schlossberg
Mike Tully
Michael Bradley
Pete Palmer
Tom Owens

Publications International, Ltd.

Dan Schlossberg is a baseball editor for the *Americana Encyclopedia Annual* and a freelance contributor to *Petersen's Pro Baseball Yearbook, Street & Smith's Baseball Yearbook,* and many other baseball periodicals. A former Associated Press sports editor, he is the author of 12 books, including *The Baseball Catalog* and *The Baseball Book of Why.*

Mike Tully is a former national baseball writer for United Press International. He has written six books, including *Leagues and Barons* and *1990-91 Baseball's Hottest Rookies.* His freelance work has appeared in *The National* sports daily, *Sports Illustrated,* and *The New York Times.*

Michael Bradley is a freelance writer whose work has appeared in *The Sporting News,* the *Philadelphia Inquirer,* and a variety of national sports publications. He is the coauthor of *1992-1993 Basketball Almanac.*

Pete Palmer edited both *Total Baseball* and *The Hidden Game of Baseball* with John Thorn. He was the statistician for *1992 Baseball Almanac* and *1992-1993 Basketball Almanac.* Palmer, a renowned sports statistician, is a member of the Society for American Baseball Research (SABR).

Tom Owens is the author of *Greatest Baseball Players of All Time, Collecting Sports Autographs,* and the *1992 Illustrated Baseball Card Price Guide.* He is a former editor of *Sports Collectors Digest.*

Special thanks to Jay Virshbo and Howe SportsData for minor league statistics.

CONTENTS

CONTENTS

CONTENTS

CONTENTS

CONTENTS

Current Players and Rookie Prospects

In this section you'll find profiles of 800 professional players—first 600 current players and then 200 rookie prospects. The current players and rookie prospects are in alphabetical order.

Full major league statistics are included with the current players. If a player played with two teams in both the American League and the National League in one season, both lines are presented in the "Major League Register." If the player played with two teams in one league during a season, the statistics were combined to give you accurate information of how each player performed against one league in one season. At the bottom of most of the Major League Registers you'll find a "3 AVE" line. Players who qualified had their last three seasons' statistics averaged for each of the 10 categories. For batters to qualify for this line, they had to accumulate 150 at bats in each season. For pitchers who had most of their last season's innings in a starting role to qualify, they had to pitch at least 60 innings each season. For pitchers who had most of their last season's innings in a relief role to qualify, they had to pitch at least 30 innings each season. If the player did not qualify for all three seasons but for only two years out of the last three, you'll find a "2 AVE" line. These lines give you a simple, straightforward way to help you better predict how these players will do next summer.

The rookie prospects each have a "Professional Register," listing minor league and major league stats. Included are statistics from each year that the player has been in organized baseball, from the Rookie leagues (**R**), Class-A (**A**), Double-A (**AA**), and Triple-A (**AAA**). If the player has played in the major leagues, each league's performance is also shown (**AL** and **NL**). If during one season a player played with more than one team on one minor league level, or if a player played with more than one AL or NL team, the statistics were combined to give you accurate information of how that player did against one level or against one major league.

The abbreviations for batters are: **BA** = batting average; **G** = games played; **AB** = at bats; **R** = runs scored; **H** = hits; **2B** = doubles; **3B** = triples; **HR** = home runs; **RBI** = runs batted in; **SB** = stolen bases. The abbreviations for pitchers are: **W** = wins; **L** = losses; **ERA** = earned run average; **G** = games; **CG** = complete games; **S** = saves; **IP** = innings pitched; **H** = hits; **ER** = earned runs; **BB** = bases on balls; **SO** = strikeouts.

The "Player Summary" box that accompanies each profile is an at-a-glance look at each player. The "Fantasy Value" line suggests a draft price for fantasy baseball players. The price range is based on a standard $260 budget for a 23-player roster. The "Card Value" line is a general estimate in determining the worth of a Mint 1993 regular-issue (base set) baseball card of that player. This estimate is based mostly on the future value gain of that player's card. Any error, variation, or specialty cards are not taken into account.

JIM ABBOTT

Position: Pitcher
Team: New York Yankees
Born: Sept. 19, 1967 Flint, MI
Height: 6'3" **Weight:** 200 lbs.
Bats: left **Throws:** left
Acquired: Traded from Angels for J.T. Snow, Russ Springer, and Jerry Nielsen, 12/92

Player Summary	
Fantasy Value	$8 to $12
Card Value	10¢ to 15¢
Will	paint the plate
Can't	always get the curve over
Expect	at least 10 wins
Don't Expect	K an inning

After posting an 18-11 record in 1991, when he finished third in the American League's Cy Young Award voting, Abbott lifted his three-year, won-lost record above .500. A lack of hitting support in 1992 left him shy of the break-even point again, even though his ERA was below 3.00. If he allowed three runs in nine innings, he probably lost. Typical of his season was a July 1 game against Minnesota: He pitched his fifth complete game, but also lost his fourth complete game, going down 2-1. He yields about three earned runs per game and generally has good control. Idled with a strained lower right rib cage in midseason, he is working on being more precise with the curve and has been developing a forkball and changeup. Even with all his pitches working, the former University of Michigan standout is the only southpaw in the majors who has a tougher time with lefty hitters than righthanded batters.

Major League Pitching Register

	W	L	ERA	G	CG	IP	H	ER	BB	SO
89 AL	12	12	3.92	29	4	181.1	190	79	74	115
90 AL	10	14	4.51	33	4	211.2	246	106	72	105
91 AL	18	11	2.89	34	5	243.0	222	78	73	158
92 AL	7	15	2.77	29	7	211.0	208	65	68	130
Life	47	52	3.49	125	20	847.0	866	328	287	508
3 AVE	12	13	3.37	32	5	222.1	225	83	71	131

KYLE ABBOTT

Position: Pitcher
Team: Philadelphia Phillies
Born: Feb. 18, 1968 Newbury Port, MA
Height: 6'4" **Weight:** 195 lbs.
Bats: left **Throws:** left
Acquired: Traded from Angels with Ruben Amaro for Von Hayes, 12/91

Player Summary	
Fantasy Value	$2 to $4
Card Value	3¢ to 4¢
Will	intimidate with fastballs
Can't	complete many games
Expect	lower ERA in '93
Don't Expect	consistent losing record

After posting the best record on the Philadelphia pitching staff during 1992 spring training exhibition play, Abbott was hailed as the answer to the club's pitching problems. Instead, the rookie lost 11 straight before beating the Dodgers, 14-3, on July 18. During his losing streak, which fell one short of the club record for futility, Abbott's ERA had approached 6.00, and he had yielded nine homers. He also allowed more than a hit per inning without completing a game. He even made a brief trip back to the minors. Although he has a good fastball, Abbott's strikeout-to-walk ratio was less than 2-to-1. Abbott could have sued his club for nonsupport, however: The Phillies averaged less than three runs a game when he was on the mound during the first three months. With Triple-A Edmonton in 1991, he was among the Angel organization's leaders in wins, strikeouts, and ERA. That year, he was 14-10 with a 3.99 ERA and 120 strikeouts in 180 innings pitched. With more experience and run support, he should become a capable big league starter.

Major League Pitching Register

	W	L	ERA	G	CG	IP	H	ER	BB	SO
91 AL	1	2	4.58	5	0	19.2	22	10	13	12
92 NL	1	14	5.13	31	0	133.1	147	76	45	88
Life	2	16	5.06	36	0	153.0	169	86	58	100

SHAWN ABNER

Position: Outfield
Team: Chicago White Sox
Born: June 17, 1966 Hamilton, OH
Height: 6'1" **Weight:** 194 lbs.
Bats: right **Throws:** right
Acquired: Signed as a free agent, 4/92

Player Summary	
Fantasy Value	$1 to $3
Card Value	3¢ to 4¢
Will	show range in outfield
Can't	always hit for average
Expect	platoon role
Don't Expect	more than 70 games

Highly touted as a prospect ever since the Mets made him the No. 1 pick in the nation in 1984, Abner made very few major league appearances until 1989. He showed some pop in the minors, leading the Carolina League with a .301 batting average, 89 RBI, 30 doubles, and 163 hits in 1985. He showed enough promise to be considered Kevin McReynolds's replacement by the San Diego front office in 1986. While Abner's glove, range, and arm have been better than average, his bat was disappointing over his first five years. Abner hit only .210 in 632 plate appearances. The White Sox took a chance on him, however, and he did well. He was better the first half of 1992, hitting .333 in his first 75 at bats, while helping to fill in for injured White Sox right fielder Dan Pasqua. Abner platooned with Pasqua in right when Pasqua returned. Although hitting coach Walt Hriniak helped Abner in 1992, he will not play regularly until he proves he can hit big league pitching consistently.

Major League Batting Register

	BA	G	AB	R	H	2B	3B	HR	RBI	SB
87 NL	.277	16	47	5	13	3	1	2	7	1
88 NL	.181	37	83	6	15	3	0	2	5	0
89 NL	.176	57	102	13	18	4	0	2	14	1
90 NL	.245	91	184	17	45	9	0	1	15	2
91 NL	.165	53	115	15	19	4	1	1	5	0
91 AL	.228	41	101	12	23	6	1	2	9	1
92 AL	.279	97	208	21	58	10	1	1	16	1
Life	.227	392	840	89	191	39	4	11	71	6
3 AVE	.238	94	203	22	48	10	1	2	15	1

RICK AGUILERA

Position: Pitcher
Team: Minnesota Twins
Born: Dec. 31, 1961 San Gabriel, CA
Height: 6'5" **Weight:** 205 lbs.
Bats: right **Throws:** right
Acquired: Traded from Mets with Kevin Tapani, Tim Drummond, Jack Savage, and David West for Frank Viola, 7/89

Player Summary	
Fantasy Value	$27 to $32
Card Value	4¢ to 7¢
Will	challenge 40-save barrier
Can't	hold runners on
Expect	All-Star performance
Don't Expect	long outings

A control pitcher whose strikeout-to-walk ratio is superb, Aguilera is one of baseball's premier closers. He throws a sinking fastball, slider, and forkball, but sometimes surprises hitters with a curve. Few relief pitchers have such large repertoires. Aguilera sometimes experiences problems holding runners on base—a potentially fatal flaw for a reliever. The bearded righthander has also had periodic elbow problems. He had started his career in dual roles of reliever and spot starter. After arriving in Minnesota, Aguilera became the Twins' closer in 1989. Two years later, he earned an All-Star berth—an honor he won again in 1992. Aguilera got off to a strong start for the '92 Twins, posting his 28th save (and 21st in 22 chances) by July 19. Drafted as a third baseman, Aguilera is an excellent fielder who can throw with lightning accuracy to any base.

Major League Pitching Register

	W	L	ERA	G	S	IP	H	ER	BB	SO
85 NL	10	7	3.24	21	0	122.1	118	44	37	74
86 NL	10	7	3.88	28	0	141.2	145	61	36	104
87 NL	11	3	3.60	18	0	115.0	124	46	33	77
88 NL	0	4	6.93	11	0	24.2	29	19	10	16
89 NL	6	6	2.34	36	7	69.1	59	18	21	80
89 AL	3	5	3.21	11	0	75.2	71	27	17	57
90 AL	5	3	2.76	56	32	65.1	55	20	19	61
91 AL	4	5	2.35	63	42	69.0	44	18	30	61
92 AL	2	6	2.83	64	41	66.2	60	21	17	52
Life	51	46	3.29	308	122	749.2	705	274	220	582
3 AVE	4	5	2.64	61	38	67.1	53	20	22	58

SCOTT ALDRED

Position: Pitcher
Team: Colorado Rockies
Born: June 12, 1968 Flint, MI
Height: 6'4" **Weight:** 215 lbs.
Bats: left **Throws:** left
Acquired: First-round pick from Tigers in 11/92 expansion draft

Player Summary	
Fantasy Value	$2 to $4
Card Value	5¢ to 10¢
Will	eventually earn starting spot
Can't	avoid walks
Expect	run-of-field ERA
Don't Expect	double-digit Ks

Aldred becomes the early favorite to be Colorado's No. 1 lefthander. He was 2-4 in 1991, but didn't make the cut in the first half of 1992, as the Tigers thought it best to return him to Triple-A Toledo to hone his skills. His physical size and repertoire of pitches should eventually earn him a place on the roster. He needs to improve his anemic strikeouts-to-innings ratio. His ERA has been adequate in his first few years as a pro, and his strikeout-to-walk ratio good, but the Rockies are hoping for improvement in both categories. His best year in pro ball was in 1989, when he was 10-6 for Double-A London of the Eastern League. Don't be surprised if he matches or betters that mark for the Rockies once he settles down and becomes part of the starting rotation. In 1991, Aldred was 8-8 for Triple-A Toledo, with a 3.92 ERA, 95 strikeouts, and 72 walks in 135 innings. He was 6-15 in 1990 for Toledo, with a 4.90 ERA.

LUIS ALICEA

Position: Second base
Team: St. Louis Cardinals
Born: July 29, 1965 Santurce, Puerto Rico
Height: 5'10" **Weight:** 150 lbs.
Bats: both **Throws:** right
Acquired: First-round pick in 6/86 free-agent draft

Player Summary	
Fantasy Value	$1 to $4
Card Value	3¢ to 4¢
Will	play good defense
Can't	hit for power
Expect	continued improvement at bat
Don't Expect	full-time role unless he hits

Before 1992, Alicea was regarded as a good-field, no-hit performer destined to be no more than a utility player in the major leagues. The switch-hitter made his major league debut in 1988, when he hit .212 in 93 games for St. Louis, but had a .970 fielding average. The second baseman on *The Sporting News* All-American team in 1986, Alicea hit .270 in 101 games for Double-A Arkansas of the Texas League that summer, but his average dropped with every move up in the ranks. He failed two big league chances before seeing more action after Jose Oquendo got hurt early in the '92 campaign. Alicea hit well enough to keep the job but was sidelined in midseason by a pulled rib-cage muscle. He singled and tripled in his first game back, in late July. By the end of the 1992 season, he compiled a .320 on-base average and a .385 slugging percentage; he used his bat and his slick glove to prove that he was a legitimate contender to be St. Louis' full-time second baseman in 1993.

Major League Pitching Register

	W	L	ERA	G	CG	IP	H	ER	BB	SO
90 AL	1	2	3.77	4	0	14.1	13	6	10	7
91 AL	2	4	5.18	11	1	57.1	58	33	30	35
92 AL	3	8	6.78	16	0	65.0	80	49	33	34
Life	6	14	5.80	31	1	136.2	151	88	73	76

Major League Batting Register

	BA	G	AB	R	H	2B	3B	HR	RBI	SB
88 NL	.212	93	297	20	63	10	4	1	24	1
91 NL	.191	56	68	5	13	3	0	0	0	0
92 NL	.245	85	265	26	65	9	11	2	32	2
Life	.224	234	630	51	141	22	15	3	56	3

ROBERTO ALOMAR

Position: Second base
Team: Toronto Blue Jays
Born: Feb. 5, 1968 Ponce, Puerto Rico
Height: 6' **Weight:** 175 lbs.
Bats: both **Throws:** right
Acquired: Traded from Padres with Joe Carter for Fred McGriff and Tony Fernandez, 12/90

Player Summary	
Fantasy Value	.................................$32 to $40
Card Value	.....................................10¢ to 18¢
Will	.................................challenge for MVP
Can't	.... clear SkyDome fences often
Expect	.... bid for batting title
Don't Expect	.... another trade

At the tender age of 25, Alomar is regarded as one of the game's premier performers. The younger brother of Cleveland catcher Sandy, Roberto is a smooth-fielding, wide-ranging second baseman who has also made a niche for himself at the plate. The No. 2 hitter in a potent Toronto lineup last summer, Alomar had fine on-base and slugging percentages and won universal respect for his base-running. Called the most complete player in the majors by Detroit manager Sparky Anderson, Alomar is a Gold Glove second baseman capable of stealing more than 50 bases a year. In 1991, he even stole third 21 times in 22 attempts. He hits well from both sides, and he made such a dramatic improvement against righties last year that he challenged for the league batting crown. He had more hits after his first four seasons than Joe Morgan or Rod Carew at the same stage. And why not? Tony Gwynn once helped Alomar perfect his swing.

Major League Batting Register

	BA	G	AB	R	H	2B	3B	HR	RBI	SB
88 NL	.266	143	545	84	145	24	6	9	41	24
89 NL	.295	158	623	82	184	27	1	7	56	42
90 NL	.287	147	586	80	168	27	5	6	60	24
91 AL	.295	161	637	88	188	41	11	9	69	53
92 AL	.310	152	571	105	177	27	8	8	76	49
Life	.291	761	2962	439	862	146	31	39	302	192
3 AVE	.297	153	598	91	178	32	8	8	68	42

SANDY ALOMAR

Position: Catcher
Team: Cleveland Indians
Born: June 18, 1966 Salinas, Puerto Rico
Height: 6'5" **Weight:** 200 lbs.
Bats: right **Throws:** right
Acquired: Traded from Padres with Chris James and Carlos Baerga for Joe Carter, 12/89

Player Summary	
Fantasy Value	...............................$10 to $16
Card Value	....6¢ to 10¢
Will	.... throw out runners
Can't	.... hit homers
Expect	.... fine defense
Don't Expect	.... Roberto's offense

Unlike younger brother Roberto, Sandy Alomar has yet to realize his potential. Defensively, he guns down runners with a rocket arm, blocks errant pitches, and works well with his pitchers. At the plate, however, he remains an enigma after three big league seasons. The 1990 AL Rookie of the Year with a .290 average and 66 runs batted in, he missed 111 games in 1991 with a shoulder injury, knee problem, and severe cut on his hand. Because rotator cuff surgery on the shoulder could have been career-threatening, Alomar opted for rest. The regimen worked: He erased 23 of his first 52 potential basestealers (44 percent) in 1992. At the plate, however, he got off to a sluggish start—even though he hit the first grand slam of his career. Alomar has trouble with outside fastballs thrown by righthanders. The starting catcher for the AL All-Stars in each of the last three seasons, he is a former two-time winner of the Minor League Player of the Year Award.

Major League Batting Register

	BA	G	AB	R	H	2B	3B	HR	RBI	SB
88 NL	.000	1	1	0	0	0	0	0	0	0
89 NL	.211	7	19	1	4	1	0	1	6	0
90 AL	.290	132	445	60	129	26	2	9	66	4
91 AL	.217	51	184	10	40	9	0	0	7	0
92 AL	.251	89	299	22	75	16	0	2	26	3
Life	.262	280	948	93	248	52	2	12	105	7
3 AVE	.263	91	309	31	81	17	1	4	33	2

13

MOISES ALOU

Position: Outfield
Team: Montreal Expos
Born: July 3, 1966 Atlanta, GA
Height: 6'3" **Weight:** 180 lbs.
Bats: right **Throws:** right
Acquired: Traded from Pirates with Scott Ruskin and Willie Greene for Zane Smith, 8/90

Player Summary	
Fantasy Value	$6 to $10
Card Value	10¢ to 15¢
Will	hit for average
Can't	worry about shoulder woes
Expect	strong defense
Don't Expect	switch to first base

If you're not going to carry your weight in the major leagues, you aren't going to be around for long, even if your father is the manager. If 1992 is any indication, Moises Alou will have nothing to worry about, dad or no dad. The son of former big league outfielder Felipe Alou (who became manager of the Montreal Expos in 1992), Moises filled in for the injured Ivan Calderon with a solid bat and strong left field defense. By mid-June, the rookie was hitting .385 with runners in scoring position, .333 against righthanded pitching, and .341 against lefties. He finished the year with a .328 on-base average and a .455 slugging average. Alou got a late start in his baseball career, never having organized ball until college. His progress in the majors was also delayed: He suffered a shoulder injury that kept him out of action for the entire 1991 season, and a hamstring problem that kept him out of action for two weeks in July in '92. He batted .264 in Triple-A in 1990 and .295 that year in Double-A.

Major League Batting Register

	BA	G	AB	R	H	2B	3B	HR	RBI	SB
90 NL	.200	16	20	4	4	0	1	0	0	0
92 NL	.282	115	341	53	96	28	2	9	56	16
Life	.277	131	361	57	100	28	3	9	56	16

WILSON ALVAREZ

Position: Pitcher
Team: Chicago White Sox
Born: March 24, 1970 Maracaibo, Venezuela
Height: 6'1" **Weight:** 175 lbs.
Bats: left **Throws:** left
Acquired: Traded from Rangers with Scott Fletcher and Sammy Sosa for Harold Baines and Fred Manrique, 7/89

Player Summary	
Fantasy Value	$3 to $5
Card Value	7¢ to 10¢
Will	have control problems
Can't	keep ERA below 4.00
Expect	occasional starts
Don't Expect	a return to minors

Alvarez broke into the White Sox starting rotation in the early part of the 1992 season. The southpaw had control problems, however, which pushed him back to the bullpen. He stayed there until June 22, when the Sox switched him back to starting following the exile of Alex Fernandez to Triple-A. While working in relief, Alvarez yielded a hit per inning and posted a shaky strikeout-to-walk ratio; in fact, he issued more passes than he had strikeouts. Of the first 14 runners he inherited, however, only two scored. The Texas Rangers now realize they gave up on Alvarez too early: In his second big league start (his first start for the White Sox), on Aug. 11, 1991, he threw a 7-0 no-hitter against the Baltimore Orioles. In 1992, he allowed a .272 batting average, a .381 on-base percentage, and a .401 slugging average. Lefty batters hit .220 against Alvarez, while righties batted .288. In 1991, he was 10-6 with a 1.83 ERA in Double-A. Just 23, the hard-throwing Alvarez figures to return to the regular rotation if he learns to harness his control.

Major League Pitching Register

	W	L	ERA	G	S	IP	H	ER	BB	SO
89 AL	0	1	0.00	1	0	0.0	3	3	2	0
91 AL	3	2	3.51	10	0	56.1	47	22	29	32
92 AL	5	3	5.20	34	1	100.1	103	58	65	66
Life	8	6	4.77	45	1	156.2	153	83	96	98

RUBEN AMARO

Position: Infield; outfield
Team: Philadelphia Phillies
Born: Feb. 12, 1965 Philadelphia, PA
Height: 5'10" **Weight:** 170 lbs.
Bats: both **Throws:** right
Acquired: Traded from Angels with Kyle Abbott for Von Hayes, 12/91

Player Summary	
Fantasy Value	$3 to $6
Card Value	5¢ to 7¢
Will	steal bases
Can't	hit for power
Expect	a few trips to the minors
Don't Expect	a full-time role

Unlike many young prospects, Ruben Amaro Jr. put his baseball career behind his education. He earned a B.S. in human biology from Stanford in 1987. In pro ball, he showed he was a decent hitter, particularly in 1991 when he led the Triple-A Pacific Coast League with 95 runs and 42 doubles while collecting a .326 batting average and 154 hits. In 1990 at Double-A Midland, Amaro batted .357 with 50 runs and four homers in 224 at bats before he was promoted to Triple-A Edmonton. Like Kyle Abbott, who joined Amaro on the Phillies as a result of the Von Hayes trade, Ruben was sent back to the minors in mid-1992. Although he got off to a hot start, his figures at the time of his exile included a .199 average, five homers, and 22 RBI. At the end of the season, he compiled a .303 on-base average and a .348 slugging percentage. The son of former major leaguer Ruben Amaro Sr., Junior has a good glove and respectable range in the infield, but is best defensively in the outfield.

Major League Batting Register

	BA	G	AB	R	H	2B	3B	HR	RBI	SB
91 AL	.217	10	23	0	5	1	0	0	2	0
92 NL	.219	126	374	43	82	15	6	7	34	11
Life	.219	136	397	43	87	16	6	7	36	11

LARRY ANDERSEN

Position: Pitcher
Team: Philadelphia Phillies
Born: May 6, 1953 Portland, OR
Height: 6'3" **Weight:** 205 lbs.
Bats: right **Throws:** right
Acquired: Signed as a free agent, 12/92

Player Summary	
Fantasy Value	$1 to $3
Card Value	3¢ to 4¢
Will	fool batters with a slider
Can't	go many innings
Expect	part-time closing role
Don't Expect	double-digit saves

Throughout his 22 years of professional baseball, Andersen has disheartened opposing batters with his wicked slider while keeping teammates entertained with his clubhouse and dugout antics. This control pitcher had been one of the game's best set-up men before the Padres decided to use him as an occasional closer—a move that may prolong his career. Extremely tough on righthanded hitters, he doesn't throw wild pitches, walk many batters, or give up home runs. His strikeout-to-walk ratios have always been good. Andersen's weaknesses are his fielding, his inability to keep runners close, and his tendency to land on the DL. He missed large chunks of the '91 season with a herniated disc in his neck.

Major League Pitching Register

	W	L	ERA	G	S	IP	H	ER	BB	SO
75 AL	0	0	4.76	3	0	5.2	4	3	2	4
77 AL	0	1	3.14	11	0	14.1	10	5	9	8
79 AL	0	0	7.56	8	0	16.2	25	14	4	7
81 AL	3	3	2.66	41	5	67.2	57	20	18	40
82 AL	0	0	5.99	40	1	79.2	100	53	23	32
83 NL	1	0	2.39	17	0	26.1	19	7	9	14
84 NL	3	7	2.38	64	4	90.2	85	24	25	54
85 NL	3	3	4.32	57	3	73.0	78	35	26	50
86 NL	2	1	3.03	48	1	77.1	83	26	26	42
87 NL	9	5	3.45	67	5	101.2	95	39	41	94
88 NL	2	4	2.94	53	5	82.2	82	27	20	66
89 NL	4	4	1.54	60	3	87.2	63	15	24	85
90 NL	5	2	1.95	50	6	73.2	61	16	24	68
90 AL	0	0	1.23	15	1	22.0	18	3	3	25
91 NL	3	4	2.30	38	13	47.0	39	12	13	40
92 NL	1	1	3.34	34	2	35.0	26	13	8	35
Life	36	35	3.12	606	49	901.0	845	312	275	664
3 AVE	3	2	2.23	46	7	59.1	48	15	16	56

BRADY ANDERSON

Position: Outfield
Team: Baltimore Orioles
Born: Jan. 18, 1964 Silver Spring, MD
Height: 6'1" **Weight:** 195 lbs.
Bats: left **Throws:** left
Acquired: Traded from Red Sox with Curt Schilling for Mike Boddicker, 7/88

Player Summary	
Fantasy Value	$12 to $20
Card Value	6¢ to 12¢
Will	reach base
Can't	hit lefties
Expect	acrobatic defense
Don't Expect	a home run crown

It's hard to believe Anderson was only a .219 career hitter before 1992. After winning Baltimore's left field job in spring training, he went on a batting tear that made him the most productive leadoff man in the AL East. He had reached a career high in runs batted in by Memorial Day and had a .286 average, 28 stolen bases, 15 homers, and 57 RBI at the All-Star break. The last leadoff man with as many RBI at the break was Bobby Bonds, who had 63 in 1973. Although Anderson cooled a bit, he still ended with a .373 on-base percentage and a .449 slugging average in '92. He attributed his success to off-season eye exercises, a mechanical adjustment in his swing, less crouch in his batting stance, and tips from former teammate Rene Gonzales, who urged Brady to relax. Once known as a stubborn player who didn't like advice, Anderson responded so well that he made the All-Star Team. A fine fielder, he is also a great baserunner.

Major League Batting Register

	BA	G	AB	R	H	2B	3B	HR	RBI	SB
88 AL	.212	94	325	31	69	13	4	1	21	10
89 AL	.207	94	266	44	55	12	2	4	16	16
90 AL	.231	89	234	24	54	5	2	3	24	15
91 AL	.230	113	256	40	59	12	3	2	27	12
92 AL	.271	159	623	100	169	28	10	21	80	53
Life	.238	549	1704	239	406	70	21	31	168	106
3 AVE	.253	120	371	55	94	15	5	9	44	27

DAVE ANDERSON

Position: Infield
Team: Los Angeles Dodgers
Born: Aug. 1, 1960 Louisville, KY
Height: 6'2" **Weight:** 191 lbs.
Bats: right **Throws:** right
Acquired: Signed as a free agent, 1/92

Player Summary	
Fantasy Value	$1 to $2
Card Value	3¢ to 4¢
Will	play several positions
Can't	hit for high average
Expect	timely pinch-hits
Don't Expect	a full-time role

A utility man who has bounced back and forth between the minors, the Dodgers, and the Giants since L.A. drafted him in 1981, Anderson is a solid fielder who saves more runs with his glove than he knocks in with his bat. He began the 1992 season in Triple-A but returned to the Dodgers May 1 after hitting .321 at Albuquerque. He plays second base and shortstop on occasion—and first base when the need arises—but he's most at home protecting the hot corner. Good at turning double plays, he'll get his share of assists and putouts. Because he's pushing 35, Anderson does not have the range he once did. He remains a productive pinch-hitter, however. He rarely hits for power but did hit two homers in six days for the first time in his career last May.

Major League Batting Register

	BA	G	AB	R	H	2B	3B	HR	RBI	SB
83 NL	.165	61	115	12	19	4	2	1	2	6
84 NL	.251	121	374	51	94	16	2	3	34	15
85 NL	.199	77	221	24	44	6	0	4	18	5
86 NL	.245	92	216	31	53	9	0	1	15	5
87 NL	.234	108	265	32	62	12	3	1	13	9
88 NL	.249	116	285	31	71	10	2	2	20	4
89 NL	.229	87	140	15	32	2	0	1	14	2
90 NL	.350	60	100	14	35	5	1	1	6	1
91 NL	.248	100	226	24	56	5	2	2	13	2
92 NL	.286	51	84	10	24	4	0	3	8	0
Life	.242	873	2026	244	490	73	12	19	143	49

ERIC ANTHONY

Position: Outfield
Team: Houston Astros
Born: Nov. 8, 1967 San Diego, CA
Height: 6'2" **Weight:** 195 lbs.
Bats: left **Throws:** left
Acquired: 34th-round pick in 6/86 free-agent draft

Player Summary	
Fantasy Value	$3 to $5
Card Value	3¢ to 4¢
Will	combine speed and power
Can't	connect as much as he should
Expect	homers in double-digits
Don't Expect	high batting average

After failing three previous big league trials, Anthony finally lived up to his advance billing in 1992. He discarded his old upper-cut swing, showed better awareness of the strike zone, and started using the whole park instead of just pulling the ball. He hit two homers on July 26 against the Cubs and a game-winning, two-out, 11th-inning grand-slam against the Braves the next night. Earlier, he had 31 RBI over a 40-game stretch that started in mid-June. One of those RBI was the result of a leadoff, first-pitch, ninth-inning homer against Cincinnati's Scott Bankhead on July 1. Anthony compiled a .298 on-base percentage and a .407 slugging average in 1992. He also batted .212 against lefties and .254 against righties. Although Pete Incaviglia opened the season as Houston's right fielder, Anthony inherited the job after Incaviglia replaced struggling left fielder Luis Gonzalez. A former San Diego schoolboy football star who got into baseball late, Anthony won two minor league homer titles, in 1988 and 1989.

Major League Batting Register

	BA	G	AB	R	H	2B	3B	HR	RBI	SB
89 NL	.180	25	61	7	11	2	0	4	7	0
90 NL	.192	84	239	26	46	8	0	10	29	5
91 NL	.153	39	118	11	18	6	0	1	7	1
92 NL	.239	137	440	45	105	15	1	19	80	5
Life	.210	285	858	89	180	31	1	34	123	11
2 AVE	.222	111	340	36	76	12	1	15	55	5

KEVIN APPIER

Position: Pitcher
Team: Kansas City Royals
Born: Dec. 6, 1967 Lancaster, CA
Height: 6'2" **Weight:** 190 lbs.
Bats: right **Throws:** right
Acquired: First-round pick in 6/87 free-agent draft

Player Summary	
Fantasy Value	$14 to $20
Card Value	4¢ to 6¢
Will	keep enemy hitters at bay
Can't	prevent stolen bases
Expect	route-going efforts
Don't Expect	many walks

The Sporting News chose Appier as the Rookie Pitcher of the Year in 1990, and he hasn't let up since. Armed with the ability to pitch the ball where he wants it, he is a fastball-and-slider hurler who averages six and one-half strikeouts per nine innings. His pickoff move and fielding ability, however, leave much to be desired, but he is improving both with experience. Lefthanded hitters had posed problems for him, but he controlled them more effectively in 1992. Lefties batted only .205 against him, while righties had a .227 average. Overall, he allowed a .217 batting average, a .281 slugging percentage, and a .319 slugging average. Appier had 10 wins by midseason and a 6-0 record and 1.15 ERA over eight starts through July 30. Clearly Kansas City's No. 1 starter, he was overlooked for the 1992 AL All-Star squad. He's determined not to let that happen again. He had increased his win total in each of his three seasons in the majors.

Major League Pitching Register

	W	L	ERA	G	CG	IP	H	ER	BB	SO
89 AL	1	4	9.14	6	0	21.2	34	22	12	10
90 AL	12	8	2.76	32	3	185.2	179	57	54	127
91 AL	13	10	3.42	34	6	207.2	205	79	61	158
92 AL	15	8	2.46	30	3	208.1	167	57	68	150
Life	41	30	3.10	102	12	623.1	585	215	195	445
3 AVE	13	9	2.89	32	4	200.2	184	64	61	145

LUIS AQUINO

Position: Pitcher
Team: Kansas City Royals
Born: May 19, 1965 Santurce, Puerto Rico
Height: 6'1" **Weight:** 190 lbs.
Bats: right **Throws:** right
Acquired: Traded from Blue Jays for Juan Beniquez, 7/87

Player Summary	
Fantasy Value	$1 to $3
Card Value	3¢ to 4¢
Will	be an occasional starter
Can't	fan many batters
Expect	good control
Don't Expect	many runs yielded

Perhaps the most versatile pitcher on the Royals, Aquino has impressed with his ability to produce as both a starter and reliever. A strained shoulder and sore right rib cage kept him sidelined for virtually all of the first half in 1992, but he returned to regular action in July. When he's right, Aquino does not chalk up many strikeouts, even during good outings. He throws a fastball, slider, and curve and generally can spot the baseball. He does have occasional control lapses, however. He allowed a .303 batting average, a .351 on-base percentage, and a .412 slugging average in 1992. A rubber-armed righthander who twice worked more than 50 times while in the minors, Aquino can be deployed as a starter, reliever, or swing man, depending on his team's needs. He compiled 20 saves in each of two seasons in the minors, in 1984 and '85. If he's healthy, Aquino can be a capable big league performer.

Major League Pitching Register

	W	L	ERA	G	CG	IP	H	ER	BB	SO
86 AL	1	1	6.35	7	0	11.1	14	8	3	5
88 AL	1	0	2.79	7	1	29.0	33	9	17	11
89 AL	6	8	3.50	34	2	141.1	148	55	35	68
90 AL	4	1	3.16	20	1	68.1	59	24	27	28
91 AL	8	4	3.44	38	1	157.0	152	60	47	80
92 AL	3	6	4.52	15	0	67.2	81	34	20	11
Life	23	20	3.60	121	5	474.2	487	190	149	203
3 AVE	5	4	3.62	24	1	97.1	97	39	31	40

JACK ARMSTRONG

Position: Pitcher
Team: Florida Marlins
Born: March 7, 1965 Englewood, NJ
Height: 6'5" **Weight:** 220 lbs.
Bats: right **Throws:** right
Acquired: Second-round pick from Indians in 11/92 expansion draft

Player Summary	
Fantasy Value	$2 to $4
Card Value	3¢ to 4¢
Will	have hot and cold streaks
Can't	post steady wins
Expect	hard throwing
Don't Expect	many complete games

Many things happened to Armstrong between his starting the 1990 All-Star Game and the 1992 All-Star break: He went 8-23, returned to the minors for a time, and went from being a tough starter with the Reds to a hopeful starter with the Indians. Perhaps it was his sore elbow. Perhaps opposing hitters read him like a batting instruction book. Perhaps both factors contributed. When he's on, Armstrong throws a fastball and a slider—and a change-up, suggested by Cleveland pitching coach Rick Adair after Armstrong's 2-12 start in 1992. He allowed a .269 batting average, a .337 on-base average, and a .430 slugging percentage in '92. He clearly wasn't the same pitcher who went 11-3 during the first half of 1990. Scouts say he hasn't lost anything off his pitches but has been hampered by poor control. Armstrong is a former first-round draft choice (1987) who is still trying to justify that selection. At Triple-A Nashville in 1989, he led his loop with 13 wins.

Major League Pitching Register

	W	L	ERA	G	CG	IP	H	ER	BB	SO
88 NL	4	7	5.79	14	0	65.1	63	42	38	45
89 NL	2	3	4.64	9	0	42.2	40	22	21	23
90 NL	12	9	3.42	29	2	166.0	151	63	59	110
91 NL	7	13	5.48	27	1	139.2	158	85	54	93
92 AL	6	15	4.64	35	1	166.2	176	86	67	114
Life	31	47	4.62	114	4	580.1	588	298	239	385
3 AVE	8	12	4.46	30	1	157.1	162	78	60	106

ANDY ASHBY

Position: Pitcher
Team: Colorado Rockies
Born: July 11, 1967 Kansas City, MO
Height: 6'5" **Weight:** 180 lbs.
Bats: Right **Throws:** Right
Acquired: First-round pick from Phillies in 11/92 expansion draft

Player Summary	
Fantasy Value	$1 to $3
Card Value	5¢ to 7¢
Will	be used as starter
Can't	go the distance
Expect	occasional control problems
Don't Expect	many complete games

Ashby becomes a member of the Colorado rotation. He had been heralded as the Phillies' best prospect since the team signed him nearly seven years ago. In 1991, he tied for the Triple-A International League lead with six complete games and three shutouts. That year he was 11-11 with a 3.46 ERA; he had 113 strikeouts and 60 walks in 161⅓ innings. At 6'5", he's an imposing figure on the mound. He worked his way into the majors in 1991 but posted a disappointing 1-5 record with an ERA of 6.00. He's not exactly a strikeout pitcher, though he tied the major league record of striking out the side on nine pitches (June 15, 1991, in the fourth inning). Projected as a Philadelphia starter in 1992, Ashby broke the thumb of his pitching hand in his third start. When healthy, he'll whiff about a half-dozen batters in nine innings. Ashby doesn't always have great control, and he's much more effective against righties than lefties. In seven games for Triple-A Scranton in 1992, he was 0-3 with a 3.00 ERA.

Major League Pitching Register

	W	L	ERA	G	CG	IP	H	ER	BB	SO
91 NL	1	5	6.00	8	0	42.0	41	28	19	26
92 NL	1	3	7.54	10	0	37.0	42	31	21	24
Life	2	8	6.72	18	0	79.0	83	59	40	50

PAUL ASSENMACHER

Position: Pitcher
Team: Chicago Cubs
Born: Dec. 10, 1960 Detroit, MI
Height: 6'3" **Weight:** 200 lbs.
Bats: left **Throws:** left
Acquired: Traded from Braves for Kelly Mann and Pat Gomez, 8/89

Player Summary	
Fantasy Value	$3 to $5
Card Value	3¢ to 4¢
Will	use curve as premier pitch
Can't	throw fastball past hitters
Expect	many relief appearances
Don't Expect	much late-inning work

Although he has been used in a variety of relief roles during his career, Assenmacher is most often deployed as a set-up man, capable of mowing down lefthanded hitters while working several innings at a time. Regardless of when he enters a game, this workhorse control pitcher (he's appeared in at least 63 games in each of the last five seasons) can be counted on to chalk up about a strikeout per inning. His specialty is the curveball—or, it should be said, curveballs—and he is a real nemesis for lefthanded hitters. Working often and rarely losing time with an injury, he doesn't throw hard (his fastball is ordinary), and his stuff either breaks the backs of batters or leaves them frozen with their bats in their hands. His fielding is passable, as is his move to first base, but his strengths elsewhere make him one of the game's most formidable relievers.

Major League Pitching Register

	W	L	ERA	G	S	IP	H	ER	BB	SO
86 NL	7	3	2.50	61	7	68.1	61	19	26	56
87 NL	1	1	5.10	52	2	54.2	58	31	24	39
88 NL	8	7	3.06	64	5	79.1	72	27	32	71
89 NL	3	4	3.99	63	0	76.2	74	34	28	79
90 NL	7	2	2.80	74	10	103.0	90	32	36	95
91 NL	7	8	3.24	75	15	102.2	85	37	31	117
92 NL	4	4	4.10	70	8	68.0	72	31	26	67
Life	37	29	3.44	459	47	552.2	512	211	203	524
3 AVE	6	5	3.29	73	11	91.1	82	33	31	93

STEVE AVERY

Position: Pitcher
Team: Atlanta Braves
Born: April 14, 1970 Trenton, MI
Height: 6'4" **Weight:** 180 lbs.
Bats: left **Throws:** left
Acquired: First-round pick in 6/88 free-agent draft

Player Summary	
Fantasy Value	$12 to $16
Card Value	5¢ to 10¢
Will	help himself at bat
Can't	shake blister problems
Expect	future Cy Young Award
Don't Expect	a losing season

After a killer year in 1991—when he went 18-8, won Championship Series MVP honors, and pitched Atlanta into the World Series—reality set in for Avery the first half of '92. His record stayed at .500, though he had a good ERA (3.20) that suggested a lack of offensive support. Like many young pitchers, Avery sometimes experiences problems in the middle innings, getting his otherwise excellent fastball up in the strike zone. He usually has good control of all his pitches—fastball, changeup, and overhand curve. He likes to keep righties off-balance with low-inside and high-outside pitches, while also coming inside on them with the curve. Righties are occasionally fooled with a change. With lefties, he works the corners with fastballs, but consistently rings up strikes low-and-outside with the curve. He has a fair pickoff move, but is easy to steal against. Opposing baserunners in '92 stole 42 bases and were caught only 14 times. Avery allowed a .246 batting average, a .300 on-base average, and a .343 slugging percentage in 1992.

Major League Pitching Register

	W	L	ERA	G	CG	IP	H	ER	BB	SO
90 NL	3	11	5.64	21	1	99.0	121	62	45	75
91 NL	18	8	3.38	35	3	210.1	189	79	65	137
92 NL	11	11	3.20	35	2	233.2	216	83	71	129
Life	32	30	3.71	91	6	543.0	526	224	181	341
3 AVE	11	10	3.71	30	2	181.1	175	75	60	114

WALLY BACKMAN

Position: Infield
Team: Philadelphia Phillies
Born: Sept. 22, 1959 Hillsboro, OR
Height: 5'9" **Weight:** 168 lbs.
Bats: both **Throws:** right
Acquired: Signed as a free agent, 1/91

Player Summary	
Fantasy Value	$1 to $3
Card Value	3¢ to 4¢
Will	bunt to get on
Can't	hit ball out of park
Expect	platoon role
Don't Expect	many swipes

Backman's production has been declining since his glory days with the 1986 Mets. One year after batting .292 for the 1990 Pirates, his batting average sagged 50 points, and he lost the Phils' second base job to rookie Mickey Morandini. Backman's average has been on a downward trend ever since. He'll probably play in less than 100 games, and in a platoon role. Although a switch-hitter, he is much better batting lefthanded than right. A player with a good eye and patience at the plate, he'll garner his share of walks, and he's quick enough to bunt for hits and beat out infield singles. Backman is a good baserunner, but he doesn't steal often. In the field, he's only adequate but is capable of playing both second and third.

Major League Batting Register

	BA	G	AB	R	H	2B	3B	HR	RBI	SB
80 NL	.323	27	93	12	30	1	1	0	9	2
81 NL	.278	26	36	5	10	2	0	0	0	1
82 NL	.272	96	261	37	71	13	2	3	22	8
83 NL	.167	26	42	6	7	0	1	0	3	0
84 NL	.280	128	436	68	122	19	2	1	26	32
85 NL	.273	145	520	77	142	24	5	1	38	30
86 NL	.320	124	387	67	124	18	2	1	27	13
87 NL	.250	94	300	43	75	6	1	1	23	11
88 NL	.303	99	294	44	89	12	0	0	17	9
89 AL	.231	87	299	33	69	9	2	1	26	1
90 NL	.292	104	315	62	92	21	3	2	28	6
91 NL	.243	94	185	20	45	12	0	0	15	3
92 NL	.271	42	48	6	13	1	0	0	6	1
Life	.276	1092	3216	480	889	138	19	10	240	117
2 AVE	.274	99	250	41	69	17	2	1	22	5

CARLOS BAERGA

Position: Infield
Team: Cleveland Indians
Born: Nov. 4, 1968 San Juan, Puerto Rico
Height: 5'11" **Weight:** 165 lbs.
Bats: both **Throws:** right
Acquired: Traded from Padres with Sandy Alomar and Chris James for Joe Carter, 12/89

Player Summary	
Fantasy Value	$12 to $20
Card Value	10¢ to 15¢
Will	produce power
Can't	get deserved publicity
Expect	vacuum glove at second
Don't Expect	many walks

At the time of his trade to the Indians from the Padres in the Sandy Alomar deal, many considered Baerga to be merely "the other player." In 1992, he proved them wrong. He became the first Indian with 100 hits at the All-Star break since Julio Franco and Pat Tabler in 1987. Baerga also won a spot on the American League squad. On July 19, he got his second four-hit game of the season and boosted his average during a 23-game hot streak to .460. A durable player who rarely misses a game, Baerga had a .323 average at midseason, and he challenged for the hit crown before settling down to a .312 mark. He had a .354 on-base average and a .455 slugging percentage in '92. Before 1992, he had experienced some trouble with high-outside fastballs, low-outside fastballs, and slightly inside fastballs when delivered by righthanders. Though he can also play shortstop and third base, Baerga has found a home at second and has become a fine fielder.

Major League Batting Register

	BA	G	AB	R	H	2B	3B	HR	RBI	SB
90 AL	.260	108	312	46	81	17	2	7	47	0
91 AL	.288	158	593	80	171	28	2	11	69	3
92 AL	.312	161	657	92	205	32	1	20	105	10
Life	.293	427	1562	218	457	77	5	38	221	13
3 AVE	.293	142	521	73	152	26	2	13	74	4

JEFF BAGWELL

Position: First base
Team: Houston Astros
Born: May 27, 1968 Boston, MA
Height: 6' **Weight:** 195 lbs.
Bats: Right **Throws:** Right
Acquired: Traded from Red Sox for Larry Andersen, 8/90

Player Summary	
Fantasy Value	$10 to $16
Card Value	10¢ to 15¢
Will	hit for average
Can't	avoid frequent Ks
Expect	good homer totals
Don't Expect	many swipes

Bagwell was a bargain. When the 'Stros sent Larry Andersen to the Red Sox for Bagwell, the former was in his option year, while Bagwell was just about to blossom. He was 1991 NL Rookie of the Year (the first in Astro history) when he lead all rookies in batting average, hits, on-base average, RBI, walks, games, and plate appearances. He finished 1991 with 48 consecutive errorless games at first base (in 155 games), even though he just started playing there that spring. In 1992, he compiled a .368 on-base average and a .444 slugging percentage. The former University of Hartford star had been moved across the diamond to allow third baseman Ken Caminiti to remain in the lineup. Bagwell has hit several tape-measure homers during his brief big league career but might connect more frequently if he cut down on his swing (and high strikeout total). He was MVP of the Double-A Eastern League in 1990 and has the potential to win a similar honor on the major league level.

Major League Batting Register

	BA	G	AB	R	H	2B	3B	HR	RBI	SB
91 NL	.294	156	554	79	163	26	4	15	82	7
92 NL	.273	162	586	87	160	34	6	18	96	10
Life	.283	318	1140	166	323	60	10	33	178	17
2 AVE	.283	159	570	83	162	30	5	17	89	9

HAROLD BAINES

Position: Designated hitter; outfield
Team: Oakland Athletics
Born: March 15, 1959 Easton, MD
Height: 6'2" **Weight:** 195 lbs.
Bats: left **Throws:** left
Acquired: Traded from Rangers for Joe Bitker and Scott Chiamparino, 8/90

Player Summary	
Fantasy Value	$12 to $15
Card Value	4¢ to 6¢
Will	go the other way
Can't	run like he used to
Expect	double-digit homers if healthy
Don't Expect	much outfield time

Baines had been Mr. Steady for more than a decade, compiling a lifetime batting average near .290. But persistent knee problems and advancing age threaten to severely affect these numbers. Still, he can be dangerous to the opposition. Pitchers have long known that if they throw him high inside fastballs, they may develop whiplash from watching the ball sail out of the park. When they pitch him away, he has responded with frequent opposite-field hits. Baines is also capable of pulling any pitch. While the knee has prevented his playing the outfield, his role as designated hitter has been a boon to his hitting and could keep him employed for a few more years, if he stays healthy. He had a .331 on-base percentage and a .391 slugging average.

Major League Batting Register

	BA	G	AB	R	H	2B	3B	HR	RBI	SB
80 AL	.255	141	491	55	125	23	6	13	49	2
81 AL	.286	82	280	42	80	11	7	10	41	6
82 AL	.271	161	608	89	165	29	8	25	105	10
83 AL	.280	156	596	76	167	33	2	20	99	7
84 AL	.304	147	569	72	173	28	10	29	94	1
85 AL	.309	160	640	86	198	29	3	22	113	1
86 AL	.296	145	570	72	169	29	2	21	88	2
87 AL	.293	132	505	59	148	26	4	20	93	0
88 AL	.277	158	599	55	166	39	1	13	81	0
89 AL	.309	146	505	73	156	29	1	16	72	0
90 AL	.284	135	415	52	118	15	1	16	65	0
91 AL	.295	141	488	76	144	25	1	20	90	0
92 AL	.253	140	478	58	121	18	0	16	76	1
Life	.286	1844	6744	865	1930	334	46	241	1066	30
3 AVE	.277	139	460	62	128	19	1	17	77	0

SCOTT BANKHEAD

Position: Pitcher
Team: Boston Red Sox
Born: July 31, 1963 Raleigh, NC
Height: 5'10" **Weight:** 185 lbs.
Bats: right **Throws:** right
Acquired: Signed as a free agent, 12/92

Player Summary	
Fantasy Value	$2 to $6
Card Value	3¢ to 4¢
Will	pitch with great control
Can't	escape shoulder problems
Expect	good whiff-walk ratio
Don't Expect	rotation return

Even though Bankhead's history of shoulder problems had made his future uncertain, switching to the NL was the cure for this 1984 U.S. Olympian. Deployed in middle relief by the Reds, Bankhead posted an 8-1 record by the end of June. His ERA was a hair above 2.00, and his strikeout-to-walk ratio was nearly 3-to-1. By the end of the year, he held opponents to a .218 batting average, a .301 on-base percentage, and a .333 slugging percentage. A control pitcher who yields few walks, Bankhead does give up his share of dingers. He throws a slider and fastball that move, and a curve that doubles as a changeup. Before 1992, Bankhead's best year was as a starter for the 1989 Mariners. He submitted to shoulder surgery a year later, however, and was written off by Seattle. Bankhead, a bargain signing at $400,000 plus incentives, mastered the job of middle reliever by learning how to prepare himself between assignments.

Major League Pitching Register

	W	L	ERA	G	S	IP	H	ER	BB	SO
86 AL	8	9	4.61	24	0	121.0	121	62	37	94
87 AL	9	8	5.42	27	0	149.1	168	90	37	95
88 AL	7	9	3.07	21	0	135.0	115	46	38	102
89 AL	14	6	3.34	33	0	210.1	187	78	63	140
90 AL	0	2	11.08	4	0	13.0	18	16	7	10
91 AL	3	6	4.90	17	0	60.2	73	33	21	28
92 NL	10	4	2.93	54	1	70.2	57	23	29	53
Life	51	44	4.12	180	1	760.0	739	348	232	522
2 AVE	7	5	3.84	36	1	65.2	65	28	25	41

WILLIE BANKS

Position: Pitcher
Team: Minnesota Twins
Born: Feb. 27, 1969 Jersey City, NJ
Height: 6'1" **Weight:** 190 lbs
Bats: right **Throws:** right
Acquired: First-round pick in 6/87 free-agent draft

Player Summary	
Fantasy Value	$3 to $6
Card Value	8¢ to 12¢
Will	become consistent winner
Can't	always rely on fastball
Expect	some bouts of wildness
Don't Expect	200 Ks, yet

Banks began 1992 in Triple-A after losing a spring training duel with Pat Mahomes for the No. 5 job in the Minnesota starting rotation. Recalled June 3 after Mahomes faltered, Banks struggled to an 8.79 ERA in three outings before beating Seattle, 5-0, on June 21 for his first win. He ended the season by allowing a .288 batting average, a .370 on-base average, and a .428 slugging percentage. When he first reached the majors in 1991, Banks threw too many pitches, but he learned from his mistakes. The highest pro baseball draft pick in New Jersey history, Banks was once too dependent on his 95 mph fastball. He has learned to blend it with his curveball and changeup. He had a 6-1 record with a 1.92 ERA, two complete games, and 41 Ks in 75 innings at Triple-A Portland in 1992 before his June promotion to the Twins. In 1990 at Portland, he was 9-8 with a 4.55 ERA and 63 Ks in 146 innings. Banks left behind a string of schoolboy pitching records, including a pair of 19-strikeout performances in seven-inning games.

Major League Pitching Register

	W	L	ERA	G	CG	IP	H	ER	BB	SO
91 AL	1	1	5.71	5	0	17.1	21	11	12	16
92 AL	4	4	5.70	16	0	71.0	80	45	37	37
Life	5	5	5.71	21	0	88.1	101	56	49	53

BRET BARBERIE

Position: Second base
Team: Florida Marlins
Born: Aug. 16, 1967 Long Beach, CA
Height: 5'11" **Weight:** 185 lbs.
Bats: both **Throws:** right
Acquired: First-round pick from Expos in 11/92 expansion draft

Player Summary	
Fantasy Value	$5 to $8
Card Value	8¢ to 12¢
Will	display occasional power
Can't	hit many home runs
Expect	gradual development
Don't Expect	Gold Glove

Barberie has every chance to solidify the middle infield for the Florida Marlins. He made such a strong impression on the Expos during his half-season with the club in 1991 that they decided to move Tim Wallach from third to first, handing Barberie the third base job during 1992 spring training. He quickly played his way off the bag, however, by failing to provide adequate defense or to compensate for defense lapses with his bat. After hitting .353—and playing all four infield positions—in 57 games for the '91 club, he folded his tent early in 1992. Producing neither offensively nor defensively, he received a ticket back to Triple-A Indianapolis. There, he batted .395 while playing mostly second base. By the time he returned, Wallach was back at third, and the Expos were playing winning baseball without Barberie. By the end of the 1992 season, he had a .354 on-base average and a .281 slugging percentage. A 1988 Olympian—whose father played in the minors—he broke into pro ball as a second baseman in 1989.

Major League Batting Register

	BA	G	AB	R	H	2B	3B	HR	RBI	SB
91 NL	.353	57	136	16	48	12	2	2	18	0
92 NL	.232	111	285	26	66	11	0	1	24	9
Life	.271	168	421	42	114	23	2	3	42	9

BRIAN BARNES

Position: Pitcher
Team: Montreal Expos
Born: March 25, 1967 Roanoke Rapids, NC
Height: 5'9" **Weight:** 170 lbs.
Bats: left **Throws:** left
Acquired: Fourth-round pick in 6/89 free-agent draft

Player Summary

Fantasy Value	$4 to $7
Card Value	4¢ to 7¢
Will	use curve for strikeouts
Can't	always throw strikes
Expect	struggle to stay in majors
Don't Expect	any relief roles

Barnes is a little lefty with a big curveball. He used the pitch as his No. 1 strikeout pitch when he led the Double-A Southern League with 213 strikeouts in 201 innings pitched in 1990. That performance advanced him to Montreal. He divided his time between the majors and minors in 1991 and opened 1992 in Triple-A. At Triple-A Indianapolis in '92, he was 4-4 with a 3.69 ERA, two complete games, 77 strikeouts, and 30 walks in 83 innings. Recalled on June 20, he showed he had improved the control that kept him from establishing a big league niche in previous trials. Although he gave up just over four walks per nine innings in '92, he allowed only a .253 batting average, a .306 on-base average, and a .329 slugging average. On July 20, his 2-1 victory over San Francisco included eight strikeouts, two walks, and only three hits in eight-plus innings pitched. Barnes was a Clemson All-American who broke into pro ball in 1989. In 1991 at Indianapolis, Barnes was 2-0 with a 1.64 ERA.

Major League Pitching Register

	W	L	ERA	G	CG	IP	H	ER	BB	SO
90 NL	1	1	2.89	4	1	28.0	25	9	7	23
91 NL	5	8	4.22	28	1	160.0	135	75	84	117
92 NL	6	6	2.97	21	0	100.0	77	33	46	65
Life	12	15	3.66	53	2	288.0	237	117	137	205
2 AVE	6	7	3.74	25	1	130.0	106	54	65	91

SKEETER BARNES

Position: Infield; outfield
Team: Detroit Tigers
Born: March 7, 1957 Cincinnati, OH
Height: 5'10" **Weight:** 180 lbs.
Bats: right **Throws:** right
Acquired: Signed as a free agent, 1/91

Player Summary

Fantasy Value	$2 to $3
Card Value	3¢ to 4¢
Will	play various positions
Can't	hit for high average
Expect	good defense
Don't Expect	full-time role

Although he broke into pro ball in 1978, Barnes had never enjoyed a full season in the majors before 1992. Although he is one of the most versatile players in the game, he has been on a perpetual rollercoaster that included only brief stops in Cincinnati, St. Louis, and Montreal before stopping in Detroit halfway through the 1991 campaign. Given more at bats by Tiger manager Sparky Anderson than he had received in parts of five National League seasons, Barnes responded with a .289 average and five homers in 75 games. His production fell a bit in '92 but was still sufficient to gain him playing time, often in a right-left platoon with the slump-ridden Scott Livingstone. Barnes compiled a .318 on-base percentage and a .388 slugging average in 1992. He is capable of playing any position except shortstop, catcher, or pitcher. While he doesn't have great range at third or in the outfield, he doesn't make mistakes.

Major League Batting Register

	BA	G	AB	R	H	2B	3B	HR	RBI	SB
83 NL	.206	15	34	5	7	0	0	1	4	2
84 NL	.119	32	42	5	5	0	0	1	3	0
85 NL	.154	19	26	0	4	1	0	0	0	0
87 NL	.250	4	4	1	1	0	0	1	3	0
89 NL	.000	5	3	1	0	0	0	0	0	0
91 AL	.289	75	159	28	46	13	2	5	17	10
92 AL	.273	95	165	27	45	8	1	3	25	3
Life	.249	245	433	67	108	22	3	11	52	15
2 AVE	.281	85	162	28	46	11	2	4	21	7

KEVIN BASS

Position: Outfield
Team: Houston Astros
Born: May 12, 1959 Redwood City, CA
Height: 6′ **Weight:** 180 lbs.
Bats: both **Throws:** right
Acquired: Signed as a free agent, 1/93

Player Summary	
Fantasy Value	$3 to $5
Card Value	3¢ to 4¢
Will	provide occasional pop
Can't	shake knee woes
Expect	good defense
Don't Expect	production of past

Bass returns to Houston, where he played from 1982 to '89. The Mets were short on outfielders and traded for Bass last summer to fill a gap. When the Giants signed him on Nov. 16, 1989, they were hoping to plug a right field gap with the player who hit .311 with 20 homers for the '86 Astros. The Giants, though, were bitterly disappointed. Instead of approximating those numbers, the rifle-armed switch-hitter spent large chunks of the next three years on the disabled list and rarely displayed the hitting form that had made him such a standout in Houston. When healthy, Bass, an NL All-Star in 1986, has speed, power, and runs the bases well. Even sessions with then San Francisco hitting coach Dusty Baker didn't help Bass. He hasn't been the same since 1990 knee surgery, and his future is as a fourth outfielder.

Major League Batting Register

	BA	G	AB	R	H	2B	3B	HR	RBI	SB
82 AL	.000	18	9	4	0	0	0	0	0	0
82 NL	.042	12	24	2	1	0	0	0	1	0
83 NL	.236	88	195	25	46	7	3	2	18	2
84 NL	.260	121	331	33	86	17	5	2	29	5
85 NL	.269	150	539	72	145	27	5	16	68	19
86 NL	.311	157	591	83	184	33	5	20	79	22
87 NL	.284	157	592	83	168	31	5	19	85	21
88 NL	.255	157	541	57	138	27	2	14	72	31
89 NL	.300	87	313	42	94	19	4	5	44	11
90 NL	.252	61	214	25	54	9	1	7	32	2
91 NL	.233	124	361	43	84	10	4	10	40	7
92 NL	.269	135	402	40	108	23	5	9	39	14
Life	.269	1267	4112	509	1106	203	39	104	507	134
3 AVE	.252	107	326	36	82	14	3	9	37	8

ROD BECK

Position: Pitcher
Team: San Francisco Giants
Born: Aug. 3, 1968 Burbank, CA
Height: 6′1″ **Weight:** 215 lbs.
Bats: right **Throws:** right
Acquired: Traded from Athletics for Charlie Corbell, 3/88

Player Summary	
Fantasy Value	$6 to $10
Card Value	4¢ to 6¢
Will	post share of Ks
Can't	break into rotation
Expect	many hits yielded
Don't Expect	superior ERA

Like many before him, Beck was a starter in the minors who reached the majors only after moving to the bullpen. Near the All-Star break in '92, he had struck out an average of a batter an inning, while yielding only a little more than one base on balls per nine innings. Slightly better against lefties than righthanded batters, he gave up about six hits per nine innings pitched, and opposing hitters could manage only a paltry .190 batting average, a .228 on-base percentage, and a .257 slugging average. He struck out eight and one-half and walked only one and one-half batters per nine innings. The busiest reliever in the San Francisco bullpen last summer, Beck had six blown saves and four holds. Although he broke into pro ball in 1986, he did not become a full-time reliever until making the switch with Triple-A Phoenix of the Pacific Coast League in 1991. That year, he was 4-3 with a 2.02 ERA, six saves, 35 strikeouts, and 13 walks in 71 innings pitched.

Major League Pitching Register

	W	L	ERA	G	S	IP	H	ER	BB	SO
91 NL	1	1	3.78	31	1	52.1	53	22	13	38
92 NL	3	3	1.76	65	17	92.0	62	18	15	87
Life	4	4	2.49	96	18	144.1	115	40	28	125
2 AVE	2	2	2.49	48	9	72.1	58	20	14	63

TIM BELCHER

Position: Pitcher
Team: Cincinnati Reds
Born: Oct. 19, 1961 Mount Gilead, OH
Height: 6'3" **Weight:** 210 lbs.
Bats: right **Throws:** right
Acquired: Traded from Dodgers with John Wetteland for Eric Davis and Kip Gross, 11/91

Player Summary	
Fantasy Value	$8 to $12
Card Value	3¢ to 4¢
Will	keep runners off base
Can't	post big K numbers
Expect	low averages by hitters
Don't Expect	inflated ERA

Belcher carried a 2.99 earned run average into the 1992 season, his first with the Cincinnati Reds. Not a strikeout pitcher, but stingy with walks, he was named the righthanded pitcher on *The Sporting News* College All-America Team in 1983 and National League Rookie Pitcher of the Year by the same publication five years later. Excellent in sticky predicaments, he has held batters to a .180 career average with runners on base in late-game pressure situations. His fastball has been clocked in the low 90s, and he also throws a splitter, slider, and curve. He is a fine fielder and has a good pickoff move. He had not allowed more than one homer in his last 47 starts between 1990 and 1991, but '92 was not nearly as productive: playing half the schedule in Riverfront Stadium, where the ball flies, he gave up 17 dingers in 1992. Opponents in '92 compiled a .238 batting average, a .303 on-base average, and a .368 slugging percentage.

Major League Pitching Register

	W	L	ERA	G	CG	IP	H	ER	BB	SO
87 NL	4	2	2.38	6	0	34.0	30	9	7	23
88 NL	12	6	2.91	36	4	179.2	143	58	51	152
89 NL	15	12	2.82	39	10	230.0	182	72	80	200
90 NL	9	9	4.00	24	5	153.0	136	68	48	102
91 NL	10	9	2.62	33	2	209.1	189	61	75	156
92 NL	15	14	3.91	35	2	227.2	201	99	80	149
Life	65	52	3.20	173	23	1033.2	881	367	341	782
3 AVE	11	11	3.48	31	3	196.1	175	76	68	136

STAN BELINDA

Position: Pitcher
Team: Pittsburgh Pirates
Born: Aug. 6, 1966 Huntington, PA
Height: 6'3" **Weight:** 200 lbs.
Bats: right **Throws:** right
Acquired: 10th-round pick in 6/86 free-agent draft

Player Summary	
Fantasy Value	$8 to $12
Card Value	3¢ to 4¢
Will	post big save numbers
Can't	break into starting rotation
Expect	low rival batting averages
Don't Expect	big K numbers

After saving 16 games for the 1991 Pirates, Belinda became the club's top closer in 1992. He had double figures in saves by midseason, thanks to an unorthodox sidearm delivery. He relies on a fastball, forkball, and breaking ball—an arsenal that keeps opposing batting averages near the Mendoza Line. Righties had hit .212 against him, while lefties only managed an anemic .209 before the 1992 season. In 1992, righties batted .256 against him, but lefties hit only .193. Overall, he allowed a .223 batting average, a .295 on-base percentage, and a .381 slugging percentage. His strikeout-to-walk ratio of slightly more than 2-to-1 is okay, but he is capable of a better ERA. He carried a three-year mark of 3.67 into the 1992 campaign. Belinda, who pitches his best baseball at home, did not yield a Three Rivers homer in 1992 before Chicago's Ryne Sandberg beat him with a two-run shot in the ninth on July 19. Belinda usually yields an average of one home run per nine innings.

Major League Pitching Register

	W	L	ERA	G	S	IP	H	ER	BB	SO
89 NL	0	1	6.10	8	0	10.1	13	7	2	10
90 NL	3	4	3.55	55	8	58.1	48	23	29	55
91 NL	7	5	3.45	60	16	78.1	50	30	35	71
92 NL	6	4	3.15	59	18	71.1	58	25	29	57
Life	16	14	3.50	182	42	218.1	169	85	95	193
3 AVE	5	4	3.38	58	14	69.1	52	26	31	61

DEREK BELL

Position: Outfield
Team: Toronto Blue Jays
Born: Dec. 11, 1968 Tampa, FL
Height: 6'2" **Weight:** 200 lbs.
Bats: right **Throws:** right
Acquired: Second-round pick in 6/87 free-agent draft

Player Summary	
Fantasy Value	$5 to $10
Card Value	5¢ to 10¢
Will	show RBI potential
Can't	hit home runs regularly
Expect	big speed
Don't Expect	return to minors

Blessed with quick wrists that have led to comparisons with Eric Davis and Dave Winfield, Bell bid for a full-time big league berth in 1991 but was sidetracked early when he suffered a fractured wrist during the first week of the season. Veteran Candy Maldonado spent most of the season in left field for the Jays, while Bell managed only a single home run by June 23. Bell has some power but is more of a line-drive hitter. He had a .324 on-base average and a .354 slugging percentage in '92. He owns a strong outfield arm, and is a good enough fielder to play both right and center fields. He helps his defensive game with good running speed. Bell's .346 average, 93 RBI, 12 triples, 158 hits, and 89 runs for Triple-A Syracuse led the International League in 1991 and were enough to make him the league's Most Valuable Player. He was also chosen as that year's Minor League Player of the Year by *Baseball America*. In 1990 at Syracuse, he hit .261 with seven homers, 56 RBI, and 57 runs scored.

Major League Batting Register

	BA	G	AB	R	H	2B	3B	HR	RBI	SB
91 AL	.143	18	28	5	4	0	0	0	1	3
92 AL	.242	61	161	23	39	6	3	2	15	7
Life	.228	79	189	28	43	6	3	2	16	10

GEORGE BELL

Position: Outfield
Team: Chicago White Sox
Born: Oct. 21, 1959 San Pedro de Macoris, Dominican Republic
Height: 6'1" **Weight:** 202 lbs.
Bats: right **Throws:** right
Acquired: Traded from Cubs for Ken Patterson and Sammy Sosa, 3/92

Player Summary	
Fantasy Value	$18 to $22
Card Value	5¢ to 7¢
Will	drive in runs
Can't	regain old form
Expect	power to all fields
Don't Expect	another MVP Award

Returning to the AL after a brief visit to the senior loop seemed to revive Bell's RBI stroke in '92. He had more RBI at the All-Star break (65) than any White Sox since Greg Luzinski in 1983. Early in the season, Bell had been swinging at bad pitches, but his bat came around after he moved into the cleanup slot June 6. He immediately collected seven home runs and 29 RBI in 16 games. His home run bat also revived after a streak of 165 at bats without one. Serving as a full-time designated hitter—a role he disdained in Toronto—probably helped Bell's bat, since he didn't have to worry about his left field play. While still a potent RBI man, Bell is no longer the slugger who once delivered 47 homers (and an MVP Award) for the '87 Jays.

Major League Batting Register

	BA	G	AB	R	H	2B	3B	HR	RBI	SB
81 AL	.233	60	163	19	38	2	1	5	12	3
83 AL	.268	39	112	5	30	5	4	2	17	1
84 AL	.292	159	606	85	177	39	4	26	87	11
85 AL	.275	157	607	87	167	28	6	28	95	21
86 AL	.309	159	641	101	198	38	6	31	108	7
87 AL	.308	156	610	111	188	32	4	47	134	5
88 AL	.269	156	614	78	165	27	5	24	97	4
89 AL	.297	153	613	88	182	41	2	18	104	4
90 AL	.265	142	562	67	149	25	0	21	86	3
91 NL	.285	149	558	63	159	27	0	25	86	2
92 AL	.255	155	627	74	160	27	0	25	112	5
Life	.282	1485	5713	778	1613	291	32	252	938	66
3 AVE	.268	149	582	68	156	26	0	24	95	3

JAY BELL

Position: Shortstop
Team: Pittsburgh Pirates
Born: Dec. 11, 1965 Eglin Air Force Base, FL
Height: 6'1" **Weight:** 180 lbs.
Bats: right **Throws:** right
Acquired: Traded from Indians for Felix Fermin, 3/89

Player Summary	
Fantasy Value	$6 to $10
Card Value	3¢ to 4¢
Will	turn many double plays
Can't	hit more than .280
Expect	solid defense at short
Don't Expect	tons of homers

Though he teamed with Jose Lind to give the Pirates one of the top double-play tandems in the NL, Bell's future may lie at third base—a Pittsburgh void created by the midseason swap of Steve Buechele last year. Though Bell has only adequate range at short, he has a strong arm and excellent instincts (his sharp eye led to the appeal play that negated an Atlanta run when David Justice missed third base in the 1991 NLCS). Bell's bat has some pop, but he didn't display the same kind of power that was obvious in 1991. His '92 batting average, however, was a respectable .264, and he also had a .326 on-base percentage and a .383 slugging average. He remains a force to be reckoned with, both with the glove and with the bat. He is an excellent No. 2 hitter whose bunting skills are among the best in the game.

Major League Batting Register

	BA	G	AB	R	H	2B	3B	HR	RBI	SB
86 AL	.357	5	14	3	5	2	0	1	4	0
87 AL	.216	38	125	14	27	9	1	2	13	2
88 AL	.218	73	211	23	46	5	1	2	21	4
89 NL	.258	78	271	33	70	13	3	2	27	5
90 NL	.254	159	583	93	148	28	7	7	52	10
91 NL	.270	157	608	96	164	32	8	16	67	10
92 NL	.264	159	632	87	167	36	6	9	55	7
Life	.257	669	2444	349	627	125	26	39	239	38
3 AVE	.263	158	608	92	160	32	7	11	58	9

ALBERT BELLE

Position: Designated hitter
Team: Cleveland Indians
Born: Aug. 25, 1966 Shreveport, LA
Height: 6'2" **Weight:** 200 lbs.
Bats: right **Throws:** right
Acquired: Second-round pick in 6/87 free-agent draft

Player Summary	
Fantasy Value	$15 to $25
Card Value	5¢ to 15¢
Will	hit tape-measure shots
Can't	control temper
Expect	good RBI production
Don't Expect	an off-year

If Belle would let his talent supersede his temper, he could become baseball's best slugger. In American League history, only Babe Ruth, Joe DiMaggio, and Rudy York produced as many home runs and RBI in so few games. Belle began the 1992 season as Cleveland's DH but complained about the assignment and was restored to his old left field job on May 23. He responded with a 14-for-24 tear that included seven home runs and a dozen RBI in six games—giving him the boost for his first 100-RBI season. He had a .320 on-base average and a .477 slugging percentage. One of the game's strongest players, he is especially dangerous to righthanded pitchers who work him high-and-outside. Temper tantrums have hampered his progress, however. He's been suspended for throwing a ball at a heckler, exiled to the minors for not running out a grounder, and ejected for charging the mound. He has also had problems with alcoholism (10 weeks in rehab in 1990).

Major League Batting Register

	BA	G	AB	R	H	2B	3B	HR	RBI	SB
89 AL	.225	62	218	22	49	8	4	7	37	2
90 AL	.174	9	23	1	4	0	0	1	3	0
91 AL	.282	123	461	60	130	31	2	28	95	3
92 AL	.260	153	585	81	152	23	1	34	112	8
Life	.260	347	1287	164	335	62	7	70	247	13
2 AVE	.270	138	523	71	141	27	2	31	104	6

RAFAEL BELLIARD

Position: Shortstop
Team: Atlanta Braves
Born: Oct. 24, 1961 Pueblo Nuevo, Mao,
    Dominican Republic
Height: 5'6" **Weight:** 150 lbs.
Bats: right **Throws:** right
Acquired: Signed as a free agent, 12/90

Player Summary	
Fantasy Value	$1 to $2
Card Value	3¢ to 4¢
Will	provide strong defense
Can't	hit for power or average
Expect	removal for pinch-hitter
Don't Expect	poor throws

Belliard's glove, range, and arm have kept him in the majors for more than a decade. His defense was so good, in fact, that he earned his first chance to play regularly in 1991 after the Braves had signed him as a utility infielder. He responded with a career-best .249 batting average and played his position well enough to help the team win the pennant. Despite that performance, he still has only one home run in 1,689 at bats. Some writers suggested only half-jokingly that manager Bobby Cox bat Belliard ninth rather than eighth when strong-hitting pitchers Tom Glavine or Steve Avery were starting. Belliard has good hands and a powerful throwing arm that is one of the best in the game. He also turns the double-play as well as anybody.

Major League Batting Register

	BA	G	AB	R	H	2B	3B	HR	RBI	SB
82 NL	.500	9	2	3	1	0	0	0	0	1
83 NL	.000	4	1	1	0	0	0	0	0	0
84 NL	.227	20	22	3	5	0	0	0	0	4
85 NL	.200	17	20	1	4	0	0	0	1	0
86 NL	.233	117	309	33	72	5	2	0	31	12
87 NL	.207	81	203	26	42	4	3	1	15	5
88 NL	.213	122	286	28	61	0	4	0	11	7
89 NL	.214	67	154	10	33	4	0	0	8	5
90 NL	.204	47	54	10	11	3	0	0	6	1
91 NL	.249	149	353	36	88	9	2	0	27	3
92 NL	.211	144	285	20	60	6	1	0	14	0
Life	.223	777	1689	171	377	31	12	1	113	38
2 AVE	.232	147	319	28	74	8	2	0	21	2

FREDDIE BENAVIDES

Position: Shortstop
Team: Colorado Rockies
Born: April 7, 1966 Laredo, TX
Height: 6'2" **Weight:** 185 lbs
Bats: right **Throws:** right
Acquired: Second-round pick from Reds in
    11/92 expansion draft

Player Summary	
Fantasy Value	$2 to $4
Card Value	4¢ to 7¢
Will	utilize speed
Can't	hit for power or average
Expect	defensive lapses
Don't Expect	many walks

Benavides gets a shot to prove he's an every-day major league shortstop. With Barry Larkin ahead of him at shortstop in Cincinnati, Benavides spent most of the 1992 campaign on the bench. He filled when Larkin was hurt or in need of a rest and also got to play some second base. While Benavides's stick is showing improvement over time, he'll never be a long-ball threat. At bat, he's much more effective against lefties than he is against right-handed pitchers. He had a .277 on-base average and a .318 slugging percentage in 1992. Benavides should continue to impress management with his glove and hands, though he falls victim to occasional defensive lapses. He has the range and the arm to be a big league shortstop, and he also plays second base. A product of Texas Christian University, Benavides broke into pro ball in 1987 and reached the majors four years later. In 1991 at Triple-A Nashville, he batted .242 with no homers and 21 RBI.

Major League Batting Register

	BA	G	AB	R	H	2B	3B	HR	RBI	SB
91 NL	.286	24	63	11	18	1	0	0	3	1
92 NL	.231	74	173	14	40	10	1	1	17	0
Life	.246	98	236	25	58	11	1	1	20	1

ANDY BENES

Position: Pitcher
Team: San Diego Padres
Born: Aug. 20, 1967 Evansville, IN
Height: 6'6" **Weight:** 235 lbs.
Bats: right **Throws:** right
Acquired: First-round pick in 6/88 free-agent draft

Player Summary	
Fantasy Value	$14 to $18
Card Value	8¢ to 12¢
Will	show continued growth
Can't	notch many complete games
Expect	at least a dozen wins
Don't Expect	any relief roles

After winning 11 of his last 12 decisions in 1991, Benes was the preseason pick of several writers for the National League's 1992 Cy Young Award. But that was before he was routinely battered by opposing batters. By dropping nine of his first 16 decisions last summer, Benes proved to be one of the biggest disappointments among the Padres. Of course, San Diego provided only three runs per nine innings for him. A 1988 Olympian who was the first choice in baseball's 1988 amateur draft, he spent less than a year in the minors. Though his lack of experience shows at times, he can be a tough opponent, displaying excellent control of his slider, change-of-pace, and fastball. His strikeout-to-walk ratio is good, but his ERA could be better. He yields too many home runs, giving up 14 in 1992. Opponents compiled a .264 batting average, a .314 on-base percentage, and a .371 slugging percentage. Benes is a good fielder, and he is a better hitter than most pitchers.

Major League Pitching Register

	W	L	ERA	G	CG	IP	H	ER	BB	SO
89 NL	6	3	3.51	10	0	66.2	51	26	31	66
90 NL	10	11	3.60	32	2	192.1	177	77	69	140
91 NL	15	11	3.03	33	4	223.0	194	75	59	167
92 NL	13	14	3.35	34	2	231.1	230	86	61	169
Life	44	39	3.33	109	8	713.1	652	264	220	542
3 AVE	13	12	3.31	33	3	215.1	200	79	63	159

TODD BENZINGER

Position: Outfield; first base
Team: Los Angeles Dodgers
Born: Feb. 11, 1963 Dayton, KY
Height: 6'1" **Weight:** 190 lbs.
Bats: both **Throws:** right
Acquired: Traded from Royals for Chris Gwynn and Domingo Mota, 12/91

Player Summary	
Fantasy Value	$3 to $5
Card Value	3¢ to 4¢
Will	sometimes show power
Can't	hit for high average
Expect	spot roles
Don't Expect	many stolen bases

Six and one-half years in the minor leagues taught Benzinger patience. He's developed a keen eye, spraying pitches around the field for hits. A switch-hitter who is better from the right side, his best year was 1989, when he led the National League with 628 at bats and led the Reds in games, runs, hits, and doubles—and was second on the team in homers and RBI. He also had a .995 fielding average at first base that season. He continues to be decent defensively at first, and in the outfield when duty calls there. Though his hitting had been slightly above average, it is beginning to slip. He sometimes displays power, but don't count on him to muscle balls over the fence too often. He's also slow. Although he began last season splitting time at first base with Eric Karros, Benzinger spent most of his summer filling in for injured right fielder Darryl Strawberry.

Major League Batting Register

	BA	G	AB	R	H	2B	3B	HR	RBI	SB
87 AL	.278	73	223	36	62	11	1	8	43	5
88 AL	.254	120	405	47	103	28	1	13	70	2
89 NL	.245	161	628	79	154	28	3	17	76	3
90 NL	.253	118	376	35	95	14	2	5	46	3
91 NL	.187	51	123	7	23	3	2	1	11	2
91 AL	.294	78	293	29	86	15	3	2	40	2
92 NL	.239	121	293	24	70	16	2	4	31	2
Life	.253	722	2341	257	593	115	14	50	317	19
3 AVE	.253	123	362	32	91	16	3	4	43	3

JUAN BERENGUER

Position: Pitcher
Team: Kansas City Royals
Born: Nov. 30, 1954 Aqualdulce, Panama
Height: 5'11" **Weight:** 225 lbs
Bats: right **Throws:** right
Acquired: Traded from Braves for Mark Davis, 7/92

Player Summary	
Fantasy Value	$2 to $4
Card Value	3¢ to 4¢
Will	work often
Can't	always master control
Expect	fevered performances
Don't Expect	20 saves

Before suffering a stress fracture of the right forearm in August 1991, Berenguer was doing a bang-up job in his first season as a closer after years of set-up work. He had converted 17 of 18 save opportunities and allowed only 3 percent of inherited runners to score—the best figure in the major leagues. In 1992, however, he proved he was really a set-up pitcher. By midseason, he was pitching so poorly for the Braves that he was used very sparingly. He asked for—and received—a trade. Berenguer throws a fastball, forkball, and curveball but doesn't always throw strikes. When he misses the strike zone, he tends to get frazzled and throw his heater down the middle. He is more effective against righties.

Major League Pitching Register

	W	L	ERA	G	S	IP	H	ER	BB	SO
78 NL	0	2	8.31	5	0	13.0	17	12	11	8
79 NL	1	1	2.93	5	0	30.2	28	10	12	25
80 NL	0	1	5.79	6	0	9.1	9	6	10	7
81 AL	2	11	5.24	20	0	91.0	84	53	51	49
82 AL	0	0	6.75	2	0	6.2	5	5	9	8
83 AL	9	5	3.14	37	1	157.2	110	55	71	129
84 AL	11	10	3.48	31	0	168.1	146	65	79	118
85 AL	5	6	5.59	31	0	95.0	96	59	48	82
86 NL	2	3	2.70	46	4	73.1	64	22	44	72
87 AL	8	1	3.94	47	4	112.0	100	49	47	110
88 AL	8	4	3.96	57	2	100.0	74	44	61	99
89 AL	9	3	3.48	56	3	106.0	96	41	47	93
90 AL	8	5	3.41	51	0	100.1	85	38	58	77
91 NL	0	3	2.24	49	17	64.1	43	16	20	53
92 NL	1	5	5.13	28	1	33.1	35	19	16	19
92 AL	1	4	5.64	19	0	44.2	42	28	20	26
Life	67	62	3.90	490	32	1205.1	1034	522	604	975
3 AVE	4	4	3.75	49	6	80.2	68	34	38	58

DAVE BERGMAN

Position: First base; designated hitter
Team: Detroit Tigers
Born: June 6, 1953 Evanston, IL
Height: 6'2" **Weight:** 190 lbs.
Bats: left **Throws:** left
Acquired: Traded from Phillies with Willie Hernandez for Glenn Wilson and John Wockenfuss, 3/84

Player Summary	
Fantasy Value	$1 to $2
Card Value	3¢ to 4¢
Will	provide good defense
Can't	hit for power or average
Expect	some outfield play
Don't Expect	stolen bases

Although he turns 40 in June, Bergman has been able to prolong his big league career because of his versatility. He can play first base, outfield, and designated hitter—or provide a quality lefthanded pinch-hitter. A contact hitter who executes the hit-and-run well, Bergman does not provide much power. He hit his first home run of 1992 on July 4 in a pinch-hitting role against Seattle. It was his first pinch-homer since 1984. Because he no longer runs well, he is a candidate to hit into a double-play—especially because he often produces ground balls. Playing his home games at Tiger Stadium doesn't help, because the infield grass slows grounders.

Major League Batting Register

	BA	G	AB	R	H	2B	3B	HR	RBI	SB
75 AL	.000	7	17	0	0	0	0	0	0	0
77 AL	.250	5	4	1	1	0	0	0	1	0
78 NL	.231	104	186	15	43	5	1	0	12	2
79 NL	.400	13	15	4	6	0	0	1	2	0
80 NL	.256	90	78	12	20	6	1	0	3	1
81 NL	.252	69	151	17	38	9	0	4	14	2
82 NL	.273	100	121	22	33	3	1	4	14	3
83 NL	.286	90	140	16	40	4	1	6	24	2
84 AL	.273	120	271	42	74	8	5	7	44	3
85 AL	.179	69	140	8	25	2	0	3	7	0
86 AL	.231	65	130	14	30	6	1	1	9	0
87 AL	.273	91	172	25	47	7	3	6	22	0
88 AL	.294	116	289	37	85	14	0	5	35	0
89 AL	.268	137	385	38	103	13	1	7	37	1
90 AL	.278	100	205	21	57	10	1	2	26	3
91 AL	.237	86	194	23	46	10	1	7	29	1
92 AL	.232	87	181	17	42	3	0	1	10	1
Life	.258	1349	2679	312	690	100	16	54	289	19
3 AVE	.250	91	193	20	48	8	1	3	22	2

DAMON BERRYHILL

Position: Catcher
Team: Atlanta Braves
Born: Dec. 3, 1963 Laguna, CA
Height: 6' **Weight:** 210 lbs.
Bats: both **Throws:** right
Acquired: Traded from Cubs with Mike Bielecki for Turk Wendell and Yorkis Perez, 9/91

Player Summary	
Fantasy Value	$2 to $4
Card Value	3¢ to 4¢
Will	produce power
Can't	throw out runners regularly
Expect	solid defense
Don't Expect	return to old form

Berryhill found a moment of glory in the '92 World Series, homering to win game one. He proved during 1992 spring training that he had shelved the shoulder problems that nearly shattered his career in Chicago. He not only was able to swing the bat with power from both sides of the plate, he also showed improved ability to snare would-be basestealers. Alternating with Greg Olson while with Atlanta last year, Berryhill got off to a good start in 1992 with a half-dozen homers before the All-Star break. He handled all the Braves catching duties in the stretch run and in the postseason because Olson was on the disabled list. Berryhill's strengths are calling good games, handling pitchers, and blocking pitches. Before his ailments, he was respected around the league for nailing his share of runners. He nailed 20 while allowing 71 in 1992, however. At bat, he had a .268 on-base average and a .384 slugging percentage.

Major League Batting Register

	BA	G	AB	R	H	2B	3B	HR	RBI	SB
87 NL	.179	12	28	2	5	1	0	0	1	0
88 NL	.259	95	309	19	80	19	1	7	38	1
89 NL	.257	91	334	37	86	13	0	5	41	1
90 NL	.189	17	53	6	10	4	0	1	9	0
91 NL	.188	63	160	13	30	7	0	5	14	1
92 NL	.228	101	307	21	70	16	1	10	43	0
Life	.236	379	1191	98	281	60	2	28	146	3
2 AVE	.214	82	234	17	50	12	1	8	29	1

DANTE BICHETTE

Position: Outfield
Team: Colorado Rockies
Born: Nov. 18, 1963 West Palm Beach, FL
Height: 6'3" **Weight:** 212 lbs.
Bats: right **Throws:** right
Acquired: Traded from Brewers for Kevin Reimer, 11/92

Player Summary	
Fantasy Value	$4 to $10
Card Value	3¢ to 4¢
Will	strike out frequently
Can't	show patience at bat
Expect	excellent outfield play
Don't Expect	high average

Bichette gets a chance to test the Mile High air during the Rockies' first season. After being pegged for years as an impatient, first-ball, fastball hitter whose average suffered as a consequence, he caught fire in the first half of the 1992 season. That earned him a share of Milwaukee's right field job, in a right-left platoon with Darryl Hamilton. Though Bichette still strikes out (74 times in '92) far more often than he walks (16 times in '92), he is not as anxious at the plate. He waits on pitches better and avoids the tendency to swing at everything. A dead pull hitter who fairs better against righties than southpaws, he is still inclined to swing at balls out of the strike zone. He compiled a .318 on-base average and a .406 slugging percentage in 1992. He has always had excellent defensive skills, and his arm was one of the best in the AL. He should continue to chalk up more than his share of assists.

Major League Batting Register

	BA	G	AB	R	H	2B	3B	HR	RBI	SB
88 AL	.261	21	46	1	12	2	0	0	8	0
89 AL	.210	48	138	13	29	7	0	3	15	3
90 AL	.255	109	349	40	89	15	1	15	53	5
91 AL	.238	134	445	53	106	18	3	15	59	14
92 AL	.287	112	387	37	111	27	2	5	41	18
Life	.254	424	1365	144	347	69	6	38	176	40
3 AVE	.259	118	394	43	102	20	2	12	51	12

MIKE BIELECKI

Position: Pitcher
Team: Cleveland Indians
Born: July 31, 1959 Baltimore, MD
Height: 6'3" **Weight:** 195 lbs.
Bats: right **Throws:** right
Acquired: Signed as a free agent, 12/92

Player Summary	
Fantasy Value	$2 to $6
Card Value	3¢ to 4¢
Will	keep batters guessing
Can't	avoid yielding hits
Expect	improved ERA
Don't Expect	20 wins

After winning a spring training duel with Pete Smith for the No. 5 spot in Atlanta's starting rotation last year, Bielecki adopted well to swing shift. Often skipped in the rotation, he took several turns in the bullpen between starts—and also went for long periods without pitching at all. He did surprisingly well, maintaining an ERA below 3.00 after taking a career mark of 4.19 into the campaign. Bielecki's season ended on July 28, however, when he tore a ligament in his elbow while pitching. When healthy, he relies on good control of his fastball, split-finger fastball, curve, and changeup to keep runners off base. Therefore, if he is going to win, he must give up less than one hit per inning, which is sometimes a problem for him. Opponents in '92 compiled a .254 batting average, a .315 on-base percentage, and a .360 slugging percentage.

Major League Pitching Register

	W	L	ERA	G	CG	IP	H	ER	BB	SO
84 NL	0	0	0.00	4	0	4.1	4	0	0	1
85 NL	2	3	4.53	12	0	45.2	45	23	31	22
86 NL	6	11	4.66	31	0	148.2	149	77	83	83
87 NL	2	3	4.73	8	2	45.2	43	24	12	25
88 NL	2	2	3.35	19	0	48.1	55	18	16	33
89 NL	18	7	3.14	33	4	212.1	187	74	81	147
90 NL	8	11	4.93	36	0	168.0	188	92	70	103
91 NL	13	11	4.46	41	0	173.2	171	86	56	75
92 NL	2	4	2.57	19	1	80.2	77	23	27	62
Life	53	52	4.05	203	7	927.1	919	417	376	551
3 AVE	8	9	4.28	32	0	140.1	145	67	51	80

CRAIG BIGGIO

Position: Second base
Team: Houston Astros
Born: Dec. 14, 1965 Smithtown, NY
Height: 5'11" **Weight:** 180 lbs.
Bats: right **Throws:** right
Acquired: First-round pick in 6/87 free-agent draft

Player Summary	
Fantasy Value	$10 to $14
Card Value	3¢ to 4¢
Will	steal bases
Can't	hit many homers
Expect	stellar career
Don't Expect	return to catching

Never again will Biggio be plagued with the old baseball cliche: "He's fast for a catcher." He's fast—period. Because his speed was better than his throwing arm, the Astros made him their second baseman in 1992. Helped in the switch by incumbent infielders Rafael Ramirez and Casey Candaele, Biggio did not feel comfortable until the season was a month old. By July 4, he had made only four errors and was not letting his offense suffer, leading the league in runs scored. A good leadoff man, he draws more than his share of walks, bunts for base hits, beats out grounders, and is always a threat to steal. Biggio was hitting .284 at the All-Star break and was selected to the NL team for the second year in a row (he went as a catcher in '91). His .295 batting average was a team high in '91, when he had 48 multihit games. A high school shortstop, Biggio also was an All-American catcher at Seton Hall.

Major League Batting Register

	BA	G	AB	R	H	2B	3B	HR	RBI	SB
88 NL	.211	50	123	14	26	6	1	3	5	6
89 NL	.257	134	443	64	114	21	2	13	60	21
90 NL	.276	150	555	53	153	24	2	4	42	25
91 NL	.295	149	546	79	161	23	4	4	46	19
92 NL	.277	162	613	96	170	32	3	6	39	38
Life	.274	645	2280	306	624	106	12	30	192	109
3 AVE	.282	154	571	76	161	26	3	5	42	27

BUD BLACK

Position: Pitcher
Team: San Francisco Giants
Born: June 30, 1957 San Mateo, CA
Height: 6'2" **Weight:** 185 lbs.
Bats: left **Throws:** left
Acquired: Signed as a free agent, 11/90

Player Summary

Fantasy Value	$7 to $10
Card Value	3¢ to 4¢
Will	start frequently
Can't	win ERA crown
Expect	12 to 15 wins
Don't Expect	many Ks

In his first National League season in 1991, Black led the National League with 16 losses. He blamed a bad elbow and strained forearm muscle—compensating in '92 by modifying his between-starts regimen. The result was an 8-2 record and 2.90 ERA by July 16. Black won seven straight Candlestick Park decisions (with a 1.29 ERA). He usually has good control of a slider, change, two heaters, and a curve that can make batters look like amateurs. Not a strikeout pitcher, he has some games where the walks and strikeouts are about equal. He gives up slightly less than one hit per inning. Opponents compiled a .263 batting average, a .321 on-base average, and a .422 slugging percentage in 1992. He keeps runners close. A fine fielder, he didn't make an error during the entire 1991 season.

Major League Pitching Register

	W	L	ERA	G	CG	IP	H	ER	BB	SO
81 AL	0	0	0.00	2	0	1.0	2	0	3	0
82 AL	4	6	4.58	22	0	88.1	92	45	34	40
83 AL	10	7	3.79	24	3	161.1	159	68	43	58
84 AL	17	12	3.12	35	8	257.0	226	89	64	140
85 AL	10	15	4.33	33	5	205.2	216	99	59	122
86 AL	5	10	3.20	56	0	121.0	100	43	43	68
87 AL	8	6	3.60	29	0	122.1	126	49	35	61
88 AL	4	4	5.00	33	0	81.0	82	45	34	63
89 AL	12	11	3.36	33	6	222.1	213	83	52	88
90 AL	13	11	3.57	32	5	206.2	171	82	61	106
91 NL	12	16	3.99	34	3	214.1	201	95	71	104
92 NL	10	12	3.97	28	2	177.0	178	78	59	82
Life	105	110	3.76	361	32	1858.0	1776	776	558	932
3 AVE	12	13	3.84	31	3	199.1	187	85	64	97

LANCE BLANKENSHIP

Position: Infield; outfield
Team: Oakland Athletics
Born: Dec. 6, 1963, Portland, Ore.
Height: 6' **Weight:** 185 lbs.
Bats: right **Throws:** right
Acquired: 10th-round pick in 6/86 free-agent draft

Player Summary

Fantasy Value	$2 to $4
Card Value	3¢ to 4¢
Will	provide good defense
Can't	hit above .255
Expect	many deep counts
Don't Expect	more than 60 RBI

In his first full big league season, Blankenship played a vital role as an all-purpose player for Oakland in 1992. Never one with a big stick, his best previous year in pro ball came in 1988 with Tacoma of the Pacific Coast League, where he hit .265 in 131 games. Always a good fielder, he was named the third baseman on The Sporting News All-America team in 1985 from the University of California, and has made appearances at shortstop and in the outfield. In 1988, he led Pacific Coast league second basemen in assists while sporting a .969 fielding average. He got off to a good start last season, with a .253 average and 15 doubles (ranking among the league's leaders) in his first 70 games. He has a good eye, and walks more than he whiffs—an asset for a player who generally does not hit for average. He compiled a .393 on-base average and a .341 slugging percentage in 1992. His average is about the same against lefties and righties.

Major League Batting Register

	BA	G	AB	R	H	2B	3B	HR	RBI	SB
88 AL	.000	10	3	1	0	0	0	0	0	0
89 AL	.232	58	125	22	29	5	1	1	4	5
90 AL	.191	86	136	18	26	3	0	0	10	3
91 AL	.249	90	185	33	46	8	0	3	21	12
92 AL	.241	123	349	59	84	24	1	3	34	21
Life	.232	367	798	133	185	40	2	7	69	41
2 AVE	.243	107	267	46	65	16	1	3	28	17

JEFF BLAUSER

Position: Shortstop
Team: Atlanta Braves
Born: Nov. 8, 1965 Los Gatos, CA
Height: 6'1" **Weight:** 180 lbs.
Bats: right **Throws:** right
Acquired: First-round pick in secondary phase of 6/84 free-agent draft

Player Summary

Fantasy Value	$5 to $8
Card Value	3¢ to 4¢
Will	play part time
Can't	hit for high average
Expect	some fielding mistakes
Don't Expect	power

For Blauser, the 1992 All-Star break came around too soon: On July 12—the last day before the break—he hit three homers. Although he had seven homers and 27 RBI in his first 176 at bats, his .210 average was a bitter disappointment. He had been working at becoming a more selective hitter. He still strikes out far more than he walks and takes too many pitches. Although he's a steady fielder at shortstop, his best position, he could not match the good hands, range, or arm of Rafael Belliard, who spent most of last summer playing that position for the Braves. Blauser did get into some games at second base, pinch-hit frequently, and stood ready to back Terry Pendleton at third—a position he played (though not well) in the past. Blauser started all the postseason games at shortstop. A clubhouse comic, he also helped keep the team loose during the heat of the pennant race.

Major League Batting Register

	BA	G	AB	R	H	2B	3B	HR	RBI	SB
87 NL	.242	51	165	11	40	6	3	2	15	7
88 NL	.239	18	67	7	16	3	1	2	7	0
89 NL	.270	142	456	63	123	24	2	12	46	5
90 NL	.269	115	386	46	104	24	3	8	39	3
91 NL	.259	129	352	49	91	14	3	11	54	5
92 NL	.262	123	343	61	90	19	3	14	46	5
Life	.262	578	1769	237	464	90	15	49	207	25
3 AVE	.264	122	360	52	95	19	3	11	46	4

BERT BLYLEVEN

Position: Pitcher
Team: Minnesota Twins
Born: April 6, 1951 Zeist, Netherlands
Height: 6'3" **Weight:** 220 lbs.
Bats: right **Throws:** right
Acquired: Signed as a free agent, 1/93

Player Summary

Fantasy Value	$2 to $4
Card Value	5¢ to 10¢
Will	remain in rotation
Can't	prevent rival home runs
Expect	steady diet of curveballs
Don't Expect	glory days

For 22 summers, Blyleven has thrown his famous curveball for the Indians, the Twins twice, the Rangers, the Pirates, and the Angels. He missed all of 1991 after rotator cuff surgery and began '92 in the minors. He won his first three decisions after returning to California. While not as impenetrable as he once was, he still has excellent control, a curveball that looks like a balloon, and a decent low-and-away fastball. He often looks like he's setting hitters up for the heater but still brings the bender. Because he's always around the plate, Blyleven surrenders many homers. He yielded a record 50 in 1986.

Major League Pitching Register

	W	L	ERA	G	CG	IP	H	ER	BB	SO
70 AL	10	9	3.18	27	5	164.0	143	58	47	135
71 AL	16	15	2.81	38	17	278.1	267	87	59	224
72 AL	17	17	2.73	39	11	287.1	247	87	69	228
73 AL	20	17	2.52	40	25	325.0	296	91	67	258
74 AL	17	17	2.66	37	19	281.0	244	83	77	249
75 AL	15	10	3.00	35	20	275.2	219	92	84	233
76 AL	13	16	2.87	36	18	297.2	283	95	81	219
77 AL	14	12	2.72	30	15	234.2	181	71	69	182
78 NL	14	10	3.03	34	11	243.2	217	82	66	182
79 NL	12	5	3.60	37	4	237.1	238	95	92	172
80 NL	8	13	3.82	34	5	216.2	219	92	59	168
81 AL	11	7	2.88	20	9	159.1	145	51	40	107
82 AL	2	2	4.87	4	0	20.1	16	11	11	19
83 AL	7	10	3.91	24	5	156.1	160	68	44	123
84 AL	19	7	2.87	33	12	245.0	204	78	74	170
85 AL	17	16	3.16	37	24	293.2	264	103	75	206
86 AL	17	14	4.01	36	16	271.2	262	121	58	215
87 AL	15	12	4.01	37	8	267.0	249	119	101	196
88 AL	10	17	5.43	33	7	207.1	240	125	51	145
89 AL	17	5	2.73	33	8	241.0	225	73	44	131
90 AL	8	7	5.24	23	2	134.0	163	78	25	69
92 AL	8	12	4.74	25	1	133.0	150	70	29	70
Life	287	250	3.31	692	242	4970.0	4632	1830	1322	3701
2 AVE	8	10	4.99	24	2	134.0	157	74	27	70

MIKE BODDICKER

Position: Pitcher
Team: Kansas City Royals
Born: Aug. 23, 1957 Cedar Rapids, IA
Height: 5'11" **Weight:** 186 lbs.
Bats: right **Throws:** right
Acquired: Signed as a free agent, 11/90

Player Summary	
Fantasy Value	$1 to $2
Card Value	3¢ to 4¢
Will	toss softly
Can't	strike out many batters
Expect	continued bullpen role
Don't Expect	return to old form

Boddicker's tenure as a starting pitcher in the major leagues may have ended when Rickey Henderson rammed him with a line drive on Sept. 25, 1991. When Boddicker returned to the Royals in 1992, he was assigned to middle relief by manager Hal McRae. Boddicker did not shine; his ERA was off, and he was 1-4. He gave up more than one hit per inning, and his strikeout-to-walk ratio was almost equal. Such statistics may be the result of a back problem that sent him to the disabled list in July. Relying on a good fastball and the ability to change speeds, Boddicker's best pitch is his "foshball," a blooping fastball that behaves like a screwball. He had posted wins in double figures for nine consecutive seasons before 1992.

Major League Pitching Register

	W	L	ERA	G	S	IP	H	ER	BB	SO
80 AL	0	1	6.14	1	0	7.1	6	5	5	4
81 AL	0	0	4.76	2	0	5.2	6	3	2	2
82 AL	1	0	3.51	7	0	25.2	25	10	12	20
83 AL	16	8	2.77	27	0	179.0	141	55	52	120
84 AL	20	11	2.79	34	0	261.1	218	81	81	128
85 AL	12	17	4.07	32	0	203.1	227	92	89	135
86 AL	14	12	4.70	33	0	218.1	214	114	74	175
87 AL	10	12	4.18	33	0	226.0	212	105	78	152
88 AL	13	15	3.39	36	0	236.0	234	89	77	156
89 AL	15	11	4.00	34	0	211.2	217	94	71	145
90 AL	17	8	3.36	34	0	228.0	225	85	69	143
91 AL	12	12	4.08	30	0	180.2	188	82	59	79
92 AL	1	4	4.98	29	3	86.2	92	48	37	47
Life	131	111	3.75	332	3	2069.2	2005	863	706	1306
3 AVE	10	8	3.91	31	1	165.1	168	72	55	90

JOE BOEVER

Position: Pitcher
Team: Houston Astros
Born: Oct. 4, 1960 St. Louis, MO
Height: 6'1" **Weight:** 200 lbs.
Bats: right **Throws:** right
Acquired: Signed as a free agent, 1/92

Player Summary	
Fantasy Value	$2 to $4
Card Value	3¢ to 4¢
Will	lean on palmball
Can't	always throw strikes
Expect	middle-relief work
Don't Expect	closer role

After signing a minor league contract with the Houston Astros, Boever won a job during spring training and continued pitching well after the 1992 season opened. By July 4, the palmball specialist was leading the league in both appearances and stranding inherited runners. His palmball often serves as a change, keeping batters off balance, and breaks like an overhand curve. However, he can't always throw it for strikes. His strikeout-to-walk ratio is unsatisfactory, so he'll have to continue to give up less than a hit per inning in order to keep his ERA respectable. Opponents had a .248 batting average, a .324 on-base average, and a .310 slugging percentage in 1992. When used as a closer in previous seasons, he led four leagues in saves. He posted a big league peak in that department with 21 for the 1989 Braves.

Major League Pitching Register

	W	L	ERA	G	S	IP	H	ER	BB	SO
85 NL	0	0	4.41	13	0	16.1	17	8	4	20
86 NL	0	1	1.66	11	0	21.2	19	4	11	8
87 NL	1	0	7.36	14	0	18.1	29	15	12	18
88 NL	0	2	1.77	16	1	20.1	12	4	1	7
89 NL	4	11	3.94	66	21	82.1	78	36	34	68
90 NL	3	6	3.36	67	14	88.1	77	33	51	75
91 NL	3	5	3.84	68	0	98.1	90	42	54	89
92 NL	3	6	2.51	81	2	111.1	103	31	45	67
Life	14	31	3.41	336	38	457.0	425	173	212	352
3 AVE	3	6	3.20	72	5	99.1	90	35	50	77

WADE BOGGS

Position: Third base
Team: New York Yankees
Born: June 15, 1958 Omaha, NE
Height: 6'2" **Weight:** 197 lbs.
Bats: left **Throws:** right
Acquired: Signed as a free agent, 12/92

Player Summary	
Fantasy Value	$20 to $30
Card Value	8¢ to 12¢
Will	be future Hall of Famer
Can't	win homer crown
Expect	bid for batting crown
Don't Expect	dazzling defense

Boggs helps plug a gap for the Yankees, his rivals for 11 years as a Red Sox. He took six batting titles into the 1992 campaign, but after collecting at least 200 hits a season from 1983 to '89, he has failed to reach that level in each of the last three years. Unhappy at Boston's reluctance to sign him to a long-term contract during 1992 spring training, the eight-time All-Star pressed at the plate for the first time in his career. The result was a .259 batting average, a .353 on-base average, and a .358 slugging percentage. He tried glasses and contact lenses and even shaved his trademark mustache as corrective measures. Superb against fastballs, Boggs has a hard time handling curves from lefties. A lighter bat helped, but age may be starting to take its toll. In the field, he has limited range but a strong, accurate arm.

Major League Batting Register

	BA	G	AB	R	H	2B	3B	HR	RBI	SB
82 AL	.349	104	338	51	118	14	1	5	44	1
83 AL	.361	153	582	100	210	44	7	5	74	3
84 AL	.325	158	625	109	203	31	4	6	55	3
85 AL	.368	161	653	107	240	42	3	8	78	2
86 AL	.357	149	580	107	207	47	2	8	71	0
87 AL	.363	147	551	108	200	40	6	24	89	1
88 AL	.366	155	584	128	214	45	6	5	58	2
89 AL	.330	156	621	113	205	51	7	3	54	2
90 AL	.302	155	619	89	187	44	5	6	63	0
91 AL	.332	144	546	93	181	42	2	8	51	1
92 AL	.259	143	514	62	133	22	4	7	50	1
Life	.338	1625	6213	1067	2098	422	47	85	687	16
3 AVE	.298	147	560	81	167	36	4	7	55	1

TOM BOLTON

Position: Pitcher
Team: Detroit Tigers
Born: May 6, 1962 Nashville, TN
Height: 6'3" **Weight:** 175 lbs.
Bats: left **Throws:** left
Acquired: Signed as a free agent, 12/92

Player Summary	
Fantasy Value	$1 to $2
Card Value	3¢ to 4¢
Will	get lots of ground balls
Can't	keep baserunners close
Expect	wins, with control
Don't Expect	many Ks

Bolton helps a struggling Tigers bullpen. When Tom Browning's season ended with a July 1 knee injury, the Cincinnati Reds scoured the market for another experienced southpaw who could fill the void in the rotation. They came up with Bolton, a lefty used as both a starter and reliever during his five-year tenure with the Boston Red Sox. Bolton's 1990 season impressed the Reds, who noted that Fenway Park is normally a graveyard for southpaws. Much better against lefthanded batters, he keeps his club close with a sinking fastball, curve, and changeup. Generally his control is good, but he is known to get into trouble with walks from time to time. When he's right, he gets most of his outs on ground balls. He is not regarded as a strikeout pitcher. In 1992, NL opponents compiled a .284 batting average, a .368 on-base percentage, and a .464 slugging percentage. Bolton is a fair fielder but below average in keeping runners close.

Major League Pitching Register

	W	L	ERA	G	CG	IP	H	ER	BB	SO
87 AL	1	0	4.38	29	0	61.2	83	30	27	49
88 AL	1	3	4.75	28	0	30.1	35	16	14	21
89 AL	0	4	8.31	4	0	17.1	21	16	10	9
90 AL	10	5	3.38	21	3	119.2	111	45	47	65
91 AL	8	9	5.24	25	0	110.0	136	64	51	64
92 AL	1	2	3.41	21	0	29.0	34	11	14	23
92 NL	3	3	5.24	16	0	46.1	52	27	23	27
Life	24	26	4.54	144	3	414.1	472	209	186	258
3 AVE	7	6	4.34	28	1	101.1	111	49	45	60

BARRY BONDS

Position: Outfield
Team: San Francisco Giants
Born: July 24, 1964 Riverside, CA
Height: 6'1" **Weight:** 185 lbs.
Bats: left **Throws:** left
Acquired: Signed as a free agent, 12/92

Player Summary	
Fantasy Value	$45 to $55
Card Value	15¢ to 25¢
Will	provide Gold Glove defense
Can't	keep out of trouble
Expect	30-30 performance
Don't Expect	Triple Crown

Like father, like son: Barry Bonds is one of the best players in the game, and one of the most temperamental. Unlike dad, Barry makes $7 million a year. Fast, powerful, and a superb defender, the former Pirate was the National League MVP in 1990, when he was the first player to bat .300, hit 30 homers, drive in 100 runs, score 100, and swipe 50 bases in the same season. His pace was off slightly in '91, but he still finished second to Terry Pendleton in a tight MVP race. Bonds won his second MVP Award in '92 even though he spent time on the DL with a strained muscle in his right rib cage. He has good power to both gaps and he can pull the ball against any pitcher. He and dad Bobby are the only father-and-son members of the 30-30 club, while Bonds and Eric Davis are the only players to hit 30 homers and steal 50 bases in a season. A two-way star, Bonds is the game's best defensive left fielder.

Major League Batting Register

	BA	G	AB	R	H	2B	3B	HR	RBI	SB
86 NL	.223	113	413	72	92	26	3	16	48	36
87 NL	.261	150	551	99	144	34	9	25	59	32
88 NL	.283	144	538	97	152	30	5	24	58	17
89 NL	.248	159	580	96	144	34	6	19	58	32
90 NL	.301	151	519	104	156	32	3	33	114	52
91 NL	.292	153	510	95	149	28	5	25	116	43
92 NL	.311	140	473	109	147	36	5	34	103	39
Life	.275	1010	3584	672	984	220	36	176	556	251
3 AVE	.301	148	501	103	151	32	4	31	111	45

RICKY BONES

Position: Pitcher
Team: Milwaukee Brewers
Born: April 7, 1969 Salinas, Puerto Rico
Height: 6' **Weight:** 190 lbs.
Bats: right **Throws:** right
Acquired: Traded from Padres with Jose Valentin and Matt Mieske for Gary Sheffield, 3/91

Player Summary	
Fantasy Value	$3 to $6
Card Value	5¢ to 10¢
Will	fire hard strikes
Can't	find consistency
Expect	improvement with experience
Don't Expect	many walks

In his first full big league season, Bones became the No. 4 starter in the rotation of the Milwaukee Brewers. Acquired in the spring training trade of Gary Sheffield, Bones split his first 12 decisions against American League hitters. He had made his big league bow the previous Aug. 11, when he worked seven scoreless innings against Cincinnati. A hard-throwing righthander signed by San Diego as an undrafted free agent at age 17, Bones has been a hot-and-cold performer during his brief career. From Sept. 1 to Sept. 13, 1991, for example, he went 3-0 with a 1.92 ERA. But he finished his rookie year with a 4-6 record and 4.83 log. He finished the 1992 season by allowing opponents to compile a .264 batting average, a .321 on-base percentage, and a .448 slugging percentage. Throughout his pro career, which began in 1986, he's demonstrated good control and a 2-1 ratio of strikeouts to walks. In 1991 at Triple-A Las Vegas, he went 8-6 with a 4.22 ERA, 43 walks, and 95 strikeouts in 136⅔ innings pitched.

Major League Pitching Register

	W	L	ERA	G	CG	IP	H	ER	BB	SO
91 NL	4	6	4.83	11	0	54.0	57	29	18	31
92 AL	9	10	4.57	31	0	163.1	169	83	48	65
Life	13	16	4.64	42	0	217.1	226	112	66	96

BOBBY BONILLA

Position: Outfield
Team: New York Mets
Born: Feb. 23, 1963 New York, NY
Height: 6'3" **Weight:** 230 lbs.
Bats: both **Throws:** right
Acquired: Signed as a free agent, 12/91

Player Summary	
Fantasy Value	$28 to $36
Card Value	10¢ to 15¢
Will	hit for power
Can't	win Triple Crown
Expect	numerous multiple-RBI games
Don't Expect	return to third

After signing a huge contract to play for the Mets, Bonilla suffered through the toughest season of his career in 1992. His slow start produced a chorus of boos that he answered by wearing earphones. He was lifted late in games for defensive purposes. Then he incurred a two-game suspension for charging Chicago pitcher Shawn Boskie and knocking umpire Larry Poncino off his feet in the ensuing brawl. Later, Bonilla cracked a rib while diving for a ball. He did have a career-best six RBI in a game and homered in three straight games for the first time ever in 1992. A switch-hitter who is better batting left, Bonilla has power to both fields. He's a fastball hitter who likes the ball down, but has a tendency to swing too hard at heat. He sometimes is fooled by slow stuff.

Major League Batting Register

	BA	G	AB	R	H	2B	3B	HR	RBI	SB
86 AL	.269	75	234	27	63	10	2	2	26	4
86 NL	.240	63	192	28	46	6	2	1	17	4
87 NL	.300	141	466	58	140	33	3	15	77	3
88 NL	.274	159	584	87	160	32	7	24	100	3
89 NL	.281	163	616	96	173	37	10	24	86	8
90 NL	.280	160	625	112	175	39	7	32	120	4
91 NL	.302	157	577	102	174	44	6	18	100	2
92 NL	.249	128	438	62	109	23	0	19	70	4
Life	.279	1046	3732	572	1040	224	37	135	596	32
3 AVE	.279	148	547	92	153	35	4	23	97	3

PAT BORDERS

Position: Catcher
Team: Toronto Blue Jays
Born: May 14, 1963 Columbus, OH
Height: 6'2" **Weight:** 205 lbs.
Bats: right **Throws:** right
Acquired: Sixth-round pick in 6/82 free-agent draft

Player Summary	
Fantasy Value	$4 to $8
Card Value	4¢ to 6¢
Will	throw out runners
Can't	steal bases
Expect	No. 1 job
Don't Expect	consistent power

Many experts thought that Borders was long overdue for a good year in 1992, but it didn't come off. Finally, in the 1992 World Series, he broke through, notching a .450 batting average and the fall classic MVP. He had an average first half in '92 for the Blue Jays, falling far short of expectations. He did, however, wrest the starting catcher's position from Greg Myers, who was traded to California in July. Borders still strikes out far more than he walks, though not at his appalling 4-to-1 ratio of 1991. He is anxious at the plate, swings wildly at certain pitches, and often grounds into double plays if he doesn't fan. He had a .290 on-base percentage and a .385 slugging average in 1992. A converted third baseman who is only satisfactory as a receiver, Borders compensates somewhat with a strong throwing arm. Showing more patience at the plate should pave the way for a repeat of his 1990 numbers: .286, 15 homers, and 49 runs batted in.

Major League Batting Register

	BA	G	AB	R	H	2B	3B	HR	RBI	SB
88 AL	.273	56	154	15	42	6	3	5	21	0
89 AL	.257	94	241	22	62	11	1	3	29	2
90 AL	.286	125	346	36	99	24	2	15	49	0
91 AL	.244	105	291	22	71	17	0	5	36	0
92 AL	.242	138	480	47	116	26	2	13	53	1
Life	.258	518	1512	142	390	84	8	41	188	3
3 AVE	.256	123	372	35	95	22	1	11	46	0

MIKE BORDICK

Position: Shortstop
Team: Oakland Athletics
Born: July 21, 1965 Marquette, MI
Height: 5'11" **Weight:** 175 lbs.
Bats: right **Throws:** right
Acquired: Signed as a free agent, 7/86

Player Summary	
Fantasy Value	$4 to $8
Card Value	3¢ to 4¢
Will	turn double plays
Can't	hit homers
Expect	steady improvement at bat
Don't Expect	many .300 seasons

Bordick gets his chance to win the Oakland shortstop job. Although he took a .229 career average into 1992, he became Oakland's biggest surprise. Hitting .342 as late as June 14, he slumped slightly but still took a .314 mark into the All-Star break. He credited his success to tips from batting coach Doug Rader, who urged Bordick to abandon his habit of shifting in the batter's box. Rader recommended that Bordick use the wide-spread stance that he used during his best minor league season. As he began to produce, pitchers adjusted and began throwing him lots of different pitches. He was forced to adapt to the new patterns. Bordick strikes out slightly more than he walks, evidence that more patience at the plate will lead to more points on his batting average. He had a .358 on-base percentage and a .371 slugging average in 1992. A better-than-average fielder, he is good at turning double plays. He filled in for injured Oakland shortstop Walt Weiss in both 1991 and 1992.

Major League Batting Register

	BA	G	AB	R	H	2B	3B	HR	RBI	SB
90 AL	.071	25	14	0	1	0	0	0	0	0
91 AL	.238	90	235	21	56	5	1	0	21	3
92 AL	.300	154	504	62	151	19	4	3	48	12
Life	.276	269	753	83	208	24	5	3	69	15
2 AVE	.280	122	370	42	104	12	3	2	35	8

CHRIS BOSIO

Position: Pitcher
Team: Seattle Mariners
Born: April 3, 1963 Carmichael, CA
Height: 6'3" **Weight:** 225 lbs.
Bats: right **Throws:** right
Acquired: Signed as a free agent, 12/92

Player Summary	
Fantasy Value	$7 to $14
Card Value	3¢ to 4¢
Will	mix pitches well
Can't	keep runners close
Expect	wins in double figures
Don't Expect	ERA title

Bosio's career has been plagued by injury and hot-headedness. When he has control of his slider, his changeup, and his sinking, rising, and split-fingered fastballs, he is usually effective. A control pitcher who doesn't yield many walks, he can be taken deep. He is almost unhittable when he works the corners of the plate with his hard stuff, but he sometimes has had problems with his off-speed deliveries. He always tries to throw a strike on the first pitch. Although knee problems hampered his progress in 1990, he won a combined 29 times in 1989 and 1991. In 1992, he allowed opposing batters to compile a .254 batting average, a .291 on-base average, and a .376 slugging percentage; lefties had a .273 batting average and righties compiled a .236 average. Bosio is an average fielder with a below-average pickoff move. He's also been hurt in the past by his own temperamental displays.

Major League Pitching Register

	W	L	ERA	G	CG	IP	H	ER	BB	SO
86 AL	0	4	7.01	10	0	34.2	41	27	13	29
87 AL	11	8	5.24	46	2	170.0	187	99	50	150
88 AL	7	15	3.36	38	9	182.0	190	68	38	84
89 AL	15	10	2.95	33	8	234.2	225	77	48	173
90 AL	4	9	4.00	20	4	132.2	131	59	38	76
91 AL	14	10	3.25	32	5	204.2	187	74	58	117
92 AL	16	6	3.62	33	4	231.1	223	93	44	120
Life	67	62	3.76	212	32	1190.0	1184	497	289	749
3 AVE	11	8	3.58	28	4	189.2	180	75	47	104

SHAWN BOSKIE

Position: Pitcher
Team: Chicago Cubs
Born: March 28, 1967 Hawthorne, NV
Height: 6'3" **Weight:** 205 lbs.
Bats: right **Throws:** right
Acquired: First-round pick in 1/86 free-agent draft

Player Summary	
Fantasy Value	$2 to $4
Card Value	3¢ to 4¢
Will	give up many homers
Can't	get ERA below 4.00
Expect	good fielding
Don't Expect	20 wins

Boskie was a pain-in-the-neck to the Chicago Cubs last season. Expected to be one of the mainstays of their starting rotation, Boskie managed only a 5-6 record and 3.93 ERA through July 26. He also spent time on the disabled list with a recurring neck muscle problem. A hard thrower who has had persistent control trouble, Boskie is a converted third baseman who is quick off the mound, has good hands, and guns the ball to any base. His good move keeps runners close. He hasn't forgotten how to hit and he's not bad with a bat. On the mound, however, he must nip the corners with his fastball, curve, and changeup while keeping his pitches down. In 1992, opponents compiled a .284 batting average, a .354 on-base percentage, and a .482 slugging average. Lefties batted .303, while righties hit .259. Batters hit too many flies against him—a fatal flaw for a pitcher working in Wrigley Field. In his first 11 games last year, Boskie yielded seven round-trippers.

Major League Pitching Register

	W	L	ERA	G	CG	IP	H	ER	BB	SO
90 NL	5	6	3.69	15	1	97.2	99	40	31	49
91 NL	4	9	5.23	28	0	129.0	150	75	52	62
92 NL	5	11	5.01	23	0	91.2	96	51	36	39
Life	14	26	4.69	66	1	318.1	345	166	119	150
3 AVE	5	9	4.69	22	0	106.1	115	55	40	50

DARYL BOSTON

Position: Outfield
Team: Colorado Rockies
Born: Jan. 4, 1963 Cincinnati, OH
Height: 6'3" **Weight:** 195 lbs.
Bats: left **Throws:** left
Acquired: Signed as a free agent, 12/92

Player Summary	
Fantasy Value	$2 to $5
Card Value	3¢ to 4¢
Will	use speed on bases
Can't	hit for power consistently
Expect	part-time role
Don't Expect	high average

Boston is a good veteran insurance policy for the Colorado outfield. He had to settle for a backup berth, plus pinch-hitting assignments, with the Mets last summer. He simply couldn't break into an outfield occupied by Vince Coleman, Howard Johnson, and Bobby Bonilla. When injuries occurred, however, Boston played well as a swing man. Once a wild swinger, he has developed patience at the plate and can hit to all fields. He compiled a .338 on-base average and a .426 slugging percentage in 1992. His good speed makes him a threat to take an extra base, but he would be more valuable if he stole and bunted more often. He has good range in the outfield, where he has one of the team's better throwing arms. He began his pro ball career in 1981 with the White Sox and reached the majors three years later.

Major League Batting Register

	BA	G	AB	R	H	2B	3B	HR	RBI	SB
84 AL	.169	35	83	8	14	3	1	0	3	6
85 AL	.228	95	232	20	53	13	1	3	15	8
86 AL	.266	56	199	29	53	11	3	5	22	9
87 AL	.258	103	337	51	87	21	2	10	29	12
88 AL	.217	105	281	37	61	12	2	15	31	9
89 AL	.252	101	218	34	55	3	4	5	23	7
90 AL	.000	5	1	0	0	0	0	0	0	1
90 NL	.273	115	366	65	100	21	2	12	45	18
91 NL	.275	137	255	40	70	16	4	4	21	15
92 NL	.249	130	289	37	72	14	2	11	35	12
Life	.250	882	2261	321	565	114	21	65	224	97
3 AVE	.266	129	304	47	81	17	3	9	34	15

JEFF BRANTLEY

Position: Pitcher
Team: San Francisco Giants
Born: Sept. 5, 1963 Florence, AL
Height: 5'11" **Weight:** 180 lbs.
Bats: right **Throws:** right
Acquired: Sixth-round pick in 6/85 free-agent draft

Player Summary	
Fantasy Value	$5 to $10
Card Value	3¢ to 4¢
Will	try to vary pitches
Can't	work often with bum shoulder
Expect	few outs on fly balls
Don't Expect	Fireman Award

After spending two years as the top righthanded closer in the San Francisco bullpen, Brantley lost his job to Rod Beck in 1992. In addition to his fastball and curve, Brantley throws a split-fingered fastball taught to him by Giants manager Roger Craig. Even with that pitch, Brantley has cooled somewhat since 1990, when he had 19 saves and a 1.56 ERA while making the NL All-Star Team in his second big league season. He is much more effective against righthanded hitters, though he's tough against anyone with the bases loaded (rivals were 4-for-51 in bases-loaded situations against him through last July 4). In 1992, opponents compiled a .207 batting average, a .307 on-base average, and a .319 slugging percentage. In addition, lefties batted .181 while righties hit .246. Brantley has a good pickoff move, is a good fielder, and is not a bad bunter. He can't pitch every day because he has to guard against the return of past shoulder problems.

Major League Pitching Register

	W	L	ERA	G	S	IP	H	ER	BB	SO
88 NL	0	1	5.66	9	1	20.2	22	13	6	11
89 NL	7	1	4.07	59	0	97.1	101	44	37	69
90 NL	5	3	1.56	55	19	86.2	77	15	33	61
91 NL	5	2	2.45	67	15	95.1	78	26	52	81
92 NL	7	7	2.95	56	7	91.2	67	30	45	86
Life	24	14	2.94	246	42	391.2	345	128	173	308
3 AVE	6	4	2.33	59	14	91.2	74	24	43	76

SID BREAM

Position: First base
Team: Atlanta Braves
Born: Aug. 3, 1960 Carlisle, PA
Height: 6'4" **Weight:** 220 lbs.
Bats: left **Throws:** left
Acquired: Signed as a free agent, 12/90

Player Summary	
Fantasy Value	$5 to $7
Card Value	3¢ to 4¢
Will	play good defense
Can't	run, show old power
Expect	persistent injury problems
Don't Expect	controversy

Bream seems to be settling into the role of an average hitter who can provide fine defense. While he once seemed capable of knocking in 75 to 80 runs a year, his production has decreased with his playing time. Reduced to a left-right platoon with Brian Hunter last summer, Bream has battled knee problems for several seasons. He lost considerable time in 1991 when surgery was necessary. As a result, he is one of the slowest runners in the game. He lasts in the majors because he gives his team stellar defense and strong clubhouse leadership. He is accomplished at short-hopping balls in the dirt, getting the edge on runners with long stretches, and turning the tough 3-6-3 double-play. Bream's future is jeopardized by a continuing lack of power at the plate.

Major League Batting Register

	BA	G	AB	R	H	2B	3B	HR	RBI	SB
83 NL	.182	15	11	0	2	0	0	0	2	0
84 NL	.184	27	49	2	9	3	0	0	6	1
85 NL	.230	50	148	18	34	7	0	6	21	0
86 NL	.268	154	522	73	140	37	5	16	77	13
87 NL	.275	149	516	64	142	25	3	13	65	9
88 NL	.264	148	462	50	122	37	0	10	65	9
89 NL	.222	19	36	3	8	3	0	0	4	0
90 NL	.270	147	389	39	105	23	2	15	67	8
91 NL	.253	91	265	32	67	12	0	11	45	0
92 NL	.261	125	372	30	97	25	1	10	61	6
Life	.262	925	2770	311	726	172	11	81	413	46
3 AVE	.262	121	342	34	90	20	1	12	58	5

GEORGE BRETT

Position: Designated hitter
Team: Kansas City Royals
Born: May 15, 1953 Glendale, WV
Height: 6' **Weight:** 200 lbs.
Bats: left **Throws:** right
Acquired: Second-round pick in 6/71 free-
agent draft

Player Summary	
Fantasy Value	$8 to $12
Card Value	10¢ to 20¢
Will	provide clutch hits
Can't	avoid injuries
Expect	minimal time at first
Don't Expect	another MVP

Brett went 4-for-5 at the end of the season to gain his 3,000th base hit. The only man to win batting titles in three different decades, he is no longer the hitting machine who produced a .390 average and an MVP in 1980. He is, however, a wily veteran who remains a dangerous clutch hitter. Brett began the 1992 season with a 1-for-40 slump, though. He has been a designated hitter since Kansas City signed free agent first baseman Wally Joyner. He spent most of his early years at third before shifting to first in 1987. He has made the AL All-Star team 14 times.

Major League Batting Register

	BA	G	AB	R	H	2B	3B	HR	RBI	SB
73 AL	.125	13	40	2	5	2	0	0	0	0
74 AL	.282	133	457	49	129	21	5	2	47	8
75 AL	.308	159	634	84	195	35	13	11	89	13
76 AL	.333	159	645	94	215	34	14	7	67	21
77 AL	.312	139	564	105	176	32	13	22	88	14
78 AL	.294	128	510	79	150	45	8	9	62	23
79 AL	.329	154	645	119	212	42	20	23	107	17
80 AL	.390	117	449	87	175	33	9	24	118	15
81 AL	.314	89	347	42	109	27	7	6	43	14
82 AL	.301	144	552	101	166	32	9	21	82	6
83 AL	.310	123	464	90	144	38	2	25	93	0
84 AL	.284	104	377	42	107	21	3	13	69	0
85 AL	.335	155	550	108	184	38	5	30	112	9
86 AL	.290	124	441	70	128	28	4	16	73	1
87 AL	.290	115	427	71	124	18	2	22	78	6
88 AL	.306	157	589	90	180	42	3	24	103	14
89 AL	.282	124	457	67	129	26	3	12	80	14
90 AL	.329	142	544	82	179	45	7	14	87	9
91 AL	.255	131	505	77	129	40	2	10	61	2
92 AL	.285	152	592	55	169	35	5	7	61	8
Life	.307	2562	9789	1514	3005	634	134	298	1520	194
3 AVE	.291	142	547	71	159	40	5	10	70	6

GREG BRILEY

Position: Outfield; infield
Team: Seattle Mariners
Born: May 24, 1965 Bethel, NC
Height: 5'8" **Weight:** 165 lbs.
Bats: left **Throws:** right
Acquired: First-round pick in secondary phase of 6/86 free-agent draft

Player Summary	
Fantasy Value	$2 to $4
Card Value	3¢ to 4¢
Will	play at several spots
Can't	reach outfield fences
Expect	frequent stolen base tries
Don't Expect	full-time slot

Although Briley was a solid hitter in the minors, he hit well in the majors only as a 1989 rookie with Seattle. That summer, he hit .266 with 13 homers and 52 RBI. He has lasted because of his versatility and speed; he plays second and third base as well as the outfield and is capable of stealing two-dozen bases if he gets enough playing time. Briley doesn't have the strongest arm, but uses his speed to show excellent range in the outfield, where he also has the ability to get a good jump on fly balls. His baserunning skills are excellent, and he could show them off more by bunting for base hits. Showing more patience at the plate would also help. Although the 5'8" Briley has a tiny strike zone, he rarely waits for the bases on balls he would surely get. In 1992, he had a .290 on-base average and a .400 slugging percentage. He batted .282 against righthanders, and .000, nothing, against lefties.

Major League Batting Register

	BA	G	AB	R	H	2B	3B	HR	RBI	SB
88 AL	.250	13	36	6	9	2	0	1	4	0
89 AL	.266	115	394	52	105	22	4	13	52	11
90 AL	.246	125	337	40	83	18	2	5	29	16
91 AL	.260	139	381	39	99	17	3	2	26	23
92 AL	.275	86	200	18	55	10	0	5	12	9
Life	.260	478	1348	155	351	69	9	26	123	59
3 AVE	.258	117	306	32	79	15	2	4	22	16

HUBIE BROOKS

Position: Designated hitter
Team: California Angels
Born: Sept. 24, 1956 Los Angeles, CA
Height: 6' **Weight:** 205 lbs.
Bats: right **Throws:** right
Acquired: Traded from Mets for Dave Gallagher, 12/91 ●

Player Summary	
Fantasy Value	$3 to $5
Card Value	3¢ to 4¢
Will	decline further
Can't	hit in the clutch
Expect	diminished role
Don't Expect	high average

A move to the designated hitter's spot didn't seem to help Brooks's bat much in 1992, as he was floating precariously above the .200 mark on the eve of the All-Star break. Obviously, the decline in batting numbers was due to the increase in chronological years. Also responsible was a strained neck that resulted in his being placed on the disabled list from June 20 until July 5. Nevertheless, his bat will sometimes show flashes of the pop that led to eight consecutive seasons with homers in double digits. Always an impatient hitter, Brooks strikes out more than he walks. He can no longer be counted on to deliver in the clutch. The Mets' full-time third baseman during the early 1980s, he once generated a 24-game hitting streak in 1984.

Major League Batting Register

	BA	G	AB	R	H	2B	3B	HR	RBI	SB
80 NL	.309	24	81	8	25	2	1	1	10	1
81 NL	.307	98	358	34	110	21	2	4	38	9
82 NL	.249	126	457	40	114	21	2	2	40	6
83 NL	.251	150	586	53	147	18	4	5	58	6
84 NL	.283	153	561	61	159	23	2	16	73	6
85 NL	.269	156	605	67	163	34	7	13	100	6
86 NL	.340	80	306	50	104	18	5	14	58	4
87 NL	.263	112	430	57	113	22	3	14	72	4
88 NL	.279	151	588	61	164	35	2	20	90	7
89 NL	.268	148	542	56	145	30	1	14	70	6
90 NL	.266	153	568	74	151	28	1	20	91	2
91 NL	.238	103	357	48	85	11	1	16	50	3
92 AL	.216	82	306	28	66	13	0	8	36	3
Life	.269	1536	5745	637	1546	276	31	147	786	63
3 AVE	.245	113	410	50	101	17	1	15	59	3

SCOTT BROSIUS

Position: Infield; outfield
Team: Oakland Athletics
Born: Aug. 15, 1966 Hillsboro, OR
Height: 6'1" **Weight:** 185 lbs.
Bats: right **Throws:** right
Acquired: 20th-round pick in 6/87 free-agent draft

Player Summary	
Fantasy Value	$1 to $3
Card Value	5¢ to 7¢
Will	win job with versatility
Can't	join Bash Brothers frat
Expect	surprising pop in his bat
Don't Expect	starting job

Primarily a three-position infielder in the minors, Brosius played right field in his first game for the 1992 Oakland Athletics, on July 6. He must have liked that assignment, since he slugged home runs in each of his first two at bats, drove in three runs, and scored four to help beat Cleveland. Although Oakland manager Tony LaRussa loves Brosius's versatility, LaRussa had to go without Brosius when the rookie was slowed with a viral infection that sent him to the disabled list shortly after his '92 bow. Brosius should get plenty of playing time because he has pop in his bat. In 1990, he hit 23 home runs for Double-A Huntsville and led the Southern League with 274 total bases. He had a .286 average with eight dingers and 31 RBI at Triple-A Tacoma in 1991. In 1992, he compiled a .258 on-base average and a .379 slugging percentage. Brosius began his pro ball career in 1987 and reached Oakland for a 36-game trial four years later. He makes good contact at the plate and has enough speed to swipe a dozen bases a year.

Major League Batting Register

	BA	G	AB	R	H	2B	3B	HR	RBI	SB
91 AL	.235	36	68	9	16	5	0	2	4	3
92 AL	.218	38	87	13	19	2	0	4	13	3
Life	.226	74	155	22	35	7	0	6	17	6

KEVIN BROWN

Position: Pitcher
Team: Texas Rangers
Born: March 14, 1965 McIntyre, GA
Height: 6'4" **Weight:** 188 lbs.
Bats: right **Throws:** right
Acquired: First-round pick in 6/86 free-agent draft

Player Summary	
Fantasy Value	$14 to $20
Card Value	5¢ to 10¢
Will	keep throwing heavy sinker
Can't	challenge for K crown
Expect	endless ground outs
Don't Expect	strong fielding

Brown's 95 mph sinker zooms to the plate with such force that catchers wear plastic thumb protectors inside their mitts—and still have to ice their swollen joints afterward. He throws about 10 mph faster than a typical sinkerballer, and he gets 70 percent of his outs on ground balls. A former Georgia Tech All-American, who yielded more hits than innings pitched from 1986 to 1991, Brown inadvertently changed his mechanics after hurting his elbow in an off-field accident. He also consulted a sports psychologist who convinced him not to worry about errors or blown saves that sabotaged his record. In 1992, Brown led the majors with 14 wins at the All-Star break—and was the AL's starting and winning pitcher. He became the first Ranger since Fergie Jenkins in 1974 to win 20. Brown allowed opposing batters to compile a .260 batting average, a .316 on-base average, and a .335 slugging percentage. Lefties had a .268 batting average against Brown, while righties had a .252 average.

Major League Pitching Register

	W	L	ERA	G	CG	IP	H	ER	BB	SO
86 AL	1	0	3.60	1	0	5.0	6	2	0	4
88 AL	1	1	4.24	4	1	23.1	33	11	8	12
89 AL	12	9	3.35	28	7	191.0	167	71	70	104
90 AL	12	10	3.60	26	6	180.0	175	72	60	88
91 AL	9	12	4.40	33	0	210.2	233	103	90	96
92 AL	21	11	3.32	35	11	265.2	262	98	76	173
Life	56	43	3.67	127	25	875.2	876	357	304	477
3 AVE	14	11	3.74	31	6	218.1	223	91	75	119

JERRY BROWNE

Position: Third base; second base; outfield
Team: Oakland Athletics
Born: Feb. 13, 1966 Christiansted, St. Croix, Virgin Islands
Height: 5'10" **Weight:** 170 lbs.
Bats: both **Throws:** right
Acquired: Signed as a free agent, 4/92

Player Summary	
Fantasy Value	$3 to $5
Card Value	3¢ to 4¢
Will	strike out too frequently
Can't	turn double play
Expect	sure hands
Don't Expect	full-time role

After hitting .231 for the Cleveland Indians during 1992 exhibition play, Browne received his unconditional release. Though he had hit .269 in six seasons, his failure to turn the double play well cost him any chance of retaining his position at second base. Signed by Oakland as insurance in April, Browne got his chance when injuries felled several members of the Athletics. He not only produced at the plate but also showed an ability to fill in at third base and several outfield spots. Browne strikes out more than he walks (understandable if he were a power hitter). In 1992, he compiled a .366 on-base percentage and a .364 slugging average. He also batted only .184 against lefties, while hitting .305 versus righties. He shows poor judgment on the basepaths sometimes. His range in the field is only adequate even though he has decent speed. Browne may have found his niche as a valuable utility player.

Major League Batting Register

	BA	G	AB	R	H	2B	3B	HR	RBI	SB
86 AL	.417	12	24	6	10	2	0	0	3	0
87 AL	.271	132	454	63	123	16	6	1	38	27
88 AL	.229	73	214	26	49	9	2	1	17	7
89 AL	.299	153	598	83	179	31	4	5	45	14
90 AL	.267	140	513	92	137	26	5	6	50	12
91 AL	.228	107	290	28	66	5	2	1	29	2
92 AL	.287	111	324	43	93	12	2	3	40	3
Life	.272	728	2417	341	657	101	21	17	222	65
3 AVE	.263	119	376	54	99	14	3	3	40	6

TOM BROWNING

Position: Pitcher
Team: Cincinnati Reds
Born: April 28, 1960 Casper, WY
Height: 6'1" **Weight:** 190 lbs.
Bats: left **Throws:** left
Acquired: Ninth-round pick in 6/82 free-agent draft

Player Summary	
Fantasy Value	$10 to $15
Card Value	3¢ to 4¢
Will	work 200 innings
Can't	avoid giving up homers
Expect	good control
Don't Expect	low ERA

Although Browning was the least effective member of Cincinnati's rotation when he was lost for the season last July 1, the Reds had a hard time replacing him. He's usually good for 15 wins and 200 innings a year. In '92, he had a 6-5 mark and 5.07 ERA in 16 starts when he tore a ligament in his left knee in a home-plate collision with Houston catcher Scott Servais. Because he has good control of his fastball, changeup, and curve, Browning is always around the plate—and always at risk to give up home runs. He can also be extremely effective, as he was when he became a rookie 20-game winner in 1985 (baseball's first since 1954) and the author of a perfect game three years later. He just missed another perfecto in 1990. Browning is a good hitter who sometimes sees service in a pinch-hitting role.

Major League Pitching Register

	W	L	ERA	G	CG	IP	H	ER	BB	SO
84 NL	1	0	1.54	3	0	23.1	27	4	5	14
85 NL	20	9	3.55	38	6	261.1	242	103	73	155
86 NL	14	13	3.81	39	4	243.1	225	103	70	147
87 NL	10	13	5.02	32	2	183.0	201	102	61	117
88 NL	18	5	3.41	36	5	250.2	205	95	64	124
89 NL	15	12	3.39	37	9	249.2	241	94	64	118
90 NL	15	9	3.80	35	2	227.2	235	96	52	99
91 NL	14	14	4.18	36	1	230.1	241	107	56	115
92 NL	6	5	5.07	16	0	87.0	108	49	28	33
Life	113	80	3.86	272	29	1756.1	1725	753	473	922
3 AVE	12	9	4.16	29	1	181.1	195	84	45	82

TOM BRUNANSKY

Position: Outfield
Team: Boston Red Sox
Born: Aug. 20, 1960 Covina, CA
Height: 6'4" **Weight:** 216 lbs.
Bats: right **Throws:** right
Acquired: Traded from Cardinals for Lee Smith, 6/90

Player Summary	
Fantasy Value	$5 to $8
Card Value	3¢ to 4¢
Will	homer in double figures
Can't	hit for average
Expect	decent play in right
Don't Expect	much time at first

After suffering through the worst season of his career in 1991, Brunansky blossomed into Boston's brightest surprise for a month in 1992. Used mostly as a right fielder and DH, he was at his best in July. He had 32 runs batted in, the most by a Red Sox in a single month since Nick Esasky plated 35 in August 1989. Playing half the schedule in Fenway Park, home of the Green Monster in left field, was a major factor in Brunansky's comeback. He is a streak hitter who often waves hopelessly at breaking balls. He has average speed and average range but gets a good jump on the ball. He has good instincts in the outfield and always throws to the right base.

Major League Batting Register

	BA	G	AB	R	H	2B	3B	HR	RBI	SB
81 AL	.152	11	33	7	5	0	0	3	6	1
82 AL	.272	127	463	77	126	30	1	20	46	1
83 AL	.227	151	542	70	123	24	5	28	82	2
84 AL	.254	155	567	75	144	21	0	32	85	4
85 AL	.242	157	567	71	137	28	4	27	90	5
86 AL	.256	157	593	69	152	28	1	23	75	12
87 AL	.259	155	532	83	138	22	2	32	85	11
88 AL	.184	14	49	5	9	1	0	1	6	1
88 NL	.245	143	523	69	128	22	4	22	79	16
89 NL	.239	158	556	67	133	29	3	20	85	5
90 NL	.158	19	57	5	9	3	0	1	2	0
90 AL	.267	129	461	61	123	24	5	15	71	5
91 AL	.229	142	459	54	105	24	1	16	70	1
92 AL	.266	138	458	47	122	31	3	15	74	2
Life	.248	1656	5860	760	1454	287	29	255	856	66
3 AVE	.250	143	478	56	120	27	3	16	72	3

STEVE BUECHELE

Position: Third base
Team: Chicago Cubs
Born: Sept. 26, 1961 Lancaster, CA
Height: 6'2" **Weight:** 190 lbs.
Bats: right **Throws:** right
Acquired: Traded from Pirates for Danny Jackson, 7/92

Player Summary

Fantasy Value	$6 to $8
Card Value	3¢ to 4¢
Will	top 15 homers
Can't	hit above .250
Expect	strong defense
Don't Expect	basepath speed

Known primarily for his defensive prowess at third base, Buechele has never hit for average his career peak was .267 in 1990). But he is a solid big league player who contributes home runs, as well as good glove work, to his team. The Bucs picked him up for their stretch drive in 1991 but sent him on to Chicago when pitching was perceived as a greater need last July. Buechele immediately gave the Cubs their best play at the position since the tenure of Ron Santo in the '60s. Impatience at the plate and vulnerability to fastballs from righthanders have probably shaved a dozen points off Buechele's lifetime average, but he's capable of hitting more than a dozen homers a year and topping 60 RBI. He doesn't have great speed, yet his fielding is excellent, and he can cover a lot of ground.

Major League Batting Register

	BA	G	AB	R	H	2B	3B	HR	RBI	SB
85 AL	.219	69	219	22	48	6	3	6	21	3
86 AL	.243	153	461	54	112	19	2	18	54	5
87 AL	.237	136	363	45	86	20	0	13	50	2
88 AL	.250	155	503	68	126	21	4	16	58	2
89 AL	.235	155	486	60	114	22	2	16	59	1
90 AL	.215	91	251	30	54	10	0	7	30	1
91 AL	.267	121	416	58	111	17	2	18	66	0
91 NL	.246	31	114	16	28	5	1	4	19	0
92 NL	.261	145	524	52	137	23	4	9	64	1
Life	.245	1056	3337	405	816	143	18	107	421	15
3 AVE	.253	129	435	52	110	18	2	13	60	1

JAY BUHNER

Position: Outfield
Team: Seattle Mariners
Born: Aug. 13, 1964 Louisville, KY
Height: 6'3" **Weight:** 205 lbs.
Bats: right **Throws:** right
Acquired: Traded from Yankees with Rick Balabon and Troy Evers for Ken Phelps, 7/88

Player Summary

Fantasy Value	$15 to $20
Card Value	3¢ to 4¢
Will	show strong arm
Can't	avoid swinging at bad pitches
Expect	frequent home runs
Don't Expect	high average

When he's concentrating and not leaving his feet to swing wildly at pitches, Buhner can hit the ball out of the park. Last July 3, for instance, he went 2-for-5, and knocked in four runs with a grand slam. Buhner's Achilles' heel is a tendency to strike out too often—a flaw that may have prompted his trade from the Yankees. He got even by launching seven seat-seeking missiles against his former team by last year's All-Star break. His average had been about the same against both righties and lefties, and he is one of five active players with the highest strikeout ratio. In 1992, he compiled a .333 on-base average and a .422 slugging percentage. He batted .230 against lefties and .248 against righties. On July 25, 1991, he hit a ball 479 feet over the left-center bullpen at Yankee Stadium. On the other end of his game, he's a fine defensive right fielder with a strong, accurate arm.

Major League Batting Register

	BA	G	AB	R	H	2B	3B	HR	RBI	SB
87 AL	.227	7	22	0	5	2	0	0	1	0
88 AL	.215	85	261	36	56	13	1	13	38	1
89 AL	.275	58	204	27	56	15	1	9	33	1
90 AL	.276	51	163	16	45	12	0	7	33	2
91 AL	.244	137	406	64	99	14	4	27	77	0
92 AL	.243	152	543	69	132	16	3	25	79	0
Life	.246	490	1599	212	393	72	9	81	261	4
3 AVE	.248	113	371	50	92	14	2	20	63	1

JIM BULLINGER

Position: Pitcher
Team: Chicago Cubs
Born: Aug. 21, 1965 New Orleans, LA
Height: 6'2" **Weight:** 185 lbs.
Bats: right **Throws:** right
Acquired: Ninth-round pick in 6/86 free-agent draft

Player Summary	
Fantasy Value	$2 to $4
Card Value	5¢ to 10¢
Will	get chance in bigs
Can't	hold first batters at bay
Expect	streaks of control trouble
Don't Expect	sudden success

A converted shortstop who hit .224 in four minor league seasons, Bullinger became a pitcher in 1990 and a reliever two years later. He had little minor league training as a closer before his promotion to Chicago on May 26 but had already posted 14 saves at Triple-A Iowa. He led the Chicago organization with 158 strikeouts in 1991, and converted seven of his first nine save opportunities in 1992 but had difficulty with first batters. Bullinger also had control problems that contributed to a high earned run average. Before reaching the majors, he posted a 2-1 ratio of strikeouts to walks. He'll have to maintain that level or improve it if he hopes to become a successful big league closer. In 1992 he held opposing hitters to a .233 batting average, a .350 on-base percentage, and a .382 slugging percentage. Bullinger had a 3-4 record with a 5.40 ERA, 30 Ks, and 23 walks in 47 innings in 1991 at Iowa. At Double-A Charlotte that year, he was 9-9 with a 3.53 ERA, 128 Ks, and 61 walks in 143 innings. His hitting should help him: He homered in his first Chicago at bat.

Major League Pitching Register

	W	L	ERA	G	S	IP	H	ER	BB	SO
92 NL	2	8	4.66	39	7	85.0	72	44	54	36
Life	2	8	4.66	39	7	85.0	72	44	54	36

TIM BURKE

Position: Pitcher
Team: Cincinnati Reds
Born: Feb. 19, 1959 Omaha, NE
Height: 6'3" **Weight:** 205 lbs.
Bats: right **Throws:** right
Acquired: Signed as a free agent, 12/92

Player Summary	
Fantasy Value	$2 to $4
Card Value	3¢ to 4¢
Will	suffer hot-and-cold spells
Can't	strike out many batters
Expect	reduced relief role
Don't Expect	return to 1990

Now a set-up man for the Reds, Burke is still trying to recapture the form that made him one of baseball's best closers from 1987 to 1990. A sinker-slider pitcher who also throws a changeup, he had 84 saves in those four years, all with the Montreal Expos, before he was slowed by a broken leg during the '90 campaign. He was traded to the New York Mets, where he didn't produce, and then on to the New York Yankees. A rubber-armed righthander, Burke tied for fourth in the NL with 72 appearances in 1991. It was the seventh straight year he worked at least 55 times. His short tenure with the Mets was unhappy, as he lost his confidence. When his sinker is sinking, however, Burke is a baron of the bullpen. He got off to a good start with the Yankees, holding batters to a .158 average in his first month with the team.

Major League Pitching Register

	W	L	ERA	G	S	IP	H	ER	BB	SO
85 NL	9	4	2.39	78	8	120.1	86	32	44	87
86 NL	9	7	2.93	68	4	101.1	103	33	46	82
87 NL	7	0	1.19	55	18	91.0	64	12	17	58
88 NL	3	5	3.40	61	18	82.0	84	31	25	42
89 NL	9	3	2.55	68	28	84.2	68	24	22	54
90 NL	3	3	2.52	58	20	75.0	71	21	21	47
91 NL	6	7	3.36	72	6	101.2	96	38	26	59
92 NL	1	2	5.74	15	0	15.2	26	10	3	7
92 AL	2	2	3.25	23	0	27.2	26	10	15	8
Life	49	33	2.72	498	102	699.1	624	211	219	444
3 AVE	4	5	3.23	56	9	73.2	73	26	22	40

JOHN BURKETT

Position: Pitcher
Team: San Francisco Giants
Born: Nov. 28, 1964 New Brighton, PA
Height: 6'3" **Weight:** 205 lbs.
Bats: right **Throws:** right
Acquired: Sixth-round pick in 6/83 free-agent draft

Player Summary	
Fantasy Value	$7 to $10
Card Value	3¢ to 4¢
Will	throw too many gophers
Can't	help himself with glove
Expect	regular assignments
Don't Expect	Cy Young

Burkett was one of many disappointments for the 1992 San Francisco Giants. Before posting his first shutout with a 5-0 win over Atlanta on July 30, he had split 12 decisions and fashioned an inflated earned run average. A durable control pitcher who throws a split-fingered fastball, curve, and changeup, Burkett is often victimized by the home run ball. He doesn't beat himself with walks, however. He usually whiffs twice as many as he walks. He's most effective against righthanded batters and pitches better in his home ballpark. In 1992, opponents compiled a .264 batting average, a .308 on-base average, and a .382 slugging percentage. He allowed lefty hitters to bat .295, while he allowed righthanded batters to hit .210. He also keeps baserunners close and has a good pickoff move. Possessed with great eye-hand coordination, Burkett hopes to try pro bowling when he's through with baseball. He's never pitched a perfect game, but he's turned the trick in bowling three times.

Major League Pitching Register

	W	L	ERA	G	S	IP	H	ER	BB	SO
87 NL	0	0	4.50	3	0	6.0	7	3	3	5
90 NL	14	7	3.79	33	2	204.0	201	86	61	118
91 NL	12	11	4.18	36	3	206.2	223	96	60	131
92 NL	13	9	3.84	32	3	189.2	194	81	45	107
Life	39	27	3.95	104	8	606.1	625	266	169	361
3 AVE	13	9	3.94	34	3	200.1	206	88	55	119

ELLIS BURKS

Position: Outfield
Team: Chicago White Sox
Born: Sept. 11, 1964 Vicksburg, MS
Height: 6'2" **Weight:** 202 lbs.
Bats: right **Throws:** right
Acquired: Signed as a free agent, 1/93

Player Summary	
Fantasy Value	$14 to $22
Card Value	4¢ to 8¢
Will	hit 20 homers if healthy
Can't	hit for high average
Expect	excellent right field
Don't Expect	healthy year

If healthy, Burks can plug a hole in Chicago's right field. He is a very good outfielder and speed-power package who was slowed by injury in 1992. A disc problem in his lower back resulted in a stay on the DL from late June until mid-July. Tried in various spots in the lineup, he is equally effective against righties and lefties, though breaking balls sometimes give him problems. He compiled a .327 on-base average and a .417 slugging percentage in 1992. He had 20 home runs and 27 stolen bases as a rookie in 1987, when he joined Carl Yastrzemski and Jackie Jensen in Boston's 20-20 club. In the field, Burks's excellent judgment of fly balls enables him to play a shallow center field and shag flies regardless of where they are hit—robbing batters of otherwise sure hits. He earned a Gold Glove in 1990. Burks can run, having topped 20 steals three times. Since he has been injured in recent seasons, though, he hasn't stolen too often.

Major League Batting Register

	BA	G	AB	R	H	2B	3B	HR	RBI	SB
87 AL	.272	133	558	94	152	30	2	20	59	27
88 AL	.294	144	540	93	159	37	5	18	92	25
89 AL	.303	97	399	73	121	19	6	12	61	21
90 AL	.296	152	588	89	174	33	8	21	89	9
91 AL	.251	130	474	56	119	33	3	14	56	6
92 AL	.255	66	235	35	60	8	3	8	30	5
Life	.281	722	2794	440	785	160	27	93	387	93
3 AVE	.272	116	432	60	118	25	5	14	58	7

RANDY BUSH

Position: Outfield; first base
Team: Minnesota Twins
Born: Oct. 5, 1958 Dover, DE
Height: 6'1" **Weight:** 190 lbs.
Bats: left **Throws:** left
Acquired: First-round pick in 6/79 free-agent draft

Player Summary	
Fantasy Value	$2 to $4
Card Value	3¢ to 4¢
Will	prove useful as pinch-hitter
Can't	hit for average
Expect	lefty DH role
Don't Expect	full-time play

Even though he was creaking along at a .214 pace last season, Randy Bush had a better year than George. Randy is one of those players whose career has been just good enough to keep him with one team for more than 10 years. He's been more than adequate in the outfield and at first, posting a fielding average of about .984. He is one of many pinch-hitters to share the record of two homers in consecutive at bats (June 20 and 23, 1986). Following a 1990 injury that cost him most of the season, Bush slowed a bit. He can no longer take the punishment of every-day play, which he last enjoyed in 1989. Because he still has a good lefthanded stroke, Bush is valuable coming off the bench, filling in as designated hitter, or spelling a veteran who needs a rest.

Major League Batting Register

	BA	G	AB	R	H	2B	3B	HR	RBI	SB
82 AL	.244	55	119	13	29	6	1	4	13	0
83 AL	.249	124	373	43	93	24	3	11	56	0
84 AL	.222	113	311	46	69	17	1	11	43	1
85 AL	.239	97	234	26	56	13	3	10	35	3
86 AL	.269	130	357	50	96	19	7	7	45	5
87 AL	.253	122	293	46	74	10	2	11	46	10
88 AL	.261	136	394	51	103	20	3	14	51	8
89 AL	.263	141	391	60	103	17	4	14	54	5
90 AL	.243	73	181	17	44	8	0	6	18	0
91 AL	.303	93	165	21	50	10	1	6	23	0
92 AL	.214	100	182	14	39	8	1	2	22	1
Life	.252	1184	3000	387	756	152	26	96	406	33
3 AVE	.252	89	176	17	44	9	1	5	21	0

BRETT BUTLER

Position: Outfield
Team: Los Angeles Dodgers
Born: June 15, 1957 Los Angeles, CA
Height: 5'10" **Weight:** 160 lbs.
Bats: left **Throws:** left
Acquired: Signed as a free agent, 12/90

Player Summary	
Fantasy Value	$20 to $28
Card Value	4¢ to 6¢
Will	post high on-base average
Can't	hit home runs
Expect	bunts in any situation
Don't Expect	defensive lapses

Just when critics thought Butler slowed down, he had a red-hot July. He batted .442 for the month with 18 stolen bases and 22 walks. He had moved from leadoff to second in the lineup on June 21, when his tear began, and scored the 1,000th run of his career five days later. A slap-and-slash hitter who bunts for hits and beats out infielder grounders, Butler is blessed with a keen batting eye that results in lots of walks. Not surprisingly, his on-base percentage is always among the league's best. His .413 on-base average in 1992 was third in the NL. A durable performer, Butler had played in 233 consecutive games until the streak ended in 1992. He has a weak throwing arm, but he rarely makes an error.

Major League Batting Register

	BA	G	AB	R	H	2B	3B	HR	RBI	SB
81 NL	.254	40	126	17	32	2	3	0	4	9
82 NL	.217	89	240	35	52	2	0	0	7	21
83 NL	.281	151	549	84	154	21	13	5	37	39
84 NL	.269	159	602	108	162	25	9	3	49	52
85 NL	.311	152	591	106	184	28	14	5	50	47
86 AL	.278	161	587	92	163	17	14	4	51	32
87 AL	.295	137	522	91	154	25	8	9	41	33
88 NL	.287	157	568	109	163	27	9	6	43	43
89 NL	.283	154	594	100	168	22	4	4	36	31
90 NL	.309	160	622	108	192	20	9	3	44	51
91 NL	.296	161	615	112	182	13	5	2	38	38
92 NL	.309	157	553	86	171	14	11	3	39	41
Life	.288	1678	6169	1048	1777	216	99	44	439	437
3 AVE	.304	159	597	102	182	16	8	3	40	43

GREG CADARET

Position: Pitcher
Team: Cincinnati Reds
Born: February 27, 1962 Detroit, MI
Height: 6'3" **Weight:** 205 lbs.
Bats: left **Throws:** left
Acquired: Purchased from Yankees, 11/92

Player Summary	
Fantasy Value	$2 to $4
Card Value	3¢ to 4¢
Will	keep batters off plate
Can't	get ahead in the count
Expect	many homers by rivals
Don't Expect	good ERA

Cadaret has been both a starter and reliever in the major leagues. Because he's a rubber-armed lefty capable of working often without much physical wear-and-tear, he's likely to remain assigned to the relief corps. A fastballer who likes to keep batters off the plate, an effective Cadaret will hold hitters to less than a .220 average with runners on base in the late innings. He also relies on a forkball and curve, an excellent pickoff move, and outstanding fielding skills to help his own cause. Cadaret has a good strikeout-to-walk ratio, but should have a better ERA than the career 3.83 he took into the 1992 campaign. Opponents compiled a .267 batting average, a .385 on-base percentage, and a .414 slugging average in 1992. He gets into trouble too easily by falling behind hitters. Forced to make pitches that are too fat, he yields far too many homers (12 in his first 79⅓ innings last year).

Major League Pitching Register

	W	L	ERA	G	S	IP	H	ER	BB	SO
87 AL	6	2	4.54	29	0	39.2	37	20	24	30
88 AL	5	2	2.89	58	3	71.2	60	23	36	64
89 AL	5	5	4.05	46	0	120.0	130	54	57	80
90 AL	5	4	4.15	54	3	121.1	120	56	64	80
91 AL	8	6	3.62	68	3	121.2	110	49	59	105
92 AL	4	8	4.25	46	1	103.2	104	49	74	73
Life	33	27	3.91	301	10	578.0	561	251	314	432
3 AVE	6	6	4.00	56	2	115.2	111	51	66	86

IVAN CALDERON

Position: Outfield; first base
Team: Boston Red Sox
Born: March 19, 1962 Fajardo, Puerto Rico
Height: 6'1" **Weight:** 221 lbs.
Bats: right **Throws:** right
Acquired: Traded from Expos for Mike Gardiner and Terry Powers, 12/92

Player Summary	
Fantasy Value	$12 to $20
Card Value	3¢ to 4¢
Will	produce power
Can't	avoid shoulder problems
Expect	deployment in left
Don't Expect	more walks than Ks

Persistent shoulder problems ruined the 1992 season for Calderon. Projected to be Montreal's starting first baseman, he instead endured his third shoulder operation in the last four seasons. He underwent a 75-minute arthroscopic procedure to repair a labrum tear and eliminate loose cartilage. When healthy and productive, he hits with power to all fields and is especially dangerous in the clutch. A former free swinger who has exercised more patience in recent seasons, Calderon still has problems with breaking balls and inside pitches. He's considered a dead fastball hitter. In 1992, he compiled a .323 on-base average and a .424 slugging percentage. Though he has more than enough speed to play left field, his brittle shoulder should also get him innings at first base and at bats as designated hitter.

Major League Batting Register

	BA	G	AB	R	H	2B	3B	HR	RBI	SB
84 AL	.208	11	24	2	5	1	0	1	1	1
85 AL	.286	67	210	37	60	16	4	8	28	4
86 AL	.250	50	164	16	41	7	1	2	15	3
87 AL	.293	144	542	93	159	38	2	28	83	10
88 AL	.212	73	264	40	56	14	0	14	35	4
89 AL	.286	157	622	83	178	34	9	14	87	7
90 AL	.273	158	607	85	166	44	2	14	74	32
91 NL	.300	134	470	69	141	22	3	19	75	31
92 NL	.265	48	170	19	45	14	2	3	24	1
Life	.277	842	3073	444	851	190	23	103	422	93
3 AVE	.282	113	416	58	117	27	2	12	58	21

KEN CAMINITI

Position: Third base
Team: Houston Astros
Born: April 21, 1963 Hanford, CA
Height: 6' **Weight:** 200 lbs.
Bats: both **Throws:** right
Acquired: Third-round pick in 6/84 free-agent draft

Player Summary

Fantasy Value.................................$10 to $15
Card Value...3¢ to 4¢
Will.............................get to balls at third
Can't...............................avoid throwing errors
Expect...15 home runs
Don't Expect.....................many stolen bases

In five big league seasons before 1992, Caminiti hit only .247. Needless to say, his .313 average through the first four months of last season was a major surprise. Caminiti was at his best in June, when his .349 mark for the month ranked third in the league. By the end of the 1992 season, he compiled a .350 on-base average and a .441 slugging percentage. He has good hands and a strong arm at third and gets to balls other third basemen can't reach. He doesn't always show good judgment, however, and most of his errors come on hurried throws. A switch-hitter with more power batting righthanded, he was the reason Houston switched Jeff Bagwell to first during 1991 spring training. Bagwell couldn't carry Caminiti's glove at third, but Houston wanted to get Bagwell's bat into the lineup. Caminiti, a former All-American at San Jose State, began his pro career in 1985 and reached Houston two years later.

CASEY CANDAELE

Position: Infield; outfield
Team: Houston Astros
Born: January 12, 1961 Lompoc, CA
Height: 5'9" **Weight:** 165 lbs.
Bats: both **Throws:** right
Acquired: Traded from Expos for Mark Bailey, 7/88

Player Summary

Fantasy Value.......................................$2 to $4
Card Value...3¢ to 4¢
Will.................play everything but bass fiddle
Can't.....................................hit enough to start
Expect...versatility
Don't Expect.......................................home runs

Candaele doesn't mind when hecklers tell him his mother was a better ballplayer, because she was considered the Ted Williams of the All-American Girls Professional Baseball League in the 1940s. Casey can't copy her heroics. He's content, however, to serve as a multipurpose player who can fill in at several positions and pop timely pinch-hits. A surprisingly strong clutch hitter—albeit with little power—Candaele uses his speed to run the bases well and to put in some time in the outfield. As an infielder, he has good range and is excellent at turning double-plays. After playing in a career-high 151 games in 1991, he had hoped to be Houston's regular second baseman. But the Astros moved catcher Craig Biggio there instead. Valued for his versatility, Candaele played all four infield positions and the outfield last summer. He's a better righthanded hitter, batting .266 against lefties in 1992 opposed to a .177 average versus righthanders.

Major League Batting Register

	BA	G	AB	R	H	2B	3B	HR	RBI	SB
87 NL	.246	63	203	10	50	7	1	3	23	0
88 NL	.181	30	83	5	15	2	0	1	7	0
89 NL	.255	161	585	71	149	31	3	10	72	4
90 NL	.242	153	541	52	131	20	2	4	51	9
91 NL	.253	152	574	65	145	30	3	13	80	4
92 NL	.294	135	506	68	149	31	2	13	62	10
Life	.256	694	2492	271	639	121	11	44	295	27
3 AVE	.262	147	540	62	142	27	2	10	64	8

Major League Batting Register

	BA	G	AB	R	H	2B	3B	HR	RBI	SB
86 NL	.231	30	104	9	24	4	1	0	6	3
87 NL	.272	138	449	62	122	23	4	1	23	7
88 NL	.170	57	147	11	25	8	1	0	5	1
90 NL	.286	130	262	30	75	8	6	3	22	7
91 NL	.262	151	461	44	121	20	7	4	50	9
92 NL	.213	135	320	19	68	12	1	1	18	7
Life	.250	641	1743	175	435	75	20	9	124	34
3 AVE	.253	139	348	31	88	13	5	3	30	8

JOHN CANDELARIA

Position: Pitcher
Team: Pittsburgh Pirates
Born: November 6, 1953 Brooklyn, NY
Height: 6'6" **Weight:** 225 lbs.
Bats: both **Throws:** left
Acquired: Signed as a free agent, 12/92

Player Summary	
Fantasy Value	$2 to $5
Card Value	3¢ to 4¢
Will	make frequent appearances
Can't	pitch well to righties
Expect	few rival homers
Don't Expect	return to rotation

Candelaria has been around long enough to know his limits. Once a premier starting pitcher, he has become one of the game's most effective middle relievers. Still a hard thrower, he has excellent control of a sinking fastball that induces grounders by batters. That translates to rally-killing double-plays in the late innings. When he's on, the Candy Man records a decent amount of strikeouts, but not always at the one-per-inning ratio he often displayed during his early days. Lack of work caused him to experience atypical control problems during the '92 campaign, but he still kept his earned run average below three.

Major League Pitching Register

	W	L	ERA	G	S	IP	H	ER	BB	SO
75 NL	8	6	2.76	18	0	120.2	95	37	36	95
76 NL	16	7	3.15	32	1	220.0	173	77	60	138
77 NL	20	5	2.34	33	0	230.2	197	60	50	133
78 NL	12	11	3.24	30	1	189.0	191	68	49	94
79 NL	14	9	3.22	33	0	207.0	201	74	41	101
80 NL	11	14	4.01	35	1	233.1	246	104	50	97
81 NL	2	2	3.54	6	0	40.2	42	16	11	14
82 NL	12	7	2.94	31	1	174.2	166	57	37	133
83 NL	15	8	3.23	33	0	197.2	191	71	45	157
84 NL	12	11	2.72	33	2	185.1	179	56	34	133
85 NL	2	4	3.64	37	9	54.1	57	22	14	47
85 AL	7	3	3.80	13	0	71.0	70	30	24	53
86 AL	10	2	2.55	16	0	91.2	68	26	26	81
87 AL	8	6	4.71	20	0	116.2	127	61	20	74
87 NL	2	0	5.84	3	0	12.1	17	8	3	10
88 AL	13	7	3.38	25	1	157.0	150	59	23	121
89 AL	3	3	5.14	10	0	49.0	49	28	12	37
89 NL	0	2	3.31	12	0	16.1	17	6	4	14
90 AL	7	6	3.95	47	5	79.2	87	73	20	63
91 NL	1	1	3.74	59	2	33.2	31	14	11	38
92 NL	2	5	3.50	50	5	25.1	20	8	13	23
Life	177	119	3.29	576	28	2506.0	2374	917	583	1656
2 AVE	4	4	3.89	53	4	56.2	59	25	16	51

TOM CANDIOTTI

Position: Pitcher
Team: Los Angeles Dodgers
Born: August 31, 1957 Walnut Creek, CA
Height: 6'2" **Weight:** 205 lbs.
Bats: right **Throws:** right
Acquired: Signed as free agent, 12/91

Player Summary	
Fantasy Value	$12 to $18
Card Value	3¢ to 4¢
Will	keep opposition close
Can't	muster good fastballs
Expect	long appearances
Don't Expect	inflated ERA

For three years, Candiotti couldn't buy a run. Even though he posted respectable ERAs with Cleveland and Toronto in 1990 and 1991, his won-lost record was not nearly as good as it could have been because his teammates' bats shut down whenever he took the mound. He was surprised that he encountered the same problem after signing with the Dodgers for 1992. Given better backing, he could become one of his league's winningest pitchers. He dumbfounds hitters with three different knuckleballs (slow, medium, and fast), a curve, and even an occasional fastball, cut fastball, and slider. Candiotti handles a glove well and keeps runners close—even though they're champing at the bit to steal against his slow-motion knucklers. His strikeout-to-walk ratio is good (better than 2-to-1), and he yields slightly less than one hit per inning.

Major League Pitching Register

	W	L	ERA	G	CG	IP	H	ER	BB	SO
83 AL	4	4	3.23	10	2	55.2	62	20	16	21
84 AL	2	2	5.29	8	0	32.1	38	19	10	23
86 AL	16	12	3.57	36	17	252.1	234	100	106	167
87 AL	7	18	4.78	32	7	201.2	193	107	93	111
88 AL	14	8	3.28	31	11	216.2	225	79	53	137
89 AL	13	10	3.10	31	4	206.0	188	71	55	124
90 AL	15	11	3.65	31	3	202.0	207	82	55	128
91 AL	13	13	2.65	34	6	238.0	202	70	73	167
92 NL	11	15	3.00	32	6	203.2	177	68	63	152
Life	95	93	3.45	245	56	1608.1	1526	616	524	1030
3 AVE	13	13	3.08	32	5	214.2	195	73	64	149

JOSE CANSECO

Position: Outfield
Team: Texas Rangers
Born: July 2, 1964 Havana, Cuba
Height: 6'3" **Weight:** 230 lbs.
Bats: right **Throws:** right
Acquired: Traded from Athletics for Ruben Sierra, Bobby Witt, and Jeff Russell, 8/92

Player Summary	
Fantasy Value	$40 to $50
Card Value	15¢ to 25¢
Will	crash 100-RBI barrier
Can't	win Gold Glove
Expect	controversy
Don't Expect	repeat of 40-40

Once considered the best player in baseball, Canseco was jettisoned by the A's to the Rangers for a right fielder in his class as a hitter, Ruben Sierra, and two veteran hurlers. Although Canseco has been one of the league's best power men, shoulder problems short-circuited his power production last summer. The injury sent him to the disabled list twice. He was a unanimous choice for AL MVP in 1988, when he became the first player to hit 40 homers and steal 40 bases in the same season. He holds numerous Oakland slugging records, including most RBI in a season and most 100-RBI campaigns. A pull hitter with a high strikeout frequency, Canseco tied a major league record with eight straight walks last July. He had a .344 on-base average in 1992. He's an adequate right fielder with a strong arm but sometimes misjudges fly balls.

Major League Batting Register

	BA	G	AB	R	H	2B	3B	HR	RBI	SB
85 AL	.302	29	96	16	29	3	0	5	13	1
86 AL	.240	157	600	85	144	29	1	33	117	15
87 AL	.257	159	630	81	162	35	3	31	113	15
88 AL	.307	158	610	120	187	34	0	42	124	40
89 AL	.269	65	227	40	61	9	1	17	57	6
90 AL	.274	131	481	83	132	14	2	37	101	19
91 AL	.266	154	572	115	152	32	1	44	122	26
92 AL	.244	119	439	74	107	15	0	26	87	6
Life	.266	972	3655	614	974	171	8	235	734	128
3 AVE	.262	135	497	91	130	20	1	36	103	17

CRIS CARPENTER

Position: Pitcher
Team: Florida Marlins
Born: April 5, 1965 St. Augustine, FL
Height: 6'1" **Weight:** 185 lbs.
Bats: right **Throws:** right
Acquired: Second-round pick from Cardinals in 11/92 expansion draft

Player Summary	
Fantasy Value	$4 to $7
Card Value	3¢ to 4¢
Will	have many appearances
Can't	get ERA much below 4.00
Expect	few baserunners
Don't Expect	a starter role

Carpenter has good credentials for his middle relief role, giving up less than a hit per inning and striking out almost twice as many hitters as he walks. Plus his arm can take the punishment that results from frequent use. He's especially effective in his first inning of work and, as a result, generally leaves inherited runners stranded. He had seven holds in 1992. Carpenter's days as a frequent flyer from majors to minors ended in 1991 when he earned a regular spot on the St. Louis pitching staff. The former Georgia All-American usually gets good results with his 90 mph fastball but he sometimes gets hurt when he tries to throw it down the middle after he gets behind in the count. In 1992, opponents compiled a .220 batting average, a .288 on-base percentage, and a .371 slugging percentage. Carpenter helps himself with his defense and keeps baserunners honest. He doesn't get to bat too often but is not an automatic out.

Major League Pitching Register

	W	L	ERA	G	S	IP	H	ER	BB	SO
88 NL	2	3	4.72	8	0	47.2	56	25	9	24
89 NL	4	4	3.18	36	0	68.0	70	24	26	35
90 NL	0	0	4.50	4	0	8.0	5	4	2	6
91 NL	10	4	4.23	59	0	66.0	53	31	20	47
92 NL	5	4	2.97	73	1	88.0	69	29	27	46
Life	21	15	3.66	180	1	277.2	253	113	84	158
2 AVE	8	4	3.51	66	1	77.0	61	30	24	47

MARK CARREON

Position: Outfield
Team: Detroit Tigers
Born: July 9, 1963 Chicago, IL
Height: 6' **Weight:** 195 lbs.
Bats: right **Throws:** left
Acquired: Traded from Mets with Tony Castillo for Paul Gibson, 1/92

Player Summary	
Fantasy Value	$3 to $5
Card Value	3¢ to 5¢
Will	hit a few homers
Can't	provide good defense
Expect	best work as pinch-hitter
Don't Expect	high batting average

Although he was one of the game's best pinch-hitters before a 1990 knee injury limited his playing time, Carreon always yearned to play full time. Although he got that wish with the Detroit Tigers last summer, his bat cooled the minute he received the exposure he wanted. He is a free-swinging pull hitter who fans twice as often as he walks. He also makes more contact than he would like, hitting a high number of ground balls that turn into double-plays. He had a .278 on-base percentage and a .360 slugging average in 1992. The former minor league speed merchant no longer runs well and seldom steals. Since he also has trouble in left field—the only place it's safe for him to play—Carreon is best-suited to pinch-hitting or serving as a designated hitter. Unlike his father, catcher Camilo Carreon, Mark does not have a good arm.

Major League Batting Register

	BA	G	AB	R	H	2B	3B	HR	RBI	SB
87 NL	.250	9	12	0	3	0	0	0	1	0
88 NL	.556	7	9	5	5	2	0	1	1	0
89 NL	.308	68	133	20	41	6	0	6	16	2
90 NL	.250	82	188	30	47	12	0	10	26	1
91 NL	.260	106	254	18	66	6	0	4	21	2
92 AL	.232	101	336	34	78	11	1	10	41	3
Life	.258	373	932	107	240	37	1	31	106	8
3 AVE	.246	96	259	27	64	10	0	8	29	2

JOE CARTER

Position: Outfield
Team: Toronto Blue Jays
Born: March 7, 1960 Oklahoma City, OK
Height: 6'3" **Weight:** 215 lbs.
Bats: right **Throws:** right
Acquired: Traded from Padres with Roberto Alomar for Fred McGriff and Tony Fernandez, 12/90

Player Summary	
Fantasy Value	$38 to $42
Card Value	8¢ to 12¢
Will	serve as occasional DH
Can't	avoid high K total
Expect	guaranteed total of 100 RBI
Don't Expect	Gold Glove play

Carter was the first player to start at three different positions in three consecutive World Series games in 1992. His license plate reads "JC RBIS" and that is his function. He led the American League with 121 runs batted in, a career high, in his second full season. A durable player who rarely misses a game, Carter is a fastball hitter who plays half his schedule in a sanctuary for sluggers. In 1992, he had his typical 30-homer, 100-RBI campaign. Though he strikes out more than three times as often as he walks, Carter connects when it counts—and hits with equal strength to all fields. He was a 30-30 man in 1987 and could join the club again. In the outfield, he runs well but doesn't quite have the arm for right (he's far superior in left field).

Major League Batting Register

	BA	G	AB	R	H	2B	3B	HR	RBI	SB
83 NL	.176	23	51	6	9	1	1	0	1	1
84 AL	.275	66	244	32	67	6	1	13	41	2
85 AL	.262	143	489	64	128	27	0	15	59	24
86 AL	.302	162	663	108	200	36	9	29	121	29
87 AL	.264	149	588	83	155	27	2	32	106	31
88 AL	.271	157	621	85	168	36	6	27	98	27
89 AL	.243	162	651	84	158	32	4	35	105	13
90 NL	.232	162	634	79	147	27	1	24	115	22
91 AL	.273	162	638	89	174	42	3	33	108	20
92 AL	.264	158	622	97	164	30	7	34	119	12
Life	.263	1344	5201	727	1370	264	34	242	873	181
3 AVE	.256	161	631	88	162	33	4	30	114	18

FRANK CASTILLO

Position: Pitcher
Team: Chicago Cubs
Born: April 1, 1969 El Paso, TX
Height: 6'1" **Weight:** 180 lbs.
Bats: right **Throws:** right
Acquired: Sixth-round pick in 6/87 free-agent draft

Player Summary	
Fantasy Value	$6 to $10
Card Value	5¢ to 10¢
Will	show good control
Can't	finish what he starts
Expect	batters to take him deep
Don't Expect	bullpen duty

In his first full major league season in 1992, Castillo received valuable on-the-job experience. He showed considerable improvement over 1991. That year he pitched well early, then fared poorly after riding the disabled list with a strained right shoulder. Because he does not have great velocity on his fastball, Castillo varies his speeds and pitches. He complements his sinking fastball with a slow curve but gets most of his strikeouts on a changeup. He also throws a slider. He is a control pitcher who yields less than a hit per inning, throws more than his share of gopher balls (he gave up 19 in '92), and almost never goes nine innings. Before the '92 season, he was considered especially tough on righthanded batters, but last summer he allowed righties to compile a .238 mark, but lefties had only a .228 average. In 1992, he allowed opponents to compile a .232 batting average, a .294 on-base average, and a .371 slugging percentage. Castillo helps himself by bunting and fielding well, but his hitting leaves much to be desired.

Major League Pitching Register

	W	L	ERA	G	CG	IP	H	ER	BB	SO
91 NL	6	7	4.35	18	4	111.2	107	54	33	73
92 NL	10	11	3.46	33	0	205.1	179	79	63	135
Life	16	18	3.78	51	4	317.0	286	133	96	208
2 AVE	8	9	3.78	26	2	158.2	143	67	48	104

ANDUJAR CEDENO

Position: Shortstop
Team: Houston Astros
Born: August 21, 1969 La Romana, Dominican Republic
Height: 6'1" **Weight:** 168 lbs.
Bats: right **Throws:** right
Acquired: Signed as free agent, 10/86

Player Summary	
Fantasy Value	$3 to $6
Card Value	5¢ to 10¢
Will	experience fielding problems
Can't	break into starting lineup
Expect	extra-base power to alleys
Don't Expect	long shortstop trial

Cedeno needs to put both halves of his game together. In 1991, he had nine homers, 36 RBI, and 18 errors in his first 67 big league games. In '92, however, his defense showed marked improvement (four errors) while his offense sagged (a .186 average, five RBI, and 37 strikeouts in 102 at bats when returned to the minor leagues in early June). His skid began early, as he chased bad pitches—with predictably poor results—and lost his confidence. For Houston in 1992, he finished the season with a .232 on-base percentage and a .277 slugging average. At Triple-A Tucson in 1992, he batted .293 with six homers and 56 RBI. He's had defensive problems in the past (51 errors in 132 Double-A games in 1990) but his combination of speed plus power stamps him as a prospect to watch. If he ever learns to handle balls hit right at him, Cedeno should get an extended audition. In 1991 at Tucson, he batted .303 with seven homers and 55 RBI. Perhaps a position change would help him—moving to the outfield worked for Ron Gant.

Major League Batting Register

	BA	AB	R	H	2B	3B	HR	RBI	SB
90 NL	.000	7	8	0	0	0	0	0	0
91 NL	.243	67	251	27	61	13	2	9	36	4
92 NL	.173	71	220	15	38	13	2	2	13	2
Life	.207	145	479	42	99	26	4	11	49	6
2 AVE	.210	69	236	21	50	13	2	6	25	3

WES CHAMBERLAIN

Position: Outfield
Team: Philadelphia Phillies
Born: April 13, 1966 Chicago, IL
Height: 6'2" **Weight:** 210 lbs.
Bats: right **Throws:** right
Acquired: Traded from Pirates with Julio Peguero and Tony Longmire for Carmelo Martinez, 8/90

Player Summary	
Fantasy Value	$13 to $17
Card Value	10¢ to 15¢
Will	constantly change stances
Can't	contend for Gold Glove
Expect	homers and strikeouts
Don't Expect	patience at bat

A weak start and worse attitude led to an unexpected minor league exile for Chamberlain early in the 1992 campaign. He grumbled at his departure but got good results. With encouragement from Triple-A Scranton manager Lee Elia, Chamberlain hit .331 with four homers and 26 RBI in 34 games. Recalled on June 18, he stroked 11 hits in his first 34 at bats. Although he possesses both power and speed, he still needs to refine his offense. He's an impatient free-swinger who fans seven times more often than he walks. Another flaw is his constant shifting in the batter's box—a tendency that produced the nickname "Man of 1,000 Stances." For the Phillies, he compiled a .285 on-base average and a .422 slugging percentage in 1992. At Triple-A Buffalo in 1992, he hit .250 with six homers and 52 RBI. Chamberlain runs well and would steal more bases if he learned to read rival pitchers and catchers. He also has trouble in the outfield, where his speed and arm don't always compensate for his inability to get a good jump on the ball.

Major League Batting Register

	BA	G	AB	R	H	2B	3B	HR	RBI	SB
90 NL	.283	18	46	9	13	3	0	2	4	4
91 NL	.240	101	383	51	92	16	3	13	50	9
92 NL	.258	76	275	26	71	18	0	9	41	4
Life	.250	195	704	86	176	37	3	24	95	17
2 AVE	.248	89	329	39	82	17	2	11	46	7

NORM CHARLTON

Position: Pitcher
Team: Seattle Mariners
Born: January 6, 1963 Fort Polk, LA
Height: 6'3" **Weight:** 195 lbs.
Bats: both **Throws:** left
Acquired: Traded from Reds for Kevin Mitchell, 11/92

Player Summary	
Fantasy Value	$15 to $20
Card Value	3¢ to 4¢
Will	get Ks with splitter
Can't	rely on spitter
Expect	occasional bouts of wildness
Don't Expect	rotation return

Charlton is Seattle's No. 1 closer. He broke into the 1992 season without the shoulder problems of the recent past and established himself as one of the National League's best relievers, notching his 20th save on July 7. He had a 3-0 record, 24 saves, and a 2.26 ERA before losing his first game on Terry Pendleton's two-out, two-strike, ninth-inning homer on August 4. Charlton was given the closer's job when incumbent Rob Dibble came down with shoulder tendinitis during spring training. Charlton was used as a starter early in 1991 before returning to the bullpen after the experiment failed. A power pitcher with great command of his fastball, curveball, and split-fingered fastball, this 1992 first-time All-Star averages more than a strikeout per inning. Although he's had control problems in the past, his whiff-to-walk ratio is about 4-to-1. In 1992, opponents compiled a .262 batting average, a .323 on-base average, and a .397 slugging percentage. He's a good fielder.

Major League Pitching Register

	W	L	ERA	G	S	IP	H	ER	BB	SO
88 NL	4	5	3.96	10	0	61.1	60	27	20	39
89 NL	8	3	2.93	69	0	95.1	67	31	40	98
90 NL	12	9	2.74	56	2	154.1	131	47	70	117
91 NL	3	5	2.91	39	1	108.1	92	35	34	77
92 NL	4	2	2.99	64	26	81.1	79	27	26	90
Life	31	24	3.00	238	29	500.2	429	167	190	421
3 AVE	6	5	2.85	53	10	114.1	101	36	43	95

ARCHI CIANFROCCO

Position: First base
Team: Montreal Expos
Born: Oct. 6, 1966 Rome, NY
Height: 6'5" **Weight:** 200 lbs.
Bats: right **Throws:** right
Acquired: Seventh-round pick in 6/87 free-agent draft

Player Summary	
Fantasy Value	$6 to $10
Card Value	15¢ to 20¢
Will	start to use power
Can't	carry Galarraga's glove
Expect	many strikeouts
Don't Expect	stolen bases

Cianfrocco was the major surprise of Montreal's 1992 spring training camp, hitting .282 with three homers and 11 RBI in 39 at bats. Even though he had no Triple-A experience, he opened the season in Montreal. He continued to hit—until a June slump cut the throttle. Suddenly, he found that big league pitchers could deliver a steady diet of high-and-tight fastballs. Basically an average hitter who displays occasional pop, he strikes out far too many times for a batter who belted only a half-dozen homers. At the end of the '92 season, he compiled a .276 on-base average and a .358 slugging percentage. He batted .305 with four homers and 16 RBI at Triple-A Indianapolis in 1992. At Double-A Harrisburg in 1991, he hit .316 with 71 runs, 21 doubles, 10 triples, nine homers, 77 RBI, 11 stolen bases, 38 walks, and 112 strikeouts in 456 at bats. In the field, he doesn't have the Gold Glove skills of Andres Galarraga—the man Montreal had hoped Archi would replace—but he's good at turning double plays and makes few errors. He can also fill in at third if necessary.

Major League Batting Register

	BA	G	AB	R	H	2B	3B	HR	RBI	SB
92 NL	.241	86	232	25	56	5	2	6	30	3
Life	.241	86	232	25	56	5	2	6	30	3

JACK CLARK

Position: Designated hitter; first base
Team: Boston Red Sox
Born: November 10, 1955 New Brighton, PA
Height: 6'3" **Weight:** 205 lbs.
Bats: right **Throws:** right
Acquired: Signed as a free agent, 12/90

Player Summary	
Fantasy Value	$3 to $8
Card Value	3¢ to 4¢
Will	generate power
Can't	avoid injury
Expect	constant carping
Don't Expect	1987's form

Although he's one of baseball's most devastating sluggers when healthy, back and shoulder problems sapped Clark's power during the 1992 campaign. He struggled to keep his average above .200 and had only three home runs in the first four months. A chronic complainer, he blamed his miseries not only on his ailments but also on his environment. He said Fenway Park's left field wall—"The Green Monster"—was so close that he was held to singles on hard-hit balls off the wall. In 1991, however, Clark had little trouble clearing the barrier. A five-year streak of 25-plus homers per season ended in 1992. Age and injuries seemed to be catching up to him.

Major League Batting Register

	BA	G	AB	R	H	2B	3B	HR	RBI	SB
75 NL	.235	8	17	3	4	0	0	0	2	1
76 NL	.225	26	102	14	23	6	2	2	10	6
77 NL	.252	136	413	64	104	17	4	13	51	12
78 NL	.306	156	592	90	181	46	8	25	98	15
79 NL	.273	143	527	84	144	25	2	26	86	11
80 NL	.284	127	437	77	124	20	8	22	82	2
81 NL	.268	99	385	60	103	19	2	17	53	1
82 NL	.274	157	563	90	154	30	3	27	103	6
83 NL	.268	135	492	82	132	25	0	20	66	5
84 NL	.320	57	203	33	65	9	1	11	44	1
85 NL	.281	126	442	71	124	26	3	22	87	1
86 NL	.237	65	232	34	55	12	2	9	23	1
87 NL	.286	131	419	93	120	23	1	35	106	1
88 AL	.242	150	496	81	120	14	0	27	93	3
89 NL	.242	142	455	76	110	19	1	26	94	6
90 NL	.266	115	334	59	89	12	1	25	62	4
91 AL	.249	140	481	75	120	18	1	28	87	0
92 AL	.210	81	257	32	54	11	0	5	33	1
Life	.267	1994	6847	1118	1826	332	39	340	1180	77
3 AVE	.245	112	357	55	88	14	1	19	61	2

JERALD CLARK

Position: Outfield
Team: Colorado Rockies
Born: August 10, 1963 Crockett, TX
Height: 6'4" **Weight:** 190 lbs.
Bats: right **Throws:** right
Acquired: First-round pick from Padres in
11/92 expansion draft

Player Summary

Fantasy Value	$5 to $8
Card Value	3¢ to 4¢
Will	hit occasional homers
Can't	cut down K ratio
Expect	another chance
Don't Expect	stellar defense

Clark gets another chance to prove that he is a legitimate outfielder. In five big league trials, Clark has indicated that he's the type of player who performs well in the minors but can't quite cut it in the big leagues. He topped .300 seven times in the minors but is less than a .240 hitter for the Padres. A hot July last year probably spared him from another trip to the minors. Although he does display occasional power, Clark is an impatient batter who strikes out far more often than he walks. He's vulnerable to all kinds of breaking balls and swings at any pitches that are up. Against low fastballs, however, he's extremely dangerous. He compiled a .278 on-base average and a .383 slugging percentage in 1992. Because he neither runs nor fields well, he won't be a regular until he shows more consistency at bat. San Diego had hoped for several seasons that he would become their left fielder and No. 5 hitter.

Major League Batting Register

	BA	G	AB	R	H	2B	3B	HR	RBI	SB
88 NL	.200	6	15	0	3	1	0	0	3	0
89 NL	.195	17	41	5	8	2	0	1	7	0
90 NL	.267	53	101	12	27	4	1	5	11	0
91 NL	.228	118	369	26	84	16	0	10	47	2
92 NL	.242	146	496	45	120	22	6	12	58	3
Life	.237	340	1022	88	242	45	7	28	126	5
2 AVE	.236	132	433	36	102	19	3	11	53	3

WILL CLARK

Position: First base
Team: San Francisco Giants
Born: March 13, 1964 New Orleans, LA
Height: 6'1" **Weight:** 190 lbs.
Bats: left **Throws:** left
Acquired: First-round pick in 6/85 free-agent draft

Player Summary

Fantasy Value	$45 to $50
Card Value	15¢ to 22¢
Will	top .300
Can't	throw or run well
Expect	25 homers, 100 RBI
Don't Expect	trouble with lefties

Clark remains one of baseball's top all-around performers. One of the few sluggers who also makes good contact, he walks almost as often as he strikes out. Though he bats lefthanded, he hits southpaws well. He carried a .302 career average into the 1992 season and had a .307 batting average against lefties in '92; he had a .295 batting average against righties. Though Fred McGriff won the fan election for the NL All-Star first base job, Clark played in the game for the fifth straight season and delivered a home run. On July 28, 1992, his two-run, pinch-homer in the ninth gave the Giants a 5-3 win over the Dodgers. Clark compiled a .384 on-base percentage and a .476 slugging average in 1992. He homered against Nolan Ryan in his first big league at bat in 1986, and the 1984 Olympian has averaged more than 20 homers a year since. He was the MVP in the 1989 NLCS with a .650 average and 1.200 slugging percentage.

Major League Batting Register

	BA	G	AB	R	H	2B	3B	HR	RBI	SB
86 NL	.287	111	408	66	117	27	2	11	41	4
87 NL	.308	150	529	89	163	29	5	35	91	5
88 NL	.282	162	575	102	162	31	6	29	109	9
89 NL	.333	159	588	104	196	38	9	23	111	8
90 NL	.295	154	600	91	177	25	5	19	95	8
91 NL	.301	148	565	84	170	32	7	29	116	4
92 NL	.300	144	513	69	154	40	1	16	73	12
Life	.301	1028	3778	605	1139	222	35	162	636	50
3 AVE	.299	149	559	81	167	32	4	21	95	8

ROYCE CLAYTON

Position: Shortstop
Team: San Francisco Giants
Born: January 2, 1970 Burbank, CA
Height: 6′ **Weight:** 175 lbs.
Bats: right **Throws:** right
Acquired: First-round pick in 6/88 free-agent draft

Player Summary	
Fantasy Value	$4 to $8
Card Value	5¢ to 15¢
Will	steal often if he reaches
Can't	avoid errors
Expect	surprising RBI production
Don't Expect	many homers

Clayton's arrival in the major leagues last spring was heralded as the second coming of Barry Larkin; instead, it was Barry Manilow. By the time San Francisco sent Clayton to Triple-A Phoenix in late June, he was carrying a .211 average with 34 strikeouts in 175 at bats. He had only three homers and 16 runs batted in. By the end of the season for San Fran, he compiled a .281 on-base average and a .308 slugging percentage. In the first half of 1992, he also had seven errors at shortstop. His defensive struggles continued at Phoenix, where he finally straightened out after a slow start, batting .240 with three homers and 18 RBI. The Giants made the same mistake with him that they did with catcher Steve Decker the year before, promoting him directly from Double-A to a daily job in the major leagues. Neither player was ready. Clayton has speed, range, and fielding potential; he led Texas League shortstops in double-plays in 1991. At Double-A Shreveport that year, he hit .280 with five homers, 68 RBI, and 36 stolen bases.

Major League Batting Register

	BA	G	AB	R	H	2B	3B	HR	RBI	SB
91 NL	.115	9	26	0	3	1	0	0	2	0
92 NL	.224	98	321	31	72	7	4	4	24	8
Life	.216	107	347	31	75	8	4	4	26	8

ROGER CLEMENS

Position: Pitcher
Team: Boston Red Sox
Born: August 4, 1962 Dayton, OH
Height: 6′4″ **Weight:** 220 lbs.
Bats: right **Throws:** right
Acquired: First-round pick in 6/83 free-agent draft

Player Summary	
Fantasy Value	$40 to $50
Card Value	15¢ to 25¢
Will	challenge for K crown
Can't	always keep his cool
Expect	bid for Cy Young Award
Don't Expect	long slumps

Baseball's best pitcher? Heading into 1992, Clemens had won three Cy Young Awards and narrowly missed two others. He led his league in shutouts four times, ERA three times, and wins and strikeouts twice each. In 1986, he became the only man to win MVP honors in both the All-Star Game and the regular season as well as the Cy Young. He also fanned a record 20 hitters in a nine-inning game. He throws a fastball, slider, and curve—all with command, control, and velocity. A native Texan who idolized Nolan Ryan, Clemens advanced to the majors after 18 games in the minors. His 1992 performance was slowed by an inflamed tendon in his right foot—an injury that kept him winless in six starts before the All-Star break. In 1992, opponents compiled a .224 batting average, a .279 on-base percentage, and a .308 slugging percentage.

Major League Pitching Register

	W	L	ERA	G	CG	IP	H	ER	BB	SO
84 AL	9	4	4.32	21	5	133.1	146	64	29	126
85 AL	7	5	3.29	15	3	98.1	83	36	37	74
86 AL	24	4	2.48	33	10	254.0	179	70	67	238
87 AL	20	9	2.97	36	18	281.2	248	93	83	256
88 AL	18	12	2.93	35	14	264.0	217	86	62	291
89 AL	17	11	3.13	35	8	253.1	215	88	93	230
90 AL	21	6	1.93	31	7	228.1	193	49	54	209
91 AL	18	10	2.62	35	13	271.1	219	79	65	241
92 AL	18	11	2.41	32	11	246.2	203	66	62	208
Life	152	72	2.80	273	89	2031.0	1703	631	552	1873
3 AVE	19	9	2.34	33	10	248.1	205	65	60	219

PAT CLEMENTS

Position: Pitcher
Team: Baltimore Orioles
Born: February 2, 1962 McCloud, CA
Height: 6′ **Weight:** 187 lbs.
Bats: right **Throws:** left
Acquired: Signed as a free agent, 7/92

Player Summary	
Fantasy Value	$1 to $3
Card Value	3¢ to 4¢
Will	work only in middle relief
Can't	keep runners off base
Expect	good luck against lefties
Don't Expect	one port of call

Competent lefty middle relievers are hard to find, but the Baltimore Orioles plucked one off the waiver wire in the heat of the 1992 pennant race. Clements joined the Birds on July 10 and promptly held American League hitters scoreless in five of his first six appearances. He held 1992 AL batters to a .258 batting average, a .350 on-base percentage, and a .292 slugging percentage. Earlier in the season, he posted a 2-1 mark at San Diego but wore out his welcome by yielding more hits than innings pitched and failing to throw strikes with consistency (12 walks in 23⅔ innings). Walks have always posed problems for Clements, who has pitched for five clubs in seven years after breaking into the majors in 1985. He has a rubber arm and the ability to work often. His seven-year ERA of 3.89 before 1992, however, suggests that he should keep his bags packed.

Major League Pitching Register

	W	L	ERA	G	CG	IP	H	ER	BB	SO
85 AL	5	0	3.34	41	1	62.0	47	23	25	19
85 NL	0	2	3.67	27	2	34.1	39	14	15	17
86 NL	0	4	2.80	65	2	61.0	53	19	32	31
87 AL	3	3	4.95	55	7	80.0	91	44	30	36
88 AL	0	0	6.48	6	0	8.1	12	6	4	3
89 NL	4	1	3.92	23	0	39.0	39	17	15	18
90 NL	0	0	4.15	9	0	13.0	20	6	7	6
91 NL	1	0	3.77	12	0	14.1	13	6	9	8
92 NL	2	1	2.66	27	0	23.2	25	7	12	11
92 AL	2	0	3.28	23	0	24.2	23	9	11	9
Life	17	11	3.77	288	12	360.1	362	151	160	158

DAVE COCHRANE

Position: Infield; outfield
Team: Seattle Mariners
Born: January 31, 1963 Riverside, CA
Height: 6′2″ **Weight:** 180 lbs.
Bats: both **Throws:** right
Acquired: Traded from Royals for Ken Spratke, 2/88

Player Summary	
Fantasy Value	$3 to $6
Card Value	3¢ to 4¢
Will	play anywhere
Can't	avoid strikeouts
Expect	some power
Don't Expect	one single spot

Cochrane's 1992 season ended on August 1 when he underwent surgery to remove the sesamoid bone from his right foot. Valued for his versatility, Cochrane hit a career-high .250 and hit a pair of homers in limited action for Seattle. He had a .309 on-base average and a .322 slugging percentage in 1992. He has never appeared in more than 65 games a year (65 in both '91 and '92), but has proven himself capable whenever he gets the nod. He has caught, played all four infield positions plus the outfield, and served as a designated hitter who bats from both sides. Cochrane even pitched in eight games for Hawaii of the Pacific Coast League in 1987. Because he lacks speed but has a strong arm, his best position is catcher. Given a chance to play, he might recapture the batting stroke that helped him top 15 homers in six minor league seasons. He needs to show more patience, however, because he whiffs three times more often than he walks.

Major League Batting Register

	BA	G	AB	R	H	2B	3B	HR	RBI	SB
86 AL	.194	19	62	4	12	2	0	1	2	0
89 AL	.235	54	102	13	24	4	1	3	7	0
90 AL	.150	15	20	0	3	0	0	0	0	0
91 AL	.247	65	178	16	44	13	0	2	22	0
92 AL	.250	65	152	10	38	5	0	2	12	1
Life	.235	218	514	43	121	24	1	8	43	1
2 AVE	.248	65	165	13	41	9	0	2	17	1

ALEX COLE

Position: Outfield
Team: Colorado Rockies
Born: August 17, 1965 Fayetteville, NC
Height: 6'2" **Weight:** 175 lbs.
Bats: left **Throws:** left
Acquired: First-round pick from Pirates in
11/92 expansion draft

Player Summary	
Fantasy Value	$7 to $10
Card Value	3¢ to 4¢
Will	steal often
Can't	play good defense
Expect	patience at plate
Don't Expect	100 runs

Cole is one of the fastest men in the business, and is a threat to steal bases whenever he gets on. He will patrol center field for the Rockies to utilize his speed. The Indians had high hopes for him in 1991, realigning their outfield to take advantage of his speed and sending him to Rod Carew's hitting school to master bunting and slap hitting. The Indians campaign was a failure, though, and before the '92 campaign, Cleveland brought the fences back in. Cole lost his center field job to newly acquired rookie Kenny Lofton. An opposite-field hitter with little power, Cole was hampered by a dislocated shoulder during spring training. With his .296 career average only a distant memory, Cole couldn't utilize his speed because he wasn't getting on base. Pittsburgh, searching for a leadoff man, remembered his 40 steals in 63 games as a 1990 rookie and decided to trade for him. He responded well, notching a .335 on-base average and .361 slugging percentage for the Bucs.

Major League Batting Register

	BA	G	AB	R	H	2B	3B	HR	RBI	SB
90 AL	.300	63	227	43	68	5	4	0	13	40
91 AL	.295	122	387	58	114	17	3	0	21	27
92 AL	.206	41	97	11	20	1	0	0	5	9
92 NL	.278	64	205	33	57	3	7	0	10	7
Life	.283	290	916	145	259	26	14	0	49	83
3 AVE	.283	97	305	48	86	9	5	0	16	28

VINCE COLEMAN

Position: Outfield
Team: New York Mets
Born: September 22, 1961 Jacksonville, FL
Height: 6' **Weight:** 170 lbs.
Bats: both **Throws:** right
Acquired: Signed as a free agent, 12/90

Player Summary	
Fantasy Value	$18 to $22
Card Value	3¢ to 4¢
Will	bid for stolen base crown
Can't	hit for power or average
Expect	recurring hamstring problems
Don't Expect	stellar defense

Although he was disabled three times in the first four months of the 1992 campaign, "Vincent Van Go" is still one of the game's top speed merchants. The only player to have three 100-steal seasons in the NL this century, Coleman suffered persistent hamstring problems that kept him out of all but 37 games by August 2. Once an ineffective leadoff man who fanned frequently, he has become more patient. Although he holds the record for most consecutive steals without being caught (50 in 1988 and '89) he says seasons of 100-plus steals are history, because pitchers slide their legs more toward first base while keeping runners close. Still, a walk to Coleman is like a double to anyone else. He was the winner of six consecutive stolen base crowns. Coleman's main weaknesses are in the field, where he sometimes misjudges fly balls and has a feeble throwing arm.

Major League Batting Register

	BA	G	AB	R	H	2B	3B	HR	RBI	SB
85 NL	.267	151	636	107	170	20	10	1	40	110
86 NL	.232	154	600	94	139	13	8	0	29	107
87 NL	.289	151	623	121	180	14	10	3	43	109
88 NL	.260	153	616	77	160	20	10	3	38	81
89 NL	.254	145	563	94	143	21	9	2	28	65
90 NL	.292	124	497	73	145	18	9	6	39	77
91 NL	.255	72	278	45	71	7	5	1	17	37
92 NL	.275	71	229	37	63	11	1	2	21	24
Life	.265	1021	4042	648	1071	124	62	18	255	610
3 AVE	.278	89	335	52	93	12	5	3	26	46

DARNELL COLES

Position: Infield; outfield
Team: Toronto Blue Jays
Born: June 2, 1962 San Bernardino, CA
Height: 6'1" **Weight:** 185 lbs.
Bats: right **Throws:** right
Acquired: Signed as a free agent, 11/92

Player Summary	
Fantasy Value	$2 to $4
Card Value	3¢ to 4¢
Will	swing solid bat
Can't	supply dazzling defense
Expect	service at several spots
Don't Expect	regular duty

Coles played for four big league teams before hanging his shingle in Cincinnati last summer. After failing to make the Reds' roster during spring training, he was promoted from Triple-A May 4 as a replacement for an injured player. His versatility helped, as he filled in at first, third, and the outfield and served as a valuable pinch-hitter with punch. With Chris Sabo out for a St. Louis series in late July, Coles cranked out seven straight hits with consecutive 4-for-4 and 5-for-6 games. Though he entered the 1992 season with a .243 career average, Coles hit .319 in his first 40 games. He notched a .322 on-base average and a .482 slugging percentage in 1992. Extremely dangerous against lefthanded pitching, Coles in 1992 batted .320 against lefties and .295 versus righties. He showed he has power in 1986, when he had 20 homers for Detroit.

Major League Batting Register

	BA	G	AB	R	H	2B	3B	HR	RBI	SB
83 AL	.283	27	92	9	26	7	0	1	6	0
84 AL	.161	48	143	15	23	3	1	0	6	2
85 AL	.237	27	59	8	14	4	0	1	5	0
86 AL	.273	142	521	67	142	30	2	20	86	6
87 AL	.181	53	149	14	27	5	1	4	15	0
87 NL	.227	40	119	20	27	8	0	6	24	1
88 NL	.232	68	211	20	49	13	1	5	36	1
88 AL	.292	55	195	32	57	10	1	10	34	3
89 AL	.252	146	535	54	135	21	3	10	59	5
90 AL	.209	89	215	22	45	7	1	3	20	0
91 NL	.214	11	14	1	3	0	0	0	0	0
92 NL	.312	55	141	16	44	11	2	3	18	1
Life	.247	761	2394	278	592	119	12	63	309	16
3 AVE	.245	52	123	13	31	7	1	3	13	0

DAVID CONE

Position: Pitcher
Team: Kansas City Royals
Born: January 2, 1963 Kansas City, MO
Height: 6'1" **Weight:** 190 lbs.
Bats: left **Throws:** right
Acquired: Signed as a free agent, 12/92

Player Summary	
Fantasy Value	$20 to $25
Card Value	3¢ to 4¢
Will	vie for strikeout crown
Can't	keep runners close
Expect	wins in double digits
Don't Expect	long losing spells

Cone returns home to help a struggling KC rotation. In 1992, Cone almost became the first pitcher to win three straight NL strikeout crowns since Warren Spahn (1950 to '52). Cone would have won the honor, but he was busy helping the Blue Jays win the World Series. He throws everything hard, including his slider, fastball, split-fingered fastball, and curve. He once struck out 19 batters in a game. In '92, he became the first Met since Tom Seaver to throw back-to-back shutouts twice, and he made the All-Star team for the second time. He first made it in 1988, the year he finished third in the Cy Young Award voting. His main weaknesses are an inability to keep runners close and an occasional tendency to lose his cool. A durable athlete capable of throwing high numbers of pitches in a game without wilting, Cone often completes what he starts and ranks among the league leaders in innings pitched.

Major League Pitching Register

	W	L	ERA	G	CG	IP	H	ER	BB	SO
86 AL	0	0	5.56	11	0	22.2	29	14	13	21
87 NL	5	6	3.71	21	1	99.1	87	41	44	68
88 NL	20	3	2.22	35	8	231.1	178	57	80	213
89 NL	14	8	3.52	34	7	219.2	183	86	74	190
90 NL	14	10	3.23	31	6	211.2	177	76	65	233
91 NL	14	14	3.29	34	5	232.2	204	85	73	241
92 NL	13	7	2.88	27	7	196.2	162	63	82	214
92 AL	4	3	2.55	8	0	53.0	39	15	29	47
Life	84	51	3.10	201	34	1267.0	1059	437	460	1227
3 AVE	15	11	3.10	33	6	231.2	194	80	83	245

DENNIS COOK

Position: Pitcher
Team: Cleveland Indians
Born: Oct. 4, 1962 Lamarque, TX
Height: 6'3" **Weight:** 185 lbs.
Bats: left **Throws:** left
Acquired: Traded from Dodgers with Mike Christopher for Rudy Seanez, 12/91

Player Summary	
Fantasy Value	$3 to $5
Card Value	3¢ to 4¢
Will	be around the plate
Can't	keep the ball in the park
Expect	more success if he starts
Don't Expect	many complete games

Cook spent six weeks in Cleveland's bullpen last spring before the desperate Indians gave him a chance to reclaim a big league starter's job. He responded so well that the team won his first five starts. Cook had been a successful starter with the Giants and Phillies, winning a combined 16 games in 1989 and '90, but failed to fare as well after the Dodgers assigned him to the bullpen three years ago. A control pitcher who strikes out twice as many batters as he walks, he allowed opponents to compile a .255 batting average, a .312 on-base percentage, and a .463 slugging percentage in 1992. Cook's biggest handicap is the home run ball; he threw 29 gophers in 158 innings last year. The designated hitter rule also worked against him, because he is an outstanding hitter who could help his own cause if he were allowed to bat. He hit .306 and homered against Fernando Valenzuela during the 1990 campaign.

Major League Pitching Register

	W	L	ERA	G	CG	IP	H	ER	BB	SO
88 NL	2	1	2.86	4	1	22.0	9	7	11	13
89 NL	7	8	3.78	23	2	121.0	183	50	38	67
90 NL	9	4	3.92	47	2	156.0	155	68	56	64
91 NL	1	0	0.51	20	0	17.2	12	1	7	8
92 AL	5	7	3.82	32	1	158.0	156	67	50	96
Life	24	20	3.66	126	6	474.2	442	193	162	248
2 AVE	7	6	3.87	40	2	157.2	156	68	53	80

SCOTT COOPER

Position: Third base; first base
Team: Boston Red Sox
Born: Oct. 13, 1967 St. Louis, MO
Height: 6'3" **Weight:** 205 lbs.
Bats: left **Throws:** right
Acquired: Third-round pick in 6/86 free-agent draft

Player Summary	
Fantasy Value	$5 to $8
Card Value	20¢ to 35¢
Will	dazzle at third
Can't	bring speed
Expect	rocket throws
Don't Expect	another Boggs

Cooper is an outstanding defensive third baseman whose progress to the majors has been blocked because he plays the same position as Wade Boggs. In 1992, Boston tried to get both players into the lineup by playing Cooper across the diamond at first. With Boggs gone, Cooper should get his chance. A lefthanded line-drive hitter without much power, Cooper has been coveted by many other clubs. He has a powerful throwing arm and good credentials, leading several minor leagues in putouts, assists, and total chances. He also didn't disappoint at the plate. He compiled a .346 on-base average and a .383 slugging percentage in 1992. Given daily duty, he'll probably hit about .275 with 15 homers. Cooper broke into pro ball in 1986 and reached the Red Sox for a brief trial four years later. In 1991 at Triple-A Pawtucket, he hit .277 with 15 homers and 72 RBI. He hit .266 with 56 runs, 12 homers, and 44 RBI in 1990 at Pawtucket. He hit .457 in a 14-game trial for the Red Sox at the end of the 1991 campaign.

Major League Batting Register

	BA	G	AB	R	H	2B	3B	HR	RBI	SB
90 AL	.000	2	1	0	0	0	0	0	0	0
91 AL	.457	14	35	6	16	4	2	0	7	0
92 AL	.276	123	337	34	93	21	0	5	33	1
Life	.292	139	373	40	109	25	2	5	40	1

JOEY CORA

Position: Second base
Team: Chicago White Sox
Born: May 14, 1965 Caguas, Puerto Rico
Height: 5'8" **Weight:** 150 lbs.
Bats: both **Throws:** right
Acquired: Traded from Padres with Kevin Garner and Warren Newson for Adam Peterson and Steve Rosenberg, 3/91

Player Summary	
Fantasy Value	$1 to $3
Card Value	3¢ to 4¢
Will	display great speed
Can't	hold regular job
Expect	unsteady defense
Don't Expect	high average

Cora is a former Vanderbilt University star who batted over .300 four times in the minors, but has never lived up to his advance billing in the majors. An impatient hitter who rarely walks or collects an extra-base hit, he depends on his speed to keep him in the majors. Even his running game is erratic, however. He gets thrown out more often than most base-stealers who possess his speed. He was nailed trying to steal three times in 1992. Cora's mediocre defense is another detriment (he had a .984 fielding average at second in 1992), but his versatility helps. He can fill in at shortstop and third base, pinch-run, or produce a timely bunt in a pinch-hit role. He doesn't strike out or hit into double-plays too often. He once had a 37-game hitting streak in the minors but has shown only flashes of offensive ability in the majors. He had a .317 on-base average and a .320 slugging percentage in 1992.

Major League Batting Register

	BA	G	AB	R	H	2B	3B	HR	RBI	SB
87 NL	.237	77	241	23	57	7	2	0	13	15
89 NL	.316	12	19	5	6	1	0	0	1	1
90 NL	.270	51	100	12	27	3	0	0	2	8
91 AL	.241	100	228	37	55	2	3	0	18	11
92 AL	.246	68	122	27	30	7	1	0	9	10
Life	.246	308	710	104	175	20	6	0	43	45

RHEAL CORMIER

Position: Pitcher
Team: St. Louis Cardinals
Born: April 23, 1967 Moncton, New Brunswick, Canada
Height: 5'10" **Weight:** 185 lbs.
Bats: left **Throws:** left
Acquired: Sixth-round pick in 6/88 free-agent draft

Player Summary	
Fantasy Value	$4 to $8
Card Value	3¢ to 4¢
Will	need better endurance
Can't	keep runners off base
Expect	inflated ERA
Don't Expect	ball to stay in park

A control pitcher whose strikeout-to-walk ratio is much better than average, Cormier was ineffective in threading the needle last summer. Early in the season, batters pounded him for a .300 batting average and he yielded more than a hit per inning. It was a rude awakening for him. He settled down by the end of the 1992 season and held batters to a .269 batting average, a .305 on-base percentage, and a .387 slugging percentage. He also showed flashes of great potential. One highlight was a 3-1 win over Los Angeles July 10 that included 11 strikeouts in seven innings. Cormier gets lots of ground-ball outs with his sinkerball. He usually handles lefthanded batters well but often has trouble with righties. In 1992, though, lefties hit .288 off him, while righties compiled only a .265 average. Late in the game, he has trouble against everyone and often needs quick relief. The 1988 Canadian Olympian led the Triple-A American Association with three shutouts in 1991, going 7-9 with a 4.23 ERA.

Major League Pitching Register

	W	L	ERA	G	CG	IP	H	ER	BB	SO
91 NL	4	5	4.12	11	2	67.2	74	31	8	38
92 NL	10	10	3.68	31	3	186.0	194	76	33	117
Life	14	15	3.80	42	5	253.2	268	107	41	155
2 AVE	7	8	3.80	21	3	127.1	134	54	21	78

HENRY COTTO

Position: Outfield
Team: Seattle Mariners
Born: Jan. 5, 1961 Bronx, NY
Height: 6'2" **Weight:** 178 lbs.
Bats: right **Throws:** right
Acquired: Traded from Yankees with Steve Trout for Lee Guetterman, Clay Parker, and Wade Taylor, 12/87

Player Summary

Fantasy Value..................................$3 to $5
Card Value...3¢ to 4¢
Will......................serve as superb outfield sub
Can't....................................accumulate walks
Expect ....potent pinch-hitting
Don't Expect ....solid throwing arm

Cotto is one of baseball's best substitutes. An ideal fourth outfielder who has good range at all three spots, he's also a proven pinch-hitter and a baserunner blessed with considerable speed. He is an impatient hitter who strikes out more often than he walks, even though he is not a power hitter. He should consider bunting for more base-hits to increase his on-base percentage and capitalize on his quickness. Cotto had a .294 on-base average and a .354 slugging average in 1992. He's capable of 20 steals a year, even in a part-time role, but his forte is his ability to pinch-hit. He poked eight hits in his first 13 emergency at bats of 1991. His overall offense has improved since he stopped swinging at the first pitch every time up. He'd hit .300 if given a steady diet of low pitches.

Major League Batting Register

	BA	G	AB	R	H	2B	3B	HR	RBI	SB
84 NL	.274	105	146	24	40	5	0	0	8	9
85 AL	.304	34	56	4	17	1	0	1	6	1
86 AL	.213	35	80	11	17	3	0	1	6	3
87 AL	.235	68	149	21	35	10	0	5	20	4
88 AL	.259	133	386	50	100	18	1	8	33	27
89 AL	.264	100	295	44	78	11	2	9	33	10
90 AL	.259	127	355	40	92	14	3	4	33	21
91 AL	.305	66	177	35	54	6	2	6	23	16
92 AL	.259	108	294	42	76	11	1	5	27	23
Life	.263	776	1938	271	509	79	9	39	189	114
3 AVE	.269	100	275	39	74	10	2	5	28	20

TIM CREWS

Position: Pitcher
Team: Los Angeles Dodgers
Born: April 3, 1961 Tampa, FL
Height: 6' **Weight:** 190 lbs.
Bats: right **Throws:** right
Acquired: Traded from Brewers with Tim Leary for Greg Brock, 12/86

Player Summary

Fantasy Value..................................$2 to $4
Card Value...3¢ to 4¢
Will ....control three pitches
Can't...................................always retire lefties
Expect ....frequent calls
Don't Expect.........................ERA under 3.00

A middle relief pitcher with a fastball, slider, and forkball, Crews took his lumps in 1992. Used mostly in mop-up roles by the floundering Dodgers, he was victimized by an indecent defense but also had too many ineffective outings. He yielded more than a hit per inning and was uncharacteristically wild—possibly because he didn't get enough work. Opponents compiled a .310 batting average, a .351 on-base percentage, and a .422 slugging percentage in 1992. He's generally much more effective against righthanded hitters. In 1992, righties batted .295 against him, while lefties were able to compile an incredible .327 batting average. A rubber-armed righty, he had worked 60-plus games two years in a row. Crews usually spots the ball to specific locations. When he's right, he owns the outside corner. He helps his own cause because he's a good fielder with a good pickoff move. He broke into pro ball in 1981 but didn't reach the majors for six years.

Major League Pitching Register

	W	L	ERA	G	S	IP	H	ER	BB	SO
87 NL	1	1	2.48	20	3	29.0	30	8	8	20
88 NL	4	0	3.14	42	0	71.2	77	25	16	45
89 NL	0	1	3.21	44	1	61.2	69	22	23	56
90 NL	4	5	2.77	66	5	107.1	98	33	24	76
91 NL	2	3	3.43	60	6	76.0	75	29	19	53
92 NL	0	3	5.19	49	0	78.0	95	45	20	43
Life	11	13	3.44	281	15	423.2	444	162	110	293
3 AVE	2	4	3.68	58	4	87.0	89	36	21	57

CHUCK CRIM

Position: Pitcher
Team: California Angels
Born: July 23, 1961 Van Nuys, CA
Height: 6′ **Weight:** 190 lbs.
Bats: right **Throws:** right
Acquired: Traded from Brewers for Mike Fetters and Glenn Carter, 12/91

Player Summary	
Fantasy Value	$2 to $5
Card Value	3¢ to 4¢
Will	yield more hits than frames
Can't	carry old workload
Expect	many ground outs
Don't Expect	respectable ERA

Before his effectiveness declined in 1992, Crim was one of baseball's best workhorse relievers. He appeared in more than 50 games for five straight seasons—all with Milwaukee—while recording a 3.47 career ERA. Traded to California, he struggled during the first half because he was opening his shoulder rather than maintaining his former compact delivery. After studying videos of his strong 1987 and '88 seasons, he also detected a flaw in his delivery. Switching to the three-quarters motion he saw on the tapes, Crim immediately piled up more than six hitless innings. A sinker-slider pitcher who also has a changeup, Crim works the outside part of the plate as much as possible. He yields more hits than innings pitched but has good control when his game is on. In 1992, opponents compiled a .293 batting average, a .355 on-base percentage, and a .440 slugging percentage. He has a good glove but his pickoff move is weak.

Major League Pitching Register

	W	L	ERA	G	S	IP	H	ER	BB	SO
87 AL	6	8	3.67	53	12	130.0	133	53	39	56
88 AL	7	6	2.91	70	9	105.0	95	34	28	58
89 AL	9	7	2.83	76	7	117.2	114	37	36	59
90 AL	3	5	3.47	67	11	85.2	88	33	23	39
91 AL	8	5	4.63	66	3	91.1	115	47	25	39
92 AL	7	6	5.17	57	1	87.0	100	50	29	30
Life	40	37	3.71	389	43	616.2	645	254	180	281
3 AVE	6	5	4.43	63	5	88.1	101	43	26	36

CHAD CURTIS

Position: Outfield
Team: California Angels
Born: Nov. 6, 1968 Marion, IN
Height: 5′10″ **Weight:** 175 lbs.
Bats: right **Throws:** right
Acquired: 45th-round pick in 6/89 free-agent draft

Player Summary	
Fantasy Value	$5 to $12
Card Value	15¢ to 25¢
Will	improve with time
Can't	hit for consistent power
Expect	frequent steals
Don't Expect	return to infield

After a shaky spring training in the outfield, Curtis began his rookie season as a backup for injured veterans Hubie Brooks and Von Hayes. But Curtis played so well that he quickly became a regular, dividing his time among all three outfield spots. He has both speed and power, and he collected two homers and five RBI against Seattle on June 26. He was often deployed as California's No. 5 batter. A speed merchant, he had a two-year total of 110 steals in the minors just prior to 1992. Curtis can also hit. He compiled a .341 on-base average and a .372 slugging percentage in 1992. He led the Class-A Midwest League with 223 total bases in 1990. In 1991 at Triple-A Edmonton, he had a .316 batting average with nine homers and 61 RBI. He also had 46 stolen bases that year. Though he's capable of playing both second and third base, Curtis is at his best defensively in the outfield. He has good range and throws well. Speed will keep him in the majors, but he needs to utilize it more by cutting down on his strikeouts.

Major League Batting Register

	BA	G	AB	R	H	2B	3B	HR	RBI	SB
92 AL	.259	139	441	59	114	16	2	10	46	43
Life	.259	139	441	59	114	16	2	10	46	43

MILT CUYLER

Position: Outfield
Team: Detroit Tigers
Born: Oct. 7, 1968 Macon, GA
Height: 5'10" **Weight:** 175 lbs.
Bats: both **Throws:** right
Acquired: Second-round pick in 6/86 free-agent draft

Player Summary	
Fantasy Value	$5 to $8
Card Value	5¢ to 10¢
Will	steal bases at will
Can't	match Pettis's defense
Expect	bunts and infield hits
Don't Expect	good average

After stealing 41 bases as a 1991 rookie, Cuyler had been expected to set the table for the sluggers who followed him in Detroit's lineup last summer. Instead, a sore right knee prevented the switch-hitting center fielder from stealing bases or dropping bunts for base hits. He also showed he needed considerable work at the plate, where he's one of the game's least patient hitters. His ratio of strikeouts to walks in 1991 was an alarming 8-to-1—unacceptable even from a slugger, which he is not. He had a .275 on-base average and a .316 slugging percentage in 1992. He batted only .220 against righties. He is a fine defensive player whose gift of speed turns potential gap hits into rally-stopping outs. His arm, however, is nothing to write home about. When healthy, Cuyler is an accomplished basestealer with an 80 percent success ratio. He'd be even more prolific if he mastered the art of hitting the ball on the ground; he either whiffs or hits flies far too often. He also needs to work on bunting.

Major League Batting Register

	BA	G	AB	R	H	2B	3B	HR	RBI	SB
90 AL	.255	19	51	8	13	3	1	0	8	1
91 AL	.257	154	475	77	122	15	7	3	33	41
92 AL	.241	89	291	39	70	11	1	3	28	8
Life	.251	262	817	124	205	29	9	6	69	50
2 AVE	.251	122	383	58	96	13	4	3	31	25

KAL DANIELS

Position: Outfield
Team: Chicago Cubs
Born: Aug. 20, 1963 Vienna, GA
Height: 5'11" **Weight:** 205 lbs.
Bats: left **Throws:** right
Acquired: Traded from Dodgers for Mike Sodders, 6/92

Player Summary	
Fantasy Value	$3 to $6
Card Value	3¢ to 4¢
Will	find spot for big bat
Can't	throw or field
Expect	bad news for bad knees
Don't Expect	durability

In his debut as a Cub last July 1, Daniels hit a single while batting for Paul Assenmacher. Daniels then was easily thrown out at the plate when he tried to score on Jose Vizcaino's double. The incident summarized Daniels's recent career, because he can still hit, but six knee operations make him a liability anytime he has to run. He strikes out twice as often as he walks but is unusually selective at the plate for a slugger. He led the National League with a .402 on-base percentage over the five-year span from 1986 to 1990. He had a .315 on-base average and a .377 slugging percentage in 1992. Daniels has good opposite-field power and a good batting eye, but he bothers umpires with constant complaints about called strikes. Never a good outfielder, he lacks range, misjudges fly balls, and doesn't throw well. He would make a good designated hitter, especially in a platoon role.

Major League Batting Register

	BA	G	AB	R	H	2B	3B	HR	RBI	SB
86 NL	.320	74	181	34	58	10	4	6	23	15
87 NL	.334	108	368	73	123	24	1	26	64	26
88 NL	.291	140	495	95	144	29	1	18	64	27
89 NL	.246	55	171	33	42	13	0	4	17	9
90 NL	.296	130	450	81	133	23	1	27	94	4
91 NL	.249	137	461	54	115	15	1	17	73	6
92 NL	.241	83	212	21	51	11	0	6	25	0
Life	.285	727	2338	391	666	125	8	104	360	87
3 AVE	.266	117	374	52	100	16	1	17	64	3

RON DARLING

Position: Pitcher
Team: Oakland Athletics
Born: August 19, 1960 Honolulu, HI
Height: 6'3" **Weight:** 195 lbs.
Bats: right **Throws:** right
Acquired: Traded from Expos for Matt Grott and Russell Cormier, 7/91

Player Summary	
Fantasy Value	$7 to $11
Card Value	3¢ to 4¢
Will	show good control
Can't	challenge for K crown
Expect	hot and cold streaks
Don't Expect	20-win season

After struggling for two seasons, Darling showed last summer that he had recaptured the form that made him a solid starter with the New York Mets from 1984 to 1989. By August, he had taken four potential no-hitters into the seventh inning and won more games than in any of the three previous years. A control pitcher who favors the split-fingered fastball, he also throws a fastball and a changeup. However, he has lost some velocity off his fastball. Although he's a good fielder, he's not adept at holding runners close. He also has problems keeping the ball in the park—although pitching half his games in the spacious Oakland Coliseum helped him last year. Three of his nine wins by August were shutouts. Darling broke into pro ball in 1981 and reached the Mets two years later.

Major League Pitching Register

	W	L	ERA	G	CG	IP	H	ER	BB	SO
83 NL	1	3	2.80	5	1	35.1	31	11	17	23
84 NL	12	9	3.81	33	2	205.2	179	87	104	136
85 NL	16	6	2.90	36	4	248.0	214	80	114	167
86 NL	15	6	2.81	34	4	237.0	203	74	81	184
87 NL	12	8	4.29	32	2	207.2	183	99	96	167
88 NL	17	9	3.25	34	7	240.2	218	87	60	161
89 NL	14	14	3.52	33	4	217.1	214	85	70	153
90 NL	7	9	4.50	33	1	126.0	135	63	44	99
91 NL	5	8	4.37	20	0	119.1	121	58	33	69
91 AL	3	7	4.08	12	0	75.0	64	34	38	60
92 AL	15	10	3.66	33	4	206.1	198	84	72	99
Life	117	89	3.57	305	29	1918.1	1760	762	729	1318
3 AVE	10	11	4.08	33	2	175.1	173	80	62	109

DANNY DARWIN

Position: Pitcher
Team: Boston Red Sox
Born: Oct. 25, 1955 Bonham, TX
Height: 6'3" **Weight:** 190 lbs.
Bats: right **Throws:** right
Acquired: Signed as a free agent, 12/90

Player Summary	
Fantasy Value	$4 to $8
Card Value	3¢ to 5¢
Will	continue swing service
Can't	keep runners from stealing
Expect	lots of hits
Don't Expect	return to 1990

Darwin has been a major disappointment since posting successive 11-4 campaigns as a member of the 1989 and '90 Astros. After signing a megabucks free-agent contract with the Red Sox, he missed large chunks of the '91 campaign with shoulder problems but couldn't find a level of consistency even when healthy. A bust in the bullpen, Darwin moved into the starting rotation and responded well. A fastball-and-slider pitcher who once led his league in ERA (1990), Darwin strikes out more than twice the number he walks. Because he's around the plate, the long ball sometimes hurts him. Except for the fact that he can't keep runners close, he helps his own cause in the field. He can't escape advancing age, however.

Major League Pitching Register

	W	L	ERA	G	S	IP	H	ER	BB	SO
78 AL	1	0	4.15	3	0	8.2	11	4	1	8
79 AL	4	4	4.04	20	0	78.0	50	35	30	58
80 AL	13	4	2.63	53	8	109.2	98	32	50	104
81 AL	9	9	3.64	22	0	146.0	115	59	57	98
82 AL	10	8	3.44	56	7	89.0	95	34	37	61
83 AL	8	13	3.49	28	0	183.0	175	71	62	92
84 AL	8	12	3.94	35	0	223.2	249	98	54	123
85 AL	8	18	3.80	39	2	217.2	212	92	65	125
86 AL	6	8	3.52	27	0	130.1	120	51	35	80
86 NL	5	2	2.32	12	0	54.1	50	14	9	40
87 NL	9	10	3.59	33	0	195.2	184	78	69	134
88 NL	8	13	3.84	44	3	192.0	189	82	48	129
89 NL	11	4	2.36	68	7	122.0	92	32	33	104
90 NL	11	4	2.21	48	2	162.2	136	40	31	109
91 AL	3	6	5.16	12	0	68.0	71	39	15	42
92 AL	9	9	3.96	51	3	161.1	159	71	53	124
Life	123	124	3.50	551	32	2142.0	2006	832	649	1431
3 AVE	8	6	3.44	37	2	130.1	122	50	33	92

DOUG DASCENZO

Position: Outfield
Team: Texas Rangers
Born: June 30, 1964 Cleveland, OH
Height: 5'8" **Weight:** 160 lbs.
Bats: both **Throws:** left
Acquired: Signed as a free agent, 12/92

Player Summary

Fantasy Value	$2 to $4
Card Value	3¢ to 4¢
Will	pitch on occasion
Can't	hit for power or average
Expect	strong outfield defense
Don't Expect	regular role

A little guy with a big glove, Dascenzo is a center fielder with speed, range, instincts, and good hands—abilities that compensate for a so-so throwing arm. His arm is actually more use on the mound, where he sometimes appears in one-sided games (he worked four scoreless innings in three 1991 appearances). Although he takes many bases on balls because of his small strike zone, Dascenzo isn't much of a hitter, and he possesses virtually no home run power. Best deployed as a pinch-runner or defensive replacement, he often wastes at bats by becoming over-anxious, taking big cuts that produce ground balls. Better from the left side, he could bunt more to boost his average, on-base average, steals, and runs scored. He had a .304 on-base percentage and a .311 slugging percentage in 1992. He holds the NL mark for consecutive error-less games plus the major league record for consecutive errorless games from the start of a career.

Major League Batting Register

	BA	G	AB	R	H	2B	3B	HR	RBI	SB
88 NL	.213	26	75	9	16	3	0	0	4	6
89 NL	.165	47	139	20	23	1	0	1	12	6
90 NL	.253	113	241	27	61	9	5	1	26	15
91 NL	.255	118	239	40	61	11	0	1	18	14
92 NL	.255	139	376	37	96	13	4	0	20	6
Life	.240	443	1070	133	257	37	9	3	80	47
3 AVE	.255	123	285	35	73	11	3	1	21	12

DARREN DAULTON

Position: Catcher
Team: Philadelphia Phillies
Born: Jan. 3, 1962 Arkansas City, KS
Height: 6'2" **Weight:** 190 lbs.
Bats: left **Throws:** right
Acquired: 25th-round pick in 6/80 free-agent draft

Player Summary

Fantasy Value	$10 to $20
Card Value	6¢ to 12¢
Will	collect many RBI
Can't	reach .300 level
Expect	patience at plate
Don't Expect	basestealers to run

Before 1992, Daulton had never hit higher than .268, topped 57 RBI, or hit more than 12 homers in a season. After a winter of rebuilding his body, battered in a near-fatal 1991 car crash, he quickly showed he would exceed those highs. He knocked in a run in eight straight games from June 3 to 12 and had a midseason total of 58 RBI, most by a Phillie at the All-Star break since Mike Schmidt had the same number in 1987. A former pull hitter who learned to hit to all fields, Daulton (a first-time All-Star in 1992) became the first 100-RBI catcher since Gary Carter in 1984. An off-season knee operation—Daulton's sixth—helped him concentrate by allowing him to play without pain. Behind the plate, he calls good games, blocks errant pitches, and throws well when healthy. He improved his defense dramatically in '92. He's a good but slow baserunner.

Major League Batting Register

	BA	G	AB	R	H	2B	3B	HR	RBI	SB
83 NL	.333	2	3	1	1	0	0	0	0	0
85 NL	.204	36	103	14	21	3	1	4	11	3
86 NL	.225	49	138	18	31	4	0	8	21	2
87 NL	.194	53	129	10	25	6	0	3	13	0
88 NL	.208	58	144	13	30	6	0	1	12	2
89 NL	.201	131	368	29	74	12	2	8	44	2
90 NL	.268	143	459	62	123	30	1	12	57	7
91 NL	.196	89	285	36	56	12	0	12	42	5
92 NL	.270	145	485	80	131	32	5	27	109	11
Life	.233	706	2114	263	492	105	9	75	309	32
3 AVE	.252	126	410	59	103	25	2	17	69	8

CHILI DAVIS

Position: Designated hitter
Team: California Angels
Born: Jan. 17, 1960 Kingston, Jamaica
Height: 6'3" **Weight:** 210 lbs.
Bats: both **Throws:** right
Acquired: Signed as a free agent, 12/92

Player Summary	
Fantasy Value	$14 to $20
Card Value	3¢ to 4¢
Will	slug from both sides
Can't	run like he used to
Expect	power when healthy
Don't Expect	many outfield duties

Davis returns to the Angels' DH role. The Twins spent most of 1992 wondering what happened to the home run punch Davis displayed during his first year with the club, in 1991. A switch-hitter who hits better lefthanded, he led the Twins with 29 home runs and added two more in the World Series against Atlanta. After hitting 19 of his '91 homers in the first 75 games, Davis's power began a downswing that extended into 1992. Back problems that have surfaced several times in the past have been a factor. In addition to power production, he has good speed, which helps him when he reaches base. But he hasn't stolen too often recently. Nor has he played much outfield, where he's a defensive disaster (19 errors for the '88 Angels led the AL). Davis is perfectly suited to the DH.

Major League Batting Register

	BA	G	AB	R	H	2B	3B	HR	RBI	SB
81 NL	.133	8	15	1	2	0	0	0	0	2
82 NL	.261	154	641	86	167	27	6	19	76	24
83 NL	.233	137	486	54	113	21	2	11	59	10
84 NL	.315	137	499	87	157	21	6	21	81	12
85 NL	.270	136	481	53	130	25	2	13	56	15
86 NL	.278	153	526	71	146	28	3	13	70	16
87 NL	.250	149	500	80	125	22	1	24	76	16
88 AL	.268	158	600	81	161	29	3	21	93	9
89 AL	.271	154	560	81	152	24	1	22	90	3
90 AL	.265	113	412	58	109	17	1	12	58	1
91 AL	.277	153	534	84	148	34	1	29	93	5
92 AL	.288	138	444	63	128	27	2	12	66	4
Life	.270	1590	5698	799	1538	275	28	197	818	117
3 AVE	.277	135	463	68	128	26	1	18	72	3

ERIC DAVIS

Position: Outfield
Team: Los Angeles Dodgers
Born: May 29, 1962 Los Angeles, CA
Height: 6'3" **Weight:** 185 lbs.
Bats: right **Throws:** right
Acquired: Traded from Reds with Kip Gross for Tim Belcher and John Wetteland, 11/91

Player Summary	
Fantasy Value	$10 to $16
Card Value	5¢ to 10¢
Will	steal often if healthy
Can't	avoid stints on DL
Expect	deployment in left field
Don't Expect	sudden return to form

Davis had high expectations in 1992. United with boyhood friend Darryl Strawberry in Los Angeles, Davis was determined to discover a fountain of youth in more ways than one. Both he and the Dodgers hoped for a return of his 1987 form of 37 homers, 50 steals, and a league-leading 380 outfield putouts. Instead, a worst-case scenario set in. Both Strawberry and Davis spent most of the season disabled as the Dodgers sunk to the cellar. Davis went out with a separated shoulder in May and an injured left wrist in August—keeping intact his record of never playing in more than 135 games. Plagued by hamstring and knee problems throughout his career, he has managed to win three Gold Gloves and produce two 100-RBI campaigns but his best days seem long gone. His performance has declined steadily in each of the last four seasons.

Major League Batting Register

	BA	G	AB	R	H	2B	3B	HR	RBI	SB
84 NL	.224	57	174	33	39	10	1	10	30	10
85 NL	.246	56	122	26	30	3	3	8	18	16
86 NL	.277	132	415	97	115	15	3	27	71	80
87 NL	.293	129	474	120	139	23	4	37	100	50
88 NL	.273	135	472	81	129	18	3	26	93	35
89 NL	.281	131	462	74	130	14	2	34	101	21
90 NL	.260	127	453	84	118	26	2	24	86	21
91 NL	.235	89	285	39	67	10	0	11	33	14
92 NL	.228	76	267	21	61	8	1	5	32	19
Life	.265	932	3124	575	828	127	19	182	564	266
3 AVE	.245	97	335	48	82	15	1	13	50	18

71

GLENN DAVIS

Position: Designated hitter
Team: Baltimore Orioles
Born: March 28, 1961 Jacksonville, FL
Height: 6'3" **Weight:** 200 lbs.
Bats: right **Throws:** right
Acquired: Traded from Astros for Steve Finley, Pete Harnisch, and Curt Schilling, 1/91

Player Summary	
Fantasy Value	$10 to $16
Card Value	4¢ to 6¢
Will	hit well to all fields
Can't	seem to avoid injuries
Expect	rising average
Don't Expect	40 home runs

Davis missed most of the 1991 campaign with nerve damage in his neck and started slowly in '92 when bothered by a muscle strain in his rib cage. Disabled through most of April last year, he finally regained his old hitting stroke in July. He lifted his average from .211 on June 15 to .301 on July 28 and had a career-best 15-game hitting streak. After playing first base on Opening Day, he spent most of the year as Baltimore's designated hitter. Although he's a power-hitter with a big swing, Davis is unlike other sluggers because he walks often. Once a dead pull hitter, he's now willing to go to the opposite field more often. The result has been a decline in power but a boost in batting average. He's not a bad first baseman, but he didn't play there much in '92 because of Randy Milligan.

Major League Batting Register

	BA	G	AB	R	H	2B	3B	HR	RBI	SB
84 NL	.213	18	61	6	13	5	0	2	8	0
85 NL	.271	100	350	51	95	11	0	20	64	0
86 NL	.265	158	574	91	152	32	3	31	101	3
87 NL	.251	151	578	70	145	35	2	27	93	4
88 NL	.271	152	561	78	152	26	0	30	99	4
89 NL	.269	158	581	87	156	26	1	34	89	4
90 NL	.251	93	327	44	82	15	4	22	64	8
91 AL	.227	49	176	29	40	9	1	10	28	4
92 AL	.276	106	398	46	110	15	2	13	48	1
Life	.262	985	3606	502	945	174	13	189	594	28
3 AVE	.257	83	300	40	77	13	2	15	47	4

MARK DAVIS

Position: Pitcher
Team: Atlanta Braves
Born: Oct. 19, 1960 Livermore, CA
Height: 6'4" **Weight:** 205 lbs.
Bats: left **Throws:** left
Acquired: Traded from Royals for Juan Berenguer, 7/92

Player Summary	
Fantasy Value	$2 to $4
Card Value	3¢ to 4¢
Will	work in middle innings
Can't	recapture Cy Young form
Expect	so-so K-walk ratio
Don't Expect	closer job

Davis has been unable to regain the form that propelled him to 44 saves in 48 opportunities in 1989, the year he earned the NL's Cy Young as a Padre. He had a fine three-pitch repertoire of a fastball, curve, and splitter. The curve was so good that he used it as his strikeout pitch. He had excellent rapport with pitching coach Pat Dobson in San Diego, and Davis was never the same after going to Kansas City. Even when the Royals inked Dobson to help Davis, he couldn't find his old form. He had problems with the index finger on his pitching hand, and even spent some time in the minors in '91. When his problems continued last summer, the Royals finally gave up and shipped him back to the NL.

Major League Pitching Register

	W	L	ERA	G	S	IP	H	ER	BB	SO
80 NL	0	0	2.57	2	0	7.0	4	2	5	5
81 NL	1	4	7.74	9	0	43.0	49	37	24	29
83 NL	6	4	3.49	20	0	111.0	93	43	50	83
84 NL	5	17	5.36	46	0	174.2	201	104	54	124
85 NL	5	12	3.54	77	7	114.1	89	45	41	131
86 NL	5	7	2.99	67	4	84.1	63	28	34	90
87 NL	4	5	4.71	20	0	70.2	72	37	28	51
87 NL	9	8	3.99	63	2	133.0	132	59	59	98
88 NL	5	10	2.01	62	28	98.1	70	22	42	102
89 NL	4	3	1.85	70	44	92.2	66	19	31	92
90 AL	2	7	5.11	53	6	68.2	71	39	52	73
91 AL	6	3	4.45	29	1	62.2	55	31	39	47
92 AL	1	3	7.18	13	0	36.1	42	29	28	19
92 NL	1	0	7.02	14	0	16.2	22	13	13	15
Life	50	78	4.07	525	92	1042.2	948	471	472	908
3 AVE	3	4	5.47	36	2	61.2	63	37	44	51

STORM DAVIS

Position: Pitcher
Team: Oakland Athletics
Born: Dec. 26, 1961 Dallas, TX
Height: 6'4" **Weight:** 200 lbs.
Bats: right **Throws:** right
Acquired: Signed as a free agent, 12/92

Player Summary	
Fantasy Value	$2 to $4
Card Value	3¢ to 4¢
Will	work in middle innings
Can't	throw fastball by anyone
Expect	good pickoff move
Don't Expect	return to rotation

Although he can pitch either way, Davis found relieving easier than starting in 1992. A painful heel spur and inflamed arch in his left foot caused less aggravation for the pitcher when he appeared in the shorter outings of a relief man. Troubled by the injuries since spring training, he fared well in middle relief last summer. He yielded less than a hit per inning although he had some problems with his control. In 1992, opponents compiled a .244 batting average, a .320 on-base average, and a .321 slugging percentage. Davis is normally a control pitcher who relies on the curveball, fastball, and forkball. He's a good fielder who keeps baserunners close. Davis made his pro debut in 1979 and reached Baltimore three years later. He was used mostly as a starter during his career.

Major League Pitching Register

	W	L	ERA	G	S	IP	H	ER	BB	SO
82 AL	8	4	3.49	29	0	100.2	96	39	28	67
83 AL	13	7	3.59	34	0	200.1	180	80	64	125
84 AL	14	9	3.12	35	1	225.0	205	78	71	105
85 AL	10	8	4.53	31	0	175.0	172	88	70	93
86 AL	9	12	3.62	25	0	154.0	166	62	49	96
87 NL	2	7	6.18	21	0	62.2	70	43	36	37
87 AL	1	1	3.26	5	0	30.1	28	11	11	28
88 AL	16	7	3.70	33	0	201.2	211	83	91	127
89 AL	19	7	4.36	31	0	169.1	187	82	68	91
90 AL	7	10	4.74	21	0	112.0	129	59	35	62
91 AL	3	9	4.96	51	2	114.1	140	63	46	53
92 AL	7	3	3.43	48	4	89.1	79	34	36	53
Life	109	84	3.98	364	7	1634.2	1663	722	605	937
3 AVE	6	7	4.45	40	2	105.1	116	52	39	56

ANDRE DAWSON

Position: Outfield
Team: Boston Red Sox
Born: July 10, 1954 Miami, FL
Height: 6'3" **Weight:** 195 lbs.
Bats: right **Throws:** right
Acquired: Signed as a free agent, 12/92

Player Summary	
Fantasy Value	$24 to $32
Card Value	10¢ to 16¢
Will	hit for power in clutch
Can't	avoid knee problems
Expect	strong throws from right
Don't Expect	many swipes or errors

The knee problems that plagued Dawson throughout his career resurfaced in 1992. The troublesome left knee had to be drained several times and he began wearing a lightweight brace in an effort to avoid surgery. One of the game's most respected clutch hitters, he won't repeat the 49-homer season that earned him MVP honors in 1987. Willie Mays and Dawson are the only players ever to produce 2,000 hits, 300 homers, and 300 steals. He's often aggressive at the plate, however, and strikes out two times more than he walks. He loves low fastballs that allow him to extend his arms. His right arm is still one of the league's best in right field. Few runners challenge this nine-time All-Star.

Major League Batting Register

	BA	G	AB	R	H	2B	3B	HR	RBI	SB
76 NL	.235	24	85	9	20	4	1	0	7	1
77 NL	.282	139	525	64	148	26	9	19	65	21
78 NL	.253	157	609	84	154	24	8	25	72	28
79 NL	.275	155	639	90	176	24	12	25	92	35
80 NL	.308	151	577	96	178	41	7	17	87	34
81 NL	.302	103	394	71	119	21	3	24	64	26
82 NL	.301	148	608	107	183	37	7	23	83	39
83 NL	.299	159	633	104	189	36	10	32	113	25
84 NL	.248	138	533	73	132	23	6	17	86	13
85 NL	.255	139	529	65	135	27	2	23	91	13
86 NL	.284	130	496	65	141	32	2	20	78	18
87 NL	.287	153	621	90	178	24	2	49	137	11
88 NL	.303	157	591	78	179	31	8	24	79	12
89 NL	.252	118	416	62	105	18	6	21	77	8
90 NL	.310	147	529	72	164	28	5	27	100	16
91 NL	.272	149	563	69	153	21	4	31	104	4
92 NL	.277	143	542	60	150	27	2	22	90	6
Life	.282	2310	8890	1259	2504	444	94	399	1425	310
3 AVE	.286	146	545	67	156	25	4	27	98	9

ROB DEER

Position: Outfield
Team: Detroit Tigers
Born: Sept. 29, 1960 Orange, CA
Height: 6'3" **Weight:** 225 lbs.
Bats: right **Throws:** right
Acquired: Signed as a free agent, 11/90

Player Summary	
Fantasy Value	$10 to $18
Card Value	3¢ to 4¢
Will	make better contact
Can't	steal bases
Expect	lots of home runs
Don't Expect	average over .240

Deer began making better contact in 1992 after a winter of workouts with White Sox hitting coach Walt Hriniak. Deer relies on videotapes of those sessions when he slumps, but he was slowed last summer by a badly strained ankle and an injured left hand. But the two stints on the DL didn't damage his power potential. Of his first 53 hits, 23 were homers and nine were doubles. On June 12, he hit a home run that actually bounced on Tiger Stadium's left field roof (only Cecil Fielder, Frank Howard, and Harmon Killebrew have cleared it). Deer had five two-homer games by July 19. Deer still strikes out frequently (131 times in 1992) but makes contact much more than he did in 1991, when he hit .179 with 175 strikeouts. Although he's not fast, Deer is a good right fielder who gets a good jump and throws well.

Major League Batting Register

	BA	G	AB	R	H	2B	3B	HR	RBI	SB
84 NL	.167	13	24	5	4	0	0	3	3	1
85 NL	.185	78	162	22	30	5	1	8	20	0
86 AL	.232	134	466	75	108	17	3	33	86	5
87 AL	.238	134	474	71	113	15	2	28	80	12
88 AL	.252	135	492	71	124	24	0	23	85	9
89 AL	.210	130	466	72	98	18	2	26	65	4
90 AL	.209	134	440	57	92	15	1	27	69	2
91 AL	.179	134	448	64	80	14	2	25	64	1
92 AL	.247	110	393	66	97	20	1	32	64	4
Life	.222	1002	3365	503	746	128	12	205	536	38
3 AVE	.210	126	427	62	90	16	1	28	66	2

JOSE DeJESUS

Position: Pitcher
Team: Philadelphia Phillies
Born: Jan. 6, 1965 Brooklyn, NY
Height: 6'5" **Weight:** 195 lbs.
Bats: right **Throws:** right
Acquired: Traded from Royals for Steve Jeltz, 3/90

Player Summary	
Fantasy Value	$2 to $4
Card Value	3¢ to 4¢
Will	need to shake injury
Can't	bunt or field
Expect	excessive walks
Don't Expect	over 12 wins

Surgery to repair a partially torn rotator cuff in the right shoulder ruined the 1992 season for DeJesus. The injury was a tough break for the hard-throwing righthander, who usually frightens hitters with his heat. He throws a fastball, slider, and changeup, but he can't always get the pitches over. DeJesus led the National League with 128 walks allowed in 1991 (against 118 strikeouts). While opposing hitters have low batting averages against him, they score runs because he throws too many wild pitches, in addition to issuing those bases on balls. Opponents had a .224 batting average but a .353 on-base average against him in 1991. At Triple-A Scranton in 1990, he was 1-4 with a 3.38 ERA, 45 strikeouts, and 39 walks in 56 innings pitched. He was 8-11 with a 3.78 ERA, 158 strikeouts, and 98 walks in 145⅓ innings pitched at Triple-A Omaha in 1989. Should DeJesus shake his shoulder woes and conquer his wildness, he could become one of baseball's top pitchers. If either problem persists, however, his career could end quickly.

Major League Pitching Register

	W	L	ERA	G	CG	IP	H	ER	BB	SO
88 AL	0	1	27.00	2	0	2.2	6	8	5	2
89 AL	0	0	4.50	3	0	8.0	7	4	8	2
90 NL	7	8	3.74	22	3	130.0	97	54	73	87
91 NL	10	9	3.42	31	3	181.2	147	69	128	118
Life	17	18	3.77	58	6	322.1	257	135	214	209
2 AVE	9	9	3.55	27	3	156.1	122	62	101	103

JOSE DeLEON

Position: Pitcher
Team: Philadelphia Phillies
Born: Dec. 20, 1960 Rancho Viejo, Dominican Republic
Height: 6'3" **Weight:** 215 lbs.
Bats: right **Throws:** right
Acquired: Signed as a free agent, 9/92

Player Summary	
Fantasy Value	.....................................$1 to $3
Card Value	....3¢ to 4¢
Will	....find a way to lose
Can't	.............................throw with old velocity
Expect	..............................some bullpen duty
Don't Expect	......................him to be hit hard

DeLeon can't win for losing. In his first 10 years in the major leagues, he had a winning record only twice. He led his league in strikeouts once but has also led in losses twice—losing 19 each time. He throws a fastball, slider, curve, and split-fingered fastball, but he does not have the velocity of his younger days. He still fans twice as many as he walks, however, yields less than a hit per inning, and keeps the ball in the park. He's not a bad fielder, but his move is only average and runners will test him. He's no help at all with a bat. DeLeon's struggles in the starting rotation remain one of baseball's mysteries. Despite a decent career ERA, he has a losing career record. After he had 142 consecutive starts, St. Louis moved DeLeon to the bullpen.

Major League Pitching Register

	W	L	ERA	G	CG	IP	H	ER	BB	SO
83 NL	7	3	2.83	15	3	108.0	75	34	47	118
84 NL	7	13	3.74	30	5	192.1	147	80	92	153
85 NL	2	19	4.70	31	1	162.2	138	85	89	149
86 NL	1	3	8.27	9	0	16.1	17	15	17	11
86 AL	4	5	2.96	13	1	79.0	49	26	42	68
87 AL	11	12	4.02	33	2	206.0	177	92	97	153
88 NL	13	10	3.67	34	3	225.1	198	92	86	208
89 NL	16	12	3.05	36	5	244.2	173	83	80	201
90 NL	7	19	4.43	32	0	182.2	168	90	86	164
91 NL	5	9	2.71	28	1	162.2	144	49	61	118
92 NL	2	9	4.37	32	0	117.1	111	57	48	79
Life	75	113	3.73	293	21	1697.0	1397	703	745	1422
3 AVE	5	12	3.81	31	0	154.2	141	65	65	120

RICH DeLUCIA

Position: Pitcher
Team: Seattle Mariners
Born: Oct. 7, 1964 Wyomissing, PA
Height: 6' **Weight:** 180 lbs.
Bats: right **Throws:** right
Acquired: Sixth-round pick in in 6/86 free-agent draft

Player Summary	
Fantasy Value	.....................................$3 to $6
Card Value	....3¢ to 4¢
Will	...........................help himself in the field
Can't	....................maintain respectable ERA
Expect	....gopher balls
Don't Expect	......................a winning record

After a 12-13 rookie season in 1991, DeLucia was hoping that the on-the-job training he received would help him. His struggles continued in 1992, however, and he found himself assigned to the bullpen after making 11 starts. A fastball pitcher who works upstairs, he gives up more than his share of fly balls. He lacks both the velocity and control to post a winning record—even if he was pitching with a team that would give him strong support. DeLucia yields more than a hit per inning and strikes out less than two batters for every one he walks. In 1992, opponents compiled a .293 batting average, a .361 on-base percentage, and a .490 slugging percentage. He's also prone to throwing the gopher ball. He gave up 13 homers in 1992. On the plus side, he is a fine fielder who is also adept at keeping baserunners close to the bag. The former University of Tennessee standout started his pro career in 1986 and reached Seattle four years later.

Major League Pitching Register

	W	L	ERA	G	S	IP	H	ER	BB	SO
90 AL	1	2	2.00	5	0	36.0	30	8	9	20
91 AL	12	13	5.09	32	0	182.0	176	103	78	98
92 AL	3	6	5.49	30	1	83.2	100	51	35	66
Life	16	21	4.83	67	1	301.2	306	162	122	184
2 AVE	8	10	5.22	31	1	133.1	138	77	57	82

JIM DESHAIES

Position: Pitcher
Team: Minnesota Twins
Born: June 23, 1960 Massena, NY
Height: 6'4" **Weight:** 220 lbs.
Bats: left **Throws:** left
Acquired: Signed as a free agent, 12/92

Player Summary	
Fantasy Value	$2 to $4
Card Value	3¢ to 4¢
Will	yield many fly outs
Can't	always throw strikes
Expect	endless throws to first
Don't Expect	airtight ERA

Deshaies gets to challenge for the Twins' No. 5 starter spot. He pitched well for the San Diego Padres after they rescued him from Triple-A last July. On July 20, he worked seven innings against Philadelphia in a game the Padres eventually won 2-1. The veteran southpaw throws fastballs, curves, changeups, and sliders, but he often has trouble finding the strike zone. He yields less than a hit per inning but can't even maintain a strikeout-to-walk ratio of 2-to-1. He has lost all velocity off his fastball. In addition, he yields too many fly balls—some of which sail out of the park. Deshaies is a deliberate worker who slows games to a crawl when runners reach base. He throws to first more often than anyone else in the majors. He's a decent fielder but a detriment as a batter. Deshaies began his pro career in 1982 and reached the majors two years later.

Major League Pitching Register

	W	L	ERA	G	CG	IP	H	ER	BB	SO
84 AL	0	1	11.57	2	0	7.0	14	9	7	5
85 NL	0	0	0.00	2	0	3.0	1	0	0	2
86 NL	12	5	3.25	26	1	144.0	124	52	59	128
87 NL	11	6	4.62	26	1	152.0	149	78	57	104
88 NL	11	14	3.00	31	3	207.0	164	69	72	127
89 NL	15	10	2.91	34	6	225.2	180	73	79	153
90 NL	7	12	3.78	34	2	209.1	186	88	84	119
91 NL	5	12	4.98	28	1	161.0	156	89	72	98
92 NL	4	7	3.28	15	0	96.0	92	35	33	46
Life	65	67	3.68	198	14	1205.0	1066	493	463	782
3 AVE	5	10	4.09	26	1	155.0	145	71	63	88

DELINO DeSHIELDS

Position: Second base
Team: Montreal Expos
Born: Jan. 15, 1969 Seaford, DE
Height: 6'1" **Weight:** 170 lbs.
Bats: left **Throws:** right
Acquired: First-round pick in 6/87 free-agent draft

Player Summary	
Fantasy Value	$18 to $28
Card Value	5¢ to 12¢
Will	run and field well
Can't	avoid getting caught
Expect	surprising power
Don't Expect	more walks than Ks

Although his omission from the 1992 NL All-Stars was a glaring oversight, DeShields blossomed into one of the game's best players last year. The former basketball star (once recruited for Villanova) has the potential to win the batting crown and hit 15 home runs. In July alone, he batted .376 with 11 stolen bases and 44 hits—most in the league. Montreal's leadoff man has speed, range, and a live bat. A slash-and-run player who drives balls to the gap, DeShields tied a team record with six hits in a doubleheader July 6, hit a three-run homer the next day, and got his fifth four-hit game of the season on July 28. In 1992, he had a .359 on-base average and a .398 slugging percentage. Though he strikes out almost twice as often as he walks, he compensates by stealing and scoring more than his share. He turns bunts and infield rollers into hits but often gets caught trying to steal. His season improved when the Expos hired Felipe Alou as their manager.

Major League Batting Register

	BA	G	AB	R	H	2B	3B	HR	RBI	SB
90 NL	.289	129	499	69	144	28	6	4	45	42
91 NL	.238	151	563	83	134	15	4	10	51	56
92 NL	.292	135	530	82	155	19	8	7	56	46
Life	.272	415	1592	234	433	62	18	21	152	144
3 AVE	.272	138	531	78	144	21	6	7	51	48

MIKE DEVEREAUX

Position: Outfield
Team: Baltimore Orioles
Born: April 10, 1963 Casper, WY
Height: 6′ **Weight:** 191 lbs.
Bats: right **Throws:** right
Acquired: Traded from Dodgers for Mike Morgan, 3/89

Player Summary

Fantasy Value	$18 to $26
Card Value	3¢ to 4¢
Will	save homers with glove
Can't	steal bases
Expect	extra-base power
Don't Expect	strong throws

Devereaux was Baltimore's leadoff man before Brady Anderson blossomed into a 1992 surprise. Moved down one notch, Devereaux proved even more productive. The acrobatic center fielder, who once held the Wyoming state high school jump record at 6′8″, routinely robs batters of home runs with leaps above outfield barriers. He also robs pitchers with his batting heroics. Devereaux batted .345 with 22 RBI for the month of June. Then he had the first five-hit game of his career on July 3. He took the league lead in triples 25 days later when he stroked his third in five games. A pull hitter who has trouble with outside breaking stuff, Devereaux strikes out twice as much as he walks. But his speed and extra-base power compensate. He had a .321 on-base average and a .464 slugging percentage in 1992. He gets a good jump on fly balls, has great range, and a passable throwing arm.

Major League Batting Register

	BA	G	AB	R	H	2B	3B	HR	RBI	SB
87 NL	.222	19	54	7	12	3	0	0	4	3
88 NL	.116	30	43	4	5	1	0	0	2	0
89 AL	.266	122	391	55	104	14	3	8	46	22
90 AL	.240	108	367	48	88	18	1	12	49	13
91 AL	.260	149	608	82	158	27	10	19	59	16
92 AL	.276	156	653	76	180	29	11	24	107	10
Life	.259	584	2116	272	547	92	25	63	267	64
3 AVE	.262	138	543	69	142	25	7	18	72	13

ROB DIBBLE

Position: Pitcher
Team: Cincinnati Reds
Born: Jan. 24, 1964 Bridgeport, CT
Height: 6′4″ **Weight:** 235 lbs.
Bats: left **Throws:** right
Acquired: First pick in the secondary phase of 6/83 free-agent draft

Player Summary

Fantasy Value	$25 to $30
Card Value	5¢ to 10¢
Will	win back closer job
Can't	avoid emotional explosions
Expect	great late heat
Don't Expect	self-help with glove

Although a case of shoulder tendinitis left Dibble on the disabled list when the 1992 season opened, the outspoken relief pitcher returned with a vengeance. By August, he had fully recaptured his former intimidating form. A fastball-and-slider pitcher who throws an occasional forkball, he embarked on a strikeout spree immediately after the All-Star break. In less than a month between July 16 and August 13, he fanned 23 batters in 13⅓ innings pitched (11 games). His best game of the year came on July 20, when he struck out all five Cubs he faced to post his 13th save. He has the highest ratio of strikeouts to innings pitched among active pitchers, averages one walk for every three whiffs, and rarely throws home run balls. But Dibble gave up more hits and walks than usual last summer and shared the No. 1 closer's job with lefty Norm Charlton. In 1992, Dibble allowed opposing batters to compile a .193 batting average, a .285 on-base percentage, and a .265 slugging percentage.

Major League Pitching Register

	W	L	ERA	G	S	IP	H	ER	BB	SO
88 NL	1	1	1.82	37	0	59.1	43	12	21	59
89 NL	10	5	2.09	74	2	99.0	62	23	39	141
90 NL	8	3	1.74	68	11	98.0	62	19	34	136
91 NL	3	5	3.17	67	31	82.1	67	29	25	124
92 NL	3	5	3.07	63	25	70.1	48	24	31	110
Life	25	19	2.35	309	69	409.0	282	107	150	570
3 AVE	5	4	2.59	66	22	83.1	59	24	30	123

GARY DiSARCINA

Position: Shortstop
Team: California Angels
Born: Nov. 19, 1967 Malden, MA
Height: 6'1" **Weight:** 178 lbs.
Bats: right **Throws:** right
Acquired: Sixth-round pick in 6/88 free-agent draft

Player Summary	
Fantasy Value	$2 to $4
Card Value	4¢ to 6¢
Will	play good defensive game
Can't	reach outfield fences
Expect	opposite-field hits
Don't Expect	lots of walks

When the Angels sent Dick Schofield to the Mets last spring, DiSarcina was the direct beneficiary. Handed California's shortstop job, he showed good range, a strong arm, and an ability to turn all the routine plays—plus an occasional great one. He showed a better bat than his predecessor. During a game against KC, only the lack of a triple kept him from hitting for the cycle. Not a power hitter, DiSarcina does have the ability to drive the ball into the gaps and can hit to the opposite field. A line-drive hitter who makes contact, he'll swipe about a dozen bases per year. In 1992, he compiled a .283 on-base average and a .301 slugging percentage. In 1991 at Triple-A Edmonton, he batted .310 with four homers, 58 RBI, and 16 stolen bases. Defense is DiSarcina's strong suit. He led three minor leagues in assists and ranked at the top twice in fielding percentage. He had a .967 fielding percentage with 250 putouts and 485 assists for the Angels in 1992.

Major League Batting Register

	BA	G	AB	R	H	2B	3B	HR	RBI	SB
89 AL	.000	2	0	0	0	0	0	0	0	0
90 AL	.140	18	57	8	8	1	1	0	0	1
91 AL	.211	18	57	5	12	2	0	0	3	0
92 AL	.247	157	518	48	128	19	0	3	42	9
Life	.234	195	632	61	148	22	1	3	45	10

JOHN DOHERTY

Position: Pitcher
Team: Detroit Tigers
Born: June 11, 1967 Bronx, NY
Height: 6'4" **Weight:** 190 lbs.
Bats: right **Throws:** right
Acquired: 19th-round pick in 6/89 free-agent draft

Player Summary	
Fantasy Value	$2 to $4
Card Value	5¢ to 10¢
Will	remain in relief corps
Can't	rack up many strikeouts
Expect	ground outs
Don't Expect	many gopher balls

Doherty jumped from Double-A to the bigs in 1992 and proved to be one of the better pitchers on the Tiger staff. A righthander with good control, he began the campaign in the bullpen but broke into the rotation in August. Although he does not register high K totals, the Concordia College grad allows less than a hit per inning and keeps the ball in the park—no easy feat in a bandbox like Tiger Stadium. His best pitch is a sinking fastball, but he also throws a slider and a changeup. When he's on, he gets most of his outs on ground balls. In 1992, opponents compiled a .287 batting average, a .328 on-base average, and a .346 slugging percentage; lefties batted .240 while righties batted .323. In three minor league seasons, Doherty recorded 40 saves. At Double-A London in 1991, he was 3-3 with a 2.22 ERA, 15 saves, 42 Ks, and 21 walks in 65 innings. At Class-A Lakeland in 1990, he was 5-1 with a 1.10 ERA, 10 saves, 23 strikeouts, and five walks in 41 innings pitched. He will return to the bullpen, and he could even work his way into a late-inning role.

Major League Pitching Register

	W	L	ERA	G	S	IP	H	ER	BB	SO
92 AL	7	4	3.88	47	3	116.0	131	50	25	37
Life	7	4	3.88	47	3	116.0	131	50	25	37

JOHN DOPSON

Position: Pitcher
Team: Boston Red Sox
Born: July 14, 1963 Baltimore, MD
Height: 6'4" **Weight:** 205 lbs.
Bats: left **Throws:** right
Acquired: Traded from Expos with Luis Rivera for Spike Owen and Dan Gakeler, 12/88

Player Summary	
Fantasy Value	$2 to $4
Card Value	3¢ to 4¢
Will	win a dozen if healthy
Can't	worry about elbow
Expect	some control problems
Don't Expect	many complete games

After missing two seasons because of elbow problems that required surgery, Dopson returned to the Boston rotation last spring. He wasted little time in proving that he had worked his way back to his 12-8 form of 1989. On June 15, he threw 93 pitches while working eight scoreless frames of a 1-0 Red Sox victory over the Yankees. Before yielding a run to Milwaukee in the sixth inning on June 26, Dopson had compiled 20 consecutive scoreless innings at Fenway Park, normally a graveyard for pitchers. A sinker-slider pitcher with a changeup, he is not noted for his control. He also has a tendency to throw too many gopher balls. Opponents had a .287 batting average, a .334 on-base percentage, and a .437 slugging average in 1992. He keeps runners close but otherwise doesn't help himself in the field. In addition to worrying about his elbow, the righthander also has to hope that past shoulder woes don't interfere with his baseball future.

Major League Pitching Register

	W	L	ERA	G	CG	IP	H	ER	BB	SO
85 NL	0	2	11.08	4	0	13.0	25	16	4	4
88 NL	3	11	3.04	26	1	168.2	150	57	58	101
89 AL	12	8	3.99	29	2	169.1	166	75	69	95
90 AL	0	0	2.04	4	0	17.2	13	4	9	9
91 AL	0	0	18.00	1	0	1.0	2	2	1	0
92 AL	7	11	4.08	25	0	141.1	159	64	38	55
Life	22	32	3.84	89	3	511.0	515	218	179	264

BILL DORAN

Position: Infield
Team: Cincinnati Reds
Born: May 28, 1958 Cincinnati, OH
Height: 6' **Weight:** 175 lbs.
Bats: both **Throws:** right
Acquired: Traded from Astros for Butch Henry, Keith Kaiser, and Terry McGriff, 8/90

Player Summary	
Fantasy Value	$2 to $6
Card Value	3¢ to 4¢
Will	walk more than whiff
Can't	steal anymore
Expect	occasional power
Don't Expect	starting role

After taking a .269 career average into the 1992 season, Doran proved to be one of Cincinnati's biggest disappointments last summer. He struggled with his hitting all year and divided playing time at second with Jeff Branson, Bip Roberts, and Freddie Benavides. On the plus side, Doran continued to walk more often than he struck out. A fastball hitter who uses all fields, he also provided good punch for a middle infielder. He's a better hitter lefthanded than righthanded. He is a decent defensive player and compensates for lack of range with personal experience against opposing hitters. He's no longer the basestealer he once was—primarily because of advancing age and past back problems. His workload will have to be reduced if he hopes to remain a valuable contributor.

Major League Batting Register

	BA	G	AB	R	H	2B	3B	HR	RBI	SB
82 NL	.278	26	97	11	27	3	0	0	6	5
83 NL	.271	154	535	70	145	12	7	8	39	12
84 NL	.261	147	548	92	143	18	11	4	41	21
85 NL	.287	148	578	84	166	31	6	14	59	23
86 NL	.276	145	550	92	152	29	3	6	37	42
87 NL	.283	162	625	82	177	23	3	16	79	31
88 NL	.248	132	480	66	119	18	1	7	53	17
89 NL	.219	142	507	65	111	25	2	8	58	22
90 NL	.300	126	403	59	121	29	2	7	37	23
91 NL	.280	111	361	51	101	12	2	6	35	5
92 NL	.235	132	387	48	91	16	2	8	47	7
Life	.267	1425	5071	720	1353	216	39	84	491	208
3 AVE	.272	123	384	53	104	19	2	7	40	12

KELLY DOWNS

Position: Pitcher
Team: Oakland Athletics
Born: October 25, 1960 Ogden, UT
Height: 6'4" **Weight:** 200 lbs.
Bats: right **Throws:** right
Acquired: Signed as a free agent, 6/92

Player Summary	
Fantasy Value	$2 to $4
Card Value	3¢ to 4¢
Will	start and relieve
Can't	always locate home plate
Expect	variety of pitches
Don't Expect	many home runs

Before rotator cuff problems intervened, Downs was a solid starting pitcher in the big leagues. Tried in relief for the first time in 1991, he pitched effectively as a set-up man. Once he joined Oakland last June, however, he became a full-time starter again. A fastball-and-slider pitcher, Downs's arsenal also includes a split-fingered fastball, curve, and changeup. He yields more than a hit per inning and also suffers occasional lapses of control. In 1992, opponents compiled a .237 batting average, a .341 on-base percentage, and a .326 slugging percentage. He doesn't throw too many gopher balls, giving up only four homers in his 82 innings in 1992. He is such a fine defensive player that he's like a fifth infielder when he's on the mound. If his surgically repaired shoulder stays sound, he is capable of competent pitching as either a starter or reliever, depending on team needs.

Major League Pitching Register

	W	L	ERA	G	CG	IP	H	ER	BB	SO
86 NL	4	4	2.75	14	1	88.1	78	27	30	64
87 NL	12	9	3.63	41	4	186.0	185	75	67	137
88 NL	13	9	3.32	27	6	168.0	140	62	47	118
89 NL	4	8	4.79	18	0	82.2	82	44	26	49
90 NL	3	2	3.43	13	0	63.0	56	24	20	31
91 NL	10	4	4.19	45	0	111.2	99	52	53	62
92 NL	1	2	3.47	19	0	62.1	65	24	24	33
92 AL	5	5	3.29	18	0	82.0	72	30	46	38
Life	52	43	3.60	195	11	844.0	777	338	313	532
3 AVE	6	4	3.67	32	0	106.1	97	43	48	55

DOUG DRABEK

Position: Pitcher
Team: Houston Astros
Born: July 25, 1962 Victoria, TX
Height: 6'1" **Weight:** 185 lbs.
Bats: right **Throws:** right
Acquired: Signed as a free-agent, 12/92

Player Summary	
Fantasy Value	$20 to $28
Card Value	5¢ to 10¢
Will	pitch 200 innings
Can't	lead league in Ks
Expect	minimum of 15 wins
Don't Expect	many walks

Drabek moved home to Texas after leading Pittsburgh for years. He doesn't mess around. Two years after a 22-win season that netted a Cy Young Award, he spent part of last summer perfecting a two-seam fastball to offset his cut fastball. The new pitch, designed primarily for lefthanded batters, made one of the league's toughest pitchers tougher. He also throws a curveball, slider, and changeup. He strikes out three times more batters than he walks and yields less than a hit per inning. He relies on his defense to get outs via ground balls, which may be dangerous in Houston. Opponents in 1992 compiled a .231 batting average, a .274 on-base percentage, and a .330 slugging percentage. He is a pressure pitcher who pitched the NL East title clinchers in both 1990 and 1991. Drabek helps his own cause with his bat and glove.

Major League Pitching Register

	W	L	ERA	G	CG	IP	H	ER	BB	SO
86 AL	7	8	4.10	27	0	131.2	126	60	50	76
87 NL	11	12	3.88	29	1	176.1	165	76	46	120
88 NL	15	7	3.08	33	3	219.1	194	75	50	127
89 NL	14	12	2.80	35	8	244.1	215	76	69	123
90 NL	22	6	2.76	33	9	231.1	190	71	56	131
91 NL	15	14	3.07	35	5	234.2	245	80	62	142
92 NL	15	11	2.77	34	10	256.2	218	79	54	177
Life	99	70	3.11	226	36	1494.1	1353	517	387	896
3 AVE	17	10	2.86	34	8	240.2	218	77	57	150

LEN DYKSTRA

Position: Outfield
Team: Philadelphia Phillies
Born: February 10, 1963 Santa Ana, CA
Height: 5'10" **Weight:** 167 lbs.
Bats: left **Throws:** left
Acquired: Traded from Mets with Roger McDowell for Juan Samuel, 6/89

Player Summary	
Fantasy Value	$15 to $22
Card Value	4¢ to 6¢
Will	drive opponents crazy
Can't	make strong throws
Expect	high on-base percentage
Don't Expect	many homers

When the Phillies signed Duncan to a free-agent contract, they promised he would play—albeit at several different positions. In 1992, he led the team in stolen bases and was second in at bats. An impatient free swinger who hammers lefthanded pitching, Duncan enjoyed his best game of the season on July 10. That was the day he hit two home runs against ace San Diego southpaw Bruce Hurst. Duncan has shortened his swing—and improved his power production—in recent seasons. The one-time switch-hitter would be even more effective if he were more selective at the plate; he strikes out five times more often than he walks. He had a .292 on-base percentage and a .389 slugging percentage in 1992. He has good speed, good range, and a strong arm but doesn't play great defense. At short, his natural position, he makes too many throwing errors.

Major League Batting Register

	BA	G	AB	R	H	2B	3B	HR	RBI	SB
85 NL	.244	142	562	74	137	24	6	6	39	38
86 NL	.229	109	407	47	93	7	0	8	30	48
87 NL	.215	76	261	31	56	8	1	6	18	11
89 NL	.248	94	258	32	64	15	2	3	21	9
90 NL	.306	125	435	67	133	22	11	10	55	13
91 NL	.258	100	333	46	86	7	4	12	40	5
92 NL	.267	142	574	71	153	40	3	8	50	23
Life	.255	788	2830	368	722	123	27	53	253	147
3 AVE	.277	122	447	61	124	23	6	10	48	14

DENNIS ECKERSLEY

Position: Pitcher
Team: Oakland Athletics
Born: Oct. 3, 1954 Oakland, CA
Height: 6'2" **Weight:** 195 lbs.
Bats: right **Throws:** right
Acquired: Traded from Cubs with Dan Rohn for Dave Wilder, Brian Guinn, and Mark Leonette, 4/87

Player Summary	
Fantasy Value	$35 to $40
Card Value	5¢ to 10¢
Will	slam the door
Can't	keep runners close
Expect	team to win with him
Don't Expect	anyone to walk

Surgery to repair a herniated disk in his back kept Dunston sidelined for almost all of the 1992 season. The injury was a massive blow to the Cubs' NL title hopes. They counted on him to produce at least 12 homers and 20 stolen bases, and strong defense at shortstop. Before he went down, he was considered the best-throwing shortstop in the game. He led the league with 261 putouts in 1991. Because Rey Sanchez played well during Dunston's absence, the Cubs talked about shifting Dunston to the outfield when he returns. Management reasoned that his speed and arm would allow him to master the new position with little difficulty. Although he has good pop in his bat, he is an impatient hitter who fans three times more often than he walks. He has particular trouble hitting sliders.

Major League Batting Register

	BA	G	AB	R	H	2B	3B	HR	RBI	SB
85 NL	.260	74	250	40	65	12	4	4	18	11
86 NL	.250	150	581	66	145	37	3	17	68	13
87 NL	.246	95	346	40	85	18	3	5	22	12
88 NL	.249	155	575	69	143	23	6	9	56	30
89 NL	.278	138	471	52	131	20	6	9	60	19
90 NL	.262	146	545	73	143	22	8	17	66	25
91 NL	.260	142	492	59	128	22	7	12	50	21
92 NL	.315	18	73	8	23	3	1	0	2	2
Life	.259	918	3333	407	863	157	38	73	342	133
2 AVE	.261	144	519	66	136	22	8	15	58	23

MARIANO DUNCAN

Position: Infield; outfield
Team: Philadelphia Phillies
Born: March 13, 1963 San Pedro de Macoris, Dominican Republic
Height: 6′ **Weight:** 185 lbs.
Bats: right **Throws:** right
Acquired: Signed as a free agent, 12/91

Player Summary

Fantasy Value	$5 to $8
Card Value	3¢ to 4¢
Will	produce surprising power
Can't	handle righties
Expect	swiping success
Don't Expect	great defense anywhere

When Dykstra is healthy, he's one of the game's best leadoff men. In 1992, however, he was on the disabled list twice in the first four months. Once regarded as a platoon player who could not hit lefties, he has become a force. In 1990, he led the NL in batting most of the year before finishing third with a .325 mark. That was also the year he led the majors with a .418 on-base percentage and tied for the league lead with 192 hits. A hustler who's unhappy unless his uniform is dirty from head-first slides, Dykstra can't stay out of trouble, however. He drops bunts, beats out infield hits, and rattles rivals more than any other leadoff man. He has stolen at least two-dozen bases seven years in a row and is rarely caught. Despite a weak arm, Dykstra is also an accomplished center fielder.

Major League Batting Register

	BA	G	AB	R	H	2B	3B	HR	RBI	SB
85 NL	.254	83	236	40	60	9	3	1	19	15
86 NL	.295	147	431	77	127	27	7	8	45	31
87 NL	.285	132	431	86	123	37	3	10	43	27
88 NL	.270	126	429	57	116	19	3	8	33	30
89 NL	.237	146	511	66	121	32	4	7	32	30
90 NL	.325	149	590	106	192	35	3	9	60	33
91 NL	.297	63	246	48	73	13	5	3	12	24
92 NL	.301	85	345	53	104	18	0	6	39	30
Life	.285	931	3219	533	916	190	28	52	283	220
3 AVE	.312	99	394	69	123	22	3	6	37	29

SHAWON DUNSTON

Position: Shortstop; outfield
Team: Chicago Cubs
Born: March 21, 1963 Brooklyn, NY
Height: 6′1″ **Weight:** 175 lbs.
Bats: right **Throws:** right
Acquired: First-round pick in 6/82 free-agent draft

Player Summary

Fantasy Value	$12 to $18
Card Value	3¢ to 4¢
Will	display NL's best arm
Can't	display patience at bat
Expect	a dozen long balls
Don't Expect	average over .260

In 1992, Eckersley converted 40 straight saves, a major league record. A sinker-slider pitcher who throws an occasional curve and splitter, Eckersley has a compact sidearm delivery and uncanny control. He ranks behind only Juan Marichal and Fergie Jenkins in lifetime ratio of strikeouts to innings. Eckersley is the only pitcher with 100 complete games, 200 saves, and four 40-save seasons. Arguably the No. 1 closer in history, the '92 Cy Young winner once faced 166 consecutive leadoff batters without yielding a walk.

Major League Pitching Register

	W	L	ERA	G	S	IP	H	ER	BB	SO
75 AL	13	7	2.60	34	2	186.2	147	54	90	152
76 AL	13	12	3.43	36	1	199.1	155	76	78	200
77 AL	14	13	3.53	33	0	247.1	214	97	54	191
78 AL	20	8	2.99	35	0	268.1	258	89	71	162
79 AL	17	10	2.99	33	0	246.2	234	82	59	150
80 AL	12	14	4.28	30	0	197.2	188	94	44	121
81 AL	9	8	4.27	23	0	154.0	160	73	35	79
82 AL	13	13	3.73	33	0	224.1	228	93	43	127
83 AL	9	13	5.61	28	0	176.1	223	110	39	77
84 AL	4	4	5.01	9	0	64.2	71	36	13	33
84 NL	10	8	3.03	24	0	160.1	152	54	36	81
85 NL	11	7	3.08	25	0	169.1	145	58	19	117
86 NL	6	11	4.57	33	0	201.0	226	102	43	137
87 AL	6	8	3.03	54	16	115.2	99	39	17	113
88 AL	4	2	2.35	60	45	72.2	52	19	11	70
89 AL	4	0	1.56	51	33	57.2	32	10	3	55
90 AL	4	2	0.61	63	48	73.1	41	5	4	73
91 AL	5	4	2.96	67	43	76.0	60	25	9	87
92 AL	7	1	1.91	69	51	80.0	62	17	11	93
Life	181	145	3.43	740	239	2971.1	2747	1133	679	2118
3 AVE	5	2	1.84	66	47	76.0	54	16	8	84

TOM EDENS

Position: Pitcher
Team: Houston Astros
Born: June 9, 1961 Ontario, OR
Height: 6'2" **Weight:** 185 lbs.
Bats: right **Throws:** right
Acquired: Traded from Marlins for Brian Griffiths and Hector Carrasco, 11/92

Player Summary

Fantasy Value	$2 to $4
Card Value	3¢ to 4¢
Will	be righty setup man
Can't	always locate plate
Expect	batters to hit ground balls
Don't Expect	K per inning

Edens brings experience as a righty set-up man to a young Astros bullpen. For the Minnesota Twins, he was the biggest pitching surprise of 1992. He did for the team in '92 what Carl Willis had done in '91—served as a superb set-up man for closer Rick Aguilera. During a 19-outing stretch that spanned 30⅔ innings in May and June, Edens compiled a 0.59 earned run average. He later worked 29 consecutive scoreless frames before Tom Brunansky connected for a home run—the first allowed by Edens last year—on July 16. The journeyman righthander yields less than a hit per inning and strikes out almost twice the number he walks. Opponents compiled a .236 batting average, a .329 on-base average, and a .298 slugging percentage in 1992; righties batted .229 and lefties batted .248 against him. He did not have a full season in the majors before 1992. Edens broke into pro ball in 1983, made a brief big league appearance four years later, and then spent two more years in the minors before getting another chance.

Major League Pitching Register

	W	L	ERA	G	S	IP	H	ER	BB	SO
87 NL	0	0	6.75	2	0	8.0	15	6	4	4
90 AL	4	5	4.45	35	2	89.0	89	44	33	40
91 AL	2	2	4.09	8	0	33.0	34	15	10	19
92 AL	6	3	2.83	52	3	76.1	65	24	36	57
Life	12	10	3.88	97	5	206.1	203	89	83	120
2 AVE	5	4	3.70	44	3	83.1	77	34	35	49

MARK EICHHORN

Position: Pitcher
Team: Toronto Blue Jays
Born: Nov. 21, 1960 San Jose, CA
Height: 6'3" **Weight:** 200 lbs.
Bats: right **Throws:** right
Acquired: Traded from Angels for Rob Ducey and Greg Myers, 7/92

Player Summary

Fantasy Value	$2 to $4
Card Value	3¢ to 4¢
Will	tantalize hitters
Can't	ring up many strikeouts
Expect	frequent calls
Don't Expect	control lapses

Eichhorn looks like a soft touch. He baffles batters with one of baseball's best changeups—thrown with a variety of speeds and motions. His sidearm to submarine style is especially tough on righthanded batters, whose composite batting average against him is usually less than .200. In 1992, righties batted .202 while lefties feasted on a .341 average. A control pitcher who keeps batters honest by mixing in a not-too-quick fastball, Eichhorn is adept at keeping the ball down in the strike zone. Though he strikes out twice as many as he walks, he gets most of his outs on ground balls. He yields less than a hit per inning and helps himself defensively. He's most effective when followed by a hard-throwing closer, such as Tom Henke. Eichhorn has a resilient right arm that allows him to work more than 60 times per season.

Major League Pitching Register

	W	L	ERA	G	S	IP	H	ER	BB	SO
82 AL	0	3	5.45	7	0	38.0	40	23	14	16
86 AL	14	6	1.72	69	10	157.0	105	30	45	166
87 AL	10	6	3.17	89	4	127.2	110	45	52	96
88 AL	0	3	4.18	37	1	66.2	79	31	27	28
89 NL	5	5	4.35	45	0	68.1	70	33	19	49
90 AL	2	5	3.08	60	13	84.2	98	29	23	69
91 AL	3	3	1.98	70	1	81.2	63	18	13	49
92 AL	4	4	3.08	65	2	87.2	86	30	25	61
Life	38	35	3.02	442	31	711.2	651	239	218	534
3 AVE	3	4	2.73	65	5	84.2	82	26	20	60

JIM EISENREICH

Position: Outfield
Team: Kansas City Royals
Born: April 18, 1959 St. Cloud, MN
Height: 5'11" **Weight:** 195 lbs.
Bats: left **Throws:** left
Acquired: Signed as a free agent, 10/86

Player Summary	
Fantasy Value	$3 to $6
Card Value	3¢ to 4¢
Will	play all outfield spots
Can't	hit balls over wall
Expect	solid defense
Don't Expect	average above .300

Although he's one of the game's top contact hitters, Eisenreich is also one of its most impatient. He rarely strikes out or walks—putting the ball into play almost eight times for every 10 trips. He had a .313 on-base average and a .340 slugging average in '92. He hits about two-dozen doubles every year but does not have the power to reach double figures in home runs. Because he hits lots of ground balls, he is a better hitter on artificial turf. He hits to the opposite field and produces in the clutch but has trouble with inside pitches. He took an eight-year mark of .279 into the 1992 campaign but had difficulty maintaining that level. Eisenreich stole 27 bases four years ago but doesn't run as much anymore. A solid outfielder at any of the three spots, he led AL colleagues with a .996 fielding percentage (one error in 142 games) in 1990.

Major League Batting Register

	BA	G	AB	R	H	2B	3B	HR	RBI	SB
82 AL	.303	34	99	10	30	6	0	2	9	0
83 AL	.286	2	7	1	2	1	0	0	0	0
84 AL	.219	12	32	1	7	1	0	0	3	2
87 AL	.238	44	105	10	25	8	2	4	21	1
88 AL	.218	82	202	26	44	8	1	1	19	9
89 AL	.293	134	475	64	139	33	7	9	59	27
90 AL	.280	142	496	61	139	29	7	5	51	12
91 AL	.301	135	375	47	113	22	3	2	47	5
92 AL	.269	113	353	31	95	13	3	2	28	11
Life	.277	698	2144	251	594	121	23	25	237	67
3 AVE	.283	130	408	46	116	21	4	3	42	9

CAL ELDRED

Position: Pitcher
Team: Milwaukee Brewers
Born: Nov. 24, 1967 Cedar Rapids, IA
Height: 6'4" **Weight:** 215 lbs.
Bats: right **Throws:** right
Acquired: First-round pick in 6/89 free-agent draft

Player Summary	
Fantasy Value	$8 to $16
Card Value	15¢ to 20¢
Will	get Ks with curve
Can't	always find plate
Expect	wins in double figures
Don't Expect	great velocity

Eldred failed to make the Milwaukee varsity during 1992 spring training, but he earned a midseason recall after performing well in the minors. At Triple-A Denver in 1992, he was 10-6 with a 3.00 ERA, four complete games, 99 strikeouts, and 42 walks in 141 innings. He maintained his momentum in the majors, winning his first start 6-3 over Chicago, on July 19. On Aug. 8, the rookie righthander hurled seven scoreless innings against heavy-hitting Minnesota. The former University of Iowa standout banks heavily on his curveball, which he combines with a fastball that can't quite break 90 mph on the Juggs gun. He fans twice as many as he walks and yields less than a hit per inning. For the Brew Crew in 1992, he allowed opponents to compile a .207 batting average, a .258 on-base percentage, and a .283 slugging percentage. He was 13-9 at Denver in 1991, with a 3.75 ERA, three complete games, 168 strikeouts, and 84 walks in 185 innings pitched. Coaches Tony Muser and Don Rowe helped him in the minor leagues. Eldred is now regarded as a possible future ace of the staff.

Major League Pitching Register

	W	L	ERA	G	CG	IP	H	ER	BB	SO
91 AL	2	0	4.50	3	0	16.0	20	8	6	10
92 AL	11	2	1.79	14	2	100.1	76	20	23	62
Life	13	2	2.17	17	2	116.1	96	28	29	72

SCOTT ERICKSON

Position: Pitcher
Team: Minnesota Twins
Born: Feb. 2, 1968 Long Beach, CA
Height: 6'4" **Weight:** 220 lbs.
Bats: right **Throws:** right
Acquired: Fourth-round pick in 6/89 free-agent draft

Player Summary	
Fantasy Value	$10 to $15
Card Value	5¢ to 10¢
Will	win often if healthy
Can't	bid for K crown
Expect	hot and cold streaks
Don't Expect	pinpoint control

Erickson is an enigma. He had a 12-game winning streak in 1991, survived second-half elbow problems en route to a 20-win season, then nearly slipped back to the minors after a slow start in '92. A sinker-and-slider pitcher who also throws a curve, he went 3-5 with a 5.13 ERA in his first dozen starts—mainly because the slider that serves as his changeup was mysteriously missing. When it returned, the former Arizona All-American went 4-2 with a 1.70 ERA over his next seven starts. He had a 5-0 one-hitter against Boston on July 24 and a 5-0 four-hitter against Milwaukee on Aug. 2. When he's on, Erickson keeps the ball down and stays ahead in the count. He's not noted for his control, however, and has a weak ratio of whiffs to walks. He gets outs on grounders rather than strikeouts. Opponents compiled a .252 batting average, a .328 on-base percentage, and a .371 slugging percentage in 1992. He is at his best with runners on base. He's a good fielder who keeps runners close.

Major League Pitching Register

	W	L	ERA	G	CG	IP	H	ER	BB	SO
90 AL	8	4	2.87	19	1	113.0	108	36	51	53
91 AL	20	8	3.18	32	5	204.0	189	72	71	108
92 AL	13	12	3.40	32	5	212.0	197	80	83	101
Life	41	24	3.20	83	11	529.0	494	188	205	262
3 AVE	14	8	3.20	28	4	176.0	165	63	68	87

CECIL ESPY

Position: Outfield
Team: Cincinnati Reds
Born: Jan. 20, 1963 San Diego, CA
Height: 6'3" **Weight:** 195 lbs.
Bats: both **Throws:** right
Acquired: Signed as a free agent, 11/92

Player Summary	
Fantasy Value	$1 to $3
Card Value	3¢ to 4¢
Will	remain multipurpose sub
Can't	hit enough to start
Expect	good use of speed
Don't Expect	home run power

Before 1992, Espy was known primarily for his speed and defense. Early in the '92 campaign with the Bucs, however, he showed a sudden ability to produce timely pinch-hits. With seven hits in his first 10 pinch at bats, he netted eight RBI—halfway toward Willie Stargell's 1982 club record of 16 pinch-RBI. The magic wore off after May 16, however, with Espy hitless in his next 17 at bats as a pinch-hitter after that date. By the end of the 1992 season, he compiled a .310 on-base average and a .340 slugging percentage. A .241 hitter in six seasons before 1992, he has spent most of his career as an extra outfielder, pinch-runner, and defensive replacement. Blessed with great speed, he stole 45 bases, second to Rickey Henderson in the American League's stolen base chase in 1989—the only year Espy saw extended action. He plays anywhere in the outfield, where he has good range and a strong arm.

Major League Batting Register

	BA	G	AB	R	H	2B	3B	HR	RBI	SB
83 NL	.273	20	11	4	3	1	0	0	1	0
87 AL	.000	14	8	1	0	0	0	0	0	2
88 AL	.248	123	347	46	86	17	6	2	39	33
89 AL	.257	142	475	65	122	12	7	3	31	45
90 AL	.127	52	71	10	9	0	0	0	1	11
91 NL	.244	43	82	7	20	4	0	1	11	4
92 NL	.258	112	194	21	50	7	3	1	20	6
Life	.244	506	1188	154	290	41	16	7	103	101

STEVE FARR

Position: Pitcher
Team: New York Yankees
Born: Dec. 12, 1956 Cheverly, MD
Height: 5'11" **Weight:** 200 lbs.
Bats: right **Throws:** right
Acquired: Signed as a free agent, 11/90

Player Summary

Fantasy Value.................................$8 to $12
Card Value..3¢ to 4¢
Will.............................pitch best in short relief
Can't ....fan a batter per inning
Expect ....fine ERA
Don't Expect ....many control woes

Before Farr went on the shelf with a strained lower back last July, he was leading the Yankee pitching staff with a dozen saves. He is a control pitcher who throws a fastball, slider, and curve. Farr is a bullpen bellwether who worked more than 50 times four years in a row before his back problems began. Used as a starter, middle reliever, and short man before joining the Yankees, he became a full-time closer for the first time and saved 23 games, a career peak. He yields less than a hit per inning and strikes out more than twice the number he walks. He took an eight-year ERA of 3.22 into the 1992 campaign but was considerably more effective last summer. Opponents compiled a .186 batting average, a .267 on-base average, and a .240 slugging percentage. He helps himself with fine defense and keeps baserunners close. He is at his best when used exclusively as a closer.

Major League Pitching Register

	W	L	ERA	G	S	IP	H	ER	BB	SO
84 AL	3	11	4.58	31	1	116.0	106	59	46	83
85 AL	1	4	3.11	16	1	37.2	34	13	20	36
86 AL	8	4	3.13	56	8	109.1	90	38	39	83
87 AL	4	3	4.15	47	1	91.0	97	42	44	88
88 AL	4	2	2.50	62	20	82.2	74	23	30	72
89 AL	2	5	4.12	51	18	63.1	75	29	22	56
90 AL	13	7	1.98	57	1	127.0	99	28	48	94
91 AL	5	5	2.19	60	23	70.0	57	17	20	60
92 AL	2	2	1.56	50	30	52.0	34	9	19	37
Life	44	42	3.10	430	103	749.0	666	258	288	609
3 AVE	7	5	1.95	56	18	83.0	63	18	29	64

JEFF FASSERO

Position: Pitcher
Team: Montreal Expos
Born: Jan. 5, 1963 Springfield, IL
Height: 6'1" **Weight:** 195 lbs.
Bats: left **Throws:** left
Acquired: Signed as a free agent, 1/91

Player Summary

Fantasy Value....................................$2 to $5
Card Value..3¢ to 4¢
Will...keep ball in park
Can't ....hold runners on base
Expect ....southpaw set-up roles
Don't Expect ....90 mph heat

In his first full big league season last summer, Fassero teamed with Mel Rojas to give Montreal a left-right tandem of set-up men for closer John Wetteland. Fassero is a fastball-and-slider pitcher who yields less than a hit per inning and strikes out twice the number he walks. He doesn't have a great heater, but his pitches show good movement. He throws few gopher balls or extra-base hits. In 1992, opponents compiled a .249 batting average, a .322 on-base percentage, and a .326 slugging percentage. He fields his position well but has trouble holding runners. A starter during his first four minor league seasons, Fassero switched to relief in 1988, started again the next year, then returned to the bullpen for good in 1990. He has a resilient arm that has allowed him to appear in more than 60 games three years in a row. In 1991 at Triple-A Indianapolis, he was 3-0 with a 1.47 ERA, four saves, 12 strikeouts, and seven walks in 18 innings. He was 5-4 with a 2.80 ERA, six saves, 61 strikeouts, and 24 walks in 64 innings at Double-A Canton in 1990.

Major League Pitching Register

	W	L	ERA	G	S	IP	H	ER	BB	SO
91 NL	2	5	2.44	51	8	55.1	39	15	17	42
92 NL	8	7	2.84	70	1	85.2	81	27	34	63
Life	10	12	2.68	121	9	141.0	120	42	51	105
2 AVE	5	6	2.68	61	5	70.2	60	21	26	53

MIKE FELDER

Position: Outfield
Team: Seattle Mariners
Born: Nov. 18, 1961 Vallejo, CA
Height: 5'8" **Weight:** 160 lbs.
Bats: both **Throws:** right
Acquired: Signed as a free agent, 11/92

Player Summary

Fantasy Value	$3 to $6
Card Value	3¢ to 4¢
Will	make good contact
Can't	clobber ball over wall
Expect	speed as primary weapon
Don't Expect	patience at bat

Felder moves into the leadoff spot for the Seattle Mariners. He is a contact hitter who rarely walks, strikes out, or powers a ball over the fence. He'd be an ideal leadoff man if he weren't so impatient at the plate. An opposite field hitter with speed, he could fatten his average by dropping bunts for base hits. He often beats out infield grounders and is a threat to steal when he reaches. At one time, he tried to pull every pitch. Now, however, he is content to rattle rivals with his slap-and-run approach. Given enough playing time, he'll steal more than two dozen bases. Pitchers don't have to worry about Felder beating them with a home run, because he had only nine in his first seven seasons. Because of his speed, Felder has great range at any outfield position. He also has a fairly strong arm.

Major League Batting Register

	BA	G	AB	R	H	2B	3B	HR	RBI	SB
85 AL	.196	15	56	8	11	1	0	0	0	4
86 AL	.239	44	155	24	37	2	4	1	13	16
87 AL	.266	108	289	48	77	5	7	2	31	34
88 AL	.173	50	81	14	14	1	0	0	5	8
89 AL	.241	117	315	50	76	11	3	3	23	26
90 AL	.274	121	237	38	65	7	2	3	27	20
91 NL	.264	132	348	51	92	10	6	0	18	21
92 NL	.286	145	322	44	92	13	3	4	23	14
Life	.257	732	1803	277	464	50	25	13	140	143
3 AVE	.275	133	302	44	83	10	4	2	23	18

JUNIOR FELIX

Position: Outfield
Team: Florida Marlins
Born: Oct. 3, 1967 Laguna Sabada, Dominican Republic
Height: 5'11" **Weight:** 165 lbs.
Bats: both **Throws:** right
Acquired: Third-round pick from California in 11/92 expansion draft

Player Summary

Fantasy Value	$4 to $7
Card Value	3¢ to 4¢
Will	try to use speed more
Can't	realize potential
Expect	impatience at plate
Don't Expect	much time in center

Felix has spent several seasons spinning his wheels in the major leagues. Billed as a prize package of speed-plus-power, he has delivered on neither—and instead developed a reputation as a player who is prone to mental lapses. Fined for lack of hustle in the outfield and on the basepaths last July, Felix continued to flounder. A paragon of impatience, he strikes out at an alarming rate—more than three times for every walk. That, of course, makes him a lousy leadoff man. In 1992, he compiled a .289 on-base percentage and a .361 slugging percentage. Although he has great speed, he's not a good basestealer. He was caught stealing eight times to go with his eight stolen bases in 1992. Nor is he a strong defensive outfielder. A failure in both right and center, Felix seems best suited to left field. Because he's a switch-hitter with speed, he will get another chance.

Major League Batting Register

	BA	G	AB	R	H	2B	3B	HR	RBI	SB
89 AL	.258	110	415	62	107	14	8	9	46	18
90 AL	.263	127	463	73	122	23	7	15	65	13
91 AL	.283	66	230	32	65	10	2	2	26	7
92 AL	.246	139	509	63	125	22	5	9	72	8
Life	.259	442	1617	230	419	69	22	35	209	46
3 AVE	.260	111	401	56	104	18	5	9	54	9

FELIX FERMIN

Position: Shortstop
Team: Cleveland Indians
Born: Oct. 9, 1963 Mao Valverde, Dominican Republic
Height: 5'11" **Weight:** 170 lbs.
Bats: right **Throws:** right
Acquired: Traded from Pirates with Denny Gonzales for Jay Bell, 3/89

Player Summary	
Fantasy Value	$1 to $3
Card Value	3¢ to 4¢
Will	make good contact
Can't	reach the fences
Expect	hit-and-run plays
Don't Expect	defensive difficulties

Cleveland manager Mike Hargrove last summer said that Fermin is Mark Belanger with a better bat. A talented defensive shortstop, Fermin lost his job to Mark Lewis. Fermin, however, remained a clubhouse leader who was ready to play when asked. Although he never hits homers and rarely steals, he is a contact hitter who is tough to fan. He doesn't walk much either, though. He does bunt and execute the hit-and-run play. He also produces surprisingly well in the clutch for a player who used to be an opposite-field hitter. In 1992, he compiled a .326 on-base average and a .321 slugging percentage. On April 22, 1990, he hit a home run, his first in 2,915 professional at bats. Fermin has good range, good hands, and a strong throwing arm, ensuring him a job. He had a .971 fielding percentage and 36 double plays at shortstop in 1992. But that light bat hurts.

Major League Batting Register

		G	AB	R	H	2B	3B	HR	RBI	SB
87 NL	.250	23	68	6	17	0	0	0	4	0
88 NL	.276	43	87	9	24	0	2	0	2	3
89 AL	.238	156	484	50	115	9	1	0	21	6
90 AL	.256	148	414	47	106	13	2	1	40	3
91 AL	.262	129	424	30	111	13	2	0	31	5
92 AL	.270	79	215	27	58	7	2	0	13	0
Life	.255	578	1692	169	431	42	9	1	111	17
3 AVE	.261	119	351	35	92	11	2	0	28	3

ALEX FERNANDEZ

Position: Pitcher
Team: Chicago White Sox
Born: Aug. 13, 1969 Miami Beach, FL
Height: 6'1" **Weight:** 205 lbs.
Bats: right **Throws:** right
Acquired: First-round pick in 6/90 free-agent draft

Player Summary	
Fantasy Value	$6 to $10
Card Value	5¢ to 8¢
Will	throw everything hard
Can't	always locate the plate
Expect	lots of innings
Don't Expect	fastball dependence

Rushed to the majors in 1990 after the White Sox made him a first-round draft choice, Fernandez came down to earth last summer. He lost seven of his first 10, watched his ERA balloon beyond 4.00, and even endured a minor league exile in July. Before his demotion, he found himself relying too heavily on his fastball to fish him out of trouble spots. Rival hitters, knowing what was coming, simply waited until they got the pitch. Since he also throws a curveball, slider, and changeup, he should be able to mix his pitches well. He did that on July 28, the first game after his recall, with almost eight walk-free innings. Control problems have hurt him in the past. Opponents compiled a .270 batting average, a .322 on-base average, and a .405 slugging percentage in 1992. He was 2-1 with a 0.94 ERA at Triple-A Vancouver in '92. At his age, Fernandez remains a red-hot prospect who may yet develop into a No. 1 starter. Whether he will live up to his advance billing as a Tom Seaver-type of hurler is another matter.

Major League Pitching Register

	W	L	ERA	G	CG	IP	H	ER	BB	SO
90 AL	5	5	3.80	13	3	87.2	89	37	34	61
91 AL	9	13	4.51	34	2	191.2	186	96	88	145
92 AL	8	11	4.27	29	4	187.2	199	89	50	95
Life	22	29	4.28	76	9	467.0	474	222	172	301
3 AVE	7	10	4.28	25	3	155.2	158	74	57	100

SID FERNANDEZ

Position: Pitcher
Team: New York Mets
Born: Oct. 12, 1962 Honolulu, HI
Height: 6'1" **Weight:** 230 lbs.
Bats: left **Throws:** left
Acquired: Traded from Dodgers with Ross Jones for Carlos Diaz and Bob Bailor, 12/83

Player Summary

Fantasy Value	$8 to $14
Card Value	3¢ to 4¢
Will	win big with support
Can't	last nine innings
Expect	great whiff-to-walk ratio
Don't Expect	rivals to bat .200

Although weight, knee, and control problems have plagued Fernandez in the past, he showed last summer that he is still one of the better lefthanders in the game. With his team plagued by injuries and riddled with a ridiculous defense, he managed to maintain a good ERA while posting double figures in wins for the first time in three years. A strikeout pitcher who throws a rising fastball, changeup, and curve, he whiffs nearly three times as many as he walks. He also yields far less than a hit an inning. During his career, he's held opposing hitters to an average only a few points above .200 (they hit .210 in 1992), one of the best marks in baseball history. Opponents also compiled a .273 on-base average and a .328 slugging percentage in '92. He helps himself with the bat, but he is only mediocre as a fielder.

TONY FERNANDEZ

Position: Shortstop
Team: New York Mets
Born: June 30, 1962 San Pedro de Macoris, Dominican Republic
Height: 6'2" **Weight:** 175 lbs.
Bats: both **Throws:** right
Acquired: Traded from Padres for Wally Whitehurst, D.J. Dozier, and Raul Casanova, 10/92

Player Summary

Fantasy Value	$10 to $15
Card Value	3¢ to 4¢
Will	show speed in all areas
Can't	become sporadic
Expect	standout defense
Don't Expect	much power

Fernandez is another player coming in to help plug the Mets' leaky defense. Handed San Diego's leadoff position in 1992, Fernandez responded with a strong season. A contact hitter who rarely fans, Fernandez doesn't produce as many extra-base hits as he has in the past, but he still runs well enough to take the extra base. He had a .337 on-base average and a .357 slugging percentage in '92. He has run less recently, but he's still capable of two-dozen steals per season. If the Mets keep Fernandez at leadoff, his value as a hit-and-run man may be wasted. His strength remains in the field, where he's won four Gold Gloves. He has good range and a strong throwing arm. When named to the NL All-Stars last July, he was among league leaders in hits, runs, and multihit games.

Major League Pitching Register

	W	L	ERA	G	CG	IP	H	ER	BB	SO
83 NL	0	1	6.00	2	0	6.0	7	4	7	9
84 NL	6	6	3.50	15	0	90.0	74	35	34	62
85 NL	9	9	2.80	26	3	170.1	108	53	80	180
86 NL	16	6	3.52	32	2	204.1	161	80	91	200
87 NL	12	8	3.81	28	3	156.0	130	66	67	134
88 NL	12	10	3.03	31	1	187.0	127	63	70	189
89 NL	14	5	2.83	35	6	219.1	157	69	75	198
90 NL	9	14	3.46	30	2	179.1	130	69	67	181
91 NL	1	3	2.86	8	0	44.0	36	14	9	31
92 NL	14	11	2.73	32	5	214.2	162	65	67	193
Life	93	73	3.17	239	22	1471.0	1092	518	567	1377
2 AVE	12	13	3.06	31	4	197.2	146	67	67	187

Major League Batting Register

	BA	G	AB	R	H	2B	3B	HR	RBI	SB
83 AL	.265	15	34	5	9	1	1	0	2	0
84 AL	.270	88	233	29	63	5	3	3	19	5
85 AL	.289	161	564	71	163	31	10	2	51	13
86 AL	.310	163	687	91	213	33	9	10	65	25
87 AL	.322	146	578	90	186	29	8	5	67	32
88 AL	.287	154	648	76	186	41	4	5	70	15
89 AL	.257	140	573	64	147	25	9	11	64	22
90 AL	.276	161	635	84	175	27	17	4	66	26
91 NL	.272	145	558	81	152	27	5	4	38	23
92 NL	.275	155	622	84	171	32	4	4	37	20
Life	.285	1328	5132	675	1465	251	70	48	479	181
3 AVE	.274	154	605	83	166	29	9	4	47	23

MIKE FETTERS

Position: Pitcher
Team: Milwaukee Brewers
Born: Dec. 19, 1964 Van Nuys, CA
Height: 6'4" **Weight:** 212 lbs.
Bats: right **Throws:** right
Acquired: Traded from Angels with Glenn Carter for Chuck Crim, 12/91

Player Summary	
Fantasy Value	$2 to $4
Card Value	3¢ to 4¢
Will	maintain microscopic ERA
Can't	keep rival runners close
Expect	more mound calls
Don't Expect	return of control lapses

A changed delivery made Fetters one of baseball's best set-up men last summer. Throwing more overhand than in three previous big league seasons, he allowed just one run by June 21. As late as Aug. 10, he had a 5-1 record and 0.65 ERA. A former first-round draft choice, Fetters found control to be a problem early in his major league career. The new motion helped. All of a sudden, he was striking out twice the number he walked, yielding far less than a hit per inning, and keeping the ball in the park. His only problem was keeping enemy baserunners close. Fetters throws a fastball, curve, changeup, slider, and forkball—a varied arsenal that is quite extensive for a relief pitcher. The fastball, which sinks and slides, is his best pitch. Opponents compiled a .185 batting average, a .290 on-base percentage, and a .268 slugging percentage in 1992. Last year was his first full season in the majors. He was 2-7 with a 4.87 ERA, 43 strikeouts, and 26 walks in 61 innings at Triple-A Edmonton in 1991.

Major League Pitching Register

	W	L	ERA	G	S	IP	H	ER	BB	SO
89 AL	0	0	8.10	1	0	3.1	5	3	1	4
90 AL	1	1	4.12	26	1	67.2	77	31	20	35
91 AL	2	5	4.84	19	0	44.2	53	24	28	24
92 AL	5	1	1.87	50	2	62.2	38	13	24	43
Life	8	7	3.58	96	3	178.1	173	71	73	106
3 AVE	3	2	3.50	32	1	58.2	56	23	24	34

CECIL FIELDER

Position: First base
Team: Detroit Tigers
Born: Sept. 21, 1963 Los Angeles, CA
Height: 6'3" **Weight:** 230 lbs.
Bats: right **Throws:** right
Acquired: Signed as a free agent, 1/90

Player Summary	
Fantasy Value	$40 to $50
Card Value	10¢ to 20¢
Will	generate enormous power
Can't	run a lick
Expect	unchallenged RBI crown
Don't Expect	bunts or infield hits

Fielder is the Rodney Dangerfield of sluggers. Though he led the majors in home runs and RBI in both 1990 and 1991, he finished second in American League Most Valuable Player voting both times. Then he failed to make the 1992 All-Star squad despite the best RBI total in the majors at the time. Before he did it in 1992, the last man to lead both leagues in RBI three straight years was Babe Ruth (1919 to 1921). A low-average hitter with a high strikeout total, Fielder fans more than twice as often as he walks. Rivals fear him. For example, Cleveland considered walking him with the bases loaded when he came up in the seventh with two outs and the Indians up by four. Fielder hit a grand slam—one of four homers (and 11 RBI) he collected that weekend. He had a .325 on-base average and a .458 slugging percentage in 1992. A pull hitter who'll poke an opposite-field single for an RBI, Fielder is adequate in the field.

Major League Batting Register

	BA	G	AB	R	H	2B	3B	HR	RBI	SB
85 AL	.311	30	74	6	23	4	0	4	16	0
86 AL	.157	34	83	7	13	2	0	4	13	0
87 AL	.269	82	175	30	47	7	1	14	32	0
88 AL	.230	74	174	24	40	6	1	9	23	0
90 AL	.277	159	573	104	159	25	1	51	132	0
91 AL	.261	162	624	102	163	25	0	44	133	0
92 AL	.244	155	594	80	145	22	0	35	124	0
Life	.257	696	2297	353	590	91	3	161	473	0
3 AVE	.261	159	597	95	156	24	0	43	130	0

CHUCK FINLEY

Position: Pitcher
Team: California Angels
Born: Nov. 26, 1962 Monroe, LA
Height: 6'6" **Weight:** 212 lbs.
Bats: left **Throws:** left
Acquired: First-round pick in 6/85 free-agent draft

Player Summary

Fantasy Value	$12 to $18
Card Value	3¢ to 4¢
Will	win often when healthy
Can't	keep ball in park
Expect	strong 1993 comeback
Don't Expect	self-help with glove

After posting a three-year record of 52-27, Finley was expected to be one of the mainstays of the California Angels' pitching staff in 1992. Instead, an early toe injury hampered his ability so much that he lost nine of his first 11, yielded more than five earned runs per game, and threw 18 home run balls by the All-Star break. Control, never a strong suit for Finley, was only part of the problem. He was also allowing more than a hit per inning and throwing frequent gopher balls. Opponents compiled a .278 batting average, a .359 on-base percentage, and a .425 slugging percentage in 1992. When he's right, Finley mixes a fastball, split-fingered fastball, curveball, and changeup with reasonable success and strikes out twice as many men as he walks. While not a superlative fielder, he helps himself by keeping enemy baserunners close to the bag—he allowed 21 swipes but had 18 caught stealing in 1992.

Major League Pitching Register

	W	L	ERA	G	S	IP	H	ER	BB	SO
86 AL	3	1	3.30	25	0	46.1	40	17	23	37
87 AL	2	7	4.67	35	0	90.2	102	47	43	63
88 AL	9	15	4.17	31	2	194.1	191	90	82	111
89 AL	16	9	2.57	29	9	199.2	171	57	82	156
90 AL	18	9	2.40	32	7	236.0	210	63	81	177
91 AL	18	9	3.80	34	4	227.1	205	96	101	171
92 AL	7	12	3.96	31	4	204.1	212	90	98	124
Life	73	62	3.45	217	26	1198.2	1131	460	510	839
3 AVE	14	10	3.36	32	5	222.1	209	83	93	157

STEVE FINLEY

Position: Outfield
Team: Houston Astros
Born: March 12, 1965 Union City, TN
Height: 6'2" **Weight:** 175 lbs.
Bats: left **Throws:** left
Acquired: Traded from Orioles with Pete Harnisch and Curt Schilling for Glenn Davis, 1/91

Player Summary

Fantasy Value	$10 to $16
Card Value	3¢ to 4¢
Will	excel as No. 2 hitter
Can't	be caught stealing
Expect	outstanding defense
Don't Expect	consistent power

Switching to second in the batting order made Finley a more aggressive hitter last summer. After hitting 10 triples in 1991, he reached that figure by the end of June. He was also tied for fourth in the league in extra-base hits and among league leaders with a stolen-base success ratio of 86 percent. The former Southern Illinois standout was once a washout against southpaws, but he began peppering lefthanded pitching consistently (batting .279 against lefties in '92). A contact hitter with speed, Finley is adept at the sacrifice and the hit-and-run. He stretches hits and steals more than 30 bases a year. In 1992, he had a .355 on-base average and a .407 slugging percentage. A two-way star, he is a fine center fielder with great range, good instincts, and a strong throwing arm. He drew serious consideration for the 1992 NL All-Star Team. At his age, he should remain a serious contender when future squads are selected.

Major League Batting Register

	BA	G	AB	R	H	2B	3B	HR	RBI	SB
89 AL	.249	81	217	35	54	5	2	2	25	17
90 AL	.256	142	464	46	119	16	4	3	37	22
91 NL	.285	159	596	84	170	28	10	8	54	34
92 NL	.292	162	607	84	177	29	13	5	55	44
Life	.276	544	1884	249	520	78	29	18	171	117
3 AVE	.280	154	556	71	155	24	9	5	49	33

CARLTON FISK

Position: Catcher
Team: Chicago White Sox
Born: Dec. 26, 1947 Bellow Falls, VT
Height: 6'2" **Weight:** 223 lbs.
Bats: right **Throws:** right
Acquired: Signed as a free agent, 3/81

Player Summary	
Fantasy Value	$4 to $7
Card Value	10¢ to 20¢
Will	pull everything
Can't	run to save his life
Expect	15 homers if healthy
Don't Expect	defensive deficiencies

Fisk needs to catch 25 games to break Bob Boone's record. The first half of the '92 season was a washout, because Fisk spent most of the time on the disabled list with a tendon inflammation and bone spur in his right foot. Overcoming that injury at his age is no easy matter—even for a player who practices an elaborate conditioning regimen. When healthy, he is still one of the best catchers in baseball. The only catcher with more than 100 homers and 100 stolen bases, Fisk is also the career home run leader among catchers.

Major League Batting Register

	BA	G	AB	R	H	2B	3B	HR	RBI	SB
69 AL	.000	2	5	0	0	0	0	0	0	0
71 AL	.313	14	48	7	15	2	1	2	6	0
72 AL	.293	131	457	74	134	28	9	22	61	5
73 AL	.246	135	508	65	125	21	0	26	71	7
74 AL	.299	52	187	36	56	12	1	11	26	5
75 AL	.331	79	263	47	87	14	4	10	52	4
76 AL	.255	134	487	76	124	17	5	17	58	12
77 AL	.315	152	536	106	169	26	3	26	102	7
78 AL	.284	157	571	94	162	39	5	20	88	7
79 AL	.272	91	320	49	87	23	2	10	42	3
80 AL	.289	131	478	73	138	25	3	18	62	11
81 AL	.263	96	338	44	89	12	0	7	45	3
82 AL	.267	135	476	66	127	17	3	14	65	17
83 AL	.289	138	488	85	141	26	4	26	86	9
84 AL	.231	102	359	54	83	20	1	21	43	6
85 AL	.238	153	543	85	129	23	1	37	107	17
86 AL	.221	125	457	42	101	11	0	14	63	2
87 AL	.256	135	454	68	116	22	1	23	71	1
88 AL	.277	76	253	37	70	8	1	19	50	0
89 AL	.293	103	375	47	110	25	2	13	68	1
90 AL	.285	137	452	65	129	21	0	18	65	7
91 AL	.241	134	460	42	111	25	0	18	74	1
92 AL	.229	62	188	12	43	4	1	3	21	3
Life	.270	2474	8703	1274	2346	421	47	375	1326	128
3 AVE	.257	111	367	40	94	17	0	13	53	4

MIKE FLANAGAN

Position: Pitcher
Team: Baltimore Orioles
Born: Dec. 16, 1951 Manchester, NH
Height: 6' **Weight:** 195 lbs.
Bats: left **Throws:** left
Acquired: Signed as a free agent, 3/91

Player Summary	
Fantasy Value	$1 to $2
Card Value	3¢ to 4¢
Will	serve as southpaw setup
Can't	ring up Ks
Expect	occasional sidearm
Don't Expect	return to rotation

The arrival of fellow lefthander Pat Clements in the Baltimore bullpen last summer eased some of the pressure on Flanagan. Before the second southpaw showed up, Flanagan had to endure a sink-or-swim situation. More often than not, he sank. When he's right, he fans twice the number he walks and yields less than a hit per inning. A fastball-and-curveball pitcher, he resurrected his career after turning to relief work in spring training of 1991. Especially effective against lefthanders, Flanagan helps himself with a fine pickoff move that is one of baseball's best. He is also quite capable as a fielder.

Major League Pitching Register

	W	L	ERA	G	S	IP	H	ER	BB	SO
75 AL	0	1	2.79	2	0	9.2	9	3	6	7
76 AL	3	5	4.13	20	0	85.0	83	39	33	56
77 AL	15	10	3.64	36	1	235.0	235	95	70	149
78 AL	19	15	4.03	40	0	281.1	271	126	87	167
79 AL	23	9	3.08	39	0	265.2	245	91	70	190
80 AL	16	13	4.12	37	0	251.1	278	115	71	128
81 AL	9	6	4.19	20	0	116.0	108	54	37	72
82 AL	15	11	3.97	36	0	236.0	233	104	76	103
83 AL	12	4	3.30	20	0	125.1	135	46	31	50
84 AL	13	13	3.53	34	0	226.2	213	89	81	115
85 AL	4	5	5.13	15	0	86.0	101	49	28	42
86 AL	7	11	4.24	29	0	172.0	179	81	66	96
87 AL	6	8	4.06	23	0	144.0	148	65	51	93
88 AL	13	13	4.18	34	0	211.0	220	98	80	99
89 AL	8	10	3.93	30	0	171.2	186	75	47	47
90 AL	2	2	5.31	5	0	20.1	28	12	8	5
91 AL	2	7	2.38	64	3	98.1	84	26	25	55
92 AL	0	0	8.05	42	0	34.2	50	31	23	17
Life	167	143	3.90	526	4	2770.0	2806	1199	890	1491
2 AVE	1	4	3.86	53	2	66.2	67	29	24	36

DAVE FLEMING

Position: Pitcher
Team: Seattle Mariners
Born: Nov. 7, 1969 Queens, NY
Height: 6'3" **Weight:** 200 lbs.
Bats: left **Throws:** left
Acquired: Third-round pick in 6/90 free-agent draft

Player Summary

Fantasy Value	$15 to $20
Card Value	10¢ to 20¢
Will	throw four pitches for strikes
Can't	contend for K crown
Expect	good command and control
Don't Expect	less than 12 wins

At age 22, Fleming not only jumped from Double-A to the majors but became the ace of the Seattle staff. A control pitcher who keeps hitters off-balance by changing speeds, he throws a fastball, sinker, curve, and changeup—which is the curve thrown with 5 to 10 mph less velocity. He has a 2-1 strikeout-to-walk ratio and yields less than a hit per inning. Opponents in 1992 compiled a .257 batting average, a .306 on-base percentage, and a .371 slugging percentage. Although his fastball is rated above-average, he learned at the University of Georgia that he couldn't throw it past anybody. That lesson paid off in a nine-game winning streak that tied Scott Bankhead's club record. With 11 first-half wins, Fleming was a top contender for Rookie of the Year. His exclusion from the All-Star team caused an uproar in Seattle. In 1991 at Double-A Jacksonville, he was 10-6 with a 2.64 ERA, 109 strikeouts, and 25 bases on balls in 140 innings. He was 2-0 with a 1.13 ERA, 16 strikeouts, and three walks in 16 innings at Triple-A Calgary that year.

Major League Pitching Register

	W	L	ERA	G	CG	IP	H	ER	BB	SO
91 AL	1	0	6.62	9	0	17.2	19	13	3	11
92 AL	17	10	3.39	33	7	228.1	225	86	60	112
Life	18	10	3.62	42	7	246.0	244	99	63	123

SCOTT FLETCHER

Position: Second base; shortstop
Team: Boston Red Sox
Born: July 30, 1958 Fort Walton Beach, FL
Height: 5'11" **Weight:** 173 lbs.
Bats: right **Throws:** right
Acquired: Signed as a free agent, 12/92

Player Summary

Fantasy Value	$2 to $4
Card Value	3¢ to 4¢
Will	thrive as platoon player
Can't	generate power
Expect	strong defense at second
Don't Expect	lots of walks or Ks

Fletcher moves to Beantown as insurance. The roller-coaster ride that represents Fletcher's career path took a noticeable upward turn last summer. After winning a job with the Brewers during spring training, he formed a fine righty-lefty second base platoon with Jim Gantner and produced his best batting average since 1988. Fletcher even hit a rare meaningful home run—a three-run, ninth-inning shot that beat the White Sox, 3-0, on July 25. Before 1992, Fletcher's average had diminished a little bit each season for four straight years. With the free-fall but a memory, the infielder should have several solid years left. A contact hitter who walks more than he Ks, Fletcher has some speed but little power. He's a good double-play man who handles second well but is only a backup at shortstop.

Major League Batting Register

	BA	G	AB	R	H	2B	3B	HR	RBI	SB
81 NL	.217	19	46	6	10	4	0	0	1	0
82 NL	.167	11	24	4	4	0	0	0	1	1
83 AL	.237	114	262	42	62	16	5	3	31	5
84 AL	.250	149	456	46	114	13	3	3	35	10
85 AL	.256	119	301	38	77	8	1	2	31	5
86 AL	.300	147	530	82	159	34	5	3	50	12
87 AL	.287	156	588	82	169	28	4	5	63	13
88 AL	.276	140	515	59	142	19	4	0	47	8
89 AL	.253	142	546	77	138	25	2	1	43	2
90 AL	.242	151	509	54	123	18	3	4	56	1
91 AL	.206	90	248	14	51	10	1	1	28	0
92 AL	.275	123	386	53	106	18	3	3	51	17
Life	.262	1361	4411	557	1155	193	31	25	437	74
3 AVE	.245	121	381	40	93	15	2	3	45	6

JOHN FRANCO

Position: Pitcher
Team: New York Mets
Born: Sept. 17, 1960 Brooklyn, NY
Height: 5'10" **Weight:** 185 lbs.
Bats: left **Throws:** left
Acquired: Traded from Reds with Don Brown for Kip Gross and Randy Myers, 12/89

Player Summary	
Fantasy Value	$20 to $28
Card Value	5¢ to 7¢
Will	convert most save chances
Can't	fan a hitter per inning
Expect	30 saves per season
Don't Expect	problems with control

Franco is one of the most consistent closers in baseball. He had five 30-save seasons in a row from 1987 to 1991 and might have reached that level in '92 if not for June elbow problems that forced him onto the disabled list for the first time in his career. Out from June 29 to Aug. 2, Franco registered a save in his first game back. He has converted more than 85 percent of his save opportunities since 1988 and owns the lowest lifetime ERA of any reliever with 500 innings pitched. He didn't yield a run last year until June 9. A strong contender for eventual membership in the 300-save club, Franco throws a fastball, slider, and changeup—an off-speed pitch that moves like a screwball. The former St. John's University southpaw works the corners, changes speeds, and keeps runners close with a good pickoff move.

Major League Pitching Register

	W	L	ERA	G	S	IP	H	ER	BB	SO
84 NL	6	2	2.61	54	4	79.1	74	23	36	55
85 NL	12	3	2.18	67	12	99.0	83	24	40	61
86 NL	6	6	2.94	74	29	101.0	90	33	44	84
87 NL	8	5	2.52	68	32	82.0	76	23	27	61
88 NL	6	6	1.57	70	39	86.0	60	15	27	46
89 NL	4	8	3.12	60	32	80.2	77	28	36	60
90 NL	5	3	2.53	55	33	67.2	66	19	21	56
91 NL	5	9	2.93	52	30	55.1	61	18	18	45
92 NL	6	2	1.64	31	15	33.0	24	6	11	20
Life	58	44	2.49	531	226	684.0	611	189	260	488
3 AVE	5	5	2.48	46	26	52.1	50	14	17	40

JULIO FRANCO

Position: Second base; outfield
Team: Texas Rangers
Born: Aug. 23, 1961 San Pedro de Macoris, Dominican Republic
Height: 6'1" **Weight:** 185 lbs.
Bats: right **Throws:** right
Acquired: Traded from Indians for Oddibe McDowell, Jerry Browne, and Pete O'Brien, 12/88

Player Summary	
Fantasy Value	$15 to $25
Card Value	4¢ to 8¢
Will	hit to opposite field
Can't	hit over 15 homers
Expect	great hitting in clutch
Don't Expect	good defense at second

After leading the majors with a .341 batting average in 1991, Franco fell upon hard times last summer. Disabled three times with knee problems, he played only 35 games. The Rangers tried him as a DH, then decided he should play left field—a position where the strain on his knees would be minimized. Although he had played center in high school, Franco did not appear in the outfield after going pro in 1978. But he has the speed to make the move work. When healthy, Franco is a feared hitter whose forte is definitely not defense. He led the league with 19 errors at second base in 1990. In '91, however, he became the first AL player since Paul Molitor in 1982 to produce 100 runs, 200 hits, and 30 stolen bases.

Major League Batting Register

	BA	G	AB	R	H	2B	3B	HR	RBI	SB
82 NL	.276	16	29	3	8	1	0	0	3	0
83 AL	.273	149	560	68	153	24	8	8	80	32
84 AL	.286	160	658	82	188	22	5	3	79	19
85 AL	.288	160	636	97	183	33	4	6	90	13
86 AL	.306	149	599	80	183	30	5	10	74	10
87 AL	.319	128	495	86	158	24	3	8	52	32
88 AL	.303	152	613	88	186	23	6	10	54	25
89 AL	.316	150	548	80	173	31	5	13	92	21
90 AL	.296	157	582	96	172	27	1	11	69	31
91 AL	.341	146	589	108	201	27	3	15	78	36
92 AL	.234	35	107	19	25	7	0	2	8	1
Life	.301	1402	5416	807	1630	249	40	86	679	220
2 AVE	.319	152	586	102	187	27	2	13	74	34

MARVIN FREEMAN

Position: Pitcher
Team: Atlanta Braves
Born: April 10, 1963 Chicago, IL
Height: 6'7" **Weight:** 222 lbs.
Bats: right **Throws:** right
Acquired: Traded from Phillies for Joe Boever, 7/90

Player Summary

Fantasy Value	$1 to $3
Card Value	3¢ to 4¢
Will	always throw hard
Can't	keep ball in the park
Expect	periods of wildness
Don't Expect	deployment as closer

Freeman's work as a middle reliever was marred last summer by an alarming tendency to yield walks and gopher balls. With six home runs and 18 walks allowed in his first 45 innings pitched, Freeman was fortunate that his record wasn't worse than 4-4. In 1991, his first full big league season, he threw only two gopher balls in 48 innings. His performance seems to improve with work, and he did show signs of pulling out of his skid late last summer. He is a fastball-and-slider pitcher who also throws a split-fingered fastball. In 1992, opponents compiled a .251 batting average, a .332 on-base average, and a .383 slugging percentage. The towering righthander could become a top reliever if he recaptures his 1991 form, which included three times more strikeouts than walks, less than a hit per inning, and an earned run average of three. He accomplished all that with pain caused by back problems that eventually needed surgery.

Major League Pitching Register

	W	L	ERA	G	S	IP	H	ER	BB	SO
86 NL	2	0	2.25	3	0	16.0	6	4	10	8
88 NL	2	3	6.10	11	0	51.2	55	35	43	37
89 NL	0	0	6.00	1	0	3.0	2	2	5	0
90 NL	1	2	4.31	25	1	48.0	41	23	17	38
91 NL	1	0	3.00	34	1	48.0	37	16	13	34
92 NL	7	5	3.22	58	3	64.1	61	23	29	41
Life	13	10	4.01	132	5	231.0	202	103	117	158
3 AVE	3	2	3.48	39	2	53.1	46	21	20	38

TODD FROHWIRTH

Position: Pitcher
Team: Baltimore Orioles
Born: Sept. 28, 1962 Milwaukee, WI
Height: 6'4" **Weight:** 204 lbs.
Bats: right **Throws:** right
Acquired: Signed as a free agent, 12/90

Player Summary

Fantasy Value	$3 to $5
Card Value	3¢ to 4¢
Will	bury righty hitters
Can't	register high K totals
Expect	Kent Tekulve clone
Don't Expect	snap throws to bases

Frohwirth was 17 years old when he copied Kent Tekulve's unorthodox submarine motion off a television screen. Frohwirth picked it up naturally, led four minor leagues in saves, and is still using it in the major leagues. He throws only two pitches, a fastball and a "slurve," which is a cross between a slider and a curve. But the angle is devastating—especially against righthanded hitters. When he's on, he yields less than a hit per inning, fans twice the number he walks, and keeps the ball in the park. If his release point is off, however, he encounters control problems and gives up hits. Although he's good on defense, Frohwirth has to maintain his submarine style in throwing to other fielders. Keeping runners close is tougher, however, because of his slow motion toward the plate. Such minor problems don't stand in his way, though; he's worked more than 50 times in each of the past two seasons.

Major League Pitching Register

	W	L	ERA	G	S	IP	H	ER	BB	SO
87 NL	1	0	0.00	10	0	11.0	12	0	2	9
88 NL	1	2	8.25	12	0	12.0	16	11	11	11
89 NL	1	0	3.59	45	0	62.2	56	25	18	39
90 NL	0	1	18.00	5	0	1.0	3	2	6	1
91 AL	3	1	1.87	51	3	96.1	64	20	29	77
92 AL	4	3	2.46	65	4	106.0	97	29	41	58
Life	14	9	2.71	188	7	289.0	248	87	107	195
2 AVE	6	3	2.18	58	4	101.1	81	25	35	68

TRAVIS FRYMAN

Position: Shortstop; third base
Team: Detroit Tigers
Born: March 25, 1969 Lexington, KY
Height: 6'2" **Weight:** 190 lbs.
Bats: right **Throws:** right
Acquired: Third-round pick in 6/87 free-agent draft

Player Summary	
Fantasy Value	$25 to $32
Card Value	10¢ to 15¢
Will	show off shotgun arm
Can't	play strong third
Expect	good power for shortstop
Don't Expect	300 average

One of the hottest young infielders in the game today, Fryman is a natural shortstop who shifted to third earlier in his career because his team also had Alan Trammell. Fryman returned to short last May when Trammell broke his ankle. Managers polled by *Baseball America* a few months later said Fryman had the best infield throwing arm in the American League. He can also hit. He went 3-for-4 with three runs scored, three RBI, and two home runs as the Tigers beat the Red Sox, 8-3 on June 29. With 20 homers and 90 RBI in 1991, Fryman became the youngest Tiger to reach the 20-90 level since 20-year-old Al Kaline in 1955. Fryman had a .316 on-base average and a .416 slugging percentage in 1992. His lone weakness is impatience; he fans four times more than he walks. Much better defensively at shortstop, he turns the double play well (88 in 1992), has decent range, and has that Shawon Dunston arm. Fryman was an All-Star for the first time in 1992.

Major League Batting Register

	BA	G	AB	R	H	2B	3B	HR	RBI	SB
90 AL	.297	66	232	32	69	11	1	9	27	3
91 AL	.259	149	557	65	144	36	3	21	91	12
92 AL	.266	161	659	87	175	31	4	20	96	8
Life	.268	376	1448	184	388	78	8	50	214	23
3 AVE	.268	125	483	61	129	26	3	17	71	8

GARY GAETTI

Position: Third base; first base
Team: California Angels
Born: Aug. 19, 1958 Centralia, IL
Height: 6' **Weight:** 200 lbs.
Bats: right **Throws:** right
Acquired: Signed as a free agent, 1/91

Player Summary	
Fantasy Value	$6 to $10
Card Value	3¢ to 4¢
Will	try to pull every pitch
Can't	find old slugging form
Expect	reduced playing time
Don't Expect	any more Gold Gloves

Gaetti is slowing down. A Gold Glove third baseman four straight years from 1986 to 1989, his play deteriorated so rapidly (17 first-half boots last year) that he became a platoon first baseman in midseason. His hitting also went south. Last summer, it almost slipped out of sight. He had only eight homers and 36 RBI by mid-August. By the end of the season, he had compiled a .267 on-base percentage and a .342 slugging average. An impatient pull hitter, he strikes out four times more than he walks. He adds no speed to the lineup and has lost range in the field—though he still has good instincts and reactions. Forced to first by the Wally Joyner defection and Lee Stevens flop, Gaetti took so well to the new job that he seemed like a kid with a new toy.

Major League Batting Register

	BA	G	AB	R	H	2B	3B	HR	RBI	SB
81 AL	.192	9	26	4	5	0	0	2	3	0
82 AL	.230	145	508	59	117	25	4	25	84	0
83 AL	.245	157	584	81	143	30	3	21	78	7
84 AL	.262	162	588	55	154	29	4	5	65	11
85 AL	.246	160	560	71	138	31	0	20	63	13
86 AL	.287	157	596	91	171	34	1	34	108	14
87 AL	.257	154	584	95	150	36	2	31	109	10
88 AL	.301	133	468	66	141	29	2	28	88	7
89 AL	.251	130	498	63	125	11	4	19	75	6
90 AL	.229	154	577	61	132	27	5	16	85	6
91 AL	.246	152	586	58	144	22	1	18	66	5
92 AL	.226	130	456	41	103	13	2	12	48	3
Life	.253	1643	6031	745	1523	287	28	231	872	82
3 AVE	.234	145	540	53	126	21	3	15	66	5

GREG GAGNE

Position: Shortstop
Team: Kansas City Royals
Born: Nov. 12, 1961 Fall River, MA
Height: 5'11" **Weight:** 172 lbs.
Bats: right **Throws:** right
Acquired: Signed as a free agent, 12/92

Player Summary	
Fantasy Value	$3 to $7
Card Value	3¢ to 4¢
Will	contend for Gold Glove
Can't	avoid June swoon
Expect	about 10 homers
Don't Expect	patience at bat

Gagne is one of baseball's best-kept secrets. A sterling defensive shortstop who hits with surprising punch, he's been consistently overlooked because he plays on a team of sluggers. A strong contender for the Gold Glove Award, he would get more consideration if he put up power numbers comparable to the stats that Cal Ripken compiles. In 1991, for example, Gagne went 76 games without an error—the second longest streak in AL history—and starred with his glove in postseason play. He has good speed, good range, good hands, and a strong throwing arm. He's especially good on artificial turf. No slouch with a bat, Gagne makes good contact—and is at his best with runners in scoring position. Over the last seven seasons, he's averaged about 10 home runs per year.

Major League Batting Register

	BA	G	AB	R	H	2B	3B	HR	RBI	SB
83 AL	.111	10	27	2	3	1	0	0	3	0
84 AL	.000	2	1	0	0	0	0	0	0	0
85 AL	.225	114	293	37	66	15	3	2	23	10
86 AL	.250	156	472	63	118	22	6	12	54	12
87 AL	.265	137	437	68	116	28	7	10	40	6
88 AL	.236	149	461	70	109	20	6	14	48	15
89 AL	.272	149	460	69	125	29	7	9	48	11
90 AL	.235	138	388	38	91	22	3	7	38	8
91 AL	.265	139	408	52	108	23	3	8	42	11
92 AL	.246	146	439	53	108	23	0	7	39	6
Life	.249	1140	3386	452	844	183	35	69	335	79
3 AVE	.249	141	412	48	102	23	2	7	40	8

ANDRES GALARRAGA

Position: First base
Team: Colorado Rockies
Born: June 18, 1961 Caracas, Venezuela
Height: 6'3" **Weight:** 235 lbs.
Bats: right **Throws:** right
Acquired: Signed as a free agent, 11/92

Player Summary	
Fantasy Value	$3 to $6
Card Value	3¢ to 4¢
Will	generate some power
Can't	avoid frequent strikeouts
Expect	Gold Glove defense
Don't Expect	average over .270

Before knee surgery limited his playing time in 1991, Galarraga was one of the NL's most productive sluggers. For four straight years with the Expos, he knocked in at least 85 runs and homered in double figures. In 1988, he led the league in hits and doubles. Traded for the first time to the Cards, he tried to make an immediate impression last year. Instead, he struggled. He finally cleared the fences on July 5, in his 128th at bat. Nineteen days later, Galarraga got his first Busch Stadium homer. His best shot of the season came on Aug. 15, when he hit an eighth-inning grand-slam in Montreal to beat the Expos. He is a wild swinger who fans too frequently but can post big RBI numbers. Galarraga is a two-time Gold Glove first baseman. He scoops bad throws, turns the 3-6-3 double play, and has good range.

Major League Batting Register

	BA	G	AB	R	H	2B	3B	HR	RBI	SB
85 NL	.187	24	75	9	14	1	0	2	4	1
86 NL	.271	105	321	39	87	13	0	10	42	6
87 NL	.305	147	551	72	168	40	3	13	90	7
88 NL	.302	157	609	99	184	42	8	29	92	13
89 NL	.257	152	572	76	147	30	1	23	85	12
90 NL	.256	155	579	65	148	29	0	20	87	10
91 NL	.219	107	375	34	82	13	2	9	33	5
92 NL	.243	95	325	38	79	14	2	10	39	5
Life	.267	942	3407	432	909	182	16	116	472	59
3 AVE	.242	119	426	46	103	19	1	13	53	7

DAVE GALLAGHER

Position: Outfield
Team: New York Mets
Born: Sept. 20, 1960 Trenton, NJ
Height: 6′ **Weight:** 180 lbs.
Bats: right **Throws:** right
Acquired: Traded from Angels for Hubie Brooks, 12/91

Player Summary	
Fantasy Value	$1 to $3
Card Value	3¢ to 4¢
Will	swing at bad pitches
Can't	hit with power
Expect	strong defense
Don't Expect	use as a starter

Gallagher is a fine defensive outfielder best utilized as an understudy for all three positions. He has good instincts, good range, and an arm that can make the tough throw from right field. Unlike the high-priced but error-prone regulars who were his teammates with the Mets last summer, Gallagher won't embarrass anyone. He made only six errors in five big league seasons prior to 1992, and he didn't have an error last summer. The rap against Gallagher is his bat—or lack of it. Although his average was .275 before '92, he had only seven homers in 1,380 at bats. Although he'd play more often if he were more productive, he is a contact hitter who rarely walks. He doesn't fan much either, but his hits seldom go for extra bases. Gallagher can bunt, hit-and-run, and hit to the opposite field. He's durable too, once playing 161 games in a season.

MIKE GALLEGO

Position: Second base; shortstop
Team: New York Yankees
Born: Oct. 31, 1960 Whittier, CA
Height: 5′8″ **Weight:** 160 lbs.
Bats: right **Throws:** right
Acquired: Signed as a free agent, 1/92

Player Summary	
Fantasy Value	$4 to $7
Card Value	3¢ to 4¢
Will	play best at second
Can't	hammer righthanders
Expect	half-dozen homers a year
Don't Expect	strong throws from short

Injuries marred Gallego's first year with the New York Yankees last summer. He missed the first 35 games with a strained tendon in his right heel, then lost two months after a Willie Banks pitch fractured Gallego's ulna bone above the right wrist on July 6. Although he played mostly at second for Oakland, he had been heralded as the answer to the Yankees' shortstop problems. He's better defensively at second, however, and has the range, quickness, and good hands that compensate for a so-so throwing arm. He also could see some time at third base in 1993. A better hitter than most middle infielders, he hits line drives with occasional power. He had a .343 on-base average and a .358 slugging percentage in 1992. He's patient at the plate, drawing almost as many walks as strikeouts. He should have little trouble winning a regular job if he's healthy in 1993.

Major League Batting Register

	BA	G	AB	R	H	2B	3B	HR	RBI	SB
87 AL	.111	15	36	2	4	1	1	0	1	2
88 AL	.303	101	347	59	105	15	3	5	31	5
89 AL	.266	161	601	74	160	22	2	1	46	5
90 AL	.254	68	126	12	32	4	1	0	7	1
91 AL	.293	90	270	32	79	17	0	1	30	2
92 NL	.240	98	175	20	42	11	1	1	21	4
Life	.271	533	1555	199	422	70	8	8	136	19
2 AVE	.272	94	223	26	61	14	1	1	26	3

Major League Batting Register

	BA	G	AB	R	H	2B	3B	HR	RBI	SB
85 AL	.208	76	77	13	16	5	1	1	9	1
86 AL	.270	20	37	2	10	2	0	0	4	0
87 AL	.250	72	124	18	31	6	0	2	14	0
88 AL	.209	129	277	38	58	8	0	2	20	2
89 AL	.252	133	357	45	90	14	2	3	30	7
90 AL	.206	140	389	36	80	13	2	3	34	5
91 AL	.247	159	482	67	119	15	4	12	49	6
92 AL	.254	53	173	24	44	7	1	3	14	0
Life	.234	782	1916	243	448	70	10	26	174	21
3 AVE	.233	117	348	42	81	12	2	6	32	4

RON GANT

Position: Outfield
Team: Atlanta Braves
Born: March 2, 1965 Victoria, TX
Height: 6′ **Weight:** 172 lbs.
Bats: right **Throws:** right
Acquired: Fourth-round pick in 6/83 free-agent draft

Player Summary	
Fantasy Value	$26 to $32
Card Value	5¢ to 10¢
Will	steal when he reaches
Can't	recapture .300 stroke
Expect	return to 30-30 form
Don't Expect	great outfield defense

Gant's bid to become the first player with three consecutive 30-30 seasons ended with a summer-long slump. He had only 11 homers and a .257 average in mid-August—the residue of a dive that began in June. A notorious pull hitter in previous seasons, he messed up his mechanics after deciding to return to the .300 plateau he had reached for the first time in 1990. Instead of trying to hit with power to left, Gant began trying to single to the opposite field. Things got so bad that he was benched briefly in August—giving him time to work with hitting coach Clarence Jones. The only aspect of Gant's game that didn't suffer was his baserunning, surpassing 30 steals for the third straight summer. He was even benched in the World Series in favor of Deion Sanders and Lonnie Smith. A former infielder with an iron glove, Gant uses his speed to compensate for mediocre play in left field.

Major League Batting Register

	BA	G	AB	R	H	2B	3B	HR	RBI	SB
87 NL	.265	21	83	9	22	4	0	2	9	4
88 NL	.259	146	563	85	146	28	8	19	60	19
89 NL	.177	75	260	26	46	8	3	9	25	9
90 NL	.303	152	575	107	174	34	3	32	84	33
91 NL	.251	154	561	101	141	35	3	32	105	34
92 NL	.259	153	544	74	141	22	6	17	80	32
Life	.259	701	2586	402	670	131	23	111	363	131
3 AVE	.271	153	560	94	152	30	4	27	90	33

JIM GANTNER

Position: Second base; third base
Team: Milwaukee Brewers
Born: Jan. 5, 1954 Fond du Lac, WI
Height: 5′11″ **Weight:** 175 lbs.
Bats: left **Throws:** right
Acquired: 12th-round pick in 6/74 free-agent draft

Player Summary	
Fantasy Value	$1 to $3
Card Value	3¢ to 4¢
Will	play reduced role
Can't	steal much anymore
Expect	clubhouse leader
Don't Expect	more than a homer a year

Gantner figures to spend the waning days of his baseball career as a role player. He was used mostly in a lefty-righty second base platoon with Milwaukee last summer. He delivered a 13th-inning homer against Boston's Jeff Reardon Aug. 14 to give the Brewers an 8-7 win. The blast was only Gantner's third home run since 1987. As an infielder, he has good hands and a decent arm despite limited range. Knee surgery several years ago has slowed him down. Gantner is a contact hitter who doesn't strike out much but doesn't have the patience to wait for walks. He still whiffs slightly more than he walks. Gantner is at his best in clutch situations.

Major League Batting Register

	BA	G	AB	R	H	2B	3B	HR	RBI	SB
76 AL	.246	26	69	6	17	1	0	0	7	1
77 AL	.298	14	47	4	14	1	0	1	2	2
78 AL	.216	43	97	14	21	1	0	1	8	2
79 AL	.284	70	208	29	59	10	3	2	22	3
80 AL	.282	132	415	47	117	21	3	4	40	11
81 AL	.267	107	352	35	94	14	1	2	33	3
82 AL	.295	132	447	48	132	17	2	4	43	6
83 AL	.282	161	603	85	170	23	8	11	74	5
84 AL	.282	153	613	61	173	27	1	3	56	6
85 AL	.254	143	523	63	133	15	4	5	44	11
86 AL	.274	139	497	58	136	25	1	7	38	13
87 AL	.272	81	265	37	72	14	0	4	30	6
88 AL	.276	155	539	67	149	28	2	0	47	20
89 AL	.274	116	409	51	112	18	3	0	34	20
90 AL	.263	88	323	36	85	8	5	0	25	18
91 AL	.283	140	526	63	149	27	4	2	47	4
92 AL	.246	101	256	22	63	12	1	1	18	6
Life	.274	1801	6189	726	1696	262	38	47	568	137
3 AVE	.269	110	368	40	99	16	3	1	30	9

MIKE GARDINER

Position: Pitcher
Team: Montreal Expos
Born: Oct. 19, 1965 Sarnia, Ontario, Canada
Height: 6' **Weight:** 185 lbs.
Bats: both **Throws:** right
Acquired: Traded from Red Sox with Terry Powers for Ivan Calderon, 12/92

Player Summary	
Fantasy Value	$2 to $5
Card Value	3¢ to 4¢
Will	mix pitches better
Can't	keep ball in the park
Expect	some control trouble
Don't Expect	great pickoff move

Gardiner returns north of the border. He was a major disappointment to the Red Sox last summer. After losing nine consecutive games, he was even returned to the minor leagues for a while in July. At Triple-A Pawtucket in 1992, he was 1-3 with a 3.31 ERA, 37 strikeouts, and nine walks in 33 innings pitched. Control problems contributed to his demise, but he also yielded more hits than innings pitched for the second straight summer. A fastball-and-slider pitcher who also throws a curve, Gardiner may need to reactivate the effective changeup he threw in the minors. Using the change would help, since his fastball and slider are no better than average. In 1992, opponents compiled a .253 batting average, a .330 on-base average and a .380 slugging percentage. Lefties had a .258 batting average, while righties notched a .249 mark. He showed better control in 1991 but was victimized by the gopher ball. His fielding is decent, however. He was on the 1984 Canadian Olympic baseball team.

MARK GARDNER

Position: Pitcher
Team: Kansas City Royals
Born: March 1, 1962 Los Angeles, CA
Height: 6'1" **Weight:** 190 lbs.
Bats: right **Throws:** right
Acquired: Traded from Expos with Doug Piatt for Tim Spehr and Jeff Shaw, 12/92

Player Summary	
Fantasy Value	$4 to $7
Card Value	3¢ to 4¢
Will	use curve as top pitch
Can't	walk so many
Expect	more than a dozen wins
Don't Expect	control to be perfect

Gardner joins an improving KC rotation. In 1991, Gardner hurled nine hitless innings at Los Angeles though the Expos lost in 10. He doesn't always have such great command, but he's very difficult to hit when his curveball is working. The curve is the leading lady of an arsenal that also includes a fastball and changeup. He showed better control last year than the year before but still threw his share of home run balls. He fanned more than twice the number he walked and yielded less than a hit per inning. And he kept his earned run average respectable. In 1992, opponents compiled a .259 batting average, a .324 on-base percentage, and a .386 slugging percentage. Gardner allowed 15 homers in 1992. He had serious elbow surgery in 1990 but seems to have recovered completely. In two seasons in the minors, he led the Montreal organization in strikeouts. He is adept at preventing runners from stealing. He's no better than adequate in the field.

Major League Pitching Register

	W	L	ERA	G	CG	IP	H	ER	BB	SO
90 AL	0	2	10.66	5	0	12.2	22	15	5	6
91 AL	9	10	4.85	22	0	130.0	140	70	47	91
92 AL	4	10	4.75	28	0	130.2	126	69	58	79
Life	13	22	5.07	55	0	273.1	288	154	110	176
2 AVE	7	10	4.80	25	0	130.1	133	70	53	85

Major League Pitching Register

	W	L	ERA	G	CG	IP	H	ER	BB	SO
89 NL	0	3	5.13	7	0	26.1	26	15	11	21
90 NL	7	9	3.42	27	3	152.2	129	58	61	135
91 NL	9	11	3.85	27	0	168.1	139	72	75	107
92 NL	12	10	4.36	33	0	179.2	179	87	60	132
Life	28	33	3.96	94	3	527.0	473	232	207	395
3 AVE	9	10	3.90	29	1	166.2	149	72	65	125

SCOTT GARRELTS

Position: Pitcher
Team: San Francisco Giants
Born: Oct. 30, 1961 Urbana, IL
Height: 6'4" **Weight:** 205 lbs.
Bats: right **Throws:** right
Acquired: First-round pick in 6/79 free-agent draft

Player Summary	
Fantasy Value	$1 to $2
Card Value	3¢ to 4¢
Will	attempt tough comeback
Can't	help himself with bat
Expect	more breaking balls
Don't Expect	medical miracles

Garrelts won the 1989 ERA crown in the National League, then went on the shelf with elbow problems two years later. He has not pitched in the majors since June 10, 1991. He had the "Tommy John" tendon transplant operation, and Garrelts attempted to pitch on rehabilitation assignment in the minors last summer but stopped when calcium deposits were discovered in the elbow. When healthy, he threw a 90 mph fastball, split-fingered fastball, and slider. He has experimented with new ways to throw his breaking pitches. A former reliever who became a starter in 1988, the bespectacled righthander handles a glove well but is an automatic out at the plate. He also runs well enough to be used as a pinch-runner on occasion. When effective, Garrelts keeps rivals at bay, as evidenced by his 3.29 career ERA.

Major League Pitching Register

	W	L	ERA	G	CG	IP	H	ER	BB	SO
82 NL	0	0	13.50	1	0	2.0	3	3	2	4
83 NL	2	2	2.52	5	1	35.2	33	10	19	16
84 NL	2	3	5.65	21	0	43.0	45	27	34	32
85 NL	9	6	2.30	74	0	105.2	76	27	58	106
86 NL	13	9	3.11	53	2	173.2	144	60	74	125
87 NL	11	7	3.22	64	0	106.1	70	38	55	127
88 NL	5	9	3.58	65	0	98.0	80	39	46	86
89 NL	14	5	2.28	30	2	193.1	149	49	46	119
90 NL	12	11	4.15	31	4	182.0	190	84	70	80
91 NL	1	1	6.41	8	0	19.2	25	14	9	8
Life	69	63	3.29	352	9	959.1	815	351	413	703
2 AVE	13	8	3.19	31	3	188.1	170	67	58	100

PAUL GIBSON

Position: Pitcher
Team: New York Mets
Born: Jan. 4, 1960 Southhampton, NY
Height: 6' **Weight:** 185 lbs.
Bats: right **Throws:** left
Acquired: Traded from Tigers with Randy Marshall for Mark Carreon and Tony Castillo, 1/92

Player Summary	
Fantasy Value	$1 to $3
Card Value	3¢ to 4¢
Will	give up too many runs
Can't	get first batters out
Expect	mop-up deployment
Don't Expect	respectable ERA

In his first National League season, Gibson was highly ineffective as a lefthanded setup man in the bullpen of the New York Mets. Although he fanned twice the number he walked, he yielded more than a hit per inning and threw an alarming number of home run balls. His 5.23 earned run average ranked dead-last on the New York staff. A sinker-and-slider pitcher who has worked more than 40 times five years in a row, the bespectacled southpaw sometimes falls victim to overuse. He allowed seven homers in 1992. When he's right, rivals usually drub the ball on the ground—an event that can be an adventure if the proper defensive support is lacking. Gibson himself wields a good glove and keeps runners close. But allowing so many baserunners is hardly the hallmark of a good relief pitcher. In 1992, opponents compiled a .287 batting average, a .352 on-base percentage, and a .467 slugging percentage.

Major League Pitching Register

	W	L	ERA	G	S	IP	H	ER	BB	SO
88 AL	4	2	2.93	40	0	92.0	83	30	34	50
89 AL	4	8	4.64	45	0	132.0	129	68	57	77
90 AL	5	4	3.05	61	3	97.1	99	33	44	56
91 AL	5	7	4.59	68	6	96.0	112	49	48	52
92 NL	0	1	5.23	43	0	62.0	70	36	25	49
Life	18	22	4.06	257	11	479.1	493	216	208	284
3 AVE	3	4	4.16	57	4	85.0	94	39	39	52

BERNARD GILKEY

Position: Outfield
Team: St. Louis Cardinals
Born: Sept. 24, 1966 St. Louis, MO
Height: 6′ **Weight:** 170 lbs.
Bats: right **Throws:** right
Acquired: Signed as a free agent, 8/84

Player Summary	
Fantasy Value	$7 to $10
Card Value	3¢ to 4¢
Will	show tremendous speed
Can't	rely on power
Expect	good clutch hitting
Don't Expect	defensive problems

After a disastrous 1991 rookie season, Gilkey realized his promise last summer. He not only became the every-day left fielder but also blossomed into the club's top clutch hitter. Because of his great speed and strong throwing arm, he cuts off balls hit into the gaps and nails runners on the bases. He's no slouch on the basepaths himself and is certain to steal 30 to 40 bases per year on a regular basis (he had three 40-plus years in the minors). Gilkey makes good contact, walks almost as often as he strikes out, and has some extra-base power (though not enough to hit many homers). In 1992, he compiled a .364 on-base average and a .427 slugging percentage. He also batted .352 versus lefthanders. He was deployed in the leadoff slot in the lineup most of last summer and figures to stay there. In 1990 at Triple-A Louisville, he batted .295 with 83 runs, 45 stolen bases, three homers, and 46 RBI. He batted only .146 in 11 games at Louisville in 1991, though, after he was returned from St. Louis.

Major League Batting Register

	BA	G	AB	R	H	2B	3B	HR	RBI	SB
90 NL	.297	18	64	11	19	5	2	1	3	6
91 NL	.216	81	268	28	58	7	2	5	20	14
92 NL	.302	131	384	56	116	19	4	7	43	18
Life	.270	230	716	95	193	31	8	13	66	38
2 AVE	.267	106	326	42	87	13	3	6	32	16

JOE GIRARDI

Position: Catcher
Team: Colorado Rockies
Born: Oct. 14, 1964 Peoria, IL
Height: 6′ **Weight:** 195 lbs.
Bats: right **Throws:** right
Acquired: First-round pick from Cubs in 11/92 expansion draft

Player Summary	
Fantasy Value	$2 to $4
Card Value	3¢ to 4¢
Will	call a good game
Can't	steal bases
Expect	passed balls
Don't Expect	home runs

Girardi will be responsible for handling the young Rockies pitching staff. He teamed with Rick Wilkins to give the Chicago Cubs a strong righty-lefty platoon behind the plate last summer. A year removed from back surgery, Girardi supplied little power but swung the bat the same way he had in 1990. He is a singles hitter who makes good contact, and he often takes outside pitches the other way. He is not adverse to taking a walk. In 1992, he compiled a .320 on-base percentage and a .300 slugging percentage. His claim to fame is his defense. A good handler of pitchers, he calls a good game, blocks the plate well, and has a better-than-average throwing arm. He led two minor leagues in putouts and assists and one league in fielding percentage. His lone drawback is a tendency to yield passed balls; Girardi allowed 16, tied for the NL lead in that dubious department, in 1990. A smart ballplayer, he holds an industrial engineering degree from Northwestern University.

Major League Batting Register

	BA	G	AB	R	H	2B	3B	HR	RBI	SB
89 NL	.248	59	157	15	39	10	0	1	14	2
90 NL	.270	133	419	36	113	24	2	1	38	8
91 NL	.191	21	47	3	9	2	0	0	6	0
92 NL	.270	91	270	19	73	3	1	1	12	0
Life	.262	304	893	73	234	39	3	3	70	10
2 AVE	.270	112	345	28	93	14	2	1	25	4

DAN GLADDEN

Position: Outfield
Team: Detroit Tigers
Born: July 7, 1957 San Jose, CA
Height: 5'11" **Weight:** 181 lbs.
Bats: right **Throws:** right
Acquired: Signed as a free agent, 12/91

Player Summary

Fantasy Value	$3 to $6
Card Value	3¢ to 4¢
Will	play strong defense
Can't	reach the fences
Expect	impatience at plate
Don't Expect	return to leadoff

Gladden didn't add much to the Detroit Tigers last year. He failed to match his nine-year average of .272, didn't steal with his usual frequency, and was unable to hit with any authority. Dropped to No. 2 in the lineup (he had hit leadoff for Minnesota), Gladden found his main contributions to the Tigers came on defense. He played left field well, catching everything hit his way, and turning on his speed to snare balls that initially seemed out of his reach. Gladden's arm is only adequate, though he twice had a dozen assists in a season while playing in Minnesota's covered bandbox. If he showed more patience at the plate to increase his walks and on-base percentage, Gladden would have more value. In 1992, he compiled a .304 on-base average and a .357 slugging percentage.

Major League Batting Register

	BA	G	AB	R	H	2B	3B	HR	RBI	SB
83 NL	.222	18	63	6	14	2	0	1	9	4
84 NL	.351	86	342	71	120	17	2	4	31	31
85 NL	.243	142	502	64	122	15	8	7	41	32
86 NL	.276	102	351	55	97	16	1	4	29	27
87 AL	.249	121	438	69	109	21	2	8	38	25
88 AL	.269	141	576	91	155	32	6	11	62	28
89 AL	.295	121	461	69	136	23	3	8	46	23
90 AL	.275	136	534	64	147	27	6	5	40	25
91 AL	.247	126	461	65	114	14	9	6	52	15
92 AL	.254	113	417	57	106	20	1	7	42	4
Life	.270	1106	4145	611	1120	187	38	61	390	214
3 AVE	.260	125	471	62	122	20	5	6	45	15

TOM GLAVINE

Position: Pitcher
Team: Atlanta Braves
Born: March 25, 1966 Concord, MA
Height: 6' **Weight:** 175 lbs.
Bats: left **Throws:** left
Acquired: Second-round pick in 6/84 free-agent draft

Player Summary

Fantasy Value	$28 to $36
Card Value	10¢ to 15¢
Will	contend for Cy Young
Can't	forget World Series
Expect	Gold Glove Award
Don't Expect	strikeout crown

Atlanta pitching coach Leo Mazzone said Glavine reminds him of Whitey Ford. Glavine reminds others of Warren Spahn. Glavine has good command of his fastball, curve, and slider. He also has a two-seam circle change that he throws up to 40 times per game. The 1991 Cy Young Award winner has started two straight All-Star Games for the National League. His 12th straight victory, on Aug. 14, 1992, tied a 78-year-old Braves' franchise record and increased his record to 18-3. Five of those wins were shutouts—all achieved before the All-Star break. Opponents in 1992 compiled a .235 batting average, a .293 on-base percentage, and a .310 slugging percentage. A strong candidate for a Gold Glove Award, Glavine has one of the game's best pickoff moves. As a hitter, he can sacrifice, bunt for a hit, or drive home a run with a base hit. He has been used as a pinch-hitter.

Major League Pitching Register

	W	L	ERA	G	CG	IP	H	ER	BB	SO
87 NL	2	4	5.54	9	0	50.1	55	31	33	20
88 NL	7	17	4.56	34	1	195.1	201	99	63	84
89 NL	14	8	3.68	29	6	186.0	172	76	40	90
90 NL	10	12	4.28	33	1	214.1	232	102	78	129
91 NL	20	11	2.55	34	9	246.2	201	70	69	192
92 NL	20	8	2.76	33	7	225.0	197	69	70	129
Life	73	60	3.60	172	24	1117.2	1058	447	353	644
3 AVE	17	10	3.16	33	6	228.1	210	80	72	150

LEO GOMEZ

Position: Third base
Team: Baltimore Orioles
Born: March 2, 1967 Canovanas, Puerto Rico
Height: 6' **Weight:** 202 lbs.
Bats: right **Throws:** right
Acquired: Signed as free agent, 12/85

Player Summary	
Fantasy Value	$8 to $12
Card Value	10¢ to 15¢
Will	improve with experience
Can't	steal many bases
Expect	good power production
Don't Expect	Brooks Robinson defense

Gomez's sophomore season was much better than his rookie year. His average, his run production, and his defensive play all improved. Winter workouts in the Florida Instructional League helped him. He strikes out less than twice as often as he walks—a good ratio for a power hitter—and shows more patience at the plate than he did as a 1991 rookie. In 1992, he compiled a .356 on-base average and a .425 slugging percentage. Gomez led the Triple-A International League with Rochester by notching 97 runs scored and 97 RBI in 1990. That year he also batted .277 with 26 homers and 26 doubles. In 1991 at Rochester, he hit .257 with six homers and 19 RBI. He should be good for 20 homers a year as he gains experience. He has good hands, good range, and a strong throwing arm at third base. He made only two errors in Baltimore's first 53 games last summer. He led one minor league in assists and another in double plays.

Major League Batting Register

	BA	G	AB	R	H	2B	3B	HR	RBI	SB
90 AL	.231	12	39	3	9	0	0	0	1	0
91 AL	.233	118	391	40	91	17	2	16	45	1
92 AL	.265	137	468	62	124	24	0	17	64	2
Life	.249	267	898	105	224	41	2	33	110	3
2 AVE	.250	128	430	51	108	21	1	17	55	2

RENE GONZALES

Position: Third Base
Team: California Angels
Born: Sept. 3, 1961 Austin, TX
Height: 6'3" **Weight:** 201 lbs.
Bats: right **Throws:** right
Acquired: Signed as a free agent, 1/92

Player Summary	
Fantasy Value	$2 to $4
Card Value	3¢ to 4¢
Will	make good contact
Can't	steal many bases
Expect	low error total
Don't Expect	old utility role

The versatility of Gonzales always worked against him, because he had such value as a spare part that no manager attempted to try him as a regular. In 1991, for example, he played in 71 games—appearing everywhere but pitcher and catcher—while batting in only 51 of them. Given a new life by the Angels, he got off to a better start than veteran third baseman Gary Gaetti. Given extended playing time for the first time in an eight-year career, Gonzales ranked third on the team in games, hits, homers, RBI, and total bases before breaking his left forearm in early August. He's a contact hitter with the patience to wait for walks. He compiled a .363 on-base average and a .398 slugging percentage in 1992. Always a strong fielder, Gonzales led two minor leagues in double plays by a shortstop. He also led some farm leagues in putouts, assists, and fielding percentage.

Major League Batting Register

	BA	G	AB	R	H	2B	3B	HR	RBI	SB
84 NL	.233	29	30	5	7	1	0	0	2	0
86 NL	.115	11	26	1	3	0	0	0	0	0
87 AL	.267	37	60	14	16	2	1	1	7	1
88 AL	.215	92	237	13	51	6	0	2	15	2
89 AL	.217	71	166	16	36	4	0	1	11	5
90 AL	.214	67	103	13	22	3	1	1	12	1
91 AL	.195	71	118	16	23	3	0	1	6	0
92 AL	.277	104	329	47	91	17	1	7	38	7
Life	.233	482	1069	125	249	36	3	13	91	16

JUAN GONZALEZ

Position: Outfield
Team: Texas Rangers
Born: Oct. 16, 1969 Vega Baja, Puerto Rico
Height: 6'3" **Weight:** 200 lbs.
Bats: right **Throws:** right
Acquired: Signed as free agent, 5/86

Player Summary	
Fantasy Value	$40 to $50
Card Value	15¢ to 25¢
Will	display devastating power
Can't	steal bases
Expect	shift to right field
Don't Expect	patience at the plate

In his second full season, Gonzalez blossomed into one of baseball's most prolific sluggers. He had 30 homers by mid-August and went on to lead the major leagues in home runs. He hit 11 homers—three of them in one game—in June, a 450-foot shot to dead center field at Camden Yards July 26, and a pair of homers in a 10-inning, 2-1 win at Boston two days later. But Gonzalez's defensive play sagged during a midseason batting slump, as he made more errors than any other AL center fielder. Because he has a strong arm but lacks the speed for center, Gonzalez is best-suited to Texas' right field, a spot occupied first by Ruben Sierra then by Jose Canseco last summer. Although Gonzalez fans four times more than he walks, he is a wrist hitter who has learned to lay off bad pitches and hit with power to all fields. In 1992, he had a .304 on-base average and a .529 slugging percentage. He broke into pro ball at age 16 in 1986.

Major League Batting Register

	BA	G	AB	R	H	2B	3B	HR	RBI	SB
89 AL	.150	24	60	6	9	3	0	1	7	0
90 AL	.289	25	90	11	26	7	1	4	12	0
91 AL	.264	142	545	78	144	34	1	27	102	4
92 AL	.260	155	584	77	152	24	2	43	109	0
Life	.259	346	1279	172	331	68	4	75	230	4
2 AVE	.262	149	565	78	148	29	2	35	106	2

LUIS GONZALEZ

Position: Outfield
Team: Houston Astros
Born: Sept. 3, 1967 Tampa, FL
Height: 6'2" **Weight:** 180 lbs.
Bats: left **Throws:** right
Acquired: Fourth-round pick in 6/88 free-agent draft

Player Summary	
Fantasy Value	$6 to $10
Card Value	3¢ to 4¢
Will	struggle against southpaws
Can't	escape injury plague
Expect	decent run production
Don't Expect	patience at bat

Injuries ruined the sophomore season of Gonzalez last summer. He twice hurt his nose during batting practice and later suffered a dislocated left shoulder that also forced him onto the disabled list. Returned to the minors after a slow start in '92, he batted .432 in 44 at bats with a homer, nine RBI, five walks, and four stolen bases at Triple-A Tucson. He came back to Houston and collected five homers and 19 RBI in June. By mid-August, however, Gonzalez—with only seven homers and 31 RBI for the year—had lost his left field job to Pete Incaviglia. When he's right, Gonzalez generates good power with a quick, compact swing. But his selectivity needs work: He strikes out more than twice as often as he walks. In addition, he struggles against lefthanded pitching. Gonzalez does have speed, however, and might develop into a 20-20 man. In 1992, he compiled a .289 on-base average and a .385 slugging percentage. A converted infielder, he is a competent outfielder with good range but a mediocre arm.

Major League Batting Register

	BA	G	AB	R	H	2B	3B	HR	RBI	SB
90 NL	.190	12	21	1	4	2	0	0	0	0
91 NL	.254	137	473	51	120	28	9	13	69	10
92 NL	.243	122	387	40	94	19	3	10	55	7
Life	.247	271	881	92	218	49	12	23	124	17
2 AVE	.249	130	430	46	107	24	6	12	62	9

DWIGHT GOODEN

Position: Pitcher
Team: New York Mets
Born: Nov. 16, 1964 Tampa, FL
Height: 6'3" **Weight:** 210 lbs.
Bats: right **Throws:** right
Acquired: First-round pick in 6/82 free-agent
draft

Player Summary	
Fantasy Value	$14 to $22
Card Value	7¢ to 10¢
Will	try to shake shoulder woes
Can't	recapture Cy Young form
Expect	self-help with bat and glove
Don't Expect	many complete games

Although Gooden returned from rotator cuff surgery much sooner than expected, he wasn't the same power pitcher he had been before. He dropped 10 of his first 16 decisions and allowed an average of more than four earned runs a game before getting back into his groove. He also missed three weeks after his shoulder pain resurfaced on July 17. Pitchers coming off shoulder surgery sometimes take two years to heal; 1993 should be a good gauge of Gooden's future success. Before last year, he had 16 victories a year over eight seasons. A fastball-and-curveball pitcher who depends upon changing speeds and pinpoint location, he fans three times the number he walks when he's healthy. Gooden helps himself with his hitting (he had one of the best batting averages on the '92 Mets) and fielding but has trouble keeping baserunners close.

Major League Pitching Register

		W	L	ERA	G	CG	IP	H	ER	BB	SO
84	NL	17	9	2.60	31	7	218.0	161	63	73	276
85	NL	24	4	1.53	35	16	276.2	198	47	69	268
86	NL	17	6	2.84	33	12	250.0	197	79	80	200
87	NL	15	7	3.21	25	7	179.2	162	64	53	148
88	NL	18	9	3.19	34	10	248.1	242	88	57	175
89	NL	9	4	2.89	19	0	118.1	93	38	47	101
90	NL	19	7	3.83	34	2	232.2	229	99	70	223
91	NL	13	7	3.60	27	3	190.0	185	76	56	150
92	NL	10	13	3.67	31	3	206.0	197	84	70	145
Life		142	66	2.99	269	60	1919.2	1664	638	575	1686
3 AVE		14	9	3.71	31	3	209.1	204	86	65	173

TOM GORDON

Position: Pitcher
Team: Kansas City Royals
Born: Nov. 18, 1967 Sebring, FL
Height: 5'9" **Weight:** 160 lbs.
Bats: right **Throws:** right
Acquired: Sixth-round pick in 6/86 free-agent
draft

Player Summary	
Fantasy Value	$4 to $7
Card Value	3¢ to 4¢
Will	rack up many strikeouts
Can't	always control curve
Expect	search for role
Don't Expect	return to '89 form

Gordon's performance last summer suggested his nickname was one of the most appropriate in baseball. "Flash" showed flashes of brilliance, including an eight-game streak in midseason when his earned run average was 0.76. Confusion over his role slowed his progress, however, and he dropped nine of his first 14 decisions. Used as a starter, middle reliever, and occasional late man, he never regained the form he had shown in his first two seasons. Control—or the lack of it—was a major problem. He fanned less than two hitters for every one he walked. Opponents in 1992 compiled a .258 batting average, a .340 on-base average, and a .379 slugging percentage. A fastball-and-curveball pitcher who usually handles righthanded hitters with ease, he also has a slider that breaks in either direction. Gordon has a good pickoff move and decent glove. He also has a tendency to let his temper take over. When he's throwing his curve for strikes, Gordon is at his best.

Major League Pitching Register

		W	L	ERA	G	S	IP	H	ER	BB	SO
88	AL	0	2	5.17	5	0	15.2	16	9	7	18
89	AL	17	9	3.64	49	1	163.0	122	66	86	153
90	AL	12	11	3.73	32	0	195.1	192	81	99	175
91	AL	9	14	3.87	45	1	158.0	129	68	87	167
92	AL	6	10	4.59	40	0	117.2	116	60	55	98
Life		44	46	3.93	171	2	649.2	575	284	334	611
3 AVE		9	12	3.99	39	0	157.1	146	70	80	147

GOOSE GOSSAGE

Position: Pitcher
Team: Oakland Athletics
Born: Sept. 5, 1951 Colorado Springs, CO
Height: 6'3" **Weight:** 225 lbs.
Bats: right **Throws:** right
Acquired: Signed as a free agent, 3/92

Player Summary	
Fantasy Value	$1 to $3
Card Value	5¢ to 7¢
Will	try to harness control
Can't	win old closer role
Expect	good velocity
Don't Expect	injury-free season

Yes, folks, Goose Gossage is still around. He's no longer the intimidator who saved 25 games in seven different seasons, but he is a competent middle reliever who can still throw hard for an inning or two. Age— and all those fastballs—have taken their toll. Shoulder problems shelved him twice in 1991, and tendinitis in his right arm knocked him out last year. Before he was sidelined, he posted a respectable ERA and fanned 26 hitters in 38 innings. He yielded less than a hit per inning but permitted too many walks—the young Gossage would not have tolerated that.

Major League Pitching Register

	W	L	ERA	G	S	IP	H	ER	BB	SO
72 AL	7	1	4.28	36	2	80.0	72	38	44	57
73 AL	0	4	7.43	20	0	49.2	57	41	37	33
74 AL	4	6	4.13	39	1	89.1	92	41	47	64
75 AL	9	8	1.84	62	26	141.2	99	29	70	130
76 AL	9	17	3.94	31	1	224.0	214	98	90	135
77 NL	11	9	1.62	72	26	133.0	78	24	49	151
78 AL	10	11	2.01	63	27	134.1	87	30	59	122
79 AL	5	3	2.62	36	18	58.1	48	17	19	41
80 AL	6	2	2.27	64	33	99.0	74	25	37	103
81 AL	3	2	0.77	32	20	46.2	22	4	14	48
82 AL	4	5	2.23	56	30	93.0	63	23	28	102
83 AL	13	5	2.27	57	22	87.1	82	22	25	90
84 NL	10	6	2.90	62	25	102.1	75	33	36	84
85 NL	5	3	1.82	50	26	79.0	64	16	17	52
86 NL	5	7	4.45	45	21	64.2	69	32	20	63
87 NL	5	4	3.12	40	11	52.0	47	18	19	44
88 NL	4	4	4.33	46	13	43.2	50	21	15	30
89 NL	2	1	2.68	31	4	43.2	32	13	27	24
89 AL	1	0	3.77	11	1	14.1	14	6	3	6
91 AL	4	2	3.57	44	1	40.1	33	16	16	28
92 AL	0	2	2.84	30	0	38.0	32	12	19	26
Life	117	102	2.93	927	308	1714.1	1404	559	691	1433
2 AVE	2	2	3.22	37	1	39.1	33	14	18	27

JIM GOTT

Position: Pitcher
Team: Los Angeles Dodgers
Born: Aug. 3, 1959 Hollywood, CA
Height: 6'4" **Weight:** 220 lbs.
Bats: right **Throws:** right
Acquired: Signed as a free agent, 12/89

Player Summary	
Fantasy Value	$2 to $6
Card Value	3¢ to 4¢
Will	throw low-90s heater
Can't	avoid control trouble
Expect	50 or more calls
Don't Expect	great pickoff move

Despite rotator cuff problems in 1986 and elbow woes three years later, Gott showed again last summer that he is one of the most effective multipurpose relievers in the majors. Working more than 50 times for the third season in a row, he fashioned a microscopic earned run average by keeping runners off base. Gott fanned twice the number he walked and yielded far less than a hit per inning. He also avoided throwing home run balls. No wonder he was the busiest pitcher in the Dodger bullpen. No longer the pitcher who had 34 saves in 1988, he thrives when used in the right spots. He throws a fastball, slider, and curve. He also fields well. His lone weaknesses are occasional lapses of control and an inability to keep runners close—because of his exaggerated leg kick.

Major League Pitching Register

	W	L	ERA	G	S	IP	H	ER	BB	SO
82 AL	5	10	4.43	30	0	136.0	134	67	66	82
83 AL	9	14	4.74	34	0	176.2	195	93	68	121
84 AL	7	6	4.02	35	2	109.2	93	49	49	73
85 AL	7	10	3.88	26	0	148.1	144	64	51	78
86 NL	0	0	7.62	9	1	13.0	16	11	13	9
87 NL	1	2	3.41	55	13	87.0	81	33	40	90
88 NL	6	6	3.49	67	34	77.1	68	30	22	76
89 NL	0	0	0.00	1	0	0.2	1	0	1	1
90 NL	3	5	2.90	50	3	62.0	59	20	34	44
91 NL	4	3	2.96	55	2	76.0	63	25	32	73
92 NL	3	3	2.45	68	6	88.0	72	24	41	75
Life	45	59	3.84	430	61	974.2	926	416	417	722
3 AVE	3	4	2.75	58	4	75.0	65	23	36	64

MARK GRACE

Position: First base
Team: Chicago Cubs
Born: June 28, 1964 Winston-Salem, NC
Height: 6'2" **Weight:** 190 lbs.
Bats: left **Throws:** left
Acquired: 24th-round pick in 6/85 free-agent draft

Player Summary

Fantasy Value................................$25 to $30
Card Value...5¢ to 10¢
Will........................show discipline at plate
Can't................................hit frequent homers
Expect.............................Gold Glove defense
Don't Expect..........prolonged batting slumps

Grace is an appropriate name for this fancy-fielding first baseman. He rarely makes a miscue and is an annual contender for the Gold Glove. Grace has led the league in putouts, assists, and chances. In 1992, he had a .998 fielding average. Despite a weak arm, he has good range and scoops all low throws. He also gives a one-man hitting clinic whenever he comes to bat. Though he lacks home run power, Grace is a line-drive hitter with supreme discipline at the plate. A contact hitter who walks more than he strikes out, he often cranks out long hitting streaks. He hit in 19 straight games in 1991, for example. His .404 average last June led the NL. That's not unfamiliar territory for Grace, who took a four-year mark of .297 into 1992. He compiled a .380 on-base average and a .430 slugging percentage in 1992. A big toe contusion forced him out of the lineup last June 10—ending a streak of 230 consecutive games played.

Major League Batting Register

	BA	G	AB	R	H	2B	3B	HR	RBI	SB
88 NL	.296	134	486	65	144	23	4	7	57	3
89 NL	.314	142	510	74	160	28	3	13	79	14
90 NL	.309	157	589	72	182	32	1	9	82	15
91 NL	.273	160	619	87	169	28	5	8	58	3
92 NL	.307	158	603	72	185	37	5	9	79	6
Life	.299	751	2807	370	840	148	18	46	355	41
3 AVE	.296	158	604	77	179	32	4	9	73	8

JOE GRAHE

Position: Pitcher
Team: California Angels
Born: June 14, 1967 West Palm Beach, FL
Height: 6' **Weight:** 200 lbs.
Bats: right **Throws:** right
Acquired: Second-round pick in 6/89 free-agent draft

Player Summary

Fantasy Value................................$8 to $12
Card Value...5¢ to 10¢
Will.........................perform under pressure
Can't.........................keep baserunners close
Expect............................struggle with control
Don't Expect.......................return to rotation

Before Bryan Harvey went down with an elbow injury last June, Grahe couldn't get off the shuttle that was rushing him between the majors and minors. With the hard-throwing Harvey out of action, however, the Angels turned to Grahe as a stop-gap closer. Grahe responded with three saves in June, then eight saves in nine opportunities in July. Although he was a strikeout pitcher in college, the former University of Miami standout has thrived in the majors by retiring hitters on ground balls. Opponents in 1992 compiled a .246 batting average, a .329 on-base percentage, and a .324 slugging percentage. Although he walked as many as he struck out last year, he did his best pitching with men on base. The fact that he's a good fielder helps—even though he doesn't hold baserunners close. A starter before 1992, Grahe may have found his niche in relief. In 1991 at Triple-A Edmonton, he was 9-3 with a 4.01 ERA, 55 strikeouts, and 20 walks in 94 innings.

Major League Pitching Register

	W	L	ERA	G	S	IP	H	ER	BB	SO
90 AL	3	4	4.98	8	0	43.1	51	24	23	25
91 AL	3	7	4.81	18	0	73.0	84	39	33	40
92 AL	5	6	3.52	46	21	94.2	85	37	39	39
Life	11	17	4.27	72	21	211.0	220	100	95	104
2 AVE	4	7	4.08	32	11	84.1	85	38	36	40

CRAIG GREBECK

Position: Infield
Team: Chicago White Sox
Born: Dec. 29, 1964 Johnstown, PA
Height: 5'8" **Weight:** 160 lbs.
Bats: right **Throws:** right
Acquired: Signed as a free agent, 8/86

Player Summary	
Fantasy Value	$3 to $6
Card Value	3¢ to 4¢
Will	surprise with bat
Can't	clear distant fences
Expect	best defense at second
Don't Expect	attempts to steal

When Ozzie Guillen needed major reconstructive knee surgery after a collision last April, Grebeck inherited the Chicago shortstop job. Though he is better defensively at second base, the versatile Grebeck held his own both in the field and at bat before suffering a fractured right foot at California on August 7. His best game came on July 1, when he went 5-for-5 with three doubles, two runs scored, and two RBI against Cleveland. A contact hitter who walks as often as he fans, he is also good at moving runners along. He is a little guy who occasionally swings a big bat (.311 during the second half of 1991). In 1992, he compiled a .341 on-base average and a .387 slugging percentage. At Double-A Birmingham in 1989, he batted .287 with 80 RBI. Defensively, he has good hands, good range, and a strong throwing arm. He can play third base. His lone weakness in the middle infield is turning the double play. But Ozzie Guillen is hard to replace.

Major League Batting Register

	BA	G	AB	R	H	2B	3B	HR	RBI	SB
90 AL	.168	59	119	7	20	3	1	1	9	0
91 AL	.281	107	224	37	63	16	3	6	31	1
92 AL	.268	88	287	24	77	21	2	3	35	0
Life	.254	254	630	68	160	40	6	10	75	1
2 AVE	.274	98	256	31	70	19	3	5	33	1

TOMMY GREENE

Position: Pitcher
Team: Philadelphia Phillies
Born: April 6, 1967 Lumberton, NC
Height: 6'5" **Weight:** 225 lbs.
Bats: right **Throws:** right
Acquired: Traded from Braves with Dale Murphy for Jeff Parrett, Jim Vatcher, and Victor Rosario, 8/90

Player Summary	
Fantasy Value	$4 to $8
Card Value	3¢ to 4¢
Will	help himself with bat
Can't	worry about shoulder
Expect	high strikeout total
Don't Expect	weak whiff-to-walk ratio

Greene was sidelined after six starts last season with tendinitis in his pitching shoulder, The loss of his services hit the Philadelphia Phillies hard. He had been a front-line starter for the first time in '91, when his 13-7 record included a no-hitter and a team-best 3.38 earned run average. A healthy Greene throws a rising fastball, big-breaking curve, and occasional changeup. In 1992, opponents compiled a .291 batting average, a .371 on-base percentage, and a .419 slugging percentage. A strikeout pitcher who fans more than twice the number he walks, he sometimes is prone to home runs. He is also one of the best-hitting pitchers in the game (he hit .268 with a couple of homers in 1991); he even pinch hit in 1991. Dumped prematurely by the Braves in the Dale Murphy deal, Greene is a fine fielder whose lone weakness is a poor pickoff move. He'd like to perfect both the pickoff and the change-of-pace in 1993.

Major League Pitching Register

	W	L	ERA	G	CG	IP	H	ER	BB	SO
89 NL	1	2	4.10	4	1	26.1	22	12	6	17
90 NL	3	3	5.08	15	0	51.1	50	29	26	21
91 NL	13	7	3.38	36	3	207.2	177	78	66	154
92 NL	3	3	5.32	13	0	64.1	75	38	34	39
Life	20	15	4.04	68	4	349.2	324	157	132	231
3 AVE	6	3	4.02	18	1	94.1	89	42	36	66

MIKE GREENWELL

Position: Outfield
Team: Boston Red Sox
Born: July 18, 1963 Louisville, KY
Height: 6′ **Weight:** 200 lbs.
Bats: left **Throws:** right
Acquired: Third-round pick in 6/82 free-agent draft

Player Summary	
Fantasy Value	$20 to $26
Card Value	5¢ to 8¢
Will	deliver in clutch
Can't	find former form
Expect	patience at bat
Don't Expect	strong defense

After taking a .311 career average into 1992, Greenwell hit .233 in 49 games before an elbow injury ended his season. Surgery on July 2 repaired a stretched ligament on the inner side of the elbow and removed scar tissue from his right knee. Also victimized by a strained right wrist last summer, he should be able to stage a strong comeback at his age. In his first two full seasons, 1987 and '88, he averaged more than 20 homers and 100 RBI. He also hit well in the clutch (23 game-winning RBI in 1988). Greenwell's power has declined since—probably because of a foot injury that forced him to stop using the rear foot as a springboard during his swing. When healthy, he's a patient contact hitter who walks more than he fans. He's no gem in left field, however, where he's handicapped by a weak arm and a decided lack of speed.

Major League Batting Register

	BA	G	AB	R	H	2B	3B	HR	RBI	SB
85 AL	.323	17	31	7	10	1	0	4	8	1
86 AL	.314	31	35	4	11	2	0	4	0	0
87 AL	.328	125	412	71	135	31	6	19	89	5
88 AL	.325	158	590	86	192	39	8	22	119	16
89 AL	.308	145	578	87	178	36	0	14	95	13
90 AL	.297	159	610	71	181	30	6	14	73	8
91 AL	.300	147	544	76	163	26	6	9	83	15
92 AL	.233	49	180	16	42	2	0	2	18	2
Life	.306	831	2980	418	912	167	26	84	489	60
3 AVE	.289	118	445	54	129	19	4	8	58	8

KEN GRIFFEY

Position: Outfield
Team: Seattle Mariners
Born: Nov. 21, 1969 Donora, PA
Height: 6′3″ **Weight:** 195 lbs.
Bats: left **Throws:** left
Acquired: First-round pick in 6/87 free-agent draft

Player Summary	
Fantasy Value	$45 to $55
Card Value	15¢ to 25¢
Will	continue rapid improvement
Can't	join 30-30 without running
Expect	Gold Glove defense
Don't Expect	proper recognition

It's hard to believe Griffey is only 23. He's already won three Gold Gloves, consecutive fan elections to the All-Star lineup, and an All-Star Game MVP Award. In each of the last three seasons, he's had at least 20 homers, 80 RBI, and a .300 average. Before he was slowed by a sprained right wrist that disabled him last June, Griffey was among AL leaders in homers and RBI. Back on track for the All-Star Game, he had an RBI single, double, and homer in three at bats—boosting his three-year All-Star mark to .625 (5-for-8). In 1992, he had a .361 on-base average and a .535 slugging percentage. Except for his basestealing, which stagnated last summer, he is improving in all areas. He shows more discipline at the plate, where he's cut his strikeouts, and he makes more putouts and fewer errors every year as he learns the hitters. He had 15 assists—a high total for a center fielder—in 1991 and eight in '92.

Major League Batting Register

	BA	G	AB	R	H	2B	3B	HR	RBI	SB
89 AL	.264	127	455	61	120	23	0	16	61	16
90 AL	.300	155	597	91	179	28	7	22	80	16
91 AL	.327	154	548	76	179	42	1	22	100	18
92 AL	.308	142	565	83	174	39	4	27	103	10
Life	.301	578	2165	311	652	132	12	87	344	60
3 AVE	.311	150	570	83	177	36	4	24	94	15

ALFREDO GRIFFIN

Position: Shortstop
Team: Toronto Blue Jays
Born: March 6, 1957 Santo Domingo, Dominican Republic
Height: 5'11" **Weight:** 166 lbs.
Bats: both **Throws:** right
Acquired: Signed as a free agent, 3/92

Player Summary	
Fantasy Value	$1 to $2
Card Value	3¢ to 4¢
Will	try to hit first pitch
Can't	play every day
Expect	declining range
Don't Expect	any kind of power

Ousted by Jose Offerman in Los Angeles, Griffin returned to his original club last summer to serve as veteran insurance for regular shortstop Manny Lee. Rusty from inactivity, Griffin flirted with the Mendoza Line all summer. When he does play, the switch-hitter is a spray hitter with little power who hits to all fields. A notorious first-ball hitter, he usually makes pretty good contact—but still strikes out twice as much as he walks. He doesn't steal much anymore and he's also slowed down in the field, but his experience allows him to compensate for declining range. A Gold Glove shortstop with Toronto in 1985, Griffin has not been noted for his defense in recent seasons.

Major League Batting Register

	BA	G	AB	R	H	2B	3B	HR	RBI	SB
76 AL	.250	12	4	0	1	0	0	0	0	0
77 AL	.146	14	41	5	6	1	0	0	3	2
78 AL	.500	5	4	1	2	1	0	0	0	0
79 AL	.287	153	624	81	179	22	10	2	31	21
80 AL	.254	155	653	63	166	26	15	2	41	18
81 AL	.209	101	388	30	81	19	6	0	21	8
82 AL	.241	162	539	57	130	20	8	1	48	10
83 AL	.250	162	528	62	132	22	9	4	47	8
84 AL	.241	140	419	53	101	8	2	4	30	11
85 AL	.270	162	614	75	166	18	7	2	64	24
86 AL	.285	162	594	74	169	23	6	4	51	33
87 AL	.263	144	494	69	130	23	5	3	60	26
88 NL	.199	95	316	39	63	8	3	1	27	7
89 NL	.247	136	506	49	125	27	2	0	29	10
90 NL	.210	141	461	38	97	11	3	1	35	6
91 NL	.243	109	350	27	85	6	2	0	27	5
92 AL	.233	63	150	21	35	7	0	0	10	3
Life	.250	1916	6685	744	1668	242	78	24	524	192
3 AVE	.226	104	320	29	72	8	2	0	24	5

MARQUIS GRISSOM

Position: Outfield
Team: Montreal Expos
Born: April 17, 1967 Atlanta, GA
Height: 5'11" **Weight:** 190 lbs.
Bats: right **Throws:** right
Acquired: Third-round pick in 6/88 free-agent draft

Player Summary	
Fantasy Value	$25 to $32
Card Value	5¢ to 10¢
Will	lead league in steals
Can't	avoid frequent Ks
Expect	bid for Gold Glove
Don't Expect	many homers

Grissom was once regarded as an Andre Dawson clone by the Montreal Expos. Like Dawson, Grissom is a Florida A&M product who began his career in center field. He doesn't have Dawson's power, but Grissom could develop into a 20-homer type player. He runs wild on the bases. Blessed with exceptional speed and a high confidence level, he has become baseball's best basestealer. He was successful in 42 of his first 47 tries last summer, and he was caught stealing only 13 times in 1992. He tied a club record with four steals in a game on July 21. He is a fine fielder with a good arm. Grissom is a good hitter who became better after dropping to the No. 2 slot last June 24. He notched a .322 on-base average and a .418 slugging percentage in 1992. He doesn't bunt much but legs out lots of infield hits and stretches singles into doubles. He would wreak even more havoc if he didn't strike out twice as much as he walked.

Major League Batting Register

	BA	G	AB	R	H	2B	3B	HR	RBI	SB
89 NL	.257	26	74	16	19	2	0	1	2	1
90 NL	.257	98	288	42	74	14	2	3	29	22
91 NL	.267	148	558	73	149	23	9	6	39	76
92 NL	.276	159	653	99	180	39	6	14	66	78
Life	.268	431	1573	230	422	78	17	24	136	177
3 AVE	.269	135	500	71	134	25	6	8	45	59

KEVIN GROSS

Position: Pitcher
Team: Los Angeles Dodgers
Born: June 8, 1961 Downey, CA
Height: 6'5" **Weight:** 215 lbs.
Bats: right **Throws:** right
Acquired: Signed as a free agent, 12/90

Player Summary	
Fantasy Value	$3 to $6
Card Value	3¢ to 4¢
Will	help himself as hitter
Can't	avoid wild streaks
Expect	losing record
Don't Expect	strong fielding

Gross had a better year in the batter's box than he did on the mound last summer. One of the best-hitting pitchers in baseball (he's sometimes used as a pinch-hitter), he just couldn't get it together in his second season with Los Angeles. He dropped 12 of his first 17 decisions, yielded about a hit per inning, and suffered several spells of wildness. However, he hurled a no-hitter on Aug. 17, 1992, against San Francisco. A fastball-and-slider pitcher who can't win without good location on his curve, Gross gets killed when he falls behind in the count. He fans twice the number he walks. Opponents in 1992 compiled a .241 batting average, a .311 on-base average, and a .337 slugging percentage. To compound the felony, his fielding ability isn't great and baserunners don't fear his pickoff move. Gross will hang around because of his workhorse reputation.

Major League Pitching Register

	W	L	ERA	G	CG	IP	H	ER	BB	SO
83 NL	4	6	3.56	17	1	96.0	100	38	35	66
84 NL	8	5	4.12	44	1	129.0	140	59	44	84
85 NL	15	13	3.41	38	6	205.2	194	78	81	151
86 NL	12	12	4.02	37	7	241.2	240	108	94	154
87 NL	9	16	4.35	34	3	200.2	205	97	87	110
88 NL	12	14	3.69	33	5	231.2	209	95	89	162
89 NL	11	12	4.38	31	4	201.1	188	98	88	158
90 NL	9	12	4.57	31	2	163.1	171	83	65	111
91 NL	10	11	3.58	46	0	115.2	123	46	50	95
92 NL	8	13	3.17	34	4	204.2	182	72	77	158
Life	98	114	3.89	345	33	1789.2	1752	774	710	1249
3 AVE	9	12	3.74	37	2	161.2	159	67	64	121

KELLY GRUBER

Position: Third base
Team: California Angels
Born: Feb. 26, 1962 Bellaire, TX
Height: 6' **Weight:** 185 lbs.
Bats: right **Throws:** right
Acquired: Traded from Blue Jays for Luis Sojo, 12/92

Player Summary	
Fantasy Value	$10 to $16
Card Value	3¢ to 4¢
Will	play strong defense
Can't	find '90 stroke
Expect	comeback season
Don't Expect	injury-free year

California rolls the dice with Gruber. Over the last two years, Gruber has not been the same player whose 31 homers and 118 RBI prompted a fourth-place finish in the 1990 voting for American League Most Valuable Player. Idled with a thumb injury in '91 and a knee problem last year, he missed large chunks of playing time. When a series of minor ailments made him a late scratch from the lineup on several different occasions in '92, Toronto teammates openly began to question his desire. He broke a postseason record when he endured an 0-for-23 slump, but he finally broke it with a home run in game three of the World Series. A pull hitter who fans twice as much as he walks, Gruber should have little trouble staging a comeback. He'll need to avoid major injuries, however, and play through minor ones. He is blessed with a strong arm and great range.

Major League Batting Register

	BA	G	AB	R	H	2B	3B	HR	RBI	SB
84 AL	.063	15	16	1	1	0	0	1	2	0
85 AL	.231	5	13	0	3	0	0	0	1	0
86 AL	.196	87	143	20	28	4	1	5	15	2
87 AL	.235	138	341	50	80	14	3	12	36	12
88 AL	.278	158	569	75	158	33	5	16	81	23
89 AL	.290	135	545	83	158	24	4	18	73	10
90 AL	.274	150	592	92	162	36	6	31	118	14
91 AL	.252	113	429	58	108	18	2	20	65	12
92 AL	.229	120	446	42	102	16	3	11	43	7
Life	.259	921	3094	421	800	145	24	114	434	80
3 AVE	.254	128	489	64	124	23	4	21	75	11

MARK GUBICZA

Position: Pitcher
Team: Kansas City Royals
Born: Aug. 14, 1962 Philadelphia, PA
Height: 6'5" **Weight:** 220 lbs.
Bats: right **Throws:** right
Acquired: Second-round pick in 6/81 free-agent draft

Player Summary	
Fantasy Value	$5 to $10
Card Value	3¢ to 4¢
Will	use entire array
Can't	get clean bill of health
Expect	Ks if healthy
Don't Expect	good fielding

Gubicza's medical news wasn't good last summer. After missing time in 1991 while recuperating from arthroscopic surgery on his partially torn rotator cuff, he was disabled with more shoulder trouble in '92. Inflammation in the shoulder caused him to alter his motion and forced him out of two starts by causing stiffness in his right forearm. The Royals placed him on the DL July 11. When healthy, Gubicza throws a fastball, slider, curveball, and changeup with relatively good control—plus enough velocity to rank among the league leaders in strikeouts. He fans twice the number he walks and usually yields a hit per inning. Because he does not have a good glove or good pickoff move (though he has improved both areas somewhat), Gubizca gets by purely with his pitching. He was a 20-game winner in 1988 but hasn't come close to that form since.

Major League Pitching Register

	W	L	ERA	G	CG	IP	H	ER	BB	SO
84 AL	10	14	4.05	29	4	189.0	172	85	75	111
85 AL	14	10	4.06	29	0	177.1	160	80	77	99
86 AL	12	6	3.64	35	3	180.2	155	73	84	118
87 AL	13	18	3.98	35	10	241.2	231	107	120	166
88 AL	20	8	2.70	35	8	269.2	237	81	83	183
89 AL	15	11	3.04	36	8	255.0	252	86	63	173
90 AL	4	7	4.50	16	2	94.0	101	47	38	71
91 AL	9	12	5.68	26	0	133.0	168	84	42	89
92 AL	7	6	3.72	18	2	111.1	110	46	36	81
Life	104	92	3.75	259	37	1651.2	1586	689	618	1091
3 AVE	7	8	4.71	20	1	113.0	126	59	39	80

PEDRO GUERRERO

Position: First base; outfield
Team: St. Louis Cardinals
Born: June 29, 1956 San Pedro de Macoris, Dominican Republic
Height: 6' **Weight:** 197 lbs.
Bats: right **Throws:** right
Acquired: Traded from Dodgers for John Tudor, 8/88

Player Summary	
Fantasy Value	$15 to $20
Card Value	3¢ to 4¢
Will	show some power
Can't	run or field
Expect	gradual decline
Don't Expect	regular job

The idea of playing Guerrero in the outfield wasn't a terrific brainstorm. Saddled with sore knees and a variety of other injuries that rendered him immobile, he had had a terrible time defensively at first base—leading the league in errors for three straight years from 1989 to '91. With smooth-fielding Andres Galarraga aboard, the Cardinals could only keep Guerrero's bat in the lineup by moving him to left field. Guerrero returned to first in 1992 when Galarraga faltered. Guerrero is no longer the hitter who knocked in 117 runs in 1989. He can't run at all and his throwing—never great—has been handicapped by shoulder problems. In 1992, he tried acupuncture to treat his sore shoulder.

Major League Batting Register

	BA	G	AB	R	H	2B	3B	HR	RBI	SB
78 NL	.625	5	8	3	5	0	1	0	1	0
79 NL	.242	25	62	7	15	2	0	2	9	2
80 NL	.322	75	183	27	59	9	1	7	31	2
81 NL	.300	98	347	46	104	17	2	12	48	5
82 NL	.304	150	575	87	175	27	5	32	100	22
83 NL	.298	160	584	87	174	28	6	32	103	23
84 NL	.303	144	535	85	162	29	4	16	72	9
85 NL	.320	137	487	99	156	22	2	33	87	12
86 NL	.246	31	61	7	15	3	0	5	10	0
87 NL	.338	152	545	89	184	25	2	27	89	9
88 NL	.286	103	545	40	104	14	2	10	65	4
89 NL	.311	162	570	60	177	42	1	17	117	2
90 NL	.281	136	498	42	140	31	1	13	80	1
91 NL	.272	115	427	41	116	12	1	8	70	4
92 NL	.219	43	146	10	32	6	1	1	16	2
Life	.300	1536	5392	730	1618	267	29	215	898	97
2 AVE	.277	126	463	42	128	22	1	11	75	3

LEE GUETTERMAN

Position: Pitcher
Team: New York Mets
Born: Nov. 22, 1958 Chattanooga, TN
Height: 6'8" **Weight:** 225 lbs.
Bats: left **Throws:** left
Acquired: Traded from Yankees for Tim Burke, 6/92

Player Summary	
Fantasy Value	$2 to $4
Card Value	3¢ to 4¢
Will	throw sinker for strikes
Can't	retire some righties
Expect	more than 60 summons
Don't Expect	closer job

Guetterman's size gives him a psychological advantage over his opponents. A towering lefthander who appears intimidating when standing on the mound, hitters expect nothing but heat. Instead, he unleashes an arsenal of five pitches—none overpowering—that he throws at a variety of speeds. Because he's not a power pitcher, the lanky lefty gets most of his outs on ground balls when his sinker is working. He also throws a fastball, slider, curve, and changeup. He helps his own cause with a good glove and fine pickoff move. In 1992, NL opponents compiled a .324 batting average, a .371 on-base percentage, and a .472 slugging percentage. He struggled with two teams last year, when he yielded more than a hit per inning and struggled with his control. He opened the 1989 season with 30⅔ scoreless innings, a record for a relief pitcher.

Major League Pitching Register

	W	L	ERA	G	S	IP	H	ER	BB	SO
84 AL	0	0	4.15	3	0	4.1	9	2	2	2
86 AL	0	4	7.34	41	0	76.0	108	62	30	38
87 AL	11	4	3.81	25	0	113.1	117	48	35	42
88 AL	1	2	4.65	20	0	40.2	49	21	14	15
89 AL	5	5	2.45	70	13	103.0	98	28	26	51
90 AL	11	7	3.39	64	2	93.0	80	35	26	48
91 AL	3	4	3.68	64	6	88.0	91	36	25	35
92 AL	1	1	9.53	15	0	22.2	35	24	13	5
92 NL	3	4	5.82	43	2	43.1	57	28	14	15
Life	35	31	4.37	345	23	584.1	644	284	185	251
3 AVE	6	5	4.48	62	3	82.1	88	41	26	34

OZZIE GUILLEN

Position: Shortstop
Team: Chicago White Sox
Born: Jan. 20, 1964 Ocumare del Tuy, Venezuela
Height: 5'11" **Weight:** 150 lbs.
Bats: left **Throws:** right
Acquired: Traded from Padres with Tim Lollar, Bill Long, and Luis Salazar for LaMarr Hoyt, Todd Simmons, and Kevin Kristan, 12/84

Player Summary	
Fantasy Value	$8 to $12
Card Value	3¢ to 4¢
Will	turn heads with defense
Can't	generate power
Expect	All-Star consideration
Don't Expect	walks or Ks

Guillen's career took a major detour when the acrobatic shortstop collided with left fielder Tim Raines 12 games into last season. Guillen underwent major reconstructive knee surgery, which may keep him out more than a year. The 1990 Gold Glove winner had been an All-Star in three of his first seven seasons—maintaining the White Sox tradition of star Venezuelan shortstops (along with Chico Carrasquel and Luis Aparicio). Guillen won American League Rookie of the Year honors in 1985. In 1988, he made 570 assists—erasing Aparicio's 1969 club record of 563. He has a knack for turning base hits into double plays with his glove. Guillen is a slap hitter with good speed but no power. He rarely walks or strikes out. He likes fastballs—especially on the first pitch. Despite his impatience, Guillen does produce.

Major League Batting Register

	BA	G	AB	R	H	2B	3B	HR	RBI	SB
85 AL	.273	150	491	71	134	21	9	1	33	7
86 AL	.250	159	547	58	137	19	4	2	47	8
87 AL	.279	149	560	64	156	22	7	2	51	25
88 AL	.261	156	566	58	148	16	7	0	39	25
89 AL	.253	155	597	63	151	20	8	1	54	36
90 AL	.279	160	516	61	144	21	4	1	58	13
91 AL	.273	154	524	52	143	20	3	3	49	21
92 AL	.200	12	40	5	8	4	0	0	7	1
Life	.266	1095	3841	432	1021	143	42	10	338	136
2 AVE	.276	157	520	57	144	21	4	2	54	17

BILL GULLICKSON

Position: Pitcher
Team: Detroit Tigers
Born: Feb. 20, 1959 Marshall, MN
Height: 6'3" **Weight:** 200 lbs.
Bats: right **Throws:** right
Acquired: Signed as a free agent, 12/90

Player Summary	
Fantasy Value	$10 to $14
Card Value	3¢ to 4¢
Will	make fielders work
Can't	depend upon heater
Expect	frequent gophers
Don't Expect	control trouble

Gullickson allows opposing hitters to put balls into play, where his fielders can record outs. A sinker-and-slider pitcher who also throws a curve, he is a workhorse capable of throwing 200 innings every year. When he gives up less than a hit per inning, he keeps his team in the game. Because he's always around the plate, he yields about three dozen homers per year. Given good support on offense and defense, however, he gets plenty of wins (his career-peak 20 tied for the major league lead in 1991). He is not a strikeout pitcher. Opponents in 1992 compiled a .267 batting average, a .305 on-base average, and a .447 slugging percentage. Although he's not a strong fielder, Gullickson keeps baserunners honest with two different pickoff moves.

Major League Pitching Register

	W	L	ERA	G	CG	IP	H	ER	BB	SO
79 NL	0	0	0.00	1	0	1.0	2	0	0	0
80 NL	10	5	3.00	24	5	141.0	127	47	50	120
81 NL	7	9	2.80	22	3	157.1	142	49	34	115
82 NL	12	14	3.57	34	6	236.2	231	94	61	155
83 NL	17	12	3.75	34	10	242.1	230	101	59	120
84 NL	12	9	3.61	32	3	226.2	230	91	37	100
85 NL	14	12	3.52	29	4	181.1	187	71	47	68
86 NL	15	12	3.38	37	6	244.2	245	92	60	121
87 NL	10	11	4.85	27	3	165.0	172	89	39	89
87 AL	4	2	4.88	8	1	48.0	46	26	11	28
90 NL	10	14	3.82	32	2	193.1	221	82	61	73
91 AL	20	9	3.90	35	4	226.1	256	98	44	91
92 AL	14	13	4.34	34	4	221.2	228	107	50	64
Life	145	122	3.73	349	51	2285.1	2317	947	553	1144
3 AVE	15	12	4.03	34	3	213.1	235	96	52	76

MARK GUTHRIE

Position: Pitcher
Team: Minnesota Twins
Born: Sept. 22, 1965 Buffalo, NY
Height: 6'4" **Weight:** 202 lbs.
Bats: both **Throws:** left
Acquired: Seventh-round pick in 6/87 free-agent draft

Player Summary	
Fantasy Value	$2 to $5
Card Value	3¢ to 4¢
Will	be lefty set-up man
Can't	avoid gophers
Expect	superior pickoff move
Don't Expect	control problems

Although he also has the ability to start, Guthrie spent last summer as Rick Aguilera's lefthanded set-up man in the Minnesota bullpen. Guthrie was even used to close out several games against teams loaded with lefthanded hitters. A fastball-and-forkball pitcher who relies on pinpoint control, he fans three times more men than he walks and yields less than a hit per inning. Opponents compiled a .215 batting average, a .274 on-base percentage, and a .321 slugging percentage in 1992; lefties batted .205 against him, while he held righties to a .220 batting average. He held the first batters he faced in each game to a composite .173 batting average last summer. Assigned to relief after making a strong showing in 1991 postseason play, Guthrie was one of the most effective pitchers on the Twins' staff. He helps himself with good defensive play and an outstanding pickoff move. A Louisiana State University product, Guthrie began his career in 1987 and reached the Twins two years later.

Major League Pitching Register

	W	L	ERA	G	S	IP	H	ER	BB	SO
89 AL	2	4	4.55	13	0	57.1	66	29	21	38
90 AL	7	9	3.79	24	0	144.2	154	61	39	101
91 AL	7	5	4.32	41	2	98.0	116	47	41	72
92 AL	2	3	2.88	54	5	75.0	59	24	23	76
Life	18	21	3.86	132	7	375.0	395	161	124	287
3 AVE	5	6	3.74	40	2	106.1	110	44	34	83

JOSE GUZMAN

Position: Pitcher
Team: Chicago Cubs
Born: April 9, 1963 Santa Isabel, Puerto Rico
Height: 6'3" **Weight:** 198 lbs.
Bats: right **Throws:** right
Acquired: Signed as a free agent, 12/92

Player Summary

Fantasy Value	$12 to $18
Card Value	3¢ to 4¢
Will	win in double figures
Can't	keep ERA below 3.50
Expect	lots of ground-ball outs
Don't Expect	more shoulder woes

Guzman continued to show last summer that his devastating shoulder problems should be consigned to memory. He won in double figures for the second straight season for the Rangers and averaged two and one-half strikeouts for every walk. He missed both 1989 and 1990 with a torn rotator cuff, but he showed no signs of the layoff that caused a 34-month gap between victories. A sinker-and-slider pitcher who keeps hitters honest with a change-of-pace, he gets outs by both ground out and strikeout. In 1992, opponents compiled a .268 batting average, a .327 on-base percentage, and a .399 slugging percentage. He does a good job of keeping the ball in the park, giving up 17 gophers in 1992. He's a good fielder who keeps close watch on enemy baserunners. Guzman is especially tough with runners in scoring position. He was AL Comeback Player of the Year in 1991 after posting career peaks with a 13-7 record and 3.08 ERA.

Major League Pitching Register

	W	L	ERA	G	CG	IP	H	ER	BB	SO
85 AL	3	2	2.76	5	0	32.2	27	10	14	24
86 AL	9	15	4.54	29	2	172.1	199	87	60	87
87 AL	14	14	4.67	37	6	208.1	196	108	82	143
88 AL	11	13	3.70	30	6	206.2	180	85	82	157
91 AL	13	7	3.08	25	5	169.2	152	58	84	125
92 AL	16	11	3.66	33	5	224.0	229	91	73	179
Life	66	62	3.90	159	24	1013.2	983	439	395	715
2 AVE	15	9	3.41	29	5	197.1	191	75	79	152

JUAN GUZMAN

Position: Pitcher
Team: Toronto Blue Jays
Born: Oct. 28, 1966
Height: 5'11" **Weight:** 190 lbs.
Bats: right **Throws:** right
Acquired: Traded from Dodgers for Mike Sharperson, 9/87

Player Summary

Fantasy Value	$18 to $26
Card Value	10¢ to 15¢
Will	notch a K per frame
Can't	always maintain control
Expect	numerous low-hit games
Don't Expect	less than 15 wins

Guzman was invincible in the 1992 ALCS, striking out 11 and notching two wins. He also struck out seven batters in game three of the World Series. Before his right shoulder began hurting last July, he was leading the AL in ERA, strikeouts, and winning percentage. By the end of the year, he averaged almost two and one-half strikeouts per walk, yielded 44 fewer hits than innings pitched, and threw only six home run balls. In short, the powerful but pencil-thin righthander was just about unhittable. He throws a slider that acts like a forkball, a heavy fastball with a lot of movement, and a changeup that belies his age and inexperience. A fitness fanatic whose 95 mph fastball can sink or sail, Guzman gets pop-ups on his high fastball and strikeouts on his slider. His motion leaves him in an awkward fielding position, however, and he's also subject to mental lapses (like forgetting to cover first). For someone with such pitching ability, however, such sins can be forgiven.

Major League Pitching Register

	W	L	ERA	G	CG	IP	H	ER	BB	SO
91 AL	10	3	2.99	23	1	138.2	98	46	66	123
92 AL	16	5	2.64	28	1	180.2	135	53	72	165
Life	26	8	2.79	51	2	319.1	233	99	138	288
2 AVE	13	4	2.79	26	1	159.2	117	50	69	144

CHRIS GWYNN

Position: Outfield
Team: Kansas City Royals
Born: Oct. 13, 1964 Los Angeles, CA
Height: 6' **Weight:** 210 lbs.
Bats: left **Throws:** left
Acquired: Traded from Dodgers with Domingo Mota for Todd Benzinger, 12/91

Player Summary	
Fantasy Value	$2 to $4
Card Value	3¢ to 4¢
Will	deliver pinch-hits
Can't	steal bases often
Expect	more power than Tony
Don't Expect	bid for bat crown

Gwynn lost his first crack at regular duty when he spent much of the 1992 season on the disabled list of the Kansas City Royals. He first went on the list May 29 with a torn right calf muscle, then later dislocated his right shoulder diving back to first base during a pickoff attempt. The brother of four-time NL batting king Tony, Chris carried a .256 career mark into last season but had not batted more than 141 times in any of his five big league campaigns. In 1992, he notched a .303 on-base average and a .405 slugging percentage. His good work as a pinch-hitter for the '91 Dodgers showed definite ability, as he went 13-for-56 with two homers and 13 RBI. Gwynn has more power but less speed and a weaker throwing arm than his famous sibling. An All-American at San Diego State and a 1984 Olympic Team member, Chris was the Dodgers' first-round choice in the 1985 free-agent draft.

Major League Batting Register

	BA	G	AB	R	H	2B	3B	HR	RBI	SB
87 NL	.219	17	32	2	7	1	0	0	2	0
88 NL	.182	12	11	1	2	0	0	0	0	0
89 NL	.235	32	68	8	16	4	1	0	7	1
90 NL	.284	101	141	19	40	2	1	5	22	0
91 NL	.252	94	139	18	35	5	1	5	22	1
92 AL	.286	34	84	10	24	3	2	1	7	0
Life	.261	290	475	58	124	15	5	11	60	2

TONY GWYNN

Position: Outfield
Team: San Diego Padres
Born: May 9, 1960 Los Angeles, CA
Height: 5'11" **Weight:** 205 lbs.
Bats: left **Throws:** left
Acquired: Third-round pick in 6/81 free-agent draft

Player Summary	
Fantasy Value	$35 to $40
Card Value	10¢ to 15¢
Will	produce lofty average
Can't	hit home runs
Expect	Gold Glove bid
Don't Expect	many swipes

Even after surviving a rare two-month batting slump—the result of chronic back problems—Gwynn notched a .317 batting average last year. The epitome of a contact hitter, he is the toughest strikeout in the National League. He fanned only 16 times in '92 and went strikeout-free from April 30 to June 10—a period in which Rob Deer whiffed 42 times. According to managers polled by *Baseball America*, Gwynn is the best hitter and the best hit-and-run man in the NL. A four-time batting king who took a .328 mark into 1992, he is a perfect No. 2 hitter, capable of bunting for a hit, executing a sacrifice, or slapping a hit to the opposite field. The six-time Gold Glove Award winner had two assists in the '92 All-Star Game (his eighth straight midsummer classic).

Major League Batting Register

	BA	G	AB	R	H	2B	3B	HR	RBI	SB
82 NL	.289	54	190	33	55	12	2	1	17	8
83 NL	.309	86	304	34	94	12	2	1	37	7
84 NL	.351	158	606	88	213	21	10	5	71	33
85 NL	.317	154	622	90	197	29	5	6	46	14
86 NL	.329	160	642	107	211	33	7	14	59	37
87 NL	.370	157	589	119	218	36	13	7	54	56
88 NL	.313	133	521	64	163	22	5	7	70	26
89 NL	.336	158	604	82	203	27	7	4	62	40
90 NL	.309	141	573	79	177	29	10	4	72	8
91 NL	.317	134	530	69	168	27	11	4	62	8
92 NL	.317	128	520	77	165	27	3	6	41	3
Life	.327	1463	5701	842	1864	275	75	59	591	249
3 AVE	.314	134	541	75	170	28	8	5	58	9

JOHN HABYAN

Position: Pitcher
Team: New York Yankees
Born: Jan. 29, 1964 Bayshore, NY
Height: 6'2" **Weight:** 195 lbs.
Bats: right **Throws:** right
Acquired: Traded from Orioles for Stan Jefferson, 7/89

Player Summary	
Fantasy Value	$1 to $3
Card Value	3¢ to 4¢
Will	keep the ball in the park
Can't	return to starting
Expect	outstanding control
Don't Expect	less than 60 calls

Habyan was less effective last summer than he had been in 1991. His slider seemed to lose some velocity, he yielded more than a hit per inning, and his control wasn't as sharp (his 1991 strikeout-to-walk ratio was 3.5-to-1). A sinker-and-slider pitcher who works to spots, he doubled as set-up man and closer for the Yankees in 1992. Appointed to fill in for the ailing Steve Farr in July, Habyan converted his first three save opportunities. When he's right, he is very stingy with gopher balls. In fact, he didn't yield one to a lefthanded hitter for nearly four years until Robin Ventura hit one in the ninth to pin him with a 2-1 loss last June 26. Habyan allowed opponents to compile a .295 batting average, a .344 on-base average, and a .418 slugging percentage in 1992. He helps his own cause with fine fielding and a good pickoff move. He usually handles a heavy workload.

Major League Pitching Register

	W	L	ERA	G	S	IP	H	ER	BB	SO
85 AL	1	0	0.00	2	0	2.2	3	0	0	2
86 AL	1	3	4.44	6	0	26.1	24	13	18	14
87 AL	6	7	4.80	27	1	116.1	110	62	40	64
88 AL	1	0	4.30	7	0	14.2	22	7	4	4
90 AL	0	0	2.08	6	0	8.2	10	2	2	4
91 AL	4	2	2.30	66	2	90.0	73	23	20	70
92 AL	5	6	3.84	56	7	72.2	84	31	21	44
Life	18	18	3.75	170	10	331.1	326	138	105	202
2 AVE	5	4	2.99	61	5	81.1	79	27	21	57

DARRYL HAMILTON

Position: Outfield
Team: Milwaukee Brewers
Born: Dec. 3, 1964 Baton Rouge, LA
Height: 6'1" **Weight:** 180 lbs.
Bats: left **Throws:** right
Acquired: 11th-round pick in 6/86 free-agent draft

Player Summary	
Fantasy Value	$10 to $18
Card Value	3¢ to 4¢
Will	use speed
Can't	rely on power
Expect	great defense
Don't Expect	many strikeouts

Hamilton proved that he is a legitimate top-of-the-order bat in the major leagues in 1992. He is a contact hitter who walks as often as he fans, steals more than two-dozen bases, but rarely hits the ball out of the park. He bunts for hits, moves runners over, and works the hit-and-run well. In 1992, he had a .356 on-base average and a .400 slugging percentage. A good clutch hitter who can hit some southpaws (he batted .247 against lefties in 1992, against a .310 mark versus righties), the right fielder spent most of last year in a lefty-righty platoon with Dante Bichette. With Bichette traded to Colorado, Hamilton should get more playing time. Hamilton has also played in center and left. A solid defensive player who made only one error in 1991, he uses his speed to reach balls other outfielders can't. He also has a surprisingly good arm; he had eight assists from right field in 1992. A competent baserunner, he was caught stealing 14 times in 55 attempts.

Major League Batting Register

	BA	G	AB	R	H	2B	3B	HR	RBI	SB
88 AL	.184	44	103	14	19	4	0	1	11	7
90 AL	.295	89	156	27	46	5	0	1	18	10
91 AL	.311	122	405	64	126	15	6	1	57	16
92 AL	.298	128	470	67	140	19	7	5	62	41
Life	.292	383	1134	172	331	43	13	8	148	74
3 AVE	.303	113	344	53	104	13	4	2	46	22

CHRIS HAMMOND

Position: Pitcher
Team: Cincinnati Reds
Born: Jan. 21, 1966 Atlanta, GA
Height: 6' **Weight:** 190 lbs.
Bats: left **Throws:** left
Acquired: Sixth-round pick in 1/86 free-agent draft

Player Summary	
Fantasy Value	$2 to $4
Card Value	3¢ to 4¢
Will	swing lively bat
Can't	avoid control trouble
Expect	reliance on changeup
Don't Expect	good K-to-walk ratio

If he could pitch as well as he can hit, Hammond would contend for the Cy Young Award. In 1991, his first full big league season, he hit .353 with a dozen hits. Last year, a 405-foot homer against John Burkett in June gave Hammond a career average of .288 (17-for-59). He is also a good bunter and fielder. He has one of the best changeups in baseball but only an average fastball, slider, and curve. He also lacks the consistent control he needs to be successful. Thus far in his short major league career, Hammond has allowed too many hits, too many homers (13 in '92), and too many walks. His occasional shoulder problems probably have contributed. In 1992, opponents compiled a .266 batting average, a .333 on-base percentage, and a .399 slugging percentage. On occasion, though, he flashes the form that won the Triple-A American Association Pitcher of the Year honors in 1990. He led that circuit in wins with 15 (against only one loss), strikeouts with 149, and ERA with a 2.17 mark.

Major League Pitching Register

	W	L	ERA	G	CG	IP	H	ER	BB	SO
90 NL	0	2	6.35	3	0	11.1	13	8	12	4
91 NL	7	7	4.06	20	0	99.2	92	45	48	50
92 NL	7	10	4.21	28	0	147.1	149	69	55	79
Life	14	19	4.25	51	0	258.1	254	122	115	133
2 AVE	7	9	4.15	24	0	123.2	121	57	52	65

DAVE HANSEN

Position: Third base
Team: Los Angeles Dodgers
Born: Nov. 24, 1968 Long Beach CA
Height: 6' **Weight:** 180 lbs.
Bats: left **Throws:** right
Acquired: Second-round pick in 6/86 free-agent draft

Player Summary	
Fantasy Value	$2 to $4
Card Value	3¢ to 4¢
Will	play hurt
Can't	hit with power
Expect	strong defense
Don't Expect	high average

Although Hansen never displayed much power in his six-year career in the minors, he always showed an ability to hit. That's why he was such a disappointment in his first shot at the every-day third base position in the major leagues. The best defensive player in the Dodger infield last year, Hansen had trouble staying above the Mendoza Line. Even though he kept his strikeouts to a minimum, he proved that a contact hitter doesn't always make good contact. He registered a .286 on-base percentage and a .299 slugging percentage in 1992. He also had 34 walks last summer. Hansen didn't display the same patience he had in the minors, where he led the 1990 Triple-A Pacific Coast League with 90 bases on balls. He has also led several minor leagues in third base putouts, assists, double-plays, and fielding percentage—and showed why last summer. Hansen is a sure-handed third baseman with a strong throwing arm. So far, however, he looks like the second coming of Jeff Hamilton.

Major League Batting Register

	BA	G	AB	R	H	2B	3B	HR	RBI	SB
90 NL	.143	5	7	0	1	0	0	0	1	0
91 NL	.268	53	56	3	15	4	0	1	5	1
92 NL	.214	132	341	30	73	11	0	6	22	0
Life	.220	190	404	33	89	15	0	7	28	1

ERIK HANSON

Position: Pitcher
Team: Seattle Mariners
Born: May 18, 1965 Kinnelon, NJ
Height: 6'6" **Weight:** 210 lbs.
Bats: right **Throws:** right
Acquired: Second-round pick in 6/86 free-agent draft

Player Summary	
Fantasy Value	$8 to $10
Card Value	3¢ to 4¢
Will	throw fine curveball
Can't	capture old control
Expect	record to reverse
Don't Expect	injuries to intervene

Hanson did not display his usual control, a fault that is magnified on a bad ballclub. He yielded more than a hit per inning and almost three walks a game. In earlier years, when his control was better, he had a 3-1 ratio of strikeouts to walks, but it was closer to 2-to-1 in 1992. Opponents compiled a .287 batting average, a .341 on-base percentage, and a .402 slugging percentage in '92. One of his biggest problems last summer was keeping the ball from leaving the park, allowing 14 homers. When healthy, Hanson has one of baseball's best curveballs, along with a fastball and a changeup. He finished the 1990 campaign with a seven-game winning streak to get 18 victories, the most ever recorded by a Seattle righthander. Elbow problems erupted early in 1991, however, and Hanson hasn't been the same pitcher since. The former Wake Forest All-American has also lost time due to tendinitis of the pitching shoulder. Hanson also fields well and keeps runners close.

Major League Pitching Register

	W	L	ERA	G	CG	IP	H	ER	BB	SO
88 AL	2	3	3.24	6	0	41.2	35	15	12	36
89 AL	9	5	3.18	17	1	113.1	103	40	32	75
90 AL	18	9	3.24	33	5	236.0	205	85	68	211
91 AL	8	8	3.81	27	2	174.2	182	74	56	143
92 AL	8	17	4.82	31	6	186.2	209	100	57	112
Life	45	42	3.76	114	14	752.1	734	314	225	577
3 AVE	11	11	3.90	30	4	199.1	199	86	60	155

MIKE HARKEY

Position: Pitcher
Team: Chicago Cubs
Born: Oct. 25, 1966 San Diego, CA
Height: 6'5" **Weight:** 220 lbs.
Bats: right **Throws:** right
Acquired: First-round pick in 6/87 free-agent draft

Player Summary	
Fantasy Value	$5 to $7
Card Value	3¢ to 4¢
Will	win big if healthy
Can't	avoid injuries
Expect	95 mph heater
Don't Expect	Bob Gibson numbers

The surgeons who repaired Harkey's ailing shoulder in May 1991 did a good job. He returned July 20, 1992, yielding three hits in five scoreless innings. Harkey broke into the win column—for the first time in nearly two years—five days later when he beat the Astros 8-5. He looked even better than he had in 1990, when his 12-6 record and 3.26 ERA convinced *The Sporting News* to name him NL Rookie Pitcher of the Year. Armed with a 95 mph fastball, which he mixes with a curve and a changeup, Harkey averages two whiffs for every walk. In 1992, opponents compiled a .243 batting average, a .316 on-base percentage, and a .414 slugging percentage. Harkey missed much of the 1989 season with shoulder and knee problems. In 1988, he was 9-2 with a 1.37 ERA at Double-A Pittsfield, 7-2 with a 3.55 ERA at Triple-A Iowa. At 6'5" and 220 pounds, the Cal State Fullerton product reminds some scouts of Lee Smith and Bob Gibson. But Harkey still needs the numbers and the well-being to match the appearance.

Major League Pitching Register

	W	L	ERA	G	CG	IP	H	ER	BB	SO
88 NL	0	3	2.60	5	0	34.2	33	10	15	18
90 NL	12	6	3.26	27	2	173.2	153	63	59	94
91 NL	0	2	5.30	4	0	18.2	21	11	6	15
92 NL	4	0	1.89	7	0	38.0	34	8	15	21
Life	16	11	3.12	43	2	265.0	241	92	95	148

PETE HARNISCH

Position: Pitcher
Team: Houston Astros
Born: Sept. 23, 1966 Commack, NY
Height: 6′ **Weight:** 207 lbs.
Bats: right **Throws:** right
Acquired: Traded from Orioles with Steve Finley and Curt Schilling for Glenn Davis, 1/91

Player Summary

Fantasy Value	$8 to $12
Card Value	3¢ to 4¢
Will	win big with support
Can't	avoid home run balls
Expect	gritty performances
Don't Expect	long control lapses

Harnisch doesn't count sheep at night—he counts gophers. All too often last summer, the erstwhile ace of the Astros lost games because of gopher balls. He served up 18 in 1992—four more than he yielded over the entire 1991 campaign and more than any other Astro pitcher. That was an alarming total for someone spending half the schedule in the Astrodome. In '91, his first NL season, Harnisch didn't have such problems. He yielded 47 fewer hits than innings, fashioned a 2.70 ERA, and finished with a 12-9 record on a last-place team. The first-time All-Star worked six 1-0 games—two wins, two losses, and two no-decisions. A fastball-and-slider pitcher with a good changeup, he holds hitters to under a hit per inning and fans more than two per walk. In 1992, opponents compiled a .234 batting average, a .294 on-base percentage, and a .371 slugging percentage. Harnisch also fields fairly well, and he even gets a few hits.

Major League Pitching Register

	W	L	ERA	G	CG	IP	H	ER	BB	SO
88 AL	0	2	5.54	2	0	13.0	13	8	9	10
89 AL	5	9	4.62	18	2	103.1	97	53	64	70
90 AL	11	11	4.34	31	3	188.2	189	91	86	122
91 NL	12	9	2.70	33	4	216.2	169	65	83	172
92 NL	9	10	3.70	34	0	206.2	182	85	64	164
Life	37	41	3.73	118	9	728.1	650	302	306	538
3 AVE	11	10	3.54	33	2	203.2	180	80	78	153

BRIAN HARPER

Position: Catcher
Team: Minnesota Twins
Born: Oct. 16, 1959 Los Angeles, CA
Height: 6′2″ **Weight:** 195 lbs.
Bats: right **Throws:** right
Acquired: Signed as a free agent, 12/87

Player Summary

Fantasy Value	$14 to $20
Card Value	3¢ to 4¢
Will	always make contact
Can't	wait for walks
Expect	high batting average
Don't Expect	any display of speed

Harper is one of baseball's best contact hitters. He fanned 15 times in his first 368 at bats last summer—making him the toughest strikeout in the American League. A line-drive hitter who uses all fields, he hits for average but reaches the fences only occasionally. He hits well in the clutch and handles both righties and lefties with relative ease. A good handler of pitchers, Harper blocks the plate well and has an adequate throwing arm—even though his percentage of success in nailing enemy basestealers is nothing to write home about. In addition, he's led four leagues (including the AL) in errors by a catcher and one in passed balls. Harper played in 133 games at catcher in 1992, which is sure to take a toll on his body, especially his knees.

Major League Batting Register

	BA	G	AB	R	H	2B	3B	HR	RBI	SB
79 AL	.000	1	2	0	0	0	0	0	0	0
81 AL	.273	4	11	1	3	0	0	0	1	1
82 NL	.276	20	29	4	8	1	0	2	4	0
83 NL	.221	61	131	16	29	4	1	7	20	0
84 NL	.259	46	112	4	29	4	0	2	11	0
85 NL	.250	43	52	5	13	4	0	0	8	0
86 AL	.139	19	36	2	5	1	0	0	3	0
87 AL	.235	11	17	1	4	1	0	0	3	0
88 AL	.295	60	166	15	49	11	1	3	20	0
89 AL	.325	126	385	43	125	24	0	8	57	2
90 AL	.294	134	479	61	141	42	3	6	54	3
91 AL	.311	123	441	54	137	28	1	10	69	1
92 AL	.307	140	502	58	154	25	0	9	73	0
Life	.295	788	2363	264	697	145	6	47	323	7
3 AVE	.304	132	474	58	144	32	1	8	65	1

GREG HARRIS

Position: Pitcher
Team: Boston Red Sox
Born: Nov. 2, 1955 Lynwood, CA
Height: 5'11" **Weight:** 165 lbs.
Bats: both **Throws:** right
Acquired: Signed as a free agent, 8/89

Player Summary

Fantasy Value	$5 to $8
Card Value	3¢ to 4¢
Will	stymie basestealers
Can't	avoid home run balls
Expect	frequent appearances
Don't Expect	return to rotation

Harris is a switch-hitter, so why can't he be a switch-thrower? The ambidextrous pitcher would like to know the answer. His goal is to become the first man to throw from both sides during a major league game. In the meantime, he'll continue to earn a good living as a quality set-up man. He has a rubber arm, is capable of working often, and strikes out twice the number he walks. His control was a bit off last year, when he was also hurt by too many home run balls, but he still yielded less than a hit per inning and kept his ERA respectable. Opponents compiled a .215 batting average, a .324 on-base average, and a .312 slugging percentage in '92. A curveballer who also throws a fastball and split-finger, Harris fields well and holds runners.

Major League Pitching Register

	W	L	ERA	G	S	IP	H	ER	BB	SO
81 NL	3	5	4.46	16	1	68.2	65	34	28	54
82 NL	2	6	4.83	34	1	91.1	96	49	37	67
83 NL	0	0	27.00	1	0	1.0	2	3	3	1
84 NL	2	2	2.48	34	3	54.1	38	15	25	45
85 AL	5	4	2.47	58	11	113.0	74	31	43	111
86 AL	10	8	2.83	73	20	111.1	103	35	42	95
87 AL	5	10	4.86	42	0	140.2	157	76	56	106
88 AL	4	6	2.36	66	1	107.0	80	28	52	71
89 NL	2	2	3.58	44	1	75.1	64	30	43	51
89 AL	2	2	2.57	15	0	28.0	21	8	15	25
90 AL	13	9	4.00	34	0	184.1	186	82	77	117
91 AL	11	12	3.85	53	2	173.0	157	74	69	127
92 AL	4	9	2.51	70	4	107.2	82	30	60	73
Life	63	75	3.55	540	44	1255.2	1125	495	550	943
3 AVE	9	10	3.60	52	2	155.1	142	62	69	106

GREG HARRIS

Position: Pitcher
Team: San Diego Padres
Born: Dec. 1, 1963 Greensboro, NC
Height: 6'2" **Weight:** 190 lbs.
Bats: right **Throws:** right
Acquired: 10th-round pick in 6/85 free-agent draft

Player Summary

Fantasy Value	$4 to $6
Card Value	3¢ to 4¢
Will	yield few walks
Can't	avoid injuries
Expect	excellent control
Don't Expect	perfected changeup

Injuries have hampered Harris for two straight seasons. After spending three weeks on the disabled list with a bad back, he broke his right middle finger while trying to bunt in the third inning of his first game back, on June 22. In 1991, Harris missed the first two months with a bad elbow, then returned in time to pitch the best baseball of his career during the second half. He pitched consecutive 1-0 shutouts during a 7-2 finish that featured a 1.88 ERA. A control pitcher whose curve is his best pitch, he also throws a fastball and a newly developed changeup. Harris fans four times more men than he walks. Opponents in 1992 compiled a .252 batting average, a .307 on-base percentage, and a .384 slugging percentage. He was more effective against righties in 1992, allowing a .205 batting average, against a .279 for lefthanders. A good bunter who's hardly an automatic out, Harris also helps himself in the field. Basestealers have to be careful against Harris.

Major League Pitching Register

	W	L	ERA	G	CG	IP	H	ER	BB	SO
88 NL	2	0	1.50	3	1	18.0	13	3	3	15
89 NL	8	9	2.60	56	0	135.0	106	39	52	106
90 NL	8	8	2.30	73	0	117.1	92	30	49	97
91 NL	9	5	2.23	20	3	133.0	116	33	27	95
92 NL	4	8	4.12	20	1	118.0	113	54	35	66
Life	31	30	2.74	172	5	521.1	440	159	166	379
3 AVE	7	7	2.86	38	1	123.0	107	39	37	86

LENNY HARRIS

Position: Infield
Team: Los Angeles Dodgers
Born: Oct. 28, 1964 Miami, FL
Height: 5'10" **Weight:** 195 lbs.
Bats: left **Throws:** right
Acquired: Traded from Reds with Kal Daniels for Tim Leary and Mariano Duncan, 7/89

Player Summary	
Fantasy Value	$6 to $9
Card Value	3¢ to 4¢
Will	play against righties
Can't	generate power
Expect	baserunning blunders
Don't Expect	decent defense

The versatility of Harris hurts his chances of winning a regular position anywhere. Capable of filling in anywhere but the battery, he handles second base best but can also sustain long spells at third. Although his speed gives him good range, he's not known for his fielding and has led four leagues in errors. He formed a left-right platoon with Mike Sharperson at both second and third for the Dodgers over the past several seasons but lost his job last year because of his defense. Despite limited playing time, Harris had 15 errors—second on the team to Jose Offerman—by mid-August. Harris might make someone a good platoon DH, because he is a contact hitter who rarely strikes out. He hits to all fields, and he can hit all pitchers except for lefty curveballers. He offers good speed but no power. He had a .318 on-base average and a .303 slugging percentage in 1992.

MIKE HARTLEY

Position: Pitcher
Team: Minnesota Twins
Born: Aug. 31, 1961 Hawthorne, CA
Height: 6'1" **Weight:** 197 lbs.
Bats: right **Throws:** right
Acquired: Traded from Phillies for David West, 12/92

Player Summary	
Fantasy Value	$2 to $4
Card Value	3¢ to 4¢
Will	bank on off-speed stuff
Can't	keep runners close
Expect	middle relief service
Don't Expect	bouts of bad control

Hartley moves to the Minnesota bullpen. He found his niche as an effective set-up man for the Phillies last summer. A control pitcher who does not throw hard, he relies heavily on a blend of curves and split-fingered fastballs thrown at various speeds. He fans more than twice the number he walks and allows an average of a hit per inning. He needs to throw strikes to stay effective. Opponents in 1992 compiled a .255 batting average, a .332 on-base percentage, and a .401 slugging percentage. Although he pitched half the schedule in a park conducive to the long ball, Hartley's ability to keep the ball in play made him the most effective member of the Philadelphia bullpen. He allowed only five home runs in 1992. He's a very good fielder but considerably less effective at holding runners close. He is no help at all as a hitter but doesn't bat much in his middle relief role. The durable righthander is capable of working more than 50 times in a season.

Major League Batting Register

	BA	G	AB	R	H	2B	3B	HR	RBI	SB
88 NL	.372	16	43	7	16	1	0	0	8	4
89 NL	.236	115	335	36	79	10	1	3	26	14
90 NL	.304	137	431	61	131	16	4	2	29	15
91 NL	.287	145	429	59	123	16	1	3	38	12
92 NL	.271	135	347	28	94	11	0	0	30	19
Life	.279	548	1585	191	443	54	6	8	131	64
3 AVE	.288	139	402	49	116	14	2	2	32	15

Major League Pitching Register

	W	L	ERA	G	S	IP	H	ER	BB	SO
89 NL	0	1	1.50	5	0	6.0	2	1	0	4
90 NL	6	3	2.95	32	1	79.1	58	26	30	76
91 NL	4	1	4.21	58	2	83.1	74	39	47	63
92 NL	7	6	3.44	46	0	55.0	54	21	23	53
Life	17	11	3.50	141	3	223.2	188	87	100	196
3 AVE	6	3	3.56	45	1	72.1	62	29	33	64

BRYAN HARVEY

Position: Pitcher
Team: Florida Marlins
Born: June 2, 1963 Chattanooga, TN
Height: 6'2" **Weight:** 215 lbs.
Bats: right **Throws:** right
Acquired: First-round pick from Angels in 11/92 expansion draft

Player Summary

Fantasy Value	$20 to $26
Card Value	3¢ to 4¢
Will	blaze ball past hitters
Can't	hold runners on
Expect	exceptional control
Don't Expect	righties to hit him

Angels' management was shocked when the Marlins plucked Harvey in the expansion draft. Throwing too many split-fingered fastballs may have caught up with Harvey in 1992. He was placed on the disabled list in June with elbow problems. When healthy, he is one of the game's premier relief specialists. Harvey throws high heat at 95 miles an hour. He also can throw a breaking ball and the split-fingered fastball for strikes, confounding hitters. Opponents compiled a .208 batting average, a .275 on-base percentage, and a .340 slugging percentage in 1992. In 1991, he had an average of 11.6 strikeouts per nine innings and 46 saves in 52 chances; opposing batters managed a measly .178 mark against him. A 1991 All-Star and Angel co-MVP, Harvey's ability to harness his once-erratic control was a major factor in his strong 1991 season. His ratio of strikeouts to walks was nearly 6-to-1. He's terrible at holding runners but seldom sees any when he starts an inning.

Major League Pitching Register

	W	L	ERA	G	S	IP	H	ER	BB	SO
87 AL	0	0	0.00	3	0	5.0	6	0	2	3
88 AL	7	5	2.13	50	17	76.0	59	18	20	67
89 AL	3	3	3.44	51	25	55.0	36	21	41	78
90 AL	4	4	3.22	54	25	64.1	45	23	35	82
91 AL	2	4	1.60	67	46	78.2	51	14	17	101
92 AL	0	4	2.83	25	13	28.2	22	9	11	34
Life	16	20	2.49	250	126	307.2	219	85	126	365
2 AVE	3	4	2.33	61	36	71.2	48	19	26	92

BILLY HATCHER

Position: Outfield
Team: Boston Red Sox
Born: Oct. 4, 1960 Williams, AZ
Height: 5'9" **Weight:** 185 lbs.
Bats: right **Throws:** right
Acquired: Traded from Reds for Tom Bolton, 7/92

Player Summary

Fantasy Value	$4 to $7
Card Value	3¢ to 4¢
Will	ignite the offense
Can't	wait for walks
Expect	strong defense
Don't Expect	power production

After spinning his wheels with the 1992 Reds, Hatcher blossomed into a spark plug after joining the Red Sox. He went 6-for-17 in his first four contests and had three doubles. He was even more of a catalyst on the bases. Given a constant green light, he became the first Sox player to steal home at Fenway Park since 1968. He had a .283 on-base average and a .311 slugging percentage in the AL in '92. A speedy spray hitter with only occasional power, Hatcher spent most of the summer as Boston's No. 2 hitter and left fielder. He has the range but not the arm to play center or right. He not only brought much-needed speed to Boston but also a positive clubhouse personality. In addition, he also brought a bat that does its best under pressure; he owns a .300 average for two playoffs and a .750 World Series mark.

Major League Batting Register

	BA	G	AB	R	H	2B	3B	HR	RBI	SB
84 NL	.111	8	9	1	1	0	0	0	0	2
85 NL	.245	53	163	24	40	12	1	2	10	2
86 NL	.258	127	419	55	108	15	4	6	36	38
87 NL	.296	141	564	96	167	28	3	11	63	53
88 NL	.268	145	530	79	142	25	4	7	52	32
89 NL	.231	135	481	59	111	19	3	4	51	24
90 NL	.276	139	504	68	139	28	5	5	25	30
91 NL	.262	138	442	45	116	25	3	4	41	11
92 NL	.287	43	94	10	27	3	0	2	10	0
92 AL	.238	75	315	37	75	16	2	1	23	4
Life	.263	1004	3521	474	926	171	25	42	311	196
3 AVE	.263	132	452	53	119	24	3	4	33	15

CHARLIE HAYES

Position: Third base
Team: Colorado Rockies
Born: May 29, 1965 Hattiesburg, MS
Height: 6' **Weight:** 205 lbs.
Bats: right **Throws:** right
Acquired: First-round pick from Yankees in 11/92 expansion draft

Player Summary	
Fantasy Value	$5 to $7
Card Value	3¢ to 4¢
Will	play solid third base
Can't	work pitchers for walks
Expect	strong clutch hitting
Don't Expect	many steal attempts

They are not happy in the Bronx. It took the Yankees years to find a third baseman like Hayes, and then they lost him in the expansion draft. Although he couldn't fill the shoes of Mike Schmidt in Philadelphia, Hayes had looked like the second coming of Clete Boyer to the Yankees. After the eight Yankee third basemen of '91 combined for more errors (38) than RBI (37), Hayes was like a breath of fresh air. He has better range than most of his AL hot-corner colleagues, good lateral movement to both sides, and a fine throwing arm. He was playing the best third base in the Bronx since Graig Nettles. Hayes erred only 10 times in his first 112 games, and he finished with 31 double plays. Although he hits with power, he would be more productive if he showed patience at the plate. He had 20 two-out RBI—tops on the team—by July 28. He had a .297 on-base average and a .409 slugging percentage in 1992.

Major League Batting Register

	BA	G	AB	R	H	2B	3B	HR	RBI	SB
88 NL	.091	7	11	0	1	0	0	0	0	0
89 NL	.257	87	304	26	78	15	1	8	43	3
90 NL	.258	152	561	56	145	20	0	10	57	4
91 NL	.230	142	460	34	106	23	1	12	53	3
92 AL	.257	142	509	52	131	19	2	18	66	3
Life	.250	530	1845	168	461	77	4	48	219	13
3 AVE	.250	145	510	47	127	21	1	13	59	3

DAVE HENDERSON

Position: Outfield
Team: Oakland Athletics
Born: July 21, 1958 Merced, CA
Height: 6'2" **Weight:** 210 lbs.
Bats: right **Throws:** right
Acquired: Signed as a free agent, 12/87

Player Summary	
Fantasy Value	$8 to $12
Card Value	3¢ to 4¢
Will	hit well in clutch
Can't	steal many bases
Expect	strong comeback
Don't Expect	poor defense

Before injuries ruined his 1992 season, Henderson was one of baseball's best all-around center fielders. A fine defensive player with decent speed and a strong arm, he swung the bat so well that he was a 1991 All-Star. He had a five-hit game and a three-homer game that season. It was a different story in 1992, however. A strained right hamstring cost him all but three games in the first half before he injured his right calf while on rehabilitation assignment for the original injury. Henderson should have no trouble staging a comeback if he's sound. He has power to all fields. He produces in the clutch; his two-out, two-strike, ninth-inning game five homer for Boston against California was the biggest blow in the 1986 ALCS.

Major League Batting Register

	BA	G	AB	R	H	2B	3B	HR	RBI	SB
81 AL	.167	59	126	17	21	3	0	6	13	2
82 AL	.253	104	324	47	82	17	1	14	48	2
83 AL	.269	137	484	50	130	24	5	17	55	9
84 AL	.280	112	350	42	98	23	0	14	43	5
85 AL	.241	139	502	70	121	28	2	14	68	6
86 AL	.265	139	388	59	103	22	4	15	47	2
87 AL	.234	75	184	30	43	10	0	8	25	1
87 NL	.238	15	21	2	5	2	0	0	1	2
88 AL	.304	146	507	100	154	38	1	24	94	2
89 AL	.250	152	579	77	145	24	3	15	80	8
90 AL	.271	127	450	65	122	28	0	20	63	3
91 AL	.276	150	572	86	158	33	0	25	85	6
92 AL	.143	20	63	1	9	1	0	0	2	0
Life	.262	1375	4550	646	1191	253	16	172	624	48
2 AVE	.274	139	511	76	140	31	0	23	74	5

RICKEY HENDERSON

Position: Outfield
Team: Oakland Athletics
Born: Dec. 25, 1958 Chicago, IL
Height: 5'10" **Weight:** 190 lbs.
Bats: right **Throws:** left
Acquired: Traded from Yankees for Luis Polonia, Greg Cadaret, and Eric Plunk, 6/89

Player Summary	
Fantasy Value	$30 to $38
Card Value	10¢ to 15¢
Will	display super speed
Can't	heal hamstring woes
Expect	ambivalent attitude
Don't Expect	strong throws

Although Henderson led the AL in stolen bases 11 times in 12 seasons, injuries interfered with his chances for another title. Disabled twice by persistent hamstring problems, the fleet left fielder found himself flooded with competition for league honors. He holds single-season and career records for steals, and he used to run away with the title. In fact, he had stolen more than 55 bases four years in a row before 1992. His steal totals have declined for five straight seasons. The 1990 AL MVP is still the game's best leadoff man who's always a threat to start a game with a home run. A contact hitter with patience, Henderson walks far more than he fans. He has great range in the outfield but doesn't throw well.

Major League Batting Register

	BA	G	AB	R	H	2B	3B	HR	RBI	SB
79 AL	.274	89	351	49	96	13	3	1	26	33
80 AL	.303	158	591	111	179	22	4	9	53	100
81 AL	.319	108	423	89	135	18	7	6	35	56
82 AL	.267	149	536	119	143	24	4	10	51	130
83 AL	.292	145	513	105	150	25	7	9	48	108
84 AL	.293	142	502	113	147	27	4	16	58	66
85 AL	.314	143	547	146	172	28	5	24	72	80
86 AL	.263	153	608	130	160	31	5	28	74	87
87 AL	.291	95	358	78	104	17	3	17	37	41
88 AL	.305	140	554	118	169	30	2	6	50	93
89 AL	.274	150	541	113	148	26	3	12	57	77
90 AL	.325	136	489	119	159	33	3	28	61	65
91 AL	.268	134	470	105	126	17	1	18	57	58
92 AL	.283	117	396	77	112	18	3	15	46	48
Life	.291	1859	6879	1472	2000	329	54	199	725	1042
3 AVE	.293	129	452	100	132	23	2	20	55	57

TOM HENKE

Position: Pitcher
Team: Texas Rangers
Born: Dec. 21, 1957 Kansas City, MO
Height: 6'5" **Weight:** 225 lbs.
Bats: right **Throws:** right
Acquired: Signed as a free agent, 12/92

Player Summary	
Fantasy Value	$25 to $32
Card Value	3¢ to 4¢
Will	top 25 saves
Can't	defend his position
Expect	lots of strikeouts
Don't Expect	injury-free year

Henke returns from Toronto to Texas, where he began his career. His ability to snuff out opponents has earned him the nickname, "The Terminator." He is a man who eliminates rivals as effectively as Arnold Schwarzenegger does in the movies. Henke mixes a cross-seam fastball with a forkball that dips as it crosses the plate. Add his dependable slider and Henke has a mix that allows him to save more than 25 games a season. The bespectacled closer had two saves in the '92 World Series and notched his 200th career save last July 4. When he's on, he fans four times more hitters than he walks, fans more than a batter per inning, and gets his outs on strikeouts or fly balls. Although he doesn't hold runners well, few try stealing because he has a quick delivery and throws so hard. He's not a strong fielder.

Major League Pitching Register

	W	L	ERA	G	S	IP	H	ER	BB	SO
82 AL	1	0	1.15	8	0	15.2	14	2	8	9
83 AL	1	0	3.38	8	1	16.0	16	6	4	17
84 AL	1	1	6.35	25	2	28.1	36	20	20	25
85 AL	3	3	2.03	28	13	40.0	29	9	8	42
86 AL	9	5	3.35	63	27	91.1	63	34	32	118
87 AL	0	6	2.49	72	34	94.0	62	26	25	128
88 AL	4	4	2.91	52	25	68.0	60	22	24	66
89 AL	8	3	1.92	64	20	89.0	66	19	25	116
90 AL	2	4	2.17	61	32	74.2	58	18	19	75
91 AL	0	2	2.32	49	32	50.1	33	13	11	53
92 AL	3	2	2.26	57	34	55.2	40	14	22	46
Life	32	30	2.64	487	220	623.0	477	183	198	695
3 AVE	2	3	2.24	56	33	60.2	44	15	17	58

MIKE HENNEMAN

Position: Pitcher
Team: Detroit Tigers
Born: Dec. 11, 1961 St. Charles, MO
Height: 6'4" **Weight:** 205 lbs.
Bats: right **Throws:** right
Acquired: Third-round pick in 6/84 free-agent draft

Player Summary	
Fantasy Value	$16 to $20
Card Value	3¢ to 4¢
Will	work at least 60 games
Can't	escape shoulder woes
Expect	tough time on turf
Don't Expect	30-save season

Although Henneman took a five-year ERA of 2.90 into the 1992 campaign, he didn't come close to matching that level of effectiveness. Deployed as Detroit's closer for the sixth straight season, he struggled to record his fourth 20-save summer. His control was sharp, with three strikeouts to every walk, but he yielded about a hit per inning and had trouble keeping the ball in the park. After yielding only two home runs for the entire 1991 campaign, he threw six last year. Henneman complements his sinker with a forkball and a slider. As a result, he gets most of his outs on ground balls—an easy task on the long natural grass in Detroit but tough on artificial turf. Opponents in 1992 compiled a .256 batting average, a .299 on-base percentage, and a .369 slugging percentage. A first-rate fielder, he's only average at holding runners. Henneman also has to worry about recurring shoulder problems.

Major League Pitching Register

	W	L	ERA	G	S	IP	H	ER	BB	SO
87 AL	11	3	2.98	55	7	96.2	86	32	30	75
88 AL	9	6	1.87	65	22	91.1	72	19	24	58
89 AL	11	4	3.70	60	8	90.0	84	37	51	69
90 AL	8	6	3.05	69	22	94.1	90	32	33	50
91 AL	10	2	2.88	60	21	84.1	81	27	34	61
92 AL	2	6	3.96	60	24	77.1	75	34	20	58
Life	51	27	3.05	369	104	534.0	488	181	192	371
3 AVE	7	5	3.27	63	22	85.1	82	31	29	56

BUTCH HENRY

Position: Pitcher
Team: Colorado Rockies
Born: Oct. 7, 1968 El Paso, TX
Height: 6'1" **Weight:** 195 lbs.
Bats: left **Throws:** left
Acquired: Second-round pick from Astros in 11/92 expansion draft

Player Summary	
Fantasy Value	$2 to $5
Card Value	5¢ to 7¢
Will	help himself at bat
Can't	yield so many hits
Expect	more gopher balls
Don't Expect	compact ERA

Henry has a chance to become the top lefthander of the Colorado starting rotation. He spent five years in the minors before winning a big league berth with the Houston Astros last spring. After getting off to a slow start, he fired a 5-0 shutout at Chicago Aug. 15. He struck out eight and did not walk anyone in that game. He gets outs with a change-of-pace that he holds like a dead fish but throws like a fastball. He complements the pitch with a fastball that he throws at various speeds. Henry strikes out twice as many as he walks but has a tendency to yield more than a hit per inning. And although he played half of his games in the Astrodome, an exorbitant 16 of those hits went over the fence in '92. Opponents compiled a .285 batting average, a .325 on-base percentage, and a .433 slugging percentage. At Triple-A Tucson in 1991, he was 10-11 with a 4.80 ERA, 97 strikeouts, and 42 walks in 153⅔ innings. He is a good-hitting pitcher capable of helping his own cause. Elbow problems helped keep him from reaching the majors sooner.

Major League Pitching Register

	W	L	ERA	G	CG	IP	H	ER	BB	SO
92 NL	6	9	4.02	28	2	165.2	185	74	41	96
Life	6	9	4.02	28	2	165.2	185	74	41	96

DOUG HENRY

Position: Pitcher
Team: Milwaukee Brewers
Born: Dec. 10, 1963 Sacramento, CA
Height: 6'4" **Weight:** 185 lbs.
Bats: right **Throws:** right
Acquired: Eight-round pick in 6/85 free-agent draft

Player Summary

Fantasy Value	$14 to $20
Card Value	3¢ to 4¢
Will	always throw hard
Can't	shake invisible image
Expect	better '93 ERA
Don't Expect	control problems

Henry deserves better. He gets so little publicity that even avid followers of baseball seem only dimly aware of his presence. He's well-known in Milwaukee, however. A hard-throwing relief pitcher who surfaced in the summer of '91, he made an immediate impression with 15 saves and a microscopic 1.00 ERA in 32 appearances. In 1992, his ratio of hits to innings wasn't as good, but he still had more than two-dozen saves before Labor Day. In 1992, opponents compiled a .256 batting average, a .319 on-base percentage, and a .400 slugging percentage. A rubber-armed righthander with a fastball, forkball, and slider, Henry was especially good at keeping the ball in the park in 1991, yielding one; he gave up six last year. Although he is righthanded, in 1992 he held lefthanded batters to a .208 average, while righthanders were able to bat .292 against him. At Triple-A Denver in 1991, he notched 14 saves, a 2.18 ERA, 20 walks, and 47 strikeouts in 57⅔ innings pitched. In 1990, he had eight saves but a 4.44 ERA at Denver, and nine saves and a 2.93 ERA at Double-A El Paso.

Major League Pitching Register

	W	L	ERA	G	S	IP	H	ER	BB	SO
91 AL	2	1	1.00	32	15	36.0	16	4	14	28
92 AL	1	4	4.02	68	29	65.0	64	29	24	52
Life	3	5	2.94	100	44	101.0	80	33	38	80
2 AVE	2	3	2.94	50	22	51.0	40	17	19	40

DWAYNE HENRY

Position: Pitcher
Team: Cincinnati Reds
Born: Feb. 16, 1962 Elkton, MD
Height: 6'3" **Weight:** 205 lbs.
Bats: right **Throws:** right
Acquired: Signed as a free agent, 11/91

Player Summary

Fantasy Value	$1 to $2
Card Value	3¢ to 4¢
Will	stay in middle relief
Can't	find the strike zone
Expect	less hits than innings
Don't Expect	definite job

If Henry could pitch the way he eats, he'd be an All-Star. On a road trip to St. Louis last summer, he devoured a 33-ounce steak, three pieces of bread, four oysters, and three clams—a feast fit for King Henry VIII but not Dwayne Henry I, who said he was still hungry. Henry's managers feel hunger too, because he fails to feed them strikes. A fastball-slider pitcher with terrific stuff but erratic control, Henry had shuttled between the majors and minors before spending his first full year with the '91 Astros. He improved his career ERA with the Reds last summer but still struggled with his control. Almost unhittable at times, Henry should also have many more whiffs than walks. Unless he corrects that flaw, he'll never work in pressure spots. Opponents in '92 compiled a .199 batting average, a .301 on-base average, and a .313 slugging percentage.

Major League Pitching Register

	W	L	ERA	G	S	IP	H	ER	BB	SO
84 AL	0	1	8.31	3	0	4.1	5	4	7	2
85 AL	2	2	2.57	16	3	21.0	16	6	7	20
86 AL	1	0	4.66	19	0	19.1	14	10	22	17
87 AL	0	0	9.00	5	0	10.0	12	10	9	7
88 AL	0	1	8.71	11	1	10.1	15	10	9	10
89 NL	0	2	4.26	12	1	12.2	12	6	5	16
90 NL	2	2	5.63	34	0	38.1	41	24	25	34
91 NL	3	2	3.19	52	2	67.2	51	24	39	51
92 NL	3	3	3.33	60	0	83.2	59	31	44	72
Life	11	13	4.21	212	7	267.1	225	125	167	229
3 AVE	3	2	3.75	49	1	63.2	50	26	36	52

CARLOS HERNANDEZ

Position: Catcher
Team: Los Angeles Dodgers
Born: May 24, 1967 Bolivar, Venezuela
Height: 5'11" **Weight:** 185 lbs.
Bats: right **Throws:** right
Acquired: Signed as free agent, 10/84

Player Summary	
Fantasy Value	$3 to $6
Card Value	5¢ to 10¢
Will	show off strong arm
Can't	wait for walks
Expect	good batting average
Don't Expect	homers in double figures

After signing as a 17-year-old third base-man in 1984, Hernandez needed seven years to reach the major leagues as a catcher. After a .345 season at Triple-A Albuquerque, he succeeded Gary Carter as the right half of a catching platoon with veteran lefthanded hitter Mike Scioscia. Hernandez is a contact hitter with occasional power and more speed than the typical catcher. He had a .316 on-base average and a .335 slugging percentage in 1992. He had eight homers, 60 runs, five swipes, and 44 RBI at Albuquerque in '91. In 1990, he batted .315 with no homers and 16 RBI there. His fielding is his forte. He has led minor leagues in putouts, assists, total chances, and dou-ble-plays. In two seasons in the minors, he also finished first in errors—the result of showing off his strong arm. He made seven errors last summer. Hernandez nailed 41 percent of would-be basesteal-ers in '91 at Albuquerque. In 1992, he nailed 25 percent, but that figure should increase with more experience. In 1993, he should be ready to play every day.

ROBERTO HERNANDEZ

Position: Pitcher
Team: Chicago White Sox
Born: Nov. 11, 1964 Santurce, Puerto Rico
Height: 6'4" **Weight:** 220 lbs.
Bats: right **Throws:** right
Acquired: Traded from Angels with Mark Doran for Mark Davis, 8/89

Player Summary	
Fantasy Value	$5 to $10
Card Value	8¢ to 12¢
Will	decimate rivals
Can't	perfect changeup
Expect	full shot as closer
Don't Expect	more arm trouble

When Bobby Thigpen proved unreliable as the White Sox closer last summer, manager Gene Lamont replaced him with the lefty-righty tandem of Scott Radinsky and Hernandez. A former starter, Hernan-dez responded well. In one contest, he fanned six of the nine Twins he faced. He throws a sinking fastball that sometimes hits 95 mph. Hernandez also has a slider, plus a changeup that he added two win-ters ago. He fans three times more men than he walks, yields half as many hits as innings pitched, and keeps the ball in the park. Opponents compiled a .180 batting average, a .249 on-base average, and a .272 slugging percentage in 1992. Because of his quick delivery, he's hard on basestealers. Working in pressure situ-ations doesn't faze him. In 1991, he need-ed surgery to alleviate a life-threatening blockage in an artery of his right forearm. In 1991 at Triple-A Vancouver, he was 4-1 with a 3.22 ERA, 23 walks, and 40 strike-outs in 44⅔ innings. He was 2-1 that year at Double-A Birmingham, with a 1.99 ERA, six walks, and 25 strikeouts in 22⅔ innings.

Major League Batting Register

	BA	G	AB	R	H	2B	3B	HR	RBI	SB
90 NL	.200	10	20	2	4	1	0	0	1	0
91 NL	.214	15	14	1	3	1	0	0	1	1
92 NL	.260	69	173	11	45	4	0	3	17	0
Life	.251	94	207	14	52	6	0	3	19	1

Major League Pitching Register

	W	L	ERA	G	S	IP	H	ER	BB	SO
91 AL	1	0	7.80	9	0	15.0	18	13	7	6
92 AL	7	3	1.65	43	12	71.0	45	13	20	68
Life	8	3	2.72	52	12	86.0	63	26	27	74

XAVIER HERNANDEZ

Position: Pitcher
Team: Houston Astros
Born: Aug. 16, 1965 Port Arthur, TX
Height: 6'2" **Weight:** 185 lbs.
Bats: left **Throws:** right
Acquired: Drafted from Blue Jays, 12/89

Player Summary
Fantasy Value	$4 to $10
Card Value	4¢ to 6¢
Will	keep batters off base
Can't	always throw strikes
Expect	frequent appearances
Don't Expect	exile to minors

Hernandez wasn't quite ready for his first extended major league tour in 1990. He struggled with his control, failed to maintain a respectable ERA, and yielded a hit per inning. When things failed to improve in '91, the Astros shipped him back to Triple-A Tucson. The move worked wonders. He harnessed his control, improved his repertoire, and became one of baseball's better middle men. He was 2-1 at Tucson, with a 2.75 ERA, four saves, nine walks, and 34 strikeouts in 36 innings. In 1992, he worked frequently, winning nine of 10, striking out twice the number he walked, allowing less hits than innings, keeping the ball in the park, and posting a trim ERA. Opponents compiled a .200 batting average, a .279 on-base percentage, and a .275 slugging percentage in 1992. The rubber-armed righty is a sinker-slider pitcher who also throws a curve and forkball. That arsenal should be sufficient; when one or two pitches don't work on a given day, the others usually do. He is a good glove man.

Major League Pitching Register
	W	L	ERA	G	S	IP	H	ER	BB	SO
89 AL	1	0	4.76	7	0	22.2	25	12	8	7
90 NL	2	1	4.62	34	0	62.1	60	32	24	24
91 NL	2	7	4.71	32	3	63.0	66	33	32	55
92 NL	9	1	2.11	77	7	111.0	81	26	42	96
Life	14	9	3.58	150	10	259.0	232	103	106	182
3 AVE	4	3	3.47	48	3	79.0	69	30	33	58

OREL HERSHISER

Position: Pitcher
Team: Los Angeles Dodgers
Born: Sept. 16, 1958 Buffalo, NY
Height: 6'3" **Weight:** 192 lbs.
Bats: right **Throws:** right
Acquired: 17th-round pick in 6/79 free-agent draft

Player Summary
Fantasy Value	$8 to $12
Card Value	5¢ to 10¢
Will	continue comeback effort
Can't	resume workhorse ways
Expect	good bat and glove
Don't Expect	Cy Young form

Hershiser hasn't been the same since submitting to rotator cuff surgery early in the 1990 campaign. Although the 1988 Cy Young Award winner pitched well after returning during the second half of 1991, his performance declined sharply last summer. His 4-1 victory over San Diego on Aug. 2 was his first complete game since 1989. A sinkerballer who also throws a curve and a cut fastball, he uses computers to stay on top of NL batters' tendencies. Hershiser is an intense competitor who could return to form if he ever gains full strength in his damaged shoulder. He's not likely to be the same pitcher who topped 200 innings five years in a row from 1985 to 1989, however. In 1988, he broke Don Drysdale's consecutive scoreless innings streak by hurling 59 straight scoreless frames. Hershiser still has a good pickoff move and solid bat.

Major League Pitching Register
	W	L	ERA	G	CG	IP	H	ER	BB	SO
83 NL	0	0	3.38	8	0	8.0	7	3	6	5
84 NL	11	8	2.66	45	8	189.2	160	56	50	150
85 NL	19	3	2.03	36	9	239.2	179	54	68	157
86 NL	14	14	3.85	35	8	231.1	213	99	86	153
87 NL	16	16	3.06	37	10	264.2	247	90	74	190
88 NL	23	8	2.26	35	15	267.0	208	67	73	178
89 NL	15	15	2.31	35	8	256.2	226	66	77	178
90 NL	1	1	4.26	4	0	25.1	26	12	4	16
91 NL	7	2	3.46	21	0	112.0	112	43	32	73
92 NL	10	15	3.67	33	1	210.2	209	86	69	130
Life	116	82	2.87	289	59	1805.0	1587	576	539	1230
2 AVE	9	9	3.60	27	1	161.1	161	65	51	102

JOE HESKETH

Position: Pitcher
Team: Boston Red Sox
Born: Feb. 15, 1959 Lackawanna, NY
Height: 6'2" **Weight:** 170 lbs.
Bats: left **Throws:** left
Acquired: Signed as a free agent, 7/90

Player Summary
Fantasy Value	$2 to $4
Card Value	3¢ to 4¢
Will	allow too many runners
Can't	escape injury jinx
Expect	more gopher balls
Don't Expect	return to '91 form

The difference between the Joe Hesketh of 1991 and the Joe Hesketh of 1992 was painfully obvious. Last year's model yielded too many hits and too many home runs. When he surprised the baseball world with a 12-4 record and 3.29 ERA in his first full AL season in '91, the Red Sox figured he had regained the form he had shown as a 1985 rookie with the Montreal Expos. They also figured he had fully recovered from serious shoulder problems. But he hobbled out of the starting gate last year like he knew he shouldn't spend half the schedule in Fenway Park. Hammered consistently, the sinker-and-slider pitcher still managed to strike out twice the number he walked but gave up many more hits than innings pitched. A dozen had sailed out of the park by mid-August. Hesketh helps himself with a good glove.

Major League Pitching Register
	W	L	ERA	G	CG	IP	H	ER	BB	SO
84 NL	2	2	1.80	11	1	45.0	38	9	15	32
85 NL	10	5	2.49	25	2	155.1	125	43	45	113
86 NL	6	5	5.01	15	0	82.2	92	46	31	67
87 NL	0	0	3.14	18	0	28.2	23	10	15	31
88 NL	4	3	2.85	60	0	72.2	63	23	35	64
89 NL	6	4	5.77	43	0	48.1	54	31	26	44
90 NL	1	2	5.29	33	0	34.0	32	20	14	24
90 AL	0	4	3.51	12	0	25.2	37	10	11	26
91 AL	12	4	3.29	39	0	153.1	142	56	53	104
92 AL	8	9	4.36	30	1	148.2	162	72	58	104
Life	49	38	3.63	286	4	794.1	768	320	303	609
3 AVE	7	6	3.93	38	0	120.2	124	53	45	86

GREG HIBBARD

Position: Pitcher
Team: Chicago Cubs
Born: Sept. 13, 1964 New Orleans, LA
Height: 6' **Weight:** 190 lbs.
Bats: left **Throws:** left
Acquired: Traded from Marlins for Alex Arias and Gary Scott, 11/92

Player Summary
Fantasy Value	$5 to $8
Card Value	3¢ to 4¢
Will	yield hits and homers
Can't	always make sinker sink
Expect	another shot as starter
Don't Expect	high K totals

When he's on, Hibbard is a sinkerballer who changes speeds well, throws strikes, and gets batters to hit ground balls. He was at his best in 1990, when he surprised baseball with a 3.16 ERA in 211 innings for the Chicago White Sox, but he's been pretty much of an enigma since. Hibbard also throws a curveball, change-up, and slider, but he struggled so much as a starter last summer that the Sox even gave him a look as a reliever. Hibbard's problems were in yielding too many hits, home runs, and walks while striking out one man for every one he walked. He's had problems with walks and gopher balls in the past—especially when his sinker didn't sink. In 1992, opponents compiled a .277 batting average, a .337 on-base percentage, and a .404 slugging percentage. Because of his unorthodox delivery, Hibbard is unusually tough on righthanded hitters for a lefty; righties batted .285 in '92, however. He fields the ground balls he produces and holds baserunners close.

Major League Pitching Register
	W	L	ERA	G	CG	IP	H	ER	BB	SO
89 AL	6	7	3.21	23	2	137.1	142	49	41	55
90 AL	14	9	3.16	33	3	211.0	202	74	55	92
91 AL	11	11	4.31	32	5	194.0	196	93	57	71
92 AL	10	7	4.40	31	0	176.0	187	86	57	69
Life	41	34	3.78	119	10	718.1	727	302	210	287
3 AVE	12	9	3.92	32	3	194.0	195	84	56	77

BRYAN HICKERSON

Position: Pitcher
Team: San Francisco Giants
Born: Oct. 13, 1963 Bemidji, MN
Height: 6'2" **Weight:** 195 lbs.
Bats: left **Throws:** left
Acquired: Traded from Twins with Jose Domingues and Ray Velasquez for David Blakely and Dan Gladden, 3/87

Player Summary	
Fantasy Value	$2 to $4
Card Value	5¢ to 10¢
Will	serve in middle relief
Can't	avoid gopher balls
Expect	success versus southpaws
Don't Expect	starting assignments

Hickerson was a busy middle reliever during his first full season in the majors last summer. A control pitcher who fans three times more than he walks, the southpaw yields less than a hit per inning. Opponents in 1992 compiled a .236 batting average, a .282 on-base percentage, and a .369 slugging percentage. His only weakness is a tendency to throw home run balls more frequently than a good reliever should. He gave up seven homers in 87 innings. Hickerson still managed a good won-lost record and respectable ERA last summer, however. He was used as both a starter and a reliever during the 1991 stretch drive. Hickerson broke into pro ball in 1986 and spent five years in the minors. He has been a middle man throughout his career. In 1990 at Triple-A Phoenix, he was 1-1 with two saves, a 3.80 ERA, five walks, and 21 strikeouts in 12 games and 21⅓ innings. He was 3-4 that year at Double-A Shreveport, with two saves, 14 bases on balls, and 41 strikeouts in 23 games and 39 innings.

Major League Pitching Register

	W	L	ERA	G	S	IP	H	ER	BB	SO
91 NL	2	2	3.60	17	0	50.0	53	20	17	43
92 NL	5	3	3.09	61	0	87.1	74	30	21	68
Life	7	5	3.28	78	0	137.1	127	50	38	111
2 AVE	4	3	3.28	39	0	69.1	64	25	19	56

GLENALLEN HILL

Position: Outfield
Team: Cleveland Indians
Born: March 22, 1965 Santa Cruz, CA
Height: 6'2" **Weight:** 205 lbs.
Bats: right **Throws:** right
Acquired: Traded from Blue Jays with Mark Whiten for Tom Candiotti and Turner Ward, 6/90

Player Summary	
Fantasy Value	$8 to $14
Card Value	4¢ to 6¢
Will	show speed plus power
Can't	realize great promise
Expect	hot and cold streaks
Don't Expect	patience at plate

Hill shared Cleveland's left field job last summer with Albert Belle and Thomas Howard. Hill is a package of speed plus power, he has no patience at the plate, and he strikes out four times more than he walks. If he showed more selectivity, he might resemble the hitter who won two minor league home run crowns. In 1992, he had a .287 on-base average and a .436 slugging percentage. Last June 10, his fourth homer in two days gave Cleveland a 4-2, 11-inning win. In 1989, he batted .321 with 21 home runs, 72 RBI, 31 doubles, and 21 stolen bases at Triple-A Syracuse. He batted .264 with 12 homers and 38 RBI at Double-A Knoxville in 1988. He has the range, arm, and instincts to play center but couldn't unseat rookie speed merchant Kenny Lofton last year. Hill led four leagues in strikeouts and two leagues in errors but is still regarded as a prospect. He needs to stay in the lineup and avoid any more injuries.

Major League Batting Register

	BA	G	AB	R	H	2B	3B	HR	RBI	SB
89 AL	.288	19	52	4	15	0	0	1	7	2
90 AL	.231	84	260	47	60	11	3	12	32	8
91 AL	.253	35	99	14	25	5	2	3	11	2
91 AL	.258	72	221	29	57	8	2	8	25	6
92 AL	.241	102	369	38	89	16	1	18	49	9
Life	.245	277	902	118	221	35	6	39	113	25
3 AVE	.242	86	283	38	69	12	2	13	35	8

KEN HILL

Position: Pitcher
Team: Montreal Expos
Born: Dec. 14, 1965 Lynn, MA
Height: 6'2" **Weight:** 175 lbs.
Bats: right **Throws:** right
Acquired: Traded from Cardinals for Andres Galarraga, 11/91

Player Summary	
Fantasy Value	$10 to $18
Card Value	3¢ to 4¢
Will	not allow many hits
Can't	avoid wild pitches
Expect	continued improvement
Don't Expect	losing record

After two so-so seasons in St. Louis, Hill showed in 1991 that he could be a successful big league starter. He not only fanned twice the number he walked but allowed less hits per inning than anyone other than Pete Harnisch. Using his arsenal of a fastball, curveball, and forkball, Hill was even better after coming to Montreal last summer. On June 8, he pitched his best game, a 6-0 one-hitter (the first of his career) against the Mets. A power pitcher who had never topped 11 wins in a season before '92, Hill still has problems when he falls behind in the count. His losses are packed with walks and wild pitches. Opponents in 1992 compiled a .230 batting average, a .297 on-base percentage, and a .335 slugging percentage. He makes a satisfactory No. 2 starter in a one-two punch with Dennis Martinez for the Montreal staff. Although Hill is a good fielder, he has trouble holding runners on. He's no automatic out as a batter.

Major League Pitching Register

	W	L	ERA	G	CG	IP	H	ER	BB	SO
88 NL	0	1	5.14	4	0	14.0	16	8	6	6
89 NL	7	15	3.80	33	2	196.2	186	83	99	112
90 NL	5	6	5.49	17	1	78.2	79	48	33	58
91 NL	11	10	3.57	30	0	181.1	147	72	67	121
92 NL	16	9	2.68	33	3	218.0	187	65	75	150
Life	39	41	3.61	117	6	688.2	615	276	280	447
3 AVE	11	8	3.48	27	1	159.1	138	62	58	110

CHRIS HOILES

Position: Catcher
Team: Baltimore Orioles
Born: March 20, 1965 Bowling Green, OH
Height: 6' **Weight:** 213 lbs.
Bats: right **Throws:** right
Acquired: Traded from Tigers with Cesar Mejia and Robinson Garces for Fred Lynn, 9/88

Player Summary	
Fantasy Value	$8 to $16
Card Value	3¢ to 4¢
Will	hit with authority
Can't	throw out runners
Expect	selective strike zone
Don't Expect	any modicum of speed

Hoiles carries a big stick but a weak wing. He was leading the Orioles in homers when the Yankees' Tim Leary hurled an errant pitch that fractured Hoiles's wrist on June 21. Hoiles was also among AL leaders in the dubious department of allowing enemy baserunners to steal successfully; he nailed only 20 percent in '92. Hardly a defensive liability, he led all AL receivers in fielding percentage in 1991, his rookie season. He made only one error in his first 136 games and established a good rapport with the young pitchers on the Baltimore staff. Once a practitioner of bad habits behind the plate, he calls good games, prevents wild pitches, and blocks the plate well. Hitting is the best aspect of his game. As a sophomore, he became more selective and earned a reputation as a contact hitter. In 1992, he collected a .384 on-base average and a .506 slugging percentage. He had almost as many walks (55) as whiffs (60).

Major League Batting Register

	BA	G	AB	R	H	2B	3B	HR	RBI	SB
89 AL	.111	6	9	0	1	0	0	1	0	0
90 AL	.190	23	63	7	12	3	0	1	6	0
91 AL	.243	107	341	36	83	15	0	11	31	0
92 AL	.274	96	310	49	85	10	1	20	40	0
Life	.250	232	723	92	181	29	1	32	78	0
2 AVE	.258	102	326	43	84	13	1	16	36	0

DAVE HOLLINS

Position: Third base
Team: Philadelphia Phillies
Born: May 25, 1966 Buffalo, NY
Height: 6'1" **Weight:** 195 lbs.
Bats: both **Throws:** right
Acquired: Drafted from Padres, 12/89

Player Summary	
Fantasy Value	$14 to $22
Card Value	5¢ to 10¢
Will	show some power
Can't	worry about shoulder
Expect	patience at plate
Don't Expect	Mike Schmidt clone

Like Shane Mack, Hollins was allowed to escape from the San Diego system as a Rule 5 draft choice. The Padres have regretted both moves. The switch-hitting Hollins showed home run power last summer for the first time in a six-year pro career. Though he'll never make Philly fans forget Mike Schmidt, Hollins has one advantage over the future Hall of Famer, in that he won't whiff as frequently. He had a .369 on-base average and a .469 slugging percentage in '92. A line-drive hitter with patience, Hollins is a fastball hitter who handles lefthanded pitching well, hitting .322 against lefties in 1992. Hollins also gave the Phils steady defensive play at third base last summer, compiling a .954 fielding average. The former University of South Carolina standout once led a minor league in putouts, assists, chances, and fielding percentage. He suffered a shoulder injury since that reduced the power of his throwing arm. He has some speed but not good judgment, getting nailed too often.

Major League Batting Register

	BA	G	AB	R	H	2B	3B	HR	RBI	SB
90 NL	.184	72	114	14	21	0	0	5	15	0
91 NL	.298	56	151	18	45	10	2	6	21	1
92 NL	.270	156	586	104	158	28	4	27	93	9
Life	.263	284	851	136	224	38	6	38	129	10
2 AVE	.275	106	369	61	102	19	3	17	57	5

BRIAN HOLMAN

Position: Pitcher
Team: Seattle Mariners
Born: Jan. 25, 1965 Denver, CO
Height: 6'4" **Weight:** 185 lbs.
Bats: right **Throws:** right
Acquired: Traded from Expos with Gene Harris and Randy Johnson for Mark Langston and Mike Campbell, 5/89

Player Summary	
Fantasy Value	$2 to $4
Card Value	3¢ to 4¢
Will	make comeback bid
Can't	avoid gopher balls
Expect	a dozen wins if healthy
Don't Expect	runners to steal

Surgery to repair a torn right rotator cuff ruined the 1992 season for Holman. An effective starting pitcher when healthy, he had made a successful recovery from previous elbow surgery. Though he's never had a winning season, Holman had two shutouts among his 13 wins for Seattle in '91 and posted a decent 3.69 ERA before his shoulder succumbed. By that time, he had allowed too many walks, hits, and homers. He was, however, the workhorse of the Seattle starting rotation, and his 200 innings of quality work were hard to replace. The year before, he finished with less hits than innings pitched and twice as many walks as strikeouts. A sinker-and-slider pitcher who also throws a slurve—a cross between a slider and a curve—Holman keeps the ball down and tries to coax ground balls from batters. One of the game's more articulate athletes, Holman is a good competitor who helps himself as a fielder. Few runners steal against him.

Major League Pitching Register

	W	L	ERA	G	CG	IP	H	ER	BB	SO
88 NL	4	8	3.23	18	1	100.1	101	36	34	58
89 NL	1	2	4.83	10	0	31.2	34	17	15	23
89 AL	8	10	3.44	23	6	159.2	160	61	62	82
90 AL	11	11	4.03	28	3	189.2	188	85	66	121
91 AL	13	14	3.69	30	5	195.1	199	80	77	108
Life	37	45	3.71	109	15	676.2	682	279	254	392
3 AVE	11	12	3.79	30	5	191.2	194	81	73	111

DARREN HOLMES

Position: Pitcher
Team: Colorado Rockies
Born: April 25, 1966 Asheville, NC
Height: 6' **Weight:** 200 lbs.
Bats: right **Throws:** right
Acquired: First-round pick from Brewers in 11/92 expansion draft

Player Summary	
Fantasy Value	$3 to $7
Card Value	3¢ to 4¢
Will	retire first batters
Can't	work as starter
Expect	pinpoint control
Don't Expect	gopher balls

Holmes will vie for the Rockies' closer job. He spent his second major league summer in the bullpen of the Brewers last year and proved a mystery to American League batters. The rubber-armed righthander was used primarily in set-up roles. In 1992, he held the first batters he faced to an incredible .171 average. He showed exceptional control, yielded less hits than innings pitched, and kept the ball in the park. He is especially effective on artificial turf. He handles righties (allowing a .225 average in '92) and lefthanded batters (a .224 average) equally well. In 1992, opponents compiled a .224 batting average, a .284 on-base percentage, and a .308 slugging percentage. At Triple-A Albuquerque in 1990, he was 12-2 with a 3.11 ERA, 13 saves, 99 strikeouts, and 39 walks in 92⅔ innings and 56 games. At Double-A San Antonio in 1989, he was 5-8, with a 3.83 ERA, one save, 81 Ks, and 44 bases on balls in 110⅓ innings and 17 games. He was 1-4 with a 7.45 ERA at Albuquerque that season.

Major League Pitching Register

	W	L	ERA	G	S	IP	H	ER	BB	SO
90 NL	0	1	5.19	14	0	17.1	15	10	11	19
91 AL	1	4	4.72	40	3	76.1	90	40	27	59
92 AL	4	4	2.55	41	6	42.1	35	12	11	31
Life	5	9	4.10	95	9	136.0	140	62	49	109
2 AVE	3	4	3.94	41	5	59.1	63	26	19	45

RICK HONEYCUTT

Position: Pitcher
Team: Oakland Athletics
Born: June 29, 1954 Chattanooga, TN
Height: 6'1" **Weight:** 190 lbs.
Bats: left **Throws:** left
Acquired: Traded from Dodgers for Tim Belcher, 8/87

Player Summary	
Fantasy Value	$1 to $3
Card Value	3¢ to 4¢
Will	coax ground-ball outs
Can't	return to rotation
Expect	strong set-up service
Don't Expect	runners to swipe

Honeycutt ripped a page from the Dennis Eckersley control book last summer when he struck out three times more men than he walked. Honeycutt is a sinker-and-slider pitcher who also uses a curve and change. He has been a successful set-up man for five seasons—since Oakland followed the Eckersley formula of moving a National League starter to an American League bullpen. Honeycutt has a lifetime losing record because he pitched for poor teams in Seattle and Texas. He missed the first few months of the 1991 season with a bad shoulder. A decent fielder, Honeycutt's strong suit on defense is his ability to keep runners close.

Major League Pitching Register

	W	L	ERA	G	S	IP	H	ER	BB	SO
77 AL	0	1	4.34	10	0	29.0	26	14	11	17
78 AL	5	11	4.89	26	0	134.1	150	73	49	50
79 AL	11	12	4.04	33	0	194.0	201	87	67	83
80 AL	10	17	3.94	30	0	203.1	221	89	60	79
81 AL	11	6	3.31	20	0	127.2	120	47	17	40
82 AL	5	17	5.27	30	0	164.0	201	96	54	64
83 AL	14	8	2.42	25	0	174.2	168	47	37	56
83 NL	2	3	5.77	9	0	39.0	46	25	13	18
84 AL	10	9	2.84	29	0	183.2	180	58	51	75
85 AL	8	12	3.42	31	1	142.0	141	54	49	67
86 AL	11	9	3.32	32	0	171.0	164	63	45	100
87 AL	2	12	4.59	27	0	115.2	133	59	45	92
87 AL	1	4	5.32	7	0	23.2	25	14	9	10
88 AL	3	2	3.50	55	7	79.2	74	31	25	47
89 AL	2	2	2.35	64	12	76.2	56	20	26	52
90 AL	2	2	2.70	63	7	63.1	46	19	22	38
91 AL	2	4	3.58	43	0	37.2	37	15	20	26
92 AL	1	4	3.69	54	3	39.0	41	16	10	32
Life	100	135	3.72	588	30	1998.1	2030	827	610	946
3 AVE	2	3	3.21	53	3	46.1	41	17	17	32

SAM HORN

Position: Designated hitter; first base
Team: Baltimore Orioles
Born: Nov. 2, 1963 Dallas, TX
Height: 6'5" **Weight:** 240 lbs.
Bats: left **Throws:** left
Acquired: Signed as a free agent, 2/90

Player Summary	
Fantasy Value	$4 to $6
Card Value	3¢ to 4¢
Will	make dynamic DH
Can't	run at all
Expect	power to all fields
Don't Expect	appearance at first

Horn spent most of last summer on the Baltimore bench, watching Randy Milligan play first base and Glenn Davis serve as the every-day designated hitter. Horn played only early in the season, when Davis was disabled. A one-dimensional player who provides immense power potential, Horn has no speed, range, or fielding acumen—even though there are other lumbering first basemen in the majors. In 1991, when he squeezed into 121 games, more than half of Horn's hits went for extra bases. He's a risk as a pinch-hitter, however, because any grounder he hits with men on base usually results in a double-play. Horn strikes out less than he once did because he's cut down on his swing. Used against righties in recent years, he can hit lefties too. And he's strong enough to hit home runs to the opposite field. In 1992, he compiled a .324 on-base average and a .401 slugging percentage.

Major League Batting Register

	BA	G	AB	R	H	2B	3B	HR	RBI	SB
87 AL	.278	46	158	31	44	7	0	14	34	0
88 AL	.148	24	61	4	9	0	0	2	8	0
89 AL	.148	33	54	1	8	2	0	0	4	0
90 AL	.248	79	246	30	61	13	0	14	45	0
91 AL	.233	121	317	45	74	16	0	23	61	0
92 AL	.235	63	162	13	38	10	1	5	19	0
Life	.234	366	998	124	234	48	1	58	171	0
3 AVE	.239	88	242	29	58	13	0	14	42	0

VINCE HORSMAN

Position: Pitcher
Team: Oakland Athletics
Born: March 9, 1967 Halifax, Nova Scotia
Height: 6'2" **Weight:** 180 lbs.
Bats: right **Throws:** left
Acquired: Signed as a free agent, 3/92

Player Summary	
Fantasy Value	$2 to $4
Card Value	3¢ to 4¢
Will	keep ball in park
Can't	count on experience
Expect	quality relief work
Don't Expect	severe control problems

Horsman spent seven summers in the farm system of the Toronto Blue Jays before hooking onto the Oakland varsity after a waiver sale in 1992. A lefthanded middle reliever who showed excellent control in the minors, he made the most of his opportunity. Working often, he yielded less than a hit per inning and compiled one of the best earned run averages on the Athletics' staff. Opponents in 1992 compiled a .252 batting average, a .339 on-base percentage, and a .335 slugging percentage. Horsman broke into pro ball in 1985 but did not reach the majors until the waning weeks of the 1991 campaign. In four fleeting appearances with Toronto in 1991, he did not allow a run. At Double-A Knoxville that season, he was 4-1 with a 2.34 ERA, three saves, 19 walks, and 80 strikeouts in 42 games and 80⅔ innings. Horsman has a couple of things in his favor to remain a major leaguer, including being lefthanded and being only 26 years old. Although he was somewhat stingy with the gopher ball in 1992, giving up just three, he led the Class-A Sally League with 20 in 1987.

Major League Pitching Register

	W	L	ERA	G	S	IP	H	ER	BB	SO
91 AL	0	0	0.00	4	0	4.0	2	0	3	2
92 AL	2	1	2.49	58	1	43.1	39	12	21	18
Life	2	1	2.28	62	1	47.1	41	12	24	20

CHARLIE HOUGH

Position: Pitcher
Team: Florida Marlins
Born: Jan. 5, 1948 Honolulu, HI
Height: 6'2" **Weight:** 190 lbs.
Bats: right **Throws:** right
Acquired: Signed as a free agent, 12/92

Player Summary	
Fantasy Value	$3 to $5
Card Value	3¢ to 4¢
Will	try to tame knuckler
Can't	avoid home run balls
Expect	more walks than whiffs
Don't Expect	inflated ERA

Hough turned in an ordinary year in 1992. He baffles batters more often than not, but when the knuckleball doesn't knuckle, Hough gets hit. Hough's problems with the unpredictable pitch are an inability to keep it in the strike zone and the tendency of "flat" knucklers to become home runs. Hough has fanned as many as 223 but has also topped 100 walks three times in the last six years. Hough learned the tricks of the trade from Hall of Fame knuckleballer Hoyt Wilhelm when both were with the Dodgers in 1971.

Major League Pitching Register

	W	L	ERA	G	CG	IP	H	ER	BB	SO
70 NL	0	0	5.29	8	0	17.0	18	10	11	8
71 NL	0	0	4.15	4	0	4.1	3	2	3	4
72 NL	0	0	3.38	2	0	2.2	2	1	2	4
73 NL	4	2	2.76	37	0	71.2	52	22	45	70
74 NL	9	4	3.75	49	0	96.0	65	40	40	63
75 NL	3	7	2.95	38	0	61.0	43	20	34	34
76 NL	12	8	2.21	77	0	142.2	102	35	77	81
77 NL	6	12	3.32	70	0	127.1	98	47	70	105
78 NL	5	5	3.28	55	0	93.1	69	34	48	66
79 NL	7	5	4.76	42	0	151.1	152	80	66	76
80 NL	1	3	5.57	19	0	32.1	37	20	21	25
80 AL	2	2	3.96	16	2	61.1	54	27	37	47
81 AL	4	1	2.96	21	2	82.0	61	27	31	69
82 AL	16	13	3.95	34	12	228.0	217	100	72	128
83 AL	15	13	3.18	34	11	252.0	219	89	95	152
84 AL	16	14	3.76	36	17	266.0	260	111	94	164
85 AL	14	16	3.31	34	14	250.1	198	92	83	141
86 AL	17	10	3.79	33	7	230.1	188	97	89	146
87 AL	18	13	3.79	40	13	285.1	238	120	124	223
88 AL	15	16	3.32	34	10	252.0	202	93	126	174
89 AL	10	13	4.35	30	5	182.0	168	88	95	94
90 AL	12	12	4.07	32	5	218.2	190	99	119	114
91 AL	9	10	4.02	31	4	199.1	167	89	94	107
92 AL	7	12	3.93	27	4	176.1	160	77	66	76
Life	202	191	3.67	803	106	3483.1	2963	1420	1542	2171
3 AVE	9	11	4.01	30	4	198.1	172	88	93	99

DAVID HOWARD

Position: Shortstop
Team: Kansas City Royals
Born: Feb. 26, 1967 Sarasota, FL
Height: 6' **Weight:** 165 lbs.
Bats: both **Throws:** right
Acquired: 32nd-round pick in 6/86 free-agent draft

Player Summary	
Fantasy Value	$1 to $3
Card Value	3¢ to 4¢
Will	show great range
Can't	hit the ball
Expect	some running speed
Don't Expect	any hint of power

Howard was disabled by a back injury during the first half of the 1992 campaign. He returned in time to reclaim Kansas City's shortstop job, which had been shared by veteran Curtis Wilkerson and rookie Rico Rossy in his absence. Howard is a superior defensive shortstop whose biggest asset is great range. He notched eight errors and a .976 fielding percentage in '92. In 1991 as a rookie, he ousted the better-hitting Kurt Stillwell from the position when Royals manager Hal McRae decided that he wanted a superior defensive club. Howard is a weak hitter with virtually no power, but he excels as a bunter who can move runners along. When he does connect, however, he makes his rare long hits count: He beat California with an inside-the-park homer with two men on last Aug. 4. He strikes out more than twice as often as he walks. Howard twice reached a dozen steals in the minors and could make himself more valuable by bunting and running more. He bats in the No. 9 slot because that's where he belongs.

Major League Batting Register

	BA	G	AB	R	H	2B	3B	HR	RBI	SB
91 AL	.216	94	236	20	51	7	0	1	17	3
92 AL	.224	74	219	19	49	6	2	1	18	3
Life	.220	168	455	39	100	13	2	2	35	6
2 AVE	.220	84	228	20	50	7	1	1	18	3

TOM HOWARD

Position: Outfield
Team: Cleveland Indians
Born: Dec. 11, 1964 Middletown, OH
Height: 6'2" **Weight:** 200 lbs.
Bats: both **Throws:** right
Acquired: Traded from Padres for Jason Hardtke and Chris Maffett, 4/92

Player Summary	
Fantasy Value	$2 to $4
Card Value	3¢ to 4¢
Will	play fine left field
Can't	generate power
Expect	more stolen bases
Don't Expect	every-day job

While the San Diego Padres searched for a left fielder last summer, this former Padre left fielder found his niche with the Cleveland Indians. A speedy switch-hitter, assigned to share left field with Albert Belle and Glenallen Hill, Howard kept his average near .300 (50 points above his career mark) most of the season before falling to a .277 mark. He produced four .300 seasons in the San Diego farm system. In 1990 at Triple-A Las Vegas, he batted .328. For the Tribe in '92, he didn't supply any power but did help the defense with a strong arm and outstanding range (good enough to play center if needed). A fastball hitter who is more productive left-handed, Howard has the speed to beat out bunts or infield hits. He is not patient at the plate, where he strikes out three times more than he walks. In 1992, he had a .308 on-base average and a .346 slugging percentage. Because he doesn't add much power, Howard figures to be no better than a fourth outfielder.

Major League Batting Register

	BA	G	AB	R	H	2B	3B	HR	RBI	SB
90 NL	.273	20	44	4	12	2	0	0	0	0
91 NL	.249	106	281	30	70	12	3	4	22	10
92 NL	.333	5	3	1	1	0	0	0	0	0
92 AL	.277	117	358	36	99	15	2	2	32	15
Life	.265	248	686	71	182	29	5	6	54	25
2 AVE	.265	114	321	34	85	14	3	3	27	13

JAY HOWELL

Position: Pitcher
Team: Los Angeles Dodgers
Born: Nov. 26, 1955 Miami, FL
Height: 6'3" **Weight:** 205 lbs.
Bats: right **Throws:** right
Acquired: Traded from Athletics with Alfredo Griffin and Jesse Orosco for Bob Welch, Jack Savage, and Matt Young, 12/87

Player Summary	
Fantasy Value	$8 to $14
Card Value	3¢ to 4¢
Will	seek closer job
Can't	stave off injuries
Expect	good control
Don't Expect	gopher balls

Before 1992, Howell was a successful closer in the major leagues for seven straight seasons. He hit a career peak with 29 saves for Oakland in 1985. Last year, a sore shoulder hobbled him early. Roger McDowell took over as the closer, with occasional help from Jim Gott and John Candelaria. Used sparingly to protect the shoulder, he recorded only one save in his first 30 appearances. He has also had past elbow, knee, and back problems. Howell throws a fastball, curveball, slider, and changeup. He keeps the ball in the park and fans more than twice the number he walks. He can't work every day, however, or throw more than an inning per stint. Despite his strong pitching last summer, his closer days might be over.

Major League Pitching Register

	W	L	ERA	G	S	IP	H	ER	BB	SO
80 NL	0	0	13.50	5	0	3.1	8	5	0	1
81 NL	2	0	4.84	10	0	22.1	23	12	10	10
82 AL	2	3	7.71	6	0	28.0	42	24	13	21
83 AL	1	5	5.38	19	0	82.0	89	49	35	61
84 AL	9	4	2.69	61	7	103.2	86	31	34	109
85 AL	9	8	2.85	63	29	98.0	98	31	31	68
86 AL	3	6	3.38	38	16	53.1	53	20	23	42
87 AL	3	4	5.89	36	16	44.1	48	29	21	35
88 NL	5	3	2.08	50	21	65.0	44	15	21	70
89 NL	5	3	1.58	56	28	79.2	60	14	22	55
90 NL	5	5	2.18	45	16	66.0	59	16	20	59
91 NL	6	5	3.18	44	16	51.0	39	18	11	40
92 NL	1	3	1.54	41	4	46.2	41	8	18	36
Life	51	49	3.29	474	153	743.1	690	272	259	607
3 AVE	4	4	2.31	43	12	54.1	46	14	16	45

KENT HRBEK

Position: First base
Team: Minnesota Twins
Born: May 21, 1960 Minneapolis, MN
Height: 6'4" **Weight:** 240 lbs.
Bats: left **Throws:** right
Acquired: 17th-round pick in 6/78 free-agent draft

Player Summary	
Fantasy Value	$14 to $22
Card Value	5¢ to 7¢
Will	top 20 homers
Can't	steal a lot
Expect	Gold Glove bid
Don't Expect	more Ks than walks

Hrbek is a hitter who can break up a game with a single swing. Before 1992, he had eight seasons of 20 homers and five years with at least 90 RBI. Hrbek had a dislocated shoulder that sent him to the disabled list early last season. He worked hard to trim 15 pounds from his 6'4" frame. Without the excess baggage, he had better mobility around first base, where he's one of the league's best fielders, and better running speed. A rare power hitter with patience, Hrbek has no trouble with southpaws and also hits to all fields. He had a .357 on-base average and a .409 slugging percentage in 1992. For a big man, he has good range at first—especially when chasing pop fouls or diving for low linedrives. Hrbek has good hands and scoops and stretches well. He's overdue for a Gold Glove.

Major League Batting Register

	BA	G	AB	R	H	2B	3B	HR	RBI	SB
81 AL	.239	24	67	5	16	5	0	1	7	0
82 AL	.301	140	532	82	160	21	4	23	92	3
83 AL	.297	141	515	75	153	41	5	16	84	4
84 AL	.311	149	559	80	174	31	3	27	107	1
85 AL	.278	158	593	78	165	31	2	21	93	1
86 AL	.267	149	550	85	147	27	1	29	91	2
87 AL	.285	143	477	85	136	20	1	34	90	5
88 AL	.312	143	510	75	159	31	0	25	76	0
89 AL	.272	109	375	59	102	17	0	25	84	3
90 AL	.287	143	492	61	141	26	0	22	79	5
91 AL	.284	132	462	72	131	20	1	20	89	4
92 AL	.244	112	394	52	96	20	0	15	58	5
Life	.286	1543	5526	809	1580	290	17	258	950	33
3 AVE	.273	129	449	62	123	22	0	19	75	5

MIKE HUFF

Position: Outfield
Team: Chicago White Sox
Born: Aug. 11, 1963 Honolulu, HI
Height: 6'1" **Weight:** 180 lbs.
Bats: right **Throws:** right
Acquired: Signed as a free agent, 6/91

Player Summary	
Fantasy Value	$2 to $4
Card Value	3¢ to 4¢
Will	make living with speed
Can't	hammer home runs
Expect	strong outfield play
Don't Expect	lots of Ks

Huff's 1992 season was ruined when he fractured his left shoulder on June 17. The former Dodger farmhand had teamed with Warren Newson in a right-left platoon that filled the gap created when regular White Sox right fielder Dan Pasqua suffered disabling hamstring injuries. Huff is a speed merchant who can man all three outfield spots. He has excellent range and a strong throwing arm, making center field his best position, although he is good enough to be a late-inning defensive replacement anywhere in the outfield. He's also a contact hitter with enough patience to coax his share of walks. He fans only slightly more often than he walks. Huff doesn't have much power but does have the ability to line hits to the opposite field. In 1992, he had a .273 onbase average and a .252 slugging percentage. Huff holds out hope of playing every day, but his lack of power hurts his chances of being more than a platoon player. He did have five .300 seasons in the minors, however, and could make someone a competent leadoff man.

Major League Batting Register

	BA	G	AB	R	H	2B	3B	HR	RBI	SB
89 NL	.200	12	25	4	5	1	0	1	2	0
91 AL	.251	102	243	42	61	10	2	3	25	14
92 AL	.209	60	115	13	24	5	0	0	8	1
Life	.235	174	383	59	90	16	2	4	35	15

TIM HULETT

Position: Second base; third base
Team: Baltimore Orioles
Born: Jan. 12, 1960 Springfield, IL
Height: 6′ **Weight:** 185 lbs.
Bats: right **Throws:** right
Acquired: Signed as a free agent, 11/88

Player Summary	
Fantasy Value	$1 to $3
Card Value	3¢ to 4¢
Will	man two spots
Can't	steal bases
Expect	some power
Don't Expect	daily duty

Hulett's 1992 season was saddened by the accidental death of his 6-year-old son Sam. The utility infielder took some time off, then returned to his job as a Baltimore backup at second and third base. Hulett, who in 1992 had the best batting average of his nine-year career, hangs onto a big league berth because of his versatility and his ability to deliver a big hit off the bench. He also had a .340 on-base percentage and a .408 slugging average last summer. He lacks speed and range but still shows some power (he hit 17 homers as the regular third baseman for the 1986 White Sox). Second base is his best position; he has led his league in putouts, assists, chances, double-plays, and fielding percentage while playing the keystone sack. At age 33, however, don't expect him to become a regular.

Major League Batting Register

	BA	G	AB	R	H	2B	3B	HR	RBI	SB
83 AL	.200	6	5	0	1	0	0	0	0	1
84 AL	.000	8	7	1	0	0	0	0	0	1
85 AL	.268	141	395	52	106	19	4	5	37	6
86 AL	.231	150	520	53	120	16	5	17	44	4
87 AL	.217	68	240	20	52	10	0	7	28	0
89 AL	.278	33	97	12	27	5	0	3	18	0
90 AL	.255	53	153	16	39	7	1	3	16	1
91 AL	.204	79	206	29	42	9	0	7	18	0
92 AL	.289	57	142	11	41	7	2	2	21	0
Life	.242	595	1765	194	428	73	12	44	182	13
2 AVE	.226	66	180	23	41	8	1	5	17	1

TODD HUNDLEY

Position: Catcher
Team: New York Mets
Born: May 27, 1969 Martinsville, VA
Height: 5′11″ **Weight:** 185 lbs.
Bats: both **Throws:** right
Acquired: Second-round pick in 6/87 free-agent draft

Player Summary	
Fantasy Value	$3 to $7
Card Value	15¢ to 25¢
Will	nail would-be stealers
Can't	hit for average
Expect	occasional power
Don't Expect	instant Gold Glove

At age 16, Todd Hundley showed up his dad at Randy's fantasy camp and impressed a collection of 1969 Cubs with his powerful throwing arm. Hundley had obviously inherited his father's bloodlines. Like Randy, who was a Gold Glove catcher, Todd is a fine defensive receiver with occasional home run power. He nailed almost half the runners who tried to steal against him in the minors. He led one minor league in assists and chances and another in double plays. He also led in errors—an occupational risk for any strong-armed catcher who likes to throw. He showed solid major league receiving ability in '92, especially with his game-calling, pitch-blocking, and throwing. As a 1992 rookie, Hundley struck out three times more than he walked, delivered less than a dozen homers, and hardly hit more than his weight. He had a .256 on-base average and a .316 slugging percentage in 1992. He can hit, though. In 1991 at Triple-A Tidewater, he had a .273 batting average with 14 homers, 66 RBI, and 24 doubles in 454 at bats.

Major League Batting Register

	BA	G	AB	R	H	2B	3B	HR	RBI	SB
90 NL	.209	36	67	8	14	6	0	0	2	0
91 NL	.133	21	60	5	8	0	1	1	7	0
92 NL	.209	123	358	32	75	17	0	7	32	3
Life	.200	180	485	45	97	23	1	8	41	3

BRIAN HUNTER

Position: First base; outfield
Team: Atlanta Braves
Born: March 4, 1968 El Toro, CA
Height: 6' **Weight:** 195 lbs.
Bats: right **Throws:** left
Acquired: Eighth-round pick in 6/87 free-agent draft

Player Summary	
Fantasy Value	$6 to $12
Card Value	3¢ to 4¢
Will	generate good power
Can't	escape platoon role
Expect	fine first base play
Don't Expect	average above .260

Hunter's immense power potential has been masked the last two years because of Atlanta's refusal to remove him from a righthander-lefthander first base platoon with Sid Bream. Hunter, though, had a .181 batting average against righties in 1992. Although he played some outfield during 1991 postseason play, he was unable to do that last summer because of a sore left shoulder. First hurt as a minor leaguer in 1988, Hunter aggravated the injury while throwing from the outfield during the '91 World Series. He hurt it again during batting practice last June. As a hitter, he had the best ratio of home runs per at bats of any member of the '92 Braves. Although he strikes out three times more than he walks, he makes better contact than most sluggers. He had a .292 on-base average and a .487 slugging percentage in 1992. In 1991 at Triple-A Richmond, he batted .260 with 10 homers and 30 RBI. Often used as a pinch-hitter, he can deliver big hits off the bench. Hunter has decent speed but doesn't run much. He's a fine-fielding first baseman.

Major League Batting Register

	BA	G	AB	R	H	2B	3B	HR	RBI	SB
91 NL	.251	97	271	32	68	16	1	12	50	0
92 NL	.239	102	238	34	57	13	2	14	41	1
Life	.246	199	509	66	125	29	3	26	91	1
2 AVE	.246	100	255	33	63	15	2	13	46	1

BRUCE HURST

Position: Pitcher
Team: San Diego Padres
Born: March 24, 1958 St. George, UT
Height: 6'3" **Weight:** 214 lbs.
Bats: left **Throws:** left
Acquired: Signed as a free agent, 12/88

Player Summary	
Fantasy Value	$16 to $22
Card Value	3¢ to 4¢
Will	win 15 games
Can't	avoid gophers
Expect	superb control
Don't Expect	losing streaks

Hurst is a power pitcher with outstanding control. When he pitched an 8-0 seven-hitter against San Francisco last June 25, he fanned a season-high 11 batters and walked only one. Hurst throws strikes with four pitches: a fastball, curve, forkball, and slider. In 1992, opponents compiled a .267 batting average, a .308 on-base percentage, and a .390 slugging percentage. A fine fielder with a feared pickoff move, Hurst also helps himself as a hitter. He's adept at moving runners with well-placed bunts and can also poke base hits—especially with runners in scoring position. Hurst has had past elbow problems, plus problems with management, but he deserves his reputation as a strong clubhouse presence. He was the ace of the San Diego staff last summer.

Major League Pitching Register

	W	L	ERA	G	CG	IP	H	ER	BB	SO
80 AL	2	2	9.10	12	0	30.2	39	31	16	16
81 AL	2	0	4.30	5	0	23.0	23	11	12	11
82 AL	3	7	5.77	28	0	117.0	161	75	40	53
83 AL	12	12	4.09	33	6	211.1	241	96	62	115
84 AL	12	12	3.92	33	9	218.0	232	95	88	136
85 AL	11	13	4.51	35	6	229.1	243	115	70	189
86 AL	13	8	2.99	25	11	174.1	169	58	50	167
87 AL	15	13	4.41	33	15	238.2	239	117	76	190
88 AL	18	6	3.66	33	7	216.2	222	88	65	166
89 NL	15	11	2.69	33	10	244.2	214	73	66	179
90 NL	11	9	3.14	33	9	223.2	188	78	63	162
91 NL	15	8	3.29	31	4	221.2	201	81	59	141
92 NL	14	9	3.85	32	6	217.1	223	92	51	131
Life	143	110	3.85	366	83	2366.1	2395	1011	718	1656
3 AVE	13	9	3.42	32	6	220.2	204	84	58	145

JEFF HUSON

Position: Infield
Team: Texas Rangers
Born: Aug. 15, 1964 Scottsdale, AZ
Height: 6'3" **Weight:** 170 lbs.
Bats: left **Throws:** right
Acquired: Traded from Expos for Drew Hall, 4/90

Player Summary	
Fantasy Value	$2 to $5
Card Value	3¢ to 4¢
Will	show good speed
Can't	turn into slugger
Expect	bunts and infield hits
Don't Expect	quick return to bench

Huson surprised even himself when he turned sudden slugger last summer. Two weeks before Labor Day, he had hit more 1992 home runs than he had in four previous years. With Dickie Thon disabled by a sore shoulder, Huson spent most of the season as the Texas shortstop. He showed good speed, good defensive skills, and patience at the plate. He is a contact hitter who will also wait for walks. He had a .342 on-base average and a .362 slugging percentage in 1992. Huson once led the Double-A Southern League with 56 steals, and he had several 30-steal years in the minors. He was the top runner on the Rangers last summer, when he led in both stolen bases and success ratio. His speed translates to good range, but he sometimes makes careless errors on throws. His defense improved with regular duty, however. Although Huson can also play second and third, his work last season cemented his reputation as a decent No. 1 shortstop.

Major League Batting Register

	BA	G	AB	R	H	2B	3B	HR	RBI	SB
88 NL	.310	20	42	7	13	2	0	0	3	2
89 NL	.162	32	74	1	12	5	0	0	2	3
90 AL	.240	145	396	57	95	12	2	0	28	12
91 AL	.213	119	268	36	57	8	3	2	26	8
92 AL	.261	123	318	49	83	14	3	4	24	18
Life	.237	439	1098	150	260	41	8	6	83	43
3 AVE	.239	129	327	47	78	11	3	2	26	13

PETE INCAVIGLIA

Position: Outfield
Team: Philadelphia Phillies
Born: April 2, 1964 Pebble Beach, CA
Height: 6'1" **Weight:** 210 lbs.
Bats: right **Throws:** right
Acquired: Signed as a free agent, 12/92

Player Summary	
Fantasy Value	$4 to $8
Card Value	3¢ to 4¢
Will	generate power
Can't	curtail strikeouts
Expect	rising average
Don't Expect	speed on the bases

Incaviglia gives the Phils a No. 4 hitter. When he cut down on his upper-cut swing last summer, he reduced his power production but increased his value. Playing in the NL for the first time, the former Oklahoma State University star watched his batting average rise 20 points above his previous lifetime mark of .244. The new, trimmed-down Incaviglia also fared well in left field after yielding the Houston right field job to Eric Anthony. Incaviglia has a strong arm but little speed. He arrived in spring camp without a big league contract but quickly showed he could overcome his strikeout-filled .214 season with the 1991 Tigers. Determined not to let his average fall for the fourth straight year, he decided to go with the pitch rather than try to pull everything. He had a .319 on-base percentage and a .430 slugging percentage in 1992. He hit some key homers, including a first-pitch, ninth-inning shot that beat Pittsburgh 3-2 on July 8.

Major League Batting Register

	BA	G	AB	R	H	2B	3B	HR	RBI	SB
86 AL	.250	153	540	82	135	21	2	30	88	3
87 AL	.271	139	509	85	138	26	4	27	80	9
88 AL	.249	116	418	59	104	19	3	22	54	6
89 AL	.236	133	453	48	107	27	4	21	81	5
90 AL	.233	153	529	59	123	27	0	24	85	3
91 AL	.214	97	337	38	72	12	1	11	38	1
92 NL	.266	113	349	31	93	22	1	11	44	2
Life	.246	904	3135	402	772	154	15	146	470	29
3 AVE	.237	121	405	43	96	20	1	15	56	2

JEFF INNIS

Position: Pitcher
Team: New York Mets
Born: July 5, 1962 Decatur, IL
Height: 6' **Weight:** 170 lbs.
Bats: right **Throws:** right
Acquired: 13th-round pick in 6/83 free-agent draft

Player Summary	
Fantasy Value	$2 to $5
Card Value	3¢ to 4¢
Will	work often
Can't	strand inherited runners
Expect	unorthodox motion
Don't Expect	lots of Ks

Innis has a thankless job. Though he works often and finishes more than two-dozen games a year, he rarely gets saves. A versatile righthander with an unorthodox delivery and rubber arm, he serves as a middle man and a mop-up man—often completing games that his team is losing. He's a sinker-and-slider pitcher who usually fans twice the number he walks, yields less hits than innings pitched, and keeps the ball in the park. Righthanded hitters dread facing Innis because of a "Down Under" delivery that is part sidearm and part submarine. In addition to his two primary pitches, he'll mix in a curve and rising fastball to keep batters guessing. Opponents compiled a .266 batting average, a .348 on-base percentage, and a .357 slugging percentage in 1992. The former University of Illinois hurler doesn't hurt himself on defense or in holding runners close. Including Triple-A, he's worked more than 50 games in each of the past four seasons.

BO JACKSON

Position: Outfield
Team: Chicago White Sox
Born: Nov. 30, 1962 Bessemer, AL
Height: 6'1" **Weight:** 225 lbs.
Bats: right **Throws:** right
Acquired: Signed as a free agent, 4/91

Player Summary	
Fantasy Value	$1 to $3
Card Value	5¢ to 15¢
Will	try new comeback
Can't	show old speed
Expect	home run power
Don't Expect	medical miracle

The odds against Bo's comeback are astronomical, though the 30-year-old out-fielder has beaten longer odds before. After suffering a devastating hip injury in an NFL playoff game in 1991, Jackson missed all but the last month of the base-ball season. Then he sat out 1992 while recovering from surgery to implant an arti-ficial left hip. Doctors suggest that Jack-son will be able to hit again but will be no more than a designated hitter because his old speed will never return. He did have one of the strongest outfield arms in base-ball, though. His hitting may be enough, because Jackson had three straight years of 25-plus homers from 1988 to '90. If hip pain persists, or if Bo is immobilized in any way, he won't approach his old levels. If he plays at all, he'll probably produce lots of double-play balls along with the usual high strikeout totals. Bo trained incredibly hard during his layoff, so if any-one can make a comeback with an artifi-cial hip, it'll be Bo.

Major League Pitching Register

	W	L	ERA	G	S	IP	H	ER	BB	SO
87 NL	0	1	3.16	17	0	25.2	29	9	4	28
88 NL	1	1	1.89	12	0	19.0	19	4	2	14
89 NL	0	1	3.18	29	0	39.2	38	14	8	16
90 NL	1	3	2.39	18	1	26.1	19	7	10	12
91 NL	0	2	2.66	69	0	84.2	66	25	23	47
92 NL	6	9	2.86	76	1	88.0	85	28	36	39
Life	8	17	2.76	221	2	283.1	256	87	83	156
2 AVE	3	6	2.76	73	1	86.1	76	27	30	43

Major League Batting Register

	BA	G	AB	R	H	2B	3B	HR	RBI	SB
86 AL	.207	25	82	9	17	2	1	2	9	3
87 AL	.235	116	396	46	93	17	2	22	53	10
88 AL	.246	124	439	63	108	16	4	25	68	27
89 AL	.256	135	515	86	132	15	6	32	105	26
90 AL	.272	111	405	74	110	16	1	28	78	15
91 AL	.225	23	71	8	16	4	0	3	14	0
Life	.249	534	1908	286	476	70	14	112	327	81
2 AVE	.263	123	460	80	121	16	4	30	92	21

DANNY JACKSON

Position: Pitcher
Team: Philadelphia Phillies
Born: Jan. 5, 1962 San Antonio, TX
Height: 6' **Weight:** 205 lbs.
Bats: right **Throws:** left
Acquired: Traded from Marlins for Joel
    Adamson and Matt Whiseant, 11/92

Player Summary	
Fantasy Value	$5 to $9
Card Value	3¢ to 4¢
Will	search for old form
Can't	avoid disabled list
Expect	continued progress
Don't Expect	repeat of '88

Jackson is the veteran lefty the Phillies have long coveted for their rotation. He was drafted by Florida and traded to Philadelphia in a prearranged deal. He has spent the last four seasons trying to recapture his 23-8 form of 1988. A series of injuries intervened and the southpaw spent much of that time on the disabled list (seven DL stints in three years from 1989 to '91). Not until last summer did Jackson even hint at a successful comeback. He went 4-1 for the Cubs in June, then pitched even better baseball after his surprise trade to Pittsburgh a month later. Pittsburgh pitching coach Ray Miller said Jackson threw harder than any of his other starters. Jackson averages about a hit per inning but manages to keep the ball from leaving the park. His control, however, has failed him on occasion.

Major League Pitching Register

	W	L	ERA	G	CG	IP	H	ER	BB	SO
83 AL	1	1	5.21	4	0	19.0	26	11	6	9
84 AL	2	6	4.26	15	1	76.0	84	36	35	40
85 AL	14	12	3.42	32	4	208.0	209	79	76	114
86 AL	11	12	3.20	32	4	185.2	177	66	79	115
87 AL	9	18	4.02	36	11	224.0	219	100	109	152
88 NL	23	8	2.73	35	15	260.2	206	79	71	161
89 NL	6	11	5.60	20	1	115.2	122	72	57	70
90 NL	6	6	3.61	22	0	117.1	119	47	40	76
91 NL	1	5	6.75	17	0	70.2	89	53	48	31
92 NL	8	13	3.84	34	0	201.1	211	86	77	97
Life	81	92	3.83	247	36	1478.1	1462	629	598	865
3 AVE	5	8	4.30	24	0	129.1	140	62	55	68

DARRIN JACKSON

Position: Outfield
Team: San Diego Padres
Born: Aug. 22, 1963 Los Angeles, CA
Height: 6' **Weight:** 185 lbs.
Bats: right **Throws:** right
Acquired: Traded from Cubs with Calvin
    Schiraldi and Phil Stephenson for Luis
    Salazar and Marvell Wynne, 8/89

Player Summary	
Fantasy Value	$6 to $12
Card Value	3¢ to 4¢
Will	surprise with his power
Can't	show patience at plate
Expect	at least 15 homers
Don't Expect	high average

Jackson gave San Diego a third home run threat in their '92 lineup behind Gary Sheffield and Fred McGriff. Jackson became a power-hitter only a year earlier—after he learned how to handle a steady diet of breaking balls. He would be even more productive if he were more patient at the plate. Jackson fans four times more than he walks and often swings at pitches out of the strike zone. He compiled a .283 on-base average and a .392 slugging percentage in 1992. Because of his speed, the fleet center fielder has good range in the outfield and on the bases. He's rarely caught when attempting to steal but doesn't try often. Last year was the first time in seven seasons that he reached a dozen stolen bases. Jackson doesn't make many errors but is not a great center fielder. He does have an above-average arm, however.

Major League Batting Register

	BA	G	AB	R	H	2B	3B	HR	RBI	SB
85 NL	.091	5	11	0	1	0	0	0	0	0
87 NL	.800	7	5	2	4	1	0	0	0	0
88 NL	.266	100	188	29	50	11	3	6	20	4
89 NL	.218	70	170	17	37	7	0	4	20	1
90 NL	.257	58	113	10	29	3	0	3	9	3
91 NL	.262	122	359	51	94	12	1	21	49	5
92 NL	.249	155	587	72	146	23	5	17	70	14
Life	.252	517	1433	181	361	57	9	51	168	27
AVE 2	.254	139	473	62	120	18	3	19	60	10

MIKE JACKSON

Position: Pitcher
Team: San Francisco Giants
Born: Dec. 22, 1964 Houston, TX
Height: 6′ **Weight:** 185 lbs.
Bats: right **Throws:** right
Acquired: Traded from Mariners with Bill Swift and Dave Burba for Kevin Mitchell and Mike Remlinger, 12/91

Player Summary	
Fantasy Value	$3 to $5
Card Value	3¢ to 4¢
Will	work 60-plus times
Can't	stop steals
Expect	solid middle relief
Don't Expect	return to closer

Jackson was a major addition to the San Francisco bullpen last summer. The rubber-armed righthander has worked at least 60 times five straight seasons. He blends a fastball with one of baseball's best sliders. He has better control than most other power pitchers. Jackson had three times more strikeouts than walks last summer and was among a handful of pitchers who averaged better than a strikeout per inning. Since he also yields less than a hit per inning, he does a good job of keeping his ERA respectable. He's much better as a set-up man than a closer. He was used the wrong way by Seattle in 1991, and he blew eight save opportunities in 22 chances. He was much more effective last year, when he served as set-up man for Rod Beck. A former infielder, Jackson never forgot how to field. But he never learned how to prevent runners from stealing.

CHRIS JAMES

Position: Outfield
Team: Houston Astros
Born: Oct. 4, 1962 Rusk, TX
Height: 6′1″ **Weight:** 190 lbs.
Bats: right **Throws:** right
Acquired: Signed as free agent, 1/93

Player Summary	
Fantasy Value	$2 to $4
Card Value	3¢ to 4¢
Will	play reserve role
Can't	find old power
Expect	aggressive play
Don't Expect	much speed

James did his best hitting of 1992 when he got substantial playing time with the Giants in July. Deployed previously as a fourth outfielder and pinch-hitter, he said he performed better as a starter because he got enough at bats to adjust to the opposing pitcher. In 1992, he had a .285 on-base average and a .375 slugging percentage. Last summer, though, he batted just .189 against righties. James hit 44 home runs over the three-year span he played regularly from 1988 to 1990. He also played well in the outfield, going 140 games without an error for the 1990 Indians. Three years earlier, James was second in the NL in chances and third in fielding percentage. Some scouts suggest he lost his power when he submitted to arthroscopic rotator cuff surgery in September of 1991. The operation certainly did not help his throwing, which was not great beforehand. He is an aggressive outfielder, however.

Major League Pitching Register

	W	L	ERA	G	S	IP	H	ER	BB	SO
86 NL	0	0	3.38	9	0	13.1	12	5	4	3
87 NL	3	10	4.20	55	1	109.1	88	51	56	93
88 AL	6	5	2.63	62	4	99.1	74	29	43	76
89 AL	4	6	3.17	65	7	99.1	81	35	54	94
90 AL	5	7	4.54	63	3	77.1	64	39	44	69
91 AL	7	7	3.25	72	14	88.2	64	32	34	74
92 NL	6	6	3.73	67	2	82.0	76	34	33	80
Life	31	41	3.56	393	31	569.1	459	225	268	489
3 AVE	6	7	3.81	67	6	82.1	68	35	37	74

Major League Batting Register

	BA	G	AB	R	H	2B	3B	HR	RBI	SB
86 NL	.283	16	46	5	13	3	0	1	5	0
87 NL	.293	115	358	48	105	20	6	17	54	3
88 NL	.242	150	566	57	137	24	1	19	66	7
89 NL	.243	132	482	55	117	17	2	13	65	5
90 AL	.299	140	528	62	158	32	4	12	70	4
91 AL	.238	115	437	31	104	16	2	5	41	3
92 NL	.242	111	248	25	60	10	4	5	32	2
Life	.260	779	2665	283	694	122	19	72	333	24
3 AVE	.265	122	404	39	107	19	3	7	48	3

DION JAMES

Position: Outfield
Team: New York Yankees
Born: Nov. 9, 1962 Philadelphia, PA
Height: 6'1" **Weight:** 180 lbs.
Bats: left **Throws:** left
Acquired: Signed as free agent, 1/91

Player Summary	
Fantasy Value	$1 to $3
Card Value	3¢ to 4¢
Will	be extra outfielder
Can't	generate much power
Expect	pinch-hitting duty
Don't Expect	strong outfield arm

James got good advice when he read Hall of Famer Rod Carew's book *The Art and Science of Hitting*. James then applied some of its lessons to his own game. He took a .284 lifetime average into 1992, and he showed last summer that the Carew book helped. After missing a year with a shoulder injury and another with elbow surgery, James began to hit the ball consistently in July. He credited the surge to an exchange of bats. He traded his heavy-barreled model for a smaller, lighter one belonging to teammate Jim Leyritz. James also said he was waiting longer on his swing. A good contact hitter with patience, he walks more than he strikes out. He doesn't have much power but will clear the fence on occasion. James is an ideal fourth outfielder because he can play all three positions. He has good speed and a fair arm, but he will never be a Gold Glover.

Major League Batting Register

	BA	G	AB	R	H	2B	3B	HR	RBI	SB
83 AL	.100	11	20	1	2	0	0	0	1	1
84 AL	.295	128	387	52	114	19	5	1	30	10
85 AL	.224	18	49	5	11	1	0	0	3	0
87 AL	.312	134	494	80	154	37	6	10	61	10
88 AL	.256	132	386	46	99	17	5	3	30	9
89 NL	.259	63	170	15	44	7	0	1	11	1
89 AL	.306	71	245	26	75	11	0	4	29	1
90 AL	.274	87	248	28	68	15	2	1	22	5
92 AL	.262	67	145	24	38	8	0	3	17	1
Life	.282	711	2144	277	605	115	18	23	204	38

STAN JAVIER

Position: Outfield
Team: Philadelphia Phillies
Born: Sept. 1, 1965 San Pedro de Macoris, Dominican Republic
Height: 6' **Weight:** 185 lbs.
Bats: both **Throws:** right
Acquired: Traded from Dodgers for Steve Searcy and Julio Peguero, 7/92

Player Summary	
Fantasy Value	$2 to $5
Card Value	3¢ to 4¢
Will	get some steals
Can't	hit for average
Expect	strong defense
Don't Expect	power production

Javier is a speedy contact hitter best known as a strong defensive outfielder. A solid center fielder who can run and throw, he got more playing time after his trade to Philadelphia last July 2. His hitting picked up a bit but he failed to reach the friendlier fences of Veterans Stadium. He had a .327 on-base percentage and a .314 slugging percentage last summer. Before 1992, Javier had only nine home runs in 1,464 at bats, spread over seven seasons. The son of former big league second baseman Julian Javier, Stan is often called upon to pinch-hit, pinch-run, or serve as a defensive replacement. He has a high success ratio as a basestealer and would have more opportunities if he showed more selectivity at the plate. Javier still strikes out more often than he walks. He's much better against righthanded pitchers.

Major League Batting Register

	BA	G	AB	R	H	2B	3B	HR	RBI	SB
84 AL	.143	7	7	1	1	0	0	0	0	0
86 AL	.202	59	114	13	23	8	0	0	8	8
87 AL	.185	81	151	22	28	3	1	2	9	3
88 AL	.257	125	397	49	102	13	3	2	35	20
89 AL	.248	112	310	42	77	12	3	1	28	12
90 AL	.242	19	33	4	8	0	2	0	3	0
90 NL	.304	104	276	56	84	9	4	3	24	15
91 NL	.205	121	176	21	36	5	3	1	11	7
92 NL	.249	130	334	42	83	17	1	1	29	29
Life	.246	758	1798	250	442	67	17	10	147	83
3 AVE	.258	125	273	41	70	10	3	2	22	13

GREGG JEFFERIES

Position: Third base
Team: Kansas City Royals
Born: Aug. 1, 1967 Burlingame, CA
Height: 5'10" **Weight:** 180 lbs.
Bats: both **Throws:** right
Acquired: Traded from Mets with Kevin McReynolds and Keith Miller for Bret Saberhagen and Bill Pecota, 12/91

Player Summary	
Fantasy Value	$18 to $25
Card Value	3¢ to 4¢
Will	relish leadoff spot
Can't	avoid errors
Expect	very solid offense
Don't Expect	return to second base

After the Mets traded him, Jefferies felt like Atlas after the world had been lifted from his shoulders. Jefferies wasted little time responding to Kansas City. He was AL Player of the Month in June, when he had an 18-game hitting streak, and KC Player of the Month in May, June, and July. He had five RBI in an 11-4 win over Toronto June 19 and his 12th multihit game in 14 starts Aug. 9. That lifted his mark as a leadoff man to .523 (23-for-44). As Labor Day approached, he was leading the Royals with a .311 average, before settling down. He had a .329 on-base average and a .404 slugging percentage in 1992. He is an excellent contact hitter who walks more than he strikes out. Jefferies also adds speed. He makes more errors than most of his third base colleagues but also has more assists because he gets to more balls. His arm is fairly good.

Major League Batting Register

	BA	G	AB	R	H	2B	3B	HR	RBI	SB
87 NL	.500	6	6	0	3	1	0	0	2	0
88 NL	.321	29	109	19	35	8	2	6	17	5
89 NL	.258	141	508	72	131	28	2	12	56	21
90 NL	.283	153	604	96	171	40	3	15	68	11
91 NL	.272	136	486	59	132	19	2	9	62	26
92 AL	.285	152	604	66	172	36	3	10	75	19
Life	.278	617	2317	312	644	132	12	52	280	82
3 AVE	.280	147	565	74	158	32	3	11	68	19

REGGIE JEFFERSON

Position: First base
Team: Cleveland Indians
Born: Sept. 25, 1968 Tallahassee, FL
Height: 6'4" **Weight:** 210 lbs.
Bats: both **Throws:** left
Acquired: Traded from Reds for Tim Costo, 6/91

Player Summary	
Fantasy Value	$2 to $7
Card Value	5¢ to 7¢
Will	kill fastballs
Can't	steal bases
Expect	good power
Don't Expect	great defense

Jefferson never got the chance to make good on his promise last summer. He missed the first half with a severely sprained elbow, then spent the rest of the summer regaining his stroke in the minors. At Triple-A Colorado Springs in 1992, he batted .312 with 11 homers, 44 RBI, 29 bases on balls, and 50 strikeouts in 218 at bats. A slugging switch-hitter who remains a red-hot prospect, Jefferson is a fastball hitter with more power from the left side. He had a .352 on-base average and a .483 slugging percentage in 1992. He had three homers and 13 RBI for Cleveland and Cincy in a 31-game trial during the 1991 campaign. Originally Cincinnati property, he was traded from the Reds in a 1991 waiver wire snafu. During his long minor league apprenticeship, he won one RBI title and also led his league in putouts, assists, and total chances. He does not run well and needs work turning the tough 3-6-3 double play. At his young age, Jefferson should be able to make his mark this season at least in a platoon situation.

Major League Batting Register

	BA	G	AB	R	H	2B	3B	HR	RBI	SB
91 NL	.143	5	7	1	1	0	0	1	1	0
91 AL	.198	26	101	10	20	3	0	2	12	0
92 AL	.337	24	89	8	30	6	2	1	6	0
Life	.259	55	197	19	51	9	2	4	19	0

HOWARD JOHNSON

Position: Outfield; third base
Team: New York Mets
Born: Nov. 29, 1960 Clearwater, FL
Height: 5'10" **Weight:** 195 lbs.
Bats: both **Throws:** right
Acquired: Traded from Tigers for Walt Terrell, 12/84

Player Summary	
Fantasy Value	$22 to $28
Card Value	5¢ to 10¢
Will	make strong comeback
Can't	avoid strikeouts
Expect	power plus speed
Don't Expect	great defensive game

Johnson is happy 1993 is an odd-numbered season, because he is much better in such years (an average of 30 homers and 91 RBI in four odd-numbered years). All Johnson's 30-30 seasons came in odd-numbered years, while his worst years were those with even numbers. Placed in center field for the first time in his career in 1992, he staggered at bat and in the field before suffering a hairline fracture of the right wrist on Aug. 1. The NL's home run and RBI leader in 1991, he is a pull hitter with patience. Johnson hammers righties' pitching. He spent 1991 at third before moving to right field. He has also tried short. He is safest in right field, where he can not only run but also air out his strong but erratic arm without risk of repeating his 31-error season of 1991. The move to center was ill-advised, at best.

Major League Batting Register

	BA	G	AB	R	H	2B	3B	HR	RBI	SB
82 AL	.316	54	155	23	49	5	0	4	14	7
83 AL	.212	27	66	11	14	0	0	3	5	0
84 AL	.248	116	355	43	88	14	1	12	50	10
85 NL	.242	126	389	38	94	18	4	11	46	6
86 NL	.245	88	220	30	54	14	0	10	39	8
87 NL	.265	157	554	93	147	22	1	36	99	32
88 NL	.230	148	495	85	114	21	1	24	68	23
89 NL	.287	153	571	104	164	41	3	36	101	41
90 NL	.244	154	590	89	144	37	3	23	90	34
91 NL	.259	156	564	108	146	34	4	38	117	30
92 NL	.223	100	350	48	78	19	0	7	43	22
Life	.253	1279	4309	672	1092	225	17	204	672	213
3 AVE	.245	137	501	82	123	30	2	23	83	29

LANCE JOHNSON

Position: Outfield
Team: Chicago White Sox
Born: July 7, 1963 Cincinnati, OH
Height: 5'11" **Weight:** 159 lbs.
Bats: left **Throws:** left
Acquired: Traded from Cardinals with Ricky Horton for Jose DeLeon, 2/88

Player Summary	
Fantasy Value	$7 to $11
Card Value	3¢ to 4¢
Will	show super speed
Can't	hit leadoff
Expect	Gold Glove defense
Don't Expect	any kind of power

Before uncorking a 25-game hitting streak last summer, Johnson had been known primarily for his speed and defense. He had a five-year average of .271 with only one home run in 1,492 trips going into '92. That's when the league discovered the other Lance Johnson. Playing with back spasms—the residue of a 1990 expressway accident—he hit .439 during his streak, which ended on Aug. 12. A contact hitter with speed, he legs out infield hits and drops occasional bunts. He also showed more patience and took more walks last year. He had a .318 on-base average and a .363 slugging percentage in 1992. He's topped 30 steals in three of the last six seasons, and he rarely gets thrown out stealing. A standout defensive center fielder, Johnson became a Gold Glove candidate last summer. He has great lateral range and an accurate, though not powerful, throwing arm. He should be just coming into his prime.

Major League Batting Register

	BA	G	AB	R	H	2B	3B	HR	RBI	SB
87 NL	.220	33	59	4	13	2	1	0	7	6
88 AL	.185	33	124	11	23	4	1	0	6	6
89 AL	.300	50	180	28	54	8	2	0	16	16
90 AL	.285	151	541	76	154	18	9	1	51	36
91 AL	.274	159	588	72	161	14	13	0	49	26
92 AL	.279	157	567	67	158	15	12	3	47	41
Life	.273	583	2059	258	563	61	38	4	176	131
3 AVE	.279	156	565	72	158	16	11	1	49	34

RANDY JOHNSON

Position: Pitcher
Team: Seattle Mariners
Born: Sept. 10, 1963 Walnut Creek, CA
Height: 6'10" **Weight:** 225 lbs.
Bats: right **Throws:** left
Acquired: Traded from Expos with Gene Harris and Brian Holman for Mark Langston and Mike Campbell, 5/89

Player Summary	
Fantasy Value	$16 to $20
Card Value	3¢ to 4¢
Will	throw white heat
Can't	conquer wildness
Expect	high K total
Don't Expect	good glovework

Johnson uses his size well. The 6'10" southpaw is the tallest player in baseball history and the hardest thrower. In a 13-strikeout win last Aug. 15, he threw a 102 mph pitch to Kirby Puckett. Johnson threw six other pitches timed at 99 mph during that game. Six days later, he fanned 11 for his third straight double-digit performance. Cy Young Award voters won't give him a second look, however, because he beats himself with walks. He averages more than a strikeout an inning but walks nearly seven hitters per game. Opponents in 1992 compiled a .206 batting average, a .344 on-base average, and a .307 slugging percentage. Johnson doesn't yield many hits or homers but gets frustrated by all those runners. He got into an argument with his manager last May after asking out of a game. That same month, he was disabled when a Mike Greenwell liner struck his elbow. Johnson's repertoire includes a fastball, curve, and change.

Major League Pitching Register

	W	L	ERA	G	CG	IP	H	ER	BB	SO
88 NL	3	0	2.42	4	1	26.0	23	7	7	25
89 NL	0	4	6.67	7	0	29.2	29	22	26	26
89 AL	7	9	4.40	22	2	131.0	118	64	70	104
90 AL	14	11	3.65	33	5	219.2	174	89	120	194
91 AL	13	10	3.98	33	2	201.1	151	89	152	228
92 AL	12	14	3.77	31	6	210.1	154	88	144	241
Life	49	48	3.95	130	16	818.0	649	359	519	818
3 AVE	13	12	3.79	32	4	210.1	160	89	139	221

BARRY JONES

Position: Pitcher
Team: New York Mets
Born: Feb. 15, 1963 Centerville, IN
Height: 6'4" **Weight:** 225 lbs.
Bats: right **Throws:** right
Acquired: Signed as a free agent, 8/92

Player Summary	
Fantasy Value	$1 to $3
Card Value	3¢ to 4¢
Will	try to find 1990 form
Can't	keep ball in park
Expect	lapses of control
Don't Expect	deployment as closer

Jeff Torborg was manager of the Chicago White Sox when Jones went 11-4 with a 2.31 ERA as set-up man for record-setting closer Bobby Thigpen in 1990. Torborg, recalling that Jones set up 32 of Thigpen's 57 saves that summer, was quick to sign Jones for the Mets after the Phillies released him last August. A sinker-and-slider pitcher capable of working often, Jones has been plagued by control problems since coming to the National League in 1991. When he's right, he gets outs on grounders rather than strikeouts. When the sinker doesn't sink, however, he has trouble keeping the ball in the park. He has to fool hitters to be effective. A dismal failure when tried as a closer by the '91 Expos, Jones handles righthanded hitters much better than lefties. He has an adequate pickoff move but is a liability in the field. Fortunately, he doesn't bat too often.

Major League Pitching Register

	W	L	ERA	G	S	IP	H	ER	BB	SO
86 NL	3	4	2.89	26	3	37.1	29	12	21	29
87 NL	2	4	5.61	32	1	43.1	55	27	23	28
88 NL	1	1	3.04	42	2	56.1	57	19	21	31
88 AL	2	2	2.42	17	1	26.0	15	7	17	17
89 AL	3	2	2.37	22	1	30.1	22	8	8	17
90 AL	11	4	2.31	65	1	74.0	62	19	33	45
91 NL	4	9	3.35	77	13	88.2	76	33	33	46
92 NL	7	6	5.68	61	1	69.2	85	44	35	30
Life	33	32	3.57	342	23	425.2	401	169	191	243
3 AVE	7	6	3.72	68	5	77.1	74	32	34	40

DOUG JONES

Position: Pitcher
Team: Houston Astros
Born: June 24, 1957 Covina, CA
Height: 6'2" **Weight:** 195 lbs.
Bats: right **Throws:** right
Acquired: Signed as a free agent, 1/92

Player Summary	
Fantasy Value	$15 to $18
Card Value	3¢ to 4¢
Will	count on changeup
Can't	blaze ball by hitters
Expect	exceptional control
Don't Expect	blown saves

Although he hit age 35 last summer, Jones reacted to his first National League season like a kid with a new toy. Rebounding from a dreadful year in Cleveland, which included an exile to the minors and trial as a starter, Jones inflicted his baffling changeup on NL hitters. Given steady work, he made the NL All-Star team and broke Dave Smith's Houston club record of 33 saves in a season. Jones also throws a fastball besides his change, but he needs ample work to stay sharp. He had appeared at least 50 times five straight years before suffering sporadic use in '91. Used as a starter to get innings, he had a 13-strikeout game after his recall. He spent a decade on the farm before '87. When he's right, Jones strikes out five times more men than he walks, yields less hits than innings, and keeps the ball in the park.

Major League Pitching Register

	W	L	ERA	G	S	IP	H	ER	BB	SO
82 AL	0	0	10.13	4	0	2.2	5	3	1	1
86 AL	1	0	2.50	11	1	18.0	18	5	6	12
87 AL	6	5	3.15	49	8	91.1	101	32	24	87
88 AL	3	4	2.27	51	37	83.1	69	21	16	72
89 AL	7	10	2.34	59	32	80.2	76	21	13	65
90 AL	5	5	2.56	66	43	84.1	66	24	22	55
91 AL	4	8	5.54	36	7	63.1	87	39	17	48
92 AL	11	8	1.85	80	36	111.2	96	23	17	93
Life	37	40	2.82	356	164	535.1	518	168	116	433
3 AVE	7	7	2.98	61	29	86.1	83	29	19	65

JIMMY JONES

Position: Pitcher
Team: Houston Astros
Born: April 20, 1964 Dallas, TX
Height: 6'2" **Weight:** 190 lbs.
Bats: right **Throws:** right
Acquired: Signed as a free agent, 3/91

Player Summary	
Fantasy Value	$3 to $6
Card Value	3¢ to 4¢
Will	work in rotation
Can't	always throw strikes
Expect	ERA over 4.00
Don't Expect	lots of Ks

After recovering from a 1991 elbow ailment, Jones spent last summer as a regular starter for the Astros. Though he's not a strikeout pitcher, Jones can be tough when he has command of his pitches—including a fastball, changeup, and two curves. Lapses of control have hurt him over the years, however. Jones usually yields more than a hit per inning and manages to strike out less than twice the number he walks. Opponents compiled a .258 batting average, a .313 on-base average, and a .403 slugging percentage in '92. He also has a tendency to throw home run balls. He gave up 13 four-baggers in 1992. Pitching half the schedule in the spacious Astrodome has helped him the last two years; he would be less effective if he were on another home field. Jones took a 4.42 career ERA into the '92 campaign and lowered it only a little. He doesn't help himself much as a hitter or fielder, but he does have a decent move to first.

Major League Pitching Register

	W	L	ERA	G	CG	IP	H	ER	BB	SO
86 NL	2	0	2.50	3	1	18.0	10	5	3	15
87 NL	9	7	4.14	30	2	145.2	154	67	54	51
88 NL	9	14	4.12	29	3	179.0	192	82	44	82
89 AL	2	1	5.25	11	0	48.0	56	28	16	25
90 AL	1	2	6.30	17	0	50.0	72	35	23	25
91 NL	6	8	4.39	26	1	135.1	143	66	51	88
92 NL	10	6	4.07	25	0	139.1	135	63	39	69
Life	39	38	4.35	141	7	715.1	762	346	230	355
3 AVE	6	5	4.55	23	0	108.1	117	55	38	61

BRIAN JORDAN

Position: Outfield
Team: St. Louis Cardinals
Born: March 26, 1967 Baltimore, MD
Height: 6'1" **Weight:** 205 lbs.
Bats: right **Throws:** right
Acquired: First-round pick in 6/88 free-agent draft

Player Summary	
Fantasy Value	$2 to $4
Card Value	10¢ to 20¢
Will	try to realize potential
Can't	produce consistent power
Expect	speed in all phases
Don't Expect	Lou Brock look-alike

Jordan made his big league debut sooner than anticipated last summer. Called up as an injury replacement, he performed well in left field, convincing the Cardinals to offer him a long-term contract that mandated he play baseball only. He had been a defensive back for the Atlanta Falcons, where he was a teammate of another two-sport star, Deion Sanders. No sooner did Jordan give up football than he encountered a prolonged big league baseball slump. During his brief big league career, he showed speed and power. He had a .250 on-base average and a .373 slugging percentage in 1992. To stay in the majors, he'll need to get better knowledge of the strike zone and avoid injuries. Heel, ankle, and wrist problems cost Jordan considerable playing time over the past few seasons. At Triple-A Louisville in 1991, he had a .264 batting average, with four homers, 24 RBI, and 10 stolen bases in 212 at bats. He has shown good instincts, good range, and a decent throwing arm in the outfield. Although he had only seven stolen bases last summer, he has speed to burn.

Major League Batting Register

	BA	G	AB	R	H	2B	3B	HR	RBI	SB
92 NL	.207	55	193	17	40	9	4	5	22	7
Life	.207	55	193	17	40	9	4	5	22	7

RICKY JORDAN

Position: First base
Team: Philadelphia Phillies
Born: May 26, 1965 Richmond, CA
Height: 6'3" **Weight:** 210 lbs.
Bats: right **Throws:** right
Acquired: First-round pick in 6/83 free-agent draft

Player Summary	
Fantasy Value	$5 to $10
Card Value	3¢ to 4¢
Will	swing at anything
Can't	throw well
Expect	some homers
Don't Expect	any steals

Jordan is one of baseball's least patient sluggers. He struck out about eight times more often than he walked in '92. He had a .313 on-base average and a .417 slugging percentage in 1992. In 1989, his best year, Jordan had a dozen homers and 75 RBI in 144 games. A first-ball, fastball hitter, he fares much better against lefthanded pitchers. He batted .371 versus lefties last summer and .243 against righties. He lacks both speed and a strong throwing arm but is otherwise capable on the field. His best position is first base, but he got some playing time in left field last summer for the first time in his five-year major league career. Although he is a better-fielding first sacker than John Kruk, who played first for the Phils last summer, Jordan does not deliver the same power or consistency at the plate. Jordan had two errors and 415 putouts in 1992 at first. He homered in his first big league at bat on July 17, 1988.

Major League Batting Register

	BA	G	AB	R	H	2B	3B	HR	RBI	SB
88 NL	.308	69	273	41	84	15	1	11	43	1
89 NL	.285	144	523	63	149	22	3	12	75	4
90 NL	.241	92	324	32	78	21	0	5	44	2
91 NL	.272	101	301	38	82	21	3	9	49	0
92 NL	.304	94	276	33	84	19	0	4	34	3
Life	.281	500	1697	207	477	98	7	41	245	10
3 AVE	.271	96	300	34	81	20	1	6	42	2

FELIX JOSE

Position: Outfield
Team: St. Louis Cardinals
Born: May 8, 1965 Santo Domingo, Dominican Republic
Height: 6'1" **Weight:** 190 lbs.
Bats: both **Throws:** right
Acquired: Traded from Athletics with Stan Royer and Daryl Green for Willie McGee, 8/90

Player Summary	
Fantasy Value	$17 to $26
Card Value	4¢ to 6¢
Will	show off strong arm
Can't	wait for walks
Expect	extra-base power
Don't Expect	outfield misplays

Improved patience at the plate paid off for Jose last summer. Showing better selectivity at the plate, he was NL Player of the Month in May with a .346 average. His 36 hits (in 104 at bats) included four doubles, two triples, four homers, 25 RBI, 15 runs scored, and five stolen bases. He should be a strong candidate for the 20-20 club every year, but playing in St. Louis has hurt his homer potential in the past. Jose is a good clutch performer with extra-base power (his 40 doubles in '91 ranked second in the NL). In 1992, he had a .347 on-base average and a .432 slugging percentage. He's a rifle-armed right fielder whose 15 assists in 1991 tied Marquis Grissom for the National League lead. Jose couldn't dislodge incumbent right fielder Jose Canseco in Oakland, but Jose found his niche in St. Louis two years ago. Because he can run, hit, and throw, he has a bright future ahead.

Major League Batting Register

	BA	G	AB	R	H	2B	3B	HR	RBI	SB
88 AL	.333	8	6	2	2	1	0	0	1	1
89 AL	.193	20	57	3	11	2	0	0	5	0
90 AL	.264	101	341	42	90	12	0	8	39	8
90 NL	.271	25	85	12	23	4	1	3	13	4
91 NL	.305	154	568	69	173	40	6	8	77	20
92 NL	.295	131	509	62	150	22	3	14	75	28
Life	.287	439	1566	190	449	81	10	33	210	61
3 AVE	.290	137	501	62	145	26	3	11	68	20

WALLY JOYNER

Position: First base
Team: Kansas City Royals
Born: June 16, 1962 Atlanta, GA
Height: 6'2" **Weight:** 198 lbs.
Bats: left **Throws:** left
Acquired: Signed as a free agent, 12/91

Player Summary	
Fantasy Value	$14 to $24
Card Value	3¢ to 4¢
Will	play good first base
Can't	find lost power
Expect	solid batting average
Don't Expect	third 100-RBI season

After spending six seasons in California, Wally's World moved to Kansas City last summer. He got off to a hot start, with a .340 average by May 5, before skidding below .300 on June 17. He rebounded in time to collect his 1,000th career hit on July 2. He did not hit with his usual authority for the Royals. Part of the reason Joyner did not approach his '91 homer mark for Kansas City is that his new home park is bigger. He did, however, give Kansas City a steady No. 2 hitter. He had a .336 on-base percentage and a .386 slugging percentage last summer. In 1992, he also provided the Royals with better defense at first than George Brett. Joyner has led AL first basemen in putouts and chances three times and assists, double plays, and fielding percentage once each. He has little speed and range. He's a contact hitter who walks almost as often as he strikes out. Joyner replaced Rod Carew in California and Brett in KC.

Major League Batting Register

	BA	G	AB	R	H	2B	3B	HR	RBI	SB
86 AL	.290	154	593	82	172	27	3	22	100	5
87 AL	.285	149	564	100	161	33	1	34	117	8
88 AL	.295	158	597	81	176	31	2	13	85	8
89 AL	.282	159	593	78	167	30	2	16	79	3
90 AL	.268	83	310	35	83	15	0	8	41	2
91 AL	.301	143	551	79	166	34	3	21	96	2
92 AL	.269	149	572	66	154	36	2	9	66	11
Life	.285	995	3780	521	1079	206	13	123	584	39
3 AVE	.281	125	478	60	134	28	2	13	68	5

DAVID JUSTICE

Position: Outfield
Team: Atlanta Braves
Born: April 14, 1966 Cincinnati, OH
Height: 6'3" **Weight:** 200 lbs.
Bats: left **Throws:** left
Acquired: Fourth-round pick in 6/85 free-agent draft

Player Summary

Fantasy Value	$25 to $32
Card Value	10¢ to 20¢
Will	show good power
Can't	win Gold Glove
Expect	success against lefties
Don't Expect	50-homer season

Worried about his ailing back, Justice did not perform his usual off-season preparation before 1992. Not only did the back buckle again, but the rusty slugger took forever to recover. After collecting 13 RBI in his first 40 games, he came alive in June. He hit .331 between May 29 and July 24 as the team went 35-10. That was before the slugger—plagued by new back and shoulder problems—went into another snooze that sapped his power. A Justice homer was the only Atlanta hit in a 1-0 win over Pittsburgh July 25. A line-drive hitter, Justice walks almost as often as he fans. He hits lefties well, getting a .283 batting average versus southpaws in 1992, as opposed to .243 against righthanders. He notched a .359 on-base average and a .446 slugging percentage in 1992. He has one of the sweetest swings in all of baseball. He runs and throws well but doesn't always hit the cut-off man. Too many catchable pop-ups fall between Justice and his infielders.

Major League Batting Register

	BA	G	AB	R	H	2B	3B	HR	RBI	SB
89 NL	.235	16	51	7	12	3	0	1	3	2
90 NL	.282	127	439	76	124	23	2	28	78	11
91 NL	.275	109	396	67	109	25	1	21	87	8
92 NL	.256	144	484	78	124	19	5	21	72	2
Life	.269	396	1370	228	369	70	8	71	240	23
3 AVE	.271	127	440	74	119	22	3	23	79	7

SCOTT KAMIENIECKI

Position: Pitcher
Team: New York Yankees
Born: April 19, 1964 Mt. Clemens, MI
Height: 6' **Weight:** 195 lbs.
Bats: right **Throws:** right
Acquired: 14th-round pick in 6/86 free-agent draft

Player Summary

Fantasy Value	$5 to $9
Card Value	3¢ to 4¢
Will	stay in rotation
Can't	keep yielding walks
Expect	six strong innings
Don't Expect	strikeout spree

Kamieniecki's best game last summer was one he lost. He blanked Boston for 7⅔ innings before yielding the runs that tagged him with a 4-2 loss. On Aug. 19, he hurled six no-hit innings against Oakland before Jose Canseco tagged Kamieniecki for a home run. He is the holder of a physical education degree from the University of Michigan, where he roomed with Jim Abbott. Kamieniecki did show last summer that had recovered from the back and neck problems that plagued him in 1991. A fastball-and-slider pitcher who also throws a curve and a changeup, Kamieniecki yields more than a hit per inning and walks almost as many as he fans. In 1992, opponents compiled a .269 batting average, a .340 on-base average, and a .379 slugging percentage. At Triple-A Columbus in 1991, he was 6-3 with a 2.36 ERA and three complete games in 11 starts. He also had a better than 3-1 ratio of strikeouts to walks in Triple-A. The former schoolboy shortstop is like a fifth infielder when he's working. His pickoff move isn't so hot, however.

Major League Pitching Register

	W	L	ERA	G	CG	IP	H	ER	BB	SO
91 AL	4	4	3.90	9	0	55.1	54	24	22	34
92 AL	6	14	4.36	28	4	188.0	193	91	74	88
Life	10	18	4.25	37	4	243.1	247	115	96	122

RON KARKOVICE

Position: Catcher
Team: Chicago White Sox
Born: Aug. 8, 1963 Union, NJ
Height: 6'1" **Weight:** 215 lbs.
Bats: right **Throws:** right
Acquired: First-round pick in 6/82 free-agent draft

Player Summary	
Fantasy Value	$3 to $5
Card Value	3¢ to 4¢
Will	nail enemy runners
Can't	hit for average
Expect	occasional power
Don't Expect	patience at plate

When Carlton Fisk fell victim to a foot problem last spring, Karkovice answered the casting call. Of course, he had been waiting in the wings for years. Karkovice delights in displaying the rocket arm for which he is famous. In the five years just prior to 1992, Karkovice erased an incredible 49 percent of the runners who tried to steal against him. He gunned down 32.4 percent in 1992. He's also skilled at game-calling, handling pitchers, and blocking errant tosses—even those thrown by knuckleballer Charlie Hough. As a hitter, Karkovice has some power. He had three homers during a stretch of 10 at bats last June. He can also bunt to move runners along. His bat froze again following a three-year warming trend, however. Karkovice had a .302 on-base average and a .392 slugging percentage in 1992. He has deceptive speed and will pull off an occasional steal; he was caught only four times in 1992.

Major League Batting Register

	BA	G	AB	R	H	2B	3B	HR	RBI	SB
86 AL	.247	37	97	13	24	7	0	4	13	1
87 AL	.071	39	85	7	6	0	0	2	7	3
88 AL	.174	46	115	10	20	4	0	3	9	4
89 AL	.264	71	182	21	48	9	2	3	24	0
90 AL	.246	68	183	30	45	10	0	6	20	2
91 AL	.246	75	167	25	41	13	0	5	22	0
92 AL	.237	123	342	39	81	12	1	13	50	10
Life	.226	459	1171	145	265	55	3	36	145	20
3 AVE	.241	89	231	31	56	12	0	8	31	4

ERIC KARROS

Position: First base
Team: Los Angeles Dodgers
Born: Nov. 4, 1967 Hackensack, NJ
Height: 6'4" **Weight:** 205 lbs.
Bats: right **Throws:** right
Acquired: Sixth-round pick in 6/88 free-agent draft

Player Summary	
Fantasy Value	$16 to $24
Card Value	15¢ to 25¢
Will	hit with power
Can't	avoid strikeouts
Expect	good batting eye
Don't Expect	Gil Hodges clone

The defection of free agent Eddie Murray did not devastate the Los Angeles Dodgers, because they knew Karros could replace him as first baseman and cleanup hitter. At age 24, Karros proved to be a beacon in the Chavez Ravine fog. The 1992 NL Rookie of the Year hit more home runs than any Dodger rookie since Greg Brock had 20 in 1983. Although Karros takes a big swing that results in frequent strikeouts, he has a keen batting eye and will wait out walks. He had a .304 on-base average and a .426 slugging percentage in 1992. The former UCLA All-American has the capacity to hit for both average and power. In 1991 at Triple-A Albuquerque, he batted .316 with 22 homers, 101 RBI, 88 runs, and 33 doubles in 488 at bats. He batted .352 with 18 homers, 78 RBI, 90 runs, and 45 doubles at Double-A San Antonio in 1990. During a four-year tenure in the minors, he twice led his league in hits, twice in doubles, and once in batting. He also led in putouts, assists, chances, double plays, and fielding percentage.

Major League Batting Register

	BA	G	AB	R	H	2B	3B	HR	RBI	SB
91 NL	.071	14	14	0	1	1	0	0	1	0
92 NL	.257	149	545	63	140	30	1	20	88	2
Life	.252	163	559	63	141	31	1	20	89	2

PAT KELLY

Position: Second base
Team: New York Yankees
Born: Oct. 10, 1967 Philadelphia, PA
Height: 6′ **Weight:** 180 lbs.
Bats: right **Throws:** right
Acquired: Ninth-round pick in 6/88 free-agent draft

Player Summary	
Fantasy Value	$2 to $4
Card Value	3¢ to 4¢
Will	field well
Can't	coax walks
Expect	good speed
Don't Expect	home run power

Kelly is an excellent defensive second baseman who needs to hit more to play regularly in the major leagues. With Andy Stankiewicz and Randy Velarde providing more offense and veteran Mike Gallego also available between stints on the disabled list last year, Kelly watched his playing time evaporate. When he does play, he collects more bunts and infield hits than line drives, but he doesn't reach base often enough. The only Yankee regular with a lower batting average last summer was Matt Nokes. An opposite-field spray hitter with lots of speed but little patience, Kelly could improve his value by drawing more walks. He had a .301 on-base average and a .374 slugging percentage in 1992. In the field, he led various minor leagues in assists, chances, and double plays twice each and putouts once. He was drafted as a shortstop, but he was converted to second base in his first pro season. He played third base in 1991. Kelly also stole at least 25 bases in three different minor league seasons.

Major League Batting Register

	BA	G	AB	R	H	2B	3B	HR	RBI	SB
91 AL	.242	96	298	35	72	12	4	3	23	12
92 AL	.226	106	318	38	72	22	2	7	27	8
Life	.234	202	616	73	144	34	6	10	50	20
2 AVE	.234	101	308	37	72	17	3	5	25	10

ROBERTO KELLY

Position: Outfield
Team: Cincinnati Reds
Born: Oct. 1, 1964 Panama City, Panama
Height: 6′4″ **Weight:** 185 lbs.
Bats: right **Throws:** right
Acquired: Traded from Yankees for Paul O'Neill and Joe DeBerry, 11/92

Player Summary	
Fantasy Value	$22 to $27
Card Value	3¢ to 4¢
Will	use good speed
Can't	earn enough walks
Expect	speed plus power
Don't Expect	shoddy outfield play

Kelly is expected to take over center field or right field for the 1993 Reds. He spent the first four months of 1992 as the center fielder of the Yankees, then shifted to left when Bernie Williams was recalled. Although Kelly was not happy with the move, he continued to provide the speed and power that had made him one of the Yankees' best players. A line-drive hitter with power to the opposite field, Kelly hit career peaks with 20 homers and 69 RBI in 1991 even though he was idled more than a month with a sprained right wrist. That showing—which placed him with Jose Canseco and Joe Carter in the AL's 20-20 club that year—gave Kelly a two-year total of 35 homers and 74 steals. He had a .322 on-base percentage and a .384 slugging percentage in 1992. He's rarely thrown out when he tries to steal; he was caught five times in 1992. He is a fine outfielder, with an average arm for a center fielder.

Major League Batting Register

	BA	G	AB	R	H	2B	3B	HR	RBI	SB
87 AL	.269	23	52	12	14	3	0	1	7	9
88 AL	.247	38	77	9	19	4	1	1	7	5
89 AL	.302	137	441	65	133	18	3	9	48	35
90 AL	.285	162	641	85	183	32	4	15	61	42
91 AL	.267	126	486	68	130	22	2	20	69	32
92 AL	.272	152	580	81	158	31	2	10	66	28
Life	.280	638	2277	320	637	110	12	56	258	151
3 AVE	.276	147	569	78	157	28	3	15	65	34

JEFF KENT

Position: Second base; third base
Team: New York Mets
Born: March 7, 1968 Bellflower, CA
Height: 6'1" **Weight:** 185 lbs.
Bats: right **Throws:** right
Acquired: Traded from Blue Jays with Ryan Thompson for David Cone, 8/92

Player Summary	
Fantasy Value	$1 to $4
Card Value	5¢ to 10¢
Will	display more speed
Can't	wait for walks
Expect	best work at second
Don't Expect	lofty batting mark

When the Mets decided that they had little chance of re-signing David Cone for the 1993 season, they jettisoned him for a couple of prospects, including Kent. Although he spent much of last summer filling in for third baseman Kelly Gruber in Toronto, Kent is actually more comfortable at second, where he spent most of his time in New York. He lacks the quick reactions required for a guardian of the hot corner but has no trouble making the double-play pivot at second. In three years in the minors, Kent led his league in chances, double plays, and assists twice each and putouts once. He also led in errors once but only because he reached balls his colleagues couldn't even consider. With eight homers in his 192 at bats in the AL, he showed pop for a middle infielder. He didn't use his speed much last summer, however. When he swiped 25 bases in Double-A in 1991, he was caught only six times. He should show more patience at the plate as he gains experience. He had a .324 on-base average in the NL in 1992.

Major League Batting Register

	BA	G	AB	R	H	2B	3B	HR	RBI	SB
92 AL	.240	65	192	36	46	13	1	8	35	2
92 NL	.239	37	113	16	27	8	1	3	15	0
Life	.239	102	305	52	73	21	2	11	50	2

JIMMY KEY

Position: Pitcher
Team: New York Yankees
Born: April 22, 1961 Huntsville, AL
Height: 6'1" **Weight:** 190 lbs.
Bats: right **Throws:** left
Acquired: Signed as a free agent, 11/92

Player Summary	
Fantasy Value	$10 to $15
Card Value	3¢ to 4¢
Will	find lost control
Can't	avoid gophers
Expect	at least 15 wins
Don't Expect	wild pitches

Key was one of Toronto's biggest pitching heroes in the 1992 World Series, winning two games, including the finale, pitching nine innings, and giving up only one earned run. He didn't have his usual control during the regular season last summer, however. He yielded more than a hit per inning, yielded far too many home runs, and failed to maintain a 2-1 ratio of strikeouts to walks. That was unusual for Key, who usually fans three times more than he passes. During a 74-start span that started in 1989, he threw only one wild pitch. His pickoff move was rated by AL managers as the league's best in a *Baseball America* poll. Key owns a four-pitch arsenal that includes a fastball, curve, slider, and changeup. He's a finesse pitcher. A fine fielder, Key also helps himself by keeping runners close to the bag.

Major League Pitching Register

	W	L	ERA	G	CG	IP	H	ER	BB	SO
84 AL	4	5	4.65	63	0	62.0	70	32	32	44
85 AL	14	6	3.00	35	3	212.2	188	71	50	85
86 AL	14	11	3.57	36	4	232.0	222	92	74	141
87 AL	17	8	2.76	36	8	261.0	210	80	66	161
88 AL	12	5	3.29	21	2	131.1	127	48	30	65
89 AL	13	14	3.88	33	5	216.0	226	93	27	118
90 AL	13	7	4.25	27	0	154.2	169	73	22	88
91 AL	16	12	3.05	33	2	209.1	207	71	44	125
92 AL	13	13	3.53	33	4	216.2	205	85	59	117
Life	116	81	3.42	317	28	1695.2	1624	645	404	944
3 AVE	14	11	3.55	31	2	193.2	194	76	42	110

DARRYL KILE

Position: Pitcher
Team: Houston Astros
Born: Dec. 2, 1968 Garden Grove, CA
Height: 6'5" **Weight:** 185 lbs.
Bats: right **Throws:** right
Acquired: 30th-round pick in 6/87 free-agent draft

Player Summary	
Fantasy Value	$2 to $5
Card Value	3¢ to 4¢
Will	get Ks with curve
Can't	always find plate
Expect	no help with bat
Don't Expect	20-win season

When Kile was sent back to Triple-A Tucson last June, his shoulder was hurting, his velocity was off, and his confidence was shot. But the pitcher returned in August to throw strikes and prove himself sound. Control problems killed Kile early last year, when he couldn't throw the curve—his No. 1 pitch—over the plate. He also throws a fastball and a changeup. Opponents in 1992 compiled a .261 batting average, a .348 on-base percentage, and a .391 slugging percentage. Righties hit .268 off Kile last summer. He found the strike zone in the minors and returned to resume his role in the Houston rotation. He was 4-1 with a 3.99 ERA, 43 strikeouts, and 32 walks in 56 innings at Tucson in 1992. In 1990 at Tucson, he was 5-10 with a 6.64 ERA. Kile is an uncertain fielder but guards rival runners like a hawk. As a hitter, he's inept. He hit a single last April 14 that ended both an 0-for-38 drought and Kile's descent toward breaking Nolan Ryan's Houston club record of 57 at bats without a hit.

Major League Pitching Register

	W	L	ERA	G	CG	IP	H	ER	BB	SO
91 NL	7	11	3.69	37	0	153.2	144	63	84	100
92 NL	5	10	3.95	22	2	125.1	124	55	63	90
Life	12	21	3.81	59	2	279.0	268	118	147	190
2 AVE	6	11	3.81	30	1	139.2	134	59	74	95

ERIC KING

Position: Pitcher
Team: Detroit Tigers
Born: April 10, 1964 Oxnard, CA
Height: 6'2" **Weight:** 218 lbs.
Bats: right **Throws:** right
Acquired: Signed as free agent, 1/92

Player Summary	
Fantasy Value	$2 to $4
Card Value	3¢ to 4¢
Will	seek '90 form
Can't	throw strikes
Expect	more shoulder woes
Don't Expect	winning season

King missed more than two months of the 1992 season with a sore pitching shoulder. Before succumbing to the injury, he failed to pitch well enough to keep his rotation berth with the pitching-poor Tigers. Yielding too many hits, too many home runs, and too many walks left King with the worst ERA on the Tiger staff in the early part of the season. A righthander with a fastball, curveball, and changeup, he allowed opponents to compile a .285 batting average, a .343 on-base percentage, and a .449 slugging percentage in 1992. He has never pitched more than 159 innings in a season. Four stints on the disabled list in as many seasons hasn't done much for his stamina. Never a strong strikeout pitcher, King can't maintain a strikeout-to-walk ratio of 2-to-1. Even in 1990, when he went 12-4 for the White Sox, he failed to fan twice as many men as he walked.

Major League Pitching Register

	W	L	ERA	G	CG	IP	H	ER	BB	SO
86 AL	11	4	3.51	33	3	138.1	108	54	63	79
87 AL	6	9	4.89	55	0	116.0	111	63	60	89
88 AL	4	1	3.41	23	0	68.2	60	26	34	45
89 AL	9	10	3.39	25	1	159.1	144	60	64	72
90 AL	12	4	3.28	25	2	151.0	135	55	40	70
91 AL	6	11	4.60	25	2	150.2	166	77	44	59
92 AL	4	6	5.22	17	0	79.1	90	46	28	45
Life	52	45	3.97	203	8	863.1	814	381	333	459
3 AVE	7	7	4.20	22	1	127.1	130	59	37	58

JEFF KING

Position: Third base; second base
Team: Pittsburgh Pirates
Born: Dec. 26, 1964 Marion, IN
Height: 6'1" **Weight:** 180 lbs.
Bats: right **Throws:** right
Acquired: First-round pick in 6/86 free-agent draft

Player Summary	
Fantasy Value	$4 to $10
Card Value	3¢ to 4¢
Will	play strong defense
Can't	steal much
Expect	15-plus homers
Don't Expect	utility role

A July exile to the minors did wonders to wake up the sleeping bat of King last year. Although he had helped the team by starting at five different positions, his inability to clobber the ball convinced Pittsburgh manager Jim Leyland that the wake-up call was necessary. At Triple-A Buffalo, King batted .345 with two homers in 29 at bats. When he returned, he spent long hours on mechanics with batting coach Milt May. Able to see the ball longer before swinging, King produced immediate results. Playing every day at third base also helped (the Pirates had traded incumbent Steve Buechele to the Cubs for pitcher Danny Jackson). Swinging more aggressively than he had before, King watched his numbers rise slowly from oblivion. He had a .272 on-base average and a .371 slugging percentage in 1992. The former Arkansas All-American is a fine fielder at third base, but is only adequate at second. He has a strong, accurate arm.

Major League Batting Register

	BA	G	AB	R	H	2B	3B	HR	RBI	SB
89 NL	.195	75	215	31	42	13	3	5	19	4
90 NL	.245	127	371	46	91	17	1	14	53	3
91 NL	.239	33	109	16	26	1	1	4	18	3
92 NL	.231	130	480	56	111	21	2	14	65	4
Life	.230	365	1175	149	270	52	7	37	155	14
2 AVE	.237	129	426	51	101	19	2	14	59	4

CHUCK KNOBLAUCH

Position: Second base
Team: Minnesota Twins
Born: July 7, 1968 Houston, TX
Height: 5'9" **Weight:** 175 lbs.
Bats: right **Throws:** right
Acquired: First-round pick in 6/89 free-agent draft

Player Summary	
Fantasy Value	$15 to $22
Card Value	5¢ to 10¢
Will	make good contact
Can't	hit with power
Expect	stolen bases
Don't Expect	sloppy defense

Knoblauch was no one-year wonder. After he won the AL Rookie of the Year Award in 1991, he showed marked improvement in all areas last summer. The No. 2 hitter in the Minnesota lineup, he is a contact hitter with patience. He walks more than he fans, hits well in the clutch, and executes sacrifices and hit-and-run plays on demand. He had a .384 on-base average and a .358 slugging percentage in 1992. He filled a big void when he jumped from Double-A to the majors during 1991 spring training. A converted shortstop, he batted .350 in the '91 Championship Series and .308 in the World Series. Knoblauch's 15 postseason hits shattered the old rookie record shared by Fred Lynn (1975) and Jimmy Sebring (1903). Knoblauch saved game one of the Series with his glove and game seven with a timely bunt. In 1990 at Double-A Orlando, he batted .289 with a couple of homers, 53 RBI, 23 stolen bases, and 74 runs scored. The former Texas A&M player steals bases and handles himself well in the field.

Major League Batting Register

	BA	G	AB	R	H	2B	3B	HR	RBI	SB
91 AL	.281	151	565	78	159	24	6	1	50	25
92 AL	.297	155	600	104	178	19	6	2	56	34
Life	.289	306	1165	182	337	43	12	3	106	59
2 AVE	.289	153	583	91	169	22	6	2	53	30

BILL KRUEGER

Position: Pitcher
Team: Detroit Tigers
Born: April 24, 1958 Waukegan, IL
Height: 6'5" **Weight:** 205 lbs.
Bats: left **Throws:** left
Acquired: Signed as a free agent, 12/92

Player Summary	
Fantasy Value	$6 to $10
Card Value	3¢ to 4¢
Will	win a dozen
Can't	avoid gophers
Expect	hot and cold streaks
Don't Expect	complete games

Krueger goes to Detroit to strengthen the Tigers' rotation. When the Twins put Krueger in the bullpen after a slump, the Expos took a chance on the tall lefty during their pennant chase; he didn't do much for Montreal, however. Krueger had taken an instant liking to Minnesota after the Twins signed him to a free-agent deal at the beginning of the 1992 season. His hot start last year (8-2 and a 2.60 ERA through June) boosted the Twins' early pennant drive. He twirled a two-hit shutout of the Angels on June 30, his first in 116 starts—12 short of the major league record. An intense competitor, Krueger endured several months of alternating good and bad starts. His problems included yielding more hits than innings, throwing gopher balls, and erratic control.

Major League Pitching Register

	W	L	ERA	G	CG	IP	H	ER	BB	SO
83 AL	7	6	3.61	17	2	109.2	104	44	53	58
84 AL	10	10	4.75	26	1	142.0	156	75	85	61
85 AL	9	10	4.52	32	2	151.1	165	76	69	56
86 AL	1	2	6.03	11	0	34.1	40	23	13	10
87 AL	0	3	9.53	9	0	5.2	9	6	8	2
87 NL	0	0	0.00	2	0	2.1	3	0	1	2
88 NL	0	0	11.57	1	0	2.1	4	3	2	1
89 AL	3	2	3.84	34	0	93.2	96	40	33	72
90 AL	6	8	3.98	30	0	129.0	137	57	54	64
91 AL	11	8	3.60	35	1	175.0	194	70	60	91
92 AL	10	6	4.30	27	2	161.1	166	77	46	86
92 NL	0	2	6.75	9	0	17.1	23	13	7	13
Life	57	57	4.25	233	8	1024.0	1097	484	431	516
3 AVE	9	8	4.05	34	1	161.1	173	72	56	85

JOHN KRUK

Position: Outfield; first base
Team: Philadelphia Phillies
Born: Feb. 9, 1961 Charleston, WV
Height: 5'10" **Weight:** 204 lbs.
Bats: left **Throws:** left
Acquired: Traded from Padres with Randy Ready for Chris James, 6/89

Player Summary	
Fantasy Value	$23 to $28
Card Value	4¢ to 6¢
Will	pound righthanders
Can't	steal often
Expect	high average
Don't Expect	home run crown

Kruk spent most of the season leading the NL in hitting before finishing third. A contact hitter who walks as often as he strikes out, he owns an inside-out swing that makes him more likely to hit to the opposite field. He has no trouble against left-handed pitchers and is especially dangerous in the clutch. He had a .423 on-base average and a .458 slugging percentage in 1992. He also hit .330 against righthanders and .314 versus lefties last summer. An NL All-Star squad member in each of the last two seasons, Kruk has 20-homer power. He has deceptive running speed—especially because his physique looks like baseball's answer to Homer Simpson. It's hard to picture him as a graceful fielder, but Kruk is a standout first baseman who also holds his own in right and left field. Kruk has a strong arm and plays well on artificial turf.

Major League Batting Register

	BA	G	AB	R	H	2B	3B	HR	RBI	SB
86 NL	.309	122	278	33	86	16	2	4	38	2
87 NL	.313	138	447	72	140	14	2	20	91	18
88 NL	.241	120	378	54	91	17	1	9	44	5
89 NL	.300	112	357	53	107	13	6	8	44	3
90 NL	.291	142	443	52	129	25	8	7	67	10
91 NL	.294	152	538	84	158	27	6	21	92	7
92 NL	.323	144	507	86	164	30	4	10	70	3
Life	.297	930	2948	434	875	142	29	79	446	48
3 AVE	.303	146	496	74	150	27	6	13	76	7

STEVE LAKE

Position: Catcher
Team: Chicago Cubs
Born: March 14, 1957 Inglewood, CA
Height: 6'1" **Weight:** 199 lbs.
Bats: right **Throws:** right
Acquired: Signed as a free agent, 12/92

Player Summary	
Fantasy Value	$1 to $2
Card Value	3¢ to 4¢
Will	play great defense
Can't	run a lick
Expect	understudy role
Don't Expect	extra-base power

Lake returns to the Cubs as a defensive specialist. He is an outstanding defensive catcher who does not hit for average or power. After carrying a nine-year mark of .238 into 1992, he saw little action behind Philadelphia All-Star Darren Daulton, one of the game's most durable receivers. With 13 homers in 1,005 lifetime at bats, Lake is rarely used as a pinch-hitter when the game is on the line. He's never used as a pinch-runner, since he has one stolen base in his career. He earns all of his money on defense. He's a good handler of pitchers who calls good games, prevents wild pitches, blocks the plate, and relishes the chance to show off his powerful throwing arm. Lake is a singles hitter who's adequate against southpaws but dreadful against righties. Not selective at the plate, he walks about as often as he steals.

Major League Batting Register

	BA	G	AB	R	H	2B	3B	HR	RBI	SB
83 NL	.259	38	85	9	22	4	1	1	7	0
84 NL	.222	25	54	4	12	4	0	2	7	0
85 NL	.151	58	119	5	18	2	0	1	11	1
86 NL	.294	36	68	4	20	2	0	2	14	0
87 NL	.251	74	179	19	45	7	2	2	19	0
88 NL	.278	36	54	5	15	3	0	1	4	0
89 NL	.252	58	155	9	39	5	1	2	14	0
90 NL	.250	29	80	4	20	2	0	0	6	0
91 NL	.228	58	158	12	36	4	1	1	11	0
92 NL	.245	20	53	3	13	2	0	1	2	0
Life	.239	432	1005	78	240	35	5	13	95	1

LES LANCASTER

Position: Pitcher
Team: Detroit Tigers
Born: April 21, 1962 Dallas, TX
Height: 6'2" **Weight:** 200 lbs.
Bats: right **Throws:** right
Acquired: Signed as a free agent, 4/92

Player Summary	
Fantasy Value	$1 to $3
Card Value	3¢ to 4¢
Will	start or relieve
Can't	throw hard
Expect	frequent gophers
Don't Expect	great control

A dozen teams bid for the services of Lancaster when the Cubs cut him last spring. The Tigers won, but then they weren't thrilled with the production they received. He gave up three grand slams in the first half—one short of the record for a full season. He limped into the winter with an ERA above 6.00—hardly what was expected from a pitcher whose five-year mark before '92 was 3.82. Lancaster's problems included more walks than strikeouts, more hits than innings, and the second-worst ratio of home runs to innings on the Tiger staff. Opponents compiled a .294 batting average, a .386 on-base average, and a .451 slugging percentage in 1992. Because he doesn't throw hard, he gets killed when he doesn't have control. He throws a fastball, cut fastball, curve, slider, change, and forkball. He'd be better if he reduced his repertoire and perfected three of those pitches. It's a good thing Lancaster is a good fielder with a good pickoff move, otherwise his ERA would be worse.

Major League Pitching Register

	W	L	ERA	G	S	IP	H	ER	BB	SO
87 NL	8	3	4.90	27	0	132.1	138	72	51	78
88 NL	4	6	3.78	44	5	85.2	89	36	34	36
89 NL	4	2	1.36	42	8	72.2	60	11	15	56
90 NL	9	5	4.62	55	6	109.0	121	56	40	65
91 NL	9	7	3.52	64	3	156.0	150	61	49	102
92 AL	3	4	6.33	41	0	86.2	101	61	51	35
Life	37	27	4.16	273	22	642.1	659	297	240	372
3 AVE	7	5	4.56	53	3	117.1	124	59	47	67

MARK LANGSTON

Position: Pitcher
Team: California Angels
Born: Aug. 20, 1960 San Diego, CA
Height: 6'2" **Weight:** 190 lbs.
Bats: right **Throws:** left
Acquired: Signed as a free agent, 12/89

Player Summary	
Fantasy Value	$16 to $24
Card Value	4¢ to 6¢
Will	lead rotation
Can't	avoid gophers
Expect	lots of strikeouts
Don't Expect	losing record

Given weak support last summer, Langston did not come close to duplicating his fine 1991 season. His strikeout totals declined while his ratio of hits to innings rose. One bright spot occurred on June 18, however, when he became the first Angel to throw consecutive shutouts since Ken Forsch in 1981. Langston is a power pitcher with a fastball, slider, changeup, and curveball. He fans twice the number he walks, and he yields less than a hit an inning. His walk total is too high, and too many of the hits that he gives up sail out of the park. Opponents in 1992 compiled a .242 batting average, a .305 on-base average, and a .343 slugging percentage; he gave up 14 homers. Langston has won three strikeout crowns and earned three Gold Gloves. When he gets into trouble, he helps himself by preventing stolen bases.

Major League Pitching Register

	W	L	ERA	G	CG	IP	H	ER	BB	SO
84 AL	17	10	3.40	35	5	225.0	188	85	118	204
85 AL	7	14	5.47	24	2	126.2	122	77	91	72
86 AL	12	14	4.85	37	9	239.1	234	129	123	245
87 AL	19	13	3.84	35	14	272.0	242	116	114	262
88 AL	15	11	3.34	35	9	261.1	222	97	110	235
89 AL	4	5	3.56	10	2	73.1	60	29	19	60
89 NL	12	9	2.39	24	6	176.2	138	47	93	175
90 AL	10	17	4.40	33	5	223.0	215	109	104	195
91 AL	19	8	3.00	34	7	246.1	190	82	96	183
92 AL	13	14	3.66	32	9	229.0	206	93	74	174
Life	128	115	3.75	299	68	2072.2	1817	864	942	1805
3 AVE	14	13	3.66	33	7	233.0	204	95	91	184

RAY LANKFORD

Position: Outfield
Team: St. Louis Cardinals
Born: June 5, 1967 Modesto, CA
Height: 5'11" **Weight:** 180 lbs.
Bats: left **Throws:** left
Acquired: Third-round pick in 6/87 free-agent draft

Player Summary	
Fantasy Value	$25 to $32
Card Value	5¢ to 10¢
Will	flash fine speed
Can't	avoid strikeouts
Expect	great defense
Don't Expect	patience at bat

After the Cardinals realized last June that Lankford fanned too frequently to bat leadoff, they made him their No. 3 hitter. He responded by becoming the club's top power producer. Though he still fans far too often (about two and one-half times more often than he walks), he has proven valuable in the new role. With Felix Jose following Lankford in the lineup, Lankford gets a steady diet of fastballs—his favorite pitch. In 1992, he compiled a .371 on-base average and a .480 slugging percentage. On the down side, he could accumulate more bases on balls, which would increase the impact of his exceptional speed; if Lankford reached more, he'd run more. He's topped 40 steals in both of his big league summers and has enough power to be considered a dark-horse candidate for the 30-30 club. In 1990 at Triple-A Louisville, he batted .260 with 10 homers, 29 swipes, and 72 RBI. Except for a mediocre arm, he is a strong defensive center fielder who uses his speed to snare possible extra-base hits.

Major League Batting Register

	BA	G	AB	R	H	2B	3B	HR	RBI	SB
90 NL	.286	39	126	12	36	10	1	3	12	8
91 NL	.251	151	566	83	142	23	15	9	69	44
92 NL	.293	153	598	87	175	40	6	20	86	42
Life	.274	343	1290	182	353	73	22	32	167	94
2 AVE	.272	152	582	85	159	32	11	15	78	43

BARRY LARKIN

Position: Shortstop
Team: Cincinnati Reds
Born: April 28, 1964 Cincinnati, OH
Height: 6′ **Weight:** 185 lbs.
Bats: right **Throws:** right
Acquired: First-round pick in 6/85 free-agent draft

Player Summary	
Fantasy Value	$28 to $35
Card Value	8¢ to 12¢
Will	make All-Star team
Can't	escape Ozzie Smith
Expect	MVP bid if healthy
Don't Expect	average to decline

Ozzie Smith may win the annual fan election as All-Star shortstop, but insiders insist Larkin is better as an overall hitter, a baserunner, and even a fielder. After straining his left knee in an April 15 collision with Glenn Braggs, Larkin missed almost a month of '92. He started 74 of 75 games after returning on May 8 and kept the Reds in contention with a .380 late-season spurt. A contact hitter who uses all fields, he also has power. He walks almost as often as he strikes out. His batting average has gone up in each of the last three years, thanks in part to private sessions with Cincinnati batting coach and now manager Tony Perez. Larkin murders lefties and thrives on high heat. He had a .377 on-base percentage and a .454 slugging percentage in 1992. He didn't steal as much last year because of the knee, but he still played strong defense. He has excellent range and a powerful arm.

Major League Batting Register

	BA	G	AB	R	H	2B	3B	HR	RBI	SB
86 NL	.283	41	159	27	45	4	3	3	19	8
87 NL	.244	125	439	64	107	16	2	12	43	21
88 NL	.296	151	588	91	174	32	5	12	56	40
89 NL	.342	97	325	47	111	14	4	4	36	10
90 NL	.301	158	614	85	185	25	6	7	67	30
91 NL	.302	123	464	88	140	27	4	20	69	24
92 NL	.304	140	533	76	162	32	6	12	78	15
Life	.296	835	3122	478	924	150	30	70	368	148
3 AVE	.302	140	537	83	162	28	5	13	71	23

GENE LARKIN

Position: First base; outfield
Team: Minnesota Twins
Born: Oct. 24, 1962, Astoria, NY
Height: 6′3″ **Weight:** 205 lbs.
Bats: both **Throws:** right
Acquired: 20th-round pick in 6/84 free-agent draft

Player Summary	
Fantasy Value	$2 to $4
Card Value	3¢ to 4¢
Will	serve as spare part
Can't	produce much power
Expect	good contact hitting
Don't Expect	any show of speed

Larkin has two claims to fame. He produced the base hit that won the 1991 World Series, and he was graduated from the same university that produced Lou Gehrig. Although both Gehrig and Larkin were star first basemen at Columbia, the comparison ends there. Larkin is, however, a valuable spare part who fills in at first base, right field, left field, pinch-hitter, and designated hitter. A contact hitter who walks as often as he fans, he spent much of 1992 platooning in right field with sophomore Pedro Munoz and filling in for Kent Hrbek at first. The switch-hitting Larkin was used primarily against southpaws because he hits lefties better, although he batted only .218 against lefties in '92. He had a .308 on-base average and a .359 slugging percentage last summer. He's best defensively at first base, though his range is limited by his lack of speed. He has the same problem in the outfield.

Major League Batting Register

	BA	G	AB	R	H	2B	3B	HR	RBI	SB
87 AL	.266	85	233	23	62	11	2	4	28	1
88 AL	.267	149	505	56	135	30	2	8	70	3
89 AL	.267	136	446	61	119	25	1	6	46	5
90 AL	.269	119	401	46	108	26	4	5	42	5
91 AL	.286	98	255	34	73	14	1	2	19	2
92 AL	.246	115	337	38	83	18	1	6	42	7
Life	.266	702	2177	258	580	124	11	31	247	23
3 AVE	.266	111	331	39	88	19	2	4	34	5

MIKE LaVALLIERE

Position: Catcher
Team: Pittsburgh Pirates
Born: Aug. 18, 1960 Charlotte, NC
Height: 5'10" **Weight:** 205 lbs.
Bats: left **Throws:** right
Acquired: Traded from Cardinals with Mike Dunne and Andy Van Slyke for Tony Pena, 4/87

Player Summary	
Fantasy Value	$3 to $5
Card Value	3¢ to 4¢
Will	show strong defense
Can't	steal a base
Expect	opposite-field singles
Don't Expect	any long balls

Although he's formed a lefty-righty platoon with Don Slaught for several seasons, LaValliere could easily hold his own as an every-day big league catcher. A contact hitter who walks twice as often as he strikes out, he lacks both power and speed. He never gets infield hits, nor does he take an extra base on a single. LaValliere is a good clutch hitter, however, and he is hard to defend because he can hit to the off-field. He also provides strong defense; in 1987, he won a Gold Glove. He handles pitchers well, prevents wild pitches, protects the plate against enemy baserunners, and still throws better than most of his contemporaries. Weight has been a problem for "Spanky," but he's kept it down the last two years. At 32, LaValliere remains one of the game's top receivers.

TERRY LEACH

Position: Pitcher
Team: Chicago White Sox
Born: March 13, 1954 Selma, AL
Height: 6' **Weight:** 191 lbs.
Bats: right **Throws:** right
Acquired: Signed as a free agent, 4/92

Player Summary	
Fantasy Value	$1 to $2
Card Value	3¢ to 5¢
Will	work 50 games
Can't	handle all lefties
Expect	Down Under delivery
Don't Expect	high strikeout total

After signing with the ChiSox last April, Leach proved to be a pleasant surprise. The 39-year-old submariner, pitching the best baseball of his career, kept his ERA down to 1.95, second only to Roberto Hernandez among the hurlers in the White Sox bullpen. A sinkerball specialist who has had problems with lefthanded hitters, Leach handcuffed all comers in his role as a middle reliever and set-up man for the Sox. He yielded far less hits than innings pitched and was especially stingy with the home run ball. He does not yield many strikeouts or walks but coaxes ground balls from hitters. When those balls are hit to him, however, he sometimes has problems; his awkward delivery leaves him in lousy fielding position. Not surprisingly, because of all his slow stuff, Leach is easy to steal against.

Major League Batting Register

	BA	G	AB	R	H	2B	3B	HR	RBI	SB
84 NL	.000	6	7	0	0	0	0	0	0	0
85 NL	.147	12	34	2	5	1	0	0	6	0
86 NL	.234	110	303	18	71	10	2	3	30	0
87 NL	.300	121	340	33	102	19	0	1	36	0
88 NL	.261	120	352	24	92	18	0	2	47	3
89 NL	.316	68	190	15	60	10	0	2	23	0
90 NL	.258	96	279	27	72	15	0	3	31	0
91 NL	.289	108	336	25	97	11	2	3	41	2
92 NL	.256	95	293	22	75	13	1	2	29	0
Life	.269	736	2134	166	574	97	5	16	243	5
3 AVE	.269	100	303	25	81	13	1	3	34	1

Major League Pitching Register

	W	L	ERA	G	S	IP	H	ER	BB	SO
81 NL	1	1	2.55	21	0	35.1	26	10	12	16
82 NL	2	1	4.17	21	1	45.1	46	21	18	30
85 NL	3	4	2.91	22	1	55.2	48	18	14	30
86 NL	0	0	2.70	6	0	6.2	6	2	3	4
87 NL	11	1	3.22	44	0	131.1	132	47	29	61
88 NL	7	2	2.54	52	3	92.0	95	26	24	51
89 NL	0	0	4.22	10	0	21.1	19	10	4	2
89 AL	5	6	4.15	30	0	73.2	78	34	36	34
90 AL	2	5	3.20	55	2	81.2	84	29	21	46
91 AL	1	2	3.61	50	0	67.1	82	27	14	32
92 AL	6	5	1.95	51	0	73.2	57	16	20	22
Life	38	27	3.16	362	6	684.0	673	240	195	328
3 AVE	3	4	2.91	52	1	74.2	74	24	18	33

TIM LEARY

Position: Pitcher
Team: Seattle Mariners
Born: Dec. 23, 1958 Santa Monica, CA
Height: 6'3" **Weight:** 205 lbs.
Bats: right **Throws:** right
Acquired: Traded from Yankees for Sean Twitty, 8/92

Player Summary	
Fantasy Value	$3 to $5
Card Value	3¢ to 4¢
Will	try new comeback
Can't	find strike zone
Expect	bloated ERA
Don't Expect	spot in rotation

Some players can't survive the pressure of pitching in New York, and Leary was one of them. Two years after posting a 17-11 record and 2.91 ERA for the World Series-winning Dodgers of 1988, he came to the Yankees in a trade. He then proceeded to lose 39 games in less than three years and finish his Bronx tenure as a bullpen outcast. Leary throws a fastball, curve, forkball, and slider, but he has not been able to control those pitches in recent seasons. Opponents compiled a .256 batting average, a .367 on-base percentage, and a .386 slugging percentage in 1992. He walked nearly twice the number he fanned and threw more than his share of wild pitches last year. When Leary did find the strike zone, enemy batters often found the fences. Leary attended UCLA, not Emory University.

Major League Pitching Register

	W	L	ERA	G	CG	IP	H	ER	BB	SO
81 NL	0	0	0.00	1	0	2.0	0	0	1	3
83 NL	1	1	3.38	2	1	10.2	15	4	4	9
84 NL	3	3	4.02	20	0	53.2	61	24	18	29
85 AL	1	4	4.05	5	0	33.1	40	15	8	29
86 AL	12	12	4.21	33	3	188.1	216	88	53	110
87 NL	3	11	4.76	39	0	107.2	121	57	36	61
88 NL	17	11	2.91	35	9	228.2	201	74	56	180
89 NL	8	14	3.52	33	2	207.0	205	81	68	123
90 AL	9	19	4.11	31	6	208.0	202	95	78	138
91 AL	4	10	6.49	28	1	120.2	150	87	57	83
92 AL	8	10	5.36	26	3	141.0	131	84	87	46
Life	66	95	4.21	253	25	1301.0	1342	609	466	811
3 AVE	7	13	5.10	28	3	156.1	161	89	74	89

MANNY LEE

Position: Shortstop
Team: Texas Rangers
Born: June 17, 1965 San Pedro de Macoris, Dominican Republic
Height: 5'9" **Weight:** 161 lbs.
Bats: both **Throws:** right
Acquired: Signed as a free agent, 12/92

Player Summary	
Fantasy Value	$3 to $6
Card Value	3¢ to 4¢
Will	improve at bat
Can't	reach .300
Expect	strong defense
Don't Expect	extra-base hits

Lee fills a huge gap in the Texas middle infield. According to Toronto general manager Pat Gillick, Lee was the club's biggest surprise in the first half of the 1992 season. Known for his glove rather than his bat, he showed sudden confidence at the plate and drove in some big runs early. By July 19, he had reached 30 RBI—surpassing his '91 total. He concentrated on hitting the ball on the ground, and he also showed better selectivity at the plate. A player who used to swing at everything, Lee hiked his walk total and reduced his strikeouts. As a result, his batting and on-base averages went up, and he even hit some home runs—something he did not do in '91. He steals a half-dozen times a year but has only average speed. A strong glove man, Lee keeps his errors to a minimum. He has great lateral range and a decent arm.

Major League Batting Register

	BA	G	AB	R	H	2B	3B	HR	RBI	SB
85 AL	.200	64	40	9	8	0	0	0	0	1
86 AL	.205	35	78	8	16	0	1	1	7	0
87 AL	.256	56	121	14	31	2	3	1	11	2
88 AL	.291	116	381	38	111	16	3	2	38	3
89 AL	.260	99	300	27	78	9	2	3	34	4
90 AL	.243	117	391	45	95	12	4	6	41	3
91 AL	.234	138	445	41	104	18	3	0	29	7
92 AL	.263	128	396	49	104	10	1	3	39	6
Life	.254	753	2152	231	547	67	17	16	199	26
3 AVE	.246	128	411	45	101	13	3	3	36	5

CRAIG LEFFERTS

Position: Pitcher
Team: Baltimore Orioles
Born: Sept. 29, 1957 Munich, West Germany
Height: 6'1" **Weight:** 210 lbs.
Bats: left **Throws:** left
Acquired: Traded from Padres for Erik Schullstrom and Ricky Gutierrez, 9/92

Player Summary	
Fantasy Value	$8 to $12
Card Value	3¢ to 4¢
Will	show good control
Can't	avoid gopher balls
Expect	starting assignments
Don't Expect	complete games

Before last summer, Lefferts had made five career starts—all as a rookie in 1983. After the arrival of Randy Myers bumped Lefferts from his job as San Diego's closer, however, he had no qualms about trying to fill a void in the front line. He succeeded beyond his wildest dreams, before he was traded to the Orioles for their pennant drive. A fastball-slider pitcher who also throws a screwball, he took a no-hitter into the seventh on June 26 before Cory Snyder homered. Although Lefferts yielded more than a hit per inning and threw his share of home run balls, he won with good control. His immediate future is as a starter. He rings up about two and one-half strikeouts per walk. He keeps runners close and helps himself with his glove.

Major League Pitching Register

	W	L	ERA	G	CG	IP	H	ER	BB	SO
83 NL	3	4	3.13	56	0	89.0	80	31	29	60
84 NL	3	4	2.13	62	0	105.2	88	25	24	56
85 NL	7	6	3.35	60	0	83.1	75	31	30	48
86 NL	9	8	3.09	83	0	107.2	98	37	44	72
87 NL	5	5	3.83	77	0	98.2	92	42	33	57
88 NL	3	8	2.92	64	0	92.1	74	30	23	58
89 NL	2	4	2.69	70	0	107.0	93	32	22	71
90 NL	7	5	2.52	56	0	78.2	68	22	22	60
91 NL	1	6	3.91	54	0	69.0	74	30	14	48
92 NL	13	9	3.69	27	0	163.1	180	67	35	81
92 AL	1	3	4.09	5	1	33.0	34	15	6	23
Life	54	62	3.17	614	1	1027.2	956	362	282	634
3 AVE	7	8	3.51	47	0	114.1	119	45	26	71

CHARLIE LEIBRANDT

Position: Pitcher
Team: Texas Rangers
Born: Oct. 4, 1956 Chicago, IL
Height: 6'3" **Weight:** 200 lbs.
Bats: right **Throws:** left
Acquired: Traded from Braves with Pat Gomez for Jose Oliva, 12/92

Player Summary	
Fantasy Value	$8 to $14
Card Value	3¢ to 4¢
Will	stay sharp
Can't	help himself at bat
Expect	slow stuff to baffle
Don't Expect	control trouble

Not the luckiest pitcher in baseball, Leibrandt has lost two game sixes in two consecutive World Series. But Atlanta followers know that the Braves pennant hopes would have been sorry without Charlie. When he beat Montreal 5-1 with a complete-game four-hitter last Aug. 18, his record rose to 10-4—not bad for a veteran considered to be his team's No. 4 starter. Opponents in 1992 compiled a .258 batting average, a .301 on-base average, and a .351 slugging percentage. A master of control and off-speed deliveries, Leibrandt always pitches around the strike zone. He yields less hits than innings pitched and keeps the ball in the park. Leibrandt doesn't post many complete games or shutouts but always seems to keep his team in the game.

Major League Pitching Register

	W	L	ERA	G	CG	IP	H	ER	BB	SO
79 NL	0	0	0.00	3	0	4.1	2	0	2	1
80 NL	10	9	4.25	36	5	173.2	200	82	54	62
81 NL	1	1	3.60	7	1	30.0	28	12	15	9
82 NL	5	7	5.10	36	0	107.2	130	61	48	34
84 AL	11	7	3.63	23	0	143.2	158	58	38	53
85 AL	17	9	2.69	33	8	237.2	223	71	68	108
86 AL	14	11	4.09	35	8	231.1	238	105	63	108
87 AL	16	11	3.41	35	8	240.1	235	91	74	151
88 AL	13	12	3.19	35	7	243.0	244	86	62	125
89 AL	5	11	5.14	33	3	161.0	196	92	54	73
90 NL	9	11	3.16	24	5	162.1	164	57	35	76
91 NL	15	13	3.49	36	1	229.2	212	89	56	128
92 NL	15	7	3.36	32	5	193.0	191	72	42	104
Life	131	109	3.65	368	51	2157.2	2221	876	611	1032
3 AVE	13	10	3.35	31	4	195.1	189	73	44	103

MARK LEITER

Position: Pitcher
Team: Detroit Tigers
Born: April 13, 1963 Joliet, IL
Height: 6'3" **Weight:** 210 lbs.
Bats: right **Throws:** right
Acquired: Traded from Yankees for Torey Lovullo, 4/91

Player Summary	
Fantasy Value	$3 to $5
Card Value	3¢ to 4¢
Will	keep job
Can't	think about shoulder
Expect	more hits than innings
Don't Expect	pinpoint control

Will the real Mark Leiter please stand up? After winning six straight decisions en route to a 9-7 rookie record with the 1991 Tigers, the pitcher had trouble finding the plate early in '92. At one point, he issued 16 walks in 12⅔ innings. Leiter eventually recovered and boosted his ratio of strikeouts to walks to 2-to-1. He yielded more hits than innings pitched, however, and threw his share of home run balls. Armed with an average fastball, plus a curve, slider, and change, he held the first batter he faced to a .111 batting average. Opponents compiled a .277 batting average, a .342 on-base percentage, and a .415 slugging percentage in 1992. He has overcome serious shoulder problems that sidelined him for three full years, 1986 to 1988. He broke into pro ball in '83 but didn't reach the majors until 1990. In 1990 at Triple-A Columbus, he was 9-4 with a 3.60 ERA, nine walks, and 21 strikeouts in 26⅓ innings. His brother, Al, pitched in the Toronto organization in 1992. Mark should be a decent, not sensational, pitcher in 1993.

Major League Pitching Register

	W	L	ERA	G	S	IP	H	ER	BB	SO
90 AL	1	1	6.84	8	0	26.1	33	20	9	21
91 AL	9	7	4.21	38	1	134.2	125	63	50	103
92 AL	8	5	4.18	35	0	112.0	116	52	43	75
Life	18	13	4.45	81	1	273.0	274	135	102	199
2 AVE	9	6	4.20	37	1	123.1	121	58	47	89

SCOTT LEIUS

Position: Third base; shortstop
Team: Minnesota Twins
Born: Sept. 24, 1965 Yonkers, NY
Height: 6'3" **Weight:** 185 lbs.
Bats: right **Throws:** right
Acquired: 13th-round pick in 6/86 free-agent draft

Player Summary	
Fantasy Value	$3 to $6
Card Value	3¢ to 4¢
Will	ruin lefties
Can't	find the fences
Expect	platoon at third
Don't Expect	fielding lapses

For the last two seasons, Leius formed a right-left platoon with Mike Pagliarulo for Minnesota at third base. At the beginning of the 1992 season, however, Leius manned the position on a full-time basis before Pagliarulo returned from a fractured wrist on July 22. Leius makes his living against lefthanders and has also proven more productive on his home turf at the Metrodome. He hit .314 against lefties and .223 versus righties last summer. He had a .309 on-base percentage and a .318 slugging average in 1992. A contact hitter with little power, Leius smacked an eighth-inning solo homer against Tom Glavine that won game two of the 1991 World Series. He steals a half-dozen bases a year. He really shows his speed in the field, where he has better range than most other third basemen. A converted shortstop, he also has a decent arm and good reflexes. Leius is hoping to get a chance at a full-time position soon. He just has to prove he can handle righthanded pitching.

Major League Batting Register

	BA	G	AB	R	H	2B	3B	HR	RBI	SB
90 AL	.240	14	25	4	6	1	0	1	4	0
91 AL	.286	109	199	35	57	7	2	5	20	5
92 AL	.249	129	409	50	102	18	2	2	35	6
Life	.261	252	633	89	165	26	4	8	59	11
2 AVE	.262	119	304	43	80	13	2	4	28	6

MARK LEMKE

Position: Second base; third base
Team: Atlanta Braves
Born: Aug. 13, 1965 Utica, NY
Height: 5'9" **Weight:** 167 lbs.
Bats: both **Throws:** right
Acquired: 27th-round pick in 6/83 free-agent draft

Player Summary	
Fantasy Value	$2 to $5
Card Value	3¢ to 4¢
Will	play solid defense
Can't	steal bases
Expect	clutch hits
Don't Expect	strong throws

Lemke is one of the best defensive second basemen in baseball. Rated right behind Ryne Sandberg and Jose Lind in the NL last year, Lemke spent most of the season as Atlanta's No. 1 man at that spot. He also filled in at third. Although his playing time was reduced after Jeff Treadway returned from the DL, Lemke gave the Braves more offense than they expected. He hit three homers during a 10-day August hot streak en route to a career high. A contact hitter who walks more often than he fans, he had a .307 on-base average and a .304 slugging percentage last summer. Lemke is subject to sudden hot streaks (he just missed the 1991 World Series MVP Award with a .417 average, .708 slugging mark, and three triples). In the field, he has quick reactions, good hands, and no trouble making the double-play pivot or snaring over-his-head liners. Lemke lacks only speed and a strong arm.

Major League Batting Register

	BA	G	AB	R	H	2B	3B	HR	RBI	SB
88 NL	.224	16	58	8	13	4	0	0	2	0
89 NL	.182	14	55	4	10	2	1	2	10	0
90 NL	.226	102	239	22	54	13	0	0	21	0
91 NL	.234	136	269	36	63	11	2	2	23	1
92 NL	.227	155	427	38	97	7	4	6	26	0
Life	.226	423	1048	108	237	37	7	10	82	1
3 AVE	.229	131	312	32	71	10	2	3	23	0

DARREN LEWIS

Position: Outfield
Team: San Francisco Giants
Born: Aug. 28, 1967 Berkeley, CA
Height: 6' **Weight:** 175 lbs.
Bats: right **Throws:** right
Acquired: Traded from Athletics with Pedro Pena for Ernest Riles, 12/90

Player Summary	
Fantasy Value	$4 to $8
Card Value	3¢ to 4¢
Will	use speed as weapon
Can't	hit consistently
Expect	great range
Don't Expect	extra-base hits

Speed alone should guarantee Lewis a long tenure in the major leagues. A center fielder with a strong arm and enormous range, he also has the makings of a first-rate leadoff man—capable of collecting infield hits, bunting his way on, or coaxing walks. He had .295 on-base average and a .272 slugging percentage in 1992. Any way he gets on first, he is a threat to steal second to get a man in scoring position. He spent much of last year sharing San Francisco's center field job with Mike Felder and Cory Snyder, before the Giants decided Lewis needed more seasoning. At Triple-A Phoenix in '92, he batted .228 with 22 runs scored, nine stolen bases, 11 walks, and 15 strikeouts in 158 at bats. His total of 28 big league stolen bases is impressive for someone who doesn't play every day or hit for a high average. Lewis should enjoy his first full big league season in '93. He'll need to overcome a pattern of quick starts and fast fades.

Major League Batting Register

	BA	G	AB	R	H	2B	3B	HR	RBI	SB
90 AL	.229	25	35	4	8	0	0	0	1	2
91 NL	.248	72	222	41	55	5	3	1	15	13
92 NL	.231	100	320	38	74	8	1	1	18	28
Life	.237	197	577	83	137	13	4	2	34	43
2 AVE	.238	86	271	40	65	7	2	1	17	21

MARK LEWIS

Position: Shortstop
Team: Cleveland Indians
Born: Nov. 30, 1969 Hamilton, OH
Height: 6'1" **Weight:** 190 lbs.
Bats: right **Throws:** right
Acquired: First-round pick in 6/88 free-agent draft

Player Summary	
Fantasy Value	$5 to $10
Card Value	5¢ to 10¢
Will	hammer southpaws
Can't	wait for walks
Expect	better power
Don't Expect	shaky fielding

At age 23, Lewis is still learning. He struggled on both offense and defense last year but made adjustments along the way that improved his performance in both areas. Plagued by frequent errors early in the season, Lewis cut down on his throwing errors by charging balls better—reducing the need to rush his throws. Because of his range, he'll reach balls other shortstops can't—and make more miscues. He has good hands and a strong arm but has some trouble on pop-ups. Lewis also junked a junk-food diet for healthier fare that made him feel stronger at the plate. Late in the season, he had boosted his average above .270 and was showing more punch at the plate. An impatient hitter who won't wait for walks, he spent part of 1992 trying to put more trigger into his swing. If he succeeds, his power should improve. He had a .308 on-base average and a .351 slugging percentage in 1992. In '91, he batted .279 with two homers and 31 RBI at Triple-A Colorado Springs. Lewis was named the Double-A Eastern League's top prospect in 1990.

JIM LEYRITZ

Position: Designated hitter; catcher
Team: New York Yankees
Born: Dec. 27, 1963 Lakewood, OH
Height: 6' **Weight:** 190 lbs.
Bats: right **Throws:** right
Acquired: Signed as free agent, 8/85

Player Summary	
Fantasy Value	$2 to $4
Card Value	3¢ to 4¢
Will	man several spots
Can't	swipe a base
Expect	occasional power
Don't Expect	Gold Glove defense

In the last three years, Leyritz has played every position but pitcher. Signed as a catcher, he was moved to third base when the Yankees wondered whether his behind-the-plate defense would be adequate. He has a very strong arm, but his glove needs work. Leyritz has always made his living as a hitter. He won the Double-A Eastern League batting title in 1989 and topped .300 in two other minor league seasons. He batted .267 with 11 homers and 48 RBI at Triple-A Columbus in '91. He got off to a strong start with the Yankees last year, hitting .320 with five home runs in his first 50 at bats. He compiled a .341 on-base average and a .444 slugging percentage by the end of the season. Used most often in '92 as a righthanded designated hitter, Leyritz started only 18 games behind the plate. He nailed seven of the first 18 runners who tried to steal against him. He also appeared at all three bases and in right field. Leyritz is a contact hitter who doesn't always wait for walks. He does not have much speed.

Major League Batting Register

	BA	G	AB	R	H	2B	3B	HR	RBI	SB
91 AL	.264	84	314	29	83	15	1	0	30	2
92 AL	.264	122	413	44	109	21	0	5	30	4
Life	.264	206	727	73	192	36	1	5	60	6
2 AVE	.264	103	364	37	96	18	1	3	30	3

Major League Batting Register

	BA	G	AB	R	H	2B	3B	HR	RBI	SB
90 AL	.257	92	303	28	78	13	1	5	25	2
91 AL	.182	32	77	8	14	3	0	0	4	0
92 AL	.257	63	144	17	37	6	0	7	26	0
Life	.246	187	524	53	129	22	1	12	55	2

DEREK LILLIQUIST

Position: Pitcher
Team: Cleveland Indians
Born: Feb. 20, 1966 Winter Park, FL
Height: 6' **Weight:** 214 lbs.
Bats: left **Throws:** left
Acquired: Signed as a free agent, 11/91

Player Summary

Fantasy Value............................$5 to $8
Card Value...3¢ to 4¢
Will..provide solid relief
Can't...pose as a DH
Expect.................................at least 60 outings
Don't Expect...........................control trouble

After three uneventful years as a struggling big league starter, Lilliquist found his niche as a reliever last summer. A fastball-and-curveball pitcher, he solved two big past problems: poor location of pitches and an alarming tendency to telegraph what he was about to throw. American League hitters managed only a .187 batting average, a .253 on-base percentage, and a .306 slugging against him in '92. Used as a set-up man and occasional closer by the Indians, Lilliquist fanned more than twice the number he walked and yielded less than five hits for every nine innings pitched. He held the first batter that he faced to a .237 batting average in '92. He also kept the ball in the yard. He had five blown saves, however. The pitcher's big frustration was the designated hitter rule, which kept him from batting. One of the game's best-hitting pitchers, he once homered twice in a game against David Cone. Lilliquist won All-America honors at the University of Georgia.

JOSE LIND

Position: Second base
Team: Kansas City Royals
Born: May 1, 1964 Toabaja, Puerto Rico
Height: 5'11" **Weight:** 170 lbs.
Bats: right **Throws:** right
Acquired: Traded from Pirates for Dennis Moeller and Joel Johnston, 11/92

Player Summary

Fantasy Value............................$5 to $8
Card Value...3¢ to 4¢
Will..go opposite way
Can't...wait for walks
Expect.................................Gold Glove defense
Don't Expect.....................extra-base power

Lind moves to Kansas City to help the Royals shore up their sagging defense. He is in the lineup because he plays his position like an All-Star. With Ryne Sandberg in the league, Lind had never won a Gold Glove until 1992—an oversight that Pittsburgh manager Jim Leyland said was a miscarriage of justice. Although Lind can't come close to Sandberg as a hitter, Lind has better range, greater leaping ability, and the skills needed to turn double plays. Lind's speed helps him mostly in the field because he's not on base often enough to steal. Even when he reaches, No. 8 hitters don't run much. A slap hitter with no power, Lind would be more valuable if he waited for walks. He swings at everything—often hitting to the opposite field. A singles hitter who makes good contact, Lind can bunt or pull the hit-and-run. He didn't do that much in 1992, when his offense fell to its lowest level in his five-year career.

Major League Pitching Register

	W	L	ERA	G	S	IP	H	ER	BB	SO
89 NL	8	10	3.97	32	0	165.2	202	73	34	79
90 NL	5	11	5.31	30	0	122.0	136	72	42	63
91 NL	0	2	8.79	6	0	14.1	25	14	4	7
92 AL	5	3	1.75	71	6	61.2	39	12	18	47
Life	18	26	4.23	137	6	363.2	402	171	98	196
2 AVE	5	7	4.12	50	3	91.3	88	42	30	55

Major League Batting Register

	BA	G	AB	R	H	2B	3B	HR	RBI	SB
87 NL	.322	35	143	21	46	8	4	0	11	2
88 NL	.262	154	611	82	160	24	4	2	49	15
89 NL	.232	153	578	52	134	21	3	2	48	15
90 NL	.261	152	514	46	134	28	5	1	48	8
91 NL	.265	150	502	53	133	16	6	3	54	7
92 NL	.235	135	468	38	110	14	1	0	39	3
Life	.255	779	2816	292	717	111	23	8	249	50
3 AVE	.254	146	495	46	126	19	4	1	47	6

PAT LISTACH

Position: Shortstop; second base
Team: Milwaukee Brewers
Born: Sept. 12, 1967 Natchitoches, LA
Height: 5'9" **Weight:** 170 lbs.
Bats: right **Throws:** right
Acquired: Fifth-round pick in 6/88 free-agent draft

Player Summary	
Fantasy Value	$15 to $24
Card Value	10¢ to 25¢
Will	steal often
Can't	hit homers
Expect	steady job
Don't Expect	weak defense

Listach won Milwaukee's shortstop job last spring after Bill Spiers underwent back surgery. By the end of the season, Listach won the AL Rookie of the Year Award by spurring the previously sleepy Brewers into a pennant race. He ranked No. 2 among the league leaders in stolen bases, trailing only Cleveland's Kenny Lofton, whom Listach beat out for ROY honors. Listach relies on savvy rather than speed to get his swipes. He became a leadoff man when Milwaukee moved Paul Molitor down to the No. 3 spot. Listach pumped the veteran Molitor for information, then applied the lessons. Listach compiled a .352 on-base average and a .349 slugging percentage last summer. After spending his minor league career at second, Listach made a smooth transition to short and showed good range. In 1991 at Triple-A Denver, he batted .252 with 51 runs scored, 45 bases on balls, 23 swipes in 286 at bats. He had a .253 average with 40 runs, 25 walks, and 14 stolen bases at Double-A El Paso that year. Listach was not considered a prospect before spring training in 1992, and he did not start the season in the bigs.

Major League Batting Register

	BA	G	AB	R	H	2B	3B	HR	RBI	SB
92 AL	.290	149	579	93	168	19	6	1	47	54
Life	.290	149	579	93	168	19	6	1	47	54

GREG LITTON

Position: Infield
Team: San Francisco Giants
Born: July 13, 1964 New Orleans, LA
Height: 6' **Weight:** 190 lbs.
Bats: right **Throws:** right
Acquired: First-round pick in 1/84 free-agent draft

Player Summary	
Fantasy Value	$1 to $2
Card Value	3¢ to 4¢
Will	play anywhere
Can't	provide punch
Expect	seat on bench
Don't Expect	stolen bases

Because of his versatility, Litton is a perfect utility man. A natural second baseman, he played all nine positions for the Giants against the Twins in the 1991 Hall of Fame Game, the only man ever to play all nine positions in the Cooperstown classic. Litton has filled in at all nine during the last two seasons. He led two minor leagues in fielding during his career, and he had a .992 fielding average in the big leagues in 1992 at second base. Though he's not known for his bat, he hit a two-run pinch-homer against Oakland's Gene Nelson in the 1989 World Series. Litton's bat is usually not so explosive. In 1992, he had a .285 on-base percentage and a .350 slugging percentage. He had a .255 batting average against lefties last year, while batting .215 against righthanders. His light hitting and periodic knee problems have resulted in returns to the minors four straight summers. He batted .306 with four homers and 19 RBI at Triple-A Phoenix in 1992.

Major League Batting Register

	BA	G	AB	R	H	2B	3B	HR	RBI	SB
89 NL	.252	71	143	12	36	5	3	4	17	0
90 NL	.245	93	204	17	50	9	1	1	24	1
91 NL	.181	59	127	13	23	7	1	1	15	0
92 NL	.229	68	140	9	32	5	0	4	15	0
Life	.230	291	614	51	141	26	5	10	71	1

SCOTT LIVINGSTONE

Position: Third base
Team: Detroit Tigers
Height: 6′ **Weight:** 190 lbs.
Bats: left **Throws:** right
Acquired: Second-round pick in 6/88 free-agent draft

Player Summary	
Fantasy Value	$4 to $7
Card Value	3¢ to 4¢
Will	stroke line drives
Can't	produce with power
Expect	good contact hitting
Don't Expect	any kind of speed

Though he doesn't produce the power expected from his position, Livingstone plays every day because he rarely strikes out. A contact hitter in a sea of strikeout-prone Tiger sluggers last summer, he started the season in a lefty-righty platoon with Skeeter Barnes but soon won the job outright. Livingstone got an unwanted assist from Alan Trammell's broken ankle, which forced Travis Fryman to shift from third to shortstop in May. A lefthanded hitter with little patience to wait for walks, Livingstone hits line drives to all fields. He's especially good at poking two-out safeties with runners in scoring position. He had a .319 on-base average and a .376 slugging percentage in 1992. When the Tigers called him up in 1991, he was leading the Triple-A International League in RBI. He batted .302 at Toledo that year, with three homers and 62 RBI. Livingstone holds the Southwest Conference record with 50 college homers for Texas A&M, but that power now seems dormant. The former All-American does carry a capable glove, however.

Major League Batting Register

	BA	G	AB	R	H	2B	3B	HR	RBI	SB
91 AL	.291	44	127	19	37	5	0	2	11	2
92 AL	.282	117	354	43	100	21	0	4	46	1
Life	.285	161	481	62	137	26	0	6	57	3

KENNY LOFTON

Position: Outfield
Team: Cleveland Indians
Born: May 31, 1967 East Chicago, IN
Height: 6′ **Weight:** 180 lbs.
Bats: left **Throws:** left
Acquired: Traded from Astros with Dave Rohde for Willie Blair and Eddie Taubensee, 12/91

Player Summary	
Fantasy Value	$15 to $20
Card Value	20¢ to 30¢
Will	run rivals ragged
Can't	clear the fences
Expect	patience at plate
Don't Expect	lapses on defense

Like Pat Listach, who beat him out for AL Rookie of the Year honors last summer, Lofton smashed the old AL mark for steals by a rookie. Managers polled by *Baseball America* named Lofton the AL's best bunter and fastest baserunner. On Aug. 3, only a single stopped him from hitting for the cycle against the Yankees. Lofton went 3-for-4 with three runs, three RBI, a stolen base, and a spectacular catch in center field. He had a .362 on-base average and a .365 slugging percentage in 1992. He stole 66 bases and was caught only 12 times. Long sessions with baserunning coach Dave Nelson speeded Lofton's learning process on the basepaths. To complicate things for opposing pitchers, he is a contact hitter who walks more than he fans and bunts for hits. The former University of Arizona basketball point guard led the Triple-A Pacific Coast League in 1991 with 545 at bats, 168 hits, and 17 triples. He also batted .308 with two homers, 50 RBI, and 40 stolen bases that year, while leading loop outfielders with 308 putouts and 27 assists.

Major League Batting Register

	BA	G	AB	R	H	2B	3B	HR	RBI	SB
91 NL	.203	20	74	9	15	1	0	0	0	2
92 AL	.285	148	576	96	164	15	8	5	42	66
Life	.275	168	650	105	179	16	8	5	42	68

KEVIN MAAS

Position: Designated hitter; first base
Team: New York Yankees
Born: Jan. 20, 1965 Castro Valley, CA
Height: 6'3" **Weight:** 205 lbs.
Bats: left **Throws:** left
Acquired: 22nd-round pick in 6/86 free-agent draft

Player Summary	
Fantasy Value	$10 to $15
Card Value	3¢ to 4¢
Will	show some power
Can't	handle lefthanders
Expect	some play at first
Don't Expect	return to rookie form

Maas broke into the big leagues like Babe Ruth in 1990, before back problems led to a quick fade over the two subsequent seasons. Maas hit his first homer against Bret Saberhagen on July 4, then went on a tear, setting the record for fewest at bats from the beginning of a career (77) needed to reach 10 homers and fewest (133) needed for 15. He outhomered all rookies but NL Rookie of the Year David Justice. A year later, Maas managed 23 homers but his average fell and strikeouts rose. He worked to make better contact last year but served only as a platoon designated hitter against righthanded pitchers. He had a .305 on-base average and a .406 slugging percentage in 1992. A graduate of the University of California at Berkeley, Maas can also play first, where he is just adequate. There has been some thought of making him a platoon outfielder, but he was not a good player there in the past. He strikes out twice as much as he walks and adds little speed.

Major League Batting Register

	BA	G	AB	R	H	2B	3B	HR	RBI	SB
90 AL	.252	79	254	42	64	9	0	21	41	1
91 AL	.220	148	500	69	110	14	1	23	63	5
92 AL	.248	98	286	35	71	12	0	11	35	3
Life	.236	325	1040	146	245	35	1	55	139	9
3 AVE	.236	108	347	49	82	12	0	18	46	3

MIKE MACFARLANE

Position: Catcher
Team: Kansas City Royals
Born: April 12, 1964 Stockton, CA
Height: 6'1" **Weight:** 200 lbs.
Bats: right **Throws:** right
Acquired: Fourth-round pick in 6/85 free-agent draft

Player Summary	
Fantasy Value	$10 to $14
Card Value	3¢ to 4¢
Will	hit homers in spurts
Can't	nail basestealers
Expect	extra-base hits
Don't Expect	any hint of speed

While watching TV, Macfarlane noticed Darren Daulton relax while batting. The light bulb went on. Macfarlane had an August home run spree that included six circuit clouts in 10 days. By Aug. 24, Macfarlane had matched his previous single-season high of 13 homers. His month-long spurt included a .276 average and seven homers in 58 at bats. Overall, however, Macfarlane struggled to reach .234 because he struck out three times more often than he walked. When he connected, extra-base hits were often the result; only 32 of his first 68 hits were singles. A fastball hitter who tries to pull everything, Macfarlane hits lefties well but suffers against off-speed stuff. He had a .310 on-base average and a .445 slugging percentage in 1992. He nailed only 29.5 percent of those who tried to steal against him last year. Overall, however, he is a sound receiver whose strength is blocking the plate. He does not possess any running speed.

Major League Batting Register

	BA	G	AB	R	H	2B	3B	HR	RBI	SB
87 AL	.211	8	19	0	4	1	0	0	3	0
88 AL	.265	70	211	25	56	15	0	4	26	0
89 AL	.223	69	157	13	35	6	0	2	19	0
90 AL	.255	124	400	37	102	24	4	6	58	1
91 AL	.277	84	267	34	74	18	2	13	41	1
92 AL	.234	129	402	51	94	28	3	17	48	1
Life	.251	484	1456	160	365	92	9	42	195	3
3 AVE	.253	112	356	41	90	23	3	12	49	1

SHANE MACK

Position: Outfield
Team: Minnesota Twins
Born: Dec. 7, 1963 Los Angeles, CA
Height: 6' **Weight:** 190 lbs.
Bats: right **Throws:** right
Acquired: Drafted from Padres, 12/89

Player Summary

Fantasy Value	$18 to $25
Card Value	3¢ to 6¢
Will	kill lefthanders
Can't	learn art of stealing
Expect	hot second half
Don't Expect	defensive lapses

Mack's sessions with Minnesota hitting coach Terry Crowley obviously helped, because Mack uncorked a 22-game hitting streak after the coach shortened his stroke. Mack has blossomed into one of baseball's best outfielders. He had a .394 on-base average and a .467 slugging percentage in 1992. Although he once had 16 straight hits as a high school shortstop, the former UCLA All-American and 1984 U.S. Olympic team performer struggled during a five-year tenure in the San Diego farm system. Left unprotected after 1989 elbow surgery, Mack came to Minnesota in the Rule 5 draft. During his time with the Twins, he's evolved from an opposite-field singles hitter into a home run threat who can turn on the ball. He is as effective against righties as lefties. Although Mack has good speed, he's caught stealing too often. He was nailed 14 times in his 40 attempts in 1992. He's a fine left fielder with good range and a decent arm.

GREG MADDUX

Position: Pitcher
Team: Atlanta Braves
Born: April 14, 1966 San Angelo, TX
Height: 6' **Weight:** 170 lbs.
Bats: right **Throws:** right
Acquired: Signed as a free agent, 12/92

Player Summary

Fantasy Value	$28 to $35
Card Value	5¢ to 8¢
Will	keep club in game
Can't	complete every game
Expect	self-help with bat
Don't Expect	Gold Glove to tarnish

Maddux joins the best rotation in baseball. With the Cubs, he finally received some of his due when he won the NL Cy Young Award in 1992. He is a control pitcher who rarely misses a start. The No. 1 starter for the Cubs over the past five seasons, he has never won less than 15 games (the only other Cub starter to do that in the last 50 years was Ferguson Jenkins). Maddux allowed opponents to compile a .210 batting average, a .272 on-base percentage, and a .279 slugging percentage last year. He usually ranks among the league leaders in strikeouts (he was third in '92)—even though he insists he is not a power pitcher. He owns a powerful arsenal that includes a fastball, split-fingered fastball, slider, curveball, and circle-change (his best pitch). With all those pitches working, Maddux played the best baseball of his career in 1992. He swings the bat very well and is such a fine fielder that he has won three Gold Gloves.

Major League Batting Register

	BA	G	AB	R	H	2B	3B	HR	RBI	SB
87 NL	.239	105	238	28	57	11	3	4	25	4
88 NL	.244	56	119	13	29	3	0	0	12	5
90 AL	.326	125	313	50	102	10	4	8	44	13
91 AL	.310	143	442	79	137	27	8	18	74	13
92 AL	.315	156	600	101	189	31	6	16	75	26
Life	.300	585	1712	271	514	82	21	46	230	61
3 AVE	.316	141	452	77	143	23	6	14	64	17

Major League Pitching Register

	W	L	ERA	G	CG	IP	H	ER	BB	SO
86 NL	2	4	5.52	6	1	31.0	44	19	11	20
87 NL	6	14	5.61	30	1	155.2	181	97	74	101
88 NL	18	8	3.18	34	9	249.0	230	88	81	140
89 NL	19	12	2.95	35	7	238.1	222	78	82	135
90 NL	15	15	3.46	35	8	237.0	242	91	71	144
91 NL	15	11	3.35	37	7	263.0	232	98	66	198
92 NL	20	11	2.18	35	9	268.0	201	65	70	199
Life	95	75	3.35	212	42	1442.0	1352	536	455	937
3 AVE	17	12	2.98	36	8	256.0	225	85	69	180

MIKE MADDUX

Position: Pitcher
Team: New York Mets
Born: Aug. 27, 1961 Dayton, OH
Height: 6'2" **Weight:** 180 lbs.
Bats: right **Throws:** right
Acquired: Traded from Padres for Roger Mason and Mike Freitas, 12/92

Player Summary	
Fantasy Value	$3 to $5
Card Value	3¢ to 4¢
Will	give quality relief
Can't	ditch Greg's shadow
Expect	less hits than innings
Don't Expect	bouts of wildness

Cy Young Award winner Greg Maddux's older brother Mike was San Diego's most effective righthanded reliever last summer. Like his sibling, Mike is a righthanded control pitcher who yields less hits than innings pitched and keeps the ball in the park. A curveball specialist who also throws a fastball and a slider, he fans almost three times as many batters as he walks. Given a chance to close a few games when Randy Myers was struggling last summer, Maddux managed to post enough saves to rank second on the San Diego staff. Opponents compiled a .210 batting average, a .272 on-base percentage, and a .279 slugging percentage in 1992. Once a victim of wobbly control, he conquered the problem in '91 while working in a career-high 64 games for the Padres. Like his brother, he helps himself with his fielding. His pickoff move is mediocre, however, and he's not much of a hitter.

Major League Pitching Register

	W	L	ERA	G	S	IP	H	ER	BB	SO
86 NL	3	7	5.42	16	0	78.0	88	47	34	44
87 NL	2	0	2.65	7	0	17.0	17	5	5	15
88 NL	4	3	3.76	25	0	88.2	91	37	34	59
89 NL	1	3	5.15	16	1	43.2	52	25	14	26
90 NL	0	1	6.53	11	0	20.2	24	15	4	11
91 NL	7	2	2.46	64	5	98.2	78	27	27	57
92 NL	2	2	2.37	50	5	79.2	71	21	24	60
Life	19	18	3.74	189	11	426.1	421	177	142	272
2 AVE	5	2	2.42	57	5	89.2	75	24	26	59

DAVE MAGADAN

Position: Third base
Team: Florida Marlins
Born: Sept. 30, 1962 Tampa, FL
Height: 6'3" **Weight:** 195 lbs.
Bats: left **Throws:** right
Acquired: Signed as a free agent, 12/92

Player Summary	
Fantasy Value	$5 to $8
Card Value	3¢ to 4¢
Will	post high average
Can't	add speed to lineup
Expect	line-drive singles
Don't Expect	great fielding

Magadan moves to the Marlins to patrol the hot corner. Third basemen generally produce more power than Magadan. A contact hitter who hits line-drive singles, he moved to third last spring after the Mets signed free-agent first baseman Eddie Murray. Magadan spent the early part of the campaign in a lefty-righty platoon with Bill Pecota, then won the job full-time with steady hitting that boosted his average to a team-best .283. On Aug. 8, however, Magadan was sidelined when he was struck on the wrist by a ball thrown by Rey Sanchez. The fractured wrist curtailed a season in which Magadan walked more than he fanned but delivered only 13 extra-base hits, along with 78 singles. He had a .390 on-base percentage and a .346 slugging percentage in 1992. He has little speed. He plays best defensively at first, where he led the NL in fielding percentage in 1990. At third, however, he ranked near the bottom in that department (.941) last season.

Major League Batting Register

	BA	G	AB	R	H	2B	3B	HR	RBI	SB
86 NL	.444	10	18	3	8	0	0	0	3	0
87 NL	.318	85	192	21	61	13	1	3	24	0
88 NL	.277	112	314	39	87	15	0	1	35	0
89 NL	.286	127	374	47	107	22	3	4	41	1
90 NL	.328	144	451	74	148	28	6	6	72	2
91 NL	.258	124	418	58	108	23	0	4	51	1
92 NL	.283	99	321	33	91	9	1	3	28	1
Life	.292	701	2088	275	610	110	11	21	254	5
3 AVE	.292	122	397	55	116	20	2	4	50	1

JOE MAGRANE

Position: Pitcher
Team: St. Louis Cardinals
Born: July 2, 1964 Des Moines, IA
Height: 6'6" **Weight:** 230 lbs.
Bats: right **Throws:** left
Acquired: First-round pick in 6/85 free-agent draft

Player Summary

Fantasy Value	$2 to $4
Card Value	3¢ to 4¢
Will	hit comeback trail
Can't	baby his elbow
Expect	good control
Don't Expect	lots of strikeouts

Though he's only 28, Magrane must feel a lot older. The former pitching ace of the St. Louis Cardinals has spent the last two seasons on the sidelines battling to come back from elbow surgery. A control pitcher who once led the National League in ERA, Magrane won 28 games in the two seasons immediately before his injury. A fastball-slider pitcher who also throws a curve, he fans twice as many hitters as he walks and yields less hits than innings pitched. Last summer, opponents compiled a .279 batting average, a .364 on-base percentage, and a .385 slugging percentage. He is not a strikeout pitcher but usually has little trouble keeping men off base. Those who reach often fall victim to his fine pickoff move—one of the game's best. Magrane is a fine fielder and even swings a solid bat. He's sometimes used as a pinch-hitter. Should he stage a full comeback in 1993, he could win more than 15 games. His return would be a major boost to the Cardinals' pennant hopes.

Major League Pitching Register

	W	L	ERA	G	CG	IP	H	ER	BB	SO
87 NL	9	7	3.54	27	4	170.1	157	67	60	101
88 NL	5	9	2.18	24	4	165.1	133	40	51	100
89 NL	18	9	2.91	34	9	234.2	219	76	72	127
90 NL	10	17	3.59	31	3	203.1	204	81	59	100
92 NL	1	2	4.02	5	0	31.1	34	14	15	20
Life	43	44	3.11	121	20	805.0	747	278	257	448

PAT MAHOMES

Position: Pitcher
Team: Minnesota Twins
Born: Aug. 9, 1970 Bryan, TX
Height: 6'1" **Weight:** 175 lbs.
Bats: right **Throws:** right
Acquired: Sixth-round pick in 6/88 free-agent draft

Player Summary

Fantasy Value	$3 to $7
Card Value	5¢ to 10¢
Will	reclaim rotation job
Can't	get by with heater
Expect	lapses of control
Don't Expect	embarrassing ERA

Control trouble ended Mahomes's first major league tour last summer. After beating out Willie Banks to win Minnesota's No. 5 starting job during spring training, Mahomes found it hard to cope with his erratic work schedule. Bypassed when the team had off days or rainouts, he couldn't keep sharp. He had a 3-2 record but inflated 5.23 ERA early in the season before getting his return ticket to Triple-A Portland. By the end of the year, opponents compiled a .279 batting average, a .364 on-base average, and a .439 slugging percentage. Guilty of relying too much on his fastball in the majors, Mahomes became more of a pitcher after returning to Portland. Mixing a curveball and a changeup with his newly developed slider helped Mahomes keep batters off balance. He recovered both his control and his confidence. He was 9-5 with a 3.41 ERA, three complete games, 43 walks, and 87 Ks in 111 innings pitched at Portland last year. At 22, he's expected to make a strong bid to rejoin the varsity rotation in 1993. He's still considered a major prospect.

Major League Pitching Register

	W	L	ERA	G	CG	IP	H	ER	BB	SO
92 AL	3	4	5.04	14	0	69.2	73	39	37	44
Life	3	4	5.04	14	0	69.2	73	39	37	44

CANDY MALDONADO

Position: Outfield
Team: Chicago Cubs
Born: Sept. 5, 1960 Humacao, Puerto Rico
Height: 6′ **Weight:** 195 lbs.
Bats: right **Throws:** right
Acquired: Signed as a free agent, 12/92

Player Summary	
Fantasy Value	$8 to $12
Card Value	3¢ to 4¢
Will	enjoy hot streaks
Can't	steal a base
Expect	power if he plays
Don't Expect	great range

Maldonado moves to Wrigley's friendly confines. He drove a game-winning, two-out, ninth-inning RBI single for the Blue Jays to win game three of the '92 World Series. After opening the season as Toronto's fourth outfielder, he got an immediate break when heralded rookie Derek Bell broke his wrist on Opening Day. Given a chance, Maldonado responded with his usual slugging performance. He hit a 451-foot homer—the fifth to reach Yankee Stadium's center field bleachers since the 1976 renovation. He was so productive that he held onto the regular left field job even after Bell returned. Maldonado has power to all fields; he also has little speed but throws well enough to play right. He is not a good outfielder, though.

Major League Batting Register

	BA	G	AB	R	H	2B	3B	HR	RBI	SB
81 NL	.083	11	12	0	1	0	0	0	0	0
82 NL	.000	6	4	0	0	0	0	0	0	0
83 NL	.194	42	62	5	12	1	1	0	6	0
84 NL	.268	116	254	25	68	14	0	5	28	0
85 NL	.225	121	213	20	48	7	1	5	19	1
86 NL	.252	133	405	49	102	31	3	18	85	4
87 NL	.292	118	442	69	129	28	4	20	85	8
88 NL	.255	142	499	53	127	23	1	12	68	6
89 NL	.217	129	345	39	75	23	0	9	41	4
90 AL	.273	155	590	76	161	32	2	22	95	3
91 AL	.250	86	288	37	72	15	0	12	48	4
92 AL	.272	137	489	64	133	25	4	20	66	2
Life	.258	1196	3603	437	928	199	16	124	541	32
3 AVE	.268	126	456	59	122	24	2	18	70	3

KIRT MANWARING

Position: Catcher
Team: San Francisco Giants
Born: July 15, 1965 Elmira, NY
Height: 5′11″ **Weight:** 190 lbs.
Bats: right **Throws:** right
Acquired: Second-round pick in 6/86 free-agent draft

Player Summary	
Fantasy Value	$1 to $3
Card Value	3¢ to 4¢
Will	intimidate rival runners
Can't	produce extra-base power
Expect	bid for Gold Glove
Don't Expect	hitting against righties

Manwaring was baseball's toughest catcher to steal against last summer. He nailed 26 of the first 52 runners who tried to steal against him, including a string of seven straight before league leader Marquis Grissom swiped third. By late August, Manwaring's 51.8 success ratio led both leagues, and he finished with a 50.5 percent mark. He calls a good game, prevents wild pitches, guards the plate against incoming runners, and works especially well with young pitchers. He was one of the top defensive backstoppers in the NL. Though he's a contact hitter who walks almost as often as he fans, Manwaring rarely produces an extra-base hit. He had a .311 on-base average and a .335 slugging percentage in 1992. He's a good bunter who's seldom asked to bunt because the pitcher follows him in the lineup. Manwaring hit lefties at a .305 clip in '92, but he struggles against right-handers (.206). Speed is not part of his game.

Major League Batting Register

	BA	G	AB	R	H	2B	3B	HR	RBI	SB
87 NL	.143	6	7	0	1	0	0	0	0	0
88 NL	.250	40	116	12	29	7	0	1	15	0
89 NL	.210	85	200	14	42	4	2	0	18	2
90 NL	.154	8	13	0	2	0	1	0	1	0
91 NL	.225	67	178	16	40	9	0	0	19	1
92 NL	.244	109	349	24	85	10	5	4	26	2
Life	.231	315	863	66	199	30	8	5	79	5
2 AVE	.237	88	264	20	63	10	3	2	23	2

CARLOS MARTINEZ

Position: First base; third base
Team: Cleveland Indians
Born: Aug. 11, 1965 La Guaira, Venezuela
Height: 6'5" **Weight:** 175 lbs.
Bats: right **Throws:** right
Acquired: Signed as a free agent, 3/91

Player Summary	
Fantasy Value	$4 to $6
Card Value	3¢ to 4¢
Will	rip lefthanders
Can't	steal bases
Expect	occasional power
Don't Expect	strong defense

After recovering from back surgery last spring, Martinez teamed with Paul Sorrento to give the Cleveland Indians a productive righty-lefty platoon at first base. A line-drive hitter with some power, Martinez believes in hacking away at everything. He doesn't walk much but usually makes good contact. He walked only seven times last season. A fastball hitter who usually feasts on lefthanders, he only batted .260 against them last summer. Martinez had a .283 on-base average and a .377 slugging percentage in 1992. He had a 16-game hitting streak, best of his career, in 1991. He also hit .360 with runners in scoring position that summer. He hopes to recapture the stroke that produced a .300 season for the 1989 White Sox. He's versatile enough to fill in at third base or the outfield, although past elbow problems have reduced the velocity of his throws. Martinez once stole 25 times in a minor league season but no longer runs much. His defense—even at first—needs work.

Major League Batting Register

	BA	G	AB	R	H	2B	3B	HR	RBI	SB
88 AL	.164	17	55	5	9	1	0	0	0	1
89 AL	.300	109	350	44	105	22	0	5	32	4
90 AL	.224	92	272	18	61	6	5	4	24	0
91 AL	.284	72	257	22	73	14	0	5	30	3
92 AL	.263	69	228	23	60	9	1	5	35	1
Life	.265	359	1162	112	308	52	6	19	121	9
3 AVE	.256	78	252	21	65	10	2	5	30	1

CHITO MARTINEZ

Position: Outfield
Team: Baltimore Orioles
Born: Dec. 19, 1965 Belize
Height: 5'10" **Weight:** 180 lbs.
Bats: left **Throws:** left
Acquired: Signed as a free agent, 11/90

Player Summary	
Fantasy Value	$5 to $8
Card Value	5¢ to 10¢
Will	seek '91 form
Can't	hit southpaws
Expect	power if he plays
Don't Expect	strong defense

Lack of playing time hurt Martinez last summer. Although he got to play in August after Joe Orsulak went on the shelf with a sprained thumb, Martinez spent most of the year on the bench. Part of the problem for Martinez was power production—or lack of it. He suffers a power drought when he doesn't see regular action. In 1992, he had a .366 on-base average and a .404 slugging percentage; he batted over .300 against lefties. A fastball hitter with little patience to wait for walks, Martinez topped 20 homers three years in a row in the minors and actually hit a combined 33 in 1991. He batted .322 at Triple-A Rochester that year, with 20 homers and 50 RBI, but only eight doubles. He batted .264 with 21 homers, eight triples, 12 doubles, and 67 RBI in 364 at bats at Triple-A Omaha in 1990. He was in the Kansas City system until 1990, when KC freed him. If Martinez finds his stroke from 1991 again, he'll find a big league job somewhere. He lacks good speed and defensive ability, but he does have a strong arm.

Major League Batting Register

	BA	G	AB	R	H	2B	3B	HR	RBI	SB
91 AL	.269	67	216	32	58	12	1	13	33	1
92 AL	.268	83	198	26	53	10	1	5	25	0
Life	.268	150	414	58	111	22	2	18	58	1
2 AVE	.268	75	207	29	56	11	1	9	29	1

DAVE MARTINEZ

Position: Outfield
Team: San Francisco Giants
Born: Sept. 26, 1964 New York, NY
Height: 5'10" **Weight:** 170 lbs.
Bats: left **Throws:** left
Acquired: Signed as a free agent, 12/92

Player Summary

Fantasy Value	$4 to $8
Card Value	3¢ to 4¢
Will	provide strong defense
Can't	hit lefthanders
Expect	good contact hitting
Don't Expect	frequent homers

Martinez is one of the most underrated players in the majors. A strong defensive outfielder who can play all three positions, he's also a dependable batsman. A contact hitter with occasional pop in his bat, he is a good clutch hitter who's especially tough with a two-strike count. He had a .323 on-base average and a .354 slugging percentage for Cincinnati in 1992. Martinez doesn't hit lefthanders all that well and rarely plays against them. When not in the lineup, however, he's often used as a pinch-runner or defensive replacement. Martinez has good speed and usually steals more than a dozen bases a year. Cincinnati used him as its leadoff man at times last summer. Best known for his defense, he has good instincts, exceptional range, and an accurate arm. His best position is center field, but he also does an adequate job filling in at first base.

Major League Batting Register

	BA	G	AB	R	H	2B	3B	HR	RBI	SB
86 NL	.139	53	108	13	15	1	1	1	7	4
87 NL	.292	142	459	70	134	18	8	8	36	16
88 NL	.255	138	447	51	114	13	6	6	46	23
89 NL	.274	126	361	41	99	16	7	3	27	23
90 NL	.279	118	391	60	109	13	5	11	39	13
91 NL	.295	124	396	47	117	18	5	7	42	16
92 NL	.254	135	393	47	100	20	5	3	31	12
Life	.269	836	2555	329	688	99	37	39	228	107
3 AVE	.276	126	393	51	109	17	5	7	37	14

DENNIS MARTINEZ

Position: Pitcher
Team: Montreal Expos
Born: May 14, 1955 Granada, Nicaragua
Height: 6'1" **Weight:** 180 lbs.
Bats: right **Throws:** right
Acquired: Traded from Orioles for Rene Gonzales, 6/86

Player Summary

Fantasy Value	$12 to $22
Card Value	4¢ to 7¢
Will	earn All-Star berth
Can't	bid for strikeout crown
Expect	curve at critical moments
Don't Expect	sloppy ERA

NL managers told *Baseball America* last year that Martinez has the league's best curveball. Since his fastball, slider, and changeup aren't too shabby either, it's no surprise that he ranks among the best pitchers in the game. He fans twice the number he walks, yields less hits than innings, and doesn't throw too many home run balls. The three-time All-Star won his league's ERA title with a career-best 2.39 in 1991, the same year he pitched a perfect game at Los Angeles. Martinez helps himself with strong defensive skills, including a good pickoff move. He can also swing the bat. Martinez has won in double figures six straight years.

Major League Pitching Register

	W	L	ERA	G	CG	IP	H	ER	BB	SO
76 AL	1	2	2.60	4	1	27.2	23	8	8	18
77 AL	14	7	4.10	42	5	166.2	157	76	64	107
78 AL	16	11	3.52	40	15	276.1	257	108	93	142
79 AL	15	16	3.66	40	18	292.1	279	119	78	132
80 AL	6	4	3.97	25	2	99.2	103	44	44	42
81 AL	14	5	3.32	25	9	179.0	173	66	62	88
82 AL	16	12	4.21	40	10	252.0	262	118	87	111
83 AL	7	16	5.53	32	4	153.0	209	94	45	71
84 AL	6	9	5.02	34	2	141.2	145	79	37	77
85 AL	13	11	5.15	33	3	180.0	203	103	63	68
86 AL	0	0	6.75	4	0	6.2	11	5	2	2
86 NL	3	6	4.59	19	1	98.0	103	50	28	63
87 NL	11	4	3.30	22	2	144.2	133	53	40	84
88 NL	15	13	2.72	34	9	235.1	215	71	55	120
89 NL	16	7	3.18	34	5	232.0	227	82	49	142
90 NL	10	11	2.95	32	7	226.0	191	74	49	156
91 NL	14	11	2.39	31	9	222.0	187	59	62	123
92 NL	16	11	2.47	32	6	226.1	172	62	60	147
Life	193	156	3.62	523	108	3159.1	3050	1271	926	1693
3 AVE	13	11	2.60	32	7	225.0	183	65	57	142

EDGAR MARTINEZ

Position: Third base
Team: Seattle Mariners
Born: Jan. 2, 1963 New York, NY
Height: 5'11" **Weight:** 175 lbs.
Bats: right **Throws:** right
Acquired: Signed as a free agent, 12/82

Player Summary	
Fantasy Value	$20 to $26
Card Value	4¢ to 8¢
Will	pursue bat crown
Can't	gain fan appeal
Expect	MVP credentials
Don't Expect	weak defense

Martinez was the winner of the 1992 AL batting crown by 14 points. Since speed doesn't sweeten his batting average, he managed to improve as the 1992 season wore on. He hit .388 in July to win AL Player of the Month honors, took the league lead in hitting on Aug. 1, and hit his first career grand slam 18 days later. Martinez reached career highs in homers and steals by July 26. Overlooked in the All-Star voting, he was added to the AL squad anyway. He walks almost as often as he fans, and in '92 he accomplished a trifecta: a .300 batting average, .400 on-base average (.404), and .500 slugging average (.544). He batted .376 against righties in '92. Now a good third baseman, he once led the AL with 27 errors—many the result of a sore right knee that prevented him from bending quickly. After lifting weights and taking infield drills, his defense improved. He charges and throws with the best in the league. He ran more in '92, although he is not too swift.

Major League Batting Register

	BA	G	AB	R	H	2B	3B	HR	RBI	SB
87 AL	.372	13	43	6	16	5	2	0	5	0
88 AL	.281	14	32	0	9	4	0	0	5	0
89 AL	.240	65	171	20	41	5	0	2	20	2
90 AL	.302	144	487	71	147	27	2	11	49	1
91 AL	.307	150	544	98	167	35	1	14	52	0
92 AL	.343	135	528	100	181	46	3	18	73	14
Life	.311	521	1805	295	561	122	8	45	204	17
3 AVE	.318	143	520	90	165	36	2	14	58	5

RAMON MARTINEZ

Position: Pitcher
Team: Los Angeles Dodgers
Born: March 22, 1968 Santo Domingo, Dominican Republic
Height: 6'4" **Weight:** 173 lbs.
Bats: right **Throws:** right
Acquired: Signed as a free agent, 9/84

Player Summary	
Fantasy Value	$12 to $20
Card Value	5¢ to 10¢
Will	seek comeback
Can't	show old speed
Expect	control lapses
Don't Expect	complete games

Although he entered the 1992 campaign as the No. 1 pitcher of the Dodgers, Martinez did not pitch with the consistency that made him an All-Star in '91. In the two starts that followed his 1-0 shutout of the Cubs May 29, he failed to last a combined total of nine innings. On July 29, however, he no-hit San Francisco until Will Clark doubled with one out in the seventh. Martinez won his third straight on Aug. 10 but came out of the month with a losing record for the season. He once fanned 18 hitters in a game. Martinez lost some velocity on his fastball. He also throws a curve and a changeup but has trouble keeping them in the strike zone. He yielded less hits than innings but didn't have a 2-1 ratio of strikeouts to walks. Opponents compiled a .245 batting average, a .331 on-base average, and a .362 slugging percentage in 1992. Look for a strong rebound in 1993. He's a so-so fielder but not a bad hitter.

Major League Pitching Register

	W	L	ERA	G	CG	IP	H	ER	BB	SO
88 NL	1	3	3.79	9	0	35.2	27	15	22	23
89 NL	6	4	3.19	15	2	98.2	79	35	41	89
90 NL	20	6	2.92	33	12	234.1	191	76	67	223
91 NL	17	13	3.27	33	6	220.1	190	80	69	150
92 NL	8	11	4.00	25	1	150.2	141	67	69	101
Life	52	37	3.32	115	21	739.2	628	273	268	586
3 AVE	15	10	3.32	30	6	201.1	174	74	68	158

TINO MARTINEZ

Position: First base
Team: Seattle Mariners
Born: Dec. 7, 1967 Tampa FL
Height: 6'2" **Weight:** 205 lbs.
Bats: left **Throws:** left
Acquired: First-round pick in 6/88 free-agent draft

Player Summary	
Fantasy Value	$12 to $18
Card Value	5¢ to 12¢
Will	powder righthanders
Can't	generate speed
Expect	hitting to improve
Don't Expect	defensive problems

Martinez knocked on the door for several seasons before he finally found a home last summer. He was named *USA Today's* Minor League Player of the Year in 1990, and was the Triple-A Pacific Coast League's MVP a year later. He became Seattle's first baseman after veteran Pete O'Brien plunged into a slump. Used as the cleanup man against righthanders, Martinez helped No. 3 hitter Ken Griffey see a steady diet of fastballs. On June 29, Martinez had his first five-hit game. He had a .316 on-base average and a .411 slugging percentage last summer. Though he struck out twice as often as he walked, he should decrease that ratio with experience; he had more walks than strikeouts in the minors. In 1991 at Triple-A Calgary, he batted .326 with 18 homers and 86 RBI. He batted .320 with 17 homers and 93 RBI in 1990 at Calgary. Although he has no speed, Martinez is no lumbering first baseman. He's an agile gloveman with good range, good hands, and a good scoop.

Major League Batting Register

	BA	G	AB	R	H	2B	3B	HR	RBI	SB
90 AL	.221	24	68	4	15	4	0	0	5	0
91 AL	.205	36	112	11	23	2	0	4	9	0
92 AL	.257	136	460	53	118	19	2	16	66	2
Life	.244	196	640	68	156	25	2	20	80	2

ROGER MASON

Position: Pitcher
Team: San Diego Padres
Born: Sept. 18, 1958 Bellaire, MI
Height: 6'6" **Weight:** 220 lbs.
Bats: right **Throws:** right
Acquired: Traded from Mets with Mike Freitas for Mike Maddux, 12/92

Player Summary	
Fantasy Value	$2 to $4
Card Value	3¢ to 4¢
Will	handcuff righties
Can't	always throw strikes
Expect	frequent appearances
Don't Expect	deployment as closer

Mason moves to Padre middle relief. He spent parts of six seasons in the majors before spending all of 1992 in Pittsburgh. Rescued from Triple-A Buffalo for the '91 stretch drive, he gave the Pirates solid middle relief. Mixing a fastball with a split-fingered fastball that he used as a changeup, Mason held hitters at bay in the clutch and allowed just one of 21 inherited runners to score. He wasn't as effective last summer, however. The good control evaporated, too many balls disappeared over the fence, and batters averaged more than a hit per inning. As a result, Mason's ERA ballooned to 4.22 and he lost six of his first 10. The rubber-armed righthander proved, however, that he's over his past elbow problems. Opponents in 1992 compiled a .246 batting average, a .320 on-base average, and a .409 slugging percentage. He gave Pirate skipper Jim Leyland much-needed relief innings. Mason can't hit or field very well.

Major League Pitching Register

	W	L	ERA	G	S	IP	H	ER	BB	SO
84 AL	1	1	4.50	5	1	22.0	23	11	10	15
85 NL	1	3	2.12	5	0	29.2	28	7	11	26
86 NL	3	4	4.80	11	0	60.0	56	32	30	43
87 NL	1	1	4.50	5	0	26.0	30	13	10	18
89 NL	0	0	20.25	2	0	1.1	2	3	2	3
91 NL	3	2	3.03	24	3	29.2	21	10	6	21
92 NL	5	7	4.09	65	8	88.0	80	40	33	56
Life	14	18	4.07	117	12	256.2	240	116	102	182

DON MATTINGLY

Team: New York Yankees
Position: First base
Born: April 20, 1961 Evansville, IN
Height: 6' **Weight:** 192 lbs.
Bats: left **Throws:** left
Acquired: 19th-round pick in 6/79 free-agent draft

Player Summary

Fantasy Value	$20 to $25
Card Value	5¢ to 15¢
Will	seek former power
Can't	steal bases
Expect	Gold Glove defense
Don't Expect	another bat title

Mattingly didn't like it when a national magazine listed him in the Over the Hill Club prior to the 1992 season. The writer apparently failed to realize that the back problems that limited Mattingly to a 102 games in 1990 also sapped the slugger's strength in '91. Last summer, his stroke gradually returned. A contact hitter who walks as often as he fans, Mattingly moved from second to fourth in the lineup after leading the team with 17 RBI in May. He later returned to his customary No. 3 spot. The six-time All-Star hit .403 during a 15-game streak that ended July 4 and was flirting with .300 as August ended. Mattingly hit well above .300 against lefties during that stretch. He also played well in the field, where his Aug. 7 bobble ended a string of 819 errorless chances. He's won seven Gold Gloves.

Major League Batting Register

	BA	G	AB	R	H	2B	3B	HR	RBI	SB
82 AL	.167	7	12	0	2	0	0	0	1	0
83 AL	.283	91	279	34	79	15	4	4	32	0
84 AL	.343	153	603	91	207	44	2	23	110	1
85 AL	.324	159	652	107	211	48	3	35	145	2
86 AL	.352	162	677	117	238	53	2	31	113	0
87 AL	.327	141	569	93	186	38	2	30	115	1
88 AL	.311	144	599	94	186	37	0	18	88	1
89 AL	.303	158	631	79	191	37	2	23	113	3
90 AL	.256	102	394	40	101	16	0	5	42	1
91 AL	.288	152	587	64	169	35	0	9	68	2
92 AL	.287	157	640	89	184	40	0	14	86	3
Life	.311	1426	5643	808	1754	363	15	192	913	14
3 AVE	.280	137	540	64	151	30	0	9	65	2

DERRICK MAY

Position: Outfield
Team: Chicago Cubs
Born: July 14, 1968 Rochester, NY
Height: 6'4" **Weight:** 205 lbs.
Bats: left **Throws:** right
Acquired: First-round pick in 6/86 free-agent draft

Player Summary

Fantasy Value	$8 to $12
Card Value	8¢ to 12¢
Will	slash line drives
Can't	show frequent power
Expect	improvement over time
Don't Expect	patience at bat

May reported to 1992 spring training camp with an inside-out swing that produced power to the left-center field gap. The Cubs convinced him to close his stance and pull the ball to right. Suddenly able to hit any pitch, he made his presence felt. On June 20, he became the first Cub rookie to hit two homers in a game since Darrin Jackson in 1988. May hit .314 with 13 RBI for the month, then came into his own in August. With a .352 spurt over the 23-game stretch that ended Aug. 25, he knocked Kal Daniels out of left field. May had a .306 on-base average and a .373 slugging percentage in 1992. In 1991 at Triple-A Iowa, he batted .297 with three homers and 39 RBI; he missed about two months of the season with an injury. He is an overly aggressive hitter who fanned twice as much as he walked. The son of former big leaguer Dave May, Derrick has decent speed, range, and arm, plus healthy knees. May batted .296 with eight homers and 69 RBI at Iowa in 1990.

Major League Batting Register

	BA	G	AB	R	H	2B	3B	HR	RBI	SB
90 NL	.246	17	61	8	15	3	0	1	11	1
91 NL	.227	15	22	4	5	2	0	1	3	0
92 NL	.274	124	351	33	96	11	0	8	45	5
Life	.267	156	434	45	116	16	0	10	59	6

BRENT MAYNE

Position: Catcher
Team: Kansas City Royals
Born: April 19, 1968 Loma Linda, CA
Height: 6'1" **Weight:** 190 lbs.
Bats: left **Throws:** right
Acquired: First-round pick in 6/89 free-agent draft

Player Summary

Fantasy Value	$1 to $3
Card Value	5¢ to 8¢
Will	hit 3-1 pitch
Can't	steal bases
Expect	good contact
Don't Expect	every-day job

Before Mike Macfarlane started imitating Babe Ruth last August, Mayne spent the summer teaming with him in a lefty-righty platoon. A .250 hitter with little power, he showed better selectivity at the plate last summer and rarely struck out. He had fewer RBI than strikeouts—and he's not a big run-producer. Mayne won't wait for walks, but in 1991 he led both the Royals and all AL catchers in batting average with a 3-1 count. He had a .260 on-base average and a .272 slugging percentage in 1992. He received his most extensive work in 1990 at Double-A Memphis; he batted .267 with two homers and 61 RBI in 412 at bats. A solid defensive catcher, Mayne reduced his errors and increased his success ratio against potential base-stealers. The former Cal-State Fullerton athlete erased 40.9 percent of opponents trying to steal. His stealing belongs in the same category as his power potential. Without a better bat, Mayne doesn't figure to be more than a lefty complement to a righty-hitting regular.

Major League Batting Register

	BA	G	AB	R	H	2B	3B	HR	RBI	SB
90 AL	.231	5	13	2	3	0	0	0	1	0
91 AL	.251	85	231	22	58	8	0	3	31	2
92 AL	.225	82	213	16	48	10	0	0	18	0
Life	.239	172	457	40	109	18	0	3	50	2
2 AVE	.239	84	222	19	53	9	0	2	25	1

KIRK McCASKILL

Position: Pitcher
Team: Chicago White Sox
Born: April 9, 1961 Kapuskasing, Ontario, Canada
Height: 6'1" **Weight:** 196 lbs.
Bats: right **Throws:** right
Acquired: Signed as a free agent, 12/91

Player Summary

Fantasy Value	$8 to $12
Card Value	3¢ to 4¢
Will	bank on curveball
Can't	find strike zone
Expect	success against righties
Don't Expect	frequent gophers

In his first season with the White Sox, McCaskill learned how to change speeds on the curve, his No. 1 pitch. The tips—relayed by pitching coach Jackie Brown—did not pay immediate dividends, though. McCaskill's ERA was almost the same as it was during his 19-loss campaign of 1991. Though McCaskill yielded less hits than innings and kept the ball in the park, he was plagued by control problems that wouldn't quit. He walked almost as many men as he fanned and was the wildest pitcher on the White Sox staff. He has a fastball, slider, and changeup in addition to the curve. His off-speed stuff is less effective when the velocity vanishes on his heater, however. The one-time hockey prospect is much more effective against righthanded batters; they hit .209 against him in 1992. He helps himself with solid defense and a fine pickoff move.

Major League Pitching Register

	W	L	ERA	G	CG	IP	H	ER	BB	SO
85 AL	12	12	4.70	30	6	189.2	189	99	64	102
86 AL	17	10	3.36	34	10	246.1	207	92	92	202
87 AL	4	6	5.67	14	1	74.2	84	47	34	56
88 AL	8	6	4.31	23	4	146.1	155	70	61	98
89 AL	15	10	2.93	32	6	212.0	202	69	59	107
90 AL	12	11	3.25	29	2	174.1	161	63	72	78
91 AL	10	19	4.26	30	1	177.2	193	84	66	71
92 AL	12	13	4.18	34	0	209.0	193	97	95	109
Life	90	87	3.91	226	30	1430.0	1384	621	543	823
3 AVE	11	14	3.91	31	1	187.1	182	81	78	86

LLOYD McCLENDON

Position: Outfield; first base
Team: Pittsburgh Pirates
Born: July 11, 1959 Gary, IN
Height: 5'11" **Weight:** 195 lbs.
Bats: right **Throws:** right
Acquired: Traded from Cubs for Mike
  Pomeranz, 9/90

Player Summary	
Fantasy Value	$2 to $6
Card Value	3¢ to 4¢
Will	slaughter southpaws
Can't	add speed to attack
Expect	power in the pinch
Don't Expect	good defense

McClendon spent last summer playing several roles for the Pirates. Used primarily against lefthanded pitching, he played first base, right field, and left field, but he never returned to his original position, catcher. Sandwiched into the cleanup spot between Andy Van Slyke and Barry Bonds last summer, McClendon was supposed to provide more power than he did. His home run on Aug. 20 was only his first since April 19 and his second of the season. He makes good contact, however, and walks more than he fans. He had a .350 on-base average and a .353 slugging percentage in 1992. A lumbering slugger who rarely runs, McClendon is hardly a gazelle in the field. He squeaks by as an outfielder but is safest at first base. An ideal designated hitter, he could also earn a living as a pinch-hitter. He's the type who can come off the bench and turn a game around.

Major League Batting Register

	BA	G	AB	R	H	2B	3B	HR	RBI	SB
87 NL	.208	45	72	8	15	5	0	2	13	1
88 NL	.219	72	137	9	30	4	0	3	14	4
89 NL	.286	92	259	47	74	12	1	12	40	6
90 NL	.164	53	110	6	18	3	0	2	12	1
91 NL	.288	85	163	24	47	7	0	7	24	2
92 NL	.253	84	190	26	48	8	1	3	20	1
Life	.249	431	931	120	232	39	2	29	123	15
2 AVE	.269	85	177	25	48	8	1	5	22	2

BOB McCLURE

Position: Pitcher
Team: Florida Marlins
Born: April 29, 1953 Oakland, CA
Height: 5'11" **Weight:** 188 lbs.
Bats: right **Throws:** left
Acquired: Signed as a free agent, 12/92

Player Summary	
Fantasy Value	$1 to $2
Card Value	3¢ to 4¢
Will	work against lefties
Can't	pile up strikeouts
Expect	middle relief chores
Don't Expect	pinpoint control

McClure is a journeyman relief pitcher best deployed exclusively against left-handed hitters. Used carefully by St. Louis manager Joe Torre last summer, McClure had more appearances than innings pitched and allowed less hits than innings. He did have control problems, however, and walked more men than he fanned. He is a fastball-curveball pitcher. Even with all his mileage, he's still capable of working 60 games in a season, albeit an inning or fraction at a time. At the ripe old athletic age of 39, McClure is still an agile fielder who keeps runners close. He should find work as a middle man again.

Major League Pitching Register

	W	L	ERA	G	S	IP	H	ER	BB	SO
75 AL	1	0	0.00	12	1	15.1	4	0	14	15
76 AL	0	0	9.00	8	0	4.0	3	4	8	3
77 AL	2	1	2.52	68	6	71.1	64	20	34	57
78 AL	2	6	3.74	44	9	65.0	53	27	30	47
79 AL	5	2	3.88	36	5	51.0	53	24	24	37
80 AL	5	8	3.08	52	10	90.2	83	31	37	47
81 AL	0	0	3.52	4	0	7.2	7	3	4	6
82 AL	12	7	4.22	34	0	172.2	160	81	74	99
83 AL	9	9	4.50	24	0	142.0	152	71	68	68
84 AL	4	8	4.38	39	1	139.2	154	68	52	68
85 AL	4	1	4.31	38	3	85.2	91	41	30	57
86 AL	2	1	3.86	13	0	16.1	18	7	10	11
86 NL	2	5	3.02	52	6	62.2	53	21	23	42
87 NL	6	1	3.44	52	5	52.1	47	20	20	33
88 NL	2	3	5.40	33	3	30.0	35	18	8	19
89 AL	6	1	1.55	48	3	52.1	39	9	15	36
90 AL	0	6	6.43	11	0	7.0	7	5	3	6
91 AL	0	0	9.31	13	0	9.2	13	10	5	5
91 NL	1	1	3.13	32	0	23.0	24	8	8	15
92 NL	2	3	3.17	71	0	54.0	52	19	25	24
Life	67	56	3.79	684	52	1152.1	1112	485	492	695
2 AVE	2	2	3.84	58	0	43.1	45	19	19	22

BEN McDONALD

Position: Pitcher
Team: Baltimore Orioles
Born: Nov. 24, 1967 Baton Rouge, LA
Height: 6'7" **Weight:** 212 lbs.
Bats: right **Throws:** right
Acquired: First-round pick in 6/89 free-agent draft

Player Summary	
Fantasy Value	$15 to $20
Card Value	5¢ to 10¢
Will	throw mid-90s heat
Can't	win without curve
Expect	frequent gophers
Don't Expect	control trouble

When McDonald was at Louisiana State University, he received the highest rating ever given to a pitcher by the major league scouting bureau. Although he has yet to justify that evaluation, he made some movement in that direction last summer. His two-hit 7-0 win at Texas July 18 was probably the best game of his short career. Plagued by elbow and shoulder problems before 1992, McDonald was a victim of the long ball last year. Although he yielded less hits than innings and averaged two and one-half strikeouts per walk, he was among the top of the list in the AL for home runs allowed, with 32. Opponents compiled a .247 batting average, a .311 on-base percentage, and a .421 slugging percentage in 1992. When he can't throw his curveball for strikes or get it to break properly, McDonald tends to lean too heavily on his fastball. Though he does mix in an occasional changeup, McDonald without his curveball is like Popeye without spinach.

Major League Pitching Register

	W	L	ERA	G	CG	IP	H	ER	BB	SO
89 AL	1	0	8.59	6	0	7.1	8	7	4	3
90 AL	8	5	2.43	21	3	118.2	88	32	35	65
91 AL	6	8	4.84	21	1	126.1	126	68	43	85
92 AL	13	13	4.24	35	4	227.0	213	107	74	158
Life	28	26	4.02	83	8	479.1	435	214	156	311
3 AVE	9	9	3.95	26	3	157.1	142	69	51	103

JACK McDOWELL

Position: Pitcher
Team: Chicago White Sox
Born: Jan. 16, 1966 Van Nuys, CA
Height: 6'5" **Weight:** 179 lbs.
Bats: right **Throws:** right
Acquired: First-round pick in 6/87 free-agent draft

Player Summary	
Fantasy Value	$24 to $32
Card Value	5¢ to 10¢
Will	finish what he starts
Can't	keep ball in park
Expect	good location
Don't Expect	many shutouts

McDowell's split-fingered fastball is like three pitches in one, because he throws it at three different speeds. He also has a fine fastball. Like White Sox Hall of Famer Ed Walsh, whose picture in McDowell's locker provides inspiration, the former Stanford star is not only the staff ace but one of his league's best. An All-Star two years in a row (the first Sox pitcher to do that since Goose Gossage in 1975 and '76), McDowell retired NL hitters on 10 pitches in his one inning of work last year. He has a strikeout-to-walk ratio of nearly 3-to-1 and can place his pitches wherever he wants. He always keeps his team in the game and ranks among the leaders in complete games. His 17th win last Aug. 23 was his fourth complete game in a row. He won 20 games, but failed in his last five starts to win a 21st. Opponents compiled a .251 batting average, a .307 on-base average, and a .379 slugging percentage in '92. He's an outstanding fielder with a quick pickoff move.

Major League Pitching Register

	W	L	ERA	G	CG	IP	H	ER	BB	SO
87 AL	3	0	1.93	4	0	28.0	16	6	6	15
88 AL	5	10	3.97	26	1	158.2	147	70	68	84
90 AL	14	9	3.82	33	4	205.0	189	87	77	165
91 AL	17	10	3.41	35	15	253.2	212	96	82	191
92 AL	20	10	3.18	34	13	260.2	247	92	75	178
Life	59	39	3.49	132	33	906.0	811	351	308	633
3 AVE	17	10	3.44	34	11	239.1	216	92	78	178

ROGER McDOWELL

Position: Pitcher
Team: Los Angeles Dodgers
Born: Dec. 21, 1960 Cincinnati, OH
Height: 6'1" **Weight:** 185 lbs.
Bats: right **Throws:** right
Acquired: Traded from Phillies for Mike Hartley and Braulio Castillo, 7/91

Player Summary	
Fantasy Value	$6 to $10
Card Value	3¢ to 4¢
Will	improve with more work
Can't	always throw strikes
Expect	exploding sinkerball
Don't Expect	high K totals

When his sinker doesn't sink, McDowell is ravaged by rival hitters. That's what happened last year, when the man slated to be the closer for the Dodgers gave up more hits than innings pitched and yielded an average of four earned runs per game. That was hardly vintage McDowell. He had saved at least 22 games in a season four times. Part of McDowell's problem last year was the reduced workload caused by his team's poor showing. He needs work to stay sharp and did not match his 101⅓ innings of the year before. He was hit hard last year and subjected to spells of wildness. McDowell averaged about four and one-half walks per nine innings. Opponents in 1992 compiled a .306 batting average, a .381 on-base average, and a .374 slugging percentage. The noted clubhouse comic helps himself with the glove and guards enemy runners well.

Major League Pitching Register

	W	L	ERA	G	S	IP	H	ER	BB	SO
85 NL	6	5	2.83	62	17	127.1	108	40	37	70
86 NL	14	9	3.02	75	22	128.0	107	43	42	65
87 NL	7	5	4.16	56	25	88.2	95	41	28	32
88 NL	5	5	2.63	62	16	89.0	80	26	31	46
89 NL	4	8	1.96	69	23	92.0	79	20	38	47
90 NL	6	8	3.86	72	22	86.1	92	37	35	39
91 NL	9	9	2.93	71	10	101.1	100	33	48	50
92 NL	6	10	4.09	65	14	83.2	103	38	42	50
Life	57	59	3.14	532	149	796.1	764	278	301	399
3 AVE	7	9	3.58	69	15	90.1	98	36	42	46

CHUCK McELROY

Position: Pitcher
Team: Chicago Cubs
Born: Oct. 1, 1967 Galveston, TX
Height: 6' **Weight:** 160 lbs.
Bats: left **Throws:** left
Acquired: Traded from Phillies with Bob Scanlan for Mitch Williams, 4/91

Player Summary	
Fantasy Value	$3 to $5
Card Value	3¢ to 4¢
Will	handle heavy workload
Can't	always keep control
Expect	better luck against lefties
Don't Expect	more hits than frames

For the second straight season, McElroy provided the Chicago bullpen with strong southpaw relief. Used as both a closer and set-up man, he mixed a fastball, slider, and changeup with a split-fingered fastball. The results were good: He averaged almost a strikeout an inning while yielding less hits than innings pitched. He fanned nearly twice the number he walked and kept the ball in the park. Opponents compiled a .237 batting average, a .341 on-base percentage, and a .367 slugging average in 1992; the first batters he faced had a .286 average. McElroy, whose 1.95 ERA in '91 led NL relievers, was not quite as effective last year—primarily because he struggled against lefthanded batters. Southpaws hit about a hundred points higher against him last summer than they did the previous year. Despite that phenomenon, he pitched more effectively than veteran lefty Paul Assenmacher, the team's former lefty closer. Though he had five blown saves in 1992, McElroy has a bright future ahead of him.

Major League Pitching Register

	W	L	ERA	G	S	IP	H	ER	BB	SO
89 NL	0	0	1.74	11	0	10.1	12	2	4	8
90 NL	0	1	7.71	16	0	14.0	24	12	10	16
91 NL	6	2	1.95	71	3	101.1	73	22	57	92
92 NL	4	7	3.55	72	6	83.2	73	33	51	83
Life	10	10	2.97	170	9	209.1	182	69	122	199
2 AVE	5	5	2.68	72	5	92.2	73	28	54	88

WILLIE McGEE

Position: Outfield
Team: San Francisco Giants
Born: Nov. 2, 1958 San Francisco, CA
Height: 6'1" **Weight:** 195 lbs.
Bats: both **Throws:** right
Acquired: Signed as a free agent, 12/90

Player Summary

Fantasy Value................................$15 to $20
Card Value..3¢ to 4¢
Will ....maintain .300 average
Can't..........................work way on with walks
Expect ....opposite-field singles
Don't Expect...........................same old speed

McGee is no longer the hitter, runner, or fielder who won an MVP Award, two batting titles, and three Gold Gloves. On the other hand, he's still good enough in all three areas to command a regular spot in the lineup. McGee is a switch-hitter who uses a slash-and-run hitting style that's almost totally devoid of power. He strikes out three times more often than he walks—thus negating the speed he could use to turn walks into doubles—but still keeps his average at the .300 mark. He compiled a .339 on-base average and a .354 slugging percentage in 1992. He hits well in the clutch and—except for a throwing arm that is only average—handles himself well in the field. He moved from center field to right for the Giants to make way for Darren Lewis.

Major League Batting Register

	BA	G	AB	R	H	2B	3B	HR	RBI	SB
82 NL	.296	123	422	43	125	12	8	4	56	24
83 NL	.286	147	601	75	172	22	8	5	75	39
84 NL	.291	145	571	82	166	19	11	6	50	43
85 NL	.353	152	612	114	216	26	18	10	82	56
86 NL	.256	124	497	65	127	22	7	7	48	19
87 NL	.285	153	620	76	177	37	11	11	105	16
88 NL	.292	137	562	73	164	24	6	3	50	41
89 NL	.236	58	199	23	47	10	2	3	17	8
90 NL	.335	125	501	76	168	32	5	3	62	28
90 AL	.274	29	113	23	31	3	2	0	15	3
91 NL	.312	131	497	67	155	30	3	4	43	17
92 NL	.297	138	474	56	141	20	2	1	36	13
Life	.298	1462	5669	773	1689	257	83	57	639	307
3 AVE	.312	141	528	74	165	28	4	3	52	20

FRED McGRIFF

Position: First base
Team: San Diego Padres
Born: Oct. 31, 1963 Tampa, FL
Height: 6'3" **Weight:** 215 lbs.
Bats: left **Throws:** left
Acquired: Traded from Blue Jays with Tony Fernandez for Joe Carter and Roberto Alomar, 12/90

Player Summary

Fantasy Value................................$40 to $45
Card Value......................................10¢ to 18¢
Will ....hit lefthanders
Can't ....avoid strikeouts
Expect ....explosive power
Don't Expect ....average of .300

McGriff spent the winter before the '92 season sharpening his stroke against lefty pitchers at the University of Tampa. On April 10, it paid off with a grand slam against John Candelaria, who had held McGriff to one hit in 21 previous trips. One of the most consistent sluggers in the game (and the only one with five straight 30-homer seasons), '92 NL homer king McGriff spent the season contending with new teammate Gary Sheffield for the league lead in homers and RBI. Because pitchers didn't want to walk Sheffield with McGriff batting next, Sheffield saw mostly fastballs. In addition to lending a helping hand in the lineup, McGriff gave Sheffield advice that resurrected his career. Feared by pitchers, McGriff walks as much as he strikes out. He had a .394 on-base average and a .556 slugging percentage in '92. He runs well for a big man, steals on occasion, and has good range and good hands.

Major League Batting Register

	BA	G	AB	R	H	2B	3B	HR	RBI	SB
86 AL	.200	3	5	1	1	0	0	0	0	0
87 AL	.247	107	295	58	73	16	0	20	43	3
88 AL	.282	154	536	100	151	35	4	34	82	6
89 AL	.269	161	551	98	148	27	3	36	92	7
90 AL	.300	153	557	91	167	21	1	35	88	5
91 NL	.278	153	528	84	147	19	1	31	106	4
92 NL	.286	152	531	79	152	30	4	35	104	8
Life	.279	883	3003	511	839	148	13	191	515	33
3 AVE	.288	153	539	85	155	23	2	34	99	6

MARK McGWIRE

Position: First base
Team: Oakland Athletics
Born: Oct. 1, 1963 Pomona, CA
Height: 6'5" **Weight:** 225 lbs.
Bats: right **Throws:** right
Acquired: First-round pick in 6/84 free-agent draft

Player Summary	
Fantasy Value	$35 to $44
Card Value	10¢ to 18¢
Will	scale 40-homer level
Can't	avoid 100 strikeouts
Expect	Gold Glove defense
Don't Expect	any display of speed

Before he was hurt diving for a ground ball in mid-August, McGwire was on pace for 52 homers—a record for a man who plays in the Oakland-Alameda County Coliseum, a tough home run park. He had a .385 on-base average and a .585 slugging percentage in 1992. The only man to top 30 homers in his first four seasons, he credited his '92 showing to winter weight training that added 25 pounds of muscle to his 6'5" frame. He also performed eye exercises that allowed him to see the ball better. McGwire returned to his old reliable 34.5-inch, 33-ounce bat. He worked more easily with new Oakland batting coach Doug Rader than predecessor Rick Burleson. Erasing the memory of a nightmare '91 campaign, McGwire had 28 homers and 69 RBI at the All-Star break, then hit 12 homers to win the All-Star workout home run contest.

Major League Batting Register

	BA	G	AB	R	H	2B	3B	HR	RBI	SB
86 AL	.189	18	53	10	10	1	0	3	9	0
87 AL	.289	151	557	97	161	28	4	49	118	1
88 AL	.260	155	550	87	143	22	1	32	99	0
89 AL	.231	143	490	74	113	17	0	33	95	1
90 AL	.235	156	523	87	123	16	0	39	108	2
91 AL	.201	154	483	62	97	22	0	22	75	2
92 AL	.268	139	467	87	125	22	0	42	104	0
Life	.247	916	3123	504	772	128	5	220	608	6
3 AVE	.234	150	491	79	115	20	0	34	96	1

MARK McLEMORE

Position: Second base
Team: Baltimore Orioles
Born: Oct. 4, 1964 San Diego, CA
Height: 5'11" **Weight:** 195 lbs.
Bats: both **Throws:** right
Acquired: Signed as free agent, 2/92

Player Summary	
Fantasy Value	$2 to $4
Card Value	3¢ to 4¢
Will	hit well on turf
Can't	reach the fences
Expect	excellent speed
Don't Expect	high average

After spending three previous seasons in the minors, McLemore worked himself back to the major league level last summer. He spent most of the year playing second fiddle to Baltimore second baseman Bill Ripken. Though McLemore offered superior speed and offense, he could not match Ripken's glovework. A better hitter against lefthanders, the switch-hitting McLemore is also a solid producer on artificial turf, where speed helps. He beats out bunts and infield hits, then tries to advance by stealing. McLemore usually has a high success rate when he runs, but he was caught stealing five times in 16 attempts in 1992. He had stolen 25 bases as the every-day second baseman for the 1987 Angels. A contact hitter with little power, McLemore walks as often as he fans. He had a .308 on-base average and a .294 slugging percentage in 1992. He's okay on defense—range and quickness are his best assets—but he's no Ripken.

Major League Batting Register

	BA	G	AB	R	H	2B	3B	HR	RBI	SB
86 AL	.000	5	4	0	0	0	0	0	0	0
87 AL	.236	138	433	61	102	13	3	3	41	25
88 AL	.240	77	233	38	56	11	2	2	16	13
89 AL	.243	32	103	12	25	3	1	0	14	6
90 AL	.150	28	60	6	9	2	0	0	2	1
91 NL	.148	21	61	6	9	1	0	0	2	0
92 AL	.246	101	228	40	56	7	2	0	27	11
Life	.229	402	1122	163	257	37	8	5	102	56

BRIAN McRAE

Position: Outfield
Team: Kansas City Royals
Born: Aug. 27, 1967 Bradenton, FL
Height: 6' **Weight:** 180 lbs.
Bats: both **Throws:** right
Acquired: First-round pick in 6/85 free-agent draft

Player Summary	
Fantasy Value	$8 to $12
Card Value	3¢ to 4¢
Will	bid for full-time job
Can't	reclaim leadoff spot
Expect	fine fielding
Don't Expect	more than 10 homers

Next to the 1-16 start that crippled his club's title chances, Kansas City skipper Hal McRae's biggest disappointment last summer was the poor performance of his son Brian. After opening the year as the Royals leadoff man and center fielder, he finished as No. 8 batter and center field platoon partner for lefty-hitting rookie Kevin Koslofski. Although McRae got hot around Memorial Day, producing a .351 average over a 14-game stretch that ended June 10, he limped into September with the lowest average among the Royals. His production was also off in home runs and stolen bases. He had a .285 on-base average and a .308 slugging percentage in 1992. He's still a sterling center fielder, however, and even made the first unassisted double play by an outfielder in 17 years on Aug. 22. He flags down balls in the gaps and rarely makes errors, but his throwing is only average. In 1990 at Double-A Memphis, he batted .268 with 10 homers, 64 RBI, 72 runs scored, and 21 stolen bases. He had an inside-the-park homer in 1991.

Major League Batting Register

	BA	G	AB	R	H	2B	3B	HR	RBI	SB
90 AL	.286	46	168	21	48	8	3	2	23	4
91 AL	.261	152	629	86	164	28	9	8	64	20
92 AL	.223	149	533	63	119	23	5	4	52	18
Life	.249	347	1330	170	331	59	17	14	139	42
3 AVE	.249	116	443	57	110	20	6	5	46	14

KEVIN McREYNOLDS

Position: Outfield
Team: Kansas City Royals
Born: Oct. 16, 1959 Little Rock, AR
Height: 6'1" **Weight:** 215 lbs.
Bats: right **Throws:** right
Acquired: Traded from Mets with Gregg Jefferies and Keith Miller for Bret Saberhagen and Bill Pecota, 12/91

Player Summary	
Fantasy Value	$8 to $12
Card Value	3¢ to 4¢
Will	lift batting average
Can't	turn on old power stroke
Expect	selectivity at bat
Don't Expect	defensive lapses

McReynolds should have had a part in the movie *Escape from New York*. After spending five years coping with the Mets' media circus, he appreciated the restraint of Kansas City. He even showed signs of recapturing the swing that once produced five straight 20-homer seasons. After his career-best 17-game hitting streak ended June 13, however, McReynolds had trouble maintaining his stroke. As August ended, he was hitting 30 points below his .269 mark of nine previous seasons. With his power also below expectations—13 homers—he was a major disappointment. A rare pull hitter who makes contact, McReynolds walks more than he strikes out. He might have been too patient last year, his first in the AL. He had a .357 on-base average and a .418 slugging percentage in 1992. He's one of the game's premier defensive left fielders.

Major League Batting Register

	BA	G	AB	R	H	2B	3B	HR	RBI	SB
83 NL	.221	39	140	15	31	3	1	4	14	2
84 NL	.278	147	525	68	146	26	6	20	75	3
85 NL	.234	152	564	61	132	24	4	15	75	4
86 NL	.287	158	560	89	161	31	6	26	96	8
87 NL	.276	151	590	86	163	32	5	29	95	14
88 NL	.288	147	552	82	159	30	2	27	99	21
89 NL	.272	148	545	74	148	25	3	22	85	15
90 NL	.269	147	521	75	140	23	1	24	82	9
91 NL	.259	143	522	65	135	32	1	16	74	6
92 AL	.247	109	373	45	92	25	0	13	49	7
Life	.267	1341	4892	660	1307	251	29	196	744	89
3 AVE	.259	133	472	62	122	27	1	18	68	7

RUSTY MEACHAM

Position: Pitcher
Team: Kansas City Royals
Born: Jan. 27, 1968 Stuart, FL
Height: 6'2" **Weight:** 165 lbs.
Bats: right **Throws:** right
Acquired: Signed as a free agent, 10/91

Player Summary	
Fantasy Value	$2 to $4
Card Value	4¢ to 6¢
Will	work often
Can't	rely on heat
Expect	good control
Don't Expect	closer job soon

The pitching-poor Tigers gave up on Meacham too soon. He showed last summer that he could be one of baseball's most effective relief pitchers. Deployed as a starter by Detroit, Meacham struggled. Kansas City handed him the key to the bullpen and reaped the rewards. A man of many movements on the mound, Meacham is a skinny righthander who blends forkballs, changeups, fastballs, and sliders—all thrown at different speeds from a variety of arm angles. He fans three times more men than he walks, yields less hits than innings pitched, and keeps the ball in the park. A perfect set-up man for Jeff Montgomery last year, Meacham made his mark with excellent location. He averaged less than two walks per nine innings in 1992, and opponents compiled a .233 batting average, a .269 on-base percentage, and a .328 slugging percentage. The first hitters he faced had a .250 batting average. At 25, he could have a future as a big league closer. He was 9-7 at Triple-A Toledo in 1991, with a 3.09 ERA, two saves, 40 walks, and 70 strikeouts in 125⅓ innings.

Major League Pitching Register

	W	L	ERA	G	S	IP	H	ER	BB	SO
91 AL	2	1	5.20	10	0	27.2	35	16	11	14
92 AL	10	4	2.74	64	2	101.2	88	31	21	64
Life	12	5	3.27	74	2	129.1	123	47	32	78

JOSE MELENDEZ

Position: Pitcher
Team: Boston Red Sox
Born: Sept. 2, 1965 Naguabo, Puerto Rico
Height: 6'2" **Weight:** 175 lbs.
Bats: right **Throws:** right
Acquired: Traded from Padres for Phil Plantier, 12/92

Player Summary	
Fantasy Value	$1 to $3
Card Value	4¢ to 6¢
Will	bank on sinker
Can't	avoid gophers
Expect	superb control
Don't Expect	rotation duty

Melendez moves to the BoSox' pen. He shows more promise as a middle reliever than he does as a starter. Given a dozen starts in the last two years, he's responded with so-so statistics. In the bullpen, however, he's been a virtual terror. Because he has great control (he averages nearly four Ks per walk), Melendez yields his share of home run balls. But he yields less hits than innings pitched, works often, and keeps his ERA at respectable levels. A sinkerballer who also throws a curveball, changeup, and split-fingered fastball, Melendez is particularly tough on righthanded hitters. Righties batted only .219 in '92, while lefties tagged him at a .281 clip. He has an easy motion and a rubber arm, and he is capable of working often. He's good for more than 50 appearances per season. In 1992, opponents compiled a .249 batting average, a .295 on-base percentage, and a .359 slugging percentage. Melendez helps himself with fine fielding and a good pickoff move. At Triple-A Las Vegas in 1991, he was 7-0 with a 3.99 ERA, 45 Ks, and 11 walks in 59 innings.

Major League Pitching Register

	W	L	ERA	G	CG	IP	H	ER	BB	SO
90 AL	0	0	11.81	3	0	5.1	8	7	3	7
91 NL	8	5	3.27	31	3	93.2	77	34	24	60
92 NL	6	7	2.92	56	0	89.1	82	29	20	82
Life	14	12	3.35	90	3	188.1	167	70	47	149
2 AVE	7	6	3.10	44	2	91.2	80	32	22	71

BOB MELVIN

Position: Catcher
Team: Boston Red Sox
Born: Oct. 28, 1961 Palo Alto, CA
Height: 6'4" **Weight:** 210 lbs.
Bats: right **Throws:** right
Acquired: Signed as a free agent, 12/92

Player Summary	
Fantasy Value	$1 to $2
Card Value	3¢ to 4¢
Will	ride bench quietly
Can't	hit for power
Expect	quality defense
Don't Expect	any hint of speed

Melvin is a strong defensive catcher who spent most of last summer serving as insurance for Kansas City's righty-lefty platoon of Mike Macfarlane and Brent Mayne. Melvin also filled in for Wally Joyner at first base, an unfamiliar position for him. When Melvin played, he hit. The seldom-used backstop had a .351 on-base average and a .386 slugging percentage in 1992. On the down side, he hit with his usual power—none—and showed equal inability to steal a base. Melvin's strengths are game-calling, plate-blocking, and protecting his pitchers from wild pitches and passed balls. He handles pitchers well and rarely makes an error. He caught 30 percent of the base thieves who tried to steal against him in 1992. An ideal backup, Melvin has now spent eight years in the majors without ever working in 100 games. But he's never complained.

Major League Batting Register

	BA	G	AB	R	H	2B	3B	HR	RBI	SB
85 AL	.220	41	82	10	18	4	1	0	4	0
86 NL	.224	89	268	24	60	14	2	5	25	3
87 NL	.199	84	246	31	49	8	0	11	31	0
88 NL	.234	92	273	23	64	13	1	8	27	0
89 NL	.241	85	278	22	67	10	1	1	32	1
90 AL	.243	93	301	30	73	14	1	5	37	0
91 AL	.250	79	228	11	57	10	0	1	23	0
92 AL	.314	32	70	5	22	5	0	0	6	0
Life	.235	595	1746	156	410	78	6	31	185	4
2 AVE	.246	86	265	21	65	12	1	3	30	0

ORLANDO MERCED

Position: First base; outfield
Team: Pittsburgh Pirates
Born: Nov. 2, 1966 San Juan, Puerto Rico
Height: 5'11" **Weight:** 170 lbs.
Bats: both **Throws:** right
Acquired: Signed as a free agent, 2/85

Player Summary	
Fantasy Value	$5 to $10
Card Value	3¢ to 4¢
Will	poke timely hits
Can't	add strong glove
Expect	improved average
Don't Expect	end of platoon

Although he is a switch-hitter, Merced has spent the last two summers as the lefty-swinging half of a first base platoon for Pittsburgh. One good reason is that he batted only .190 versus lefties in 1992, as opposed to .262 against righthanders. Alternating with Gary Redus, Merced managed to provide some timely hits. He had only five homers by September, for example, but each gave the Pirates the lead in games they eventually won. A contact hitter who walks almost as often as he strikes out, he hits line drives to all fields. He had a .332 on-base average and a .385 slugging percentage in 1992. He has some speed and usually bats in the lead-off slot. The versatile Merced can play any position but pitcher and shortstop. He doesn't provide stalwart defense at any, however. His best spot is right field, but he spent most of last year at first base. He batted .262 with nine homers, 55 RBI, and 14 stolen bases at Triple-A Buffalo in 1991. Merced hopes to boost his production in 1993.

Major League Batting Register

	BA	G	AB	R	H	2B	3B	HR	RBI	SB
90 NL	.208	25	24	3	5	1	0	0	0	0
91 NL	.275	120	411	83	113	17	2	10	50	8
92 NL	.247	134	405	50	100	28	5	6	60	5
Life	.260	279	840	136	218	46	7	16	110	13
2 AVE	.261	127	408	67	107	23	4	8	55	7

KENT MERCKER

Position: Pitcher
Team: Atlanta Braves
Born: Feb. 1, 1968 Dublin, OH
Height: 6'2" **Weight:** 195 lbs.
Bats: left **Throws:** left
Acquired: First-round pick in 6/86 free-agent draft

Player Summary	
Fantasy Value	$4 to $8
Card Value	3¢ to 4¢
Will	keep hits to minimum
Can't	always throw strikes
Expect	lots of hard stuff
Don't Expect	fewer Ks than frames

Mercker is a hard-throwing lefthander who is extremely difficult to hit. He pitched the first six innings of a three-man no-hitter late in '91, then hurled 25 straight scoreless relief innings last year and held opponents to less than a .200 average for the season. Mercker learned the changeup from fellow lefty Charlie Leibrandt, and the new pitch helped. The veteran Leibrandt also convinced Mercker to go after hitters more aggressively. Mercker became more effective by adding the change to a repertoire that already included a fastball, slider, and curve. He yielded fewer hits than innings pitched and kept the ball in the park. His only problem was an occasional inability to locate the strike zone. Opponents in 1992 compiled a .207 batting average, a .312 on-base percentage, and a .297 slugging percentage. He is a good fielder, but he needs work on his pickoff move. Mercker came up through the Atlanta organization as a starter, and he could return to the rotation again.

JOSE MESA

Position: Pitcher
Team: Cleveland Indians
Born: May 22, 1966 Azua, Dominican Republic
Height: 6'3" **Weight:** 222 lbs.
Bats: right **Throws:** right
Acquired: Traded from Orioles for Kyle Washington, 7/92

Player Summary	
Fantasy Value	$3 to $6
Card Value	3¢ to 4¢
Will	yield many hits
Can't	locate strike zone
Expect	streaks of excellence
Don't Expect	winning record

After the Orioles traded Mesa to the Tribe last July, he thought that he would be able to improve substantially. He had complained that he was a victim of misuse, because he was unable to keep sharp with 10 days between starting assignments. After a brief flurry of success with the Indians, however, he managed to fall back into predictable patterns. He allowed more hits than innings pitched, more walks than strikeouts, and more than his share of home run balls. As a result, his earned run average remained well over four, and clouds began to obscure his future. Opponents compiled a .273 batting average, a .348 on-base average, and a .397 slugging percentage in 1992. Mesa failed to make a substantial reduction in his high career ERA. Since he throws a fastball, slider, curve, and changeup, he should be able to keep batters off balance. But the minute his concentration wavers, his control fails. Defensive lapses have also hurt.

Major League Pitching Register

	W	L	ERA	G	S	IP	H	ER	BB	SO
89 NL	0	0	12.46	2	0	4.1	8	6	6	4
90 NL	4	7	3.17	36	7	48.1	43	17	24	39
91 NL	5	3	2.58	50	6	73.1	56	21	35	62
92 NL	3	2	3.42	53	6	68.1	51	26	35	49
Life	12	12	3.24	141	19	194.1	158	70	100	154
3 AVE	4	4	3.03	46	6	63.1	50	21	31	50

Major League Pitching Register

	W	L	ERA	G	CG	IP	H	ER	BB	SO
87 AL	1	3	6.03	6	0	31.1	38	21	15	17
90 AL	3	2	3.86	7	0	46.2	37	20	27	24
91 AL	6	11	5.97	23	2	123.2	151	82	62	64
92 AL	7	12	4.54	28	1	160.2	169	82	70	62
Life	17	28	5.09	64	3	362.1	395	205	174	167
2 AVE	7	12	5.19	26	2	142.2	160	82	66	63

BOB MILACKI

Position: Pitcher
Team: Baltimore Orioles
Born: July 28, 1964 Trenton, NJ
Height: 6'4" **Weight:** 225 lbs.
Bats: right **Throws:** right
Acquired: Second-round pick in 6/83 free-
agent draft

Player Summary	
Fantasy Value	$2 to $5
Card Value	3¢ to 4¢
Will	seek rotation job
Can't	pile up strikeouts
Expect	comeback season
Don't Expect	pinpoint control

Milacki was a solid major league starter for two seasons before the roof fell in last summer. He lost the No. 4 slot in the Baltimore rotation after the Brewers blasted him June 29, increasing his ERA to an unattractive 5.65. When a stint in the bullpen failed to straighten him out, Milacki received a ticket to Triple-A Rochester. He won seven of his eight decisions, with a 4.57 ERA, 21 walks, and 35 Ks in 61 innings at Rochester—as he tried to work his way back to the majors. Milacki throws two fastballs and a slider, curve, and changeup. He doesn't always put them in the strike zone, however. Even when he won 14 games in 1989, he failed to fan twice as many as he walked. He walked four per nine innings in 1992. He knows how to keep runners close and how to play the field. Every little bit helps, since he is not a power pitcher and usually has more than his share of baserunners to worry about.

Major League Pitching Register

	W	L	ERA	G	CG	IP	H	ER	BB	SO
88 AL	2	0	0.72	3	1	25.0	9	2	9	18
89 AL	14	12	3.74	37	3	243.0	233	101	88	113
90 AL	5	8	4.46	27	1	135.1	143	67	61	60
91 AL	10	9	4.01	31	3	184.0	175	82	53	108
92 AL	6	8	5.84	23	0	115.2	140	75	44	51
Life	37	37	4.19	121	8	703.0	700	327	255	350
3 AVE	7	8	4.63	27	1	145.1	153	75	53	73

KEITH MILLER

Position: Outfield; second base
Team: Kansas City Royals
Born: June 12, 1963 Midland, MI
Height: 5'11" **Weight:** 180 lbs.
Bats: right **Throws:** right
Acquired: Traded from Mets with Kevin
McReynolds and Greg Jefferies for Bret
Saberhagen and Bill Pecota, 12/91

Player Summary	
Fantasy Value	$4 to $8
Card Value	3¢ to 4¢
Will	top 20 steals
Can't	clear fences
Expect	strong defense
Don't Expect	many Ks

After starting last season in the outfield, Miller displaced Terry Shumpert as Kansas City's regular second baseman. A speedy contact hitter and a tough, gutsy player in his first AL season, Miller gave the Royals far better offense and passable defense at the position. He was hitting .304 in mid-July when he fractured a bone below his left knee and suffered a deep bruise of his left leg. The injury kept Miller out of action more than a month. The Royals missed his bat even more than his glove. Twenty-five of Miller's first 84 hits went for extra bases. He's an excellent bunter who can pull the hit-and-run play and leg out infield hits. He had a .352 on-base average and a .389 slugging percentage in 1992. He's also versatile enough to fill in at other positions when needed. Miller's throwing arm is one of the strongest of big league second basemen, and is adequate for the outfield.

Major League Batting Register

	BA	G	AB	R	H	2B	3B	HR	RBI	SB
87 NL	.373	25	51	14	19	2	2	0	1	8
88 NL	.214	40	70	9	15	1	1	1	5	0
89 NL	.231	57	143	15	33	7	0	1	7	6
90 NL	.258	88	233	42	60	8	0	1	12	16
91 NL	.280	98	275	41	77	22	1	4	23	14
92 AL	.284	106	416	57	118	24	4	4	38	16
Life	.271	414	1188	178	322	64	8	11	86	60
3 AVE	.276	97	308	47	85	18	2	3	24	15

RANDY MILLIGAN

Position: First base
Team: Baltimore Orioles
Born: Nov. 27, 1961 San Diego, CA
Height: 6'2" **Weight:** 225 lbs.
Bats: right **Throws:** right
Acquired: Traded from Pirates for Pete Blohm, 11/88

Player Summary	
Fantasy Value	$10 to $15
Card Value	3¢ to 4¢
Will	reach base often
Can't	steal bases
Expect	some home runs
Don't Expect	strong defense

After a sudden power vacuum left Milligan with one home run in 54 games last summer, he consulted Baltimore batting coach Greg Biagini. The result was a more erect stance, coupled with a slight leg kick that enabled Milligan to drive the ball. He responded with consecutive-inning homers—one of them a game-winner—against California Aug. 26. He had already moved from fifth to second in the lineup, and he retained his sharp batting eye and penchant for patience. He ranked among the league leaders in on-base percentage because he walked about 30 times more than he fanned and reached base nearly 40 percent of the time. He had a .383 on-base average and a .361 slugging percentage in 1992. Milligan can hit with power to all fields and is toughest in clutch situations. He's an above-average first baseman who rarely makes an error. He does not have great range, however.

Major League Batting Register

	BA	G	AB	R	H	2B	3B	HR	RBI	SB
87 NL	.000	3	1	0	0	0	0	0	0	0
88 NL	.220	40	82	10	18	5	0	3	8	1
89 AL	.268	124	365	56	98	23	5	12	45	9
90 AL	.265	109	362	64	96	20	1	20	60	6
91 AL	.263	141	483	57	127	17	2	16	70	0
92 AL	.240	137	462	71	111	21	1	11	53	0
Life	.256	554	1755	258	450	86	9	62	236	16
3 AVE	.256	129	436	64	111	19	1	16	61	2

ALAN MILLS

Position: Pitcher
Team: Baltimore Orioles
Born: Oct. 18, 1966 Lakeland, FL
Height: 6'1" **Weight:** 190 lbs.
Bats: both **Throws:** right
Acquired: Traded from Yankees for Francisco de la Rosa, 2/92

Player Summary	
Fantasy Value	$2 to $5
Card Value	3¢ to 4¢
Will	work in any role
Can't	always find plate
Expect	outstanding stuff
Don't Expect	high K totals

Mills proved last summer he can handle a variety of pitching assignments. Recalled from Triple-A Rochester on April 17, he was used as a middle reliever and set-up man. By the All-Star break, he ranked among American League leaders in relief innings and lowest batting average by opposing hitters. Kevin Seitzer said Mills had the best stuff he saw in the first half. Although he throws hard, Mills is not a strikeout pitcher. He lets hitters put the ball in play but keeps them from hitting it hard. He saw some starting service during the second half and picked up his first win in that role on Aug. 11, when he pitched five scoreless innings against Toronto, increasing his record to 8-2. Opponents in 1992 compiled a .215 batting average, a .315 on-base average, and a .312 slugging percentage. At Rochester in 1992, he was 0-1 with a 5.40 ERA. At Triple-A Columbus in 1991, he was 7-5 with a 4.43 ERA, 75 walks, and 77 strikeouts in 113⅓ innings. The Yankees may have abandoned Mills too soon.

Major League Pitching Register

	W	L	ERA	G	S	IP	H	ER	BB	SO
90 AL	1	5	4.10	36	0	41.2	48	19	33	24
91 AL	1	1	4.41	6	0	16.1	16	8	11	8
92 AL	10	4	2.61	35	2	103.1	78	30	54	60
Life	12	10	3.18	77	2	161.1	142	57	95	95
2 AVE	6	5	3.04	36	1	72.2	63	25	44	42

KEVIN MITCHELL

Position: Outfield
Team: Cincinnati Reds
Born: Jan. 13, 1962 San Diego, CA
Height: 5'11" **Weight:** 210 lbs.
Bats: right **Throws:** right
Acquired: Traded from Mariners for Norm Charlton, 11/92

Player Summary	
Fantasy Value	$16 to $20
Card Value	3¢ to 4¢
Will	try to find old power
Can't	stay healthy
Expect	great power
Don't Expect	return to third base

Mitchell moves to fill Cincy's power vacuum. Injuries interfered with Mitchell's AL debut last summer. Slowed by wrist and knee problems early, he went on the disabled list Aug. 7 with a strained left rib cage. Critics charged that Mitchell was too heavy and had lost his old bat speed. He answered those charges with 29 RBI in 27 games through July 30. He hit his third homer in five games that day, then hit a three-run shot against Roger Clemens Aug. 23—his first day back from the DL. Mitchell also hit his first career grand slam last summer. His nine-homer performance in 1992 was a far cry from the 47-homer form that won the NL MVP Award in 1989. Mitchell won't rebound unless he stays healthy. If his offense won't carry him, nothing will. Mitchell is a liability in left field, and he is no great shakes on the bases.

Major League Batting Register

	BA	G	AB	R	H	2B	3B	HR	RBI	SB
84 NL	.214	7	14	0	3	0	0	0	1	0
86 NL	.277	108	328	51	91	22	2	12	43	3
87 NL	.280	131	328	68	130	20	2	22	70	9
88 NL	.251	148	505	60	127	25	7	19	80	5
89 NL	.291	154	543	100	158	34	6	47	125	3
90 NL	.290	140	524	90	152	24	2	35	93	4
91 NL	.256	113	371	52	95	13	1	27	69	2
92 AL	.286	99	360	48	103	24	0	9	67	0
Life	.276	900	3109	469	859	162	20	171	548	26
3 AVE	.279	117	418	63	117	20	1	24	76	2

PAUL MOLITOR

Position: Designated hitter; infield
Team: Toronto Blue Jays
Born: Aug. 22, 1956 St. Paul, MN
Height: 6' **Weight:** 185 lbs.
Bats: right **Throws:** right
Acquired: Signed as a free agent, 12/92

Player Summary	
Fantasy Value	$22 to $28
Card Value	3¢ to 4¢
Will	reach base often
Can't	avoid injury bug
Expect	liners with power
Don't Expect	much use in field

The Jays valued Molitor's versatility. He's one of eight players to appear 50 times at all four infield spots as well as the outfield. After Milwaukee moved Molitor from leadoff to third in the lineup last May, the team began to contend for the AL East title. Discarding his habit of first-ball swinging, he worked deeper counts with good results. He hit .360 in May and June combined. He finished the season with a career high in RBI. He runs hard, stretches singles into doubles, and steals two-dozen bases a year. Managers told *Baseball America* last summer that Molitor is still the league's top baserunner. He's stolen home seven times. He had a 39-game hitting streak in 1987. Molitor has missed 500 games since 1978.

Major League Batting Register

	BA	G	AB	R	H	2B	3B	HR	RBI	SB
78 AL	.273	125	521	73	142	26	4	6	45	30
79 AL	.322	140	584	88	188	27	16	9	62	33
80 AL	.304	111	450	81	137	29	2	9	37	34
81 AL	.267	64	251	45	67	11	0	2	19	10
82 AL	.302	160	666	136	201	26	8	19	71	41
83 AL	.270	152	608	95	164	28	6	15	47	41
84 AL	.217	13	46	3	10	1	0	0	6	1
85 AL	.297	140	576	93	171	28	3	10	48	21
86 AL	.281	105	437	62	123	24	6	9	55	20
87 AL	.353	118	465	114	164	41	5	16	75	45
88 AL	.312	154	609	115	190	34	6	13	60	41
89 AL	.315	155	615	84	194	35	4	11	56	27
90 AL	.285	103	418	64	119	27	6	12	45	18
91 AL	.325	158	665	133	216	32	13	17	75	19
92 AL	.320	158	609	89	195	36	7	12	89	31
Life	.303	1856	7520	1275	2281	405	86	160	790	412
3 AVE	.313	140	564	95	177	32	9	14	70	23

RICH MONTELEONE

Position: Pitcher
Team: New York Yankees
Born: March 22, 1963 Tampa, FL
Height: 6'2" **Weight:** 236 lbs.
Bats: right **Throws:** right
Acquired: Traded from Angels with Claudell Washington for Louis Polonia, 4/90

Player Summary	
Fantasy Value	$1 to $3
Card Value	3¢ to 4¢
Will	appear 50 times
Can't	rack up Ks
Expect	middle relief work
Don't Expect	lapses of control

After bouncing between the majors and minors for five years, Monteleone became a valuable middle reliever for the Yankees last summer. Working primarily as a righthanded set-up man for Steve Farr, Monteleone yielded fewer hits than innings pitched, fanned twice as many men as he walked, and kept his ERA respectable. He won seven of his 10 decisions but did not post any saves. Opponents in 1992 compiled a .235 batting average, a .289 on-base percentage, and a .355 slugging percentage. Monteleone broke into pro ball in 1982 and reached the majors with the Mariners five years later. In 1991, his best year, he posted 17 saves for Triple-A Columbus before earning a promotion to the Yankee bullpen. He also notched a 1-3 record, 2.12 ERA, seven walks, and 52 strikeouts in 46⅔ innings pitched at Columbus in '91. In 1990 at Columbus, he was 4-4 with a 2.24 ERA, nine saves, 23 walks, and 50 Ks in 64⅓ innings.

JEFF MONTGOMERY

Position: Pitcher
Team: Kansas City Royals
Born: Jan. 7, 1962 Wellston, OH
Height: 5'11" **Weight:** 180 lbs.
Bats: right **Throws:** right
Acquired: Traded from Reds for Van Snider, 2/88

Player Summary	
Fantasy Value	$28 to $36
Card Value	3¢ to 4¢
Will	top 60 appearances
Can't	win Gold Glove
Expect	at least 30 saves
Don't Expect	righties to hit him

Montgomery is making Royals fans forget Dan Quisenberry. Montgomery adds to his save totals every year, stamping himself as a strong candidate to approach Quisenberry's club record of 45 saves in a season. Unlike Quisenberry, Montgomery averages nearly a strikeout per inning. He fans more than twice the number he walks, yields fewer hits than innings pitched, and keeps the ball in the park. To complement a fastball that moves over 90 mph, Montgomery throws a slow curve that he uses as a changeup. He is particularly difficult for righthanded hitters. Opponents compiled a .205 batting average, a .277 on-base percentage, and a .279 slugging percentage in 1992. A first-time All-Star in 1992, Montgomery would have had more save opportunities had the Royals been in contention. He's only average in the field but keeps baserunners close. The Marshall University graduate held the first batter he faced each game to a .142 batting average in '92.

Major League Pitching Register

	W	L	ERA	G	S	IP	H	ER	BB	SO
87 AL	0	0	6.43	3	0	7.0	10	5	4	2
88 AL	0	0	0.00	3	0	4.1	4	0	1	3
89 AL	2	2	3.18	24	0	39.2	39	14	13	27
90 AL	0	1	6.14	5	0	7.1	8	5	2	8
91 AL	3	1	3.64	26	0	47.0	42	19	19	34
92 AL	7	3	3.30	47	0	92.2	82	34	27	62
Life	12	7	3.50	108	0	198.0	185	77	66	136
2 AVE	5	2	3.42	37	0	70.1	62	27	23	48

Major League Pitching Register

	W	L	ERA	G	S	IP	H	ER	BB	SO
87 NL	2	2	6.52	14	0	19.1	25	14	9	13
88 AL	7	2	3.45	45	1	62.2	54	24	30	47
89 AL	7	3	1.37	63	18	92.0	66	14	25	94
90 AL	6	5	2.39	73	24	94.1	81	25	34	94
91 AL	4	4	2.90	67	33	90.0	83	29	28	77
92 AL	1	6	2.18	65	39	82.2	61	20	27	69
Life	27	22	2.57	327	115	441.0	370	126	153	394
3 AVE	4	5	2.49	68	32	89.1	75	25	30	80

MIKE MOORE

Position: Pitcher
Team: Detroit Tigers
Born: Nov. 26, 1959 Eakly, OK
Height: 6'4" **Weight:** 205 lbs.
Bats: right **Throws:** right
Acquired: Signed as a free agent, 12/92

Player Summary	
Fantasy Value	$10 to $15
Card Value	3¢ to 4¢
Will	seek 1991 form
Can't	avoid gophers
Expect	lots of runners
Don't Expect	ERA below 4.00

Moore moves to Motown. For the last four seasons with th A's, he recorded alternating good and bad years. In 1992, he couldn't come close to duplicating his 2.96 ERA of the year before. One of the slowest workers in the league, he managed to win a lot but also averaged more than four earned runs per game. His problems included more hits than innings pitched, too many gopher balls, and more than four walks per nine innings. A sinker-slider pitcher who also throws a split-fingered fastball, Moore tries to get ground balls with the sinker and strikeouts with his other pitches. Opponents had a .269 batting average, a .349 on-base average, and a .399 slugging percentage. Although he usually handles righthanded batters well, that was not the case last year. Moore helps himself with his glove and is good at holding runners.

Major League Pitching Register

	W	L	ERA	G	CG	IP	H	ER	BB	SO
82 AL	7	14	5.36	28	1	144.1	159	86	79	73
83 AL	6	8	4.71	22	3	128.0	130	67	60	108
84 AL	7	17	4.97	34	6	212.0	236	117	85	158
85 AL	17	10	3.46	35	14	247.0	230	95	70	155
86 AL	11	13	4.30	38	11	266.0	279	127	94	146
87 AL	9	19	4.71	33	12	231.0	268	121	84	115
88 AL	9	15	3.78	37	9	228.2	196	96	63	182
89 AL	19	11	2.61	35	6	241.2	193	70	83	172
90 AL	13	15	4.65	33	3	199.1	204	103	84	73
91 AL	17	8	2.96	33	3	210.0	176	69	105	153
92 AL	17	12	4.12	36	2	223.0	229	102	103	117
Life	132	142	4.07	364	70	2331.0	2300	1053	910	1452
3 AVE	16	12	3.90	34	3	211.0	203	91	97	114

MICKEY MORANDINI

Position: Second base
Team: Philadelphia Phillies
Born: April 22, 1966 Kittanning, PA
Height: 5'11" **Weight:** 170 lbs.
Bats: left **Throws:** right
Acquired: Fifth-round pick in 6/88 free-agent draft

Player Summary	
Fantasy Value	$4 to $8
Card Value	3¢ to 4¢
Will	run bases well
Can't	hit lefthanders
Expect	strong defense
Don't Expect	extra-base hits

Morandini failed in his attempt to prove that he was more than a platoon player. An easy out for lefthanded pitchers, he batted .198 against lefties in 1992. Early in the season he lost Philadelphia's regular second base job, which went instead to Mariano Duncan. Morandini got the job back when Duncan moved to the outfield. Blessed with speed but not power, Morandini strikes out too much for a singles hitter (he had 64 Ks in 1992). He'd be more valuable if he worked his way on base with walks, but he averages only one walk to every two and one-half strikeouts. Morandini had a .305 on-base average and a .344 slugging percentage in 1992. He has enough speed to steal two-dozen times a year—provided he gets the opportunities. He stole 25 bases one year in the minors. The former Indiana University star and 1988 Team USA member is a converted shortstop with good range and the ability to turn the double play. He made only one error in his first 58 games last year.

Major League Batting Register

	BA	G	AB	R	H	2B	3B	HR	RBI	SB
90 NL	.241	25	79	9	19	4	0	1	3	3
91 NL	.249	98	325	38	81	11	4	1	20	13
92 NL	.265	127	422	47	112	8	8	3	30	8
Life	.257	250	826	94	212	23	12	5	53	24
2 AVE	.258	113	374	43	97	10	6	2	25	11

MIKE MORGAN

Position: Pitcher
Team: Chicago Cubs
Born: Oct. 8, 1959 Tulare, CA
Height: 6'2" **Weight:** 215 lbs.
Bats: right **Throws:** right
Acquired: Signed as a free agent, 12/91

Player Summary

Fantasy Value	$14 to $20
Card Value	3¢ to 4¢
Will	thrive on grass
Can't	always find zone
Expect	lots of grounders
Don't Expect	too many gophers

The long infield grass of Wrigley Field helped Morgan last year. After losing his first two starts, he launched a personal-best seven-game winning streak. He was NL Pitcher of the Month for May with a 5-0 record and 2.32 ERA in six starts. He won his first seven decisions at Wrigley and posted a 1.41 ERA in the process. An All-Star for the second straight year, Morgan boosted his record six games over .500—a career first—on Aug. 23. He gives his team 200 quality innings a year. Morgan throws a sinker, slider, and split-fingered fastball with fairly good control. He gets lots of grounders and usually ranks among the league leaders in inducing double plays. He allowed 14 homers last season. Morgan has a good glove but average pickoff move. He's a mediocre hitter.

Major League Pitching Register

	W	L	ERA	G	CG	IP	H	ER	BB	SO
78 AL	0	3	7.30	3	1	12.1	19	10	8	0
79 AL	2	10	5.94	13	2	77.1	102	51	50	17
82 AL	7	11	4.37	30	2	150.1	167	73	67	71
83 AL	0	3	5.16	16	0	45.1	48	26	21	22
85 AL	1	1	12.00	2	0	6.0	11	8	5	2
86 AL	11	17	4.53	37	9	216.1	243	109	86	116
87 AL	12	17	4.65	34	8	207.0	245	107	53	85
88 AL	1	6	5.43	22	2	71.1	70	43	23	29
89 AL	8	11	2.53	40	0	152.2	130	43	33	72
90 NL	11	15	3.75	33	6	211.0	216	88	60	106
91 NL	14	10	2.78	34	5	236.1	197	73	61	140
92 NL	16	8	2.55	34	6	240.0	203	68	79	123
Life	83	112	3.87	298	41	1626.0	1651	699	546	783
3 AVE	14	11	3.00	34	6	229.0	205	76	67	123

HAL MORRIS

Position: First base
Team: Cincinnati Reds
Born: April 9, 1965 Fort Rucker, AL
Height: 6'4" **Weight:** 215 lbs.
Bats: left **Throws:** left
Acquired: Traded from Yankees with Rodney Imes for Tim Leary and Van Snider, 12/89

Player Summary

Fantasy Value	$12 to $16
Card Value	3¢ to 4¢
Will	rip righthanders
Can't	reach the fences
Expect	contact at plate
Don't Expect	sterling defense

After nearly winning the NL batting title in 1991, Morris suffered through an injury-riddled season in 1992. On April 15, he suffered a broken right hand when hit by a Charlie Leibrandt pitch in the first inning. Morris went back on the disabled list in August after pulling a hamstring muscle while swinging a bat in the on-deck circle. He was also slowed all season by a sore knee. When he's right, he is a line-drive hitter who makes good contact, walking almost as often as he strikes out. A solid .281 hitter against righthanders in 1992, he's not as effective against southpaws, notching a .252 batting average. Morris hit .340 as a 1990 rookie, then followed with a .318 mark. He came within one hit of the '91 batting crown. In 1992, he had a .347 on-base average and a .385 slugging percentage. He's only average as a baserunner and defensive first baseman, though he did improve his fielding a lot last year. He notched a .999 fielding percentage.

Major League Batting Register

	BA	G	AB	R	H	2B	3B	HR	RBI	SB
88 AL	.100	15	20	1	2	0	0	0	0	0
89 AL	.278	15	18	2	5	0	0	4	0	
90 NL	.340	107	309	50	105	22	3	7	36	9
91 NL	.318	136	478	72	152	33	1	14	59	10
92 NL	.271	115	395	41	107	21	3	6	53	6
Life	.304	388	1220	166	371	76	7	27	152	25
3 AVE	.308	119	394	54	121	25	2	9	49	8

JACK MORRIS

Position: Pitcher
Team: Toronto Blue Jays
Born: May 16, 1955 St. Paul, MN
Height: 6'3" **Weight:** 200 lbs.
Bats: right **Throws:** right
Acquired: Signed as a free agent, 12/91

Player Summary	
Fantasy Value	$22 to $28
Card Value	5¢ to 10¢
Will	rack up wins
Can't	avoid gophers
Expect	inflated ERA
Don't Expect	poor fielding

Even though he'll hit 39 years of age before Memorial Day, Morris has a chance to win 300 games. A workhorse righthander, he always manages to pitch well enough to win. The score of his 14th win last summer, for example, was 15-11. Backed by Toronto's solid offense and defense in 1992, Morris yielded more than four earned runs per game. When necessary, Morris can be miserly with runs. He went all the way in the 10-inning, 1-0 thriller that won the 1991 World Series for Minnesota. He did not have such a good 1992 World Series for Toronto, however. A fastball-forkball pitcher with a high leg kick, Morris is an exceptional fielder. He allows plenty of baserunners and has trouble keeping them close.

Major League Pitching Register

	W	L	ERA	G	CG	IP	H	ER	BB	SO
77 AL	1	1	3.74	7	1	45.2	38	19	23	28
78 AL	3	5	4.33	28	0	106.0	107	51	49	48
79 AL	17	7	3.28	27	9	197.2	179	72	59	113
80 AL	16	15	4.18	36	11	250.0	252	116	87	112
81 AL	14	7	3.05	25	15	198.0	153	67	78	97
82 AL	17	16	4.06	37	17	266.1	247	120	96	135
83 AL	20	13	3.34	37	20	293.2	257	109	83	232
84 AL	19	11	3.60	35	9	240.1	221	96	87	148
85 AL	16	11	3.33	35	13	257.0	212	95	110	191
86 AL	21	8	3.27	35	15	267.0	229	97	82	223
87 AL	18	11	3.38	34	13	266.0	227	100	93	208
88 AL	15	13	3.94	34	10	235.0	225	103	83	168
89 AL	6	14	4.86	24	10	170.1	189	92	59	115
90 AL	15	18	4.51	36	11	249.2	231	125	97	162
91 AL	18	12	3.43	35	10	246.2	226	94	92	163
92 AL	21	6	4.04	34	6	240.2	222	108	80	132
Life	237	168	3.73	499	170	3530.0	3215	1464	1258	2275
3 AVE	18	12	3.99	35	9	245.2	226	109	90	152

TERRY MULHOLLAND

Position: Pitcher
Team: Philadelphia Phillies
Born: March 9, 1963 Uniontown, PA
Height: 6'3" **Weight:** 200 lbs.
Bats: right **Throws:** left
Acquired: Traded from Giants with Dennis Cook and Charlie Hayes for Steve Bedrosian and Rick Parker, 6/89

Player Summary	
Fantasy Value	$16 to $20
Card Value	3¢ to 4¢
Will	become big winner
Can't	ring up strikeouts
Expect	frequent pickoffs
Don't Expect	lapses of control

Although he's lefthanded, Mulholland uses Tom Seaver as a role model. Like Seaver, Mulholland is a control specialist who hides the ball from the hitters and drives off his legs. Working more than 200 innings a year, he throws four pitches for strikes and often finishes what he starts. A durable performer who rarely misses a start, he is a master at keeping baserunners glued to the bag. His pickoff move—taught to him by Rick Reuschel—is so good that Mulholland set a record in that department last season. A sinker-and-slider pitcher who also throws a curveball and a changeup, Mulholland gets most of his outs on ground balls. He averages about five strikeouts per nine innings, but he also allows fewer than two walks per nine innings. Opponents in 1992 compiled a .261 batting average, a .298 on-base average, and a .365 slugging percentage. Mulholland doesn't give himself much help as a fielder or hitter.

Major League Pitching Register

	W	L	ERA	G	CG	IP	H	ER	BB	SO
86 NL	1	7	4.94	15	0	54.2	51	30	35	27
88 NL	2	1	3.72	9	2	46.0	50	19	7	18
89 NL	4	7	4.92	25	2	115.1	137	63	36	66
90 NL	9	10	3.34	33	6	180.2	172	67	42	75
91 NL	16	13	3.61	34	8	232.0	231	93	49	142
92 NL	13	11	3.81	32	12	229.0	227	97	46	125
Life	45	49	3.87	148	30	857.2	868	369	215	453
3 AVE	13	11	3.60	33	9	214.1	210	86	46	114

PEDRO MUNOZ

Position: Outfield
Team: Minnesota Twins
Born: Sept. 19, 1968, Ponce, Puerto Rico
Height: 5'11" **Weight:** 170 lbs.
Bats: right **Throws:** right
Acquired: Traded from Blue Jays with Nelson Liriano for John Candelaria, 7/90

Player Summary	
Fantasy Value	$5 to $8
Card Value	5¢ to 10¢
Will	stroke line drives
Can't	wait out walks
Expect	occasional power
Don't Expect	Gold Glove defense

Because he hits lefthanders better than righthanders, Munoz was platooned in right field by Minnesota much of 1992. He batted .295 against southpaws and .260 versus righties. He showed some extra-base power and kept his average respectable but displayed extreme impatience at the plate. Munoz fanned five times more than he walked, thus negating the value of speed that could be exploited if he waited out bases on balls. A line-drive hitter who lives for fastballs, he notched a .298 on-base average and a .409 slugging percentage in 1992. Once considered a defensive liability, Munoz managed to shake that reputation. Even though he shifted between right field and left, he made only a handful of errors and showed decent range and a competent throwing arm. Munoz had consecutive .300-plus seasons at Triple-A Portland before reaching Minnesota in mid-1991. He batted .316 with five homers and 28 RBI at Portland in 1991, and he hit .318 with five homers and 21 RBI there in 1990. He also hit .319 with seven homers and 56 RBI at Double-A Syracuse in '90.

Major League Batting Register

	BA	G	AB	R	H	2B	3B	HR	RBI	SB
90 AL	.271	22	85	13	23	4	1	0	5	3
91 AL	.283	51	138	15	39	7	1	7	26	3
92 AL	.270	127	418	44	113	16	3	12	71	4
Life	.273	200	641	72	175	27	5	19	102	10

DALE MURPHY

Position: Outfield
Team: Philadelphia Phillies
Born: March 12, 1956, Portland, OR
Height: 6'4" **Weight:** 215 lbs.
Bats: right **Throws:** right
Acquired: Traded from Braves with Tommy Greene for Jeff Parrett, Jim Vatcher, and Victor Rosario, 8/90

Player Summary	
Fantasy Value	$8 to $12
Card Value	5¢ to 8¢
Will	seek medical miracle
Can't	roll back the clock
Expect	good bat versus lefties
Don't Expect	same speed

For Murphy, the 1992 season was a total loss. Four months before spring training, he underwent arthroscopic knee surgery. The same knee had to be drained three times during the six-week training period. After playing 17 games in pain, Murphy went on the shelf again. He had arthroscopic surgery twice as doctors removed scar tissue and other debris. His future is clouded. Even if he gets a clean bill of health, Murphy is only a shadow of the player who won MVP awards in 1982 and '83. Murphy still hits lefthanders and has a fine arm in right field, so he might finish out as a platoon player.

Major League Batting Register

	BA	G	AB	R	H	2B	3B	HR	RBI	SB
76 NL	.262	19	65	3	17	6	0	0	9	0
77 NL	.316	18	76	5	24	8	1	2	14	0
78 NL	.226	151	530	66	120	14	3	23	79	11
79 NL	.276	104	384	53	106	7	2	21	57	6
80 NL	.281	156	569	98	160	27	2	33	89	9
81 NL	.247	104	369	43	91	12	1	13	50	14
82 NL	.281	162	598	113	168	23	2	36	109	23
83 NL	.302	162	589	131	178	24	4	36	121	30
84 NL	.290	162	607	94	176	32	8	36	100	19
85 NL	.300	162	616	118	185	32	2	37	111	10
86 NL	.265	160	614	89	163	29	7	29	83	7
87 NL	.295	159	566	115	167	27	1	44	105	16
88 NL	.226	156	592	77	134	35	4	24	77	3
89 NL	.228	154	574	60	131	16	0	20	84	3
90 NL	.245	154	563	60	138	23	1	24	83	9
91 NL	.252	153	544	66	137	33	1	18	81	1
92 NL	.161	18	62	5	10	1	0	2	7	0
Life	.266	2154	7918	1196	2105	349	39	398	1259	161
2 AVE	.248	154	554	63	138	28	1	21	82	5

ROB MURPHY

Position: Pitcher
Team: Houston Astros
Born: May 26, 1960 Miami, FL
Height: 6'2" **Weight:** 215 lbs.
Bats: left **Throws:** left
Acquired: Signed as a free agent, 1/92

Player Summary	
Fantasy Value	$1 to $3
Card Value	3¢ to 4¢
Will	work against lefties
Can't	always locate plate
Expect	frequent appearances
Don't Expect	gopher balls

After going to spring training as a non-roster invitee, Murphy gave the 1992 Astros an extra southpaw arm in the bullpen. After taking a seven-year ERA of 3.15 into the season, the veteran left-hander struggled with his control and also yielded more hits than innings pitched. On the plus side, however, he was extremely stingy in throwing home run balls. Opponents compiled a .260 batting average, a .322 on-base average, and a .353 slugging percentage in 1992, and Murphy allowed the first batter he faced each game to notch a .296 batting average. He usually has better control of his fastball, slider, and forkball. Years of overuse may have caught up with him. He worked 87 times for the 1987 Reds, then less often in every season since. In many of his outings, he's used only to retire a single left-handed hitter. Murphy's deficient defensive play detracts from his game.

Major League Pitching Register

	W	L	ERA	G	S	IP	H	ER	BB	SO
85 NL	0	0	6.00	2	0	3.0	2	2	2	1
86 NL	6	0	0.72	34	1	50.1	26	4	21	36
87 NL	8	5	3.04	87	3	100.2	91	34	32	99
88 NL	0	6	3.08	76	3	84.2	69	29	38	74
89 NL	5	7	2.74	74	9	105.0	97	32	41	107
90 AL	0	6	6.32	68	7	57.0	85	40	32	54
91 AL	0	1	3.00	57	4	48.0	47	16	19	34
92 NL	3	1	4.04	59	0	55.2	56	25	21	42
Life	22	26	3.25	457	27	504.1	473	182	206	447
3 AVE	1	3	4.54	61	4	53.1	63	27	24	43

EDDIE MURRAY

Position: First base
Team: New York Mets
Born: Feb. 24, 1956 Los Angeles, CA
Height: 6'2" **Weight:** 224 lbs.
Bats: right **Throws:** right
Acquired: Signed as a free agent, 11/91

Player Summary	
Fantasy Value	$20 to $25
Card Value	5¢ to 10¢
Will	knock in runs
Can't	steal bases
Expect	clutch hitting
Don't Expect	great fielding

Even though the Mets struggled last summer, Murray reached 75 RBI for the 16th consecutive season. He is bettered only by Hank Aaron, who notched at least 75 RBI for 19 straight seasons. Murray, who ranks second in home runs by active players, hit his 17th career grand slam to beat the Reds on Sept. 4. The switch-hitting slugger has not reached 30 homers since 1987 or 100 RBI since 1985 and may not reach those levels again. Nor is he likely to repeat the Gold Gloves he won from 1982 to '84. Though he turns the 3-6-3 double play well, Murray's range has declined and he has trouble on pop-ups. He doesn't run well, rarely steals, and hits into more than his share of double plays.

Major League Batting Register

	BA	G	AB	R	H	2B	3B	HR	RBI	SB
77 AL	.283	160	611	81	173	29	2	27	88	0
78 AL	.285	161	610	85	174	32	3	27	95	6
79 AL	.295	159	606	90	179	30	2	25	99	10
80 AL	.300	158	621	100	186	36	2	32	116	7
81 AL	.294	99	378	57	111	21	2	22	78	2
82 AL	.316	151	550	87	174	30	1	32	110	7
83 AL	.306	156	582	115	178	30	3	33	111	5
84 AL	.306	162	588	97	180	26	3	29	110	10
85 AL	.297	156	583	111	173	37	1	31	124	5
86 AL	.305	137	495	61	151	25	1	17	84	3
87 AL	.277	160	618	89	171	28	3	30	91	1
88 AL	.284	161	603	75	171	27	2	28	84	5
89 NL	.247	160	594	66	147	29	1	20	88	7
90 NL	.330	155	558	96	184	22	3	26	95	8
91 NL	.260	153	576	69	150	23	1	19	96	10
92 NL	.261	156	551	64	144	37	2	16	93	4
Life	.290	2444	9124	1343	2646	462	32	414	1562	90
3 AVE	.284	155	562	76	159	27	2	20	95	7

MIKE MUSSINA

Position: Pitcher
Team: Baltimore Orioles
Born: Dec. 8, 1968 Williamsport, PA
Height: 6′ **Weight:** 182 lbs.
Bats: right **Throws:** right
Acquired: First-round pick in 6/90 free-agent draft

Player Summary

Fantasy Value	$20 to $32
Card Value	10¢ to 25¢
Will	make All-Star team
Can't	avoid gopher balls
Expect	exceptional control
Don't Expect	fewer than 15 wins

Mussina took only three and one-half years to earn his economics degree from Stanford. He's still practicing what he learned, because he is the American League's most economical pitcher in doling out walks. He has total command of his fastball, slider, and knuckle-curve. He changes speeds well and displays the poise of a much more experienced pitcher. He was on the AL All-Star squad for the July 14 game, then pitched a one-hitter against Texas three days later. Mussina strikes out three times more men than he walks, yields fewer hits than innings pitched, fields his position well, and keeps runners close. Opponents in 1992 compiled a .239 batting average, a .278 on-base percentage, and a .348 slugging percentage. Three of his first 12 wins last year were shutouts. He pitched only 28 games in the minors. At Triple-A Rochester in 1991, he was 10-4 with a 2.87 ERA, 31 walks, and 107 strikeouts in 122⅓ innings. He was named the '91 International League's Pitcher of the Year. One of baseball's smartest players, his locker overflows with books.

Major League Pitching Register

	W	L	ERA	G	CG	IP	H	ER	BB	SO
91 AL	4	5	2.87	12	2	87.2	77	28	21	52
92 AL	18	5	2.54	32	8	241.0	212	68	48	130
Life	22	10	2.63	44	10	328.2	289	96	69	182
2 AVE	11	5	2.63	22	5	164.1	145	48	35	91

GREG MYERS

Position: Catcher
Team: California Angels
Born: April 14, 1966 Riverside, CA
Height: 6′2″ **Weight:** 206 lbs.
Bats: left **Throws:** right
Acquired: Traded from Blue Jays with Rob Ducey for Mark Eichhorn, 7/92

Player Summary

Fantasy Value	$2 to $4
Card Value	3¢ to 4¢
Will	make contact
Can't	clear fences
Expect	weak defense
Don't Expect	stolen bases

Good catchers are hard to find, but those that hit lefthanded are at a premium. They're even more valuable when they hit well. Myers hinted in 1991 that he might qualify. Used in a lefty-righty platoon with Pat Borders by the Toronto Blue Jays, Myers hit .262 with eight home runs in 107 games. He regressed last year, however, and was traded. Slowed by a sore wrist that sent him to the disabled list in late August, Myers saw minimal action last summer. When healthy, he makes decent contact but fans twice as much as he walks. He had a .271 on-base average and a .359 slugging percentage in 1992. Equipped with the speed of a loaded oil truck, Myers never steals, rarely takes extra bases, and often grounds into double plays. He's also a weak defensive catcher—thanks in part to past elbow and shoulder injuries that have hampered his throwing. In 1992, Myers could be entering a crossroads season.

Major League Batting Register

	BA	G	AB	R	H	2B	3B	HR	RBI	SB
87 AL	.111	7	9	1	1	0	0	0	0	0
89 AL	.114	17	44	0	5	2	0	0	1	0
90 AL	.236	87	250	33	59	7	1	5	22	0
91 AL	.262	107	309	25	81	22	0	8	36	0
92 AL	.231	30	78	4	18	7	0	1	13	0
Life	.238	248	690	63	164	38	1	14	72	0
2 AVE	.250	97	280	29	70	15	1	7	29	0

RANDY MYERS

Position: Pitcher
Team: Chicago Cubs
Born: Sept. 19, 1962 Vancouver, WA
Height: 6'1" **Weight:** 210 lbs.
Bats: left **Throws:** left
Acquired: Signed as a free agent, 12/92

Player Summary	
Fantasy Value	$23 to $28
Card Value	3¢ to 4¢
Will	hope heater works
Can't	avoid gopher balls
Expect	ninth-inning calls
Don't Expect	pinpoint control

Myers is the closer the Cubs have longed for. In his first year as the No. 1 closer for the Padres, he had a rough start but a strong finish. Hitters belted him for a .307 average in the first half, when he blew five saves in 20 chances and yielded 51 hits in 41 innings. Then he started a string of 16 straight saves. His primary problem last year was giving up more hits than innings pitched and keeping the ball in the park. Sometimes considered headstrong and unreceptive to coaching, Myers averages almost a strikeout per inning and fans two batters for every walk. He's strictly a power pitcher who relies on mixing his fastball and slider. Opponents in 1992 compiled a .279 batting average, a .349 on-base percentage, and a .402 slugging percentage. As a hitter, Myers is no automatic out but strikes out a lot. He's a mediocre fielder whose best asset is keeping runners close.

Major League Pitching Register

	W	L	ERA	G	S	IP	H	ER	BB	SO
85 NL	0	0	0.00	1	0	2.0	0	0	1	2
86 NL	0	0	4.22	10	0	10.2	11	5	9	13
87 NL	3	6	3.96	54	6	75.0	61	33	30	92
88 NL	7	3	1.72	55	26	68.0	45	13	17	69
89 NL	7	4	2.35	65	24	84.1	62	22	40	88
90 NL	4	6	2.08	66	31	86.2	59	20	38	98
91 NL	6	13	3.55	58	6	132.0	116	52	80	108
92 NL	3	6	4.29	66	38	79.2	84	38	34	66
Life	30	38	3.06	375	131	538.1	438	183	249	536
3 AVE	4	8	3.32	63	25	99.1	86	37	51	91

CHRIS NABHOLZ

Position: Pitcher
Team: Montreal Expos
Born: Jan. 5, 1967 Harrisburg, PA
Height: 6'5" **Weight:** 210 lbs.
Bats: left **Throws:** left
Acquired: Third-round pick in 6/88 free-agent draft

Player Summary	
Fantasy Value	$2 to $6
Card Value	3¢ to 4¢
Will	improve with time
Can't	always find zone
Expect	ground-ball outs
Don't Expect	home run balls

Although he has only one full season under his belt, Nabholz is already one of the NL's leading lefties. He's improving as he gains experience, and he has a bright future. A sinkerballer who also throws a curve and a changeup, Nabholz has a deceptive delivery that is especially tough on lefthanded hitters. He averages about eight hits, three and one-half walks, and six strikeouts per nine innings. He gets most of his outs on ground balls. Although he would like to sharpen his control and increase his strikeout totals, Nabholz needs no help in keeping gopher balls to a minimum. Opponents in 1992 compiled a .244 batting average, a .317 on-base percentage, and a .349 slugging percentage. He has a decent pickoff move but is only average as a fielder and below average as a hitter and bunter. In 1991 at Triple-A Indianapolis, he was 2-2 with a 1.86 ERA, five walks, and 16 strikeouts in 19⅓ innings. He was 8-7 with a 3.63 ERA, 57 walks, and 99 strikeouts in 153⅔ innings at Indianapolis in 1990.

Major League Pitching Register

	W	L	ERA	G	CG	IP	H	ER	BB	SO
90 NL	6	2	2.83	11	1	70.0	43	22	32	53
91 NL	8	7	3.63	24	1	153.2	134	62	57	99
92 NL	11	12	3.32	32	1	195.0	176	72	74	130
Life	25	21	3.35	67	3	418.2	353	156	163	282
3 AVE	8	7	3.35	22	1	139.1	118	52	54	94

TIM NAEHRING

Position: Infield
Team: Boston Red Sox
Born: Feb. 1, 1967 Cincinnati, OH
Height: 6'2" **Weight:** 190 lbs.
Bats: right **Throws:** right
Acquired: Eighth-round pick in 6/88 free-agent draft

Player Summary	
Fantasy Value	$2 to $4
Card Value	3¢ to 4¢
Will	try for comeback
Can't	worry about back
Expect	surprising power
Don't Expect	display of speed

The bright promise Naehring showed several springs ago is quickly fading into memory. Once regarded as a red-hot shortstop prospect because of his power, he was slowed by a sprained right wrist last summer. He had a .308 on-base average and a .323 slugging percentage in 1992. He also spent time in the minor leagues, trying to recapture his home run stroke. At Triple-A Pawtucket last year, he batted .294 with two homers and five RBI, in 34 at bats. He missed most of the 1991 season with serious back problems, which required surgery. In 1990, Naehring hit 15 homers in 82 games for Pawtucket, then added two more in a 24-game look with the Red Sox. He hit .275 with three homers and 31 RBI in 273 at bats at Pawtucket in 1989. Naehring has played all three infield positions since turning pro in 1988. He's best at short but will have to prove totally recovered from his back surgery. He played 23 games at second base. A contact hitter who doesn't strike out too much, Naehring once stole 16 bases in Triple-A.

Major League Batting Register

	BA	G	AB	R	H	2B	3B	HR	RBI	SB
90 AL	.271	24	85	10	23	6	0	2	12	0
91 AL	.109	20	55	1	6	1	0	0	3	0
92 AL	.231	72	186	12	43	8	0	3	14	0
Life	.221	116	326	23	72	15	0	5	29	0

CHARLES NAGY

Position: Pitcher
Team: Cleveland Indians
Born: May 5, 1967 Bridgeport, CT
Height: 6'3" **Weight:** 200 lbs.
Bats: left **Throws:** right
Acquired: First-round pick in 6/88 free-agent draft

Player Summary	
Fantasy Value	$20 to $30
Card Value	5¢ to 10¢
Will	make All-Star team
Can't	carry club alone
Expect	Cy Young bid
Don't Expect	control lapses

In his second full big league season, Nagy blossomed into one of the best pitchers in the American League. On June 17, he notched his fifth straight win to increase his record to 9-3, drop his ERA to 2.20, and extend his walkless streak to 28⅔ innings. Nagy credited his performance to better control and confidence in a newly developed forkball. He'll throw the forkball at any time in the count, and he also throws a fastball and a slider. Opponents in 1992 compiled a .260 batting average, a .300 on-base percentage, and a .346 slugging percentage. The 1992 All-Star authored all six of Cleveland's complete games in the first half and ended Indian losing streaks with eight of his first 11 wins. Only a seventh-inning Glenn Davis single kept Nagy from a no-hitter at Baltimore Aug. 8. He also notched three shutouts. Though he yields an average of a hit per inning, Nagy keeps the ball in the park; he allowed 11 homers in 1992. He averages two walks and six whiffs per nine innings.

Major League Pitching Register

	W	L	ERA	G	CG	IP	H	ER	BB	SO
90 AL	2	4	5.91	9	0	45.2	58	30	21	26
91 AL	10	15	4.13	33	6	211.1	228	97	66	109
92 AL	17	10	2.96	33	10	252.0	245	83	57	169
Life	29	29	3.71	75	16	509.0	531	210	144	304
2 AVE	14	13	3.50	33	8	232.1	237	90	62	139

JAIME NAVARRO

Position: Pitcher
Team: Milwaukee Brewers
Born: March 27, 1967 Bayamon, Puerto Rico
Height: 6'4" **Weight:** 210 lbs.
Bats: right **Throws:** right
Acquired: Third-round pick in 6/87 free-agent draft

Player Summary	
Fantasy Value	$12 to $16
Card Value	3¢ to 4¢
Will	top 200 frames
Can't	get strikeouts
Expect	superb control
Don't Expect	losing streaks

Navarro doesn't get very many strikeouts. All he does is win. Told last season to take something off his fastball and let the defense record the outs, he won 11 of his first 17, notched his first shutout July 27, and posted a 2.35 ERA for the month of August. A control pitcher who can hit certain spots, Navarro credited his improvement to better control and better concentration. He averages about two walks and eight hits per nine innings. He can be much tougher, however, yielding only three hits in a 17-inning stretch last July and posting a 1.11 ERA between the All-Star break and Aug. 16. A sinker-and-slider pitcher who also throws a changeup, Navarro pitches most effectively in tight games. Opponents compiled a .246 batting average, a .295 on-base percentage, and a .351 slugging percentage in 1992. He's not good at keeping runners close but he does hold his own in the field. Navarro is coming off consecutive big years and has a bright future.

Major League Pitching Register

	W	L	ERA	G	CG	IP	H	ER	BB	SO
89 AL	7	8	3.12	19	1	109.2	119	38	32	56
90 AL	8	7	4.46	32	3	149.1	176	74	41	75
91 AL	15	12	3.92	34	10	234.0	237	102	73	114
92 AL	17	11	3.33	34	5	246.0	224	91	64	100
Life	47	38	3.71	119	19	739.0	756	305	210	345
3 AVE	13	10	3.82	33	6	210.0	212	89	59	96

DENNY NEAGLE

Position: Pitcher
Team: Pittsburgh Pirates
Born: Sept. 13, 1968 Prince Georges County, MD
Height: 6'4" **Weight:** 209 lbs.
Bats: left **Throws:** left
Acquired: Traded from Twins for John Smiley and Midre Cummings, 3/92

Player Summary	
Fantasy Value	$4 to $8
Card Value	5¢ to 10¢
Will	seek rotation berth
Can't	avoid gopher balls
Expect	excellent changeup
Don't Expect	steady relief work

During his three-year tenure in the minors, Neagle was a control pitcher who fanned three times more batters than he walked. As a rookie with the 1992 Pirates, however, he failed to maintain that ratio. The Pirates felt he was such a good prospect that they were willing to give up a former 20-game winner in John Smiley to obtain him. After making a half-dozen starts, Neagle was assigned to the bullpen. He averaged eight strikeouts and eight hits per nine innings but also allowed an average of nearly four and one-half walks per nine innings. Though he yielded fewer hits than innings, he threw too many home run balls. As a result, Neagle had neither a good record nor a respectable ERA. Opponents in 1992 compiled a .247 batting average, a .335 on-base percentage, and a .387 slugging percentage. He has a good changeup that he mixes with an average fastball. When he throws both pitches for strikes, he can be effective. Neagle has a good glove and knows how to hold runners on. In 1991 at Triple-A Portland, he was 9-4 with a 3.24 ERA.

Major League Pitching Register

	W	L	ERA	G	S	IP	H	ER	BB	SO
91 AL	0	1	4.05	7	0	20.0	28	9	7	14
92 NL	4	6	4.48	55	2	86.1	81	43	43	77
Life	4	7	4.40	62	2	106.1	109	52	50	91

AL NEWMAN

Position: Second base; shortstop
Team: Texas Rangers
Born: June 30, 1960 Kansas City, MO
Height: 5'9" **Weight:** 188 lbs.
Bats: left **Throws:** right
Acquired: Signed as a free agent, 4/92

Player Summary	
Fantasy Value	$1 to $2
Card Value	3¢ to 4¢
Will	fill in well
Can't	hit with power
Expect	low average
Don't Expect	daily duty

Newman's versatility and defensive ability keep him in the big leagues. A light-hitting utility man, he has exactly one home run in 2,107 at bats. Signed by Texas to fill in for injured second baseman Julio Franco, Newman provided better speed and defense at the position. A spray hitter who hits 100 points higher against lefthanders, Newman walks more often than he strikes out. He had a .317 on-base average and a .240 slugging percentage in 1992. He has the speed to steal when he reaches (which isn't often), but he was caught stealing six times in '92. Second base is Newman's best spot, but he can fill in at shortstop or third without hurting the defense. He's also played the outfield on occasion. Newman broke into pro ball in 1982 and reached the majors three years later. The former San Diego State University player has participated in two World Series.

Major League Batting Register

	BA	G	AB	R	H	2B	3B	HR	RBI	SB
85 NL	.172	25	29	7	5	1	0	0	1	2
86 NL	.200	95	185	23	37	3	0	1	8	11
87 AL	.221	110	307	44	68	15	5	0	29	15
88 AL	.223	105	260	35	58	7	0	0	19	12
89 AL	.253	141	446	62	113	18	2	0	38	25
90 AL	.242	144	388	43	94	14	0	0	30	13
91 AL	.191	118	246	25	47	5	0	0	19	4
92 AL	.220	116	246	25	54	5	0	0	12	9
Life	.226	854	2107	264	476	68	7	1	156	91
3 AVE	.222	126	293	31	65	8	0	0	20	9

ROD NICHOLS

Position: Pitcher
Team: Cleveland Indians
Born: Dec. 29, 1964 Burlington, IA
Height: 6'2" **Weight:** 190 lbs.
Bats: right **Throws:** right
Acquired: Fifth-round pick in 6/85 free-agent draft

Player Summary	
Fantasy Value	$2 to $4
Card Value	3¢ to 4¢
Will	try to find role
Can't	avoid gophers
Expect	live fastball
Don't Expect	ERA below 4.00

Nichols began last year in the Cleveland bullpen, then spent some time in the minors before returning to take the rotation spot of Jack Armstrong. The velocity on Nichols's fastball had fallen to 84 mph at the time of his exile but was 7 mph faster when he returned. He throws a fastball, curveball, slider, and changeup, but he doesn't always find the strike zone. Opponents in 1992 compiled a .273 batting average, a .323 on-base average, and a .429 slugging percentage. The first batters he faced compiled a .389 average. Nichols yields more hits than innings pitched and has trouble keeping the ball in the park. At Triple-A Colorado Springs in 1992, he was 3-3 with a 5.67 ERA, 16 walks, and 35 strikeouts in 54 innings pitched. Used as both a starter and reliever over the last five seasons, Nichols has yet to find his niche in the major leagues. He might still be a productive pitcher if given a specified role. The keys are more control and fewer gopher balls.

Major League Pitching Register

	W	L	ERA	G	S	IP	H	ER	BB	SO
88 AL	1	7	5.06	11	0	69.1	73	39	23	31
89 AL	4	6	4.40	15	0	71.2	81	35	24	42
90 AL	0	3	7.87	4	0	16.0	24	14	6	3
91 AL	2	11	3.54	31	1	137.1	145	54	30	76
92 AL	4	3	4.53	30	0	105.1	114	53	31	56
Life	11	30	4.39	91	1	399.2	437	195	114	208
2 AVE	3	7	3.97	31	1	121.1	130	54	31	66

DAVE NILSSON

Position: Catcher
Team: Milwaukee Brewers
Born: Dec. 14, 1969 Queensland, Australia
Height: 6'3" **Weight:** 185 lbs.
Bats: left **Throws:** right
Acquired: Signed as free agent, 2/87

Player Summary	
Fantasy Value	$3 to $5
Card Value	10¢ to 15¢
Will	play if healthy
Can't	inject speed
Expect	good contact
Don't Expect	poor defense

Nilsson is a catcher with a strong lefthanded bat. His statistics during five minor league seasons prior to 1992 included a .418 performance in 65 games for Double-A El Paso in 1991. After earning a promotion to Triple-A Denver that year, Nilsson's season was shortened by surgery on his left shoulder. Last summer wasn't much better for the native Australian. His progress was slowed by a sprained left wrist and an unexpected return to Denver. He batted .317 with three homers, 39 RBI, 16 doubles, seven triples, 10 stolen bases, 23 walks, and 19 strikeouts in 240 at bats in Denver last summer. When he's right, he is a fine defensive catcher who has a stronger arm than B.J. Surhoff, the veteran incumbent who played ahead of Nilsson in Milwaukee last year. He calls games like a veteran and blocks the plate well. He nailed 36.4 percent of runners trying to steal last summer. He's also capable of filling in at first, third, and designated hitter. Nilsson is a contact hitter who walked more than he fanned in the minors. He compiled a .304 on-base average and a .354 slugging percentage for Milwaukee in 1992.

Major League Batting Register

	BA	G	AB	R	H	2B	3B	HR	RBI	SB
92 AL	.232	51	164	15	38	8	0	4	25	2
Life	.232	51	164	15	38	8	0	4	25	2

OTIS NIXON

Position: Outfield
Team: Atlanta Braves
Born: Jan. 9, 1959 Evergreen, NC
Height: 6'2" **Weight:** 180 lbs.
Bats: both **Throws:** right
Acquired: Traded from Expos for Jimmy Kremers, 4/91

Player Summary	
Fantasy Value	$13 to $21
Card Value	3¢ to 4¢
Will	use great speed
Can't	generate power
Expect	contact hitting
Don't Expect	erratic defense

Although he is a switch-hitter, Nixon hits nearly 100 points higher against lefthanded pitchers. He is no slouch against righties either and will try to bunt his way on when he feels overmatched. He batted .343 against lefties in 1992, and he hit .263 against righties. A career .228 hitter before meeting Atlanta batting coach Clarence Jones, Nixon was batting .300 much of the season. He has little extra-base power but makes up in speed what he lacks in strength. Nixon has swiped 30 bases five years in a row and fattens his average with infield hits. His speed also helps in the outfield, where center is his best position. He runs down balls in the gaps and sometimes makes superhuman leaps to flag down potential homers. Nixon hit .435 during an 11-game hitting streak from Aug. 5 to 16.

Major League Batting Register

	BA	G	AB	R	H	2B	3B	HR	RBI	SB
83 AL	.143	13	14	2	2	0	0	0	0	2
84 AL	.154	49	91	16	14	0	0	0	1	12
85 AL	.235	104	162	34	38	4	0	3	9	20
86 AL	.263	105	95	33	25	4	1	0	8	23
87 AL	.059	19	17	2	1	0	0	0	1	2
88 NL	.244	90	271	47	66	8	2	0	15	46
89 NL	.217	126	258	41	56	7	2	0	21	37
90 NL	.251	119	231	46	58	6	2	1	20	50
91 NL	.297	124	401	81	119	10	1	0	26	72
92 NL	.294	120	456	79	134	14	2	2	22	41
Life	.257	869	1996	381	513	53	10	6	123	305
3 AVE	.286	121	363	69	104	10	2	1	23	54

206

MATT NOKES

Position: Catcher
Team: New York Yankees
Born: Oct. 31, 1963 San Diego, CA
Height: 6'1" **Weight:** 185 lbs.
Bats: left **Throws:** right
Acquired: Traded from Tigers for Clay Parker and Lance McCullers, 6/90

Player Summary

Fantasy Value	$13 to $16
Card Value	3¢ to 4¢
Will	show some power
Can't	hit lefthanders
Expect	runners to steal
Don't Expect	same anemic average

After making enormous career strides in 1991, Nokes went backward last summer. His defense deteriorated, and his bat went along for the ride. Once so weak behind the plate that Sparky Anderson made him a designated hitter, Nokes worked with special instructor Marc Hill to improve his defense. Nokes is a good game-caller and handler of pitchers, but he needs more work on blocking the plate and throwing. In '92, his success ratio in nailing would-be basestealers plunged below 25 percent. At the same time, Nokes became an automatic out against lefthanded pitchers (he batted .197 versus lefties) and didn't do much better against righties (.230). His swing, however, is ideally suited to Yankee Stadium's dimensions. He had a .293 on-base average and a .424 slugging percentage in 1992. Though he's hit 20 homers three times, Nokes must focus on his fielding to retain a regular job.

Major League Batting Register

	BA	G	AB	R	H	2B	3B	HR	RBI	SB
85 NL	.208	19	53	3	11	2	0	2	5	0
86 AL	.333	7	24	2	8	1	0	1	2	0
87 AL	.289	135	461	69	133	14	2	32	87	2
88 AL	.251	122	382	53	96	18	0	16	53	0
89 AL	.250	87	268	15	67	10	0	9	39	1
90 AL	.248	136	351	33	87	9	1	11	40	2
91 AL	.268	135	456	52	122	20	0	24	77	3
92 AL	.224	121	384	42	86	9	1	22	59	0
Life	.256	762	2379	269	610	83	4	117	362	8
3 AVE	.248	131	397	42	98	13	1	19	59	2

EDWIN NUNEZ

Position: Pitcher
Team: Texas Rangers
Born: May 27, 1963 Humacao, Puerto Rico
Height: 6'5" **Weight:** 240 lbs.
Bats: right **Throws:** right
Acquired: Traded from Brewers, 5/92

Player Summary

Fantasy Value	$1 to $3
Card Value	3¢ to 4¢
Will	throw hard
Can't	avoid injury
Expect	set-up role
Don't Expect	gopher balls

Nunez spent last summer as a middle reliever in the bullpen of the Rangers. A rubber-armed righthander who throws hard, he served mainly in a set-up role. Nunez mixes a fastball and a forkball, and he averages more than seven strikeouts per nine innings but only a little more than three walks per nine innings. Though he yields almost a hit per inning, he keeps the ball in the park. Opponents compiled a .268 batting average, a .331 on-base percentage, and a .426 slugging percentage in 1992. For some reason, Nunez had more success against lefthanded hitters than righties last summer. His career progress has been slowed by 1991 back surgery and assorted other injuries. Nunez has been a starter and closer at various times in his career. He broke into pro ball in 1979.

Major League Pitching Register

	W	L	ERA	G	S	IP	H	ER	BB	SO
82 AL	1	2	4.58	8	0	35.1	36	18	16	27
83 AL	0	4	4.38	14	0	37.0	40	18	22	35
84 AL	2	2	3.19	37	7	67.2	55	24	21	57
85 AL	7	3	3.09	70	16	90.1	79	31	34	58
86 AL	1	2	5.82	14	0	21.2	25	14	5	17
87 AL	3	4	3.80	48	12	47.1	45	20	18	34
88 AL	1	4	7.98	14	0	29.1	45	26	14	19
88 NL	1	0	4.50	10	0	14.0	21	7	3	8
89 AL	3	4	4.17	27	1	54.0	49	25	36	41
90 AL	3	1	2.24	42	6	80.1	65	20	37	66
91 AL	2	1	6.04	23	8	25.1	28	17	13	24
92 AL	1	3	4.85	49	3	59.1	63	32	22	49
Life	25	30	4.04	356	53	561.2	551	252	241	435
2 AVE	2	2	3.35	46	5	69.3	64	26	30	58

CHARLIE O'BRIEN

Position: Catcher
Team: New York Mets
Born: May 1, 1961 Tulsa, OK
Height: 6'2" **Weight:** 190 lbs.
Bats: right **Throws:** right
Acquired: Traded from Brewers for Julio Machado and Kevin Brown, 8/90

Player Summary	
Fantasy Value	$1 to $2
Card Value	3¢ to 4¢
Will	nail rival runners
Can't	build good average
Expect	great glove work
Don't Expect	long-ball production

O'Brien has proven to be a survivor. He had hit under .200 two years in a row, but he kept his spot in the major leagues because he's so valuable behind the plate. His throwing arm is like a howitzer. He nailed 15 of the first 25 runners who tried to steal last year, a 60 percent success rate that led both leagues. His season mark stood at 45.5 percent—just a notch above his career ratio. Behind the plate, O'Brien gets high marks for handling pitchers, blocking the plate, and snaring wild pitches. At bat, he doesn't strike out a lot. O'Brien hits routine grounders, pop-ups, and fly balls with alarming frequency, however. He actually hit six homers in 62 games for the '89 Brewers but then hit none the next year. He had a .289 on-base average and a .327 slugging percentage in 1992.

Major League Batting Register

	BA	G	AB	R	H	2B	3B	HR	RBI	SB
85 AL	.273	16	11	3	3	1	0	0	1	0
87 AL	.200	10	35	2	7	3	1	0	0	0
88 AL	.220	40	118	12	26	6	0	2	9	0
89 AL	.234	62	188	22	44	10	0	6	35	0
90 NL	.186	46	145	11	27	7	2	0	11	0
90 NL	.162	28	68	6	11	3	0	0	9	0
91 NL	.185	69	168	16	31	6	0	2	14	0
92 NL	.212	68	156	15	33	12	0	2	13	0
Life	.205	339	889	87	182	48	3	12	92	0
3 AVE	.190	70	179	16	34	9	1	1	16	0

PETE O'BRIEN

Position: First base; designated hitter
Team: Seattle Mariners
Born: Feb. 9, 1958 Santa Monica, CA
Height: 6'2" **Weight:** 195 lbs.
Bats: left **Throws:** left
Acquired: Signed as a free agent, 12/89

Player Summary	
Fantasy Value	$6 to $12
Card Value	3¢ to 4¢
Will	show some power
Can't	handle lefthanders
Expect	good glove at first
Don't Expect	frequent Ks

O'Brien began last season as Seattle's regular first baseman but ended it in a lefty-righty designated hitter platoon with Lance Parrish. The emergence of highly touted youngster Tino Martinez pushed O'Brien off first. The veteran's failure to hit contributed even more to his reduced playing time. After taking a 10-year mark of .265 into the 1992 campaign, O'Brien hovered around the Mendoza Line all year. He did provide some power but his home run and RBI totals, like his average, were down from 1991. Even in a bad year, however, O'Brien is a good contact hitter who walks more often than he strikes out. He's a good-fielding first baseman, but he adds no speed to the lineup. He led AL first basemen in assists twice and fielding percentage once. At 35, O'Brien has seen his better days.

Major League Batting Register

	BA	G	AB	R	H	2B	3B	HR	RBI	SB
82 AL	.239	20	67	13	16	4	1	4	13	1
83 AL	.237	154	524	53	124	24	5	8	53	5
84 AL	.287	142	520	57	149	26	2	18	80	3
85 AL	.267	159	573	69	153	34	3	22	92	5
86 AL	.290	156	551	86	160	23	3	23	90	4
87 AL	.286	159	569	84	163	26	1	23	88	0
88 AL	.272	156	547	57	149	24	1	16	71	1
89 AL	.260	155	554	75	144	24	1	12	55	3
90 AL	.224	108	366	32	82	18	0	5	27	0
91 AL	.248	152	560	58	139	29	3	17	88	0
92 AL	.222	134	396	40	88	15	1	14	52	2
Life	.262	1495	5227	624	1367	247	21	162	709	24
3 AVE	.234	131	441	43	103	21	1	12	56	1

JOSE OFFERMAN

Position: Shortstop
Team: Los Angeles Dodgers
Born: Nov. 8, 1968 San Pedro de Macoris, Dominican Republic
Height: 6' **Weight:** 160 lbs.
Bats: both **Throws:** right
Acquired: Signed as a free agent, 7/86

Player Summary

Fantasy Value.................................$4 to $10
Card Value..4¢ to 6¢
Will.......................................like leadoff spot
Can't................................avoid bad throws
Expect...............................world class speed
Don't Expect..........................long-ball hitting

Pee Wee Reese, the Hall of Fame short-stop who played for the Dodgers, once made 47 errors in a season. With that fact in mind, club management hopes Offerman will show steady improvement after becoming the first National Leaguer since 1978 (Garry Templeton) to make 40 miscues in a season. Offerman has good range and a strong arm. After flunking two previous trials, Offerman spent all of 1992 in Los Angeles. He got off to a slow start with the bat, but he burst out after Tommy Lasorda moved Offerman to the top of the lineup on July 11. In his first 10 days as the leadoff man, the switch-hitting speed merchant had a .457 on-base percentage. He ended the season with a .331 on-base average and a .333 slugging percentage. He has a better swing batting righthanded but shows more patience batting lefthanded. He batted .269 versus lefties and .255 against righties in 1992. Although he homered in his first big league at bat, he lacks in power what he has in speed. He topped 50 steals three years in a row in the minors.

Major League Batting Register

	BA	G	AB	R	H	2B	3B	HR	RBI	SB
90 NL	.155	29	58	7	9	0	0	1	7	1
91 NL	.195	52	113	10	22	2	0	0	3	3
92 NL	.260	149	534	67	139	20	8	1	30	23
Life	.241	230	705	84	170	22	8	2	40	27

BOB OJEDA

Position: Pitcher
Team: Cleveland Indians
Born: Dec. 17, 1957 Los Angeles, CA
Height: 6'1" **Weight:** 195 lbs.
Bats: left **Throws:** left
Acquired: Signed as a free agent, 12/92

Player Summary

Fantasy Value.....................................$4 to $8
Card Value...3¢ to 4¢
Will.............................post a winning record
Can't..............................finish what he starts
Expect.........................outstanding changeup
Don't Expect............................perfect control

Although he retained his reputation as a solid southpaw starter last summer, Ojeda endured uncharacteristic control problems. He walked almost as many hitters as he fanned—a far cry from his 1985 career year, when he went 18-5 and had a 3-1 ratio of strikeouts to walks. He banks on a changeup as his best pitch. He also throws a fastball, slider, and curve. Ojeda stifles lefthanded hitters, and he rarely yields gopher balls. He averages fewer than six strikeouts but more than eight hits per nine innings. Ojeda throws to first base frequently, showing several different moves that keep runners guessing. He thrives on the pressure of difficult situations. He also helps himself as a hitter and fielder. He broke into the big leagues with Boston in 1980.

Major League Pitching Register

	W	L	ERA	G	CG	IP	H	ER	BB	SO
80 AL	1	1	6.92	7	0	26.0	39	20	14	12
81 AL	6	2	3.12	10	2	66.1	50	23	25	28
82 AL	4	6	5.63	22	0	78.1	95	49	29	52
83 AL	12	7	4.04	29	5	173.2	173	78	73	94
84 AL	12	12	3.99	33	8	216.2	211	96	96	137
85 AL	9	11	4.00	39	5	157.2	166	70	48	102
86 NL	18	5	2.57	32	7	217.1	185	62	52	148
87 NL	3	5	3.88	10	0	46.1	45	20	10	21
88 NL	10	13	2.88	29	5	190.1	158	61	33	133
89 NL	13	11	3.47	31	5	192.0	179	74	78	95
90 NL	7	6	3.66	38	0	118.0	123	48	40	62
91 NL	12	9	3.18	31	2	189.1	181	67	70	120
92 NL	6	9	3.63	29	2	166.1	169	67	81	94
Life	113	97	3.60	340	41	1838.1	1774	735	649	1098
3 AVE	8	8	3.46	33	1	158.1	158	61	64	92

JOHN OLERUD

Position: First base
Team: Toronto Blue Jays
Born: Aug. 5, 1968 Seattle, WA
Height: 6'5" **Weight:** 205 lbs.
Bats: left **Throws:** left
Acquired: Third-round pick in 6/89 free-agent draft

Player Summary

Fantasy Value	$20 to $25
Card Value	4¢ to 6¢
Will	show great patience
Can't	add speed to lineup
Expect	liners to all fields
Don't Expect	defensive problems

Like a younger Don Mattingly, Olerud is a lefthanded slugger with patience. He makes good contact, walks more than he strikes out, and hits for a good average. He also piles up some home runs and RBI. Olerud batted .291 against righthanded pitching in 1992, and hit a respectable .258 versus lefties. While recuperating from a hamstring problem last Aug. 5, he came off the bench to stroke a two-out, game-winning single against Boston's Jeff Reardon with the bases loaded in the eighth inning. A line-drive hitter who uses all fields, Olerud had a .375 on-base average and a .450 slugging percentage in 1992. He advanced directly to Toronto from the Washington State campus in 1989 without stopping in the minor leagues first. Initially used as a designated hitter, he became the full-time first baseman after Fred McGriff was traded to San Diego in December 1990. Olerud is a fine fielder with an unusually strong arm. He doubled as a pitcher in college.

Major League Batting Register

	BA	G	AB	R	H	2B	3B	HR	RBI	SB
89 AL	.375	6	8	2	3	0	0	0	0	0
90 AL	.265	111	358	43	95	15	1	14	48	0
91 AL	.256	139	454	64	116	30	1	17	68	0
92 AL	.284	138	458	68	130	28	0	16	66	1
Life	.269	394	1278	177	344	73	2	47	182	1
3 AVE	.269	129	423	58	114	24	1	16	61	0

STEVE OLIN

Position: Pitcher
Team: Cleveland Indians
Born: Oct. 10, 1965 Portland, OR
Height: 6'2" **Weight:** 190 lbs.
Bats: right **Throws:** right
Acquired: 16th-round pick in 6/87 free-agent draft

Player Summary

Fantasy Value	$18 to $22
Card Value	3¢ to 4¢
Will	remain good closer
Can't	quell lefthanders
Expect	deceptive delivery
Don't Expect	bouts of wildness

If Olin ever learns to retire lefthanded hitters, he'll become one of baseball's top closers. Lefties were able to notch a .324 batting average against him, while righties batted only .188 in 1992. Even though lefties hit him well last summer, Olin became the fifth Indian to vault the 20-save barrier. He yielded fewer hits than innings pitched. He showed good control, but he averaged fewer than five strikeouts per nine innings. Opponents in 1992 compiled a .249 batting average, a .314 on-base average, and a .355 slugging percentage. A sinker-and-slider pitcher with a deceptive submarine delivery, he picked up where Doug Jones left off in the Cleveland pen. Olin converts a healthy percentage of his save opportunities, failing only when an opposing hitter takes him deep. That's what happens when the sinker doesn't sink. Olin's delivery must confuse baserunners as much as batters, because few try to steal on him. He is an okay fielder, helping his own cause with quick reactions.

Major League Pitching Register

	W	L	ERA	G	S	IP	H	ER	BB	SO
89 AL	1	4	3.75	25	1	36.0	35	15	14	24
90 AL	4	4	3.41	50	1	92.1	96	35	26	64
91 AL	3	6	3.36	48	17	56.1	61	21	23	38
92 AL	8	5	2.34	72	29	88.1	80	23	27	47
Life	16	19	3.10	195	48	273.0	272	94	90	173
3 AVE	5	5	3.00	57	16	79.1	79	26	25	50

OMAR OLIVARES

Position: Pitcher
Team: St. Louis Cardinals
Born: July 6, 1967 Mayaguez, Puerto Rico
Height: 6'1" **Weight:** 185 lbs.
Bats: right **Throws:** right
Acquired: Traded from Padres for Alex Cole
and Steve Peters, 2/90

Player Summary	
Fantasy Value	$6 to $10
Card Value	3¢ to 4¢
Will	improve with experience
Can't	avoid home run balls
Expect	self-help with the bat
Don't Expect	lots of complete games

Last year, in his first full major league season, Olivares became one of the mainstays of the pitching rotation of the St. Louis Cardinals. A righthander with a fastball, slider, and split-fingered fastball, he yielded fewer hits than innings pitched and showed better control than he had in the past. Olivares might have been around the plate too often, however, because he gave up more gopher balls (20) than anyone else on the staff. Opponents in 1992 compiled a .257 batting average, a .316 on-base percentage, and a .394 slugging percentage. A victim of spotty run support last summer, Olivares split his 18 decisions despite a decent ERA. In 1990 at Triple-A Louisville, he was 10-11 with a 2.82 ERA. He rarely finishes what he starts but often works deep into games. He lacks both a good glove and a winning pickoff move (he throws to first often anyway) but swings the bat well. In fact, he's one of the best-hitting pitchers in the National League. He hit .370 in 1989 at Triple-A Tucson.

JOE OLIVER

Position: Catcher
Team: Cincinnati Reds
Born: July 24, 1965 Memphis, TN
Height: 6'3" **Weight:** 210 lbs.
Bats: right **Throws:** right
Acquired: Second-round pick in 6/83 free-
agent draft

Player Summary	
Fantasy Value	$4 to $8
Card Value	3¢ to 4¢
Will	demolish lefties
Can't	win Gold Glove
Expect	a dozen homers
Don't Expect	any hint of speed

Oliver showed last summer that he had made a full recovery from his shoulder problems of the year before. He homered in double figures for the second straight season and scorched southpaw pitching, hitting some 58 points better against lefties (.307) than righties (.249). A pull hitter who disdains curves and inside fastballs, Oliver doesn't have much patience, striking out twice as often as he walks. He had a .316 on-base average and a .388 slugging percentage in 1992. He shouldered a heavier workload last year because lefty-hitting platoon partner Jeff Reed was idled by elbow surgery. Darren Daulton was the only receiver in the National League who donned the tools of ignorance as often as did Oliver, both with 141 games. Although Oliver has his share of throwing errors and passed balls, he is a durable receiver who calls a good game, handles pitchers well, and knows how to block the plate. He erased 35 percent of potential base-stealers in 1992.

Major League Pitching Register

	W	L	ERA	G	CG	IP	H	ER	BB	SO
90 NL	1	1	2.92	9	0	49.1	45	16	17	20
91 NL	11	7	3.71	28	0	167.1	148	69	61	91
92 NL	9	9	3.84	32	1	197.0	189	84	63	124
Life	21	17	3.68	69	1	413.2	382	169	141	235
2 AVE	10	8	3.78	30	1	182.1	169	77	62	108

Major League Batting Register

	BA	G	AB	R	H	2B	3B	HR	RBI	SB
89 NL	.272	49	151	13	41	8	0	3	23	0
90 NL	.231	121	364	34	84	23	0	8	52	1
91 NL	.216	94	269	21	58	11	0	11	41	0
92 NL	.270	143	485	42	131	25	1	10	57	2
Life	.247	407	1269	110	314	67	1	32	173	3
3 AVE	.244	119	373	32	91	20	0	10	50	1

GREG OLSON

Position: Catcher
Team: Atlanta Braves
Born: Sept. 6, 1960 Marshall, MN
Height: 6′ **Weight:** 200 lbs.
Bats: right **Throws:** right
Acquired: Signed as a free agent, 11/89

Player Summary

Fantasy Value	$3 to $6
Card Value	3¢ to 4¢
Will	play solid defense
Can't	clear the fences
Expect	more walks than Ks
Don't Expect	any show of speed

In his third year as the every-day catcher for the Braves, Olson solidified his reputation as a strong defensive player and clubhouse leader who doesn't deliver much punch. He handles pitchers well and calls a good game. He saves wild pitches better than most of his colleagues, and he blocks the plate well. Though he's had past problems with throwing, Olson improved his success rate against basestealers to nearly 40 percent last summer. At the same time, however, his batting average continued its three-year downward spiral. His power production—already minimal—also declined. A contact hitter who walks more often than he fans, Olson's lack of speed leads to a lot of double plays. He had a .316 on-base average and a .328 slugging percentage in 1992. He usually hits better with runners in scoring position. Olson is also more productive against lefthanded pitchers. At the end of the 1992 season, he fractured his leg, missing all of the postseason.

GREGG OLSON

Position: Pitcher
Team: Baltimore Orioles
Born: Oct. 11, 1966 Omaha, NE
Height: 6′4″ **Weight:** 210 lbs.
Bats: right **Throws:** right
Acquired: First-round pick in 6/88 free-agent draft

Player Summary

Fantasy Value	$24 to $30
Card Value	5¢ to 10¢
Will	get Ks with curve
Can't	avoid bad streaks
Expect	at least 30 saves
Don't Expect	frequent gophers

Before yielding a game-tying, ninth-inning homer to Roberto Kelly last June 22, Olson had converted 19 straight save opportunities. His ERA fell to 1.59 on July 1. Seven days later, however, he strained a muscle in his side and plunged into a slump. Unable to throw strikes with men on base, he blew six of 15 save chances through Aug. 15. The youngest pitcher to post 100 saves, Olson complements a curve—his best pitch—with a fastball and a change. Jose Canseco rates Olson's curve the AL's best. Olson averages nearly a strikeout an inning but fewer than eight hits per nine innings. Opponents compiled a .211 batting average, a .287 on-base average, and a .280 slugging percentage in 1992. The first batters he faced last summer had a .245 batting average. He has good control, keeps the ball in the park, and is especially effective at Camden Yards. Olson once worked 41 straight scoreless innings, a relief record. The former All-American from Auburn pitched only 16 games in the minor leagues.

Major League Batting Register

	BA	G	AB	R	H	2B	3B	HR	RBI	SB
89 AL	.500	3	2	0	1	0	0	0	0	0
90 NL	.262	100	298	36	78	12	1	7	36	1
91 NL	.241	133	411	46	99	25	0	6	44	1
92 NL	.238	95	302	27	72	14	2	3	27	2
Life	.247	331	1013	109	250	51	3	16	107	4
3 AVE	.246	109	337	36	83	17	1	5	36	1

Major League Pitching Register

	W	L	ERA	G	S	IP	H	ER	BB	SO
88 AL	1	1	3.27	10	0	11.0	10	4	10	9
89 AL	5	2	1.69	64	27	85.0	57	16	46	90
90 AL	6	5	2.42	64	37	74.1	57	20	31	74
91 AL	4	6	3.18	72	31	73.2	74	26	29	72
92 AL	1	5	2.05	60	36	61.1	46	14	24	58
Life	17	19	2.36	270	131	305.1	244	80	140	303
3 AVE	4	5	2.58	65	35	69.1	59	20	28	68

PAUL O'NEILL

Position: Outfield
Team: New York Yankees
Born: Feb. 25, 1963 Columbus, OH
Height: 6'4" **Weight:** 210 lbs.
Bats: left **Throws:** left
Acquired: Traded from Reds with Joe DeBerry for Roberto Kelly, 11/92

Player Summary

Fantasy Value	$11 to $18
Card Value	5¢ to 10¢
Will	show off powerful arm
Can't	tolerate platoon role
Expect	better power
Don't Expect	production against lefties

In 1993, O'Neill will be given the opportunity to patrol right field for the Yankees on a full-time basis. Platooning for the Reds didn't agree with him last summer. Upset that then-Cincy manager Lou Piniella played O'Neill primarily against righthanded pitchers, he became enraged when the manager pinch-hit for him with the bases loaded in the eighth inning July 6; a 25-minute, closed-door meeting followed. When he maintained a .225 average against southpaws last summer, O'Neill watched Glenn Braggs take over in right field against lefties. In addition to the platoon situation, O'Neill also was pained by a sore right wrist last year. When healthy, he makes good contact for a slugger and shows patience at the plate, walking as much as he fans. He has a rifle arm in right field and is always among league leaders in assists.

Major League Batting Register

	BA	G	AB	R	H	2B	3B	HR	RBI	SB
85 NL	.333	5	12	1	4	1	0	0	1	0
86 NL	.000	3	2	0	0	0	0	0	0	0
87 NL	.256	84	160	24	41	14	1	7	28	2
88 NL	.252	145	485	58	122	25	3	16	73	8
89 NL	.276	117	428	49	118	24	2	15	74	20
90 NL	.270	145	503	59	136	28	0	16	78	13
91 NL	.256	152	532	71	136	36	0	28	91	12
92 NL	.246	148	496	59	122	19	1	14	66	6
Life	.259	799	2618	321	679	147	7	96	411	61
3 AVE	.257	148	510	63	131	28	0	19	78	10

JOSE OQUENDO

Position: Second base; shortstop
Team: St. Louis Cardinals
Born: July 4, 1963 Rio Piedras, Puerto Rico
Height: 5'10" **Weight:** 160 lbs.
Bats: both **Throws:** right
Acquired: Traded from Mets with Mark Davis for Argenis Salazar and John Young, 4/85

Player Summary

Fantasy Value	$3 to $7
Card Value	3¢ to 4¢
Will	flash fine glove
Can't	generate power
Expect	patience at plate
Don't Expect	any stolen bases

Injuries ruined Oquendo's season in 1992. First, he suffered a partial dislocation of the left shoulder that cost him seven weeks of playing time. After returning in June, he was sidelined with a heel spur that kept him out much longer than he had expected. As a result, the Cardinals tried Geronimo Pena, Luis Alicea, and Rex Hudler at second base, Oquendo's best position. The versatile Oquendo, who pitched four relief innings in an extra-inning game, also plays a fine game at shortstop. A patient contact hitter, he walks more often than he strikes out. He had a .350 on-base average and a .400 slugging percentage in 1992. Although he doesn't translate his speed into steals, Oquendo has fine range at both short and second, plus a strong arm. He makes very few errors (a record-low three as a second baseman in 1990).

Major League Batting Register

	BA	G	AB	R	H	2B	3B	HR	RBI	SB
83 NL	.213	120	328	29	70	7	0	1	17	8
84 NL	.222	81	189	23	42	5	0	0	10	10
86 NL	.297	76	138	20	41	4	1	0	13	2
87 NL	.286	116	248	43	71	9	0	1	24	4
88 NL	.277	148	451	36	125	10	1	7	46	4
89 NL	.291	163	556	59	162	28	7	1	48	3
90 NL	.252	156	469	38	118	17	5	1	37	1
91 NL	.240	127	366	37	88	11	4	1	26	1
92 NL	.257	14	35	3	9	3	1	0	3	0
Life	.261	1001	2780	288	726	94	19	12	224	33
2 AVE	.247	142	418	38	103	14	5	1	32	1

JESSE OROSCO

Position: Pitcher
Team: Milwaukee Brewers
Born: April 21, 1957 Santa Barbara, CA
Height: 6'2" **Weight:** 185 lbs.
Bats: right **Throws:** left
Acquired: Traded from Indians for a player to be named later, 12/91

Player Summary	
Fantasy Value	$1 to $2
Card Value	3¢ to 4¢
Will	enter action often
Can't	retire lefty hitters
Expect	more Ks than innings
Don't Expect	deployment as closer

Orosco was one of the busiest members of the Milwaukee bullpen last summer. A former closer who once had a 31-save summer, Orosco has worked at least 47 times per year for 11 consecutive seasons. Because he had trouble with left-handed hitters, Orosco served mostly in mop-up or set-up roles in 1992. Considered too unreliable for the late innings, he got only two opportunities and blew one of them. A fastball-slider pitcher whose concentration tends to waver, Orosco strikes out three times more men than he walks. He also produces more strikeouts than innings pitched. He allowed 7.5 hits per nine innings in 1992, but too many of those cleared the fences (four in his first 30 innings last year). Orosco is an accomplished fielder with a good pickoff move.

Major League Pitching Register

	W	L	ERA	G	S	IP	H	ER	BB	SO
79 NL	1	2	4.89	18	0	35.0	33	19	22	22
81 NL	0	1	1.56	8	1	17.1	13	3	6	18
82 NL	4	10	2.72	54	4	109.1	92	33	40	89
83 NL	13	7	1.47	62	17	110.0	76	18	38	84
84 NL	10	6	2.59	60	31	87.0	58	25	34	85
85 NL	8	6	2.73	54	17	79.0	66	24	34	68
86 NL	8	6	2.33	58	21	81.0	64	21	35	62
87 NL	3	9	4.44	58	16	77.0	78	38	31	78
88 NL	3	2	2.72	55	9	53.0	41	16	30	43
89 AL	3	4	2.08	69	3	78.0	54	18	26	79
90 AL	5	4	3.90	55	2	64.2	58	28	38	55
91 AL	2	0	3.74	47	0	45.2	52	19	15	36
92 AL	3	1	3.23	59	1	39.0	33	14	13	40
Life	63	58	2.84	657	122	876.0	718	276	362	759
3 AVE	3	2	3.68	54	1	49.1	48	20	22	44

JOE ORSULAK

Position: Outfield
Team: New York Mets
Born: May 31, 1962 Glen Ridge, NJ
Height: 6'1" **Weight:** 196 lbs.
Bats: left **Throws:** left
Acquired: Signed as a free agent, 12/92

Player Summary	
Fantasy Value	$3 to $6
Card Value	3¢ to 4¢
Will	make good contact
Can't	wait for walks
Expect	great outfield arm
Don't Expect	power production

Orsulak was hitting just .216 last May 20 when he replaced the struggling Chito Martinez as Baltimore's right fielder. Orsulak, a vastly superior defensive player, rewarded his club's confidence with an offensive explosion. From June 8 through July 3, he hit .383 (31-for-81). When he notched his seventh assist of the season July 28, it pushed his two-year total to 29, five more than any other AL outfielder. Orsulak hit .370 in July and was going great guns when he suffered a sprained thumb that sent him to the disabled list. Though he doesn't provide much power, Orsulak is a good contact hitter who hits righthanders hard and holds his own against southpaws. He rarely walks, strikes out, steals a base, or makes an error. He had a .342 on-base average and a .381 slugging percentage in 1992. But his batting average has gone up three years in a row.

Major League Batting Register

	BA	G	AB	R	H	2B	3B	HR	RBI	SB
83 NL	.182	7	11	0	2	0	0	0	1	0
84 NL	.254	32	67	12	17	1	2	0	3	3
85 NL	.300	121	397	54	119	14	6	0	21	24
86 NL	.249	138	401	60	100	19	6	2	19	24
88 AL	.288	125	379	48	109	21	3	8	27	9
89 AL	.285	123	390	59	111	22	5	7	55	5
90 AL	.269	124	413	49	111	14	3	11	57	6
91 AL	.278	143	486	57	135	22	1	5	43	6
92 AL	.289	117	391	45	113	18	3	4	39	5
Life	.278	930	2935	384	817	131	29	37	265	82
3 AVE	.278	128	430	50	120	18	2	7	46	6

JUNIOR ORTIZ

Position: Catcher
Team: Cleveland Indians
Born: Oct. 24, 1959 Humacao, Puerto Rico
Height: 5'11" **Weight:** 176 lbs.
Bats: right **Throws:** right
Acquired: Signed as free agent, 12/91

Player Summary	
Fantasy Value	$1 to $2
Card Value	3¢ to 4¢
Will	make good contact
Can't	win every-day job
Expect	line-drive singles
Don't Expect	extra-base hits

In 11 major league seasons, Ortiz has established several predictable patterns. He rarely homers, walks, or steals a base, but he makes contact often enough to produce a respectable career batting average. He also supplies solid defense whenever he's called upon in his role as backup catcher. Playing behind Sandy Alomar at Cleveland last summer, Ortiz hit below his lifetime average, but he did nail 33 percent of the runners who tried to steal against him. He handled the club's young pitchers well, saved wild pitches, and blocked the plate when necessary. A line-drive singles hitter who fares better against righthanders, Ortiz had a .296 on-base average and a .279 slugging percentage in 1992. He hit .335 for Minnesota in '90 and .336 for Pittsburgh in '86. He began his professional career in 1977.

Major League Batting Register

	BA	G	AB	R	H	2B	3B	HR	RBI	SB
82 NL	.200	7	15	1	3	1	0	0	0	0
83 NL	.249	73	193	11	48	5	0	0	12	1
84 NL	.198	40	91	6	18	3	0	0	11	1
85 NL	.292	23	72	4	21	2	0	1	5	1
86 NL	.336	49	110	11	37	6	0	0	14	0
87 NL	.271	75	192	16	52	8	1	1	22	0
88 NL	.280	49	118	8	33	6	0	2	18	1
89 NL	.217	91	230	16	50	6	1	1	22	2
90 AL	.335	71	170	18	57	7	1	0	18	0
91 AL	.209	61	134	9	28	5	1	0	11	0
92 AL	.250	86	244	20	61	7	0	0	24	1
Life	.260	625	1569	120	408	56	4	5	157	7
2 AVE	.285	79	207	19	59	7	1	0	21	1

DONOVAN OSBORNE

Position: Pitcher
Team: St. Louis Cardinals
Born: June 21, 1969 Roseville, CA
Height: 6'2" **Weight:** 195 lbs.
Bats: both **Throws:** left
Acquired: First-round pick in 6/90 free-agent draft

Player Summary	
Fantasy Value	$8 to $14
Card Value	5¢ to 15¢
Will	show good control
Can't	keep lefties down
Expect	key rotation role
Don't Expect	many gopher balls

Osborne made the St. Louis varsity last spring only because Rheal Cormier caught the flu. By the All-Star break, Osborne had seven wins, more than any other NL rookie, and had shown unusual poise for a pitcher of his age. Banished to the bullpen briefly in July, Osborne returned to the rotation later in the summer and pitched well again. Osborne has exceptional control of his fastball, curveball, slider, and changeup. He yields fewer than two walks per nine innings, compensating for his average of slightly more than a hit per inning. Opponents compiled a .275 batting average, a .312 on-base percentage, and a .404 slugging percentage in 1992. The former UNLV standout needs to perfect his pickoff move—a problem for a pitcher with such a distinctive leg kick. He also needs to be more effective against lefthanded batters, who had a .318 batting average against him in 1992, while righties batted .263. In 1991 at Double-A Arkansas, he was 8-12 with a 3.63 ERA, three complete games, 43 walks, and 130 strikeouts in 166 innings. In 1990, he was 2-4 with a 2.93 ERA in Class-A.

Major League Pitching Register

	W	L	ERA	G	CG	IP	H	ER	BB	SO
92 NL	11	9	3.77	34	0	179.0	193	75	38	104
Life	11	9	3.77	34	0	179.0	193	75	38	104

AL OSUNA

Position: Pitcher
Team: Houston Astros
Born: Aug. 10, 1965 Inglewood, CA
Height: 6'3" **Weight:** 200 lbs.
Bats: right **Throws:** left
Acquired: 16th-round pick in 6/87 free-agent draft

Player Summary	
Fantasy Value	$3 to $5
Card Value	3¢ to 4¢
Will	rely on screwball
Can't	locate the plate
Expect	more set-up roles
Don't Expect	luck against righties

If Osuna had better control, his stock as a relief pitcher would rise through the roof. In his second NL season last summer, he had trouble finding the strike zone, yielding an average of five walks per nine innings. His average of more than seven hits per nine innings was much more palatable to Houston management, although the top brass couldn't understand why the lefthanded Osuna had so much trouble with lefthanded hitters. He is a screwball specialist who also throws a fastball and two sliders. Opponents compiled a .236 batting average, a .343 on-base average, and a .377 slugging percentage in 1992. He was more impressive in 1991. Working for a last-place club, he had seven wins and 12 saves in 71 outings, a record for a Houston rookie. The former Stanford University standout, who has never started since turning pro in 1987, is a solid fielder who holds runners well. In 1990, he was 7-5 with a 3.38 ERA, six saves, 33 walks, and 82 Ks in 69 innings at Double-A Columbus.

DAVE OTTO

Position: Pitcher
Team: Pittsburgh Pirates
Born: Nov. 12, 1964 Chicago, IL
Height: 6'7" **Weight:** 210 lbs.
Bats: left **Throws:** left
Acquired: Drafted from Indians, 11/92

Player Summary	
Fantasy Value	$1 to $3
Card Value	3¢ to 4¢
Will	seek starting job
Can't	keep ball in park
Expect	embarrassing ERA
Don't Expect	a winning record

Otto pitched so well early last spring that he left spring training in Tucson as Cleveland's No. 2 starter. Then he developed tendinitis in his shoulder, spent time on the disabled list, and lost his momentum. The lefty lost four straight and was sent to the minors with a 4-7 mark on June 25. He wasn't much better when he returned, but the Indians held out hope Otto would return to his spring training form. As September started, however, he had allowed more walks than strikeouts, more hits than innings (an average of 12.3 hits per nine innings), and too many home runs. He had an ERA over seven and a weak won-lost mark. Such erratic statistics explain why Otto has bounced between the majors and minors for six straight summers. A fastball-and-slider pitcher who also throws a forkball, Otto needs location since he doesn't have velocity. At Triple-A Colorado Springs in 1992, he was 3-2 with a 2.89 ERA, 11 strikeouts, and 10 walks in 44 innings.

Major League Pitching Register

	W	L	ERA	G	S	IP	H	ER	BB	SO
90 NL	2	0	4.76	12	0	11.1	10	6	6	6
91 NL	7	6	3.42	71	12	81.2	59	31	46	68
92 NL	6	3	4.23	66	0	61.2	52	29	38	37
Life	15	9	3.84	149	12	154.2	121	66	90	111
2 AVE	7	5	3.77	69	6	71.2	56	30	42	53

Major League Pitching Register

	W	L	ERA	G	CG	IP	H	ER	BB	SO
87 AL	0	0	9.00	3	0	6.0	7	6	1	3
88 AL	0	0	1.80	3	0	10.0	9	2	6	7
89 AL	0	0	2.70	1	0	6.2	6	2	2	4
90 AL	0	0	7.71	2	0	2.1	3	2	3	2
91 AL	2	8	4.23	18	1	100.0	108	47	27	47
92 AL	5	9	7.06	18	0	80.1	110	63	33	32
Life	7	17	5.35	45	1	205.1	243	122	72	95
2 AVE	4	9	5.49	18	1	90.1	109	55	30	40

SPIKE OWEN

Position: Shortstop
Team: New York Yankees
Born: April 19, 1961 Cleburne, TX
Height: 5'10" **Weight:** 170 lbs.
Bats: both **Throws:** right
Acquired: Signed as a free agent, 12/92

Player Summary	
Fantasy Value	$4 to $8
Card Value	3¢ to 4¢
Will	make good contact
Can't	rip righthanders
Expect	sure hands at short
Don't Expect	10-plus homers

Owen moves to a shortstop job in the Bronx. He was the unsung hero of the Expos' surprise season in 1992. He enjoyed the best offensive display of his 10-year career. A contact hitter who walks more often than he strikes out, Owen also packs some punch. He reached a personal peak in home runs, hit .286 against left-handed pitching, and was even more effective with runners in scoring position. He had a .348 on-base average and a .381 slugging percentage in 1992. A switch-hitter who batted .258 against righties in 1992, Owen has a little speed. He is best known for his glove, however. A sure-handed shortstop who twice led the NL in fielding percentage, he holds the NL single-season record for consecutive errorless games by a shortstop (63 in 1990). His range and arm are only average, but nobody has better hands.

Major League Batting Register

	BA	G	AB	R	H	2B	3B	HR	RBI	SB
83 AL	.196	80	306	36	60	11	3	2	21	10
84 AL	.245	152	530	67	130	18	8	3	43	16
85 AL	.259	118	352	41	91	10	6	6	37	11
86 AL	.231	154	528	67	122	24	7	1	45	4
87 AL	.259	132	437	50	113	17	7	2	48	11
88 AL	.249	89	257	40	64	14	1	5	18	0
89 NL	.233	142	437	52	102	17	4	6	41	3
90 NL	.234	149	453	55	106	24	5	5	35	8
91 NL	.255	139	424	39	108	22	8	3	26	2
92 NL	.269	122	386	52	104	16	3	7	40	9
Life	.243	1277	4110	499	1000	173	52	40	354	74
3 AVE	.252	137	421	49	106	21	5	5	34	6

MIKE PAGLIARULO

Position: Third base
Team: Minnesota Twins
Born: March 15, 1960 Medford, MA
Height: 6'2" **Weight:** 195 lbs.
Bats: left **Throws:** right
Acquired: Signed as a free agent, 1/91

Player Summary	
Fantasy Value	$1 to $4
Card Value	3¢ to 4¢
Will	platoon at third
Can't	wait for walks
Expect	decent defense
Don't Expect	return of power

Pagliarulo needs to rebound to keep his job in the majors. He broke his right wrist during batting practice in Seattle last April. The injury kept him out until July 22, then interfered with his swing afterward, totally neutralizing his power. He had a .213 on-base average and a .238 slugging percentage in 1992. The healthy Pagliarulo plays almost exclusively against righthanded pitching (Scott Leius was Pags's platoon partner for the past two seasons with Minnesota). Pagliarulo hits line drives to all fields. He doesn't have the patience to earn bases on balls, striking out about two and one-half times per walk. He's no longer the pull hitter who hit a total of 60 homers for the Yankees in 1986 and '87. In the field, Pagliarulo has little speed and mediocre range but has quick reactions, good hands, and a strong, accurate arm. Pags broke into pro ball in 1981.

Major League Batting Register

	BA	G	AB	R	H	2B	3B	HR	RBI	SB
84 AL	.239	67	201	24	48	15	3	7	34	0
85 AL	.239	138	380	55	91	16	2	19	62	0
86 AL	.238	149	504	71	120	24	3	28	71	4
87 AL	.234	150	522	76	122	26	3	32	87	1
88 AL	.216	125	444	46	96	20	1	15	67	1
89 AL	.197	74	223	19	44	10	0	4	16	1
89 NL	.196	50	148	12	29	7	0	3	14	2
90 NL	.254	128	398	29	101	23	2	7	38	1
91 NL	.279	121	365	38	102	20	0	6	36	1
92 AL	.200	42	105	10	21	4	0	0	9	1
Life	.235	1044	3290	380	774	165	14	121	434	12
2 AVE	.266	125	382	34	102	22	1	7	37	1

TOM PAGNOZZI

Position: Catcher
Team: St. Louis Cardinals
Born: July 30, 1962 Tucson, AZ
Height: 6'1" **Weight:** 190 lbs.
Bats: right **Throws:** right
Acquired: Eighth-round pick in 6/83 free-agent draft

Player Summary	
Fantasy Value	$6 to $12
Card Value	3¢ to 4¢
Will	make All-Star team
Can't	display any speed
Expect	Gold Glove defense
Don't Expect	long-ball hitting

Putting both halves of his game together is proving difficult for Pagnozzi. A Gold Glove catcher in 1991, his defense declined in the first half of the season last summer—just as his offense improved. At one point in June, he came under fire from St. Louis manager Joe Torre, a former catcher himself, for poor game-calling. Pagnozzi's 1991 success ratio of 45 percent against enemy basestealers also dropped sharply. On the plus side, he had only one error all season. He is good at blocking the plate, preventing wild pitches, and handling the pitching staff. He was good enough defensively in 1992 to win his second consecutive Gold Glove. He also tripled his home run production while maintaining the .257 mark he had compiled over five previous seasons. He had a .290 on-base average and a .359 slugging percentage in 1992. Pagnozzi is likely to repeat his 1992 All-Star selection many times.

Major League Batting Register

	BA	G	AB	R	H	2B	3B	HR	RBI	SB
87 NL	.188	27	48	8	9	1	0	2	9	1
88 NL	.282	81	195	17	55	9	0	0	15	0
89 NL	.150	52	80	3	12	2	0	0	3	0
90 NL	.277	69	220	20	61	15	0	2	23	1
91 NL	.264	140	459	38	121	24	5	2	57	9
92 NL	.249	139	485	33	121	26	3	7	44	2
Life	.255	508	1487	119	379	77	8	13	151	13
3 AVE	.260	116	388	30	101	22	3	4	41	4

DONN PALL

Position: Pitcher
Team: Chicago White Sox
Born: Jan. 11, 1962 Chicago, IL
Height: 6'1" **Weight:** 180 lbs.
Bats: right **Throws:** right
Acquired: 23rd-round pick in 6/85 free-agent draft

Player Summary	
Fantasy Value	$2 to $4
Card Value	3¢ to 4¢
Will	bank on splitter
Can't	get lefties out
Expect	comeback season
Don't Expect	more wild spells

After three strong seasons as a middle reliever in the White Sox bullpen, Pall encountered hard times in 1992. Used sparingly by rookie manager Gene Lamont, Pall had as many walks as strikeouts and more hits allowed than innings pitched. He also had an inflated ERA. When he's right, Pall uses his split-fingered fastball to fan twice as many men as he walks. He also yields fewer hits than innings. Opponents compiled a .272 batting average, a .335 on-base percentage, and a .410 slugging percentage in 1992. Inability to control his splitter, slider, and curve cost him last season. He had his usual problems against lefthanded hitters, as they compiled a .291 batting average in 1992. He was repeatedly victimized by basestealers. Plagued by periodic arm problems, Pall's 1992 performance may have resulted from overwork. He had appeared more than 50 times in each of three previous years. At age 31, he will have to be monitored carefully if he is to make a complete comeback.

Major League Pitching Register

	W	L	ERA	G	S	IP	H	ER	BB	SO
88 AL	0	2	3.45	17	0	28.2	39	11	8	16
89 AL	4	5	3.31	53	6	87.0	90	32	19	58
90 AL	3	5	3.32	56	2	76.0	63	28	24	39
91 AL	7	2	2.41	51	0	71.0	59	19	20	40
92 AL	5	2	4.93	39	1	73.0	79	40	27	27
Life	19	16	3.49	216	9	335.2	330	130	98	180
3 AVE	5	3	3.56	49	1	73.0	67	29	24	35

RAFAEL PALMEIRO

Position: First base
Team: Texas Rangers
Born: Sept. 24, 1964 Havana, Cuba
Height: 6′ **Weight:** 180 lbs.
Bats: left **Throws:** left
Acquired: Traded from Cubs with Drew Hall and Jamie Moyer for Curtis Wilkerson, Steve Wilson, Mitch Williams, Paul Kilgus, Luis Benitez, and Pablo Delgado, 12/88

Player Summary	
Fantasy Value	$25 to $32
Card Value	5¢ to 15¢
Will	get extra-base hits
Can't	add speed to lineup
Expect	big batting comeback
Don't Expect	dazzling defense

Palmeiro was hurt because he found himself swinging at some bad pitches last summer. After compiling a .302 average in six previous seasons, he had trouble making the necessary adjustments when pitchers began working him differently. Although he won some games with his glove, his average and power production fell dramatically. The only part of his hitting that pleased Palmeiro was his .281 batting average against lefthanded pitchers. He should be at the peak of his career. He had a .352 on-base average and a .434 slugging percentage in 1992. When he's right, Palmeiro makes good contact, walks almost as much as he fans, and delivers both a high average and extra-base power. In 1991, when he began to pull the ball more, he notched 336 total bases, which ranked second in the AL. He's adequate but not brilliant as a defensive first baseman.

Major League Batting Register

	BA	G	AB	R	H	2B	3B	HR	RBI	SB
86 NL	.247	22	73	9	18	4	0	3	12	1
87 NL	.276	84	221	32	61	15	1	14	30	2
88 NL	.307	152	580	75	178	41	5	8	53	12
89 AL	.275	156	559	76	154	23	4	8	64	4
90 AL	.319	154	598	72	191	35	6	14	89	3
91 AL	.322	159	631	115	203	49	3	26	88	4
92 AL	.268	159	608	84	163	27	4	22	85	2
Life	.296	886	3270	463	968	194	23	95	421	28
3 AVE	.303	157	612	90	186	37	4	21	87	3

DEAN PALMER

Position: Third base
Team: Texas Rangers
Born: Dec. 27, 1968 Tallahassee, FL
Height: 6′1″ **Weight:** 190 lbs.
Bats: right **Throws:** right
Acquired: Third-round pick in 6/86 free-agent draft

Player Summary	
Fantasy Value	$14 to $22
Card Value	4¢ to 6¢
Will	improve with time
Can't	avoid strikeouts
Expect	hefty power numbers
Don't Expect	high batting average

If Palmer ever learns the strike zone, he could become one of baseball's most prolific power hitters. At the moment, however, he rates as an all-or-nothing slugger more likely to lead the league in strikeouts than home runs. Although he improved his batting average last season, he still had 154 strikeouts. Before the arrival of Jose Canseco in September, Palmer stood second only to Juan Gonzalez in home runs by a Ranger. Palmer notched a .311 on-base average and a .420 slugging percentage in 1992. He is far more productive against lefthanded pitching; he had a .252 batting average against lefthanders in 1992 and a .221 average versus righties. He has excellent long-range potential, considering that he has more home runs than Mike Schmidt did at the same stage of his career. Though Palmer has a strong arm and decent range, he makes his share of miscues. He can't erase the memory of former Texas third baseman Steve Buechele, one of the best fielders at the position.

Major League Batting Register

	BA	G	AB	R	H	2B	3B	HR	RBI	SB
89 AL	.105	16	19	0	2	2	0	0	1	0
91 AL	.187	81	268	38	50	9	2	15	37	0
92 AL	.229	152	541	74	124	25	0	26	72	10
Life	.213	249	828	112	176	36	2	41	110	10
2 AVE	.215	117	405	56	87	17	1	21	55	5

JEFF PARRETT

Position: Pitcher
Team: Oakland Athletics
Born: Aug. 26, 1961 Indianapolis, IN
Height: 6'3" **Weight:** 193 lbs.
Bats: right **Throws:** right
Acquired: Signed as a free agent, 3/92

Player Summary	
Fantasy Value	$2 to $4
Card Value	3¢ to 4¢
Will	dominate righty batters
Can't	always find strike zone
Expect	more middle relief work
Don't Expect	more whiffs than frames

Parrett prospered from his first look at American League hitters. After earning his release with a poor performance in Atlanta, he hooked on with the Athletics in spring training and contributed a strong season in middle relief. Used primarily as one of several set-up men for Dennis Eckersley, Parrett got his ninth win in 10 decisions Aug. 22 by retiring nine of the 11 Orioles he faced—five of them on strikeouts. He averaged seven hits and more than seven strikeouts per nine innings, with occasional control trouble his primary weakness. Opponents compiled a .226 batting average, a .308 on-base percentage, and a .344 slugging percentage in 1992. He throws a fastball, slider, and split-fingered fastball—rendering right-handed hitters helpless. He held righty hitters to a .192 batting average in 1992, though lefties had a .278 batting average against him. He throws to first base often, but runners still run wild on him. Parrett is adequate as a fielder.

Major League Pitching Register

	W	L	ERA	G	S	IP	H	ER	BB	SO
86 NL	0	1	4.87	12	0	20.1	19	11	13	21
87 NL	7	6	4.21	45	6	62.0	53	29	30	56
88 NL	12	4	2.65	61	6	91.2	66	27	45	62
89 NL	12	6	2.98	72	6	105.2	90	35	44	98
90 NL	5	10	4.64	67	2	108.2	119	56	55	86
91 NL	1	2	6.33	18	1	21.1	31	15	12	14
92 AL	9	1	3.02	66	0	98.1	81	33	42	78
Life	46	30	3.65	341	21	508.0	459	206	241	415
2 AVE	7	6	3.87	67	1	103.2	100	45	49	82

LANCE PARRISH

Position: Catcher
Team: Seattle Mariners
Born: June 15, 1956 Clairton, PA
Height: 6'3" **Weight:** 220 lbs.
Bats: right **Throws:** right
Acquired: Signed as a free agent, 6/92

Player Summary	
Fantasy Value	$4 to $8
Card Value	3¢ to 4¢
Will	hit with power
Can't	avoid strikeouts
Expect	decent defense
Don't Expect	any kind of speed

Signing with Seattle last summer gave Parrish a fresh start. An eight-time All-Star, his average had tumbled far below his 15-year mark of .254 in 1991, and he received a pink slip from the economy-minded Angels. The Mariners picked him up, and he was a backup for Dave Valle. Parrish fans three times more than he walks and has hit 30 points higher against lefthanders than righties in his career. He had a .294 on-base average and a .418 slugging average in 1992. A three-time Gold Glover who's still a good receiver at 36, Parrish led AL catchers in fielding percentage (.997) and runners caught stealing (42.4 percent) in 1991. His fielding slipped a bit in 1992, however.

Major League Batting Register

	BA	G	AB	R	H	2B	3B	HR	RBI	SB
77 AL	.196	12	46	10	9	2	0	3	7	0
78 AL	.219	85	288	37	63	11	3	14	41	0
79 AL	.276	143	493	65	136	26	3	19	65	6
80 AL	.286	144	553	79	158	34	6	24	82	6
81 AL	.244	96	348	39	85	18	2	10	46	2
82 AL	.284	133	486	75	138	19	2	32	87	3
83 AL	.269	155	605	80	163	42	3	27	114	1
84 AL	.237	147	578	75	137	16	2	33	98	2
85 AL	.273	140	549	64	150	27	1	28	98	2
86 AL	.257	91	327	53	84	6	1	22	62	0
87 NL	.245	130	466	42	114	21	0	17	67	0
88 NL	.215	123	424	44	91	17	2	15	60	0
89 AL	.238	124	433	48	103	12	1	17	50	1
90 AL	.268	133	470	54	126	14	0	24	70	2
91 AL	.216	119	402	38	87	12	0	19	51	0
92 AL	.233	93	275	26	64	13	1	12	32	1
Life	.253	1868	6743	829	1708	290	27	316	1030	26
3 AVE	.241	115	382	39	92	13	0	18	51	1

DAN PASQUA

Position: Outfield; first base
Team: Chicago White Sox
Born: Oct. 17, 1961 Yonkers, NY
Height: 6' **Weight:** 203 lbs.
Bats: left **Throws:** left
Acquired: Traded from Yankees with Mark Salas and Steve Rosenberg for Richard Dotson and Scott Nielsen, 11/87

Player Summary	
Fantasy Value	$3 to $6
Card Value	3¢ to 4¢
Will	try for comeback
Can't	hit lefthanders
Expect	power production
Don't Expect	stellar defense

The White Sox missed Pasqua's power last season. Twice disabled by hamstring problems, the lefty-hitting right fielder missed large chunks of the season. When he returned, he had trouble finding his stroke and wound up platooning with righthanded hitter Shawn Abner. When he's right, Pasqua provides a .250 average and more than 15 home runs a season. He might hit considerably more if he saw more southpaws but is usually held out against them. He batted .219 versus righties in '92. Pasqua has a good batting eye and enough patience to wait out walks. He had a .305 batting average and a .347 slugging percentage in 1992. He adds no speed to the lineup. His best position is first base, since his outfield range is poor. Last year, however, he played almost exclusively in right field. At 31, he should supply lefty power if healthy.

Major League Batting Register

	BA	G	AB	R	H	2B	3B	HR	RBI	SB
85 AL	.209	60	148	17	31	3	1	9	25	0
86 AL	.293	102	280	44	82	17	0	16	45	2
87 AL	.233	113	318	42	74	7	1	17	42	0
88 AL	.227	129	422	48	96	16	2	20	50	1
89 AL	.248	73	246	26	61	9	1	11	47	1
90 AL	.274	112	325	43	89	27	3	13	58	1
91 AL	.259	134	417	71	108	22	5	18	66	0
92 AL	.211	93	265	26	56	16	1	6	33	0
Life	.247	816	2421	317	597	117	14	110	366	5
3 AVE	.251	113	336	47	84	22	3	12	52	0

BOB PATTERSON

Position: Pitcher
Team: Texas Rangers
Born: May 16, 1959 Jacksonville, FL
Height: 6'2" **Weight:** 192 lbs.
Bats: right **Throws:** left
Acquired: Signed as a free agent, 12/92

Player Summary	
Fantasy Value	$4 to $6
Card Value	3¢ to 4¢
Will	rely on location
Can't	help cause with bat
Expect	some closing roles
Don't Expect	return to starting

It's hard to believe that Patterson was once the Opening Day starter for the Pirates, in 1987. He's made only 21 starts in seven seasons and has become a valuable bullpen arm—with some success as a southpaw closer. He has worked at least 50 times three years in a row, and he was Pittsburgh's most effective reliever last summer. He averaged about eight hits, three walks, and six strikeouts per nine innings. Opponents compiled a .246 batting average, a .309 on-base percentage, and a .400 slugging percentage in 1992. He kept the ball in the park and was equally effective against righties and lefties. Against Patterson, righties batted .241 while lefties notched a .256 mark last summer. A fastball-and-curveball pitcher who dominated lefties in previous years, Patterson had a 4-1 ratio of strikeouts to walks in 1991. He holds runners close and fields his position well. Patterson doesn't hit much, but he rarely gets the chance.

Major League Pitching Register

	W	L	ERA	G	S	IP	H	ER	BB	SO
85 NL	0	0	24.75	3	0	4.0	13	11	3	1
86 NL	2	3	4.95	11	0	36.1	49	20	5	20
87 NL	1	4	6.70	15	0	43.0	49	32	22	27
89 NL	4	3	4.05	12	1	26.2	23	12	8	20
90 NL	8	5	2.95	55	5	94.2	88	31	21	70
91 NL	4	3	4.11	54	2	65.2	67	30	15	57
92 NL	6	3	2.92	60	9	64.2	59	21	23	43
Life	25	21	4.22	210	17	335.0	348	157	97	238
3 AVE	6	4	3.28	56	5	74.2	71	27	20	57

BILL PECOTA

Position: Infield
Team: Atlanta Braves
Born: Feb. 16, 1960 Redwood City, CA
Height: 6'2" **Weight:** 190 lbs.
Bats: right **Throws:** right
Acquired: Signed as a free agent, 1/93

Player Summary	
Fantasy Value	$3 to $5
Card Value	3¢ to 4¢
Will	make decent contact
Can't	generate much power
Expect	speed and defense
Don't Expect	repeat of low average

Pecota has played all nine positions since reaching the majors in 1986. When spring training broke last year, he was expected to form a righty-lefty platoon with Dave Magadan at third base for the Mets. Instead, Pecota was a three-position infielder, pinch-hitter, and defensive replacement. A slap hitter with little power, he usually walks as much as he strikes out, though he was burned a little more by NL pitching. He had a .293 on-base average and a .297 slugging percentage in 1992. He's at his best against lefthanded pitchers and in clutch situations. Although he took a six-year average of .254 into last season, Pecota's main claims to fame are his speed and defense. He had a long errorless streak as a third baseman in 1991 and can also hold his own at second. He's a little weaker at short but has a strong throwing arm from any of the three positions.

Major League Batting Register

	BA	G	AB	R	H	2B	3B	HR	RBI	SB
86 AL	.207	12	29	3	6	2	0	0	2	0
87 AL	.276	66	156	22	43	5	1	3	14	5
88 AL	.208	90	178	25	37	3	3	1	15	7
89 AL	.205	65	83	21	17	4	2	3	5	5
90 AL	.242	87	240	43	58	15	2	5	20	8
91 AL	.286	125	398	53	114	23	2	6	45	16
92 NL	.227	117	269	28	61	13	0	2	26	9
Life	.248	562	1353	195	336	65	10	20	127	50
3 AVE	.257	110	302	41	78	17	1	4	30	11

ALEJANDRO PENA

Position: Pitcher
Team: Pittsburgh Pirates
Born: June 25, 1959 Cambiaso, Dominican Republic
Height: 6'1" **Weight:** 203 lbs.
Bats: right **Throws:** right
Acquired: Signed as a free agent, 12/92

Player Summary	
Fantasy Value	$5 to $10
Card Value	3¢ to 4¢
Will	depend on fastball
Can't	avoid gopher balls
Expect	lots of strikeouts
Don't Expect	bouts of wildness

The hero of Atlanta's 1991 stretch drive, Pena was hit hard by injuries last season. Bouts with bronchitis and strep throat sapped his strength during the first half, while tendinitis of the elbow disabled him again in mid-August. Early in the year, Pena lost velocity on his fastball by rushing his delivery and dragging his arm behind his leg-kick. Watching 1991 videotapes helped Pena revive in time to convert all of nine save chances in July. When he's right, he is a power pitcher who relies almost totally on his fastball, which has great movement. He also throws a slider and a palmball that he uses as a changeup. Opponents compiled a .255 batting average, a .310 on-base percentage, and a .420 slugging percentage in 1992.

Major League Pitching Register

	W	L	ERA	G	S	IP	H	ER	BB	SO
81 NL	1	1	2.84	14	2	25.1	18	8	11	14
82 NL	0	2	4.79	29	0	35.2	37	19	21	20
83 NL	12	9	2.75	34	1	177.0	152	54	51	120
84 NL	12	6	2.48	28	0	199.1	186	55	46	135
85 NL	0	1	8.31	2	0	4.1	7	4	3	2
86 NL	1	2	4.89	24	1	70.0	74	38	30	46
87 NL	2	7	3.50	37	11	87.1	82	34	37	76
88 NL	6	7	1.91	60	12	94.1	75	20	27	83
89 NL	4	3	2.13	53	5	76.0	62	18	18	75
90 NL	3	3	3.20	52	5	76.0	71	27	22	76
91 NL	8	1	2.40	59	15	82.1	74	22	22	62
92 NL	1	6	4.07	41	15	42.0	40	19	13	34
Life	50	48	2.95	433	67	969.2	878	318	301	743
3 AVE	4	3	3.05	51	12	67.0	62	23	19	57

GERONIMO PENA

Position: Second base
Team: St. Louis Cardinals
Born: March 29, 1967 Distrito Nacional, Dominican Republic
Height: 6'1" **Weight:** 170 lbs.
Bats: both **Throws:** right
Acquired: Signed as a free agent, 8/84

Player Summary

Fantasy Value	$6 to $12
Card Value	3¢ to 4¢
Will	slaughter southpaws
Can't	move over to third
Expect	better use of speed
Don't Expect	defensive problems

Pena's progress was slowed by injuries in 1992. He started the season on the disabled list after breaking his collarbone during spring training, then did well as the St. Louis leadoff man when he returned. He returned to the DL with a nerve problem in his right shoulder on June 29. He had a .386 on-base average and a .478 slugging percentage in 1992. A switch-hitter who murders lefthanded pitching (he batted .328 against lefties in 1992), he batted .248 with three homers, 12 RBI, four stolen bases, 13 walks, and 27 strikeouts in 101 at bats at Triple-A Louisville in 1992. Pena offers a package of speed, defense, and some power potential. He once stole 80 bases in a 134-game minor league season. Pena has also led various leagues in putouts, assists, chances, double plays, and fielding percentage. He is a better hitter and faster runner than Jose Oquendo, Rex Hudler, or Luis Alicea, who shared Pena's second base job last summer. At age 26, Pena is a strong candidate for daily duty if he stays healthy.

Major League Batting Register

	BA	G	AB	R	H	2B	3B	HR	RBI	SB
90 NL	.244	18	45	5	11	2	0	0	2	1
91 NL	.243	104	185	38	45	8	3	5	17	15
92 NL	.305	62	203	31	62	12	1	7	31	13
Life	.273	184	433	74	118	22	4	12	50	29
2 AVE	.276	83	194	35	54	10	2	6	24	14

TONY PENA

Position: Catcher
Team: Boston Red Sox
Born: June 4, 1957 Monte Cristi, Dominican Republic
Height: 6' **Weight:** 184 lbs.
Bats: right **Throws:** right
Acquired: Signed as a free agent, 11/89

Player Summary

Fantasy Value	$4 to $6
Card Value	3¢ to 4¢
Will	give good defense
Can't	reach the fences
Expect	off-field singles
Don't Expect	offense to revive

Durability is Pena's middle name. The sturdy backstop has not been on the disabled list since 1987. A noted defensive star who has won Gold Gloves in both leagues, he is also a competent hitter. He failed to supply any speed or power to the lackluster Red Sox lineup. An opposite-field fastball hitter with no patience, Pena fans two and one-half times for every walk. He hits lefties better than righties but didn't scare either group last summer. He notched a .284 on-base average and a .305 slugging percentage in 1992. The years of catching 140 games have taken a toll. He remains a regular primarily because of his defense. He handles pitchers well, calls good games, prevents wild pitches, and guns down a third of the runners who test him.

Major League Batting Register

	BA	G	AB	R	H	2B	3B	HR	RBI	SB
80 NL	.429	8	21	1	9	1	0	1	0	0
81 NL	.300	66	210	16	63	9	1	2	17	1
82 NL	.296	138	497	53	147	28	4	11	63	2
83 NL	.301	151	542	51	163	22	3	15	70	6
84 NL	.286	147	546	77	156	27	2	15	78	12
85 NL	.249	147	546	53	136	27	2	10	59	12
86 NL	.288	144	510	56	147	26	2	10	52	9
87 NL	.214	116	384	40	82	13	4	5	44	6
88 NL	.263	149	505	55	133	23	1	10	51	6
89 NL	.259	141	424	36	110	17	2	4	37	5
90 AL	.263	143	491	62	129	19	1	7	56	8
91 AL	.231	141	464	45	107	23	2	5	48	8
92 AL	.241	133	410	39	99	21	1	1	38	3
Life	.267	1624	5550	584	1481	256	26	95	614	78
3 AVE	.245	139	455	49	112	21	1	4	47	6

TERRY PENDLETON

Position: Third base
Team: Atlanta Braves
Born: July 16, 1960 Los Angeles, CA
Height: 5'9" **Weight:** 195 lbs.
Bats: both **Throws:** right
Acquired: Signed as a free agent, 12/90

Player Summary

Fantasy Value	$28 to $36
Card Value	8¢ to 18¢
Will	lead team by example
Can't	shake knee problems
Expect	All-Star performance
Don't Expect	trouble in the field

After winning a surprise batting title and MVP Award in 1991, Pendleton made a valiant try for a repeat performance last summer. Even though aching knees and a right groin pull caused him constant pain, he conceded only his ability to run. Rarely missing a game, he played third base well enough to win his third Gold Glove, while proving himself the best clutch hitter in the NL. During one stretch, he went 13-for-17 with runners in scoring position. He finished the season with the loop's best batting average with runners in scoring position, hitting .391. A switch-hitter who clobbers lefthanders, Pendleton had a .345 on-base average and a .473 slugging percentage in 1992. He hit game-winning, ninth-inning homers against Mitch Williams and Norm Charlton in 1992. Pendleton was voted the starting third baseman in the All-Star Game last year.

Major League Batting Register

	BA	G	AB	R	H	2B	3B	HR	RBI	SB
84 NL	.324	67	262	37	85	16	3	1	33	20
85 NL	.240	149	559	56	134	16	3	5	69	17
86 NL	.239	159	578	56	138	26	5	1	59	24
87 NL	.286	159	583	82	167	29	4	12	96	19
88 NL	.253	110	391	44	99	20	2	6	53	3
89 NL	.264	162	613	83	162	28	5	13	74	9
90 NL	.230	121	447	46	103	20	2	6	58	7
91 NL	.319	153	586	94	187	34	8	22	86	10
92 NL	.311	160	640	98	199	39	1	21	105	5
Life	.273	1240	4659	596	1274	228	33	87	633	114
3 AVE	.292	145	558	79	163	31	4	16	83	7

MELIDO PEREZ

Position: Pitcher
Team: New York Yankees
Born: Feb. 15, 1966 San Cristobal, Dominican Republic
Height: 6'4" **Weight:** 180 lbs.
Bats: right **Throws:** right
Acquired: Traded from Sox for Steve Sax, 1/92

Player Summary

Fantasy Value	$16 to $24
Card Value	4¢ to 6¢
Will	seek strikeout crown
Can't	always locate plate
Expect	low earned run mark
Don't Expect	more hits than frames

Given a chance to start by the pitching-poor Yankees, Perez responded with his finest season. He was handed only 23 runs in his first 13 losses. So on Aug. 11, he got his seventh complete game—four more than the 1991 Yankee staff—and took the league lead in strikeouts. Perez then blanked Minnesota 5-0 on Aug. 27 for his first shutout in two years, extending his scoreless streak to 17 innings. Though he sometimes struggles in the first inning and has some bouts of wildness, Perez has become one of the league's premier pitchers. He averages almost eight Ks and fewer than eight hits per nine innings. Perez dominates righthanded batters (who batted only .225 against him in '92), and keeps the ball in the park. He throws a fastball, curve, and splitter. Opponents in 1992 compiled a .235 batting average, a .308 on-base percentage, and a .332 slugging percentage in 1992. Perez fields his position well and keeps runners close.

Major League Pitching Register

	W	L	ERA	G	S	IP	H	ER	BB	SO
87 AL	1	1	7.84	3	0	10.1	18	9	5	5
88 AL	12	10	3.79	32	3	197.0	186	83	72	138
89 AL	11	14	5.01	31	2	183.1	187	102	90	141
90 AL	13	14	4.61	35	3	197.0	177	101	86	161
91 AL	8	7	3.12	49	0	135.2	111	47	52	128
92 AL	13	16	2.87	33	10	247.2	212	79	93	218
Life	58	62	3.90	183	18	971.0	891	421	398	791
3 AVE	11	12	3.52	39	4	193.1	167	76	77	169

MIKE PEREZ

Position: Pitcher
Team: St. Louis Cardinals
Born: Oct. 19, 1964 Yauco, Puerto Rico
Height: 6′ **Weight:** 185 lbs.
Bats: right **Throws:** right
Acquired: 12th-round pick in 6/86 free-agent draft

Player Summary	
Fantasy Value	$3 to $7
Card Value	5¢ to 10¢
Will	keep ball in park
Can't	avoid wild streaks
Expect	frequent outings
Don't Expect	righties to hit

When Perez posted a minor league record 41 saves and an 0.85 ERA for Class-A Springfield in 1987, the Cardinals realized a future bullpen standout was on his way. They gave him two brief looks before keeping him for a full season last summer. Working as one of several set-up men for closer Lee Smith, Perez responded with a fine rookie year. He handcuffed righthanded hitters while averaging seven hits and almost five strikeouts per nine innings. Perez was also extremely stingy with the long ball, yielding only four. Opponents compiled a .210 batting average, a .278 on-base percentage, and a .276 slugging percentage in 1992. Righthanded batters compiled a paltry .181 average against him. Blessed with a resilient arm, Perez has worked at least 50 games four years in a row, including a career high for the 1992 Cardinals. The transition from closer to set-up man isn't easy, but Perez had no problems. In 1991 at Triple-A Louisville, he was 3-5 with a 6.13 ERA, four saves, 25 walks, and 39 strikeouts in 47 innings pitched. Mark him down as a future closer.

Major League Pitching Register

	W	L	ERA	G	S	IP	H	ER	BB	SO
90 NL	1	0	3.95	13	1	13.2	12	6	3	5
91 NL	0	2	5.82	14	0	17.0	19	11	7	7
92 NL	9	3	1.84	77	0	93.0	70	19	32	46
Life	10	5	2.62	104	1	123.2	101	36	42	58

GERALD PERRY

Position: First base
Team: St. Louis Cardinals
Born: Oct. 30, 1960 Savannah, GA
Height: 6′ **Weight:** 190 lbs.
Bats: left **Throws:** right
Acquired: Signed as a free agent, 12/90

Player Summary	
Fantasy Value	$1 to $3
Card Value	3¢ to 4¢
Will	struggle against lefties
Can't	provide power
Expect	pinch-hit roles
Don't Expect	strong fielding

Perry is a better performer when he plays more often. Reduced to fill-in roles in St. Louis, he has not been the same player who stole 42 bases for the 1987 Braves and hit .300 the same club a year later. He's had some RBI as a pinch-hitter, but his average has hovered in the .240 range for consecutive seasons. He can't handle lefthanded pitching and seldom gets more than singles against righthanders. He had a .200 batting average against lefties last summer, opposed to a .246 average versus righties. He's more likely to strike out than walk. He had a .311 on-base average and a .315 slugging percentage in 1992. No longer the speed merchant he once was, Perry had some problems on the bases last season. He also had trouble in the field; he is not a good defensive first baseman. In 1988, his last year as a regular, he led loop first sackers in errors.

Major League Batting Register

	BA	G	AB	R	H	2B	3B	HR	RBI	SB
83 NL	.359	27	39	5	14	2	0	1	6	0
84 NL	.265	122	347	52	92	12	2	7	47	15
85 NL	.214	110	238	22	51	5	0	3	13	9
86 NL	.271	29	70	6	19	2	0	2	11	0
87 NL	.270	142	533	77	144	35	2	12	74	42
88 NL	.300	141	547	61	164	29	1	8	74	29
89 NL	.252	72	266	24	67	11	0	4	21	10
90 AL	.254	133	465	57	118	22	2	8	57	17
91 NL	.240	109	242	29	58	8	4	6	36	15
92 NL	.238	87	143	13	34	8	0	1	18	3
Life	.263	972	2890	346	761	134	11	52	357	140
2 AVE	.249	121	354	43	88	15	3	7	47	16

GENO PETRALLI

Position: Catcher
Team: Texas Rangers
Born: Sept. 25, 1959 Sacramento, CA
Height: 6'2" **Weight:** 180 lbs.
Bats: left **Throws:** right
Acquired: Signed as a free agent, 5/85

Player Summary

Fantasy Value	$1 to $2
Card Value	3¢ to 4¢
Will	play several spots
Can't	add speed or power
Expect	fairly good contact
Don't Expect	Gold Glove defense

Although Petralli carried a 10-year average of .278 into the 1992 campaign, the advent of Ivan Rodriguez sharply curtailed Petralli's playing time. Rusting on the bench, he suffered through the worst season of his career. Never a robust hitter against southpaws, he didn't do much with righthanders either. Petralli has no power or speed. In 1992, he had a .274 on-base average and a .276 slugging percentage. When he plays enough to stay sharp, Petralli makes fairly good contact. But he doesn't have the patience to wait for walks. In fact, the only thing keeping him in the major leagues is his versatility. In addition to being a lefty-hitting catcher, Petralli can play second and third base in a pinch. He is only average behind the plate. He's a good game-caller with a mediocre arm. He'll win no Gold Gloves in the infield, either.

Major League Batting Register

	BA	G	AB	R	H	2B	3B	HR	RBI	SB
82 AL	.364	16	44	3	16	2	0	0	1	0
83 AL	.000	6	4	0	0	0	0	0	0	0
84 AL	.000	3	3	0	0	0	0	0	0	0
85 AL	.270	42	100	7	27	2	0	0	11	1
86 AL	.255	69	137	17	35	9	3	2	18	3
87 AL	.302	101	202	28	61	11	2	7	31	0
88 AL	.282	129	351	35	99	14	2	7	36	0
89 AL	.304	70	184	18	56	7	0	4	23	0
90 AL	.255	133	325	28	83	13	1	0	21	0
91 AL	.271	87	199	21	54	8	1	2	20	2
92 AL	.198	94	192	11	38	12	0	1	18	0
Life	.269	750	1741	168	469	78	9	23	179	6
3 AVE	.244	105	239	20	58	11	1	1	20	1

GARY PETTIS

Position: Outfield
Team: Oakland Athletics
Born: April 3, 1958 Oakland, CA
Height: 6'1" **Weight:** 160 lbs.
Bats: both **Throws:** left
Acquired: Signed as a free agent, 12/92

Player Summary

Fantasy Value	$2 to $4
Card Value	3¢ to 4¢
Will	play great defense
Can't	hit for average
Expect	good use of speed
Don't Expect	any hint of power

Pettis is Oakland's insurance for Dave Henderson. Pettis has always been a wonderful fielder with a woeful bat. A gifted center fielder, he won the Gold Glove for fielding excellence five times. In one of those seasons, 1986, he led the American League in putouts and total chances. Although he took a 10-year mark of .237 into 1992, Pettis has watched his average shrink for four years in a row. He hit lefthanders well, and he had a .338 on-base average and a .302 slugging percentage in 1992. Pettis has great speed but no power. He's stolen more than 40 bases in a season four times and could reach that again if he ever learned how to reach base. Pettis fans far too frequently for a singles hitter. That light bat also precludes any chance he'll return to the lineup on a regular basis.

Major League Batting Register

	BA	G	AB	R	H	2B	3B	HR	RBI	SB
82 AL	.200	10	5	5	1	0	0	1	0	4
83 AL	.294	22	85	19	25	2	3	3	6	8
84 AL	.227	140	397	63	90	11	6	2	29	48
85 AL	.257	125	443	67	114	10	8	1	32	56
86 AL	.258	154	539	93	139	23	4	5	58	50
87 AL	.208	133	394	49	82	13	2	1	17	24
88 AL	.210	129	458	65	96	14	4	3	36	44
89 AL	.257	119	444	77	114	8	6	1	18	43
90 AL	.239	136	423	66	101	16	3	3	31	38
91 AL	.216	137	282	37	61	7	5	0	19	29
92 NL	.200	30	30	0	6	1	0	0	0	1
92 AL	.222	48	129	27	26	3	1	3	12	13
Life	.236	1183	3629	568	855	109	49	21	259	354
3 AVE	.225	117	288	43	65	9	5	1	21	27

TONY PHILLIPS

Position: Infield; outfield
Team: Detroit Tigers
Born: April 15, 1959 Atlanta, GA
Height: 5'10" **Weight:** 175 lbs.
Bats: both **Throws:** right
Acquired: Signed as a free agent, 12/89

Player Summary	
Fantasy Value	$12 to $20
Card Value	3¢ to 4¢
Will	reach base often
Can't	keep arguing calls
Expect	good glove anywhere
Don't Expect	20-20 campaign

In his 11-year career in the majors, Phillips has played every position but catcher and pitcher. He spent most of last year at second base for Detroit but also played more than 20 games at third base and right field. Though solid at every spot, Phillips is best at second, where he shows good hands, great range, and a strong arm. He rarely makes an error. He is a switch-hitter who usually hits best against lefties. Because he ranks among the league leaders in walks, he is a fine lead-off man. He had a .387 on-base average and a .388 slugging percentage in 1992. A battler who's never satisfied, he argues ball-and-strike calls frequently—not winning friends among the umpires. His only weakness is a tendency to be overaggressive on the bases; Phillips was caught trying to steal 10 times last summer.

Major League Batting Register

	BA	G	AB	R	H	2B	3B	HR	RBI	SB
82 AL	.210	40	81	11	17	2	2	0	8	2
83 AL	.248	148	412	54	102	12	3	4	35	16
84 AL	.266	154	451	62	120	24	3	4	37	10
85 AL	.280	42	161	23	45	12	2	4	17	3
86 AL	.256	118	441	76	113	14	5	5	52	15
87 AL	.240	111	379	48	91	20	0	10	46	7
88 AL	.203	79	212	32	43	8	4	2	17	0
89 AL	.262	143	451	48	118	15	6	4	47	3
90 AL	.251	152	573	97	144	23	5	8	55	19
91 AL	.284	146	564	87	160	28	4	17	72	10
92 AL	.276	159	606	114	167	32	3	10	64	12
Life	.259	1292	4331	652	1120	190	37	68	450	97
3 AVE	.270	152	581	99	157	28	4	12	64	14

HIPOLITO PICHARDO

Position: Pitcher
Team: Kansas City Royals
Born: Aug. 22, 1969 Jicome Esperanza, Dominican Republic
Height: 6'1" **Weight:** 160 lbs.
Bats: right **Throws:** right
Acquired: Signed as a free agent, 12/87

Player Summary	
Fantasy Value	$4 to $8
Card Value	3¢ to 4¢
Will	get ground-ball outs
Can't	keep runners close
Expect	success versus righties
Don't Expect	problems with control

Pichardo pitched an 8-0 one-hitter against Boston last July 21. He was almost perfect that day. With his nasty sinkerball in sync, he coaxed 17 ground outs. He is primarily a sinkerballer who also throws a forkball, changeup, and slider. Pichardo had a career record of 9-21 in the minors when he was promoted from Double-A Memphis in April. He had not gone longer than six and one-third innings in any of 18 previous big league appearances. He averages about a hit per inning and fewer than three walks and four strikeouts per nine innings. Opponents compiled a .267 batting average, a .327 on-base percentage, and a .379 slugging percentage in 1992. He is much more effective against righthanded hitters. Righties batted .252 against him, while lefties tagged him for a .287 average last summer. Pichardo needs to improve his pickoff move, because baserunners took advantage of him in '92. At Memphis in 1991, he was 3-11 with a 4.27 ERA, 38 bases on balls, and 75 strikeouts in 99 innings pitched. A pro since 1988, he has a bright future ahead of him.

Major League Pitching Register

	W	L	ERA	G	CG	IP	H	ER	BB	SO
92 AL	9	6	3.95	31	1	143.2	148	63	49	59
Life	9	6	3.95	31	1	143.2	148	63	49	59

PHIL PLANTIER

Position: Outfield
Team: San Diego Padres
Born: Jan. 27, 1969 Manchester, NH
Height: 5'11" **Weight:** 195 lbs.
Bats: left **Throws:** right
Acquired: Traded from Red Sox for Jose Melendez, 12/92

Player Summary	
Fantasy Value	$8 to $12
Card Value	5¢ to 15¢
Will	hit with power
Can't	steal often
Expect	strong rebound
Don't Expect	great throwing

The Padres fill their left field hole with Plantier. Injuries ruined his 1992 season. Heralded as the next great Red Sox slugger after a brilliant rookie year in 1991, Plantier managed only five homers in his first 215 at bats. He had a sore knee plus a sore elbow that was slow to recover from off-season surgery. He had a .332 on-base average and a .361 slugging percentage in 1992. He was bitter when the Red Sox returned him to the minors on Aug. 12. He said he ran into problems only because he was willing to play hurt at the team's request. At Triple-A Pawtucket last year, he batted .425 with five homers, 14 RBI, six walks, and six Ks in 40 at bats. At age 24, Plantier has plenty of time to recapture his 1991 form. He batted .305 with 16 homers and 61 RBI at Pawtucket in 1991. In 1990 at Pawtucket, he batted .253, had 79 RBI, and led the International League with 33 home runs. Because of his injuries, Plantier's defense suffered last year. Despite an average arm, he is a decent defensive outfielder.

Major League Batting Register

	BA	G	AB	R	H	2B	3B	HR	RBI	SB
90 AL	.133	14	15	1	2	1	0	0	3	0
91 AL	.331	53	148	27	49	7	1	11	35	1
92 AL	.246	108	349	46	86	19	0	7	30	2
Life	.268	175	512	74	137	27	1	18	68	3

DAN PLESAC

Position: Pitcher
Team: Chicago Cubs
Born: Feb. 4, 1962 Gary, IN
Height: 6'5" **Weight:** 215 lbs.
Bats: left **Throws:** left
Acquired: Signed as a free agent, 12/92

Player Summary	
Fantasy Value	$6 to $10
Card Value	3¢ to 4¢
Will	seek closer job
Can't	always throw strikes
Expect	lots of strikeouts
Don't Expect	trouble with lefties

Although he made the All-Star team as a closer three times, Plesac spent last summer as a middle reliever in the Milwaukee bullpen. He even made four starts. Plesac had a 95 mph fastball and a slider that devoured lefthanded hitters before running into arm problems in 1990. After admitting to the ailment, he agreed to a cortisone shot and even tried starting in '91 after 331 consecutive relief outings. A winter workout regimen helped, and Plesac regained some of his zip last year. He averaged nearly six and one-half strikeouts and gave up seven hits per nine innings. He had trouble locating the strike zone consistently, giving up four walks per nine innings. Opponents compiled a .229 batting average, a .317 on-base percentage, and a .343 slugging percentage in 1992. Plesac handles both right- and lefthanded hitters, fields his position well, and holds runners close. At 31, he will bid to win a job as Chicago's closer in 1993.

Major League Pitching Register

	W	L	ERA	G	S	IP	H	ER	BB	SO
86 AL	10	7	2.97	51	14	91.0	81	30	29	75
87 AL	5	6	2.61	57	23	79.1	63	23	23	89
88 AL	1	2	2.41	50	30	52.1	46	14	12	52
89 AL	3	4	2.35	52	33	61.1	47	16	17	52
90 AL	3	7	4.43	66	24	69.0	67	34	31	65
91 AL	2	7	4.29	45	8	92.1	92	44	39	61
92 AL	5	4	2.96	44	1	79.0	64	26	35	54
Life	29	37	3.21	365	133	524.1	460	187	186	448
3 AVE	3	6	3.89	52	11	80.0	74	35	35	60

ERIC PLUNK

Position: Pitcher
Team: Cleveland Indians
Born: Sept. 3, 1963 Wilmington, CA
Height: 6'5" **Weight:** 210 lbs.
Bats: right **Throws:** right
Acquired: Signed as a free agent, 4/92

Player Summary	
Fantasy Value	$2 to $4
Card Value	3¢ to 4¢
Will	retire first batters
Can't	find strike zone
Expect	poor self-defense
Don't Expect	fence-clearing shots

Wildness was Plunk's biggest problem last year. The hard-throwing middle reliever averaged seven hits and seven strikeouts but almost five walks per nine innings. He has an advantage over other relievers because of his five-pitch arsenal: a fastball, slider, curve, changeup, and split-fingered fastball. Opponents compiled a .229 batting average, a .324 on-base percentage, and a .320 slugging percentage in 1992. Righthanded batters don't get around on his hard stuff. Righties batted just .223 against him in 1992, and lefties managed only a .237 batting average. An effective set-up man who is sometimes used in save situations, Plunk made a habit of retiring first batters last summer. He was also stingier than Jack Benny when it came to throwing home run balls. The former Yankee, once the world's greatest benefactor of would-be basestealers, improved his pickoff move dramatically in 1992. He sabotages his own cause with sloppy fielding, however.

LUIS POLONIA

Position: Outfield
Team: California Angels
Born: Oct. 12, 1964 Santiago City, Dominican Republic
Height: 5'8" **Weight:** 155 lbs.
Bats: both **Throws:** left
Acquired: Traded from Yankees for Claudell Washington, 4/90

Player Summary	
Fantasy Value	$16 to $24
Card Value	3¢ to 4¢
Will	turn speed into weapon
Can't	belt balls over fences
Expect	solid batting average
Don't Expect	awards for fielding

Pain plagued Polonia all of last season. He was forced to get his at bats as a designated hitter for a month when a sore left hand prevented him from playing left field. He also endured knee, hand, shoulder, and hamstring problems. Polonia still had a strong season as a leadoff man. One of the game's best basestealers, he succeeds about 70 percent of the time. He's on base often enough to try, since he's a contact hitter who walks as much as he strikes out. He had a .337 on-base average and a .329 slugging percentage in 1992. Polonia rips righthanded pitching but holds his own against southpaws. A singles hitter who sometimes reaches the gaps for doubles, he hits best on artificial turf. He fattens his average on infield hits. Even if he hadn't been hurt last year, Polonia would have been a DH often, because he is an erratic outfielder with a mediocre arm.

Major League Pitching Register

	W	L	ERA	G	S	IP	H	ER	BB	SO
86 AL	4	7	5.31	26	0	120.1	91	71	102	98
87 AL	4	6	4.74	32	2	95.0	91	50	62	90
88 AL	7	2	3.00	49	5	78.0	62	26	39	79
89 AL	8	6	3.28	50	1	104.1	82	38	64	85
90 AL	6	3	2.72	47	0	72.2	58	22	43	67
91 AL	2	5	4.76	43	0	111.2	128	59	62	103
92 AL	9	6	3.64	58	4	71.2	61	29	38	50
Life	40	35	4.06	305	12	653.2	573	295	410	572
3 AVE	6	5	3.87	49	1	85.2	82	37	48	73

Major League Batting Register

	BA	G	AB	R	H	2B	3B	HR	RBI	SB
87 AL	.287	125	435	78	125	16	10	4	49	29
88 AL	.292	84	288	51	84	11	4	2	27	24
89 AL	.286	59	206	31	59	6	4	1	17	13
89 AL	.313	66	227	39	71	11	2	2	29	9
90 AL	.335	120	403	52	135	7	9	2	35	21
91 AL	.296	150	604	92	179	28	8	2	50	48
92 AL	.286	149	577	83	165	17	4	0	35	51
Life	.299	753	2740	426	818	96	41	13	242	195
3 AVE	.302	140	528	76	160	17	7	1	40	40

MARK PORTUGAL

Position: Pitcher
Team: Houston Astros
Born: Oct. 30, 1962 Los Angeles, CA
Height: 6' **Weight:** 190 lbs.
Bats: right **Throws:** right
Acquired: Traded from Twins for Todd McClure, 12/88

Player Summary	
Fantasy Value	$4 to $6
Card Value	3¢ to 4¢
Will	keep ball in park
Can't	compete for K crown
Expect	some control problems
Don't Expect	righties to hit him

Injuries interfered with Houston's plan to let Portugal lend veteran experience to a young staff last summer, as he went on the shelf with a shoulder problem. He pitched brilliantly in 15 games when he returned. Bone chips in the right elbow, however, sent him to the disabled list again. Portugal averaged fewer than seven hits and almost five and one-half strikeouts per nine innings last year. He had scattered control trouble (almost four walks per nine innings). Opponents in 1992 compiled a .213 batting average, a .295 on-base percentage, and a .331 slugging average. The owner of a change-up that serves as the perfect complement to his fastball, slider, and curve, Portugal usually dominates righthanded hitters. He's very good at keeping runners close enough for his catchers to thwart any steal attempts. He is a fine fielder and an excellent hitter.

Major League Pitching Register

	W	L	ERA	G	CG	IP	H	ER	BB	SO
85 AL	1	3	5.55	6	0	24.1	24	15	14	12
86 AL	6	10	4.31	27	3	112.2	112	54	50	67
87 AL	1	3	7.77	13	0	44.0	58	38	24	28
88 AL	3	3	4.53	26	0	57.2	60	29	17	31
89 NL	7	1	2.75	20	2	108.0	91	33	37	86
90 NL	11	10	3.62	32	1	196.2	187	79	67	136
91 NL	10	12	4.49	32	1	168.1	163	84	59	120
92 NL	6	3	2.66	18	1	101.1	76	30	41	62
Life	45	45	4.01	174	8	813.0	771	362	309	542
3 AVE	9	8	3.72	27	1	155.1	142	64	56	106

DENNIS POWELL

Position: Pitcher
Team: Seattle Mariners
Born: Aug. 13, 1963 Moultrie, GA
Height: 6'3" **Weight:** 200 lbs.
Bats: right **Throws:** left
Acquired: Signed as a free agent, 4/91

Player Summary	
Fantasy Value	$1 to $3
Card Value	3¢ to 4¢
Will	get first hitter
Can't	locate the plate
Expect	progress versus lefties
Don't Expect	closer job

If Powell could learn to throw strikes, he would make a much better reliever. A three-pitch lefthander who has bounced from majors to minors since breaking in with the 1985 Dodgers, he spent the entire 1991 season in the Triple-A Calgary rotation, going 9-8 with a 4.15 ERA. He had been tried as a starter and as a closer before being put in middle relief. Although he yielded fewer hits than innings last year, Powell also averaged more than five walks per nine innings. The best aspect of his game was consistent success at retiring first batters. The first batters he faced each game compiled only a .100 batting average. Powell needs to concentrate more against lefthanders—who hit him at a .250 clip last summer. Opponents compiled a .238 batting average, a .340 on-base percentage, and a .374 slugging percentage in 1992. At age 29, his career could be in jeopardy if he doesn't show quick improvement.

Major League Pitching Register

	W	L	ERA	G	S	IP	H	ER	BB	SO
85 NL	1	1	5.22	16	1	29.1	30	17	13	19
86 NL	2	7	4.27	27	0	65.1	65	31	25	31
87 AL	1	3	3.15	16	0	34.1	32	12	15	17
88 AL	1	3	8.68	12	0	18.2	29	18	11	15
89 AL	2	2	5.00	43	2	45.0	49	25	21	27
90 AL	0	4	7.02	11	0	42.1	64	33	21	23
92 AL	4	2	4.58	49	0	57.0	49	29	29	35
Life	11	22	5.09	174	3	292.0	318	165	135	167
2 AVE	2	1	4.80	26	0	30.0	27	16	16	18

TED POWER

Position: Pitcher
Team: Cleveland Indians
Born: Jan. 31, 1955 Guthrie, OK
Height: 6'4" **Weight:** 220 lbs.
Bats: right **Throws:** right
Acquired: Signed as a free agent, 4/92

Player Summary	
Fantasy Value	$2 to $4
Card Value	3¢ to 4¢
Will	keep the ball in park
Can't	win unless sinker sinks
Expect	many middle relief calls
Don't Expect	first batters to reach

Although 1992 was his 12th season in the big leagues, Power produced his most effective performance. En route to a career-best ERA, he proved the perfect set-up man for Cleveland relief ace Steve Olin. Power even converted some save chances himself. A sinker-slider pitcher who also throws a changeup, he averages almost six strikeouts and three walks per nine innings. He keeps the ball in the park but yields about a hit per inning. Opponents compiled a .248 batting average, a .316 on-base percentage, and a .346 slugging percentage in 1992. Power does well against first batters and usually fares better against righthanded hitters—but not last year. Righthhanded hitters compiled a .261 batting average in '92. He preserved more than a dozen wins in 1992. Power knows how to field and keep runners close.

Major League Pitching Register

	W	L	ERA	G	S	IP	H	ER	BB	SO
81 NL	1	3	3.14	5	0	14.1	16	5	7	7
82 NL	1	1	6.68	12	0	33.2	38	25	23	15
83 NL	5	6	4.54	49	2	111.0	120	56	49	57
84 NL	9	7	2.82	78	11	108.2	93	34	46	81
85 NL	8	6	2.70	64	27	80.0	65	24	45	42
86 NL	10	6	3.70	56	1	129.0	115	53	52	95
87 NL	10	13	4.50	34	0	204.0	213	102	71	133
88 AL	6	7	5.91	26	0	99.0	121	65	38	57
89 NL	7	7	3.71	23	0	97.0	96	40	21	43
90 NL	1	3	3.66	40	7	51.2	50	21	17	42
91 NL	5	3	3.62	68	3	87.0	87	35	31	51
92 AL	3	3	2.54	64	6	99.1	88	28	35	51
Life	66	65	3.94	519	57	1114.2	1102	488	435	674
3 AVE	3	3	3.18	57	5	79.1	75	28	28	48

KIRBY PUCKETT

Position: Outfield
Team: Minnesota Twins
Born: March 14, 1961 Chicago, IL
Height: 5'8" **Weight:** 213 lbs.
Bats: right **Throws:** right
Acquired: First-round pick in 6/82 free-agent draft

Player Summary	
Fantasy Value	$36 to $45
Card Value	10¢ to 35¢
Will	bid for MVP
Can't	wait for good pitches
Expect	Gold Glove defense
Don't Expect	any hint of decline

Puckett can do it all. He is a seven-time All-Star with six Gold Gloves, and he's hit for power and average over the past seven seasons. His career-best .356 average in 1988 was the AL's best by a righthanded hitter since Joe DiMaggio's .357 average in 1941. Puckett's biggest hit was the 11th-inning homer in game six of the 1991 World Series. A notorious bad-ball hitter with no patience, he had a .374 on-base percentage and a .490 slugging average in 1992. Puckett powders lefthanded pitching, hitting .328 against lefties last summer. He's no slouch against righties—he actually had a better average, .329, against righthanders in '92. He had four straight 200-hit campaigns from 1986 to 1989 and reached 24 homers three different times. Though shaped like a tapir, he plays like a gazelle. Puckett patrols center field with excellent range, fine instincts, and a strong arm.

Major League Batting Register

	BA	G	AB	R	H	2B	3B	HR	RBI	SB
84 AL	.296	128	557	63	165	12	5	0	31	14
85 AL	.288	161	691	80	199	29	13	4	74	21
86 AL	.328	161	680	119	223	37	6	31	96	20
87 AL	.332	157	624	96	207	32	5	28	99	12
88 AL	.356	158	657	109	234	42	5	24	121	6
89 AL	.339	159	635	75	215	45	4	9	85	11
90 AL	.298	146	551	82	164	40	3	12	80	5
91 AL	.319	152	611	92	195	29	6	15	89	11
92 AL	.329	160	639	104	210	38	4	19	110	17
Life	.321	1382	5645	820	1812	304	51	142	785	117
3 AVE	.316	153	600	93	190	36	4	15	93	11

CARLOS QUINTANA

Position: First base; outfield
Team: Boston Red Sox
Born: Aug. 26, 1965 Estado Miranda, Venezuela
Height: 6′2″ **Weight:** 195 lbs.
Bats: right **Throws:** right
Acquired: Signed as a free agent, 11/84

Player Summary	
Fantasy Value	$4 to $6
Card Value	3¢ to 4¢
Will	seek comeback
Can't	help with speed
Expect	hits in the clutch
Don't Expect	steady power stroke

After showing much promise as the regular first baseman for the Red Sox in 1991, Quintana missed the entire '92 campaign while recovering from an off-season automobile accident in Venezuela. The mishap left him with a broken left arm and nerve damage to the left wrist. Since Quintana bats and throws righthanded, he should be able to make a comeback at age 27. If he makes a full comeback, he is a talented hitter who walks almost as much as he strikes out. He has a good stroke with some power and he's willing to hit to all fields. In '91, he had a .375 on-base average and a .412 slugging percentage. A former singles hitter who began to pull in 1991, Quintana is an accomplished bunter and a good clutch hitter. He murders lefthanders. Although he's a converted outfielder, Quintana lacks the speed and range needed to play a strong left or right field. He is a fine-fielding first baseman, however.

Major League Batting Register

	BA	G	AB	R	H	2B	3B	HR	RBI	SB
88 AL	.333	5	6	1	2	0	0	0	2	0
89 AL	.208	34	77	6	16	5	0	0	6	0
90 AL	.287	149	512	56	147	28	0	7	67	1
91 AL	.295	149	478	69	141	21	1	11	71	1
Life	.285	337	1073	132	306	54	1	18	146	2
2 AVE	.291	149	495	63	144	25	1	9	69	1

JAMIE QUIRK

Position: Catcher; infield
Team: Oakland Athletics
Born: Oct. 22, 1954 Whittier, CA
Height: 6′4″ **Weight:** 200 lbs.
Bats: left **Throws:** right
Acquired: Signed as free agent, 11/90

Player Summary	
Fantasy Value	$1 to $3
Card Value	3¢ to 4¢
Will	try any position
Can't	hit for average
Expect	some pinch-hits
Don't Expect	home run power

In 18 big league seasons, Quirk has done everything but pitch. Primarily a backup catcher and pinch-hitter, he is only a .240 hitter with little power and no speed. Nevertheless, he is valued for his experience and his ability to come off the bench and stroke a key hit. He had five hits in his first 13 trips as a pinch-hitter last season. Quirk strikes out twice as often as he walks and hits primarily to the opposite field. He had a .294 on-base average and a .305 slugging percentage last year. A good game-caller who handles pitchers well, he surprises runners with his throwing arm. He nailed about 33 percent of would-be stealers in 1992. Quirk became a part-time catcher in 1979.

Major League Batting Register

	BA	G	AB	R	H	2B	3B	HR	RBI	SB
75 AL	.256	14	39	2	10	0	0	1	5	0
76 AL	.246	64	114	11	28	6	0	1	15	0
77 AL	.217	93	221	16	48	14	1	3	13	0
78 AL	.207	17	29	3	6	2	0	0	2	0
79 AL	.304	51	79	8	24	6	1	1	11	0
80 AL	.276	62	163	13	45	5	0	5	21	3
81 AL	.250	46	100	8	25	7	0	0	10	0
82 AL	.231	36	78	8	18	3	0	1	5	0
83 NL	.209	48	86	3	18	2	1	2	11	0
84 AL	.333	4	3	1	1	0	0	1	2	0
85 AL	.281	19	57	3	16	3	1	0	4	0
86 AL	.215	80	219	24	47	10	0	8	26	0
87 AL	.236	109	296	24	70	17	0	5	33	1
88 AL	.240	84	196	22	47	7	1	8	25	1
89 AL	.176	47	85	6	15	2	0	1	10	0
90 AL	.281	56	121	12	34	5	1	3	26	0
91 AL	.261	76	203	16	53	4	0	1	17	0
92 AL	.220	78	177	13	39	7	1	2	11	0
Life	.240	984	2266	193	544	100	7	43	247	5
2 AVE	.242	77	190	15	46	6	1	2	14	0

SCOTT RADINSKY

Position: Pitcher
Team: Chicago White Sox
Born: March 3, 1968 Glendale, CA
Height: 6'3" **Weight:** 190 lbs.
Bats: left **Throws:** left
Acquired: Third-round pick in 6/86 free-agent draft

Player Summary	
Fantasy Value	$10 to $16
Card Value	3¢ to 4¢
Will	rack up Ks
Can't	keep full control
Expect	more use as closer
Don't Expect	hits by lefties

When Bobby Thigpen struggled last summer, rookie White Sox manager Gene Lamont tried a righty-lefty closer platoon of Roberto Hernandez and Radinsky. A fastball-and-slider pitcher used primarily as a set-up man previously, Radinsky responded with his finest season. He decimated lefthanded hitters (who had only a .182 batting average against him in 1992) and kept the ball in the park while averaging seven hits and more than eight strikeouts per nine innings. Opponents compiled a .243 batting average, a .347 on-base percentage, and a .351 slugging percentage in 1992. His lone weakness was a tendency to let home plate wander on occasion. The first batters he faced in '92 notched a .288 batting average. Radinsky, who went into a brief June slump when his velocity dropped, has a resilient arm that responds to frequent work. He's registered more than 60 games in each of his three seasons with the Sox. Runners don't challenge him. He is also a good fielder. At 25, Radinsky could shed the platoon and become a full-time closer this season.

Major League Pitching Register

	W	L	ERA	G	S	IP	H	ER	BB	SO
90 AL	6	1	4.82	62	4	52.1	47	28	36	46
91 AL	5	5	2.02	67	8	71.1	53	16	23	49
92 AL	3	7	2.73	68	15	59.1	54	18	34	48
Life	14	13	3.05	197	27	183.0	154	62	93	143
3 AVE	5	4	3.05	66	9	61.1	51	21	31	48

TIM RAINES

Position: Outfield
Team: Chicago White Sox
Born: Sept. 16, 1959 Sanford, FL
Height: 5'8" **Weight:** 185 lbs.
Bats: both **Throws:** right
Acquired: Traded from Expos with Jeff Carter and Mario Brito for Barry Jones and Ivan Calderon, 12/90

Player Summary	
Fantasy Value	$18 to $24
Card Value	5¢ to 10¢
Will	provide solid offense
Can't	hit ball over fence
Expect	patience at bat
Don't Expect	catchers to nail him

After moving from leadoff to second in the White Sox lineup last July 28, Raines embarked on his best stretch of the year. He collected 37 hits in his first 98 at bats for a .378 average. He used the hot streak to improve his running game. He was caught stealing only six times last year. A switch-hitter who's better against righties, Raines is no longer the speedster who swiped 70 bases seven years in a row. But he's a formidable force when his hamstrings are healthy. A contact hitter with a great eye, Raines walks much more often than he fans. He had a .380 on-base average and a .405 slugging percentage in 1992. Despite his speed, he's an erratic left fielder with a weak arm.

Major League Batting Register

	BA	G	AB	R	H	2B	3B	HR	RBI	SB
79 NL	.000	6	0	3	0	0	0	0	0	2
80 NL	.050	15	20	5	1	0	0	0	0	5
81 NL	.304	88	313	61	95	13	7	5	37	71
82 NL	.277	156	647	90	179	32	8	4	43	78
83 NL	.298	156	615	133	183	32	8	11	71	90
84 NL	.309	160	622	106	192	38	9	8	60	75
85 NL	.320	150	575	115	184	30	13	11	41	70
86 NL	.334	151	580	91	194	35	10	9	62	70
87 NL	.330	139	530	123	175	34	8	18	68	50
88 NL	.270	109	429	66	116	19	7	12	48	33
89 NL	.286	145	517	76	148	29	6	9	60	41
90 NL	.287	130	457	65	131	11	5	9	62	49
91 AL	.268	155	609	102	163	20	6	5	50	51
92 AL	.294	144	551	102	162	22	9	7	54	45
Life	.297	1704	6465	1138	1923	315	96	108	656	730
3 AVE	.282	143	539	90	152	18	7	7	55	48

WILL RANDOLPH

Position: Second base
Team: New York Mets
Born: July 6, 1954 Holly Hill, SC
Height: 5'11" **Weight:** 163 lbs.
Bats: right **Throws:** right
Acquired: Signed as a free agent, 12/91

Player Summary	
Fantasy Value	$2 to $4
Card Value	3¢ to 4¢
Will	turn double plays
Can't	hit the long ball
Expect	good on-base mark
Don't Expect	many stolen bases

Even at his age, Randolph proved last summer he can still play defense. His range has declined with his speed, but he had only eight errors last year. He was the Mets regular second baseman until aching knees hampered his running and limited his playing time. His season was shortened for good on Aug. 12, when a pitch from Pittsburgh's Bob Walk broke Randolph's wrist. At the time of the fracture, Randolph was giving the Mets strong defense. Still blessed with a sharp batting eye, he walks more than he strikes out, giving him a high on-base percentage. In 1992, he had a .352 on-base percentage and a .318 slugging percentage.

Major League Batting Register

	BA	G	AB	R	H	2B	3B	HR	RBI	SB
75 NL	.164	30	61	9	10	1	0	0	3	1
76 AL	.267	125	430	59	115	15	4	1	40	37
77 AL	.274	147	551	91	151	28	11	4	40	13
78 AL	.279	134	499	87	139	18	6	3	42	36
79 AL	.270	153	574	98	155	15	13	5	61	33
80 AL	.294	138	513	99	151	23	7	7	46	30
81 AL	.232	93	357	59	83	14	3	2	24	14
82 AL	.280	144	553	85	155	21	4	3	36	16
83 AL	.279	104	420	73	117	21	1	2	38	12
84 AL	.287	142	564	86	162	24	2	2	31	10
85 AL	.276	143	497	75	137	21	2	5	40	16
86 AL	.276	141	492	76	136	15	2	5	50	15
87 AL	.305	120	449	96	137	24	2	7	67	11
88 AL	.230	110	404	43	93	20	1	2	34	8
89 AL	.282	145	549	62	155	18	0	2	36	7
90 NL	.271	26	96	15	26	4	0	1	9	1
90 AL	.257	93	292	37	75	9	3	1	21	6
91 AL	.327	124	431	60	141	14	3	0	54	4
92 NL	.252	90	286	29	72	11	1	2	15	1
Life	.276	2202	8018	1239	2210	316	65	54	687	271
3 AVE	.284	111	368	47	105	13	2	1	33	4

RANDY READY

Position: Infield; outfield
Team: Oakland Athletics
Born: Jan. 8, 1960 San Mateo, CA
Height: 5'11" **Weight:** 180 lbs.
Bats: right **Throws:** right
Acquired: Signed as a free agent, 1/92

Player Summary	
Fantasy Value	$1 to $3
Card Value	3¢ to 4¢
Will	walk more than whiff
Can't	handle righthanders
Expect	use at several spots
Don't Expect	long-ball production

Ready was one of several valuable extra parts who plugged the dam when a tidal wave of injuries felled Oakland's regulars last summer. He played second, third, left field, and right field while also serving as a part-time DH. Although he has shown some power and speed during his 10-year career, Ready's hitting and running have fallen off sharply in recent seasons. He still hits lefthanders well but has trouble with righties. A good two-strike hitter, Ready makes contact. He has patience at the plate, walking more than he fans. Defensively, Ready's best positions are second base—despite his limited range—and third. He has no trouble turning the double play, has good instincts and good hands, and rarely makes errors. In 1992, Ready played left field more than any other position.

Major League Batting Register

	BA	G	AB	R	H	2B	3B	HR	RBI	SB
83 AL	.405	12	37	8	15	3	2	1	6	0
84 AL	.187	37	123	13	23	6	1	3	13	0
85 AL	.265	48	181	29	48	9	5	1	21	0
86 AL	.190	23	79	8	15	4	0	1	4	2
86 NL	.000	1	3	0	0	0	0	0	0	0
87 NL	.309	124	350	69	108	26	6	12	54	7
88 NL	.266	114	331	43	88	16	2	7	39	6
89 NL	.264	100	254	37	67	13	2	8	24	4
90 NL	.241	101	217	26	53	9	1	1	26	3
91 NL	.249	76	205	32	51	10	1	1	20	2
92 AL	.200	61	125	17	25	2	0	3	17	1
Life	.259	697	1905	282	493	98	20	38	226	25
2 AVE	.246	89	211	29	52	10	1	1	23	3

JEFF REARDON

Position: Pitcher
Team: Atlanta Braves
Born: Oct. 1, 1955 Dalton, MA
Height: 6′ **Weight:** 200 lbs.
Bats: right **Throws:** right
Acquired: Traded from Red Sox for Nate Minchey and Sean Ross, 8/92

Player Summary

Fantasy Value	$18 to $26
Card Value	4¢ to 6¢
Will	bank on breaking ball
Can't	blaze ball by hitters
Expect	exceptional control
Don't Expect	lots of baserunners

Reardon has saved more games than any reliever in baseball history. He notched No. 342 to pass Hall of Famer Rollie Fingers last summer. At age 36, Reardon notched his 11th straight 20-save season while splitting the year between the Red Sox and Braves, who acquired him for the stretch drive. Before arriving in Atlanta, Reardon had complained about lack of work—the result of the poor Red Sox season. That situation changed immediately. A former power pitcher who now relies on throwing his curveball for strikes, Reardon gives up a lot of hits but averages nearly seven strikeouts per nine innings. He hurts his own cause with shaky defense. He also has a poor pickoff move, and baserunners often take advantage of him.

Major League Pitching Register

	W	L	ERA	G	S	IP	H	ER	BB	SO
79 NL	1	2	1.74	18	2	20.2	12	4	9	10
80 NL	8	7	2.61	61	6	110.1	96	32	47	101
81 NL	3	0	2.18	43	8	70.1	48	17	21	49
82 NL	7	4	2.06	75	26	109.0	87	25	36	86
83 NL	7	9	3.03	66	21	92.0	87	31	44	78
84 NL	7	7	2.90	68	23	87.0	70	28	37	79
85 NL	2	8	3.18	63	41	87.2	68	31	26	67
86 NL	7	9	3.94	62	35	89.0	83	39	26	67
87 AL	8	8	4.48	63	31	80.1	70	40	28	83
88 AL	2	4	2.47	63	42	73.0	68	20	15	56
89 AL	5	4	4.07	65	31	73.0	68	33	12	46
90 AL	5	3	3.16	47	21	51.1	39	18	19	33
91 AL	1	4	3.03	57	40	59.1	54	20	16	44
92 AL	2	2	4.25	46	27	42.1	53	20	7	32
92 NL	3	0	1.15	14	3	15.2	14	2	2	7
Life	68	71	3.05	811	357	1061.0	917	360	345	838
3 AVE	4	3	3.20	55	30	56.2	53	20	15	39

GARY REDUS

Position: First base; outfield
Team: Pittsburgh Pirates
Born: Nov. 1, 1956 Tanner, AL
Height: 6′1″ **Weight:** 185 lbs.
Bats: right **Throws:** right
Acquired: Traded from White Sox for Mike Diaz, 8/88

Player Summary

Fantasy Value	$4 to $8
Card Value	3¢ to 4¢
Will	save job with speed
Can't	get extra-base hits
Expect	decline to continue
Don't Expect	dynamic defense

Redus has seen his better days. He is no longer the player who was considered a pretty good leadoff man. He is barely hanging on as a platoon first baseman. He struggled against southpaws for the second straight season in '92, as he had the lowest seasonal runs scored total in his major league career. A contact hitter who walks as much as he fans, he contributed only speed to the Pittsburgh offense last summer. He had a .321 on-base average and a .381 slugging percentage in 1992. He was successful in 11 of his 15 steal attempts. Redus, who also played the outfield in '92, is not a good defensive player anywhere—despite great range. Low throws at first give him as much trouble as outfield flies over his head.

Major League Batting Register

	BA	G	AB	R	H	2B	3B	HR	RBI	SB
82 NL	.217	20	83	12	18	3	2	1	7	11
83 NL	.247	125	453	90	112	20	9	17	51	39
84 NL	.254	123	394	69	100	21	3	7	22	48
85 NL	.252	101	246	51	62	14	4	6	28	48
86 NL	.247	90	340	62	84	22	4	11	33	25
87 AL	.236	130	475	78	112	26	6	12	48	52
88 AL	.263	77	262	42	69	10	4	6	34	26
88 NL	.197	30	71	12	14	2	0	2	4	5
89 NL	.283	98	279	42	79	18	7	6	33	25
90 NL	.247	96	227	32	56	15	3	6	23	11
91 NL	.246	98	252	45	62	12	2	7	24	17
92 NL	.256	76	176	26	45	7	3	3	12	11
Life	.250	1064	3258	561	813	170	47	84	319	318
3 AVE	.249	90	218	34	54	11	3	5	20	13

JODY REED

Position: Second base
Team: Los Angeles Dodgers
Born: July 26, 1962 Tampa, FL
Height: 5'9" **Weight:** 160 lbs.
Bats: right **Throws:** right
Acquired: Traded from Rockies for Rudy Seanez, 11/92

Player Summary	
Fantasy Value	$5 to $9
Card Value	3¢ to 4¢
Will	provide good defense
Can't	hit frequent homers
Expect	good contact hitting
Don't Expect	average to stay low

Reed moves to solidify an otherwise terrible Dodgers defense and provide a No. 2 hitter. Although he took a five-year average of .288 into last season, he stumbled out of the gate for the Red Sox and never recovered. He finished more than 30 points off his lifetime mark. Because he's a contact hitter who walks more than he strikes out, Reed compiled a respectable on-base percentage. He had a .321 on-base percentage and a .316 slugging average. The former Florida State star hits lefthanders well and produces in the clutch, though he sometimes hurts himself by trying to pull the ball. A traditional slow starter, Reed offers a smattering of power and speed. He led the AL in doubles in 1990 but has never hit more than five homers in a season. Reed has also played shortstop, and he is a fine fielder who has good range and a better throwing arm than most of his colleagues. He turns the twin killing and makes diving stops.

Major League Batting Register

	BA	G	AB	R	H	2B	3B	HR	RBI	SB
87 AL	.300	9	30	4	9	1	1	0	8	1
88 AL	.293	109	338	60	99	23	1	1	28	1
89 AL	.288	146	524	76	151	42	2	3	40	4
90 AL	.289	155	598	70	173	45	0	5	51	4
91 AL	.283	153	618	87	175	42	2	5	60	6
92 AL	.247	143	550	64	136	27	1	3	40	7
Life	.280	715	2658	361	743	180	7	17	227	23
3 AVE	.274	150	589	74	161	38	1	4	50	6

KEVIN REIMER

Position: Designated hitter; outfield
Team: Milwaukee Brewers
Born: June 28, 1964 Macon, GA
Height: 6'2" **Weight:** 215 lbs.
Bats: left **Throws:** right
Acquired: Traded from Rockies for Dante Bichette, 11/92

Player Summary	
Fantasy Value	$8 to $12
Card Value	3¢ to 4¢
Will	hit righties hard
Can't	give good defense
Expect	good run production
Don't Expect	any show of speed

The designated hitter rule was made for Reimer. He had eight errors in the first three months of 1992 and finished the year with 11; he is a definite liability in left field. Though he's improved a lot since making 32 errors in the Class-A Carolina League in 1986, Reimer still lacks speed, range, and the throwing arm required for adequate outfield play. He also doesn't have the instincts to play the position. He has played some first base and could move there eventually. Or he could remain a DH, able to concentrate on his hitting. Reimer in '92 was able to notch a .272 batting average against righthanders, while batting .247 against lefties. He had a .336 on-base average and a .437 slugging percentage in 1992. He's good for about 20 homers and 70 RBI a year—probably more if he gets more playing time. Reimer is a first-ball, fastball hitter who hits well in the clutch. A former amateur hockey player, he was a member of Canada's 1984 Olympic baseball team.

Major League Batting Register

	BA	G	AB	R	H	2B	3B	HR	RBI	SB
88 AL	.120	12	25	2	3	0	0	1	2	0
89 AL	.000	3	5	0	0	0	0	0	0	0
90 AL	.260	64	100	5	26	9	1	2	15	0
91 AL	.269	136	394	46	106	22	0	20	69	0
92 AL	.267	148	494	56	132	32	2	16	58	2
Life	.262	363	1018	109	267	63	3	39	144	2
2 AVE	.268	142	444	51	119	27	1	18	64	1

HAROLD REYNOLDS

Position: Second base
Team: Baltimore Orioles
Born: Nov. 26, 1960 Eugene, OR
Height: 5'11" **Weight:** 165 lbs.
Bats: both **Throws:** right
Acquired: Signed as a free agent, 12/92

Player Summary	
Fantasy Value	$5 to $9
Card Value	3¢ to 4¢
Will	make contact
Can't	get proper publicity
Expect	great range at second
Don't Expect	hits that clear fence

Reynolds moves to Baltimore to provide some offense from second base. Before Seattle decided to sit him to look at rookie hot-shot Bret Boone, Reynolds was on course for his sixth straight season of 150 games and 25 steals. One of the game's most underappreciated stars, Reynolds is a three-time Gold Glove winner who has also led the American League in triples and stolen bases. A contact hitter with patience, he walks more than he fans. Reynolds usually hits lefthanders better but last year was equally productive from both sides. He's a fine bunter who is also adept at the hit-and-run play. As a baserunner, Reynolds was thrown out almost as often as he stole. Defensively, he's led his league in putouts, assists, chances, double plays, and also errors—but only because he gets to balls other second basemen couldn't consider.

Major League Batting Register

	BA	G	AB	R	H	2B	3B	HR	RBI	SB
83 AL	.203	20	59	8	12	4	1	0	1	0
84 AL	.300	10	10	3	3	0	0	0	0	1
85 AL	.144	67	104	15	15	3	1	0	6	3
86 AL	.222	126	445	46	99	19	4	1	24	30
87 AL	.275	160	530	73	146	31	8	1	35	60
88 AL	.283	158	598	61	169	26	11	4	41	35
89 AL	.300	153	613	87	184	24	9	0	43	25
90 AL	.252	160	642	100	162	36	5	5	55	31
91 AL	.254	161	631	95	160	34	6	3	57	28
92 AL	.247	140	458	55	113	23	3	3	33	15
Life	.260	1155	4090	543	1063	200	48	17	295	228
3 AVE	.251	154	577	83	145	31	5	4	48	25

ARTHUR LEE RHODES

Position: Pitcher
Team: Baltimore Orioles
Born: Oct. 24, 1969 Waco, TX
Height: 6'2" **Weight:** 204 lbs.
Bats: left **Throws:** left
Acquired: Second-round pick in 6/88 free-agent draft

Player Summary	
Fantasy Value	$6 to $12
Card Value	10¢ to 25¢
Will	get Ks with curve
Can't	always find plate
Expect	command over lefties
Don't Expect	a losing record

When Rhodes got his first taste of the big leagues in 1991, his inexperience and anxiety got the best of his control. Last year was different. Recalled July 8 when Storm Davis was disabled, Rhodes won four straight decisions. He topped Texas July 24 for the first complete game by a Baltimore southpaw since Jeff Ballard in 1989. Rhodes changes speeds well and gets ahead in the count. He throws a low-90s fastball that moves, a sharp-breaking curve that often gets strikeouts, and a slider. He was second in strikeouts in the Triple-A International League at the time of his promotion. He was 6-6 at Rochester, with a 3.72 ERA, 46 walks, and 115 strikeouts in 102 innings. Rhodes averages eight hits and seven strikeouts per nine innings but has occasional problems with location and gopher balls. Major league opponents compiled a .250 batting average, a .325 on-base percentage, and a .382 slugging percentage in 1992. He also needs to improve his performance against lefties. In 1991 at Double-A Hagerstown, he was 7-4 with a 2.70 ERA, 47 walks, and 115 strikeouts in 107 innings.

Major League Pitching Register

	W	L	ERA	G	CG	IP	H	ER	BB	SO
91 AL	0	3	8.00	8	0	36.0	47	32	23	23
92 AL	7	5	3.63	15	2	94.1	87	38	38	77
Life	7	8	4.83	23	2	130.1	134	70	61	100

DAVE RIGHETTI

Position: Pitcher
Team: San Francisco Giants
Born: Nov. 28, 1958 San Jose, CA
Height: 6'4" **Weight:** 210 lbs.
Bats: left **Throws:** left
Acquired: Signed as a free agent, 12/90

Player Summary	
Fantasy Value	$3 to $6
Card Value	3¢ to 4¢
Will	struggle to stick
Can't	always find plate
Expect	mop-up assignments
Don't Expect	fastball to sizzle

Righetti had made 522 straight relief outings before the Giants gave him a start last June. Returning to the rotation did not help him, however. After an 0-2 record and 8.68 ERA in four starts, Righetti returned to the bullpen, where he had 248 saves before last season. The author of a 1983 no-hitter has obviously seen better days. He yielded almost a hit an inning last year, averaged more than four walks per nine innings, and fanned fewer than six batters per nine innings. Opponents compiled a .269 batting average, a .344 on-base percentage, and a .374 slugging percentage in 1992. Righetti has fallen far from his 46-save form of 1986. Even though he still throws a sinker, slider, curveball, and changeup, Righetti has lost velocity on his once-feared fastball.

Major League Pitching Register

	W	L	ERA	G	S	IP	H	ER	BB	SO
79 AL	0	1	3.63	3	0	17.1	10	7	10	13
81 AL	8	4	2.05	15	0	105.1	75	24	38	89
82 AL	11	10	3.79	33	1	183.0	155	77	108	163
83 AL	14	8	3.44	31	0	217.0	194	83	67	169
84 AL	5	6	2.34	64	31	96.1	79	25	37	90
85 AL	12	7	2.78	74	29	107.0	96	33	45	92
86 AL	8	8	2.45	74	46	106.2	88	29	35	83
87 AL	8	6	3.51	60	31	95.0	95	37	44	77
88 AL	5	4	3.52	60	25	87.0	86	34	37	70
89 AL	2	6	3.00	55	25	69.0	73	23	26	51
90 AL	1	1	3.57	53	36	53.0	48	21	26	43
91 NL	2	7	3.39	61	24	71.2	64	27	28	51
92 NL	2	7	5.06	54	3	78.1	79	44	36	47
Life	78	75	3.25	637	251	1286.2	1142	464	537	1038
3 AVE	2	5	4.08	56	21	67.1	64	31	30	47

JOSE RIJO

Position: Pitcher
Team: Cincinnati Reds
Born: May 13, 1965 San Cristobal, Dominican Republic
Height: 6'2" **Weight:** 210 lbs.
Bats: right **Throws:** right
Acquired: Traded from Athletics with Tim Birtsas for Dave Parker, 12/87

Player Summary	
Fantasy Value	$16 to $22
Card Value	4¢ to 6¢
Will	mix pitches well
Can't	escape injury jinx
Expect	self-help with bat
Don't Expect	control problems

Problems with his pitching elbow in 1992 kept Rijo from winning his first game until May 23. Working with a sore arm, he yielded six hits in six innings to beat Bob Tewksbury 3-2 on July 18. By Aug. 23, when he turned his forkball against Montreal, Rijo had returned to form. He allowed five hits in seven innings in that 1-0 win. Rijo was MVP of the 1990 World Series. When Rijo's on, his slider is the league's best, according to managers polled by *Baseball America*. He also throws a fastball and a changeup that he'll throw at any time in the count. Opponents in 1992 compiled a .238 batting average, a .281 on-base percentage, and a .340 slugging percentage. He is a pretty good-hitting pitcher, and he is a fine fielder. Rijo has also been disabled by elbow, back, shoulder, and ankle injuries.

Major League Pitching Register

	W	L	ERA	G	CG	IP	H	ER	BB	SO
84 AL	2	8	4.76	24	0	62.1	74	33	33	47
85 AL	6	4	3.53	12	0	63.2	57	25	28	65
86 AL	9	11	4.65	39	4	193.2	172	100	108	176
87 AL	2	7	5.90	21	1	82.1	106	54	41	67
88 NL	13	8	2.39	49	0	162.0	120	43	63	160
89 NL	7	6	2.84	19	1	111.0	101	35	48	86
90 NL	14	8	2.70	29	7	197.0	151	59	78	152
91 NL	15	6	2.51	30	3	204.1	165	57	55	172
92 NL	15	10	2.56	33	2	211.0	185	60	44	171
Life	83	68	3.26	256	18	1287.1	1131	466	498	1096
3 AVE	15	8	2.59	31	4	204.0	167	59	59	165

BILL RIPKEN

Position: Second base
Team: Baltimore Orioles
Born: Dec. 16, 1964 Havre de Grace, MD
Height: 6'1" **Weight:** 185 lbs.
Bats: right **Throws:** right
Acquired: 11th-round pick in 6/82 free-agent draft

Player Summary

Fantasy Value	$2 to $5
Card Value	3¢ to 4¢
Will	show great glove
Can't	copy Cal's power
Expect	average below .250
Don't Expect	errors in the field

Ripken is still trying to convince people that his .291 batting average of 1990 was no fluke. The younger brother of Cal Ripken, Bill does not have his sibling's hitting ability. He took a five-year average of .247 into the 1992 campaign and failed to match it. Even though he hit a career high in home runs last summer, his lack of an improved on-base average disappointed. In 1992, he had a .275 on-base average and a .312 slugging percentage. A contact hitter who knows how to bunt, he is a good man to work the hit-and-run play—especially because he delivers more than his share of ground outs. He doesn't strike out or walk much. He is first and foremost a glove man. A standout second baseman who rarely makes an error, he and Cal have formed one of the game's finest double-play combinations over the last six seasons. Bill has good hands and good range.

Major League Batting Register

	BA	G	AB	R	H	2B	3B	HR	RBI	SB
87 AL	.308	58	234	27	72	9	0	2	20	4
88 AL	.207	150	512	52	106	18	1	2	34	8
89 AL	.239	115	318	31	76	11	2	2	26	1
90 AL	.291	129	406	48	118	28	1	3	38	5
91 AL	.216	104	287	24	62	11	1	0	14	0
92 AL	.230	111	330	35	76	15	0	4	36	2
Life	.244	667	2087	217	510	92	5	13	168	20
3 AVE	.250	115	341	36	85	18	1	2	29	2

CAL RIPKEN

Position: Shortstop
Team: Baltimore Orioles
Born: Aug. 24, 1960 Havre de Grace, MD
Height: 6'4" **Weight:** 220 lbs.
Bats: right **Throws:** right
Acquired: Second-round pick in 6/78 free-agent draft

Player Summary

Fantasy Value	$34 to $42
Card Value	10¢ to 20¢
Will	seek old stroke
Can't	show any speed
Expect	Gold Glove
Don't Expect	slump to linger

Even though 1992 was the least productive of his 12 major league seasons, Ripken received a five-year contract extension on his birthday. The $30.5 million deal keeps him in Baltimore through 1997—long after he will have superseded Lou Gehrig's 2,130 consecutive games played (Ripken could do that in 1995). Ripken managed a career-best 17-game hitting streak and started his eighth straight All-Star Game, but his numbers were far off his MVP form of 1991. Even a slumping Ripken is dangerous, however. He walks more than he strikes out and often delivers clutch hits. He had a .323 on-base average and a .366 slugging percentage last summer. Ripken is a Gold Glover who usually leads the league in putouts, assists, and percentage. He lacks great range but has a strong arm.

Major League Batting Register

	BA	G	AB	R	H	2B	3B	HR	RBI	SB
81 AL	.128	23	39	1	5	0	0	0	0	0
82 AL	.264	160	598	90	158	32	5	28	93	3
83 AL	.318	162	663	121	211	47	2	27	102	0
84 AL	.304	162	641	103	195	37	7	27	86	2
85 AL	.282	161	642	116	181	32	5	26	110	2
86 AL	.282	162	627	98	177	35	1	25	81	4
87 AL	.252	162	624	97	157	28	3	27	98	3
88 AL	.264	161	575	87	152	25	1	23	81	2
89 AL	.257	162	646	80	166	30	0	21	93	3
90 AL	.250	161	600	78	150	28	4	21	84	3
91 AL	.323	162	650	99	210	46	5	34	114	6
92 AL	.251	162	637	73	160	29	1	14	72	4
Life	.277	1800	6942	1043	1922	369	34	273	1014	32
3 AVE	.276	162	629	83	173	34	3	23	90	4

BEN RIVERA

Position: Pitcher
Team: Philadelphia Phillies
Born: Jan. 11, 1969 San Pedro de Macoris, Dominican Republic
Height: 6'6" **Weight:** 210 lbs.
Bats: right **Throws:** right
Acquired: Traded from Braves for Donnie Elliott, 5/92

Player Summary	
Fantasy Value	$4 to $6
Card Value	5¢ to 10¢
Will	throw curve for strikes
Can't	rely on experience
Expect	bright future
Don't Expect	too many gophers

After opening the 1992 season as the extra man in the Atlanta bullpen, Rivera finished it as a front-line starter for the Phillies. Traded because he was out of options, he got a chance to start when several veterans got hurt. He made the most of his opportunity. He substituted a curveball and a changeup for the slider and the split-fingered fastball that he used to throw, then he added a four-seam fastball to his arsenal. He proved he could throw the curve for strikes on Aug. 14 when he fanned five straight Mets—some of whom compared him with a young Doc Gooden. Rivera, though, is not a strikeout pitcher but a control hurler. He is stingy with the long ball, giving up nine homers in 1992. He yields fewer hits than innings pitched and averages about six strikeouts per nine innings. Opponents compiled a .230 batting average, a .307 on-base percentage, and a .357 slugging percentage in 1992. At Double-A Greenville in 1991, he was 11-8 with a 3.57 ERA, 75 walks, and 116 strikeouts in 158⅔ innings pitched.

Major League Pitching Register

	W	L	ERA	G	CG	IP	H	ER	BB	SO
92 NL	7	4	3.07	28	4	117.1	99	40	45	77
Life	7	4	3.07	28	4	117.1	99	40	45	77

LUIS RIVERA

Position: Shortstop; second base
Team: Boston Red Sox
Born: Jan. 3, 1964 Cidra, Puerto Rico
Height: 5'10" **Weight:** 170 lbs.
Bats: right **Throws:** right
Acquired: Traded from Expos with John Dopson for Spike Owen and Dan Gakeler, 12/88

Player Summary	
Fantasy Value	$1 to $3
Card Value	3¢ to 4¢
Will	resume utility role
Can't	maintain good stroke
Expect	decent throwing arm
Don't Expect	Gold Glove defense

Before hot prospect John Valentin reached the majors late last summer, Rivera was the regular Red Sox shortstop. Although his defense improved from 1991, when he led AL shortstops with 24 errors, Rivera lost his job when he failed to hit with the same authority he had shown the previous season. His power vanished; he had a .287 on-base percentage and a .260 slugging percentage in 1992. His production against lefthanded pitchers fell far below .200. He failed to add any speed to the lineup. In addition, his defense, though better, was still below average. In seven years, Rivera has never played in 130 games—perhaps because his hitting has been so sporadic. He topped .255 in two of the three seasons before 1992, but he still is less than a .235 hitter in his career. Rivera's fall from grace is somewhat of a surprise, since he had shown an ability to hit hard line-drives to the opposite field in '91.

Major League Batting Register

	BA	G	AB	R	H	2B	3B	HR	RBI	SB
86 NL	.205	55	166	20	34	11	1	0	13	1
87 NL	.156	18	32	0	5	2	0	0	1	0
88 NL	.224	123	371	35	83	17	3	4	30	3
89 AL	.257	93	323	35	83	17	1	5	29	2
90 AL	.225	118	346	38	78	20	0	7	45	4
91 AL	.258	129	414	64	107	22	3	8	40	4
92 AL	.215	102	288	17	62	11	1	0	29	4
Life	.233	638	1940	209	452	100	9	24	187	18
3 AVE	.236	116	349	40	82	18	1	5	38	4

BIP ROBERTS

Position: Infield; outfield
Team: Cincinnati Reds
Born: Oct. 27, 1963 Berkeley, CA
Height: 5'7" **Weight:** 165 lbs.
Bats: both **Throws:** right
Acquired: Traded from Padres with Craig Pueschner for Randy Myers, 12/91

Player Summary	
Fantasy Value	$18 to $24
Card Value	3¢ to 4¢
Will	rip righties
Can't	provide consistent power
Expect	excellent leadoff
Don't Expect	strong outfield throws

Even after their late-summer fade knocked the Reds out of contention for the 1992 NL West title, Roberts continued his job as the catalyst at the top of the batting order. The switch-hitting speed merchant not only led the teams in runs scored and stolen bases, but also made the All-Star team for the first time. He had a .393 on-base average and a .432 slugging percentage in 1992. Though he spent most of his time in left field, he also played second base, third base, and center field—manning at least two spots in the same game more than two dozen times. A little guy who plays hurt, Roberts battled a chronic sore shoulder, a sore wrist, and a neck sprain last year. The NL's best every-day utility player, he has speed that translates to great range in the outfield, but his throwing arm is suspect. His best position is probably second base, which is where Cincinnati plans on using him in the 1993 season.

Major League Batting Register

	BA	G	AB	R	H	2B	3B	HR	RBI	SB
86 NL	.253	101	241	34	61	5	2	1	12	14
88 NL	.333	5	9	1	3	0	0	0	0	0
89 NL	.301	117	329	81	99	15	8	3	25	21
90 NL	.309	149	556	104	172	36	3	9	44	46
91 NL	.281	117	424	66	119	13	3	3	32	26
92 NL	.323	147	532	92	172	34	6	4	45	44
Life	.299	636	2091	378	626	103	22	20	158	151
3 AVE	.306	138	504	87	154	28	4	5	40	39

JEFF ROBINSON

Position: Pitcher
Team: Chicago Cubs
Born: Dec. 13, 1960 Santa Ana, CA
Height: 6'4" **Weight:** 200 lbs.
Bats: right **Throws:** right
Acquired: Signed as a free agent, 1/92

Player Summary	
Fantasy Value	$2 to $3
Card Value	3¢ to 4¢
Will	see middle relief work
Can't	rack up many Ks
Expect	wild pitches
Don't Expect	first batters to reach

Used as both a starter and reliever in his nine-year career, Robinson has found more success in the bullpen. For five straight years, he has had more than 50 appearances. He even had his first start in nearly two years last July. He wasn't so fortunate with the rest of his outings, however. He yielded more hits than innings pitched and had control problems and trouble with lefties. Robinson throws a fastball, curve, and split-fingered fastball, but doesn't get many strikeouts (an average of about five per nine innings). He throws too many wild pitches, lacks a good pickoff move, and is not a strong fielder. Opponents in 1992 compiled a .263 batting average, a .354 on-base percentage, and a .388 slugging percentage in 1992. On the plus side, he handles first batters well—holding them to a .175 batting average last summer.

Major League Pitching Register

	W	L	ERA	G	S	IP	H	ER	BB	SO
84 NL	7	15	4.56	34	0	171.2	195	87	52	102
85 NL	0	0	5.11	8	0	12.1	16	7	10	8
86 NL	6	3	3.36	64	8	104.1	92	39	32	90
87 NL	8	9	2.85	81	14	123.1	89	39	54	101
88 NL	11	5	3.03	75	9	124.2	113	42	39	87
89 NL	7	13	4.58	50	4	141.1	161	72	59	95
90 AL	3	6	3.45	54	0	88.2	82	34	34	43
91 AL	0	3	5.37	39	3	57.0	56	34	29	57
92 NL	4	3	3.00	49	1	78.0	76	26	40	46
Life	46	57	3.79	454	39	901.1	880	380	349	629
3 AVE	2	4	3.78	47	1	74.1	71	31	34	49

RON ROBINSON

Position: Pitcher
Team: Milwaukee Brewers
Born: March 24, 1962 Woodlake, CA
Height: 6'4" **Weight:** 235 lbs.
Bats: right **Throws:** right
Acquired: Traded from Reds with Bob Sebra for Glenn Braggs and Billy Bates, 6/90

Player Summary
Fantasy Value	$1 to $3
Card Value	3¢ to 4¢
Will	need medical miracle
Can't	pile up strikeouts
Expect	pretty good control
Don't Expect	bases to stay clear

After he spent months in rehab, Robinson's chronic elbow troubles resurfaced after the All-Star break last summer. The victim of five previous elbow operations, he managed one victory—a 10-0 decision over Oakland in June—in five 1992 decisions. When he's right, he is a control pitcher who mixes a fastball, slider, curve, and changeup. He also holds runners close and fields his position well. Though he keeps the ball in the park, he always yields a lot of hits. In 1990, for example, he went 12-5 with a 2.91 ERA as the ace of the Milwaukee staff, but he yielded 10 more hits than innings pitched. Never a power pitcher, Robinson records outs by changing speeds and coaxing ground outs and pop-ups. After winning one game in two years, however, the 31-year-old righthander may need a medical miracle to stage another comeback.

Major League Pitching Register
	W	L	ERA	G	CG	IP	H	ER	BB	SO
84 NL	1	2	2.72	12	1	39.2	35	12	13	24
85 NL	7	3	3.99	33	0	108.1	107	48	32	76
86 NL	10	3	3.24	70	0	116.2	110	42	43	117
87 NL	7	5	3.68	48	0	154.0	148	63	43	99
88 NL	3	7	4.12	17	0	78.2	88	36	26	38
89 NL	5	3	3.35	15	0	83.1	80	31	28	36
90 NL	2	2	4.88	6	0	31.1	36	17	14	14
90 AL	12	5	2.91	22	7	148.1	158	48	37	57
91 AL	0	1	6.23	1	0	4.1	6	3	3	2
92 AL	1	4	5.86	8	0	35.1	51	23	14	12
Life	48	39	3.63	232	8	800.0	819	323	253	473

IVAN RODRIGUEZ

Position: Catcher
Team: Texas Rangers
Born: Nov. 30, 1971 Vega Baja, Puerto Rico
Height: 5'9" **Weight:** 165 lbs.
Bats: right **Throws:** right
Acquired: Signed as a free agent, 7/88

Player Summary
Fantasy Value	$10 to $16
Card Value	5¢ to 15¢
Will	nail basestealers
Can't	wait out walks
Expect	occasional power
Don't Expect	batting discipline

At age 20, Rodriguez was the youngest of baseball's 1992 All-Stars. If he maintains his present level of play, he'll be back for multiple encores. The first All-Star born in the 1970s, Rodriguez is quickly becoming baseball's best catcher. A durable performer who prevents wild pitches, absorbs collisions, and has a howitzer arm, Rodriguez needs only to improve his handling of the pitching staff—an area of expertise that comes with experience. He already has a Gold Glove. After losing three weeks in June with a stress fracture of his lower back, Rodriguez rebounded in a big way—with a single and upper-deck home run in his first game back. Though he led all catchers in errors, he erased more than 50 percent of would-be basestealers—also leading the league. He is nicknamed "Pudge" after his childhood favorite player, Pudge Fisk. Rodriguez is an improving hitter who has some power. He had a .300 on-base average and a .360 slugging percentage in 1992. In 1991 at Double-A Tulsa, he batted .274 with three homers and 28 RBI.

Major League Batting Register
	BA	G	AB	R	H	2B	3B	HR	RBI	SB
91 AL	.264	88	280	24	74	16	0	3	27	0
92 AL	.260	123	420	39	109	16	1	8	37	0
Life	.261	211	700	63	183	32	1	11	64	0
2 AVE	.261	106	350	32	92	16	1	6	32	0

RICH RODRIGUEZ

Position: Pitcher
Team: San Diego Padres
Born: March 1, 1963 Los Angeles, CA
Height: 5'11" **Weight:** 200 lbs.
Bats: left **Throws:** left
Acquired: Traded from Mets for Brad Pounders and Bill Stevenson, 1/89

Player Summary	
Fantasy Value	$2 to $4
Card Value	3¢ to 4¢
Will	work often
Can't	hold runners
Expect	good control
Don't Expect	gopher balls

Though Randy Myers reeled in most of the save opportunities last summer, Rodriguez played an important role in the San Diego bullpen. A fastball-slider pitcher who also throws a curve, Rodriguez had the thankless job of serving as middle reliever and set-up man. Working more than 50 times for the second straight year, he averaged fewer than eight hits and three walks per nine innings, while fanning nearly six batters over the same span. Opponents compiled a .229 batting average, a .289 on-base percentage, and a .313 slugging percentage in 1992. The first batters he faced batted only .218 last year. Rodriguez kept the ball in the park (allowing only four home runs all year) and held righties at bay by adding a screwball to his repertoire. Righties batted .227 against him in 1992, while lefties hit .233. He is adept at coaxing double plays in critical situations. Rodriguez is a decent fielder who improved his pickoff move last summer. He has been used as a pinch-runner on occasion.

Major League Pitching Register

	W	L	ERA	G	S	IP	H	ER	BB	SO
90 NL	1	1	2.83	32	1	47.2	52	15	16	22
91 NL	3	1	3.26	64	0	80.0	66	29	44	40
92 NL	6	3	2.37	61	0	91.0	77	24	29	64
Life	10	5	2.80	157	1	218.2	195	68	89	126
3 AVE	3	2	2.80	52	0	73.1	65	23	30	42

KENNY ROGERS

Position: Pitcher
Team: Texas Rangers
Born: Nov. 10, 1964 Savannah, GA
Height: 6'1" **Weight:** 200 lbs.
Bats: left **Throws:** left
Acquired: 39th-round pick in 6/82 free-agent draft

Player Summary	
Fantasy Value	$4 to $6
Card Value	3¢ to 4¢
Will	retain set-up role
Can't	prevent gopher balls
Expect	frequent appearances
Don't Expect	return to rotation

Rogers has been a heavy-duty reliever for the Rangers for four straight seasons. A fine set-up man, he hit a personal peak in appearances last summer—even though he yielded more hits than innings pitched. He is a fastball-and-curveball pitcher who also throws a good changeup. Rogers did not have good luck against righties, lefties, or first batters in 1992. Righthanded hitters had a .262 batting average, lefties hit .261, and the first batters he faced had a .241 batting average. But he survived by fanning nearly eight men per nine innings and walking an average of three per nine innings. Overall, in 1992 opponents compiled a .261 batting average, a .318 on-base average, and a .392 slugging percentage. He did throw more than his share of home run balls, however, and blew four of his 10 save opportunities. He was a starter at the open of the '91 season, but he is now a committed reliever. A capable fielder, Rogers has a strong pick-off move and is a tough target for base-stealers.

Major League Pitching Register

	W	L	ERA	G	S	IP	H	ER	BB	SO
89 AL	3	4	2.93	73	2	73.2	60	24	42	63
90 AL	10	6	3.13	69	15	97.2	93	34	42	74
91 AL	10	10	5.42	63	5	109.2	121	66	61	73
92 AL	3	6	3.09	81	6	78.2	80	27	26	70
Life	26	26	3.78	286	28	359.2	354	151	171	280
3 AVE	8	7	4.00	71	9	95.2	98	42	43	72

MEL ROJAS

Position: Pitcher
Team: Montreal Expos
Born: Dec. 10, 1966 Haina, Dominican Republic
Height: 5'11" **Weight:** 185 lbs.
Bats: right **Throws:** right
Acquired: Signed as free agent, 11/85

Player Summary	
Fantasy Value	$6 to $12
Card Value	3¢ to 4¢
Will	stifle rival rallies
Can't	stop basestealers
Expect	first batters to fail
Don't Expect	gophers to beat him

Rojas stretches his index and middle fingers on a softball for five minutes every day, gripping the ball as hard as he can. That makes it easier for him to throw his forkball, a strikeout pitch he blends with a 90 mph fastball and a slider. Rojas started last year at Triple-A Indianapolis, where he tried to slow the forkball to just over 80 mph. Returning with a vengeance, he posted the best ERA of any NL reliever. Righties, lefties, and first batters all failed to hit .200 against him, as he averaged six hits, six strikeouts, and three walks per nine innings. Opponents compiled a .199 batting average, a .271 on-base percentage, and a .269 slugging percentage in 1992. Used as both a set-up man and closer, the hard-throwing Rojas converted all of his first 10 save chances and proved extremely stingy with the gopher ball. He could be a closer in 1993. The nephew of Montreal manager Felipe Alou, Rojas has an inability to keep runners from stealing.

SCOTT RUSKIN

Position: Pitcher
Team: Cincinnati Reds
Born: June 6, 1963 Jacksonville, FL
Height: 6'2" **Weight:** 185 lbs.
Bats: right **Throws:** left
Acquired: Traded from Expos with Dave Martinez and Willie Greene for John Wetteland and Bill Risley, 12/91

Player Summary	
Fantasy Value	$1 to $3
Card Value	3¢ to 4¢
Will	ring up strikeouts
Can't	always control curve
Expect	regular relief calls
Don't Expect	runners left stranded

Inability to strand inherited runners hurt Ruskin last summer, his first as a member of the Cincinnati bullpen. First hitters hammered Ruskin for a .346 batting average. He yielded more than nine hits and three walks per nine innings. A curveball specialist who also throws a fastball and a changeup, he averages seven and one-half strikeouts per nine innings and doesn't throw too many home run balls. Opponents compiled a .275 batting average, a .339 on-base percentage, and a .412 slugging percentage in 1992. His biggest problem is throwing the curve for strikes—especially when first brought in from the bullpen. He might be better off as a starter, despite a reputation as a reliever who can work often (he appeared in a total of 131 games in 1990 and '91). Though Ruskin holds runners close and fields his position well, he could help himself most as a hitter. He is a converted outfielder who once hit .297 in the minors. He was a pitcher and an outfielder at the University of Florida.

Major League Pitching Register

	W	L	ERA	G	S	IP	H	ER	BB	SO
90 NL	3	1	3.60	23	1	40.0	34	16	24	26
91 NL	3	3	3.75	37	6	48.0	42	20	13	37
92 NL	7	1	1.43	68	10	100.2	71	16	34	70
Life	13	5	2.48	128	17	188.2	147	52	71	133
3 AVE	4	2	2.48	43	6	63.1	49	17	24	44

Major League Pitching Register

	W	L	ERA	G	S	IP	H	ER	BB	SO
90 NL	3	2	2.75	67	2	75.1	75	23	38	57
91 NL	4	4	4.24	64	6	63.2	57	30	30	46
92 NL	4	3	5.03	57	0	53.2	56	30	20	43
Life	11	9	3.88	188	8	192.2	188	83	88	146
3 AVE	4	3	3.88	63	3	63.3	63	28	29	49

JEFF RUSSELL

Position: Pitcher
Team: Oakland Athletics
Born: Sept. 2, 1961 Cincinnati, OH
Height: 6'3" **Weight:** 210 lbs.
Bats: right **Throws:** right
Acquired: Traded from Rangers with Ruben Sierra and Bobby Witt for Jose Canseco, 8/92

Player Summary	
Fantasy Value	$16 to $24
Card Value	3¢ to 4¢
Will	slam door on righties
Can't	always locate plate
Expect	return to closer role
Don't Expect	many home runs

Russell started last year as a Texas closer but finished it as an Oakland set-up man. He finished with the best earned run average of his 10-year career. Traded only because free agency loomed, Russell converted 29 of 38 save opportunities before the trade. He dominated righthanded batters, fared well against first hitters, and kept the ball in the park. He averaged fewer than eight hits and nearly seven strikeouts per nine innings, while yielding almost three and one-half walks over that span. A fastball-slider pitcher who also brandishes a changeup, Russell has regained his form of 1989, when he led the AL with 38 saves (in 71 games). He keeps runners close, fields his position well, and seems totally healed from 1990 elbow surgery. Despite his early problems of 1992, he should be a closer again.

Major League Pitching Register

	W	L	ERA	G	S	IP	H	ER	BB	SO
83 NL	4	5	3.03	10	0	68.1	58	23	22	40
84 NL	6	18	4.26	33	0	181.2	186	86	65	101
85 AL	3	6	7.55	13	0	62.0	85	52	27	44
86 AL	5	2	3.40	37	2	82.0	74	31	31	54
87 AL	5	4	4.44	52	3	97.1	109	48	52	56
88 AL	10	9	3.82	34	0	188.2	183	80	66	88
89 AL	6	4	1.98	71	38	72.2	45	16	24	77
90 AL	1	5	4.26	27	10	25.1	23	12	16	16
91 AL	6	4	3.29	68	30	79.1	71	29	26	52
92 AL	4	3	1.63	59	30	66.1	55	12	25	48
Life	50	60	3.79	404	113	923.2	889	389	354	576
2 AVE	5	4	2.53	64	30	72.3	63	21	26	50

NOLAN RYAN

Position: Pitcher
Team: Texas Rangers
Born: Jan. 31, 1947 Refugio, TX
Height: 6'2" **Weight:** 210 lbs.
Bats: right **Throws:** right
Acquired: Signed as a free agent, 12/88

Player Summary	
Fantasy Value	$12 to $20
Card Value	10¢ to 35¢
Will	keep strikeouts coming
Can't	avoid nagging injuries
Expect	some control problems
Don't Expect	runners to be held

Ryan suffered through his most disappointing season in 1992. He failed to win until June 28—giving him a career-worst streak of 13 winless starts. He endured various injuries and showed only flashes of his old form. Ryan won five straight in July with a 1.65 ERA over six starts. He then went 0-4 in August, walking 19 in 28 innings. At age 46, Ryan is entering his 27th season, a record. His fastball hasn't lost its steam.

Major League Pitching Register

	W	L	ERA	G	CG	IP	H	ER	BB	SO
66 NL	0	1	15.00	2	0	3.0	5	5	3	6
68 NL	6	9	3.09	21	3	134.0	93	46	75	133
69 NL	6	3	3.53	25	2	89.1	60	35	53	92
70 NL	7	11	3.42	27	5	131.2	86	50	97	125
71 NL	10	14	3.97	30	3	152.0	125	67	116	137
72 AL	19	16	2.28	39	20	284.0	166	72	157	329
73 AL	21	16	2.87	41	26	326.0	238	104	162	383
74 AL	22	16	2.89	42	26	332.2	221	107	202	367
75 AL	14	12	3.45	28	10	198.0	152	76	132	186
76 AL	17	18	3.36	39	21	284.1	193	106	183	327
77 AL	19	16	2.77	37	22	299.0	198	92	204	341
78 AL	10	13	3.72	31	14	234.2	183	97	148	260
79 AL	16	14	3.60	34	17	222.2	169	89	114	223
80 NL	11	10	3.35	35	4	233.2	205	87	98	200
81 NL	11	5	1.69	21	5	149.0	99	28	68	140
82 NL	16	12	3.16	35	10	250.1	196	88	109	245
83 NL	14	9	2.98	29	5	196.1	134	65	101	183
84 NL	12	11	3.04	30	5	183.2	143	62	69	197
85 NL	10	12	3.80	35	4	232.0	205	98	95	209
86 NL	12	8	3.34	30	1	178.0	119	66	82	194
87 NL	8	16	2.76	34	0	211.2	154	65	87	270
88 NL	12	11	3.52	33	4	220.0	186	86	87	228
89 AL	16	10	3.20	32	6	239.1	162	85	98	301
90 AL	13	9	3.44	30	5	204.0	137	78	74	232
91 AL	12	6	2.91	27	2	173.0	102	56	72	203
92 AL	5	9	3.72	27	2	157.1	138	65	69	157
Life	319	287	3.17	794	222	5319.2	3869	1875	2755	5668
3 AVE	10	8	3.35	28	3	178.0	126	66	72	197

BRET SABERHAGEN

Position: Pitcher
Team: New York Mets
Born: April 11, 1964 Chicago Heights, IL
Height: 6'1" **Weight:** 195 lbs.
Bats: right **Throws:** right
Acquired: Traded from Royals with Bill Pecota for Kevin McReynolds, Gregg Jefferies, and Keith Miller, 12/91

Player Summary	
Fantasy Value	$8 to $15
Card Value	3¢ to 4¢
Will	keep men off base
Can't	avoid injuries
Expect	complete comeback
Don't Expect	bouts of wildness

The odd-year/even-year jinx that has followed him since 1984 continued to dog Saberhagen last summer. The two-time Cy Young Award winner and one-time World Series MVP (all in odd-numbered years) lost most of last season to tendinitis in the right index finger. He had a losing record for the fifth time in as many even-numbered years. When he's right, Saberhagen fans three times more men than he walks, yields less hits than innings, and keeps the ball in the park. Even last year, his fastball was clocked at 93 mph. Saberhagen, who also throws a curve and change, is a quick worker with pinpoint control. Opponents in 1992 compiled a .233 batting average, a .292 on-base average, and a .344 slugging percentage. The one-time Gold Glove winner backs up the bases, fields his position, and owns an outstanding pickoff move.

Major League Pitching Register

	W	L	ERA	G	CG	IP	H	ER	BB	SO
84 AL	10	11	3.48	38	2	157.2	138	61	36	73
85 AL	20	6	2.87	32	10	235.1	211	75	38	158
86 AL	7	12	4.15	30	4	156.0	165	72	29	112
87 AL	18	10	3.36	33	15	257.0	246	96	53	163
88 AL	14	16	3.80	35	9	260.2	271	110	59	171
89 AL	23	6	2.16	36	12	262.1	209	63	43	193
90 AL	5	9	3.27	20	5	135.0	146	49	28	87
91 AL	13	8	3.07	28	7	196.1	165	67	45	136
92 NL	3	5	3.50	17	1	97.2	84	38	27	81
Life	113	83	3.23	269	65	1758.0	1635	631	358	1174
3 AVE	7	7	3.23	22	4	143.1	132	51	33	101

CHRIS SABO

Position: Third base
Team: Cincinnati Reds
Born: Jan. 19, 1962 Detroit, MI
Height: 6'1" **Weight:** 185 lbs.
Bats: right **Throws:** right
Acquired: Second-round pick in 6/83 free-agent draft

Player Summary	
Fantasy Value	$12 to $18
Card Value	4¢ to 6¢
Will	make strong comeback
Can't	win Gold Glove
Expect	bid for 30-30 club
Don't Expect	injuries to linger

An ankle injury that required postseason arthroscopic surgery sapped Sabo's strength last summer. Hampered by calcification on the outside of his right ankle and an injury to the navicular bone on the inside, Sabo couldn't push off his back foot. That neutralized his usual home run power, negated his ability to steal bases, and limited his mobility in the field. He also suffered back problems last summer. Sabo usually gives his team power, speed, defense, and a pesky bat that produces from any position in the lineup. He's known for an all-out aggressive style punctuated by head-first slides. A pull hitter who usually devours southpaws, Sabo batted only .247 against them in his injury-plagued year. He lives for fastballs. He had a .302 on-base average and a .422 slugging percentage in 1992. He's a former 25-25 man who could join the 30-30 club with pitching diluted by expansion. In the field, Sabo has good range and a strong arm.

Major League Batting Register

	BA	G	AB	R	H	2B	3B	HR	RBI	SB
88 NL	.271	137	538	74	146	40	2	11	44	46
89 NL	.260	82	304	40	79	21	1	6	29	14
90 NL	.270	148	567	95	153	38	2	25	71	25
91 NL	.301	153	582	91	175	35	3	26	88	19
92 NL	.244	96	344	42	84	19	3	12	43	4
Life	.273	616	2335	342	637	153	11	80	275	108
3 AVE	.276	132	498	76	137	31	3	21	67	16

LUIS SALAZAR

Position: Infield; outfield
Team: Chicago Cubs
Born: May 19, 1956 Barcelona, Venezuela
Height: 5'9" **Weight:** 180 lbs.
Bats: right **Throws:** right
Acquired: Traded from Padres with Marvell Wynne for Calvin Schiraldi, Phil Stephenson, and Darrin Jackson, 8/89

Player Summary	
Fantasy Value	$1 to $3
Card Value	3¢ to 4¢
Will	play any position
Can't	add speed to game
Expect	success against southpaws
Don't Expect	much playing time

When Gary Scott failed last summer to provide offense at third for the Cubs, Salazar was supposed to provide insurance. Salazar's slump prompted the Cubs to trade for veteran third baseman Steve Buechele. The deal returned Salazar to his former utility role, and he wound up playing five different positions, including first base, third base, shortstop, and the outfield corners. His playing time has decreased in each of the last five seasons, and his production fell sharply last year. Salazar hits southpaws well but won't wait for walks, fanning three times more often. Because he lacks speed, Salazar hits into frequent double plays and has only average range in the outfield. His versatility plus his occasional power maintain his value.

Major League Batting Register

	BA	G	AB	R	H	2B	3B	HR	RBI	SB
80 NL	.337	44	169	28	57	4	7	1	25	11
81 NL	.303	109	400	37	121	19	6	3	38	11
82 NL	.242	145	524	55	127	15	5	8	62	32
83 NL	.258	134	481	52	124	16	2	14	45	24
84 NL	.241	93	228	20	55	7	2	3	17	11
85 AL	.245	122	327	39	80	18	2	10	45	14
86 AL	.143	4	7	1	1	0	0	0	0	0
87 NL	.254	84	189	13	48	5	0	3	17	3
88 AL	.270	130	452	61	122	14	1	12	62	6
89 NL	.282	121	326	34	92	12	2	9	34	1
90 NL	.254	115	410	44	104	13	3	12	47	3
91 NL	.258	103	333	34	86	14	1	14	38	0
92 NL	.208	98	255	20	53	7	2	5	25	1
Life	.261	1302	4101	438	1070	144	33	94	455	117
3 AVE	.243	105	333	33	81	11	2	10	37	1

BILL SAMPEN

Position: Pitcher
Team: Kansas City Royals
Born: Jan. 18, 1963 Lincoln, IL
Height: 6'1" **Weight:** 185 lbs.
Bats: right **Throws:** right
Acquired: Traded from Expos with Chris Haney for Sean Berry and Archie Corbin, 8/92

Player Summary	
Fantasy Value	$1 to $3
Card Value	3¢ to 4¢
Will	try to earn job
Can't	prevent gophers
Expect	control trouble
Don't Expect	respectable ERA

After showing considerable promise during his first two big league seasons, Sampen regressed last year. Unable to harness his erratic control or add to a thin repertoire, he fell out of favor in Montreal and was shipped across league lines in late summer. A fastball-and-slider pitcher, Sampen yields more hits than innings pitched and walks almost as many men as he fans. He also has trouble keeping the ball in the park. He has been used as both a starter and reliever, though with his heater he is best suited to come out of the bullpen. Opponents in the American League in 1992 compiled a .292 batting average, a .338 on-base percentage, and a .333 slugging percentage. National League opponents in 1992 compiled a .268 batting average, a .351 on-base percentage, and a .368 slugging percentage. Although he's a good fielder, Sampen is not good at keeping runners close—a potentially fatal flaw for a relief pitcher. He either shows some improvement soon or returns permanently to the minors.

Major League Pitching Register

	W	L	ERA	G	S	IP	H	ER	BB	SO
90 NL	12	7	2.99	59	2	90.1	94	30	33	69
91 NL	9	5	4.00	43	0	92.1	96	41	46	52
92 NL	1	4	3.13	44	0	63.1	62	22	29	23
92 AL	0	2	3.66	8	0	19.2	21	8	3	14
Life	22	18	3.42	154	2	265.2	273	101	111	158
3 AVE	7	6	3.42	51	1	88.2	91	34	37	53

JUAN SAMUEL

Position: Outfield; second base
Team: Cincinnati Reds
Born: Dec. 9, 1960 San Pedro de Macoris, Dominican Republic
Height: 5'11" **Weight:** 170 lbs.
Bats: right **Throws:** right
Acquired: Signed as a free agent, 12/92

Player Summary	
Fantasy Value	$2 to $4
Card Value	3¢ to 4¢
Will	display good speed
Can't	find former power
Expect	too many strikeouts
Don't Expect	awards for fielding

Samuel will play outfield for the Reds in 1993. Injuries interfered with his 1992 performance even before the season started. He suffered two broken fingers on his left hand when hit by a pitch during spring training and got off to a poor start. He made his second career start in right field on June 27, dropped a fly ball, and said he felt uncomfortable. But he wasn't much better at second base, his original position. The Dodgers decided to release him July 30. Samuel liked his first look at AL pitching but did not produce his usual power. He did, however, show that his running game remained intact. He not only stole bases for the Royals but also displayed good range in right field. He also spent some time at second base. He had a .336 on-base average and a .392 slugging percentage for the Royals in 1992.

Major League Batting Register

	BA	G	AB	R	H	2B	3B	HR	RBI	SB
83 NL	.277	18	65	14	18	1	2	2	5	3
84 NL	.272	160	701	105	191	36	19	15	69	72
85 NL	.264	161	663	101	175	31	13	19	74	53
86 NL	.266	145	591	90	157	36	12	16	78	42
87 NL	.272	160	655	113	178	37	15	28	100	35
88 NL	.243	157	629	68	153	32	9	12	67	33
89 NL	.235	137	532	69	125	16	2	11	48	42
90 NL	.242	143	492	62	119	24	3	13	52	38
91 NL	.271	153	594	74	161	22	6	12	58	23
92 NL	.262	47	122	7	32	3	1	0	15	2
92 AL	.284	29	102	15	29	5	3	0	8	6
Life	.260	1310	5146	718	1338	243	85	128	574	349
3 AVE	.260	124	437	53	114	18	4	8	44	23

REY SANCHEZ

Position: Shortstop
Team: Chicago Cubs
Born: Oct. 5, 1967 Rio Piedras, Puerto Rico
Height: 5'9" **Weight:** 165 lbs.
Bats: right **Throws:** right
Acquired: Traded from Rangers for Bryan House, 1/90

Player Summary	
Fantasy Value	$1 to $4
Card Value	4¢ to 6¢
Will	make good contact
Can't	wait out walks
Expect	decent defense
Don't Expect	home run power

The fine play of Sanchez lessened the impact of the back problems that kept Shawon Dunston sidelined most of last season. Although Dunston's throwing arm is better, Sanchez is a fine fielder with good instincts, good range, and good hands. Sanchez had a .974 fielding percentage in 1992 and turned 52 double plays. He lacks power, but he is a contact hitter who rarely strikes out. Since he doesn't display much patience, he doesn't walk much, either. He is a solid hitter against southpaws but needs work against righthanders. He had a .285 on-base average and a .341 slugging percentage in 1992. He needs to improve his running game, which mysteriously disappeared last season. Sanchez topped a dozen steals in the minors three times and would increase his value if he could do the same in the majors. At Triple-A Iowa in 1992, he was .342 in 76 at bats. In 1991, he batted .290 with two homers, 46 RBI, 13 stolen bases, and 60 runs scored. His 1992 season ended early when he suffered a bulging disc in his lower back.

Major League Batting Register

	BA	G	AB	R	H	2B	3B	HR	RBI	SB
91 NL	.261	13	23	1	6	0	0	0	2	0
92 NL	.251	74	255	24	64	14	3	1	19	2
Life	.252	87	278	25	70	14	3	1	21	2

RYNE SANDBERG

Position: Second base
Team: Chicago Cubs
Born: Sept. 18, 1959 Spokane, WA
Height: 6'2" **Weight:** 180 lbs.
Bats: right **Throws:** right
Acquired: Traded from Phillies with Larry Bowa for Ivan DeJesus, 1/82

Player Summary

Fantasy Value	$36 to $46
Card Value	10¢ to 25¢
Will	hammer lefty pitching
Can't	keep average at .300
Expect	power in the clutch
Don't Expect	mistakes in the field

Sandberg owns nine Gold Gloves, nine All-Star rings, one MVP trophy, and a home run crown. At 33, he's the most popular member of the Cubs and one of the best players in the game. He does it all, at an All-Star level: hit, hit with power, run, field, and throw. Last Aug. 1, for example, his third-inning single in game two of a doubleheader was his eighth straight hit. The next day, however, his 60-game errorless streak came to an end. Sandberg once went 123 games without an error—a record for a second baseman. He posts more RBI than strikeouts and walks almost as much as he he fans. He had a .371 on-base average and a .510 slugging percentage in 1992. He's also a good basestealer who succeeds 75 percent of the time.

Major League Batting Register

	BA	G	AB	R	H	2B	3B	HR	RBI	SB
81 NL	.167	13	6	2	1	0	0	0	0	0
82 NL	.271	156	635	103	172	33	5	7	54	32
83 NL	.261	158	633	94	165	25	4	8	48	37
84 NL	.314	156	636	114	200	36	19	19	84	32
85 NL	.305	153	609	113	186	31	6	26	83	54
86 NL	.284	154	627	68	178	28	5	14	76	34
87 NL	.294	132	523	81	154	25	2	16	59	21
88 NL	.264	155	618	77	163	23	8	19	69	25
89 NL	.290	157	606	104	176	25	5	30	76	15
90 NL	.306	155	615	116	188	30	3	40	100	25
91 NL	.291	158	585	104	170	32	2	26	100	22
92 NL	.304	158	612	100	186	32	8	26	87	17
Life	.289	1705	6705	1076	1939	320	67	231	836	314
3 AVE	.300	157	604	107	181	31	4	31	96	21

DEION SANDERS

Position: Outfield
Team: Atlanta Braves
Born: Aug. 9, 1967 Fort Myers, FL
Height: 6'1" **Weight:** 195 lbs.
Bats: left **Throws:** left
Acquired: Signed as a free agent, 1/91

Player Summary

Fantasy Value	$16 to $20
Card Value	5¢ to 20¢
Will	run like a deer
Can't	wait out walks
Expect	flair for drama
Don't Expect	good-bye to football

Suddenly, Sanders realized his potential. After taking a three-year average of .183 into the season, the two-sport star made the most of the opportunity created by Otis Nixon's season-opening drug-abuse suspension. Handed Atlanta's center field job and leadoff spot, Sanders hit .407 during a 14-game hitting streak from April 7 to 20. He led the majors with 14 triples (he had 13 by the All-Star break), and he had a .346 on-base average and a .495 slugging percentage. He was named the NL's fastest player in a *Baseball America* poll. When Nixon returned, he was platooned with Sanders. Sanders batted .533 in the World Series, getting the nod as the starting left fielder against righthanders over Ron Gant. On Sunday, Oct. 11, Neon Deion played football in the afternoon for the Atlanta Falcons, then flew to Pittsburgh before game five of the NLCS for the Braves. After the Braves clinched, he threw water on broadcaster Tim McCarver, earning a fine. Sanders hit less than .250 after July 3 but still managed to finish above .300.

Major League Batting Register

	BA	G	AB	R	H	2B	3B	HR	RBI	SB
89 AL	.234	14	47	7	11	2	0	2	7	1
90 AL	.158	57	133	24	21	2	2	3	9	8
91 NL	.191	54	110	16	21	1	2	4	13	11
92 NL	.304	97	303	54	92	6	14	8	28	26
Life	.245	222	593	101	145	11	18	17	57	46

REGGIE SANDERS

Position: Outfield
Team: Cincinnati Reds
Born: Dec. 1, 1967 Florence, SC
Height: 6'1" **Weight:** 180 lbs.
Bats: right **Throws:** right
Acquired: Seventh-round pick in 6/87 free-
agent draft

Player Summary	
Fantasy Value	$8 to $16
Card Value	5¢ to 8¢
Will	improve with experience
Can't	stop fanning frequently
Expect	speed and power
Don't Expect	success against righties

As a 1992 rookie, Sanders showed the
speed-plus-power package that made him
a worthy successor to Eric Davis as a
Cincinnati outfielder. Sanders might have
made a run at Rookie of the Year honors
if injuries hadn't intervened. He missed 36
games early in the season with a pulled
left hamstring and bruised right rib cage. A
converted shortstop who moved in part to
protect previous ankle and shoulder
injuries, he never played on the Triple-A
level. That inexperience sometimes shows
in the outfield, when he misplays balls hit
over his head. He has great range, however, and a fairly good arm. He may see
more action in right field in 1993. As a hitter, Sanders fans too frequently to maxi-
mize his blinding speed. He also hurts
himself by trying to pull too many pitches.
He had a .356 on-base percentage and a
.462 slugging percentage in 1992. In
1991, he batted .315 with eight homers,
49 RBI, and 15 stolen bases at Double-A
Chattanooga before being called up.
Sanders gets good advice from his mom,
since she was a standout in softball.

Major League Batting Register

	BA	G	AB	R	H	2B	3B	HR	RBI	SB
91 NL	.200	9	40	6	8	0	0	1	3	1
92 NL	.270	116	385	62	104	26	6	12	36	16
Life	.264	125	425	68	112	26	6	13	39	17

SCOTT SANDERSON

Position: Pitcher
Team: New York Yankees
Born: July 22, 1956 Dearborn, MI
Height: 6'5" **Weight:** 200 lbs.
Bats: right **Throws:** right
Acquired: Purchased from Athletics, 12/90

Player Summary	
Fantasy Value	$6 to $10
Card Value	3¢ to 4¢
Will	seek old control
Can't	stop basestealers
Expect	frequent gophers
Don't Expect	huge turnaround

After winning 33 games in two previous
campaigns, Sanderson failed to find consistency last summer. He yielded more
hits than innings, threw more gophers
than any other Yankee, and had occasional control problems. When he's right, the
former Vanderbilt University star has complete control of his fastball, curve, and
split-fingered fastball. In 1992, opponents
compiled a .286 batting average, a .340
on-base percentage, and a .464 slugging
percentage. He had a K-to-walk ratio of
4.5-to-1 in 1991, the only time he made
the All-Star squad. Because neither his
pitch nor his delivery is quick, he is an
easy mark for basestealers. He fields his
position well, though. He styles his
approach to pitching after Hall of Famer
Catfish Hunter, Sanderson's longtime
hero.

Major League Pitching Register

	W	L	ERA	G	CG	IP	H	ER	BB	SO
78 NL	4	2	2.51	10	1	61.0	52	17	21	50
79 NL	9	8	3.43	34	5	168.0	148	64	54	138
80 NL	16	11	3.11	33	7	211.1	206	73	56	125
81 NL	9	7	2.95	22	4	137.1	122	45	31	77
82 NL	12	12	3.46	32	7	224.0	212	86	58	158
83 NL	6	7	4.65	18	0	81.1	98	42	20	55
84 NL	8	5	3.14	24	3	140.2	140	49	24	76
85 NL	5	6	3.12	19	2	121.0	100	42	27	80
86 NL	9	11	4.19	37	1	169.2	165	79	37	124
87 NL	8	9	4.29	32	0	144.2	156	69	50	106
88 NL	1	2	5.28	11	0	15.1	13	9	3	6
89 NL	11	9	3.94	37	2	146.1	155	64	31	86
90 AL	17	11	3.88	34	2	206.1	205	89	66	128
91 AL	16	10	3.81	34	2	208.0	200	88	29	130
92 AL	12	11	4.93	33	2	193.1	220	106	64	104
Life	143	121	3.72	410	38	2228.1	2192	922	571	1443
3 AVE	15	11	4.19	34	2	202.1	208	94	53	121

BENITO SANTIAGO

Position: Catcher
Team: Florida Marlins
Born: March 9, 1965 Ponce, Puerto Rico
Height: 6'1" **Weight:** 185 lbs.
Bats: right **Throws:** right
Acquired: Signed as a free agent, 12/92

Player Summary	
Fantasy Value	$10 to $16
Card Value	5¢ to 8¢
Will	show off shotgun arm
Can't	handle pitching staff
Expect	decent production
Don't Expect	patience at bat

Santiago gives the Marlins a star to handle their young pitching staff. Even though he made the NL All-Star team for the fourth straight season, Santiago did not enjoy the 1992 campaign. He cracked the little finger on his right hand while sliding into second May 30, barely returning in time for the San Diego All-Star Game. He then grumbled about playing left field so rookie Dan Walters could catch. Normally a fan favorite who shows off his rifle arm by throwing from his knees, he is often guilty of poor game-calling. Santiago also makes some errors, however, when trying to nail baserunners. He has won three Gold Gloves. He gives his team run production and some speed, but he is an undisciplined hitter. He had a .287 on-base average and a .383 slugging percentage in 1992. During his 1987 Rookie-of-the-Year season, he set a major league rookie record with a 37-game hitting streak.

Major League Batting Register

	BA	G	AB	R	H	2B	3B	HR	RBI	SB
86 NL	.290	17	62	10	18	2	0	3	6	0
87 NL	.300	146	546	64	164	33	2	18	79	21
88 NL	.248	139	492	49	122	22	2	10	46	15
89 NL	.236	129	462	50	109	16	3	16	62	11
90 NL	.270	100	344	42	93	8	5	11	53	5
91 NL	.267	152	580	60	155	22	3	17	87	8
92 NL	.251	106	386	37	97	21	0	10	42	2
Life	.264	789	2872	312	758	124	15	85	375	62
3 AVE	.263	119	437	46	115	17	3	13	61	5

MACKEY SASSER

Position: Catcher; first base; outfield
Team: Seattle Mariners
Born: Aug. 3, 1962 Fort Gaines, GA
Height: 6'1" **Weight:** 210 lbs.
Bats: left **Throws:** right
Acquired: Signed as a free agent, 12/92

Player Summary	
Fantasy Value	$2 to $3
Card Value	3¢ to 4¢
Will	make good contact
Can't	improve throwing
Expect	pinch-hitter role
Don't Expect	any hint of speed

Sasser becomes the Mariners' lefty bat off the bench. He did not escape the malaise that enveloped the 1992 Mets. The veteran utility man, often deployed as a left-handed pinch-hitter, failed to perform his usual heroics against righthanded pitching. He had a .244 batting average against righties in 1992, almost matching his .222 average versus lefties. His power disappeared, and his playing time was reduced as a result. He had a .248 on-base average and a .326 slugging percentage last summer. Even after a crash course on catching with coach Barry Foote, Sasser remained a defensive liability—nailing less than 15 percent of those who tried to steal against him. He wasn't much better at first base, right field, or left field, the other positions where he was used. Sasser has a strong but inaccurate arm and poor range, but the Mets figured he was safer in the outfield than behind the plate, where he once fell on his face because of poor footwork.

Major League Batting Register

	BA	G	AB	R	H	2B	3B	HR	RBI	SB
87 NL	.185	14	27	2	5	0	0	0	2	0
88 NL	.285	60	123	9	35	10	1	1	17	0
89 NL	.291	72	182	17	53	14	2	1	22	0
90 NL	.307	100	270	31	83	14	0	6	41	0
91 NL	.272	96	228	18	62	14	2	5	35	0
92 NL	.241	92	141	7	34	6	0	2	18	0
Life	.280	434	971	84	272	58	5	15	135	0
2 AVE	.291	98	249	25	73	14	1	6	38	0

STEVE SAX

Position: Second base
Team: Chicago White Sox
Born: Jan. 29, 1960 West Sacramento, CA
Height: 6' **Weight:** 182 lbs.
Bats: right **Throws:** right
Acquired: Traded from Yankees for Melido Perez, 1/92

Player Summary	
Fantasy Value	$16 to $22
Card Value	3¢ to 4¢
Will	make comeback bid
Can't	hit the long ball
Expect	more walks than Ks
Don't Expect	Gold Glove defense

In his first year with the White Sox, Sax suffered some dramatic declines. His average fell some 70 points—leaving him with the worst mark of his 12-year career—and he led the majors in errors by a second baseman. He got hot briefly in August after his switch from No. 2 to lead-off in the lineup; he was also tried in the No. 7 spot. The fleet contact hitter walked more than he fanned but didn't come close to his 1991 numbers. His stolen base totals have declined three years in a row. Sax is usually a clutch hitter who's tough to defense because he hits liners to all fields and sometimes over the fence. He had also shaken a reputation as an erratic fielder before regressing last summer. The White Sox are depending on a comeback by Sax in 1993.

Major League Batting Register

	BA	G	AB	R	H	2B	3B	HR	RBI	SB
81 NL	.277	31	119	15	33	2	0	2	9	5
82 NL	.282	150	638	88	180	23	7	4	47	49
83 NL	.281	155	623	94	175	18	5	5	41	56
84 NL	.243	145	569	70	138	24	4	1	35	34
85 NL	.279	136	488	62	136	8	4	1	42	27
86 NL	.332	157	633	91	210	43	4	6	56	40
87 NL	.280	157	610	84	171	22	7	6	46	37
88 NL	.277	160	632	70	175	19	4	5	57	42
89 AL	.315	158	651	88	205	26	3	5	63	43
90 AL	.260	155	615	70	160	24	2	4	42	43
91 AL	.304	158	652	85	198	38	2	10	56	31
92 AL	.236	143	567	74	134	26	4	4	47	30
Life	.282	1705	6797	891	1915	273	46	53	541	437
3 AVE	.268	152	611	76	164	29	3	6	48	35

BOB SCANLAN

Position: Pitcher
Team: Chicago Cubs
Born: Aug. 9, 1966 Los Angeles, CA
Height: 6'7" **Weight:** 215 lbs.
Bats: right **Throws:** right
Acquired: Traded from Phillies with Chuck McElroy for Mitch Williams, 4/91

Player Summary	
Fantasy Value	$2 to $6
Card Value	3¢ to 4¢
Will	bid for closer role
Can't	ring up Ks
Expect	good work versus lefties
Don't Expect	starting assignments

In his first full major league season last summer, Scanlan became the No. 1 closer for the Cubs. The towering righthander responded well to regular relief work. Mixing a live fastball with a slider and a changeup, Scanlan converted all of his first six save opportunities after the All-Star break and eventually led the team in saves, even though he had opened the season as a set-up man. He averages less than seven hits per nine innings and more than four strikeouts per nine innings, keeps the ball in the park, and has overcome past control problems. Opponents compiled a .235 batting average, a .301 on-base percentage, and a .319 slugging percentage in 1992. Even though he's a righthander, he's more effective against lefty batters—making him especially valuable in late relief. He was initially used as a starter after his 1991 trade from Philadelphia and was a starter throughout his seven years in the Phillies' minor league organization. Though he holds runners on, Scanlan does not help his cause as a fielder or hitter.

Major League Pitching Register

	W	L	ERA	G	S	IP	H	ER	BB	SO
91 NL	7	8	3.89	40	1	111.0	114	48	40	44
92 NL	3	6	2.89	69	14	87.1	76	28	30	42
Life	10	14	3.45	109	15	198.1	190	76	70	86
2 AVE	5	7	3.45	55	8	99.1	95	38	35	43

CURT SCHILLING

Position: Pitcher
Team: Philadelphia Phillies
Born: Nov. 14, 1966 Anchorage, AK
Height: 6'4" **Weight:** 215 lbs.
Bats: right **Throws:** right
Acquired: Traded from Astros for Jason Grimsley, 4/92

Player Summary

Fantasy Value	$10 to $16
Card Value	3¢ to 4¢
Will	show good control
Can't	worry about weight
Expect	few baserunners
Don't Expect	return to relief

Curt was worth much more than a Schilling to the Phillies last summer. He came out of nowhere to become the club's top starter. Acquired in a spring training trade, he reported overweight and acted as if he had the club made. After watching him throw on the sidelines before a spring-training game, manager Jim Fregosi moved Schilling from the bullpen to the rotation. The move paid quick dividends. He launched a 29-inning scoreless streak July 22, then pitched a one-hitter against the Mets Sept. 9. Schilling averaged about six and one-half hits and six strikeouts per nine innings while showing good control and keeping the ball in the park. He gave up 11 homers in 1992. An intense competitor, Schilling is a fastball-and-slider pitcher who uses a splitter as a changeup. Opponents compiled a .201 batting average, a .254 on-base percentage, and a .288 slugging percentage in 1992. He holds runners on, fields his position, and gets occasional hits.

Major League Pitching Register

	W	L	ERA	G	CG	IP	H	ER	BB	SO
88 AL	0	3	9.82	4	0	14.2	22	16	10	4
89 AL	0	1	6.23	5	0	8.2	10	6	3	6
90 AL	1	2	2.54	35	0	46.0	38	13	19	32
91 NL	3	5	3.81	56	0	75.2	79	32	39	71
92 NL	14	11	2.35	42	10	226.1	165	59	59	147
Life	18	22	3.05	142	10	371.1	314	126	130	260
3 AVE	6	6	2.69	44	3	116.1	94	35	39	83

DICK SCHOFIELD

Position: Shortstop
Team: New York Mets
Born: Nov. 21, 1962 Springfield, IL
Height: 5'10" **Weight:** 175 lbs.
Bats: right **Throws:** right
Acquired: Traded from Angels for Julio Valera, 4/92

Player Summary

Fantasy Value	$2 to $4
Card Value	3¢ to 4¢
Will	provide strong defense
Can't	provide power
Expect	more bench time
Don't Expect	healthy batting average

When the 1992 season opened, the Mets thought Kevin Elster would be their best defensive infielder. With Elster idled by shoulder surgery, however, the team had to look to Schofield. He arrived in an April trade and never looked back. A fine fielder with some speed, he was the lone beacon in the club's defensive fog last summer. Flashing exceptional range, reliable hands, and a good arm, he led NL shortstops in fielding. Between Oct. 1, 1991, and May 27, 1992, he went 44 games without an error. He even provided some big hits, including a career-best six RBI against the Giants July 19. Overall, though, Schofield's bat was a washout. Though he draws a lot of walks, he fans too often for a singles hitter. He had a .309 on-base average and a .286 slugging percentage in 1992.

Major League Batting Register

	BA	G	AB	R	H	2B	3B	HR	RBI	SB
83 AL	.204	21	54	4	11	2	0	3	4	0
84 AL	.192	140	400	39	77	10	3	4	21	5
85 AL	.219	147	438	50	96	19	3	8	41	11
86 AL	.249	139	458	67	114	17	6	13	57	23
87 AL	.251	134	479	52	120	17	3	9	46	19
88 AL	.239	155	527	61	126	11	6	6	34	20
89 AL	.228	91	302	42	69	11	2	4	26	9
90 AL	.255	99	310	41	79	8	1	1	18	3
91 AL	.225	134	427	44	96	9	3	0	31	8
92 AL	.333	1	3	0	1	0	0	0	0	0
92 NL	.205	142	420	52	86	18	2	4	36	11
Life	.229	1203	3818	452	875	122	29	52	314	109
3 AVE	.226	125	387	46	87	12	2	2	28	7

MIKE SCHOOLER

Position: Pitcher
Team: Seattle Mariners
Born: Aug. 10, 1962 Anaheim, CA
Height: 6'3" **Weight:** 220 lbs.
Bats: right **Throws:** right
Acquired: Second-round pick in 6/85 free-agent draft

Player Summary	
Fantasy Value	$2 to $4
Card Value	3¢ to 4¢
Will	seek closer job
Can't	escape injury jinx
Expect	fewer saves
Don't Expect	as many gopher balls

After saving a total of 63 games for Seattle in 1989 and '90, Schooler has struggled to find himself. Plagued by shoulder problems in '91, he had a strained right biceps last year. In addition, his arm has troubled him off and on the past three seasons. The injuries took their toll; for example, four of the seven homers Schooler yielded last summer lost games and two others produced ties. Three of the shots came with the bases loaded. At age 30, it's not too late for him to rebound, but he will probably move to more of a middle relief role with Norm Charlton moving to Seattle. A fastball-slider pitcher who keeps hitters honest with a curve, Schooler has been known to yield less hits than innings, keep the ball in the park, and fan three times more men than he walks. In 1992, however, his ERA went up for the third year in a row. Opponents compiled a .275 batting average, a .351 on-base percentage, and a .420 slugging percentage last summer.

Major League Pitching Register

	W	L	ERA	G	S	IP	H	ER	BB	SO
88 AL	5	8	3.54	40	15	48.1	45	19	24	54
89 AL	1	7	2.81	67	33	77.0	81	24	19	69
90 AL	1	4	2.25	49	30	56.0	47	14	16	45
91 AL	3	3	3.67	34	7	34.1	25	14	10	31
92 AL	2	7	4.70	53	13	51.2	55	27	24	33
Life	12	29	3.30	243	98	267.1	253	98	93	232
3 AVE	2	5	3.49	45	17	47.1	42	18	17	36

PETE SCHOUREK

Position: Pitcher
Team: New York Mets
Born: May 10, 1969 Austin, TX
Height: 6'5" **Weight:** 195 lbs.
Bats: left **Throws:** left
Acquired: Second-round pick in 6/87 free-agent draft

Player Summary	
Fantasy Value	$4 to $8
Card Value	3¢ to 4¢
Will	make good starts
Can't	win without control
Expect	runners to steal
Don't Expect	lots of strikeouts

Although he's been used as a starter and reliever since coming to the majors in 1991, Schourek seems better suited for a starting role. He hurled a one-hitter late in the '91 campaign and gave a consistent performance last year after replacing the injured Bret Saberhagen in the rotation. Schourek is a fastball-and-curveball pitcher who also throws a changeup. He depends upon good control, coupled with support from his offense and defense. Though he averaged less than three walks per nine innings last year, he was often the victim of nonsupport by his teammates. Schourek yields more hits than innings pitched and about four strikeouts per nine innings, while keeping the ball in the park. Opponents compiled a .261 batting average, a .319 on-base percentage, and a .385 slugging percentage in 1992. In 1991 at Triple-A Tidewater, he was 1-1 with a 2.52 ERA. He was 11-4 with a 3.04 ERA at Double-A Jackson in 1990. The former high school first baseman can hit, but his fielding is only fair and his ability to stop basestealers is virtually nonexistent.

Major League Pitching Register

	W	L	ERA	G	CG	IP	H	ER	BB	SO
91 NL	5	4	4.27	35	1	86.1	82	41	43	67
92 NL	6	8	3.64	22	0	136.0	137	55	44	60
Life	11	12	3.89	57	1	222.1	219	96	87	127
2 AVE	6	6	3.89	29	1	111.1	110	48	44	64

MIKE SCIOSCIA

Position: Catcher
Team: Los Angeles Dodgers
Born: Nov. 27, 1958 Upper Darby, PA
Height: 6'2" **Weight:** 223 lbs.
Bats: left **Throws:** right
Acquired: First-round pick in 6/76 free-agent draft

Player Summary	
Fantasy Value	$2 to $4
Card Value	3¢ to 4¢
Will	work hit-and-run play
Can't	run for any reason
Expect	strong defense
Don't Expect	power production

Scioscia picked a terrible time for the worst of his 13 big league seasons. In 1992, he stumbled out of the gate and never recovered. Scioscia is usually a solid lefthanded hitter who has both patience and the ability to make contact. When he's right, he walks more often than he strikes out and hammers righthanded pitching. He had a .286 on-base average and a .282 slugging percentage in 1992. Though he sometimes seems like an immovable object on the basepaths, Scioscia strikes the same appearance to oncoming baserunners; no one blocks the plate better. Despite an average arm, he's a fine defensive catcher who prevents wild pitches and handles his pitchers well. He nailed 33.1 percent of would-be basestealers last year.

Major League Batting Register

	BA	G	AB	R	H	2B	3B	HR	RBI	SB
80 NL	.254	54	134	8	34	5	1	1	8	1
81 NL	.276	93	290	27	80	10	0	2	29	0
82 NL	.219	129	365	31	80	11	1	5	38	2
83 NL	.314	12	35	3	11	3	0	1	7	0
84 NL	.273	114	341	29	93	18	0	5	38	2
85 NL	.296	141	429	47	127	26	3	7	53	3
86 NL	.251	122	374	36	94	18	1	5	26	3
87 NL	.265	142	461	44	122	26	1	6	38	7
88 NL	.257	130	408	29	105	18	0	3	35	0
89 NL	.250	133	408	40	102	16	0	10	44	0
90 NL	.264	135	435	46	115	25	0	12	66	4
91 NL	.264	119	345	39	91	16	2	8	40	4
92 NL	.221	117	348	19	77	6	3	3	24	3
Life	.259	1441	4373	398	1131	198	12	68	446	29
3 AVE	.251	124	376	35	94	16	2	8	43	4

SCOTT SCUDDER

Position: Pitcher
Team: Cleveland Indians
Born: Feb. 14, 1968 Paris, TX
Height: 6'2" **Weight:** 180 lbs.
Bats: right **Throws:** right
Acquired: Traded from Reds with Jack Armstrong for Greg Swindell, 11/91

Player Summary	
Fantasy Value	$2 to $5
Card Value	3¢ to 4¢
Will	bid for starting job
Can't	stymie basestealers
Expect	more control problems
Don't Expect	high strikeout ratio

Control—or lack of it—has always stood between Scudder and major league success. In three of his four seasons, he's walked almost as many men as he's fanned. In the fourth season, he actually walked more than he struck out. Given a full crack at starting by the Indians last year, he not only struggled with his control but yielded more hits than innings pitched. Lefties batted .299 against him, while righties batted .309. He threw 10 home run balls. Scudder uses a fastball, slider, changeup, and curveball, but he can't throw all of them for strikes. When he can't target his breaking stuff, batters—knowing what's coming—tee off on the fastball. Opponents compiled a .303 batting average, a .380 on-base percentage, and a .432 slugging percentage in 1992. His pickoff move seems to be regressing, but he is a fine fielder and a good athlete. Scudder, at age 25, is at the point where he has to step up and show if he has major league ability.

Major League Pitching Register

	W	L	ERA	G	CG	IP	H	ER	BB	SO
89 NL	4	9	4.49	23	0	100.1	91	50	61	66
90 NL	5	5	4.90	21	0	71.2	74	39	30	42
91 NL	6	9	4.35	27	0	101.1	91	49	56	51
92 AL	6	10	5.28	23	0	109.0	134	64	55	66
Life	21	33	4.76	94	0	382.1	390	202	202	225
3 AVE	6	8	4.85	24	0	94.1	100	51	47	53

DAVID SEGUI

Position: First base; outfield
Team: Baltimore Orioles
Born: July 19, 1966 Kansas City, KS
Height: 6'1" **Weight:** 195 lbs.
Bats: both **Throws:** left
Acquired: 18th-round pick in 6/87 free-agent draft

Player Summary

Fantasy Value	$2 to $6
Card Value	3¢ to 4¢
Will	show good glove
Can't	hit with power
Expect	better average
Don't Expect	extra-base hits

Segui spent last summer as Baltimore's understudy to Randy Milligan at first base and Joe Orsulak in right field. A switch-hitter with little power or speed, Segui rarely strikes out or walks. The son of former big league pitcher Diego Segui, David could break into the lineup if he recaptures the stroke that produced three .300 seasons in the minors. Last year, he limped to the finish line some 30 points below his career mark. He had a .306 on-base average and a .296 slugging percentage in 1992. He had a .252 batting average versus righthanders last year, while batting .205 against lefties. He's valuable as a pinch-hitter because of an ability to hit well in the clutch and as defensive replacement at first base. A better gloveman than Milligan, Segui has good instincts, decent range, and a good scoop at the position. He's less polished—but learning—in the outfield, where he made some good catches last year. He doesn't have great speed or a great outfield arm.

Major League Batting Register

	BA	G	AB	R	H	2B	3B	HR	RBI	SB
90 AL	.244	40	123	14	30	7	0	2	15	0
91 AL	.278	86	212	15	59	7	0	2	22	1
92 AL	.233	115	189	21	44	9	0	1	17	1
Life	.254	241	524	50	133	23	0	5	54	2
2 AVE	.257	101	201	18	52	8	0	2	20	1

KEVIN SEITZER

Position: Third base
Team: Milwaukee Brewers
Born: March 26, 1962 Springfield, IL
Height: 5'11" **Weight:** 180 lbs.
Bats: right **Throws:** right
Acquired: Signed as a free agent, 4/92

Player Summary

Fantasy Value	$6 to $10
Card Value	3¢ to 4¢
Will	show patience at plate
Can't	provide consistent power
Expect	decent defensive game
Don't Expect	falling batting average

Healthy knees helped Seitzer restore his reputation last summer. Able to bend easily for grounders that eluded him in 1991, he made a big impression during his first year with Milwaukee—even though he was bothered by a tight muscle in his neck. Seitzer slammed a pair of homers against Chicago July 17 and produced many other important hits. His final average was a bit of a disappointment, however, because the Brewers hoped Seitzer would continue the hot hitting he showed at the beginning of the 1992 season. He did show patience at the plate, however, and wound up with more walks than strikeouts. He had a .337 on-base average and a .367 slugging percentage in 1992; he also batted .313 against lefties. Even if he fails to hike his average, Seitzer's improved glovework will guarantee his job. His poor fielding led to his job loss in KC in 1991.

Major League Batting Register

	BA	G	AB	R	H	2B	3B	HR	RBI	SB
86 AL	.323	28	96	16	31	4	1	2	11	0
87 AL	.323	161	641	105	207	33	8	15	83	12
88 AL	.304	149	559	90	170	32	5	5	60	10
89 AL	.281	160	597	78	168	17	2	4	48	17
90 AL	.275	158	622	91	171	31	5	6	38	7
91 AL	.265	85	234	28	62	11	3	1	25	4
92 AL	.270	148	540	74	146	35	1	5	71	13
Life	.290	889	3289	482	955	163	25	38	336	63
3 AVE	.271	130	465	64	126	26	3	4	45	8

FRANK SEMINARA

Position: Pitcher
Team: San Diego Padres
Born: May 16, 1967 Brooklyn, NY
Height: 6'2" **Weight:** 205 lbs.
Bats: right **Throws:** right
Acquired: Drafted from Yankees, 12/90

Player Summary	
Fantasy Value	$4 to $8
Card Value	5¢ to 10¢
Will	get ground outs
Can't	always throw strikes
Expect	rotation job
Don't Expect	gophers to beat him

Jose Rijo, Bob Tewksbury, and Doug Drabek were rejected by the Yankees before they realized their potential. The Padres hope Seminara is another pitcher that the Bronx Bombers prematurely let go. A Rule 5 draft choice who was once offered back to the Yankees—who declined—Seminara justified San Diego's selection after moving into the rotation last June. He dropped his first two but then won five straight. He is a hard-throwing sinkerballer with a three-quarters delivery. Opponents in 1992 compiled a .258 batting average, a .341 on-base percentage, and a .345 slugging percentage. Though he yields more hits than innings, he keeps the ball in the park, and he averages more than five strikeouts per nine innings. Seminara dominates righties, holding them to a .216 batting average in 1992. He has trouble preventing runners from stealing. Occasional control problems stopped him from making even more progress as a 1992 rookie. In 1991 at Double-A Wichita, he was 15-10 with a 3.38 ERA, 68 walks, and 107 strikeouts in 176 innings pitched. He was 16-8 with a 1.90 ERA, 52 walks, and 132 strikeouts at Class-A Prince William in 1990.

Major League Pitching Register

	W	L	ERA	G	CG	IP	H	ER	BB	SO
92 NL	9	4	3.68	19	0	100.1	98	41	46	61
Life	9	4	3.68	19	0	100.1	98	41	46	61

SCOTT SERVAIS

Position: Catcher
Team: Houston Astros
Born: June 4, 1967 LaCrosse, WI
Height: 6'2" **Weight:** 195 lbs.
Bats: right **Throws:** right
Acquired: Third-round pick in 6/88 free-agent draft

Player Summary	
Fantasy Value	$2 to $5
Card Value	4¢ to 6¢
Will	provide sound defense
Can't	hike anemic average
Expect	improved throwing
Don't Expect	long-distance hits

Servais was a 1992 Houston rookie who spent the season in a righty-lefty catching platoon with Eddie Taubensee. Servais lived up to his reputation as a strong defensive receiver, but he rendered an inadequate average with no power or speed. Servais has also succumbed to big league pitching—especially righties—in his brief career. He batted .217 against righties in 1992 and had a .248 average versus lefties. He doesn't strike out or walk much and almost never produces an extra-base hit. He had a .294 on-base average and a .283 slugging percentage in 1992. He is a good handler of pitchers who snares wild pitches, blocks the plate, and has a better arm than his 1992 success ratio of 23.8 percent suggests. A member of the 1988 Olympic Team out of Creighton University, he has shown flashes of hitting ability. He hit .324, with two homers, 27 RBI, 19 strikeouts, and 13 bases on balls in 60 games and 219 at bats at Triple-A Tucson in 1991. He batted only .218 for the same Tucson club in 89 games a year earlier.

Major League Batting Register

	BA	G	AB	R	H	2B	3B	HR	RBI	SB
91 NL	.162	16	37	0	6	3	0	0	6	0
92 NL	.239	77	205	12	49	9	0	0	15	0
Life	.227	93	242	12	55	12	0	0	21	0

MIKE SHARPERSON

Position: Infield
Team: Los Angeles Dodgers
Born: Oct. 4, 1961 Orangeburg, SC
Height: 6'3" **Weight:** 190 lbs.
Bats: right **Throws:** right
Acquired: Traded from Toronto for Juan Guzman, 9/87

Player Summary	
Fantasy Value	$4 to $8
Card Value	3¢ to 4¢
Will	kill lefties
Can't	produce power
Expect	best defense at second
Don't Expect	another All-Star trip

Sharperson enjoyed the best of his six big league seasons in 1992. He earned the Dodger spot on the NL All-Star team with a .328 midseason average. He went on to enjoy his first .300 year in the majors. Deployed primarily in a righty-lefty platoon with Lenny Harris over recent seasons, Sharperson played more as his bat remained red-hot. He split his time last year almost equally between second and third base. Though he once beat Cecil Fielder and Fred McGriff in a Triple-A home run derby, Sharperson has never hit for power in the majors. A contact hitter with patience, he walks more often than he fans and maintains a high on-base percentage. He had a .387 on-base average and a .394 slugging percentage in 1992. He's best deployed as a No. 2 hitter and second baseman but spent much of last year as a No. 3 hitter and third baseman. His defense at either position is erratic.

Major League Batting Register

	BA	G	AB	R	H	2B	3B	HR	RBI	SB
87 AL	.208	32	96	4	20	4	1	0	9	2
87 NL	.273	10	33	7	9	2	0	0	1	0
88 NL	.271	46	59	8	16	1	0	0	4	0
89 NL	.250	27	28	2	7	3	0	0	5	0
90 NL	.297	129	357	42	106	14	2	3	36	15
91 NL	.278	105	216	24	60	11	2	2	20	1
92 NL	.300	128	317	48	95	21	0	3	36	2
Life	.283	477	1106	135	313	56	5	8	111	20
3 AVE	.293	121	297	38	87	15	1	3	31	6

GARY SHEFFIELD

Position: Third base
Team: San Diego Padres
Born: Nov. 18, 1968 Tampa, FL
Height: 5'11" **Weight:** 190 lbs.
Bats: right **Throws:** right
Acquired: Traded from Brewers with Geoff Kellogg for Ricky Bones, Jose Valentin, and Matt Mieske, 3/92

Player Summary	
Fantasy Value	$34 to $40
Card Value	8¢ to 16¢
Will	destroy rival pitchers
Can't	become big basestealer
Expect	more walks than whiffs
Don't Expect	erratic defensive play

Sheffield made a serious bid last season to become the first NL Triple Crown winner since Joe Medwick in 1937. Healed from 1991 wrist and shoulder injuries, plus a history of controversy in Milwaukee, Sheffield responded warmly to the San Diego climate. Sandwiched between Tony Gwynn and Fred McGriff in the lineup, Sheffield filled two long-standing Padre voids—third base and third in the lineup. San Diego's seventh third baseman in as many seasons, Sheffield supplied such a strong bat that his fine defense was overlooked. A natural shortstop, he had a .961 fielding percentage in 1992. In the first half alone, he hit .325 with 18 homers and 61 RBI—making the All-Star squad for the first time. He didn't let up, winning NL Player of the Month honors in August. He ended the season with the NL batting title. He had a .385 on-base average and a .580 slugging percentage in 1992. Sheffield is the nephew of Doc Gooden.

Major League Batting Register

	BA	G	AB	R	H	2B	3B	HR	RBI	SB
88 AL	.237	24	80	12	19	1	0	4	12	3
89 AL	.247	95	368	34	91	18	0	5	32	10
90 AL	.294	125	487	67	143	30	1	10	67	25
91 AL	.194	50	175	25	34	12	2	2	22	5
92 NL	.330	146	557	87	184	34	3	33	100	5
Life	.283	440	1667	225	471	95	6	54	233	48
3 AVE	.296	107	406	60	120	25	2	15	63	12

CRAIG SHIPLEY

Position: Second base; shortstop
Team: San Diego Padres
Born: Jan. 7, 1963 Parramatta, Australia
Height: 6'1" **Weight:** 185 lbs.
Bats: right **Throws:** right
Acquired: Drafted from Mets, 12/90

Player Summary	
Fantasy Value	$2 to $4
Card Value	3¢ to 4¢
Will	bid for regular job
Can't	get hits or homers
Expect	good glove anywhere
Don't Expect	patience at plate

Shipley spent last summer on the San Diego bench, entertaining teammates with his Crocodile Dundee imitation. A native Australian whose baseball talents were discovered at the University of Alabama, Shipley served the Padres in 1991 as a three-position infielder, pinch-hitter, and pinch-runner. While his batting statistics weren't sensational, he did fare well against lefthanders. He batted .294 against lefties in 1992. Valued almost entirely for his versatility, he adds little to the offense. He has no power, speed, or patience at the plate. Men walk on the moon more often than Shipley walks to first base. He had a .262 on-base average and a .305 slugging percentage last summer. At Triple-A Las Vegas in 1991, he batted .300 with five homers and 34 RBI in 230 at bats. Strong fielding keeps him in the majors. He's best at shortstop but does not embarrass himself at second or third. Shipley has good range, good instincts, and a good arm and can also turn the double play.

Major League Batting Register

	BA	G	AB	R	H	2B	3B	HR	RBI	SB
86 NL	.111	12	27	3	3	1	0	0	4	0
87 NL	.257	26	35	3	9	1	0	0	2	0
89 NL	.143	4	7	3	1	0	0	0	0	0
91 NL	.275	37	91	6	25	3	0	1	6	0
92 NL	.248	52	105	7	26	6	0	0	7	1
Life	.242	131	265	22	64	11	0	1	19	1

RUBEN SIERRA

Position: Outfield
Team: Oakland Athletics
Born: Oct. 6, 1965 Rio Piedras, Puerto Rico
Height: 6'1" **Weight:** 175 lbs.
Bats: both **Throws:** right
Acquired: Traded from Rangers with Bobby Witt and Jeff Russell for Jose Canseco, 8/92

Player Summary	
Fantasy Value	$40 to $48
Card Value	10¢ to 20¢
Will	rebound big
Can't	vie for 30-30 club
Expect	return of power
Don't Expect	defense to win awards

Sierra suffered through his toughest season last summer. Since reaching the majors, he had played 99.4 percent of the time before a strained hamstring sent him to the sidelines in June. Later, he was sidelined with chicken pox. Though Sierra's play improved following his swap to Oakland, he finished far below his usual form. When he's right, the switch-hitting slugger is one of baseball's best run producers. He had five straight seasons with more than 90 RBI before 1992. A clutch hitter who uses all fields, Sierra has hit more than two-dozen homers three times. He's increased his walks and cut his strikeouts in recent years. He had a .323 on-base average and a .448 slugging percentage in 1992. He batted .339 against lefthanders last summer. Sierra steals a dozen bases a year. In the field, he makes some careless errors, and he doesn't nail as many runners as he should with his cannon arm.

Major League Batting Register

	BA	G	AB	R	H	2B	3B	HR	RBI	SB
86 AL	.264	113	382	50	101	13	10	16	55	7
87 AL	.263	158	643	97	169	35	4	30	109	16
88 AL	.254	156	615	77	156	32	2	23	91	18
89 AL	.306	162	634	101	194	35	14	29	119	8
90 AL	.280	159	608	70	170	37	2	16	96	9
91 AL	.307	161	661	110	203	44	5	25	116	16
92 AL	.278	151	601	83	167	34	7	17	87	14
Life	.280	1060	4144	588	1160	230	44	156	673	88
3 AVE	.289	157	623	88	180	38	5	19	100	13

DON SLAUGHT

Position: Catcher
Team: Pittsburgh Pirates
Born: Sept. 11, 1958 Long Beach, CA
Height: 6'1" **Weight:** 190 lbs.
Bats: right **Throws:** right
Acquired: Traded from Yankees for Willie
  Smith and Jeff Robinson, 12/89

Player Summary	
Fantasy Value	$2 to $4
Card Value	3¢ to 4¢
Will	produce in platoon
Can't	hit the long ball
Expect	fine clutch hitting
Don't Expect	another career year

The righty-lefty catching platoon of Don Slaught and Mike LaValliere continued to pay dividends for the Pirates in 1992. After taking a 10-year mark of .274 into the season, Slaught produced a career year at age 33. A contact hitter with little power but great bunting and hit-and-run skills, he topped .300 against both lefties and righties. Though known as a fastball hitter who uses all fields, he can also handle off-speed deliveries. He doesn't deliver many extra-base hits or stolen bases but he's a good clutch performer. Slaught doesn't strike out or walk much. He had a .384 on-base average and a .482 slugging percentage in 1992. Behind the plate, he can't match LaValliere's defense, but Slaught ranks as a respectable receiver. He nailed 35.7 percent of would-be base-stealers last summer.

Major League Batting Register

	BA	G	AB	R	H	2B	3B	HR	RBI	SB
82 AL	.278	43	115	14	32	6	0	3	8	0
83 AL	.312	83	276	21	86	13	4	0	28	3
84 AL	.264	124	409	48	108	27	4	4	42	0
85 AL	.280	102	343	34	96	17	4	8	35	5
86 AL	.264	95	314	39	83	17	1	13	46	3
87 AL	.224	95	237	25	53	15	2	8	16	0
88 AL	.283	97	322	33	91	25	1	9	43	1
89 AL	.251	117	350	34	88	21	3	5	38	1
90 NL	.300	84	230	27	69	18	3	4	29	0
91 NL	.295	77	220	19	65	17	1	1	29	1
92 NL	.345	87	255	26	88	17	3	4	37	2
Life	.280	1004	3071	320	859	193	26	59	351	16
3 AVE	.315	83	235	24	74	17	2	3	32	1

JOE SLUSARSKI

Position: Pitcher
Team: Oakland Athletics
Born: Dec. 19, 1966 Indianapolis, IN
Height: 6'4" **Weight:** 195 lbs.
Bats: right **Throws:** right
Acquired: Second-round pick in 6/88 free-
  agent draft

Player Summary	
Fantasy Value	$2 to $4
Card Value	3¢ to 4¢
Will	bank on fastball
Can't	harness off-speed pitch
Expect	too many gophers
Don't Expect	many Ks

After finishing spring training as Oakland's most effective starter, Slusarski couldn't maintain his momentum into the regular season last year. The sinker that he used as his out pitch mysteriously vanished, and he was exiled to the minors. At Triple-A Tacoma, he had a 2-4 record with a 3.77 ERA, 18 walks, and 26 strikeouts in 57 innings pitched. A fastball pitcher who still needs to develop a quality off-speed delivery, Slusarski has yet to realize the promise that sent him to the 1988 Olympics. He averaged more than 10 hits but less than five strikeouts per nine innings last year; however, he improved his control from the previous season. Opponents compiled a .284 batting average, a .350 on-base percentage, and a .512 slugging percentage in 1992. His biggest problem in 1992 was keeping the ball in the park. Slusarski is a fine fielder with a quick pickoff move. In 1991 at Tacoma, the former University of New Orleans hurler was 4-2 with a 2.72 ERA, 10 walks, and 25 strikeouts in 46 innings. He was also 4-2 (with a 3.40 ERA) in 1990 at Tacoma.

Major League Pitching Register

	W	L	ERA	G	CG	IP	H	ER	BB	SO
91 AL	5	7	5.27	20	1	109.1	121	64	52	60
92 AL	5	5	5.45	15	0	76.0	85	46	27	38
Life	10	12	5.34	35	1	185.1	206	110	79	98
2 AVE	5	6	5.34	18	1	93.1	103	55	40	49

JOHN SMILEY

Position: Pitcher
Team: Cincinnati Reds
Born: March 17, 1965 Phoenixville, PA
Height: 6'4" **Weight:** 200 lbs.
Bats: left **Throws:** left
Acquired: Signed as a free agent, 11/92

Player Summary	
Fantasy Value	$16 to $26
Card Value	3¢ to 4¢
Will	win most starts
Can't	avoid gophers
Expect	fine control
Don't Expect	complete games

Smiley replaces Greg Swindell as the Reds' top lefty. After getting used to the American League strike zone, Smiley recovered from his slow start last spring. He was AL Pitcher of the Month in June with a 4-0 record and 1.34 ERA, capping a two-month performance that included eight wins in nine decisions and a 2.39 earned run mark. Slowed by a sore arm in April, he finished with the second-best win total of his seven-year career. He has excellent control of his fastball, changeup, and curve. He averaged about two and one-half walks, six strikeouts, and eight hits per nine innings last year. He gives up his share of gopher balls. Opponents in 1992 compiled a .231 batting average, a .286 on-base percentage, and a .356 slugging percentage. Smiley fields his position well and holds runners close—a technique he perfected after working on his mechanics two years ago. At age 28, Smiley should remain one of baseball's premier southpaw starters.

Major League Pitching Register

	W	L	ERA	G	CG	IP	H	ER	BB	SO
86 NL	1	0	3.86	12	0	11.2	4	5	4	9
87 NL	5	5	5.76	63	0	75.0	69	48	50	58
88 NL	13	11	3.25	34	5	205.0	185	74	46	129
89 NL	12	8	2.81	28	8	205.1	174	64	49	123
90 NL	9	10	4.64	26	2	149.1	161	77	36	86
91 NL	20	8	3.08	33	2	207.2	194	71	44	129
92 AL	16	9	3.21	34	5	241.0	205	86	65	163
Life	76	51	3.49	230	22	1095.0	992	425	294	697
3 AVE	15	9	3.52	31	3	199.1	187	78	48	126

BRYN SMITH

Position: Pitcher
Team: Colorado Rockies
Born: Aug. 11, 1955 Marietta, GA
Height: 6'2" **Weight:** 205 lbs.
Bats: right **Throws:** right
Acquired: Signed as a free agent, 11/92

Player Summary	
Fantasy Value	$2 to $4
Card Value	3¢ to 4¢
Will	reclaim rotation job
Can't	blaze ball by batter
Expect	bat to help own cause
Don't Expect	lapses of control

Smith adds veteran help to Colorado's staff. His 1992 season was almost a total loss. He underwent elbow surgery after injuring himself in his first start and spent most of the summer recovering before making a brief return in September. At 37, he still throws well enough to be a fourth or fifth starter, if healthy. A finesse pitcher with good control, his best pitches are a sinker and a palmball. When he's on, Smith gets outs on ground balls rather than strikeouts. Opponents compiled a .247 batting average, a .315 on-base percentage, and a .383 slugging percentage in 1992. He needs to work on his pickoff move because baserunners have made him an easy mark. Smith helps his own cause with outstanding fielding and a competent bat; he is one of baseball's better-hitting pitchers.

Major League Pitching Register

	W	L	ERA	G	CG	IP	H	ER	BB	SO
81 NL	1	0	2.77	7	0	13.0	14	4	3	9
82 NL	2	4	4.20	47	0	79.1	81	37	23	50
83 NL	6	11	2.49	49	5	155.1	142	43	43	101
84 NL	12	13	3.32	28	4	179.0	178	66	51	101
85 NL	18	5	2.91	32	4	222.1	193	72	41	127
86 NL	10	8	3.94	30	1	187.1	182	82	63	105
87 NL	10	9	4.37	26	2	150.1	164	73	31	94
88 NL	12	10	3.00	32	1	198.0	179	66	32	122
89 NL	10	11	2.84	33	3	215.2	177	68	54	129
90 NL	9	8	4.27	26	0	141.1	160	67	30	78
91 NL	12	9	3.85	31	3	198.2	188	85	45	94
92 NL	4	2	4.64	13	0	21.1	20	11	5	9
Life	106	90	3.44	354	23	1761.2	1678	674	421	1019
2 AVE	11	9	4.02	29	2	170.2	174	76	38	86

DWIGHT SMITH

Position: Outfield
Team: Chicago Cubs
Born: Nov. 8, 1963 Tallahassee, FL
Height: 5'11" **Weight:** 175 lbs.
Bats: left **Throws:** right
Acquired: Third-round pick in secondary phase
of 6/84 free-agent draft

Player Summary

Fantasy Value	$4 to $8
Card Value	3¢ to 4¢
Will	pinch-hit against righties
Can't	provide solid defense
Expect	spot duty in outfield
Don't Expect	return to rookie form

After finishing second in 1989 NL Rookie of the Year voting, Smith has not performed at the same level. His average fell for two straight years before reviving a bit last summer. His playing time has fallen sharply, however. He rusted on the Cub bench most of 1992 before returning to the lineup in September after center fielder Sammy Sosa fractured his ankle. Sharing the spot with Doug Dascenzo, Smith served well in limited action as Chicago's leadoff man—a peculiar task for an impatient hitter who hardly walks. Though he adds some speed to the lineup, Smith fans too often to hit first on an extended basis. Nor is he a home run threat. He had a .318 on-base average and a .392 slugging percentage in 1992. He batted .284 against righthanded pitchers last year. Smith's defense is mediocre at best, and his arm is only fair. At 29, however, he's not too old to resurrect his career as a lefty pinch-hitter and fourth outfielder.

Major League Batting Register

	BA	G	AB	R	H	2B	3B	HR	RBI	SB
89 NL	.324	109	343	52	111	19	6	9	52	9
90 NL	.262	117	290	34	76	15	0	6	27	11
91 NL	.228	90	167	16	38	7	2	3	21	2
92 NL	.276	109	217	28	60	10	3	3	24	9
Life	.280	425	1017	130	285	51	11	21	124	31
3 AVE	.258	105	225	26	58	11	2	4	24	7

LEE SMITH

Position: Pitcher
Team: St. Louis Cardinals
Born: Dec. 4, 1957 Jamestown, LA
Height: 6'6" **Weight:** 250 lbs.
Bats: right **Throws:** right
Acquired: Traded from Red Sox for Tom
Brunansky, 5/90

Player Summary

Fantasy Value	$38 to $46
Card Value	5¢ to 10¢
Will	slam the door
Can't	stop basestealers
Expect	high save totals
Don't Expect	first batters to reach

After saving an NL-record 47 games in 1991, Smith was slowed by shoulder problems last summer. He still pitched well enough to make the All-Star team for the fourth time and to move into second place on the all-time saves list. He blew eight saves, but most were in the first half. He was best in August, when his dozen saves were one short of the major league mark for a single month. A model of consistency, he could be even better if he stays healthy, but he has been plagued by bad knees throughout his career. He is a hard thrower with good command of his fastball, slider, and splitter. Opponents compiled a .221 batting average, a .286 on-base percentage, and a .320 slugging percentage in 1992.

Major League Pitching Register

	W	L	ERA	G	S	IP	H	ER	BB	SO
80 NL	2	0	2.91	18	0	21.2	21	7	14	17
81 NL	3	6	3.51	40	1	66.2	57	26	31	50
82 NL	2	5	2.69	72	17	117.0	105	35	37	99
83 NL	4	10	1.65	66	29	103.1	70	19	41	91
84 NL	9	7	3.65	69	33	101.0	98	41	35	86
85 NL	7	4	3.04	65	33	97.2	87	33	32	112
86 NL	9	9	3.09	66	31	90.1	69	31	42	93
87 NL	4	10	3.12	62	36	83.2	84	29	32	96
88 AL	4	5	2.80	64	29	83.2	72	26	37	96
89 AL	6	1	3.57	64	25	70.2	53	28	33	96
90 AL	2	1	1.88	11	4	14.1	13	3	9	17
90 NL	4	4	2.10	53	27	68.2	58	16	20	70
91 NL	6	3	2.34	67	47	73.0	70	19	13	67
92 NL	4	9	3.12	70	43	75.0	62	26	26	60
Life	65	74	2.86	787	355	1066.2	919	339	402	1050
3 AVE	5	6	2.49	67	40	77.1	68	21	23	71

LONNIE SMITH

Position: Outfield
Team: Pittsburgh Pirates
Born: Dec. 22, 1955 Chicago, IL
Height: 5'9" **Weight:** 170 lbs.
Bats: right **Throws:** right
Acquired: Signed as a free agent, 1/93

Player Summary	
Fantasy Value	$2 to $4
Card Value	3¢ to 4¢
Will	produce in clutch
Can't	flash former speed
Expect	occasional power
Don't Expect	strong throwing arm

Smith made up for his baserunning error in the 1991 World Series by hitting a grand slam in game five of the 1992 fall classic. After getting off to a 3-for-33 start (.091) in the regular season last summer, Smith revived in time to become a valuable spare part during Atlanta's 1992 stretch drive. He got more playing time when Ron Gant slumped, and Smith was so productive that manager Bobby Cox changed his nickname from "Skates" to "Stretch Drive." Smith had earned the former name with erratic play in left field. He is not likely to be a regular again but is a fine clutch hitter who murders lefthanders. He brings occasional power and some of his old speed to the Pirates' lineup.

Major League Batting Register

	BA	G	AB	R	H	2B	3B	HR	RBI	SB
78 NL	.000	17	4	6	0	0	0	0	0	4
79 NL	.167	17	30	4	5	2	0	0	3	2
80 NL	.339	100	298	69	101	14	4	3	20	33
81 NL	.324	62	176	40	57	14	3	2	11	21
82 NL	.307	156	592	120	182	35	8	8	69	68
83 NL	.321	130	492	83	158	31	5	8	45	43
84 NL	.250	145	504	77	126	20	4	6	49	50
85 NL	.260	28	96	15	25	2	2	0	7	12
85 AL	.257	120	448	77	115	23	4	6	41	40
86 AL	.287	134	508	80	146	25	7	8	44	26
87 AL	.251	48	167	26	42	7	1	3	8	9
88 NL	.237	43	114	14	27	3	0	3	9	4
89 NL	.315	134	482	89	152	34	4	21	79	25
90 NL	.305	135	466	72	142	27	9	9	42	10
91 NL	.275	122	353	58	97	19	1	7	44	9
92 NL	.247	84	158	23	39	8	2	6	33	4
Life	.289	1475	4888	853	1414	264	54	90	504	360
3 AVE	.285	114	326	51	93	18	4	7	40	8

OZZIE SMITH

Position: Shortstop
Team: St. Louis Cardinals
Born: Dec. 26, 1954 Mobile, AL
Height: 5'10" **Weight:** 160 lbs.
Bats: both **Throws:** right
Acquired: Traded from Padres for Garry Templeton, 2/82

Player Summary	
Fantasy Value	$18 to $26
Card Value	10¢ to 20¢
Will	reach base often
Can't	generate old speed
Expect	Gold Glove defense
Don't Expect	game-winning homers

In a poll of managers conducted by *Baseball America* in 1990, Smith was named the NL's smartest player. Though he no longer has blinding speed, his understanding of opposing pitchers lets him get jumps that others don't. Smith remains an acrobatic infielder who compensates for a lost step with great instincts, plus knowledge of rival hitters. A 12-time All-Star who's won 13 consecutive Gold Gloves, only Barry Larkin comes close to carrying Smith's glove at short. Though he lacks power, Smith is a good contact hitter with patience. An ideal No. 2 hitter, he walks much more often than he fans, works the hit-and-run to perfection, and is one of baseball's best bunters. He had a .367 on-base average and a .342 slugging percentage in 1992.

Major League Batting Register

	BA	G	AB	R	H	2B	3B	HR	RBI	SB
78 NL	.258	159	590	69	152	17	6	1	46	40
79 NL	.211	156	587	77	124	18	6	0	27	28
80 NL	.230	158	609	67	140	18	5	0	35	57
81 NL	.222	110	450	53	100	11	2	0	21	22
82 NL	.248	140	488	58	121	24	1	2	43	25
83 NL	.243	159	552	69	134	30	6	3	50	34
84 NL	.257	124	412	53	106	20	5	1	44	35
85 NL	.276	158	537	70	148	22	3	6	54	31
86 NL	.280	153	514	67	144	19	4	0	54	31
87 NL	.303	158	600	104	182	40	4	0	75	43
88 NL	.270	153	575	80	155	27	1	3	51	57
89 NL	.273	155	593	82	162	30	8	2	50	29
90 NL	.254	143	512	61	130	21	1	1	50	32
91 NL	.285	150	550	96	157	30	3	3	50	35
92 NL	.295	132	518	73	153	20	2	0	31	43
Life	.261	2208	8087	1079	2108	347	57	22	681	542
3 AVE	.278	142	527	77	147	24	2	1	44	37

PETE SMITH

Position: Pitcher
Team: Atlanta Braves
Born: Feb. 27, 1966 Abington, MA
Height: 6'2" **Weight:** 185 lbs.
Bats: right **Throws:** right
Acquired: Traded from Phillies with Ozzie Virgil for Milt Thompson and Steve Bedrosian, 12/85

Player Summary	
Fantasy Value	$6 to $12
Card Value	3¢ to 4¢
Will	stifle righty hitters
Can't	prevent basestealing
Expect	improved changeup
Don't Expect	control problems

Will the real Pete Smith please stand up? The pitcher who took a 19-40 career record and 4.37 ERA into the 1992 campaign was simply not the same one who pitched so well as Atlanta's No. 5 starter after Mike Bielecki's late-July elbow injury. After starting the season at Triple-A Richmond, Smith showed he had totally recovered from his 1990 rotator cuff surgery. His 7-0 win over Houston Sept. 12 was his first big league shutout since August 1988. The "new" Pete Smith is a faster worker with a better changeup. He's a fastball-and-slider pitcher who also throws a curve in addition to the circle change. Smith doesn't get as many strikeouts as he once did, but he yields less hits than innings pitched, has better control, and keeps the ball in the park. Opponents compiled a .217 batting average, a .285 on-base percentage, and a .300 slugging percentage in 1992. He's particularly tough on righthanded hitters. He was 7-4 with a 2.14 ERA at Richmond last summer.

Major League Pitching Register

	W	L	ERA	G	CG	IP	H	ER	BB	SO
87 NL	1	2	4.83	6	0	31.2	39	17	14	11
88 NL	7	15	3.69	32	5	195.1	183	80	88	124
89 NL	5	14	4.75	28	1	142.0	144	75	57	115
90 NL	5	6	4.79	13	3	77.0	77	41	24	56
91 NL	1	3	5.06	14	0	48.0	48	27	22	29
92 NL	7	0	2.05	12	2	79.0	63	18	28	43
Life	26	40	4.05	105	11	573.0	554	258	233	378
2 AVE	6	3	3.40	13	3	78.0	70	30	26	50

ZANE SMITH

Position: Pitcher
Team: Pittsburgh Pirates
Born: Dec. 28, 1960 Madison, WI
Height: 6'2" **Weight:** 195 lbs.
Bats: left **Throws:** left
Acquired: Traded from Expos for Scott Ruskin, Moises Alou, and Willie Greene, 8/90

Player Summary	
Fantasy Value	$6 to $10
Card Value	3¢ to 4¢
Will	win when healthy
Can't	hold runners on
Expect	stellar control
Don't Expect	high K numbers

Shoulder problems sent Smith to the sidelines last July. After two stints on the disabled list, he finally agreed to an operation that repaired a torn muscle in the left shoulder. The premature end to his season was disappointing for him. When he's on, Smith is a sinkerballer known for his pinpoint control. He yields about a hit per inning but only about one walk per nine innings. One of the league's fastest workers, Smith complements the sinker with a slider, curve, and changeup. He's extremely effective against lefthanded hitters and stingy with the long ball. Opponents in 1992 compiled a .261 batting average, a .287 on-base percentage, and a .365 slugging percentage. Smith helps his own cause with his hitting, bunting, running, and fielding. He's even used as a pinch-hitter on occasion. He is not exceptionally good at keeping runners close.

Major League Pitching Register

	W	L	ERA	G	CG	IP	H	ER	BB	SO
84 NL	1	0	2.25	3	0	20.0	16	5	13	16
85 NL	9	10	3.80	42	2	147.0	135	62	80	85
86 NL	8	16	4.05	38	3	204.2	209	92	105	139
87 NL	15	10	4.09	36	9	242.0	245	110	91	130
88 NL	5	10	4.30	23	3	140.1	159	67	44	59
89 NL	1	13	3.49	48	0	147.0	141	57	52	93
90 NL	12	9	2.55	33	4	215.1	196	61	50	130
91 NL	16	10	3.20	35	6	228.0	234	81	29	120
92 NL	8	8	3.06	23	4	141.0	138	48	19	56
Life	75	86	3.53	281	31	1485.1	1473	583	483	828
3 AVE	12	9	2.93	30	5	195.0	189	63	33	102

JOHN SMOLTZ

Position: Pitcher
Team: Atlanta Braves
Born: May 15, 1967 Detroit, MI
Height: 6'3" **Weight:** 185 lbs.
Bats: right **Throws:** right
Acquired: Traded from Tigers for Doyle
   Alexander, 8/87

Player Summary

Fantasy Value	$20 to $28
Card Value	5¢ to 10¢
Will	seek 20-win season
Can't	avoid wild pitches
Expect	lots of strikeouts
Don't Expect	long losing streak

Smoltz was the NLCS MVP in 1992, winning two of his three starts. After a 14-6 start during the regular season last summer, Smoltz suffered a nagging groin pull that hampered his effectiveness. Though he finished with the first 200-strikeout season of his career, he wasn't the same pitcher after the injury until he reached postseason play. When Smoltz is healthy, he is one of baseball's best pitchers. He won 25 of his first 33 decisions after the 1991 All-Star break—thanks in part to the counsel of sports psychologist Jack Llewellyn. Smoltz also enjoyed a 30-inning scoreless streak last summer. Opponents compiled a .224 batting average, a .287 on-base average, and a .332 slugging percentage in 1992. He throws a fastball, curve, and slider, plus a forkball that he uses as a changeup against lefties. Though his control is usually good, he has periodic bouts of wildness (he lost some games on wild pitches last year). He holds runners on, fields well, and helps himself with the bat.

Major League Pitching Register

	W	L	ERA	G	CG	IP	H	ER	BB	SO
88 NL	2	7	5.48	12	0	64.0	74	39	33	37
89 NL	12	11	2.94	29	5	208.0	160	68	72	168
90 NL	14	11	3.85	34	6	231.1	206	99	90	170
91 NL	14	13	3.80	36	5	229.2	206	97	77	148
92 NL	15	12	2.85	35	9	246.2	206	78	80	215
Life	57	54	3.50	146	25	979.2	852	381	352	738
3 AVE	14	12	3.48	35	7	235.2	206	91	82	178

CORY SNYDER

Position: Outfield; infield
Team: Los Angeles Dodgers
Born: Nov. 11, 1962 Inglewood, CA
Height: 6'3" **Weight:** 185 lbs.
Bats: right **Throws:** right
Acquired: Signed as a free agent, 12/92

Player Summary

Fantasy Value	$6 to $10
Card Value	3¢ to 4¢
Will	play any position
Can't	avoid striking out
Expect	howitzer throwing arm
Don't Expect	production to fizzle

The Dodgers signed Snyder for his versatility and pop. After coming to the Giants' 1992 camp hoping to hook on as a utility player, he used his booming bat to become the club's cleanup hitter. Responding well to tips provided by batting coach Dusty Baker, Snyder was most likely the Giants' most valuable player in the first half of the 1992 season. He finished the year with a .311 on-base percentage and a .444 slugging average in 1992. In previous years, Snyder had always been a high-power, low-average performer who fanned frequently. The victim of back problems, bad habits, and conflicting advice in the past, Snyder studied highlight films and spent hours in a backyard batting cage prior to joining the Giants. He still fans four times more than he walks. Snyder plays anywhere but catcher and pitcher without embarrassment. An All-American shortstop at BYU, he was on the 1984 U.S. Olympic baseball team.

Major League Batting Register

	BA	G	AB	R	H	2B	3B	HR	RBI	SB
86 AL	.272	103	416	58	113	21	1	24	69	2
87 AL	.236	157	577	74	136	24	2	33	82	5
88 AL	.272	142	511	71	139	24	3	26	75	5
89 AL	.215	132	489	49	105	17	0	18	59	6
90 AL	.233	123	438	46	102	27	3	14	55	1
91 AL	.188	50	117	10	22	4	0	3	11	0
91 AL	.143	21	49	4	7	0	1	0	6	0
92 NL	.269	124	390	48	105	22	2	14	57	4
Life	.244	852	2987	360	729	139	12	132	414	23
3 AVE	.237	106	331	36	79	18	2	10	43	2

LUIS SOJO

Position: Infield
Team: Toronto Blue Jays
Born: Jan. 3, 1966 Barquisimeto, Venezuela
Height: 5'11" **Weight:** 174 lbs.
Bats: right **Throws:** right
Acquired: Traded from Angels for Kelly Gruber and cash, 12/92

Player Summary	
Fantasy Value	$2 to $4
Card Value	3¢ to 4¢
Will	make good contact
Can't	wait for walks
Expect	decent fielding
Don't Expect	success versus lefties

Sojo moves to the Jays in a utility role. Although Bobby Rose started last year as California's regular second baseman, Sojo regained the job after Rose was hurt in the club's May bus crash in New Jersey. Sojo hit well enough to hold the job all year, even though veteran Ken Oberkfell provided second-half insurance. A contact hitter with little patience, Sojo rarely strikes out or walks. He is more than an opposite-field singles hitter, however. He can bunt, beat out infield hits, execute the hit-and-run, and even clear the fences once in awhile. He had a .299 on-base percentage and a .378 slugging percentage in 1992. Despite his speed, Sojo's baserunning needs work. His fielding, however, is fine. He turns the double play well, shows better than average range, and owns a decent arm. Though second base is his best position, he can fill in at short and third. In 1992 at Triple-A Edmonton, Sojo batted .297 with one homer, 24 RBI, nine bases on balls, 17 strikeouts, and four stolen bases in 145 at bats.

Major League Batting Register

	BA	G	AB	R	H	2B	3B	HR	RBI	SB
90 AL	.225	33	80	14	18	3	0	1	9	1
91 AL	.258	113	364	38	94	14	1	3	20	4
92 AL	.272	106	368	37	100	12	3	7	43	7
Life	.261	252	812	89	212	29	4	11	72	12
2 AVE	.265	110	366	38	97	13	2	5	32	6

PAUL SORRENTO

Position: First base
Team: Cleveland Indians
Born: Nov. 17, 1965 Somerville, MA
Height: 6'2" **Weight:** 223 lbs.
Bats: left **Throws:** right
Acquired: Traded from Twins for Oscar Munoz and Curtis Leskanic, 3/92

Player Summary	
Fantasy Value	$6 to $12
Card Value	3¢ to 4¢
Will	show power
Can't	hit lefties
Expect	platoon work
Don't Expect	stolen bases

Reggie Jefferson's elbow injury gave Sorrento his first chance to be a big league regular. After an agonizingly slow start that included a .217 average on July 4, Sorrento's bat awakened in time to make him Cleveland's lefthanded platoon partner for Carlos Martinez at first base. As Sorrento learns the pitchers, he should be able to boost his power production by reducing his strikeouts. He should also draw more walks, though he already shows a good eye for a 27-year-old with limited experience. He had a .341 on-base average and a .443 slugging percentage in 1992. He struggled against southpaws in 1992, batting only .156, but he ripped righthanders, batting .281. Sorrento lacks speed and defensive polish. He's not a bad first baseman, but his best position might be designated hitter. Before coming to the Indians in 1992, he was stuck in the Twins' organization behind Kent Hrbek. In 1991 at Triple-A Portland, he batted .308 with 13 homers and 79 RBI. He batted .302 with 19 homers and 72 RBI at Portland in 1990.

Major League Batting Register

	BA	G	AB	R	H	2B	3B	HR	RBI	SB
89 AL	.238	14	21	2	5	0	0	0	1	0
90 AL	.207	41	121	11	25	4	1	5	13	1
91 AL	.255	26	47	6	12	2	0	4	13	0
92 AL	.269	140	458	52	123	24	1	18	60	0
Life	.255	221	647	71	165	30	2	27	87	1

SAMMY SOSA

Position: Outfield
Team: Chicago Cubs
Born: Nov. 10, 1968 San Pedro de Macoris, Dominican Republic
Height: 6' **Weight:** 175 lbs.
Bats: right **Throws:** right
Acquired: Traded from White Sox with Ken Patterson for George Bell, 3/92

Player Summary	
Fantasy Value	$8 to $12
Card Value	3¢ to 4¢
Will	deliver in clutch
Can't	avoid frequent Ks
Expect	strong throwing arm
Don't Expect	patience at bat

Look up "free swinger" in the dictionary and you'll find a picture of Sammy Sosa. The author of an exaggerated swing that never changes, he resembles the all-or-nothing hitter who either homers or strikes out; he actually contributes much more, however. Though he does whiff four times more often than he walks, Sosa hits lefties for a solid average (he had a .280 average versus lefthanders in 1992), steals successfully 70 percent of the time, and gets a surprising number of clutch hits. In his first three games back from the disabled list last July, he delivered one game-winning hit (an 11th-inning homer) and two game-tying hits. He stayed on the active list only nine days, however, between DL assignments for a broken hand and then a broken ankle. He had a .317 on-base average and a .393 slugging percentage in 1992. Sosa is a smooth center fielder with considerable range and a powerful throwing arm; he has lessened the number of mistakes he makes.

Major League Batting Register

	BA	G	AB	R	H	2B	3B	HR	RBI	SB
89 AL	.257	58	183	27	47	8	0	4	13	7
90 AL	.233	153	532	72	124	26	10	15	70	32
91 AL	.203	116	316	39	64	10	1	10	33	13
92 NL	.260	67	262	41	68	7	2	8	25	15
Life	.234	394	1293	179	303	51	13	37	141	67
3 AVE	.231	112	370	51	85	14	4	11	43	20

BILL SPIERS

Position: Shortstop; second base
Team: Milwaukee Brewers
Born: June 5, 1966 Orangeburg, SC
Height: 6'2" **Weight:** 190 lbs.
Bats: left **Throws:** right
Acquired: First-round pick in 6/87 free-agent draft

Player Summary	
Fantasy Value	$4 to $8
Card Value	3¢ to 4¢
Will	mount comeback
Can't	hit lefthanders
Expect	decent defense
Don't Expect	average of .300

Spiers missed the first 134 games of the 1992 season while recuperating from back surgery. By the time he returned, Pat Listach had not only taken the Milwaukee shortstop job but won the AL Rookie of the Year Award. Spiers's surgery, which repaired a herniated disc in his back, was performed in November 1991—a month after he finished his best year in the majors. When healthy, Spiers is a line-drive hitter with occasional power. He had a .353 on-base percentage and a .438 slugging percentage in 1992. He's a competent but not brilliant shortstop. He strikes out more often than he should but draws his share of walks. He's also good for a dozen steals. In the field, Spiers has good instincts, good hands, and the ability to turn the double play. His errors often come on throws. At 26, he could be a regular again. Where he'll play is the big question, but the 1987 Clemson All-American played all four infield positions as a rookie in 1989.

Major League Batting Register

	BA	G	AB	R	H	2B	3B	HR	RBI	SB
89 AL	.255	114	345	44	88	9	3	4	33	10
90 AL	.242	112	363	44	88	15	3	2	36	11
91 AL	.283	133	414	71	117	13	6	8	54	14
92 AL	.313	12	16	2	5	2	0	0	2	1
Life	.262	371	1138	161	298	39	12	14	125	36
2 AVE	.264	123	389	58	103	14	5	5	45	13

ANDY STANKIEWICZ

Position: Shortstop; second base
Team: New York Yankees
Born: Aug. 10, 1964 Inglewood, CA
Height: 5'9" **Weight:** 165 lbs.
Bats: right **Throws:** right
Acquired: 12th-round pick in 6/86 free-agent draft

Player Summary	
Fantasy Value	$2 to $5
Card Value	8¢ to 15¢
Will	make good contact
Can't	clear the fences
Expect	more basestealing
Don't Expect	lapses on defense

Promoted to the Yankees last year after Mike Gallego and Pat Kelly went down with injuries, Stankiewicz did so well that he never left the lineup. His gutsy playing also made him a fan favorite among a tough Bronx crowd. Capable of playing both second and short, Stankiewicz is a contact hitter who walks almost as often as he strikes out. Though he has some power to the gaps, he is better known for his speed. He led the team in infield hits last year and also showed he's a good bunter. He'll steal more often as he learns the pitchers. Used as a leadoff man early last year, Stankiewicz finished the year as the No. 8 hitter. He sought advice from Randy Velarde and Pat Kelly and added daily entries to his black book immediately after every game. Stankiewicz had a .338 on-base average and a .347 slugging percentage in 1992. Though he has good range and a decent arm at shortstop, he's better at second, his original position. At Triple-A Columbus in 1991, he batted .272 with one homer, 41 RBI, 47 runs, 29 walks, 45 strikeouts, and 29 stolen bases in 372 at bats.

Major League Batting Register

	BA	G	AB	R	H	2B	3B	HR	RBI	SB
92 AL	.268	116	400	52	107	22	2	2	25	9
Life	.268	116	400	52	107	22	2	2	25	9

MIKE STANLEY

Position: Catcher; first base
Team: New York Yankees
Born: June 25, 1963 Fort Lauderdale, FL
Height: 6' **Weight:** 190 lbs.
Bats: right **Throws:** right
Acquired: Signed as a free agent, 1/92

Player Summary	
Fantasy Value	$2 to $5
Card Value	3¢ to 4¢
Will	retain utility role
Can't	avoid strikeouts
Expect	pinch-hitting duty
Don't Expect	world-class defense

Stanley's versatility helps keep him in the majors. He's not only caught but played first, third, and the outfield during his seven-year sojourn in the majors. Though he's not known for his bat, he comes up with big hits on occasion. His third career grand slam, in the first inning last July 9 against the Mariners, led the Yankees to a 7-6 victory. He had eight homers in his 173 at bats—an impressive power ratio. Stanley also draws more than his share of walks. He had a .372 on-base average and a .428 slugging percentage in 1992. Though he usually destroys lefthanders, he was more effective against righties last year. Stanley adds no speed to the lineup. He doesn't bring much defense either, though he did nail 31.7 percent of would-be basestealers last year. Pitchers like to work to him, however; he was behind the plate for Nolan Ryan's seventh no-hitter. Stanley also plays first on occasion.

Major League Batting Register

	BA	G	AB	R	H	2B	3B	HR	RBI	SB
86 AL	.333	15	30	4	10	3	0	1	1	1
87 AL	.273	78	216	34	59	8	1	6	37	3
88 AL	.229	94	249	21	57	8	0	3	27	0
89 AL	.246	67	122	9	30	3	1	1	11	1
90 AL	.249	103	189	21	47	8	1	2	19	1
91 AL	.249	95	181	25	45	13	1	3	25	0
92 AL	.249	68	173	24	43	7	0	8	27	0
Life	.251	520	1160	138	291	50	4	24	147	6
3 AVE	.249	89	181	23	45	9	1	4	24	0

MIKE STANTON

Position: Pitcher
Team: Atlanta Braves
Born: June 2, 1967 Houston, TX
Height: 6'1" **Weight:** 190 lbs.
Bats: left **Throws:** left
Acquired: 13th-round pick in 6/87 free-agent draft

Player Summary
Fantasy Value......................................$4 to $8
Card Value...3¢ to 4¢
Will..................................work as lefty closer
Can't................................always locate plate
Expect ....high strikeout count
Don't Expect ....trouble with lefties

Although the first half of the 1992 season was a struggle for Stanton, his brilliant work during Atlanta's September stretch drive superseded the early struggle. A combination of poor location and ill-timed gopher balls hurt him before the All-Star break. He found that even a good fastball couldn't fool big league batters. When he couldn't throw his slider or curve for strikes, Stanton resorted to a heater that hitters knew was coming. By late August, however, the lefty's control returned, enabling him to resume his red-hot rookie form of 1991. Stanton averaged more than six strikeouts and eight hits per nine innings in 1992; he usually gives up more than three walks per nine innings, but he fell below that mark by the end of the year. Opponents compiled a .247 batting average, a .308 on-base percentage, and a .368 slugging percentage in 1992. His high leg-kick allows baserunners an extra step but he has a good move to first base. Stanton knows how to field and isn't a bad hitter.

Major League Pitching Register
	W	L	ERA	G	S	IP	H	ER	BB	SO
89 NL	0	1	1.50	20	7	24.0	17	4	8	27
90 NL	0	3	18.00	7	2	7.0	16	14	4	7
91 NL	5	5	2.88	74	7	78.0	62	25	21	54
92 NL	5	4	4.10	65	8	63.2	59	29	20	44
Life	10	13	3.75	166	24	172.2	154	72	53	132
2 AVE	5	5	3.43	70	8	71.1	61	27	21	49

TERRY STEINBACH

Position: Catcher
Team: Oakland Athletics
Born: March 2, 1962 New Ulm, MN
Height: 6'1" **Weight:** 195 lbs.
Bats: right **Throws:** right
Acquired: Ninth-round pick in 6/83 free-agent draft

Player Summary
Fantasy Value...............................$8 to $13
Card Value...3¢ to 4¢
Will....................................erase basestealers
Can't ....steal many bases
Expect ....some home run power
Don't Expect ....hits against righties

Steinbach is one of baseball's best all-around catchers. He hits for a solid average, produces some long balls, handles his pitchers well, and shows off a strong throwing arm. A former third baseman who converted to catching in 1986, Steinbach has made the AL All-Star team twice. He is the only player ever to homer in his first regular-season at bat as well as his first All-Star at bat. Steinbach, who hits for a higher average against lefties, is a selective hitter who walks almost as much as he strikes out. He's prone to streaks and did his best work last year after the All-Star break. In 1992, he had a .345 on-base average and a .411 slugging percentage. An aggressive player in all phases, Steinbach doesn't think twice about taking charge of the defense. He calls good games, blocks the plate, prevents wild pitches, and nails more than 40 percent of enemy basestealers.

Major League Batting Register
	BA	G	AB	R	H	2B	3B	HR	RBI	SB
86 AL	.333	6	15	3	5	0	0	2	4	0
87 AL	.284	122	391	66	111	16	3	16	56	1
88 AL	.265	104	351	42	93	19	1	9	51	3
89 AL	.273	130	454	37	124	13	1	7	42	1
90 AL	.251	114	379	32	95	15	2	9	57	0
91 AL	.274	129	456	50	125	31	1	6	67	2
92 AL	.279	128	438	48	122	20	1	12	53	2
Life	.272	733	2484	278	675	114	9	61	330	9
3 AVE	.269	124	424	43	114	22	1	9	59	1

LEE STEVENS

Position: First base
Team: California Angels
Born: July 10, 1967 Kansas City, MO
Height: 6'4" **Weight:** 219 lbs.
Bats: left **Throws:** left
Acquired: First-round pick in 6/86 free-agent draft

Player Summary	
Fantasy Value	$2 to $6
Card Value	3¢ to 4¢
Will	hope for platoon
Can't	hit lefthanders
Expect	occasional power
Don't Expect	strong fielding

After improving for three straight years on the Triple-A level, Stevens convinced the Angels that he might fill the void created by the free agent departure of Wally Joyner. Stevens didn't live up to that promise, however—even after veteran Alvin Davis left in June to pursue his career in Japan. Stevens struggled against southpaws, did only slightly better against righthanders, and wound up in a temporary lefty-righty platoon with Gary Gaetti. Until Stevens learns to reduce his strikeout total, he is not likely to play every day in the majors. Because of his long stroke, he has trouble with inside breaking balls—a weakness AL pitchers exploited. He had a .288 on-base average and a .349 slugging percentage in 1992. He doesn't have much speed and is not good defensively—especially when compared to Joyner. Stevens must prove he's more of a prospect than a suspect. In 1991 at Triple-A Edmonton, he batted .314 with 19 homers and 96 RBI. He batted .293 with 16 homers and 66 RBI at Edmonton in 1990.

Major League Batting Register

	BA	G	AB	R	H	2B	3B	HR	RBI	SB
90 AL	.214	67	248	28	53	10	0	7	32	1
91 AL	.293	18	58	8	17	7	0	0	9	1
92 AL	.221	106	312	25	69	19	0	7	37	1
Life	.225	191	618	61	139	36	0	14	78	3
2 AVE	.218	87	280	27	61	15	0	7	35	1

DAVE STEWART

Position: Pitcher
Team: Toronto Blue Jays
Born: Feb. 19, 1957 Oakland, CA
Height: 6'2" **Weight:** 200 lbs.
Bats: right **Throws:** right
Acquired: Signed as a free agent, 12/92

Player Summary	
Fantasy Value	$8 to $12
Card Value	4¢ to 8¢
Will	keep rotation role
Can't	avoid gopher balls
Expect	control to improve
Don't Expect	return to 20-win form

Stewart wasn't the same pitcher in '92 that he was winning 20 games a year from 1987 to 1990, nor the same as his lousy 1991. He showed he could still be an important member of a rotation if not the leader of the staff. Before a tender right elbow sent him to the disabled list for 24 days in July, he had won four in a row with a 1.40 ERA. When he returned in July, he used a new no-windup delivery designed to place less pressure on the tender elbow. Opponents compiled a .237 batting average, a .315 on-base percentage, and a .393 slugging percentage in '92. He also neutralized righthanded hitters with his repertoire of a fastball, forkball, and curveball.

Major League Pitching Register

	W	L	ERA	G	CG	IP	H	ER	BB	SO
78 NL	0	0	0.00	1	0	2.0	1	0	0	1
81 AL	4	3	2.49	32	0	43.1	40	12	14	29
82 NL	9	8	3.81	45	0	146.1	137	62	49	80
83 NL	5	2	2.96	46	0	76.0	67	25	33	54
83 AL	5	2	2.14	8	2	59.0	50	14	17	24
84 AL	7	14	4.73	32	3	192.1	193	101	87	119
85 AL	0	6	5.42	42	0	81.1	86	49	37	64
85 NL	0	0	6.23	4	0	4.1	5	3	4	2
86 NL	0	0	6.57	8	0	12.1	15	9	4	9
86 AL	9	5	3.74	29	4	149.1	137	62	65	102
87 AL	20	13	3.68	37	8	261.1	224	107	105	205
88 AL	21	12	3.23	37	14	275.2	240	99	110	192
89 AL	21	9	3.32	36	8	257.2	260	95	69	155
90 AL	22	11	2.56	36	11	267.0	226	76	83	166
91 AL	11	11	5.18	35	2	226.0	245	130	105	144
92 AL	12	10	3.66	31	2	199.1	175	81	79	130
Life	146	106	3.69	459	54	2253.1	2101	925	861	1476
3 AVE	15	11	3.73	34	5	231.0	215	96	89	147

DAVE STIEB

Position: Pitcher
Team: Chicago White Sox
Born: July 22, 1957 Santa Ana, CA
Height: 6'1" **Weight:** 195 lbs.
Bats: right **Throws:** right
Acquired: Signed as a free agent, 12/92

Player Summary	
Fantasy Value	$3 to $6
Card Value	3¢ to 4¢
Will	renew comeback bid
Can't	escape injury jinx
Expect	berth in rotation
Don't Expect	bouts of wildness

Stieb was one of baseball's most successful and durable starting pitchers, for the Blue Jays, before he was sidelined with a herniated disc on May 22, 1991. Unable to recapture his former form, he went on the shelf again in August with pain in his elbow. Though he is 35, he is an intense competitor who could stage a comeback with the Pale Hose through sheer determination. A fastball-slider pitcher who also throws a curve and changeup, he has appeared in seven All-Star games, tying Early Wynn's record for an AL pitcher. Stieb has thrown a no-hitter and five one-hitters. When he's right, he strikes out twice as many men as he walks, yields less hits than innings pitched, and keeps the ball from leaving the park.

Major League Pitching Register

	W	L	ERA	G	CG	IP	H	ER	BB	SO
79 AL	8	8	4.31	18	7	129.1	139	62	48	52
80 AL	12	15	3.71	34	14	242.2	232	100	83	108
81 AL	11	10	3.19	25	11	183.2	148	65	61	89
82 AL	17	14	3.25	38	19	288.1	271	104	75	141
83 AL	17	12	3.04	36	14	278.0	223	94	93	187
84 AL	16	8	2.83	35	11	267.0	215	84	88	198
85 AL	14	13	2.48	36	8	265.0	206	73	96	167
86 AL	7	12	4.74	37	1	205.0	239	108	87	127
87 AL	13	9	4.09	33	3	185.0	164	84	87	115
88 AL	16	8	3.04	32	8	207.1	157	70	79	147
89 AL	17	8	3.35	33	3	206.2	164	77	76	101
90 AL	18	6	2.93	33	2	208.2	179	68	64	125
91 AL	4	3	3.17	9	1	59.2	52	21	23	29
92 AL	4	6	5.04	21	1	96.1	98	54	43	45
Life	174	132	3.39	420	103	2822.2	2487	1064	1003	1631
2 AVE	11	6	3.60	27	2	152.2	139	61	54	85

KURT STILLWELL

Position: Second base; shortstop
Team: San Diego Padres
Born: June 4, 1965 Glendale, CA
Height: 5'11" **Weight:** 175 lbs.
Bats: both **Throws:** right
Acquired: Signed as a free agent, 2/92

Player Summary	
Fantasy Value	$2 to $5
Card Value	3¢ to 4¢
Will	fight for job
Can't	hit with power
Expect	lousy fielding
Don't Expect	extra-base hits

Stillwell did not deliver as advertised to the Padres. He didn't come close to duplicating his career batting average, nor did he deliver the defense expected after his shift from shortstop to second base. Though he did his best hitting after returning from a sore back that disabled him in late summer, he contributed little power or speed to the lineup. He had a .274 on-base average and a .298 slugging percentage in 1992. He wound up batting eighth and sharing his position with Tim Teufel, Jeff Gardner, and Craig Shipley. Stillwell is a switch-hitter who usually fares better against lefties. He batted .250 versus lefthanders in 1992. He has to improve his offense to retain a regular job. His defense was supposed to be above-average for league second basemen, but he is not a great defensive player. He makes too many errors and misses too many other balls because of poor range, almost precluding the option of moving him back to shortstop.

Major League Batting Register

	BA	G	AB	R	H	2B	3B	HR	RBI	SB
86 NL	.229	104	279	31	64	6	1	0	26	6
87 NL	.258	131	395	54	102	20	7	4	33	4
88 AL	.251	128	459	63	115	28	5	10	53	6
89 AL	.261	130	463	52	121	20	7	7	54	9
90 AL	.249	144	506	60	126	35	4	3	51	0
91 AL	.265	122	385	44	102	17	1	6	51	3
92 AL	.227	114	379	35	86	15	3	2	24	4
Life	.250	873	2866	339	716	141	28	32	292	32
3 AVE	.247	127	423	46	105	22	3	4	42	2

TODD STOTTLEMYRE

Position: Pitcher
Team: Toronto Blue Jays
Born: May 20, 1965 Sunnyside, WA
Height: 6'3" **Weight:** 190 lbs.
Bats: left **Throws:** right
Acquired: First-round pick in secondary phase of 6/85 free-agent draft

Player Summary	
Fantasy Value	$8 to $12
Card Value	3¢ to 4¢
Will	seek 1991 form
Can't	stop stealers
Expect	gopher balls
Don't Expect	great control

In the wake of his strong 1991 campaign, Stottlemyre was expected to become one of the aces of the Toronto pitching staff. Except for brief flashes of brilliance, however, the promise of '91 evaporated quickly. Stottlemyre, slowed by a tender knee and bad shoulder in June, yielded a hit per inning and struggled with his control. He also allowed 20 home runs. He did manage to break an ignominious streak; he had thrown no shutouts in his first 104 career starts (worst among active pitchers). He survives by changing speeds on his fastball, slider, and curve. Opponents in 1992 compiled a .262 batting average, a .329 on-base percentage, and a .398 slugging percentage. He pitched in four games in the 1992 World Series, all in relief roles. The son of Mets pitching coach Mel Stottlemyre, Todd is much more effective against righthanded batters. Righties batted .247 against him, and lefthanders batted .282. His biggest weakness is an inability to stop basestealers. His fielding also needs work.

Major League Pitching Register

	W	L	ERA	G	CG	IP	H	ER	BB	SO
88 AL	4	8	5.69	28	0	98.0	109	62	46	67
89 AL	7	7	3.88	27	0	127.2	137	55	44	63
90 AL	13	17	4.34	33	4	203.0	214	98	69	115
91 AL	15	8	3.78	34	1	219.0	194	92	75	116
92 AL	12	11	4.50	28	6	174.0	175	87	63	98
Life	51	51	4.32	150	11	821.2	829	394	297	459
3 AVE	13	12	4.18	32	4	199.0	194	92	69	110

DARRYL STRAWBERRY

Position: Outfield
Team: Los Angeles Dodgers
Born: March 12, 1962 Los Angeles, CA
Height: 6'6" **Weight:** 200 lbs.
Bats: left **Throws:** left
Acquired: Signed as a free agent, 11/90

Player Summary	
Fantasy Value	$22 to $30
Card Value	8¢ to 16¢
Will	go for the downs
Can't	boost his average
Expect	success against lefties
Don't Expect	great glove

If experience is the best teacher, Strawberry won't make any more predictions. After boasting last spring that he'd hit 45 home runs, he spent most of the season on the sidelines, recuperating from a herniated disc in his back, which eventually required surgery. He had a .322 on-base average and a .385 slugging percentage in 1992. Playing in just 43 games, he hit five homers—26 short of the Los Angeles team record; at age 31, however, a healthy Strawberry could challenge that mark, especially in an expansion year. He's hit at least 37 homers three times. He could boost his average by using his speed but prefers to swing for the fences—a game plan that produces many strikeouts. He does walk often, however. The former 30-30 man doesn't steal much anymore. His arm is strong enough for right, but he's not a good outfielder.

Major League Batting Register

	BA	G	AB	R	H	2B	3B	HR	RBI	SB
83 NL	.257	122	420	63	108	15	7	26	74	19
84 NL	.251	147	522	75	131	27	4	26	97	27
85 NL	.277	111	393	78	109	15	4	29	79	26
86 NL	.259	136	475	76	123	27	5	27	93	28
87 NL	.284	154	532	108	151	32	5	39	104	36
88 NL	.269	153	543	101	146	27	3	39	101	29
89 NL	.225	134	476	69	107	26	1	29	77	11
90 NL	.277	152	542	92	150	18	1	37	108	15
91 NL	.265	139	505	86	134	22	4	28	99	10
92 NL	.237	43	156	20	37	8	0	5	25	3
Life	.262	1291	4564	768	1196	217	34	285	857	204
3 AVE	.267	111	401	66	107	16	2	23	77	9

FRANKLIN STUBBS

Position: First base; outfield
Team: Milwaukee Brewers
Born: Oct. 21, 1960 Laurinburg, NC
Height: 6'2" **Weight:** 209 lbs.
Bats: left **Throws:** left
Acquired: Signed as a free agent, 12/90

Player Summary

Fantasy Value	$4 to $8
Card Value	3¢ to 4¢
Will	seek old power
Can't	make contact
Expect	fight for job
Don't Expect	good defense

Stubbs continues to be long on potential and short on results. He stumbled through his second straight poor season with the Brewers last summer. If it's too late to teach an old dog new tricks, he could be through at 32. Stubbs strikes out three times more than he walks, gets caught almost as often as he steals, and doesn't deliver the long ball as often as he should. In addition, he's a defensive liability at both first base and the outfield (he should be a DH). His job was saved last summer solely because he was the only legitimate lefthanded power-hitter in the lineup. For the last two years, however, he performed so poorly against righthanded pitchers that it didn't matter which way he batted. In 1992, he batted .224 against righthanders and .256 versus lefties; he had a .297 on-base average and a .368 slugging percentage.

Major League Batting Register

	BA	G	AB	R	H	2B	3B	HR	RBI	SB
84 NL	.194	87	217	22	42	2	3	8	17	2
85 NL	.222	10	9	0	2	0	0	0	2	0
86 NL	.226	132	420	55	95	11	1	23	58	7
87 NL	.233	129	386	48	90	16	3	16	52	8
88 NL	.223	115	242	30	54	13	0	8	34	11
89 NL	.291	69	103	11	30	6	0	4	15	3
90 NL	.261	146	448	59	117	23	2	23	71	19
91 NL	.213	103	362	48	77	16	2	11	38	11
92 NL	.229	92	288	37	66	11	1	9	42	11
Life	.232	883	2475	310	573	98	12	102	329	74
3 AVE	.237	114	366	48	87	17	2	14	50	14

B.J. SURHOFF

Position: Catcher; third base
Team: Milwaukee Brewers
Born: Aug. 4, 1964 Bronx, NY
Height: 6'1" **Weight:** 200 lbs.
Bats: left **Throws:** right
Acquired: First-round pick in 6/85 free-agent draft

Player Summary

Fantasy Value	$6 to $10
Card Value	3¢ to 4¢
Will	deliver in clutch
Can't	reach 10 homers
Expect	slap-and-run style
Don't Expect	throwing problems

Surhoff is different than most catchers. A contact hitter with speed, he walks as much as he strikes out, steals a dozen bases a year, and fills in at first base, third base, and the outfield. A hot second-half hitter in each of the last two years, he has adopted the speed merchant technique of hitting the ball on the ground and running all-out. That approach helped his average but hurt his power production. He had a .314 on-base average and a .321 slugging percentage in 1992. He had a .270 batting average against lefties last summer and a .246 average versus righthanders. Surhoff worked hard to improve his throwing last year and succeeded handsomely, erasing more than 40 percent of would-be base-stealers. Because he's such an intelligent player, pitchers like to work with him. He blocks wild pitches and incoming runners and handles the staff well. The former College Player of the Year from North Carolina was a 1984 Olympian.

Major League Batting Register

	BA	G	AB	R	H	2B	3B	HR	RBI	SB
87 AL	.299	115	395	50	118	22	3	7	68	11
88 AL	.245	139	493	47	121	21	0	5	38	21
89 AL	.248	126	436	42	108	17	4	5	55	14
90 AL	.276	135	474	55	131	21	4	6	59	18
91 AL	.289	143	505	57	146	19	4	5	68	5
92 AL	.252	139	480	63	121	19	1	4	62	14
Life	.268	797	2783	314	745	119	16	32	350	83
3 AVE	.273	139	486	58	133	20	3	5	63	12

RICK SUTCLIFFE

Position: Pitcher
Team: Baltimore Orioles
Born: June 21, 1956 Independence, MO
Height: 6'7" **Weight:** 215 lbs.
Bats: left **Throws:** right
Acquired: Signed as free agent, 12/91

Player Summary	
Fantasy Value	$4 to $9
Card Value	3¢ to 4¢
Will	rely on location
Can't	throw old heater
Expect	respectable job
Don't Expect	another Cy Young

After posting a 4.41 ERA over two seasons for the 1990 and '91 Cubs, Sutcliffe knew he'd have to prove his shoulder sound to the Orioles. He wasted little time justifying the judgment of manager Johnny Oates, who had caught Sutcliffe's first big league win in 1979. Oates knew Sutcliffe could help Ben McDonald and Mike Mussina and also knew Sutcliffe could become a rotation mainstay himself. Except for an 0-5 streak that ended Aug. 4, Sutcliffe succeeded. He blanked Cleveland 2-0 Opening Day, then enjoyed his best month with a 4-0 record and 2.57 ERA in August. Sutcliffe changes speeds and pinpoints the location of his curve and his slider—his primary pitches. He also throws a fastball and a changeup.

Major League Pitching Register

	W	L	ERA	G	CG	IP	H	ER	BB	SO
76 NL	0	0	0.00	1	0	5.0	2	0	1	3
78 NL	0	0	0.00	2	0	1.2	2	0	1	0
79 NL	17	10	3.46	39	5	242.0	217	93	97	117
80 NL	3	9	5.56	42	1	110.0	122	68	55	59
81 NL	2	2	4.02	14	0	47.0	41	21	20	16
82 AL	14	8	2.96	34	6	216.0	174	71	98	142
83 AL	17	11	4.29	36	10	243.1	251	116	102	160
84 AL	4	5	5.15	15	2	94.1	111	54	46	58
84 NL	16	1	2.69	20	7	150.1	123	45	39	155
85 NL	8	8	3.18	20	6	130.0	119	46	44	102
86 NL	5	14	4.64	28	4	176.2	166	91	96	122
87 NL	18	10	3.68	34	6	237.1	223	97	106	174
88 NL	13	14	3.86	32	12	226.0	232	97	70	144
89 NL	16	11	3.66	35	5	229.0	202	93	69	153
90 NL	0	2	5.91	5	0	21.1	25	14	12	7
91 NL	6	5	4.10	19	0	96.2	96	44	45	52
92 AL	16	15	4.47	36	5	237.1	251	118	74	109
Life	155	125	3.90	412	69	2464.0	2357	1068	975	1573
2 AVE	11	10	4.37	28	3	167.2	174	81	60	81

RUSS SWAN

Position: Pitcher
Team: Seattle Mariners
Born: Jan. 3, 1964 Fremont, CA
Height: 6'4" **Weight:** 215 lbs.
Bats: left **Throws:** left
Acquired: Traded from Giants for Gary Eave, 5/90

Player Summary	
Fantasy Value	$2 to $4
Card Value	3¢ to 4¢
Will	need strong comeback
Can't	thwart basestealers
Expect	problems with control
Don't Expect	low ERA

Even though he dominated lefthanded batters, Swan was hardly graceful in his role as Seattle's southpaw closer last summer. He walked as many men as he fanned, yielded a hit per inning, and threw too many gopher balls. That combination spelled trouble, as he yielded nearly five earned runs per game. The season was especially disappointing because it came in the wake of Swan's fine 1991 work as a set-up man. A sinker-and-slider pitcher who also throws a split-fingered fastball, he gets ground-ball outs when all his pitches are working. He yields walks and homers when they're not. Opponents in 1992 notched a .262 batting average, a .338 on-base percentage, and a .398 slugging average. He has trouble holding runners on—a fatal flaw for a reliever. Swan acquits himself well as a fielder. His pitching needs considerable improvement if he hopes to stay in the majors, even in a set-up role. The fact that he's lefthanded helps his cause.

Major League Pitching Register

	W	L	ERA	G	S	IP	H	ER	BB	SO
89 NL	0	2	10.80	2	0	6.2	11	8	4	2
90 NL	0	1	3.86	2	0	2.1	6	1	4	1
90 AL	2	3	3.64	11	0	47.0	42	19	18	15
91 AL	6	2	3.43	63	2	78.2	81	30	28	33
92 AL	3	10	4.74	55	9	104.1	104	55	45	45
Life	11	18	4.26	133	11	239.0	244	113	99	96
3 AVE	3	4	4.18	40	4	61.1	64	29	26	26

BILL SWIFT

Position: Pitcher
Team: San Francisco Giants
Born: Oct. 27, 1961 South Portland, ME
Height: 6' **Weight:** 180 lbs.
Bats: right **Throws:** right
Acquired: Traded from Mariners with Mike Jackson and Dave Burba for Kevin Mitchell and Mike Remlinger, 12/91

Player Summary	
Fantasy Value	$8 to $16
Card Value	3¢ to 4¢
Will	bank on sharp sinker
Can't	worry about shoulder
Expect	ground-ball outs
Don't Expect	return to rotation

After making 71 relief appearances for the 1991 Mariners, Swift was the Opening Day starter for the 1992 Giants. He won six straight—two of them shutouts—before missing a month with shoulder problems. He later went on the shelf again after an overdeveloped muscle pinched an artery in his shoulder. Unable to pitch for prolonged periods, Swift returned as a reliever in September. He was also told to reduce his rigorous weight-lifting regimen. Swift had no trouble as a college starter at the University of Maine, where he had a 26-7 career record before joining the 1984 U.S. Olympic Team. A sinker-slider pitcher who gets ground balls, he is a control pitcher. Opponents compiled a .239 batting average, a .292 on-base percentage, and a .314 slugging percentage in 1992. He keeps the ball in the park. Swift has a swift pickoff move and has no trouble fielding his position.

GREG SWINDELL

Position: Pitcher
Team: Houston Astros
Born: Jan. 2, 1965 Fort Worth, TX
Height: 6'3" **Weight:** 225 lbs.
Bats: both **Throws:** left
Acquired: Signed as a free agent, 12/92

Player Summary	
Fantasy Value	$12 to $18
Card Value	3¢ to 4¢
Will	become big winner
Can't	think about elbow
Expect	consistent performance
Don't Expect	control to falter

Swindell rarely has to worry about baserunners, because he yields less than a hit per inning and two walks per nine innings while averaging four strikeouts for every walk. Given the support of a strong ballclub at Cincinnati last summer, he posted the best ERA of his seven-year career. Swindell's 6-0 win at Philadelphia Aug. 18 was his third shutout and fifth complete game. His success wasn't surprising, considering that Swindell had a 43-8 record at the University of Texas, made the All-America team three times, and was drafted by Cleveland in the first round of the amateur draft. He pitched only three games in the minors before making the majors in 1986. Swindell has excellent command of his fastball, slider, changeup, and curve. Opponents in 1992 compiled a .260 batting average, a .295 on-base percentage, and a .365 slugging percentage. He is a good fielder who keeps runners close.

Major League Pitching Register

	W	L	ERA	G	CG	IP	H	ER	BB	SO
85 AL	6	10	4.77	23	0	120.2	131	64	48	55
86 AL	2	9	5.46	29	1	115.1	148	70	55	55
88 AL	8	12	4.59	38	6	174.2	199	89	65	47
89 AL	7	3	4.43	17	0	130.0	140	64	38	45
90 AL	6	4	2.39	55	0	128.0	135	34	21	42
91 AL	1	2	1.99	71	0	90.1	74	20	26	48
92 NL	10	4	2.08	30	3	164.2	144	38	43	77
Life	40	44	3.69	283	10	923.2	971	379	296	369
3 AVE	6	3	2.16	52	1	127.1	118	31	30	56

Major League Pitching Register

	W	L	ERA	G	CG	IP	H	ER	BB	SO
86 AL	5	2	4.23	9	1	61.2	57	29	15	46
87 AL	3	8	5.10	16	4	102.1	112	58	37	97
88 AL	18	14	3.20	33	12	242.0	234	86	45	180
89 AL	13	6	3.37	28	5	184.1	170	69	51	129
90 AL	12	9	4.40	34	3	214.2	245	105	47	135
91 AL	9	16	3.48	33	7	238.0	241	92	31	169
92 NL	12	8	2.70	31	5	213.2	210	64	41	138
Life	72	63	3.60	184	37	1256.2	1269	503	267	894
3 AVE	11	11	3.53	33	5	222.1	232	87	40	147

JEFF TACKETT

Position: Catcher
Team: Baltimore Orioles
Born: Dec. 1, 1965 Fresno, CA
Height: 6'2" **Weight:** 206 lbs.
Bats: right **Throws:** right
Acquired: Second-round pick in 6/84 free-agent draft

Player Summary	
Fantasy Value	$2 to $5
Card Value	5¢ to 10¢
Will	show strong arm
Can't	hit for average
Expect	terrific defense
Don't Expect	trouble against lefties

During an eight-year tenure in the minors, Tackett built a reputation as a hard-working young receiver with a strong glove (he led several leagues in putouts, assists, chances, and double plays) but a weak bat. He also earned renown as a practical joker who enjoys hard rock and slam dancing. In two of his three seasons in the Triple-A International League, Tackett finished first in the loop in gunning down would-be basestealers. He also caught Baltimore hurlers Mike Mussina and Ben McDonald on the farm. Promoted to the Orioles as understudy to Chris Hoiles last summer, Tackett erased more than one-third of the runners who tried to steal against him. Tackett provided unexpected punch with five homers in his first 51 at bats (after hitting none in his first five minor league seasons). He then went homerless the rest of the season. He had a .307 on-base average and a .380 slugging percentage last year. Tackett also had a .288 batting average versus left-handers. At Rochester in '91, he batted .236 with six homers and 50 RBI.

Major League Batting Register

	BA	G	AB	R	H	2B	3B	HR	RBI	SB
91 AL	.125	6	8	1	1	0	0	0	0	0
92 AL	.240	66	179	21	43	8	1	5	24	0
Life	.235	72	187	22	44	8	1	5	24	0

FRANK TANANA

Position: Pitcher
Team: New York Mets
Born: July 3, 1953 Detroit, MI
Height: 6'3" **Weight:** 195 lbs.
Bats: left **Throws:** left
Acquired: Signed as a free agent, 12/92

Player Summary	
Fantasy Value	$3 to $6
Card Value	3¢ to 4¢
Will	win with finesse
Can't	blaze ball by hitters
Expect	frequent gopher balls
Don't Expect	high K totals

Like the TV rabbit, Tanana keeps going and going and going. . . . Since he no longer throws hard, he succeeds through a combination of guile and experience. Tanana changes speeds deftly on his fastball and his curveball while keeping batters guessing when they might see his third pitch—a cross between a screwball and changeup. Though Tanana's control has been off the last couple of years, he's one of the league's best lefties when he's on. He stifles lefthanded hitters, holds runners well, and fields adeptly. Tanana's biggest problem recently has been giving up gophers.

Major League Pitching Register

	W	L	ERA	G	CG	IP	H	ER	BB	SO
73 AL	2	2	3.08	4	2	26.1	20	9	8	22
74 AL	14	19	3.12	39	12	268.2	262	93	77	180
75 AL	16	9	2.62	34	16	257.1	211	75	73	269
76 AL	19	10	2.43	34	23	288.1	212	78	73	261
77 AL	15	9	2.54	31	20	241.1	201	68	61	205
78 AL	18	12	3.65	33	10	239.0	239	97	60	137
79 AL	7	5	3.89	18	2	90.1	93	39	25	46
80 AL	11	12	4.15	32	7	204.0	223	94	45	113
81 AL	4	10	4.01	24	5	141.1	142	63	43	78
82 AL	7	18	4.21	30	7	194.1	199	91	55	87
83 AL	7	9	3.16	29	3	159.1	144	56	49	108
84 AL	15	15	3.25	35	9	246.1	234	89	81	141
85 AL	12	14	4.27	33	4	215.0	220	102	57	159
86 AL	12	9	4.16	32	3	188.1	196	87	65	119
87 AL	15	10	3.91	34	5	218.2	216	95	56	146
88 AL	14	11	4.21	32	2	203.0	213	95	64	127
89 AL	10	14	3.58	33	6	223.2	227	89	74	147
90 AL	9	8	5.31	34	1	176.1	190	104	66	114
91 AL	13	12	3.77	33	3	217.1	217	91	78	107
92 AL	13	11	4.39	32	3	186.2	188	91	90	91
Life	233	219	3.63	606	143	3985.2	3847	1606	1200	2657
3 AVE	12	10	4.44	33	2	193.1	198	95	78	104

KEVIN TAPANI

Position: Pitcher
Team: Minnesota Twins
Born: Feb. 18, 1964 Des Moines, IA
Height: 6′ **Weight:** 180 lbs.
Bats: right **Throws:** right
Acquired: Traded from Mets with David West, Jack Savage, Rick Aguilera, and Tim Drummond for Loy McBride and Frank Viola, 7/89

Player Summary

Fantasy Value	$12 to $18
Card Value	3¢ to 4¢
Will	show good control
Can't	avoid gophers
Expect	results against righties
Don't Expect	long losing streaks

After leading the Twins with an average of over seven innings per start in 1991, Tapani had trouble getting past the sixth early last season. After solving the stamina problem, the pitcher's performance improved. He went 9-1 with a 3.39 ERA in 13 starts before losing to Cleveland July 21—his first defeat since May 6. A control pitcher, Tapani throws a fastball, curve, changeup, and forkball. The club's No. 1 starter after the free agent defection of Jack Morris, Tapani did not pitch as effectively as he had in '91 but still managed to surpass the 15-win plateau. Opponents compiled a .269 batting average, a .309 on-base percentage, and a .405 slugging percentage in 1992. He threw too many gopher balls (he allowed 17 homers) and failed to perform as well as expected against righthanded hitters. Righties batted .259 against him last year. Although he's a fine fielder, Tapani sometimes has trouble holding runners on.

Major League Pitching Register

	W	L	ERA	G	CG	IP	H	ER	BB	SO
89 NL	0	0	3.68	3	0	7.1	5	3	4	2
89 AL	2	2	3.86	5	0	32.2	34	14	8	21
90 AL	12	8	4.07	28	1	159.1	164	72	29	101
91 AL	16	9	2.99	34	4	244.0	225	81	40	135
92 AL	16	11	3.97	34	4	220.0	226	97	48	138
Life	46	30	3.62	104	9	663.1	654	267	129	397
3 AVE	15	9	3.61	32	3	208.0	205	83	39	125

DANNY TARTABULL

Position: Outfield
Team: New York Yankees
Born: Oct. 30, 1962 San Juan, Puerto Rico
Height: 6′1″ **Weight:** 205 lbs.
Bats: right **Throws:** right
Acquired: Signed as a free agent, 1/92

Player Summary

Fantasy Value	$32 to $40
Card Value	5¢ to 12¢
Will	produce great power
Can't	avoid strikeouts
Expect	patience at plate
Don't Expect	polished defense

Injuries have cost Tartabull an average of 44 games missed over the last three seasons. In 1992, his first year with the Yankees, he was slowed by wrist and hamstring problems early and lower-back problems later. Once he got going, however, Tartabull terrorized AL pitchers. In his best offensive explosion, he went 5-for-5 with two homers and a career-best 9 RBI—best by a Yankee in 56 years—at Baltimore Sept. 8. He had a .409 on-base average and a .489 slugging percentage in 1992. The son of former big leaguer Jose Tartabull, Danny has topped 100 RBI three times. Though he strikes out frequently, he is a selective hitter who walks almost as often as he fans. He hits about 40 points higher against lefties than righties. Tartabull steals a half-dozen bases a year but is not noted for his speed or defense. He's a mediocre right fielder.

Major League Batting Register

	BA	G	AB	R	H	2B	3B	HR	RBI	SB
84 AL	.300	10	20	3	6	1	0	2	7	0
85 AL	.328	19	61	8	20	7	1	1	7	1
86 AL	.270	137	511	76	138	25	6	25	96	4
87 AL	.309	158	582	95	180	27	3	34	101	9
88 AL	.274	146	507	80	139	38	3	26	102	8
89 AL	.268	133	441	54	118	22	0	18	62	4
90 AL	.268	88	313	41	84	19	0	15	60	1
91 AL	.316	132	484	78	153	35	3	31	100	6
92 AL	.266	123	421	72	112	19	0	25	85	2
Life	.284	946	3340	507	950	193	16	177	620	35
3 AVE	.287	114	406	64	116	24	1	24	82	3

EDDIE TAUBENSEE

Position: Catcher
Team: Houston Astros
Born: Oct. 31, 1968 Beeville, TX
Height: 6'4" **Weight:** 205 lbs.
Bats: left **Throws:** right
Acquired: Traded from Indians with Willie Blair for Kenny Lofton and Dave Rohde, 12/91

Player Summary

Fantasy Value	$2 to $5
Card Value	3¢ to 4¢
Will	show some pop
Can't	add speed to lineup
Expect	strong throwing arm
Don't Expect	luck against lefties

Catchers who can both hit and throw are rare finds. Lefty-hitting catchers who do both are on the list of endangered species. Though Houston sacrificed Kenny Lofton to get Taubensee, the Astros were happy they had him last summer. After hitting .162 in his first stint with the team, Taubensee returned to Triple-A Tucson for a refresher course. He batted .338 with one homer, 10 RBI, eight walks, and 17 strikeouts in 74 at bats there. More relaxed when he came back, the catcher went 14-for-31 his first three weeks back. Used mainly in a lefty-righty platoon with Scott Servais, Taubensee enjoyed a strong finish. He showed some power at the plate, notching a .299 on-base average and a .323 slugging percentage. He also displayed a powerful throwing arm during his tenure with the team, gunning down 34.3 percent of would-be basestealers. He's a fine defensive receiver. In 1991 at Triple-A Colorado Springs, he batted .310 with 13 homers, 39 RBI, and 23 doubles in 287 at bats. He batted .259 with 16 homers and 62 RBI at Class-A Cedar Rapids in 1990.

Major League Batting Register

	BA	G	AB	R	H	2B	3B	HR	RBI	SB
91 AL	.242	26	66	5	16	2	1	0	8	0
92 NL	.222	104	297	23	66	15	0	5	28	2
Life	.226	130	363	28	82	17	1	5	36	2

WALT TERRELL

Position: Pitcher
Team: Detroit Tigers
Born: May 11, 1958 Jeffersonville, IN
Height: 6'1" **Weight:** 215 lbs.
Bats: right **Throws:** right
Acquired: Signed as free agent, 7/90

Player Summary

Fantasy Value	$2 to $4
Card Value	3¢ to 4¢
Will	need good sinkerball
Can't	prevent gopher balls
Expect	plenty of baserunners
Don't Expect	ERA to deflate

Terrell had so much trouble with the home run ball last summer that he lost his job in Detroit's starting rotation. He allowed 14 home runs in 1992. Though used sparingly after his switch to the bullpen, he was much more effective in that role. His sinker didn't always sink when he started, and Terrell faced an endless parade of baserunners. He yields too many hits and walks to pitch in a hitters' ballpark, such as Tiger Stadium. Terrell also has a tough time with righthanded hitters, who shouldn't find him such easy pickings. They batted .308 against him last year. Overall, opponents compiled a .298 batting average, a .354 on-base percentage, and a .431 slugging percentage in 1992. Terrell sometimes sabotages his own efforts with sloppy fielding and failing to hold baserunners.

Major League Pitching Register

	W	L	ERA	G	CG	IP	H	ER	BB	SO
82 NL	0	3	3.43	3	0	21.0	22	8	14	8
83 NL	8	8	3.57	21	4	133.2	123	53	55	59
84 NL	11	12	3.52	33	3	215.0	232	84	80	114
85 AL	15	10	3.85	34	5	229.0	221	98	95	130
86 AL	15	12	4.56	34	9	217.1	199	110	98	93
87 AL	17	10	4.05	35	10	244.2	254	110	94	143
88 AL	7	16	3.97	29	11	206.1	199	91	78	84
89 NL	5	13	4.01	19	4	123.1	134	55	26	63
89 AL	6	5	5.20	13	1	83.0	102	48	24	30
90 NL	2	7	5.88	16	0	82.2	98	54	33	34
90 AL	6	4	4.54	13	0	75.1	86	38	24	30
91 AL	12	14	4.24	35	8	218.2	257	103	79	80
92 AL	7	10	5.20	36	1	136.2	163	79	48	61
Life	111	124	4.22	321	56	1986.2	2090	931	748	929
3 AVE	9	12	4.80	33	3	170.2	201	91	61	68

MICKEY TETTLETON

Position: Catcher
Team: Detroit Tigers
Born: Sept. 16, 1960 Oklahoma, OK
Height: 6'2" **Weight:** 214 lbs.
Bats: both **Throws:** right
Acquired: Traded from Orioles for Jeff Robinson, 1/91

Player Summary	
Fantasy Value	$23 to $28
Card Value	3¢ to 4¢
Will	produce power
Can't	steal bases
Expect	frequent walks
Don't Expect	high average

Tettleton produces more power than any other catcher in the major leagues. In three of the last four seasons, he's topped 25 homers—some of them memorable clouts that cleared the roof at Tiger Stadium. He has a high strikeout total, high power production, and low batting average. The switch-hitting receiver is a selective hitter who draws more than 100 walks a year—giving him a high on-base percentage. In 1992, he had a .379 on-base average and a .469 slugging percentage. Tettleton is a slightly better hitter against lefties, but he's a horrible runner against everyone (18 steals in nine years). As a catcher, he is a good game-caller who handles a staff well, blocks most of the balls in the dirt, and has a solid throwing arm (he nails 35 percent of would-be basestealers). As a plate-blocker, he's no Mike Scioscia.

Major League Batting Register

	BA	G	AB	R	H	2B	3B	HR	RBI	SB
84 AL	.263	33	76	10	20	2	1	1	5	0
85 AL	.251	78	211	23	53	12	0	3	15	2
86 AL	.204	90	211	26	43	9	0	10	35	7
87 AL	.194	82	211	19	41	3	0	8	26	1
88 AL	.261	86	283	31	74	11	1	11	37	0
89 AL	.258	117	411	72	106	21	2	26	65	3
90 AL	.223	135	444	68	99	21	2	15	51	2
91 AL	.263	154	501	85	132	17	2	31	89	3
92 AL	.238	157	525	82	125	25	0	32	83	0
Life	.241	932	2873	416	693	121	8	137	406	18
3 AVE	.242	149	490	78	119	21	1	26	74	2

TIM TEUFEL

Position: Infield
Team: San Diego Padres
Born: July 7, 1958 Greenwich, CT
Height: 6' **Weight:** 175 lbs.
Bats: right **Throws:** right
Acquired: Traded from Mets for Garry Templeton, 5/91

Player Summary	
Fantasy Value	$2 to $4
Card Value	3¢ to 4¢
Will	play every base
Can't	hit righthanders
Expect	occasional power
Don't Expect	dynamite defense

For the second straight season in 1992, Teufel hit well below his career batting average. He was still valuable to the Padres, however, because he played three infield positions and delivered several timely homers. Because he shows patience at the plate, Teufel walks almost as often as he strikes out. He makes good contact even though he has a tendency to overswing—especially when he sees a fastball he likes. Teufel thrives against lefthanded pitching and spent much of the 1992 season as part of a righty-lefty platoon with Kurt Stillwell, who also played second base for San Diego. Teufel has a little speed (nine steals in '91) but lacks defensive skills—especially range and arm strength. Because of his power, he often pinch-hits. Teufel's playing time will drop unless he gets back on track.

Major League Batting Register

	BA	G	AB	R	H	2B	3B	HR	RBI	SB
83 AL	.308	21	78	11	24	7	1	3	6	0
84 AL	.262	157	568	76	149	30	3	14	61	1
85 AL	.260	138	434	58	113	24	3	10	50	4
86 NL	.247	93	279	35	69	20	1	4	31	1
87 NL	.308	97	299	55	92	29	0	14	61	3
88 NL	.234	90	273	35	64	20	0	4	31	0
89 NL	.256	83	219	27	56	7	2	2	15	1
90 NL	.246	80	175	28	43	11	0	10	24	0
91 NL	.217	117	341	41	74	16	0	12	44	9
92 NL	.224	101	246	23	55	10	0	6	25	2
Life	.254	977	2912	389	739	174	10	79	348	21
3 AVE	.226	99	254	31	57	12	0	9	31	4

BOB TEWKSBURY

Position: Pitcher
Team: St. Louis Cardinals
Born: Nov. 30, 1960 Concord, NH
Height: 6'4" **Weight:** 200 lbs.
Bats: right **Throws:** right
Acquired: Signed as a free agent, 12/88

Player Summary

Fantasy Value	$16 to $22
Card Value	3¢ to 4¢
Will	always throw strikes
Can't	get by with fastball
Expect	15 victories
Don't Expect	high K total

Tewksbury doesn't throw hard but he does throw strikes. A fast worker who has better control than any other big league starter, he relies on location, movement, and changes of speed rather than velocity. His fastball hits 86 mph on a good day and his slider, curve, and change are only average. An artist whose work has been featured in *Sports Illustrated,* Tewksbury is also an artist when it comes to painting the corners. Because batters know he can hit the corners at any count, he gets lots of outs on fastballs down the middle. After making the NL All-Stars for the first time in 1992, he became a Cy Young Award candidate by winning 16 of his 21 decisions and leading the league in ERA all season. He almost finished with more wins than walks. Opponents compiled a .248 batting average, a .265 on-base average, and a .353 slugging percentage. Tewksbury can hit, field, and keep baserunners close.

Major League Pitching Register

	W	L	ERA	G	CG	IP	H	ER	BB	SO
86 AL	9	5	3.31	23	2	130.1	144	48	31	49
87 AL	1	4	6.75	8	0	33.1	47	25	7	12
87 NL	0	4	6.50	7	0	18.0	32	13	13	10
88 NL	0	0	8.10	1	0	3.1	6	3	2	1
89 NL	1	0	3.30	7	1	30.0	25	11	10	17
90 NL	10	9	3.47	28	3	145.1	151	56	15	50
91 NL	11	12	3.25	30	3	191.0	206	69	38	75
92 NL	16	5	2.16	33	5	233.0	217	56	20	91
Life	48	39	3.22	137	14	784.1	828	281	136	305
3 AVE	12	9	2.86	30	4	190.0	191	60	24	72

BOBBY THIGPEN

Position: Pitcher
Team: Chicago White Sox
Born: July 17, 1963 Tallahassee, FL
Height: 6'3" **Weight:** 195 lbs.
Bats: right **Throws:** right
Acquired: Fourth-round pick in 6/85 free-agent draft

Player Summary

Fantasy Value	$20 to $28
Card Value	3¢ to 4¢
Will	seek old closer role
Can't	find the strike zone
Expect	lots of baserunners
Don't Expect	return to 1990 form

In 1992, for the second year in a row, Thigpen's statistics fell sharply from the previous season. Two years after saving a record 57 games and posting a career-best 1.83 ERA, he pitched so poorly that he lost his job as White Sox closer. He incurred the wrath of the Comiskey Park faithful by blowing seven of his first 26 save opportunities. The victim of severe control problems, Thigpen posted only one save in the month between the All-Star Game and Aug. 14. On Sept. 20, however, he did manage to become the youngest pitcher to reach 200 career saves when he got the last four outs in a 10-8 game. He is a fastball-slider pitcher who mixes in a changeup and a curve. Opponents in 1992 compiled a .275 batting average, a .375 on-base average, and a .374 slugging percentage. Thigpen thrives on a heavy workload. He didn't get it—or deserve it—in '92, when his string of four straight 60-game seasons ended.

Major League Pitching Register

	W	L	ERA	G	S	IP	H	ER	BB	SO
86 AL	2	0	1.77	20	7	35.2	26	7	12	20
87 AL	7	5	2.73	51	16	89.0	86	27	24	52
88 AL	5	8	3.30	68	34	90.0	96	33	33	62
89 AL	2	6	3.76	61	34	79.0	62	33	40	47
90 AL	4	6	1.83	77	57	88.2	60	18	32	70
91 AL	7	5	3.49	67	30	69.2	63	27	38	47
92 AL	1	3	4.75	55	22	55.0	58	29	33	45
Life	28	33	3.09	399	200	507.0	451	174	212	343
3 AVE	4	5	3.12	66	36	71.1	60	25	34	54

FRANK THOMAS

Position: First base
Team: Chicago White Sox
Born: May 27, 1968 Columbus, GA
Height: 6'5" **Weight:** 240 lbs.
Bats: right **Throws:** right
Acquired: First-round pick in 6/89 free-agent draft

Player Summary	
Fantasy Value	$44 to $52
Card Value	10¢ to 30¢
Will	exceed 100 RBI
Can't	steal too much
Expect	MVP credentials
Don't Expect	dazzling defense

It's hard to believe Thomas is only 24. In 1992, his second full season in the majors, he became the eighth player in big league history to produce a .300 average, 20 homers, 100 RBI, and 100 walks in consecutive seasons. He also had his first five-hit game and a 19-game hitting streak while becoming the first White Sox player with consecutive 100-RBI seasons since Minnie Minoso in 1953 and '54. Because Thomas is a student of the strike zone who seldom swings at a bad pitch, he walks more than he fans. The former Auburn All-American wreaked havoc on lefthanded pitching all year. He had a .357 batting average versus lefties and "only" a .312 average against righthanders. He also had a league-leading .439 on-base average and a .536 slugging percentage. He teamed with George Bell to become the third tandem to notch 20 homers and 100 RBI in White Sox history. Thomas even stole a half-dozen bases. His lone weakness is defense; only Mo Vaughn made more errors among AL first basemen last year.

Major League Batting Register

	BA	G	AB	R	H	2B	3B	HR	RBI	SB
90 AL	.330	60	191	39	63	11	3	7	31	0
91 AL	.318	158	559	104	178	31	2	32	109	1
92 AL	.323	160	573	108	185	46	2	24	115	6
Life	.322	378	1323	251	426	88	7	63	255	7
3 AVE	.322	126	441	84	142	29	2	21	85	2

JIM THOME

Position: Third base
Team: Cleveland Indians
Born: Aug. 27, 1990 Peoria, IL
Height: 6'3" **Weight:** 200 lbs.
Bats: left **Throws:** right
Acquired: 13th-round pick in 6/89 free-agent draft

Player Summary	
Fantasy Value	$2 to $5
Card Value	10¢ to 20¢
Will	go opposite way
Can't	wait for walks
Expect	decent defense
Don't Expect	consistent power

Thome never lived up to his advance billing as the second coming of Wade Boggs. Like Boggs, Thome is a lefty-hitting third baseman with a line-drive stroke and inside-out swing. But Thome got off to a slow start last year because of a sprained wrist; he failed to hit and was finally sent to the minors Aug. 25 after making 11 errors in 40 games. At Triple-A Colorado Springs in 1992, he batted .313 with two homers and 14 RBI in 48 at bats. He's an aggressive hitter with good bat speed and the ability to make contact. He had a .275 on-base average and a .299 slugging percentage in 1992. Also like Boggs, Thome has overcome an early reputation as a weak defensive player to become an above-average defender. His arm is average but accurate. Signed as a shortstop, he moved to third base in 1990. In 1991, he batted .285 with two homers and 28 RBI at Colorado Springs, and .337 with five home runs and 45 RBI at Double-A Canton. He batted .373 in rookie ball in 1990 and won the Lou Boudreau Award as Cleveland's top minor leaguer.

Major League Batting Register

	BA	G	AB	R	H	2B	3B	HR	RBI	SB
91 AL	.255	27	98	7	25	4	2	1	9	1
92 AL	.205	40	117	8	24	3	1	2	12	2
Life	.228	67	215	15	49	7	3	3	21	3

MILT THOMPSON

Position: Outfield
Team: Philadelphia Phillies
Born: Jan. 5, 1959 Washington, DC
Height: 5'11" **Weight:** 170 lbs.
Bats: left **Throws:** right
Acquired: Signed as a free agent, 12/92

Player Summary	
Fantasy Value	$5 to $8
Card Value	3¢ to 4¢
Will	get pinch-hits
Can't	play every day
Expect	running attack
Don't Expect	the long ball

Thompson brings his speed back to Philly. He played all three outfield positions for St. Louis last summer. A speed merchant who usually murders righthanded pitching, Thompson actually did better against lefties last year. He gets occasional extra-base hits, enjoys a 75 percent success ratio on steal attempts, and provides strong defense because of his exceptional range. He also served as a lefthanded pinch-hitter. Though he's willing to wait for walks, Thompson is an aggressive hitter who likes to swing—one reason why he strikes out more than other singles hitters. Thompson's slap-and-run formula works especially well on artificial turf because he hits the ball on the ground. Because he hits to all fields, Thompson is tough to defense. He had a .350 on-base average and a .404 slugging percentage in 1992. He has the throwing arm of a left fielder.

Major League Batting Register

	BA	G	AB	R	H	2B	3B	HR	RBI	SB
84 NL	.303	25	99	16	30	1	0	2	4	14
85 NL	.302	73	182	17	55	7	2	0	6	9
86 NL	.251	96	299	38	75	7	1	6	23	19
87 NL	.302	150	527	86	159	26	9	7	43	46
88 NL	.288	122	378	53	109	16	2	2	33	17
89 NL	.290	155	545	60	158	28	8	4	68	27
90 NL	.218	135	418	42	91	14	7	6	30	25
91 NL	.307	115	326	55	100	16	5	6	34	16
92 NL	.293	109	208	31	61	9	1	4	17	18
Life	.281	980	2982	398	838	124	35	37	258	191
3 AVE	.265	120	317	43	84	13	4	5	27	20

ROBBY THOMPSON

Position: Second base
Team: San Francisco Giants
Born: May 10, 1962 West Palm Beach, FL
Height: 5'11" **Weight:** 170 lbs.
Bats: right **Throws:** right
Acquired: First-round pick in secondary phase of 6/83 free-agent draft

Player Summary	
Fantasy Value	$12 to $18
Card Value	3¢ to 4¢
Will	show some power
Can't	avoid strikeouts
Expect	great glove work
Don't Expect	return to leadoff

With the singular exception of Ryne Sandberg, Thompson produces more power than any National League second baseman. He's hit more than a dozen home runs four years in a row and once led the league with 11 triples. Though he's only a .260 hitter who strikes out more than he should, Thompson draws his share of walks, steals a dozen or so bases per season, and is one of baseball's best bunters. He fans too much to bat first—an experiment that fizzled in 1991—but Thompson is a solid No. 6 hitter. He's especially productive against lefthanded pitching, batting .280 last year against lefties. He had a .333 on-base average and a .415 slugging percentage in 1992. More than a one-dimensional player, Thompson is a solid fielder with good hands, good instincts, and the ability to turn the double play. He led NL second basemen in double plays in 1991 and tied for the lead the year before.

Major League Batting Register

	BA	G	AB	R	H	2B	3B	HR	RBI	SB
86 NL	.271	149	549	73	149	27	3	7	47	12
87 NL	.262	132	420	62	110	26	5	10	44	16
88 NL	.264	138	477	66	126	24	6	7	48	14
89 NL	.241	148	547	91	132	26	11	13	50	12
90 NL	.245	144	498	67	122	22	3	15	56	14
91 NL	.262	144	492	74	129	24	5	19	48	14
92 NL	.260	128	443	54	115	25	1	14	49	5
Life	.258	983	3426	487	883	174	34	85	342	87
3 AVE	.255	139	478	65	122	24	3	16	51	11

DICKIE THON

Position: Shortstop
Team: Texas Rangers
Born: June 20, 1958 South Bend, IN
Height: 5'11" **Weight:** 175 lbs.
Bats: right **Throws:** right
Acquired: Signed as a free agent, 12/91

Player Summary	
Fantasy Value	$2 to $4
Card Value	3¢ to 4¢
Will	hit lefthanders
Can't	find old stroke
Expect	declining defense
Don't Expect	patience at bat

Thon was a promising young shortstop in 1984 when a Mike Torrez pitch hit him in the face. Even after Thon returned, lingering eye problems—plus the fear of being hit again—stood between him and his chance to recapture his preinjury form. In 1983, Thon collected 57 extra-base hits and went to the All-Star Game. He's never come close since. Though he's still an aggressive hitter who won't wait for walks, Thon can't hit fastballs with his old authority. He had a .293 on-base average and a .367 slugging percentage in 1992. He still steals a dozen bases a year (and rarely gets caught). Thon's defense has also declined. An average shortstop at best, he sometimes encounters throwing problems. He was bothered by a sore shoulder late last summer.

Major League Batting Register

	BA	G	AB	R	H	2B	3B	HR	RBI	SB
79 AL	.339	35	56	6	19	3	0	0	8	0
80 AL	.255	80	267	32	68	12	2	0	15	7
81 AL	.274	49	95	13	26	6	0	0	3	6
82 NL	.276	136	496	73	137	31	10	3	36	37
83 NL	.286	154	619	81	177	28	9	20	79	34
84 NL	.353	5	17	3	6	0	1	0	1	0
85 NL	.251	84	251	26	63	6	1	6	29	8
86 NL	.248	106	278	24	69	13	1	3	21	6
87 NL	.212	32	66	6	14	1	0	1	3	3
88 NL	.264	95	258	36	68	12	2	1	18	19
89 NL	.271	136	435	45	118	18	4	15	60	6
90 NL	.255	149	552	54	141	20	4	8	48	12
91 NL	.252	146	539	44	136	18	4	9	44	11
92 NL	.247	95	275	30	68	15	3	4	37	12
Life	.264	1302	4204	473	1110	183	41	70	402	161
3 AVE	.253	130	455	43	115	18	4	7	43	12

GARY THURMAN

Position: Outfield
Team: Kansas City Royals
Born: Nov. 12, 1964 Indianapolis, IN
Height: 5'10" **Weight:** 175 lbs.
Bats: right **Throws:** right
Acquired: First-round pick in 6/83 free-agent draft

Player Summary	
Fantasy Value	$1 to $3
Card Value	3¢ to 4¢
Will	slap and run
Can't	produce power
Expect	some steals
Don't Expect	regular job

Thurman played all three outfield positions and served as a part-time designated hitter for the 1992 Royals. Used most often in right field, he supplied speed and defense but no power in limited action. An overly aggressive hitter who fans four times more than he walks, Thurman succeeds when he hits down on the ball—producing grounders that skip through the artificial turf infield. He had a .281 on-base average and a .305 slugging percentage in 1992. He is slightly more productive against lefthanded pitchers. Because he has great range, he's a decent outfielder who throws well enough to man right field on occasion. His best position is center field. In four-dozen outfield starts last year, he made only a couple of errors. Thurman is one of those players who's too good to linger in Triple-A but not quite good enough for the majors. He had three .300 years in the minors but has never come close to that figure in the majors.

Major League Batting Register

	BA	G	AB	R	H	2B	3B	HR	RBI	SB
87 AL	.296	27	81	12	24	2	0	0	5	7
88 AL	.167	35	66	6	11	1	0	0	5	2
89 AL	.195	72	87	24	17	2	1	0	5	16
90 AL	.233	23	60	5	14	3	0	0	3	1
91 AL	.277	80	184	24	51	9	0	2	13	15
92 AL	.245	88	200	25	49	6	3	0	20	9
Life	.245	325	678	96	166	23	4	2	48	53
2 AVE	.260	84	192	25	50	8	2	1	17	12

MIKE TIMLIN

Position: Pitcher
Team: Toronto Blue Jays
Born: March 10, 1966 Midland, TX
Height: 6'4" **Weight:** 205 lbs.
Bats: right **Throws:** right
Acquired: Fifth-round pick in 6/87 free-agent draft

Player Summary	
Fantasy Value	$1 to $3
Card Value	3¢ to 4¢
Will	land set-up job
Can't	retire lefties
Expect	few gophers
Don't Expect	perfect control

After a fine rookie year in 1991, Timlin was slow to heal from off-season elbow surgery. He spent some time at Triple-A Syracuse trying to recapture his rookie form. He had an 0-1 record with an 8.74 ERA, five walks, and seven strikeouts in 11 innings and seven games at Syracuse. A fastball-and-slider pitcher who averages seven strikeouts per nine innings, Timlin had control trouble last year. He also yielded more hits than innings pitched—something he did not do when healthy. Opponents in 1992 compiled a .271 batting average, a .351 on-base percentage, and a .307 slugging percentage. Although Timlin fares well when facing first batters, he often has problems with lefty hitters. He'll need to improve in that department to retain a prominent relief role. He could become a closer if healthy. At Class-A Dunedin in 1990, he had a 7-2 record with a 1.43 ERA and 22 saves. He had a 1-2 record with a 1.73 ERA and eight saves at Double-A Knoxville that same year. Timlin holds runners and fields well.

Major League Pitching Register

	W	L	ERA	G	CG	IP	H	ER	BB	SO
91 AL	11	6	3.16	63	3	108.1	94	38	50	85
92 AL	0	2	4.12	26	1	43.2	45	20	20	35
Life	11	8	3.43	89	4	152.0	139	58	70	120
2 AVE	6	4	3.43	45	2	76.2	70	29	35	60

RANDY TOMLIN

Position: Pitcher
Team: Pittsburgh Pirates
Born: June 14, 1966 Bainbridge, MD
Height: 5'11" **Weight:** 179 lbs.
Bats: left **Throws:** left
Acquired: 18th-round pick in 6/88 free-agent draft

Player Summary	
Fantasy Value	$6 to $12
Card Value	3¢ to 4¢
Will	change speeds well
Can't	ring up strikeouts
Expect	success against southpaws
Don't Expect	bouts of wildness

Tomlin responded well last year when asked to inherit John Smiley's position as the top Pittsburgh lefthander. A finesse pitcher who depends upon pinpoint control, Tomlin survives by staying ahead in the count and keeping batters off balance. He changes speeds on his fastball and curveball, and keeps the ball in the park. He yields a hit an inning but fewer than two walks per nine innings. He fans about four per nine innings. Opponents compiled a .282 batting average, a .320 on-base average, and a .397 slugging percentage in 1992. He throws across his body and dominates lefthanded hitters, who batted .250 against him in '92. Once told his size would prevent him from making the majors, Tomlin answered by winning NL Pitcher of the Month honors in June with a 5-1 record, 2.22 ERA, five walks, and 22 strikeouts in 44⅔ innings. He was the first Pirate with more than 10 wins at the All-Star break since Jim Bibby in 1980. A good fielder with a fine pickoff move, Tomlin also can hit.

Major League Pitching Register

	W	L	ERA	G	CG	IP	H	ER	BB	SO
90 NL	4	4	2.55	12	2	77.2	62	22	12	42
91 NL	8	7	2.98	31	4	175.0	170	58	54	104
92 NL	14	9	3.41	35	1	208.2	226	79	42	90
Life	26	20	3.10	78	7	461.1	458	159	108	236
3 AVE	9	7	3.10	26	2	153.1	153	53	36	79

ALAN TRAMMELL

Position: Shortstop; third base
Team: Detroit Tigers
Born: Feb. 21, 1958 Garden Grove, CA
Height: 6' **Weight:** 180 lbs.
Bats: right **Throws:** right
Acquired: Second-round pick in 6/76 free-agent draft

Player Summary	
Fantasy Value	$4 to $8
Card Value	5¢ to 10¢
Will	plot comeback course
Can't	hit with old power
Expect	switch of position
Don't Expect	end of injury jinx

Although Trammell has been Detroit's shortstop since 1977, chances are good that he won't be playing the position in 1993. He went on the shelf with a broken ankle last May 15, and in Trammell's stead Travis Fryman played so well that he made the All-Star team. As a result, Trammell will stage his comeback at either third base or the outfield, according to Tiger manager Sparky Anderson. Trammell is a contact hitter who walks as much as he fans. He had a .370 on-base average and a .392 slugging percentage in 1992. He's been a 20-20 man twice but is not likely to reach that mark again, especially in stolen bases. Because of his experience, Trammell is still very valuable.

Major League Batting Register

	BA	G	AB	R	H	2B	3B	HR	RBI	SB
77 AL	.186	19	43	6	8	0	0	0	0	0
78 AL	.268	139	448	49	120	14	6	2	34	3
79 AL	.276	142	460	68	127	11	4	6	50	17
80 AL	.300	146	560	107	168	21	5	9	65	12
81 AL	.258	105	392	52	101	15	3	2	31	10
82 AL	.258	157	489	66	126	34	3	9	57	19
83 AL	.319	142	505	83	161	31	2	14	66	30
84 AL	.314	139	555	85	174	34	5	14	69	19
85 AL	.258	149	605	79	156	21	7	13	57	14
86 AL	.277	151	574	107	159	33	7	21	75	25
87 AL	.343	151	597	109	205	34	3	28	105	21
88 AL	.311	128	466	73	145	24	1	15	69	7
89 AL	.243	121	449	54	109	20	3	5	43	10
90 AL	.304	146	559	71	170	37	1	14	89	12
91 AL	.248	101	375	57	93	20	0	9	55	11
92 AL	.275	29	102	11	28	7	1	1	11	2
Life	.286	1965	7179	1077	2050	356	51	162	876	212
2 AVE	.282	124	467	64	132	29	1	12	72	12

JEFF TREADWAY

Position: Second base
Team: Cleveland Indians
Born: Jan. 22, 1963 Columbus, GA
Height: 5'11" **Weight:** 170 lbs.
Bats: left **Throws:** right
Acquired: Signed as a free agent, 12/92

Player Summary	
Fantasy Value	$2 to $4
Card Value	3¢ to 4¢
Will	mount comeback
Can't	bid for Gold Glove
Expect	line-drive singles
Don't Expect	too many strikeouts

Hand surgery handicapped Treadway's performance last summer. He missed the first half of the year, then had trouble regaining the stroke that had produced a career-best .320 average in 1991. As a result, he couldn't unseat former platoon partner Mark Lemke, who is a much better fielder. At age 30, Treadway is young enough to make a strong comeback. When he's right, he's a line-drive hitter with some power who makes an excellent No. 2 hitter. Because he makes good contact, Treadway is a fine hit-and-run man. In 1991, he walked more often than he fanned. Treadway also has occasional power, getting three home runs in one game in 1990. He had a .274 batting average and a .286 slugging percentage in 1992. As a fielder, Treadway's only advantage over Lemke was his height. At best, Treadway is a mediocre defensive player, but he's not the league's worst second sacker by a long shot. He has little speed, especially considering the fact that he is a second baseman.

Major League Batting Register

	BA	G	AB	R	H	2B	3B	HR	RBI	SB
87 NL	.333	23	84	9	28	4	0	2	4	1
88 NL	.252	103	301	30	76	19	4	2	23	2
89 NL	.277	134	473	58	131	18	3	8	40	3
90 NL	.283	128	474	56	134	20	2	11	59	3
91 NL	.320	106	306	41	98	17	2	3	32	2
92 NL	.222	61	126	5	28	6	1	0	5	1
Life	.281	555	1764	199	495	84	12	26	163	12
2 AVE	.297	117	390	49	116	19	2	7	46	3

JOSE URIBE

Position: Shortstop
Team: Houston Astros
Born: Jan. 21, 1960 San Cristobal, Dominican Republic
Height: 5'10" **Weight:** 165 lbs.
Bats: both **Throws:** right
Acquired: Signed as a free agent, 1/93

Player Summary	
Fantasy Value	$1 to $2
Card Value	3¢ to 4¢
Will	supply decent defense
Can't	hit the long ball
Expect	less playing time
Don't Expect	high batting average

Uribe provides depth at short for Houston. Although highly regarded rookie Royce Clayton opened and closed the 1992 season as the San Francisco shortstop, Uribe spent much of the year at the position when neither Clayton nor fellow youngster Mike Benjamin produced enough offense. Uribe is a switch-hitter who is much more productive against lefties; he had a .302 batting average against southpaws in 1992. Though he does not add any power or speed to the lineup, Uribe is a spray hitter who makes fairly good contact. He also drew a surprising share of walks. He had a .299 on-base average and a .346 slugging percentage in 1992. Though he lacks range in the field, he's still a better-than-average shortstop because of good instincts, good hands, and a strong arm. He once led NL shortstops in turning double plays.

Major League Batting Register

	BA	G	AB	R	H	2B	3B	HR	RBI	SB
84 NL	.211	8	19	4	4	0	0	0	3	1
85 NL	.237	147	476	46	113	20	4	3	26	8
86 NL	.223	157	453	46	101	15	1	3	43	22
87 NL	.291	95	309	44	90	16	5	5	30	12
88 NL	.252	141	493	47	124	10	7	3	35	14
89 NL	.221	151	453	34	100	12	6	1	30	6
90 NL	.248	138	415	35	103	8	6	1	24	5
91 NL	.221	90	231	23	51	8	4	1	12	3
92 NL	.241	66	162	24	39	9	1	2	13	2
Life	.241	993	3011	303	725	98	34	19	216	73
3 AVE	.239	98	269	27	64	8	4	1	16	3

JULIO VALERA

Position: Pitcher
Team: California Angels
Born: Oct. 13, 1968 San Sebastian, Puerto Rico
Height: 6'2" **Weight:** 215 lbs.
Bats: right **Throws:** right
Acquired: Traded from Mets for Dick Schofield, 4/92

Player Summary	
Fantasy Value	$2 to $6
Card Value	3¢ to 4¢
Will	give team innings
Can't	worry about weight
Expect	control to improve
Don't Expect	low strikeout count

Although weight problems have slowed his progress in the past, Valera made the most of his first opportunity to become a big league starter. Though given sporadic support by the weak-hitting Angels last summer, he showed flashes of brilliance. He four-hit Oakland for his second shutout of the season on June 20. A sinker-and-slider pitcher who also throws a curveball and split-fingered fastball, Valera yields a hit per inning and walks about three batters per nine innings. His control was better in the minors, when he had a 3-1 ratio of strikeouts to walks. With a year of experience under his belt, he might revert to that ratio—especially if his strikeout total goes up as expected. He finished the year as the top righty in the Angel rotation. Opponents compiled a .262 batting average, a .323 on-base percentage, and a .386 slugging percentage in 1992. Valera fields his position well but needs work in holding runners. He was 10-10 with a 3.83 ERA, 70 walks, and 117 strikeouts in 176 innings at Triple-A Tidewater in 1991.

Major League Pitching Register

	W	L	ERA	G	CG	IP	H	ER	BB	SO
90 NL	1	1	6.92	3	0	13.0	20	10	7	4
91 NL	0	0	0.00	2	0	2.0	1	0	4	3
92 AL	8	11	3.73	30	4	188.0	188	78	64	113
Life	9	12	3.90	35	4	203.0	209	88	75	120

DAVE VALLE

Position: Catcher
Team: Seattle Mariners
Born: Oct. 30, 1960 Bayside, NY
Height: 6'2" **Weight:** 200 lbs.
Bats: right **Throws:** right
Acquired: Second-round pick in 6/78 free-agent draft

Player Summary	
Fantasy Value	$2 to $5
Card Value	3¢ to 4¢
Will	play good defense
Can't	hit righthanders
Expect	occasional power
Don't Expect	any type of speed

After finishing below the Mendoza Line in 1991, Valle surged well above his career average last summer. He shared the Seattle catching chores with veteran Lance Parrish for much of the year. Valle fattened his average against lefthanders while adding some power to the batting order. Though he draws more than his share of walks, he strikes out too frequently. He had a .305 on-base average and a .362 slugging percentage in 1992. His primary value to the club is defensive. Valle has a fine arm and handles pitchers well. He's also adept at preventing wild pitches and blocking the plate. He led AL catchers in fielding percentage in 1990 and previously led several minor leagues in assists and double plays by a catcher. He broke into pro ball in 1978 and reached Seattle six years later. Valle can play first base in a pinch.

Major League Batting Register

	BA	G	AB	R	H	2B	3B	HR	RBI	SB
84 AL	.296	13	27	4	8	1	0	1	4	0
85 AL	.157	31	70	2	11	1	0	0	4	0
86 AL	.340	22	53	10	18	3	0	5	15	0
87 AL	.256	95	324	40	83	16	3	12	53	2
88 AL	.231	93	290	29	67	15	2	10	50	0
89 AL	.237	94	316	32	75	10	3	7	34	0
90 AL	.214	107	308	37	66	15	0	7	33	1
91 AL	.194	132	324	38	63	8	1	8	32	0
92 AL	.240	124	367	39	88	16	1	9	30	0
Life	.230	711	2079	231	479	85	10	59	255	3
3 AVE	.217	121	333	38	72	13	1	8	32	0

JOHN VanderWAL

Position: Outfield
Team: Montreal Expos
Born: April 29, 1966 Grand Rapids, MI
Height: 6'2" **Weight:** 190 lbs.
Bats: left **Throws:** left
Acquired: Third-round pick in 6/87 free-agent draft

Player Summary	
Fantasy Value	$2 to $4
Card Value	10¢ to 20¢
Will	improve with experience
Can't	avoid strikeouts
Expect	power to the gaps
Don't Expect	luck against lefties

When veteran slugger Ivan Calderon went down with shoulder problems last summer, VanderWal was one of several youngsters who filled in. Used awhile in a lefty-righty platoon with Moises Alou, VanderWal also played some first base and right field and came off the bench to serve as a lefty pinch-hitter. Though he didn't show it last summer in limited playing time, the former Western Michigan University standout has some power and speed. VanderWal is a selective hitter who is willing to wait for walks. If he succeeds in reducing his strikeouts, his line-drive stroke and gap power—developed after a winter weight-lifting regimen two years ago—could make him a regular. He had a .316 on-base average and a .352 slugging percentage in 1992. In 1991 at Triple-A Indianapolis, he batted .293 with 15 homers, eight triples, 36 doubles, 71 RBI, and 84 runs in 478 at bats. He batted .303 with eight homers and 40 RBI at Double-A Jacksonville in 1990, and had a .296 batting average, two homers, and 14 RBI that year at Indianapolis.

Major League Batting Register

	BA	G	AB	R	H	2B	3B	HR	RBI	SB
91 NL	.213	21	61	4	13	4	1	1	8	0
92 NL	.239	105	213	21	51	8	2	4	20	3
Life	.234	126	274	25	64	12	3	5	28	3

ANDY VAN SLYKE

Position: Outfield
Team: Pittsburgh Pirates
Born: Dec. 21, 1960 Utica, NY
Height: 6'2" **Weight:** 192 lbs.
Bats: left **Throws:** right
Acquired: Traded from Cardinals with Mike Dunne and Mike LaValliere for Tony Pena, 4/87

Player Summary	
Fantasy Value	$22 to $30
Card Value	5¢ to 10¢
Will	bury righthanders
Can't	deliver old power
Expect	Gold Glove defense
Don't Expect	trouble with lefties

Van Slyke headed into the 1992 season with an average of 18 homers a year since playing for Pittsburgh. After he was diagnosed with three degenerative discs in his lower back, however, Van Slyke switched to a lighter, shorter bat and altered his swing. The result was less power, but a higher average and selection to the NL All-Stars for the second time. Never a .300 hitter in a big league career that began in 1983, Van Slyke finished second in NL in batting last summer. He was the first NL player to reach double figures in doubles, triples, homers, and steals. He had a .381 on-base average and a .505 slugging percentage in 1992. His defensive play is tops, including great instincts, fine range, and the best center field arm in the game. He has won five consecutive Gold Gloves.

Major League Batting Register

	BA	G	AB	R	H	2B	3B	HR	RBI	SB
83 NL	.262	101	309	51	81	15	5	8	38	21
84 NL	.244	137	361	45	88	16	4	7	50	28
85 NL	.259	146	424	61	110	25	6	13	55	34
86 NL	.270	137	418	48	113	23	7	13	61	21
87 NL	.293	157	564	93	165	36	11	21	82	34
88 NL	.288	154	587	101	169	23	15	25	100	30
89 NL	.237	130	476	64	113	18	9	9	53	16
90 NL	.284	136	493	67	140	26	6	17	77	14
91 NL	.265	138	491	87	130	24	7	17	83	10
92 NL	.324	154	614	103	199	45	12	14	89	12
Life	.276	1390	4737	720	1308	251	82	144	688	220
3 AVE	.293	143	533	86	156	32	8	16	83	12

GARY VARSHO

Position: Outfield
Team: Cincinnati Reds
Born: June 20, 1961 Marshfield, WI
Height: 5'11" **Weight:** 190 lbs.
Bats: left **Throws:** right
Acquired: Signed as a free agent, 11/92

Player Summary	
Fantasy Value	$2 to $3
Card Value	3¢ to 4¢
Will	stroke pinch-hits
Can't	handle southpaws
Expect	good throwing arm
Don't Expect	consistent power

Varsho becomes Cincy's top lefty bat off the bench. He was one of several players who filled in for free-agent defector Bobby Bonilla as Pittsburgh's right fielder last summer. A lefty hitter with some sting in his swing, Varsho also plays the other outfield positions, fills in at first base, and makes a capable pinch-hitter against righthanded pitchers. He has some speed and steals on occasion. The speed translates to good range in the outfield, where he also has a strong arm but sometimes misjudges fly balls. An aggressive hitter who rarely walks, Varsho needs to cut his strikeout rate to retain his big league job. He made better contact in '91 than he did last year, and the averages reflect the decline. He had only a .221 batting average against righties last summer. He had a .266 on-base average and a .370 slugging percentage in 1992. Varsho broke into the pros in 1982 and made the majors six years later. Signed as a second baseman, he moved to the outfield because of poor defense.

Major League Batting Register

	BA	G	AB	R	H	2B	3B	HR	RBI	SB
88 NL	.274	46	73	6	20	3	0	0	5	5
89 NL	.184	61	87	10	16	4	2	0	6	3
90 NL	.250	46	48	10	12	4	0	0	1	2
91 NL	.273	99	187	23	51	11	2	4	23	9
92 NL	.222	103	162	22	36	6	3	4	22	5
Life	.242	355	557	71	135	28	7	8	57	24
2 AVE	.249	101	175	23	44	9	3	4	23	7

GREG VAUGHN

Position: Outfield
Team: Milwaukee Brewers
Born: July 3, 1965 Sacramento, CA
Height: 6' **Weight:** 195 lbs.
Bats: right **Throws:** right
Acquired: Fourth-round pick in 6/86 free-agent draft

Player Summary	
Fantasy Value	$10 to $18
Card Value	4¢ to 6¢
Will	hit with power
Can't	escape slumps
Expect	higher average
Don't Expect	strong throws

The glittering promise left by his 1991 performance disappeared early last season for Vaughn. He hurt his ribs and back yanking luggage out of his car trunk, then aggravated the problem diving for a fly ball in left field. By the end of June, he was still 20 points below the Mendoza Line. Moved lower in the order to reduce the pressure, Vaughn showed some signs of life, including his two five-RBI games. Though he draws his share of walks, Vaughn fans frequently. He has good bat speed and a short stroke but is subject to prolonged slumps. He had a .313 on-base average and a .409 slugging percentage in 1992. He has some running speed and should steal upwards of a dozen times a year, but he was caught stealing 15 times last year. As an outfielder, he has good range and good hands but a weak arm. He belongs in left field. Vaughn began his pro career in 1986 and reached Milwaukee three years later.

Major League Batting Register

	BA	G	AB	R	H	2B	3B	HR	RBI	SB
89 AL	.265	38	113	18	30	3	0	5	23	4
90 AL	.220	120	382	51	84	26	2	17	61	7
91 AL	.244	145	542	81	132	24	5	27	98	2
92 AL	.228	141	501	77	114	18	2	23	78	15
Life	.234	444	1538	227	360	71	9	72	260	28
3 AVE	.232	135	475	70	110	23	3	22	79	8

MO VAUGHN

Position: First base
Team: Boston Red Sox
Born: Dec. 15, 1967 Norwalk, CT
Height: 6'1" **Weight:** 225 lbs.
Bats: left **Throws:** right
Acquired: First-round pick in 6/89 free-agent draft

Player Summary	
Fantasy Value	$4 to $10
Card Value	5¢ to 10¢
Will	show more power
Can't	hit lefthanders
Expect	dreadful defense
Don't Expect	inkling of speed

Contradicting the hype, Vaughn was a failure for the Red Sox last summer. Given a full shot at first base following Carlos Quintana's preseason car crash, Vaughn delivered neither the power nor the defense to hold the position. After leading all AL first basemen in errors—most of them on dropped throws—he finished the year in a lefty-righty DH platoon with Eric Wedge. Sent to Triple-A Pawtucket during the year, he batted .282 with six homers and 28 RBI in 149 at bats there. Vaughn's inside-out swing had been projected as the perfect match for the friendly confines of Fenway Park's Green Monster. AL pitchers proved to be more of a beast, however. Vaughn died against lefties, failed to hit on the road, and fanned too frequently for a man who produced only a dozen homers. He had a .326 on-base average and a .400 slugging percentage last year. He's willing to wait for walks but never steals a base. At age 25, the former Seton Hall star needs to start producing. In 1991 at Pawtucket, he batted .274 with 14 home runs and 50 RBI in 234 at bats.

Major League Batting Register

	BA	G	AB	R	H	2B	3B	HR	RBI	SB
91 AL	.260	74	219	21	57	12	0	4	32	2
92 AL	.234	113	355	42	83	16	2	13	57	3
Life	.244	187	574	63	140	28	2	17	89	5
2 AVE	.244	94	287	32	70	14	1	9	45	3

RANDY VELARDE

Position: Infield; outfield
Team: New York Yankees
Born: Nov. 24, 1962 Midland, TX
Height: 6′ **Weight:** 190 lbs.
Bats: right **Throws:** right
Acquired: Traded from White Sox with Pete Filson for Scott Nielsen and Mike Soper, 1/87

Player Summary	
Fantasy Value	$2 to $5
Card Value	3¢ to 4¢
Will	play any position
Can't	reduce strikeouts
Expect	luck against southpaws
Don't Expect	regular home runs

If he weren't so versatile, Velarde would be a regular because of his bat. Playing everything but the bass fiddle last year (he also missed pitcher, catcher, and first), he overcame a slow start to become one of the best hitters in Yankee pinstripes. On a July trip to the West Coast, Velarde went 16-for-26 (.615) with seven doubles, a triple, two homers, six RBI, and eight runs. In his first 22 games after becoming a part-timer, he hit .395. Though he has some power and some speed, Velarde's running needs refinement. He's been guilty of sloppy defense in the past, though his fielding has improved greatly at shortstop, his primary position. If he continues to hit second, Velarde could hike his value by waiting out more walks. He fans twice as much as he walks and should make better contact. He had a .333 on-base average and a .386 slugging percentage in 1992.

Major League Batting Register

	BA	G	AB	R	H	2B	3B	HR	RBI	SB
87 AL	.182	8	22	1	4	0	0	0	1	0
88 AL	.174	48	115	18	20	6	0	5	12	1
89 AL	.340	33	100	12	34	4	2	2	11	0
90 AL	.210	95	229	21	48	6	2	5	19	0
91 AL	.245	80	184	19	45	11	1	1	15	3
92 AL	.272	121	412	57	112	24	1	7	46	7
Life	.248	385	1062	128	263	51	6	20	104	11
3 AVE	.248	99	275	32	68	14	1	4	27	3

ROBIN VENTURA

Position: Third base
Team: Chicago White Sox
Born: July 14, 1967 Santa Maria, CA
Height: 6′1″ **Weight:** 185 lbs.
Bats: left **Throws:** right
Acquired: First-round pick in 6/88 free-agent draft

Player Summary	
Fantasy Value	$24 to $32
Card Value	5¢ to 10¢
Will	join All-Stars
Can't	generate speed
Expect	power to return
Don't Expect	defensive lapses

Though Ventura failed to match his 1991 home run production last summer, he remained one of the premier all-around third basemen in the American League. Batting No. 5 in the White Sox lineup behind George Bell, Ventura remained a major run producer and used his keen batting eye to forge a high on-base percentage. He notched a .375 on-base average and a .431 slugging percentage in 1992. A patient hitter who walks much more than he strikes out, Ventura hit some 35 points higher against righties but was no automatic out against southpaws. Though he hits into a lot of double plays, his lack of speed does not hurt in the field. He has good reactions, good hands, and a strong arm at third, where he has won two straight Gold Gloves. Like Brooks Robinson, Ventura covers a lot of ground for a man who doesn't run well. The former College Player of the Year from Oklahoma State led both leagues in chances and putouts in '91.

Major League Batting Register

	BA	G	AB	R	H	2B	3B	HR	RBI	SB
89 AL	.178	16	45	5	8	3	0	0	7	0
90 AL	.249	150	493	48	123	17	1	5	54	1
91 AL	.284	157	606	92	172	25	1	23	100	2
92 AL	.282	157	592	85	167	38	1	16	93	2
Life	.271	480	1736	230	470	83	3	44	254	5
3 AVE	.273	155	564	75	154	27	1	15	82	2

FRANK VIOLA

Position: Pitcher
Team: Boston Red Sox
Born: April 19, 1960 Hempstead, NY
Height: 6'4" **Weight:** 209 lbs.
Bats: left **Throws:** left
Acquired: Signed as a free agent, 12/92

Player Summary	
Fantasy Value	$8 to $14
Card Value	3¢ to 4¢
Will	bank on changeup
Can't	find old velocity
Expect	improved control
Don't Expect	frequent gophers

Ever since he won World Series MVP honors in 1987 and the AL Cy Young Award a year later, Viola has been searching for consistency. Traded by the Twins in 1989 because management felt he had lost velocity off his fastball, Viola rallied for a 20-win season in 1990. He dropped 10 of his last 11 in '91 when his changeup suddenly became hittable. Last year, his usually good control vanished and his strikeout total plunged—negating his ability to yield fewer hits than innings pitched. Viola vanquished lefties and kept the ball from leaving the park. He still relies on his changeup, once baseball's best. Opponents compiled a .242 batting average, a .313 on-base percentage, and a .331 slugging percentage in 1992. He helps his own cause with his fielding and ability to hold runners on.

Major League Pitching Register

	W	L	ERA	G	CG	IP	H	ER	BB	SO
82 AL	4	10	5.21	22	3	126.0	152	73	38	84
83 AL	7	15	5.49	35	4	210.0	242	128	92	127
84 AL	18	12	3.21	35	10	257.2	225	92	73	149
85 AL	18	14	4.09	36	9	250.2	262	114	68	135
86 AL	16	13	4.51	37	7	245.2	257	123	83	191
87 AL	17	10	2.90	36	7	251.2	230	81	66	197
88 AL	24	7	2.64	35	7	255.1	236	75	54	193
89 AL	8	12	3.79	24	7	175.2	171	74	47	138
89 NL	5	5	3.38	12	2	85.1	75	32	27	73
90 NL	20	12	2.67	35	7	249.2	227	74	60	182
91 NL	13	15	3.97	35	3	231.1	259	102	54	132
92 AL	13	12	3.44	35	6	238.0	214	91	89	121
Life	163	137	3.70	377	72	2577.0	2550	1059	751	1722
3 AVE	15	13	3.34	35	5	239.1	233	89	68	145

JOSE VIZCAINO

Position: Infield
Team: Chicago Cubs
Born: March 26, 1968 Palenque, Dominican Republic
Height: 6'1" **Weight:** 150 lbs.
Bats: both **Throws:** right
Acquired: Traded from Dodgers for Greg Smith, 12/90

Player Summary	
Fantasy Value	$1 to $2
Card Value	3¢ to 4¢
Will	play good defense
Can't	reach the fences
Expect	more show of speed
Don't Expect	big batting average

In his first full major league season last year, Vizcaino served the Cubs as a three-position infielder. He mostly shared shortstop with Rey Sanchez after incumbent Shawon Dunston went down with a bad back. Vizcaino also saw lots of action at third, and he even served as Ryne Sandberg's chief understudy at second. Vizcaino didn't add much punch to the offense. His homer Aug. 1 was his first in 446 career at bats. Nor did Vizcaino take advantage of his natural speed. He made decent contact but poked few extra-base hits and struggled against southpaws. He had a .260 on-base average and a .298 slugging percentage in 1992. A fine defensive player, Vizcaino has good range and a capable arm. Shortstop is his best position, but he's more than adequate at second base. He was voted the best second baseman in the Triple-A Pacific Coast League in 1990. If he boosts his on-base average by waiting for walks and starts stealing some bases, he'll improve his value.

Major League Batting Register

	BA	G	AB	R	H	2B	3B	HR	RBI	SB
89 NL	.200	7	10	2	2	0	0	0	0	0
90 NL	.275	37	51	3	14	1	1	0	2	1
91 NL	.262	93	145	7	38	5	0	0	10	2
92 NL	.225	86	285	25	64	10	4	1	17	3
Life	.240	223	491	37	118	16	5	1	29	6

OMAR VIZQUEL

Position: Shortstop
Team: Seattle Mariners
Born: April 24, 1967 Caracas, Venezuela
Height: 5'9" **Weight:** 165 lbs.
Bats: both **Throws:** right
Acquired: Signed as a free agent, 4/84

Player Summary	
Fantasy Value	$3 to $7
Card Value	3¢ to 4¢
Will	murder righthanders
Can't	hit the long ball
Expect	Gold Glove fielding
Don't Expect	'92 bubble to burst

Even if his bat hadn't come alive last summer, Vizquel would have kept his job as Seattle's shortstop because his fielding percentage at the position led the major leagues. He made only seven errors last summer. A wide-ranging shortstop who can turn the double play, he has very good hands and a strong arm. His fielding inspired images of fellow Venezuelan acrobats Luis Aparicio, Dave Concepcion, and Ozzie Guillen. Until 1992, Vizquel had no chance to join their ranks among the All-Stars. Then Seattle batting coach Gene Clines convinced Vizquel to go with the pitch, hit to all fields, and take advantage of his artificial home field. He became the Mariners' leadoff man with a .351 burst in July and seemed headed for his first .300 season before a September slump did him in. He had a .340 on-base average and a .354 slugging percentage in 1992. He was still Seattle's most pleasant surprise: a .230 career hitter who found the Midas touch.

Major League Batting Register

	BA	G	AB	R	H	2B	3B	HR	RBI	SB
89 AL	.220	143	387	45	85	7	3	1	20	1
90 AL	.247	81	255	19	63	3	2	2	18	4
91 AL	.230	142	426	42	98	16	4	1	41	7
92 AL	.294	136	483	49	142	20	4	0	21	15
Life	.250	502	1551	155	388	46	13	4	100	27
3 AVE	.260	120	388	37	101	13	3	1	27	9

TIM WAKEFIELD

Position: Pitcher
Team: Pittsburgh Pirates
Born: Aug. 2, 1966 Melbourne, FL
Height: 6'2" **Weight:** 195 lbs.
Bats: right **Throws:** right
Acquired: Eighth-round pick in 6/88 free-agent draft

Player Summary	
Fantasy Value	$8 to $18
Card Value	10¢ to 25¢
Will	baffle rival batters
Can't	always locate plate
Expect	fewer hits than innings
Don't Expect	balls to leave park

Wakefield delivered the Pirates back from the brink twice in the NLCS last fall, winning two games and riveting the baseball world. He was a Class-A first baseman in 1989 when a manager saw Wakefield throwing some knuckleballs to a teammate and made him a pitcher. By 1992 spring training, he was ready. He talked shop with veteran Charlie Hough, and Wakefield's confidence level soared. He began the year at Triple-A Buffalo, where he was 10-3 with a 3.06 ERA, 71 strikeouts, and 51 walks in 135 innings. He made an immediate impression after his promotion. In his July 31 debut, he not only won 3-2 but also fanned 10 Cards. Wakefield averaged over seven hits, three walks, and five strikeouts per nine innings. Opponents compiled a .232 batting average, a .305 on-base percentage, and a .309 slugging percentage in 1992. He showed an exceptional pickoff move—especially for a righthander. Wakefield's dad taught him the trick pitch, and he throws it up to 80 percent of the time. He had a 15-8 record in 1991 at Double-A Carolina, with a 2.90 ERA, 51 walks, and 120 strikeouts in 183 innings.

Major League Pitching Register

	W	L	ERA	G	CG	IP	H	ER	BB	SO
92 NL	8	1	2.15	13	4	92.0	76	22	35	51
Life	8	1	2.15	13	4	92.0	76	22	35	51

BOB WALK

Position: Pitcher
Team: Pittsburgh Pirates
Born: Nov. 26, 1955 Van Nuys, CA
Height: 6'4" **Weight:** 217 lbs.
Bats: right **Throws:** right
Acquired: Signed as a free agent, 4/84

Player Summary	
Fantasy Value	$2 to $6
Card Value	3¢ to 4¢
Will	win money games
Can't	avoid injuries
Expect	superb control
Don't Expect	return to pen

Though troubled with groin pulls on three occasions in 1992, Walk did a creditable job as both a starter and a reliever for the Pirates. One of the team's top pitchers after the All-Star break, he worked 14 times in relief (with a 4-0 record and 2.74 ERA) before returning to the rotation Aug. 19. A favorite of Pittsburgh manager Jim Leyland, Walk was hot down the stretch. He's the only pitcher in the majors with a winning record in each of the last six seasons (minimum 10 decisions). He is a fastball-curveball pitcher who works in occasional sliders and changeups. Opponents compiled a .258 batting average, a .322 on-base percentage, and a .379 slugging percentage in 1992. He's extremely effective against righthanders. Walk's biggest weakness is an inability to stop basestealers.

Major League Pitching Register

	W	L	ERA	G	CG	IP	H	ER	BB	SO
80 NL	11	7	4.57	27	2	151.2	163	77	71	94
81 NL	1	4	4.57	12	0	43.1	41	22	23	16
82 NL	11	9	4.87	32	3	164.1	179	89	59	84
83 NL	0	0	7.36	1	0	3.2	7	3	2	4
84 NL	1	1	2.61	2	0	10.1	8	3	4	10
85 NL	2	3	3.68	9	1	58.2	60	24	18	40
86 NL	7	8	3.75	44	1	141.2	129	59	64	78
87 NL	8	2	3.31	39	1	117.0	107	43	51	78
88 NL	12	10	2.71	32	1	212.2	183	64	65	81
89 NL	13	10	4.41	33	2	196.0	208	96	65	83
90 NL	7	5	3.75	26	1	129.2	136	54	36	73
91 NL	9	2	3.60	25	0	115.0	104	46	35	67
92 NL	10	6	3.20	36	1	135.0	132	48	43	60
Life	92	67	3.82	318	13	1479.0	1457	628	536	768
3 AVE	9	4	3.51	29	1	126.1	124	49	38	67

CHICO WALKER

Position: Third base; outfield
Team: New York Mets
Born: Nov. 25, 1957 Jackson, MS
Height: 5'9" **Weight:** 170 lbs.
Bats: both **Throws:** right
Acquired: Signed as a free agent, 5/92

Player Summary	
Fantasy Value	$1 to $3
Card Value	3¢ to 4¢
Will	tattoo lefthanders
Can't	win spot in lineup
Expect	good pinch-hitting
Don't Expect	big power display

Throughout a professional career that began in 1976, Walker has always shown speed, power, and versatility. His ability to play so many spots so well worked against him, creating a utility label he couldn't shake. He played all three outfield positions, plus second and third. He was also the Mets' most successful pinch-hitter. He did his best work, however, after Mets skipper Jeff Torborg gave him a crack at the every-day third base job in August. Walker went 4-for-4 Aug. 12, knocked in three runs Aug. 20, and hit .350 in his first 26 starts. He was thrown out only once in his first 16 steal attempts. A contact hitter who walks almost as much as he fans, he had a .351 on-base average and a .391 slugging percentage in 1992. Walker is deadly against left-handed pitching. His best positions are second base and center field.

Major League Batting Register

	BA	G	AB	R	H	2B	3B	HR	RBI	SB
80 AL	.211	19	57	3	12	0	0	1	5	3
81 AL	.353	6	17	3	6	0	0	0	2	0
83 AL	.400	4	5	2	2	0	2	0	1	0
84 AL	.000	3	2	0	0	0	0	0	1	0
85 AL	.083	21	12	3	1	0	0	0	0	1
86 AL	.277	28	101	21	28	3	2	1	7	15
87 AL	.200	47	105	15	21	4	0	0	7	11
88 AL	.154	33	78	8	12	1	0	0	2	2
91 NL	.257	124	374	51	96	10	1	6	34	13
92 NL	.289	126	253	26	73	12	1	4	38	15
Life	.250	411	1004	132	251	30	6	12	97	60
2 AVE	.270	125	314	39	85	11	1	5	36	14

LARRY WALKER

Position: Outfield
Team: Montreal Expos
Born: Dec. 1, 1966 Maple Ridge, British Columbia, Canada
Height: 6'2" **Weight:** 205 lbs.
Bats: left **Throws:** right
Acquired: Signed as a free agent, 11/84

Player Summary	
Fantasy Value	$24 to $32
Card Value	5¢ to 10¢
Will	make great throws
Can't	get press notices
Expect	good clutch power
Don't Expect	trouble against lefties

Twice last season, Walker nailed a runner at first on a routine base hit to right. Though fans of Tony Gwynn or Andre Dawson might argue, Walker has no peer as a defensive right fielder. He has good hands, exceptional range, and an arm as powerful and precise as a rifle. He led NL right fielders in assists in 1992, with 16. Last season, he waltzed to his first All-Star Game by handling lefties as well as he hit righties. Walker has speed, power, and the ability to hit in the clutch. He had a .353 on-base average and a .506 slugging percentage. He led the Expos in average, home runs, and RBI—not bad for a player plagued by a strained left quadriceps, strained left groin, and strained muscle in his side. Walker gave the young Expos a legit No. 4 hitter. He foretold of his big 1992 season with a .331 batting average in the second half of 1991—the best in the NL. He said he improved after copying Jose Canseco's open stance.

Major League Batting Register

	BA	G	AB	R	H	2B	3B	HR	RBI	SB
89 NL	.170	20	47	4	8	0	0	0	4	1
90 NL	.241	133	419	59	101	18	3	19	51	21
91 NL	.290	137	487	59	141	30	2	16	64	14
92 NL	.301	143	528	85	159	31	4	23	93	18
Life	.276	433	1481	207	409	79	9	58	212	54
3 AVE	.280	138	478	68	134	26	3	19	69	18

TIM WALLACH

Position: Third base
Team: Los Angeles Dodgers
Born: Sept. 14, 1957 Huntington Park, CA
Height: 6'3" **Weight:** 200 lbs.
Bats: right **Throws:** right
Acquired: Traded from Expos for Tim Barker, 11/92

Player Summary	
Fantasy Value	$6 to $12
Card Value	3¢ to 4¢
Will	seek old power
Can't	help with speed
Expect	good defense
Don't Expect	decent average

The Dodgers got a former All-Star to solve their third base problems. For the third straight season in 1992, Wallach's power production took a precipitous drop. He reached career lows in both home runs and RBI, which prompted the Expos to audition Bret Barberie and Sean Berry as successors at third. Wallach had a .296 batting average and a .331 slugging percentage in 1992. Though he showed flashes of his old power with more than two-dozen doubles, he proved hapless against lefties. Only his strong fielding kept Montreal's team captain in the lineup. Though he lacks speed, Wallach has quick reactions, good hands, and a strong arm. The three-time Gold Glove winner has reduced his errors each year during the same three-year span that his home run total has fallen.

Major League Batting Register

	BA	G	AB	R	H	2B	3B	HR	RBI	SB
80 NL	.182	5	11	1	2	0	0	1	2	0
81 NL	.236	71	212	19	50	9	1	4	13	0
82 NL	.268	158	596	89	160	31	3	28	97	6
83 NL	.269	156	581	54	156	33	3	19	70	0
84 NL	.246	160	582	55	143	25	4	18	72	3
85 NL	.260	155	569	70	148	36	3	22	81	9
86 NL	.233	134	480	50	112	22	1	18	71	8
87 NL	.298	153	593	89	177	42	4	26	123	9
88 NL	.257	159	592	52	152	32	5	12	69	2
89 NL	.277	154	573	76	159	42	0	13	77	3
90 NL	.296	161	626	69	185	37	5	21	98	6
91 NL	.225	151	577	60	130	22	1	13	73	2
92 NL	.223	150	537	53	120	29	1	9	59	2
Life	.259	1767	6529	737	1694	360	31	204	905	50
3 AVE	.250	154	580	61	145	29	2	14	77	3

DAN WALTERS

Position: Catcher
Team: San Diego Padres
Born: Aug. 15, 1966 Brunswick, ME
Height: 6'4" **Weight:** 225 lbs.
Bats: right **Throws:** right
Acquired: Traded from Astros for Ed Vosberg, 12/88

Player Summary	
Fantasy Value	$2 to $6
Card Value	5¢ to 12¢
Will	hit lefthanders
Can't	show much speed
Expect	respectable bat
Don't Expect	Benito Santiago

When Padres incumbent catcher Benito Santiago went on the shelf with a broken pinky last June, the Padres made Walters their starting catcher. A good receiver with a quick release and a strong arm, Walters responded by collecting 16 RBI in his first 29 games. He hit nearly .300 against left-handed pitchers, produced occasional long-ball power, and showed an aggressive baserunning style for a big man. He makes decent contact but needs to show more patience at the plate. He had a .295 on-base percentage and a .391 slugging percentage in 1992. At Triple-A Las Vegas last summer, he batted .394 with two homers, 25 RBI, 10 walks, and 12 strikeouts in 127 at bats. He hit .317 with four home runs, 44 RBI, 22 walks, and 35 strikeouts in 293 at bats for Las Vegas in 1991. Although he does not throw as well as Santiago, Walters has won the praise of his pitching staff for excellent game-calling. In addition, he presents a formidable obstacle at the plate when he protects the plate against baserunners. Walters will have a good shot at seeing more duty in the big leagues in 1993.

Major League Batting Register

	BA	G	AB	R	H	2B	3B	HR	RBI	SB
92 NL	.251	57	179	14	45	11	1	4	22	1
Life	.251	57	179	14	45	11	1	4	22	1

DUANE WARD

Position: Pitcher
Team: Toronto Blue Jays
Born: May 28, 1964 Parkview, NM
Height: 6'4" **Weight:** 215 lbs.
Bats: right **Throws:** right
Acquired: Traded from Braves for Doyle Alexander, 7/86

Player Summary	
Fantasy Value	$10 to $18
Card Value	3¢ to 4¢
Will	handcuff hitters
Can't	hold runners on
Expect	many strikeouts
Don't Expect	the long ball

Heat and durability have been the hallmarks of Ward's career. One of the hardest-throwing relievers in baseball, he gets more than a strikeout per inning with a two-pitch repertoire that consists of a 95 mph fastball and an 87 mph slider. He had been used most often as a set-up man, but Ward can also be a competent closer when he has control. He may get the chance for more late-inning work in 1993. He managed a 3-1 ratio of whiffs to walks last year, when he averaged over three and one-half walks per nine innings. Ward yields fewer than seven hits per nine innings and keeps the ball in the park. Opponents in 1992 compiled a .207 batting average, a .282 on-base percentage, and a .286 slugging average. Though Ward had a microscopic ERA last year, he had problems with first batters and basestealers. He fields all the grounders he can reach.

Major League Pitching Register

	W	L	ERA	G	S	IP	H	ER	BB	SO
86 NL	0	1	7.31	10	0	16.0	22	13	8	8
86 AL	0	1	13.50	2	0	2.0	3	3	4	1
87 AL	1	0	6.94	12	0	11.2	14	9	12	10
88 AL	9	3	3.30	64	15	111.2	101	41	60	91
89 AL	4	10	3.77	66	15	114.2	94	48	58	122
90 AL	2	8	3.45	73	11	127.2	101	49	42	112
91 AL	7	6	2.77	81	23	107.1	80	33	33	132
92 AL	7	4	1.95	79	12	101.1	76	22	39	103
Life	30	33	3.31	387	76	592.1	491	218	256	579
3 AVE	5	6	2.78	78	15	112.1	86	35	38	116

MITCH WEBSTER

Position: Outfield
Team: Los Angeles Dodgers
Born: May 16, 1959 Larned, KS
Height: 6'1" **Weight:** 185 lbs.
Bats: both **Throws:** left
Acquired: Traded from Pirates for Jose
Gonzalez, 7/91

Player Summary	
Fantasy Value	$2 to $4
Card Value	3¢ to 4¢
Will	retain reserve role
Can't	reach .300 average
Expect	pinch-hitting luck
Don't Expect	success against righties

Injuries to Darryl Strawberry and Eric Davis gave Webster more playing time than expected last summer. A switch-hitter who is most productive as a righthanded batter, he did his best work in a pinch-hitting role. Primarily a singles hitter who makes decent contact, he sometimes shows some extra-base power. He had a .334 on-base average and a .420 slugging percentage in 1992. He'll use his speed to steal or take an extra base whenever possible. That speed helps Webster in the outfield, where his arm is only average. He's much better at catching the ball than throwing it. Webster spent most of last year in right field but also played a lot of left field and some center. He is a valuable sub.

Major League Batting Register

	BA	G	AB	R	H	2B	3B	HR	RBI	SB
83 AL	.182	11	11	2	2	0	0	0	0	0
84 AL	.227	26	22	9	5	2	1	0	4	0
85 AL	.000	4	1	0	0	0	0	0	0	0
85 NL	.274	74	212	32	58	8	2	11	30	15
86 NL	.290	151	576	89	167	31	13	8	49	36
87 NL	.281	156	588	101	165	30	8	15	63	33
88 NL	.260	151	523	69	136	16	8	6	39	22
89 NL	.257	98	272	40	70	12	4	3	19	14
90 AL	.252	128	437	58	110	20	6	12	55	22
91 AL	.125	13	32	2	4	0	0	0	0	2
91 NL	.222	94	171	21	38	8	5	2	19	0
92 NL	.267	135	262	33	70	12	5	6	35	11
Life	.266	1041	3107	456	825	139	52	63	313	155
3 AVE	.251	119	290	37	73	13	5	7	36	11

BILL WEGMAN

Position: Pitcher
Team: Milwaukee Brewers
Born: Dec. 19, 1962 Cincinnati, OH
Height: 6'5" **Weight:** 220 lbs.
Bats: right **Throws:** right
Acquired: Fifth-round pick in 6/81 free-agent
draft

Player Summary	
Fantasy Value	$6 to $12
Card Value	3¢ to 4¢
Will	get ground balls
Can't	notch many Ks
Expect	frequent gophers
Don't Expect	control problems

The home run ball hurt Wegman last summer. Though he yielded fewer hits than innings pitched, Wegman didn't come close to duplicating 1991 numbers, primarily because he allowed 28 dingers. Known for his nasty slider, Wegman also throws a fastball and changeup. Because he keeps the ball down but throws without high velocity, Wegman gets outs on ground balls rather than strikeouts. Opponents in 1992 compiled a .250 batting average, a .294 on-base percentage, and a .387 slugging percentage. His control is so good (fewer than two walks per nine innings) that he can change his game plan from inning to inning. Wegman had problems with many righthanded hitters last year, as they compiled a .286 batting average against him. He proved, though, that he was over his old shoulder woes. The former schoolboy shortstop helps himself with fine fielding but has some trouble stopping basestealers.

Major League Pitching Register

	W	L	ERA	G	CG	IP	H	ER	BB	SO
85 AL	2	0	3.57	3	0	17.2	17	7	3	6
86 AL	5	12	5.13	35	2	198.1	217	113	43	82
87 AL	12	11	4.24	34	7	225.0	229	106	53	102
88 AL	13	13	4.12	32	4	199.0	207	91	50	84
89 AL	2	6	6.71	11	0	51.0	69	38	21	27
90 AL	2	4	4.85	8	1	29.2	37	16	6	20
91 AL	15	7	2.84	28	7	193.1	176	61	40	89
92 AL	13	14	3.20	35	7	261.2	251	93	55	127
Life	64	65	4.02	186	28	1175.2	1203	525	271	537
2 AVE	14	11	3.05	32	7	227.2	214	77	48	108

WALT WEISS

Position: Shortstop
Team: Florida Marlins
Born: Nov. 28, 1963 Tuxedo, NY
Height: 6′ **Weight:** 175 lbs.
Bats: both **Throws:** right
Acquired: Traded from Athletics for Eric Helfand and Scott Baker, 11/92

Player Summary	
Fantasy Value	$2 to $4
Card Value	3¢ to 4¢
Will	supply good glove
Can't	avoid injury jinx
Expect	good batting eye
Don't Expect	power production

Weiss becomes the anchor of the Marlins' infield at shortstop. The A's decided that Mike Bordick could handle shortstop duties for them and traded Weiss. Though he took a batting average of .254 into 1992, he hit well below that level. For the second straight year, he failed to hit .200 against lefthanded pitching. A brittle athlete who has missed large chunks of playing time in four of his six seasons in the majors, Weiss is a usually a productive performer. He is a contact hitter who walks more than he strikes out, and he's adept at bunting, squeezing, and working the hit-and-run. He had a .305 on-base average and a .241 slugging average in 1992. No matter what Weiss hits, he's valued more for his defense. He's a smooth-fielding shortstop with quick reactions, good range, and a fine throwing arm. His speed hasn't been diminished by the knee problems that have plagued him throughout his career.

Major League Batting Register

	BA	G	AB	R	H	2B	3B	HR	RBI	SB
87 AL	.462	16	26	3	12	4	0	0	1	1
88 AL	.250	147	452	44	113	17	3	3	39	4
89 AL	.233	84	236	30	55	11	0	3	21	6
90 AL	.265	138	445	50	118	17	1	2	35	9
91 AL	.226	40	133	15	30	6	1	0	13	6
92 AL	.212	103	316	36	67	5	2	0	21	6
Life	.246	528	1608	178	395	60	7	8	130	32
2 AVE	.243	121	381	43	93	11	2	1	28	8

BOB WELCH

Position: Pitcher
Team: Oakland Athletics
Born: Nov. 3, 1956 Detroit, MI
Height: 6′3″ **Weight:** 195 lbs.
Bats: right **Throws:** right
Acquired: Traded from Dodgers with Matt Young for Alfredo Griffin and Jay Howell, 12/87

Player Summary	
Fantasy Value	$10 to $18
Card Value	3¢ to 4¢
Will	try to avoid injuries
Can't	blaze ball by batters
Expect	best work against righties
Don't Expect	Cy Young season

A variety of injuries sliced large portions off the 1992 campaign for Welch. He began the year on the DL with shoulder tendinitis, a strained back, and a sore knee. The knee problems resurfaced after five May starts, while a sore elbow disabled him in August. When Welch worked, he showed flashes of the 27-win form that produced a Cy Young Award in 1990. Though he used mostly fastballs and curves that year, he now relies more on a changeup. Opponents compiled a .247 batting average, a .312 on-base percentage, and a .360 slugging percentage in 1992. He relies on his defense to get batters out. Welch fields his position well and has a fine pickoff move for a righthander.

Major League Pitching Register

	W	L	ERA	G	CG	IP	H	ER	BB	SO
78 NL	7	4	2.02	23	4	111.1	92	25	26	66
79 NL	5	6	3.98	25	1	81.1	82	36	32	64
80 NL	14	9	3.29	32	3	213.2	190	78	79	141
81 NL	9	5	3.44	23	2	141.1	141	54	41	88
82 NL	16	11	3.36	36	9	235.2	199	88	81	176
83 NL	15	12	2.65	31	4	204.0	164	60	72	156
84 NL	13	13	3.78	31	3	178.2	191	75	58	126
85 NL	14	4	2.31	23	8	167.1	141	43	35	96
86 NL	7	13	3.28	33	7	235.2	227	86	55	183
87 NL	15	9	3.22	35	6	251.2	204	90	86	196
88 AL	17	9	3.64	36	4	244.2	237	99	81	158
89 AL	17	8	3.00	33	1	209.2	191	70	78	137
90 AL	27	6	2.95	35	2	238.0	214	78	77	127
91 AL	12	13	4.58	35	7	220.0	220	112	91	101
92 AL	11	7	3.27	20	0	123.2	114	45	43	47
Life	199	129	3.27	451	61	2856.2	2607	1039	935	1862
3 AVE	17	9	3.64	30	3	194.1	183	78	70	92

297

DAVID WELLS

Position: Pitcher
Team: Toronto Blue Jays
Born: May 20, 1963 Torrance, CA
Height: 6'4" **Weight:** 225 lbs.
Bats: left **Throws:** left
Acquired: Second-round pick in 6/82 free-agent draft

Player Summary	
Fantasy Value	$2 to $6
Card Value	3¢ to 4¢
Will	throw strikes
Can't	avoid gophers
Expect	lots of runners
Don't Expect	starter's berth

Wells is coming off a difficult year. Ineffective in 14 starts for Toronto last summer, he was banished to the bullpen after the Jays acquired David Cone in August. Wells's season was embodied by a single game: On Aug. 20, he yielded 13 earned runs in the first four and one-third innings of a 16-3 loss to Milwaukee. Opponents compiled a .289 batting average, a .346 on-base percentage, and a .471 slugging percentage in 1992. Wells showed good control, giving up fewer than three walks per nine innings. Nevertheless, he showed an alarming tendency to yield home run balls, giving up 16. He had one of the worst ratios of home runs to innings pitched in the league. Since Wells also yielded more hits than innings, the gopher balls often came with men on base. Lefties—his chief patsies in 1991—hit him hard. It's a good thing he holds runners well, because he had lots of them.

Major League Pitching Register

	W	L	ERA	G	S	IP	H	ER	BB	SO
87 AL	4	3	3.99	18	1	29.1	37	13	12	32
88 AL	3	5	4.62	41	4	64.1	65	33	31	56
89 AL	7	4	2.40	54	2	86.1	66	23	28	78
90 AL	11	6	3.14	43	3	189.0	165	66	45	115
91 AL	15	10	3.72	40	1	198.1	188	82	49	106
92 AL	7	9	5.40	41	2	120.0	138	72	36	62
Life	47	37	3.78	237	13	687.1	659	289	201	449
3 AVE	11	8	3.90	41	2	169.0	164	73	43	94

JOHN WETTELAND

Position: Pitcher
Team: Montreal Expos
Born: Aug. 21, 1966 San Mateo, CA
Height: 6'2" **Weight:** 195 lbs.
Bats: right **Throws:** right
Acquired: Traded from Reds with Bill Risley for Dave Martinez, Scott Ruskin, and Willie Greene, 12/91

Player Summary	
Fantasy Value	$24 to $32
Card Value	3¢ to 4¢
Will	blow batters away
Can't	keep good control
Expect	great saves total
Don't Expect	timid baserunners

Wetteland was the only major leaguer traded twice during the 1991-92 off-season. The Expos, seeking a closer, obviously knew what they were doing. Given his first chance to close in the majors, he pitched the Expos into contention. A fastball-and-slider pitcher who's still learning how to set up hitters, Wetteland blew a few saves early before settling into a groove. He converted 10 of 11 in July and won two others, netting the most Rolaids Relief Man points (32) for a single month since Mark Davis had 35 in September 1989. Blessed with a fearless psyche and a rubber arm, Wetteland works his way out of trouble with strikeouts. In 1992, opponents compiled a .213 batting average, a .304 on-base percentage, and a .306 slugging percentage. Wetteland handles first batters well and keeps the ball in the park. His main weakness is holding runners. He had 20 saves, a 4-3 record, a 2.79 ERA, 26 walks, and 55 strikeouts in 61⅓ innings at Triple-A Albuquerque in 1991.

Major League Pitching Register

	W	L	ERA	G	S	IP	H	ER	BB	SO
89 NL	5	8	3.77	31	1	102.2	81	43	34	96
90 NL	2	4	4.81	22	0	43.0	44	23	17	36
91 NL	1	0	0.00	6	0	9.0	5	0	3	9
92 NL	4	4	2.92	67	37	83.1	64	27	36	99
Life	12	16	3.52	126	38	238.0	194	93	90	240
2 AVE	3	4	3.56	45	19	63.1	54	25	27	68

LOU WHITAKER

Position: Second base
Team: Detroit Tigers
Born: May 12, 1957 Brooklyn, NY
Height: 5'11" **Weight:** 180 lbs.
Bats: left **Throws:** right
Acquired: Fifth-round pick in 6/75 free-agent draft

Player Summary	
Fantasy Value	$12 to $20
Card Value	5¢ to 10¢
Will	put wood on the ball
Can't	show speed of youth
Expect	high on-base average
Don't Expect	defensive difficulty

Whitaker could give lessons in contact hitting. He is one of the toughest strikeouts in the game, and he walks more than twice as much as he fans. Whitaker still manages to generate plenty of power. At age 35, last summer he had his best average since 1984 and hit well over .350 against lefthanded pitching (no mean feat for a lefty hitter). He had a .386 on-base average and a .461 slugging percentage in 1992. His numbers might have been better had he not shared second base with versatile switch-hitter Tony Phillips. Whitaker is no longer as quick as he once was, but he substitutes experience for lost range. Whitaker still turns the double play and plays the hitters perfectly.

Major League Batting Register

	BA	G	AB	R	H	2B	3B	HR	RBI	SB
77 AL	.250	11	32	5	8	1	0	0	2	2
78 AL	.285	139	484	71	138	12	7	3	58	7
79 AL	.286	127	423	75	121	14	8	3	42	20
80 AL	.233	145	477	68	111	19	1	1	45	8
81 AL	.263	109	335	48	88	14	4	5	36	5
82 AL	.286	152	560	76	160	22	8	15	65	11
83 AL	.320	161	643	94	206	40	6	12	72	17
84 AL	.289	143	558	90	161	25	1	13	56	6
85 AL	.279	152	609	102	170	29	8	21	73	6
86 AL	.269	144	584	95	157	26	6	20	73	13
87 AL	.265	149	604	110	160	38	6	16	59	13
88 AL	.275	115	403	54	111	18	2	12	55	2
89 AL	.251	148	509	77	128	21	1	28	85	6
90 AL	.237	132	472	75	112	22	2	18	60	8
91 AL	.279	138	470	94	131	26	2	23	78	4
92 AL	.278	130	453	77	126	26	0	19	71	6
Life	.274	2095	7616	1211	2088	353	62	209	930	134
3 AVE	.265	133	465	82	123	25	1	20	70	6

DEVON WHITE

Position: Outfield
Team: Toronto Blue Jays
Born: Dec. 29, 1962 Kingston, Jamaica
Height: 6'2" **Weight:** 178 lbs.
Bats: both **Throws:** right
Acquired: Traded from Angels with Willie Fraser and Marcus Moore for Junior Felix, Luis Sojo, and Ken Rivers, 12/90

Player Summary	
Fantasy Value	$18 to $24
Card Value	4¢ to 6¢
Will	run like a gazelle
Can't	stop striking out
Expect	brilliant defense
Don't Expect	throws to nail him

White showed that he was the best defensive center fielder in the game in the 1992 World Series when he made a sensational leaping back-handed catch in game three of the 1992 World Series, starting what should have been only the second triple play in Series' history. Managers polled by *Baseball America* said White was the best defensive outfielder in the American League. He has a very strong arm, and his great speed enables him to flag down balls other outfielders can only dream about. White also used his speed in the leadoff slot. He wasn't as productive last year as he was in '91, but he still topped 30 steals for the fourth time and homered in double figures for the fifth year in a row. He still needs to cut his strikeouts and improve against lefties. He had a .303 on-base average and a .390 slugging percentage last summer.

Major League Batting Register

	BA	G	AB	R	H	2B	3B	HR	RBI	SB
85 AL	.143	21	7	7	1	0	0	0	0	3
86 AL	.235	29	51	8	12	1	1	1	3	6
87 AL	.263	159	639	103	168	33	5	24	87	32
88 AL	.259	122	455	76	118	22	2	11	51	17
89 AL	.245	156	636	86	156	18	13	12	56	44
90 AL	.217	125	443	57	96	17	3	11	44	21
91 AL	.282	156	642	110	181	40	10	17	60	33
92 AL	.248	153	641	98	159	26	7	17	60	37
Life	.254	921	3514	545	891	157	41	93	361	193
3 AVE	.253	145	575	88	145	28	7	15	55	30

WALLY WHITEHURST

Position: Pitcher
Team: San Diego Padres
Born: April 11, 1964 Shreveport, LA
Height: 6'3" **Weight:** 185 lbs.
Bats: right **Throws:** right
Acquired: Traded from Mets with D.J. Dozier and Raul Casanova for Tony Fernandez, 10/92

Player Summary	
Fantasy Value	$2 to $5
Card Value	3¢ to 4¢
Will	get rotation shot
Can't	retire first batters
Expect	exceptional control
Don't Expect	gophers to beat him

Whitehurst moves to San Diego, where he might get a shot at the starting rotation. Most of his numbers for the Mets were good last year—except for his won-lost record. Splitting the season between the bullpen and starting rotation for the second straight year, he yielded a hit per inning but fewer than three walks per nine innings. He was extremely stingy with the home run ball and averaged six and one-half strikeouts per nine innings. A curve-ball specialist who also throws a fastball and a slider, Whitehurst has a much better career record as a reliever. His main problem in the pen last year, however, was an inability to retire first batters, who compiled a .333 batting average. Whitehurst is also weak at holding runners on base. Opponents compiled a .264 batting average, a .328 on-base percentage, and a .384 slugging percentage in 1992. He helps himself in the field and at the plate. Whitehurst began his pro career in 1985.

MARK WHITEN

Position: Outfield
Team: Cleveland Indians
Born: Nov. 25, 1966 Pensacola, FL
Height: 6'3" **Weight:** 215 lbs.
Bats: both **Throws:** right
Acquired: Traded from Blue Jays with Glenallen Hill and Denis Boucher for Tom Candiotti and Turner Ward, 6/91

Player Summary	
Fantasy Value	$8 to $14
Card Value	4¢ to 6¢
Will	intimidate runners
Can't	cut his strikeouts
Expect	power to increase
Don't Expect	high batting mark

Though he's been in the majors only two full years, Whiten has already attracted the attention of American League managers. They told *Baseball America* last year that his right field throwing arm is the league's best. He has made more than a dozen assists in each of the last two years. He owns fine defensive tools but shows even more promise on offense. A package of speed plus power, he hits for a higher average righthanded but has more power lefthanded. Though he showed more selectivity last summer, when he doubled his walk total, Whiten still needs to reduce his strikeout count. When he does, he could realize his power potential. He had a .347 on-base average and a .360 slugging percentage last summer. He made great strides as a runner last year but was still thrown out trying to steal far too often. At age 26, Whiten should start to refine his game this year. At Triple-A Syracuse in 1990, he batted .290 with 14 homers and 48 RBI.

Major League Pitching Register

	W	L	ERA	G	S	IP	H	ER	BB	SO
89 NL	0	1	4.50	9	0	14.0	17	7	5	9
90 NL	1	0	3.29	38	2	65.2	63	24	9	46
91 NL	7	12	4.18	36	1	133.1	142	62	25	87
92 NL	3	9	3.62	44	0	97.0	99	39	33	70
Life	11	22	3.83	127	3	310.0	321	132	72	212
3 AVE	4	7	3.80	39	1	98.1	101	42	22	68

Major League Batting Register

	BA	G	AB	R	H	2B	3B	HR	RBI	SB
90 AL	.273	33	88	12	24	1	1	2	7	2
91 AL	.243	116	407	46	99	18	7	9	45	4
92 AL	.254	148	508	73	129	19	4	9	43	16
Life	.251	297	1003	131	252	38	12	20	95	22
2 AVE	.249	132	458	60	114	19	6	9	44	10

KEVIN WICKANDER

Position: Pitcher
Team: Cleveland Indians
Born: Jan. 4, 1965 Fort Dodge, IA
Height: 6'2" **Weight:** 202 lbs.
Bats: left **Throws:** left
Acquired: Second-round pick in 6/86 free-agent draft

Player Summary	
Fantasy Value	$1 to $3
Card Value	3¢ to 4¢
Will	keep ball in park
Can't	learn strike zone
Expect	bouts of wildness
Don't Expect	lefties to thrive

Wickander was one of the most effective but least publicized members of the Cleveland bullpen in 1992. Deployed as a set-up man, he averaged more than eight strikeouts per nine innings while yielding just under a hit per inning. He threw only one home run ball all season. Wickander's weakness was wildness. He yielded almost six walks per nine innings—hardly the kind of control any big league reliever should have. First batters also gave Wickander trouble. He should do better against southpaws, since he's lefthanded, but he was actually more effective against righties last year. Opponents compiled a .260 batting average, a .386 on-base percentage, and a .327 slugging percentage in 1992. He was 0-0 with a 1.64 ERA, two saves, 18 strikeouts, and six walks in 11 innings at Triple-A Colorado Springs in 1992. Wickander had a 1-0 record, 16 saves, and 0.63 ERA at Double-A Williamsport in 1989. That season, his ratio of strikeouts to walks was 4-to-1. Should he recapture that form, he could play a more prominent role in the relief corps.

Major League Pitching Register

	W	L	ERA	G	S	IP	H	ER	BB	SO
89 AL	0	0	3.38	2	0	2.2	6	1	2	0
90 AL	0	1	3.65	10	0	12.1	14	5	4	10
92 AL	2	0	3.07	44	1	41.0	39	14	28	38
Life	2	1	3.21	56	1	56.0	59	20	34	48

RICK WILKINS

Position: Catcher
Team: Chicago Cubs
Born: July 4, 1967 Jacksonville, FL
Height: 6'2" **Weight:** 210 lbs.
Bats: left **Throws:** right
Acquired: 23rd-round pick in 6/86 free-agent draft

Player Summary	
Fantasy Value	$2 to $6
Card Value	3¢ to 4¢
Will	deliver some homers
Can't	attain high average
Expect	more at bats
Don't Expect	runners to test arm

Wilkins is one of baseball's best young catchers. He not only hits with power but throws out 40 percent of the runners who try to steal. A good game-caller who handles pitchers well, he improved his ability to prevent wild pitches after working with Cubs' coach Tom Trebelhorn last summer. A lefthanded hitter, he was used in platoon with the righthanded Joe Girardi last summer. Since Girardi is off to the Rockies, Wilkins should receive more at bats this year. He had a strong year despite a weak finish. He hit righthanders well, showed some patience at the plate, and displayed fine defensive skills. He had a .344 on-base average and a .414 slugging percentage in 1992. He batted .280 against lefties and .268 versus righthanders. He even revealed a trace of speed—an unusual trait for a big league catcher. Wilkins has led several minor leagues in putouts, assists, total chances, and double plays. He notched a 37.2 percent success rate in gunning down potential basestealers in 1992. He broke into pro ball in 1987.

Major League Batting Register

	BA	G	AB	R	H	2B	3B	HR	RBI	SB
91 NL	.222	86	203	21	45	9	0	6	22	3
92 NL	.270	83	244	20	66	9	1	8	22	0
Life	.248	169	447	41	111	18	1	14	44	3
2 AVE	.248	85	224	21	56	9	1	7	22	2

BERNIE WILLIAMS

Position: Outfield
Team: New York Yankees
Born: Sept. 13, 1968 San Juan, Puerto Rico
Height: 6'2" **Weight:** 180 lbs.
Bats: both **Throws:** right
Acquired: Signed as a free agent, 9/85

Player Summary

Fantasy Value	$6 to $14
Card Value	5¢ to 15¢
Will	relish fastball diet
Can't	show consistent power
Expect	gradual improvement
Don't Expect	Mickey Mantle clone

Williams was hitting .306 with eight homers, 50 RBI, 52 walks, 61 strikeouts, and 20 steals in 363 at bats at Triple-A Columbus when he was promoted to the Yankees last July 31. He quickly justified the call with a flurry of hitting and fielding gems. On Aug. 2, he went 2-for-3 with two walks, two runs scored, and a runner doubled off first against Toronto. Later, he hit a 444-foot homer against Detroit's John Doherty. Williams is a switch-hitter who has a higher average righthanded but more power lefthanded. He spent the last half of '91 in the Bronx but struggled. In 1992, he was ready. Handed the leadoff spot and center field job, Williams showed patience at the plate. He had a .354 on-base average and a .406 slugging percentage in 1992. He walked almost as much as he fanned. Williams is a fastball hitter who hits to all fields. He has plenty of range in the outfield, and his arm is strong enough. He batted .294 with eight homers and 37 RBI in 1991 at Columbus. He was named the International League's No. 8 prospect in '91, and its No. 4 prospect last year.

Major League Batting Register

	BA	G	AB	R	H	2B	3B	HR	RBI	SB
91 AL	.237	85	320	43	76	19	4	3	34	10
92 AL	.280	62	261	39	73	14	2	5	26	7
Life	.256	147	581	82	149	33	6	8	60	17
2 AVE	.256	74	291	41	75	17	3	4	30	9

BRIAN WILLIAMS

Position: Pitcher
Team: Houston Astros
Born: Feb. 15, 1969 Lancaster, SC
Height: 6'2" **Weight:** 195 lbs.
Bats: right **Throws:** right
Acquired: First-round pick in 6/90 free-agent draft

Player Summary

Fantasy Value	$6 to $12
Card Value	5¢ to 12¢
Will	become big winner
Can't	always find plate
Expect	improved control
Don't Expect	batting problems

In three of his first five starts in the majors, Williams threw at least five scoreless innings. He has poise, doesn't panic with runners on base, and has unusually good command for an inexperienced pitcher. He won his first three decisions last summer, lost three straight, and then recovered to become one of Houston's more dependable starters. Williams throws two-seam and four-seam fastballs, along with a curve and a changeup. He yields fewer hits than innings and averages five strikeouts per nine innings. Opponents in 1992 compiled a .255 batting average, a .330 on-base percentage, and a .393 slugging percentage. His control needs work. At Triple-A Tucson in 1992, he had a 6-1 record with a 4.50 ERA, 26 walks, and 58 strikeouts in 70 innings. Williams helps himself with his glove, bat, and legs. The college outfielder did not switch to pitching until his junior year at the University of South Carolina. He played for Team USA in 1989. In 1991, he was 0-1 with a 4.93 ERA at Tucson, 2-1 with a 4.20 ERA at Double-A Jackson, and 6-4 with a 2.91 ERA at Class-A Osceola.

Major League Pitching Register

	W	L	ERA	G	CG	IP	H	ER	BB	SO
91 NL	0	1	3.75	2	0	12.0	11	5	4	4
92 NL	7	6	3.92	16	0	96.1	92	42	42	54
Life	7	7	3.90	18	0	108.1	103	47	46	58

MATT WILLIAMS

Position: Third base
Team: San Francisco Giants
Born: Nov. 28, 1965 Bishop, CA
Height: 6'2" **Weight:** 205 lbs.
Bats: right **Throws:** right
Acquired: First-round pick in 6/86 free-agent draft

Player Summary	
Fantasy Value	$22 to $28
Card Value	5¢ to 10¢
Will	come back
Can't	avoid strikeouts
Expect	tremendous power
Don't Expect	defensive lapses

In his first three big league seasons, Williams swung at bad pitches, fanned frequently, and failed to hit his weight. Though two strong years followed, Williams reverted to old habits in 1992, especially during the first half. Plagued from a sore right thumb, sore right foot, and bruised left knee, he was often pathetic. Between May 22 and July 6, he went 124 at bats without a home run—an amazing drought for someone who had two-year totals of 67 homers and 220 RBI. The former UNLV All-American led the Giants in strikeouts. Williams, who tries to pull every pitch over the fence, fans three times more than he walks. He had a .286 on-base average and a .384 slugging percentage in 1992. His defense suffered during his hitting drought. Williams led NL third basemen in errors one year after winning a Gold Glove. He did lead in double plays, however. He steals on occasion but often gets thrown out.

MITCH WILLIAMS

Position: Pitcher
Team: Philadelphia Phillies
Born: Nov. 17, 1964 Santa Ana, CA
Height: 6'4" **Weight:** 205 lbs.
Bats: left **Throws:** left
Acquired: Traded from Cubs for Bob Scanlan and Chuck McElroy, 4/91

Player Summary	
Fantasy Value	$20 to $28
Card Value	3¢ to 4¢
Will	get strikeouts
Can't	master control
Expect	runners on base
Don't Expect	home run balls

"Wild Thing" is a fitting nickname for Williams. The hard-throwing lefty closer has been known to walk the bases loaded, then strike out the side. He averages almost eight strikeouts per nine innings and keeps the ball in the park. He still finds ways to sabotage his own efforts, nonetheless. In 1992, for example, Williams averaged more than seven walks per nine innings—by far the worst control of any relief pitcher in the majors. Opponents compiled a .240 batting average, a .386 on-base percentage, and a .359 slugging percentage last year. A durable performer, who has topped 60 appearances in six of the last seven years, Williams needs to conquer his own flamboyance. A power pitcher who walks as many men as he fans can't be a winner. A fastball-slider pitcher who puts his entire body into every pitch, Williams falls off the mound—leaving him in poor fielding position. His pickoff move is adequate.

Major League Batting Register

	BA	G	AB	R	H	2B	3B	HR	RBI	SB
87 NL	.188	84	245	28	46	9	2	8	21	4
88 NL	.205	52	156	17	32	6	1	8	19	0
89 NL	.202	84	292	31	59	18	1	18	50	1
90 NL	.277	159	617	87	171	27	2	33	122	7
91 NL	.268	157	589	72	158	24	5	34	98	5
92 NL	.227	146	529	58	120	13	5	20	66	7
Life	.241	682	2428	293	586	97	16	121	376	24
3 AVE	.259	154	578	72	150	21	4	29	95	6

Major League Pitching Register

	W	L	ERA	G	S	IP	H	ER	BB	SO
86 AL	8	6	3.58	80	8	98.0	69	39	79	90
87 AL	8	6	3.23	85	6	108.2	63	39	94	129
88 AL	2	7	4.63	67	18	68.0	48	35	47	61
89 NL	4	4	2.76	76	36	81.2	71	25	52	67
90 NL	1	8	3.93	59	16	66.1	60	29	50	55
91 NL	12	5	2.34	69	30	88.1	56	23	62	84
92 NL	5	8	3.78	66	29	81.0	69	34	64	74
Life	40	44	3.41	502	143	592.0	436	224	448	560
3 AVE	6	7	3.28	65	25	78.1	62	29	59	71

CARL WILLIS

Position: Pitcher
Team: Minnesota Twins
Born: Dec. 28, 1960 Danville, VA
Height: 6'4" **Weight:** 212 lbs.
Bats: left **Throws:** right
Acquired: Signed as a free agent, 12/90

Player Summary

Fantasy Value	$1 to $3
Card Value	3¢ to 4¢
Will	supply strong set-up
Can't	take over closer job
Expect	frequent appearances
Don't Expect	trouble with control

After an agonizingly slow start, Willis recaptured the form that made him the main set-up man in the 1991 Minnesota bullpen. Throwing a heater and split-fingered fastball with pinpoint control, he averaged more than five strikeouts and just over eight hits per nine innings. He also kept the ball in the park—no easy feat for anyone who spends half his time in the Metrodome. Opponents compiled a .246 batting average, a .270 on-base percentage, and a .347 slugging percentage in 1992. Willis, who never had a full season in the majors before 1992, succeeds by staying ahead in the count. Two years ago, he did that so well that he ranked second in the AL in efficiency against first batters. Though he didn't do as well last year, he still managed to maintain a respectable ERA while setting a career high in appearances. Willis usually handcuffs righthanded batters, fields his position well, and keeps baserunners honest.

Major League Pitching Register

	W	L	ERA	G	S	IP	H	ER	BB	SO
84 AL	0	2	7.31	10	0	16.0	25	13	5	4
84 NL	0	1	3.72	7	1	9.2	8	4	2	3
85 NL	1	0	9.22	11	1	13.2	21	14	5	6
86 NL	1	3	4.47	29	0	52.1	54	26	32	24
88 AL	0	0	8.25	6	0	12.0	17	11	7	6
91 AL	8	3	2.63	40	2	89.0	76	26	19	53
92 AL	7	3	2.72	59	1	79.1	73	24	11	45
Life	17	12	3.90	162	5	272.0	274	118	81	141
2 AVE	8	3	2.67	50	2	84.1	75	25	15	49

TREVOR WILSON

Position: Pitcher
Team: San Francisco Giants
Born: June 7, 1966 Torrance, CA
Height: 6' **Weight:** 175 lbs.
Bats: left **Throws:** left
Acquired: Eighth-round pick in 6/85 free-agent draft

Player Summary

Fantasy Value	$10 to $14
Card Value	3¢ to 4¢
Will	dominate lefthanders
Can't	prevent gopher balls
Expect	giant-sized comeback
Don't Expect	runners to test him

Wilson could have sued his teammates for nonsupport last summer. He was given fewer than three runs per nine innings all year, so it is not surprising that he led the Giants in losses. Wilson had hoped to maintain the momentum of his strong 1991 finish but ran into trouble before Opening Day. During surgery to remove a benign cyst from his ribs, surgeons sliced portions of two healthy ribs. Wilson later encountered elbow problems that knocked him out of action in September. In between, he had more than five strikeouts per nine innings. He threw too many home run balls and did not enjoy his usual success against lefthanded hitters. Wilson's main pitches are a rising fastball and big curveball, though he also throws a changeup and a slider. Opponents compiled a .265 batting average, a .342 on-base percentage, and a .416 slugging percentage in 1992. Basestealers rarely test Wilson's proven pickoff move. He also helps himself as a hitter, bunter, and fielder.

Major League Pitching Register

	W	L	ERA	G	CG	IP	H	ER	BB	SO
88 NL	0	2	4.09	4	0	22.0	25	10	8	15
89 NL	2	3	4.35	14	0	39.1	28	19	24	22
90 NL	8	7	4.00	27	3	110.1	87	49	49	66
91 NL	13	11	3.56	44	2	202.0	173	80	77	139
92 NL	8	14	4.21	26	1	154.0	152	72	64	88
Life	31	37	3.92	115	6	527.2	465	230	222	330
3 AVE	10	11	3.88	32	2	155.0	137	67	63	98

WILLIE WILSON

Position: Outfield
Team: Chicago Cubs
Born: July 9, 1955 Montgomery, AL
Height: 6'3" **Weight:** 200 lbs.
Bats: both **Throws:** right
Acquired: Signed as a free agent, 12/92

Player Summary	
Fantasy Value	$2 to $6
Card Value	3¢ to 4¢
Will	use running game
Can't	avoid strikeouts
Expect	great range
Don't Expect	display of power

Two years after he was given up for dead, Wilson proved to be a lifesaver to the Athletics last season. Pressed into regular service in center field after Dave Henderson was sidelined by injury, Wilson not only played the position well but topped 20 steals for the 15th year in succession. His lifetime success ratio stealing bases exceeds 80 percent. Wilson runs like a deer on the bases but still strikes out too much for a singles hitter. Were he willing to wait for walks, Wilson would increase his value in direct proportion to his on-base percentage. He had a .329 on-base percentage and a .333 slugging percentage in 1992. His range is impressive but his arm is not.

Major League Batting Register

	BA	G	AB	R	H	2B	3B	HR	RBI	SB
76 AL	.167	12	6	0	1	0	0	0	0	2
77 AL	.324	13	34	10	11	2	0	0	1	6
78 AL	.217	127	198	43	43	8	2	0	16	46
79 AL	.315	154	588	113	185	18	13	6	49	83
80 AL	.326	161	705	133	230	28	15	3	49	79
81 AL	.303	102	439	54	133	10	7	1	32	34
82 AL	.332	136	585	87	194	19	15	3	46	37
83 AL	.276	137	576	90	159	22	8	2	33	59
84 AL	.301	128	541	81	163	24	9	2	44	47
85 AL	.278	141	605	87	168	25	21	4	43	43
86 AL	.269	156	631	77	170	20	7	9	44	34
87 AL	.279	146	610	97	170	18	15	4	30	59
88 AL	.262	147	591	81	155	17	11	1	37	35
89 AL	.253	112	383	58	97	17	7	3	43	24
90 AL	.290	115	307	49	89	13	3	2	42	24
91 AL	.238	113	294	38	70	14	4	0	28	20
92 AL	.270	132	396	38	107	15	5	0	37	28
Life	.286	2032	7489	1136	2145	270	142	40	574	660
3 AVE	.267	120	332	42	89	14	4	1	36	24

DAVE WINFIELD

Position: Designated hitter; outfield
Team: Minnesota Twins
Born: Oct. 3, 1951 St. Paul, MN
Height: 6'6" **Weight:** 220 lbs.
Bats: right **Throws:** right
Acquired: Signed as a free agent, 12/92

Player Summary	
Fantasy Value	$20 to $25
Card Value	10¢ to 20¢
Will	knock in runs
Can't	run like a kid
Expect	home run power
Don't Expect	speed on bases

Winfield is finally coming home. In 1992, Winfield not only provided veteran leadership to the World Champion Blue Jays, he provided the World Series-winning RBI. He proved in 1992 that life begins at 40. On Sept. 24, he became the first player of that age with 100 RBI when he hit a two-run homer off Ben McDonald. Signed to serve as DH, outfield backup, and unofficial coach for Toronto's younger players, his presence in the lineup as Toronto's cleanup hitter helped No. 3 man Joe Carter get a steady diet of pitches to hit. When Carter missed RBI chances, Winfield cashed in: His 32 RBI in August were a club record for a month.

Major League Batting Register

	BA	G	AB	R	H	2B	3B	HR	RBI	SB
73 NL	.277	56	141	9	39	4	1	3	12	0
74 NL	.265	145	498	57	132	18	4	20	75	9
75 NL	.267	143	509	74	136	20	2	15	76	23
76 NL	.283	137	492	81	139	26	4	13	69	26
77 NL	.275	157	615	104	169	29	7	25	92	16
78 NL	.308	158	587	88	181	30	5	24	97	21
79 NL	.308	159	597	97	184	27	10	34	118	15
80 NL	.276	162	558	89	154	25	6	20	87	23
81 AL	.294	105	388	52	114	25	1	13	68	11
82 AL	.280	140	539	84	151	24	8	37	106	5
83 AL	.283	152	598	99	169	26	8	32	116	15
84 AL	.340	141	567	106	193	34	4	19	100	6
85 AL	.275	155	633	105	174	34	6	26	114	19
86 AL	.262	154	565	90	148	31	5	24	104	6
87 AL	.275	156	575	83	158	22	1	27	97	5
88 AL	.322	149	559	96	180	37	2	25	107	9
90 AL	.213	20	61	7	13	3	0	2	6	0
90 AL	.275	112	414	63	114	18	2	19	72	0
91 AL	.262	150	568	75	149	27	4	28	86	7
92 AL	.290	156	583	92	169	33	3	26	108	2
Life	.285	2707	10047	1551	2866	493	83	432	1710	218
3 AVE	.274	146	542	79	148	27	3	25	91	3

305

BOBBY WITT

Position: Pitcher
Team: Oakland Athletics
Born: May 11, 1964 Arlington, VA
Height: 6'2" **Weight:** 205 lbs.
Bats: right **Throws:** right
Acquired: Traded from Rangers with Ruben Sierra and Jeff Russell for Jose Canseco, 8/92

Player Summary	
Fantasy Value	$8 to $16
Card Value	3¢ to 4¢
Will	throw sizzling heater
Can't	avoid control trouble
Expect	fewer hits than frames
Don't Expect	second coming of 1990

Witt has walked more than 100 batters in a season four times in the last five years. Last Aug. 15, he walked 10 in less than five innings against Detroit. Wildness cost Witt his job in Texas, which included him in the package for Jose Canseco two weeks after the Tiger fiasco. Told to relax by Oakland pitching coach Dave Duncan, Witt prospered with Oakland before his old control troubles resurfaced. If his problems stem from mechanical flaws—as some scouts suggest—he may be able to recapture his 1990 form. At age 28, his raw talent is obvious. Witt's fastball tops 95 mph; his slider and curve are perfect complements. Witt yields fewer hits than innings and averages six strikeouts per nine innings. Opponents compiled a .256 batting average, a .356 on-base percentage, and a .371 slugging percentage last summer. He allowed five walks per nine innings in '92. He has a mediocre pickoff move and is a good fielder.

Major League Pitching Register

	W	L	ERA	G	CG	IP	H	ER	BB	SO
86 AL	11	9	5.48	31	0	157.2	130	96	143	174
87 AL	8	10	4.91	26	1	143.0	114	78	140	160
88 AL	8	10	3.92	22	13	174.1	134	76	101	148
89 AL	12	13	5.14	31	5	194.1	182	111	114	166
90 AL	17	10	3.36	33	7	222.0	197	83	110	221
91 AL	3	7	6.09	17	1	88.2	84	60	74	82
92 AL	10	14	4.29	31	0	193.0	183	92	114	125
Life	69	73	4.57	191	27	1173.0	1024	596	796	1076
3 AVE	10	10	4.20	27	3	167.2	155	78	99	143

MARK WOHLERS

Position: Pitcher
Team: Atlanta Braves
Born: Jan. 23, 1970 Holyoke, MA
Height: 6'4" **Weight:** 205 lbs.
Bats: right **Throws:** right
Acquired: Eighth-round pick in 6/88 free-agent draft

Player Summary	
Fantasy Value	$4 to $8
Card Value	5¢ to 10¢
Will	throw blue darters
Can't	keep runners close
Expect	control to improve
Don't Expect	ball to leave park

After spending two years trying to justify a closer-of-the-future tag, Wohlers started to realize that potential during the 1992 stretch drive. After opening the year in the minors, he came up May 28 but didn't get enough work to stay sharp. Returned to Triple-A Richmond on Aug. 2, Wohlers got two starts—giving him the innings he needed to find his form. Sensational after Atlanta called again, Wohlers yielded fewer hits than innings, refused to give up gophers, and conquered previous control problems. The power pitcher's fastball hit 99 mph on the radar gun. Wohlers also works in a slider and a cut fastball that he uses as a changeup. Opponents in 1992 compiled a .235 batting average, a .319 on-base percentage, and a .261 slugging percentage. He's effective against first batters. He wields a good glove but needs work in holding runners. Wohlers was 0-2 with nine saves, 17 walks, and 33 strikeouts in 34 innings last summer at Richmond. In 1991, he had a 1.03 ERA and 11 saves at Richmond and a 0.57 ERA with 21 saves at Double-A Greenville.

Major League Pitching Register

	W	L	ERA	G	S	IP	H	ER	BB	SO
91 NL	3	1	3.20	17	2	19.2	17	7	13	13
92 NL	1	2	2.55	32	4	35.1	28	10	14	17
Life	4	3	2.78	49	6	55.0	45	17	27	30

TODD WORRELL

Position: Pitcher
Team: Los Angeles Dodgers
Born: Sept. 28, 1959 Arcadia, CA
Height: 6'5" **Weight:** 222 lbs.
Bats: right **Throws:** right
Acquired: Signed as a free agent, 12/92

Player Summary	
Fantasy Value	.....................................$4 to $8
Card Value	....3¢ to 4¢
Will	................................seek closer role
Can't	.............................prevent stolen bases
Expect	....high K total
Don't Expect	.................first batters to reach

Worrell is the new closer for LA. He showed last summer that he had made a full recovery from two elbow operations and arthroscopic shoulder surgery. Sidelined between Labor Day 1989 and spring training last year, he worked his way back as the set-up man for St. Louis closer Lee Smith. Once the Cardinal closer himself, Worrell did not get many save opportunities in 1992. When he did, however, he capitalized. On Sept. 5, he broke Bruce Sutter's club record when he notched his 128th career save. The hard-throwing Worrell averaged a strikeout an inning and seven hits per nine innings. His control was shaky at times (more than three walks per nine innings), but he kept the ball in the park, handled first hitters well, and decimated lefthanded batters, who had only a .174 batting average against him last summer. Opponents compiled a .198 batting average, a .281 on-base percentage, and a .282 slugging percentage in 1992. Worrell's weakness was stopping basestealers, who ran wild against him.

Major League Pitching Register

	W	L	ERA	G	S	IP	H	ER	BB	SO
85 NL	3	0	2.91	17	5	21.2	17	7	7	17
86 NL	9	10	2.08	74	36	103.2	86	24	41	73
87 NL	8	6	2.66	75	33	94.2	86	28	34	92
88 NL	5	9	3.00	68	32	90.0	69	30	34	78
89 NL	3	5	2.96	47	20	51.2	42	17	26	41
92 NL	5	3	2.11	67	3	64.0	45	15	25	64
Life	33	33	2.56	348	129	425.2	345	121	167	365

ANTHONY YOUNG

Position: Pitcher
Team: New York Mets
Born: Jan. 19, 1966 Houston, TX
Height: 6'2" **Weight:** 200 lbs.
Bats: right **Throws:** right
Acquired: First-round pick in 6/87 free-agent draft

Player Summary	
Fantasy Value	......................................$3 to $7
Card Value	....5¢ to 12¢
Will	..........................yield a hit per inning
Can't	...............................keep job in rotation
Expect	..........................problems with lefties
Don't Expect	...................streaks of wildness

Young was an enigma as a 1992 rookie with the Mets. After going 2-8 as a starter, he moved to the bullpen and did well before the bottom fell out again. He got his first save in six years of pro ball July 1, then worked 18 more consecutive appearances (23⅔ innings) without yielding a run through Aug. 26. Young notched eight straight saves while filling in for closer John Franco but then blew four ninth-inning leads in two weeks. Young looked so good when he first moved to the pen that he's likely to stay there. He's fine against first batters but has to improve against lefties. Young has the repertoire of a starter. He is a sinkerball pitcher with a slider, curve, and changeup. The former defensive back from the University of Houston can hit, field, and hold runners. In 1991 at Triple-A Tidewater, he was 7-9 with a 3.73 ERA, 67 walks, and 93 strikeouts in 164 innings. He was the Texas League Pitcher of the Year in 1990, when he went 15-3 with a 1.65 ERA, 52 walks, and 95 strikeouts in 158 innings.

Major League Pitching Register

	W	L	ERA	G	S	IP	H	ER	BB	SO
91 NL	2	5	3.10	10	0	49.1	48	17	12	20
92 NL	2	14	4.17	52	15	121.0	134	56	31	64
Life	4	19	3.86	62	15	170.1	182	73	43	84

MATT YOUNG

Position: Pitcher
Team: Boston Red Sox
Born: Aug. 9, 1958 Pasadena, CA
Height: 6'3" **Weight:** 205 lbs.
Bats: left **Throws:** left
Acquired: Signed as a free agent, 12/90

Player Summary	
Fantasy Value	$1 to $3
Card Value	3¢ to 4¢
Will	have losing year
Can't	curb runaway ERA
Expect	control problems
Don't Expect	another contract

Young may not have been the worst free-agent signing in baseball history, but he comes close. Signed before the 1991 season to replace Mike Boddiker in the BoSox rotation, Young has won three games in two seasons—hardly justifying a three-year, $6.35 million contract that still has a year to run. He's had a winning record in only one of his nine seasons and has a career ERA that's as big as the federal deficit. He's had periodic elbow and shoulder problems but his biggest headache last year was control—or lack of it. He yielded a hit per inning but too many of those hits went all the way (seven). Opponents compiled a .257 batting average, a .360 on-base percentage, and a .379 slugging percentage in 1992. Young's best pitch is a curve, but he has trouble throwing it for strikes. He even has trouble throwing to first.

Major League Pitching Register

	W	L	ERA	G	S	IP	H	ER	BB	SO
83 AL	11	15	3.27	33	0	203.2	178	74	79	130
84 AL	6	8	5.72	22	0	113.1	141	72	57	73
85 AL	12	19	4.91	37	1	218.1	242	119	76	136
86 AL	8	6	3.82	65	13	103.2	108	44	46	82
87 NL	5	8	4.47	47	11	54.1	62	27	17	42
89 AL	1	4	6.75	26	0	37.1	42	28	31	27
90 AL	8	18	3.51	34	0	225.1	198	88	107	176
91 AL	3	7	5.18	19	0	88.2	92	51	53	69
92 AL	0	4	4.58	28	0	70.2	69	36	42	57
Life	54	89	4.35	311	25	1115.1	1132	539	508	792
3 AVE	4	10	4.09	27	0	128.2	120	58	67	101

ROBIN YOUNT

Position: Outfield
Team: Milwaukee Brewers
Born: Sept. 16, 1955 Danville, IL
Height: 6' **Weight:** 180 lbs.
Bats: right **Throws:** right
Acquired: First-round pick in 6/73 free-agent draft

Player Summary	
Fantasy Value	$14 to $20
Card Value	10¢ to 25¢
Will	hit in clutch
Can't	find old power
Expect	a dozen steals
Don't Expect	high average

Yount has managed to spend his entire career with Milwaukee. He began as the club's 18-year-old shortstop in 1974 but switched to center field in 1985 after shoulder surgery. One of three players to win MVP awards at two different positions, Yount enjoyed several great moments last summer. He singled against Jose Mesa for his 3,000th hit Sept. 9, then enjoyed his best game of the year six days later with a two-run homer, two runs scored, and an outfield assist. He had a .325 on-base average and a .390 slugging percentage in 1992. He played a solid center field.

Major League Batting Register

	BA	G	AB	R	H	2B	3B	HR	RBI	SB
74 AL	.250	107	344	48	86	14	5	3	26	7
75 AL	.267	147	558	67	149	28	2	8	52	12
76 AL	.252	161	638	59	161	19	3	2	54	16
77 AL	.288	154	605	66	174	34	4	4	49	16
78 AL	.293	127	502	66	147	23	9	9	71	16
79 AL	.267	149	577	72	154	26	5	8	51	11
80 AL	.293	143	611	121	179	49	10	23	87	20
81 AL	.273	96	377	50	103	15	5	10	49	4
82 AL	.331	156	635	129	210	46	12	29	114	14
83 AL	.308	149	578	102	178	42	10	17	80	12
84 AL	.298	160	624	105	186	27	7	16	80	14
85 AL	.277	122	466	76	129	26	3	15	68	10
86 AL	.312	140	522	82	163	31	7	9	46	14
87 AL	.312	158	635	99	198	25	9	21	103	19
88 AL	.306	162	621	92	190	38	11	13	91	22
89 AL	.318	160	614	101	195	38	9	21	103	19
90 AL	.247	158	587	98	145	17	5	17	77	15
91 AL	.260	130	503	66	131	20	4	10	77	6
92 AL	.264	150	557	71	147	40	3	8	77	15
Life	.287	2729	10554	1570	3025	558	123	243	1355	262
3 AVE	.257	146	549	78	141	26	4	12	77	12

TODD ZEILE

Position: Third base
Team: St. Louis Cardinals
Born: Sept. 9, 1965 Van Nuys, CA
Height: 6'1" **Weight:** 190 lbs.
Bats: right **Throws:** right
Acquired: Third-round pick in 6/86 free-agent draft

Player Summary	
Fantasy Value	$6 to $14
Card Value	3¢ to 4¢
Will	show more power
Can't	ignore advice
Expect	better defense
Don't Expect	lots of steals

The Cardinals decreased the distance to their outfield fences to accommodate Zeile. The move backfired, however, when his power vanished after a three-homer burst in the opening week. Batting coach Don Baylor dropped a bushel of hints about extra batting practice, but Zeile failed to respond. The Cards reacted by shipping him to Triple-A Louisville on Aug. 11. He batted .311 with five homers and 13 RBI there. Zeile's attitude and actions differed sharply after his return. Though his power still lagged, his strong finish created optimism for 1993. He had a .352 on-base average and a .364 slugging percentage in 1992. The converted catcher makes decent contact, walks as much as he fans, steals a few bases, and projects 20-homer power. He's much more dangerous against lefthanders. Zeile is still learning to play third but has made great strides. He'll never play it as well as the man he replaced, but there's only one Terry Pendleton.

Major League Batting Register

	BA	G	AB	R	H	2B	3B	HR	RBI	SB
89 NL	.256	28	82	7	21	3	1	1	8	0
90 NL	.244	144	495	62	121	25	3	15	57	2
91 NL	.280	155	565	76	158	36	3	11	81	17
92 NL	.257	126	439	51	113	18	4	7	48	7
Life	.261	453	1581	196	413	82	11	34	194	26
3 AVE	.262	142	500	63	131	26	3	11	62	9

BOB ZUPCIC

Position: Outfield
Team: Boston Red Sox
Born: Aug. 18, 1966 Pittsburgh, PA
Height: 6'4" **Weight:** 225 lbs.
Bats: right **Throws:** right
Acquired: First-round pick in 6/87 free-agent draft

Player Summary	
Fantasy Value	$4 to $8
Card Value	5¢ to 12¢
Will	improve with experience
Can't	maintain average
Expect	fielding to get better
Don't Expect	more late-inning slams

With Ellis Burks idled by back problems much of last season, Boston needed a ready replacement in center field; they found one at Triple-A Pawtucket in the person of Bob Zupcic. He was hitting .320 with a couple of homers and five ribbies at the time of his recall. On June 30, he hit a one-out, ninth-inning grand slam to beat Detroit 8-5. On July 10, he connected with the bases loaded in the eighth to tie the White Sox. Zupcic made the headlines again with a leaping catch that robbed Mickey Tettleton of a Fenway Park homer Sept. 13; Tony Phillips called it the best catch he had ever seen. Zupcic was a bright spot on a bad team. Though he played all three outfield spots, he finished the year in a righty-lefty center field platoon with Herm Winningham. Zupcic has limited range but an above-average outfield arm. He had a .322 on-base average and a .352 slugging percentage in 1992. In 1991 at Pawtucket, he batted .240 with 18 homers, 70 RBI, and 11 stolen bases. He was an All-American outfielder from Oral Roberts in '87.

Major League Batting Register

	BA	G	AB	R	H	2B	3B	HR	RBI	SB
91 AL	.160	18	25	3	4	0	0	1	3	0
92 AL	.276	124	392	46	108	19	1	3	43	2
Life	.269	142	417	49	112	19	1	4	46	2

BOB ABREU

Position: Outfield
Team: Houston Astros
Born: March 11, 1974 Avaguа, Venezuela
Height: 6′ **Weight:** 160 lbs.
Bats: left **Throws:** right
Acquired: Signed as a free agent, 8/90

Player Summary	
Fantasy Value	$2 to $4
Card Value	10¢ to 15¢
Will	make contact
Can't	see limits yet
Expect	good offense
Don't Expect	a fizzle

Abreu may be one of the most intriguing hitting prospects in all of baseball. He played two pro seasons before his 19th birthday and hit strongly both times. He spent 1992 at Class-A Asheville and was one of the South Atlantic League's batting leaders. He opened the second half with an 0-for-7 slump, then went 11-for-18 to raise his average to a league-leading .344. At one point, he had five straight multihit games. Abreu knows how to knock in a run, will take a walk, and can steal a base. After collecting just 10 extra-base hits in his first pro season, Abreu showed some power in 1992 and, when he fills out, he could hit his share of home runs. He took 63 walks and had a .375 on-base average in 1992. By getting off to such a fine start on his pro career, he has left himself some time for the inevitable adjustments. One immediate improvement he will have to make is his play in the outfield. He has a strong arm, he just needs to stop making so many errors (he had 11 in '92). He could spend another year or so at the Class-A level and still be considered a very young prospect.

Professional Batting Register

	BA	G	AB	R	H	2B	3B	HR	RBI	SB
91 R	.301	56	183	21	55	7	3	0	20	10
92 A	.292	135	480	81	140	21	4	8	48	15

MANNY ALEXANDER

Position: Shortstop
Team: Baltimore Orioles
Born: March 20, 1971 San Padro de Macoris, Dominican Republic
Height: 5′10″ **Weight:** 150 lbs.
Bats: right **Throws:** right
Acquired: Signed as a free agent, 2/88

Player Summary	
Fantasy Value	$2 to $5
Card Value	10¢ to 15¢
Will	dazzle with glove
Can't	unseat Ripken yet
Expect	strong arm
Don't Expect	big slugging average

Cal Ripken is a future Hall of Famer who shows no signs of slowing down, but Alexander gives the Orioles insurance for the time when Ripken can't play every day. Alexander is a superb glove man in the tradition of Mark Belanger, but Alexander will hit more than Belanger did and could steal 30 bases a year in the majors. Alexander played at Double-A Hagerstown in 1992, was voted the Eastern League's best defensive shortstop, and started for the American League farmhands in the Double-A All-Star Game. It was the third time in four pro seasons that Alexander captured one honor or another. In 1991, he made both the midseason and postseason All-Star teams, and was named by *Baseball America* as the top prospect in the Class-A Carolina League. Alexander broke into pro ball by making the Appalachian League All-Star team in 1989. He was tabbed as the best shortstop in all five rookie leagues. Alexander won't hit with any power, but he'll put the ball in play.

Professional Batting Register

	BA	G	AB	R	H	2B	3B	HR	RBI	SB
89 R	.310	65	274	49	85	13	2	2	34	19
90 A	.178	44	152	16	27	3	1	0	11	8
91 A	.261	134	548	81	143	17	3	3	42	47
91 AA	.333	3	9	3	3	1	0	0	2	0
92 AA	.259	127	499	70	129	22	8	2	41	43
92 AAA	.292	6	24	3	7	1	0	0	3	2
92 AL	.200	4	5	1	1	0	0	0	0	0

JEFF ALKIRE

Position: Pitcher
Team: St. Louis Cardinals
Born: Nov. 15, 1969 Cols, OH
Height: 6'1" **Weight:** 200 lbs.
Bats: right **Throws:** left
Acquired: Fifth-round pick in 6/92 free-agent draft

Player Summary	
Fantasy Value	$1 to $3
Card Value	10¢ to 25¢
Will	take a challenge
Can't	overpower people
Expect	a craftsman
Don't Expect	automatic major leaguer

Alkire spent the 1992 season with the U.S. Olympic Team and became the first man to start an official game for the United States. He responded with one of his best efforts of the season, going seven and one-third innings against Spain while striking out 10. He pitched four seasons for the University of Miami, going 14-3 with a 2.62 ERA in his senior year. He was named to several All-America teams. He had a 3-0 record on the United States' Olympic tour, with one of the wins coming in a three-game series in Cuba. At 22 years of age, Alkire will be trailing most of his peers in pro experience, but his four years at an outstanding program should help him compensate. His international experience won't hurt, either. He was 4-2 with a 2.95 ERA for Hyannis in the Cape Cod League, a summer college circuit. The Cardinals will probably want him to challenge for a big league spot in two years at the most, however. Alkire's stats indicate he won't overpower many people, and his control was a little shaky on the Olympic trail. However, he has shown an ability to pitch well in big games, and his ability to grow into situations makes him a prospect to watch.

No minor league experience

RON ALLEN

Position: Pitcher
Team: Philadelphia Phillies
Born: May 10, 1970 Palo Alto, CA
Height: 5'11" **Weight:** 185 lbs.
Bats: right **Throws:** right
Acquired: Third-round pick in 6/91 free-agent draft

Player Summary	
Fantasy Value	$1 to $4
Card Value	10¢ to 15¢
Will	take the ball
Can't	blow people away
Expect	steady performance
Don't Expect	press clippings

One of the most gratifying things to a major league club is to see its picks rise steadily through the system, making the proper adjustments as the competition grows tougher. This is certainly the case with Allen, who has been at several levels in just two years without looking out of place in any of them. He went to Texas A&M, where he was 8-3 with a 3.28 ERA in '91. After being drafted, Allen broke in with Batavia of the Class-A New York-Penn League, where he was 3-3 with a 3.13 ERA. He then was promoted to Spartanburg of the South Atlantic League, where he won his only two starts. He finished his first year of pro ball with a 5-3 mark in just 10 outings. The Phils started him in high Class-A ball at Clearwater in 1992. Despite being one of the youngest players on the club, Allen was 6-6 with a 2.86 ERA in the Florida State League and earned another advancement. His first look at Double-A was a success, a victory over Harrisburg. Allen's stats won't knock you out, but every step brings him closer to the major leagues.

Professional Pitching Register

	W	L	ERA	G	CG	IP	H	ER	BB	SO
91 A	5	3	3.15	10	2	60.0	47	21	11	46
92 A	6	6	2.86	15	1	91.1	87	29	24	49
92 AA	1	3	4.94	5	1	31.0	35	17	9	17

TAVO ALVAREZ

Position: Pitcher
Team: Montreal Expos
Born: Nov. 25, 1971 Obregon, Mexico
Height: 6'3" **Weight:** 185 lbs.
Bats: right **Throws:** right
Acquired: Second-round pick in 6/90 free-agent draft

Player Summary	
Fantasy Value	$3 to $6
Card Value	10¢ to 20¢
Will	stay on fast track
Can't	lose breaking ball
Expect	strikes
Don't Expect	missed starts

Montreal's former brain trust, now with the Florida Marlins, was justifiably proud of the way it acquired Alvarez, because you don't see many players drafted out of Mexico. However, the Expos spotted Alvarez while he was playing high school ball in Tucson, Arizona. In 1992, he was one of the top pitchers in the minors. He notched 17 victories, which was tops of any pitcher in the Montreal organization. He also was among the leaders in ERA and had his share of strikeouts. Last summer, Alvarez was named the best control pitcher in the Class-A Florida State League in a *Baseball America* poll, and he held opposing hitters to a .242 batting average. He made the loop's All-Star team. He earned a promotion to Double-A Harrisburg in the middle of the season, beating Binghamton 3-1 in his debut. Alvarez throws a fastball and a change, and his breaking ball is coming around. His matchup against former first-round pick Brien Taylor was one of the highlights of the Florida State League season.

Professional Pitching Register

	W	L	ERA	G	CG	IP	H	ER	BB	SO
90 R	5	2	2.60	11	0	52.0	42	15	16	47
91 A	12	10	3.24	25	3	152.2	151	55	58	158
92 A	13	4	1.49	19	7	139.0	124	23	24	83
92 AA	4	1	2.85	7	2	47.1	48	15	9	42

GARRET ANDERSON

Position: Outfield
Team: California Angels
Born: June 30, 1972 Los Angeles, CA
Height: 6'3" **Weight:** 190 lbs.
Bats: left **Throws:** left
Acquired: Fourth-round pick in 6/90 free-agent draft

Player Summary	
Fantasy Value	$2 to $4
Card Value	10¢ to 15¢
Will	drive in runs
Can't	steal bases
Expect	some doubles
Don't Expect	home runs

Anderson didn't do much in his first two pro seasons, but he signed just out of high school. He blossomed in 1992, helping Palm Springs to the first-half title in the Class-A California League. Anderson went on a 52-for-129 tear that placed him well above .300 and among the batting leaders in the California chain. He then was boosted to Double-A Midland of the Texas League. Anderson is somewhat unusual in that he has shown virtually no power or basestealing speed. In view of his size, however, it may be a bit too early to write him off as a power threat. Besides, he has driven home his share of runs, especially in '92, when he had 62 in his 322 at bats for Palm Springs. He also had a .366 on-base average and a .391 slugging percentage there. Anderson also has made some adjustments, cutting down on his strikeouts and drawing a few more walks. Whether he can hit .300 as he climbs the ladder remains to be seen, but Anderson could have a niche as the lefty bat every club needs.

Professional Batting Register

	BA	G	AB	R	H	2B	3B	HR	RBI	SB
90 R	.213	32	127	5	27	2	0	0	14	3
90 A	.253	25	83	11	21	3	1	1	8	0
91 A	.260	105	392	40	102	22	2	2	42	5
92 A	.323	81	322	46	104	15	2	1	62	1
92 AA	.274	39	146	16	40	5	0	2	19	2

SHANE ANDREWS

Position: Third base
Team: Montreal Expos
Born: Aug. 28, 1971 Dallas, TX
Height: 6'1" **Weight:** 205 lbs.
Bats: right **Throws:** right
Acquired: First-round pick in 6/90 free-agent draft

Player Summary	
Fantasy Value	$2 to $4
Card Value	10¢ to 15¢
Will	produce runs
Can't	make consistent contact
Expect	swinging at bad balls
Don't Expect	overnight delivery

There are few players a manager desires more than a good defensive third base-man with power, and that's the promise Andrews offers. Although it is still very early in his career, he shows the potential to be a top player both with the glove and with the bat. *Baseball America* named him best defensive third baseman in the Class-A South Atlantic League in 1992. He had a .922 fielding percentage last summer. He was also among the top power hitters in all of the minor leagues, ranking near the top of the Expos' organization in both homers and RBI. Andrews had a .439 slugging percentage and a .382 on-base average in 1992. He also is described as having excellent speed, though his baserunning is not polished. Andrews will have to improve on his knowledge of the strike zone; he struck out 173 times in 453 at bats in 1992. Major league clubs will put up with the strikeouts if the power is there. However, the major leagues are still far away for Andrews. Figure him to play Double-A in 1993.

Professional Batting Register

	BA	G	AB	R	H	2B	3B	HR	RBI	SB
90 R	.242	56	190	31	46	7	1	3	24	11
91 A	.208	105	356	46	74	16	7	11	49	5
92 A	.230	136	453	76	104	18	1	25	87	8

MARCOS ARMAS

Position: First base
Team: Oakland Athletics
Born: Aug. 5, 1969 Puerto Pirtu, Puerto Rico
Height: 6'5" **Weight:** 190 lbs.
Bats: right **Throws:** right
Acquired: Signed as a free agent, 12/87

Player Summary	
Fantasy Value	$2 to $4
Card Value	8¢ to 12¢
Will	hit it far
Can't	shed brother's specter
Expect	strikeouts
Don't Expect	many stolen bases

The A's signed Armas at the age of 18 and brought him along very steadily, and this approach seems to have worked. The younger brother of former Oakland slug-ger Tony Armas, Marcos is showing more and more power. Last summer he achieved his second straight season in double figures in homers. He made the 1992 Double-A All-Star team, and went 3-for-4 with a homer in the game. Like most young sluggers, Armas strikes out fre-quently and can have trouble with the breaking ball. He must improve his eye and his discipline at the plate; his path to the majors may depend on how much he lets pitchers expand the strike zone. Armas has played third base and outfield in the past, but for Huntsville he played first base only. His biggest problem may be the comparisons to his brother, but a few home runs such as the one he hit in the All-Star Game will give him his own niche.

Professional Batting Register

	BA	G	AB	R	H	2B	3B	HR	RBI	SB
88 R	.293	17	58	14	17	2	1	0	10	0
89 A	.316	36	136	18	43	5	2	3	22	1
90 A	.238	75	260	32	62	13	0	7	33	3
91 A	.279	36	140	21	39	7	0	8	33	0
91 AA	.226	81	305	40	69	16	1	8	53	2
92 AA	.283	132	509	83	144	30	6	17	85	9

RENE AROCHA

Position: Pitcher
Team: St. Louis Cardinals
Born: Feb. 24, 1966 Havana, Cuba
Height: 6′ **Weight:** 180 lbs.
Bats: right **Throws:** right
Acquired: Signed as a free agent, 11/91

Player Summary	
Fantasy Value	$4 to $8
Card Value	10¢ to 20¢
Will	pitch with savvy
Can't	hit much
Expect	occasional knuckleballs
Don't Expect	amateur play

Arocha is one of the oldest prospects in baseball, but there are unusual circumstances. He defected from Cuba in 1991, and the Cardinals won his rights in a lottery, beating out six other teams. His skills and maturity are at such an advanced level that even with no mainland experience, he was deemed ready for Triple-A ball. Arocha spent the 1992 season with Louisville, and he was voted the best pitching prospect and owner of the best breaking pitch in the American Association. He was voted the No. 3 prospect in the league. Opponents compiled only a .234 batting average against him in 1992. He hurled two innings in the Triple-A All-Star Game, allowing three hits and one run. His repertoire includes a fastball, slider, curve, change, and forkball. Arocha played with three title teams in Cuba: 1985, 1986, and 1988, plus a World Cup winner in 1987. In April of 1991, he notched his 100th career victory, joining 14 other Cuban pitchers who had reached the milestone. He also collected more than 1,000 strikeouts in Cuba. Arocha planned to play winter ball in Puerto Rico after the 1992 season.

Professional Pitching Register

	W	L	ERA	G	CG	IP	H	ER	BB	SO
92 AAA	12	7	2.70	25	3	166.2	145	50	65	128

BILLY ASHLEY

Position: Outfield
Team: Los Angeles Dodgers
Born: July 11, 1970 Taylor, MI
Height: 6′7″ **Weight:** 220 lbs.
Bats: right **Throws:** right
Acquired: Third-round pick in 6/88 free-agent draft

Player Summary	
Fantasy Value	$2 to $4
Card Value	10¢ to 15¢
Will	tear up PCL
Can't	hit .300
Expect	lots of strikeouts
Don't Expect	good eye at bat

Ashley blossomed as a big-time power hitter in 1992, and his emergence must have been a bit of a relief for the Dodgers. He had spent four years in pro ball, never reaching double figures in homers and never getting beyond Class-A. He also suffered through three trips to the disabled list in 1991 with back and elbow injuries. Ashley responded to Double-A, however, showing enough to be named the best power prospect in the Texas League. He ranked among the leaders in the Dodgers' organization in both home runs and RBI, and hit for a respectable average. He still doesn't walk as much as a man with his power should, but at least he seems to have outgrown his 1990 season, when he struck out 135 times. Ashley used to be a high percentage basestealer, but he doesn't run anymore. With the Triple-A Pacific Coast League's tendency to pad power totals, you could be hearing quite a bit about him at Albuquerque in 1993.

Professional Batting Register

	BA	G	AB	R	H	2B	3B	HR	RBI	SB
88 R	.154	9	26	3	4	0	0	0	0	1
89 R	.238	48	160	23	38	6	2	1	19	9
90 A	.218	99	331	48	72	13	1	9	40	17
91 A	.252	61	206	18	52	11	2	7	42	9
92 AA	.279	101	380	60	106	23	1	24	66	13
92 AAA	.211	25	95	11	20	7	0	2	10	1
92 NL	.221	29	95	6	21	5	0	2	6	0

BRETT BACKLUND

Position: Pitcher
Team: Pittsburgh Pirates
Born: Dec. 16, 1969 Salem, OR
Height: 6′ **Weight:** 190 lbs.
Bats: right **Throws:** right
Acquired: Fifth-round pick in 1992 free-agent draft

Player Summary	
Fantasy Value	$4 to $7
Card Value	20¢ to 35¢
Will	adjust well
Can't	get overconfident
Expect	more time at Triple-A
Don't Expect	only good times

Backlund is the kind of success story that makes a scouting department smile. Drafted in a fairly high round, he progressed so quickly he could not be held back. Selected out of the University of Iowa, he raced through three levels of pro ball within a matter of months. He has impressed the Pirates with his composure, and nothing illustrates that as well as his Triple-A debut. Hurling in front of a crowd of approximately 20,000 at Buffalo's Pilot Field, he went seven innings and allowed just one hit. Triple-A batters compiled only a .167 batting average last summer. Backlund throws four pitches: a fastball in the high 80s, plus a curve, changeup, and slider. And he throws them for strikes, as his puny walk totals indicate. In college, Backlund also played the infield, and so his swing is not a bad one. Considering how he has performed this season, there's no way of judging how he might react in 1993. He might need a year in one place, or he could jump right to the majors.

CORY BAILEY

Position: Pitcher
Team: Boston Red Sox
Born: Jan. 24, 1971 Herrin, IL
Height: 6′1″ **Weight:** 208 lbs.
Bats: right **Throws:** right
Acquired: 15th-round pick in 6/91 free-agent draft

Player Summary	
Fantasy Value	$1 to $2
Card Value	10¢ to 15¢
Will	throw hard stuff
Can't	be ruled out for '93
Expect	lots of appearances
Don't Expect	any starts

Bailey is among a new breed of pitchers who are relief specialists from the moment they enter pro ball. He broke into pro ball in 1991, and both stops that season testify to his role as a closer. In the rookie Gulf Coast League, he saved the only game in which he appeared. He led the Class-A New York-Penn League with 15 saves and 25 games finished. He is still a couple of years from pitching in the majors, but in the meantime he is making an impression. Bailey throws hard, and has a good slider and good command. Class-A Carolina League batters compiled a .185 batting average against him in 1992. He enjoys the challenge of closing; he picked it up easily, and is well suited for the job, which means a great deal. He is also said to possess a rubber arm—another requirement—and his size won't hurt, either. He played both basketball and football in high school, then attended Southeastern Illinois Junior College, where he was All-Conference in baseball in 1991. Bailey attended the Florida Instructional League in 1991.

Professional Pitching Register

	W	L	ERA	G	CG	IP	H	ER	BB	SO
92 A	3	0	0.36	5	0	25.0	10	1	4	31
92 AA	1	1	1.89	3	0	19.0	11	4	3	17
92 AAA	3	0	2.16	4	2	25.0	15	6	11	9

Professional Pitching Register

	W	L	ERA	G	S	IP	H	ER	BB	SO
91 R	0	0	0.00	1	1	2.0	2	0	1	1
91 A	2	4	1.85	28	15	39.0	19	8	12	54
92 A	5	7	2.44	49	23	66.1	43	18	30	87

ROGER BAILEY

Position: Pitcher
Team: Colorado Rockies
Born: Oct. 3, 1970 Chattahoochee, FL
Height: 6′ **Weight:** 180 lbs.
Bats: right **Throws:** right
Acquired: Third-round pick in 6/92 free-agent draft

Player Summary	
Fantasy Value	$1 to $3
Card Value	8¢ to 12¢
Will	climb a notch
Can't	blow it by
Expect	wide repertoire
Don't Expect	majors in '93

Born on the 29th anniversary of Bobby Thomson's historic home run against the Brooklyn Dodgers, Bailey has already been part of history himself. He was a member of the outstanding stable of pitchers assembled in Colorado's first draft, and is in on the ground floor of what the Rockies hope will be a quick rise to respectability. He has great command of four pitches. His fastball is only average, but it has some run to it. Bailey has an outstanding change and also throws a curve and a slider. Most importantly, he can pitch. A Florida State University product, he was listed among *Baseball America's* top 100 college prospects entering the 1992 season, and he helped put his team into the College World Series. Upon turning pro, Bailey entered the rotation for the Rockies' farm club in Bend, Oregon. He didn't have much luck in the victory column at first, but he quickly became one of the rookie Northwest League's strikeout leaders. He needs to improve his endurance. Opponents were able to take him deep four times, and they compiled a .205 batting average last summer.

BRIAN BARBER

Position: Pitcher
Team: St. Louis Cardinals
Born: March 4, 1973 Hamilton, Ontario
Height: 6′1″ **Weight:** 175 lbs.
Bats: right **Throws:** right
Acquired: First-round pick in 6/91 free-agent draft

Player Summary	
Fantasy Value	$2 to $6
Card Value	10¢ to 25¢
Will	be worth Coleman's loss
Can't	count on breaking ball
Expect	arrival in 1994
Don't Expect	another year in Class-A

Barber has been working his way up the chain, gaining valuable experience that included a Class-A game played in Busch Stadium. His stats haven't been eye-popping yet, but there's plenty of time for that. Right now, all Barber needs to do is pitch and learn his way around the game. Acquired with the pick given St. Louis for the Mets' signing of free agent Vince Coleman, Barber was just age 18 when he turned pro in 1991. He had a slow start at Johnson City of the rookie Appalachian League but finished strongly, recording a 4-1 mark with a 1.72 ERA in August. He allowed just three earned runs in his last 25⅔ innings, and worked eight and one-third hitless innings on Aug. 20. Barber was a nonroster invitee to spring training in 1992, the youngest player in camp, and he impressed vets with his fastball and control. He opened the season with Springfield of the Class-A Midwest League, holding opposing batters to a .207 batting average in his eight starts there. His next step was St. Petersburg of the Class-A Florida State League.

Professional Pitching Register

	W	L	ERA	G	CG	IP	H	ER	BB	SO
92 R	5	2	2.20	11	1	65.1	48	16	30	81

Professional Pitching Register

	W	L	ERA	G	CG	IP	H	ER	BB	SO
91 R	4	6	5.40	14	0	73.1	62	44	38	84
92 A	8	9	3.40	27	1	164.0	138	62	70	158

JASON BATES

Position: Shortstop
Team: Colorado Rockies
Born: Jan. 5, 1971 Yorba Linda, CA
Height: 5'11" **Weight:** 180 lbs.
Bats: both **Throws:** right
Acquired: Seventh-round pick in 6/92 free-agent draft

Player Summary

Fantasy Value	$1 to $3
Card Value	8¢ to 12¢
Will	understand game
Can't	match college power
Expect	enthusiasm
Don't Expect	All-Star shortstop

Bates's play in the rookie Northwest League in 1992 made the Rockies feel they had one of the best first-year pro shortstops in the game. He was voted the No. 7 prospect in the loop. He had a .419 on-base average and a .420 slugging percentage last summer. Bates has great quickness and a feel for playing defense. He sees the ball off the bat well and has good anticipation; he impressed the staff in Bend, Oregon, with his range. This assessment rates him higher than the school of thought that wonders if shortstop is Bates's ticket to the majors. His manager at Bend, Gene Glynn, said Bates had all the tools to play shortstop at a higher level. He loves to play, and he has been involved in more than one winning situation as an amateur. That poise may come from his college experience. He played at the University of Arizona, one of the best programs in the country, and the level of competition he faced in the Pacific-10 South helped him as he began his pro career. A switch-hitter, Bates was one of the top batters in the conference. How quickly he advances will depend mostly on his adjustment to the wooden bat.

Professional Batting Register

	BA	G	AB	R	H	2B	3B	HR	RBI	SB
92 R	.286	70	255	57	73	10	3	6	31	18

MIGUEL BATISTA

Position: Pitcher
Team: Montreal Expos
Born: Feb. 19, 1971 Santo Domingo, Dominican Republic
Height: 6' **Weight:** 160 lbs.
Bats: right **Throws:** right
Acquired: Signed as a free agent, 2/88

Player Summary

Fantasy Value	$1 to $3
Card Value	8¢ to 12¢
Will	be back in majors
Can't	throw with command yet
Expect	lots of personality
Don't Expect	quick results

Batista's talent led Pittsburgh to grab him in the 1991 Rule 5 draft with hopes of carrying him on the major league roster. But the demands of being a contender made it impossible for the Pirates to afford Batista's lack of experience, and so he was returned to the Expos' organization on April 23. Armed with a taste of the major leagues, he became a member of the rotation at West Palm Beach of the Class-A Florida State League. He can deliver a fastball above 90 mph, but he doesn't always have control of it. That helps account for the so-so results he turned in at West Palm, where he was 7-7 and allowed opponents to compile a .251 batting average. Batista broke into the pros in 1990 with Bradenton of the rookie Gulf Coast League, then moved on to Rockford of the Class-A Midwest League, compiling a 4-4 overall mark with a 3.59 ERA. He worked at extended spring training in 1991, then spent the season at Rockford, going 11-5 and winning five of his last six.

Professional Pitching Register

	W	L	ERA	G	CG	IP	H	ER	BB	SO
90 R	4	3	2.06	9	0	39.1	33	9	17	21
90 A	0	1	8.76	3	0	12.1	16	12	5	7
91 A	11	5	4.04	23	2	133.2	126	60	57	90
92 A	7	7	3.79	24	1	135.1	130	57	54	92
92 NL	0	0	9.00	1	0	2.0	4	2	3	1

317

HOWARD BATTLE

Position: Third base
Team: Toronto Blue Jays
Born: March 25, 1972 Ocean Springs, MS
Height: 6'1" **Weight:** 197 lbs.
Bats: right **Throws:** right
Acquired: Fifth-round pick in 6/90 free-agent draft

Player Summary	
Fantasy Value	$1 to $2
Card Value	8¢ to 12¢
Will	hit it out
Can't	forget overall game
Expect	production
Don't Expect	Brooks Robinson

Battle was named the Class-A Florida State League's best infield arm in 1992 in a poll by *Baseball America.* It is interesting that this third baseman should be honored for a defensive tool. In 1991, there were some doubts about his ability with the glove. Battle's real claim to a major league job rests in his power potential. For two straight years, he has ranked among the leaders of the Toronto chain in home runs and RBI. Battle was named the No. 5 prospect in the FSL last summer. He made the Florida State League All-Star team last summer, following up a similar feat in the Class-A Sally League in 1991. He'll strike out a bit, but no more than the usual power hitter and less than some. A true slugger, Battle will also get his share of doubles. That means he carries the threat of a long ball without the likelihood of being an easy out. He has even flashed some basestealing speed. Battle was named the rookie Pioneer League's eighth-best prospect in 1990. *Baseball America* ranked him 70th in its list of the 100 top major league prospects before 1992.

Professional Batting Register

	BA	G	AB	R	H	2B	3B	HR	RBI	SB
90 R	.266	61	233	25	62	17	1	5	32	5
91 A	.279	138	520	82	145	33	4	20	87	15
92 A	.254	136	520	76	132	27	3	17	85	6

RICH BECKER

Position: Outfield
Team: Minnesota Twins
Born: Feb. 1, 1972 Aurora, IL
Height: 5'10" **Weight:** 180
Bats: both **Throws:** left
Acquired: Third-round pick in 6/90 free-agent draft

Player Summary	
Fantasy Value	$1 to $3
Card Value	10¢ to 20¢
Will	help build runs
Can't	forget contact
Expect	speed in outfield
Don't Expect	boring at bats

Imagine a player who could switch-hit for average, steal a base, and hit home runs. Now imagine him on the artificial surface of the Metrodome, within distance of those inviting fences. That's what the Twins envision in Becker. He played for Visalia of the Class-A California League in 1992, his third year of pro ball, and did nothing to hurt the impression he can be quite an offensive threat. He wasn't a team leader in homers, RBI, or stolen bases, but he had his share of all three. He also knows how to draw a walk (he had 114 last summer) and how to score runs. Becker strikes out too much; he went down 122 times last summer and 108 times in 1991. At one point in '92 he was a .406 hitter when putting the ball in play. He had a .441 on-base average and a .486 slugging percentage in 1992. Warning: Some of his offensive totals may be misleading because Visalia's fences are just 320 down the foul lines. Then again, if he makes it to Minnesota, he'll be in a nice hitter's park, too. Becker was also named the top defensive flycatcher in the loop and the No. 9 prospect.

Professional Batting Register

	BA	G	AB	R	H	2B	3B	HR	RBI	SB
90 R	.289	56	194	54	56	5	1	6	24	18
91 A	.267	130	494	100	132	38	3	13	53	19
92 A	.316	136	506	118	160	37	2	15	82	29

SEAN BERGMAN

Position: Pitcher
Team: Detroit Tigers
Born: April 11, 1970 Joliet, IL
Height: 6'4" **Weight:** 205 lbs.
Bats: right **Throws:** right
Acquired: Fourth-round pick in 6/91 free-agent draft

Player Summary	
Fantasy Value	$1 to $3
Card Value	10¢ to 15¢
Will	need more seasoning
Can't	throw ball past hitters
Expect	another pitch
Don't Expect	lack of toughness

Bergman is one of Detroit's better pitching prospects, and he took a major step in 1992 when he worked his way into Double-A. He had some trouble there, despite winning his first start, but the Tigers like him a great deal. Bergman throws an 87 mph fastball, just slightly above major league average, but it's a live one. He is a good competitor who merely needs to pitch. He was inconsistent with his breaking ball last summer, but that may be due to inexperience more than anything else. Double-A opponents compiled a .257 batting average in 1992. Bergman attended Southern Illinois University, and he was an All-Missouri Conference pick in 1991. He broke into the pros with Detroit's Class-A New York-Penn League entry in Niagara Falls, and went 5-7 with a 4.46 ERA. Detroit promoted him to Lakeland to open the '92 season, and he quickly moved through the Class-A Florida State League, going 5-2. In his 171 innings of work last summer, he gave up only four home runs, but he did have six wild pitches.

Professional Pitching Register

	W	L	ERA	G	CG	IP	H	ER	BB	SO
91 A	5	7	4.46	15	0	84.2	87	42	42	77
92 A	5	2	2.49	13	0	83.0	61	23	14	67
92 AA	4	7	4.28	14	1	88.1	85	42	45	59

BEN BLOMDAHL

Position: Pitcher
Team: Detroit Tigers
Born: Dec. 30, 1970 Long Beach, CA
Height: 6'2" **Weight:** 185 lbs.
Bats: right **Throws:** right
Acquired: 14th-round pick in 6/90 free-agent draft

Player Summary	
Fantasy Value	$1 to $3
Card Value	8¢ to 12¢
Will	throw to spots
Can't	overuse changeup
Expect	ball in play
Don't Expect	another perfect game

Blomdahl provided one of the highlights of the minor league season on June 4, 1992, when he hurled a perfect game to lead Fayetteville to a 1-0 victory over Spartanburg in the second game of a South Atlantic League doubleheader. He didn't rest on his laurels, either, going 10-4 with a 2.70 ERA in his 17 starts. Sally League opponents compiled a .240 batting average against him last year. His work earned him a trip to Detroit's high Class-A club in Lakeland. Blomdahl, who attended Riverside Community College in California, is not overpowering. He has good command, a good changeup, and mixes his pitches. He improved his won-lost record in 1992, and he can credit that to having sharpened his control. When Blomdahl broke in with Niagara Falls in 1991, he walked 50 in just 78⅔ innings. With Fayetteville, he issued only 26 walks in his first 103 innings. As a pitcher who neither walks nor strikes out many, he'll have the ball in play a lot. His chances of reaching the majors will depend on his ability to keep hitters from sitting on one pitch.

Professional Pitching Register

	W	L	ERA	G	CG	IP	H	ER	BB	SO
91 A	6	6	4.46	16	0	78.2	72	39	50	30
92 A	15	7	3.43	27	4	165.1	171	63	31	106

GREG BLOSSER

Position: Outfield
Team: Boston Red Sox
Born: June 26, 1971 Bradenton, FL
Height: 6'3" **Weight:** 200 lbs.
Bats: left **Throws:** left
Acquired: First-round pick in 6/89 free-agent draft

Player Summary	
Fantasy Value	$2 to $4
Card Value	10¢ to 20¢
Will	hit shots
Can't	forget contact
Expect	more seasoning
Don't Expect	high average

The Red Sox could have used someone like Blosser in 1992, when they struggled throughout the season without the benefit of much power. He was tabbed the best power-hitting prospect in the Double-A Eastern League by *Baseball America* in 1992, and he set a New Britain franchise record for homers. He had a .465 slugging percentage. He was among the leaders in home runs and RBI in the Red Sox organization, and Boston's front office considers his power potential to be outstanding. As a lefthanded hitter, he won't be shooting at the Green Monster in left field, but his problem right now is distance—it's contact. He struck out 114 times in 1991 while driving home just 46 runs, not nearly the ratio a team needs. He was the 16th overall pick in the draft, and came with a selection gained through San Diego's signing of Type-A free agent Bruce Hurst. Blosser's power began to show one year later, when he led the Carolina League with 18 homers and made the All-Star team, but he also struck out 99 times.

Professional Batting Register

	BA	G	AB	R	H	2B	3B	HR	RBI	SB
89 R	.288	40	146	17	42	7	3	2	20	3
89 A	.255	28	94	6	24	1	1	2	14	1
90 A	.282	119	447	63	126	23	1	18	62	5
91 AA	.217	134	452	47	98	21	3	8	46	9
92 AA	.242	129	434	59	105	23	4	22	71	0

ROD BOLTON

Position: Pitcher
Team: Chicago White Sox
Born: Sept. 23, 1968 Chattanooga, TN
Height: 6'2" **Weight:** 190 lbs.
Bats: right **Throws:** right
Acquired: 13th-round pick in 6/90 free-agent draft

Player Summary	
Fantasy Value	$4 to $8
Card Value	15¢ to 25¢
Will	reach majors soon
Can't	be judged on '92 wins
Expect	fielders to stay busy
Don't Expect	false advertising

Bolton was named the White Sox organization's minor league Pitcher of the Year after the 1991 season, and he provided an impressive follow-up in '92. His won-loss record won't knock you over, but he managed a stingy ERA in the Triple-A Pacific Coast League, which with its high altitudes and occasional small parks generally favors hitters. Bolton appeared as a reliever for the American League farmhands in the Triple-A All-Star Game, and hurled two innings of no-hit relief, striking out two. He has established himself as someone who can throw the ball over the plate with something on it. In his first five pro stops, he has posted a strong hits-to-innings ratio. In 1991, he was named the White Sox organization's Pitcher of the Month for July, going 5-1 with an 0.60 ERA for Birmingham of the Double-A Southern League. He could be in the bigs to stay as early as '93. Bolton played baseball four years for the University of Kentucky, and holds a marketing degree.

Professional Pitching Register

	W	L	ERA	G	CG	IP	H	ER	BB	SO
90 A	10	2	1.23	13	4	95.0	61	13	23	95
91 A	7	6	1.91	15	5	103.2	81	22	23	77
91 AA	8	4	1.62	12	3	89.0	73	16	21	57
92 AAA	11	9	2.93	27	3	187.1	174	61	59	111

BRET BOONE

Position: Second base
Team: Seattle Mariners
Born: April 6, 1969 El Cajon, CA
Height: 5'10" **Weight:** 180 lbs.
Bats: right **Throws:** right
Acquired: Fifth-round pick in 6/90 free-agent
draft

Player Summary	
Fantasy Value	$4 to $8
Card Value	10¢ to 20¢
Will	drive in runs
Can't	do more in minors
Expect	references to dad
Don't Expect	a Boone-doggle

Boone has pretty much accomplished all he can at the minor league level, and so the only remaining question is how well his career will stack up against that of his bloodlines. Boone's father, Bob, caught in the majors for 19 years and his grandfather, Ray, was an infielder with six major league teams for 13 years. Bret played three years at the University of Southern California, then stepped into a pro career in which he has improved every season. He has been selected to play in both the Double-A and Triple-A All-Star Games. A power-hitting second baseman who will steal an occasional base, Boone may hit for average, too. He has done a good job of cutting down on his strikeouts and has suffered no apparent loss of power in the process. He had a .398 on-base average and a .485 slugging percentage for Triple-A Calgary in 1992. He was named the Pacific Coast League's No. 2 prospect last summer. If he can get to the Kingdome and put the ball in play, he will add to the reputation of the Boone line.

Professional Batting Register

	BA	G	AB	R	H	2B	3B	HR	RBI	SB
90 A	.267	74	255	42	68	13	2	8	38	5
91 AA	.255	139	475	64	121	18	1	19	75	9
92 AAA	.314	118	439	73	138	26	5	13	73	17
92 AL	.194	33	129	15	25	4	0	4	15	1

RICO BROGNA

Position: First base
Team: Detroit Tigers
Born: April 18, 1970 Turner Falls, MA
Height: 6'2" **Weight:** 202
Bats: left **Throws:** left
Acquired: First-round pick in 6/88 free-agent
draft

Player Summary	
Fantasy Value	$2 to $6
Card Value	10¢ to 20¢
Will	make plays at first
Can't	run
Expect	more time in minors
Don't Expect	unseating of Fielder

Brogna is regarded as one of the Tigers' top prospects, but he'll have to do a lot more than he has if he wants to win a job. For one thing, he has Cecil Fielder ahead of him at the major league level, and there's probably no player in baseball who could unseat the home run and RBI machine. Second, Brogna simply hasn't responded to Triple-A competition. After being a home run champion for London of the Double-A Eastern League in 1990, he has failed to impress in more than one try at Triple-A Toledo, especially with regards to power. There's a school of thought that says Brogna is starting to put it together, and that too much was expected of him too soon. He is a below average runner but not a bad performer with the glove; he was voted the Class-A Florida State League's top fielding first baseman in 1989 by *Baseball America*. He got the call to the bigs in August 1992.

Professional Batting Register

	BA	G	AB	R	H	2B	3B	HR	RBI	SB
88 R	.254	60	209	37	53	11	2	7	33	3
89 A	.235	128	459	47	108	20	7	5	51	2
90 AA	.262	137	488	70	128	21	3	21	77	1
91 AAA	.220	41	132	13	29	6	1	2	13	2
91 AA	.273	77	293	40	80	13	1	13	51	0
92 AAA	.261	121	387	45	101	19	4	10	58	1
92 AL	.192	9	26	3	5	1	0	1	3	0

JOE BROWNHOLTZ

Position: Pitcher
Team: Texas Rangers
Born: Dec. 6, 1969 Miami, FL
Height: 6'1" **Weight:** 195 lbs.
Bats: right **Throws:** left
Acquired: 31st-round pick in 6/91 free-agent draft

Player Summary	
Fantasy Value	$1 to $2
Card Value	10¢ to 20¢
Will	keep team close
Can't	offer great fastball
Expect	good ratios
Don't Expect	many walks

Lefthanders who can throw the ball over the plate have a chance to win, and Brownholtz is a good example. He broke into the pros out of the draft and walked just 15 batters in 46 innings. He was even better in 1992. As a result, Brownholtz was among the organization's leaders in both victories and ERA. He was also moving rapidly up the ladder. He received a promotion from the Class-A Sally League, and nearly had a masterpiece while pitching for Charlotte of the high Class-A Florida State League. He took a no-hitter into the ninth inning against Fort Lauderdale on July 5. He was 6-2 with a 2.12 ERA for Gastonia in the Sally League, and 6-5 with a 3.11 ERA for Charlotte. He held Sally League hitters to a .226 batting average last summer. Brownholtz will need more than that, though. He will be age 23 entering the 1993 season, and his fastball is just borderline. He is an off-speed, finesse type of pitcher, the so-called crafty lefthander, who will be around the plate. As a low-round draft choice, he may not get the same look more prominent pitchers might.

DAMON BUFORD

Position: Outfield
Team: Baltimore Orioles
Born: June 12, 1970 Baltimore, MD
Height: 5'10" **Weight:** 170 lbs.
Bats: right **Throws:** right
Acquired: 10th-round pick in 6/90 free-agent draft

Player Summary	
Fantasy Value	$2 to $4
Card Value	15¢ to 25¢
Will	steal bases
Can't	switch-hit like dad
Expect	so-so on-base percentage
Don't Expect	name to carry him

Buford comes from a baseball family, his father, Don, having played for the Orioles and his brother having been a Baltimore farmhand. With bloodlines like that, and with his speed and basestealing ability, he's got a chance to reach the majors. Buford spent part of the 1992 season with Hagerstown of the Double-A Eastern League, where at least he didn't have to get to know the manager; it was his father. He was a whiz on the basepaths for the third straight season and was leading the organization in steals when promoted to Triple-A. Buford got six hits and four stolen bases in his first five games in Triple-A. However, he undermines his own strengths when he strikes out as often as he does. He will have to learn to put the ball in play, and preferably on the ground. He was a switch-hitter for a while in college and did some experimenting with it in the Florida Instructional League, but he appears to be staying with his natural righthanded style. Buford has played winter ball in Australia.

Professional Pitching Register

	W	L	ERA	G	CG	IP	H	ER	BB	SO
91 R	4	2	3.72	9	1	46.0	43	19	15	42
92 A	12	7	2.61	25	1	144.2	133	42	30	104

Professional Batting Register

	BA	G	AB	R	H	2B	3B	HR	RBI	SB
90 A	.300	41	160	31	48	7	2	1	14	15
91 A	.273	133	505	71	138	25	6	8	54	50
92 AA	.239	101	373	53	89	17	3	1	30	41
92 AAA	.284	45	155	29	44	10	2	1	12	23

SCOTT BULLETT

Position: Outfield
Team: Pittsburgh Pirates
Born: Dec. 25, 1968 Martinsburg, WV
Height: 6'2" **Weight:** 190 lbs.
Bats: left **Throws:** left
Acquired: Signed as a free agent, 6/88

Player Summary	
Fantasy Value	$2 to $5
Card Value	10¢ to 20¢
Will	play right or center
Can't	steal first base
Expect	good shot at Bucs
Don't Expect	power

The old television show said that Superman could move faster than a speeding bullet. In the Pittsburgh organization, that would make him fast indeed. Bullett is a prospect who seems on the verge of a big league job, and his gifts include a strong arm and blurring speed. Like Superman, Bullett can make great leaps in a single bound. In 1991, for instance, he started the season at low Class-A, was promoted to high Class-A, then zoomed straight to the majors. He was back in the minors in 1992, but his quick rise gives you a sense of the kind of tools the Pirates see in him. Bullett has stolen 25 or more bases in three of five seasons. However, his success rate entering 1992 was just 73 percent, and it didn't get any better in '92; he was caught stealing 20 times. Bullett has not shown any power as a pro, even though his size suggests he could have some. He had a .316 on-base average and a .375 slugging percentage in Double-A in 1992. He must cut down on his strikeouts.

Professional Batting Register

	BA	G	AB	R	H	2B	3B	HR	RBI	SB
88 R	.180	21	61	6	11	1	0	0	8	2
89 R	.255	46	165	24	42	7	3	1	16	15
90 A	.302	74	255	46	77	11	4	3	33	30
91 A	.298	134	540	83	161	29	11	3	51	63
91 NL	.000	11	4	2	0	0	0	0	0	1
92 AA	.270	132	518	60	140	20	5	8	45	29

JOHN BURKE

Position: Pitcher
Team: Colorado Rockies
Born: Feb. 9, 1970 Englewood, CO
Height: 6'4" **Weight:** 215 lbs.
Bats: both **Throws:** right
Acquired: First-round pick in 6/92 free-agent draft

Player Summary	
Fantasy Value	$1 to $3
Card Value	8¢ to 12¢
Will	light up radar gun
Can't	hurt marketing
Expect	occasional injuries
Don't Expect	rush to majors

Burke is one of the more intriguing picks of the 1992 talent grab bag. For one thing, he is the first pick the new franchise ever made, and it didn't hurt the publicity (or the team's insight into him) that he was a local boy. Second, Burke has had some troubles with injuries, and there was some perception he was brittle. Third, he had already turned down the Astros after having been picked as the No. 6 player in the nation the previous season. Finally, there is the matter of talent. Quite simply, the Rockies believe they got one of the best arms in the country. Burke throws a fastball clocked at about 95 mph. He also throws a good downer curveball and a changeup. Burke started off slowly at rookie league Bend in his first pro year as the club put him on a 50-pitch limit. Northwest League hitters compiled a .247 batting average last summer. He used to use an overhead delivery, but the organization is working on trying to drop his arm angle. As for the shoulder and arm problems, the Rockies obviously didn't think that the problem was anything too major.

Professional Pitching Register

	W	L	ERA	G	CG	IP	H	ER	BB	SO
92 R	2	0	2.41	10	0	41.0	38	11	18	32

JEROMY BURNITZ

Position: Outfield
Team: New York Mets
Born: April 14, 1969 Westminster, CA
Height: 6′ **Weight:** 190 lbs.
Bats: left **Throws:** right
Acquired: First-round pick in 6/90 free-agent draft

Player Summary	
Fantasy Value	$4 to $8
Card Value	10¢ to 25¢
Will	be power threat
Can't	make consistent contact
Expect	great tools
Don't Expect	a relaxed player

Burnitz emerged as a top prospect in 1991, delivering one of the most spectacular minor league seasons since Greg Vaughn became a 30-30 man in 1987. Burnitz's 31 homers were second only to Howard Johnson's 38 in the Mets' organization, and Burnitz paced Double-A Williamsport in RBI with 13 more than his closest pursuer. He was named the top power hitter in the Eastern League by *Baseball America* for his accomplishments that year. He fell short of repeating that performance in '92, as pitchers in Triple-A controlled his power much better than those in Double-A ever did. He had a .298 on-base average and a .357 slugging percentage in 1992. Burnitz's basestealing didn't suffer quite as much, reflecting the axiom that speed doesn't slump. Making contact at bat is another matter, however, and Burnitz will have to work on. Even in his 30-30 season, he batted just .225, and major league pitchers will find even more holes. Burnitz, who attended Oklahoma State, is a hard-working player who demands a lot of himself. He has sometimes tried too hard; he must stay relaxed.

Professional Batting Register

	BA	G	AB	R	H	2B	3B	HR	RBI	SB
90 A	.278	62	205	43	57	7	5	6	25	13
91 AA	.225	135	457	80	103	16	10	31	85	31
92 AAA	.243	121	445	56	108	21	3	8	40	30

TERRY BURROWS

Position: Pitcher
Team: Texas Rangers
Born: Nov. 28, 1968 Lake Charles, LA
Height: 6′1″ **Weight:** 185
Bats: left **Throws:** left
Acquired: Seventh-round pick in 6/90 free-agent draft

Player Summary	
Fantasy Value	$2 to $5
Card Value	8¢ to 12¢
Will	improve
Can't	stop working on control
Expect	fine hit-to-frame ratio
Don't Expect	great heater

Ranger fans have been treated to some strikeout artists in the last couple of years, most notably Nolan Ryan and Bobby Witt. Burrows won't be in their class—his fastball is merely average to plus—but his stock has risen in his first three seasons as a pro. Upon breaking in, he averaged more than a strikeout per inning for Butte of the rookie Pioneer League in 1990. The next year, Burrows led all Rangers' minor leaguers with 151 whiffs. In 1992, he ranked among the organization's top men in strikeouts. His repertoire includes a slider and a change. Unfortunately, he does not always throw the ball over the plate, and so the Texas front office must have been pleased to see Burrows cut down on his walks in 1992. His improved control no doubt contributed to his enhanced stock in the organization. In 1992, Class-A batters compiled a .241 batting average, and Double-A batters hit .237 against him. Burrows attended McNeese State University, where he was named Southland Conference Player of the Year and Pitcher of the Year in 1990.

Professional Pitching Register

	W	L	ERA	G	CG	IP	H	ER	BB	SO
90 R	3	6	4.02	14	1	62.2	56	28	35	64
91 A	12	8	4.45	27	0	147.2	108	73	78	151
92 A	4	2	2.03	14	0	80.0	71	18	25	66
92 AA	6	3	2.13	14	1	76.0	66	18	35	59
92 AAA	1	0	1.13	1	0	8.0	3	1	5	0

ESSEX BURTON

Position: Outfield
Team: Chicago White Sox
Born: May 16, 1969 Arlington, TX
Height: 5'9" **Weight:** 160 lbs.
Bats: both **Throws:** right
Acquired: 26th-round pick in 6/91 free-agent draft

Player Summary	
Fantasy Value	$1 to $2
Card Value	10¢ to 15¢
Will	steal bases
Can't	give away at bats
Expect	excitement
Don't Expect	extra-base hits

Burton ran away with the basestealing title among White Sox minor leaguers in 1992, which shouldn't surprise anyone who has seen him play. *Baseball America* called him not only the fastest baserunner in the Class-A Midwest League, but also the best. Now what he must do is translate that speed into more base hits. The first step is better contact. Burton's size tells you he won't hit many homers, but his strikeout totals in '92 were more in line with a slugger's ratio than with a speed-ster's. He went down 109 times on strikes. He hurts himself every time he lets a team get him out without a throw. His switch-hitting ability puts him closer to first base for the possibility of some infield hits. Burton does a good job of drawing walks (he had 67 last summer), and that can help the whole offense because there's something especially frustrating about walking a fast man. He had a .351 on-base average in 1992. One further note about speed: Burton better move quickly. He'll turn 24 in '93, and the edge could come off his main asset.

Professional Batting Register

	BA	G	AB	R	H	2B	3B	HR	RBI	SB
91 R	.278	50	194	37	54	5	2	0	17	21
91 A	.276	15	58	11	16	0	0	0	4	6
92 A	.253	122	459	78	116	6	3	0	29	65

ROB BUTLER

Position: Outfield
Team: Toronto Blue Jays
Born: April 10, 1970 East York, Ontario
Height: 5'11" **Weight:** 185 lbs.
Bats: left **Throws:** left
Acquired: Signed as a free agent, 9/90

Player Summary	
Fantasy Value	$1 to $2
Card Value	8¢ to 12¢
Will	hit for average
Can't	worry bout foot
Expect	runs scored
Don't Expect	lots of walks

A stress fracture in his foot put a big dent in Butler's 1992 season, but he still managed to win the Class-A Florida State League batting title and lead all Toronto minor leaguers. He has made the All-Star team in each of his first two pro seasons, hitting at least .338 and winning awards both times. He was also named the No. 6 prospect in the loop. None of this can guarantee he will be a sure-fire major leaguer, but you do have to wonder when he'll find a league that will level him off. He is a leadoff type of hitter who gets his bat on the ball, and his swing suggests he could hit anywhere. You'd like him to walk a bit more at the top of the order, but that can be overlooked if he continues to hit for average. He had a .394 on-base average and a .458 slugging percentage in 1992. His speed helps in center field, where he can track down balls in the gap. Track was among his four sports in high school, and it is reflected in his stolen base totals. Butler played for the Canadian Youth team. In 1991, Butler was chosen as the Topps Player of the Month for August.

Professional Batting Register

	BA	G	AB	R	H	2B	3B	HR	RBI	SB
91 A	.338	76	311	71	105	16	5	7	45	33
92 A	.358	92	391	67	140	13	7	4	41	19

PAUL BYRD

Position: Pitcher
Team: Cleveland Indians
Born: Dec. 3, 1970 Louisville, KY
Height: 6'1" **Weight:** 180 lbs.
Bats: right **Throws:** right
Acquired: Fourth-round pick in 6/91 free-agent draft

Player Summary

Fantasy Value	$3 to $5
Card Value	10¢ to 20¢
Will	get look soon
Can't	neglect control
Expect	good curveball
Don't Expect	lingering in minors

Byrd has a style that may remind you of Mike Boddicker: intelligent, with a good feel for pitching and an overhand curveball. Byrd could be a third or fourth starter in the big leagues some day, and it could be sooner rather than later. After all, he broke into the pros at the high Class-A level, and one year later, was one of the best starters in the Double-A Eastern League. He picked up 20 decisions in his 24 starts of 1992, indicating an instinct for being around when the game is decided. Four of those starts resulted in complete games. Byrd could use some work on his control; if he gets behind and walks roughly one man every two innings in Triple-A, his won-loss mark will look nothing like it did in '92. His hits-to-innings ratio, however, has looked pretty good in his first two pro seasons, and he knows how to turn good stats into victories. Eastern League hitters compiled a .219 batting average against him last summer. Another pitch will make him even better, so don't be surprised to see him in the big leagues. He is another talented hurler that Louisiana State has produced in recent years, including fellow Indian prospect Chad Ogea.

Professional Pitching Register

	W	L	ERA	G	CG	IP	H	ER	BB	SO
91 A	4	3	3.16	14	0	62.2	40	22	36	62
92 AA	14	6	3.01	24	4	152.1	124	51	74	118

GARY CARABALLO

Position: Third base
Team: Kansas City Royals
Born: July 11, 1971 Brooklyn, NY
Height: 6' **Weight:** 180 lbs.
Bats: right **Throws:** right
Acquired: 12th-round pick in 6/89 free-agent draft

Player Summary

Fantasy Value	$1 to $2
Card Value	8¢ to 12¢
Will	play top defense
Can't	make KC forget Brett
Expect	honest at bats
Don't Expect	double figures in homers

Caraballo plays third base, a position at which the Royals seem well-stocked, and he may be as good as any of his fellow hopefuls. He had some trouble adjusting to Double-A in 1992 but part of that can be explained by his age and by the fact he received an in-season move for the third time in four pro campaigns. Caraballo led Royals' farmhands with 68 RBI in 1991, and was named the organization's sixth-best prospect by *Baseball America*. That publication also tabbed him as the best defensive third baseman in the Class-A Florida State League in 1992. He compiled a .363 on-base average and a .410 slugging percentage in Class-A last summer. He was named Baseball City's Player of the Month for June for a fine performance at the plate. Shortly after that, he was moved up to Double-A. If Caraballo develops into the best defensive third baseman in the league, keeps the ball in play, and puts a few in the gaps, he could be quite a player. Look for him to start '93 in Double-A, and then move up.

Professional Batting Register

	BA	G	AB	R	H	2B	3B	HR	RBI	SB
89 R	.238	46	160	18	38	6	0	1	25	4
89 A	.333	3	9	0	3	0	0	0	0	0
90 A	.214	123	406	37	87	14	3	6	50	6
91 A	.240	129	454	67	109	25	4	5	68	17
92 A	.289	67	239	30	69	9	4	4	40	6
92 AA	.210	58	195	17	41	6	2	3	17	1

PEDRO CASTELLANO

Position: Third base
Team: Colorado Rockies
Born: March 11, 1970 Lara, Venezuela
Height: 6'1" **Weight:** 175 lbs.
Bats: right **Throws:** right
Acquired: Third-round pick from Cubs in 11/92 expansion draft

Player Summary	
Fantasy Value	$1 to $3
Card Value	10¢ to 20¢
Will	collect some doubles
Can't	duplicate MVP year
Expect	shot in spring training
Don't Expect	Gold Glove winner

Castellano was coveted by the Rockies' management, several of whom came out of the Cubs' organization. He had some bumps in 1992 after an award-winning season the previous year. He made it to Triple-A and hit in the .250 range, but was dropped back a notch when the Cubs needed some help at their Double-A club in Charlotte. Castellano is a third baseman who will hit for average and have an adequate glove. He can also play some short, though that would probably be in an emergency. The first man on the Cubs' 40-man roster to be born in the 1970s, he won the Most Valuable Player Award in the Class-A Carolina League in 1991. He was selected to both the midseason and postseason All-Star clubs and to the Topps-National Association Class-A squad. His .956 fielding percentage was the highest by a league third baseman with a minimum of 50 appearances. Castellano hit 10 homers in 1991, but he probably won't hit with that kind of power again.

Professional Batting Register

	BA	G	AB	R	H	2B	3B	HR	RBI	SB
89 R	.311	66	244	55	76	17	4	9	42	5
90 A	.265	136	483	67	128	27	4	3	52	8
91 A	.303	129	459	59	139	25	3	10	87	11
91 AA	.421	7	19	2	8	0	0	0	2	0
92 AA	.224	45	147	16	33	3	0	1	15	0
92 AAA	.248	74	238	25	59	14	4	2	20	2

DAN CHOLOWSKY

Position: Second base; third base
Team: St. Louis Cardinals
Born: Oct. 30, 1970 Yonkers, NY
Height: 6' **Weight:** 195 lbs.
Bats: right **Throws:** right
Acquired: First-round pick in 6/91 free-agent draft

Player Summary	
Fantasy Value	$1 to $2
Card Value	10¢ to 15¢
Will	run bases well
Can't	match Cards' blazers
Expect	line drives
Don't Expect	a second baseman

Cholowsky came to the Cardinals as a sandwich pick off Toronto's signing of free-agent Ken Dayley. Cholowsky is a speedy, hard-nosed player in the Cardinals' mold, and his aggressiveness could help him get to the majors. He made the Class-A South Atlantic League All-Star team while he was playing for Savannah in 1992. He has some offensive tools, though his average fell off when he was promoted to the high Class-A Florida State League in the middle of the season. He has played quite a bit of second, but his position could change; it's possible he may not be nimble enough for the keystone. He could wind up at third, since his arm is good enough for that spot. Cholowsky wouldn't be a classic bat as a third baseman, as his style inclines more toward line drive and RBI power. However, he can deliver the occasional home run. He had a .491 slugging average at Savannah. He has good speed and, though he is not a burner in the Vince Coleman mold, Cholowsky is intelligent on the bases.

Professional Batting Register

	BA	G	AB	R	H	2B	3B	HR	RBI	SB
91 A	.232	20	69	9	16	1	1	1	6	6
92 A	.307	128	433	63	133	14	4	9	51	48

327

JOE CICCARELLA

Position: Pitcher
Team: Boston Red Sox
Born: Dec. 29, 1969 Cincinnati, OH
Height: 6'3" **Weight:** 200 lbs.
Bats: left **Throws:** left
Acquired: Fourth-round pick in 6/91 free-agent draft

Player Summary	
Fantasy Value	$1 to $2
Card Value	8¢ to 12¢
Will	throw live fastball
Can't	walk first batter
Expect	inexperience to show
Don't Expect	return to first

Ciccarella is one pitcher who should understand how a hitter thinks, for the simple reason that he himself was one not too long ago. In his second pro season, he made the transition from first base to closer. Out of Loyola Marymount, Ciccarella pitched and played first base in school and was a second-team All-American according to *Baseball America* in 1991. The Red Sox liked his arm and decided they had better prospects at first base, so into the bullpen he went. His .232 batting average and .263 slugging percentage in '91 at Class-A Winter Haven helped expedite the decision. Ciccarella throws a live fastball, a split-fingered pitch, and a sharp breaking ball. He'll have to cut down on his walks if he means to be an effective closer on a higher level, but he's demonstrated the ability to get a strikeout. Opponents compiled a .241 batting average in 1992. He played first base in both the Gulf Coast League and Florida State League in his first pro season. He was a member of Team USA in 1990. In 1991 at Loyola Marymount, he batted .435 with 13 homers and 67 RBI.

Professional Pitching Register

	W	L	ERA	G	S	IP	H	ER	BB	SO
92 A	2	1	2.66	38	12	40.2	35	12	27	46

JEFF CIRILLO

Position: Third base; second base
Team: Milwaukee Brewers
Born: Sept. 23, 1969 Pasadena, CA
Height: 6'2" **Weight:** 190 lbs.
Bats: right **Throws:** right
Acquired: 11th-round pick in 6/91 free-agent draft

Player Summary	
Fantasy Value	$1 to $2
Card Value	8¢ to 12¢
Will	get better at third
Can't	be big power hitter
Expect	good eye at bat
Don't Expect	another .350 average

Cirillo probably could have handled a higher level of ball in 1992, but he managed to excel where circumstances put him. He opened with Milwaukee's high Class-A team in Stockton, California, and had some troubles at the plate early in the season. He went to Class-A Beloit to fill an injury at third base there. He responded with a nifty campaign that found him on the Midwest League All-Star team and among the top run-producers in Milwaukee's minor league system. He had a .304 batting average and a .439 slugging percentage for Beloit. Cirillo has extremely quick hands with good reactions down the line. He also showed some knack for pulling the hidden ball trick. He does a lot of things to help on offense: hitting for average, stealing a base, producing an extra-base hit or the occasional home run, and drawing a walk. With two years of pro ball, including a full season at Class-A, Cirillo could well be headed for Double-A in 1993. It sure doesn't look like it would be too much for him.

Professional Batting Register

	BA	G	AB	R	H	2B	3B	HR	RBI	SB
91 R	.350	70	286	60	100	16	2	10	51	3
92 A	.301	133	468	67	141	28	3	9	76	21

JEFF CONINE

Position: First base
Team: Florida Marlins
Born: June 27, 1966 Tacoma, WA
Height: 6'1" **Weight:** 220 lbs.
Bats: right **Throws:** right
Acquired: First-round pick from Royals in 11/92 expansion draft

Player Summary

Fantasy Value	$5 to $10
Card Value	10¢ to 25¢
Will	put up numbers
Can't	make himself younger
Expect	many fans in Florida
Don't Expect	a lumbering runner

Conine is the perfect type of player for Florida to draft. He has plenty of professional experience, he is talented, and he is young enough to stick around for years. Not only was Conine a 58th-round draft pick in 1987, he has overcome injuries to regain his former star status. In fact, Conine might already be a star in the majors if not for the hamate bone in his left wrist. He appeared briefly in the majors in 1990 when he was called up from Triple-A Memphis, and he was in big league camp in 1991. But trouble from wrist surgery he had undergone that year pushed back his timetable for reaching the majors. Conine reinjured the wrist in May and went on the disabled list in late June. He bounced back in 1992, ranking among the home run and RBI leaders in the Royals' chain. Conine in 1990 was the Royals' Minor League Player of the Year and was voted the Triple-A American Association's No. 2 prospect behind Frank Thomas.

Professional Batting Register

	BA	G	AB	R	H	2B	3B	HR	RBI	SB
88 A	.272	118	415	63	113	23	9	10	59	26
89 A	.273	113	425	68	116	12	7	14	60	32
90 AA	.320	137	487	89	156	37	8	15	95	21
90 AL	.250	9	20	3	5	2	0	0	2	0
91 AAA	.257	51	171	23	44	9	1	3	15	0
92 AAA	.302	110	397	69	120	24	5	20	72	4
92 AL	.253	28	91	10	23	5	2	0	9	0

JIM CONVERSE

Position: Pitcher
Team: Seattle Mariners
Born: Aug. 17, 1971 San Francisco, CA
Height: 5'9" **Weight:** 180 lbs.
Bats: left **Throws:** right
Acquired: 16th-round pick in 6/90 free-agent draft

Player Summary

Fantasy Value	$1 to $4
Card Value	10¢ to 25¢
Will	advance again
Can't	make himself taller
Expect	skeptics
Don't Expect	lack of heart

If Converse makes it to the majors for any length of time, he will have overcome a certain scouting bias. There are those in baseball who won't even look at a righthander under 6'. Not only does he seem to be making it, but he's doing so in style. In just three pro seasons, he worked his way up to Double-A, where he made the 1992 All-Star team. He allowed only five earned runs in the month of July, and he allowed hitters to bat only .231. His walks will have to come down, but there is nothing wrong with his ratio of hits to innings. He was one of the top strikeout artists in the Mariners' organization in 1992. Converse was part of the U.S. squad that toured Japan in 1988, and he played for the West in the U.S. Olympic Festival in 1989. He got off to a slow start in the Class-A Carolina League in 1991, but compiled a 3.64 ERA over his last 16 starts. He was named Peninsula's MVP and was tabbed as the ninth-best prospect in the Carolina League by *Baseball America*. And remember, he's only 21 years old.

Professional Pitching Register

	W	L	ERA	G	CG	IP	H	ER	BB	SO
90 A	2	4	3.92	12	0	66.2	50	29	32	75
91 A	6	15	4.97	26	1	137.2	143	76	97	137
92 AA	12	7	2.66	27	2	159.0	134	47	82	157

STEVE COOKE

Position: Pitcher
Team: Pittsburgh Pirates
Born: Jan. 14, 1970 Kanai, HI
Height: 6'6" **Weight:** 220 lbs.
Bats: right **Throws:** left
Acquired: 35th-round pick in 6/89 free-agent draft

Player Summary	
Fantasy Value	$2 to $5
Card Value	10¢ to 20¢
Will	adjust well
Can't	rule out more seasoning
Expect	member of rotation
Don't Expect	ERA under 4.00

Talent and circumstances pushed Cooke into the majors more quickly than you would have expected for a low-round choice who only began pro ball in 1990. The talent was evident by the fact he was among the farm system's leaders in wins, ERA, and strikeouts when he was called up from the minors in July of '92. The circumstances were that the Pirates were battling a slump and injuries to their staff in the heat of a pennant race. He made his debut on July 28. Cooke put himself in position to be called up by advancing quickly through the Pirates' system and having success at every level. He made 11 starts in the Class-A New York-Penn League in 1990. He was a real workhorse in '91, pitching in the Class-A South Atlantic and Carolina leagues and the Double-A Southern League. He still must work on his control a bit, but he has been stingy with hits. He may need some refining in the minors after such a quick rise.

WIL CORDERO

Position: Shortstop
Team: Montreal Expos
Born: Oct. 3, 1971 Mayaguez, Puerto Rico
Height: 6'2" **Weight:** 185 lbs.
Bats: right **Throws:** right
Acquired: Signed as a free agent, 5/88

Player Summary	
Fantasy Value	$3 to $8
Card Value	5¢ to 10¢
Will	make big plays
Can't	relax on routine plays
Expect	good bat
Don't Expect	stolen bases

Cordero made it to the majors July 23, 1992, and has a chance to be around a long time. He has been in the Expos' organization since he was age 16, and the buildup to his arrival made it somehow seem that he was late getting to the big club. However, he'll be just 21 as the 1993 season starts, giving him time to grow into one of the league's dominant shortstops. In 1992, Cordero was named the top defensive shortstop in the Triple-A American Association by *Baseball America,* the latest in a series of laurels he has received. That honor came shortly after he became the youngest MVP of the Puerto Rican Winter League. Cordero has a chance to hit for a solid average in the majors, and he may reach double figures in home runs. He still has some trouble with the routine play, but his biggest problem may be staying healthy. A fracture to the fifth metacarpal bone on his left hand ended his 1991 season early, and he had a variety of hurts in 1992.

Professional Pitching Register

	W	L	ERA	G	CG	IP	H	ER	BB	SO
90 A	2	3	2.35	11	0	46.0	36	12	17	43
91 A	6	4	3.18	13	1	73.2	64	26	37	57
91 AA	3	3	2.26	9	1	55.2	39	14	19	46
92 AA	2	2	3.00	6	0	36.0	31	12	12	38
92 AAA	6	3	3.75	13	0	74.1	71	31	36	52
92 NL	2	0	3.52	11	0	23.0	22	9	4	10

Professional Batting Register

	BA	G	AB	R	H	2B	3B	HR	RBI	SB
88 A	.258	52	190	18	49	3	0	2	22	3
89 A	.277	78	289	37	80	12	2	6	29	2
89 AA	.215	39	121	9	26	6	1	3	17	1
90 AA	.234	131	444	63	104	18	4	7	40	9
91 AAA	.261	98	360	48	94	16	4	11	52	9
92 AAA	.314	52	204	32	64	11	1	6	27	6
92 NL	.302	45	126	17	38	4	1	2	8	0

MARTY CORDOVA

Position: Outfield
Team: Minnesota Twins
Born: July 10, 1969 Las Vegas, NV
Height: 6′ **Weight:** 195 lbs.
Bats: right **Throws:** right
Acquired: 10th-round pick in 6/89 free-agent draft

Player Summary	
Fantasy Value	$1 to $2
Card Value	10¢ to 20¢
Will	provide offense
Can't	afford much backsliding
Expect	bit of speed
Don't Expect	more Class-A

It's a good bet that this native of Las Vegas got the attention of the Twins with his slugging in 1992. Cordova was named the Class-A California League's top power prospect by *Baseball America* and was among the leaders in several offensive categories. He had a .589 slugging percentage and a .431 on-base average last summer. It was a breakthrough season for Cordova, a four-year pro who was coming off a year that made him seem like he was on the way out not on the way up. He gave a hint of his power potential in his first pro season (in 1989) when, while playing for Elizabethton in the rookie Appalachian League, he hit eight homers in 148 at bats. That's one homer every 18.5 trips and translates into 30 over a full season. He seemed to stall in his next two seasons, however, producing neither power nor average. He generated just 14 extra-base hits in 189 at bats for Class-A Visalia in 1991, a .365 slugging average. Cordova's showing in 1992 ensures that the Twins will be watching him.

TIM COSTO

Position: First base
Team: Cincinnati Reds
Born: Feb. 16, 1969 Melrose Park, IL
Height: 6′5″ **Weight:** 220 lbs.
Bats: right **Throws:** right
Acquired: Traded from Indians for Reggie Jefferson, 6/91

Player Summary	
Fantasy Value	$3 to $6
Card Value	5¢ to 10¢
Will	bring out tape measure
Can't	put wood on ball
Expect	all-or-nothing at bats
Don't Expect	defensive position

Costo came to the Reds when a front office mistake exposed top prospect Reggie Jefferson to a trade, but Costo looks like more than just a consolation prize. He played first base for Double-A Chattanooga in 1992 and battled Willie Greene for the home run title among Reds' farmhands. Costo's at bats were all-or-nothing affairs, though; his RBI totals failed to keep pace with the home run output, and at one point he had 20 homers and just 11 doubles and triples combined. Costo will have to work on that aspect of his game, and he can start by cutting down his strikeouts, which have been in triple figures. None of this should obscure the fact Costo had a breakthrough season, more than doubling his home run totals of his first two pro campaigns. He can play first base, third base, and shortstop, but if he reaches the majors, it will be at one of the corners. Costo was Cleveland's first-round draft choice in 1990 out of the University of Iowa.

Professional Batting Register

	BA	G	AB	R	H	2B	3B	HR	RBI	SB
89 R	.284	38	148	32	42	2	3	8	29	2
90 A	.216	81	269	35	58	7	5	7	25	6
91 A	.212	71	189	31	40	6	1	7	19	2
92 A	.341	134	513	103	175	31	6	28	131	13

Professional Batting Register

	BA	G	AB	R	H	2B	3B	HR	RBI	SB
90 A	.316	56	206	34	65	13	1	4	42	4
91 AA	.276	137	485	59	134	29	6	6	53	13
92 AA	.241	121	424	63	102	18	2	28	71	4
92 NL	.222	12	36	3	8	2	0	0	2	0

MIDRE CUMMINGS

Position: Outfield
Team: Pittsburgh Pirates
Born: Oct. 14, 1971 St. Croix, Virgin Islands
Height: 6'1" **Weight:** 195 lbs.
Bats: both **Throws:** right
Acquired: Traded from Twins with Denny Neagle for John Smiley, 3/92

Player Summary	
Fantasy Value	$1 to $2
Card Value	15¢ to 30¢
Will	be key to trade
Can't	do more in Class-A
Expect	power and speed
Don't Expect	decline in '93

Sharp fans may recall hearing of Cummings before the 1992 season when he was part of a deal that sent lefthander John Smiley to the Twins. Cummings was considered a key to the trade, and his play since then shows why. He was sent to the Pirates' Carolina League team in Salem and, at age 20, more than held his own in the strong Class-A circuit. After slumping at the start, Cummings showed both power and speed and was MVP of the All-Star Game. He used a red-hot July, including back-to-back four-hit games, to get his average up near the .300 mark. He also was among the RBI leaders in the Pittsburgh system. He had a .361 on-base average and a .479 slugging percentage last summer. His ability to switch-hit makes him even more potent as an offensive weapon. Cummings was the Twins' second pick, and the 29th overall, in the 1990 draft. In his first two seasons, he hit well over .300. It's possible he may fill out a little more, which should make his extra-base hit totals even higher.

Professional Batting Register

	BA	G	AB	R	H	2B	3B	HR	RBI	SB
90 R	.316	47	177	28	56	3	4	5	28	14
91 A	.322	106	382	59	123	20	4	4	54	28
92 A	.305	113	420	55	128	21	5	14	75	23

CARLOS DELGADO

Position: Catcher
Team: Toronto Blue Jays
Born: June 25, 1972 Aguadilla, Puerto Rico
Height: 6'3" **Weight:** 215 lbs.
Bats: left **Throws:** right
Acquired: Signed a free agent, 10/88

Player Summary	
Fantasy Value	$1 to $2
Card Value	10¢ to 35¢
Will	crush the ball
Can't	stop learning
Expect	Johnny Bench bat
Don't Expect	Johnny Bench glove

Delgado showed little respect for the pitching in the Class-A Florida State League in 1992, putting up numbers that made him a candidate for the Triple Crown. It was his third straight year with one honor or another. In 1990, Delgado was the most outstanding player of St. Catharines of the rookie New York-Penn League; in 1991 he was named to the Class-A South Atlantic League All-Star team. He was just flat-out one of the best prospects in all of baseball in 1992. He made the Florida State League All-Star team, *Baseball America* named him the best hitting and power prospect in the league, and included him in its list of the 100 top prospects. He became the first FSL player to hit 25 homers since Steve Balboni did it in 1979. Delgado had a .402 on-base average and a .579 slugging percentage last summer. One area of concern could be Delgado's defense. Nowhere in any of the praise do you hear about that aspect of Delgado's game, and this could become more of a concern as he gets closer to the big leagues.

Professional Batting Register

	BA	G	AB	R	H	2B	3B	HR	RBI	SB
89 A	.180	31	89	9	16	5	0	0	11	0
90 A	.281	67	228	30	64	13	0	6	39	2
91 A	.286	132	441	72	126	18	2	18	70	9
91 AAA	.000	1	3	0	0	0	0	0	0	0
92 A	.324	133	485	83	157	30	2	30	100	2

JERRY DiPOTO

Position: Pitcher
Team: Cleveland Indians
Born: May 24, 1968 Jersey City, NJ
Height: 6'2" **Weight:** 203 lbs.
Bats: right **Throws:** right
Acquired: Third-round pick in 6/89 free agent draft

Player Summary	
Fantasy Value	$2 to $4
Card Value	8¢ to 12¢
Will	enjoy bullpen more
Can't	thrive in rotation
Expect	wild pitches
Don't Expect	pinpoint control

After being a starter virtually all his pro career, DiPoto may have found his niche in 1992 when he went to the bullpen. His temperament seems better suited to pitching on call rather than waiting four days between starts. He may have a future as a setup man in the majors, but there could be an obstacle with his control. DiPoto has walked roughly one man every two innings as a pro, and the number one rule for a reliever is to throw strikes. In 1991, he led Double-A Canton-Akron with 74 walks and 15 wild pitches. After the season, DiPoto participated in the team's Florida Instructional League program, permitting one earned run in 28 innings. He then played winter ball with Aguilas of the Dominican League. DiPoto throws a two-seam and a four-seam fastball, plus a hard slider. He had a changeup as a starter, but now goes with the fastball and the slider. DiPoto played three years at Virginia Commonwealth University and was named to two All-Sun Belt squads.

Professional Pitching Register

	W	L	ERA	G	S	IP	H	ER	BB	SO
89 A	6	5	3.61	14	0	87.1	75	35	39	98
90 A	11	4	3.78	24	0	145.1	129	61	77	143
90 AA	1	0	2.57	3	0	14.0	11	4	4	12
91 AA	6	11	3.81	28	0	156.0	143	66	74	97
92 AAA	9	9	4.94	50	2	122.0	148	67	66	62

STEVE DREYER

Position: Pitcher
Team: Texas Rangers
Born: Nov. 19, 1969 Ames, IA
Height: 6'3" **Weight:** 180 lbs.
Bats: right **Throws:** right
Acquired: Eighth-round pick in 6/90 free-agent draft

Player Summary	
Fantasy Value	$1 to $2
Card Value	10¢ to 15¢
Will	change speeds
Can't	match flame-throwers
Expect	comfortable collars
Don't Expect	huge jump in '93

Dreyer will never be compared to some of the flame-throwers who have graced the mound in Arlington but, then again, the object of the game is to get people out and that is what he seems to do. He has pitched three years in pro ball, and three times he has recorded a fine hits-to-innings ratio. All three times he has thrown the ball over the plate. Dreyer fares by changing speeds and by challenging the hitters. His stuff is average. You have to beat him; he won't beat himself. Dreyer pitched for Charlotte in the Class-A Florida State League in 1992 and ranked among the Ranger organization's leaders in victories, ERA, and strikeouts. He was especially sharp during a stretch in July, when he hurled a shutout then followed with eight innings for another victory. Right now, he is a secondary prospect, but as long as he keeps getting people out he can advance to a higher level. Dreyer played for the University of Northern Iowa and made all-conference in 1990.

Professional Pitching Register

	W	L	ERA	G	CG	IP	H	ER	BB	SO
90 R	1	1	4.54	8	0	35.2	32	18	10	29
91 A	7	10	2.33	25	3	162.0	137	42	62	122
92 A	11	7	2.40	26	4	168.2	164	45	37	111

DAMION EASLEY

Position: Infield
Team: California Angels
Born: Nov. 11, 1969 New York, NY
Height: 5'11" **Weight:** 155 lbs.
Bats: right **Throws:** right
Acquired: 30th-round pick in 6/88 free-agent draft

Player Summary
Fantasy Value	$3 to $6
Card Value	10¢ to 20¢
Will	get good shot in '93
Can't	play short in bigs
Expect	second or third base
Don't Expect	high slugging percentage

Easley was one of the few things that went right in an otherwise disappointing 1992 season for the Angels. He came to the majors and made his debut Aug. 13, playing third base. Easley has played second, short, and third in his pro career. With Gary DiSarcina at short, Easley would have to break in at one of the other two positions, and the Angels seem inclined to give him that chance. Easley was headed for the best offensive season of his career when summoned to the majors last summer; he had a .340 on-base average and a .366 slugging percentage at Triple-A Edmonton. He looks like he'll be able to hold his own at the plate, and may reach double figures both in home runs and in stolen bases. He can draw a walk and doesn't strike out too often. Easley attended Long Beach City College and was named All-South Coast Conference in 1989. He made the Class-A Midwest League All-Star team in 1990, helped Quad City to the title, and was named one of the league's top-10 prospects.

Professional Batting Register
	BA	G	AB	R	H	2B	3B	HR	RBI	SB
89 A	.298	36	131	34	39	5	1	4	21	9
90 A	.274	103	365	59	100	19	3	10	56	25
91 AA	.254	127	452	73	115	24	5	6	57	23
92 AAA	.289	108	429	61	124	18	3	3	44	26
92 AL	.258	47	151	14	39	5	0	1	12	9

TOMMY EASON

Position: Catcher
Team: Philadelphia Phillies
Born: July 8, 1970 Kinston, NC
Height: 6' **Weight:** 200 lbs.
Bats: right **Throws:** left
Acquired: Sixth-round pick in 6/91 free-agent draft

Player Summary
Fantasy Value	$1 to $2
Card Value	8¢ to 12¢
Will	put bat on ball
Can't	overtake Lieberthal
Expect	extra-base hits
Don't Expect	above-average arm

Eason showed lots of potential in 1992, when he wasn't getting injured. He was hitting nearly .400 early in the year when he tore a ligament in his back. Later, he was named to the Class-A South Atlantic League All-Star Game, but never made it. He was hit in the face by a pitch from Columbia's Brad Schorr. Eason was on a roll at the time, having hit in 18 of 22 games. The interruptions didn't seem to bother Eason all that much, as he was one of the top bats in the entire Philadelphia organization. He is a contact hitter who still manages a nice percentage of extra-base hits. He was behind Mike Lieberthal on the Phils' depth chart in 1992 but is said to have enough tools to have a fine chance in the big leagues. Eason is described as having good mechanics behind the plate, a good attitude, and an arm that is major league average. Eason, who attended East Carolina University, broke into the pros with Class-A Batavia of the New York-Penn League in 1991 and was promoted to the Class-A Sally League that year.

Professional Batting Register
	BA	G	AB	R	H	2B	3B	HR	RBI	SB
91 A	.314	15	51	8	16	3	0	1	4	1
91 A	.292	42	137	18	40	12	0	2	14	2
92 A	.298	73	262	41	78	20	1	7	37	2

DONNIE ELLIOTT

Position: Pitcher
Team: Atlanta Braves
Born: Sept. 20, 1968 Pasadena, TX
Height: 6'4" **Weight:** 190 lbs.
Bats: right **Throws:** right
Acquired: Traded from Phillies for Ben Rivera, 5/92

Player Summary	
Fantasy Value	$2 to $4
Card Value	10¢ to 20¢
Will	be wild at times
Can't	offer big repertoire
Expect	Triple-A in 1993
Don't Expect	top changeup

Elliott has been on the move a great deal in the last year or so. First he was drafted from Philadelphia by Seattle in the 1991 Rule 5 draft and was returned to the Phillies the next spring. Then he was acquired in the deal that sent pitcher Ben Rivera to the Phillies. Elliott began the season with the Phils' high Class-A club in Clearwater and was promoted to Double-A Reading before the trade. Atlanta assigned him to Double-A Greenville, where, after a shaky start, he helped the Braves become one of the top teams in the minors. Elliott compiled a 4-0 mark in July. He is a power pitcher with above-average arm strength, and an average slider. He also has a change, but relies primarily on the other two pitches. While pitching for Class-A Spartanburg in 1991, he fanned 17 men in seven and two-thirds innings on May 25; it was the best single-game performance in the minors all season. Elliott was picked by the Phillies in the seventh round of the 1987 draft.

Professional Pitching Register

	W	L	ERA	G	CG	IP	H	ER	BB	SO
88 R	4	2	3.66	15	0	59.0	47	24	31	77
89 A	6	4	1.89	15	1	100.2	91	21	28	84
90 A	4	8	3.50	20	0	105.1	101	41	46	109
91 A	11	9	3.24	28	1	158.0	120	57	87	184
92 A	1	1	3.00	3	0	18.0	12	6	8	12
92 AA	10	5	2.20	25	0	139.1	113	34	46	123

ALAN EMBREE

Position: Pitcher
Team: Cleveland Indians
Born: Jan. 23, 1970 Vancouver, WA
Height: 6'2½" **Weight:** 185 lbs.
Bats: left **Throws:** left
Acquired: Fifth-round pick in 6/89 free-agent draft

Player Summary	
Fantasy Value	$4 to $8
Card Value	10¢ to 25¢
Will	throw hard
Can't	hit spots yet
Expect	advancement in '93
Don't Expect	command of craft

The Indians feel Embree has one of the finest arms in all of the minor leagues, and he may rank as their top lefthanded prospect. He has a plus fastball, but still has a way to go in his command of the strike zone, in his knowledge of pitching, and in his approach. He did seem to sharpen his control a bit in 1992. *Baseball America* called him the top pitching prospect in the Class-A Carolina League last summer. Embree jumped from Kinston to Double-A Canton-Akron to Cleveland, and he was among the top Cleveland farmhands in wins, ERA, and strikeouts. Embree broke into the pros in 1990, and finished eighth in the Appalachian League with a 2.64 ERA. He got a look at full-season Class-A at the South Atlantic League in 1991, and led Columbus with 10 wins, 155⅓ innings, 137 strikeouts, and three complete games. He fanned the third-most of any member of the Indians' system and, in his last 12 starts, struck out 80 in 81 innings. He played four sports in high school.

Professional Pitching Register

	W	L	ERA	G	CG	IP	H	ER	BB	SO
90 R	4	4	2.64	15	0	81.2	87	24	30	58
91 A	10	8	3.59	27	3	155.1	126	62	77	137
92 A	10	5	3.30	15	1	101.0	89	37	32	115
92 AA	7	2	2.28	12	0	79.0	61	20	28	56
92 AL	0	2	7.00	4	0	18.0	19	14	8	12

CARL EVERETT

Position: Outfield
Team: Florida Marlins
Born: June 3, 1971 Tampa, FL
Height: 6′ **Weight:** 190 lbs.
Bats: both **Throws:** right
Acquired: Second-round pick from Yankees in 11/92 expansion draft

Player Summary	
Fantasy Value	$1 to $4
Card Value	10¢ to 15¢
Will	star on defense
Can't	start '92 over again
Expect	speed
Don't Expect	tough out

Everett was one of the reasons Yankees fans are so upset with the front office; they thought they might lose him, but losing both him and Charlie Hayes was alarming. Everett's speed and style in center made him one of the more interesting prospects in the Yankees' organization. *Baseball America* called him the best defensive center fielder and the top arm in the Class-A Florida State League in 1992. His over-the-shoulder catch helped Fort Lauderdale beat West Palm Beach on June 9. All in all, though, it wasn't a year Everett could savor. He got off to a slow start at the plate, and he also spent some time on the disabled list. His assignment for the Marlins in 1993 will be tough to judge, given his limited amount of at bats in '92. He is out of Hillsborough High School in Tampa, also attended by Doc Gooden. Everett scored 96 runs in 1991 for Class-A Greensboro, second in the Yanks' minor league chain. Nicknamed "Poochy," Everett is a switch-hitter but gives away a lot of that advantage by striking out too frequently.

Professional Batting Register

	BA	G	AB	R	H	2B	3B	HR	RBI	SB
90 R	.259	48	185	28	48	8	5	1	14	15
91 A	.271	123	468	96	127	18	0	4	40	28
92 A	.230	46	183	30	42	8	2	2	9	11
92 A	.318	6	22	7	7	0	0	4	9	1

JORGE FABREGAS

Position: Catcher
Team: California Angels
Born: March 13, 1970 Miami Beach, FL
Height: 6′3″ **Weight:** 205 lbs.
Bats: left **Throws:** right
Acquired: First-round pick in 6/91 free-agent draft

Player Summary	
Fantasy Value	$1 to $2
Card Value	8¢ to 12¢
Will	eventually show power
Can't	learn it overnight
Expect	play at other spots
Don't Expect	smooth glove

Fabregas kept his head above water in 1992 despite having to make several adjustments. Not only was he in his first pro season, having missed 1991 in a contract dispute, but he was learning what was virtually a new position for him. He also had to put up with injury problems. Fabregas had played the infield at the University of Miami, his only catcher's duty coming as a backup to the Marlins' 1992 first-round draft choice, Charles Johnson. The Angels had Fabregas try catching full-time, but it wasn't an easy year. He suffered a sprained ankle early in the season and was out for 10 days. Later, he strained ligaments in his left wrist and was in a cast. He has a lot to learn about catching, and Angels instructors were trying to help him keep the ball in front of him. The arm is there, but Fabregas rushed some of his throws. He is a line-drive batter who didn't show much power in 1992. He had a .356 on-base average and a .333 slugging percentage last summer. He showed a better stick when he was in college. Figure on him being two years away.

Professional Batting Register

	BA	G	AB	R	H	2B	3B	HR	RBI	SB
92 A	.283	70	258	35	73	13	0	0	40	0

MIKE FARRELL

Position: Pitcher
Team: Milwaukee Brewers
Born: Jan. 28, 1969 Logansport, IN
Height: 6'2" **Weight:** 184 lbs.
Bats: left **Throws:** left
Acquired: Signed as a free agent, 6/91

Player Summary	
Fantasy Value	$2 to $4
Card Value	8¢ to 12¢
Will	deliver innings
Can't	match draftees' stuff
Expect	poise
Don't Expect	lots of attention

Farrell was only 22 years old when he thought his career might be over. He had not been drafted out of Indiana State University, and he had resigned himself to getting on with his life. Then came a call from the Brewers, and Farrell got his shot. He made three stops in the low minors in 1991, getting more starts as he advanced. He compiled an 8-4 record with a 2.21 ERA and just 19 walks in 89⅔ innings. Farrell got bumped up to Class-A Stockton in 1992, made the All-Star team and was named top control pitcher in the California League by *Baseball America*. Class-A batters compiled a .243 batting average against him in 1992. Another promotion took him to El Paso of the Double-A Texas League, where he made a string of low-run starts. He was among the leaders in the Brewers' minor league system in wins, ERA, and strikeouts. Equipped with a fastball, slider, and changeup, he has impressed the Brewers with his composure. It also won't hurt if he keeps allowing only about two walks per nine innings.

Professional Pitching Register

	W	L	ERA	G	CG	IP	H	ER	BB	SO
91 R	6	2	2.36	11	2	53.1	42	14	11	39
91 A	2	1	1.98	6	0	36.1	33	8	8	38
92 A	8	4	2.33	13	3	92.2	82	24	21	67
92 AA	7	6	2.62	14	5	106.1	95	31	25	66

KENNY FELDER

Position: Outfield
Team: Milwaukee Brewers
Born: Feb. 9, 1971 Harrisburg, PA
Height: 6'3" **Weight:** 230 lbs.
Bats: right **Throws:** right
Acquired: First-round pick in 6/92 free-agent draft

Player Summary	
Fantasy Value	$1 to $2
Card Value	7¢ to 15¢
Will	provoke oohs and aahs
Can't	chase bad balls
Expect	trouble with off-speed
Don't Expect	consistent contact

Felder owns, in the words of one person who has seen him, "tremendous power, overwhelming power." He showed it at the College World Series when he hit a ball out of Rosenblatt Stadium, more than 450 feet from home plate. One experienced baseball man claims he has more power than White Sox slugger Frank Thomas. Another observer compared Felder's raw ability to Bo Jackson's. Felder was assigned to Helena of the rookie Pioneer League, where he showed some of this strength but had trouble with his batting average. As you might expect from a slugger, he had to learn some patience; he was having trouble with the breaking ball, and was striking out a lot—swinging. He had a .335 on-base average and a .417 slugging percentage last summer. Felder has an above-average arm, but he played left field in Helena. His agility and speed for the position are more than adequate, as his status as a backup quarterback in college would attest. The Brew Crew needs power, and Felder may be the one who can provide it.

Professional Batting Register

	BA	G	AB	R	H	2B	3B	HR	RBI	SB
92 R	.217	74	276	58	60	8	1	15	48	11

337

CLIFF FLOYD

Position: Outfield; first base
Team: Montreal Expos
Born: Dec. 5, 1972 Markham, IL
Height: 6'4" **Weight:** 220 lbs.
Bats: left **Throws:** left
Acquired: First-round pick in 6/91 free-agent draft

Player Summary	
Fantasy Value	$1 to $2
Card Value	10¢ to 15¢
Will	bring great skills
Can't	forget defense
Expect	some time in outfield
Don't Expect	long stay in Class-A

Floyd may be one of the top power prospects in all of baseball, and his talents are not limited to swinging the bat. He runs very well for someone his size, and can steal more than the occasional base. He also has a good arm. However, it will be Floyd's bat that will garner him the most headlines as he zooms toward the majors. In 1992, *Baseball America* named him the best hitting prospect, the best power prospect, and the most exciting player in the Class-A South Atlantic League. He made the All-Star team, but as a reserve, not a starter, at first base. He was named the No. 1 prospect in the loop, however. His work in the field has not always been the smoothest, but he has the time and skill to improve. Floyd's season included a 20-game hitting streak, with most of it coming in July, when he hit .340. He ranked among the Sally League leaders in RBI and batting average. Putting up these numbers in the low minors is one thing, in higher levels it is another—but Floyd has the tools.

Professional Batting Register

	BA	G	AB	R	H	2B	3B	HR	RBI	SB
91 R	.262	56	214	35	56	9	3	6	30	13
92 A	.301	135	521	83	157	24	16	16	98	32

BROOK FORDYCE

Position: Catcher
Team: New York Mets
Born: May 7, 1970 New London, CT
Height: 6'1" **Weight:** 185 lbs.
Bats: right **Throws:** right
Acquired: Third-round pick in 6/89 free-agent draft

Player Summary	
Fantasy Value	$3 to $6
Card Value	10¢ to 20¢
Will	hit for extra bases
Can't	match Hundley defensively
Expect	switch to first
Don't Expect	speed on bases

Fordyce has Todd Hundley ahead of him in the major leagues, a situation that represents both an obstacle and an opportunity. If Hundley starts to hit a little, no one can take his job. However, if he remains near the .200 mark, someone like Fordyce could enter the picture. Fordyce has been in pro ball four years and distinguished himself at most levels. He made the Appalachian League All-Star squad in rookie ball in 1989; led the Class-A South Atlantic League with a .478 slugging percentage and was an All-Star in 1990; was selected to play in the Class-A Florida State League All-Star Game in 1991; and in 1992 was among the top hitters on his club in his first exposure to Double-A ball. Fordyce offers a little bit of power without giving away the contact that many batters do. He is still working on his defensive game, and didn't do a bad job handling Binghamton's staff in 1992. But it would take quite an effort for him to top Hundley behind the plate.

Professional Batting Register

	BA	G	AB	R	H	2B	3B	HR	RBI	SB
89 R	.327	69	226	45	74	15	0	9	38	10
90 A	.315	104	372	45	117	29	1	10	54	4
91 A	.239	115	406	42	97	19	3	7	55	4
92 AA	.278	118	425	59	118	28	0	11	61	1

BRENT GATES

Position: Second base
Team: Oakland Athletics
Born: March 14, 1970 Grand Rapids, MI
Height: 6'1" **Weight:** 180 lbs.
Bats: both **Throws:** right
Acquired: First-round pick in 6/91 free-agent draft

Player Summary	
Fantasy Value	$1 to $3
Card Value	10¢ to 25¢
Will	pound the ball
Can't	let draft slot burden him
Expect	fixture in lineup
Don't Expect	shortstop in majors

When the Athletics made Gates the 26th player taken in the '91 draft, they felt they had selected one of the top offensive middle infielders in the game. As for position, even though he had played shortstop as an amateur, his future was probably at another spot. One year later, Gates has proven the A's correct about their evaluation of his offense. And the position has taken care of itself, as Gates was named by *Baseball America* as the top defensive second baseman in the Class-A California League. However, he will either succeed or fail on the basis of his offense. At age 22, he was one of the top run-producers in the Oakland system. In 1992, Gates had a .414 on-base average and a .465 slugging percentage. He can be both consistent and explosive, as shown when he broke a 43-year-old Cal League record with his 35-game hitting streak—during which he hit .436. At the University of Minnesota, Gates never missed a start in 179 games. He became the first Gopher to hit .400 since Terry Steinbach did it in 1982.

STEVE GIBRALTER

Position: Outfield
Team: Cincinnati Reds
Born: Oct. 9, 1970 Dallas, TX
Height: 6' **Weight:** 180 lbs.
Bats: right **Throws:** right
Acquired: Sixth-round pick in 6/90 free-agent draft

Player Summary	
Fantasy Value	$1 to $3
Card Value	10¢ to 20¢
Will	hit lots of doubles
Can't	fan 100 times a year
Expect	work ethic
Don't Expect	domination at every level

Gibralter was a rock of consistency in his third pro season, seldom going more than a game or two without a hit. This quality is all the more impressive when found in a power hitter, and a young one at that. He has emerged as one of the more intriguing bats in the Reds' system, and he has done so before his 20th birthday. He made the Class-A Midwest League All-Star team in 1992, when he was among the leaders in the Triple Crown categories for both the Reds' system and the league. Gilbralter got his feet wet in pro ball in 1990, but really began making noise in 1991. That's when he led the Class-A South Atlantic League with 36 doubles. Gibralter's homers really began coming in 1992, though he may have benefited from fences that are just 325 feet down the line and 385 in center. He had a .378 on-base average and a .486 slugging percentage last summer. He can steal a base now and then, and he covers a lot of ground in the outfield. He has shown the ability to make adjustments, such as going to the opposite field.

Professional Batting Register

	BA	G	AB	R	H	2B	3B	HR	RBI	SB
91 A	.290	62	231	45	67	13	0	3	27	9
92 A	.321	133	505	94	162	39	2	10	88	9

Professional Batting Register

	BA	G	AB	R	H	2B	3B	HR	RBI	SB
90 R	.259	52	174	26	45	11	3	4	27	9
91 A	.267	140	544	72	145	36	7	6	71	11
92 A	.306	137	529	92	162	32	3	19	99	12

BENJI GIL

Position: Shortstop
Team: Texas Rangers
Born: Oct. 6, 1972 Tijuana, Mexico
Height: 6'2" **Weight:** 182 lbs.
Bats: right **Throws:** right
Acquired: First-round pick in 6/91 free-agent draft

Player Summary	
Fantasy Value	$1 to $2
Card Value	10¢ to 15¢
Will	steal bases
Can't	pick it
Expect	strong arm
Don't Expect	majors in '93

Gil is one of the top prospects in the organization, an all-around shortstop who the Rangers believe can one day occupy a premium spot in the major league lineup. He has good hands, a great arm, good to above-average speed, and occasional power. The 19th player selected in the draft, Gil made the Class-A South Atlantic League All-Star team in 1992 and went 1-for-3 in the game. He had a .343 on-base average and a .378 slugging percentage last year. On May 25, he alertly scored the winning run in extra innings when the Columbus catcher failed to call time before going to the mound. Gil had a rough time in the field during his first pro season, making 14 errors in 163 total chances. He went to the Florida Instructional League after the season, where he hit .254, and also played for Mexicali in the Mexican winter league. Gil played four seasons of high school ball, and went 9-4 with an 0.58 ERA with a no-hitter while batting .430 with seven homers. Gil has plenty of time to develop, and the Rangers have said they will not rush him.

Professional Batting Register

	BA	G	AB	R	H	2B	3B	HR	RBI	SB
91 R	.287	32	129	25	37	4	3	2	15	9
92 A	.274	132	482	75	132	21	1	9	55	26

DOUG GLANVILLE

Position: Outfield
Team: Chicago Cubs
Born: Aug. 25, 1970 Hackensack, NJ
Height: 6'2" **Weight:** 170 lbs.
Bats: right **Throws:** right
Acquired: First-round pick in 6/91 free-agent draft

Player Summary	
Fantasy Value	$1 to $2
Card Value	8¢ to 12¢
Will	steal bases
Can't	ease up on intensity
Expect	line drives
Don't Expect	home run power

Glanville was the 12th overall pick in the draft in 1991 and has shown the tools to justify such a status. He runs well, can throw, and is a line-drive hitter. He is making progress, but there are some balls he doesn't get to in center, and one school of thought says Glanville still must learn the value of playing hard every day. He played at Winston-Salem in 1992, Chicago's Class-A affiliate in the Carolina League. Though his average was not the best, he was among the organization's leaders in stolen bases. He had a .318 on-base average and a .336 slugging percentage last summer. Glanville attended the University of Pennsylvania, hit .414, and was a GTE Academic All-American. He played for Wareham and was named to the Cap Cod Summer League All-Star team in 1990. Glanville made a big impression in the Class-A New York-Penn League after the draft, playing 36 error-less games. He went 5-for-7 in just his sixth pro game, and had a 4-for-5, three-steal outing against Pittsfield. *Baseball America* named Glanville the second-best prospect in the circuit that year.

Professional Batting Register

	BA	G	AB	R	H	2B	3B	HR	RBI	SB
91 A	.303	36	152	29	46	8	0	2	12	17
92 A	.258	120	485	72	125	18	4	4	36	32

GREG GOHR

Position: Pitcher
Team: Detroit Tigers
Born: Oct. 29, 1967 Santa Clara, CA
Height: 6'3" **Weight:** 205 lbs.
Bats: right **Throws:** right
Acquired: First-round pick in 6/89 free-agent
draft

Player Summary	
Fantasy Value	$1 to $4
Card Value	7¢ to 10¢
Will	take his turn
Can't	overuse slider
Expect	smarts
Don't Expect	consistency yet

Gohr did not begin to pitch until he reached college, but he has made up for it by moving quickly through the minors. He attended Santa Clara University, where among other things he beat No. 1 Fresno State in 1989, ending a 32-game winning streak. The Tigers project Gohr as a 15-game winner in the big leagues; they like his baseball smarts. His fastball is in the high 80s and sometimes reaches 90 mph. The organization made him quit throwing his slider for part of 1992, in order for him to gain command of his curve. When he accomplished that, they let him throw the slider again. Gohr entered the pros in 1989, but a hip injury kept him to just four starts. He emerged in 1990, making 25 starts. In 1991, he needed just two outings in Double-A to prove he was ready for another promotion. He adjusted well to the Triple-A International League, where opposing batters hit just .230 against him. Gohr is the Tigers' top mound prospect, and he should be in the majors to stay soon.

Professional Pitching Register

	W	L	ERA	G	CG	IP	H	ER	BB	SO
89 A	0	2	7.15	4	0	11.1	11	9	6	10
90 A	13	5	2.62	25	0	137.2	125	40	50	90
91 AA	0	0	0.00	2	0	11.0	9	0	2	10
91 AAA	10	8	4.61	26	2	148.1	125	76	66	96
92 AAA	8	10	3.99	22	2	130.2	124	58	46	94

ALEX GONZALEZ

Position: Shortstop
Team: Toronto Blue Jays
Born: April 8, 1973 Miami, FL
Height: 6' **Weight:** 185 lbs.
Bats: right **Throws:** right
Acquired: 13th-round pick in 6/91 free-agent
draft

Player Summary	
Fantasy Value	$1 to $2
Card Value	8¢ to 12¢
Will	develop more power
Can't	be top glove man
Expect	Double-A in '93
Don't Expect	rush to majors

The Blue Jays certainly had no bad luck with the 13th pick in 1991. In just one year, Gonzalez has gone from a gamble to one of Toronto's top prospects. At draft time, there were some doubts about his willingness to sign a contract, since he had a scholarship to the University of Miami. However, the Blue Jays took the chance and got him. Gonzalez has shown more than a bit of punch in his bat and has the infield tools to go along with it. He was rated the best infield arm in the Class-A South Atlantic League by *Baseball America* in 1992. He had a .932 fielding average last summer. He has surprised some people with his power, especially coming off a 1991 season in which he had just nine extra-base hits in 192 at bats. In 1992, Gonzalez finished third on Myrtle Beach in home runs, RBI, and stolen bases. He had a .322 on-base average and a .402 slugging percentage last summer. Since he will be just 20 years old as the 1993 season begins, he could get even stronger, which would make him a real find.

Professional Batting Register

	BA	G	AB	R	H	2B	3B	HR	RBI	SB
91 R	.209	53	191	29	40	5	4	0	10	7
92 A	.271	134	535	82	145	22	9	10	62	26

SHAWN GREEN

Position: Outfield
Team: Toronto Blue Jays
Born: Nov. 10, 1972 Des Plaines, IL
Height: 6'4" **Weight:** 180 lbs.
Bats: left **Throws:** left
Acquired: First-round pick in 6/92 free-agent draft

Player Summary	
Fantasy Value	$1 to $2
Card Value	10¢ to 15¢
Will	continue education
Can't	play for Stanford
Expect	steady development
Don't Expect	him to be overwhelmed

Don't put too much importance on Green's stats for 1992. For one thing, he suffered a fractured thumb while sliding, which cost him some time and at bats. Second, the Florida State League was pretty fast company for a young man of 19 years of age who had never played in pro ball. Finally, Green is carrying a pretty unwieldy schedule at this stage of his life, playing ball in the Blue Jays organization and attending Stanford. He is obviously a very talented young man, an opinion the Blue Jays no doubt shared when they made him the 16th overall pick and paid him a reported $700,000 in 1991. Green was an academic star at Tustin High School in California. His athletic showing wasn't too bad, either. He tied the California Interscholastic Federation record with 147 hits as a senior. *USA Today* named Green to its All-USA High School first team. Green showed line-drive power last summer, and with his size he should develop plenty more pop. He faces a lot of adjustments, such as the wooden bat, but he will be fun to follow.

Professional Batting Register

	BA	G	AB	R	H	2B	3B	HR	RBI	SB
92 A	.273	110	417	44	114	21	3	1	49	22

TYLER GREEN

Position: Pitcher
Team: Philadelphia Phillies
Born: Feb. 18, 1970 Inglewood, CO
Height: 6'5" **Weight:** 185 lbs.
Bats: right **Throws:** right
Acquired: First-round pick in 6/91 free-agent draft

Player Summary	
Fantasy Value	$2 to $4
Card Value	8¢ to 12¢
Will	blow people away
Can't	overuse knuckle curve
Expect	one year at Triple-A
Don't Expect	injury-free season

Perhaps the top pitching prospect in the Phillies' organization, Green has a fastball in the 90s, a changeup, and what one member of the front office calls the best knuckle curve in pro baseball. Green suffered some shoulder problems in 1992, but the Phils hope that can be corrected with weight training. It was his second straight season with arm trouble, however. His 1991 campaign ended with a mild strain in his elbow. Green has passed most of the pitching tests in his brief career. He went 3-0 in five starts in his first season of pro ball, starting in the New York-Penn League then moving to high Class-A Florida State League. Promoted to Double-A Reading in 1992, he promptly went 6-3. He was considered to have the best breaking pitch in the Eastern League, and was an alternate to the All-Star Game. He ran into some problems at Triple-A Scranton, but he should rebound as long as he is healthy. Green led Wichita State University into the 1991 College World Series. He was also a member of the 1988 Junior Olympic Team.

Professional Pitching Register

	W	L	ERA	G	CG	IP	H	ER	BB	SO
91 A	3	0	1.29	5	0	28.0	10	4	14	39
92 AA	6	3	1.88	12	0	62.1	46	13	20	67
92 AAA	0	1	6.10	2	0	10.1	7	7	12	15

RICKY GREENE

Position: Pitcher
Team: Detroit Tigers
Born: Jan. 2, 1971 Fort Knox, KY
Height: 6'5" **Weight:** 200 lbs.
Bats: right **Throws:** right
Acquired: First-round pick in 6/91 free-agent draft

Player Summary	
Fantasy Value	$1 to $2
Card Value	10¢ to 20¢
Will	work out of bullpen
Can't	intimidate big leaguers
Expect	broken bats
Don't Expect	big league closer

Greene has had an eventful baseball career, even though he only signed in August of 1992. He owns a College World Series title, having helped Louisiana State University to the honor in 1991. He was the 16th overall pick in the 1992 draft, and he played for the U.S. Olympic Team in Barcelona, where he went 1-0 in five appearances. Upon returning to the United States, he signed with the Tigers, and went to their minor league system. Greene is a closer who intimidated college hitters and led Division I with 14 saves in 1991. He throws in the high 80s and may be able to get it into the 90s with big league instruction and conditioning. The Tigers also like the way his ball moves. His fastball rides up on righthanders. Greene might have moved along a bit more quickly had he gone straight to the pros, but exposure to the Olympic spotlight and competition might prove just as beneficial in the long run. He has had some knee problems that had him headed for surgery in the fall of 1992.

No minor league experience

WILLIE GREENE

Position: Third base
Team: Cincinnati Reds
Born: Sept. 23, 1971 Milledgeville, GA
Height: 5'11" **Weight:** 160 lbs.
Bats: left **Throws:** right
Acquired: Traded from Expos with Dave Martinez and Scott Ruskin for John Wetteland and Bill Risley, 12/91

Player Summary	
Fantasy Value	$3 to $7
Card Value	10¢ to 20¢
Will	produce power
Can't	depend on speed
Expect	diet of breaking balls
Don't Expect	return to shortstop

There are two intriguing questions about Greene. The first is how someone of his size generates such sock. His 1992 figures stamped him as one of the top power hitters not only in the Reds' chain but in all of the minors. His bat produces a distinctive crack when it meets ball. Yet Green's height and weight are those of an average-sized infielder; he apparently compensates with strong hips and good wrists. The second question is whether he's finally found a home. He has been in three organizations and reached double figures in homers for each. Originally drafted by the Pirates as their No. 1 choice in 1989, Greene was traded to Montreal as part of the deal that brought Zane Smith to Pittsburgh in '90. Then on Dec. 11, 1991, Greene came to Cincinnati in a transaction that sent John Wetteland to Montreal. Wetteland worked out very well for the Expos, but they may one day regret having had to part with Greene. He was drafted as a shortstop, but played third base in 1992.

Professional Batting Register

	BA	G	AB	R	H	2B	3B	HR	RBI	SB
89 R	.306	62	222	39	68	9	7	7	35	8
90 A	.259	114	386	72	100	16	5	14	58	11
91 A	.217	99	322	46	70	9	3	12	43	10
92 A	.283	34	120	26	34	8	2	12	40	2
92 AA	.278	96	349	47	97	19	2	15	66	8
92 NL	.269	29	93	10	25	5	2	2	13	0

KEN GRUNDT

Position: Pitcher
Team: San Francisco Giants
Born: Aug. 26, 1969 Melrose Park, IL
Height: 6'4" **Weight:** 195 lbs.
Bats: left **Throws:** left
Acquired: 53rd-round pick in 6/91 free-agent draft

Player Summary	
Fantasy Value	$1 to $2
Card Value	7¢ to 10¢
Will	get ahead of hitters
Can't	afford bad location
Expect	breaking balls
Don't Expect	good fastball

Grundt was taken so deep into the draft that he could have a future as a skin diver; he certainly didn't spend much time in the depths of the San Francisco organization, however. Despite his low draft status, Grundt has made two All-Star teams and quickly worked his way into the higher Class-A levels. He is not an overpowering pitcher. His off-speed stuff even at this stage of his career is his strength. But he has a knack for coming out of the bullpen and getting ahead in the count. He also has responded to the role of closer. In 1992, Grundt was one of the Class-A Midwest League's save leaders before being promoted to the high Class-A California League. On Aug. 4, he combined with Rich Hyde on a one-hitter—Grundt's first save in high Class-A. His lack of pure stuff suggests that he has some tougher times ahead, but he has earned a great shot at the next level. With his size and ability to throw strikes, the Giants' organization would be making a mistake by not paying attention.

Professional Pitching Register

	W	L	ERA	G	S	IP	H	ER	BB	SO
91 A	4	5	2.33	29	4	54.0	55	14	16	58
92 A	6	3	0.72	51	19	75.1	48	6	18	76

BILLY HALL

Position: Second base
Team: San Diego Padres
Born: June 17, 1969 Wichita, KS
Height: 5'9" **Weight:** 180 lbs.
Bats: both **Throws:** right
Acquired: 17th-round pick in 6/91 free-agent draft

Player Summary	
Fantasy Value	$1 to $2
Card Value	7¢ to 10¢
Will	pressure the defense
Can't	waste time advancing
Expect	stretched base hits
Don't Expect	pure power

Hall fell short after his brief flirtation with the .400 mark in 1992, but the effort certainly called attention to his skills. *Baseball Weekly* noticed, naming Hall its Player of the Week for July 28-Aug. 4. And *Baseball America* called him the fastest baserunner in the Class-A California League. He carried a .400 average into July before settling for his very respectable finish. A second baseman who was a walk-on at Wichita State University, Hall complements his quickness with the ability to switch-hit, thus making him a formidable force at the top of the lineup. He was among the stolen base leaders in the Padres' organization in 1992. Hall will never hit with power, and he doesn't put the ball in play as often as someone with his speed should—every strikeout is a missed chance to put pressure on the defense. After two straight seasons over .300, Hall has shown he can compete in pro ball. He had a .418 on-base average and a .432 slugging percentage last year. His biggest obstacle is that he will be 23 years old in 1993, and he has to make his impact soon.

Professional Batting Register

	BA	G	AB	R	H	2B	3B	HR	RBI	SB
91 A	.301	72	279	41	84	6	5	2	28	25
92 A	.356	119	495	92	176	22	5	2	39	49

BOB HAMELIN

Position: First base; designated hitter
Team: Kansas City Royals
Born: Nov. 29, 1967 Elizabeth, NJ
Height: 6' **Weight:** 230 lbs.
Bats: left **Throws:** left
Acquired: Second-round pick in 6/88 free-agent draft

Player Summary

Fantasy Value	$2 to $6
Card Value	10¢ to 15¢
Will	excel if healthy
Can't	regain lost time
Expect	job as DH
Don't Expect	many more chances

Hamelin was one of the top power prospects in baseball before back problems cut short three straight seasons. Now he has returned, having undergone back surgery, and the hope in Kansas City is that there is still enough time for this first baseman-designated hitter to get to the majors. To get an idea of his physical tools, consider he was recruited out of high school as a linebacker. Hamelin broke into pro ball in 1988 and led the Class-A Northwest League with 17 homers. By 1989, he was in Double-A, making the All-Star squad and being named the seventh-best prospect according to league managers. That's when Hamelin's back problems started, and his 16 homers came despite a pair of trips to the disabled list, including one that ended his season Aug. 3. Hamelin played at Triple-A in 1990 before being diagnosed as having a stress fracture in his back. More problems hit him in 1991, and he underwent disc fusion surgery June 28.

Professional Batting Register

	BA	G	AB	R	H	2B	3B	HR	RBI	SB
88 A	.298	70	235	42	70	19	1	17	61	9
89 AA	.308	68	211	45	65	12	5	16	47	3
90 AAA	.232	90	271	31	63	11	2	8	30	2
91 AAA	.189	37	127	13	24	3	1	4	19	0
92 A	.273	11	44	7	12	0	1	1	6	0
92 AA	.333	35	120	23	40	8	0	6	22	0
92 AAA	.200	27	95	9	19	3	1	5	15	0

JOEY HAMILTON

Position: Pitcher
Team: San Diego Padres
Born: Sept. 9, 1970 Statesboro, GA
Height: 6'4" **Weight:** 215 lbs.
Bats: right **Throws:** right
Acquired: First-round pick in 6/91 free-agent draft

Player Summary

Fantasy Value	$1 to $4
Card Value	8¢ to 12¢
Will	have trouble with weight
Can't	offer polished curve yet
Expect	good hard fastball
Don't Expect	complicated repertoire

Hamilton no doubt has big league talent and could have been one of those college players who take a fast track to the majors, but a combination of circumstances has held him back. For one, he held out in contract talks, missing at least a half-year of what would have been his first pro season. He also came down with some tenderness in his elbow. Along the way, he endured personal tragedy when his father died after a long illness. For all of the problems, Hamilton remains one of the top prospects in the organization. He began the 1992 campaign in the Class-A South Atlantic League, and quickly outclassed the competition there before moving on to the high Class-A California League and then into Double-A ball. He has said he believes he can be in the majors by 1993, and it's not out of the question. Hamilton, out of Georgia Southern University, throws a fastball and a changeup. He has to watch his weight. *Baseball America* ranked him 36th among its top 100 before the 1992 season.

Professional Pitching Register

	W	L	ERA	G	CG	IP	H	ER	BB	SO
92 A	6	5	3.00	16	0	84.0	83	28	22	78
92 AA	3	0	2.86	6	0	34.2	33	11	11	26

JEFFREY HAMMONDS

Position: Outfield
Team: Baltimore Orioles
Born: March 5, 1971 Scotch Plains, NJ
Height: 6' **Weight:** 185 lbs.
Bats: right **Throws:** right
Acquired: First-round pick in 6/92 free-agent draft

Player Summary	
Fantasy Value	$1 to $4
Card Value	15¢ to 50¢
Will	be a star
Can't	escape spotlight
Expect	complete package
Don't Expect	long stay in minors

Hammonds is one of a growing list of players (whose numbers include Todd Van Poppel and Brien Taylor) reflecting baseball's finances as well as their own talent. Hammonds, who possesses the complete baseball package, might have been the first overall pick in the 1992 draft, but Houston had some doubts about being able to sign him; Cleveland and Montreal also passed. Not until Baltimore stepped up with the fifth pick of the draft did Hammonds get his name called. A two-time All-American from Stanford, Hammonds was the first outfielder chosen. As a freshman, he compiled a 37-game hitting streak. He was a member of the United States Olympic Team, hitting .414 in the round-robin and going 3-for-7 in the medal round. He was honored by *Baseball Weekly* as the team's MVP. Olympic Coach Ron Fraser has said he thinks Hammonds can be a superstar. He was originally drafted out of high school by Toronto, but accepted a scholarship to Stanford. He became only the third player from New Jersey to be tabbed in the top five since the draft began in 1965.

No minor league experience

MIKE HAMPTON

Position: Pitcher
Team: Seattle Mariners
Born: Sept. 9, 1972 Brooksville, FL
Height: 5'10" **Weight:** 180 lbs.
Bats: right **Throws:** left
Acquired: Sixth-round pick in 6/90 free-agent draft

Player Summary	
Fantasy Value	$1 to $3
Card Value	10¢ to 20¢
Will	see Double-A in '93
Can't	stop throwing strikes
Expect	good curve
Don't Expect	another no-hitter

Hampton has bounced back from an unusual 1991 season in which a no-hitter seemed to bring him nothing but bad luck for a while. He rebounded to rank among the win and ERA leaders in the Seattle system. He is one of the Mariners' best pitching prospects, especially from the left side. Hampton opened the 1991 season with San Bernardino of the Class-A California League, and his highlight came May 31 with a no-hitter against Visalia. But he couldn't produce any quality outings in subsequent starts, and he was demoted, leaving him as the first pitcher in Cal League history to throw a no-hitter for his only win. Hampton turned things around in the Class-A Northwest League, posting a 1.58 ERA and seven decisions in nine starts. In 1992, he seemed more at home in his second crack at the Cal League, and he roared off to a 9-6 start. He needed four shots at his 10th win, and finally got it against his old friends at Visalia, fanning 12 in seven innings. Class-A opponents in 1992 compiled a .255 batting average.

Professional Pitching Register

	W	L	ERA	G	CG	IP	H	ER	BB	SO
90 R	7	2	2.66	14	0	64.1	52	19	40	59
91 A	6	9	3.65	27	1	130.2	103	53	73	122
92 A	13	8	3.12	25	6	170.0	163	59	66	132
92 AA	0	1	4.35	2	1	10.1	13	5	1	6

GREG HANSELL

Position: Pitcher
Team: Los Angeles Dodgers
Born: March 12, 1971 Bellflower, CA
Height: 6'4" **Weight:** 200 lbs.
Bats: right **Throws:** right
Acquired: Traded from Mets with Bob Ojeda for Hubie Brooks, 12/90

Player Summary	
Fantasy Value	$2 to $5
Card Value	10¢ to 20¢
Will	sink his fastball
Can't	command curve yet
Expect	durable starter
Don't Expect	real heat

Hansell has done his share of moving around in his four years in pro ball. Lately, however, there's an important difference: Now he's making his moves within the Dodger family, whereas earlier he was moving from organization to organization. He was originally drafted by the Red Sox, and was acquired by the Mets during the 1990 season as part of a deal that sent Mike Marshall to Boston. Just as quickly, the Mets shipped Hansell to Los Angeles as a throw-in in the Bob Ojeda-Hubie Brooks trade. In his first full campaign with his new club, Hansell pitched for the Dodgers' affiliate in Bakersfield and wound up making the Class-A California League All-Star Team. Hansell started the '92 season at Double-A San Antonio, but he soon got a promotion to Triple-A Albuquerque. He didn't fare well there and was returned to the Texas League, where he put together a fine record. Double-A opponents compiled a .235 batting average last summer. He has a sinking fastball that produces grounders.

Professional Pitching Register

	W	L	ERA	G	CG	IP	H	ER	BB	SO
89 A	3	2	2.53	10	0	57.0	51	16	23	44
90 A	9	14	3.30	27	2	153.1	129	58	79	95
91 A	14	5	2.87	25	0	150.2	142	48	42	132
92 AA	6	4	2.83	14	0	92.1	80	29	33	66
92 AAA	1	5	5.24	13	0	68.2	84	40	35	38

ANDY HARTUNG

Position: First base
Team: Chicago Cubs
Born: Feb. 12, 1969 Melrose, MA
Height: 6'1" **Weight:** 205 lbs.
Bats: right **Throws:** right
Acquired: 30th-round pick in 6/90 free-agent draft

Player Summary	
Fantasy Value	$1 to $2
Card Value	8¢ to 12¢
Will	drive in runs
Can't	unseat Grace
Expect	high strikeouts
Don't Expect	slow runner

Hartung is in the unfortunate situation of having Mark Grace ahead of him at the major league level. If Hartung has another season like he did in 1992, however, he may prove hard to ignore. Playing most of the season in the Class-A Carolina League, he led Cubs farmhands both in home runs and in RBI. He compiled a .347 on-base average and a .484 slugging percentage. He also got a late-season call-up to Double-A Charlotte, and hit a three-run homer in a 4-3 win over Jacksonville. A fine all-around athlete, Hartung comes out of New England, where he was a fine hockey player and an all-state high school shortstop in Massachusetts. He became a first-team All-American at the University of Maine, where he hit .414 and led his team to a 42-20 mark. Hartung was an impressive slugger the moment he set foot in pro ball, leading the Class-A New York-Penn league with 70 RBI, a .544 slugging percentage, and 143 total bases. His exploits will earn him a shot at Double-A and maybe higher in 1993.

Professional Batting Register

	BA	G	AB	R	H	2B	3B	HR	RBI	SB
90 A	.331	74	263	48	87	19	2	11	70	1
91 A	.254	81	260	29	66	6	2	9	33	0
92 A	.278	132	496	76	138	25	4	23	94	10
92 AA	.333	2	9	1	3	1	0	1	3	0

HILLY HATHAWAY

Position: Pitcher
Team: California Angels
Born: Sept. 12, 1969 Jacksonville, FL
Height: 6'4" **Weight:** 195 lbs.
Bats: left **Throws:** left
Acquired: 35th-round pick in 6/89 free-agent draft

Player Summary

Fantasy Value.............................$2 to $5
Card Value.................................10¢ to 20¢
Will...get decisions
Can't...overuse curve
Expect......................................good competitor
Don't Expect ....many walks

Hathaway is the kind of player who just keeps coming at you, whether it's from a low draft position, an injury, or on the ladder from the low minors to the majors. He has been a pro three years now, and just keeps collecting starts and wins. An injury kept Hathaway in extended spring training in 1992, but when he emerged, he quickly passed a test in the high Class-A California League. He went on to be an important starter for Double-A Midland. He is a stopper in a rotation, someone who can go to the mound after a losing streak or in a tough situation and give his team a chance. Hathaway has an outstanding curve, perhaps the best one in the Texas League in '92; it can freeze a batter. He also throws a fastball and a change, and Double-A opponents compiled a .251 batting average. Most impressive of all, though, may be Hathaway's control. In 125 innings in 1992, he walked just 16 batters. Any lefty who can do that has a great chance to make it.

Professional Pitching Register

	W	L	ERA	G	CG	IP	H	ER	BB	SO
90 A	8	2	1.47	15	0	86.0	56	14	25	113
91 A	9	6	3.35	20	1	129.0	126	48	41	110
92 A	2	1	1.50	3	2	24.0	25	4	3	17
92 AA	7	2	3.21	14	1	95.1	90	34	10	69
92 AL	0	0	7.94	2	0	5.2	8	5	3	1

SCOTT HATTEBERG

Position: Catcher
Team: Boston Red Sox
Born: Dec. 14, 1969 Salem, OR
Height: 6'1" **Weight:** 185 lbs.
Bats: left **Throws:** right
Acquired: First-round pick in 6/92 free-agent draft

Player Summary

Fantasy Value...................................$1 to $3
Card Value......................................7¢ to 10¢
Will ....handle staff well
Can't ....reach bleachers in Fenway
Expect ....good makeup
Don't Expect ....running speed

Hatteberg was acquired with a sandwich pick the Red Sox earned from Kansas City as compensation for the signing of Mike Boddicker. Hatteberg has moved quickly up the ladder, though he has not established much power or run production. Some of his rapid ascent can likely be ascribed to his college and international experience; he played for Washington State University and the 1990 American squad for the Goodwill Games. Hatteberg is a fine defensive receiver, calls a good game, and throws well. A fine all-around athlete with good makeup, Hatteberg also played both football and basketball in college. He was a college teammate of Boston's prospect righthander Aaron Sele, who was taken in the same round. Hatteberg played in the Alaska League in 1989 and '90. He also attended the Florida Instructional League in 1991. Hatteberg has the tools to make himself useful in the majors—and perhaps quickly—but he won't cure Boston's power shortage. He had a .327 on-base percentage and a .300 slugging average in 1992 at Double-A New Britain. He walked more than he struck out, indicating that he has a developed batting eye.

Professional Batting Register

	BA	G	AB	R	H	2B	3B	HR	RBI	SB
91 A	.269	64	216	25	58	9	3	1	27	1
92 AA	.232	103	297	28	69	13	2	1	30	1

RYAN HAWBLITZEL

Position: Pitcher
Team: Colorado Rockies
Born: April 30, 1971 West Palm Beach, FL
Height: 6'2" **Weight:** 170 lbs.
Bats: right **Throws:** right
Acquired: Second-round pick from Cubs in
11/92 expansion draft

Player Summary	
Fantasy Value	$2 to $5
Card Value	8¢ to 12¢
Will	sink his fastball
Can't	overpower hitters
Expect	four pitches
Don't Expect	another 15-2 campaign

Hawblitzel has a chance to make an impact on the major league level with the Rockies much sooner than if he would have stayed in the Cubs' organization. Although he failed in 1992 to dominate to the extent that he did in 1991, no one really expected him to duplicate the 15-2 mark he hung up in the Class-A Carolina League. Instead, the slender righty put in his first full year at Double-A, and once again was among the win and strikeout leaders in the Cubs' farm system. Hawblitzel has an average fastball that may gain a yard or two as he gains strength. His success will depend on making sure it sinks, and in throwing his curve for strikes. Hawblitzel went to pro ball right out of high school, where he played on three championship teams. He was the *Sun-Sentinel's* 1990 Player of the Year in Ft. Lauderdale, and was picked for the Florida Athletic Coaches All-Star team. One year later, he was the starting pitcher in the Carolina League All-Star Game.

ERIC HELFAND

Position: Catcher
Team: Oakland Athletics
Born: March 25, 1969 Erie, PA
Height: 6' **Weight:** 195 lbs.
Bats: left **Throws:** right
Acquired: Traded from Marlins for Walt Weiss,
11/92

Player Summary	
Fantasy Value	$1 to $2
Card Value	7¢ to 15¢
Will	improve power figures
Can't	run much
Expect	more All-Star appearances
Don't Expect	majors in 1993

The A's are so impressed with Helfand that they drafted him, lost him in the expansion draft, and then traded for him. He received his first promotion to Double-A in 1992, but not until he had left his mark on the Class-A California League. Helfand singled and homered to become the MVP of the All-Star Game. That performance came roughly one year after a broken collar bone interrupted what was shaping up as an impressive 1991 season. Helfand was originally picked by Seattle in the eighth round of the 1987 draft, but instead went to Nebraska on a baseball scholarship. In 1990, the A's made him the 65th overall selection, and the first position player they took, using the pick obtained as compensation for Kansas City's signing of free agent Storm Davis. Helfand spent most of his first pro year with Southern Oregon of the Northwest League, where he was named the team's co-MVP. In 1991, Helfand was hitting .248 when he broke his collar bone while trying to score. He returned in time to play 22 games.

Professional Pitching Register

	W	L	ERA	G	CG	IP	H	ER	BB	SO
90 R	6	5	3.93	14	2	75.2	72	33	25	71
91 A	15	2	2.42	20	5	134.0	110	36	47	103
91 AA	1	2	3.21	5	1	33.2	31	12	12	25
92 AA	12	8	3.76	28	3	174.2	180	73	38	119

Professional Batting Register

	BA	G	AB	R	H	2B	3B	HR	RBI	SB
90 A	.285	57	207	29	59	12	0	2	39	4
91 A	.256	67	242	35	62	15	1	7	38	0
92 A	.289	72	249	40	72	15	0	10	44	0
92 AA	.228	37	114	13	26	7	0	2	9	0

FERNANDO HERNANDEZ

Position: Pitcher
Team: Cleveland Indians
Born: June 16, 1971 Santiago, Dominican Republic
Height: 6'2" **Weight:** 170 lbs.
Bats: right **Throws:** right
Acquired: Signed as free agent, 1/90

Player Summary	
Fantasy Value	.... $1 to $2
Card Value	.... 8¢ to 12¢
Will	.... get better
Can't	..............................lapse on control
Expect	.... nearly a K per inning
Don't Expect	.... majors in '93

Cleveland's pitching is suddenly better than it's been in a while, and Hernandez is a prospect who can help strengthen the movement. The organization likes him a great deal, describing him as being very "projectable." The Indians believe he could get bigger and perhaps stronger. Hernandez already owns a fastball that is average to slightly above average, and he has an outstanding slider. His progress has been steady rather than flashy, as the Indians nurse him because of his age. Even so, the pace picked up a bit in 1992. Hernandez was the Opening Day starter for Columbus of the Class-A South Atlantic League and helped the Indians take the first-half title. On June 7, he hurled a shutout against Savannah, his club's second straight whitewash. He held Sally League hitters to a .184 batting average. Later he was promoted to the Class-A Carolina League. All the while, Hernandez was among the Indians' farmhands in ERA and strikeouts per innings pitched. His ratios have been good to outstanding, especially in 1991.

Professional Pitching Register

	W	L	ERA	G	CG	IP	H	ER	BB	SO
90 R	4	4	4.00	11	2	69.2	61	31	30	43
91 R	4	4	2.92	14	0	77.0	74	25	19	86
92 A	5	8	1.57	19	2	110.1	78	33	55	102

KIKI HERNANDEZ

Position: Catcher
Team: New York Yankees
Born: Oct. 3, 1969 Arecibo, Puerto Rico
Height: 5'11" **Weight:** 195 lbs.
Bats: right **Throws:** right
Acquired: Signed as a free agent, 7/88

Player Summary	
Fantasy Value	..................................$2 to $4
Card Value	.... 10¢ to 20¢
Will	.... put ball in play
Can't	.... sustain power
Expect	.... shot somewhere
Don't Expect	.... regular in majors

Hernandez continued his development in 1992, making the Eastern League All-Star squad as a reserve and getting two at bats in the Double-A classic. It was his second straight All-Star berth after three years of laboring without distinction in the lower regions of the Yankee organization. His breakthrough campaign came in 1991, when he led the Class-A South Atlantic League with a .535 slugging percentage, compiled the top batting average in the entire organization, and was named league MVP. Hernandez failed to match this admittedly high standard in 1992, when his power became a casualty of the Eastern League. Without this pop, Hernandez becomes less of a prospect, especially since his other position, first base, also requires some sock. However, any catcher has a chance these days, since the ranks generally are thin. He had a .372 slugging average and a .358 on-base percentage at Double-A Albany in 1992. Hernandez was the roommate of 1991's first overall pick Brien Taylor during the Instructional League in 1991.

Professional Batting Register

	BA	G	AB	R	H	2B	3B	HR	RBI	SB
88 R	.160	9	25	2	4	1	0	0	2	0
89 A	.223	29	94	12	21	4	0	2	7	1
90 A	.250	107	360	39	90	20	2	6	47	0
91 A	.328	115	415	58	136	31	2	16	83	2
92 A	.111	3	9	1	1	0	0	0	1	0
92 AA	.280	99	328	46	92	18	0	4	40	0

TYRONE HILL

Position: Pitcher
Team: Milwaukee Brewers
Born: March 7, 1972 Yucaipa, CA
Height: 6'6" **Weight:** 195 lbs.
Bats: left **Throws:** left
Acquired: First-round pick in 6/91 free-agent draft

Player Summary	
Fantasy Value	$1 to $2
Card Value	10¢ to 20¢
Will	blow people away
Can't	get by on two pitches
Expect	Brewers to hold breath
Don't Expect	lefties to hit him

Hill had some nice moments in what should have been his first full pro season, but the club shut him down in early August with a sore left triceps. At the time, he was tied with Mark Kiefer for first in the minor league chain with 133 strikeouts. Entering the season, *Baseball America* named Hill the third-best lefty prospect in baseball and the 20th best prospect overall. The paper also tabbed him as the best pitching prospect and owner of the best breaking ball in the Class-A Midwest League. He allowed Class-A hitters to compile only a .184 batting average. He made the league's All-Star squad, too. Hill's size, the fact that he is lefthanded, and the way he can strike out hitters has produced comparisons to John Candelaria. Hill throws a fastball that has been clocked into the 90s, plus a breaking ball. With Hill being so talented, and with the Brewers having such a high pick invested in him, they will feel some concern until he proves his triceps is sound. It could delay his arrival a half-year.

Professional Pitching Register

	W	L	ERA	G	CG	IP	H	ER	BB	SO
91 R	4	2	3.15	11	0	60.0	43	21	35	76
92 A	9	5	3.25	20	1	113.2	76	41	74	133

STERLING HITCHCOCK

Position: Pitcher
Team: New York Yankees
Born: April 29, 1971 Fayetteville, NC
Height: 6'1" **Weight:** 200 lbs.
Bats: left **Throws:** left
Acquired: Ninth-round pick in 6/89 free-agent draft

Player Summary	
Fantasy Value	$1 to $3
Card Value	10¢ to 20¢
Will	strike out hitters
Can't	stop the puns
Expect	pretty good control
Don't Expect	automatic berth with Yanks

Headline writers are already making puns with this prospect's last name, since it's the same as the famous filmmaker's. There's just one problem with this—there may be no suspense. The Yankee Hitchcock seems to be the real thing, and his call-up in 1992 shows as much. He made his debut on Sept. 11 against the Royals, and permitted just one run in six innings. He should get a long look in spring training, along with fellow phenoms Sam Militello and Bob Wickman. The fact that Hitchcock is lefthanded is all the better. Yankee Stadium is not quite the heaven for lefties that it used to be, but every club loves a southpaw who can throw the ball over the plate. Hitchcock signed out of Armwood High School in Florida and dominated in his first look at the pros. He was named the Gulf Coast League "Star of Stars," and was tabbed Topps Player of the Month for August. Hitchcock pitched a no-hitter while working in the Class-A Sally League in 1990.

Professional Pitching Register

	W	L	ERA	G	CG	IP	H	ER	BB	SO
89 R	9	1	1.53	13	0	76.2	48	13	27	98
90 A	12	12	2.91	27	6	173.1	122	56	60	171
91 A	7	7	2.64	19	2	119.1	111	35	26	101
92 AA	6	9	2.58	24	2	147.0	116	42	42	156
92 AL	0	2	8.31	3	0	13.0	23	12	6	6

DENNY HOCKING

Position: Shortstop
Team: Minnesota Twins
Born: April 2, 1970 Torrance, CA
Height: 5'10" **Weight:** 165 lbs.
Bats: Both **Throws:** right
Acquired: 52nd-round pick in 6/89 free-agent draft

Player Summary	
Fantasy Value	$1 to $2
Card Value	8¢ to 12¢
Will	use speed on offense
Can't	easily judge bat
Expect	good arm
Don't Expect	easy out

Hocking seemed to blossom during the 1992 season. In the coziness of the Visalia ballpark, where the fences are just 320 feet down the lines, it can be hard to tell. At one point during the season, Class-A Visalia players accounted for the top five batting averages in Minnesota's minor league system, and Hocking was right up there in second place. So how to judge? Well, a small park had nothing to do with the fact that *Baseball America* said that Hocking had the California League's best infield arm. And a small park doesn't account for Hocking increasing his stolen-base total two consecutive years. When he notched six hits in 11 at bats in a series against Reno in mid-August, he did so on the road. Hocking does not owe his excellent walk totals to the distance to the fence. He had a .415 on-base average and a .464 slugging percentage in 1992. Finally, is there any law against taking advantage of a good situation? After all, if Hocking reaches the Twins, he won't exactly be playing in a hitter's nightmare.

AARON HOLBERT

Position: Shortstop
Team: St. Louis Cardinals
Born: Jan. 9, 1973 Torrance, CA
Height: 6' **Weight:** 160 lbs.
Bats: right **Throws:** right
Acquired: First-round pick in 6/90 free-agent draft

Player Summary	
Fantasy Value	$1 to $2
Card Value	10¢ to 25¢
Will	make dazzling plays
Can't	drive ball
Expect	Cards to have patience
Don't Expect	stolen bases

Heaven help the shortstops who must perform in St. Louis in the days after Ozzie Smith's departure. They will be judged against his Gold Glove standards, a burden for any player, much less a rookie. Holbert is one of the candidates for such a spotlight, though. As the 18th player drafted in 1990, he clearly possesses the skills that attracted the Cardinals. In 1992, he was among the nonroster players invited to spring training. He was assigned to Savannah of the Class-A South Atlantic League, and made the All-Star team as a reserve. Holbert still makes too many errors and, like other players, he can pull off the spectacular play, only to have trouble with the routine ones. He had the best year of his career at the plate, but did so at a level where it is still hard to see how much he'll hit. He had a .335 on-base average and a .330 slugging percentage last summer. Since he has shown no record of stealing bases or piling up the total bases, he had better become more consistent at short.

Professional Batting Register

	BA	G	AB	R	H	2B	3B	HR	RBI	SB
90 R	.294	54	201	45	59	6	2	6	30	14
91 A	.255	125	432	72	110	17	8	2	36	22
92 A	.331	135	550	117	182	34	9	7	81	38

Professional Batting Register

	BA	G	AB	R	H	2B	3B	HR	RBI	SB
90 R	.172	54	174	27	30	4	1	1	18	4
91 A	.223	59	215	22	48	5	1	1	24	5
92 A	.267	119	439	53	117	17	4	1	34	62

JESSE HOLLINS

Position: Pitcher
Team: Chicago Cubs
Born: Jan. 27, 1970 Conroe, TX
Height: 6'3" **Weight:** 200 lbs.
Bats: right **Throws:** right
Acquired: 40th-round pick in 6/88 free-agent draft

Player Summary	
Fantasy Value	$1 to $3
Card Value	7¢ to 10¢
Will	reach the 90s
Can't	always find plate
Expect	more bullpen work
Don't Expect	another Lee Smith

Hollins is one of the better pitching prospects in the Cubs' organization, and he seemed to come into his own in 1992. After his first three pro years, during which he moved between the rotation and the bullpen, Hollins came into his own as a closer. Pitching at the highest level of his career, he became the runaway save leader in the Cubs' minor league system. Hollins reached the 20-save mark in late July by escaping a bases-loaded jam in the ninth. He has been compared to Lee Smith and, though not as big as Smith, Hollins does throw extremely hard—both a fastball and a slider. However, he has not always thrown the ball over the plate; he walked nearly one man per inning in 1991. Hollins attended San Jacinto Junior College in Houston, where he pitched a perfect game and won the Junior College World Series in 1989. He had some success as a starter in 1990 when he led the Class-A New York-Penn League with his 10 wins. He was Topps Player of the Month for August that year.

Professional Pitching Register

	W	L	ERA	G	S	IP	H	ER	BB	SO
89 R	3	1	4.84	22	0	48.1	59	26	23	31
90 A	10	3	2.77	22	0	107.0	99	36	54	123
91 A	4	8	5.67	41	5	98.1	107	62	83	74
92 AA	3	4	3.20	63	25	70.1	60	25	32	73
92 NL	0	0	13.50	4	0	4.2	8	7	5	0

STEVE HOSEY

Position: Outfield
Team: San Francisco Giants
Born: April 2, 1969 Oakland, CA
Height: 6'3" **Weight:** 215 lbs.
Bats: right **Throws:** right
Acquired: First-round pick in 6/89 free-agent draft

Player Summary	
Fantasy Value	$2 to $5
Card Value	10¢ to 25¢
Will	make impact in bigs
Can't	make consistent contact
Expect	great arm
Don't Expect	25 homers

Hosey could be the starting right fielder for the Giants in 1993, and well beyond that. He made his major league debut on Aug. 29, 1992, and played quite a bit over the last month. His numbers weren't spectacular, but it was a chance for him to get the feel of the big leagues. Once he does that, he'll likely be just the kind of player he was in the minors—good average, solid extra-base power, and more than a few stolen bases. He'll get even better as he works on making more consistent contact. He led the Class-A California League with 139 strikeouts in 1990. Hosey attended Fresno State University where he hit .336 with 21 homers, 123 RBI, and 30 stolen bases; he was a member of the squad that went to the 1988 College World Series. He made an impact in his first pro season, being named to the Topps-National Association short season Class-A All-Star squad. In 1991, he helped Shreveport win the Texas League title, getting four hits in game two of the finals.

Professional Batting Register

	BA	G	AB	R	H	2B	3B	HR	RBI	SB
89 A	.288	72	285	44	82	14	3	13	59	14
90 A	.232	139	479	85	111	13	6	16	78	16
91 AA	.293	126	409	79	120	21	5	17	74	24
92 AAA	.286	126	462	64	132	28	7	10	65	15
92 NL	.250	21	56	6	14	1	0	1	6	1

MIKE HOSTETLER

Position: Pitcher
Team: Atlanta Braves
Born: June 5, 1970 Marietta, GA
Height: 6'2" **Weight:** 195 lbs.
Bats: right **Throws:** right
Acquired: 21st-round pick in 6/91 free-agent draft

Player Summary	
Fantasy Value	$1 to $2
Card Value	8¢ to 12¢
Will	work on changeup
Can't	get overconfident
Expect	quick healer
Don't Expect	another quick jump

Considering the kind of year the Braves had in 1992, it's quite an assertion to say a Double-A pitcher was one of the system's best. Yet, not many pitchers dominated to the extent that Hostetler did. He opened the season in the Class-A Carolina League and won nine games there. He was promoted to Double-A Greenville, where he enjoyed the same kind of success in terms of winning percentage; his strikeout-to-innings ratio, however, suffered with the tougher competition at the higher level. At season's end, Hostetler was one of the top winners and strikeout artists in the whole organization, the majors included. The season was all the more remarkable considering Hostetler had been involved in a 1991 car wreck that put him into the hospital. The injuries no doubt account for the fact no team selected him until the 21st round. But he showed no problems in his first exposure to pro ball in '91, averaging 11.68 strikeouts per nine innings. After his rapid ascent, Hostetler could use a solid year at Triple-A.

Professional Pitching Register

	W	L	ERA	G	CG	IP	H	ER	BB	SO
91 R	3	2	1.91	9	0	47.0	35	10	9	61
92 A9	3	2.15	12			388.0	75	21	19	88
92 AA	6	2	3.90	16	1	81.0	78	35	23	57

BUTCH HUSKEY

Position: Third base
Team: New York Mets
Born: Nov. 10, 1971 Lawton, OK
Height: 6'3" **Weight:** 244 lbs.
Bats: right **Throws:** right
Acquired: Seventh-round pick in 6/89 free-agent draft

Player Summary	
Fantasy Value	$1 to $2
Card Value	10¢ to 20¢
Will	be noticed at third
Can't	field with the best
Expect	clean-cut image
Don't Expect	quickness on bunts

You can bet that Huskey will use his body to block a few balls at third base. It's possible that bigger men have played the position, but none leap to mind. Huskey looks like a defensive end out there, and that's no exaggeration—he was once offered a football scholarship by Oklahoma. He loves baseball, though, and it shows in his approach. He plays hurt, doesn't miss games, and is a positive influence and team leader. His mind is made up he's going to make the majors. It would be a mistake to bet against him, since he's one of the highest-rated players in the Mets' farm system. Huskey's got some pop in his bat, not surprising for his size. Time will tell if he can became a genuine power hitter. He made the Class-A Florida State League All-Star team in 1992, and was right up there with the leading Mets' farmhands in the power stats. He had a .299 on-base average and a .402 slugging percentage in 1992. Look for him to start in Double-A in 1993.

Professional Batting Register

	BA	G	AB	R	H	2B	3B	HR	RBI	SB
89 R	.263	54	190	27	50	14	2	6	34	4
90 R	.269	72	279	39	75	13	0	14	53	7
91 A	.287	134	492	88	141	27	5	26	99	22
92 A	.254	134	493	65	125	17	1	18	75	7

MARK HUTTON

Position: Pitcher
Team: New York Yankees
Born: Feb. 6, 1970 Adelaide, Australia
Height: 6'6" **Weight:** 225 lbs.
Bats: right **Throws:** right
Acquired: Signed as a free agent, 12/88

Player Summary
Fantasy Value	$2 to $5
Card Value	10¢ to 15¢
Will	add to Australia's input
Can't	find pinpoint control
Expect	fastball in the 90s
Don't Expect	top curveball

More and more natives of Australia seem to be arriving in North America, and Hutton has a chance to be one of the best yet. He was rated as one of New York's top prospects entering the 1992 campaign. He did a nice job for Albany of the Double-A Eastern League last year, holding EL hitters to a .235 batting average. He was among the victory leaders in the Yankees' minor league system. Hutton gets points for his size alone, but he also makes good use of it. A starting pitcher, he throws a fastball that can get well into the 90s, plus a slider and a changeup. He appeared in the Double-A All-Star Game and hurled two scoreless innings, allowing two hits and striking out one. Hutton still walks a few too many; if he can improve on that, his ERA will drop a bit. Hutton has come a long way in the transition from a thrower to a pitcher. He has begun to do his best work at a time when the Yanks can really use some young arms. Sam Militello gave the big club a lift in August of 1992; Hutton will likely get a shot sometime in 1993.

Professional Pitching Register
	W	L	ERA	G	CG	IP	H	ER	BB	SO
89 A	6	2	4.07	12	0	66.1	70	30	24	62
90 A	1	10	6.31	21	0	81.1	77	57	62	72
91 A	5	8	2.45	24	3	147.0	98	40	65	117
91 AAA	1	0	1.50	1	0	6.0	3	1	5	5
92 AA	13	7	3.59	25	1	165.1	146	66	66	128
92 AAA	0	1	5.40	1	0	5.0	7	3	2	4

ADAM HYZDU

Position: Outfield
Team: San Francisco Giants
Born: Dec. 6, 1971 San Jose, CA
Height: 6'3" **Weight:** 210 lbs.
Bats: right **Throws:** right
Acquired: First-round pick in 6/90 free-agent draft

Player Summary
Fantasy Value	$1 to $2
Card Value	8¢ to 12¢
Will	cover ground in right
Can't	project as 15-homer man
Expect	above average arm
Don't Expect	blazing speed

The man with the Scrabble™ name can spell success for himself if he learns how to make more consistent contact. Hyzdu's defense is superb right now, and he has improved his batting average. He also reached career highs in home runs, stolen bases, and RBI—reflecting an ability to improve even against tougher competition. So there's a feeling that Hyzdu could really be something if he can trim his strikeouts by a third, and add that amount to his bases on balls. He had 134 Ks in 1992, with 55 walks; he also had a .353 on-base average and a .416 slugging percentage. He positions himself well in the outfield and gets a good jump on the ball; he always seems to be where the ball is. Not many people test his arm. He is still having some trouble with the curve, which is not unusual for someone in Class-A ball. Hyzdu has never hit a great deal of homers in pro ball, but San Jose is not an easy park. He has the talent to help in the majors, and if he keeps improving, he could be even better than that.

Professional Batting Register
	BA	G	AB	R	H	2B	3B	HR	RBI	SB
90 A	.245	69	253	31	62	16	1	6	34	2
91 A	.234	124	410	47	96	13	5	5	50	4
92 A	.279	128	457	60	127	25	5	9	60	10

RICK IRELAND

Position: Pitcher
Team: Florida Marlins
Born: Nov. 11, 1974 Medford, OR
Height: 5'11" **Weight:** 195 lbs.
Bats: left **Throws:** left
Acquired: Third-round pick in 6/92 free-agent draft

Player Summary	
Fantasy Value	.....................$1 to $2
Card Value	.............................8¢ to 12¢
Will	........................thrive with changeup
Can't	...............................let wildness stop him
Expect	...........................toughness on mound
Don't Expect	...............................super fastball

Ireland was just 17 years old when drafted out of Crater High School in Oregon by the Marlins, but the word is that he has a couple of tools that go beyond years. For one thing, he possesses a great feel for pitching. His changeup, too, is described as being great for his age. Ireland throws an average fastball, but lefties usually take longer to develop a good one, and he has many years to work on adding velocity and movement. He is very competitive. He was 10-2 with an 0.26 ERA during the 1992 scholastic season; his résumé for '92 included three no-hitters and 138 strikeouts in 80 innings. One of Ireland's high school games was a 19-strikeout masterpiece over seven innings. He also fanned 18 on two occasions. He comes from the same high school conference as fellow Marlins draftee Andy Larkin. Ireland was assigned to Osceola of the Gulf Coast League, where he was immediately inserted into the rotation. Early indications are that, like other young lefties, Ireland will have some trouble throwing strikes. Golf Coast League opponents compiled a .263 batting average last season.

Professional Pitching Register

	W	L	ERA	G	CG	IP	H	ER	BB	SO
92 R	4	3	4.57	10	0	43.1	42	22	28	26

JOHN JAHA

Position: First base
Team: Milwaukee Brewers
Born: March 12, 1966 Portland, OR
Height: 6'1" **Weight:** 195 lbs.
Bats: right **Throws:** right
Acquired: 14th-round pick in 6/84 free-agent draft

Player Summary	
Fantasy Value	...................................$5 to $10
Card Value	.................................10¢ to 25¢
Will	............................need time to adjust
Can't	...........................drive in 134 again
Expect	............................trouble with curve
Don't Expect	..................................poor fielder

They say that with hard work and talent, you can get to the big leagues but, in Jaha's case, the hard work may have actually interrupted his rise to "the show." He appeared to be on a laser for the majors until the off-season between 1989 and 1990, when he suffered a knee injury during a workout. The resulting surgery kept him out until mid-July of 1990. His comeback was complete, as he became the MVP in the Double-A Texas League. It marked the second time Jaha captured such an award, having taken the trophy in the Class-A California League in 1989. Jaha has been an All-Star in the Northwest, California, and Texas leagues as well as the American Association. The first baseman had his major league debut on July 9, 1992, putting him in the fire of a pennant race in his rookie season. Jaha has not yet shown what he can do in the big leagues, but don't be surprised if he is a factor in '93.

Professional Batting Register

	BA	G	AB	R	H	2B	3B	HR	RBI	SB
85 R	.265	24	68	13	18	3	0	2	14	4
86 A	.318	73	258	65	82	13	2	15	67	9
87 A	.269	122	376	68	101	22	0	7	47	10
88 A	.255	99	302	58	77	14	6	8	54	10
89 A	.292	140	479	83	140	26	5	25	91	8
90 A	.262	26	84	12	22	5	0	4	19	0
91 AA	.344	130	486	121	167	38	3	30	134	12
92 AAA	.321	79	274	61	88	18	2	18	69	6
92 AL	.226	47	133	17	30	3	1	2	10	10

LANCE JENNINGS

Position: Catcher
Team: Kansas City Royals
Born: Oct. 3, 1971 Redlands, CA
Height: 6′ **Weight:** 190 lbs.
Bats: right **Throws:** right
Acquired: Second-round pick in 6/89 free-agent draft

Player Summary

Fantasy Value	$1 to $2
Card Value	8¢ to 12¢
Will	adjust well
Can't	steal a base
Expect	frequent flyer miles
Don't Expect	Royals Stadium power

A sandwich pick as compensation for the loss of free-agent Jamie Quirk, the Royals hope Jennings will prove to be nourishment for the organization's hunger for catching prospects. Signed out of high school, he has been a pro for four seasons, and has been on the move in three of them. He split the 1990 season between Kansas City's two short-season Class-A clubs. He began 1991 with Appleton, where he caught 77 games with a .987 fielding percentage, and was assigned to Baseball City of the Florida State League in August. *Baseball America* named him the Royals' seventh-best prospect that year. In '92, he put up the best numbers of his pro career at Baseball City, and he was named to the FSL All-Star squad. He had a .323 on-base average and a .420 slugging percentage in Class-A last season. He got the call to Double-A Memphis midway through the season, and his numbers there show that he has to do a better job of making contact. That may come when he spends some time in the same place.

Professional Batting Register

	BA	G	AB	R	H	2B	3B	HR	RBI	SB
89 R	.238	47	164	15	39	3	0	1	15	0
90 R	.292	15	48	4	14	4	0	0	5	0
90 A	.185	31	92	8	17	3	1	4	9	0
91 A	.236	92	318	26	75	23	0	5	47	0
92 A	.259	51	174	16	45	7	0	7	24	0
92 AA	.145	52	145	5	21	5	0	1	8	0

DEREK JETER

Position: Shortstop
Team: New York Yankees
Born: June 26, 1974 Kalamazoo, MI
Height: 6′3″ **Weight:** 175 lbs.
Bats: right **Throws:** right
Acquired: First-round pick in 6/92 free-agent draft

Player Summary

Fantasy Value	$1 to $2
Card Value	8¢ to 12¢
Will	show Dunston-like arm
Can't	force him to bigs
Expect	speed and range
Don't Expect	him to forget signs

Jeter's talent is so overwhelming that even an ankle injury did not scare off the Yankees when the sixth overall pick in the draft came. Jeter was the top high school player taken last year, and the Yankees say they did not hesitate before tabbing him. He is said to have a powerful arm at short, with good range and above-average speed. He needs to improve his footwork around the bag, especially taking throws from the catcher. He began to show some power in his junior year in high school, and his size indicates he may be able to drive the ball. He's an honor student as well. The Yankees assigned him to Tampa of the rookie Gulf Coast League, where he stumbled a bit in his first look at the pros. But he also collected three homers and a .318 slugging percentage, a further indication that power could be part of his repertoire. The Yankees then moved him up to the Class-A South Atlantic League. Despite his rough initiation into the pros, Jeter, with his intelligence and skill, should advance quickly.

Professional Batting Register

	BA	G	AB	R	H	2B	3B	HR	RBI	SB
92 R	.202	47	173	19	35	9	1	3	25	2
92 A	.243	11	37	4	9	0	0	1	4	0

BOBBY JONES

Position: Pitcher
Team: New York Mets
Born: Feb. 10, 1970 Fresno, CA
Height: 6'4" **Weight:** 210 lbs.
Bats: right **Throws:** right
Acquired: First-round pick in 6/91 free-agent draft

Player Summary	
Fantasy Value	$2 to $4
Card Value	10¢ to 15¢
Will	pitch not throw
Can't	get heat in 90s
Expect	good shot in '93
Don't Expect	another 16-2 mark

Jones had the honor of starting the Double-A All-Star Game in 1992, and he went an inning, allowing no runs, hits, or walks. Chances are it won't be the last time he will be in the spotlight. Jones was one of the top starters not only in the Double-A Eastern League, but in the entire Mets' organization. He pitched six and one-third perfect innings in a triumph over the White Sox in the Hall of Fame game. He beat Hagerstown 1-0 on July 28, his fourth shutout of the season. Jones throws a fastball that is far from exceptional, but he complements it with a great breaking pitch and a changeup. Double-A opponents compiled a meager .209 batting average in 1992. His ratio of walks to innings in his first two pro seasons tells you all you need to know about why he enjoys the success he does. Victory is nothing new to Jones, as he went 16-2 for Fresno State in 1991. With the injuries that ravaged New York's staff in 1992, the Mets may be more than willing to give Jones a shot in '93.

CHIPPER JONES

Position: Shortstop
Team: Atlanta Braves
Born: April 24, 1972 Deland, GA
Height: 6'3" **Weight:** 185 lbs.
Bats: both **Throws:** right
Acquired: First-round pick in 6/90 free-agent draft

Player Summary	
Fantasy Value	$4 to $10
Card Value	10¢ to 35¢
Will	produce slugging average
Can't	rule out '93 arrival
Expect	homestate boy to make good
Don't Expect	weight from No. 1 pick

Jones is among the highest-rated prospects in a Braves' organization that has already used its farm system to climb into baseball's top echelons. He was the first overall pick in the 1990 draft, and he retains the look of a future major leaguer. Entering the 1992 season, *Baseball America* named Jones the fourth-best prospect in baseball, and first among position players. The publication also tabbed Jones best defensive shortstop in the Class-A Carolina League after the '92 season, quite a tribute considering his problems in the field one year earlier. His high draft status gave him an excuse to wilt under pressure, and he did have some problems in his first pro season. But he bounced back in 1991, pacing Braves' farmhands in all three Triple Crown departments. He also made a smooth transition to Double-A in '92. Last year, he had a .353 on-base average and a .413 slugging average in Class-A, and a .367 on-base average and a .594 slugging percentage in Double-A. Jones has the bat to make it, and it would be a bonus if his glove keeps improving.

Professional Pitching Register

	W	L	ERA	G	CG	IP	H	ER	BB	SO
91 A	3	1	1.85	5	0	24.1	20	5	3	35
92 AA	12	4	1.88	24	4	158.0	118	33	43	144

Professional Batting Register

	BA	G	AB	R	H	2B	3B	HR	RBI	SB
90 R	229	44	140	20	32	1	1	1	18	5
91 A	326	136	473	104	154	24	11	15	98	40
92 A	277	70	264	43	73	22	1	4	31	10
92 AA	346	67	266	43	92	17	11	9	42	14

TODD JONES

Position: Pitcher
Team: Houston Astros
Born: April 24, 1968 Marietta, GA
Height: 6'3" **Weight:** 200 lbs.
Bats: left **Throws:** right
Acquired: First-round pick in 6/89 free-agent draft

Player Summary	
Fantasy Value	$1 to $2
Card Value	8¢ to 12¢
Will	intimidate hitters
Can't	match Ryan
Expect	more bullpen work
Don't Expect	great breaking ball

Jones was taken as the compensation pick for the Astros when they lost Nolan Ryan via free agency. Fittingly enough, Jones is a hard thrower. However, the similarity ends around there; after three mediocre years as a starter, Jones seems to have found a niche in the bullpen. He zoomed past the 20-save mark in his first whack at closing, thereby earning a shot at Triple-A Tucson or even better in 1993. Jones can throw in the low 90s, and his heater has some movement. This fastball, plus his size, can make him very intimidating. He throws a bit of a curve. A perfectionist who is his own biggest critic, Jones is also a bit of a character. He'll talk to himself and do some occasional stomping around on the mound. He's also been known to come to home plate and pick out a ball he likes. His lowest ERA entering 1992 was the 3.51 mark he compiled in Class-A ball in 1990. He split the 1991 season between Class-A and Double-A, winning just eight times in 24 starts.

Professional Pitching Register

	W	L	ERA	G	S	IP	H	ER	BB	SO
89 A	2	3	5.44	11	0	49.2	47	30	42	71
90 A	12	10	3.51	27	0	151.1	124	59	109	106
91 A	4	4	4.35	14	0	72.1	69	35	35	51
91 AA	4	3	4.88	10	0	55.1	51	30	39	37
92 AA	3	7	3.14	61	25	66.0	53	23	44	60
92 AAA	0	1	4.50	3	0	4.0	1	2	10	4

ANDRE KEENE

Position: First base
Team: San Francisco Giants
Born: March 11, 1971 Washington, DC
Height: 6'5" **Weight:** 265 lbs.
Bats: left **Throws:** left
Acquired: 32nd-round pick in 6/90 free-agent draft

Player Summary	
Fantasy Value	$1 to $2
Card Value	8¢ to 12¢
Will	generate runs
Can't	unseat Will Clark
Expect	lots of ink
Don't Expect	pivot men to hang in

He has already been called Andre "The Giant" Keene, and he should certainly get the attention of fielders who must cover bases or block the plate. He combines his size with basestealing speed, and fielders will need courage to wait for a throw while he bears down on them. Keene looks like he'll have the potential to intimidate at the plate as well. He was named top power prospect in the Class-A Midwest League by *Baseball America*. He is listed as a first baseman in the Giants' press guide, but made the All-Star team in the designated hitter slot. He played first base in only 10 games last summer. He was mostly a DH, and he will have to adjust to left field or find another organization. In 1992, Keene was either at or near the top in homers, RBI, and steals both for Clinton and the entire Giants' minor league system. On Aug. 2, he hit a pinch-hit grand slam in a victory over Waterloo. Out of the University of South Carolina, Keene broke into the pros with Scottsdale of the Arizona League, and led the team with a .478 slugging percentage and .466 on-base average.

Professional Batting Register

	BA	G	AB	R	H	2B	3B	HR	RBI	SB
91 R	.348	44	138	30	48	11	2	1	30	12
92 A	.272	128	438	67	119	19	3	14	70	28

JASON KENDALL

Position: Catcher
Team: Pittsburgh Pirates
Born: June 26, 1974 San Diego, CA
Height: 6' **Weight:** 180 lbs.
Bats: right **Throws:** right
Acquired: First-round pick in 6/92 free-agent draft

Player Summary	
Fantasy Value	$1 to $2
Card Value	8¢ to 12¢
Will	catch and throw well
Can't	make position change
Expect	good bloodlines
Don't Expect	immediate power

Kendall is the son of former big league catcher Fred Kendall, whose 12-year career was spent mostly with the Padres. The younger Kendall has also chosen catching as a profession, and the Pirates obviously believe he has a future at the position. He tied a national scholastic mark by hitting in 43 straight games and became the 23rd overall pick in the country. He signed with the Pirates for a reported $336,000. Kendall is described as a very good defensive catcher with an above-average throwing arm. He gets excellent grades for his leadership qualities, his makeup, and his overall athletic ability. He looked fine in his first pro season at bat, but the most important aspect of the game for a young catcher is defense, and he has many years to learn how to play behind the plate. Right now there doesn't seem to be much latitude for a position change, so Kendall will either make it or not as a backstopper. The Pirates would love to see it happen; a couple of late-season trades have thinned out their farm system, and they need this draft to be a productive one.

MIKE KELLY

Position: Outfield
Team: Atlanta Braves
Born: June 2, 1970 Los Angeles, CA
Height: 6'4" **Weight:** 195 lbs.
Bats: right **Throws:** right
Acquired: First-round pick in 6/91 free-agent draft

Player Summary	
Fantasy Value	$2 to $5
Card Value	15¢ to 25¢
Will	add power and speed
Can't	maintain strikeout pace
Expect	good coverage in center
Don't Expect	rush job to bigs

One of the big stories on the 1992 Atlanta Braves was the difficulty in getting playing time for an overcrowded outfield; imagine the extent of the problem if Kelly had been ready. There doesn't seem to be much doubt he has the tools to be an above average player in the majors, maybe a good deal better than average. He is a very good center fielder, with power, basestealing speed, and a good makeup. Out of Arizona State, he was the second overall pick, and first nonpitcher, of the '91 draft. He still needs to play to develop his tools, and the Braves' success at the big league level should give him the time he needs. A reserve in the 1992 Double-A All-Star Game, Kelly showed his mixture of power and speed by reaching the 20-homer, 20-stolen base plateau for Greenville. He also had a .328 on-base average and a .442 slugging percentage last summer. If he could carry those numbers to the big leagues, the Braves would take a step further toward certifying themselves as the team of the '90s.

Professional Batting Register

	BA	G	AB	R	H	2B	3B	HR	RBI	SB
92 R	.252	34	7	28	2	0	0	0	10	2

Professional Batting Register

	BA	G	AB	R	H	2B	3B	HR	RBI	SB
91 A	.250	35	124	29	31	6	1	6	17	6
92 AA	.229	134	475	83	109	18	4	25	71	22

RYAN KLESKO

Position: First base
Team: Atlanta Braves
Born: June 12, 1971 Westminster, CA
Height: 6'3" **Weight:** 220 lbs.
Bats: left **Throws:** left
Acquired: Sixth-round pick in 6/89 free-agent
    draft

Player Summary

Fantasy Value	$5 to $9
Card Value	20¢ to 50¢
Will	get a shot in '93
Can't	stop upgrading defense
Expect	extra-base hits
Don't Expect	immediate impact

Klesko is an intriguing prospect who has shown power and speed, but who registered a disappointing season in his first look at Triple-A pitching. The Braves concede that he had some problems adjusting in 1992, but they believe he still is improving and can be an outstanding power hitter in the majors. They also say his work around first base is getting better. Drafted as a pitcher, Klesko had arm trouble and was shifted to first to because of his pop. He has received a lot of attention; *Baseball America* listed him eighth on its list of baseball's top 100 prospects. So far, though, in five pro seasons, he has not put together an eye-popping home run total. Part of the reason in '92 was a hyperextension of the right elbow suffered in batting practice. Klesko did notch a .323 on-base average and a .435 slugging percentage last summer. He should get a legitimate shot to win a big league job in '93, but don't be surprised if he starts slowly.

Professional Batting Register

	BA	G	AB	R	H	2B	3B	HR	RBI	SB
89 R	.404	17	57	14	23	5	4	1	16	4
89 A	.289	25	90	17	26	6	0	1	12	1
90 A	.316	140	523	81	165	31	2	17	85	23
91 AA	.291	126	419	64	122	22	3	14	67	14
92 AAA	.251	123	418	63	105	22	2	17	59	3
92 NL	.000	13	14	0	0	0	0	0	1	0

TIM LAKER

Position: Catcher
Team: Montreal Expos
Born: Nov. 27, 1969 Encino, CA
Height: 6'2" **Weight:** 175 lbs.
Bats: right **Throws:** right
Acquired: Sixth-round pick in 6/88 free-agent
    draft

Player Summary

Fantasy Value	$3 to $8
Card Value	15¢ to 50¢
Will	progress steadily
Can't	rule out '93 arrival
Expect	good arm
Don't Expect	consistent contact

Laker enjoyed the finest power season of his career in 1992, ranking among the top home run and RBI men in the Expos' minor league system. It was the latest step taken by a player who has made steady, though not spectacular, progress since coming out of Oxnard Community College in California. Laker put himself on track for the majors with his 1990 season, in which he made the Class-A Midwest League All-Star team and led loop catchers with 125 assists. He also paced his own club with 57 RBI and was second with seven homers. Laker took another step in 1991, when he received his first promotion to Double-A and hit respectably there. But the highlight of Laker's '91 campaign came when he hit .310 over seven playoff games to help West Palm Beach capture the Class-A Florida State League title. The Expos describe him as a good defensive catcher with a great arm. If he lives up to that, and keeps improving his hitting, he will play in Triple-A and maybe beyond in '93.

Professional Batting Register

	BA	G	AB	R	H	2B	3B	HR	RBI	SB
88 A	.224	47	152	14	34	9	0	0	17	2
89 A	.224	72	264	29	59	10	2	2	26	9
90 A	.220	122	428	46	94	18	3	7	57	7
91 A	.231	100	333	35	77	15	2	5	33	10
91 AA	.286	11	35	4	10	1	0	1	5	0
92 AA	.242	117	409	55	99	19	3	15	68	2
92 NL	.217	28	46	8	10	3	0	0	4	1

PAT LEAHY

Position: Pitcher
Team: Florida Marlins
Born: Oct. 31, 1970 Kennewick, WA
Height: 6'7" **Weight:** 245 lbs.
Bats: right **Throws:** right
Acquired: Sixth-round pick in 6/92 free-agent draft

Player Summary	
Fantasy Value	$1 to $2
Card Value	8¢ to 12¢
Will	have size going for him
Can't	punt on 3-and-2
Expect	relief duty
Don't Expect	greatness

In a departure from family tradition, Leahy holds his huddles on the mound instead of near the line of scrimmage. He is the grandson of legendary Notre Dame football coach Frank Leahy and the son of Jim, who played football at the university. Pat's brother Ryan currently is a lineman there. There are certainly bloodlines for athletic achievement. Leahy won 25 games in his three years at Notre Dame. He went 9-3 with a 3.16 ERA as a junior, striking out 80 and walking 30 in 91 innings, and leading the Irish to the NCAA Regional Tournament. Leahy was originally picked by the Blue Jays in the 16th round of the 1989 draft. Leahy was neither a starter nor a closer in his first pro season, which suggests that the Marlins feel that they have other pitchers with more promise. Leahy allowed Class-A opponents to compile a .274 batting average, but he had a good K-to-innings ratio. He also has a tradition of success. On size alone, not to mention the athletic tradition in his family and his good ERA in 1992, Leahy is one to watch.

Professional Pitching Register

	W	L	ERA	G	S	IP	H	ER	BB	SO
92 A	2	0	1.70	26	5	37.0	37	7	12	27

MIKE LIEBERTHAL

Position: Catcher
Team: Philadelphia Phillies
Born: Jan. 18, 1972 Glendale, CA
Height: 6' **Weight:** 170 lbs.
Bats: right **Throws:** right
Acquired: First-round pick in 6/90 free-agent draft

Player Summary	
Fantasy Value	$1 to $4
Card Value	8¢ to 12¢
Will	go far with arm
Can't	hit for power
Expect	arrival in '93
Don't Expect	him to flop

Lieberthal is making a rocket-like trip to the majors, even though he defies some textbook attributes of a catcher; he doesn't hit with much power and is a bit small at 170 pounds. The Phils think he will get bigger, however, which should help in the power department. As for defense, one observer watching Lieberthal play in the Class-A South Atlantic League says he throws runners out at second from a crouch. That, no doubt, is what makes him such a comer. Lieberthal is a very smart catcher who plays a good defensive game. He doesn't strike out much, and can be a .260 to .280 hitter, maybe a little more. Lieberthal got his feet wet in 1990 with Martinsville of the Appalachian League, but really took off in 1991, when he made the Sally League All-Star team and then was promoted to Clearwater. He continued his rise in 1992, appearing in the Double-A All-Star Game as a DH. He had a .343 on-base average and a .364 slugging percentage against Double-A pitching last season. He also was named the Eastern League's top defensive catcher by *Baseball America*.

Professional Batting Register

	BA	G	AB	R	H	2B	3B	HR	RBI	SB
90 R	.228	49	184	26	42	9	0	4	22	2
91 A	.302	88	295	41	89	19	0	0	38	1
92 AA	.286	86	308	30	88	16	1	2	37	4
92 AAA	.200	16	45	4	9	1	0	0	4	0

JOSE LIMA

Position: Pitcher
Team: Detroit Tigers
Born: Sept. 30, 1972 Santiago, Dominican Republic
Height: 6'2" **Weight:** 170 lbs.
Bats: right **Throws:** right
Acquired: Signed as a free agent, 7/89

Player Summary	
Fantasy Value	$1 to $2
Card Value	8¢ to 12¢
Will	throw strikes
Can't	always stay cool
Expect	average fastball
Don't Expect	big win totals

Lima had all his ratios together in 1992 except the one that has to be the bottom line—wins and losses. He has superb control of his pitches, allows fewer hits than innings pitched, and strikes out nearly one batter per inning. Despite all of this, Lima did not win a whole lot in 1992. In fact, he has had trouble translating his starts into wins for all three of his pro seasons. Lima has been described as having a tendency to get a bit hyper on the mound, and this may be a factor in his not achieving the victories that Detroit would prefer. He did earn one of the Class-A Florida State League's Pitcher of the Week designations for shutout victories over Winter Haven and the Miracle, and he had a 3-5 record with a 2.58 ERA through early July. Then he went into an extended victory drought. By the end of the season, he allowed FSL opponents to compile a .239 batting average. Lima is still very young, but the '93 season could be a big one for him.

ALBIE LOPEZ

Position: Pitcher
Team: Cleveland Indians
Born: Aug. 18, 1971 Mesa, AZ
Height: 6'2" **Weight:** 205 lbs.
Bats: right **Throws:** right
Acquired: 20th-round pick in 6/91 free-agent draft

Player Summary	
Fantasy Value	$1 to $2
Card Value	8¢ to 12¢
Will	be around at finish
Can't	throw in 90s
Expect	great K-to-walk ratio
Don't Expect	return to Sally League

Cleveland scouts did a good job of finding this husky righthander in the lower rounds. After two years in pro ball, Lopez shapes up as a legitimate prospect, one who will throw the ball over the plate with something on it. He made the Class-A South Atlantic League All-Star team in 1992, held Sally loop hitters to a .221 batting average, continued his success after a promotion to the high Class-A Carolina League, and finished the season among the ERA and strikeout leaders in the Indians' chain. Lopez seems to have a tenacious streak, as he is involved—win or lose—in a nice percentage of his starts. He had nine decisions in 13 starts in 1991, and captured his last six Sally League starts in '92. Lopez hurled a three-hitter on July 18 to beat Salem 1-0. In midsummer he earned one of Cleveland's Pitcher of the Week awards, going 2-0 and allowing just seven hits in 15 innings. Lopez can throw in the high 80s, and he offers a curveball and a changeup as well. Look for him in Double-A and beyond in 1993.

Professional Pitching Register

	W	L	ERA	G	CG	IP	H	ER	BB	SO
90 R	3	8	5.02	14	1	75.1	89	42	22	64
91 A	1	4	5.73	22	0	66.2	69	42	27	65
92 A	6	11	3.06	26	6	156.0	138	53	21	143

Professional Pitching Register

	W	L	ERA	G	CG	IP	H	ER	BB	SO
91 R	4	5	3.44	13	0	73.1	61	28	23	81
92 A	12	4	3.13	26	2	161.0	136	56	59	161

JAVIER LOPEZ

Position: Catcher
Team: Atlanta Braves
Born: Nov. 5, 1970 Ponce, Puerto Rico
Height: 6'3" **Weight:** 185 lbs.
Bats: right **Throws:** right
Acquired: Signed as a free agent, 11/87

Player Summary	
Fantasy Value	$2 to $4
Card Value	10¢ to 20¢
Will	hit for average
Can't	stop refining defense
Expect	bit of speed
Don't Expect	RBI champion

In an age where catching seems to be more than a bit thin, Lopez has a chance to really stand out. He has nice size, hits for average and power, and can even run a little. His work behind the plate has come along to the point that he was named the top defensive catcher in the Double-A Southern League by *Baseball America* in 1992. He was part of the reason Greenville dominated to the extent it did in 1992. He was the starting catcher in the Double-A All-Star Game, going 2-for-2 with a run scored. As the regular season wound down, Lopez owned a lead of more than 10 percentage points over his closest pursuer for the batting title among Braves' minor leaguers, which is remarkable for a catcher. He also had a .362 on-base average and a .507 slugging percentage. He has shown an ability to homer in double figures, and playing in Atlanta wouldn't hurt that. His RBI totals were a little low in '92, though. Unseating Greg Olson, a big part of the Braves' success, may not be easy for Lopez.

Professional Batting Register

	BA	G	AB	R	H	2B	3B	HR	RBI	SB
88 R	.191	31	94	8	18	4	0	1	9	1
89 R	.261	51	153	27	40	8	1	3	27	3
90 A	.265	116	422	48	112	17	3	11	55	0
91 A	.245	113	384	43	94	14	2	11	51	10
92 AA	.321	115	442	64	142	28	3	16	60	7
92 NL	.375	9	16	3	6	2	0	0	2	0

LUIS LOPEZ

Position: Shortstop
Team: San Diego Padres
Born: Sept. 4, 1970 Cidra, Puerto Rico
Height: 5'11" **Weight:** 155 lbs.
Bats: both **Throws:** right
Acquired: Signed as a free agent, 9/87

Player Summary	
Fantasy Value	$2 to $4
Card Value	8¢ to 12¢
Will	strike out a lot
Can't	hit with power
Expect	more Triple-A
Don't Expect	old quickness

Lopez overcame one obstacle to playing in the big leagues—knee surgery. He doesn't have the kind of numbers that would push him into the San Diego picture yet, but he is still young and he has shown hints of offensive ability. Unfortunately for him, his best showing at the plate came in 1990, just before he went down for the season with knee surgery. At the time, Lopez was hitting .370 over 14 games and seemed headed for the year of his life. He rebounded well in 1991, making the adjustment despite having spent little time in high Class-A ball. He continued the ascent in '92, playing in Triple-A for the first time. His production stalled, but he may need more time to get acclimated. He had a .271 on-base average and a .301 slugging percentage last summer. Lopez doesn't steal many bases anymore; maybe surgery took some aggressiveness and speed. If so, any lost step might hurt his chances at shortstop. His range seemed to be lessened, but he was more consistent.

Professional Batting Register

	BA	G	AB	R	H	2B	3B	HR	RBI	SB
88 A	.304	70	312	50	95	13	1	0	35	14
89 A	.222	127	460	50	102	15	1	1	29	12
90 A	.370	14	46	5	17	3	1	1	4	4
91 A	.268	125	452	43	121	17	1	1	41	6
92 AAA	.233	120	395	44	92	8	8	1	31	6

DEREK LOWE

Position: Pitcher
Team: Seattle Mariners
Born: June 1, 1973 Dearborn, MI
Height: 6'6" **Weight:** 170 lbs.
Bats: right **Throws:** right
Acquired: Eighth-round pick in 6/91 free-agent draft

Player Summary	
Fantasy Value	$1 to $2
Card Value	8¢ to 12¢
Will	throw a curve
Can't	get overconfident
Expect	him to get bigger
Don't Expect	long stint in Class-A ball

Though not taken in the very top rounds, Lowe put himself in the same class as some of Seattle's brightest pitching prospects with his performance in the Northwest League in 1992. He won five of his first nine starts in the short-season Class-A circuit, compiling one of the stingiest ERAs both in the league and in the Seattle organization. He was named the No. 6 prospect in the loop and was the youngest player on the list. Opponents compiled just a .216 batting average against him last year. He throws a fastball in the 90s and a curve, and he can throw them for strikes. Lowe graduated in 1991 from Ford High School in Dearborn, where he was a standout in golf, basketball, baseball, and soccer. Instead of playing basketball in college, which was a viable option, Lowe signed with the Mariners and began his career with Tempe in rookie ball. He led the Arizona League by allowing just 10.27 baserunners per nine innings, and he ranked fourth in opponents' batting average, .217. His soccer background suggests a dexterity that should help him field his position. If he combines good mechanics with his size, look out.

Professional Pitching Register

	W	L	ERA	G	CG	IP	H	ER	BB	SO
91 R	5	3	2.41	12	0	71.0	58	19	21	60
92 A	7	3	2.42	14	2	85.2	69	23	22	66

LOU LUCCA

Position: Third base
Team: Florida Marlins
Born: Oct. 13, 1970 San Francisco, CA
Height: 5'11" **Weight:** 205 lbs.
Bats: right **Throws:** right
Acquired: 32nd-round pick in 6/92 free-agent draft

Player Summary	
Fantasy Value	$1 to $2
Card Value	8¢ to 12¢
Will	show decent eye
Can't	duplicate college numbers
Expect	adjustment at Triple-A
Don't Expect	tools of high-rounders

Lucca was one of the reasons that Florida's farm team in Erie enjoyed such a fine first season, reaching the championship round of the Class-A New York-Penn League playoffs. He made the circuit's postseason All-Star team at third base, and was among the league leaders in home runs. He also was a club leader in doubles, and he showed a nice eye at the plate. He compiled a .370 on-base average and a .498 slugging percentage in 1992. Lucca came out of Oklahoma State, a school with a strong baseball tradition, and he did nothing to diminish it. Lucca was twice selected to the all-Big Eight team. He led the Cowboys with 17 homers and 73 RBI in 1992 and hit .357 to collect third-team All-America honors. Three of his homers came in a single game against Northwest Louisiana. Lucca hit .368 at Oklahoma State. The fact that 31 rounds went past before any club selected him makes Lucca a definite long shot to reach the majors, but it's tough to rule someone out when they react to pro ball the way Lucca did.

Professional Batting Register

	BA	G	AB	R	H	2B	3B	HR	RBI	SB
92 A	.281	76	263	51	74	16	1	13	44	6

365

RYAN LUZINSKI

Position: Catcher
Team: Los Angeles Dodgers
Born: Aug. 22, 1973 Medford, NJ
Height: 6'1" **Weight:** 225 lbs.
Bats: right **Throws:** right
Acquired: First-round pick in 6/92 free-agent draft

Player Summary	
Fantasy Value	$1 to $2
Card Value	15¢ to 50¢
Will	block balls and plate
Can't	live off dad's feats
Expect	baseball instincts
Don't Expect	quick arrival

The son of former Phils' power hitter Greg Luzinski, Ryan is built along similar lines, and the Dodgers are hoping he can give them some of the power his father once produced. The younger Luzinski is already somewhat of a prize for the Dodgers because of how they got him. They made him the 32nd overall pick—a supplemental choice—even though there were rumors that he would be hard to sign. A deal worth a reported $500,000 ended those rumors for good. Unlike his father, who played outfield, Ryan is a catcher. This will make his road to the big leagues a long one, though it could bring great reward if he makes it. Luzinski has his father's build, and this gives him a good start toward being the power-hitting catcher so coveted by all teams. Luzinski flashed a bit of that long-ball potential with Great Falls of the rookie Pioneer League. He had a .321 on-base average and a .401 slugging percentage. He also had a .987 fielding average and showed ability behind the plate. It was a good start, but bridging the chasm between high school and pros will take work.

Professional Batting Register

	BA	G	AB	R	H	2B	3B	HR	RBI	SB
92 R	.251	61	227	26	57	14	4	4	29	2

SCOTT LYDY

Position: Outfield
Team: Oakland Athletics
Born: Oct. 26, 1968 Mesa, AZ
Height: 6'5" **Weight:** 190 lbs.
Bats: Right **Throws:** Right
Acquired: Second-round pick in 6/89 free-agent draft

Player Summary	
Fantasy Value	$2 to $5
Card Value	10¢ to 15¢
Will	show speed and pop
Can't	stop adjusting
Expect	time with big club
Don't Expect	basher-type power

Things came together very quickly for Lydy in 1992. After three years of slow progress through the Oakland farm system, he suddenly played his way into *Baseball America's* Player of the Year Watch. Lydy began the season with Reno of the Class-A California League, where he notched a .500 on-base average and a .581 slugging percentage. He then zoomed his way into the Southern League's batting race. He finished the season at Double-A Huntsville with a .409 on-base average and a .442 slugging percentage. Lydy has speed, power, and an arm good enough that he played right field on Opening Day. His RBI total ranked with that of anyone in the A's organization, and three of them came on one Aug. 2 swing when his eighth-inning homer beat Knoxville. Another pair came on consecutive nights when Lydy delivered RBI hits in extra innings. Lydy had consistent problems making contact, but a sizzling start at Reno quickly got him promoted. He'll be 24 during the '93 season, and there could be room for him in Oakland.

Professional Batting Register

	BA	G	AB	R	H	2B	3B	HR	RBI	SB
89 A	.209	67	230	37	48	11	2	3	28	8
90 A	.190	54	174	33	33	6	2	4	19	7
90 R	.340	18	50	8	17	6	0	2	11	0
91 A	.259	127	464	64	120	26	2	12	69	24
92 A	.395	33	124	29	49	13	2	2	27	9
92 AA	.305	109	387	64	118	20	3	9	65	16

JOHN LYNCH

Position: Pitcher
Team: Florida Marlins
Born: Sept. 25, 1971 Hinsdale, IL
Height: 6'2" **Weight:** 210 lbs.
Bats: right **Throws:** right
Acquired: Second-round pick in 6/92 free-agent draft

Player Summary

Fantasy Value	$1 to $2
Card Value	8¢ to 12¢
Will	bring athletic ability
Can't	win with football approach
Expect	long road
Don't Expect	strikeout pitcher

The Marlins were clearly looking at Lynch's size and athletic skills, not his baseball experience, when they made him such a high priority in their first draft. He was a high school quarterback and attended Stanford on a football scholarship, where he was listed as a starter at safety entering the university's 1992 season. He did play some baseball there, making 18 pitching appearances in three seasons for the Cardinal and hitting five homers as a designated hitter. Lynch broke into the pros with Erie and went 0-3 with a 2.15 ERA and a lousy K-to-walk ratio there. While opposing batters only hit .222 against him, the 17 walks he allowed hurt him; he should cut his walks allowed ratio with experience. He left after seven starts to return to Stanford, where he hoped to get to the Rose Bowl; he also had some irritation between his shoulder blades. Lynch's father, John, also played football and made it to the pros as a linebacker for the Steelers. One of the potential pitfalls for the Marlins is that football and baseball involve a different mentality. How well Lynch can make the transition could determine how far he goes.

Professional Pitching Register

	W	L	ERA	G	CG	IP	H	ER	BB	SO
92 A	0	3	2.15	7	0	29.1	24	7	17	16

PEDRO MARTINEZ

Position: Pitcher
Team: Los Angeles Dodgers
Born: July 25, 1971 Manoguayabo, Dominican Republic
Height: 5'11" **Weight:** 150 lbs.
Bats: right **Throws:** right
Acquired: Signed as a free agent, 6/88

Player Summary

Fantasy Value	$5 to $10
Card Value	10¢ to 35¢
Will	compete for starting job
Can't	let comparisons bother him
Expect	good fastball
Don't Expect	strikeout title

Martinez leveled off in 1992, one year after making it look easy. He failed to approach the previous season's victory total, he battled some shoulder problems, and he certainly wasn't named *The Sporting News* Minor League Player of the Year, as he was in '91. Still, the season wasn't a total loss for the younger brother of Dodgers pitcher Ramon Martinez. Pedro still had a mean strikeout pitch going, he was called owner of the Pacific Coast League's best fastball by *Baseball America,* and he went to the Triple-A All-Star Game, though he did not pitch in it. Martinez entered the '92 season 22 games over .500, which explains his quick ascent. His most spectacular year was '91, when he zoomed from high Class-A ball to Triple-A, all the while under the strain of being Ramon's brother. Pedro could compete for a job in Los Angeles in '93, but remember that though the PCL isn't kind to pitching stats, he faced little adversity until '92. It will be interesting to see how he reacts.

Professional Pitching Register

	W	L	ERA	G	CG	IP	H	ER	BB	SO
90 R	8	3	3.62	14	0	77.0	74	31	40	82
91 A	8	0	2.05	10	0	61.1	41	14	19	83
91 AA	7	5	1.76	12	4	76.2	57	15	31	74
91 AAA	3	3	3.66	6	0	39.1	28	16	16	35
92 AAA	7	6	3.81	20	3	125.1	104	53	57	124
92 NL	0	1	2.25	2	0	8.0	6	2	1	8

DAVID McCARTY

Position: Outfield
Team: Minnesota Twins
Born: Nov. 23, 1969 Houston, TX
Height: 6'5" **Weight:** 210 lbs.
Bats: right **Throws:** left
Acquired: First-round pick in 6/91 free-agent draft

Player Summary	
Fantasy Value	$6 to $12
Card Value	15¢ to 50¢
Will	produce runs
Can't	steal bases
Expect	chance for majors in '93
Don't Expect	consistent contact

It looks like the Twins chose wisely when they made McCarty the third overall pick in the nation in 1991. In just his second pro season, he was a run-producer to be reckoned with in the Double-A Southern League. He had a .356 on-base average and a .433 slugging percentage, and he also hit the long ball. McCarty's baseball résumé was a long one even before he pulled on a pro uniform and included both college and international experience. McCarty was a member of the USA Junior National Team that visited Japan in 1988, and he led Team USA with a .445 average in 1990. He led Stanford to third place in the College World Series in his sophomore year, and starred for the Cardinal in 1991. His feats that season included a .490 average over a 26-game hitting streak and homers in six consecutive games. McCarty spent the first 15 games of his pro career with Visalia of the Class-A California League, hitting .380. Promoted to Double-A, he hit .321 with six RBI in the playoffs as Huntsville took the Southern League title.

RAY McDAVID

Position: Outfield
Team: San Diego Padres
Born: July 20, 1971 San Diego, CA
Height: 6'3" **Weight:** 190 lbs.
Bats: left **Throws:** right
Acquired: Ninth-round pick in 6/89 free-agent draft

Player Summary	
Fantasy Value	$1 to $2
Card Value	8¢ to 12¢
Will	decide on a position
Can't	disappoint on defense
Expect	tape-measure homers
Don't Expect	bigs in '93

McDavid was one of the reasons why the High Desert Mavericks set a franchise attendance record in 1992. His blend of power and speed make him worth the price of admission; *Baseball America* named him the most exciting player in the Class-A California League. Not only is McDavid one of the top prospects in the Padres chain, he is a charismatic player who gives fans something to appreciate every time they come to the park. He strikes out a lot, but he also walks a lot. He had a .519 slugging average and set career highs in doubles, home runs, and RBI. He had a high on-base percentage (.409), and has the speed both to steal bases and to stretch base hits. That speed comes in handy in center field, too. McDavid hit .330 during the month of July 1992. Out of Arizona Western University, he is a good student of the game who is making adjustments as he climbs the ladder. A promotion seems assured, and it may not be too long before McDavid brings his excitement to the majors.

Professional Batting Register

	BA	G	AB	R	H	2B	3B	HR	RBI	SB
91 A	.380	15	50	16	19	3	0	3	8	3
91 AA	.261	28	88	18	23	4	0	3	11	0
92 AA	.271	130	457	75	124	16	2	18	79	6
92 AAA	.500	7	26	7	13	2	0	1	8	1

Professional Batting Register

	BA	G	AB	R	H	2B	3B	HR	RBI	SB
90 R	.146	13	41	4	6	0	2	0	1	3
91 A	.247	127	425	93	105	16	9	10	45	60
92 A	.276	123	428	94	118	22	5	24	94	43

KEVIN McGEHEE

Position: Pitcher
Team: San Francisco Giants
Born: Jan. 18, 1969 Alexandria, LA
Height: 6′ **Weight:** 190 lbs.
Bats: right **Throws:** right
Acquired: Eighth-round pick in 6/90 free-agent draft

Player Summary	
Fantasy Value	$2 to $4
Card Value	8¢ to 12¢
Will	sink the fastball
Can't	regress on control
Expect	lots of strikeouts
Don't Expect	Giants to open '93

McGehee's victory total fell a bit in 1992, but he made a successful jump to Double-A and once again ranked in his league's top 10 in ERA, so he remains on track for the majors. He finished sixth in the Texas League with a 2.96 ERA, one year after his 2.33 gave him the third-lowest ERA in the Class-A California League. McGehee throws a sinking fastball that can give him either a strikeout or a ground ball. He has also done a good job of sharpening his control, bringing his walks down from one per every two innings to less than one every three innings. McGehee was among the leaders in strikeouts and ERA among Giants farmhands in 1992. In midseason, he compiled a scoreless streak of 16⅔ innings. Opponents compiled a .245 batting average in 1992. He has posted excellent strikeout ratios all three of his pro seasons. A starting pitcher virtually all his pro career, the former Louisiana Tech standout could well get a long look in spring training in 1993, though he could use some development time in Triple-A.

Professional Pitching Register

	W	L	ERA	G	CG	IP	H	ER	BB	SO
90 A	4	8	4.76	15	1	73.2	74	39	38	86
91 A	13	6	2.33	26	2	174.0	129	45	87	171
92 AA	9	7	2.96	25	1	158.1	146	52	42	140

JEFF McNEELY

Position: Outfield
Team: Boston Red Sox
Born: Oct. 18, 1969 Monroe, NC
Height: 6′2″ **Weight:** 190 lbs.
Bats: right **Throws:** right
Acquired: Second-round pick in 6/89 free-agent draft

Player Summary	
Fantasy Value	$1 to $3
Card Value	10¢ to 15¢
Will	cover ground in center
Can't	succeed without hams
Expect	good on-base percentage
Don't Expect	Boston lineup in '93

McNeely followed a season to remember with a year to forget. After leading the Class-A Carolina League with a .322 average in 1991, McNeely last year suffered some hamstring problems that robbed him of some of the at bats and experience he needs. He had a .294 on-base average and a .303 slugging percentage in 1992. His busiest campaign came in '91 when he played 106 games, 28 fewer than the club did. McNeely was an effective player when in the lineup, though. He was named the Player of the Month for July in the Carolina League, played errorless ball in the outfield after July 8, finished with a league-leading .436 on-base percentage and was named to the postseason All-Star team. Though taken in the second round, McNeely was the fourth player drafted by the Red Sox in '89. He was named to the Class-A New York-Penn League All-Star team in 1990, leading the loop in stolen bases. McNeely is a table-setting kind of player who won't hit for much power. His game depends on speed, which is why hamstrings pose a concern.

Professional Batting Register

	BA	G	AB	R	H	2B	3B	HR	RBI	SB
89 R	.406	9	32	10	13	1	1	0	4	5
89 A	.250	61	208	20	52	7	0	2	21	16
90 A	.282	89	308	44	87	4	5	6	40	46
91 A	.322	106	382	58	123	16	5	4	38	38
92 AA	.218	85	261	30	57	8	4	2	11	10

LUIS MERCEDES

Position: Outfield
Team: Baltimore Orioles
Born: Feb. 20, 1969 Walnut Creek, MA
Height: 6'3" **Weight:** 193 lbs.
Bats: right **Throws:** right
Acquired: Signed as an undrafted free agent, 2/87

Player Summary	
Fantasy Value	.....................$2 to $5
Card Value	..........................8¢ to 12¢
Will	.................................hit for average
Can't	................................crack the outfield
Expect	................................quick temper
Don't Expect	............................great defense

At the rate Mercedes is hitting, he'll only fall out of the top 10 in batting if he plays another 16 years. Mercedes won the Class-A Carolina League batting title in 1989 and the Double-A Eastern League crown in 1990. Then he posted consecutive second-place finishes in the Triple-A International League, missing the 1992 championship by one base hit. Mercedes also was one of the top basestealers in the Baltimore farm system. A leadoff hitter with a high on-base percentage, he has done all he can in the minors, and has every right to look at the bigs. Unfortunately for him, the Orioles outfield is an impressive one both at bat and in the field. Mercedes may lack the power, production, and defensive skills to force himself into the picture soon. He has appeared in the big leagues both in '91 and '92, but never with enough at bats to establish what he did in the minors. Mercedes has a quick temper; he was involved in an on-field fight with an opponent in 1991.

Professional Batting Register

	BA	G	AB	R	H	2B	3B	HR	RBI	SB
88 R	.274	59	215	36	59	8	4	0	20	16
89 A	.309	108	401	62	124	12	5	3	36	29
90 AA	.334	108	416	71	139	12	4	3	37	38
91 AAA	.334	102	374	68	125	14	5	2	36	23
91 AL	.204	19	54	10	11	2	0	0	2	0
92 AAA	.313	111	62	128	15	1	3	29	35	
92 AL	.140	23	50	7	7	2	0	0	4	0

MATT MIESKE

Position: Outfield
Team: Milwaukee Brewers
Born: Feb. 13, 1968 Auburn, MI
Height: 6' **Weight:** 185 lbs.
Bats: right **Throws:** right
Acquired: Traded from Padres with Ricky Bones and Jose Valentin for Gary Sheffield and Geoff Kellogg, 3/92

Player Summary	
Fantasy Value	....................$4 to $8
Card Value	..........................10¢ to 35¢
Will	.................................drive in runs
Can't	................let Sheffield burden him
Expect	................................good arm in right
Don't Expect	............................MVP in bigs

Pressure will be Mieske's companion until he establishes himself in the big leagues. He brought some of it on himself with consecutive MVP seasons in the Class-A Northwest and California leagues. The rest came the day he arrived in the Milwaukee system as part of a deal that sent Gary Sheffield to the Padres. Sheffield's success in San Diego guarantees that Mieske will be looked upon to help make the trade a good one for the Brewers. He failed to duplicate his '90 and '91 heroics, but he still looms as the key to the deal. The Brewers have to be happy with the way he fought back after a tough initiation in Triple-A. He wound up among the most effective power hitters in the Milwaukee organization. He had a .319 on-base average and a .473 slugging percentage last summer. Mieske is a right fielder with a good arm and a knack for producing runs. He can also steal a base, though his total fell in '92. Mieske could probably use a little more time in Triple-A, but only an injury or a major backslide can keep him from the majors.

Professional Batting Register

	BA	G	AB	R	H	2B	3B	HR	RBI	SB
90 A	.340	76	291	59	99	20	0	12	63	26
91 A	.341	133	492	108	168	36	6	15	119	39
92 AAA	.267	134	524	80	140	29	11	19	77	13

SAM MILITELLO

Position: Pitcher
Team: New York Yankees
Born: Nov. 26, 1969 Tampa, FL
Height: 6'3" **Weight:** 200 lbs.
Bats: right **Throws:** right
Acquired: Sixth-round pick in 6/90 free-agent draft

Player Summary	
Fantasy Value	$5 to $10
Card Value	15¢ to 35¢
Will	get ahead in count
Can't	judge on a few outings
Expect	classy starter
Don't Expect	him to be traded

Militello made his major league debut on Aug. 9, 1992, in front of a big Sunday crowd at Yankee Stadium, and he made as good an impression as any pitcher on the Yankee scene for some time. He allowed just one hit over seven innings against the Red Sox before a rain delay took him out of the game. The excitement didn't wear off quickly, either. He became the first Yankee rookie starter to go 3-0 since Ray Fontenot in 1983. Militello throws a decent fastball and an above-average slider. He comes from an unusual angle, three-quarters to sidearm, and he hides the ball well. He throws strikes, has good concentration, and does the little things a pitcher should, like cover empty bases. Triple-A hitters batted just .205 against him in 1992, and he was the No. 1 prospect in the International League. When summoned to the majors, Militello was leading Yankee farmhands in victories, ERA, and strikeouts. His wins included a 12-strikeout, 3-0 whitewash of Scranton/Wilkes-Barre on July 30. He pitched two innings in the Triple-A All-Star Game.

Professional Pitching Register

	W	L	ERA	G	CG	IP	H	ER	BB	SO
90 A	8	2	1.22	13	3	88.2	53	12	24	119
91 A	12	2	1.22	16	1	103.1	65	14	27	113
91 AA	2	2	2.35	7	0	46.0	40	12	19	55
92 AAA	12	2	2.29	22	3	141.1	105	36	46	152
92 AL	3	3	3.45	9	0	60.0	43	23	32	42

KURT MILLER

Position: Pitcher
Team: Texas Rangers
Born: Aug. 24, 1972 Tucson, AZ
Height: 6'5" **Weight:** 200 lbs.
Bats: right **Throws:** right
Acquired: Traded from Pirates with Hector Fajardo for Steve Buechele, 8/91

Player Summary	
Fantasy Value	$2 to $4
Card Value	8¢ to 12¢
Will	throw plus fastball
Can't	regress on control
Expect	three good pitches
Don't Expect	prolonged Double-A

Miller came to the Rangers in one of those deals that beef up a contender for a stretch run, and he may end up fortifying Texas for pennant races of its own. He arrived on Aug. 30, 1991, in a trade that sent third baseman Steve Buechele to the Pirates. Miller throws a fastball, curve, and changeup that are all above average. He also had a nice year in the minors; he was the Opening Day starter for Port Charlotte of the Class-A Florida State League and received a June promotion to Double-A. He wound up the season as one of the top winners and strikeout artists in the Texas chain. Miller was originally a first-round pick of the Pirates in 1990. He went right from high school to a spot in the rotation for Welland of the Class-A New York-Penn League, and followed up with more success for Augusta of the Class-A South Atlantic League in '91. Miller needed some work on throwing strikes in his first two pro stops, but he seems to have handled that in Double-A.

Professional Pitching Register

	W	L	ERA	G	CG	IP	H	ER	BB	SO
90 A	3	2	3.29	14	0	65.2	59	24	37	62
91 A	6	7	2.50	21	2	115.1	89	32	57	103
92 A	5	4	2.39	12	0	75.1	51	20	29	58
92 AA	7	5	3.68	16	0	88.0	82	36	35	73

RAUL MONDESI

Position: Outfield
Team: Los Angeles Dodgers
Born: March 12, 1971 San Cristobal, Dominican Republic
Height: 5'11" **Weight:** 150 lbs.
Bats: right **Throws:** right
Acquired: Signed as a free agent, 6/88

Player Summary

Fantasy Value	$2 to $5
Card Value	10¢ to 15¢
Will	bring great tools
Can't	sulk
Expect	extra-base hits
Don't Expect	injury-free season

Mondesi entered the 1992 season as one of the top prospects in the Dodgers' chain, but didn't enjoy the most successful year of his career. He hurt his knee in a slide, injured a wrist, and required surgery. Furthermore, he had some attitude problems that the organization didn't appreciate. Some of that can be attributed to his still-tender years; if his maturity catches up to his physical skills, watch out. In 1991, Mondesi enjoyed the best year of his pro career, performing at the Class-A, Double-A, and Triple-A levels. He was tabbed as one of the top 50 minor league prospects by *The Sporting News,* even though he missed two months with a knee injury. Mondesi also enjoyed a fine first season in 1990, when he led Great Falls to a championship and made the rookie Pioneer League All-Star team. After the trouble the Dodgers endured in 1992, they will welcome all the help they can get. Mondesi will need the health and the outlook to respond.

BOO MOORE

Position: Outfield
Team: Boston Red Sox
Born: Jan. 23, 1970 Augusta, GA
Height: 6'4" **Weight:** 200 lbs.
Bats: right **Throws:** right
Acquired: 10th-round pick in 6/88 free-agent draft

Player Summary

Fantasy Value	$1 to $2
Card Value	8¢ to 12¢
Will	strike out a lot
Can't	linger in Class-A
Expect	good speed
Don't Expect	hit for average

Moore is a power prospect who could give the Red Sox some help in taking advantage of the Green Monster in Fenway Park. Then again, his chances of getting to the big leagues may depend on not trying to pull the ball too much. He is learning to hit to all fields, a skill that could help him break through to the high minors after years of playing in various rookie and Class-A leagues. Moore has played mostly the outfield as a pro, with extremely rare duty at first; he also can serve as a DH. In 1992, Moore was among the better home run and RBI men in the Boston chain. He hit a home run in the Class-A Carolina League All-Star Game. His season included a 24-for-70 hot streak. He had a .300 on-base average and a .453 slugging percentage last season. Moore's breakthrough as a power hitter came in 1991, when he led Lynchburg with 30 doubles, but he also struck out 135 times, a pretty high price to pay for just 14 homers.

Professional Batting Register

	BA	G	AB	R	H	2B	3B	HR	RBI	SB
90 R	.303	44	175	35	53	10	4	8	31	30
91 A	.283	28	106	23	30	7	2	3	13	9
91 AA	.272	53	213	32	58	11	5	5	26	8
91 AAA	.333	2	9	3	3	0	1	0	0	1
92 AAA	.312	35	138	23	43	4	7	4	15	2
92 AA	.265	18	68	8	18	2	2	2	14	3

Professional Batting Register

	BA	G	AB	R	H	2B	3B	HR	RBI	SB
88 R	.276	28	87	12	24	2	2	0	5	6
89 A	.074	12	27	0	2	0	0	0	0	1
89 R	.267	28	86	10	23	4	1	2	13	2
90 A	.255	123	431	46	110	19	7	4	33	17
91 A	.249	132	502	63	125	30	3	14	69	8
92 A	.240	106	371	50	89	16	3	19	58	3

KERWIN MOORE

Position: Outfield
Team: Florida Marlins
Born: Oct. 29, 1970 Detroit, MI
Height: 6'1" **Weight:** 190 lbs.
Bats: right **Throws:** right
Acquired: Third-round pick from Royals in
11/92 expansion draft

Player Summary	
Fantasy Value	$1 to $2
Card Value	8¢ to 12¢
Will	use his wheels
Can't	depend on bat
Expect	more patience in Florida
Don't Expect	infinite patience

Moore probably has joined a more crowd-
ed center field situation in Florida than he
left in Kansas City. The Royals, feeling
that his progress was too slow and that
Brian McRae is the center fielder of the
future, chose not to protect Moore through
three rounds of the expansion draft. He
has shown conclusively that he can steal
bases, but he is approaching the point
where he must start hitting. Despite the
high opinion he has engendered, Moore
has seldom done much with the bat as a
pro. His main problem has been a lack of
contact: In 1990, Moore scored a Class-A
Midwest League-leading 93 runs, despite
striking out 139 times. His Ks climbed in
'91 as he got a full year in the Class-A
Florida State League. He still managed to
lead the FSL with 61 stolen bases, the
seventh-highest total among Class-A players. He also committed just four errors in
the outfield. You can't teach speed, and
Moore may yet find a way to build an
offense on it.

Professional Batting Register

	BA	G	AB	R	H	2B	3B	HR	RBI	SB
88 R	.176	53	165	19	29	5	0	0	14	20
89 A	.228	69	237	47	54	9	2	3	27	20
90 A	.222	128	451	93	100	17	7	2	36	57
91 A	.210	130	485	67	102	14	2	1	23	61
92 A	.238	66	248	39	59	2	1	1	10	26
92 AA	.235	58	179	27	42	4	3	4	17	16

GARY MOTA

Position: Outfield
Team: Houston Astros
Born: Oct. 6, 1970 Santo Domingo, Dominican
Republic
Height: 6' **Weight:** 195 lbs.
Bats: right **Throws:** right
Acquired: Second-round pick in 6/90 free-
agent draft

Player Summary	
Fantasy Value	$1 to $2
Card Value	10¢ to 25¢
Will	have name recognition
Can't	tackle Astrodome yet
Expect	good arm
Don't Expect	another 20-20 year

Gary is one of six baseball-playing sons of
long-time Dodger pinch-hitting specialist
Manny Mota. Entering the 1992 season,
Gary was the youngest of Mota's offspring
in the pros, with two others playing in high
school. Unlike his father, who hit only 31
lifetime homers, Gary is shaping up as a
power hitter, which the Astros would welcome. He was a 20-homer, 20-steal man
for Asheville in 1992, and he made the
Class-A South Atlantic League All-Star
team. He was named the game's MVP,
going 3-for-4. Mota dominated the home
run and RBI departments among Houston
farmhands, and did it without sacrificing
his batting average, ranking in the top 10
for much of the year. He had a .367 on-
base average and a .500 slugging percentage last summer. He also throws well
enough to play right field. Out of Fullerton
Junior College in California, he has now
spent three years in the lower minors and
should be ready to test himself in high
Class-A or Double-A. Power and speed
are two of the most valued skills in baseball, and Mota has them both.

Professional Batting Register

	BA	G	AB	R	H	2B	3B	HR	RBI	SB
90 A	.258	69	248	39	64	12	4	3	19	12
91 A	.197	22	71	10	14	2	2	0	3	4
92 A	.291	137	484	92	141	21	4	24	90	22

CHAD MOTTOLA

Position: Outfield
Team: Cincinnati Reds
Born: Oct. 15, 1971 Augusta, GA
Height: 6'3" **Weight:** 220 lbs.
Bats: right **Throws:** right
Acquired: First-round pick in 6/92 free-agent draft

Player Summary	
Fantasy Value	$1 to $2
Card Value	8¢ to 12¢
Will	adjust to wood bat
Can't	dive into bases
Expect	good instincts
Don't Expect	rapid promotions

Mottola's pro career got off to a slow start in the rookie Pioneer League when he injured a finger going into a base and wound up on the disabled list. He rebounded quickly and began showing the skills—speed, power, arm strength—that made him the fifth overall pick in the draft. He had a .361 on-base average and a .521 slugging percentage in 1992. Mottola's arm, good enough to gun down 14 runners in his junior year at Central Florida, made him a right fielder in Billings and is of major league caliber. Mottola runs well for a man his size, and has good baseball instincts. He had some limited experience with a wooden bat, which may help ease a transition that bothers some college players. Mottola hit .329 in his junior year and led the club in homers and RBI. He didn't hurt his draft position with his performance in an exhibition game against Kansas City, when he had three hits and threw out two runners. Mottola is working hard at improving, and has impressed scouts with his intelligence and polish.

JAMES MOUTON

Position: Second base
Team: Houston Astros
Born: Dec. 29, 1968 Denver, CO
Height: 5'9" **Weight:** 175 lbs.
Bats: right **Throws:** right
Acquired: Seventh-round pick in 6/91 free-agent draft

Player Summary	
Fantasy Value	$1 to $2
Card Value	10¢ to 15¢
Will	stretch base hits
Can't	overswing
Expect	balls in gaps
Don't Expect	Gold Glove

Mouton was born right around Christmas time, and he has proven to be quite a package. The second baseman broke into the pros in spectacular style in 1991, and he followed up by prospering in a tough league in '92. Mouton builds his game on speed, but has extra-base pop and can stretch base hits. A leadoff man who can put a lot of pressure on defenses, Mouton has a knack for scoring runs and for drawing walks. He would be an ideal Astrodome player, provided he concentrates on meeting the ball and doesn't let his swing get too big. Mouton led all players in the various rookie leagues with 60 steals in 1991, and his 10 triples paced the New York-Penn League. In 1992, he fought Buck McNabb of Burlington for the stolen base title among Houston farmhands. Mouton also had a .376 on-base average and a .430 slugging average last season. His defensive game is not on par with what he can do on offense, but if he pays attention to his glove, his natural tools could take him far. Look for Mouton in Double-A in 1993.

Professional Batting Register

	BA	G	AB	R	H	2B	3B	HR	RBI	SB
92 R	.286	57	213	53	61	8	3	12	37	12

Professional Batting Register

	BA	G	AB	R	H	2B	3B	HR	RBI	SB
91 A	.264	76	288	71	76	15	10	2	40	60
92 A	.282	133	507	110	143	30	6	11	62	50

MIKE NEILL

Position: Outfield
Team: Oakland Athletics
Born: April 27, 1970 Martinsville, VA
Height: 6'2" **Weight:** 190 lbs.
Bats: left **Throws:** left
Acquired: Second-round pick in 6/91 free-agent draft

Player Summary	
Fantasy Value	$2 to $4
Card Value	8¢ to 12¢
Will	hit over .300
Can't	be a basher
Expect	good speed
Don't Expect	another 6-for-6

Neill's play has begun to pose a question that the A's hope has no answer: Is there a league in which he will not be able to hit? He made the Class-A California League the latest full-season stop, and those pitchers were no match for him. Granted, the Cal League is a rung or three away from the bigs, but it's also true that some people can flat-out hit. And Neill's career, from high school and Villanova University all the way to Double-A Huntsville, suggests he will do damage anywhere he plays. Neill was listed No. 43 on *Baseball America's* preseason look at the top 100 prospects, and the publication also named him the best batting prospect in the Cal League. He had a .437 on-base average and a .452 slugging percentage in Class-A last summer. Neill was at his best on May 4, 1992, when he went 6-for-6 in a game against Modesto. He improved his basestealing in 1992, joining the leaders in the Athletics' system; he was caught stealing only 11 times. Despite pretty good size, Neill may not hit many home runs. But that hasn't stopped him from being a solid run-producer his first two years.

Professional Batting Register

	BA	G	AB	R	H	2B	3B	HR	RBI	SB
91 A	.350	63	240	42	84	14	0	5	42	9
92 A	.336	130	473	101	159	26	7	5	76	23
92 AA	.313	5	16	4	5	0	0	0	2	1

TOM NEVERS

Position: Shortstop
Team: Houston Astros
Born: Sept. 13, 1971 Edina, MN
Height: 6'1" **Weight:** 175 lbs.
Bats: right **Throws:** right
Acquired: First-round pick in 6/90 free-agent draft

Player Summary	
Fantasy Value	$1 to $2
Card Value	10¢ to 15¢
Will	hit occasional homer
Can't	go back to hockey
Expect	poor K-to-walk ratio
Don't Expect	routine outs

Nevers has had some defensive problems that could get in the way of an otherwise promising career. He was part of a porous Class-A Osceola infield that averaged almost an error per game over the first three months of the 1992 season. Nevers had 35 over that span, four of them coming in one game. This streak came one year after Nevers was named the best defensive shortstop in the Class-A South Atlantic League by *Baseball America*. He was also tabbed for the midseason All-Star team. Nevers is a two-sport star who was selected in the fifth round of the 1989 NHL draft by the Pittsburgh Penguins. Instead, he chose baseball, and was named the 10th-best prospect in the rookie Gulf Coast League that year. Nevers has a little pop in his bat, but he has topped 100 strikeouts for two straight years. He had a .289 on-base average and a .382 slugging percentage in 1992. His father, Gordy, reached Triple-A during his career. Though impressive for a young shortstop, Tom's batting is not overpowering enough to get him to the bigs, so he had better learn to catch the ball.

Professional Batting Register

	BA	G	AB	R	H	2B	3B	HR	RBI	SB
90 R	.238	50	185	23	44	10	5	2	32	13
91 A	.251	129	442	59	111	26	4	16	71	10
92 A	.251	125	455	49	114	24	6	8	55	6

PHIL NEVIN

Position: Third base
Team: Houston Astros
Born: Jan. 19, 1971 Fullerton, CA
Height: 6'2" **Weight:** 180 lbs.
Bats: right **Throws:** right
Acquired: First-round pick in 6/92 free-agent draft

Player Summary	
Fantasy Value	$1 to $2
Card Value	15¢ to 50¢
Will	adjust to wood bat
Can't	duplicate college numbers
Expect	extra-base hits
Don't Expect	quick arrival in bigs

It's a sign of the times that getting drafted first overall can somehow turn out as a backhanded compliment. The word was the Astros picked Nevin because he was considered to be easier to sign than some of the other players available, especially Jeffrey Hammonds of Stanford, who was taken by the Orioles with the fourth pick of the draft. That should in no way reflect poorly on Nevin's talents or his chances of being an impact player in the big leagues. He had a very eventful 1992, going to the College World Series and the Olympics in addition to being the top pick. He hit .347 with a team-leading 10 doubles, nine homers, and 31 RBI during the Olympic tour, but went 0-for-4 in the bronze medal game against Japan. He went 1-for-3 in the College World Series title game as Cal State Fullerton lost to Pepperdine 3-2. He led all hitters with a .526 average, had 11 RBI, and was tabbed as the tournament's Most Valuable Player. Nevin was also named *Baseball America's* College Player of the Year. He showed a good glove as a third baseman; Nevin will likely be in high Class-A or Double-A in 1993.

No minor league experience

MARK NEWFIELD

Position: Outfield
Team: Seattle Mariners
Born: Oct. 19, 1972 Sacramento, CA
Height: 6'4" **Weight:** 205 lbs.
Bats: right **Throws:** right
Acquired: First-round pick in 6/90 free-agent draft

Player Summary	
Fantasy Value	$3 to $6
Card Value	10¢ to 20¢
Will	require tape measure
Can't	get '92 back
Expect	dominating power
Don't Expect	quick move to bigs

Newfield missed quite a bit of the 1992 season due to surgery on his left big toe. The injury cost him what would have been a full campaign in Double-A. Now the Mariners must watch 1993 to see if he is as good a prospect as they think he is. Newfield is a power hitter who has been known to launch a tape-measure homer. In his first pro game, he hit a 500-foot shot. Topps named him Player of the Month for August of 1990 in the rookie Arizona League. He wound up as first baseman on the All All-Star squad and was selected league Most Valuable Player. Newfield got his first full pro season in 1991, playing his way up from the high Class-A California League to Double-A Jacksonville. He was voted best batting prospect by Cal League managers, made the All-Star team, and was named San Bernardino's MVP. He had a .391 on-base average and a .439 slugging percentage in Class-A that year. Losing almost a full season is bound to cost Newfield some development time, but he is young enough to rate as a prime prospect.

Professional Batting Register

	BA	G	AB	R	H	2B	3B	HR	RBI	SB
90 R	.313	51	192	34	60	13	2	6	38	4
91 A	.300	125	440	64	132	22	3	11	68	12
91 AA	.231	6	26	4	6	3	0	0	2	0
92 AA	.247	45	162	15	40	12	0	4	19	0

DAVID NIED

Position: Pitcher
Team: Colorado Rockies
Born: Dec. 22, 1968 Dallas, TX
Height: 6'2" **Weight:** 175 lbs.
Bats: right **Throws:** right
Acquired: First-round pick from Braves in 11/92 expansion draft

Player Summary	
Fantasy Value	$7 to $14
Card Value	10¢ to 25¢
Will	win games
Can't	learn more in Triple-A
Expect	Denver in '93
Don't Expect	many walks

The first player taken in the expansion draft, Nied is the kind of pitcher to anchor a starting staff. He has learned to pitch in the last couple of years, and that development has made him one of the top prospects in all of baseball. In fact, Nied should assume the role of the No. 1 starter on Colorado's staff in 1993. He pitched at Richmond of the Triple-A International League in '92, and was a member of the All-Star team. He was among the victory, strikeout, and ERA leaders in the Atlanta system, including the major leaguers. He averaged about a strikeout per inning, very impressive for a starter, and walked only about two batters per start. IL batters compiled a .233 batting average against Nied last summer. *Baseball America* included Nied in its minor leaguer Player of the Year Watch. He fired a three-hitter against Syracuse July 25, then flirted with a no-hitter for seven and two-thirds innings in a 9-0 rout of Rochester. Nied throws a fastball, slider, and change, and all are quality pitches.

Professional Pitching Register

	W	L	ERA	G	CG	IP	H	ER	BB	SO
88 A	12	9	3.76	27	3	165.1	156	69	53	133
89 A	10	8	5.00	25	2	138.2	152	77	46	111
90 A	6	4	2.87	20	1	106.1	93	34	24	93
91 A	8	3	1.56	13	2	80.2	46	14	23	77
91 AA	7	3	2.41	15	1	89.2	79	24	20	101
92 AAA	14	9	2.84	26	7	168.0	144	53	44	159
92 NL	3	0	1.17	6	0	23.0	10	3	5	19

MELVIN NIEVES

Position: Outfield
Team: Atlanta Braves
Born: Dec. 28, 1971 San Juan, Puerto Rico
Height: 6'2" **Weight:** 186 lbs.
Bats: both **Throws:** right
Acquired: Signed as a free agent, 5/88

Player Summary	
Fantasy Value	$1 to $4
Card Value	8¢ to 12¢
Will	produce runs
Can't	steal bases
Expect	great tools
Don't Expect	perfect discipline

If Nieves is not the top power prospect in Atlanta's organization, he's got to be up there. Coming back from a leg injury that limited his 1991 season to 64 games, he rocked the Class-A Carolina League and the Double-A Southern League in '92. By the time he was finished, he was runaway leader for the RBI title among Atlanta farmhands, and ranked with the leaders in batting average and RBI, too. He won a Howe Player of the Week award in mid-season, batting .500 with nine RBI. *Baseball America* included him in its Minor League Player of the Year Watch. In 1992, Nieves in Class-A compiled a .395 on-base average and a .632 slugging percentage, and at Double-A he had a .381 on-base average and a .531 slugging percentage. His ability to switch-hit could make him a formidable obstacle late in games when managers start to bring in lefties or righties. He will likely kill more than one rally with an undisciplined at bat, however. If Nieves were to arrive now, he would face a crunch in the outfield.

Professional Batting Register

	BA	G	AB	R	H	2B	3B	HR	RBI	SB
88 R	.170	56	176	16	30	6	0	1	12	5
89 R	.277	64	231	43	64	16	3	9	46	6
90 A	.283	126	459	60	130	24	7	9	59	10
91 A	.264	64	201	31	53	11	0	9	25	3
92 A	.302	31	106	18	32	9	1	8	32	4
92 AA	.283	100	350	61	99	23	5	18	76	6
92 NL	.211	12	19	0	4	1	0	0	1	0

ALEX OCHOA

Position: Outfield
Team: Baltimore Orioles
Born: March 29, 1972 Miami Lakes, FL
Height: 6' **Weight:** 175 lbs.
Bats: right **Throws:** right
Acquired: Third-round pick in 6/91 free-agent draft

Player Summary

Fantasy Value	$1 to $2
Card Value	8¢ to 12¢
Will	play left or right
Can't	hit for power
Expect	good eye at plate
Don't Expect	center field speed

It's still early, but the Orioles must be pleased with the way Ochoa has adjusted to pro ball in his first two seasons. He broke into pro ball in 1991 by finishing seventh in the rookie Gulf Coast League in hitting. He then followed that up last summer by making the Class-A Midwest League All-Star team. Ochoa played shortstop in high school, where twice he was the most valuable player on his team. Now he is in the outfield, with an arm good enough to play right. One of Ochoa's biggest assets is the ability to improve. In his first year of pro ball, for example, he hit .233 in June, .292 in July, and .367 in August. In 1992, he raised his stolen base totals from the previous year, and also sharpened his ratio between walks and strikeouts. Ochoa so far has shown no home run power and little of the extra-base variety, so he may have to make his impact with a high average and an ability to reach base. He compiled a .371 on-base average and a .373 slugging percentage in 1992. It's reasonable to think Ochoa has earned a shot at a higher Class-A league in 1993.

Professional Batting Register

	BA	G	AB	R	H	2B	3B	HR	RBI	SB
91 R	.307	53	179	26	55	8	3	1	30	11
92 A	.295	133	499	65	147	22	7	1	59	31

JOHN O'DONOGHUE

Position: Pitcher
Team: Baltimore Orioles
Born: May 26, 1969 Wilmington, DE
Height: 6'6" **Weight:** 198 lbs.
Bats: left **Throws:** left
Acquired: Signed as a free agent, 6/90

Player Summary

Fantasy Value	$2 to $5
Card Value	10¢ to 15¢
Will	give quality starts
Can't	forget baseball card
Expect	more progress
Don't Expect	McDonald-type buildup

O'Donoghue has a background filled with major leaguers. He played against Montreal's Delino DeShields in Little League, was a teammate of Orioles righty Ben McDonald at Louisiana State University, and is the son of John O'Donoghue, who pitched nine years in the majors. It may not be long before John Jr. is surrounded by major leaguers all the time. Despite not being drafted, he has enjoyed lots of success in a quick rise through the Orioles' farm system. He opened 1992 on the Hagerstown roster, made the Double-A All-Star team, and kept winning after a promotion to Triple-A. Double-A opponents in 1992 compiled a .188 batting average against him, while Triple-A opposition had only a .232 batting average. O'Donoghue is a lefthander who may not have great stuff but he throws the ball over the plate and doesn't beat himself. He is a workhorse of a starter, pitching three complete games in his first five Triple-A starts. He has a superstition of pitching with his father's baseball card in his back pocket.

Professional Pitching Register

	W	L	ERA	G	CG	IP	H	ER	BB	SO
90 R	4	2	2.01	10	2	49.1	50	11	10	67
90 A	0	1	4.50	1	0	4.0	5	2	0	3
91 A	7	8	2.90	22	2	133.2	131	43	50	128
92 AA	7	4	2.24	17	2	112.1	77	28	40	86
92 AAA	5	4	3.23	13	3	69.2	60	25	19	47

CHAD OGEA

Position: Pitcher
Team: Cleveland Indians
Born: Nov. 9, 1970 Lake Charles, LA
Height: 6'2" **Weight:** 200 lbs.
Bats: right **Throws:** right
Acquired: Third-round pick in 6/91 free-agent draft

Player Summary
Fantasy Value	$1 to $2
Card Value	10¢ to 15¢
Will	arrive quickly
Can't	wait for another World Series
Expect	lots of polish
Don't Expect	flat fastball

Ogea will always be remembered in his home state for pitching Louisiana State University to the 1991 College World Series title. He would love to make his mark elsewhere, as well. Ogea got off to a good start in his first pro season, emerging as one of Cleveland's very best pitching prospects. He began the season at Kinston in the Class-A Carolina League and was a big winner there. Class-A opponents compiled a .255 batting average against him, but he helped himself with almost a K per inning. Then he got a promotion to Double-A Canton-Akron, where he had a 3-0 record with a 1.77 ERA in his first three starts. Eastern League opponents compiled a .219 batting average against him last summer. Ogea is very polished—in part due to his college career—and throws an average major league fastball with good life on it. He has tremendous command of his breaking ball, and also throws a change of pace. The Indians believe he could come quickly, and he certainly might if he keeps throwing strikes; he walked just 41 batters in his 188⅓ innings pitched.

Professional Pitching Register
	W	L	ERA	G	CG	IP	H	ER	BB	SO
92 A	13	3	3.49	21	5	139.1	135	54	29	123
92 AA	6	1	2.20	7	1	49.0	39	12	12	40

JOSE OLIVA

Position: Third base
Team: Atlanta Braves
Born: March 3, 1971 San Pedro de Macoris, Dominican Republic
Height: 6'1" **Weight:** 160 lbs.
Bats: right **Throws:** right
Acquired: Traded from Rangers for Charlie Leibrandt and Pat Gomez, 12/92

Player Summary
Fantasy Value	$1 to $2
Card Value	8¢ to 12¢
Will	drive in runs
Can't	play short in bigs
Expect	all or nothing at bats
Don't Expect	consistency

Oliva has several years to learn how to become a major league third baseman, now that ahead of him at Atlanta he finds Terry Pendleton. Oliva has a lot of rough edges that must be smoothed before he gets to the big leagues. Oliva can be dishearteningly inconsistent however. He has struck out more than 100 times for three straight seasons, and must work to get the most of his talent. He doesn't walk a great deal and has shown little skill in stealing bases. But slugging he can provide: He has increased his RBI and home run totals in every pro season. Last summer, he had a .328 on-base average and a .467 slugging percentage. In '91, he tied for the Class-A Florida State League lead with 14 homers despite being sidelined 10 days with a fractured hand. Oliva broke into pro ball as a shortstop, but don't expect him to get near the majors at that position. He will be a third baseman, though some see him at first base.

Professional Batting Register
	BA	G	AB	R	H	2B	3B	HR	RBI	SB
88 R	.214	27	70	5	15	3	0	1	11	0
89 R	.211	41	114	18	24	2	3	4	13	4
90 A	.209	120	387	43	81	25	1	10	52	9
91 A	.240	108	383	55	92	17	4	14	59	9
91 R	.091	3	11	0	1	0	0	0	1	0
92 AA	.270	124	445	57	120	28	6	16	75	3

STEVE OLSEN

Position: Pitcher
Team: Chicago White Sox
Born: Nov. 2, 1969 Louisville, KY
Height: 6'4" **Weight:** 225 lbs.
Bats: right **Throws:** right
Acquired: Seventh-round pick in 6/91 free-agent draft

Player Summary	
Fantasy Value	$1 to $3
Card Value	8¢ to 12¢
Will	throw good change
Can't	duplicate '92 stats
Expect	command of three pitches
Don't Expect	return to Class-A ball

Olsen has come a long way in just two years, from playing ball in Eastern Kentucky University to being one of the top pitching prospects in the White Sox' system. His 1992 campaign included a winning streak that extended well over two months. He started in the Class-A Florida State League and dominated there before being promoted to the Double-A Southern league, where his success continued. *Baseball America* called Olsen the owner of the best breaking pitch in the FSL. He was among the victory, strikeout, and ERA leaders in the Chicago organization. Class-A opponents compiled a .209 batting average against him last summer, and Double-A hitters had a .235 batting average. While pitching in Double-A, Olsen went eight scoreless innings against Huntsville on Aug. 4, raising his record to 17-3, best in North American pro ball at that juncture. He throws a fastball, a curveball, and a good change, which he says he picked up in his first year in pro ball. Aggressive and able to throw strikes, Olsen could reach the bigs in '93, and he wouldn't even have to match 1992.

Professional Pitching Register

	W	L	ERA	G	CG	IP	H	ER	BB	SO
91 A	6	2	3.20	15	0	95.2	83	34	32	96
92 A	11	1	1.94	13	3	88.0	68	19	32	85
92 AA	6	4	3.03	12	1	77.1	68	26	29	46

LUIS ORTIZ

Position: Third base; designated hitter
Team: Boston Red Sox
Born: May 25, 1970 Santo Domingo, Dominican Republic
Height: 6' **Weight:** 188 lbs.
Bats: right **Throws:** right
Acquired: Eighth-round pick in 6/91 free-agent draft

Player Summary	
Fantasy Value	$1 to $2
Card Value	8¢ to 12¢
Will	homer in double figures
Can't	run well
Expect	play in New England
Don't Expect	Hobson-type power

The Red Sox may have come up with something special with their 11th pick (but in the eighth round) of the '91 draft. A power-hitting third baseman always intrigues a ballclub, especially when the hitter is righthanded and would play in Fenway Park. That's getting a bit ahead of the game, but Ortiz has not hurt his chances in his first two years as a pro. He was voted the best hitting prospect in the Class-A Carolina League in 1992, and was among the top run-producers in the Red Sox' system. He has the very attractive ability to supply pop while not giving up at bats; in 1991 he owned the second-highest slugging percentage (.510) in the rookie Gulf Coast League while being the second-toughest to strike out (nine Ks in 153 at bats). That ratio will diminish as Ortiz gets closer to the bigs, but the approach is an intelligent one. He had a .331 on-base average and a .454 slugging percentage last summer. He attended Union University in Jackson, Tennessee, and is a two-time nominee to Who's Who Among International Students in American Universities.

Professional Batting Register

	BA	G	AB	R	H	2B	3B	HR	RBI	SB
91 R	.333	42	153	21	51	11	2	4	29	2
92 A	.290	94	355	43	103	26	1	10	61	4

JEFF PATTERSON

Position: Pitcher
Team: Philadelphia Phillies
Born: Oct. 1, 1968 Anaheim, CA
Height: 6'2" **Weight:** 200 lbs.
Bats: right **Throws:** right
Acquired: 58th-round pick in 6/88 free-agent draft

Player Summary

Fantasy Value	$2 to $4
Card Value	8¢ to 12¢
Will	throw strikes
Can't	succeed as starter
Expect	some setbacks
Don't Expect	30 saves

Patterson has a chance to become one of those long shots who give hope to those picked in the lower rounds. Coming from deep within the draft, he changed his role and now may be just a phone call from the majors. He began his pro career as a starter, but never really put anything together until 1991, when converted to a reliever. At Class-A Spartanburg in the South Atlantic League, he finished with a 9-8 record and 4.42 in 35 games, but the key stat was his nine saves. Patterson was named the Phils' Pitcher of the Month in Aug. 1991. The Phillies' organization likes his arm, rates his fastball above average for the majors, and is hoping he can close in the bigs. He turned in quite a few innings in 1992 and one key will be seeing how well his arm responds to the workload and to the change from a starter's routine to a reliever's. Last summer, Class-A opponents compiled a .216 batting average, while Double-A hitters had a .258 mark.

Professional Pitching Register

	W	L	ERA	G	S	IP	H	ER	BB	SO
89 R	2	4	3.61	7	0	42.1	35	17	12	44
89 A	2	4	2.87	9	1	53.1	44	17	11	41
90 A	3	6	2.96	11	0	67.0	63	22	22	28
91 A	9	8	4.42	35	9	114.0	103	56	41	114
92 A	2	1	1.98	30	14	36.1	29	8	11	33
92 AA	3	1	4.60	26	13	31.1	30	16	14	22
92 AAA	2	1	2.63	11	1	13.2	10	4	8	11

LLOYD PEEVER

Position: Pitcher
Team: Colorado Rockies
Born: Sept. 15, 1971 Stonewall, OK
Height: 5'11" **Weight:** 185 lbs.
Bats: right **Throws:** right
Acquired: Fourth-round pick in 6/92 free-agent draft

Player Summary

Fantasy Value	$1 to $2
Card Value	8¢ to 12¢
Will	throw good breaking ball
Can't	match college won-lost
Expect	good change
Don't Expect	quick arrival

Peever came up with an outstanding junior year to lead Louisiana State University into the South I Regional of the NCAA tournament. Shortly thereafter, the Rockies drafted him. Peever is stocky and a little short for a righthander, but he has impressed the scouts with his pitches and his style. They love the way he can throw a breaking ball or a change when behind in the count, something pitchers must do on the major league level. His curveball has tight spin, good tilt, and good depth. He also throws a fastball and an outstanding changeup. One of the keys to his success in college was his control, and this asset did not desert him once he turned pro. Peever was assigned to Bend of the rookie Northwest League, and walked only ten batters in his first 43⅓ innings there; he compiled an outstanding strike-out-to-walk ratio. Used both as a starter and reliever, Peever came up with three victories and one save, with a 2.91 ERA, in his 11 outings. Opponents compiled a .267 batting average last summer. Being with an expansion club can only help Peever reach the big leagues sooner.

Professional Pitching Register

	W	L	ERA	G	CG	IP	H	ER	BB	SO
92 R	3	2	2.91	11	0	43.1	44	14	10	48

BRAD PENNINGTON

Position: Pitcher
Team: Baltimore Orioles
Born: April 14, 1969 Salem, IN
Height: 6'5" **Weight:** 205 lbs.
Bats: left **Throws:** left
Acquired: 12th-round pick in 6/89 free-agent draft

Player Summary
Fantasy Value	$1 to $4
Card Value	8¢ to 12¢
Will	strike people out
Can't	stop refining control
Expect	three good pitches
Don't Expect	big league no-nos

Pennington has shown considerable wildness in his career. He has time to harness some control, and there was evidence in 1992 that he has started. After three pro seasons in which he averaged more walks than innings, he began to throw strikes a bit more consistently. While he unfailingly used to allow more than one walk per inning earlier in his career, he cut that rate down to four walks in nine innings at Frederick in the Class-A Carolina League and 17 bases on balls in 28⅓ innings at Hagerstown of the Double-A Eastern League. This progress earned him a promotion to Triple-A Rochester, where he allowed just 12 hits in his first 39 innings. Pennington broke into the pros as a starter, but his wildness prevented him from having much success. He never allowed many base hits; in fact, in 1992 the highest batting average his opponents were able to muster was from Eastern League hitters, who batted only .215.

Professional Pitching Register
	W	L	ERA	G	S	IP	H	ER	BB	SO
89 R	2	7	6.58	15	0	64.1	50	47	74	81
90 A	4	9	5.18	32	0	106.0	81	61	121	142
91 A	1	6	4.59	59	17	66.2	48	34	69	101
92 A	1	0	2.00	8	2	9.0	5	2	4	16
92 AA	1	2	2.54	19	7	28.1	20	8	17	32
92 AAA	1	3	2.08	29	5	39.0	12	9	33	56

TROY PERCIVAL

Position: Pitcher
Team: California Angels
Born: Aug. 9, 1969 Fontana, CA
Height: 6'3" **Weight:** 200 lbs.
Bats: right **Throws:** right
Acquired: Sixth-round pick in 6/90 free-agent draft

Player Summary
Fantasy Value	$2 to $4
Card Value	8¢ to 12¢
Will	overpower hitters
Can't	assume good elbow
Expect	breaking ball mixed in
Don't Expect	return to catching

Now that closer Bryan Harvey is a Marlin, Percival's stock with California has risen higher. He is considered one of the top prospects in the Angels' organization, but calcium deposits and inflammation in the elbow not only held him back but raised the specter of surgery. In 1992, he nevertheless pitched at Palm Springs in the Class-A California League and got promoted to Double-A Midland. But he still was not at full strength. Percival pitched well in the Arizona Fall League after the '92 season, and he was named the No. 4 prospect in that circuit by *Baseball America*. He throws a fastball that can get well into the 90s, and he has a good breaking ball that can set it up. Out of the University of California Riverside, Percival broke into pro ball as a catcher, but hit just .200 at Boise in 1990. His arm strength, however, made him an obvious candidate for the pitching staff, and he made the transition with results that shot up his stock. In a return to Boise in 1991, Percival fanned 63 batters in 38⅓ innings. If he has put his elbow trouble behind him, he could be ready for the majors sometime in '93.

Professional Pitching Register
	W	L	ERA	G	S	IP	H	ER	BB	SO
91 A	2	0	1.41	28	12	38.1	23	6	18	63
92 A	1	1	5.06	11	2	10.2	6	6	8	16
92 AA	3	0	2.37	20	5	19.0	18	5	11	21

EDUARDO PEREZ

Position: Third base
Team: California Angels
Born: Sept. 11, 1969 Cincinnati, OH
Height: 6'4" **Weight:** 215 lbs.
Bats: right **Throws:** right
Acquired: First-round pick in 6/91 free-agent draft

Player Summary
Fantasy Value....................................$1 to $4
Card Value....................................15¢ to 35¢
Will ....hit line drives
Can't ....allow pressure about his dad
Expect ....improvement at third
Don't Expect ....smoothest glove

Perez is one of the many second-generation baseball players in the game today, but few must follow the legacy he does. He was born when his father, Tony, was on his way to becoming one of Cincinnati's sports heroes. Now Eduardo must carve a career for himself, and he is working his way up the California chain. In fact, he survived a freak accident at the plate to get a promotion in 1992; the injury occurred when Perez bunted a pitch into his contact lens, temporarily blurring his vision. He returned from the disabled list, helped Palm Springs take the first-half crown in the Class-A California League, then was promoted to Midland in the Double-A Texas League. Last summer, he had a .386 on-base average and a .436 slugging percentage in Class-A, and a .295 on-base percentage and a .311 slugging percentage at Midland. Perez has played first base and outfield, but has been switched to the hot corner and is improving daily. He hasn't hit for much power; he's a line drive type of player. Given his size, though, the home runs may come with time. Perez could be in Triple-A in 1993.

Professional Batting Register

	BA	G	AB	R	H	2B	3B	HR	RBI	SB
91 A	.288	46	160	35	46	13	0	1	22	12
92 A	.314	54	204	37	64	8	4	3	35	14
92 AA	.230	62	235	27	54	8	1	3	23	19

MATT PETERSEN

Position: Pitcher
Team: Florida Marlins
Born: May 21, 1970 Rochester, MN
Height: 6'4" **Weight:** 190 lbs.
Bats: right **Throws:** right
Acquired: 27th-round pick in 6/92 free-agent draft

Player Summary
Fantasy Value....................................$1 to $2
Card Value....................................8¢ to 12¢
Will...................................get promoted
Can't...............................get ink of high picks
Expect ....great numbers
Don't Expect ....high ERA

Petersen was one of the real achievers in the first year the Marlins put their organization on the field. Despite his low draft position, he emerged as one of the surprise stalwarts of the Erie staff during the regular season, and helped bring the Sailors past Hamilton and into the championship round of the Class-A New York-Penn League. Out of Iowa State University, Petersen won his first four pro decisions and five of six, taking a regular turn in the rotation and posting a 2.68 ERA through his 14 starts. It was quite a performance coming from someone whose college stats would not make you take notice. Petersen went 5-4 with a 4.09 ERA as a senior for the Cyclones. He twice was selected as the Big Eight Player of the Week, however, and he was honored as an Academic All-Big Eight performer. Petersen was originally drafted in the 32nd round by the Minnesota Twins in 1991. He graduated from ISU with a degree in finance. If he keeps pitching the way he did last summer, his personal finances will be fine.

Professional Pitching Register

	W	L	ERA	G	CG	IP	H	ER	BB	SO
91 A	5	1	2.68	14	1	81.0	56	24	29	44

JOSE PETT

Position: Pitcher
Team: Toronto Blue Jays
Born: Jan. 8, 1976 São Paulo, Brazil
Height: 6'6" **Weight:** 195 lbs.
Bats: right **Throws:** right
Acquired: Signed as a free agent, 6/92

Player Summary	
Fantasy Value	$1 to $2
Card Value	8¢ to 12¢
Will	be closely followed
Can't	rely on heat only
Expect	90 mph fastball
Don't Expect	North American instincts

In Pett, the Blue Jays have landed a truly unusual prospect. His acquisition reflects both the growing international scope of baseball and the lengths to which clubs go to find talent. Pett comes from Brazil, not exactly known as a baseball breeding ground. But the Blue Jays have already spent a reported $700,000 on signing him, so they must feel they have found something. He was able to take all $700,000 home with him under a Brazilian-Canadian taxation agreement; Pett would have had to pay taxes if a team from the United States had signed him, and reportedly four U.S. teams were outbid. Just 16 when he signed, he has represented his country in international competition, and his résumé includes a no-hitter over Chinese Taipei. A hard thrower, Pett has already worked out in the SkyDome, and the Blue Jays had him work out with St. Catharines of the Class-A New York-Penn League to get the feel of pro ball. He then went on to more international competition, playing for a Brazilian national team. Toronto's assumption is that the intensive instruction he can get in North America will only enhance his formidable natural gifts. If Pett comes through for the Jays, international scouting budgets all over baseball will increase.

No minor league experience

MIKE PIAZZA

Position: Catcher
Team: Los Angeles Dodgers
Born: Sept. 4, 1968 Norristown, PA
Height: 6'3" **Weight:** 200 lbs.
Bats: right **Throws:** right
Acquired: 62nd-round pick in 6/88 free-agent draft

Player Summary	
Fantasy Value	$6 to $10
Card Value	15¢ to 35¢
Will	hit for average
Can't	run much
Expect	good shot in '93
Don't Expect	preferred treatment

Piazza may have gone from godson to godsend. His father is a friend to Dodgers' manager Tommy Lasorda, and Lasorda is the young man's godfather. But even if that relationship got Piazza an extra look, it didn't get him to the major leagues—talent did. Piazza has become one of the top power prospects in the Los Angeles organization, and it may be just a matter of time before he's behind the plate in Dodger Stadium. Piazza has shown punch ever since he turned pro in 1989, but the last two seasons have been special. In 1991, he topped all Class-A players with a .540 slugging percentage and with 58 extra-base hits. He followed that performance with big numbers in 1992; that year he had a .441 on-base average and a .658 slugging average at Double-A San Antonio, and he had a .405 on-base average and a .564 slugging percentage at Triple-A Albuquerque. Piazza made the Class-A Northwest League All-Star team in 1989, and helped Vero Beach win the Class-A Florida State League title in 1990.

Professional Batting Register

	BA	G	AB	R	H	2B	3B	HR	RBI	SB
89 A	.268	57	198	22	53	11	0	8	25	0
90 A	.250	88	272	27	68	20	0	6	45	0
91 A	.277	117	448	71	124	27	2	29	80	0
92 AA	.377	31	114	18	43	11	0	7	20	0
92 AAA	.341	94	358	54	122	22	5	16	69	1
92 NL	.232	21	69	5	16	3	0	1	7	0

ED PIERCE

Position: Pitcher
Team: Kansas City Royals
Born: Oct. 6, 1968 Arcadia, CA
Height: 6'1" **Weight:** 185 lbs.
Bats: left **Throws:** left
Acquired: Seventh-round pick in 6/89 free-
  agent draft

Player Summary	
Fantasy Value	$1 to $3
Card Value	8¢ to 12¢
Will	strike people out
Can't	fault role change
Expect	good hits-innings ratio
Don't Expect	quick return to bullpen

Give the Royals credit for winning what appears to have been a very unorthodox gamble. They took Pierce, who didn't look bad in the bullpen, and made him a starter. They couldn't have been too far wrong because he made his major league debut on Sept. 6, 1992, and got no decision in a 3-2 victory over the White Sox. Pierce had delivered some effective work out of the bullpen in his first two pro seasons, showing good strikeout and base hit ratios. In 1991, however, he started for the first time in his pro career and, even though he only went 4-11 in his first 20 starts for Memphis of the Double-A Southern League, the Royals must have liked something. He spent a second year at Memphis and, working only as a starter, reached double figures in wins and was one of the top strikeout artists in the Kansas City organization. Double-A opponents last summer compiled a .266 batting average. Pierce seems to have worked on his control, which might make his 1992 cup of coffee a prelude to a shot at Kansas City's starting rotation in 1993.

Professional Pitching Register

	W	L	ERA	G	CG	IP	H	ER	BB	SO
89 A	2	2	2.77	27	0	39.0	24	12	26	71
90 A	3	1	3.24	37	0	50.0	49	18	32	53
90 AA	0	0	0.00	1	0	1.0	0	0	1	1
91 A	5	11	3.84	31	2	136.0	136	58	61	90
92 AA	10	10	3.81	25	1	153.2	159	65	51	131
92 AL	0	0	3.38	2	0	5.1	9	2	4	3

GREG PIRKL

Position: First base; catcher
Team: Seattle Mariners
Born: Aug. 7, 1970 Long Beach, CA
Height: 6'5" **Weight:** 225 lbs.
Bats: right **Throws:** right
Acquired: Second-round pick in 6/88 free-
  agent draft

Player Summary	
Fantasy Value	$1 to $3
Card Value	8¢ to 12¢
Will	hit home runs
Can't	reach majors as catcher
Expect	many RBI
Don't Expect	patient hitter

Pirkl was listed as a catcher in Seattle's 1992 press guide, but he played a lot of first base as he marched closer to the big leagues. Pirkl began the season with Jacksonville of the Double-A Southern League and did well, notching a .332 on-base percentage and a .480 slugging average. He then advanced to Calgary of the Triple-A Pacific Coast League, notching a .305 on-base percentage and a .423 slugging percentage at the Triple-A level last season. Despite a power slump that began in mid-July, Pirkl ranked with the top home run hitters in Seattle's farm system. In 1991, he led the Mariners' minor league chain with 20 homers and 94 RBI. Pirkl turned pro after a successful high school career in which, among other things, he was named player of the year by two Southern California papers. In his first two pro stops, Pirkl led or tied for most RBI on the club. He suffered a strained knee at San Bernardino of the Class-A California League in 1990 and twice went on the disabled list.

Professional Batting Register

	BA	G	AB	R	H	2B	3B	HR	RBI	SB
88 A	.240	65	246	22	59	6	0	6	35	1
89 A	.257	70	265	31	68	6	0	8	36	4
90 A	.295	58	207	37	61	10	0	5	28	3
91 A	.289	127	478	52	138	29	1	20	94	4
92 AA	.291	59	227	25	66	11	1	10	29	0
92 AAA	.266	79	286	30	76	21	3	6	32	4

TODD PRIDY

Position: First base
Team: Florida Marlins
Born: Feb. 28, 1971 Napa, CA
Height: 5'11" **Weight:** 225 lbs.
Bats: left **Throws:** left
Acquired: 23rd-round pick in 6/92 free-agent draft

Player Summary	
Fantasy Value	$1 to $2
Card Value	10¢ to 15¢
Will	drive in runs
Can't	kill with speed
Expect	below-average glove
Don't Expect	infield hits

Todd Pridy has done nothing to hurt Gary Hughes's reputation for finding talent throughout a draft pool. Despite being selected in the 23rd round, Pridy quickly became one of the best players in the organization. He fortified his reputation as a run producer and helped the Erie Sailors into the finals of the Class-A New York-Penn League playoffs. A first baseman, he does not present a big target to the infielders, but he falls into the category of "the better he hits, the better he fields," meaning his bat will be his ticket. A very productive hitter, Pridy is in the mold of John Kruk. Pridy had a .383 on-base average and a .526 slugging percentage last summer at Erie. His last season in college, he led Long Beach State University with 12 homers while hitting .291 with 47 RBI. He earned junior college All-America honors in 1990 after hitting 21 homers at Napa Valley JC. He once drove in nine runs in a junior college game. Pridy will likely receive a chance to test his bat against some tougher competition in 1993, but he should try to improve his glove so it doesn't hold him back.

MANNY RAMIREZ

Position: Outfield
Team: Cleveland Indians
Born: May 30, 1972 Santo Domingo, Dominican Republic
Height: 6' **Weight:** 190 lbs.
Bats: right **Throws:** right
Acquired: First-round pick in 6/91 free-agent draft

Player Summary	
Fantasy Value	$1 to $2
Card Value	8¢ to 12¢
Will	provide power
Can't	steal bases
Expect	center fielder
Don't Expect	great arm

Ramirez was the 13th overall pick in the 1991 draft, and a bruised hand meant nothing but bad luck for him in '92. Playing for Kinston of the Class-A Carolina League, Ramirez put up tolerable numbers, garnering a .379 on-base average and a .502 slugging percentage. His biggest assignment over the winter was making sure his hand was ready for the '93 season. If it is, look for a big campaign, because he is one of the Indians' top power prospects. He is only a fair fielder, because he makes too many mistakes. He had six errors last summer and a .956 fielding average. Ramirez broke into pro ball in 1991, and nearly won the Triple Crown in the rookie Appalachian League. His 19 homers and 63 RBI led the league, and his .326 put him third in the batting race. Ramirez also led the league with a .679 slugging percentage and 146 total bases, was third with a .426 on-base percentage, and was fifth with 70 hits. All this was more than enough to get him named the league's Most Valuable Player. *Baseball America* tabbed Ramirez as Player of the Year for all short-season leagues.

Professional Batting Register

	BA	G	AB	R	H	2B	3B	HR	RBI	SB
92 R	.310	75	274	42	85	15	1	14	60	2

Professional Batting Register

	BA	G	AB	R	H	2B	3B	HR	RBI	SB
91 R	.326	59	215	44	70	11	4	19	63	7
92 A	.278	81	291	52	81	18	4	13	63	1

JOE RANDA

Position: Third base
Team: Kansas City Royals
Born: Dec. 18, 1969 Milwaukee, WI
Height: 6′ **Weight:** 190 lbs.
Bats: right **Throws:** right
Acquired: 11th-round pick in 6/91 free-agent
  draft

Player Summary	
Fantasy Value	$1 to $2
Card Value	8¢ to 12¢
Will	hit for average
Can't	duplicate '91
Expect	good on-base percentage
Don't Expect	power in KC

Randa suffered a drop in power in his second year of pro ball, but still made progress in the Royals' chain and remains one of their prospects at third base. Most of the problems came after Randa was promoted from the Class-A Midwest League to the Class-A Florida League, generally a tough place to hit homers. Still, Randa has made the All-Star team and hit for average in both of his pro campaigns, and he is moving up the ladder. Out of the University of Tennessee, Randa made a spectacular entrance into the pros. He was named Most Valuable Player in the rookie Northwest League in 1991, and was tabbed for the Topps Class-A Short-Season Rookie All-Star team. He led the league with 93 hits, 150 total bases, and a .438 on-base percentage. His .338 average was the highest among Royals' farmhands. Randa made the Midwest League All-Star team in 1992 as an extra player. He had a .301 batting average and hit five of his six homers for Appleton last summer. Look for him to move up to the Double-A level in 1993, and watch to see if his power comes back.

Professional Batting Register

	BA	G	AB	R	H	2B	3B	HR	RBI	SB
91 A	.338	72	275	53	93	20	2	11	59	6
92 A	.290	123	455	77	132	20	0	6	55	10

STEVE REED

Position: Pitcher
Team: Colorado Rockies
Born: March 11, 1966 Los Angeles, CA
Height: 6′2″ **Weight:** 200 lbs.
Bats: right **Throws:** right
Acquired: Third-round pick from Giants in
  11/92 expansion draft

Player Summary	
Fantasy Value	$4 to $10
Card Value	15¢ to 40¢
Will	offer different look
Can't	afford bad sinker
Expect	advantage in count
Don't Expect	classic closer

Reed set a minor league record by gathering 43 saves last summer while pitching in the San Francisco organization. Drafted by the Rockies, he has the inside line to become Colorado's closer in 1993, an assignment that would have eluded him for several years if he stayed with the Giants. He is a submariner with below-average velocity, but his ball sinks, and his unusual delivery gives him an advantage. He throws strikes, and is a big believer in a good mental approach, which helps in the tight spots a closer must face. Reed attended Lewis & Clark College in Idaho, then began a long trip through the minors. He was the 1988 Rolaids Relief Pitcher of the Year in the rookie Pioneer League, and a 1989 Class-A Midwest League All-Star. In 1992, Reed began at Double-A Shreveport, where he picked up 23 saves in his first 24 chances. Promoted to Phoenix, he was effective there as well. Reed was a *Baseball Weekly* Player of the Week in early August.

Professional Pitching Register

	W	L	ERA	G	S	IP	H	ER	BB	SO
88 R	4	1	2.54	31	13	46.0	42	13	8	49
89 A	5	3	1.02	62	26	96.2	54	11	39	107
90 AA	3	1	1.64	45	8	60.1	53	11	20	59
91 AA	2	0	0.83	15	7	21.2	17	2	3	26
91 AAA	2	3	4.31	41	6	56.1	62	27	12	46
92 AA	1	0	0.62	27	23	29.0	18	2	0	33
92 AAA	0	1	3.48	29	20	31.0	27	12	10	30
92 NL	1	0	2.30	18	0	15.2	13	4	3	11

CALVIN REESE

Position: Shortstop
Team: Cincinnati Reds
Born: June 10, 1973 Columbia, SC
Height: 5'11" **Weight:** 160 lbs.
Bats: right **Throws:** right
Acquired: First-round pick in 6/91 free-agent draft

Player Summary	
Fantasy Value	$1 to $2
Card Value	10¢ to 20¢
Will	contribute in lineup
Can't	rely on glove only
Expect	ability to adjust
Don't Expect	quick rise

Reese has been paid a very high compliment; scouts have compared him to Ozzie Smith, an acrobat with flair. *Baseball America* tabbed Reese the top defensive shortstop in the Class-A South Atlantic League in 1992. Whether that can get him to the majors, especially with the likes of Barry Larkin currently manning the position for the Reds, is questionable. Just as Smith had to when he was a younger man, Reese must work on his offense. So far, he has made some adjustments and, while not an offensive force, he held his own in the Charleston lineup and delivered occasional power. He notched a .315 on-base average and a .382 slugging percentage last summer. He also did this before the age of 20, suggesting that with experience and some extra muscle, Reese could reach double figures in home runs. He has to cut down on his strikeouts, however. He had 76 Ks last season, and he notched 24 bases on balls. He has the speed to steal bases. If Reese can keep improving at the plate, his glove will assure him a spot. Otherwise, no amount of acrobatic skill will vault him past Larkin.

Professional Batting Register

	BA	G	AB	R	H	2B	3B	HR	RBI	SB
91 R	.238	62	231	30	55	8	3	3	27	10
92 A	.268	106	380	50	102	19	3	6	53	19

TODD REVENIG

Position: Pitcher
Team: Oakland Athletics
Born: June 28, 1969 Brainerd, MN
Height: 6'1" **Weight:** 185 lbs.
Bats: right **Throws:** right
Acquired: 37th-round pick in 6/90 free-agent draft

Player Summary	
Fantasy Value	$1 to $4
Card Value	15¢ to 35¢
Will	throw strikes
Can't	beat out Eckersley
Expect	few baserunners
Don't Expect	any starting duty

That's quite a pitcher the Oakland Athletics have, the righthander who piles up the saves and hardly walks anyone. No, not Dennis Eckersley. This reliever is Todd Revenig, who emerged as one of the top closers in Double-A in 1992. Revenig pitched for the Huntsville Stars of the Southern League and surpassed the former league record of 31 saves set in 1988 by German Gonzalez. Technically, Revenig did not break the record, because Chattanooga's Jerry Spradlin beat him to it. But that doesn't detract from what Revenig did. One of his saves helped to cap a 10-inning no-hitter against Birmingham. He is not a classic late-inning reliever in that he is not a strikeout artist. The way that he succeeds is by allowing few baserunners. Double-A opponents compiled only a .147 batting average against him last summer, and he allowed only 11 walks. Out of Mankato State University, Revenig has been a reliever all his pro career. The A's sent him to Phoenix for additional work in the Arizona Fall League.

Professional Pitching Register

	W	L	ERA	G	S	IP	H	ER	BB	SO
90 A	3	2	0.81	24	6	44.2	33	4	9	46
91 A	1	0	0.94	26	13	28.2	13	3	10	27
91 AA	1	2	0.98	12	0	18.1	11	2	4	10
92 AA	1	1	1.70	53	33	63.2	32	12	11	49
92 AL	0	0	0.00	2	0	2.0	2	0	0	1

TODD RITCHIE

Position: Pitcher
Team: Minnesota Twins
Born: Nov. 7, 1971 Portsmouth, VA
Height: 6'3" **Weight:** 185 lbs.
Bats: right **Throws:** right
Acquired: First-round pick in 6/90 free-agent draft

Player Summary	
Fantasy Value	$1 to $2
Card Value	8¢ to 12¢
Will	make his starts
Can't	stop refining breaking ball
Expect	double figures in wins
Don't Expect	big leap in '93

There may have been more than a touch of anxiety in the Minnesota front office early in 1992, when Ritchie was getting battered in the Class-A California League. Through his first 15 starts, Ritchie had a 6.22 ERA. That's not the way clubs like to see their top draft choices treated, but Minnesota had to be pleased with the way Ritchie responded. He won nine of his last 11 decisions, getting his won-loss record in shape and bringing his ERA down more than a run per game. Ritchie's turnaround was a big factor in Visalia winning the second half of the Southern Division. In fact, he opened the finals by hurling a 1-0 victory over Stockton for what proved to be Visalia's last triumph of the season. Ritchie, the 12th overall pick in the 1990 draft, has advanced steadily through the Minnesota farm system. His control could use a little sharpening, but he made some progress on that in 1992. One other problem is that batters averaged more than one hit per inning, but he didn't have a problem with that in his previous two seasons, and the Cal League is a good hitters' circuit.

MARIANO RIVERA

Position: Pitcher
Team: New York Yankees
Born: Nov. 29, 1969 Panama City, Panama
Height: 6'4" **Weight:** 168 lbs.
Bats: right **Throws:** right
Acquired: Signed as a free agent, 2/90

Player Summary	
Fantasy Value	$1 to $2
Card Value	8¢ to 12¢
Will	combine power and control
Can't	afford more limited seasons
Expect	domination
Don't Expect	Taylor's ink

In judging Rivera's prospects, you must choose between two stats from 1992—the limited number of starts he made, or what he accomplished in those starts. Rivera was on the disabled list for part of the season, which helps explain the low start totals. But look at the walk, strikeout, and hit ratios, and you'll see the Yankees may have themselves an intriguing prospect. Anyone who compiles an 8-1 strikeout-to-walk ratio in two loops is someone to look at. Through three years of pro ball, Rivera's victory totals have been very modest, but he knows how to throw in some spectacular outings. On Aug. 31, 1990, Rivera celebrated his first pro start with a seven-inning no-hitter. He finished the season with an 0.17 ERA, which led the rookie Gulf Coast League, and was named the circuit's "Star of Stars." In 1992, he opened with a 3-0 record and a 0.00 ERA over 22 innings and at one point was named the Class-A Florida State League Pitcher of the Week. FSL opponents compiled a .191 batting average last season. Rivera will be 23 years old in 1993, and the Yanks must see if he can handle a load at a higher level.

Professional Pitching Register

	W	L	ERA	G	CG	IP	H	ER	BB	SO
90 R	5	2	1.94	11	1	65.0	45	14	24	49
91 A	7	6	3.55	21	0	117.0	113	46	50	101
92 A	11	9	5.06	28	3	172.2	193	97	65	129

Professional Pitching Register

	W	L	ERA	G	CG	IP	H	ER	BB	SO
90 R	5	1	0.17	22	1	52.0	17	1	7	58
91 A	4	9	2.75	29	1	114.2	103	35	36	123
92 A	5	3	2.28	10	3	59.1	40	15	5	42

MIKE ROBERTSON

Position: First base
Team: Chicago White Sox
Born: Oct. 9, 1970 Norwich, CT
Height: 6′ **Weight:** 180 lbs.
Bats: both **Throws:** left
Acquired: Third-round pick in 6/91 free-agent draft

Player Summary	
Fantasy Value	$1 to $3
Card Value	8¢ to 12¢
Will	make good contact
Can't	beat out Thomas
Expect	run production
Don't Expect	rush job

Robertson showed the ability to hit the long ball in 1992, thus adding power to what had already been a pretty impressive package. After launching just one homer in his first professional season, the switch-hitting first baseman ranked among the home run and RBI leaders in the White Sox system in '92. This power, combined with a good glove and a solid batting average, makes Robertson a player to watch. He compiled a .343 on-base percentage and a .395 slugging average at Sarasota in the Class-A Florida State League last summer; he had a little trouble when promoted to Birmingham of the Double-A Southern League, notching a .267 on-base average and a .333 slugging percentage. *Collegiate Baseball* selected Robertson as one of the nation's top 50 seniors in high school. He was also a member of the San Pedro Connie Mack squad that won the 1987 World Series. Robertson attended the University of Southern California and was named an All-Pac-10 infielder in 1991. He is the son of Mike Robertson, a major leaguer who played for the Washington-Texas franchise in the late 1960s and early 1970s.

Professional Batting Register

	BA	G	AB	R	H	2B	3B	HR	RBI	SB
91 A	.296	67	264	36	78	18	3	1	34	8
92 A	.251	106	395	50	99	21	3	10	59	5
92 AA	.189	27	90	6	17	8	1	1	9	0

FRANK RODRIGUEZ

Position: Pitcher
Team: Boston Red Sox
Born: Dec. 11, 1972 Brooklyn, NY
Height: 6′ **Weight:** 175 lbs.
Bats: right **Throws:** right
Acquired: Second-round pick in 6/90 free-agent draft

Player Summary	
Fantasy Value	$1 to $2
Card Value	15¢ to 50¢
Will	pitch in '93
Can't	allow bat to rust
Expect	94-mph fastball
Don't Expect	final decision yet

Rodriguez is in a good position as he moves into the third year of his pro career. He has spent one season as a position player, and another as a pitcher, and thus has two ways in which to reach the majors. As a pitcher, he throws a 94-mph fastball; as a shortstop, he hits for average and a little power. Right now, he seems to be doing well in his preferred role, which is pitching. He played for Lynchburg of the Class-A Carolina League in 1992, and was among the win, strikeout, and ERA leaders in the Red Sox' organization. Rodriguez was the 41st overall pick in the draft in 1990, and came to the Red Sox as compensation for free agent Nick Esasky having gone to Atlanta. Rodriguez attended Howard Junior College in Big Springs, Texas, and was the 1991 Junior College Player of the Year with a .464 batting average and a 12-1 pitching record. Rodriguez was named to the 1991 New York-Penn League All-Star team as a shortstop. That year in Class-A, he batted .271 with six homers, 31 RBI, 13 bases on balls, and 38 strikeouts in 255 at bats, and he compiled a .927 fielding percentage at shortstop.

Professional Pitching Register

	W	L	ERA	G	CG	IP	H	ER	BB	SO
92 A	12	7	3.09	25	1	148.2	125	11	65	129

KEVIN ROGERS

Position: Pitcher
Team: San Francisco Giants
Born: Aug. 20, 1968 Cleveland, MS
Height: 6'2" **Weight:** 190 lbs.
Bats: both **Throws:** left
Acquired: 11th-round pick in 6/88 free-agent draft

Player Summary	
Fantasy Value	$2 to $5
Card Value	10¢ to 15¢
Will	show live arm
Can't	skip Triple-A
Expect	high strikeouts
Don't Expect	behind in count

Rogers was perhaps the best pitching prospect the Double-A Texas League had to offer in 1992. Hurling for Shreveport, he was named the circuit's No. 2 hopeful, trailing only Dodger outfielder Raul Mondesi. Rogers is one of those specimens you love to see, an overpowering lefty who is sharpening his control as he climbs higher on the ladder. His good work in Shreveport earned him a promotion to Triple-A Phoenix and to San Francisco, where he found the going a little rougher. But regular work in the majors could beckon as quickly as April of 1993. Out of Mississippi Delta Community College, where he forged a 19-3 mark over two years, Rogers had a rough initiation to the pros, winning just two of 13 starts. He asserted himself in 1989, holding his Class-A Midwest League opponents to a .203 batting average. Rogers made the Class-A California League All-Star squad in 1990, and opened the playoffs with a four-hit victory over Stockton. Shoulder soreness kept him out of part of 1991.

Professional Pitching Register

	W	L	ERA	G	CG	IP	H	ER	BB	SO
88 R	2	6	6.20	13	1	69.2	73	48	35	71
89 A	13	8	2.55	29	4	169.1	128	48	78	168
90 A	14	5	3.61	28	1	172.0	143	69	68	186
91 AA	4	6	3.36	22	2	118.0	124	44	54	108
92 AA	8	5	2.58	16	2	101.0	87	29	29	110
92 AAA	3	3	4.00	11	1	70.0	63	31	22	62
92 NL	0	2	4.24	6	0	34.0	37	16	13	26

JOHN ROPER

Position: Pitcher
Team: Cincinnati Reds
Born: Nov. 21, 1971 Moore County, NC
Height: 6' **Weight:** 170 lbs.
Bats: right **Throws:** right
Acquired: 12th-round pick in 6/90 free-agent draft

Player Summary	
Fantasy Value	$1 to $4
Card Value	10¢ to 15¢
Will	use great knuckle curve
Can't	get impatient
Expect	K per inning
Don't Expect	total command

Roper was headed for another superb season—perhaps a career high in victories—in 1992 at Double-A Chattanooga when he was injured in an accident while in teammate Ty Griffin's BMW. Roper suffered a strained back and was put on the disabled list. At the time, he was among the strikeout and victory leaders in the Cincinnati system, and had also been named to pitch in the Double-A All-Star Game. In his second start after returning from the injury, Roper hurled a seven-inning no-hitter. Although he had a high earned run average, he was named the No. 7 prospect in the Southern League last summer by *Baseball America*. Double-A opponents compiled a .249 batting average against him last summer. A starting pitcher who came to the pros right out of high school, Roper throws a fastball that can get to 90 mph, with control that is average. Roper's biggest weapon may be a knuckle curve. Using this pitch, Roper led the Class-A South Atlantic League with 189 strikeouts in 1991. The Reds must now decide how much the injury lay-off hurt Roper, if at all. Look for him to start the 1993 season in Double-A.

Professional Pitching Register

	W	L	ERA	G	CG	IP	H	ER	BB	SO
90 R	7	2	0.97	13	0	74.0	41	8	31	76
91 A	14	9	2.27	27	5	186.2	135	47	67	189
92 AA	10	9	4.03	20	1	120.2	115	54	36	98

JOE ROSSELLI

Position: Pitcher
Team: San Francisco Giants
Born: May 28, 1972 Woodlands Hills, CA
Height: 6'1" **Weight:** 170 lbs.
Bats: right **Throws:** left
Acquired: Second-round pick in 6/89 free-agent draft

Player Summary	
Fantasy Value	$1 to $2
Card Value	10¢ to 15¢
Will	throw in high 80s
Can't	go with two pitches
Expect	big slider
Don't Expect	many walks

Rosselli made his third season in pro ball a highly successful one, being named Pitcher of the Year in the Class-A California League. He led the league in ERA, and he ranked near the top of the Giants' farm system in both victories and ERA. He showed exceptional control for a young lefthander, walking only about one man per four innings. Cal League opponents last season compiled a .258 batting average. Rosselli throws a hard fastball in the high 80s, maybe even 90 mph. He also throws an excellent slider that may be his No. 1 pitch; he can make a lefthanded batter look silly using it. Rosselli probably needs another pitch to take the next step, and he is working on a change. He is also working on being a little bit more of a pitcher, instead of just a thrower. He had a little tenderness in his shoulder, and that may be something to keep an eye on. It may have been tendinitis or just fatigue. San Jose has produced the Cal League Pitcher of the Year five straight seasons, and so Rosselli may owe some success to the park. The test will be when he moves up to Double-A ball.

SCOTT RUFFCORN

Position: Pitcher
Team: Chicago White Sox
Born: Dec. 29, 1969 New Braunfels, TX
Height: 6'4" **Weight:** 210 lbs.
Bats: right **Throws:** right
Acquired: First-round pick in 6/91 free-agent draft

Player Summary	
Fantasy Value	$1 to $2
Card Value	10¢ to 15¢
Will	overpower hitters
Can't	reach ChiSox in '93
Expect	ability to adjust
Don't Expect	first-round bust

Ruffcorn was the 25th overall pick in the 1991 draft, signing for a reported $185,000. Last summer, he did nothing to contradict Chicago's high opinion of him. He was one of the top winners in the entire White Sox system and made the Class-A Florida State League All-Star team. One of his early victories came at the expense of Brien Taylor, the top overall pick in '91. Ruffcorn was named the No. 10 prospect in the circuit by *Baseball America*. FSL opponents in 1992 compiled a .206 batting average last year. He also pitched for the White Sox in the Hall of Fame Game in Cooperstown, though he emerged as the loser. He is coming off an outstanding college career at Baylor University, where he was the Bears' most valuable player as a sophomore and went 7-1 with a 2.37 ERA in his junior season. He broke into pro ball in 1991 and showed his ability to overpower hitters, averaging more than one K per inning. He also sharpened his control over his first pro season. Ruffcorn has conquered the Florida State League, so expect to see him at one level higher in 1993.

Professional Pitching Register

	W	L	ERA	G	CG	IP	H	ER	BB	SO
90 A	4	4	4.71	15	0	78.1	87	41	29	90
91 A	8	7	3.10	22	2	153.2	144	53	49	127
92 A	11	4	2.41	22	4	149.2	145	40	46	111

Professional Pitching Register

	W	L	ERA	G	CG	IP	H	ER	BB	SO
91 R	0	0	3.18	4	0	11.1	8	4	5	15
91 A	1	3	3.92	9	0	43.2	35	19	25	45
92 A	14	5	2.19	25	2	160.1	122	39	39	140

JOHNNY RUFFIN

Position: Pitcher
Team: Chicago White Sox
Born: July 29, 1971 Butler, AL
Height: 6'3" **Weight:** 172 lbs.
Bats: Right **Throws:** Right
Acquired: Fourth-round pick in 6/88 free-agent draft

Player Summary	
Fantasy Value	$1 to $2
Card Value	8¢ to 12¢
Will	get behind hitters
Can't	delay much longer
Expect	another shot at Double-A
Don't Expect	Sox to wait forever

Ruffin entered the 1992 season as perhaps the top White Sox pitching prospect, but he suffered some mechanical problems, lost some confidence, and was demoted to the bullpen in a dreary season. A hard thrower, Ruffin began the season at Double-A Birmingham, but wound up having trouble getting anyone out in the Class-A Florida State League. Double-A hitters compiled a .273 batting average last summer, while Class-A opponents had a .232 batting average. Since Ruffin is just 21 years old, there would normally be plenty of time to get his career back on track. However, this was his fifth pro season, and he's really only been a star in one of them. His control has never been superb, and he will have to harness it eventually, or else his great arm strength will do him little good. He posted his best season in 1991, when he won a career-high 11 games. He was named the organization's Pitcher of the Month for June, and also earned a Florida State League Pitcher of the Week Award.

Professional Pitching Register

	W	L	ERA	G	CG	IP	H	ER	BB	SO
88 R	4	2	2.30	13	1	58.2	43	15	22	31
89 A	4	8	3.36	15	0	88.1	67	33	46	92
90 A	7	6	4.17	24	0	123.0	117	57	82	92
91 A	11	4	3.23	26	6	158.2	126	57	62	117
92 AA	0	7	6.04	10	0	47.2	51	32	34	44
92 A	3	7	5.89	23	0	62.2	56	41	41	61

PAUL RUSSO

Position: Third base; first base
Team: Minnesota Twins
Born: Aug. 26, 1969 Tampa, FL
Height: 6' **Weight:** 215 lbs.
Bats: right **Throws:** right
Acquired: 16th-round pick in 6/90 free-agent draft

Player Summary	
Fantasy Value	$2 to $5
Card Value	8¢ to 12¢
Will	play first or third
Can't	make consistent contact
Expect	home runs
Don't Expect	speed merchant

If Russo keeps on the pace he has established, he should be hitting 20 homers in the majors either in 1993 or '94. That's because he has hit 20 or more in each of his three pro seasons, starting in rookie ball, then Class-A, and then Double-A. You can never assume any player can keep on pace, especially when moving up, but Russo seems to have the size and the knack. Playing against his toughest competition yet, he didn't flinch in 1992. Russo went 0-for-1 as a designated hitter for the American League farmhands in the Double-A All-Star Game. He had a .329 on-base average and a .452 slugging percentage in 1992. He passed 100 Ks for the second straight year, but managers can live with that as long as the production is there. In Russo's case, the RBI totals fell, and he'll have to get that number back closer to the 100 he delivered in '91. Russo played third base and first base for Orlando last summer; he has the arm for third, having been a catcher before he turned pro. His ticket to the majors, however, resides in his ability to hit those 20 homers.

Professional Batting Register

	BA	G	AB	R	H	2B	3B	HR	RBI	SB
90 R	.335	62	221	58	74	10	3	22	67	4
91 A	.271	125	421	60	114	20	3	20	100	4
92 AA	.255	126	420	63	107	13	2	22	74	0

ROGER SALKELD

Position: Pitcher
Team: Seattle Mariners
Born: March 6, 1971 Burbank, CA
Height: 6'5" **Weight:** 215 lbs.
Bats: right **Throws:** right
Acquired: First-round pick in 6/89 free-agent draft

Player Summary
Fantasy Value	$1 to $2
Card Value	10¢ to 25¢
Will	blow away hitters
Can't	pencil him in
Expect	several walks
Don't Expect	perfect arm health

Salkeld was the third player taken overall in the 1989 draft, but so far things have not worked out for him. Seattle's top pitching prospect, he spent the '92 season on the disabled list with a sore shoulder. The Mariners were hoping that rest, and not surgery, would be the answer. Their plan was to have him undergo rehab in the fall and winter. Salkeld's arm is the kind that no franchise can afford to lose. He came right out of high school, where he posted a 30-7 career record with 404 strikeouts in 264 innings, and he has shown a little of this ability in pro ball. In 1989, Salkeld held Class-A Northwest League batters to a .176 average. He made the All-Star team in the Class-A California League in 1990, and reached the Triple-A level in 1991. That year, Double-A hitters compiled a .234 batting average, while Triple-A hitters notched a .250 batting average against him. Salkeld has averaged more strikeouts than innings at every level of pro ball. But right now the issue is not Salkeld's talent, it's the health of his arm. The Mariners will have their fingers crossed for 1993.

Professional Pitching Register
	W	L	ERA	G	S	IP	H	ER	BB	SO
89 A	2	2	1.29	8	0	42.0	27	6	10	55
90 A	11	5	3.40	25	2	153.1	140	58	83	167
91 AA	8	8	3.05	23	5	153.2	131	52	55	159
91 AAA	2	1	5.12	4	0	19.1	18	11	13	21

TIM SALMON

Position: Outfield
Team: California Angels
Born: Aug. 24, 1968 Long Beach, CA
Height: 6'3" **Weight:** 210 lbs.
Bats: Right **Throws:** Right
Acquired: Third-round pick in 6/89 free-agent draft

Player Summary
Fantasy Value	$9 to $15
Card Value	25¢ to 55¢
Will	hit a ton
Can't	forget contact
Expect	good shot in 1993
Don't Expect	dull at bats

Salmon last year was named the Minor League Player of the Year by *Baseball America.* He was a star among stars. Salmon drove in one run and scored another to help the American League's farmhands to a 2-1 victory over the National League's in the Triple-A midsummer classic in Richmond. Salmon enjoyed his second straight power season, only this time he added consistency and contact to the raw figures he put up in 1991, when he struck out 166 times. Last summer, he cut his number of strikeouts by 50 down to 116. Salmon owned 105 RBI in his 118 Triple-A games, nearly a one-per-game pace. He also notched a .469 on-base average and a .672 slugging percentage last summer for Edmonton. Salmon played his college ball at Grand Canyon College in Phoenix, where he set career records with 51 homers and 192 RBI. In 1988, he led the squad to a second-place finish in the NAIA Tournament.

Professional Batting Register
	BA	G	AB	R	H	2B	3B	HR	RBI	SB
89 A	.245	55	196	37	48	6	5	6	31	2
90 A	.288	36	118	19	34	6	0	2	21	11
90 AA	.268	27	97	17	26	3	1	3	16	1
91 AA	.245	131	465	100	114	26	4	23	94	12
92 AAA	.347	118	409	101	142	38	4	29	105	9
92 AL	.177	23	79	8	14	1	0	2	6	1

AARON SELE

Position: Pitcher
Team: Boston Red Sox
Born: June 25, 1970 Golden Valley, MN
Height: 6'5" **Weight:** 205 lbs.
Bats: right **Throws:** right
Acquired: First-round pick in 6/91 free-agent
  draft

Player Summary	
Fantasy Value	$2 to $6
Card Value	10¢ to 20¢
Will	win games
Can't	face Cuban team again
Expect	New England in '93
Don't Expect	raw pitcher

The United States Olympians could have used someone to beat the Cuban National Team in Barcelona in 1992. Unfortunately for them, there was just such a person pitching in the Red Sox farm system. Sele had played for Team USA in 1990 and hurled a three-hit shutout over the Cubans. Now, however, his focus is on retiring pro hitters, and he showed he can do that in his second season. Sele was one of the top winners and strikeout artists in the Red Sox' system. He started the campaign at Class-A Lynchburg in the Carolina League and wound up pitching for Boston's Double-A affiliate in New Britain. Sele's 13 wins were second in the Carolina League, and his 2.88 ERA ranked fourth. He was ranked the No. 5 prospect in the Carolina League in 1992; loop opponents compiled a measly .221 batting average. He had some bumps in his first look at Double-A, but should be ready by '93. Out of Washington State University, Sele was voted a 1990 first-team All-American by the American Baseball Coaches Association. Boston made him the 23rd overall choice in the '91 draft.

Professional Pitching Register

	W	L	ERA	G	CG	IP	H	ER	BB	SO
91 A	3	6	4.96	13	4	69.0	65	38	32	51
92 A	13	5	2.88	20	2	128.0	104	41	46	112
92 AA	2	1	6.27	7	1	33.0	43	23	15	29

BASIL SHABAZZ

Position: Outfield
Team: St. Louis Cardinals
Born: Jan. 31, 1972 Little Rock, AR
Height: 6'1" **Weight:** 195 lbs.
Bats: right **Throws:** right
Acquired: Third-round pick in 6/91 free-agent
  draft

Player Summary	
Fantasy Value	$1 to $2
Card Value	7¢ to 10¢
Will	disrupt defenses
Can't	waste at bats
Expect	good arm
Don't Expect	high on-base average

Shabazz is one of those players who make scouting and player evaluation so interesting. He has been a pro for two years now, and most of his offensive stats wouldn't impress the average fan. However, he has gifts you can't teach, namely overwhelming speed and athletic ability. These talents gave him 41 stolen bases in 1992, most of any short-season player. He has been known to beat out routine ground balls to the infield. This speed would blend Shabazz in perfectly with a tradition of St. Louis burners. His arm strength is such that he can play right field. However, baseball is Shabazz's fourth sport, having refused football, track, and basketball scholarship offers to become a pro baseball player; he has a great deal to learn. He must make contact at the plate, walk more, and keep the ball out of the air, since every chopper is a potential base hit for him, and every time on base is a chance to disrupt the defense. He had a .312 on-base average and a .318 slugging percentage last summer. Shabazz will likely get a shot at Class-A in '93, and then we'll know more about his chances.

Professional Batting Register

	BA	G	AB	R	H	2B	3B	HR	RBI	SB
91 R	.205	40	117	18	24	3	0	0	11	4
92 R	.229	55	223	33	51	7	2	3	20	41

DUANE SINGLETON

Position: Outfield
Team: Milwaukee Brewers
Born: Aug. 6, 1972 Staten Island, NY
Height: 6'1" **Weight:** 170 lbs.
Bats: left **Throws:** right
Acquired: Fifth-round pick in 6/90 free-agent draft

Player Summary	
Fantasy Value	$1 to $3
Card Value	8¢ to 12¢
Will	show quick bat
Can't	clash with manager
Expect	more pop in El Paso
Don't Expect	Brewers in '93

Singleton may be the top prospect in the Milwaukee organization, especially after a midseason disciplinary move in 1992 helped him focus. He was loaned to Class-A Salinas, an independent team in the California League after angering manager Tim Ireland of Stockton, which is the Brewers' Cal League affiliate. Singleton was one of the fastest players in the Cal League, with a very quick bat and not a bad eye at the plate. He had a .352 on-base average and a .416 slugging percentage with Stockton last summer, and he notched a .359 on-base percentage and a .472 slugging percentage with Salinas. He is still very raw, not surprising considering he only turned 20 years old during the '92 campaign. Singleton enjoyed two lengthy hitting streaks in 1992, one of 14 games and one of 21 during which he hit over .400. He has pretty good pop for his size, and he has increased his home run and RBI totals for two consecutive years. It will be interesting to see exactly how much power he can produce if his 170 pounds becomes a solid 185 pounds.

Professional Batting Register

	BA	G	AB	R	H	2B	3B	HR	RBI	SB
90 R	.238	45	126	30	30	6	1	1	12	7
91 A	.289	101	388	57	112	13	7	3	44	42
92 A	.291	116	461	79	134	20	12	6	59	38

DAN SMITH

Position: Pitcher
Team: Texas Rangers
Born: Aug. 20, 1969 St. Paul, MN
Height: 6'5" **Weight:** 190 lbs.
Bats: left **Throws:** left
Acquired: First-round pick in 6/90 free-agent draft

Player Summary	
Fantasy Value	$1 to $5
Card Value	8¢ to 12¢
Will	be around plate
Can't	repeat '91 flop
Expect	three good pitches
Don't Expect	delay in call-up

Smith assembled the best showing of his three-year pro career in 1992, coming back beautifully from a disastrous 1991. Last summer, he was named the Double-A Texas League Pitcher of the Year and captured the ERA title. Smith ranked among the win, ERA, and strikeout leaders in the Rangers' minor league system, and compiled a five-game winning streak. He appeared in the Double-A All-Star Game and pitched two-thirds of an inning without allowing a hit or a walk. Double-A opponents compiled a .212 batting average last year. Smith might have collected an extra victory or two, but he had a bout with shoulder tendinitis. His size gives him a presence on the mound, and he backs it up with an ability to throw the ball over the plate with something on it. Smith played his college ball at Creighton University, where he was named All-Conference in 1989 and '90. He played for Team USA in 1989. He throws a fastball, slider, and change. Smith seems ready for another crack at Triple-A, with a long-term call-up to the bigs likely.

Professional Pitching Register

	W	L	ERA	G	CG	IP	H	ER	BB	SO
90 R	2	0	3.65	5	0	24.2	23	10	6	27
90 AA	3	2	3.76	7	0	38.1	27	16	16	32
91 AAA	4	17	5.52	28	3	151.2	195	93	75	85
92 AA	11	7	2.52	24	4	146.1	110	41	34	122
92 AL	0	3	5.02	4	0	14.1	18	8	8	5

MARK SMITH

Position: Outfield
Team: Baltimore Orioles
Born: May 7, 1970 Pasadena, CA
Height: 6'2" **Weight:** 195 lbs.
Bats: right **Throws:** right
Acquired: First-round pick in 6/91 free-agent draft

Player Summary

Fantasy Value	$1 to $3
Card Value	8¢ to 12¢
Will	bring good skills
Can't	think of 25 homers yet
Expect	good arm
Don't Expect	rush job to majors

Smith was a bright spot for a seventh-place Hagerstown club in 1992, leading the team with 62 RBI and finishing fifth in the Double-A Eastern League in batting. It was just a little of what the Orioles hoped to see when they made him the ninth overall pick in the '91 draft. Smith earned an EL Player of the Week Award in early August with a .464 average and four RBI. His power so far has been for extra bases, not home runs, but he may get into double figures as he adjusts to pro ball. He certainly has the size for it. He had a .351 on-base average and a .407 slugging percentage in 1992. He was named the No. 8 prospect in the EL by *Baseball America*. Smith grew up in Southern California and hit .468 as a senior in high school. He attended Southern Cal and finished his college career as the Trojans' all-time leader with 168 RBI, 57 steals, and 13 triples. As a junior, he hit .338 and was named a first-team All-American by *Collegiate Baseball*. Smith will probably be given more seasoning in Triple-A, but it's not out of the question he could come to Baltimore sometime in '93.

Professional Batting Register

	BA	G	AB	R	H	2B	3B	HR	RBI	SB
91 A	.250	38	148	20	37	5	1	4	29	1
92 AA	.288	128	472	51	136	32	6	4	62	15

J.T. SNOW

Position: First base
Team: California Angels
Born: Feb. 26, 1968 Long Beach, CA
Height: 6'2" **Weight:** 202 lbs.
Bats: both **Throws:** left
Acquired: Traded from Yankees with Jerry Nielsen and Russ Springer for Jim Abbott, 12/92

Player Summary

Fantasy Value	$8 to $14
Card Value	25¢ to 75¢
Will	make adjustments
Can't	miss in California
Expect	every-day position
Don't Expect	great power

If he thought there was pressure in trying to move up to New York and challenge Don Mattingly, wait till Snow sees what is waiting for him in Anaheim. He was the key player traded for Jim Abbott, who is a national hero and Angels owner Gene Autry's favorite player. That's pressure. Snow is coming off the year of his life and had better be ready for the majors. Son of the Notre Dame and Los Angeles Rams wide receiver Jack Snow, J.T. was the Triple-A International League's Rookie of the Year and won its Most Valuable Player Award in 1992. He reached career highs in batting average, homers, and RBI. His .313 average claimed the batting title, and he notched a .395 on-base average and a .474 slugging percentage. He made the All-Star team at first base; it was the third straight year Snow made the All-Star squad. His ability to switch-hit adds flexibility to the Angels lineup. He was a fifth-round pick by the Yanks from the University of Arizona.

Professional Batting Register

	BA	G	AB	R	H	2B	3B	HR	RBI	SB
89 A	.292	73	274	41	80	18	2	8	51	4
90 A	.256	138	520	57	133	25	1	8	72	5
91 AA	.279	132	477	78	133	33	3	13	76	5
92 AAA	.313	135	492	81	154	26	4	15	78	3
92 AL	.143	7	14	1	2	1	0	0	2	0

PAUL SPOLJARIC

Position: Pitcher
Team: Toronto Blue Jays
Born: Sept. 24, 1970 Kelowna, British Columbia, Canada
Height: 6'3" **Weight:** 190 lbs.
Bats: right **Throws:** left
Acquired: Signed as a free agent, 8/89

Player Summary	
Fantasy Value	$1 to $2
Card Value	8¢ to 12¢
Will	work hard
Can't	make enemies of umps
Expect	strikeout pitch
Don't Expect	easy-going on mound

A native of British Columbia, Spoljaric has come a long way looking for a job with the Blue Jays. And his performance indicates he didn't come all this way to fail. He enjoyed a solid season in 1992, being named to the Class-A South Atlantic League All-Star team and contributing to Myrtle Beach's successful campaign. He was also judged the circuit's third-best prospect by *Baseball America*. All this indicates he has rebounded from elbow soreness that sent him home after just four starts in 1991. Spoljaric is all business on the mound, and he was once thrown out of a game for questioning the umpire. He has also been known to talk to hitters—and not pleasantries, either. Spoljaric throws three pitches: a fastball, breaking ball, and changeup. Spoljaric struck out 161 in 163 innings in '92, leading Blue Jays' farmhands in that department. Opponents compiled only a .193 batting average against him last summer. He has averaged just under one whiff per inning in his career. If the big lefty just learns to cut his walks, he will be a resident of Toronto in no time.

Professional Pitching Register

	W	L	ERA	G	CG	IP	H	ER	BB	SO
90 R	3	7	4.34	15	0	66.1	57	32	35	62
91 A	0	2	4.82	4	0	18.2	21	10	9	21
92 A	10	8	2.82	26	1	162.2	111	51	58	161

DAVE STATON

Position: Outfield
Team: San Diego Padres
Born: April 12, 1968 Seattle, WA
Height: 6'5" **Weight:** 220 lbs.
Bats: right **Throws:** right
Acquired: Fifth-round pick in 6/89 free-agent draft

Player Summary	
Fantasy Value	$5 to $10
Card Value	10¢ to 15¢
Will	produce runs
Can't	find position
Expect	trade to American League
Don't Expect	Gold Glove

The Padres are frank about where Staton fits into their picture. They love his bat, but his glove isn't on the same par. The size that gives Staton such tremendous power at the plate does not translate well in the field. And there's little chance for him in the infield, because Gary Sheffield and Fred McGriff occupy the corners. Staton has played four years of pro ball, including two straight in Triple-A, and he knocked down the fences in all of them. On July 23, 1992, he hit a ball off the scoreboard at Las Vegas' Cashman Field that was measured as traveling some 550 feet. He was among the top home run and RBI producers in the Padres' farm system. He had a .353 on-base average and a .510 slugging percentage last summer. In 1991, Staton led Las Vegas in home runs and RBI despite a stint on the disabled list with a broken nose suffered in a brawl. Staton led Spokane to the Class-A Northwest League title in 1989, and was Class-A Riverside's Player of the Year in 1990. There's a chance he could be dealt to an American League team as a DH.

Professional Batting Register

	BA	G	AB	R	H	2B	3B	HR	RBI	SB
89 A	.362	70	260	52	94	18	0	17	72	1
90 A	.290	92	335	56	97	16	1	20	64	4
90 AA	.305	45	164	26	50	11	0	6	31	0
91 AAA	.267	107	375	61	100	19	1	22	74	1
92 AAA	.281	96	335	47	94	20	0	19	76	0

KEVIN STOCKER

Position: Shortstop
Team: Philadelphia Phillies
Born: Feb. 13, 1970 Spokane, WA
Height: 6'1" **Weight:** 178 lbs.
Bats: both **Throws:** right
Acquired: Second-round pick in 6/91 free-agent draft

Player Summary
Fantasy Value	$1 to $4
Card Value	8¢ to 12¢
Will	learn in minors
Can't	chip in RBI
Expect	artificial surface player
Don't Expect	lots of homers

Stocker is a shortstop who turned in a solid season at the Class-A and Double-A levels in 1992. Since he was just one year removed from the draft, that represents excellent progress. Stocker is a speed player who can help on artificial turf. He can steal bases, and is viewed as a fundamentally sound infielder who makes all the plays. He is given a chance to hit in the majors, but the Phils don't have to rush him, since the team has several options on the big league level. Stocker began the '92 season with Class-A Clearwater and quickly became one of the basestealing, batting, and RBI leaders in the Phils' organization, making the Florida State League All-Star Team. At Clearwater, he compiled a .360 on-base average and a .381 slugging percentage. Promoted to Reading of the Double-A Eastern League, he put together a hitting streak and batted .333 over five games. By the end of the season, he had a .318 on-base average and a .317 slugging percentage at Reading. His chances of getting to the big leagues may rest in whether he can use his switch-hitting ability to get on base.

Professional Batting Register
	BA	G	AB	R	H	2B	3B	HR	RBI	SB
91 A	.220	70	250	26	55	11	1	0	20	15
92 A	.283	63	244	43	69	13	4	1	33	15
92 AA	.250	62	240	31	60	9	2	1	13	17

BRIEN TAYLOR

Position: Pitcher
Team: New York Yankees
Born: Dec. 26, 1971 Beaufort, NC
Height: 6'3" **Weight:** 195 lbs.
Bats: left **Throws:** left
Acquired: First-round pick in 6/91 free-agent draft

Player Summary
Fantasy Value	$2 to $4
Card Value	25¢ to 75¢
Will	throw heat
Can't	let pressure burden him
Expect	strikeouts
Don't Expect	David Clyde career

Taylor owns a huge fastball, but faces a challenge to match. As the top overall pick and recipient of a big contract, he is working his way toward a New York City that has heard a great deal about him. The Yankees know this, and they probably will be very careful about the pace of bringing him along. They assigned Taylor to the Class-A Florida State League, where he left an imprint. He didn't have much luck in terms of victories, but he made the All-Star team and won the strikeout crown with 187. He also was among the ERA leaders in the Yankee farm system. FSL opponents compiled a .210 batting average against him last summer. Taylor consistently throws a fastball in the low to mid 90s, and he was clocked as high as 99 mph in high school. He became only the second top overall pick by the Yankees, joining Ron Blomberg in 1967. Taylor was also the first high school pitcher taken in the top slot since David Clyde in 1973. All of this may bring its share of pressure, and it will be up to Taylor and the club to overcome it. So far the Yankees haven't been inclined to rush Taylor to New York.

Professional Pitching Register
	W	L	ERA	G	S	IP	H	ER	BB	SO
92 A	6	8	2.57	27	0	161.1	122	46	66	187

LARRY THOMAS

Position: Pitcher
Team: Chicago White Sox
Born: Oct. 25, 1969 Miami, FL
Height: 6'1" **Weight:** 190 lbs.
Bats: right **Throws:** left
Acquired: Second-round pick in 6/91 free-agent draft

Player Summary	
Fantasy Value	$2 to $6
Card Value	10¢ to 15¢
Will	be around plate
Can't	lead league in Ks
Expect	shot at Triple-A
Don't Expect	any pitching to Fisk

There were bigger White Sox prospects entering the 1992 season, but Thomas may have changed that with a fine campaign. He was the Opening Day pitcher for Sarasota of the Class-A Florida State League and wound up as one of the top hurlers in the Double-A Southern League. He was named Pitcher of the Year for Birmingham, and led the league and Chicago's farmhands in ERA. Thomas collected a Southern League Pitcher of the Week Award for a stretch in which he allowed just one run over 14⅔ innings. He did it with uncanny control, as he walked only about one man per five innings. Double-A opponents compiled a .233 batting average last summer, while Florida State hitters had just a .208 batting average against Thomas in 1992. Out of the University of Maine, Thomas finished third in the New York-Penn League in 1991 with a 1.47 ERA. Having grown up in New England, Thomas was thrilled when he joined former Red Sox catcher Carlton Fisk in the ChiSox battery for the exhibition Windy City Classic.

Professional Pitching Register

	W	L	ERA	G	CG	IP	H	ER	BB	SO
91 A	1	3	1.47	11	0	73.1	55	12	25	61
91 AA	0	0	3.00	2	0	6.0	6	2	4	2
92 A	5	0	1.62	8	0	55.2	44	10	7	50
92 AA	8	6	1.94	17	3	120.2	102	26	30	72

MARK THOMPSON

Position: Pitcher
Team: Colorado Rockies
Born: April 7, 1971 Russellville, KY
Height: 6'2" **Weight:** 205 lbs.
Bats: right **Throws:** right
Acquired: Second-round pick in 6/92 free-agent draft

Player Summary	
Fantasy Value	$1 to $2
Card Value	8¢ to 12¢
Will	get ahead of hitters
Can't	be intimidated
Expect	Triple-A in '93
Don't Expect	rush to majors

If early returns are any indication, the Rockies chose well when they made Thompson the second draft choice in franchise history. He pitched at Bend of the rookie Northwest League in 1992 and more than held his own in it. Through his first eight decisions, Thompson was leading the league with 67 strikeouts, and was among the top performers in ERA. The Rockies like Thompson both for his stuff and for his makeup. His repertoire includes what one talent evaluator described as a solid fastball, a good slider, and a changeup. Out of the University of Kentucky, he has impressed the organization with his competitiveness, his work ethic, and his durability. Thompson's first encounter with pro hitters didn't seem to faze him much; he won his first three decisions and wasn't afraid to put the ball over the plate. He also held opposing hitters to a .211 batting average last summer. *Baseball America* had listed Thompson No. 73 among the draft's top 100 prospects; he may end up being much better than that. Colorado seems to feel that the only way to build its pitching staff is through the draft, and the franchise is off to a good start with Thompson.

Professional Pitching Register

	W	L	ERA	G	CG	IP	H	ER	BB	SO
92 R	8	4	2.03	16	4	106.1	81	23	31	102

OZZIE TIMMONS

Position: Outfield
Team: Chicago Cubs
Born: Sept. 18, 1970 Tampa, FL
Height: 6'2" **Weight:** 205 lbs.
Bats: right **Throws:** right
Acquired: Fifth-round pick in 6/91 free-agent draft

Player Summary	
Fantasy Value	$1 to $4
Card Value	8¢ to 12¢
Will	play left
Can't	be rushed
Expect	start '93 at Double-A
Don't Expect	above-average glove

Timmons is another product from that seemingly limitless source of talent—Tampa. He has a chance to be a power-hitting righty who will aim at the left field wall in Wrigley Field in a couple of years. Timmons played most of the 1992 season in the Class-A Carolina League, and he was one of the most productive hitters in the Cubs' system. Only one Chicago farmhand—Andy Hartung—hit more homers than Timmons did. He had a .396 on-base percentage and a .518 slugging percentage for Class-A Winston-Salem. The Cubs tried to force Timmons a bit, sending him up a notch to Double-A Charlotte, but that didn't work well. He is a left fielder at best, because of his weak glove; his bat is his ticket to the majors. Timmons played baseball and football at Brandon High School, then went to the University of Tampa, where he was a two-time Division II All-American and an All-Sunshine Conference selection. He played for Falmouth of the Cape Cod Summer League in 1989. In his first pro season, Timmons shared the Class-A New York-Penn League home run title.

Professional Batting Register

	BA	G	AB	R	H	2B	3B	HR	RBI	SB
91 A	.221	73	294	35	65	10	1	12	47	4
92 A	.282	86	305	64	86	18	0	18	56	10
92 AA	.213	36	122	13	26	6	0	3	13	2

SALOMON TORRES

Position: Pitcher
Team: San Francisco Giants
Born: March 11, 1972 San Pedro de Macoris, Dominican Republic
Height: 5'11" **Weight:** 150 lbs.
Bats: right **Throws:** right
Acquired: Signed as a free agent, 9/89

Player Summary	
Fantasy Value	$1 to $4
Card Value	8¢ to 12¢
Will	pile up strikeouts
Can't	dwell on '92
Expect	regrouping in '93
Don't Expect	another ERA title

After a spectacular season to open his career, Torres ran into trouble in his first look at Double-A. Even though he battled Shreveport teammate Dan Carlson for the strikeout title in the Texas League, Torres couldn't put together many wins, mostly due to a dreadful second half. His hits-to-innings ratio suffered as well, and Texas League hitters compiled a fairly high .263 batting average. He certainly didn't look like the man who was named Pitcher of the Year in the Class-A Midwest League, and who led all minor leaguers in ERA in 1991. It's not that Torres lacked stuff. He was named by *Baseball America* as the best pitching prospect in the Texas League, and owner of the circuit's best breaking pitch. None of this helped him in the second half of '92, as he went 0-5 with a 6.15 ERA over one stretch. In fairness to Torres, very few pitchers cruise through the minors without some blip; he did have an okay first half, and his reaction to the slump is more important than the slide itself. For this reason, 1993 will be an interesting challenge for Torres.

Professional Pitching Register

	W	L	ERA	G	CG	IP	H	ER	BB	SO
91 A	16	5	1.41	28	8	210.1	148	33	47	214
92 AA	6	10	4.21	25	4	162.1	167	76	34	151

STEVE TRACHSEL

Position: Pitcher
Team: Chicago Cubs
Born: Oct. 31, 1970 Oxnard, CA
Height: 6'3" **Weight:** 185 lbs.
Bats: right **Throws:** right
Acquired: Eighth-round pick in 6/91 free-agent draft

Player Summary	
Fantasy Value	$2 to $4
Card Value	8¢ to 12¢
Will	throw splitter
Can't	be ruled out for '93
Expect	major league starter
Don't Expect	slow track

This Halloween prospect could one day be a scary proposition for big league hitters. Trachsel throws a split-fingered fastball and a forkball for strikes, and people in the Cubs' organization give him a chance to be a legitimate third starter for a good major league club. He doesn't beat himself by walking many batters, compiling excellent strikeout-to-walk ratios in his pro career. He notched a solid record for Charlotte of the Double-A Southern League in 1992, and was a solid contender for a "Triple Crown" of the victory, strikeout, and ERA titles in Chicago's farm system. He held Double-A hitters to a .250 batting average last summer. Trachsel played varsity baseball and basketball in high school, then attended Long Beach State, where he was a second-team All-American. He tied for sixth in the nation with 139 strikeouts, and led his school to a berth in the College World Series. Trachsel broke into pro ball in 1991, and compiled a 5-4 mark in 14 starts over two assignments. On July 12, he hurled a seven-inning no-hitter against Peninsula. With his forkball, splitter, and good control, Trachsel has an excellent future.

Professional Pitching Register

	W	L	ERA	G	CG	IP	H	ER	BB	SO
91 A	5	4	3.27	14	1	88.0	80	32	25	76
92 AA	13	8	3.06	29	5	191.0	180	65	35	135

BEN VAN RYN

Position: Pitcher
Team: Los Angeles Dodgers
Born: Aug. 9, 1971 Fort Wayne, IN
Height: 6'5" **Weight:** 185 lbs.
Bats: left **Throws:** left
Acquired: Traded from Expos for Mark Griffin, 12/91

Player Summary	
Fantasy Value	$1 to $2
Card Value	8¢ to 12¢
Will	be in rotation
Can't	let control slip
Expect	leveling out in '93
Don't Expect	overpowering stuff

Trades often take years to evaluate, but early indications are that Montreal may have given up a bit too early on Van Ryn. He was shipped to the Dodgers in the winter of 1991 for Mark Griffin, and Van Ryn blossomed in his first season with the Los Angeles organization. In his third pro campaign, the big lefthander pitched for Vero Beach of the Class-A Florida State League, made the circuit's All-Star Team, and wound up as an arm to watch for 1993. He wasn't quite as effective in the second half of the season as he was in the first, but he still finished among the ERA leaders in the Dodgers' chain. FSL hitters compiled a .243 batting average against him last summer. Van Ryn was originally signed by the Expos and began his pro career in 1990. He suffered a disastrous season in 1991, going a combined 5-16 at two stops in the low minors. His experience at Sumter of the Class-A South Atlantic League, where he lost 13 of 20 starts and compiled a 6.50 ERA, will make him a better pitcher in the long run. Van Ryn is likely headed for some higher competition in '93, high Class-A or maybe Double-A.

Professional Pitching Register

	W	L	ERA	G	CG	IP	H	ER	BB	SO
90 R	5	3	1.74	10	0	51.2	44	10	15	56
91 A	5	16	5.49	26	1	141.2	159	97	73	100
92 A	10	7	3.20	26	1	137.2	125	49	54	108

JOE VITIELLO

Position: First base; outfield
Team: Kansas City Royals
Born: April 11, 1970 Cambridge, MA
Height: 6'3" **Weight:** 215 lbs.
Bats: right **Throws:** right
Acquired: First-round pick in 6/91 free-agent draft

Player Summary	
Fantasy Value	$1 to $3
Card Value	8¢ to 12¢
Will	drive in runs
Can't	steal bases
Expect	more extra-base hits
Don't Expect	home runs in KC

Vitiello was chosen seventh overall in the 1991 draft, making him the highest Royals' pick in 20 years. Last summer, he spent his second pro season with Baseball City of the Class-A Florida State League, and was named the team's most valuable player. His stats weren't all that spectacular, but they indicate a steady development, which may be better for him and the club in the long run. Besides, Vitiello did lead his club in RBI, and was among its top home run producers, though the total was too small to justify his high strikeout total (he had 101 whiffs last season). A first baseman in '92, Vitiello has also played the outfield, picking up some assists, and served as DH. He notched a .362 on-base percentage and a .390 slugging average last summer. He played his college ball at the University of Alabama and hit 15 homers with 67 RBI in his junior season. *Baseball America* named him the best power college prospect in the '91 draft. The next stop for Vitiello is probably an extended stay at Double-A, where he must keep his line-drive stroke but show more extra-base power.

Professional Batting Register

	BA	G	AB	R	H	2B	3B	HR	RBI	SB
91 A	.328	19	64	16	21	2	0	6	21	1
91 AA	.219	36	128	15	28	4	1	0	18	0
92 A	.285	115	400	52	114	16	1	8	65	0

JOE VITKO

Position: Pitcher
Team: New York Mets
Born: Feb. 1, 1970 Somerville, NJ
Height: 6'8" **Weight:** 210 lbs.
Bats: right **Throws:** right
Acquired: 24th-round pick in 6/89 free-agent draft

Player Summary	
Fantasy Value	$1 to $3
Card Value	8¢ to 12¢
Will	take the ball
Can't	be guaranteed a spot
Expect	good competitor
Don't Expect	choke in big games

The Mets could very well have the tallest pitching staff in baseball for 1993. They already have a candidate in 6'10" Eric Hillman, and Vitko at 6'8" gives them another giant. But it's stature in baseball that he's after now, and he's getting close to the point where he can help a big league club. Vitko played a critical role to Binghamton's Double-A Eastern League title. Taking the mound with the Mets trailing two games to one, he brought a no-hitter into the eighth inning en route to a 7-2 victory. Vitko tied for the lead among Mets' minor leaguers with 12 victories. He led or tied for the club lead with 26 starts, 165 innings, and four complete games. When he received a call-up to the Mets last September, Vitko became the first player to wear the Mets' uniform who was not born during or before their "Miracle" 1969 World Series season. He has enjoyed a winning record at five straight minor league stops. His hits-to-innings ratio slid a bit in '92 as he faced better hitters, but it was still good.

Professional Pitching Register

	W	L	ERA	G	CG	IP	H	ER	BB	SO
89 R	4	1	3.29	8	1	41.0	28	15	16	33
89 A	2	1	0.91	5	1	29.2	24	3	8	29
90 A	8	1	2.49	16	4	90.1	70	25	30	72
91 A	11	8	2.24	22	5	140.1	102	35	39	105
92 AA	12	8	3.49	26	4	165.0	163	64	53	90
92 NL	0	1	13.50	3	0	4.2	12	7	1	6

SHON WALKER

Position: Outfield
Team: Pittsburgh Pirates
Born: June 9, 1974 Cynthiana, KY
Height: 6'1" **Weight:** 180 lbs.
Bats: left **Throws:** left
Acquired: First-round pick in 6/92 free-agent draft

Player Summary	
Fantasy Value	$1 to $2
Card Value	8¢ to 12¢
Will	steal occasional base
Can't	try to hit everything out
Expect	raw talent
Don't Expect	new homer marks

Walker will be one of the most closely watched players in the Pirates' organization because he was acquired with a pick awarded as compensation for the loss of free-agent Bobby Bonilla. While he has a long way to go before he achieves the stature that Bobby Bo did, Walker is off to a good start. For one thing, he set a national scholastic home run record in spring of 1992 by hitting 28 or, as the Pittsburgh front office says, "quite a bundle." Walker is described as having a lot of raw ability. He's a pretty good outfielder, he can run and throw, and he projects having some power. Walker signed for a reported $221,000 and was assigned to Pittsburgh's Bradenton affiliate in the rookie Gulf Coast League. He struck out roughly three times for every three official trips to the plate, but he also hit the first of what the Pirates hope will be many home runs on the pro level. The Pirates have several young outfield prospects, so they will probably go slow with Walker. The two most probable options for 1993 are on the Class-A level at the New York-Penn League or the South Atlantic League.

Professional Batting Register

	BA	G	AB	R	H	2B	3B	HR	RBI	SB
92 R	.295	156	42	27	46	10	2	2	15	8

ALLEN WATSON

Position: Pitcher
Team: St. Louis Cardinals
Born: Nov. 18, 1970 Jamaica, NY
Height: 6'3" **Weight:** 190 lbs.
Bats: left **Throws:** left
Acquired: First-round pick in 6/91 free-agent draft

Player Summary	
Fantasy Value	$3 to $7
Card Value	10¢ to 25¢
Will	get lefties out
Can't	throw 95 mph
Expect	no nibbling
Don't Expect	refined off-speed stuff

Watson is a New York City product who grew up idolizing Ron Guidry of the Yankees. The Cardinals would certainly be happy to have Watson develop into a pitcher of that effectiveness. The 21st player taken overall in the 1991 draft, he has now played two seasons in pro ball and received a promotion both times. He hasn't looked out of place at any level. Last summer, he held Class-A Florida State League hitters to a .232 batting average, while Double-A Texas League hitters compiled a .222 mark against him. He could very well get a long look in spring training of '93. Watson is an athlete talented enough to have played guard on a nationally ranked high school basketball team. He only played baseball in his senior year, and was named New York City Player of the Year. Watson went on to the New York Institute of Technology and earned All-American and all-region honors in baseball. He is a tall lefty who throws strikes, has a fastball in the high 80s, and a slider. He could either be at Triple-A or the majors in 1993.

Professional Pitching Register

	W	L	ERA	G	CG	IP	H	ER	BB	SO
91 A	2	2	2.89	11	0	53.0	38	17	25	58
92 A	5	4	1.91	14	2	89.2	81	19	18	80
92 AA	8	5	2.15	14	3	96.1	77	23	23	93
92 AAA	1	0	1.46	2	0	12.1	8	2	5	9

MATT WHISENANT

Position: Pitcher
Team: Florida Marlins
Born: June 8, 1971 Los Angeles, CA
Height: 6'3" **Weight:** 200 lbs.
Bats: both **Throws:** left
Acquired: Traded from Phillies with Joel Adamson for Danny Jackson, 11/92

Player Summary	
Fantasy Value	$1 to $3
Card Value	8¢ to 12¢
Will	have to learn to win
Can't	throw strikes yet
Expect	good arm
Don't Expect	Danny Jackson

Whisenant was one of two young players traded by Philadelphia to the Marlins immediately after the expansion draft in a prearranged deal so the Phillies could get Danny Jackson. Whisenant established himself as one of the premier starters in the Class-A South Atlantic League in 1992. He is a candidate to climb the ladder after a season in which he hurled two perfect innings, with four strikeouts, in the All-Star Game. Whisenant led Spartanburg in starts, and was also among leaders in strikeouts, wins, and earned run average in the Phillies' organization. Sally League hitters compiled a .214 batting average against him. Whisenant throws an above-average fastball and a change, and says he must work on his slider. He must also learn how to translate his opportunities into victory totals; he had just two wins in 10 starts in 1991, and five in his first 16 outings in 1992. It may happen when he straightens out his control. He may not have the same kind of arm that Jackson does, but Whisenant has a bright future for Florida.

Professional Pitching Register

	W	L	ERA	G	CG	IP	H	ER	BB	SO
90 R	0	0	11.40	9	0	15.0	16	19	20	25
91 A	2	1	2.45	11	0	47.2	31	13	42	55
92 A	11	7	3.23	27	2	150.2	117	54	85	151

RONDELL WHITE

Position: Outfield
Team: Montreal Expos
Born: Feb. 23, 1972 Milledgeville, GA
Height: 6'1" **Weight:** 205 lbs.
Bats: right **Throws:** right
Acquired: First-round pick in 6/90 free-agent draft

Player Summary	
Fantasy Value	$2 to $5
Card Value	10¢ to 25¢
Will	be offensive force
Can't	predict power yet
Expect	stolen bases
Don't Expect	decent arm

If you thought Montreal's 1992 season was exciting, consider that more talent is on the way from the minors. White, in fact, was named the Most Exciting Player in the Class-A Florida State League by *Baseball America*. He finished third in the batting race, and was named to the post-season All-Star team in left field. He was also named the No. 3 prospect in the FSL by league managers. White has totaled more than 100 stolen bases in his three pro seasons, and has shown some flashes of power. White was the second of Montreal's two picks in the first round in 1990, and was the 24th player taken. That year, he was named the Topps Player of the Month of July and was selected a rookie Gulf Coast League All-Star. White's 1991 campaign was even better. Playing in the Class-A South Atlantic League, White led his club in homers and RBI, and paced the Expos' minor league system in steals. He once again made the All-Star squad. That makes three All-Star teams in as many years, and White seems headed for Double-A or maybe even Triple-A in 1993.

Professional Batting Register

	BA	G	AB	R	H	2B	3B	HR	RBI	SB
90 R	.297	57	222	33	66	8	4	5	34	10
91 A	.260	123	465	80	121	23	6	12	67	51
92 A	.316	120	450	80	142	10	12	4	41	42
92 AA	.303	22	89	22	27	1	2	2	7	6

BOB WICKMAN

Position: Pitcher
Team: New York Yankees
Born: June 8, 1971 Los Angeles, CA
Height: 6'1" **Weight:** 207 lbs.
Bats: both **Throws:** left
Acquired: Traded from White Sox with Melido Perez and Domingo Jean for Steve Sax, 1/92

Player Summary	
Fantasy Value	$4 to $8
Card Value	15¢ to 50¢
Will	get a shot
Can't	stop improving
Expect	good control
Don't Expect	return to ChiSox

Wickman is a key figure in what could prove to be one of the better trades the Yankees have made recently. Wickman was acquired with Melido Perez and Domingo Jean for second baseman Steve Sax on Jan. 10, 1992. Perez became the Yankee ace in 1992, Jean owned a fine ERA in the minors, and Wickman reeled off an impressive winning streak in the Triple-A International League. Wickman held IL hitters to a .227 batting average last summer. Called to the majors late in the season and joining Sam Militello as a farmhand who brought promise for the future, Wickman won three of his first four starts with the Yankees. One of his victories completed a three-game sweep of Baltimore, hurting the Orioles' chances to win the division. All this happened despite a farm accident that cost Wickman the tip of his right index finger when he was two years old. He was originally selected by the White Sox in the second round of the June 1990 draft. Expect to have a good shot at winning a job in New York in 1993.

Professional Pitching Register

	W	L	ERA	G	CG	IP	H	ER	BB	SO
90 R	2	0	2.45	2	0	11.0	7	3	1	15
90 A	7	3	1.58	11	3	79.0	67	13	20	58
91 A	5	1	2.05	7	1	44.0	43	10	11	32
91 AA	6	10	3.56	20	4	131.1	127	52	50	81
92 AAA	12	5	2.92	23	2	157.0	131	51	55	108
92 AL	6	1	4.11	8	0	50.1	51	23	20	21

BRANDON WILSON

Position: Shortstop
Team: Chicago White Sox
Born: Feb. 26, 1969 Owensboro, KY
Height: 6'1" **Weight:** 170 lbs.
Bats: right **Throws:** right
Acquired: 18th-round pick in 6/90 free-agent draft

Player Summary	
Fantasy Value	$1 to $4
Card Value	8¢ to 12¢
Will	hit for average
Can't	hit for power
Expect	stolen bases
Don't Expect	White Sox in '93

Wilson enjoyed his second straight outstanding season in 1992, affirming his status as one of the top prospects in the White Sox' organization. He finished fifth in the Class-A Florida State League in hitting, and was named both to the FL's mid-season All-Star Game and to its postseason squad. He had a .371 on-base average and a .411 slugging average for Sarasota last summer. Wilson also stole 30 bases, giving him 71 over the past two seasons. His outstanding play came at an especially interesting time for the White Sox, who watched shortstop Ozzie Guillen go down with a severe injury. Wilson is a good fielder who needs to refine his play just a little. He has quickly improved his stature with the White Sox, who in 1990 picked him in the lower rounds. He was a member of a state title baseball team and was named to the all-tournament squad. He also played at the University of Kentucky. Wilson led the Class-A Midwest League in stolen bases in 1991, had 30 two-hit games, and was named an All-Star.

Professional Batting Register

	BA	G	AB	R	H	2B	3B	HR	RBI	SB
90 R	.268	11	41	4	11	1	0	0	5	3
90 A	.248	53	165	31	41	2	0	0	14	14
91 A	.313	125	463	75	145	18	6	2	49	41
91 AA	.400	2	10	3	4	1	0	0	2	0
92 A	.296	103	399	68	118	22	6	4	54	30
92 AA	.271	27	107	10	29	4	0	0	4	5

DAN WILSON

Position: Catcher
Team: Cincinnati Reds
Born: March 25, 1969 Arlington Heights, IL
Height: 6'3" **Weight:** 190 lbs.
Bats: right **Throws:** right
Acquired: First-round pick in 6/90 free-agent draft

Player Summary	
Fantasy Value	$2 to $6
Card Value	10¢ to 15¢
Will	be good receiver
Can't	unseat Oliver
Expect	throw out runners
Don't Expect	Johnny Bench power

Wilson reached the big leagues in just his third professional season, and the speed with which he arrived leaves him plenty of time to excel with the Reds. He made his major league debut on Sept. 7, 1992, but spent most of his time getting the feel of the majors. And while he doesn't seem likely to wrest the starting job from Joe Oliver any time soon, Wilson does give Cincinnati depth at this important position and looms as the catcher of the future. He was the seventh overall pick in the 1990 draft, and owns a reputation as a fine defensive player. He broke into the pros with Charleston of the Class-A South Atlantic League in 1990 and made just one error in 32 games. He opened the following season with Class-A Charleston, threw out 44 percent of runners trying to steal, and was named the league's top defensive receiver. He was promoted to Double-A ball in June. Wilson was drafted by the Mets in the 26th round in 1987, but chose to attend the University of Minnesota. He was named first team All-American by *Baseball America* in 1990.

NIGEL WILSON

Position: Outfield
Team: Florida Marlins
Born: Jan. 12, 1970 Oshawa, Ontario
Height: 6'1" **Weight:** 185 lbs.
Bats: left **Throws:** left
Acquired: First-round pick from Blue Jays in 11/92 expansion draft

Player Summary	
Fantasy Value	$4 to $8
Card Value	15¢ to 50¢
Will	get extra-base hits
Can't	rely on first player status
Expect	speed and power
Don't Expect	NL All-Star yet

There was a question as to what Florida was going to look for during the expansion draft; there was no question, however, when Wilson was left unprotected by Toronto—and when Colorado decided on David Nied—that the Marlins were going to snap up Wilson. While Toronto's Southern League affiliate in Knoxville suffered through a difficult season in 1992, Wilson was a highlight film in himself. He finished third in the league with 26 homers. Wilson had twice reached double figures in his pro career, and earned a spot on the Florida State League's postseason All-Star team in 1991, but he had never put things together quite the way he did in his first look at Double-A ball. He had a .325 on-base average and a .516 slugging percentage last summer. His RBI totals aren't exceptional for someone who produces so many extra-base hits, however. He was named to the Southern League's postseason All-Star team as a designated hitter; if he improves his fielding, he could be Florida's Opening Day left fielder.

Professional Batting Register

	BA	G	AB	R	H	2B	3B	HR	RBI	SB
90 A	.248	32	113	16	28	9	1	2	17	0
91 A	.315	52	197	25	62	11	1	3	29	1
91 AA	.257	81	292	32	75	19	2	2	38	2
92 AAA	.251	99	336	27	92	16	1	4	34	1
92 NL	.360	12	25	2	9	1	0	0	3	0

Professional Batting Register

	BA	G	AB	R	H	2B	3B	HR	RBI	SB
88 A	.204	40	103	12	21	1	2	2	11	8
89 A	.217	42	161	17	35	5	2	4	18	8
90 A	.273	110	440	77	120	23	9	16	62	22
91 A	.301	119	455	64	137	18	13	12	55	27
92 AA	.274	137	521	85	143	34	7	26	69	13

PRESTON WILSON

Position: Outfield; pitcher
Team: New York Mets
Born: July 19, 1974 Bamberg, SC
Height: 6'3" **Weight:** 190 lbs.
Bats: right **Throws:** right
Acquired: First-round pick in 6/92 free-agent draft

Player Summary	
Fantasy Value	$1 to $2
Card Value	10¢ to 15¢
Will	decide on a position
Can't	keep smile off face
Expect	tape measure homers
Don't Expect	Mookie's style

Preston already faces expectations in the Big Apple because his stepfather, Mookie Wilson, was one of the great favorites at Shea Stadium. Mookie played a game built on enthusiasm, speed, and occasional power. Scouts expect the younger Wilson, however, to deliver more than a sporadic long ball. One Met talent maven called Wilson the best high school bat in the 1992 draft. Picked with the ninth selection, Wilson was the second high school player taken in the draft, after the Yankees selected shortstop Derek Jeter. Wilson has used his size well in amateur baseball. He led his high school team to a South Carolina state title in 1992, hitting 22 homers with 86 RBI in just 36 games. He hit seven grand slams, tying a national scholastic mark. He went 13-0 as a pitcher, striking out 95 in 81 innings. With arm strength like that, Wilson could even make it in right field. It is doubtful that the Mets would give him much of a chance on the mound, however. Valedictorian of his high school class with a 4.0 average, Wilson is more than just an athlete. He was a member of the U.S. team that lost to Cuba in the World Junior Championships in Monterrey, Mexico, in 1992.

No minor league experience

TIM WORRELL

Position: Pitcher
Team: San Diego Padres
Born: July 5, 1967 Arcadia, CA
Height: 6'4" **Weight:** 210 lbs.
Bats: right **Throws:** right
Acquired: 20th-round pick in 6/89 free-agent draft

Player Summary	
Fantasy Value	$1 to $5
Card Value	10¢ to 15¢
Will	throw in 90s
Can't	complain about career pace
Expect	mostly strikes
Don't Expect	name to carry him

Tim is the younger brother of Cardinals' veteran reliever Todd Worrell. Unlike his brother, Tim seems headed for a career as a starter. He spent most of 1992 pitching for San Diego's Double-A affiliate in Wichita and was named the Texas League's ninth-best prospect by *Baseball America*. He worked one scoreless inning in the Double-A All-Star Game, and was named to the postseason squad as well. His 2.86 ERA placed him fourth in the league. It was the first time that he had a more-than-respectable ERA, but in fairness, he has been pitching mostly in notorious hitters' circuits. Worrell was promoted to Triple-A Las Vegas last summer and finished the season with a flourish, hurling a no-hitter. Out of Biola University in California, Worrell throws a fastball in the 90s, and his control has been good. He has moved quickly through the system, even though he did not pitch professionally in the year he was drafted. By 1991, Worrell was blazing through two Class-A stops with a combined 13-6 record and 153 Ks. He could very well pitch at two levels in 1993—one of them the majors.

Professional Pitching Register

	W	L	ERA	G	CG	IP	H	ER	BB	SO
90 A	5	8	4.64	20	3	110.2	120	57	28	68
91 A	13	6	3.72	25	5	150.0	135	62	66	153
92 AA	8	6	2.86	19	1	126.0	115	40	32	109
92 AAA	4	2	4.26	10	1	63.0	61	30	19	32

DMITRI YOUNG

Position: Third base
Team: St. Louis Cardinals
Born: Oct. 11, 1973 Vicksburg, MS
Height: 6'2" **Weight:** 215 lbs.
Bats: both **Throws:** right
Acquired: First-round pick in 6/91 free-agent draft

Player Summary

Fantasy Value	$1 to $2
Card Value	8¢ to 12¢
Will	be fearsome switch-hitter
Can't	win Gold Glove
Expect	terrific size
Don't Expect	immediate switch to first

Young is a switch-hitting third baseman who can deliver power from both sides of the plate. That's a package that brings the promise of excitement, and he has delivered it in his short pro career. In 1992, *Baseball America* named him the top prospect in the Class-A Midwest League, as well as the top hitting prospect and the most exciting player. Not just a home run slugger, he also led the loop with 36 doubles last summer. Unfortunately, there's also an element of excitement to his play around third base, where he does turn many balls into adventures. However, there's time to work on that. He is a large player, and many feel that he either needs to lose some weight or become more solid. Besides, if Young keeps hitting the way people think he might, there will be room for him somewhere else on defense, perhaps first base. Young exhibited his gift for creating excitement from the first time he entered the pros after being a first-round pick. Early in his career, he slammed a home run estimated to have traveled 450 feet. Look for Young to eventually reach at least the Double-A level in 1993.

Professional Batting Register

	BA	G	AB	R	H	2B	3B	HR	RBI	SB
91 R	.256	37	129	22	33	10	0	2	22	2
92 A	.310	120	493	74	153	36	6	14	72	14

KEVIN YOUNG

Position: Third base
Team: Pittsburgh Pirates
Born: June 16, 1969 Alpena, MI
Height: 6'3" **Weight:** 210 lbs.
Bats: right **Throws:** right
Acquired: Seventh-round pick in 6/90 free-agent draft

Player Summary

Fantasy Value	$4 to $8
Card Value	15¢ to 25¢
Will	get shot at third
Can't	match Buechele's glove
Expect	improving power
Don't Expect	more Triple-A play

Young is coming off a campaign in which *Baseball America* named him top prospect in the American Association. Young finished third in the league's batting race, his second straight season well north of the .300 mark, and was named the circuit's Rookie of the Year. His glove does not yet match his bat, but he improved as the '92 season progressed and seems to have the athletic ability to play third. He certainly has both the range and the arm, but he needs to cut down on his mistakes. Out of Southern Mississippi University, Young has raced through the Pittsburgh farm system, particularly in 1991, when he played in Class-A, Double-A, and Triple-A. Young offers extra-base as opposed to home run pop, though with his size and approach he could hit 15 or 20 in the majors some day. His RBI totals have been solid, not eye-popping. Young is no burner, but has reached double figures in steals three straight years, and that speed must be respected.

Professional Batting Register

	BA	G	AB	R	H	2B	3B	HR	RBI	SB
90 A	.244	72	238	46	58	16	2	5	30	10
91 A	.313	56	201	38	63	12	4	6	28	3
91 AA	.342	75	263	36	90	19	6	3	33	9
91 AAA	.222	4	9	1	2	1	0	0	2	1
92 AAA	.314	122	490	91	154	29	6	8	65	18
92 NL	.571	10	7	2	4	0	0	0	4	1

Team Overviews

You'll find an overview of the 26 established major league organizations in this section. The section is arranged according to the final standings of 1992, starting with the AL East, followed by the AL West, the NL West, and the NL East.

The teams are ordered as follows: Toronto Blue Jays, Milwaukee Brewers, Baltimore Orioles, Cleveland Indians, New York Yankees, Detroit Tigers, and Boston Red Sox in the AL East; Oakland Athletics, Minnesota Twins, Chicago White Sox, Texas Rangers, California Angels, Kansas City Royals, and Seattle Mariners in the AL West; Atlanta Braves, Cincinnati Reds, San Diego Padres, Houston Astros, San Francisco Giants, Los Angeles Dodgers, and Colorado Rockies in the NL West; and the Pittsburgh Pirates, Montreal Expos, St. Louis Cardinals, Chicago Cubs, New York Mets, Philadelphia Phillies, and Florida Marlins in the NL East.

Except for the Rockies and the Marlins, each team overview begins with an analysis of that club's key players (not every player on each ballclub is mentioned); the team's 1992 season is examined as well. The manager section includes the skipper's overall major league record (including all major league ballclubs he has managed), his overall record with his current team, and his record in 1992. The abbreviations for managers are: **W** = wins; **L** = losses; **PCT** = winning percentage. The executives listed make up the ownership and baseball structure for each organization.

The "Five-Year Finishes" show in what place each organization finished in its division in the last five years. If two or more clubs were tied for a position—such as the Cleveland Indians and the New York Yankees, who tied for fourth in the 1992 AL East—each ballclub gets a "T" designation; the Indians and the Yankees received a T4. Each team's overall five-year record is included; the "Rank" compares the five-year record against the other 26 established major league organizations. The ballparks that the franchise has occupied, plus the years that the organization was there, are shown. If more than one ballpark is listed for a given year, the franchise occupied both parks during that season. The seating capacity and the dimensions of the present ballpark are included, as is the team's address. A brief history of each organization is presented with an emphasis on how each franchise has done over the last 15 to 20 years.

TORONTO BLUE JAYS

96-66, .593 Manager: Cito Gaston

After years of playoff disappointment, the Toronto Blue Jays finally went out and got the veteran leadership needed to make it to the World Series. The strategy worked. Toronto staved off a late charge by Milwaukee and then dusted Oakland in six games to qualify for its first fall classic—in five tries. Though manager Cito Gaston again did a great job with the team's day-to-day progress, the World Series appearance was as much the responsibility of GM Pat Gillick as it was any player, coach, or manager. Gillick's off-season acquisitions of playoff-tested hurler Jack Morris (21-6) and veteran slugger, clubhouse leader, and medical marvel Dave Winfield (.290, 26 HR, 108 RBI), combined with a late-season trade for fireballing righty David Cone (4-3, 47 Ks in 53

IP) were the final ingredients needed to snap the team's postseason jinx. Cone and Morris teamed with immensely talented second-year man Juan Guzman (16-5, 2.64, 165 Ks), Jimmy Key (13-13), and Todd Stottlemeyer (12-11) to give the Jays a solid rotation. Together with superb relievers Duane Ward (7-4, 1.95, 12 saves) and Tom Henke (3-2, 2.26, 34 saves), they comprised the game's best overall staff. Winfield combined with emerging superstar second baseman Roberto Alomar (.310, 76 RBI, 49 SBs), RBI machine Joe Carter (34 HR, 119 RBI), outfielder Candy Maldonado (20 HR, 66 RBI), and first baseman John Olerud (.284, 16 HR, 66 RBI) to make up one of the game's most dangerous lineups—one that finally produced in the clutch.

Manager			
Cito Gaston	W	L	PCT
Major League record	323	242	.572
With Blue Jays	323	242	.572
1992 record	96	66	.593
Coaches: Bob Bailor, Galen Cisco, Rich Hacker, Larry Hisle, John Sullivan, Gene Tenace			

Ballparks

Exhibition Stadium 1977-1989;
   The SkyDome 1989-present.
1992 Attendance: 4,028,318
Capacity: 50,516
Surface: artificial turf
Retractable Dome

Left field fence: 328 feet
Center field fence: 400 feet
Right field fence: 328 feet
Left-center fence: 375 feet
Right-center fence: 375 feet

Five-Year Finishes

88	89	90	91	92
T3	1	2	1	1

Five-Year Record: 449-361; .554
Rank: 2nd in AL; 3rd in ML

Chairman: P.N.T. Widdington
President & CEO: Paul Beeston
Executive VP, Baseball: Pat Gillick
VP, Baseball: Bob Mattick
VP, Baseball: Al LaMacchia
Assistant GM: Gord Ash
Director, Development: Mel Queen
Director, Scouting: Bob Engle

Address
The Skydome
300 Bremner Boulevard
Toronto, Ontario M5V 3b3

Team History

Unlike Seattle, their 1977 expansion siblings, the Blue Jays have enjoyed growing success over the years. Toronto asserted itself in the early 1980s and became a contender. The Jays won the 1985 AL East crown but choked away the '87 title, losing their last seven games. In 1989, the Blue Jays moved from Exhibition Stadium to the SkyDome. It was that same year that Cito Gaston took over as skipper. They rebounded to a division title again in '89, but that

was as far as the Blue Jays progressed. The following season was disappointing for the Jays. After much effort, they failed to sew up their division in '90 on the final day of regular-season play. The team was developing a reputation for choking, especially in the most crucial games. They put an end to that in 1992 by becoming World Champions. By winning in six games over the Atlanta Braves, the Blue Jays took the first Series trophy through customs.

MILWAUKEE BREWERS

92-70, .569, 4 Manager: Phil Garner

In the old days, Brewer baseball was a bunch of cartoon-like characters bashing homers, some guy sliding into a vat of beer out in the outfield, and the pitching staff floundering every season. New manager Phil Garner changed all that. The 1992 Brewers were the antithesis of the old Brew Crew. They ran. They fielded. They pitched. And they contended. Milwaukee stayed close to Toronto throughout all of August and September—posting the AL's best record after the All-Star break—before finally succumbing in the season's last week. Still, a second-place finish and 92 wins aren't so bad. The Brewers' four main starters were tremendous, particularly down the stretch. Chris Bosio (16-6) posted a 10-game winning streak, and rookie Cal Eldred (11-2, 1.79) won nine in a row. Bill Wegman (13-14, 3.20) and Jaime Navarro (17-11, 3.33) were both effective much of the season, as was young closer Doug Henry (29 saves). Although the Brewers didn't dial the long ball too often, their aggressive baserunning produced runs. DH Paul Molitor (.320, 31 steals), outfielder Darryl Hamilton (.298, 41 steals), and Rookie of the Year shortstop Pat Listach (.290, 54 steals) sparked an offense that received support from Greg Vaughn (23 HR, 78 RBI), third baseman Kevin Seitzer (.270, 71 RBI) and ageless Robin Yount (.264, 77 RBI), who passed the 3,000-hit milestone in September.

Manager

Phil Garner	W	L	PCT
Major League record	92	70	.568
With Brewers	92	70	.568
1992 record	92	70	.568

Coaches: Bill Castro, Duffy Dyer, Tim Foli, Don Rowe, Gene Clines

Ballparks

Seattle: Sicks' Stadium 1969;
Milwaukee: County Stadium 1970-present
Capacity: 53,192
1992 Attendance: 1,857,351
Surface: natural grass

Left field fence: 362 feet
Center field fence: 402 feet
Right field fence: 362 feet
Left-center fence: 392 feet
Right-center fence: 392 feet

Five-Year Finishes

88	89	90	91	92
4	4	6	4	2

Five-Year Record: 417-393; .515
Rank: Tied 4th in AL; tied 7th in ML

President, CEO: Allan H. (Bud) Selig
Sr. VP-Baseball Operations: Sal Bando
Senior VP: Harry Dalton
VP-Scouting and Planning: Al Goldis
Asst. VP-Baseball Op.: Bruce Manno
Director of Player Development: Fred Stanley

Address
201 S. 46th Street
Milwaukee, WI 53214

Team History

After a one-year stint as the last-place, first-year Seattle Pilots, this franchise brought baseball back to Milwaukee in 1970. The Brewers floundered in the AL East for much of the next decade. By 1978, however, they posted their first winning season, finishing third. The Brew Crew really came alive in the early 1980s, due largely to the multi-talented Robin Yount. The Brewers won the second-half crown in strike-shortened 1981. In 1982, they took their only AL pennant, not coincidentally during Yount's MVP, All-Star, and Gold Glove season. They took the Cardinals all the way to seven games in a futile bid for the World Championship in '82. The brightest moment for the franchise in 1987 was their sprint out of the gate. The Brewers got off to a record-tying start of 13 consecutive wins. They hit the skids shortly thereafter, losing 12 games in a row. This decline continued for the next few years, until 1992. That season saw them turn around their descent and finish the season second in their division.

BALTIMORE ORIOLES
89-73, .549, 7 Manager: Johnny Oates

The preseason joke was that Baltimore's beautiful new ballpark was going to be ruined by its tenants. Four straight dismal finishes gave Oriole fans little reason for optimism. Who would have believed what happened next? The O's treated fans to an improbable run at the pennant and a season full of excitement. The Orioles hung right with Toronto throughout most of the season and entered the final month just two games back. But a dearth of quality pitching late in the season doomed the O's, and they finished seven games behind their ornithological rivals to the north. As with any Cinderella story, there were plenty of surprises. Second-year starter Mike Mussina (18-5, 2.54) was brilliant, earning an All-Star berth in the process.

Outfielder Brady Anderson (.271, 21 HR, 80 RBI, 53 steals) electrified Oriole fans all season with his aggressive play. Slugger Mike Devereaux (.276, 24 HR, 107 RBI) had a career year, while Joe Orsulak (.289) and catcher Chris Hoiles (.274, 20 HR) were impressive. Ageless Rick Sutcliffe (16-15) was steady all year, and Leo Gomez (.265, 17 HR) was a pleasant surprise. There were, of course, some disappointments. Iron man Cal Ripken (.251, 14 HR, 72 RBI) was well off his 1991 MVP numbers, and Glenn Davis (.276, 13 HR) battled injuries and inconsistency all year. Other than Mussina and Sutcliffe, the starting pitching was shaky, though the bullpen was sparked by stopper Gregg Olson (35 saves).

Manager

Johnny Oates	W	L	PCT
Major League record	143	144	.499
With Orioles	143	144	.499
1992 record	89	73	.549

Coaches: Greg Biagini, Dick Bosman, Elrod Hendricks, Davey Lopes, Sammy Snider, Mike Ferraro, Jerry Narron

Five-Year Finishes

88	89	90	91	92
5	2	5	6	3

Five-Year Record: 373-435; .462
Rank: Tied 11th in AL; tied 22nd in ML

Chairman: Eli S. Jacobs
President: Lawrence Lucchino
Exec. VP/GM: Roland A. Hemond
Senior VP: Thomas A. Daffron
Assistant GM, Director of Player Personnel: R. Douglas Melvin
Director of Scouting: Gary Nickels

Address
Oriole Park at Camden Yards
333 W. Camden Street
Baltimore, MD 21201

Ballparks

Milwaukee: Lloyd Street Grounds 1901. **St. Louis:** Sportsman's Park 1902-1953. **Baltimore:** Memorial Stadium 1954-1991; Oriole Park at Camden Yards 1992. Capacity: 48,000

1992 Attendance: 3,567,819
Surface: natural grass
Left field fence: 335 feet
Center field fence: 400 feet
Right field fence: 318 feet
Left-center fence: 410 feet
Right-center fence: 386 feet

Team History

For nearly 45 years, futility in American League baseball had a home in St. Louis. The Browns, founded in 1902, wallowed at the bottom of the standings until 1944. Winning the pennant in 1944, they lost the Series to the crosstown Cardinals. They began anew in 1954, moving to Baltimore. By developing a very productive farm system, the Orioles became pennant contenders by the 1960s. A first-ever World Series win came to the franchise in 1966, and the Orioles went on to become a force to be dealt with,

challenging for the top honors for three consecutive years (1969 to '71). Boasting the talents of players like Boog Powell, Jim Palmer, and Cal Ripken Jr., and managers and coaches like Earl Weaver and Ray Miller, the franchise is noted for its unity and strong fundamentals. They have won seven division titles, six pennants, and three world titles (1966, '70, and '83). They stumbled out of the blocks in 1984, but by '89 they had recovered, going from last place to one game out of first.

413

CLEVELAND INDIANS
76-86, .469, 20 Manager: Mike Hargrove

When more than 30,000 people showed up at creaky Cleveland Stadium for the finale of the 1992 Indians season, they weren't doing so to honor a pennant-winner or even a solid runner-up. The Tribe finished fourth in the AL East, a solid 20 games behind first-place Toronto. But the team's 76 wins represented a 19-game turnaround from 1991, when Cleveland dropped a franchise-record 105 games. So color the final-day faithful optimistic, a sentiment that hasn't exactly engulfed Indian baseball over the last two decades. After sputtering out of the gate 14-30, Cleveland finished the rest of the season 62-56, thanks to its collection of young talent. As the Tribe prepares to enter a sparkling new ballpark in 1994, it does so with high hopes. The Indians' promise starts with Carlos Baerga

(.312, 20 HR, 105 RBI), who became the first second baseman in AL history to hit over .300, with 20 homers, more than 100 RBI, and 200-plus hits. Scintillating rookie Kenny Lofton (.285, 66 SBs), who led the AL in stolen bases, and slugger Albert Belle (34 HR, 112 RBI) were both big producers, while infielders Jim Thome, Mark Lewis (.264), and Paul Sorrento (.269, 18 HR, 60 RBI) joined talented outfielders Glenallen Hill (18 HR) and Mark Whiten (.254, 73 runs) in a solid lineup. Pitching ace Charles Nagy (17-10, 2.96, 169 Ks) was one of the AL's best all year, but the rest of the Tribe's starting rotation was weak. The bullpen was tough with Steve Olin (8-5, 2.34, 29 saves), Derek Lilliquist (5-3, 1.75), and Ted Power (3-3, 2.54) providing solid performances all year.

Manager

Mike Hargrove	W	L	PCT
Major League record	108	139	.437
With Indians	108	139	.437
1992 record	76	86	.469

Coaches: Rick Adair, Ken Bolek, Dom Chiti, Ron Clark, Jose Morales, Dave Nelson, Jeff Newman

Five-Year Finishes

88	89	90	91	92
6	6	4	7	T4

Five Year Record: 361-449; .446
Rank: 14th in AL; 25th in ML

Chairman of the Board & CEO:
  Richard E. Jacobs
Vice Chairman of the Board: David H. Jacobs
VP, Baseball Operations: John Hart
Director, Player Dev.: Dan O'Dowd
Director, Scouting: Mickey White
Address
Boudreau Boulevard
Cleveland, OH 44114

Ballparks

League Park 1901-1946;
  Cleveland Stadium 1932-present.
Capacity: 74,483
1992 Attendance: 1,224,094
Surface: natural grass

Left field fence: 364 feet
Center field fence: 404 feet
Right field fence: 360 feet
Left-center fence: 375 feet
Right-center fence: 370 feet

Team History

Baseball fans of the Cleveland Indians can testify to the fact that baseball can break your heart. In their earlier days, the Tribe was an American League power. Cleveland won the AL pennant in 1920 and again in '48, taking the World Championship trophy both times. Six years later, they set a league record for wins (111), en route to the 1954 pennant. Since that time, there has been little to cheer about. Frustration has been the constant companion of the

Indians. Since 1969, the Tribe has finished in last place eight times and second to last nine times. In 1990, the Cleveland fans almost had a glimpse at the top half of the standings, finishing fourth in the AL East. Reality set in again in 1991, and the Indians plummeted to 105 losses, a new team record. Showing a little muscle in '92, they bounced back to a fourth place finish in their league.

NEW YORK YANKEES
76-86, .469, 20 Manager: Buck Showalter

He's b-a-a-a-a-a-c-k. That's right, folks, Mr. Congeniality himself, George Steinbrenner, returns to the helm of the Yankees for the 1993 season, guaranteeing some excitement in the Bronx, regardless of how poorly the Yankees play. In 1992, that was slightly less pathetically than in previous years. New York finished above fifth place (tied for fourth with Cleveland) for the first time since 1987 and was actually in contention until the summer started. Despite a pretty good job by rookie manager Buck Showalter, the Yanks were done in by an awful pitching staff (team ERA 4.21), untimely injuries, and drug problems. Only one Yankee regular starter, Scott Sanderson (12-11, 4.93), had a record above .500. The loss of Mike

Witt (elbow) for the season hurt, as did the suspensions of Pascual Perez and reliever Steve Howe for drug use. Perez's brother, Melido (13-16, 2.87), had some hard luck. The offense was fine. Don Mattingly (.288, 14 HR, 86 RBI) had a healthy year, and second-year man Bernie Williams (.280) showed promise in the outfield. Free-agent acquisition Danny Tartabull (.266, 25 HR, 85 RBI) had an off year, as did Mel Hall (.280, 15 HR, 81 RBI), but Roberto Kelly (.272) continued to impress in the outfield, while hustling infielder Andy Stankiewicz (.268) was a fan favorite. Charlie Hayes (18 HR) was adequate at third, but catcher Matt Nokes slumped, despite his 22 homers.

Manager			
Buck Showalter	W	L	PCT
Major League record	76	86	.469
With Yankees	76	86	.469
1992 record	76	86	.469

Coaches: Clete Boyer, Tony Cloninger, Mark Connor, Frank Howard, Russ "Monk" Meyer, Ed Napoleon, Rick Down

Ballparks

American League Park 1901-1902; Hilltop Park 1903-1912; Polo Grounds 1913-1922; Shea Stadium 1974-1975; Yankee Stadium 1923-1973, 1976-present
Capacity: 57,545

1992 Attendance: 1,748,737
Surface: natural grass
Left field fence: 318 feet
Center field fence: 408 feet
Right field fence: 314 feet
Left-center fence: 399 feet
Right-center fence: 385 feet

Five-Year Finishes				
88	89	90	91	92
5	5	7	5	T4

Five-Year Record: 373-435; .462
Rank: Tied 11th in AL; tied 22nd in ML

Principal Owner: George M. Steinbrenner
Man. Gen. Part.: Daniel R. McCarthy
Ex. VP & COO: Leonard L. Kleinman
Vice President: Joseph A. Malloy
Senior VP: Arthur Richman
VP and GM: Gene Michael
VP, Player Development and Scouting: Brian Sabean

Address
Yankee Stadium
Bronx, NY 10451

Team History

Easily baseball's showcase franchise, the Yankees have won a record 22 World Championships and have fielded some of the game's greatest teams, players, and managers. The 1927 "Murderer's Row" unit featured immortals Babe Ruth and Lou Gehrig, while Hall of Famers like Joe DiMaggio, Yogi Berra, and Whitey Ford dotted the rosters in the 1930s, '40s, and '50s. The 1977 and '78 championship squads boasted Reggie Jackson and Catfish Hunter. The '80s saw the Yankees twist in the

wind, partly due to the see-saw changes in managerial staff. Owner George Steinbrenner had Billy Martin on a revolving door when it came to the skipper position. During Steinbrenner's previous 17 years as an owner, there were 17 different managers. By 1990, the once-legendary Yankees were at the bottom of their division. In 1991, they had stepped up to fifth place. A tie for fourth was as good as it got in '92, but the Yankees still had not come close to being the powerhouse team of days past.

DETROIT TIGERS
75-87, .463, 21 Manager: Sparky Anderson

While the 1992 Tigers provided little drama on the field, they certainly kept things interesting off it. By midseason, the club announced that it couldn't meet payroll. Then the franchise was sold from one pizza magnate (Tom Monaghan of Domino's) to another (Mike Ilitch of Little Caesar's). To top it off, Detroit canned its president and C.E.O., Bo Schembechler, by fax. While the front office spun out of control, the team played its usual brand of ridiculous baseball. Detroit hitters smashed a majors-best 182 homers, scored 791 runs—again best in baseball—and struck out 1,055 times, another MLB superlative. Tiger pitchers posted some big numbers of their own, just in the wrong columns. Detroit hurlers combined for baseball's worst team ERA (4.60) and surrendered the most hits

in the majors (1,534). That combination stopped Detroit from contending—unlike 1991. In the end, Detroit sagged to 21 games out and sat in sixth place. Still, sluggers Cecil Fielder (35 HR, 124 RBI), Mickey Tettleton (32 HR, 83 RBI), and Rob Deer (32 HR, 64 RBI) always swung hard, and utility specialist Tony Phillips (.276, 64 RBI) was once again invaluable. Shortstop Travis Fryman (.266, 20 HR, 96 RBI) had another big year, and rookie Scott Livingstone (.282) filled in well after Alan Trammell broke his ankle. Few of the pitchers did the same. Bill Gullickson (14-13, 4.34) and Frank Tanana (13-11, 4.39) hoped for big support each time out. Rookie John Doherty (7-4, 3.88) was a little sharper, while stopper Mike Henneman (3.96, 24 saves) struggled.

Manager			
Sparky Anderson	W	L	PCT
Major League record	1996	1611	.553
With Tigers	1133	1025	.525
1992 record	75	87	.463

Coaches: Billy Consolo, Larry Herndon, Billy Muffett, Gene Roof, Dick Tracewski, Dan Whitmer

Five-Year Finishes

88	89	90	91	92
2	7	3	T2	6

Five-Year Record: 385-425; .475
Rank: 10th in AL; 20th in ML

Owner: Mike Ilitch
Chairman-Chief Executive Officer: James A. Campbell
Sr. VP-Player Procurement & Development: Joseph A. McDonald
Vice President-Scouting: Joe Klein
Sr. Vice President-Major League Personnel: Jerry A. Walker
Dir. of Player Dev.: Mike Jorgensen

Address
Tiger Stadium
Detroit, MI 48216

Ballparks

Bennett Park 1901-1911; Tiger Stadium 1912-present
Capacity: 52,416
1992 Attendance: 1,423,963
Surface: natural grass

Left field fence: 340 feet
Center field fence: 440 feet
Right field fence: 325 feet
Left-center fence: 365 feet
Right-center fence: 375 feet

Team History

With a winning percentage of over .500, the Tigers have been perennial contenders since their inception in 1901. They have finished last only five times and have never had more than four consecutive losing seasons. The franchise has won 11 titles and brought World Championships to the Motor City in 1935, 1945, 1968, and 1984. The Tigers brought a feisty manager on board in mid-'79. Sparky Anderson provided a mature, seasoned presence, shaping the De-

troit club into a formidable force in less than five years. The Tigers were a mighty power in '84, boasting big arms on offense and defense. The next two years, however, they dipped down to third in their division. In 1987, they roared back to win the AL pennant, but could not grab the grand prize. In 1989, they bottomed out, finishing last in their division. The strength shown from 1944 through '87 has yet to be apparent in the '90s.

BOSTON RED SOX

73-89, .451, 23 Manager: Butch Hobson

There is a temptation to revile the BoSox for their first last-place finish since 1932. After all, the team's offense—its long-time staple—was dreadful. And its pitching—a long-time headache—was again shaky. But this year's Sox sad song is one filled with injuries. Boston first baseman Carlos Quintana suffered a broken arm in an automobile accident before spring training and didn't play a single game. Starting outfielders Ellis Burks (back) and Mike Greenwell (elbow) together missed a total of 190 games, neither playing after June 25. Those three combined to drive in 210 runs in 1991, and their absence went a long way toward explaining why Boston finished next-to-last in runs scored in the AL. Throw in a dismal year by Wade Boggs (.259) and a poor season by bankrupt slugger Jack Clark (.210, 5 HR), and it's a wonder the Red Sox didn't fall further off the pace. Of course, Roger Clemens (18-11, 2.41, 208 Ks) was again marvelous, though he stumbled in September and cost himself another Cy Young Award. Free-agent acquisition Frank Viola (13-12, 3.44) was inconsistent, and the rest of the starting rotation was poor—as usual. Boston even gutted its bullpen by dishing closer Jeff Reardon to Atlanta for a pair of prospects. There were a few offensive highlights. Rookies Scott Cooper (.276) and Bob Zupcic (.276) had solid seasons, and Tom Brunansky (.266, 15 HR, 74 RBI) provided some power, but that was about it.

Manager:			
Butch Hobson	**W**	**L**	**PCT**
Major League record	73	89	.451
With Red Sox	73	89	.451
1992 record	73	89	.451
Coaches: Gary Allenson, Al Bumbry, Rick Burleson, Rich Gale			

Five-Year Finishes			
88	89	90	91	92
1	3	1	T2	7

Five-Year Record: 417-393; .515
Rank: Tied 4th in AL; tied 7th in ML

Ballparks

Huntington Avenue Grounds
  1901-1911; Fenway Park
  1912-present
Capacity: 33,925
1992 Attendance: 2,468,574
Surface: natural grass

Left field fence: 315 feet
Center field fence: 390 feet
Right field fence: 302 feet
Left-center fence: 379 feet
Right-center fence: 380 feet

President: John L. Harrington
Owner and General Partner:
  Haywood C. Sullivan
Sr. VP & GM: James "Lou" Gorman
VP Baseball Dev.: Edward M. Kasko
Assistant GM: Elaine C. Steward
Director of Minor League
  Operations: Edward P. Kenney
Address
4 Yawkey Way
Boston, MA 02215

Team History

Long-suffering Beantown fans wish they could be transported back to the early 1900s, when the BoSox were winners—five pennants, four world titles. But after selling Babe Ruth to the Yankees in 1920, the franchise fell fast. The Sox rebounded in the 1940s and '50s, but didn't bounce back quite enough, save a pennant in '46. The arrival of young blood in the '60s helped elevate the team to a pennant in '67. Not until 1975, and the appearance of more youngsters, did the sagging Sox get another lift. They stretched out a run at a World Championship in '75, only to lose to the Reds in the seventh game. Again in 1986, exceptional talent brought the BoSox a pennant, but not even the likes of Wade Boggs and Roger Clemens could overcome what seems to be the perpetual close-but-no-cigar syndrome. Mid-'88 saw Joe Morgan steer the Sox to a division title, only to get swept by the A's in the LCS.

OAKLAND ATHLETICS
96-66, .593 Manager: Tony LaRussa

Talk about a good month! If Oakland could have an August like it had in 1992 every season, the A's would be perpetual AL West champs. Oakland turned a half-game deficit into a seven-game lead during summer's stickiest 31 days and held off Minnesota for the division crown. Though the A's became the first-ever playoff victim of the Toronto Blue Jays, the divisional championship was their fourth in the last five years. After various player changes, 1992 may have been the Athletics' swan song. Still, manager Tony LaRussa earned his Manager of the Year award as he coaxed the title out of an injury-depleted, controversy-ridden ballclub. Of course, LaRussa can't take much credit for the superb performance of Cy Young and MVP winner Dennis Eckersley (7-1, 1.91, 51 saves). LaRussa also can't take complete credit for returning slugger Mark McGwire (.268, 42 HR, 104 RBI) to his pre-1991 production levels. LaRussa did, however, manage a team that used the disabled list a club-record 22 times and was able to shuffle outfielders, pitchers, and shortstops, all the while winning 96 games. Joining Eckersley on the hurling honor roll were Bob Welch (11-7, 3.27), Dave Stewart (12-10, 3.66), and surprising Ron Darling (15-10, 3.66). McGwire's prodigious production was supplemented by Rickey Henderson (.283, 15 HR, 48 SB), catcher Terry Steinbach (.279, 12 HR), and outfielder Willie Wilson (.270, 28 SB). Role players Jerry Browne, Lance Blankenship, Mike Bordick, and Randy Ready were also solid throughout the year.

Manager

Tony LaRussa

	W	L	PCT
Major League record	1134	949	.544
With Athletics	612	439	.582
1992 record	96	66	.593

Coaches: Dave Duncan, Art Kusnyer, Dave McKay, Tommie Reynolds, Greg Luzinski

Ballparks

Philadelphia: Columbia Park 1901-1908; Shibe Park 1909-1954. **Kansas City:** Municipal Stadium 1955-1967. **Oakland:** Oakland-Alameda County Coliseum 1968-present
Capacity: 47,313

1992 Attendance: 2,494,160
Surface: natural grass
Left field fence: 330 feet
Center field fence: 400 feet
Right field fence: 330 feet
Left-center fence: 375 feet
Right-center fence: 375 feet

Five-Year Finishes

88	89	90	91	92
1	1	1	4	1

Five-Year Record: 486-324; .600
Rank: 1st in AL; 1st in ML

Owner/Managing General Partner:
Walter A. Haas, Jr.
President & CEO: Walter J. Haas
VP, Baseball Op.: Sandy Alderson
Dir. of Player Development: Keith Lieppman
Director of Baseball Administration: Walt Jocketty
Director of Scouting: Dick Bogard

Address
Oakland-Alameda County Coliseum
Oakland, CA 94621

Team History

The Oakland Athletics have had a colorful existence. Formed in 1901 in Philadelphia, the A's captured World Championships in 1910, '11, '13, '29, and '30, before embarking on a dismal period that saw the franchise move to Kansas City. Then in 1968, Charlie Finley had a plan. He wanted to move his team to Oakland, make them a success, and sell lots of tickets. His Oakland team became a reality and the winning began—just not in front of as large an audience as had been hoped. World titles came in 1972 through '74. After winning the division championship in the strike-affected '81 season, area businesses took over the reins. Packing the team with power and talent, the Athletics won pennants from 1988 through '90, with a World Championship in 1989. Topping their division again in '92, Oakland could remain a force to be dealt with throughout the '90s.

MINNESOTA TWINS
90-72, .556, 6 Manager: Tom Kelly

There were no miracles for the 1992 Twins. Fresh off its storybook, last-to-first World Series Championship of '91, Minnesota was unable to hold its early American League West lead and slid into second place. The Twins held the lead from May into August, but their pitching sagged late. The Minnesota team found itself unable to win key games against eventual division champ Oakland. Despite a late-season charge, Minnesota fell short. Center fielder and Gold Glover Kirby Puckett (.329, 19 HR, 110 RBI), arguably the game's best player, declared his free-agency after the season. Shane Mack (.315, 16 HR, 75 RBI) had another solid season, as did catcher Brian Harper (.307,

73 RBI). Second baseman Chuck Knoblauch (.297) proved that his sensational rookie year was no fluke, and second-year outfielder Pedro Munoz (.270, 12 HR, 71 RBI) was a pleasant surprise. Though first baseman Kent Hrbek (.244, 15 HR) struggled with injuries to both shoulders, he was steady, as was outfielder Chili Davis (.288, 12 HR, 66 RBI). The pitching staff deserves an honorable mention. John Smiley (16-9, 3.21) came over in a preseason trade with Pittsburgh and became the ace, while Scott Erickson (13-12, 3.40) and Kevin Tapani (16-11, 3.97) were again reliable. Closer Rick Aguilera (2.84, 41 saves) was one of the league's best.

Manager			
Tom Kelly	**W**	**L**	**PCT**
Major League record	527	468	.530
With Twins	527	468	.530
1992 record	90	72	.556
Coaches: Terry Crowley, Ron Gardenhire, Rich Stelmaszek, Dick Such, Wayne Terwilliger			

Ballparks

Washington: American League Park 1901-1910; Griffith Stadium 1911-1960.
Minnesota: Metropolitan Stadium 1961-1981; Hubert H. Humphrey Metrodome 1982-present.
Capacity: 55,883

1992 Attendance: 2,482,428
Stationary Dome
Surface: Artificial Turf
Left field fence: 343 feet
Center field fence: 408 feet
Right field fence: 327 feet
Left-center fence: 385 feet
Right-center fence: 367 feet

Five-Year Finishes

88	89	90	91	92
2	5	7	1	2

Five-Year Record: 430-380; 531
Rank: 3rd in AL; 4th in ML

Owner: Carl R. Pohlad
President: T. Geron (Jerry) Bell
Executive VP, General Manager: Andy MacPhail
Vice President, Player Personnel: Terry Ryan
Director of Minor Leagues: Jim Rantz
Director of Scouting: Larry Corrigan

Address
501 Chicago Avenue South
Minneapolis, MN 55415

Team History

As the Washington Senators, this franchise mixed a few highs—three pennants and a 1924 World Championship—with years of deep lows. After a move to the Twin Cities in 1960, the team won the 1965 pennant but slid out of contention for most of the next two decades. Perhaps all they needed was to be sheltered from the elements. The team moved indoors and captured the World Series in '87 with a young team of sluggers. In 1990, they finished last in

their division. Then, as if a magic wand had been waved over the Metrodome, the Twins came back with a vengeance in '91. They posted a regular-season record of 95-67, and took on Toronto in the ALCS. Winning the pennant, the Twins went seven games in the World Series, overcoming the Atlanta Braves for all the marbles. Showing their strength again in '92, the Twins finished second in their division.

CHICAGO WHITE SOX

86-76, .531, 10 Manager: Gene Lamont

If Chicago had been able to start playing its 162 games on August 1, there is a good chance some postseason banners would have been flapping in the Comiskey Park breeze. Staggering out of the gate, the ChiSox had a 36-25 record after the season's first four months. They made a weak run at the AL West title but, for the second season in a row, failed to live up to their vast potential. Chicago was never downright bad, and its team statistics look pretty sharp. But the Sox' early and mid-season inconsistency rendered the late-season charge moot. Manager Gene Lamont made his first season as the White Sox' skipper at least end above .500. Though Chicago scored plenty of runs (738—sixth in baseball), the Sox pitching staff, other than Jack McDowell, was weak. McDowell (20-10, 3.18, 174 Ks), also known for his off-season rock career and menacing facial hair, posted Cy Young-like numbers. If you looked any deeper than Black Jack, though, it was bleak. Stopper extraordinaire Bobby Thigpen (22 saves, 4.75) slumped badly, and no Sox starter other than Greg Hibbard (10-7, 4.40) won more games than he lost. Of course, with guys like Frank Thomas (.323, 24 HR, 115 RBI, 108 runs, 122 BB), George Bell (25 HR, 112 RBI), and Gold Glover Robin Ventura (.282, 16 HR, 93 RBI) in the lineup, Sox pitchers couldn't sue for lack of support. Craig Grebeck (.268) filled in well for injured Ozzie Guillen, but Steve Sax (.236) faltered, and Tim Raines' (.294) production sagged until it was too late.

Manager			
Gene Lamont	**W**	**L**	**PCT**
Major League record	86	76	.531
With White Sox	86	76	.531
1992 record	86	76	.531

Coaches: Terry Bevington, Jackie Brown, Walt Hriniak, Doug Mansolino, Joe Nossek, Mike Squires

Ballparks

South Side Park 1901-1910;
  Comiskey Park 1911-1990;
  New Comiskey Park 1991-present
Capacity: 44,177
1992 Attendance: 2,681,156

Surface: natural grass
Left field fence: 347 feet
Center field fence: 400 feet
Right field fence: 347 feet
Left-center fence: 375 feet
Right-center fence: 375 feet

Five-Year Finishes

88	89	90	91	92
5	7	2	2	3

Five-Year Record: 407-401; .504
Rank: 6th in AL; 11th in ML

Chairman: Jerry Reinsdorf
Vice Chairman: Eddie Einhorn
Executive VP: Howard Pizer
Senior VP, Major League Operations: Ron Schueler
Senior VP, Baseball: Jack Gould
Director of Baseball Operations: Daniel Evans
Director of Scouting: Duane Shaffer
Address
333 W. 35th Street
Chicago, IL 60616

Team History

Although the Sox' 91-year history has been a roller coaster ride, no one could ever call it boring. They won the AL pennant in their first year (1901) and captured World Championships in 1906 and 1917. Although baseball got a black eye when the infamous "Black Sox Scandal" hit after the 1919 World Series, the Sox found themselves stripped of their stars. A drought began after this unfortunate event and the ChiSox didn't win another pennant for 40 years.

In 1959, under the ownership of Bill Veeck, the Sox experienced a resurgence and won their division title. An AL West title in 1983 is the highest level the Sox have reached in recent years, although there have been flashes of brilliance. After suffering through six less-than-stellar years, the Sox finished second in their league in 1990 and 1991. The Sox also got a new home in 1991, located just across the street from old Comiskey.

TEXAS RANGERS

77-85, .475, 19 Managers: Bobby Valentine (45-41); Toby Harrah (32-44)

The 1992 Texas Rangers story is a familiar one to AL West fans. High hopes dominate the preseason. Mediocre play dooms the regular season. The Rangers' annual slide into the middle of the division's pack was rife with all the usual suspects: poor pitching, weak defense, and a key injury or two. In 1992, the Rangers added another symptom—bad hitting. The team batting average for the Rangers dropped to .250, and no regular player hit higher than .278. The repeat performance cost manager Bobby Valentine his job—even though he had a winning record (45-41) at the time. Replacement Toby Harrah didn't last long, as he was succeeded by Kevin Kennedy at the season's end. Several Ranger regulars will no longer be part of the lineup for '93. Among them are slugger Ruben Sierra (.278, 17 HR, 87 RBI), starter Bobby Witt (10-14), and closer Jeff Russell (30 saves). They were all dealt to Oakland for mega-talent/attitude problem Jose Canseco (.244, 26 HR, 87 RBI). Who knows how long ageless iron man hurler Nolan Ryan (5-9, 3.72, 157 Ks) will labor? Kevin Brown (21-11, 3.32, 173 Ks) and Jose Guzman (16-11, 3.66, 179 Ks) each had big years in '92. So did second-year outfielder Juan Gonzalez (.260, 43 HR, 109 RBI), who led the majors in homers. But Rafael Palmeiro's production (.268, 22 HR, 85 RBI) slipped, and '91 batting champ Julio Franco was hampered by a bad right knee. Second-year man Dean Palmer (26 HR, 72 RBI) showed some pop at third base.

Manager			
Kevin Kennedy	**W**	**L**	**PCT**
Major League record	0	0	.000
With Rangers	0	0	.000
1992 record	0	0	.000
Coaches: Dave Oliver, Willie Upshaw, Mickey Hatcher, Jackie Moore, Claude Osteen			

Five-Year Finishes

88	89	90	91	92
6	4	3	3	4

Five-Year Record: 398-411; .492

Rank: 9th in AL; 18th in ML

General Partners: George W. Bush, Edward W. "Rusty" Rose

President: J. Thomas Schieffer

VP, GM: Thomas A. Grieve

Assistant GM, Player Personnel and Scouting: Sandy Johnson

Assistant GM: Wayne Krivsky

Director, Player Dev.: Marty Scott

Address
P.O. Box 91111
1250 Copeland Road
Arlington, TX 76004

Ballparks

Washington: Griffith Stadium 1961; Robert F. Kennedy Stadium 1962-1971; **Texas:** Arlington Stadium 1972-present
Capacity: 43,521
1992 Attendance: 2,198,231

Surface: natural grass
Left field fence: 330 feet
Center field fence: 400 feet
Right field fence: 330 feet
Left-center fence: 380 feet
Right-center fence: 380 feet

Team History

What can you expect from a team that began as the reincarnation of the Washington Senators? In the three decades since its inception in 1961 in the nation's capital, this franchise has won no titles and has rarely managed to sneak above .500. They circled the wagons in 1972 and headed West for Arlington. Racked by instability, the Texas Rangers have become an exercise in futility. Billy Martin, taking a stab at making something happen, took the team as far as second place in 1974. The team had been worked so hard, though, that by mid-'75 they fizzled out. In 1977, four different managers attempted to take over the helm. Lack of funds forced the talent to go elsewhere, ripping any hopes of recovery out by the seams. Since the move in '72, the team has only reached second place in the AL West four times.

CALIFORNIA ANGELS

72-90 .425, 24 Managers: John Wathan (38-47); Marcel Lachemann (3-1); Buck Rodgers (31-42)

When some teams use the word, "disaster" to describe a poor season, they do so metaphorically, in order to dramatize a season's worth of wan performances on the diamond. When the California Angels employ the term as a description for 1992, they use it literally. Fans might consider the Angels' fifth-place finish or club record 14 different disabled-list entries disastrous enough, but those pale in the light of the team's frightful bus crash May 21 along the New Jersey Turnpike. The early-morning wreck knocked manager Buck Rodgers out of the dugout for three months and shook the whole franchise. However, California stumbled through the full 162-game schedule, feeling the effects of a lousy farm system and a flock of ineffective veterans. In '92, the team's vaunted pitching staff didn't deliver. None of the regular starters posted a record above .500, and the team batting average of .243 was the lowest in the American League. Hard-luck Jim Abbott (7-15, 2.77) and Mark Langston (13-14, 3.66, 174 Ks) led the starters. Young Joe Grahe (21 saves) became the bullpen stopper while Bryan Harvey nursed a sore elbow. Outfielder Luis Polonia (.286, 51 SBs) provided some spark atop the California lineup, while Rene Gonzales (.277), Luis Sojo (.272), and rookie outfielder Chad Curtis (.259, 10 HR) showed promise. Veteran third baseman Gary Gaetti led the team in homers with 12, although this mark was hardly a cause for celebration.

Manager Buck Rodgers	W	L	PCT
Major League record	726	690	.513
With Angels	52	60	.464
1992 record	31	42	.425

Coaches: Rod Carew, Bobby Knopp, Chuck Hernandez, Ken Macha, Jimmy Reese, Rick Turner, John Wathan

Five-Year Finishes				
88	89	90	91	92
4	3	4	7	T5

Five-Year Record: 399-411; .493
Rank: 8th in AL; tied 16th in ML

Chairman of the Board: Gene Autry
Pres. & CEO: Richard M. Brown
Executive VP: Jackie Autry
VP, Treasurer & CFO: Ron Shirley
Sr. VP, Base. Op.: Daniel F. O'Brien
Sr. VP/Dir. Play. Pers.: Whitey Herzog
Director, Minor League Operations: Bill Bavasi
Director, Scouting: Bob Fontaine, Jr.

Address
P.O. Box 2000
Anaheim, CA 92803

Ballparks

Los Angeles: Wrigley Field
1961; Dodger Stadium 1962-
1965. **Anaheim:** Anaheim
Stadium 1966-present
Surface: natural grass
1992 Attendance: 2,065,444

Left field fence: 370 feet
Center field fence: 404 feet
Right field fence: 370 feet
Left-center fence: 386 feet
Right-center fence: 386 feet

Team History

Cowboy singer Gene Autry gave birth to the Angels in Los Angeles in 1961. His Halos, however, have yet to ride off into the sunset with an American League pennant—much less a World Championship title—slung over their shoulders. Although the California team managed to finish third in 1964, they faltered for the next 14 years. They spent freely when the era of free-agency began in the mid-'70s. This strategy seemed to pay off for them a few years later. In 1979, they won a divisional title, using a team core of veteran free agents. The Angels did manage to repeat the feat in 1982 and '86, but have yet to progress beyond that point. The loss in 1986 was perhaps the most painful of all as the California team was only one pitch away from clinching the pennant when fate stepped in. The Halos once again walked off empty handed, losing this time to Boston. In the '90s, the Angels have only finished as high as .500 once.

KANSAS CITY ROYALS
72-90, .444, 24 Manager: Hal McRae

Few Royals fans will be able to forget 1992—for a number of reasons. Optimists will recall George Brett rallying late and reaching the 3,000 hit plateau. They'll also think of KC's first two months of the season and how the team stood near .500. Chances are, however, that the pessimists will have more to remember. Take, for instance, KC's 72 wins, its lowest non-strike total since 1970. Also consider the Royals' fifth-place finish (tied with California), the team's third consecutive second-division performance in the AL West. Royals' batters managed only 75 homers in '92, next-to-last in the majors. Injuries also forced 11 different players to spend significant time out of action. Those who did play produced with varying success.

Pitcher Kevin Appier (15-8, 2.46, 150 Ks) was marvelous, as were relievers Jeff Montgomery (2.18, 39 saves) and Rusty Meacham (10-4, 2.74). New York Met import Gregg Jefferies (.285, 10 HR, 72 RBI) rebounded from a slow start, as did Keith Miller (.284), another former Met. Wally Joyner (.269, 9 HR, 66 RBI), acquired from California, was not nearly as productive as in previous years. Another disappointing performance was logged in by Kevin McReynolds (.247, 13 HR, 49 RBI). Catcher Mike Macfarlane's power (17 HR) was a pleasant surprise, but pitcher Mark Gubicza's DL time (75 games) was not. That left Hipolito Pichardo (9-6, 3.95) as KC's second starter—hardly reason for rejoicing.

Manager			
Hal McRae	W	L	PCT
Major League record	138	148	.483
With Royals	138	148	.483
1992 record	72	90	.444

Coaches: Glenn Ezell, Adrian Garrett, Guy Hansen, Lynn Jones, Bruce Kison, Lee May

Five-Year Finishes			
88	89	90	91	92
3	2	6	6	T5

Five-Year Record: 405-403; .501
Rank: 7th in AL; 13th in ML

Chairman of the Board/Owner: Ewing Kauffman
President: Joe Burke
Exec. VP & GM: Herk Robinson
Vice President-Director of Player Personnel: Joe Klein
Director of Scouting: Art Stewart
Director of Minor League Operations: Steve Schryver

Address
1 Royal Way
Kansas City, MO 64129

Ballparks

Municipal Stadium 1969-1972; Royals Stadium 1973-present
Capacity: 40,625
1992 Attendance: 1,867,689
Surface: artificial turf

Left field fence: 330 feet
Center field fence: 410 feet
Right field fence: 330 feet
Left-center fence: 385 feet
Right-center fence: 385 feet

Team History

The Kansas City Royals came into existence in 1968 to fill a void left by the departed A's. In no time at all, the Royals began to make themselves known. Moving quickly to the top of the AL West, they won divisional titles from 1976 through '78. The team took its first pennant in 1980. In 1984, they took another AL West crown. They went on to win a World Championship in 1985, overcoming 3-1 deficits in the playoffs and World Series. The Royals continued to show their strength from 1986 through '89 by remaining in second or third place in their division. In 1990, however, they plummeted to the sixth spot in the AL West. This fast, hard tumble came as a surprise to all who were used to the Kansas City team being contenders. The Royals hadn't finished this low in the standings since 1974. They retained this berth through 1992, having few bright stars to console them in their collapse.

SEATTLE MARINERS
64-98, .395, 32 Manager: Bill Plummer

If last season's first-ever above-.500 finish earned Jim Lefebrve the boot, guess what 1992's dismal, 64-98 record got Bill Plummer? That's right—a pink slip. The seventh-place finish was weak, even by pathetic Mariners' standards. As a matter of fact, it tied for the fourth-worst in franchise history. By season's end, the M's were the worst team in all of baseball, ending a full 19 games below their 1991 tally. The breakdown was thorough. The Mariners tried 11 different starting pitchers—before the All-Star break. Slugger Kevin Mitchell (.286, 9 HR, 67 RBI), acquired before the season from San Francisco, was a huge disappointment at the plate and missed 43 games with injuries. Fireballing pitcher

Randy Johnson (12-14, 3.77, 241 Ks) may have led the league in strikeouts but was inconsistent all year. Seattle's bullpen "stopper," Mike Schooler, posted just 13 saves, and the team ERA of 4.55 was only better than Detroit's. One of the few and far between positive aspects for 1992 was third baseman Edgar Martinez (.342, 18 HR, 73 RBI). Always dangerous AL batting champ and Gold Glover Ken Griffey Jr. (.308, 27 HR, 103 RBI,) and shortstop Omar Vizquel (.294) were two more checks on the plus side. Rookie Dave Fleming (17-10, 3.39) was a revelation on the mound for Seattle, and Jay Buhner (25 HR, 79 RBI) was a solid power source.

Manager			
Lou Piniella	W	L	PCT
Major League record	479	424	.530
With Mariners	0	0	.000
1992 record (with Reds)	90	72	.556

Coaches: Sammy Ellis, John McLaren, Lee Elia, Ken Griffey Sr., Sam Perlozzo, Sammy Mejias

Ballparks

Kingdome 1977-present
Capacity: 59,702
1992 Attendance: 1,651,367
Stationary Dome
Surface: artificial turf
Left field fence: 331 feet

Center field fence: 405 feet
Right field fence: 312 feet
Left-center fence: 372 feet
Right-center fence: 349 feet

Five-Year Finishes

88	89	90	91	92
7	6	5	5	7

Five-Year Record: 365-444; .451
Rank: 13th in AL; 24th in ML

General Partner: Hiroshi Yamauchi
Vice President, Baseball Operations:
  Woody Woodward
VP, Scouting & Player Development:
  Roger Jongewaard
Director of Baseball Administration:
  Lee Pelekoudas
Farm Director: Jim Beattie
Coordinator of Minor League
  Instruction: Jim Skaalen

Address
P.O. Box 4100
Seattle, WA 98104

Team History

When the Seattle Pilots flew out of the Pacific Northwest, Seattle was a little more than miffed to be stranded. Demanding a team to call their own, they were awarded the 1977 expansion team, the Seattle Mariners. The highest position the Mariners have achieved in the American League West standings is fourth place. They have only reached this rung twice, first in 1982 and again in 1987. In 1989, they claimed their first-ever All-Star selection, Ken Griffey Jr. The

Mariners posted their only winning season thus far in 1991. The 83-79 record was, however, still well off the division-leading Minnesota Twins' mark. In 1992, the Seattle franchise saw a complete reversal of the previous season's efforts, finishing in the cellar again. The Mariners are one of only two teams—joining the Rangers—to never win a division championship or a pennant. The Mariners have brought little joy to fans in the Pacific Northwest.

ATLANTA BRAVES
98-64, .605 Manager: Bobby Cox

In 1991, Atlanta's rise from the cellar to the World Series was considered a miracle, a fluke. The Braves' trip to the fall classic a year later was hardly surprising, rather it reflected the work of a talented, young team. Fans watched the Braves go from a slow start to a division title and another chance at baseball's highest honor. There were all kinds of heroes, but many believed the season belonged to a little-known reserve catcher named Francisco Cabrera. His two-out, two-run single in the bottom of the ninth propelled Atlanta past Pittsburgh in the seventh game of the NLCS. Of course, Cabrera wouldn't have had a chance at his heroics if the Braves hadn't been such a good team during the season. Starters Tom Glavine (20-8, 2.76), John Smoltz (15-12, 2.85, 215 Ks),

Charlie Leibrandt (15-7, 3.36), Steve Avery (11-11, 3.20), and Pete Smith (7-0, 2.15) comprised the majors' best starting rotation. Once again, third baseman Terry Pendleton (.311, 21 HR, 105 RBI) was invaluable, as was center fielder Otis Nixon (.294, 41 SBs). Right fielder David Justice (21 HR, 72 RBI) overcame a dreadful start, and Ron Gant (17 HR, 80 RBI) was productive, despite a drop in his average. There were plenty of other contributors, the products of manager Bobby Cox's shrewd personnel manipulation. Deion Sanders (.304, 26 SBs) proved he was more than just a curiosity, and second baseman Jeff Blauser (.262, 14 HR) and first baseman Sid Bream (.261, 61 RBI) fit well into their platoon assignments.

Manager			
Bobby Cox	**W**	**L**	**PCT**
Major League record	853	804	.515
With Braves	498	512	.493
1992 record	98	64	.605
Coaches: Jim Beauchamp, Pat Corrales, Clarence Jones, Leo Mazzone, Jimy Williams			

Five-Year Finishes

88	89	90	91	92
6	6	6	1	1

Five-Year Record: 374-432; .464
Rank: 11th in NL; 21st in ML

Chairman of the Board: William C. Bartholomay
President: Stanley H. Kasten
Senior VP and Assistant to the President: Henry L. Aaron
Executive VP & GM: John Schuerholz
Assistant GM: Dean Taylor
Director of Scouting and Player Development: Chuck LaMar
Address
521 Capitol Avenue SW
Atlanta, GA 30312

Ballparks

Boston: South End Grounds
1871-1914; Braves Field
1914-1952. Milwaukee:
County Stadium 1953-1965.
Atlanta: Fulton County
Stadium 1966-present
Capacity: 52,013

1992 Attendance: 3,077,400
Surface: natural grass
Left field fence: 330 feet
Center field fence: 402 feet
Right field fence: 330 feet
Left-center fence: 385 feet
Right-center fence: 385 feet

Team History

The Braves began in the National Association in 1871 as the Boston Red Stockings. After winning four NA pennants and joining the National League in 1876, the Braves flourished and dominated the NL in the 1890s (winning five pennants). Money woes (brought on in part by the AL's Red Sox) caused five decades of misery to follow, broken only by the "Miracle Braves" of 1914 and the pennant winners of 1948. Boston loved the Red Sox, so the Braves

moved to Milwaukee in 1953. The Spahn- and Aaron-led club won a World Championship in '57 and a pennant in '58. The Braves were the first club to shift twice, moving to Atlanta in 1966. Division championships in 1969 and 1982 brightened otherwise dismal years for the club down south. The worst club in the league in 1990, the Braves drove to the World Series in 1991, losing to the Twins in seven of the most exciting games in fall classic history.

CINCINNATI REDS
90-72, .556, 8 Manager: Lou Piniella

You can blame it on injuries. You can accuse unpredictable Reds owner Marge Schott and her pooch. Maybe it was that typically oppressive weather in the Queen City last August. Or perhaps the Reds just choked. Whatever the reason, the hugely talented and expectation-laden 1992 edition of the Big Red Machine faltered in late summer and staggered to a second-place finish in the NL West. Sure, the Reds made it exciting in September with a nine-game winning streak following the locker room brawl between manager Lou Piniella and wacky reliever Rob Dibble. But folks didn't expect sideshows and futility from Cincinnati. They expected a championship. Why didn't they get one? Start with the pitching. Injuries to Tom Browning (knee), Jose Rijo (elbow), and Greg Swindell (ribs) hurt the Cincinnati

cause. Though Rijo (15-10, 2.56, 171 Ks) and Swindell (12-8, 2.70) still had solid seasons, newcomer Tim Belcher (15-14) was worse than advertised. Dibble (3.07, 25 saves) was inconsistent throughout the second half, though Norm Charlton (4-2, 2.99, 26 saves) produced very well. The field was not without its problems. Third baseman Chris Sabo (.244, 12 HR, 43 RBI) was hampered all year by a bum right ankle, while Hal Morris (.271) slumped without the benefit of an injury excuse. Bip Roberts (.323), on the other hand, was a sparkplug atop the Reds order, and shortstop Barry Larkin (.304, 12 HR, 78 RBI) was again outstanding. Rookie Reggie Sanders (.270) showed promise in center, and catcher Joe Oliver (.270) improved considerably on his 1991 numbers.

Manager Tim Perez	W	L	PCT
Major League record	0	0	.000
With Reds	0	0	.000
1992 record	0	0	.000

Coaches: Larry Rothschild, Dave Bristol, Ron Oester, Dave Miley, Don Gullett

Five-Year Finishes

88	89	90	91	92
2	5	1	5	2

Five-Year Record: 417-392; .515
Rank: 3rd in NL; 6th in ML

President & CEO: Marge Schott
VP & General Manager: Jim Bowden
Assist. GM: Gene Bennett
Controller: Ernie Brubaker
Director Player Development: Chief Bender
Director Scouting: Julian Mock

Address
100 Riverfront Stadium
Cincinnati, OH 45202

Ballparks

Lincoln Park Grounds 1876;
  Avenue Grounds 1876-1879;
  Bank Street Grounds 1880;
  League Park 1890-1901;
  Palace of the Fans 1902-
  1911; Crosley Field 1912-
  1970; Riverfront Stadium
  1970-present.

Capacity: 52,952
1992 Attendance: 2,315,946
Surface: artifical turf
Left field fence: 330 feet
Center field fence: 404 feet
Right field fence: 330 feet
Left-center fence: 375 feet
Right-center fence: 375 feet

Team History

Baseball's first professional team has enjoyed recent history much more than its earlier decades. The Reds won the tainted 1919 World Series but didn't top the baseball world again until 1939. A 1961 pennant was followed by the emergence of the "Big Red Machine." During the '70s, this powerhouse organization finished in first place six times, won four National League pennants, and won the 1975 and '76 World Se-

ries. The '80s were not as kind to the franchise. To add to their woes, longtime team affiliate, Pete Rose, was shrouded in controversy over alleged gambling while involved with the game. In 1990, they proved they had put the scandal behind, rebounding from a fifth place finish the year before, bolting all the way to first. That year they won it all and brought another World Championship crown to Cincinnati.

SAN DIEGO PADRES

82-80, .506, 16 Managers: Greg Riddoch (78-72); Jim Riggleman (4-8)

Let's face it. About the only baseball drama generated in San Diego in the 1992 season was Gary Sheffield's flirtation with the Triple Crown. Granted, the Milwaukee Brewers refugee made headlines and sold tickets with his huge season, but the Padres followed their familiar, post-1984 storyline: impress early, fade late. That performance cost manager Greg Riddoch his job. Though Riddoch had fashioned an above-.500 record during his two-plus seasons near the Mexican border, San Diego never really challenged for the National League West title. And so, Jim Riggleman was appointed to head up the team that lacks pitching and a strong bench. Third baseman Sheffield (.330, 33 HR, 100 RBI), who grabbed the National League batting title for '92, and

first bagger Fred McGriff (.286, 35 HR, 104 RBI) both managed to produce magnificent '92 seasons. Add in right field hitting machine Tony Gwynn (.317), solid shortstop Tony Fernandez, All-Star catcher Benito Santiago, and emerging outfielders Darrin Jackson (17 HR, 70 RBI) and Jerald Clark (12 HR, 58 RBI), and the Padres had a dangerous lineup. The mound, however, did not boast the same magnitude of strength. Andy Benes (13-14, 3.35, 169 Ks) and Bruce Hurst (14-9) performed well, but Ed Whitson left a hole in the rotation as he missed the season with torn elbow ligaments. The Padres bullpen was pretty solid, thanks to closer Randy Myers (38 saves) and set-up men Rich Rodriguez (6-3, 2.37) and Mike Maddux (2.37).

Manager			
Jim Riggleman	W	L	PCT
Major League record	4	8	.333
With Padres	4	8	.333
1992 record	4	8	.333

Coaches: Bruce Kimm, Rob Picciolo, Merv Rettenmund, Mike Roarke, Jim Snyder

Ballpark

Jack Murphy Stadium 1969-present
Capacity: 59,700
1992 Attendance: 1,721,406
Surface: natural grass
Left field fence: 327 feet

Center field fence: 405 feet
Right field fence: 327 feet
Left-center fence: 370 feet
Right-center fence: 370 feet

Five-Year Finishes

88	89	90	91	92
3	2	5	3	3

Five-Year Record: 413-396; .511
Rank: 5th in NL; 10th in ML

Chairman/Managing Partner: Tom Werner
President: Dick Freeman
Executive VP/Baseball Operations & General Manager: Joe McIlvaine
Assistant VP/Baseball Operations & Assistant GM: John Barr
Director/Minor Leagues: Ed Lynch
Director/Scouting: Reggie Waller

Address
P.O. Box 2000
San Diego, CA 92112

Team History

A product of the 1969 expansion with Montreal, the Padres struggled below .500 for their first 15 seasons. Their first winning year—1984—they also became pennant winners. Taking three out of five games in the NLCS, the Padres put away the Chicago Cubs and faced the formidable force that was the Detroit Tigers. Unfortunately, for San Diego fans, the dream season ended in short order with the Tigers snuffing out any championship hopes the

Padres had in only five games. The rest of the '80s featured middle-division finishes. One little glimmer came in 1989, when the Padres finished second in their division, just three games behind the eventual pennant-winning San Francisco Giants. Injuries hit the San Diego team hard in 1990, and it was evidenced in their next-to-last-place finish. They rebounded somewhat in '91 and '92, but again had to settle for being in the middle of the pack both years.

HOUSTON ASTROS

81-81, .500, 17 Manager: Art Howe

If any team seemed destined for a dismal 1992 season, it was Houston. The Astros were fresh off a sixth-place showing in '91 and faced the specter of a 29-day, 26-game midseason road swing, because the Republicans booked the Astrodome for their national convention. Disaster seemed imminent. However, Houston surprised just about everyone. They survived the sojourn and posted the franchise's best record since 1989, finishing at 81-81, an even .500 for the '92 season. In the process, the 'Stros fell one game short of third place, and their 47-34 home record caused a few folks to wonder about what might have happened had the team faced a normal schedule. A solid nucleus of young talent gave Houston fans considerable hope for the future. Among the regu-

lars, only outfielder Pete Incaviglia entered the season with more than four years of big league service. Particularly strong was the Astro infield, led by third baseman Ken Caminiti (.294), second bagger Craig Biggio (.277, 38 SB), and first baseman Jeff Bagwell (.273, 18 HR, 96 RBI). Steve Finley (.292, 44 steals) and Eric Anthony (19 HR, 80 RBI) were solid outfielders, and Incaviglia resurrected his career with a strong contribution. The Astros did hurt a little on the mound, thanks in part to injuries to Jimmy Jones (10-6) and Mark Portugal (6-3 in 16 starts). Pete Harnisch (9-10, 3.70 ERA, 164 Ks) slumped a little, but the Astro bullpen was outstanding, thanks to stopper Doug Jones (11-8, 1.85, 36 saves) and Xavier Hernandez (9-1, 2.11, 7 saves).

Manager

Art Howe	W	L	PCT
Major League record	307	341	.474
With Astros	307	341	.474
1992 record	81	81	.500

Coaches: Bob Cluck, Matt Galante, Rudy Jaramillo, Ed Ott, Tom Spencer

Five-Year Finishes

88	89	90	91	92
5	3	4	6	4

Five-Year Record: 389-421; .480
Rank: 10th in NL; 19th in ML

Chairman of the Board: Drayton McLane Jr.
General Manager: Bill Wood
Assistant General Manager: Bob Watson
Director of Minor League Operations: Fred Nelson
Director of Scouting: Dan O'Brien
Vice President, Marketing: Ted Haracz

Ballparks

Colt Stadium 1962-1964; The Astrodome 1965-present
Capacity: 54,816
1992 Attendance: 1,211,412
Stationary Dome
Surface: artificial turf

Left field fence: 330 feet
Center field fence: 400 feet
Right field fence: 330 feet
Left-center fence: 380 feet
Right-center fence: 380 feet

Team History

Baseball purists may curse the arrival of baseball in Texas. After three years outdoors as the Colt .45s, the franchise became the first to play indoors. In an attempt to beat the heat, the Astrodome was built in 1965. However, growing real grass indoors presented a problem. Astro-Turf arrived the next year. Houston's play, however, hasn't been nearly so innovative. Although they contended for most of the 1970s, the Astros did not win their first division title

until 1980. In strike-split '81, Houston won the second half of the season, but lost to the Los Angeles Dodgers in postseason play. The 'Stros didn't see another division title until 1986, but failed in the attempt for a pennant when the New York Mets prevailed 4 games to 2. The team known best for starting slow and finishing strong hasn't put together a memorable season since. After finishing dead last in 1991, they rebounded to a .500 finish in '92.

SAN FRANCISCO GIANTS
72-90, .444, 26 Manager: Roger Craig

While the baseball world was treated to the season-long drama of exactly where the Giants would play in 1993, the team force-fed its fans a dismal fifth-place finish. If it truly had been the franchise's last performance in windy Candlestick Park, the players and fans would have much preferred that the curtain come down in August, rather than October. The only good thing about the season was that the Giants finished nine games ahead of longtime rival Los Angeles. After that, the pickings were slim. Few Giants were worthy of praise during this past season. Even excellent first baseman Will Clark (.300, 16 HR, 73 RBI) didn't thrill quite so much as he slumped some. The pitching staff was particularly shaky, thanks in part to prolonged arm troubles that stung starters Bill Swift (10-4, 2.08 ERA) and Trevor Wilson (8-14). There were a few highlights sprinkled here and there. Cory Snyder (14 HR, 57 RBI) staged a comeback from a few blasé seasons. In the outfield, Willie McGee (.297) and Mike Felder (.286) were solid. Second baseman Robby Thompson (.260, 14 HR, 49 RBI) had his usual sound year. But Matt Williams' production sagged at third (.227, 20 HR, 66 RBI), compounding the absence of Kevin Mitchell—traded to Seattle before the season got underway. Manager Roger Craig raved about starter John Burkett (13-9, 3.84), but Craig could not have been pleased with a bullpen that produced just 30 saves.

Manager			
Dusty Baker	**W**	**L**	**PCT**
Major League record	0	0	.000
With Giants	0	0	.000
1992 record	0	0	.000

Coaches: Bobby Bonds, Dick Pole, Bob Brenly, Wendell Kim, Bob Lillis

Five-Year Finishes

88	89	90	91	92
4	1	3	4	5

Five-Year Record: 407-403; .502
Rank: 6th in NL; 12th in ML

Chairman: Peter Magowan
General Manager: Bob Quinn
Executive VP: Larry Baer
Senior Vice President: Pat Gallagher
VP/Assistant GM: Brian Sabean
VP, Baseball Operations: Bob Kennedy
VP, Scouting: Bob Fontaine

Address
Candlestick Park
San Francisco, CA 94124

Ballparks

New York: Polo Grounds 1883-1888, 1891-1957; St. George Cricket Grounds 1889-1890. San Francisco: Seals Stadium 1958-1959; Candlestick Park 1960-present
Capacity: 58,000

1992 Attendance: 1,560,998
Surface: natural grass
Left field fence: 335 feet
Center field fence: 400 feet
Right field fence: 335 feet
Left-center fence: 365 feet
Right-center fence: 365 feet

Team History

Few dispute the economic reasons for moving this proud franchise west from New York, but many believe the Giants were never the same after coming to San Francisco. The Giants dominated the NL before 1900, and they won 15 pennants and five World Championships from 1904 through '54. Though they enjoyed 14 consecutive winning seasons after their 1958 move, the Giants won only two more pennants—1962 and '89. They also won their division in 1987, but could not progress beyond that point, losing the pennant to St. Louis in seven games. Since the '90s began, the San Francisco team has given their fans little to cheer about. Dreadful pitching and little offensive pop led the franchise down the path to mediocrity. In 1990, the pitching staff had a combined 4.08 ERA. Again in '91, the Giant hurlers were a disappointment. They were last in the league in ERA for that season. The team by the bay did not fare well in '92, posting a .444 winning percentage and finishing fifth in the NL West.

LOS ANGELES DODGERS

63-99, .389, 35 Manager: Tommy Lasorda

Talk about your disasters! Just one season before, the Dodgers battled Atlanta to the season's last weekend for the NL West title. In 1992, LA was miserable, slumping to last place for the first time since 1905 in a quagmire of ugly play. Tommy Lasorda may bleed Dodger Blue, but his team proved anemic for the '92 season. The Dodgers led the league in errors (174), suffered through 40 one-run losses, and scored a major-league low 548 runs. What galled Dodger fans even more was that high-price tag outfielders Darryl Strawberry (43 games) and Eric Davis (76 games) combined to drive in only 57 runs. Even the Dodgers' vaunted pitching staff was mediocre, boasting no one with more than 11 wins, though Kevin

Gross (8-13) did throw the majors' only no-hitter. By season's end, Lasorda was holding minor league tryouts at nearly every position. One youngster who produced all year was Eric Karros (.257, 20 HR, 88 RBI). His performance did not go unnoticed as he was named the NL Rookie of the Year. Brett Butler (.309, 39 RBI, 41 steals) had another excellent year in the leadoff spot, and Mike Sharperson (.300) played well. The "ace" of the Dodger pitching staff was Tom Candiotti (11-15, 3.00, 152 Ks), while Ramon Martinez slumped to 8-11. Orel Hershiser was simply a disappointment. The Dodger bullpen was equally weak, with Roger McDowell (4.00 ERA) leading the way with only 14 saves.

Manager

Tommy Lasorda	W	L	PCT
Major League record	1341	1201	.528
With Dodgers	1341	1201	.528
1992 record	63	99	.389

Coaches: Joe Amalfitano, Mark Cresse, Joe Ferguson, Ben Hines, Ron Perranoski

Five-Year Finishes

88	89	90	91	92
1	4	2	2	6

Five-Year Record: 413-394; .512
Rank: 4th in NL; 9th in ML

President: Peter O'Malley
Executive Vice President, Player Personnel: Fred Claire
Vice President, Communications: Tommy Hawkins
Director, Minor League Operations: Charlie Blaney
Director, Scouting: Terry Reynolds

Address
1000 Elysian Park Avenue
Los Angeles, CA 90012

Ballparks

Brooklyn: Union Grounds 1876; Washington Park 1891-1897; Ebbets Field 1913-1957. Los Angeles: Memorial Coliseum 1958-61; Dodger Stadium 1962-present
Capacity: 56,000

1992 Attendance: 2,473,266
Surface: natural grass
Left field fence: 330 feet
Center field fence: 395 feet
Right field fence: 330 feet
Left-center fence: 385 feet
Right-center fence: 385 feet

Team History

The National League's most successful franchise got its start in Brooklyn in 1884, named for the borough's Trolley Dodgers. Flatbush fans suffered until "next year" finally brought a World Championship in 1955. They cried two years later when Walter O'Malley moved the team to LA, where the Dodgers won the World Series in 1959, 1963, 1965, 1977, and 1988. In 1989, the Dodgers' winning percentage fell from .584 in '88 to .481. This dramatic dip helps explain why the team from tinseltown finished fourth in their division. They took some steps in

the right direction during 1990, regaining second place in the division, but finishing five games behind the eventual World Champion Cincinnati Reds that season. Spirits were high in '91, but the mighty Dodgers fell apart down the stretch. One must remember that this was also the year of the miracle Atlanta Braves. LA finished '91 only one game behind the tomahawk-chopping "America's Team." After coming so close, the '92 season seems to be an extra-painful reality. It looks like "wait until next year" is becoming a Dodger cry again.

COLORADO ROCKIES
Manager: Don Baylor

Colorado Rockies Expansion Draft
First Round

Overall No.	Team Pick	Player	Pos.	Drafted From
1	1	David Nied	P	Braves
3	2	Charlie Hayes	3B	Yankees
5	3	Darren Holmes	P	Brewers
7	4	Jerald Clark	OF	Padres
9	5	Kevin Reimer	OF	Rangers
11	6	Eric Young	2B	Dodgers
13	7	Jody Reed	2B	Red Sox
15	8	Scott Aldred	P	Tigers
17	9	Alex Cole	OF	Pirates
19	10	Joe Girardi	C	Cubs
21	11	Willie Blair	P	Astros
23	12	Jay Owens	C	Twins
25	13	Andy Ashby	P	Phillies

Second Round

Overall No.	Team Pick	Player	Pos.	Drafted From
28	14	Freddie Benavides	SS	Reds
30	15	Roberto Mejia	2B	Dodgers
32	16	Doug Bochtler	P	Expos
34	17	Lance Painter	P	Padres
36	18	Butch Henry	P	Astros
38	19	Ryan Hawblitzel	P	Cubs
40	20	Vinnie Castilla	SS	Braves
42	21	Brett Merriman	P	Angels
44	22	Jim Tatum	3B	Brewers
46	23	Kevin Ritz	P	Tigers
48	24	Eric Wedge	C	Red Sox
50	25	Keith Sheperd	P	Phillies
52	26	Calvin Jones	P	Mariners

Third Round

Overall No.	Team Pick	Player	Pos.	Drafted From
54	27	Brad Ausmus	C	Yankees
56	28	Marcus Moore	P	Blue Jays
58	29	Armando Reynoso	P	Braves
60	30	Steve Reed	P	Giants
62	31	Mo Sanford	P	Reds
64	32	Pedro Castellano	3B	Cubs
66	33	Curtis Leskanic	P	Twins
68	34	Scott Fredrickson	P	Padres
70	35	Braulio Castillo	OF	Phillies
72	36	Denis Boucher	P	Indians

PITTSBURGH PIRATES
96-66, .593 Manager: Jim Leyland

Under most circumstances, three consecutive division titles would be cause for euphoria. However, Pittsburgh's collapse to Atlanta in the 1992 National League playoffs drained some of the joy from the regular-season success and robbed Pirate fans of a World Series appearance for the third year in a row. NL MVP and Gold Glover Barry Bonds (.311, 34 HR, 103 RBI) along with pitcher supreme Doug Drabek (15-11, 2.77, 177 Ks), were vital in keeping the mighty Bucs on top this season. But despite the playoff disappointment, Pittsburgh had a great year. Those who thought the loss of slugger Bobby Bonilla (free agency), excellent third baseman Steve Buechele (traded to Cubs), and pitcher John Smiley (traded to Twins) would kill the Bucs were wrong. Pittsburgh made it through the year nearly injuryfree, won plenty of close games, and received clutch contributions from a slew of players. Gold Glove winner Andy Van Slyke (.324, 89 RBI) challenged for the batting title all year. Jose Lind was also awarded a Gold Glove for his play last year. The catching tandem of Don Slaught (.345) and Mike LaValliere was steady all season. There were also unsung performers like shortstop Jay Bell (.264) and third bagger Jeff King (14 HR, 65 RBI) who were constantly productive for manager Jim Leyland. Bob Walk (10-6, 3.20) and Randy Tomlin (14-9, 3.41) stepped up in place of Smiley, while rookie knuckleballer Tim Wakefield (8-1, 2.15) was a late-season and playoff revelation. The Buc bullpen, particularly Stan Belinda (6-4, 18 saves) and Bob Patterson (6-3, 2.92, 9 saves), proved effective.

Manager			
Jim Leyland	**W**	**L**	**PCT**
Major League record	595	540	.524
With Pirates	595	540	.524
1992 record	96	66	.593

Coaches: Terry Collins, Rich Donnelly, Milt May, Ray Miller, Tommy Sandt

Five-Year Finishes

88	89	90	91	92
2	5	1	1	1

Five-Year Record: 448-360; .554
Rank: 1st in NL; 2nd in ML

Chairman of the Board: Douglas D. Danforth
President and CEO: Mark Sauer
Senior VP & GM for Baseball Operations: Ted Simmons
Assistant GM: Cam Bonifay
Director of Minor League Operations: Chet Montgomery
Director of Scouting: Jack Zduriencik
Address
P.O. Box 7000
Pittsburgh, Pa 15212

Ballparks

Exposition Park 1891-1909;
  Forbes Field 1909-1970;
  Three Rivers Stadium 1970-present
Capacity: 58,729
1992 Attendance: 1,829,395

Surface: artificial turf
Left field fence: 335 feet
Center field fence: 400 feet
Right field fence: 335 feet
Left-center fence: 375 feet
Right-center fence: 375 feet

Team History

From the early 1900s, Pirate fans have enjoyed much success. Pittsburgh won five pennants from 1900 through '30 and two World Series (1909 and '25). After sagging throughout the '40s and '50s, the Bucs stunned the Yankees in the 1960 fall classic. They captured the 1971 Series as well and were on top again in 1979. The '70s were a joyous time to be a Pirate fan. The Bucs finished nine out of 10 years in the first or second slot in the NL East. As the '80s unfolded, that joy turned to pain. Instead of being a perennial contender, the highest level of success the Pirates attained was two trips to second in the division. Not happy to just slip one or two rungs, the Bucs spent three consecutive years (1984 through '86) in dead last. However, from 1990 through 1992 the Pirates have taken the division title.

MONTREAL EXPOS

87-75, .537, 9 Managers: Tom Runnels (17-20); Felipe Alou (70-55)

Although the 1992 Expos unveiled a different uniform style, it wasn't until they got a new manager that things really started humming. Felipe Alou replaced the not-so-popular Tom Runnels in May and turned the young Expos from cellar dwellers into pennant contenders. Alou combined Montreal's superior team speed (196 steals) with its excellent crop of young pitchers to keep the heat on Pittsburgh. Though the young Expos faded in the length of their drive, they showed some promise on the way. The continued development of second baseman Delino DeShields (.292, 46 steals) and center fielder Marquis Grissom (.276, 14 HR, 66 RBI, 78 steals), coupled with the emergence of rookie rightfielder Moises Alou (.282, 56 RBI), gave the Expos terrific punch at the top of the lineup. Despite the repeated injury problems of RBI man Ivan Calderon (104 games missed) and a slump by veteran third bagger Tim Wallach (.223), Les Expos still produced runs. A monster year by Gold Glover Larry Walker (.301, 23 HR, 93 RBI) is a big reason for the run scoring success. Veteran hurler Dennis Martinez (16-11, 2.47) was again magnificent, but this time, he had some help. Ex-Cardinal Ken Hill (16-9, 2.68) teamed with Chris Nabholz (11-12, 3.32 ERA) and Mark Gardner (12-10) to give Montreal a solid rotation. Closer John Wetteland (37 saves), Mel Rojas (7-1, 1.43), and Jeff Fassero (8-7, 2.84) made substantial bullpen contributions.

Manager Felipe Alou	W	L	PCT
Major League record	70	55	.560
With Expos	70	55	.560
1992 record	70	55	.560

Coaches: Tommy Harper, Joe Kerrigan, Jerry Manuel, Luis Pujols, Tim Johnson, Pierre Arsenault

Ballparks

Jarry Park 1969-1976; Stade Olympique 1977-present.
Capacity: 60,011
1992 Attendance: 1,669,127
Retractable Dome
Surface: artificial turf

Left field fence: 325 feet
Center field fence: 404 feet
Right field fence: 325 feet
Left-center fence: 375 feet
Right-center fence: 375 feet

Five-Year Finishes

88	89	90	91	92
3	4	3	6	2

Five-Year Record: 405-404; .501
Rank: 7th in NL; 14th in ML

Pres. & General Part.: Claude Brochu
Chair. of the Board: Jacques Menard
Vice President & GM: Dan Duquette
VP, Baseball Operations: Bill Stoneman
Director, Scouting: Kevin Malone
Director, Minor League Operations: Kent Qualls
Address
P.O. Box 500, Station M
Montreal, Quebec
H1V 3P2 Canada

Team History

Named for the city's world exposition in the late 1960s, the Expos have given fans very few highlights. Their humble beginnings in tiny Jarry Park were matched by equally modest performances. The Expos did not contend for the NL East title until 1973, when their fourth place finish betrayed the fact that they were only 3½ games out of first. The franchise did not come close again until 1979, finishing second by two games to the eventual World Champion Pittsburgh Pirates. Although success did not wait quite so long to make another appearance—they captured the division crown in 1981—it has been elusive since. From 1982 through '89, the Expos never went above the third rung in their division. In 1991, as if some director were setting up a dramatic foreshadowing scene, parts of the roof on Olympic Stadium came crashing down. That season, the Expos wound up dead last in the division. The Expos did, however, rebound in '92, finishing second in the NL East.

ST. LOUIS CARDINALS

83-79, .512, 13 Manager: Joe Torre

A glance at the injury listings for the 1992 St. Louis Cardinals might lead the casual observer to believe the team struggled all season, finishing near the NL East basement. The Cards missed a total of 709 games on the DL—more than any other team in the NL. Trainers for the team treated shoulders, elbows, ankles, knees, wrists, hamstrings—even the chicken pox. Somehow, St. Louis actually contended for part of the year. The Cards were even in first place in early June. Eventually, though, the bad health—and a substantial lack of power at the plate—finally left the Redbirds sitting in third place, 13 games away from the Pirates. No area was spared from injury woes. Pitchers Joe Magrane (elbow), Bryn Smith (shoulder), and Scott Terry (rotator cuff) started six games between them. Left fielder Jose Oquendo missed 120 games with an assortment of maladies, and sluggers Felix Jose, Andres Galarraga, and Pedro Guerrero each missed at least 16 games to injuries. Those who were healthy performed well. Starter Bob Tewksbury (16-5, 2.16, 20 BB) was magnificent all year, and young hurlers Rheal Cormier (10-10), Donovan Osborne (11-9), and Omar Olivares (9-9) each threw 180 innings or more. Closer Lee Smith (43 saves) was erratic at times, but set-up man Mike Perez (9-3, 1.84) was steady. Outfielders Bernard Gilkey (.302) and Milt Thompson (.293) were solid. Felix Jose (.295, 14 HR, 75 RBI) provided much of the team's power. Even though management might not think so, shortstop Ozzie Smith (.295) again proved he is one of the league's best. Smith and catcher Tom Pagnozzi both won Gold Gloves for '92.

Manager

Joe Torre	W	L	PCT
Major League record	735	840	.467
With Cardinals	212	201	.513
1992 record	83	79	.512

Coaches: Chris Chambliss, Joe Coleman, Dave Collins, Bucky Dent, Gaylen Pitts

Ballparks

Robison Field 1893-1920; Sportsman's Park 1920-1966; Busch Stadium 1966-present.
Capacity: 56,627
1992 Attendance: 2,418,483

Surface: artificial turf
Left field fence: 330 feet
Center field fence: 402 feet
Right field fence: 330 feet
Left-center fence: 375 feet
Right-center fence: 375 feet

Five-Year Finishes

88	89	90	91	92
5	3	6	2	3

Five-Year Record: 399-411; .493
Rank: 9th in NL; tied 16th in ML

Chairman of the Board: August A. Busch, III
Vice Chairman: Fred L. Kuhlmann
President & CEO: Stuart F. Meyer
Vice President/GM: Dal Maxvill
Director of Player Development: Mike Jorgensen
Director of Scouting: Marty Maier
Address
250 Stadium Plaza
St. Louis, MO 63102

Team History

Born the Browns in 1884, the St. Louis Cardinals won six World Championships from 1926 through '46, thanks mostly to Branch Rickey's fine farm system. St. Louis was back on top in 1964 and '67. The 1970s were thin on excitement for Cardinal fans, but then the tide turned. In strike-split '81, the Cards had the best winning percentage overall, but did not get to the playoffs. In 1982, they won the World Series over the Milwaukee Brewers. The St. Louis team migrated to the lower half of the standings for the next few years, but got right back in the thick of things in '85. They won pennants in '85 and again in '87. Known more for speed on the basepaths rather than long-ball prowess, the Cardinals are always a threat.

CHICAGO CUBS
78-84, .481, 18 Manager: Jim Lefebvre

After the '92 season, Cub fans probably spent most of their time repeating that familiar baseball refrain: What if? What if the Cubbies hadn't stumbled out of the gate, settling quickly into last place? What if Shawon Dunston (herniated disk) had played a full year and had continued his torrid (.315) start? What if midseason acquisition Kal Daniels had hit for power, instead of fizzling? Cy Young and Gold Glove winner Greg Maddux (20-11, 2.18, 199 Ks) and Andre Dawson (.277, 22 HR, 90 RBI) both announced their free-agency after the season. Two other familiar faces continued to perform very well, namely Ryne Sandberg (.304, 26 HR, 87 RBI) and Gold Glover Mark Grace (.307, 79 RBI). Nevertheless, Chicago's combination of young outfielders — Dwight Smith (.276),

Derrick May (.274), Doug Dascenzo (.255), and Sammy Sosa (.260)—needed more consistency. The midseason acquisition of Steve Buechele (.261, 64 RBI) made third look pretty steady, and youngster Rick Wilkins (.270) was strong at catcher. They have lost catcher Joe Girardi (.270), however, as he became a member of the Colorado Rockies in November. What about the rest of the pitching staff? Dodger outcast Mike Morgan (16-8, 2.55) was ace material, but Frank Castillo (10-11) and Shawn Boskie (5-11) were shaky. The healthy return of Mike Harkey would be a big boost, as would another successful year of bullpen-by-committee, featuring Bob Scanlan (14 saves), Jim Bullinger, and Paul Assenmacher.

Manager

Jim Lefebvre	W	L	PCT
Major League record	311	337	.480
With Cubs	78	84	.481
1992 record	78	84	.481

Coaches: Billy Connors, Chuck Cottier, Sammy Ellis, Jose Martinez, Tom Trebelhorn, Tony Musar

Five-Year Finishes

88	89	90	91	92
4	1	T4	T3	4

Five-Year Record: 402-406; .498
Rank: 8th in NL; 15th in ML

Chair. of the Board: Stanton R. Cook
Exec. VP, Baseball Op.: Larry Himes
Sr. VP/Spec. Player Cons.: Jim Frey
Assistant General Manager: Syd Thrift
VP, Scouting and Player Development: Dick Balderson
VP, Baseball Admin.: Ned Colletti
Director, Minor League Operations: Bill Harford

Address
Clark & Addison Streets
Chicago, IL 60613

Ballparks

Union Base-Ball Grounds, 23rd Street Grounds, LakeFront Park, South Side Park pre-1916; Wrigley Field 1916-present
Capacity: 38,710
1992 Attendance: 2,126,720

Surface: natural grass
Left field fence: 355 feet
Center field fence: 400 feet
Right field fence: 353 feet
Left-center fence: 368 feet
Right-center fence: 368 feet

Team History

The Cubs are notorious for having baseball's longest championship drought. Born the White Stockings in 1870, the franchise dominated National League play during the late 1800s. Chicago won the 1906 pennant and featured the likes of double-play combo Joe Tinker, Johnny Evers, and Frank Chance, as well as pitcher Three Finger Brown. They captured World Championships in 1907 and 1908, beating the Detroit Tigers both times. Despite seven

National League pennants from 1910 to '45, the Cubs couldn't win another Series. The Cubs acquired a reputation for being perpetual also-rans. There were only three seasons from 1940 through 1966 that were winning ones, and the Cubs finished dead last six times. Chicago never won another pennant, though they did take the NL East in 1984 and 1989. Joining the 20th century, night games came to Wrigley Field in 1988.

NEW YORK METS
72-90, .444, 24 Manager: Jeff Torborg

For most of the 1992 season, it seemed like the good old days in New York. Unfortunately for Met fans, that's good old days as in late 1970s, not mid-1980s. After feigning contention early in the season, the Mets slid quickly into the NL East's depths, finding themselves in a life-and-death struggle with the Phillies for fifth place. Once again, New York proved that money can't buy happiness—or division championships. High-price free agent Bobby Bonilla (.249, 19 HR, 70 RBI) was largely a bust, despite a late-season rally. Highly regarded pitcher Bret Saberhagen, acquired in a blockbuster deal with Kansas City, spent much of the year on the DL with an annoying finger injury. About the only revelation for the Mets was free agent first baseman Eddie Murray

(.261, 16 HR, 93 RBI), who comprised much of the New York run production. There were some other highlights. Chico Walker (.289) played well in the infield, while third baseman Dave Magadan (.283) rebounded from a weak '91. Outfielder Vince Coleman struggled with injuries and a bad attitude, stealing only 24 bases, and slugger Howard Johnson (.223) slumped miserably before breaking his wrist in early August. The once-proud Met pitching staff was a shadow of its former self. Only Sid Fernandez (14-11, 2.73 ERA) made good on his potential, while Dwight Gooden (10-13) sagged, and fire-balling David Cone was shipped to Toronto in late August. Closer John Franco (6-2, 1.64 ERA) battled a bad elbow for much of the season.

Manager

Jeff Torborg	W	L	PCT
Major League record	479	526	.477
With Mets	72	90	.444
1992 record	72	90	.444

Coaches: Mike Cubbage, Barry Foote, Dave LaRoche, Tom McCraw, Mel Stottlemyre

Ballparks

Polo Grounds 1962-1963; Shea Stadium 1974-present.
Capacity: 55,601
1992 Attendance: 1,779,534
Surface: natural grass

Left field fence: 338 feet
Center field fence: 410 feet
Right field fence: 338 feet
Left-center fence: 371 feet
Right-center fence: 371 feet

Five-Year Finishes

88	89	90	91	92
1	2	2	5	5

Five-Year Record: 427-380; .529
Rank: 2nd in NL; 5th in ML

Chairman of the Board: Nelson Doubleday
President & CEO: Richard Cummins
COO: Al Harazin
Senior VP: J. Frank Cashen
Assistant VP of Baseball Operations: Gerald Hunsicker

Address
126th Street & Roosevelt Avenue
Flushing, NY 11368

Team History

The 30-year history of the Big Apple's "other" franchise has been filled with meteoric highs and laughable lows. New York debuted in 1962 and lost 120 games, but the Miracle Mets stunned the baseball world in 1969 with a storybook World Series title. New York won another pennant in 1973 but was inept until a mid-'80s renaissance. The Metropolitans struggled through the first four years of the decade, finishing last or next to last. They became contenders in '84 under new manager Davey Johnson. Another second place finish was in order in 1985, as they closed the gap, finishing only three games out of first. Adding clutch-hitting and a fine offensive lineup to their sterling pitching staff, the Mets won it all in '86, bringing home their second World Championship trophy. Another division win would be theirs in 1988,. In the '90s, they have yet to duplicate the success enjoyed in the mid-'80s.

PHILADELPHIA PHILLIES
70-92, .432, 26 Manager: Jim Fregosi

Hopes were high for the 1992 Phillies, based on a third-place finish in '91. Even sharp new uniforms, though, couldn't give one of the game's weakest organizations a suitable facelift. The Phils slumped to last in the NL East, registering their sixth-consecutive losing record. Why? Look no further than weak pitching, lousy defense, and a season-long string of unfortunate injuries. Though the team scored the second most runs in the NL (686), its staff ERA of 4.11 offset the fireworks. Two separate injuries to center field sparkplug Lenny Dykstra (.301 in just 345 AB) took away much of the team's competitive fire. Other assorted bumps, bruises, sprains, and tears forced the Phils to use 48 different players in '92. There were, however, some highlights. Colorful first baseman John Kruk (.323) flirted with the batting title, and catcher Darren Daulton (.270, 27 HR, 109 RBI) won the league's RBI title. Sophomore third baseman Dave Hollins (.270, 27 HR, 93 RBI) posted Mike Schmidt-style numbers, and second baseman Mickey Morandini (.265) improved considerably. The pitching picture was not so encouraging. Injuries to starters Jose DeJesus and Tommy Greene forced manager Jim Fregosi to use all comers. Even though talented newcomers Curt Schilling (14-11, 2.35) and Ben Rivera (7-4, 3.07) emerged, they just weren't enough. Phillies 1991 ace, Terry Mulholland (13-11), slumped some in '92. Although closer Mitch Williams collected 29 saves, his 3.78 ERA and 5-8 record were sharp drops from '91.

Manager			
Jim Fregosi	W	L	PCT
Major League record	598	641	.483
With Phillies	144	167	.463
1992 record	70	92	.432

Coaches: Larry Bowa, John Vukovich, Mel Roberts, Mike Ryan, Johnny Podres, Denis Menke

Five-Year Finishes

88	89	90	91	92
6	6	T4	T3	6

Five-Year Record: 357-452; .441
Rank: 12th in NL; 26th in ML

President, CEO & General Partner: Bill Giles

Executive VP & COO: David Montgomery

Senior VP, GM: Lee Thomas

Director, Player Development: Del Unser

Director, Scouting: Jay Hankins

VP, Public Relations: Larry Shenk

Address
P.O. Box 7575
Philadelphia, PA 19148

Ballparks

Philadelphia Base Ball Grounds
1887-1894; Baker Bowl
1895-1938; Shibe
Park/Connie Mack Stadium
1938-1970; Veterans
Stadium 1971-present
Capacity: 62,382

1992 Attendance: 1,927,448
Surface: artificial turf
Left field fence: 330 feet
Center field fence: 408 feet
Right field fence: 330 feet
Left-center fence: 371 feet
Right-center fence: 371 feet

Team History

The Philadelphia Phillies have won just one World Championship in 108 years. The 1915 pennant winners lost in the Series to Boston, while the 1950 NL Champion "Whiz Kids" were dropped by the Yankees. The Phils won the NL East from 1976 through '78 but didn't reach the Series again until 1980, when they finally won. They waited a record 97 years as a franchise to gain their first World Championship. A 1983 Series appearance was not so fruitful, as they managed to win only one game against the eventual World Champion Baltimore Orioles. The rest of the '80s were an abysmal plight for Philly players and fans. Only once did they grab second place in the NL East ('86), and that year they were over 20 games behind the first place Mets. Winding up the decade with two successive last place finishes, the outlook has been grim. In the '90s, the Phillies have yet to place higher than third in their division, taking low honors again in '92.

FLORIDA MARLINS

Manager: Rene Lachemann

Florida Marlins Expansion Draft
First Round

Overall No.	Team Pick	Player	Pos.	Drafted From
2	1	Nigel Wilson	OF	Blue Jays
4	2	Jose Martinez	P	Mets
6	3	Bret Barbarie	2B	Expos
8	4	Trevor Hoffman	P	Reds
10	5	Pat Rapp	P	Giants
12	6	Greg Hibbard	P	White Sox
14	7	Chuck Carr	OF	Cardinals
16	8	Darrell Whitmore	OF	Indians
18	9	Eric Helfand	C	Athletics
20	10	Bryan Harvey	P	Angels
22	11	Jeff Conine	1B	Royals
24	12	Kip Yaughn	P	Orioles
26	13	Jesus Tavarez	OF	Mariners

Second Round

Overall No.	Team Pick	Player	Pos.	Drafted From
27	14	Carl Everett	OF	Yankees
29	15	David Weathers	P	Blue Jays
31	16	John Johnstone	P	Mets
33	17	Ramon Martinez	SS	Pirates
35	18	Steve Decker	C	Giants
37	19	Cris Carpenter	P	Cardinals
39	20	Jack Armstrong	P	Indians
41	21	Scott Chiamparino	P	Rangers
43	22	Tom Edens	P	Twins
45	23	Andres Berumen	P	Royals
47	24	Robert Person	P	White Sox
49	25	Jim Corsi	P	Athletics
51	26	Richie Lewis	P	Orioles

Third Round

Overall No.	Team Pick	Player	Pos.	Drafted From
53	27	Danny Jackson	P	Pirates
55	28	Rob Natal	C	Expos
57	29	Jamie McAndrew	P	Dodgers
59	30	Junior Felix	OF	Angels
61	31	Kerwin Moore	OF	Royals
63	32	Ryan Owen	P	Astros
65	33	Scott Baker	P	Cardinals
67	34	Chris Donnels	3B	Mets
69	35	Monty Farris	OF	Rangers
71	36	Jeff Tabaka	P	Brewers

Hall of Famers

Profiles of the players, managers, umpires, and executives who have been inducted into the National Baseball Hall of Fame and Museum comprise this section. The profiles are presented in alphabetical order.

In preparation for baseball's centennial in 1939, a National Baseball Museum was proposed, first as a matter of civic pride, and later as memorial for the greatest of those who have ever played the game.

While the rules governing election to the Hall of Fame have varied in specifics over the years, in general the criteria have remained the same. One must be named on 75 percent of ballots cast by members of the Baseball Writers' Association of America. To be eligible, players must have played for at least 10 years. The players have to be retired for at least five years but not more than 20 years. A player is eligible for 15 years in the BBWAA vote.

If the player is not named on 75 percent of the ballots in 15 years, his name becomes eligible for consideration by the Committee on Baseball Veterans. This committee also considers managers, umpires, and executives for induction to Cooperstown. The same 75 percent rule applies. Anyone on baseball's permanently ineligible list is excluded from consideration.

The Committee on the Negro Leagues was added to the selection process in 1971. This board considered players who had 10 years of service in the pre-1946 Negro Leagues, and also those who made the major leagues. The Negro League board dissolved into the Veterans' Committee in 1977.

HANK AARON
Outfielder (1954-1976)

Aaron is baseball's all-time leader in home runs with 755 and in RBI with 2,297. During a 23-year career with the Braves and the Brewers, "Hammerin' Hank" stood out as one of the game's most complete and consistent performers. He was the NL MVP in 1957 when he hit .322 with 44 home runs and 132 RBI. Inducted in 1982, Aaron hit 40 home runs or more eight times and had more than 100 RBI 11 different seasons.

GROVER ALEXANDER
Pitcher (1911-1930)

Despite battles against alcohol and epilepsy, Alexander's 373 wins is tied for the NL record. While pitching with Philadelphia in 1916, he recorded a major league record 16 shutouts on his way to a 33-12 record. "Pete" led the senior loop in wins six times, ERA five times, and shutouts seven times. His 90 shutouts are second on the all-time list. He was inducted in 1938.

WALTER ALSTON
Manager (1954-1976)
"Smokey" Alston struck out in his only big league at bat. In 23 years as manager of the Dodgers, however, all under one-year contracts, Alston led the club to seven pennants and four world championships. Under his patient leadership, the Dodgers made pitching and defense a winning combination. Inducted in 1983, his career record is 2,040 wins and 1,613 losses for a .558 winning percentage.

CAP ANSON
First baseman (1871-1897)
Manager (1879-1898)
A baseball pioneer, as player, manager, and part-owner of NL Chicago, "Pop" Anson was the game's most influential figure in the 19th century. He hit .300 or better in 20 consecutive seasons, won five pennants, and is often credited with developing the hit-and-run and other strategies. Inducted in 1939, he reached 3,000 base hits. But, in 1887, he intimidated organized baseball into banning blacks.

LUIS APARICIO
Shortstop (1956-1973)
No man played more games at shortstop—2,581—than Aparicio. The swift, sure-handed infielder played a vital role in championship seasons for the White Sox in 1959 and the Orioles in 1966. Inducted in 1984, the winner of nine Gold Gloves led the AL in stolen bases nine times en route to 506 career thefts.

LUKE APPLING
Shortstop (1930-1943; 1945-1950)
Known better for his bat than his glove, Appling nonetheless played shortstop for the White Sox for 20 seasons. Nicknamed "Old Aches and Pains," Appling led the AL in batting twice, finishing with a career average of .310. Inducted in 1964, he finished his career with 1,116 RBI and 1,319 runs scored. In 1936, he hit .388 and collected 128 RBI, despite hitting only six home runs.

EARL AVERILL
Outfielder (1929-1941)
The only outfielder selected to baseball's first six All-Star games, Averill didn't turn pro until age 23, and didn't make the major leagues, with Cleveland, until age 26. In his first 10 seasons he was one of the game's best sluggers. In a 1933 doubleheader, he hit four home runs, three consecutively. Inducted in 1975, Averill had more than 90 RBI in each of nine seasons and ended his career with 1,165 runs batted in. A congenital back condition cut his career short.

FRANK BAKER
Third baseman (1908-1922)
Despite never hitting more than 12 home runs in a season, during baseball's deadball era Baker was a slugger supreme. He led the AL in home runs from 1911 to 1914. His two 1911 World Series home runs earned him his "Home Run" nickname. In six World Series with the A's and Yankees, he hit .363. Inducted in 1955, Baker had 1,013 RBI in his career.

DAVE BANCROFT
Shortstop (1915-1930)
One of the best fielding shortstops of all time, Bancroft set a major league record in 1922 when he handled 984 chances. A heady ballplayer, "Beauty" was named captain of the Giants in 1920 and led them to four straight pennants. Inducted in 1971, he batted over .300 five times in his career.

ERNIE BANKS
Shortstop; first baseman
(1953-1971)
Known as "Mr. Cub," the irrepressible Banks combined unbridled enthusiasm with remarkable talent to become one of the most popular players of his era. As a

shortstop he won back-to-back NL MVP awards in 1958 and 1959 before switching to first base. Despite 512 career home runs and 11 All-Star appearances, the Cubs failed to win a pennant during Banks's tenure. Inducted in 1977, he had 2,583 lifetime hits and 1,636 RBI.

AL BARLICK
Umpire (1940-1971)
One of the most respected arbiters in baseball, Barlick began his career in the NL in 1940 when old-timer Bill Klem was injured. He worked in Jackie Robinson's first game. Inducted in 1989, Barlick also umpired in seven All-Star contests and in seven World Series.

ED BARROW
Executive
In 1918, Barrow was named manager of the Red Sox and led them to a World Series victory. Credited with transferring Babe Ruth from the mound to the outfield, Barrow followed Ruth to the Yankees. Under "Cousin Ed's" direction, the Yankee dynasty became legend. Inducted in 1953, he was in charge of the Bronx Bombers from 1920 to 1947.

JAKE BECKLEY
First baseman (1888-1907)
One of baseball's earliest stars, Beckley played more games at first base than any man in history. Inducted in 1971, he had 2,931 hits, 1,600 runs scored, and 1,575 RBI. His dashing handle-bar mustache made him a fan favorite. "St. Jacob's" 243 career triples are fourth on the all-time list.

COOL PAPA BELL
Outfielder (1922-1946)
Perhaps the fastest man to ever play the game, Bell starred as an outfielder in the Negro Leagues for more than two decades. Satchel Paige claimed Bell was so fast he could switch off the light and leap into bed before the room got dark.

Often credited with scoring from second on a sacrifice fly, Bell (who was inducted in 1974) hit .392 against organized major league competition.

JOHNNY BENCH
Catcher (1967-1983)
Upon his arrival in the big leagues in 1967, Bench was heralded as baseball's best defensive catcher. After his NL MVP year in 1970 at age 22, with 48 home runs and 148 RBI, he was baseball's best catcher, period. He won his second MVP in 1972. With Bench behind the plate, the Reds won four pennants and two World Series. In the 1976 Series against the Yankees, he hit .533. Inducted in 1989, he had 389 homers and 1,376 RBI.

CHIEF BENDER
Pitcher (1903-1917; 1925)
An alumni of the Carlisle Indian School, the half-Chippewa Bender overcame a series of racial slights to become one of the Philadelphia A's most valued members. In his 10 World Series appearances, Bender went 6-4. Inducted in 1953, he led the AL in winning percentage three times, including a 17-3 mark in 1914.

YOGI BERRA
Catcher (1946-1965)
If championships are the best measure of success, then Berra stands second to no one. His 14 World Series appearances, 75 Series games played, and 71 Series hits are all records. A three-time MVP, the Yankee hit 20 homers in 10 consecutive seasons. Known as well for his way with words, Berra will be remembered for the oft-quoted "it's never over till it's over." Inducted in 1972, he had 1,430 lifetime RBI to go with his 358 home runs.

JIM BOTTOMLEY
First baseman (1922-1937)
One of the first products of the famous Cardinals' farm system, Bottomley was

named NL MVP in 1928 for hitting .325, 31 homers, and driving in 136 runs. On September 16, 1924, "Sunny Jim" knocked in 12 runs with six hits against Brooklyn. Inducted in 1974, he had a career .310 batting average and 1,422 RBI.

LOU BOUDREAU
Shortstop (1938-1952)
Manager (1942-1950; 1952-1957; 1960)
Both as a fielder and a hitter, Boudreau was one of the game's great shortstops. He was named Cleveland's player-manager in 1942 at age 24. In 1948, he led the club to the AL pennant, hitting .355, scoring 116 runs, while driving in 106, easily capturing the AL MVP Award. Inducted in 1970, he led AL shortstops in fielding eight times. As a manager, he won 1,162 games.

ROGER BRESNAHAN
Catcher (1897; 1900-1915)
The first catcher elected to the Hall of Fame, Bresnahan is most famous for pioneering the use of shin guards and batting helmets. A solid hitter, Bresnahan hit .350 with the Giants in 1903. Inducted in 1945, he possessed rare speed for a catcher, stealing 34 bases in 1903 and finishing his career with 212 stolen bases.

LOU BROCK
Outfielder (1961-1979)
Brock's career totals of 938 stolen bases and 3,023 career hits, coupled with a .293 batting average, gained him admittance to the Hall. In 1974, at age 35, he stole 118 bases. He excelled in three World Series for the Cardinals, hitting .391 and scoring 16 runs. Inducted in 1985, Brock had more than 200 hits four times.

DAN BROUTHERS
First baseman (1879-1896); 1904)
Baseball's premier 19th century slugger, Brouthers toiled for nine different clubs, in three different major leagues, for 21 sea-

sons. He was the first man to win back-to-back batting titles, in 1882 and 1883. Inducted in 1945, he batted over .300 in 16 consecutive seasons, reaching .374 in 1883.

THREE FINGER BROWN
Pitcher (1903-1916)
A farm accident in a corn grinder mutilated Brown's right hand, severing most of his index finger, mangling his middle finger, and paralyzing his little finger. The injuries, however, gave his pitches a natural sink and curve. Pitching with the Cubs between 1904 and 1910, Brown's highest ERA was 1.86, helping Chicago to four pennants. Inducted in 1949, he had a career 239-129 record, with a 2.06 ERA and 57 shutouts.

MORGAN BULKELEY
NL President (1876)
Bulkeley's notoriety is in his almost complete anonymity. In 1876, He was named the first President of the new National League, because of his respectable standing in the business world. He served one year without distinction and resigned. He was inducted in 1937.

JESSE BURKETT
Outfielder (1890-1905)
In the 1890s, the lefthanded-hitting Burkett hit over .400 two times. A fine baserunner and bunter, the third-strike foul-bunt rule was created due to Burkett's prowess at the art. "Crab" won three batting titles in his career. Inducted in 1946, he scored 1,718 runs, drew 1,029 walks, and notched 2,853 base hits in his 16-year career.

ROY CAMPANELLA
Catcher (1948-1957)
Campanella, one of the great athletes of his time, had a .312 average, 41 homers, 103 runs scored, and 142 RBI in 1953—amazing marks for a backstop. In 1951,

1953, and 1955 the Dodger catcher was named the NL's MVP. Inducted in 1969, he led his team to five pennants in 10 years. A 1958 automobile accident left Campanella paralyzed, and his struggle to remain active has served as a continuing inspiration.

ROD CAREW
First baseman; second baseman (1967-1985)

An infielder with Minnesota and California, Carew was one of baseball's premiere singles hitters, slapping 3,053 hits and registering a lifetime .328 batting average. Inducted in 1991, he topped .300 in 15 consecutive seasons on his way to seven batting titles, a mark surpassed only by Ty Cobb's 12 batting titles. Carew's 1977 MVP year consisted of a .388 batting average, 239 hits, 16 triples, 128 runs scored, 100 RBI, and an on-base percentage of .415.

MAX CAREY
Outfielder (1910-1929)

A tremendous defensive center fielder, primarily with Pittsburgh, Carey took advantage of his speed and instincts to swipe 738 bases. In 1925, despite two broken ribs, "Scoops" batted .458 in the World Series as the Pirates defeated Washington. In game seven, his four hits and three runs scored beat the great Walter Johnson. Inducted in 1961, Carey scored 1,545 runs and had 2,665 base hits in his 20-year career.

ALEXANDER CARTWRIGHT
Executive

On September 23, 1845, Alexander Cartwright formed the Knickerbocker Base Ball Club and formalized a set of 20 rules that gave baseball its basic shape. While Cartwright's involvement with the game lasted only a few years, he is the man most responsible for the game that is played, and loved, today. Our national pastime is his legacy. Cartwright was inducted in 1938.

HENRY CHADWICK
Writer-Statistician

While Alexander Cartwright is baseball's inventor, Chadwick is the first man to chronicle the game. The only sportswriter enshrined in the Hall itself (in 1938), as opposed to the Writers Wing, he was the first baseball writer. Chadwick's guides and instructional booklets helped popularize the game, and his method of scoring led to the game's wealth of statistics.

FRANK CHANCE
First baseman (1898-1914)

Anchor of the Cubs' "Tinker-to-Evers-to-Chance" double-play combo, Chance helped Chicago win four pennants. While he was hardly a dominant player, he nevertheless hit .296 during his career and hit .310 in Series play. Chance's career was cut short by repeated beanings, which eventually left him deaf in one ear. Inducted in 1946, "The Peerless Leader" managed the Cubs for seven years and won at least 100 games four times.

HAPPY CHANDLER
Commissioner (1945-1951)

The former governor and U.S. senator from Kentucky, Chandler succeeded Judge Kenesaw Mountain Landis as the second Commissioner of baseball. Despite the opposition of most baseball owners, Chandler backed Branch Rickey's signing of Jackie Robinson and prevented a player strike by threatening to ban any striking player for life. Preferring a "yes-man," the owners voted Chandler out in 1951. He was inducted in 1982.

OSCAR CHARLESTON
Outfielder (1915-1941)

Blessed with speed and power in abundance, center fielder Charleston is thought by many to be greatest of all Negro League players. Superb defensively, on offense he could both steal a base and hit a home run. In 1932, he became player-manager of the Pittsburgh Crawfords, whose lineup, including Charleston, featured five Hall of Famers. The team went 99-36 that year, and Charleston hit .363. He was enshrined in 1976.

JACK CHESBRO
Pitcher (1899-1909)

Chesbro's 41 victories in 454⅔ innings in 1904 stand as one of the game's more remarkable single-season achievements. A master of the spitball, his wild pitch in the next to the last game of the 1904 season against Boston, however, cost New York the AL pennant. The winner of 199 games, "Happy Jack" (inducted in 1946) led his league in winning percentage in three different seasons.

FRED CLARKE
Outfielder (1894-1911; 1913-1915)
Manager (1897-1915)

For 19 of his 21 big league seasons, Clarke was a manager as well as a player, all for the NL Louisville-Pittsburgh franchise. As a player, he hit .312 with 2,675 base hits and 1,621 runs scored. As manager he won one World Series in 1910, four pennants, including three in a row from 1901 to 1903, and finished second five times. Inducted in 1945, "Cap" finished his managing career with 1,602 wins against 1,181 losses.

JOHN CLARKSON
Pitcher (1882-1894)

An early master of the curveball, Clarkson excelled during the years when the pitching distance was a mere 50 feet. Six times he hurled more than 400 innings, twice more than 600. In 1885 with the White Stockings, he went 53-16. With the Beaneaters in 1889, Clarkson's record was 49-19 in an incredible 73 appear-

ances. Winner of 328 games for his career, he had 485 complete games and led the NL in strikeouts four times. He was inducted in 1963.

ROBERTO CLEMENTE
Outfielder (1955-1972)

Clemente won four NL batting titles and also possessed one of the strongest outfield arms in baseball history. Intensely proud of his Puerto Rican heritage, it was not until the 1971 World Series, when Clemente led Pittsburgh to victory with a .414 average, that he began to receive his due. In 13 of his 18 seasons he hit .300 or better, topping the .350 mark three times. On New Year's Eve, 1972, Clemente died in a plane crash bringing supplies to earthquake-ravaged Nicaragua. The normal five-year waiting period was waived, and in 1973 Clemente became the first Hispanic elected to the Hall of Fame.

TY COBB
Outfielder (1905-1928)

The first man elected to the Hall of Fame, Cobb received more votes than any of his counterparts. Intense beyond belief, the daring Cobb epitomized the "scientific" style of play that dominated baseball in the first quarter of the 20th century. In 23 of his 24 seasons Cobb hit over the .320 mark, and his lifetime .366 average is still the all-time best. Inducted in 1936, he led the AL in batting average 12 seasons. The "Georgia Peach's" 2,245 runs scored are the most in history, while his 4,190 hits and 892 stolen bases rank second and third respectively.

MICKEY COCHRANE
Catcher (1925-1937)

An exceptional defensive catcher and dangerous hitter, Cochrane led the Athletics and Tigers to five pennants, including two as Detroit manager. "Black Mike" cracked the .300 mark in eight seasons, and his lifetime .320 batting average is the highest of any catcher. Inducted in 1947, Mickey was twice AL MVP. In 1937, Cochrane was beaned by Yankee pitcher Bump Hadley and suffered a fractured skull, ending his career at the relatively young age of 34.

EDDIE COLLINS
Second baseman (1906-1930)
As Connie Mack's on-field manager, Collins led the Athletics to four pennants in five years. Traded to the White Sox, he helped that club to two more. An accomplished all-around ballplayer, Collins smacked 3,310 hits for a career average of .333, yet never won a batting title. A consummate basestealer, he ranks fourth on the all-time list with 743 career swipes. Inducted in 1939, "Cocky" scored 1,818 runs and drove in 1,299 runs in his 25-year career.

JIMMY COLLINS
Third baseman (1895-1908)
Inducted in 1945, Collins revolutionized the third base position by moving around, charging in, and fielding bunts bare-handed. Playing primarily for both the Boston Beaneaters in the National League and the Boston Pilgrims in the AL, Collins hit a robust .294, topping the .300 mark five times and the 100 RBI mark four times.

EARLE COMBS
Outfielder (1924-1935)
While Babe Ruth and Lou Gehrig cleaned up at the plate, Combs set the table. As the leadoff man and center fielder for the Yankees, Combs scored 100 or more runs in eight straight seasons. Inducted in 1970, "The Kentucky Colonel" had a lifetime .325 average and scored 1,186 runs. A collision with an outfield fence in 1934 forced his retirement a year later.

CHARLES COMISKEY
Executive
Comiskey parlayed modest field success into managerial brilliance, later becoming the first former player to be sole owner of a major league franchise. Inducted in 1939, the "Old Roman" assisted Ban Johnson in the formation of the American League. As owner of the White Sox, Comiskey earned a reputation as a cheapskate, and some historians feel that his parsimonious spending habits indirectly led to the 1919 "Black Sox" scandal.

JOCKO CONLAN
Umpire (1941-1964)
A long-time minor leaguer, Conlan started umpiring by accident. In a 1935 game, when one of the regular umpires was overcome by the heat, Conlan was rushed in to pinch-ump. Remembered for his trademark polka dot tie, Conlan utilized a sharp tongue to keep order. Inducted in 1974, he umpired in six World Series and six All-Star Games.

TOMMY CONNOLLY
Umpire (1898-1931)
Although born in England, Connolly fell in love with baseball as a teenager and became an NL umpire in 1898. Frustrated with the circuit by 1900, he signed on to the AL in 1901. Thirty years later he was named chief of AL umpires, his position for another 23 years. Connolly and Bill Klem became the first umpires named to the Hall of Fame, in 1953. Connolly umpired in eight World Series, including the first in 1903.

ROGER CONNOR
First baseman (1880-1897)
Until Babe Ruth broke the mark in 1921, Connor held the lifetime record for home runs with 136. A career .317 hitter, the Giant first baseman was a bona fide deadball era slugger, smacking 233 triples, fifth all time. In his first game with the Giants in 1883, he hit such an impressive shot that the fans passed the hat and bought him a gold watch. Inducted in 1976, he scored 1,620 runs and had 1,125 RBI in his career.

STAN COVELESKI
Pitcher (1912; 1916-1928)
A coal miner at age 13, Coveleski didn't reach the majors to stay until 1916, when he was age 27. The spitball artist had his best years with Cleveland from 1918 to 1921, winning 20 games or more each season. Inducted in 1969, Coveleski won 215 games, while his brother Harry won 81. Stan lost only 142 games and retired with a lifetime 2.88 ERA.

SAM CRAWFORD
Outfielder (1899-1917)
Crawford played outfield for Detroit alongside Ty Cobb. The powerful Crawford is baseball's all-time leader in triples with 309. A native of Wahoo, Nebraska, "Wahoo Sam" retired only 39 hits shy of 3,000. Inducted in 1957, he hit .309 lifetime, with 1,393 runs scored and 1,525 RBI. He later returned to baseball as an umpire in the Pacific Coast League.

JOE CRONIN
Shortstop (1926-1945)
Manager (1933-1947)
AL President (1959-1973)
For 50 years, Cronin excelled as a player, manager, and executive. A hard-hitting shortstop, he made baseball history in 1934 when Red Sox owner Tom Yawkey purchased him from Washington owner (and Cronin's uncle-in-law) Clark Griffith for $225,000. Cronin was a .301 career batter, and he had 1,233 runs scored and 1,424 RBI to go with his 515 doubles. As a manager, Cronin led the Senators to a pennant in 1934 and the Red Sox to one in 1946. From 1959 to 1973, he served as AL President. He was inducted in 1956.

CANDY CUMMINGS
Pitcher (1872-1877)
Baseball's legendary inventor of the curveball, Cummings allegedly discovered the pitch while tossing clam shells as a youngster. Despite standing 5'9" and never weighing more than 120 pounds, from 1872 to 1877, he won 146 games before overwork forced him to retire. Inducted in 1939, he pitched for the Excelsior Club of Brooklyn before becoming a professional in the National Association.

KIKI CUYLER
Outfielder (1921-1938)
Pronounced "Cuy-Cuy," Kiki Cuyler hit a robust .354 as a Pirate rookie in 1924 and was heralded as "the next Ty Cobb." Kiki hit over .300 10 times and topped the .350 mark four times. He accumulated 2,299 hits for a lifetime mark of .321. Inducted in 1968, he had 1,305 runs, 1,065 RBI, and 328 stolen bases during his career.

RAY DANDRIDGE
Third baseman (1933-1944)
Dandridge excelled at third base in the Negro and Mexico Leagues, hitting for power and average while fielding with precision. He accumulated a .347 average against white big league pitching. In 1949, he signed with the Giants and tore apart the American Association for Minneapolis, but at age 36 never received a call to the majors. He was inducted in 1987.

DIZZY DEAN
Pitcher (1930-1941; 1947)
Baseball's most colorful pitcher, Dean threw smoke, spoke in home-spun hyperbole, and by age 26 had won 134 games for the Cardinals. After breaking his toe in the 1937 All-Star game, Dean altered his pitching motion, hurt his arm, and never approached his previous record. Inducted in 1953, he had a 150-83 career record with a 3.02 ERA. Dizzy was the last NL pitcher to notch 30 wins in a season when he went 30-7 in 1934. His brother Paul also pitched for the Cardinals. Later a broadcaster, Dizzy's folksy, broken grammar attracted the ire of English teachers and the devotion of listeners everywhere.

ED DELAHANTY
Outfielder (1888-1903)

One of five brothers to play in the majors, Delahanty was perhaps baseball's premier hitter of the 1890s. He hit .400 three times, and his .346 career mark is fourth all time. Unfortunately, he lived as hard as he played. In 1903, Delahanty was suspended for drinking. En route to his home, "Big Ed" (age 35) was kicked off a train, fell into the Niagara River, and was swept over the falls to his death. He was inducted in 1945.

BILL DICKEY
Catcher (1928-1943; 1946)

Catcher of 100 or more games for 13 consecutive seasons, in 1936 Dickey hit .363, still a record for the position. He accumulated a .313 batting average and 1,209 RBI in his career. During his 17 years, the Yankees won nine pennants and captured eight world championships. Inducted in 1954, Dickey is also credited with developing the receiving skills of Yogi Berra.

MARTIN DIHIGO
Pitcher; outfielder (1923-1950)

The first Cuban elected to the Hall, Dihigo starred as a pitcher and outfielder in Negro and Caribbean baseball from 1923 to 1950. Winner of more than 250 games from the mound, he hit over .400 three times. He was one of the most versatile players in the game's recent history; he was able to play all of the infield positions, as well as being one of the best hurlers in history. Inducted in 1977, Dihigo is also in the Cuban and Mexican Halls of Fame.

JOE DiMAGGIO
Outfielder (1936-1942; 1946-1951)

The best of the DiMaggio brothers, "Joltin' Joe" led the Yankees to nine pennants while making 13 All-Star teams in 13 seasons. A three-time MVP, the quiet, graceful center fielder is often credited with being the best player of his generation. In 1941, "The Yankee Clipper" hit in a record 56 consecutive games. He led the AL in batting average twice, slugging average twice, triples once, home runs twice, runs scored once, and RBI twice. Inducted in 1955, he retired with a .325 batting average, a .579 slugging average, 361 home runs, 1,390 runs scored, and 1,537 RBI.

BOBBY DOERR
Second baseman (1937-1944; 1946-1951)

Doerr was known for his reliable defensive play and potent bat. For 14 seasons he was one of the best second basemen in baseball, spending his entire career with the Red Sox, and never playing a game at another position. In 1944, Doerr was the AL MVP, leading the loop in slugging at .528. Inducted in 1986, Doerr had a career .288 average, 223 homers, and 1,247 RBI.

DON DRYSDALE
Pitcher (1956-1969)

In the early 1960s, Drysdale and teammate Sandy Koufax gave the Dodgers baseball's best pitching tandem. The intimidating Drysdale led the NL in Ks three times. He was 25-9 with a 2.83 ERA and a league-best 232 strikeouts in 1962, winning the Cy Young Award. In 1968, "Big D" hurled six shutouts in a row on his way to 58 consecutive scoreless innings. Inducted in 1984, he was 209-166 with a 2.95 ERA and 2,486 strikeouts.

HUGH DUFFY
Outfielder (1888-1906)

In 1894, the diminutive Duffy hit .438 for NL Boston, the highest mark ever recorded under current rules. He also captured the first-ever Triple Crown that year, with 18 homers and 145 RBI. Never again approaching .400, Duffy still compiled a career .324 average, 1,551 runs, and 1,299 RBI. Inducted in 1945, he led the NL in homers twice despite playing at 165 pounds. After his retirement, he served another 48 seasons as manager, coach, owner, and scout.

BILLY EVANS
Umpire (1906-1927)
Inducted in 1973, Evans got his start as a sportswriter and then did what many writers have always thought they could do better—be an umpire. He was one of the best in the AL, working six World Series.

JOHNNY EVERS
Second baseman (1902-1917; 1922; 1929)
Perhaps the best of the "Tinker-to-Evers-to-Chance" double play combination, second baseman Evers relied on a steady glove and just enough hitting to help lead his club to five pennants in 16 seasons. Although he played most of his career with the Cubs, in 1914 he was the NL MVP while with the "Miracle" Boston Braves. Inducted in 1946, "The Trojan" retired with 919 runs scored and 324 stolen bases.

BUCK EWING
Catcher (1880-1897)
Connie Mack called Ewing "the greatest catcher of all time." He eclipsed the .300 mark in 10 seasons, including a string of eight straight times. Inducted in 1939, Ewing had a lifetime .303 batting average and scored 1,129 runs.

RED FABER
Pitcher (1914-1933)
The last AL pitcher allowed to throw the spitball, Faber spent his entire 20-year career with the White Sox, posting a 254-213 record. An illness and injury in 1919 kept him out of the World Series, and left him untouched by the infamous "Black Sox" scandal. He led the AL in ERA and in complete games in two years. Inducted in 1964, Faber posted a career 3.15 ERA in 4,087⅔ innings, with 274 complete games.

BOB FELLER
Pitcher (1936-1941; 1945-1956)
Phenom Feller left the farm at age 17 and struck out 15 in his first official big league appearance. Amazingly, he was signed by a Cleveland scout for one dollar and an autographed baseball. Feller's fastball, once timed at over 98 mph, may have been the fastest of all time. "Rapid Robert" led the AL seven times in strikeouts, six seasons in wins, and four times in shutouts. Inducted in 1962, Feller won 266 games, all for Cleveland, and three no-hitters.

RICK FERRELL
Catcher (1929-1947)
One of the few players inducted (in 1984) primarily for his defense, Ferrell nonetheless hit .300 four times. He was a career .281 hitter and drew 931 walks. With the Red Sox, for four seasons Ferrell teamed with pitching brother Wes to form one of baseball's few brothers batteries.

ROLLIE FINGERS
Pitcher (1968-1985)
The earliest reliever to be used in a "closer" role, Fingers was the first pitcher to reach 300 saves. He was the fireman for the champion Athletics in the early 1970s, then led the NL in saves with San Diego. In 1981 with the Brewers, he won the MVP and Cy Young awards. He retired in 1985 with 341 career saves and was inducted in 1992.

ELMER FLICK
Outfielder (1898-1910)
A slick fielding, speedy outfielder for the Phillies and Indians, in 1905 Flick won the AL batting crown with a then record low average of .306. In the spring of 1907, Detroit thought so much of Flick they offered Ty Cobb in trade. The Indians turned Detroit down. That season Flick hit .302 in his last full season, Cobb hit .350 in his first. Inducted in 1963, Flick compiled a .313 career batting average.

WHITEY FORD
Pitcher (1950; 1953-1967)

Ford's winning percentage of .690 is the best of any 200-game winner. The Yankee pitcher led the AL in wins three times and ERA twice. Ford holds eight World Series pitching records, including wins (10) and strikeouts (94). His 25-4 record in 1961 earned him the Cy Young Award. Inducted in 1974, "The Chairman of the Board" was 236-106 with a 2.75 ERA and 156 complete games.

RUBE FOSTER
Executive; pitcher

As a star pitcher for a number of early black teams, and later as the first president of the Negro National League, Foster earned the title "Father of Black Baseball." Foster's efforts in organizing the NNL gave black baseball needed stability. He in effect saved the Negro League and made it a popular game. Foster was enshrined to the Hall of Fame in 1981.

JIMMIE FOXX
First baseman (1925-1942; 1944-1945)

For 12 consecutive seasons with the Athletics and Red Sox, Foxx slammed 30 or more home runs and knocked in more than 100 runs. In 1933, Foxx hit .356, swatted 48 homers, and knocked in 163 RBI to win the Triple Crown. A three-time MVP, "Double X" had a lifetime slugging average of .609, fourth all time. Inducted in 1951, Foxx had 534 career homers, 1,921 RBI, and a .325 average.

FORD FRICK
NL President (1934-1951)
Commissioner (1951-1965)

Frick served as Babe Ruth's ghost writer before being named NL President in 1934. In 1951, he was elected Commissioner. During his executive tenure he helped establish the Hall of Fame, supported Branch Rickey's signing of Jackie Robin-son, and presided over baseball's busiest period of expansion before retiring. He was inducted in 1970.

FRANKIE FRISCH
Second baseman (1919-1937)

A member of more NL pennant winners than any other player, Frisch played in four fall classics with the Giants and four with the Cardinals. He cracked the .300 mark 13 times, scored 100 runs seven times, and was the 1931 NL MVP. Named player-manager in 1933, "The Fordham Flash" led the "Gashouse Gang" to the world championship in 1934. Inducted in 1947, he scored 1,532 runs in his career while batting .316.

PUD GALVIN
Pitcher (1875; 1879-1892)

Nicknamed "Pud" because he made pudding out of hitters, Galvin was pitcher supreme for NL Buffalo in the 1880s. On his way to 364 career victories, Galvin pitched more than 400 innings nine times, and won 46 games in both 1883 and 1884. "Gentle Jeems" is 11th on the all-time list with 57 shutouts. Inducted in 1965, he is also second all time with 646 complete games and 6,003⅓ innings pitched.

LOU GEHRIG
First baseman (1923-1939)

"The Iron Horse," Gehrig played in a record 2,130 consecutive games for the Yankees. Usually batting cleanup behind Babe Ruth, Gehrig knocked 46 home runs and set the AL record for RBI with 184 in 1931. He had more than 40 home runs in five seasons, more than 150 RBI in seven seasons, and a .600 slugging percentage in nine seasons. "Columbia Lou" had a .632 career slugging percentage, a .340 batting average, 493 home runs, 1,990 RBI, and 1,888 runs scored. Although fatally ill with amyotrophic lateral sclerosis, in 1939 he bid farewell to 61,000 fans at

Yankee Stadium by saying "Today I consider myself the luckiest man on the face of the earth." The waiting period for the Hall was waived, and Gehrig was admitted in 1939.

CHARLIE GEHRINGER
Second baseman (1924-1942)

His efficient and dependable play at second base for the Tigers earned Gehringer the appellation "The Mechanical Man." He regularly led the league in fielding and hit over .300 in 13 of 16 seasons. He had over 100 RBI and 200 or more hits in seven seasons. In 1937, his loop-high .371 average made him AL MVP. Inducted in 1949, he retired with a career .320 batting average, 2,839 hits, 1,774 runs scored, and 1,427 RBI.

BOB GIBSON
Pitcher (1959-1975)

In 1968, Gibson had the second-lowest ERA in modern NL history, a stingy 1.12, while winning both Cy Young and MVP honors. He also won the Cy Young Award in 1970. In the 1967 World Series, he led St. Louis to victory over Boston, winning three times while giving up only 14 hits. A consummate power-pitcher, Gibson's blend of speed and control resulted in 251 career wins. Inducted in 1981, "Hoot" had a career 2.91 ERA, 3,117 strikeouts, and 255 complete games.

JOSH GIBSON
Catcher (1930-1946)

For 16 seasons Gibson reigned as the Negro Leagues' supreme slugger, perhaps smacking nearly 1,000 home runs and as many as 90 in a single season. The powerful catcher was often called the black Babe Ruth; in another time, Ruth may have been referred to as the poor man's Josh Gibson. One of the most dedicated players ever, Gibson would play 200 games in summer and winter leagues in a single season. In 1947, with Jackie

Robinson on the verge of breaking the big league color line, Gibson, only age 36, died of a brain hemorrhage. He was inducted in 1972.

WARREN GILES
NL President (1951-1969)

Giles's career started as president of minor league Moline in 1919 and ended 50 years later when he retired as president of the NL. During his tenure, from 1951 to 1969, he oversaw the transfer of the Giants and Dodgers to California, and the addition of franchises in New York (Mets), Houston, San Diego, and Montreal. He was inducted in 1979.

LEFTY GOMEZ
Pitcher (1930-1943)

Gomez's sense of humor was matched only by his skill on the mound. A 20-game winner four times for the Yankees of the 1930s, Gomez went undefeated in six World Series decisions. He led the AL in Ks three times and in ERA twice. His secret to success? Quipped Lefty, "Clean living and a fast outfield." Inducted in 1972, "Goofy" was 189-102 with a 3.34 ERA in his career.

GOOSE GOSLIN
Outfielder (1921-1938)

The best hitter ever to play for the Senators, Goslin led Washington to its only three appearances in the World Series. He slugged three home runs in both the 1924 and 1925 fall classics. Goose had 100 RBI or more and batted over .300 in 11 seasons. Inducted in 1968, he excelled in the clutch, and in 18 seasons had 1,609 RBI, 2,735 hits, and a .316 average.

HANK GREENBERG
First baseman (1930; 1933-1941; 1945-1947)

Despite playing only nine full seasons, Greenberg smacked 331 home runs and captured AL MVP honors in 1935 and

1940 for the Tigers. He lost three years to World War II, but came back in 1946 to lead the AL in homers and RBI. He had league- and career-high totals of 58 dingers (1938) and 183 RBI (1937). Inducted in 1956, "Hammerin' Hank" had a career .313 batting average, a .605 slugging percentage, and 1,276 RBI.

CLARK GRIFFITH
Manager (1901-1920)
A leading pitcher of the 1890s, Griffith won 20 games six straight seasons with the White Stockings. He won 240 games in his career. Over a 20-year period the cagey "Old Fox" managed, in turn, the White Sox, Yankees, Reds, and Senators. He had a 1,491-1,367 record and won but one pennant. Inducted in 1946, he was also president of the Senators from 1920 to 1955.

BURLEIGH GRIMES
Pitcher (1916-1934)
In 1934, Grimes threw the last legal spitter in baseball history. Over the preceding 19 seasons, he won 270 games with seven different teams. One of a handful of pitchers allowed to throw the spitter after its ban in 1920, Grimes was by far the most successful. Inducted in 1964, "Ol' Stubble-beard" won more than 20 games in five seasons, and led the NL in complete games four times.

LEFTY GROVE
Pitcher (1925-1941)
In an era dominated by hitting, the left-handed Grove was almost unhittable, winning 20 games or more seven straight seasons with Connie Mack's Philadelphia A's, including a remarkable 31-4 mark in 1931. That year, Grove was the AL MVP. On his way to 300 wins, he led the AL in strikeouts seven times, in ERA nine times, in complete games three times, and in winning percentage five times. "Mose" was inducted in 1947.

CHICK HAFEY
Outfielder (1924-1937)
Hafey's misfortune was to play before the advent of the batting helmet. Several beanings and a chronic sinus condition affected his vision, forcing him to wear glasses in an effort to correct the damage. Nevertheless, Chick (inducted in 1971) hit over .300 in nine seasons and captured the NL title in 1931 with a .349 mark. He was known for his rifle arm and his line drives. Ill health and vision problems, however, forced the career .317 batter to retire.

JESSE HAINES
Pitcher (1918; 1920-1937)
Knuckleballer Haines didn't make the big leagues for good until he was age 26. However, he stuck around until he was 45, winning 20 games three times and finishing with 210 victories for the Cardinals, including a no-hitter against the Braves in 1924. In 1927, he racked up a 24-10 record, leading the NL with 25 complete games and six shutouts. Inducted in 1970, "Pop" had a career .571 winning percentage and 209 complete games.

BILLY HAMILTON
Outfielder (1888-1901)
While playing with Philadelphia and Boston in the NL, "Sliding Billy" Hamilton ran into the records. He was credited with 915 stolen bases, although for most of his career a runner received credit for a base theft by advancing an extra base on a hit. Inducted in 1961, his lifetime .344 mark is the eighth best all time. In 1894, his ability on the bases brought him home a record 196 times.

WILL HARRIDGE
AL President (1931-1959)
AL President from 1931 until 1959, Harridge stayed out of the limelight and quietly led the league from the era of Babe Ruth to the era of Mickey Mantle. An early supporter of the All-Star Game and night

baseball, Harridge was a tough, conservative executive who insisted on order. He was inducted in 1972.

BUCKY HARRIS
Manager (1924-1943; 1947-1948; 1950-1956)

An above average second baseman for the Senators, Harris was a natural leader who had his greatest success as manager. In his first season as player-manager in 1924, he led the Senators to their only world championship. He went on to manage another 28 seasons with five other clubs, going 2,157-2,218. Inducted in 1975, Harris usually had little talent but was a respected strategist who drove his players to play their best.

GABBY HARTNETT
Catcher (1922-1941)

From 1922 through 1940, Hartnett was likely the NL's best catcher. A fine defensive catcher, his best season was 1930, when he hit .339 with 37 home runs and 122 RBI. Hartnett was chosen as an All-Star player from 1933 through 1938. In the 1934 game, he was the backstop when Ruth, Gehrig, Foxx, Simmons, and Cronin were put away in order. He hit .344 as the NL MVP in 1935. His late-season, ninth-inning "homer in the gloaming" against Pittsburgh won the 1938 pennant for the Cubs. Inducted in 1955, he had a .297 career batting average, with 236 homers and 1,179 RBI.

HARRY HEILMANN
Outfielder (1914; 1916-1930; 1932)

In the four seasons that Heilmann won the AL batting crown, his lowest average was .393. Inducted in 1952, he batted over .300 in 12 seasons and hit an amazing .403 in 1923. Playing mostly for Detroit, the slow-footed outfielder (nicknamed "Slug") wielded a line-drive bat that resulted in 2,660 hits, including 542 doubles, for a .342 batting average.

BILLY HERMAN
Second baseman (1931-1943; 1946-1947)

A 10-time All-Star, Herman's 227 hits and 57 doubles in 1935 were tops in the NL. The best defensive second baseman in the loop, he hit .300 or better eight times in his career. After playing most of his career for the Cubs, in 1941 he was traded to Brooklyn, prompting Dodger owner Larry MacPhail to pronounce, accurately, "I just bought a pennant." Inducted in 1975, Herman had a career .304 batting average and 486 doubles.

HARRY HOOPER
Outfielder (1909-1925)

A right field star, Hooper's arm was legendary (he averaged 20 assists a year) as he teamed with Duffy Lewis and Tris Speaker to give the BoSox the best outfield of the era. A lifetime .281 hitter, Hooper scored 1,429 runs. He was inducted in 1971.

ROGERS HORNSBY
Second baseman (1915-1937)

Perhaps the greatest righthanded hitter of all time, Hornsby's career .358 average is second only to Ty Cobb's .366. "Rajah's" .424 mark in 1924 is the best of the century. His greatest success came with the Cardinals; from 1920 to 1925 he collected six straight batting titles, as well as two Triple Crowns. Inducted in 1942, Hornsby's fierce demeanor made him one of the most disliked players of his time.

WAITE HOYT
Pitcher (1918-1938)

The Yankee pitching ace of the 1920s, Hoyt won 20 games only twice, but compiled a 6-4 record in the World Series with a 1.83 ERA. In 1927, "Schoolboy" led the AL in wins (22), winning percentage (.759), and ERA (2.63). Inducted in 1969, he won in double figures 12 seasons and had a career 237-182 record. He was one of the first ex-ballplayers to work in broadcasting.

CAL HUBBARD
Umpire (1936-1951; 1954-1962)

Hubbard is the only man in the baseball, college football, and pro football Halls of Fame. While starring as a football tackle, Cal umpired in his off-seasons, and when he retired from football became an AL umpire. He weighed 250 pounds, and few players chose to argue with Hubbard. He was inducted in 1976.

CARL HUBBELL
Pitcher (1928-1943)

Hubbell used the screwball to notch 253 career wins and a 2.97 ERA, all for the Giants. From 1933 to 1937, he posted five straight 20-win seasons, and was NL MVP in '33 and '36. Inducted in 1947, "King Carl" led the NL in wins three times, ERA three times, and in strikeouts once. In the 1934 All-Star game, the lefthanded "Meal Ticket" struck out five straight Hall-of-Famers—Babe Ruth, Lou Gehrig, Jimmie Foxx, Al Simmons, and Joe Cronin.

MILLER HUGGINS
Manager (1913-1929)

A decent second baseman with the Reds and Cardinals, Huggins is best remembered as the Yankee manager of the 1920s. Standing only 5'6", he was the one man able to temper the boisterous Babe Ruth. "The Mighty Mite's" 1927 Yankees team is widely considered the best of all time. "Hug" was 1,413-1,134 in his career, including five seasons with mediocre Cardinal clubs. Inducted in 1964, he won six pennants and three world championships in his 12 years with the Yankees.

CATFISH HUNTER
Pitcher (1965-1979)

Given his nickname by A's owner Charlie Finley, Hunter went directly from high school to the major leagues. Beginning in 1971, Catfish won 20 games or more five straight seasons and earned the Cy Young Award in 1974 with a 25-12 record. After three A's world championships (1972 to 1974), Hunter signed with the Yankees for $3.75 million in 1975, then the biggest contract in baseball history. Inducted in 1987, he had a 224-166 career record with a 3.26 ERA and 2,958 strikeouts.

MONTE IRVIN
Outfielder (Negro Leagues years 1939-1943; 1945-1948; NL years 1949-1956)

Despite twice leading the Negro National League in hitting, it was 1949 before 30-year-old Irvin was signed by the Giants. He began his Negro League career in 1939, and he also played in the Mexican League, where he won a Triple Crown in 1940. In eight NL seasons, he hit .293, leading the league in RBI with 121 in 1951. He was enshrined in 1973.

REGGIE JACKSON
Outfielder (1967-1987)

"The Straw that Stirs the Drink," Jackson was a publicity hog, a prolific slugger, a superior outfielder, and most of all, a big winner. He played on 11 division winners and five World Champions. "Mr. October's" finest moment came in game six of the 1977 Series, when he smacked three homers, each on the first pitch of the at bat. Inducted in 1993, the four-time home run king had 563 homers and 1,702 RBI, but he also compiled more Ks (2,597) than any other player.

TRAVIS JACKSON
Shortstop (1922-1936)

A solid defensive shortstop for the Giants of the 1920s and 1930s, Jackson helped the Giants to four pennants. "Stonewall" also batted over .300 in six seasons, and he had more than 90 RBI in three seasons. Inducted in 1982, he accumulated a career average of .291, peaking at .339 in 1930.

FERGUSON JENKINS
Pitcher (1965-1983)

After being traded from the Phillies to the Cubs in early 1966, Jenkins embarked on a string of six consecutive 20-plus win seasons. He won only 14 in 1973 and was traded to Texas, where he won the 1974 Cy Young Award with a 25-12 record. One of the game's most durable pitchers, Jenkins had a career 284-226 record, with a a 3.34 ERA and 3,192 Ks. He was inducted in 1991.

HUGHIE JENNINGS
Shortstop (1891-1903; 1907; 1909; 1912; 1918)
Manager (1907-1920; 1924)

From 1894 to 1896 as shortstop and captain of NL Baltimore, Jennings led the club to pennants. In his five years with Baltimore, "Hustling Hughie" never hit below .328 and was a lifetime .312 hitter. In his first three years as Detroit's manager, Jennings won pennants, from 1907 to 1909. Inducted in 1945, he was 1,163-984 as a manager.

BAN JOHNSON
AL President (1901-1927)

The founder of the American League, Johnson was arguably the most powerful man in baseball during the first quarter of the 20th century. When the minor Western League folded in 1893, Johnson revived it. He put it on solid footing and made it a major league in 1901. The Black Sox scandal of 1920 undermined his power, however, and led to the Commissioner system, leading to Johnson's retirement in 1927. He was inducted in 1937.

JUDY JOHNSON
Third baseman (1919-1936)

The greatest third baseman in Negro League history, Johnson combined steady defensive play with stellar batting performances. A line-drive hitter, Johnson hit .390 and .406 in two of his seasons with the Philadelphia Hilldales, leading them to two black World Series appearances. In later years, Judy scouted for the Philadelphia A's and Phillies. He was inducted in 1975.

WALTER JOHNSON
Pitcher (1907-1927)

One of the first five men elected to the Hall, Johnson's legendary fastball and pinpoint control enabled him to win 417 games (second on the all-time list) with the usually inferior Senators. In his 20-year career, "The Big Train" led the AL in strikeouts 12 times, shutouts seven times, and in victories six times. Johnson's 110 shutouts are the most in history. Inducted in 1936, "Barney's" 2.16 career ERA is seventh lowest, his 531 complete games rank fourth, and his 5,924 innings pitched are the third most in baseball.

ADDIE JOSS
Pitcher (1902-1910)

In only nine seasons with Cleveland, Joss won 160 games with a winning percentage of .623 and an ERA of 1.89 (second all time). A side-armer, Joss hurled two no-hitters. He struck out 926 batters and walked only 370 in 2,336 innings pitched. In 1911, he died of tubercular meningitis at age 31. Due to his spectacular record, the Hall's usual 10-year career requirement was waived for Joss, in 1978.

AL KALINE
Outfielder (1953-1974)

As a 20-year-old outfielder with Detroit in 1955, Kaline won the batting title, hitting .340, to become the youngest champion ever. Although he never duplicated that figure, he played in 18 All-Star games, won 11 Gold Gloves, and accumulated 3,007 hits. Inducted in 1980, he also had 498 doubles, 399 home runs, 1,583 RBI, 1,622 runs scored, and 1,277 bases on balls. In his only World Series, in 1968, Kaline hit .379 and had two homers.

TIM KEEFE
Pitcher (1880-1893)

In only 14 seasons, Keefe won 342 games, one of six 19th century pitchers to top the 300 mark. Remarkably, after overhand pitching was legalized in 1884, Keefe continued to pitch—and win—underhanded. Inducted in 1964, "Sir Timothy" pioneered the use of the changeup to notch a career 2.62 ERA with 553 complete games. He led his league in ERA in three seasons.

WEE WILLIE KEELER
Outfielder (1892-1910)

Keeler said, "I hit 'em where they ain't." Utilizing his good speed and batting skills, he developed the "Baltimore chop" to bounce the ball over and between infielders. From 1894 to 1901, he collected a major league record 200 hits each season. Inducted in 1939, he had 2,947 career hits, 1,719 runs, and a .341 batting average. In 1897, he hit in 44 consecutive games. That same year he notched a personal best .432 batting average, leading the league with 243 hits in only 128 games.

GEORGE KELL
Third baseman (1943-1957)

An excellent third baseman and career .306 hitter, Kell excelled for five different clubs in the 1940s and 1950s. In 1949, he edged out Ted Williams for his only batting crown, hitting .3429 to Williams's .3427. Inducted in 1983, Kell scored a lifetime 881 runs and drove in 870 runs.

JOE KELLEY
Outfielder (1891-1906; 1908)

Kelley played for the great Baltimore teams of the 1890s and later went to star with Brooklyn and Cincinnati. He batted over .300 for 11 straight years. In 1894, he hit .393 and batted a perfect 9 for 9 in a doubleheader. Kelley had a lifetime .317 average, with 194 triples, 1,424 runs scored, and 1,193 RBI. He was inducted in 1971.

GEORGE KELLY
First baseman (1915-1917; 1919-1930; 1932)

After failing in his first three seasons in the bigs, Kelly came into his own for the Giants in 1919. From 1921 to 1926, Kelly hit over .300 and averaged 108 RBI, helping the Giants capture four pennants. Inducted in 1973, he was a .297 hitter and totaled 1,020 RBI.

KING KELLY
Outfielder; catcher (1878-1893)

Baseball's first celebrity, Kelly was the subject of the popular song, "Slide, Kelly, Slide"; recited "Casey At The Bat" on stage; and off the field played the role of dandy to a tee. On the field, he perfected the hit-and-run and developed the hook and head-first slides. Inducted in 1945, he hit .308 lifetime and scored 1,357 runs.

HARMON KILLEBREW
First baseman; third baseman (1954-1975)

Killebrew hit 573 home runs; only Babe Ruth hit more in AL history. Killebrew led the league in homers five times, each time hitting more than 40. "Killer" had 40 or more homers in eight different seasons. The 1969 AL MVP also drove in more than 100 RBI in nine years, pacing the AL three times. Inducted in 1984, he hit only .256 lifetime but had 1,559 bases on balls.

RALPH KINER
Outfielder (1946-1955)

Joining Pittsburgh after World War II, in his first seven seasons Kiner led or tied for the NL lead in homers. Inducted in 1975, he had 369 lifetime dingers (for an incredible 7.1 home run percentage), 1,015 RBI, and 1,011 bases on balls in 10 years. Kiner has enjoyed a second career as a broadcaster for the Mets.

CHUCK KLEIN
Outfielder (1928-1944)

Playing five and one-half seasons in Philadelphia's cozy Baker Bowl, Klein led the NL in homers four times and never hit below .337. He was the 1932 NL MVP and won the Triple Crown in 1933 (.368 average, 28 homers, 120 RBI). Klein set an all-time record for outfield assists with 44 in 1930. Traded to the Cubs in 1934, he remained productive but didn't approach his earlier performances. Inducted in 1980, he had a lifetime .320 batting average, 300 homers, and 1,202 RBI.

BILL KLEM
Umpire (1905-1941)

Baseball's best-known umpire, Klem was active from 1905 to 1941. He revolutionized the position, and is credited with being the first to employ hand signals and don a chest protector. Inducted in 1953, he worked a record 18 World Series, and he was the umpire at the first All-Star Game in 1933.

SANDY KOUFAX
Pitcher (1955-1966)

Koufax had two careers. His best record in his first six years was an 11-11 mark. But, between 1961 and 1966, the lefty led the NL in wins and shutouts three times each and Ks four times. Koufax paced the Dodgers to pennants in '63, '65, and '66 while winning the Cy Young Award each year. His 25-5 record in 1963 earned him the NL MVP. Pitching in excruciating pain due to arthritis, Koufax led the NL in ERA his final five seasons, culminating with a 1.73 mark while going 27-9 in 1966. He retired at the peak of his profession. Inducted in 1972, he had a 165-87 record with a 2.76 career ERA and 2,396 strikeouts to only 817 walks.

NAP LAJOIE
Second baseman (1896-1916)

One of the best righty batters in history, Lajoie was the best second baseman of his era and became the first man at his position to be elected to the Hall. A graceful fielder, he hit over .300 16 times in his career. Inducted in 1937, he won the Triple Crown in 1901, the American League's debut season; he batted .422 with 14 homers and 125 RBI. His presence and outstanding performance gave the AL much-need attention and respect. Lajoie had a career .338 average, 3,242 hits, and 657 doubles.

KENESAW MOUNTAIN LANDIS
Commissioner (1920-1944)

Baseball's first Commissioner, Landis left his job as a federal judge in 1920 to take complete control of the major leagues. In cleaning up the Black Sox scandal, he restored the public's confidence in the integrity of baseball. His rule was law, and nobody dared challenge his authority. A champion of player rights, he unsuccessfully tried to halt the farm system. He died in 1944, eight days after his election for another seven-year term as "Baseball Czar." He was inducted in 1944.

TONY LAZZERI
Second baseman (1926-1939)

The second baseman on the "Murderer's Row" Yankee teams of the 1920s and '30s, Lazzeri combined power, high average, and slick fielding. A career .292 hitter who socked 178 homers, "Poosh 'Em Up" topped the .300 mark five times, and hit .354 in 1929. He was inducted in 1991.

BOB LEMON
Pitcher (1941-1942; 1946-1958)

Lemon made the big leagues as a third baseman, but he made the Hall of Fame as a pitcher. Switched to pitching during

World War II, Lemon won 20 games for the Indians seven times from 1948 to 1956. He led the AL in wins three times and complete games five times. Inducted in 1976, he had a career 207-128 record for a .618 winning percentage. As manager, he took over the Yankees in mid-1978, overtaking the bumbling Red Sox from 10½ games back and leading the Bombers to a world championship.

BUCK LEONARD
First baseman (1934-1948)
In the Negro Leagues, Walter Leonard played Lou Gehrig to teammate Josh Gibson's Babe Ruth. Leonard played for the Homestead Grays and helped lead them to nine consecutive pennants. He was a lefthanded power hitter and clutch RBI man who hit for a high average. Inducted in 1972, he twice led the NNL in hitting, peaking at .410 in 1947. In 1952, at age 45, Leonard turned down an offer from Bill Veeck to play for the St. Louis Browns.

FREDDIE LINDSTROM
Third baseman (1924-1936)
Playing in the World Series for the Giants as an 18-year-old rookie in 1924, Lindstrom survived two bad hop ground balls that helped beat New York to become one of the NL's best third basemen. He topped the .300 mark seven times, including a .379 average in 1930. A year later an injury led to a switch to the outfield. He retired in 1936, at age 31, with a .311 career batting average, 301 doubles, and 895 runs scored. He was inducted in 1976.

POP LLOYD
Shortstop (1905-1932)
The finest shortstop in Negro baseball, Lloyd's stellar performance in a 1909 exhibition series against Ty Cobb's Tigers so embarrassed Cobb he vowed never to play blacks again. In 1928, despite being age 44, Lloyd led the Negro National League in batting with an eye-popping .564 average. From his time in Cuba, his nickname was "El Cuchara," which means "scoop" in Spanish. Lloyd was inducted in 1977.

ERNIE LOMBARDI
Catcher (1931-1947)
Called "Schnozz" because of his enormous nose, Lombardi was a slow, awkward-looking catcher who could hit a ton. He surpassed the .300 mark 10 times. In 1938, his league-leading .342 average with Cincinnati earned him the NL MVP Award. Five years later with the Braves, Lombardi again led the league with a .330 average, becoming the only catcher to do so twice. Inducted in 1986, he had a career .306 batting average and 990 RBI.

AL LOPEZ
Catcher (1928; 1930-1947)
Manager (1951-1965; 1968-1969)
A workhorse behind the plate, Lopez held the major league record for games caught until 1987. He turned manager in 1951, and in 1954 led Cleveland to 111 wins. In 1959, he won another pennant with the White Sox. Inducted in 1977, he drove his 17 teams to a 1,410-1,004 record for a .584 winning percentage, eighth all time. Usually losing the pennant to the Yankees, Lopez's clubs finished second in the AL 10 times.

TED LYONS
Pitcher (1923-1942; 1946)
Lyons had the misfortune of pitching for the White Sox during some of the worst years in the history of the franchise. Inducted in 1955, he won 260 games lifetime, with 356 complete games and 27 shutouts. He led the AL in shutouts twice and wins twice. In 1942, he led the AL with a 2.10 ERA. At age 42, he served three years in the Marines during World War II, then returned to baseball for one last season in 1946, going 1-4 despite a 2.32 ERA. He managed the Sox through '48.

CONNIE MACK
Manager (1894-1896; 1901-1950)

As player, manager, and owner, Mack had a career that spanned an incredible eight decades. Manager of the Athletics from 1901 to 1950, Mack built then tore apart several championship clubs. His first dynasty was from 1910 to 1914, when the Athletics won four pennants and three world championships. He sold off many of those players and finished in last place from 1915 to 1921. His second dynasty was the 1929 to 1931 clubs—three pennants and two world champs. Known to all as "Mr. Mack," he was the last man to manage out of uniform, preferring to wear formal attire. Inducted in 1937, he was 3,731-3,948 in his 53 years as a manager.

LARRY MacPHAIL
Executive

As an executive with the Reds, the Dodgers, and the Yankees, MacPhail played a part in virtually every baseball development between the wars. He brought air travel and lights to the major leagues in 1935, and radio broadcasts to Brooklyn in 1938. He was inducted in 1978. MacPhail's son and grandson, Lee and Andy, followed him as baseball executives.

MICKEY MANTLE
Outfielder (1951-1968)

Named after Mickey Cochrane by his baseball-loving father, Mutt, Mantle was taught to switch hit and became baseball's leading switch-hitter. Succeeding Joe DiMaggio as Yankee center fielder, all Mantle did was match Joe's three MVP Awards (1956, 1957, 1962). "The Commerce Comet" hit .353, 52 homers, and drove in 130 RBI to win the Triple Crown in 1956. He led the AL in home runs four times, RBI once, runs scored six times, and walks five times. If not for a series of knee injuries, Mantle may have been the best all time. He had the most all-time

World Series homers, RBI, and runs. Inducted in 1974, lifetime he had a .298 batting average, 536 homers, 1,509 RBI, 1,677 runs scored, and 1,733 walks.

HEINIE MANUSH
Outfielder (1923-1939)

Often overlooked today, Manush was one of the best hitters in baseball during his era. Topping the .300 mark 11 times, he compiled a career average of .330. Playing for the Tigers, Browns, Senators, Braves, Pirates, and Dodgers, he led his league in hits twice. Inducted in 1964, Manush notched 1,173 career RBI and 1,287 runs.

RABBIT MARANVILLE
Shortstop (1912-1933; 1935)

A top defensive shortstop and consummate showman, Maranville was the kind of player that did the little things, on and off the field, to make his team better. A superior fielder, he ranks first among all shortstops in putouts (5,139). Inducted in 1954, Maranville collected 2,605 hits and score 1,255 runs in 23 NL seasons.

JUAN MARICHAL
Pitcher (1960-1975)

In the mid-1960s, the Giants' Marichal was one of the best and most consistent pitchers in the game. His patented high leg kick masked a multitude of pitches. A six-time 20-game winner, Marichal somehow failed to win the Cy Young Award. His 243 career wins more than made up for that omission. He led the league in shutouts and in complete games twice. Inducted in 1983, "The Dominican Dandy" had a career 243-142 record, a 2.89 ERA, 2,303 Ks, and 52 shutouts.

RUBE MARQUARD
Pitcher (1908-1925)

In 1912, Marquard won his first 19 decisions for the Giants on his way to a 26-11 record. Although he won 23 games the following season, he never again matched his earlier play. He and Christy Mathewson gave the Giants a one-two punch few teams could match. Inducted in 1971, Marquard had a 201-177 career record with 197 complete games.

EDDIE MATHEWS
Third baseman (1952-1968)
Mathews combined with Hank Aaron to form one of the best power combos ever. For 14 consecutive years, Mathews hit 23 or more home runs, hitting 40 or more four times. A steady defensive player, he was an All-Star nine times. He led the NL in bases on balls in four seasons to retire with a total of 1,444. Inducted in 1978, he also tallied 512 career homers, 1,453 RBI, and 1,509 runs scored.

CHRISTY MATHEWSON
Pitcher (1900-1916)
As baseball's most popular player in his day, Mathewson dispelled the prevalent notion at the time that ballplayers need be crude and uneducated. "Big Six" was also perhaps the game's best pitcher. For 12 consecutive seasons he won 20 or more games for the Giants, as his trademark "fadeaway," a screwball, baffled a generation of batters. In the 1905 World Series, he hurled three shutouts in six days. He led the NL in ERA in five seasons, in Ks five times, and in shutouts four times. Inducted in 1936, "Matty" had a 373-188 career record, with a 2.13 ERA and 79 shutouts.

WILLIE MAYS
Outfielder (1951-1952; 1954-1973)
Mays could do everything: hit, field, and run. While the Giant center fielder's 660 home runs rank third all time, his magnificent over-the-shoulder catch of Vic Wertz's blast to center field in the 1954 World Series has become the standard against which all other catches are compared. Inducted in 1979, "The Say Hey

Kid" led the NL in slugging percentage five times, homers and stolen bases four times, triples three times, and runs scored twice. He had 3,283 career hits, a .302 batting average, a .557 slugging percentage, 1,903 RBI, and 2,062 runs scored.

JOE McCARTHY
Manager (1926-1946; 1948-1950)
While McCarthy never played a game in the majors, in 24 years as manager he collected seven world championships and nine pennants. Inducted in 1957, his 2,125-1,333 record gives him an all-time best .615 winning percentage. Most of his success came with the Yankees, where he won four straight World Series from 1936 to 1939. After winning the NL pennant with the Cubs in 1929, McCarthy piloted the Yankees to a pennant in 1932 to become the first manager to win a pennant in both leagues.

TOMMY McCARTHY
Outfielder (1884-1896)
McCarthy made a lasting mark on the game when he perfected the fly-ball trap in order to throw out the lead runner of a double play, leading to the infield fly rule. Although he was known for his defense, in 1893 he hit a robust .361, helping Boston to the NL title. Inducted in 1946, he was a career .292 hitter and topped the .300 mark four times.

WILLIE McCOVEY
First baseman (1959-1980)
Willie McCovey joined Giants teammate Willie Mays to give opposing pitchers the willies. McCovey smashed 30 or more home runs seven times, leading the NL in dingers three times, in home run percentage five times, and in RBI twice. In 1969, "Stretch" was NL MVP with a .320 average, 45 homers, and 126 RBI. That same year he drew a record 45 intentional walks. In 1970, McCovey homered in all 12 parks, a rare feat. Inducted in 1986,

459

"Big Mac" notched 521 homers, 1,555 RBI, 1,229 runs scored, and 1,350 walks in his career.

JOE McGINNITY
Pitcher (1899-1908)

While McGinnity's nickname "Iron Man" was derived from his off-season occupation in a foundry, it well described his mound efforts. For nine straight years he pitched 300-plus innings, topping 400 twice and leading the league five times. Inducted in 1946, he had a career 247-144 record with a 2.64 ERA and 314 complete games. He pitched another 17 seasons in the minors, finally retiring at age 54.

BILL McGOWAN
Umpire (1925-1954)

Inducted in 1992, McGowan earned his "No. 1" nickname in the AL because of his renown for accuracy. Chosen to work in eight World Series games, he also worked four All-Star games, including the first, in 1933.

JOHN McGRAW
Manager (1899; 1901-1932)

As third baseman for Baltimore in the 1890s, McGraw was talented enough to make the Hall on his merits as a player. As the Giants manager from 1902 to 1932, he dominated baseball during its "scientific" era, and successfully made the transition to the power game of the 1920s. Despite capturing 10 pennants, the "Little Napoleon" won the World Series only three times. A manager for 33 years, McGraw racked up 2,784 victories in 4,801 games, both second on the all-time list to Connie Mack.

BILL McKECHNIE
Manager (1915; 1922-1926; 1928-1946)

McKechnie may have been the best-liked manager ever. Winning pennants with three different teams, the gentlemanly McKechnie refuted Leo Durocher's "nice guys finish last" notion. "The Deacon's" best effort, though, might have been with the fifth-place 1937 Braves, enough to win the Manager of the Year award. Inducted in 1962, he won two world championships and was 1,899-1,724 in 25 years.

JOE MEDWICK
Outfielder (1932-1948)

Medwick provided the power to light up the 1930s Cardinals' "Gashouse Gang." He led the NL in RBI three consecutive years and in hits twice. In 1937, "Ducky" (a nickname he loathed) batted .374 with 31 homers and 154 RBI to capture the Triple Crown. Inducted in 1968, "Muscles" was a brawler who had a career .324 average, 1,383 RBI, and 540 doubles. In the 1934 World Series against Detroit, his hard slide into third earned him the wrath of Tiger fans, who pelted him with garbage until Commissioner Landis ordered him from the field for his own safety.

JOHNNY MIZE
First baseman (1936-1942; 1946-1953)

Despite losing three prime years to World War II, Mize still connected for 359 home runs, primarily with the Cardinals and Giants. He led the NL in homers four times and RBI three times. Sold to the Yankees in 1949, Mize played in five World Series, hitting three home runs in the 1952 classic. Inducted in 1981, "The Big Cat" batted .312 lifetime, slugged .562 (eighth highest in history), and drove in 1,337.

JOE MORGAN
Second baseman (1963-1984)

Where Morgan played, championships followed. After leading Cincinnati's "Big Red Machine" of the mid-1970s to two World Series victories, Morgan led the 1980 Astros to a division title. He then helped Philadelphia capture the pennant in 1983. Inducted in 1990, "Little Joe" won back-to-back NL MVP Awards in 1975 and '76. Only 5'7", he had 268 career homers, 689 stolen bases, 1,133 RBI, 1,650 runs, and 1,865 walks.

STAN MUSIAL
Outfielder; first baseman (1941-1944; 1946-1963)

Originally signed as a pitcher, Musial hurt his arm and transferred to the outfield. Joining the Cardinals in 1941, Musial batted .426 in 12 games, and he went on to lead the NL seven times in batting average. NL MVP in 1943, '46, and '48, he used his "corkscrew" batting stance to hit over .310 for 16 seasons in a row. At the time of his retirement in 1963, "Stan the Man" held more than 50 major league and NL records. Inducted in 1969, he had a career .331 batting average, 3,630 base hits (fourth all time), 725 doubles (third), 475 home runs, 1,951 RBI, and 1,949 runs scored.

HAL NEWHOUSER
Pitcher (1939-1955)

The only pitcher to win back-to-back MVPs (in 1944 and '45), Newhouser was a Detroit native who pitched 15 seasons for the Tigers. Slighted by some as a wartime wonder, he had 275 Ks and a 26-9 record in 1946, and a 21-12 record in 1948. The lefty had 207 career wins and was inducted in 1992.

KID NICHOLS
Pitcher (1890-1901; 1904-1906)

Ranked seventh all time in wins with 361, Nichols starred in the 1890s for Boston, leading them to five NL pennants. Winner of 30 games seven times, Nichols started what he finished. In his 501 Boston starts, he was relieved only 25 times. Inducted in 1949, he had a lifetime 361-208 record and a 2.94 ERA.

JIM O'ROURKE
Outfielder (1872-1893; 1904)

In 1876, O'Rourke collected the first base hit in NL history, one of 2,304 he'd gather for his career. A lifetime .310 hitter, O'Rourke's manner of speaking earned him the nickname "Orator Jim." He was inducted in 1945.

MEL OTT
Outfielder (1926-1947)

Despite his small stature (5'9", 170 pounds), this Giant outfielder stands as a colossus among the game's sluggers. Ott's unique leg kick enabled him to generate the power for 511 home runs, the first man in NL history to hit 500. He led the NL in homers six times, in HR percentage 10 times, but in RBI only once. When he retired in 1947, he held the NL career mark for homers, runs scored (1,859), RBI (1,861), and walks (1,708). Inducted in 1951, "Master Melvin" retired with a .304 average.

SATCHEL PAIGE
Pitcher (Negro Leagues years 1926-1947; 1950; AL years 1948-1949; 1951-1953; 1965)

The first African-American ever elected to the Hall of Fame, Paige was the Negro Leagues' greatest drawing card. He started pitching for the Birmingham Black Barons in 1926 at age 20. His blazing fastball, uncanny control, and effervescent personality made him a legend by age 30. Inducted in 1971, he made his greatest mark on the game by pitching for the Kansas City Monarchs in the 1940s. In 1948, at age 42, he made his major league debut and helped Cleveland to the AL pennant. In 1965, at age 59, he was still able to pitch three scoreless innings for the Athletics.

JIM PALMER
Pitcher (1965-1967; 1969-1984)
Ace of Baltimore's powerful teams of the 1970s, Palmer won 20 games eight times on his way to three Cy Young Awards and 268 career wins. He led the AL in ERA twice and in innings pitched four times. Inducted in 1990, he had a career 2.86 ERA, 2,212 Ks, and 1,311 walks in 3,948 innings pitched.

HERB PENNOCK
Pitcher (1912-1917; 1919-1934)
Pennock finessed his way through 22 seasons to earn 240 wins. He had his greatest success with the Yankees of the 1920s, for whom he went 5-0 in World Series play, sporting a stellar 1.95 ERA. Inducted in 1948, "The Knight of Kennett Square" won in double figures for 13 seasons and completed 248 of his 421 career starts.

GAYLORD PERRY
Pitcher (1962-1983)
Though he won 314 games, struck out 3,534 batters, and registered a 3.10 ERA during a 22-year career that included tenures with eight different teams, Perry was best known for throwing—or not throwing—a spitball. He won 20 games five times in his career. He won the AL Cy Young Award in 1972 with Cleveland and the 1978 NL Cy Young Award with San Diego, making him the only pitcher to win the award in both leagues. He was inducted in 1991.

EDDIE PLANK
Pitcher (1901-1917)
A late bloomer, Plank didn't reach Connie Mack's A's until age 26. No matter, the lefthander blossomed to win 326 games. He won at least 20 games in eight seasons, with four in a row from 1902 to 1905. Inducted in 1946, "Gettysburg Eddie" compiled 69 career shutouts (fifth all time) and a 2.35 ERA.

OLD HOSS RADBOURN
Pitcher (1880-1891)
In 1884, Radbourn won 60 games for NL Providence, still an all-time record, notching a 1.38 ERA and 679 innings pitched. In only 12 seasons he chalked up 309 wins and a 2.67 ERA. Inducted in 1939, Old Hoss's 489 career complete games are eighth on the all-time list.

PEE WEE REESE
Shortstop (1940-1942; 1946-1958)
Reese led the Dodgers to seven pennants between 1941 and 1956. Despite his small size (5'10", 160 pounds), he was the acknowledged leader on the star-laden club. One of the top-fielding shortstops during the 1940s and 1950s, Pee Wee was an All-Star from 1947 to 1954. Inducted in 1984, he scored 1,338 runs in his career, leading the NL in 1947 with 132. When Branch Rickey signed Jackie Robinson, it was Reese, a Southerner, who led his teammates to accept Robinson as a player and a friend.

SAM RICE
Outfielder (1915-1934)
Rice, a fleet 150-pounder, smacked 2,987 hits on his way to a .322 career average for Washington. Inducted in 1963, he led the AL in hits twice and had 200 or more base hits six times. He scored 1,515 career runs and stole 351 bases. A master of bat control, Rice struck out only nine times in 616 at bats in 1929.

BRANCH RICKEY
Executive
One of the game's great innovators, Rickey invented the farm system and built NL dynasties in St Louis and Brooklyn. When he joined the Cardinals in 1919 as president and field manager, the franchise could not compete with richer clubs. "The Mahatma" began to buy minor league clubs, and by 1941, St. Louis had 32 minor league affiliates. He moved to

Brooklyn in 1942 to build that franchise. Rickey's most historic act, however, was to integrate the major leagues when he signed Jackie Robinson in 1947. Rickey was enshrined in 1967.

EPPA RIXEY
Pitcher (1912-1917; 1919-1933)

Rixey was a very good pitcher for some not very good teams, winning 266 games while losing 251. A workhorse and a master of control, Rixey won in double figures in 14 seasons and won 20 games four times. He was inducted in 1963. In 1922, his best season, he went a league-leading 25-13 for Cincinnati.

ROBIN ROBERTS
Pitcher (1948-1966)

Despite a penchant for throwing the gopher ball, Roberts won 20 games for six consecutive seasons from 1950 to 1955. He topped the NL in wins four straight years, and in innings pitched and complete games five times each. While not remembered as a strikeout artist, Robin did lead the NL two years in row in Ks. In 1952, he went 28-7 for the sixth-place Phillies. Inducted in 1976, Roberts was 286-245 with a 3.41 ERA in his 19 years.

BROOKS ROBINSON
Third baseman (1955-1977)

One of the greatest fielding third basemen ever, Robinson won the Gold Glove 16 times in 23 seasons. The AL MVP in 1964, Brooks turned in a .317 average, 28 homers, and a league-leading 118 RBI. He sparkled in postseason play, posting a .348 average in 18 ALCS games. In the 1970 World Series, he led the Orioles over the Reds, hitting .429 and turning in one spectacular fielding play after another. Inducted in 1983, he had 268 career homers, 1,357 RBI, and 1,232 runs.

FRANK ROBINSON
Outfielder (1956-1976)

Robinson was the first and only player to be selected MVP in both leagues. He was named NL Rookie of the Year in 1956 and the loop's MVP in 1961, when he paced the NL with a .611 slugging average and led the Reds to a pennant. Traded to Baltimore after the '65 season, Frank responded in '66 by hitting .316, 49 home runs, and knocking in 122 runs to win the Triple Crown. Inducted in 1982, he hit 30 homers in 11 seasons, and his 586 career homers rank fourth all time. He also had 1,812 career RBI and 1,829 runs scored. Named manager of the Indians in 1975, Robinson was the first African-American to manage a major league team.

JACKIE ROBINSON
Second baseman (1947-1956)

The first African-American to play major league baseball since 1884, Robinson succeeded under almost unbearable pressure to secure the black player a permanent place in the game. He endured numerous racial slights, even from his own teammates, without yielding his dignity, while leading the Dodgers to six pennants. A tremendous athlete, Robinson was a four-sport star at UCLA and served in the Army during World War II, before reaching the majors. As a 28-year-old rookie for Brooklyn in 1947, Robinson's aggressive base-running and hitting earned him Rookie of the Year honors. Two years later, in 1949, he led the NL with a .342 average and was named NL MVP. In 10 years of major league service, he accumulated a .311 batting average. He was enshrined in 1962.

WILBERT ROBINSON
Manager (1902; 1914-1931)

A catching star for Baltimore in the 1890s, Robinson coached under the Giants' John McGraw before becoming Brooklyn's manager in 1914. "Uncle Robbie" won pennants in 1916 and 1920 but never won a World Series. Inducted in 1945, he had a career 1,399-1,398 record.

EDD ROUSH
Outfielder (1913-1929; 1931)
One of the great defensive outfielders, Roush swung his 48-ounce bat with enough authority to attain two NL batting titles and a .323 lifetime average. In his 10 years in Cincinnati, he never hit lower than .321. Inducted in 1962, he had 1,099 career runs and 981 RBI. Roush habitually held out of spring training, returning only a week or so before opening day.

RED RUFFING
Pitcher (1924-1942; 1945-1947)
In six seasons with the Red Sox, Ruffing couldn't win, going 39-96 from 1924 to 1930 and leading the AL in losses twice. After he was traded to the Yankees, he couldn't lose, with a career 273-225 record and a 7-2 mark in 10 World Series games. Inducted in 1967, he won 20 games four seasons in a row from 1936 to 1939.

AMOS RUSIE
Pitcher (1889-1895; 1897-1898; 1901)
Rusie's fastball forced the rule makers to move the pitching distance from 45 feet to 60 feet 6 inches. From 1890 to 1895, the Giants pitcher led the NL in Ks five times, yet he walked nearly one man for every strikeout. "The Hoosier Thunderbolt" had eight 20-win seasons and 246 career victories in only nine full seasons, before he was traded to Cincinnati for Christy Mathewson. Rusie was inducted in 1977.

BABE RUTH
Outfielder; pitcher (1914-1935)
George Herman Ruth is arguably the greatest player of all time. A man of gargantuan appetites and ability, the Babe's mystique has transcended the sport of baseball and has become ingrained in American mythology. Starting his career as a pitcher with Boston, he was one of the best in the AL. In 1916, the Babe led the AL with a 1.75 ERA while going 23-12. He had 24 wins in '17 with a loop-high 35 complete games. Converted to the outfield part-time in 1918, he led the AL in homers with 11. After he was sold to the Yankees in 1920, he became a full-time flycatcher, and all but invented the home run, slugging 714 for his career, including a then-record 60 in 1927. Inducted in 1936, he led the AL in homers 12 seasons, RBI six seasons, slugging percentage 13 times, and bases on balls 11 times. He had a career .342 batting average, .690 slugging average (first all time), 506 doubles, 2,211 RBI (second all time), 2,174 runs (second all time), and 2,056 walks (first all time).

RAY SCHALK
Catcher (1912-1929)
Although Schalk's career average was .253, few complained when he was elected to the Hall. A superb catcher, Ray's game was defense. In 1920, he caught four 20-game winners for the White Sox, and four no-hitters, more than any other catcher. Inducted in 1955, he holds the AL record for assists by a catcher (1,811). Untainted by the 1919 Black Sox scandal, "Cracker" went on to play another decade.

RED SCHOENDIENST
Second baseman (1945-1963)
Schoendienst teamed with shortstop Marty Marion to form one of baseball's best-ever double-play combinations. Red could also hit, reaching a career-high .342 in 1953. Despite contracting tuberculosis in 1958, he returned to play parts of five more seasons. Inducted in 1989, he had 2,449 career hits and 1,223 runs scored.

TOM SEAVER
Pitcher (1967-1986)
In 1992, Seaver was named on a record 98.8 percent of the ballots for enshrine-

ment, indicating his stature among fans. A three-time Cy Young winner (1969, '73, and '75), he also finished second twice and third once. "Tom Terrific" led the Mets to a miracle world championship in 1969. He won 311 games and struck out 3,640 batters, and his .603 winning percentage was the best of any 300-game winner since Lefty Grove retired in 1941.

JOE SEWELL
Shortstop (1920-1933)
Sewell replaced Ray Chapman in the Cleveland lineup following Chapman's tragic death in 1920. One of the game's best fielding shortstops, Sewell struck out only 114 times in 7,132 at bats. Inducted in 1977, he had 1,141 career runs and 1,051 RBI.

AL SIMMONS
Outfielder (1924-1941; 1943-1944)
An unlikely looking hitter due to his "foot in the bucket" batting stance, Simmons was a leading slugger of his era. From 1929 to 1931, he helped the Athletics to three consecutive pennants, winning batting titles in both 1930 and 1931 with averages of .381 and .390. Inducted in 1953, "Bucketfoot Al" batted over .300 in the first 11 seasons of his career, racking up 2,927 hits and a career .334 batting average.

GEORGE SISLER
First baseman (1915-1922; 1924-1930)
Like Babe Ruth, Sisler's hitting was too good to be on a pitcher's schedule. He was switched to first base full-time in 1916 for the Browns and became one of the best, defensively. At bat he was simply unbelievable, hitting .407, .371, and .420 from 1920 to 1922. In 1920, "Gorgeous George" collected 257 base hits, still the all-time record. A sinus infection that affected his vision sidelined him in 1923. He returned to play seven more seasons. He was inducted in 1939.

ENOS SLAUGHTER
Outfielder (1938-1942; 1946-1959)
Slaughter would do anything—and often did—in order to win, using hustle to make up for any shortcomings in talent. His mad dash from first to home on a double won the 1946 World Series for the Cardinals. He led the NL in base hits in 1942 before going to war; he led the league in RBI when he came back. Inducted in 1985, "Country" played on four world champion clubs.

DUKE SNIDER
Outfielder (1947-1964)
Known as the "Duke of Flatbush" to his Brooklyn fans, Snider was one of a trio of Hall of Fame center fielders in New York during the 1950s. The others were named Willie Mays and Mickey Mantle. Inducted in 1980, Snider hit 40 homers from 1953 to 1957. He had 407 career homers, 1,333 RBI, and 1,259 runs scored.

WARREN SPAHN
Pitcher (1942; 1946-1965)
Baseball's winningest lefthander, Spahn didn't even stick in the majors until he was age 25. With the Braves, he won 20 games or more in 13 seasons, tying the major league record. Inducted in 1973, he led the league in wins eight times, complete games nine times, and strikeouts four times. He won the Cy Young Award in 1957, its second year of existence. After 21 years, Spahn retired with 363 wins (fifth all time), 245 losses, a 3.09 ERA, 382 complete games, and 63 shutouts (sixth all time) in 5,243⅔ innings pitched.

AL SPALDING
Pitcher (1871-1878); executive
A star pitcher in the 1870s, Spalding started a sporting goods company and took over NL Chicago. As a pitcher, he had a .787 career winning percentage. Inducted in 1939 as an executive, he helped write the new NL's constitution.

TRIS SPEAKER
Outfielder (1907-1928)

The best center fielder of his time, Speaker played close enough to the infield to take pick-off throws at second. "The Grey Eagle" hit over .300 in 18 seasons and topped .375 six times on his way to a career .344 mark (seventh all time). Traded from Boston to Cleveland in 1916, he won his only batting title, at .386. Inducted in 1937, "Spoke" hit a record 792 career doubles, and had 3,515 base hits (fifth all time).

WILLIE STARGELL
**Outfielder; first baseman
(1962-1982)**

One of the strongest players ever, Stargell made tape-measure homers common. He had 13 consecutive years of 20 or more home runs, pacing the NL in 1971 and 1973. He was named season, NLCS, and World Series MVP in 1979, when he led the world champion Bucs. Inducted in 1988, he had 475 career homers and 1,540 RBI.

CASEY STENGEL
Manager (1934-1936; 1938-1943; 1949-1960; 1962-1965)

A good outfielder, Stengel's two homers in the 1923 World Series helped the Giants beat the Yankees. As manager of Brooklyn and Boston, he earned a reputation as an entertaining, if not very effective, skipper. His creative use of the language, dubbed "Stengelese," made him a fan favorite. Named Yankee manager in 1949, "The Old Professor" won 10 pennants in 12 years, plus seven world championships. Inducted in 1966, he had a career 1,905-1,842 record.

BILL TERRY
First baseman (1923-1936)

A career .341 hitter, Terry was the last National Leaguer to hit over .400, batting .401 in 1930 with an amazing 254 hits.

Inducted in 1954, "Memphis Bill" had more than 100 RBI from 1927 to 1932. Showing long-ball power when he wanted, Terry smashed 28 homers in 1932. Generally, though, his strengths were doubles and triples. A fine defensive first baseman, he took over as Giant manager in 1932 and led the team to three pennants.

SAM THOMPSON
Outfielder (1885-1898; 1906)

Thompson was a home run hitter in an era when the talent was not much appreciated. He had his greatest success with the Phillies in the 1890s, where in 1894, he hit .404 and fellow outfielders, Billy Hamilton (.399), Ed Delahanty (.400), and Tuck Turner (.416) all had big years. "Big Sam" led the NL in base hits three times, and in homers and RBI twice each. Inducted in 1974, he had 128 career homers, with a .331 average and 1,299 RBI.

JOE TINKER
Shortstop (1902-1916)

Interestingly, Tinker, Johnny Evers, and Frank Chance were all elected to the Hall in the same year. Shortstop Tinker was a fielding whiz who keyed the success of that double-play combo. Although not a great hitter, he stole 336 career bases to augment his .263 average. His batting averages from 1902 to 1912 (the years he was with the Cubs) were better than most starting NL shortstops of the time. He was inducted in 1946.

PIE TRAYNOR
Third baseman (1920-1935; 1937)

Traynor earned his way into the Hall of Fame as the best fielding third baseman of his era. A career .320 hitter for Pittsburgh, he hit .300 or better 10 times and had more than 100 RBI seven times. He was selected in 1969 as a member of the all-time team for baseball's centennial. Inducted in 1948, Pie had 1,273 career RBI and 1,183 runs.

DAZZY VANCE
Pitcher (1915; 1918; 1922-1935)

As a 31-year-old rookie with Brooklyn in 1922, Vance won 18 games. Two years later his mark of 28-6 earned him league MVP honors. Armed with an incredible fastball, he led the major leagues in Ks each of his first seven seasons and paced the NL in ERA three times. Inducted in 1955, Dazzy had a career 197-140 record, with a 3.24 ERA and 2,045 Ks.

ARKY VAUGHAN
Shortstop (1932-1943; 1947-1948)

One of the game's best hitting shortstops, only twice in 14 seasons did Vaughan fail to hit .300. In 1935, his .385 average for Pittsburgh led the NL. Arky notched a career .406 on-base percentage, .318 batting average, 1,173 runs, and 926 RBI. Inducted in 1985, he scored more than 100 runs in five seasons, and he led the NL in putouts and assists three times.

BILL VEECK
Executive

One of baseball's most colorful showmen, Veeck integrated the AL when he signed Larry Doby while the Indians' owner. He owned three AL teams—Cleveland, St. Louis, and Chicago. His 1948 Tribe club was the first to top two million in attendance. While owner of the Browns, he sent midget Eddie Gaedel up to bat, and as the chief of the White Sox, introduced baseball's first exploding scoreboard. He was inducted in 1991.

RUBE WADDELL
Pitcher (1897; 1899-1910)

Waddell threw hard and lived even harder. In the AL's first six seasons, Rube was the circuit's best lefthander, under the watchful eye of Connie Mack, winning 20 games four straight years and leading the league in Ks six consecutive years. An eccentric, Waddell couldn't confine himself to baseball, as alligator wrestling, fire-fighting, acting, marbles, and the demon alcohol all competed for his attention. Inducted in 1946, he had a career 191-145 record with 2,316 Ks.

HONUS WAGNER
Shortstop (1897-1917)

One of the game's first five inductees to the Hall of Fame, Wagner hit over .300 17 consecutive seasons. Bowlegged and awkward looking, Wagner possessed tremendous speed and range afield. For his 21-year career, the shortstop had 722 stolen bases and a .327 batting average, highest of any shortstop. Honus led the NL in batting eight times, slugging six times, RBI four times, runs scored twice, and doubles eight times. Inducted in 1936, "The Flying Dutchman" accumulated 3,415 career hits, 640 doubles, 252 triples, 1,732 RBI, 1,736 runs scored, and 963 walks. Some consider Wagner the greatest player of all time.

BOBBY WALLACE
Shortstop (1894-1918)

The first AL shortstop elected to the Hall, Wallace was the best at his position during the first decade of the league. "Rhody" made his mark with the glove, leading the league in putouts three times and assists four times. He averaged 6.1 chances per game lifetime. Inducted in 1953, he twice notched more than 100 RBI in a season.

ED WALSH
Pitcher (1904-1917)

Perhaps no other pitcher threw the spitball as successfully as Walsh. While his arm gave out after only seven full seasons as a starter, he recorded nearly 170 of his career 195 wins during that span. In 1908, he pitched 464 innings for the White Sox on his way to 40 victories. He led the AL in games pitched five times, innings pitched four times, games started three times, and in strikeouts twice. Inducted in

1946, "Big Ed" had a career 195-126 record with a 1.82 ERA, the lowest average of all time.

LLOYD WANER
Outfielder (1927-1942; 1944-1945)

"Little Poison," to older brother Paul's "Big Poison," Lloyd Waner was to the single what Babe Ruth was to the home run. In 1927, Waner's rookie year, the little lead-off man hit 198 one-baggers. He used his speed to cover the vast Forbes Field outfield, leading the NL in putouts four times. Inducted in 1967, Waner had a .316 career batting average, 2,459 hits, and 1,201 runs scored.

PAUL WANER
Outfielder (1926-1945)

"Big Poison" didn't settle for hitting singles like his little brother; 905 of Paul Waner's 3,152 career hits were for extra bases. He led the NL in hitting three times, peaking at .380 in 1927, when he led Pittsburgh to the pennant and was named league MVP. Inducted in 1952, Waner retired with a .333 batting average, 605 doubles, 1,626 runs scored, and 1,309 RBI. When Lloyd was inducted, the Waners became the second brother combination to be so honored, after the Wrights.

MONTE WARD
Pitcher; shortstop (1878-1894)

Perhaps no figure in baseball had distinguished himself in so many areas as did Ward. As a pitcher for Providence, he led the NL in ERA in 1878 and in wins in 1879. Switched to shortstop in 1885, he became the best in the league for New York. Unhappy with the reserve clause, in 1890 he helped form the Players' League. Becoming a manager, he led the Giants to a championship in 1894. Retiring at age 34 to practice law, Ward returned to the game as part-owner of the Braves in 1911. He was inducted in 1964.

GEORGE WEISS
Executive

As farm director and general manager of the Yankees from 1932 through 1960, Weiss deserves much of the credit for creating the Yankee dynasty. He built the farm system to 21 teams, then became general manager and dealt from strength, constantly picking up precisely the player the Yankees needed in exchange for several prospects plucked from the system he created. He joined the Mets as the club's first president in 1961. He was inducted in 1971.

MICKEY WELCH
Pitcher (1880-1892)

The third man to win 300 games, Welch starred in the 1880s for Troy (New York) and New York of the NL. In 1885 he won 17 consecutive decisions on his way to 44 wins for the year. Inducted in 1973, "Smiling Mickey" won at least 20 games nine times, with four seasons of more than 30. He had a career 307-210 record with a 2.71 ERA.

ZACK WHEAT
Outfielder (1909-1927)

The Dodgers' first star, Wheat played left field in Ebbets Field for 18 seasons. A line-drive hitter, he topped the .300 mark in 14 seasons, including an NL-best .335 in 1918. He was a complete ballplayer who did everything well. Inducted in 1959, he had a career .317 average, 2,884 hits, 1,261 RBI, 1,289 runs scored, and 205 stolen bases. "Buck" was never ejected from a game during his 19-year career.

HOYT WILHELM
Pitcher (1952-1972)

Wilhelm was the first pitcher elected to the Hall (in 1985) solely on his merits as a reliever. A knuckleballer, he toiled for nine teams, pitching in a record 1,070 games and winning 124 in relief. He started only 52 games in his 21-year career, compiling

227 saves and a 2.52 ERA. "Snacks" pitched five consecutive seasons (1964 to 1968) with an ERA under 2.00. In his very first big league at bat, Wilhelm hit what would be the only homer of his entire career.

BILLY WILLIAMS
Outfielder (1959-1976)

Williams's much admired swing produced 426 career homers and a .290 batting average. The NL Rookie of the Year in 1961, he had at least 20 home runs and 84 RBI in 13 consecutive seasons. His two best seasons were in 1970 and 1972. In 1970, Billy hit .322 with 42 homers, a league-best 137 runs scored, and 129 RBI. He led the NL with a .333 batting average and a .606 slugging average, with 37 homers and 122 RBI in 1972. Playing most of his career for the Cubs, between 1963 and 1970 Williams played in an NL-record 1,117 consecutive games. He was inducted in 1987.

TED WILLIAMS
Outfielder (1939-1942; 1946-1960)

Williams's one desire was to walk down the street and have people say, "There goes the greatest hitter that ever lived." Arguably, he was. Despite missing nearly five years to the military, the Red Sox left fielder won two MVP Awards, six batting and four home run titles, and two Triple Crowns. "The Splendid Splinter" batted over .316 in each of his 19 seasons except one. In 1941, "The Kid" hit a .406 mark. He's the last player to attain that plateau. Inducted in 1966, he had 30 or more homers in eight seasons, 20 or more in 16 seasons. "Teddy Ballgame" retired with the sixth highest career batting average (.344), the second highest slugging average (.634), the second most bases on balls (2,019), and number 10 for both home runs (521) and RBI (1,839).

HACK WILSON
Outfielder (1923-1934)

For five seasons, from 1926 to 1930, the muscular, midgetlike Wilson was one of the game's greatest sluggers. In 1930, the Cub outfielder hit an NL-record 56 homers and knocked in a major league record 190 runs. Inducted in 1979, he led the NL in homers four times and in RBI twice. Liquor, nonetheless, was Wilson's downfall, and by the end of 1934, he was out of baseball.

GEORGE WRIGHT
Shortstop (1871-1882)

The star shortstop for the original Cincinnati Red Stockings team that went undefeated for the entire 1869 season, Wright played through 1882. He then started a successful sporting goods firm and helped start the Union Association in 1884. Later in life he served on baseball's Centennial Commission, and was instrumental in the creation of the National Baseball Hall of Fame, to which he was inducted in 1937.

HARRY WRIGHT
Manager (1871-1893)

Harry Wright, the older brother of George, was player-manager of the Cincinnati Red Stockings (the first overtly all-professional team), which Harry led to some 130 consecutive victories, fathering professional baseball in the process. He helped start the National Association in 1871, and later managed a number of NL teams, going 225-60 in the National Association and 1,000-825 in the National League. He was inducted in 1953.

EARLY WYNN
Pitcher (1939; 1941-1944; 1946-1963)

After a so-so career with the Senators, Wynn was traded to Cleveland in 1949 and became a big winner. He won 20 games for the Indians four times and had eight consecutive winning seasons. Traded to the White Sox after the '57 season, "Gus" led Chicago to the pennant in 1959 by winning 22 games, plus the Cy Young Award. Wynn's all-business approach was pretty well summed up when he stated he'd knock down his grandmother if she dug in against him. Inducted in 1972, he had a 300-244 career record and a 3.54 ERA.

CARL YASTRZEMSKI
Outfielder (1961-1983)
Spending his entire 23-year career with the Red Sox, Yastrzemski is the only AL player to collect over 3,000 hits and 400 home runs. "Yaz" will always be remembered for one remarkable season—1967, the year of The Impossible Dream. As a testament to his outstanding performance that year, he won the Triple Crown. During a most remarkable September that season, he single-handedly won the pennant for Boston. Taking over left field for Ted Williams, "Captain Carl" soon proved that he belonged in the same category, winning batting titles in 1963, '67, and '68. Inducted in 1989, he had 3,419 career hits, a .285 average, 646 doubles, 452 home runs, 1,844 RBI, 1,816 runs scored, and 1,845 bases on balls.

TOM YAWKEY
Executive
Yawkey is one of the few inducted to the Hall (in 1980) who neither played, coached, umpired, nor served as a general manager. In 1933, at age 30, he received his inheritance and bought the Red Sox for $1.5 million. Boston at that time was a doormat and Fenway Park was falling apart. Over the next 44 seasons he spent lavishly on the club and the stadium, doling out another $1.5 million for renovations alone. He failed in his one, singular quest: While they became winners, the Red Sox never won the World Series for Tom Yawkey.

CY YOUNG
Pitcher (1890-1911)
Young won 511 games, which is 94 victories more than runner-up Walter Johnson. In a career that bridged three decades and several eras of play, Cy was consistently superb. Blessed with speed, control, stamina, and just about every quality a successful pitcher needs, Young won 20 or more games 15 times, including nine seasons in a row from 1891 to 1899. He led his league in victories four times, and in ERA, winning percentage, and strikeouts twice each. Inducted in 1937, Cy is also first on the complete-game list with 749 and innings pitched list with 7,355. When they decided to give an award to the season's top pitcher, they named it after Young.

ROSS YOUNGS
Outfielder (1917-1926)
Youngs was a star on four straight pennant winners for John McGraw's Giants in the early 1920s. He soon was McGraw's favorite and one of the game's best hitters. On the verge of greatness, in 1925 Youngs's skills deserted him and his average fell nearly 100 points. Diagnosed with Bright's disease, a terminal kidney disorder, Youngs gamely played one more season and died in 1927. Inducted in 1972, he had a .322 career batting average with 1,491 hits and 812 runs scored.

Awards and Highlights

Baseball's top achievements and tributes are listed in this section. The all-time career leaders in several batting and pitching categories are included (with players active in 1992 in **bold**), as well as the leaders among active players. The all-time single-season leaders are next. The Most Valuable Players, the Cy Young Award winners, and the Rookies of the Year follow. Fielding excellence is acknowledged with the Gold Glove Award winners. Finally, the winners and losers of the World Series and the National League and American League Championship Series are listed.

ALL-TIME LEADERS

BATTING AVERAGE
1. Ty Cobb .... .366
2. Rogers Hornsby .... .358
3. Joe Jackson .... .356
4. Ed Delahanty .... .346
5. Tris Speaker .... .345
6. Ted Williams .... .344
7. Billy Hamilton .... .344
8. Dan Brouthers .... .342
9. Babe Ruth .... .342
10. Harry Heilmann .... .342
11. Pete Browning .... .341
12. Willie Keeler .... .341
13. Bill Terry .... .341
14. George Sisler .... .340
15. Lou Gehrig .... .340
16. Jesse Burkett .... .338
17. Nap Lajoie .... .338
18. Wade Boggs .... .338
19. Riggs Stephenson .... .336
20. Al Simmons .... .334

HITS
1. Pete Rose 4,256
2. Ty Cobb 4,190
3. Hank Aaron 3,771
4. Stan Musial 3,630
5. Tris Speaker 3,514
6. Carl Yastrzemski 3,419
7. Honus Wagner 3,415
8. Cap Anson 3,413
9. Eddie Collins 3,310
10. Willie Mays 3,283
11. Nap Lajoie 3,242
12. Paul Waner 3,152
13. Rod Carew 3,053
14. Robin Yount 3,025
15. Lou Brock 3,023
16. Al Kaline 3,007
17. George Brett 3,005
18. Roberto Clemente 3,000
19. Sam Rice 2,987
20. Sam Crawford 2,961

DOUBLES
1. Tris Speaker 792
2. Pete Rose 746
3. Stan Musial 725
4. Ty Cobb 724
5. Nap Lajoie 657
6. Carl Yastrzemski 646
7. Honus Wagner 640
8. George Brett 634
9. Hank Aaron 624
10. Paul Waner 605
11. Cap Anson 582
12. Charlie Gehringer 574
13. Robin Yount 558

14. Harry Heilmann 542
15. Rogers Hornsby 541
16. Joe Medwick 540
17. Al Simmons 539
18. Lou Gehrig 534
19. Al Oliver 529
20. Frank Robinson 528

TRIPLES
1. Sam Crawford 309
2. Ty Cobb 295
3. Honus Wagner 252
4. Jake Beckley 243
5. Roger Connor 233
6. Tris Speaker 222
7. Fred Clarke 220
8. Dan Brouthers 205
9. Joe Kelley 194
10. Paul Waner 191
11. Bid McPhee 188
12. Eddie Collins 186
13. Ed Delahanty 185
14. Sam Rice 184
15. Edd Roush 182
     Jesse Burkett 182
17. Ed Konetchy 181
18. Buck Ewing 178
19. Stan Musial 177
     Rabbit Maranville 177

HOME RUNS
1. Hank Aaron 755
2. Babe Ruth 714
3. Willie Mays 660
4. Frank Robinson 586
5. Harmon Killebrew 573
6. Reggie Jackson 563
7. Mike Schmidt 548
8. Mickey Mantle 536
9. Jimmie Foxx 534
10. Ted Williams 521
   Willie McCovey 521
12. Eddie Mathews 512
   Ernie Banks 512
14. Mel Ott.....................511
15. Lou Gehrig.................493
16. Willie Stargell............475
   Stan Musial................475
18. Carl Yastrzemski 452
19. Dave Kingman 442
20. Dave Winfield.............432

RUNS BATTED IN
1. Hank Aaron 2,297
2. Babe Ruth 2,211
3. Lou Gehrig................1,990
4. Ty Cobb 1,961
5. Stan Musial...............1,951
6. Jimmie Foxx..............1,921
7. Willie Mays 1,903
8. Mel Ott....................1,861
9. Carl Yastrzemski 1,844
10. Ted Williams 1,839
11. Al Simmons 1,827
12. Frank Robinson 1,812
13. Honus Wagner 1,732
14. Cap Anson 1,715
15. Dave Winfield..........1,710
16. Reggie Jackson 1,702
17. Tony Perez 1,652
18. Ernie Banks 1,636
19. Goose Goslin 1,609
20. Nap Lajoie 1,599

SLUGGING AVERAGE
1. Babe Ruth .... .690
2. Ted Williams .... .634
3. Lou Gehrig................. .632
4. Jimmie Foxx.............. .609
5. Hank Greenberg........ .605
6. Joe DiMaggio .... .579
7. Rogers Hornsby .... .577
8. Johnny Mize .... .562
9. Stan Musial............... .559
10. Willie Mays .... .557
11. Mickey Mantle .... .557

12. Hank Aaron .... .555
13. Ralph Kiner................ .548
14. Hack Wilson .... .545
15. Chuck Klein .... .543
16. Duke Snider .... .540
17. Frank Robinson .... .537
18. Al Simmons .... .535
19. Dick Allen .... .534
20. Earl Averill .... .534

ON-BASE PERCENTAGE
1. Ted Williams .... .483
2. Babe Ruth .... .474
3. John McGraw .... .465
4. Billy Hamilton............. .455
5. Lou Gehrig................. .447
6. Rogers Hornsby .... .434
7. Ty Cobb .... .432
8. Wade Boggs............. .432
9. Jimmie Foxx .... .428
10. Tris Speaker .... .428
11. Ferris Fain .... .425
12. Eddie Collins .... .424
13. Dan Brouthers .... .423
14. Joe Jackson .... .423
15. Max Bishop .... .423
16. Mickey Mantle .... .423
17. Mickey Cochrane........ .419
18. Stan Musial................ .418
19. Cupid Childs .... .415
20. Mel Ott..................... .414

STOLEN BASES
1. Rickey Henderson ..1,042
2. Lou Brock 938
3. Ty Cobb 892
4. Eddie Collins 743
5. Max Carey 738
6. Tim Raines 730
7. Honus Wagner 722
8. Joe Morgan 689
9. Willie Wilson 660
10. Bert Campaneris 649
11. Vince Coleman..........610
12. Maury Wills 586
13. Dave Lopes 557
14. Cesar Cedeno 550
15. Ozzie Smith 542
16. Luis Aparicio 506
17. Clyde Milan 495
18. Omar Morano 487
19. Bobby Bonds 461
20. Jimmy Sheckard 460

RUNS SCORED
1. Ty Cobb 2,245

2. Babe Ruth 2,174
   Hank Aaron 2,174
4. Pete Rose 2,165
5. Willie Mays 2,062
6. Cap Anson................1,996
7. Stan Musial..............1,949
8. Lou Gehrig................1,888
9. Tris Speaker 1,882
10. Mel Ott....................1,859
11. Frank Robinson 1,829
12. Eddie Collins 1,819
13. Carl Yastrzemski 1,816
14. Ted Williams 1,798
15. Charlie Gehringer........1,774
16. Jimmie Foxx 1,751
17. Honus Wagner 1,736
18. Jim O'Rourke 1,733
19. Jesse Burkett 1,720
20. Willie Keeler 1,719

WALKS
1. Babe Ruth 2,056
2. Ted Williams 2,019
3. Joe Morgan 1,865
4. Carl Yastrzemski 1,845
5. Mickey Mantle 1,733
6. Mel Ott....................1,708
7. Eddie Yost.................1,614
8. Darrell Evans 1,605
9. Stan Musial................1,599
10. Pete Rose 1,566
11. Harmon Killebrew 1,559
12. Lou Gehrig.................1,508
13. Mike Schmidt 1,507
14. Eddie Collins 1,499
15. Willie Mays 1,464
16. Jimmie Foxx 1,452
17. Eddie Mathews 1,444
18. Frank Robinson 1,420
19. Hank Aaron 1,402
20. Dwight Evans 1,391

GAMES
1. Pete Rose 3,562
2. Carl Yastrzemski 3,308
3. Hank Aaron 3,298
4. Ty Cobb 3,035
5. Stan Musial................3,026
6. Willie Mays 2,992
7. Rusty Staub...............2,951
8. Brooks Robinson 2,896
9. Al Kaline 2,834
10. Eddie Collins 2,826
11. Reggie Jackson 2,820
12. Frank Robinson 2,808
13. Honus Wagner 2,792

14. Tris Speaker 2,789
15. Tony Perez 2,777
16. Mel Ott 2,730
17. Robin Yount 2,729
18. Dave Winfield 2,707
19. Graig Nettles 2,700
20. Darrell Evans 2,687

WINS

1. Cy Young 511
2. Walter Johnson 417
3. Christy Mathewson 373
   Pete Alexander 373
5. Jim Galvin 364
6. Warren Spahn 363
7. Kid Nichols 361
8. Tim Keefe 342
9. Steve Carlton 329
10. John Clarkson 328
11. Eddie Plank 326
12. Don Sutton 324
13. Nolan Ryan 319
14. Phil Niekro 318
15. Gaylord Perry 314
16. Tom Seaver 311
17. Charley Radbourn 309
18. Mickey Welch 307
19. Early Wynn 300
    Lefty Grove 300

WINNING PERCENTAGE

1. Al Spalding 796
2. Dave Foutz 690
3. Whitey Ford 690
4. Bob Caruthers 688
5. Dwight Gooden 683
6. Lefty Grove 680
7. Roger Clemens 679
8. Vic Raschi 667
9. Larry Corcoran 665
10. Christy Mathewson 665
11. Sam Leever 660
12. Sal Maglie 657
13. Dick McBride 656
14. Sandy Koufax 655
15. Johnny Allen 654
16. Ron Guidry 651
17. Lefty Gomez 649
18. John Clarkson 648
19. Mordecai Brown 648
20. Dizzy Dean 644

EARNED RUN AVERAGE

1. Ed Walsh 1.82
2. Addie Joss 1.89
3. Mordecai Brown 2.06

4. John Ward 2.10
5. Christy Mathewson 2.13
6. Rube Waddell 2.16
7. Walter Johnson 2.16
8. Al Spalding 2.22
9. Orval Overall 2.23
10. Will White 2.28
11. Ed Reulbach 2.28
12. Jim Scott 2.30
13. Tommy Bond 2.31
14. Eddie Plank 2.35
15. Larry Corcoran 2.36
16. George McQuillan 2.38
17. Eddie Cicotte 2.38
18. Ed Killian 2.38
19. Doc White 2.39
20. George Bradley 2.42

STRIKEOUTS

1. Nolan Ryan 5,668
2. Steve Carlton 4,136
3. Bert Blyleven 3,701
4. Tom Seaver 3,640
5. Don Sutton 3,574
6. Gaylord Perry 3,534
7. Walter Johnson 3,509
8. Phil Niekro 3,342
9. Fergie Jenkins 3,192
10. Bob Gibson 3,117
11. Jim Bunning 2,855
12. Mickey Lolich 2,832
13. Cy Young 2,800
14. Frank Tanana 2,657
15. Warren Spahn 2,583
16. Bob Feller 2,581
17. Jerry Koosman 2,556
18. Tim Keefe 2,521
19. Christy Mathewson ...2,502
20. Don Drysdale 2,486

SAVES

1. Jeff Reardon 357
2. Lee Smith 355
3. Rollie Fingers 341
4. Goose Gossage 308
5. Bruce Sutter 300
6. Dave Righetti 251
7. Dan Quisenberry 244
8. Dennis Eckersley....239
9. Sparky Lyle 238
10. Hoyt Wilhelm 227
11. John Franco.........226
12. Tom Henke 220
13. Gene Garber 218
14. Dave Smith 216
15. Bobby Thigpen 200

16. Roy Face 193
17. Mike Marshall 188
18. Kent Tekulve 184
    Steve Bedrosian 184
20. Tug McGraw 180

COMPLETE GAMES

1. Cy Young 749
2. Jim Galvin 646
3. Tim Keefe 553
4. Kid Nichols 531
   Walter Johnson 531
6. Mickey Welch 525
   Bobby Mathews 525
8. Charley Radbourn 489
9. John Clarkson 485
10. Tony Mullane 468
11. Jim McCormick 466
12. Gus Weyhing 448
13. Pete Alexander 437
14. Christy Mathewson ...434
15. Jack Powell 422
16. Eddie Plank 410
17. Will White 394
18. Amos Rusie 392
19. Vic Willis 388
20. Tommy Bond 386

SHUTOUTS

1. Walter Johnson 110
2. Pete Alexander 90
3. Christy Mathewson 79
4. Cy Young 76
5. Eddie Plank 69
6. Warren Spahn 63
7. Tom Seaver 61
   Nolan Ryan 61
9. Bert Blyleven 60
10. Don Sutton 58
11. Ed Walsh 57
    Jim Galvin 57
13. Bob Gibson 56
14. Steve Carlton 55
    Mordecai Brown 55
16. Gaylord Perry 53
    Jim Palmer 53
18. Juan Marichal 52
19. Vic Willis 50
    Rube Waddell 50

GAMES PITCHED

1. Hoyt Wilhelm 1,070
2. Kent Tekulve 1,050
3. Lindy McDaniel 987
4. Rollie Fingers 944
5. Gene Garber 931

6. **Goose Gossage** **927**
7. Cy Young 906
8. Sparky Lyle 899
9. Jim Kaat 898
10. Don McMahon 874
11. Phil Niekro 864
12. Roy Face 848
13. Tug McGraw 824
14. **Jeff Reardon** **811**
15. **Charlie Hough** **803**
16. Walter Johnson 802
17. **Nolan Ryan** **794**
18. **Lee Smith** **787**
19. Gaylord Perry 777
20. Don Sutton 774

INNINGS PITCHED

1. Cy Young 7,355.1
2. Jim Galvin 6,003.1
3. Walter Johnson 5,923.2
4. Phil Niekro 5,404.1
5. Gaylord Perry 5,350.1
6. **Nolan Ryan** **5,319.2**
7. Don Sutton 5,282.1
8. Warren Spahn 5,243.2
9. Steve Carlton 5,217.1
10. Pete Alexander 5,189.1
11. Kid Nichols 5,056.1

12. Tim Keefe 5,052.1
13. **Bert Blyleven** **4,970.0**
14. Bobby Mathews 4,956.0
15. Mickey Welch 4,802.0
16. Tom Seaver 4,782.2
17. Christy Mathewson 4,780.2
18. Tommy John 4,710.1
19. Robin Roberts 4,688.2
20. Early Wynn 4,564.0

FEWEST WALKS PER NINE INNINGS

1. Candy Cummings 0.49
2. Al Spalding 0.49
3. Tommy Bond 0.49
4. George Bradley 0.60
5. George Zettlein 0.61
6. Terry Larkin 0.71
7. Dick McBride 0.74
8. John Ward 0.92
9. Fred Goldsmith 0.96
10. Bobby Mathews 0.97
11. Jim Whitney 1.06
12. Jim Galvin 1.12
13. Deacon Phillippe 1.25
14. Will White 1.26
15. Babe Adams 1.29
16. Jack Lynch 1.38

17. Addie Joss 1.41
18. Cy Young 1.49
19. Guy Hecker 1.51
20. Lee Richmond 1.53

GAMES STARTED

1. Cy Young 815
2. **Nolan Ryan** **760**
3. Don Sutton 756
4. Phil Niekro 716
5. Steve Carlton 709
6. Tommy John 700
7. Gaylord Perry 690
8. Jim Galvin 689
9. **Bert Blyleven** **685**
10. Walter Johnson 666
11. Warren Spahn 665
12. Tom Seaver 647
13. Jim Kaat 625
14. Early Wynn 612
15. Robin Roberts 609
16. Pete Alexander 598
17. Fergie Jenkins 594
18. Tim Keefe 593
19. **Frank Tanana** **584**
20. Bobby Mathews 568

ACTIVE LEADERS

HITS

1. Robin Yount 3,025
2. George Brett............3,005
3. Dave Winfield 2,866
4. Eddie Murray 2,646
5. Andre Dawson 2,504
6. Carlton Fisk 2,346
7. Paul Molitor 2,281
8. Willie Randolph 2,210
9. Willie Wilson 2,145
10. Ozzie Smith 2,108

HOME RUNS

1. Dave Winfield 432
2. Eddie Murray 414
3. Andre Dawson 399
4. Dale Murphy 398
5. Carlton Fisk 375
6. Jack Clark 340
7. Gary Carter 324
8. Lance Parrish 316
9. George Brett...........298
10. Darryl Strawberry 285

RUNS BATTED IN

1. Dave Winfield 1,710
2. Eddie Murray 1,562
3. George Brett............1,520
4. Andre Dawson 1,425
5. Robin Yount 1,355
6. Carlton Fisk 1,326
7. Dale Murphy 1,259
8. Gary Carter 1,225
9. Jack Clark 1,180
10. Brian Downing 1,073

BATTING AVERAGE
(Minimum 2,500 at bats)

1. Wade Boggs 338
2. Tony Gwynn 327
3. Kirby Puckett 321
4. Don Mattingly 311
5. George Brett...........307
6. Mike Greenwell 306
7. Paul Molitor 303
8. Will Clark 301
9. Julio Franco 301
10. Pedro Guerrero 300

WINS

1. Nolan Ryan 319
2. Bert Blyleven 287
3. Jack Morris 237
4. Frank Tanana 233
5. Charlie Hough 202
6. Bob Welch 199
7. Dennis Martinez 193
8. Dennis Eckersley 188
9. John Candelaria 177
10. Dave Stieb 174

GAMES PITCHED

1. Goose Gossage 927
2. Jeff Reardon...........811
3. Charlie Hough 803
4. Nolan Ryan 794
5. Lee Smith 787
6. Dennis Eckersley 740
7. Bert Blyleven 692
8. Bob McClure 684
9. Jesse Orosco 657
10. Dennis Lamp 639

STRIKEOUTS

1. Nolan Ryan 5,668
2. Bert Blyleven 3,701
3. Frank Tanana...........2,657
4. Jack Morris 2,275
5. Charlie Hough 2,171
6. Dennis Eckersley 2,118
7. Roger Clemens 1,873
8. Bob Welch...............1,862
9. Mark Langston 1,805
10. Floyd Bannister 1,723

SAVES

1. Jeff Reardon................357
2. Lee Smith 355
3. Goose Gossage 308
4. Dave Righetti.............251
5. Dennis Eckersley 239
6. John Franco..............226
7. Tom Henke.................220
8. Dave Smith................216
9. Bobby Thigpen 200
10. Doug Jones 164

SINGLE SEASON LEADERS (Since 1900)

BATTING AVERAGE

	BA	YEAR
1. Rogers Hornsby STL(NL)	.424	1924
2. Nap Lajoie PHI(AL)	.422	1901
3. George Sisler STL(AL)	.420	1922
4. Ty Cobb DET	.420	1911
5. Ty Cobb DET	.410	1912
6. Joe Jackson CLE	.408	1911
7. George Sisler STL(AL)	.407	1920
8. Ted Williams BOS(AL)	.406	1941
9. Rogers Hornsby STL(NL)	.403	1925
10. Harry Heilmann DET	.403	1923
11. Rogers Hornsby STL(NL)	.401	1922
12. Bill Terry NY(NL)	.401	1930
13. Ty Cobb DET	.401	1922
14. Lefty O'Doul PHI(NL)	.398	1929
15. Harry Heilmann DET	.398	1927
16. Rogers Hornsby STL(NL)	.397	1921
17. Joe Jackson CLE	.395	1912
18. Harry Heilmann DET	.394	1921
19. Babe Ruth NY(AL)	.393	1923
20. Harry Heilmann DET	.393	1925

HITS

	H	YEAR
1. George Sisler STL(AL)	257	1920
2. Bill Terry NY(NL)	254	1930
Lefty O'Doul PHI(NL)	254	1929
4. Al Simmons PHI(AL)	253	1925
5. Rogers Hornsby STL(NL)	250	1922
Chuck Klein PHI(NL)	250	1930
7. Ty Cobb DET	248	1911
8. George Sisler STL(AL)	246	1922
9. Babe Herman BKN	241	1930
Heinie Manush STL(AL)	241	1928
11. Wade Boggs BOS	240	1985
12. Rod Carew MIN	239	1977
13. Don Mattingly NY(AL)	238	1986
14. Harry Heilmann DET	237	1921
Paul Waner PIT	237	1927
Joe Medwick STL(NL)	237	1937
17. Jack Tobin STL(AL)	236	1921
18. Rogers Hornsby STL(NL)	235	1921
19. Lloyd Waner PIT	234	1929
Kirby Puckett MIN	234	1988

DOUBLES

	2B	YEAR
1. Earl Webb BOS(AL)	67	1931
2. George Burns CLE	64	1926
Joe Medwick STL(NL)	64	1936
4. Hank Greenberg DET	63	1934
5. Paul Waner PIT	62	1932
6. Charlie Gehringer DET	60	1936
7. Tris Speaker CLE	59	1923
Chuck Klein PHI(NL)	59	1930
9. Billy Herman CHI(NL)	57	1936
Billy Herman CHI(NL)	57	1935
11. Joe Medwick STL(NL)	56	1937
George Kell DET	56	1950
13. Gee Walker DET	55	1936
14. Hal McRae KC	54	1977
15. Don Mattingly NY(AL)	53	1986
Tris Speaker BOS(AL)	53	1912
Al Simmons PHI(AL)	53	1926
Paul Waner PIT	53	1936
Stan Musial STL(NL)	53	1953

TRIPLES

	3B	YEAR
1. Owen Wilson PIT	36	1912
2. Joe Jackson CLE	26	1912
Sam Crawford DET	26	1914
Kiki Cuyler PIT	26	1925
5. Tommy Long STL(NL)	25	1915
Larry Doyle NY(NL)	25	1911
Sam Crawford DET	25	1903
8. Ty Cobb DET	24	1911

HOME RUNS

	HR	YEAR
1. Roger Maris NY(AL)	61	1961
2. Babe Ruth NY(AL)	60	1927
3. Babe Ruth NY(AL)	59	1921
4. Jimmie Foxx PHI(AL)	58	1932
Hank Greenberg DET	58	1938
6. Hack Wilson CHI(NL)	56	1930
7. Babe Ruth NY(AL)	54	1920
Babe Ruth NY(AL)	54	1928
Ralph Kiner PIT	54	1949
Mickey Mantle NY(AL)	54	1961

11. Mickey Mantle NY(AL)	52	1956
Willie Mays SF	52	1965
George Foster CIN	52	1977
14. Ralph Kiner PIT	51	1947
Johnny Mize NY(NL)	51	1947
Willie Mays NY(NL)	51	1955
Cecil Fielder DET	51	1990
18. Jimmie Foxx BOS(AL)	50	1938

HOME RUN PERCENTAGE

	HR%	YEAR
1. Babe Ruth NY(AL)	11.8	1920
2. Babe Ruth NY(AL)	11.1	1927
3. Babe Ruth NY(AL)	10.9	1921
4. Mickey Mantle NY(AL)	10.5	1961
5. Hank Greenberg DET	10.4	1938
6. Roger Maris NY(AL)	10.3	1961
7. Babe Ruth NY(AL)	10.1	1928
8. Jimmie Foxx PHI(AL)	9.9	1932
9. Ralph Kiner PIT	9.8	1949
10. Mickey Mantle NY(AL)	9.8	1956
11. Hack Wilson CHI(NL)	9.6	1930
12. Hank Aaron ATL	9.5	1971
Babe Ruth NY(AL)	9.5	1926
14. Jim Gentile BAL	9.5	1961
15. Babe Ruth NY(AL)	9.5	1930
16. Willie Stargell PIT	9.4	1971
17. Rudy York DET	9.3	1937
18. Willie Mays SF	9.3	1965
19. Babe Ruth NY(AL)	9.2	1929
20. Willie McCovey SF	9.2	1969

RUNS BATTED IN

	RBI	YEAR
1. Hack Wilson CHI(NL)	190	1930
2. Lou Gehrig NY(AL)	184	1931
3. Hank Greenberg DET	183	1937
4. Jimmie Foxx BOS(AL)	175	1938
Lou Gehrig NY(AL)	175	1927
6. Lou Gehrig NY(AL)	174	1930
7. Babe Ruth NY(AL)	171	1921
8. Hank Greenberg DET	170	1935
Chuck Klein PHI(NL)	170	1930
10. Jimmie Foxx PHI(AL)	169	1932
11. Joe DiMaggio NY(AL)	167	1937
12. Al Simmons PHI(AL)	165	1930
Lou Gehrig NY(AL)	165	1934
14. Babe Ruth NY(AL)	164	1927
15. Babe Ruth NY(AL)	163	1931
Jimmie Foxx PHI(AL)	163	1933
17. Hal Trosky CLE	162	1936

SLUGGING AVERAGE

	SA	YEAR
1. Babe Ruth NY(AL)	.847	1920
2. Babe Ruth NY(AL)	.846	1921
3. Babe Ruth NY(AL)	.772	1927
4. Lou Gehrig NY(AL)	.765	1927
5. Babe Ruth NY(AL)	.764	1923
6. Rogers Hornsby STL(NL)	.756	1925
7. Jimmie Foxx PHI(AL)	.749	1932
8. Babe Ruth NY(AL)	.739	1924
9. Babe Ruth NY(AL)	.737	1926
10. Ted Williams BOS(AL)	.735	1941
11. Babe Ruth NY(AL)	.732	1930
12. Ted Williams BOS	.731	1957
13. Hack Wilson CHI(NL)	.723	1930
14. Rogers Hornsby STL(NL)	.722	1922
15. Lou Gehrig NY(AL)	.721	1930
16. Babe Ruth NY(AL)	.709	1928
17. Al Simmons PHI(AL)	.708	1930
18. Lou Gehrig NY(AL)	.706	1934
19. Mickey Mantle NY(AL)	.705	1956
20. Jimmie Foxx BOS(AL)	.704	1938

TOTAL BASES

	TB	YEAR
1. Babe Ruth NY(AL)	457	1921
2. Rogers Hornsby STL(NL)	450	1922
3. Lou Gehrig NY(AL)	447	1927
4. Chuck Klein PHI(NL)	445	1930
5. Jimmie Foxx PHI(AL)	438	1932
6. Stan Musial STL(NL)	429	1948
7. Hack Wilson CHI(NL)	423	1930
8. Chuck Klein PHI(NL)	420	1932
9. Lou Gehrig NY(AL)	419	1930
10. Joe DiMaggio NY(AL)	418	1937
11. Babe Ruth NY(AL)	417	1927
12. Babe Herman BKN	416	1930
13. Lou Gehrig NY(AL)	410	1931
14. Lou Gehrig NY(AL)	409	1934
Rogers Hornsby CHI(NL)	409	1929
16. Joe Medwick STL(NL)	406	1937
Jim Rice BOS	406	1978
18. Chuck Klein PHI(NL)	405	1929
Hal Trosky CLE	405	1936
20. Jimmie Foxx PHI(AL)	403	1933
Lou Gehrig NY(AL)	403	1936

BASES ON BALLS

	BB	YEAR
1. Babe Ruth NY(AL)	170	1923
2. Ted Williams BOS(AL)	162	1947
Ted Williams BOS(AL)	162	1949
4. Ted Williams BOS(AL)	156	1946
5. Eddie Yost WAS	151	1956
6. Eddie Joost PHI(AL)	149	1949
7. Babe Ruth NY(AL)	148	1920
Jimmy Wynn HOU	148	1969
Eddie Stanky BKN	148	1945
10. Jimmy Sheckard CHI(AL)	147	1911
11. Mickey Mantle NY(AL)	146	1957

12. Ted Williams BOS(AL)	145	1941
Ted Williams BOS(AL)	145	1942
Harmon Killebrew MIN	145	1969
15. Babe Ruth NY(AL)	144	1926
Eddie Stanky NY(NL)	144	1950
Babe Ruth NY(AL)	144	1921
18. Ted Williams BOS(AL)	143	1951
19. Babe Ruth NY(AL)	142	1924
20. Eddie Yost WAS	141	1950

RUNS SCORED

	RS	YEAR
1. Babe Ruth NY(AL)	177	1921
2. Lou Gehrig NY(AL)	167	1936
3. Babe Ruth NY(AL)	163	1928
Lou Gehrig NY(AL)	163	1931
5. Babe Ruth NY(AL)	158	1920
Babe Ruth NY(AL)	158	1927
Chuck Klein PHI(NL)	158	1930
8. Rogers Hornsby CHI(NL)	156	1929
9. Kiki Cuyler CHI(NL)	155	1930
10. Lefty O'Doul PHI(NL)	152	1929
Woody English CHI(NL)	152	1930
Al Simmons PHI(AL)	152	1930
Chuck Klein PHI(NL)	152	1932
14. Babe Ruth NY(AL)	151	1923
Jimmie Foxx PHI(AL)	151	1932
Joe DiMaggio NY(AL)	151	1937
17. Babe Ruth NY(AL)	150	1930
Ted Williams BOS(AL)	150	1949

STOLEN BASES

	SB	YEAR
1. Rickey Henderson OAK	130	1982
2. Lou Brock STL	118	1974
3. Vince Coleman STL	110	1985
4. Vince Coleman STL	109	1987
5. Rickey Henderson OAK	108	1983
6. Vince Coleman STL	107	1986
7. Maury Wills LA	104	1962
8. Rickey Henderson OAK	100	1980
9. Ron LeFlore MON	97	1980
10. Ty Cobb DET	96	1915
Omar Moreno PIT	96	1980
12. Maury Wills LA	94	1965
13. Rickey Henderson NY(AL)	93	1988
14. Tim Raines MON	90	1983
15. Clyde Milan WAS	88	1912
16. Rickey Henderson NY(AL)	87	1986
17. Willie Wilson KC	83	1979
Ty Cobb DET	83	1911
19. Eddie Collins PHI(AL)	81	1910
Bob Bescher CIN	81	1911
Vince Coleman STL	81	1988

WINS

	W	YEAR
1. Jack Chesbro NY(NL)	41	1904
2. Ed Walsh CHI(AL)	40	1908
3. Christy Mathewson NY(NL)	37	1908
4. Walter Johnson WAS	36	1913
5. Joe McGinnity NY(NL)	35	1904
6. Smoky Joe Wood BOS(AL)	34	1912
7. Cy Young BOS(AL)	33	1901
Grover Alexander PHI(NL)	33	1916
Christy Mathewson NY(NL)	33	1904
10. Cy Young BOS(AL)	32	1902
Walter Johnson WAS	32	1912
12. Joe McGinnity NY(NL)	31	1903
Christy Mathewson NY(NL)	31	1905
Jack Coombs PHI(AL)	31	1910
Grover Alexander PHI(NL)	31	1915
Jim Bagby CLE	31	1920
Lefty Grove PHI(AL)	31	1931
Denny McLain DET	31	1968

WINNING PERCENTAGE

	W%	YEAR
1. Roy Face PIT	.947	1959
2. Johnny Allen CLE	.938	1937
3. Ron Guidry NY(AL)	.893	1978
4. Freddie Fitzsimmons BKN	.889	1940
5. Lefty Grove PHI(AL)	.886	1931
6. Bob Stanley BOS	.882	1978
7. Preacher Roe BKN	.880	1951
8. Tom Seaver CIN	.875	1981
9. Smoky Joe Wood BOS(AL)	.872	1912
10. David Cone NY(NL)	.870	1988
11. Orel Hershiser LA	.864	1985
12. Wild Bill Donovan DET	.862	1907
Whitey Ford NY(AL)	.862	1961
14. Roger Clemens BOS	.857	1986
Dwight Gooden NY(NL)	.857	1985

EARNED RUN AVERAGE

	ERA	YEAR
1. Dutch Leonard BOS(AL)	1.01	1914
2. Three Finger Brown CHI(NL)	1.04	1906
3. Walter Johnson WAS	1.09	1913
4. Bob Gibson STL	1.12	1968
5. Christy Mathewson NY(NL)	1.14	1909
6. Jack Pfiester CHI(NL)	1.15	1907
7. Addie Joss CLE	1.16	1908
8. Carl Lundgren CHI(NL)	1.17	1907
9. Grover Alexander PHI(NL)	1.22	1915
10. Cy Young BOS(AL)	1.26	1908
11. Ed Walsh CHI(AL)	1.27	1910
12. Walter Johnson WAS	1.27	1918
13. Christy Mathewson NY(NL)	1.27	1905
14. Jack Coombs PHI(AL)	1.30	1910
15. Three Finger Brown CHI(NL)	1.31	1909

STRIKEOUTS

	SO	YEAR
1. Nolan Ryan CAL	383	1973
2. Sandy Koufax LA	382	1965
3. Nolan Ryan CAL	367	1974
4. Rube Waddell PHI(AL)	349	1904
5. Bob Feller CLE	348	1946
6. Nolan Ryan CAL	341	1977
7. Nolan Ryan CAL	329	1972
8. Nolan Ryan CAL	327	1976
9. Sam McDowell CLE	325	1965
10. Sandy Koufax LA	317	1966
11. J.R. Richard HOU	313	1979
Walter Johnson WAS	313	1910
13. Steve Carlton PHI	310	1972
14. Mickey Lolich DET	308	1971
15. Mike Scott HOU	306	1986
Sandy Koufax LA(NL)	306	1963

SHUTOUTS

	ShO	YEAR
1. Grover Alexander PHI(NL)	16	1916
2. Jack Coombs PHI(AL)	13	1910
Bob Gibson STL	13	1968
4. Grover Alexander PHI(NL)	12	1915
Christy Mathewson NY(NL)	12	1908
6. Dean Chance LA(AL)	11	1964
Walter Johnson WAS	11	1913
Sandy Koufax LA(NL)	11	1963
Ed Walsh CHI(AL)	11	1908

COMPLETE GAMES

	CG	YEAR
1. Jack Chesbro NY(NL)	48	1904
2. Vic Willis BOS(NL)	45	1902
3. Joe McGinnity NY(NL)	44	1903
4. Ed Walsh CHI(AL)	42	1908
George Mullin DET	42	1904
6. Noodles Hahn CIN	41	1901
Cy Young BOS(AL)	41	1902
Irv Young BOS(NL)	41	1905
9. Cy Young BOS(AL)	40	1904

GAMES PITCHED

	G	YEAR
1. Mike Marshall LA	106	1974
2. Kent Tekulve PIT	94	1979
3. Mike Marshall MON	92	1973
4. Kent Tekulve PIT	91	1978
5. Wayne Granger CIN	90	1969
Mike Marshall MIN	90	1979
Kent Tekulve PHI	90	1987
8. Mark Eichhorn TOR	89	1987
9. Wilbur Wood CHI(AL)	88	1968
10. Rob Murphy CIN	87	1987
11. Kent Tekulve PIT	85	1982

Mitch Williams TEX	85	1987
Frank Williams CIN	85	1987

INNINGS PITCHED

	IP	YEAR
1. Ed Walsh CHI(AL)	464	1908
2. Jack Chesbro NY(NL)	455	1904
3. Joe McGinnity NY(NL)	434	1903
4. Ed Walsh CHI(AL)	422	1907
5. Vic Willis BOS(NL)	410	1902
6. Joe McGinnity NY(NL)	408	1904
7. Ed Walsh CHI(AL)	393	1912
8. Christy Mathewson NY(NL)	391	1908
9. Jack Powell NY(NL)	390	1904
10. Togie Pittinger BOS(NL)	389	1902
Grover Alexander PHI(NL)	389	1916

SAVES

	SV	YEAR
1. Bobby Thigpen CHI(AL)	57	1990
2. Dennis Eckersley OAK	51	1992
3. Dennis Eckersley OAK	48	1990
4. Lee Smith STL	47	1991
5. Dave Righetti NY(AL)	46	1986
Bryan Harvey CAL	46	1991
7. Dan Quisenberry KC	45	1983
Bruce Sutter STL	45	1984
Dennis Eckersley OAK	45	1988
10. Dan Quisenberry KC	44	1984
Mark Davis SD	44	1989
12. Doug Jones CLE	43	1990
Dennis Eckersley OAK	43	1991
Lee Smith STL	43	1992
13. Jeff Reardon MIN	42	1988
Rick Aguilera MIN	42	1991
15. Rick Aguilera MIN	41	1992

WINS PLUS SAVES

	W+S	YEAR
1. Bobby Thigpen CHI(AL)	61	1990
2. Dennis Eckersley OAK	58	1992
3. Dave Righetti NY(AL)	54	1986
4. Lee Smith STL	53	1991
5. Dennis Eckersley OAK	52	1990
6. Dan Quisenberry KC	50	1984
Bruce Sutter STL	50	1984
Dan Quisenberry KC	50	1983
9. Dennis Eckersley OAK	49	1988
10. John Hiller DET	48	1973
Mark Davis SD	48	1989
Doug Jones CLE	48	1990
Bryan Harvey CAL	48	1991
Dennis Eckersley OAK	48	1991

MOST VALUABLE PLAYERS

NATIONAL LEAGUE

CHALMERS
1911 Wildfire Schulte CHI (OF)
1912 Larry Doyle NY (2B)
1913 Jake Daubert BKN (1B)
1914 Johnny Evers BOS (2B)
1915-21 No Selection

LEAGUE
1922-23 No Selection
1924 Dazzy Vance BKN (P)
1925 Rogers Hornsby STL (2B)
1926 Bob O'Farrell STL (C)
1927 Paul Waner PIT (OF)
1928 Jim Bottomley STL (1B)
1929 Rogers Hornsby CHI (2B)
1930 No Selection

BASEBALL WRITERS ASSOCIATION OF AMERICA
1931 Frankie Frisch STL (2B)
1932 Chuck Klein PHI (OF)
1933 Carl Hubbell NY (P)
1934 Dizzy Dean STL (P)
1935 Gabby Hartnett CHI (C)
1936 Carl Hubbell NY (P)
1937 Joe Medwick STL (OF)
1938 Ernie Lombardi CIN (C)
1939 Bucky Walters CIN (P)
1940 Frank McCormick
     CIN (1B)
1941 Dolph Camilli BKN (1B)
1942 Mort Cooper STL (P)
1943 Stan Musial STL (OF)
1944 Marty Marion STL (SS)
1945 Phil Cavarretta CHI (1B)
1946 Stan Musial STL (1B)
1947 Bob Elliott BOS (3B)
1948 Stan Musial STL (OF)
1949 Jackie Robinson
     BKN (2B)
1950 Jim Konstanty PHI (P)
1951 Roy Campanella BKN (C)
1952 Hank Sauer CHI (OF)
1953 Roy Campanella BKN (C)
1954 Willie Mays NY (OF)
1955 Roy Campanella BKN (C)
1956 Don Newcombe BKN (P)
1957 Hank Aaron MIL (OF)
1958 Ernie Banks CHI (SS)
1959 Ernie Banks CHI (SS)
1960 Dick Groat PIT (SS)
1961 Frank Robinson CIN (OF)

1962 Maury Wills LA (SS)
1963 Sandy Koufax LA (P)
1964 Ken Boyer STL (3B)
1965 Willie Mays SF (OF)
1966 Roberto Clemente
     PIT (OF)
1967 Orlando Cepeda STL (1B)
1968 Bob Gibson STL (P)
1969 Willie McCovey SF (1B)
1970 Johnny Bench CIN (C)
1971 Joe Torre STL (3B)
1972 Johnny Bench CIN (C)
1973 Pete Rose CIN (OF)
1974 Steve Garvey LA (1B)
1975 Joe Morgan CIN (2B)
1976 Joe Morgan CIN (2B)
1977 George Foster CIN (OF)
1978 Dave Parker PIT (OF)
1979 Keith Hernandez
     STL (1B)
     Willie Stargell PIT (1B)
1980 Mike Schmidt PHI (3B)
1981 Mike Schmidt PHI (3B)
1982 Dale Murphy ATL (OF)
1983 Dale Murphy ATL (OF)
1984 Ryne Sandberg CHI (2B)
1985 Willie McGee STL (OF)
1986 Mike Schmidt PHI (3B)
1987 Andre Dawson CHI (OF)
1988 Kirk Gibson LA (OF)
1989 Kevin Mitchell SF (OF)
1990 Barry Bonds PIT (OF)
1991 Terry Pendleton ATL (3B)
1992 Barry Bonds PIT (OF)

AMERICAN LEAGUE

CHALMERS
1911 Ty Cobb DET (OF)
1912 Tris Speaker BOS (OF)
1913 Walter Johnson WAS (P)
1914 Eddie Collins PHI (2B)
1915-21 No Selection

LEAGUE
1922 George Sisler STL (1B)
1923 Babe Ruth NY (OF)
1924 Walter Johnson WAS (P)
1925 Roger Peckinpaugh
     WAS (SS)
1926 George Burns CLE (1B)
1927 Lou Gehrig NY (1B)
1928 Mickey Cochrane PHI (C)
1929-30 No Selection

BASEBALL WRITERS ASSOCIATION OF AMERICA
1931 Lefty Grove PHI (P)
1932 Jimmie Foxx PHI (1B)
1933 Jimmie Foxx PHI (1B)
1934 Mickey Cochrane
     DET (C)
1935 Hank Greenberg
     DET (1B)
1936 Lou Gehrig NY (1B)
1937 Charlie Gehringer
     DET (2B)
1938 Jimmie Foxx BOS (1B)
1939 Joe DiMaggio NY (OF)
1940 Hank Greenberg
     DET (1B)
1941 Joe DiMaggio NY (OF)
1942 Joe Gordon NY (2B)
1943 Spud Chandler NY (P)
1944 Hal Newhouser DET (P)
1945 Hal Newhouser DET (P)
1946 Ted Williams BOS (OF)
1947 Joe DiMaggio NY (OF)
1948 Lou Boudreau CLE (SS)
1949 Ted Williams BOS (OF)
1950 Phil Rizzuto NY (SS)
1951 Yogi Berra NY (C)
1952 Bobby Shantz PHI (P)
1953 Al Rosen CLE (3B)
1954 Yogi Berra NY (C)
1955 Yogi Berra NY (C)
1956 Mickey Mantle NY (OF)
1957 Mickey Mantle NY (OF)
1958 Jackie Jensen BOS (OF)
1959 Nellie Fox CHI (2B)
1960 Roger Maris NY (OF)
1961 Roger Maris NY (OF)
1962 Mickey Mantle NY (OF)
1963 Elston Howard NY (C)
1964 Brooks Robinson
     BAL (3B)
1965 Zoilo Versalles MIN (SS)
1966 Frank Robinson
     BAL (OF)
1967 Carl Yastrzemski
     BOS (OF)
1968 Denny McLain DET (P)
1969 Harmon Killebrew
     MIN (3B)
1970 Boog Powell BAL (1B)
1971 Vida Blue OAK (P)
1972 Richie Allen CHI (1B)
1973 Reggie Jackson OAK (OF)

1974 Jeff Burroughs TEX (OF)
1975 Fred Lynn BOS (OF)
1976 Thurman Munson NY (C)
1977 Rod Carew MIN (1B)
1978 Jim Rice BOS (OF)
1979 Don Baylor CAL (DH)
1980 George Brett KC (3B)

1981 Rollie Fingers MIL (P)
1982 Robin Yount MIL (SS)
1983 Cal Ripken BAL (SS)
1984 Willie Hernandez DET (P)
1985 Don Mattingly NY (1B)
1986 Roger Clemens BOS (P)
1987 George Bell TOR (OF)

1988 Jose Canseco OAK (OF)
1989 Robin Yount MIL (OF)
1990 Rickey Henderson OAK (OF)
1991 Cal Ripken BAL (SS)
1992 Dennis Eckersley OAK (P)

CY YOUNG AWARD WINNERS (one selection 1956-66)

NATIONAL LEAGUE
1956 Don Newcombe BKN (RH)
1957 Warren Spahn MIL (LH)
1960 Vern Law PIT (RH)
1962 Don Drysdale LA (RH)
1963 Sandy Koufax LA (LH)
1965 Sandy Koufax LA (LH)
1966 Sandy Koufax LA (LH)
1967 Mike McCormick SF (LH)
1968 Bob Gibson STL (RH)
1969 Tom Seaver NY (RH)
1970 Bob Gibson STL (RH)
1971 Ferguson Jenkins CHI (RH)
1972 Steve Carlton PHI (LH)
1973 Tom Seaver NY (RH)
1974 Mike Marshall LA (RH)
1975 Tom Seaver NY (RH)
1976 Randy Jones SD (LH)
1977 Steve Carlton PHI (LH)
1978 Gaylord Perry SD (RH)
1979 Bruce Sutter CHI (RH)
1980 Steve Carlton PHI (LH)
1981 Fernando Valenzuela LA (LH)

1982 Steve Carlton PHI (LH)
1983 John Denny PHI (RH)
1984 Rick Sutcliffe CHI (RH)
1985 Dwight Gooden NY (RH)
1986 Mike Scott HOU (RH)
1987 Steve Bedrosian PHI (RH)
1988 Orel Hershiser LA (RH)
1989 Mark Davis SD (LH)
1990 Doug Drabek PIT (RH)
1991 Tom Glavine ATL (LH)
1992 Greg Maddux CHI (RH)

AMERICAN LEAGUE
1958 Bob Turley NY (RH)
1959 Early Wynn CHI (RH)
1961 Whitey Ford NY (LH)
1964 Dean Chance LA (RH)
1967 Jim Lonborg BOS (RH)
1968 Denny McLain DET (RH)
1969 Mike Cuellar BAL (LH)
     Denny McLain DET (RH)
1970 Jim Perry MIN (RH)
1971 Vida Blue OAK (LH)
1972 Gaylord Perry CLE (RH)
1973 Jim Palmer BAL (RH)

1974 Jim (Catfish) Hunter OAK (RH)
1975 Jim Palmer BAL (RH)
1976 Jim Palmer BAL (RH)
1977 Sparky Lyle NY (LH)
1978 Ron Guidry NY (LH)
1979 Mike Flanagan BAL (LH)
1980 Steve Stone BAL (RH)
1981 Rollie Fingers MIL (RH)
1982 Pete Vuckovich MIL (RH)
1983 LaMarr Hoyt CHI (RH)
1984 Willie Hernandez DET (LH)
1985 Bret Saberhagen KC (RH)
1986 Roger Clemens BOS (RH)
1987 Roger Clemens BOS (RH)
1988 Frank Viola MIN (LH)
1989 Bret Saberhagen KC (RH)
1990 Bob Welch OAK (RH)
1991 Roger Clemens BOS (RH)
1992 Dennis Eckersley OAK (RH)

ROOKIE OF THE YEAR (one selection 1947-48)

NATIONAL LEAGUE
1947 Jackie Robinson BKN (1B)
1948 Alvin Dark BOS (SS)
1949 Don Newcombe BKN (P)
1950 Sam Jethroe BOS (OF)
1951 Willie Mays NY (OF)
1952 Joe Black BKN (P)
1953 Junior Gilliam BKN (2B)
1954 Wally Moon STL (OF)
1955 Bill Virdon STL (OF)
1956 Frank Robinson CIN (OF)
1957 Jack Sanford PHI (P)
1958 Orlando Cepeda SF (1B)
1959 Willie McCovey SF (1B)
1960 Frank Howard LA (OF)
1961 Billy Williams CHI (OF)

1962 Ken Hubbs CHI (2B)
1963 Pete Rose CIN (2B)
1964 Richie Allen PHI (3B)
1965 Jim Lefebvre LA (2B)
1966 Tommy Helms CIN (2B)
1967 Tom Seaver NY (P)
1968 Johnny Bench CIN (C)
1969 Ted Sizemore LA (2B)
1970 Carl Morton MON (P)
1971 Earl Williams ATL (C)
1972 Jon Matlack NY (P)
1973 Gary Matthews SF (OF)
1974 Bake McBride STL (OF)
1975 Jon Montefusco SF (P)
1976 Pat Zachry CIN (P)
     Butch Metzger SD (P)
1977 Andre Dawson MON (OF)

1978 Bob Horner ATL (3B)
1979 Rick Sutcliffe LA (P)
1980 Steve Howe LA (P)
1981 Fernando Valenzuela LA (P)
1982 Steve Sax LA (2B)
1983 Darryl Strawberry NY (OF)
1984 Dwight Gooden NY (P)
1985 Vince Coleman STL (OF)
1986 Todd Worrell STL (P)
1987 Benito Santiago SD (C)
1988 Chris Sabo CIN (3B)
1989 Jerome Walton CHI (OF)
1990 Dave Justice ATL (OF)
1991 Jeff Bagwell HOU (1B)
1992 Eric Karros LA (1B)

AMERICAN LEAGUE
1949 Roy Sievers STL (OF)
1950 Walt Dropo BOS (1B)
1951 Gil McDougald NY (3B)
1952 Harry Byrd PHI (P)
1953 Harvey Kuenn DET (SS)
1954 Bob Grim NY (P)
1955 Herb Score CLE (P)
1956 Luis Aparicio CHI (SS)
1957 Tony Kubek NY (SS)
1958 Albie Pearson WAS (OF)
1959 Bob Allison WAS (OF)
1960 Ron Hansen BAL (SS)
1961 Don Schwall BOS (P)
1962 Tom Tresh NY (SS)
1963 Gary Peters CHI (P)

1964 Tony Oliva MIN (OF)
1965 Curt Blefary BAL (OF)
1966 Tommie Agee CHI (OF)
1967 Rod Carew MIN (2B)
1968 Stan Bahnsen NY (P)
1969 Lou Piniella KC (OF)
1970 Thurman Munson NY (C)
1971 Chris Chambliss CLE (1B)
1972 Carlton Fisk BOS (C)
1973 Al Bumbry BAL (OF)
1974 Mike Hargrove TEX (1B)
1975 Fred Lynn BOS (OF)
1976 Mark Fidrych DET (P)
1977 Eddie Murray BAL (DH)
1978 Lou Whitaker DET (2B)
1979 Alfredo Griffin TOR (SS)

John Castino MIN (3B)
1980 Joe Charboneau
     CLE (OF)
1981 Dave Righetti NY (P)
1982 Cal Ripken BAL (SS)
1983 Ron Kittle CHI (OF)
1984 Alvin Davis SEA (1B)
1985 Ozzie Guillen CHI (SS)
1986 Jose Canseco OAK (OF)
1987 Mark McGwire OAK (1B)
1988 Walt Weiss OAK (SS)
1989 Gregg Olson BAL (P)
1990 Sandy Alomar CLE (C)
1991 Chuck Knoblauch
     MIN (2B)
1992 Pat Listach MIL (SS)

GOLD GLOVE AWARD

COMBINED SELECTION-1957
P Bobby Shantz NY(AL)
C Sherm Lollar CHI(AL)
1B Gil Hodges BKN
2B Nellie Fox CHI(AL)
3B Frank Malzone BOS
SS Roy McMillan CIN
LF Minnie Minoso CHI(AL)
CF Willie Mays NY(NL)
RF Al Kaline DET

PITCHERS

NATIONAL LEAGUE
1958 Harvey Haddix CIN
1959-60 Harvey Haddix PIT
1961 Bobby Shantz PIT
1962-63 Bobby Shantz STL
1964 Bobby Shantz PHI
1965-73 Bob Gibson STL
1974-75 Andy Messersmith LA
1976-77 Jim Kaat PHI
1978-80 Phil Niekro ATL
1981 Steve Carlton PHI
1982-83 Phil Niekro ATL
1984 Joaquin Andujar STL
1985 Rick Reuschel PIT
1986 Fernando Valenzuela LA
1987 Rick Reuschel SF
1988 Orel Hershiser LA
1989 Ron Darling NY
1990-92 Greg Maddux CHI

AMERICAN LEAGUE
1958-60 Bobby Shantz NY
1961 Frank Lary DET
1962-72 Jim Kaat MIN

1973 Jim Kaat MIN, CHI
1974-75 Jim Kaat CHI
1976-79 Jim Palmer BAL
1980-81 Mike Norris OAK
1982-86 Ron Guidry NY
1987-88 Mark Langston SEA
1989 Bret Saberhagen KC
1990 Mike Boddicker BOS
1991-92 Mark Langston CAL

CATCHERS

NATIONAL LEAGUE
1958-60 Del Crandall MIL
1961 Johnny Roseboro LA
1962 Del Crandall MIL
1963-64 Johnny Edwards CIN
1965 Joe Torre MIL
1966 Johnny Roseboro LA
1967 Randy Hundley CHI
1968-77 Johnny Bench CIN
1978-79 Bob Boone PHI
1980-82 Gary Carter MON
1983-85 Tony Pena PIT
1986 Jody Davis CHI
1987 Mike LaValliere PIT
1988-90 Benito Santiago SD
1991-92 Tom Pagnozzi STL

AMERICAN LEAGUE
1958-59 Sherm Lollar CHI
1960 Earl Battey WAS
1961-62 Earl Battey MIN
1963-64 Elston Howard NY
1965-69 Bill Freehan DET
1970-71 Ray Fosse CLE
1972 Carlton Fisk BOS

1973-75 Thurman Munson NY
1976-81 Jim Sundberg TEX
1982 Bob Boone CAL
1983-85 Lance Parrish DET
1986-88 Bob Boone CAL
1989 Bob Boone CAL
1990 Sandy Alomar CLE
1991 Tony Pena BOS
1992 Ivan Rodriguez TEX

FIRST BASEMEN

NATIONAL LEAGUE
1958-59 Gil Hodges LA
1960-65 Bill White STL
1966 Bill White PHI
1967-72 Wes Parker LA
1973 Mike Jorgenson MON
1974-77 Steve Garvey LA
1978-82 Keith Hernandez STL
1983 Keith Hernandez STL, NY
1984-88 Keith Hernandez NY
1989-90 Andres Galarraga
     MON
1991 Will Clark SF
1992 Mark Grace CHI

AMERICAN LEAGUE
1958-61 Vic Power CLE
1962-63 Vic Power MIN
1964 Vic Power LA
1965-66 Joe Pepitone NY
1967-68 George Scott BOS
1969 Joe Pepitone NY
1970 Jim Spencer CAL
1971 George Scott BOS
1972-76 George Scott MIL

1977 Jim Spencer CHI
1978 Chris Chambliss NY
1979-80 Cecil Cooper MIL
1981 Mike Squires CHI
1982-84 Eddie Murray BAL
1985-89 Don Mattingly NY
1990 Mark McGwire OAK
1991-92 Don Mattingly NY

SECOND BASEMEN

NATIONAL LEAGUE
1958 Bill Mazeroski PIT
1959 Charlie Neal LA
1960-61 Bill Mazeroski PIT
1962 Ken Hubbs CHI
1963-67 Bill Mazeroski PIT
1968 Glenn Beckert CHI
1969 Felix Millan ATL
1970-71 Tommy Helms CIN
1972 Felix Millan ATL
1973-77 Joe Morgan CIN
1978 Davey Lopes LA
1979 Manny Trillo PHI
1980 Doug Flynn NY
1981-82 Manny Trillo PHI
1983-91 Ryne Sandberg CHI
1992 Jose Lind PIT

AMERICAN LEAGUE
1958 Frank Bolling DET
1959-60 Nellie Fox CHI
1961-65 Bobby Richardson NY
1966-68 Bobby Knoop CAL
1969-71 Dave Johnson BAL
1972 Doug Griffin BOS
1973-76 Bobby Grich BAL
1977-82 Frank White KC
1983-85 Lou Whitaker DET

1986-87 Frank White KC
1988-90 Harold Reynolds SEA
1991-92 Roberto Alomar TOR

THIRD BASEMEN

NATIONAL LEAGUE
1958-61 Ken Boyer STL
1962 Jim Davenport SF
1963 Ken Boyer STL
1964-68 Ron Santo CHI
1969 Clete Boyer ATL
1970-74 Doug Rader HOU
1975 Ken Reitz STL
1976-84 Mike Schmidt PHI
1985 Tim Wallach MON
1986 Mike Schmidt PHI
1987 Terry Pendleton STL
1988 Tim Wallach MON
1989 Terry Pendleton STL
1990 Tim Wallach MON
1991 Matt Williams SF
1992 Terry Pendleton ATL

AMERICAN LEAGUE
1958-59 Frank Malzone BOS
1960-75 Brooks Robinson BAL
1976 Aurelio Rodriguez DET
1977-78 Graig Nettles NY
1979-84 Buddy Bell TEX
1985 George Brett KC
1986-89 Gary Gaetti MIN
1990 Kelly Gruber TOR
1991-92 Robin Ventura CHI

SHORTSTOPS

NATIONAL LEAGUE
1958-59 Roy McMillan CIN

1960 Ernie Banks CHI
1961-62 Maury Wills LA
1963 Bobby Wine PHI
1964 Ruben Amaro PHI
1965 Leo Cardenas CIN
1966-67 Gene Alley PIT
1968 Dal Maxvill STL
1969-70 Don Kessinger CHI
1971 Bud Harrelson NY
1972 Larry Bowa PHI
1973 Roger Metzger HOU
1974-77 Dave Concepcion CIN
1978 Larry Bowa PHI
1979 Dave Concepcion CIN
1980-81 Ozzie Smith SD
1982-92 Ozzie Smith STL

AMERICAN LEAGUE
1958-62 Luis Aparicio CHI
1963 Zoilo Versalles MIN
1964 Luis Aparicio BAL
1965 Zoilo Versalles MIN
1966 Luis Aparicio BAL
1967 Jim Fregosi CAL
1968 Luis Aparicio CHI
1969 Mark Belanger BAL
1970 Luis Aparicio CHI
1971 Mark Belanger BAL
1972 Eddie Brinkman DET
1973-78 Mark Belanger BAL
1979 Rick Burleson BOS
1980-81 Alan Trammell DET
1982 Robin Yount MIL
1983-84 Alan Trammell DET
1985 Alfredo Griffin OAK
1986-89 Tony Fernandez TOR
1990 Ozzie Guillen CHI
1991-92 Cal Ripken BAL

NATIONAL LEAGUE OUTFIELDERS

1958
Frank Robinson CIN (LF)
Willie Mays SF (CF)
Hank Aaron MIL (RF)

1959
Jackie Brant SF (LF)
Willie Mays SF (CF)
Hank Aaron MIL (RF)

1960
Wally Moon LA (LF)
Willie Mays SF (CF)
Hank Aaron MIL (RF)

1961
Willie Mays SF
Roberto Clemente PIT
Vada Pinson CIN

1962
Willie Mays SF
Roberto Clemente PIT
Bill Virdon PIT

1963
Willie Mays SF
Roberto Clemente PIT
Curt Flood STL

1964
Willie Mays SF
Roberto Clemente PIT
Curt Flood STL

1965
Willie Mays SF
Roberto Clemente PIT
Curt Flood STL

1966
Willie Mays SF
Curt Flood STL
Roberto Clemente PIT

1967
Roberto Clemente PIT
Curt Flood STL
Willie Mays SF

1968
Willie Mays SF
Roberto Clemente PIT
Curt Flood STL

1969
Roberto Clemente PIT
Curt Flood STL
Pete Rose CIN

1970
Roberto Clemente PIT
Tommy Agee NY
Pete Rose CIN

1971
Roberto Clemente PIT
Bobby Bonds SF
Willie Davis LA

1972
Roberto Clemente PIT
Cesar Cedeno HOU
Willie Davis LA

1973
Bobby Bonds SF
Cesar Cedeno HOU
Willie Davis LA

1974
Cesar Cedeno HOU
Cesar Geronimo CIN
Bobby Bonds SF

1975
Cesar Cedeno HOU
Cesar Geronimo CIN
Garry Maddox PHI

1976
Cesar Cedeno HOU
Cesar Geronimo CIN
Garry Maddox PHI

1977
Cesar Geronimo CIN
Garry Maddox PHI
Dave Parker PIT

1978
Garry Maddox PHI
Dave Parker PIT
Ellis Valentine MON

1979
Garry Maddox PHI
Dave Parker PIT
Dave Winfield SD

1980
Andre Dawson MON
Garry Maddox PHI
Dave Winfield SD

1981
Andre Dawson MON
Garry Maddox PHI
Dusty Baker LA

1982
Andre Dawson MON
Dale Murphy ATL
Garry Maddox PHI

1983
Andre Dawson MON

Dale Murphy ATL
Willie McGee STL

1984
Dale Murphy ATL
Bob Dernier CHI
Andre Dawson MON

1985
Willie McGee STL
Andre Dawson MON
Dale Murphy ATL

1986
Dale Murphy ATL
Willie McGee STL
Tony Gwynn SD

1987
Eric Davis CIN
Tony Gwynn SD
Andre Dawson CHI

1988
Andre Dawson CHI
Eric Davis CIN
Andy Van Slyke PIT

1989
Eric Davis CIN
Tony Gwynn SD
Andy Van Slyke PIT

1990
Barry Bonds PIT
Tony Gwynn SD
Andy Van Slyke PIT

1991
Barry Bonds PIT
Tony Gwynn SD
Andy Van Slyke PIT

1992
Barry Bonds PIT
Larry Walker MON
Andy Van Slyke PIT

**AMERICAN
LEAGUE
OUTFIELDERS**

1958
Norm Siebern NY (LF)
Jimmy Piersall BOS (CF)
Al Kaline DET (RF)

1959
Minnie Minoso CLE (LF)
Al Kaline DET (CF)
Jackie Jensen BOS (RF)

1960
Minnie Minoso CHI (LF)
Jim Landis CHI (CF)
Roger Maris NY (RF)

1961
Al Kaline DET
Jimmy Piersall CLE
Jim Landis CHI

1962
Jim Landis CHI
Mickey Mantle NY
Al Kaline DET

1963
Al Kaline DET
Carl Yastrzemski BOS
Jim Landis CHI

1964
Al Kaline DET
Jim Landis CHI
Vic Davalillo CLE

1965
Al Kaline DET
Tom Tresh NY
Carl Yastrzemski BOS

1966
Al Kaline DET
Tommy Agee CHI
Tony Oliva MIN

1967
Carl Yastrzemski BOS
Paul Blair BAL
Al Kaline DET

1968
Mickey Stanley DET
Carl Yastrzemski BOS
Reggie Smith BOS

1969
Paul Blair BAL
Mickey Stanley DET
Carl Yastrzemski BOS

1970
Mickey Stanley DET
Paul Blair BAL
Ken Berry CHI

1971
Paul Blair BAL
Amos Otis KC
Carl Yastrzemski BOS

1972
Paul Blair BAL

Bobby Murcer NY
Ken Berry CAL

1973
Paul Blair BAL
Amos Otis KC
Mickey Stanley DET

1974
Paul Blair BAL
Amos Otis KC
Joe Rudi OAK

1975
Paul Blair BAL
Joe Rudi OAK
Fred Lynn BOS

1976
Joe Rudi OAK
Dwight Evans BOS
Rick Manning CLE

1977
Juan Beniquez TEX
Carl Yastrzemski BOS
Al Cowens KC

1978
Fred Lynn BOS
Dwight Evans BOS
Rick Miller CAL

1979
Dwight Evans BOS
Sixto Lezcano MIL
Fred Lynn BOS

1980
Fred Lynn BOS
Dwayne Murphy OAK
Willie Wilson KC

1981
Dwayne Murphy OAK
Dwight Evans BOS
Rickey Henderson OAK

1982
Dwight Evans BOS
Dave Winfield NY
Dwayne Murphy OAK

1983
Dwight Evans BOS
Dave Winfield NY
Dwayne Murphy OAK

1984
Dwight Evans BOS
Dave Winfield NY
Dwayne Murphy OAK

1985
Gary Pettis CAL
Dave Winfield NY
Dwight Evans BOS
Dwayne Murphy OAK

1986
Jesse Barfield TOR
Kirby Puckett MIN
Gary Pettis CAL

1987
Jesse Barfield TOR
Kirby Puckett MIN
Dave Winfield NY

1988
Devon White CAL
Gary Pettis CAL
Kirby Puckett MIN

1989
Devon White CAL
Gary Pettis DET
Kirby Puckett MIN

1990
Ken Griffey Jr. SEA
Ellis Burks BOS
Gary Pettis TEX

1991
Ken Griffey Jr. SEA
Devon White TOR
Kirby Puckett MIN

1992
Ken Griffey Jr. SEA
Devon White TOR
Kirby Puckett MIN

THE WORLD SERIES 1903-90

YEAR	WINNER	SERIES	LOSER
1903	BOS Pilgrims	5-3	PIT Pirates (NL)
1904	NO SERIES		
1905	NY Giants (NL)	4-1	PHI Athletics (AL)
1906	CHI White Sox (AL)	4-2	CHI Cubs (NL)
1907	CHI Cubs (NL)	4-0	DET Tigers (AL)
1908	CHI Cubs (NL)	4-1	DET Tigers (AL)
1909	PIT Pirates (NL)	4-3	DET Tigers (AL)
1910	PHI Athletics (AL)	4-1	CHI Cubs (NL)
1911	PHI Athletics (AL)	4-2	NY Giants (NL)
1912	BOS Red Sox (AL)	4-3	NY Giants (NL)
1913	PHI Athletics (AL)	4-1	NY Giants (NL)
1914	BOS Braves (NL)	4-0	PHI Athletics (AL)
1915	BOS Red Sox (AL)	4-1	PHI Phillies (NL)
1916	BOS Red Sox (AL)	4-1	BKN Robins (NL)
1917	CHI White Sox (AL)	4-2	NY Giants (NL)
1918	BOS Red Sox (AL)	4-2	CHI Cubs (NL)
1919	CIN Reds (NL)	5-3	CHI White Sox (AL)
1920	CLE Indians (AL)	5-2	BKN Robins (NL)
1921	NY Giants (NL)	5-3	NY Yankees (AL)
1922	NY Giants (NL)	4-0	NY Yankees (AL)
1923	NY Yankees (AL)	4-2	NY Giants (NL)
1924	WAS Senators (AL)	4-3	NY Giants (NL)
1925	PIT Pirates (NL)	4-3	WAS Senators (AL)
1926	STL Cardinals (NL)	4-3	NY Yankees (AL)
1927	NY Yankees (AL)	4-0	PIT Pirates (NL)
1928	NY Yankees (AL)	4-0	STL Cardinals (NL)
1929	PHI Athletics (AL)	4-1	CHI Cubs (NL)
1930	PHI Athletics (AL)	4-2	STL Cardinals (NL)
1931	STL Cardinals (NL)	4-3	PHI Athletics (AL)
1932	NY Yankees (AL)	4-0	CHI Cubs (NL)
1933	NY Giants (NL)	4-1	WAS Senators (AL)
1934	STL Cardinals (NL)	4-3	DET Tigers (AL)
1935	DET Tigers (AL)	4-2	CHI Cubs (NL)
1936	NY Yankees (AL)	4-2	NY Giants (NL)
1937	NY Yankees (AL)	4-1	NY Giants (NL)
1938	NY Yankees (AL)	4-0	CHI Cubs (NL)
1939	NY Yankees (AL)	4-0	CIN Reds (NL)
1940	CIN Reds (NL)	4-3	DET Tigers (AL)
1941	NY Yankees (AL)	4-1	BKN Dodgers (NL)
1942	STL Cardinals (NL)	4-1	NY Yankees (AL)
1943	NY Yankees (AL)	4-1	STL Cardinals (NL)
1944	STL Cardinals (NL)	4-2	STL Browns (AL)
1945	DET Tigers (AL)	4-3	CHI Cubs (NL)
1946	STL Cardinals (NL)	4-3	BOS Red Sox (AL)
1947	NY Yankees (AL)	4-3	BKN Dodgers (NL)
1948	CLE Indians (AL)	4-2	BOS Braves (NL)
1949	NY Yankees (AL)	4-1	BKN Dodgers (NL)
1950	NY Yankees (AL)	4-0	PHI Phillies (NL)
1951	NY Yankees (AL)	4-2	NY Giants (NL)
1952	NY Yankees (AL)	4-3	BKN Dodgers (NL)
1953	NY Yankees (AL)	4-2	BKN Dodgers (NL)
1954	NY Giants (NL)	4-0	CLE Indians (AL)
1955	BKN Dodgers (NL)	4-3	NY Yankees (AL)
1956	NY Yankees (AL)	4-3	BKN Dodgers (NL)
1957	MIL Braves (NL)	4-3	NY Yankees (AL)
1958	NY Yankees (AL)	4-3	MIL Braves (NL)
1959	LA Dodgers (NL)	4-2	CHI White Sox (AL)
1960	PIT Pirates (NL)	4-3	NY Yankees (AL)
1961	NY Yankees (AL)	4-1	CIN Reds (NL)
1962	NY Yankees (AL)	4-3	SF Giants (NL)
1963	LA Dodgers (NL)	4-0	NY Yankees (AL)
1964	STL Cardinals (NL)	4-3	NY Yankees (AL)
1965	LA Dodgers (NL)	4-3	MIN Twins (AL)
1966	BAL Orioles (AL)	4-0	LA Dodgers (NL)
1967	STL Cardinals (NL)	4-3	BOS Red Sox (AL)
1968	DET Tigers (AL)	4-3	STL Cardinals (NL)
1969	NY Mets (NL)	4-1	BAL Orioles (AL)
1970	BAL Orioles (AL)	4-1	CIN Reds (NL)
1971	PIT Pirates (NL)	4-3	BAL Orioles (AL)
1972	OAK Athletics (AL)	4-3	CIN Reds (NL)
1973	OAK Athletics (AL)	4-3	NY Mets (NL)
1974	OAK Athletics (AL)	4-1	LA Dodgers (NL)
1975	CIN Reds (NL)	4-3	BOS Red Sox (AL)
1976	CIN Reds (NL)	4-0	NY Yankees (AL)
1977	NY Yankees (AL)	4-2	LA Dodgers (NL)
1978	NY Yankees (AL)	4-2	LA Dodgers (NL)
1979	PIT Pirates (NL)	4-3	BAL Orioles (AL)
1980	PHI Phillies (NL)	4-2	KC Royals (AL)
1981	LA Dodgers (NL)	4-2	NY Yankees (AL)
1982	STL Cardinals (NL)	4-3	MIL Brewers (AL)
1983	BAL Orioles (AL)	4-1	PHI Phillies (NL)
1984	DET Tigers (AL)	4-1	SD Padres (NL)
1985	KC Royals (AL)	4-3	STL Cardinals (NL)
1986	NY Mets (NL)	4-3	BOS Red Sox (AL)
1987	MIN Twins (AL)	4-3	STL Cardinals (NL)
1988	LA Dodgers (NL)	4-1	OAK Athletics (AL)
1989	OAK Athletics (AL)	4-0	SF Giants (NL)
1990	CIN Reds (NL)	4-0	OAK Athletics (AL)
1991	MIN Twins (AL)	4-3	ATL Braves (NL)
1992	TOR Blue Jays (AL)	4-2	ATL Braves (NL)

LEAGUE CHAMPIONSHIP SERIES 1969-1990

	NLCS				ALCS		
YEAR	WINNER	SERIES	LOSER	YEAR	WINNER	SERIES	LOSER
1969	NY Mets (E)	3-0	ATL Braves (W)	1969	BAL Orioles (E)	3-0	MIN Twins (W)
1970	CIN Reds (W)	3-0	PIT Pirates (E)	1970	BAL Orioles (E)	3-0	MIN Twins (W)
1971	PIT Pirates (E)	3-1	SF Giants (W)	1971	BAL Orioles (E)	3-0	OAK Athletics (W)
1972	CIN Reds (W)	3-2	PIT Pirates (E)	1972	OAK Athletics (W)	3-2	DET Tigers (E)
1973	NY Mets (E)	3-2	CIN Reds (W)	1973	OAK Athletics (W)	3-2	BAL Orioles (E)
1974	LA Dodgers (W)	3-1	PIT Pirates (E)	1974	OAK Athletics (W)	3-1	BAL Orioles (E)
1975	CIN Reds (W)	3-0	PIT Pirates (E)	1975	BOS Red Sox (E)	3-0	OAK Athletics (W)
1976	CIN Reds (W)	3-0	PHI Phillies (E)	1976	NY Yankees (E)	3-2	KC Royals (W)
1977	LA Dodgers (W)	3-1	PHI Phillies (E)	1977	NY Yankees (E)	3-2	KC Royals (W)
1978	LA Dodgers (W)	3-1	PHI Phillies (E)	1978	NY Yankees (E)	3-1	KC Royals (W)
1979	PIT Pirates (W)	3-0	CIN Reds (W)	1979	BAL Orioles (E)	3-1	CAL Angels (W)
1980	PHI Phillies (E)	3-2	HOU Astros (W)	1980	KC Royals (W)	3-0	NY Yankees (E)
1981	NL EAST PLAYOFF			1981	AL EAST PLAYOFF		
	MON Expos	3-2	PHI Phillies		NY Yankees	3-2	MIL Brewers
	NL WEST PLAYOFF				AL WEST PLAYOFF		
	LA Dodgers	3-2	HOU Astros		OAK Athletics	3-0	KC Royals
	LCS				LCS		
	LA Dodgers (W)	3-2	MON Expos (E)		NY Yankees (E)	3-0	OAK Athletics (W)
1982	STL Cardinals (E)	3-0	ATL Braves (W)	1982	MIL Brewers (E)	3-2	CAL Angels (W)
1983	PHI Phillies (E)	3-1	LA Dodgers (W)	1983	BAL Orioles (E)	3-1	CHI White Sox (W)
1984	SD Padres (W)	3-2	CHI Cubs (E)	1984	DET Tigers (E)	3-0	KC Royals (W)
1985	STL Cardinals (E)	4-2	LA Dodgers (W)	1985	KC Royals (W)	4-3	TOR Blue Jays (E)
1986	NY Mets (E)	4-2	HOU Astros (W)	1986	BOS Red Sox (E)	4-3	CAL Angels (W)
1987	STL Cardinals (E)	4-3	SF Giants (W)	1987	MIN Twins (W)	4-1	DET Tigers (E)
1988	LA Dodgers (W)	4-3	NY Mets (E)	1988	OAK Athletics (W)	4-0	BOS Red Sox (E)
1989	SF Giants (W)	4-1	CHI Cubs (E)	1989	OAK Athletics (W)	4-1	TOR Blue Jays (E)
1990	CIN Reds (W)	4-2	PIT Pirates (E)	1990	OAK Athletics (W)	4-0	BOS Red Sox (E)
1991	ATL Braves (W)	4-3	PIT Pirates (E)	1991	MIN Twins (W)	4-2	TOR Blue Jays (E)
1992	ATL Braves (W)	4-3	PIT Pirates (E)	1992	TOR Blue Jays (E)	4-2	OAK Athletics (W)

Yearly Team and Individual Leaders

In this section, you will find how each National League and American League organization did in each season since 1900. Included also are each league's individual leaders in batting and pitching for each year.

Above the team names is a standard won-lost line. The abbreviations are: **W** = wins; **L** = losses; **PCT** = winning percentage; **GB** = games the team finished behind the league winner or the division winner; **R** = runs scored by the team; **OR** = runs scored by the team's opponents; **BA** = team batting average; **FA** = team fielding average; **ERA** = team earned run average. The league's total runs, opponents runs, batting average, fielding average, and earned run average are shown totaled below the columns. The team that won the World Series received a star (★), the team that won the LCS but not the fall classic received a bullet (●).

The year's individual leaders in each league follow, beginning with hitters' categories—batting average, hits, doubles, triples, home runs, runs batted in, slugging average, stolen bases, and runs scored. Pitchers' categories follow—wins, winning percentage, earned run average, strikeouts, saves, complete games, shutouts, games pitched, and innings pitched. Most of these categories will have the top three leaders in the league. When two or more players tied for a position, it is indicated. If there are two who were far and away the leaders in any one category, and many who either tied or were among the ordinary, only two players are listed. The minimum requirements to be considered as a league leader have changed many times over the years. As a rule, this publication lists those players who at the time were the acknowledged leaders in their categories. For example, if Ty Cobb was recognized by his contemporaries as the batting champion in 1914, he is listed as the batting average leader in 1914, even though he may not have had enough plate appearances to qualify recently. The leaders listed under a particular year would have been eligible under the rules of that year. Others who may have been eligible under current rules—or another generally accepted minimum, such as 3.1 plate appearances per scheduled game—do not appear.

1900 NL

	W	L	PCT	GB	R	OR	BA	FA	ERA
BROOKLYN	82	54	.603	—	816	722	.293	.948	3.89
PITTSBURGH	79	60	.568	4.5	733	612	.272	.945	3.06
PHILADELPHIA	75	63	.543	8	810	791	.290	.945	4.12
BOSTON	66	72	.478	17	778	739	.283	.953	3.72
CHICAGO	65	75	.464	19	635	751	.260	.933	3.23
ST. LOUIS	65	75	.464	19	743	747	.291	.943	3.75
CINCINNATI	62	77	.446	21.5	702	745	.266	.945	3.83
NEW YORK	60	78	.435	23	713	823	.279	.928	3.96
					5930	5930	.279	.942	3.69

BATTING AVERAGE
Honus Wagner PIT..... .381
Elmer Flick PHI .... .378
W. Keeler BKN .... .368

HITS
W. Keeler BKN............ 208
Elmer Flick PHI 207
Jesse Burkett STL 203

DOUBLES
Honus Wagner PIT 45
Elmer Flick PHI 33
two tied at 32

TRIPLES
Honus Wagner PIT 22
Hickman NY 17
Joe Kelley BKN............. 17

HOME RUNS
Herman Long BOS 12
Elmer Flick PHI 11
Mike Donlin STL 10

RUNS BATTED IN
Elmer Flick PHI 110
Ed Delahanty PHI 109
Honus Wagner PIT 100

SLUGGING AVERAGE
Honus Wagner PIT .... .573
Elmer Flick PHI .... .545
Nap Lajoie PHI........... .517

STOLEN BASES
Patsy Donovan STL...... 45
Van Haltren NY 45
Jimmy Barrett CIN 44

RUNS SCORED
Roy Thomas PHI 134
Jimmy Slagle PHI 115
two tied at 114

WINS
Joe McGinnity BKN....... 29
four tied at..................... 20

WINNING PERCENTAGE
Jesse Tannehill PIT ... .769
Joe McGinnity BKN.... .763
Chick Fraser PHI .... .615

EARNED RUN AVERAGE
Rube Waddell PIT...... 2.37
Ned Garvin CHI 2.41
Jack Taylor CHI 2.55

STRIKEOUTS
Rube Waddell PIT....... 130
Noodles Hahn CIN...... 127
Cy Young STL 119

SAVES
Frank Kitson BKN 4
Bill Bernhard PHI 2
five tied at 1

COMPLETE GAMES
Pink Hawley NY 34
Bill Dinneen BOS 33
four tied at..................... 32

SHUTOUTS
four tied at....................... 4

GAMES PITCHED
Bill Carrick NY............... 45
Joe McGinnity BKN....... 45
Ed Scott CIN 43

INNINGS PITCHED
Joe McGinnity BKN..... 347
Bill Carrick NY............. 342
Pink Hawley NY 329

1901 AL

	W	L	PCT	GB	R	OR	BA	FA	ERA
CHICAGO	83	53	.610	—	819	631	.276	.941	2.98
BOSTON	79	57	.581	4	759	608	.279	.943	3.04
DETROIT	74	61	.548	8.5	741	694	.279	.930	3.30
PHILADELPHIA	74	62	.544	9	805	761	.288	.942	4.00
BALTIMORE	68	65	.511	13.5	760	750	.294	.926	3.73
WASHINGTON	61	73	.455	21	678	767	.269	.943	4.09
CLEVELAND	55	82	.401	28.5	663	827	.271	.942	4.12
MILWAUKEE	48	89	.350	35.5	641	828	.261	.934	4.06
					5866	5866	.277	.938	3.66

BATTING AVERAGE
Nap Lajoie PHI............ .422
Buck Freeman BOS... .345
Mike Donlin BAL .... .341

HITS
Nap Lajoie PHI............ 229
John Anderson MIL... 190
Jimmy Collins BOS 187

DOUBLES
Nap Lajoie PHI.............. 48
John Anderson MIL...... 46
Jimmy Collins BOS 42

TRIPLES
Jimmy Williams BAL 21
Bill Keister BAL 21
Sam Mertes CHI 17

HOME RUNS
Nap Lajoie PHI.............. 13
Buck Freeman BOS...... 12
Mike Grady WAS 9

RUNS BATTED IN
Nap Lajoie PHI............. 125
Buck Freeman BOS.... 114
John Anderson MIL....... 99

SLUGGING AVERAGE
Nap Lajoie PHI............ .635
Buck Freeman BOS... .527
Socks Seybold PHI .... .499

STOLEN BASES
Frank Isbell CHI 52
Sam Mertes CHI 46
two tied at 38

RUNS SCORED
Nap Lajoie PHI............ 145
Fielder Jones CHI 120
Jimmy Williams BAL ... 113

WINS
Cy Young BOS 33
Joe McGinnity BAL 26
Clark Griffith CHI........... 24

WINNING PERCENTAGE
Clark Griffith CHI........ .774
Cy Young BOS .... .767
Nixie Callahan CHI .... .652

EARNED RUN AVERAGE
Cy Young BOS 1.62
Nixie Callahan CHI 2.42
Joe Yeager DET 2.61

STRIKEOUTS
Cy Young BOS 158
Roy Patterson CHI...... 127
Dowling CLE, MIL 124

SAVES
Bill Hoffer CLE 3
Joe McGinnity BAL 3
Ned Garvin MIL............... 2

COMPLETE GAMES
Joe McGinnity BAL 39
Cy Young BOS 38
two tied at 35

SHUTOUTS
Clark Griffith CHI.............. 5
Cy Young BOS 5
two tied at 4

GAMES PITCHED
Joe McGinnity BAL 48
P. Dowling CLE, MIL..... 43
Cy Young BOS 43

INNINGS PITCHED
Joe McGinnity BAL 382
Cy Young BOS 371
Roscoe Miller DET 332

1901 NL

	W	L	PCT	GB	R	OR	BA	FA	ERA
PITTSBURGH	90	49	.647	—	776	534	.286	.950	2.58
PHILADELPHIA	83	57	.593	7.5	668	543	.267	.954	2.87
BROOKLYN	79	57	.581	9.5	744	600	.288	.950	3.14
ST. LOUIS	76	64	.543	14.5	792	689	.285	.949	3.68
BOSTON	69	69	.500	20.5	531	556	.250	.952	2.90
CHICAGO	53	86	.381	37	578	699	.258	.943	3.33
NEW YORK	52	85	.380	37	544	755	.255	.941	3.87
CINCINNATI	52	87	.374	38	561	818	.251	.940	4.17
					5194	5194	.268	.947	3.32

BATTING AVERAGE
Jesse Burkett STL ..... .382
Ed Delahanty PHI ...... .357
W. Keeler BKN............ .355

HITS
Jesse Burkett STL 228
W. Keeler BKN............ 209
J. Sheckard BKN 197

DOUBLES
Jake Beckley CIN 39
Honus Wagner PIT 39
Ed Delahanty PHI 39

TRIPLES
Jimmy Sheckard BKN... 19
three tied at................... 17

HOME RUNS
Sam Crawford CIN........ 16
Jimmy Sheckard BKN... 11
Jesse Burkett STL 10

RUNS BATTED IN
Honus Wagner PIT 126
Ed Delahanty PHI 108
two tied at 104

SLUGGING AVERAGE
J. Sheckard BKN 536
Ed Delahanty PHI 533
Sam Crawford CIN...... 528

STOLEN BASES
Honus Wagner PIT 49
Topsy Hartsel CHI 41
Sammy Strang NY 40

RUNS SCORED
Jesse Burkett STL 139
W. Keeler BKN............ 123
G. Beaumont PIT 120

WINS
B. Donovan BKN........... 25
Jack Harper STL 23
two tied at 22

WINNING PERCENTAGE
Jack Chesbro PIT 677
Jack Harper STL 657
D. Phillippe PIT 647

EARNED RUN AVERAGE
Jesse Tannehill PIT ... 2.18
D. Phillippe PIT 2.22
Al Orth PHI................. 2.27

STRIKEOUTS
Noodles Hahn CIN...... 239
B. Donovan BKN.......... 226
T. Hughes CHI 225

SAVES
Jack Powell STL 3
three tied at..................... 2

COMPLETE GAMES
Noodles Hahn CIN........ 41
Dummy Taylor NY 37
two tied at 36

SHUTOUTS
Vic Willis BOS................. 6
Jack Chesbro PIT 6
Al Orth PHI..................... 6

GAMES PITCHED
B. Donovan BKN........... 45
Jack Powell STL 45
Dummy Taylor NY 45

INNINGS PITCHED
Noodles Hahn CIN...... 375
Dummy Taylor NY 353
B. Donovan BKN......... 351

1902 AL

	W	L	PCT	GB	R	OR	BA	FA	ERA
PHILADELPHIA	83	53	.610	—	775	636	.287	.953	3.29
ST. LOUIS	78	58	.574	5	619	607	.265	.953	3.34
BOSTON	77	60	.562	6.5	664	600	.278	.955	3.02
CHICAGO	74	60	.552	8	675	602	.268	.955	3.41
CLEVELAND	69	67	.507	14	686	667	.289	.950	3.28
WASHINGTON	61	75	.449	22	707	790	.283	.945	4.36
DETROIT	52	83	.385	30.5	566	657	.251	.943	3.56
BALTIMORE	50	88	.362	34	715	848	.277	.938	4.33
					5407	5407	.275	.949	3.57

BATTING AVERAGE
Ed Delahanty WAS .... .376
N. Lajoie PHI, CLE..... .366
Hickman BOS, CLE ... .363

HITS
Hickman BOS, CLE 195
Lave Cross PHI........... 191
Bill Bradley CLE.......... 187

DOUBLES
Ed Delahanty WAS 43
Harry Davis PHI 43
two tied at 39

TRIPLES
Jimmy Williams BAL 21
Buck Freeman BOS...... 19
two tied at 14

HOME RUNS
Socks Seybold PHI 16
three tied at................... 11

RUNS BATTED IN
Buck Freeman BOS.... 121
Hickman BOS, CLE 110
Lave Cross PHI........... 108

SLUGGING AVERAGE
Ed Delahanty WAS .... .590
N. Lajoie PHI, CLE..... .551
Hickman BOS, CLE ... .541

STOLEN BASES
Topsy Hartsel PHI......... 47
Sam Mertes CHI 46
Dave Fultz PHI.............. 44

RUNS SCORED
Topsy Hartsel PHI...... 109
Dave Fultz PHI............ 109
Sammy Strang CHI..... 108

WINS
Cy Young BOS 32
Rube Waddell PHI 24
two tied at 22

WINNING PERCENTAGE
B. Bernhard PHI, CLE.. .783
Rube Waddell PHI ..... .774
Cy Young BOS .... .744

EARNED RUN AVERAGE
Ed Siever DET 1.91
Rube Waddell PHI 2.05
two tied at 2.15

STRIKEOUTS
Rube Waddell PHI 210
Cy Young BOS 160
Jack Powell STL 137

SAVES
Jack Powell STL 3

COMPLETE GAMES
Cy Young BOS 41
Bill Dinneen BOS 39
two tied at 36

SHUTOUTS
Addie Joss CLE 5
three tied at.................... 4

GAMES PITCHED
Cy Young BOS 45
Jack Powell STL 42
Bill Dinneen BOS.......... 42

INNINGS PITCHED
Cy Young BOS 385
Bill Dinneen BOS........ 371
Jack Powell STL 328

1902 NL

	W	L	PCT	GB	R	OR	BA	FA	ERA
PITTSBURGH	103	36	.741	—	775	440	.287	.958	2.30
BROOKLYN	75	63	.543	27.5	564	519	.257	.952	2.69
BOSTON	73	64	.533	29	572	516	.250	.959	2.61
CINCINNATI	70	70	.500	33.5	633	566	.282	.945	2.67
CHICAGO	68	69	.496	34	530	501	.251	.946	2.21
ST. LOUIS	56	78	.418	44.5	517	695	.258	.944	3.47
PHILADELPHIA	56	81	.409	46	484	649	.247	.946	3.50
NEW YORK	48	88	.353	53.5	401	590	.238	.943	2.82
					4476	4476	.259	.949	2.78

BATTING AVERAGE
G. Beaumont PIT .... .357
W. Keeler BKN .... .338
Sam Crawford CIN..... .333

HITS
G. Beaumont PIT 194
W. Keeler BKN............ 188
Sam Crawford CIN...... 185

DOUBLES
Honus Wagner PIT 33
Fred Clarke PIT 27
Duff Cooley BOS 26

TRIPLES
Sam Crawford CIN....... 23
Tommy Leach PIT 22
Honus Wagner PIT 16

HOME RUNS
Tommy Leach PIT 6
Jake Beckley CIN 5
two tied at 4

RUNS BATTED IN
Honus Wagner PIT 91
Tommy Leach PIT 85
Sam Crawford CIN........ 78

SLUGGING AVERAGE
Honus Wagner PIT .... .467
Sam Crawford CIN..... .461
Fred Clarke PIT .... .453

STOLEN BASES
Honus Wagner PIT 42
Jimmy Slagle CHI 40
Patsy Donovan STL...... 34

RUNS SCORED
Honus Wagner PIT 105
Fred Clarke PIT 104
G. Beaumont PIT 100

WINS
Jack Chesbro PIT 28
Togie Pittinger BOS 27
Vic Willis BOS............... 27

WINNING PERCENTAGE
Jack Chesbro PIT ...... .824
Ed Doheny PIT .... .800
Jesse Tannehill PIT ... .769

EARNED RUN AVERAGE
Jack Taylor CHI 1.33
Noodles Hahn CIN 1.76
Jesse Tannehill PIT ... 1.95

STRIKEOUTS
Vic Willis BOS............. 225
Doc White PHI 185
Togie Pittinger BOS ... 174

SAVES
Vic Willis BOS................ 3
Sam Leever PIT.............. 2
nine tied at 1

COMPLETE GAMES
Vic Willis BOS............... 45
Togie Pittinger BOS...... 36
two tied at 34

SHUTOUTS
Christy Mathewson NY ... 8
Jack Chesbro PIT 8
Jack Taylor CHI 8

GAMES PITCHED
Vic Willis BOS............... 51
Togie Pittinger BOS...... 46
Stan Yerkes STL............ 39

INNINGS PITCHED
Vic Willis BOS............. 410
Togie Pittinger BOS 389
Jack Taylor CHI 325

1903 AL

	W	L	PCT	GB	R	OR	BA	FA	ERA
★BOSTON	91	47	.659	—	708	504	.272	.959	2.57
PHILADELPHIA	75	60	.556	14.5	597	519	.264	.960	2.97
CLEVELAND	77	63	.550	15	639	579	.270	.946	2.66
NEW YORK	72	62	.537	17	579	573	.250	.953	3.08
DETROIT	65	71	.478	25	567	539	.268	.950	2.75
ST. LOUIS	65	74	.468	26.5	500	525	.242	.953	2.77
CHICAGO	60	77	.438	30.5	516	613	.247	.949	3.02
WASHINGTON	43	94	.314	47.5	437	691	.231	.954	3.82
					4543	4543	.256	.953	2.95

BATTING AVERAGE
Nap Lajoie CLE.......... .355
Sam Crawford DET.... .335
P. Dougherty BOS ..... .331

HITS
P. Dougherty BOS 195
Sam Crawford DET..... 184
Nap Lajoie CLE........... 173

DOUBLES
Socks Seybold PHI 45
Nap Lajoie CLE............. 40
Buck Freeman BOS..... 39

TRIPLES
Sam Crawford DET....... 25
Bill Bradley CLE............ 22
Buck Freeman BOS..... 20

HOME RUNS
Buck Freeman BOS...... 13
Hickman CLE................ 12
Hobe Ferris BOS 9

RUNS BATTED IN
Buck Freeman BOS..... 104
Hickman CLE................ 97
Nap Lajoie CLE............. 93

SLUGGING AVERAGE
Nap Lajoie CLE.......... .533
Hickman CLE............. .502
Buck Freeman BOS... .496

STOLEN BASES
Harry Bay CLE.............. 45
Ollie Pickering PHI........ 40
two tied at 35

RUNS SCORED
P. Dougherty BOS 108
Bill Bradley CLE.......... 103
two tied at 95

WINS
Cy Young BOS 28
Eddie Plank PHI............ 23
four tied at..................... 21

WINNING PERCENTAGE
Cy Young BOS .... .757
Tom Hughes BOS....... .741
Earl Moore CLE .... .679

EARNED RUN AVERAGE
Earl Moore CLE 1.77
Cy Young BOS 2.08
Bill Bernhard CLE 2.12

STRIKEOUTS
Rube Waddell PHI 302
Bill Donovan DET 187
two tied at 176

SAVES
five tied at 2

COMPLETE GAMES
Bill Donovan DET 34
Cy Young BOS 34
Rube Waddell PHI 34

SHUTOUTS
Cy Young BOS 7
Bill Dinneen BOS............ 6
George Mullin DET 6

GAMES PITCHED
Eddie Plank PHI............. 43
George Mullin DET 41
two tied at 40

INNINGS PITCHED
Cy Young BOS 342
Eddie Plank PHI.......... 336
Jack Chesbro NY........ 325

1903 NL

	W	L	PCT	GB	R	OR	BA	FA	ERA
PITTSBURGH	91	49	.650	—	793	613	.287	.951	2.91
NEW YORK	84	55	.604	6.5	729	567	.272	.951	2.95
CHICAGO	82	56	.594	8	695	599	.275	.942	2.77
CINCINNATI	74	65	.532	16.5	765	656	.288	.946	3.07
BROOKLYN	70	66	.515	19	667	682	.265	.951	3.44
BOSTON	58	80	.420	32	578	699	.245	.937	3.34
PHILADELPHIA	49	86	.363	39.5	617	738	.268	.947	3.97
ST. LOUIS	43	94	.314	46.5	505	795	.251	.940	3.76
					5349	5349	.269	.946	3.27

BATTING AVERAGE
Honus Wagner PIT .... .355
Fred Clarke PIT .... .351
Mike Donlin CIN.......... .351

HITS
G. Beaumont PIT 209
Cy Seymour CIN......... 191
George Browne NY..... 185

DOUBLES
Sam Mertes NY 32
Harry Steinfelt CIN........ 32
Fred Clarke PIT 32

TRIPLES
Honus Wagner PIT 19
Mike Donlin CIN............ 18
Tommy Leach PIT 17

HOME RUNS
Jimmy Sheckard BKN..... 9
six tied at........................ 7

RUNS BATTED IN
Sam Mertes NY 104
Honus Wagner PIT 101
Jack Doyle BKN............ 91

SLUGGING AVERAGE
Fred Clarke PIT .... .532
Honus Wagner PIT .... .518
Mike Donlin CIN.......... .516

STOLEN BASES
Jimmy Sheckard BKN... 67
Frank Chance CHI........ 67
two tied at 46

RUNS SCORED
G. Beaumont PIT 137
Mike Donlin CIN.......... 110
George Browne NY..... 105

WINS
Joe McGinnity NY 31
C. Mathewson NY......... 30
Sam Leever PIT............ 25

WINNING PERCENTAGE
Sam Leever PIT.......... .781
D. Phillippe PIT .... .774
Jake Weimer CHI........ .700

EARNED RUN AVERAGE
Sam Leever PIT.......... 2.06
C. Mathewson NY...... 2.26
Jake Weimer CHI....... 2.30

STRIKEOUTS
C. Mathewson NY....... 267
Joe McGinnity NY 171
Ned Garvin BKN 154

SAVES
Carl Lundgren CHI.......... 3
Roscoe Miller NY 3
six tied at......................... 2

COMPLETE GAMES
Joe McGinnity NY 44
C. Mathewson NY 37
Togie Pittinger BOS 35

SHUTOUTS
Sam Leever PIT.............. 7
Henry Schmidt BKN........ 5
Noodles Hahn CIN......... 5

GAMES PITCHED
Joe McGinnity NY 55
C. Mathewson NY......... 45
Togie Pittinger BOS 44

INNINGS PITCHED
Joe McGinnity NY 434
C. Mathewson NY....... 366
Togie Pittinger BOS.... 352

1904 AL

	W	L	PCT	GB	R	OR	BA	FA	ERA
BOSTON	95	59	.617	—	608	466	.247	.962	2.12
NEW YORK	92	59	.609	1.5	598	526	.259	.958	2.57
CHICAGO	89	65	.578	6	600	482	.242	.964	2.30
CLEVELAND	86	65	.570	7.5	647	482	.262	.959	2.22
PHILADELPHIA	81	70	.536	12.5	557	503	.249	.959	2.35
ST. LOUIS	65	87	.428	29	481	604	.239	.960	2.83
DETROIT	62	90	.408	32	505	627	.231	.959	2.77
WASHINGTON	38	113	.252	55.5	437	743	.227	.951	3.62
					4433	4433	.245	.959	2.60

BATTING AVERAGE
Nap Lajoie CLE.......... .381
W. Keeler NY .... .343
Harry Davis PHI......... .309

HITS
Nap Lajoie CLE........... 211
W. Keeler NY 186
Bill Bradley CLE.......... 182

DOUBLES
Nap Lajoie CLE............. 50
Jimmy Collins BOS 33
four tied at..................... 31

TRIPLES
Joe Cassidy WAS 19
Buck Freeman BOS...... 19
Chick Stahl BOS 19

HOME RUNS
Harry Davis PHI............. 10
Buck Freeman BOS........ 7
Danny Murphy PHI 7

RUNS BATTED IN
Nap Lajoie CLE........... 102
Buck Freeman BOS...... 84
Bill Bradley CLE............ 83

SLUGGING AVERAGE
Nap Lajoie CLE........... .554
Harry Davis PHI.......... .490
Danny Murphy PHI .... .440

STOLEN BASES
Elmer Flick CLE 42
Harry Bay CLE.............. 38
Emmet Heidrick STL..... 35

RUNS SCORED
Dougherty BOS, NY.....113
Elmer Flick CLE 97
Bill Bradley CLE............ 94

WINS
Jack Chesbro NY 41
Eddie Plank PHI............ 26
Cy Young BOS 26

WINNING PERCENTAGE
Jack Chesbro NY .... .774
J. Tannehill BOS......... .656
Frank Smith CHI .... .640

EARNED RUN AVERAGE
Addie Joss CLE 1.59
Rube Waddell PHI 1.62
Otto Hess CLE........... 1.67

STRIKEOUTS
Rube Waddell PHI 349
Jack Chesbro NY........ 239
Cy Young BOS 203

SAVES
Casey Patten WAS......... 3
eight tied at 1

COMPLETE GAMES
Jack Chesbro NY.......... 48
George Mullin DET 42
Cy Young BOS 40

SHUTOUTS
Cy Young BOS 10
Rube Waddell PHI 8
two tied at 7

GAMES PITCHED
Jack Chesbro NY.......... 55
Jack Powell NY............. 47
Rube Waddell PHI 46

INNINGS PITCHED
Jack Chesbro NY.......... 455
Jack Powell NY........... 390
Rube Waddell PHI 383

1904 NL

	W	L	PCT	GB	R	OR	BA	FA	ERA
NEW YORK	106	47	.693	—	744	476	.262	.956	2.17
CHICAGO	93	60	.608	13	599	517	.248	.954	2.30
CINCINNATI	88	65	.575	18	695	547	.255	.954	2.35
PITTSBURGH	87	66	.569	19	675	592	.258	.955	2.89
ST. LOUIS	75	79	.487	31.5	602	595	.253	.952	2.64
BROOKLYN	56	97	.366	50	497	614	.232	.945	2.70
BOSTON	55	98	.359	51	491	749	.237	.946	3.43
PHILADELPHIA	52	100	.342	53.5	571	784	.248	.937	3.39
					4874	4874	.249	.950	2.73

BATTING AVERAGE
Honus Wagner PIT .... .349
M. Donlin CIN, NY ..... .329
Jake Beckley STL .... .325

HITS
G. Beaumont PIT 185
Jake Beckley STL 179
Honus Wagner PIT 171

DOUBLES
Honus Wagner PIT 44
Sam Mertes NY 28
Joe Delahanty BOS 27

TRIPLES
Harry Lumley BKN 18
Honus Wagner PIT 14
two tied at 13

HOME RUNS
Harry Lumley BKN 9
Dave Brain STL 7
four tied at 6

RUNS BATTED IN
Bill Dahlen NY............... 80
Sam Mertes NY 78
Harry Lumley BKN 78

SLUGGING AVERAGE
Honus Wagner PIT .... .520
Mike Grady STL......... .474
M. Donlin CIN, NY ..... .457

STOLEN BASES
Honus Wagner PIT 53
Bill Dahlen NY............... 47
Sam Mertes NY 47

RUNS SCORED
George Browne NY........ 99
Honus Wagner PIT 97
Ginger Beaumont PIT ... 97

WINS
Joe McGinnity NY 35
C. Mathewson NY......... 33
Jack Harper CIN 23

WINNING PERCENTAGE
Joe McGinnity NY ...... .814
C. Mathewson NY...... .733
Jack Harper CIN .... .719

EARNED RUN AVERAGE
Joe McGinnity NY 1.61
Ned Garvin BKN 1.68
T. Brown CHI 1.86

STRIKEOUTS
C. Mathewson NY....... 212
Vic Willis BOS............. 196
Jake Weimer CHI........ 177

SAVES
Joe McGinnity NY 5
Red Ames NY 3
Hooks Wiltse NY............. 3

COMPLETE GAMES
Jack Taylor STL............. 39
Vic Willis BOS............... 39
two tied at 38

SHUTOUTS
Joe McGinnity NY 9
Jack Harper CIN 6
two tied at 5

GAMES PITCHED
Joe McGinnity NY 51
C. Mathewson NY......... 48
Oscar Jones BKN 46

INNINGS PITCHED
Joe McGinnity NY 408
Oscar Jones BKN 377
C. Mathewson NY....... 368

1905 AL

	W	L	PCT	GB	R	OR	BA	FA	ERA
PHILADELPHIA	92	56	.622	—	623	492	.255	.958	2.19
CHICAGO	92	60	.605	2	612	451	.237	.968	1.99
DETROIT	79	74	.516	15.5	512	602	.243	.957	2.83
BOSTON	78	74	.513	16	579	564	.234	.953	2.84
CLEVELAND	76	78	.494	19	567	587	.255	.963	2.85
NEW YORK	71	78	.477	21.5	586	622	.248	.952	2.93
WASHINGTON	64	87	.424	29.5	559	623	.223	.951	2.87
ST. LOUIS	54	99	.353	40.5	511	608	.232	.955	2.74
					4549	4549	.241	.957	2.65

BATTING AVERAGE
Elmer Flick CLE .... .306
W. Keeler NY .... .302
Harry Bay CLE .... .298

HITS
George Stone STL 187
Sam Crawford DET 171
Harry Davis PHI 171

DOUBLES
Harry Davis PHI 47
Sam Crawford DET 40
two tied at 37

TRIPLES
Elmer Flick CLE 19
Hobe Ferris BOS 16
Terry Turner CLE 14

HOME RUNS
Harry Davis PHI 8
George Stone STL 7
four tied at 6

RUNS BATTED IN
Harry Davis PHI 83
Lave Cross PHI 77
Jiggs Donahue CHI 76

SLUGGING AVERAGE
Elmer Flick CLE .... .466
Frank Isbell CHI .... .440
Sam Crawford DET .... .433

STOLEN BASES
Danny Hoffman PHI 46
Dave Fultz NY 44
Jake Stahl WAS 41

RUNS SCORED
Harry Davis PHI 92
Fielder Jones CHI 91
Harry Bay CLE 90

WINS
Rube Waddell PHI 26
Eddie Plank PHI 25
Ed Killian DET 23

WINNING PERCENTAGE
Andy Coakley PHI ...... .741
J. Tannehill BOS .... .710
Rube Waddell PHI ..... .703

EARNED RUN AVERAGE
Rube Waddell PHI 1.48
Doc White CHI 1.76
Cy Young BOS 1.82

STRIKEOUTS
Rube Waddell PHI 287
Eddie Plank PHI 210
Cy Young BOS 208

SAVES
Rube Waddell PHI 4
Clark Griffith NY 3
Chief Bender PHI 3

COMPLETE GAMES
Eddie Plank PHI 36
Harry Howell STL 35
George Mullin DET 35

SHUTOUTS
Ed Killian DET 8
Rube Waddell PHI 7
two tied at 6

GAMES PITCHED
Rube Waddell PHI 46
George Mullin DET 44
two tied at 42

INNINGS PITCHED
George Mullin DET 348
Eddie Plank PHI 347
Frank Owen CHI 334

1905 NL

	W	L	PCT	GB	R	OR	BA	FA	ERA
★NEW YORK	105	48	.686	—	778	505	.273	.960	2.39
PITTSBURGH	96	57	.627	9	692	570	.266	.961	2.86
CHICAGO	92	61	.601	13	667	442	.245	.962	2.04
PHILADELPHIA	83	69	.546	21.5	708	602	.260	.957	2.81
CINCINNATI	79	74	.516	26	735	698	.269	.953	3.01
ST. LOUIS	58	96	.377	47.5	535	734	.248	.957	3.59
BOSTON	51	103	.331	54.5	468	731	.234	.951	3.52
BROOKLYN	48	104	.316	56.5	506	807	.246	.936	3.76
					5089	5089	.255	.954	2.99

BATTING AVERAGE
Cy Seymour CIN .... .377
Honus Wagner PIT .... .363
Mike Donlin NY .... .356

HITS
Cy Seymour CIN 219
Mike Donlin NY 216
Honus Wagner PIT 199

DOUBLES
Cy Seymour CIN 40
John Titus PHI 36
Honus Wagner PIT 32

TRIPLES
Cy Seymour CIN 21
Sam Mertes NY 17
Sherry Magee PHI 17

HOME RUNS
Fred Odwell CIN 9
Cy Seymour CIN 8
three tied at 7

RUNS BATTED IN
Cy Seymour CIN 121
Sam Mertes NY 108
Honus Wagner PIT 101

SLUGGING AVERAGE
Cy Seymour CIN .... .559
Honus Wagner PIT ..... .505
Mike Donlin NY .... .495

STOLEN BASES
Billy Maloney CHI 59
Art Devlin NY 59
Honus Wagner PIT 57

RUNS SCORED
Mike Donlin NY 124
Roy Thomas PHI 118
Miller Huggins CIN 117

WINS
C. Mathewson NY 31
Togie Pittinger PHI........ 23
two tied at 22

WINNING PERCENTAGE
C. Mathewson NY ...... .795
Sam Leever PIT .... .760
Red Ames NY .... .733

EARNED RUN AVERAGE
C. Mathewson NY 1.27
Ed Reulbach CHI 1.42
Bob Wicker CHI 2.02

STRIKEOUTS
C. Mathewson NY 206
Red Ames NY 198
Orval Overall CIN........ 173

SAVES
Claude Elliott NY............. 6
Joe McGinnity NY 3
Hooks Wiltse NY............. 3

COMPLETE GAMES
Irv Young BOS............... 41
Vic Willis BOS............... 36
Chick Fraser BOS......... 35

SHUTOUTS
C. Mathewson NY........... 8
Irv Young BOS................. 7
two tied at 5

GAMES PITCHED
Togie Pittinger PHI........ 46
Joe McGinnity NY 46
two tied at 43

INNINGS PITCHED
Irv Young BOS............. 378
Vic Willis BOS............. 342
C. Mathewson NY 339

1906 AL

	W	L	PCT	GB	R	OR	BA	FA	ERA
★CHICAGO	93	58	.616	—	570	460	.230	.963	2.13
NEW YORK	90	61	.596	3	644	543	.266	.957	2.78
CLEVELAND	89	64	.582	5	663	482	.279	.967	2.09
PHILADELPHIA	78	67	.538	12	561	542	.247	.956	2.60
ST. LOUIS	76	73	.510	16	558	498	.247	.954	2.23
DETROIT	71	78	.477	21	518	599	.242	.959	3.06
WASHINGTON	55	95	.367	37.5	518	664	.238	.955	3.25
BOSTON	49	105	.318	45.5	462	706	.239	.949	3.41
					4494	4494	.249	.958	2.69

BATTING AVERAGE
George Stone STL..... .358
Nap Lajoie CLE.......... .355
Hal Chase NY .... .323

HITS
Nap Lajoie CLE........... 214
George Stone STL...... 208
Elmer Flick CLE 194

DOUBLES
Nap Lajoie CLE............. 49
Harry Davis PHI 42
Elmer Flick CLE 34

TRIPLES
Elmer Flick CLE 22
George Stone STL........ 20
Sam Crawford DET....... 16

HOME RUNS
Harry Davis PHI 12
Hickman WAS................. 9
George Stone STL.......... 6

RUNS BATTED IN
Harry Davis PHI 96
Nap Lajoie CLE............. 91
George Davis CHI.......... 80

SLUGGING AVERAGE
George Stone STL..... .501
Nap Lajoie CLE.......... .460
Harry Davis PHI .... .459

STOLEN BASES
Elmer Flick CLE 39
John Anderson WAS 39
two tied at 37

RUNS SCORED
Elmer Flick CLE 98
Topsy Hartsel PHI......... 96
Wee Willie Keeler NY ... 96

WINS
Al Orth NY..................... 27
Jack Chesbro NY.......... 24
two tied at 22

WINNING PERCENTAGE
Eddie Plank PHI.......... .760
Doc White CHI .... .750
Addie Joss CLE .... .700

EARNED RUN AVERAGE
Doc White CHI 1.52
Barney Pelty STL........ 1.59
Addie Joss CLE 1.72

STRIKEOUTS
Rube Waddell PHI 196
Cy Falkenberg WAS ... 178
Ed Walsh CHI 171

SAVES
Otto Hess CLE................ 3
Chief Bender PHI............ 3
seven tied at 2

COMPLETE GAMES
Al Orth NY..................... 36
George Mullin DET 35
Otto Hess CLE.............. 33

SHUTOUTS
Ed Walsh CHI 10
Addie Joss CLE 9
Rube Waddell PHI 8

GAMES PITCHED
Jack Chesbro NY.......... 49
Al Orth NY..................... 45
Otto Hess CLE.............. 44

INNINGS PITCHED
Al Orth NY................... 339
Otto Hess CLE............. 334
George Mullin DET 330

1906 NL

	W	L	PCT	GB	R	OR	BA	FA	ERA
CHICAGO	116	36	.763	—	705	381	.262	.969	1.76
NEW YORK	96	56	.632	20	625	510	.255	.963	2.49
PITTSBURGH	93	60	.608	23.5	623	470	.261	.964	2.21
PHILADELPHIA	71	82	.464	45.5	528	564	.241	.956	2.58
BROOKLYN	66	86	.434	50	496	625	.236	.955	3.13
CINCINNATI	64	87	.424	51.5	533	582	.238	.959	2.69
ST. LOUIS	52	98	.347	63	470	607	.235	.957	3.04
BOSTON	49	102	.325	66.5	408	649	.226	.947	3.17
					4388	4388	.244	.959	2.63

BATTING AVERAGE
Honus Wagner PIT .... .339
Harry Steinfeldt CHI... .327
Harry Lumley BKN ..... .324

HITS
Harry Steinfeldt CHI... 176
Honus Wagner PIT 175
Seymour CIN, NY 165

DOUBLES
Honus Wagner PIT 38
Sherry Magee PHI 36
Kitty Bransfield PHI....... 28

TRIPLES
Wildfire Schulte CHI...... 13
Fred Clarke PIT 13
two tied at 12

HOME RUNS
Tim Jordan BKN 12
Harry Lumley BKN.......... 9
Cy Seymour CIN, NY...... 8

RUNS BATTED IN
Jim Nealon PIT 83
Harry Steinfeldt CHI...... 83
Cy Seymour CIN, NY.... 80

SLUGGING AVERAGE
Harry Lumley BKN ..... .477
Honus Wagner PIT ..... .459
Sammy Strang NY ..... .435

STOLEN BASES
Frank Chance CHI........ 57
Sherry Magee PHI 55
Art Devlin NY 54

RUNS SCORED
Frank Chance CHI 103
Honus Wagner PIT 103
Jimmy Sheckard CHI.... 90

WINS
Joe McGinnity NY 27
T. Brown CHI 26
three tied at................... 22

WINNING PERCENTAGE
Ed Reulbach CHI .... .826
T. Brown CHI .... .813
Sam Leever PIT .... .759

EARNED RUN AVERAGE
T. Brown CHI 1.04
Jack Pfiester CHI 1.56
Ed Reulbach CHI 1.65

STRIKEOUTS
F. Beebe CHI, STL 171
Big Jeff Pfeffer BOS.... 158
Red Ames NY 156

SAVES
George Ferguson NY...... 6
Hooks Wiltse NY............. 5
Elmer Stricklett BKN 5

COMPLETE GAMES
Irv Young BOS.............. 37
Big Jeff Pfeffer BOS...... 33
four tied at..................... 32

SHUTOUTS
T. Brown CHI 10
Lefty Leifield PIT 8
Jake Weimer CIN............ 7

GAMES PITCHED
Joe McGinnity NY 45
Irv Young BOS.............. 43
two tied at 42

INNINGS PITCHED
Irv Young BOS............. 358
Joe McGinnity NY 340
Vic Willis PIT................ 322

1907 AL

	W	L	PCT	GB	R	OR	BA	FA	ERA
DETROIT	92	58	.613	—	694	532	.266	.959	2.33
PHILADELPHIA	88	57	.607	1.5	582	511	.255	.958	2.35
CHICAGO	87	64	.576	5.5	588	474	.237	.966	2.22
CLEVELAND	85	67	.559	8	530	525	.241	.960	2.26
NEW YORK	70	78	.473	21	605	665	.249	.947	3.03
ST. LOUIS	69	83	.454	24	542	555	.253	.959	2.61
BOSTON	59	90	.396	32.5	464	558	.234	.959	2.45
WASHINGTON	49	102	.325	43.5	506	691	.243	.952	3.11
					4511	4511	.247	.958	2.54

BATTING AVERAGE
Ty Cobb DET .... .350
Sam Crawford DET.... .323
George Stone STL..... .320

HITS
Ty Cobb DET 212
George Stone STL...... 191
Sam Crawford DET..... 188

DOUBLES
Harry Davis PHI............ 36
Sam Crawford DET....... 34
two tied at 30

TRIPLES
Elmer Flick CLE............ 18
Sam Crawford DET....... 17
Ty Cobb DET 15

HOME RUNS
Harry Davis PHI............. 8
Socks Seybold PHI 5
Ty Cobb DET 5

RUNS BATTED IN
Ty Cobb DET 116
Socks Seybold PHI 92
Harry Davis PHI............ 87

SLUGGING AVERAGE
Ty Cobb DET .... .473
Sam Crawford DET.... .460
Elmer Flick CLE......... .412

STOLEN BASES
Ty Cobb DET 49
Wid Conroy NY 41
Elmer Flick CLE............ 41

RUNS SCORED
Sam Crawford DET..... 102
Davy Jones DET......... 101
Ty Cobb DET 97

WINS
Addie Joss CLE 27
Doc White CHI 27
two tied at 25

WINNING PERCENTAGE
Bill Donovan DET .... .862
Jimmy Dygert PHI....... .724
Addie Joss CLE .... .711

EARNED RUN AVERAGE
Ed Walsh CHI 1.60
Ed Killian DET............. 1.78
Addie Joss CLE 1.83

STRIKEOUTS
Rube Waddell PHI 232
Ed Walsh CHI 206
Eddie Plank PHI.......... 183

SAVES
Ed Walsh CHI 4
Tom Hughes WAS 4
Bill Dinneen BOS, STL ... 4

COMPLETE GAMES
Ed Walsh CHI 37
George Mullin DET 35
Addie Joss CLE 34

SHUTOUTS
Eddie Plank PHI.............. 8
Doc White CHI 7
Rube Waddell PHI 7

GAMES PITCHED
Ed Walsh CHI 56
Doc White CHI 47
George Mullin DET 46

INNINGS PITCHED
Ed Walsh CHI 422
George Mullin DET 357
Eddie Plank PHI.......... 344

1907 NL

	W	L	PCT	GB	R	OR	BA	FA	ERA
★CHICAGO	107	45	.704	—	572	390	.250	.967	1.73
PITTSBURGH	91	63	.591	17	634	510	.254	.959	2.30
PHILADELPHIA	83	64	.565	21.5	512	476	.236	.957	2.43
NEW YORK	82	71	.536	25.5	574	510	.251	.963	2.45
BROOKLYN	65	83	.439	40	446	522	.232	.959	2.38
CINCINNATI	66	87	.431	41.5	526	519	.247	.963	2.41
BOSTON	58	90	.392	47	502	652	.243	.961	3.33
ST. LOUIS	52	101	.340	55.5	419	606	.232	.947	2.70
					4185	4185	.243	.959	2.46

BATTING AVERAGE
Honus Wagner PIT .... .350
Sherry Magee PHI ..... .328
G. Beaumont BOS ...... .322

HITS
G. Beaumont BOS 187
Honus Wagner PIT 180
Tommy Leach PIT 166

DOUBLES
Honus Wagner PIT 38
Sherry Magee PHI 28
two tied at 25

TRIPLES
W. Alperman BKN......... 16
John Ganzel CIN 16
two tied at 14

HOME RUNS
Dave Brain BOS 10
Harry Lumley BKN.......... 9
Red Murray STL 7

RUNS BATTED IN
Sherry Magee PHI 85
Honus Wagner PIT 82
Ed Abbaticchio PIT 82

SLUGGING AVERAGE
Honus Wagner PIT .... .513
Sherry Magee PHI ..... .455
Harry Lumley BKN ..... .425

STOLEN BASES
Honus Wagner PIT 61
Johnny Evers CHI 46
Sherry Magee PHI 46

RUNS SCORED
Spike Shannon NY 104
Tommy Leach PIT 102
Honus Wagner PIT 98

WINS
C. Mathewson NY 24
Orval Overall CHI.......... 23
two tied at 22

WINNING PERCENTAGE
Ed Reulbach CHI .... .810
T. Brown CHI .... .769
Orval Overall CHI........ .742

EARNED RUN AVERAGE
Jack Pfiester CHI 1.15
Carl Lundgren CHI..... 1.17
T. Brown CHI 1.39

STRIKEOUTS
C. Mathewson NY 178
Buck Ewing CIN.......... 147
Red Ames NY 146

SAVES
Joe McGinnity NY 4
T. Brown CHI 3
Orval Overall CHI............ 3

COMPLETE GAMES
Stoney McGlynn STL.... 33
Buck Ewing CIN............ 32
C. Mathewson NY......... 31

SHUTOUTS
Christy Mathewson NY ... 8
Orval Overall CHI............ 8
Carl Lundgren CHI.......... 7

GAMES PITCHED
Joe McGinnity NY 47
Stoney McGlynn STL.... 45
two tied at 41

INNINGS PITCHED
S. McGlynn STL.......... 352
Buck Ewing CIN.......... 333
C. Mathewson NY....... 316

1908 AL

	W	L	PCT	GB	R	OR	BA	FA	ERA
DETROIT	90	63	.588	—	647	547	.264	.953	2.40
CLEVELAND	90	64	.584	.5	568	457	.239	.962	2.02
CHICAGO	88	64	.579	1.5	537	470	.224	.966	2.22
ST. LOUIS	83	69	.546	6.5	544	483	.245	.964	2.15
BOSTON	75	79	.487	15.5	564	513	.246	.955	2.27
PHILADELPHIA	68	85	.444	22	486	562	.223	.957	2.57
WASHINGTON	67	85	.441	22.5	479	539	.235	.958	2.34
NEW YORK	51	103	.331	39.5	459	713	.236	.947	3.16
					4284	4284	.239	.958	2.39

BATTING AVERAGE
Ty Cobb DET .... .324
Sam Crawford DET.... .311
Doc Gessler BOS ...... .308

HITS
Ty Cobb DET 188
Sam Crawford DET.... 184
two tied at 168

DOUBLES
Ty Cobb DET 36
Sam Crawford DET....... 33
C. Rossman DET.......... 33

TRIPLES
Ty Cobb DET 20
Sam Crawford DET....... 16
Jake Stahl BOS, NY 16

HOME RUNS
Sam Crawford DET......... 7
Bill Hinchman CLE.......... 6
three tied at.................... 5

RUNS BATTED IN
Ty Cobb DET 108
Sam Crawford DET....... 80
two tied at 74

SLUGGING AVERAGE
Ty Cobb DET .... .475
Sam Crawford DET.... .457
Doc Gessler BOS ...... .423

STOLEN BASES
Patsy Dougherty CHI.... 47
Charlie Hemphill NY 42
G. Schaefer DET 40

RUNS SCORED
Matty McIntyre DET 105
Sam Crawford DET..... 102
G. Schaefer DET 96

WINS
Ed Walsh CHI 40
Addie Joss CLE 24
Ed Summers DET......... 24

WINNING PERCENTAGE
Ed Walsh CHI .... .727
Bill Donovan DET ...... .720
Addie Joss CLE .... .686

EARNED RUN AVERAGE
Addie Joss CLE 1.16
Cy Young BOS 1.26
Ed Walsh CHI 1.42

STRIKEOUTS
Ed Walsh CHI 269
Rube Waddell STL...... 232
Tom Hughes WAS...... 165

SAVES
Ed Walsh CHI 6
Tom Hughes WAS.......... 4
two tied at 3

COMPLETE GAMES
Ed Walsh CHI 42
Cy Young BOS 30
Addie Joss CLE 29

SHUTOUTS
Ed Walsh CHI 11
Addie Joss CLE 9
two tied at 6

GAMES PITCHED
Ed Walsh CHI 66
Rube Vickers PHI 53
Jack Chesbro NY.......... 45

INNINGS PITCHED
Ed Walsh CHI 464
Addie Joss CLE 325
Harry Howell STL........ 324

1908 NL

	W	L	PCT	GB	R	OR	BA	FA	ERA
★CHICAGO	99	55	.643	—	624	461	.249	.969	2.14
NEW YORK	98	56	.636	1	652	456	.267	.962	2.14
PITTSBURGH	98	56	.636	1	585	469	.247	.964	2.12
PHILADELPHIA	83	71	.539	16	504	445	.244	.963	2.10
CINCINNATI	73	81	.474	26	489	544	.227	.959	2.37
BOSTON	63	91	.409	36	537	622	.239	.962	2.79
BROOKLYN	53	101	.344	46	377	516	.213	.961	2.47
ST. LOUIS	49	105	.318	50	371	626	.223	.946	2.64
					4139	4139	.239	.961	2.35

BATTING AVERAGE
Honus Wagner PIT .... .354
Mike Donlin NY .... .334
Larry Doyle NY .... .308

HITS
Honus Wagner PIT 201
Mike Donlin NY 198
two tied at 167

DOUBLES
Honus Wagner PIT 39
Sherry Magee PHI 30
Frank Chance CHI 27

TRIPLES
Honus Wagner PIT 19
Hans Lobert CIN 18
two tied at 16

HOME RUNS
Tim Jordan BKN 12
Honus Wagner PIT 10
Red Murray STL 7

RUNS BATTED IN
Honus Wagner PIT 109
Mike Donlin NY 106
Cy Seymour NY 92

SLUGGING AVERAGE
Honus Wagner PIT .... .542
Mike Donlin NY .... .452
Sherry Magee PHI ..... .417

STOLEN BASES
Honus Wagner PIT 53
Red Murray STL 48
Hans Lobert CIN 47

RUNS SCORED
Fred Tenney NY 101
Honus Wagner PIT 100
Tommy Leach PIT 93

WINS
C. Mathewson NY 37
T. Brown CHI 29
Ed Reulbach CHI 24

WINNING PERCENTAGE
Ed Reulbach CHI .... .774
C. Mathewson NY ...... .771
T. Brown CHI .... .763

EARNED RUN AVERAGE
C. Mathewson NY 1.43
T. Brown CHI 1.47
G. McQuillan PHI 1.53

STRIKEOUTS
C. Mathewson NY 259
Nap Rucker BKN 199
Orval Overall CHI........ 167

SAVES
T. Brown CHI 5
Christy Mathewson NY ... 5
Joe McGinnity NY 4

COMPLETE GAMES
C. Mathewson NY 34
Kaiser Wilhelm BKN 33
G. McQuillan PHI 32

SHUTOUTS
C. Mathewson NY 12
T. Brown CHI 9
two tied at 7

GAMES PITCHED
C. Mathewson NY 56
G. McQuillan PHI 48
Bugs Raymond STL...... 48

INNINGS PITCHED
C. Mathewson NY 391
G. McQuillan PHI 360
Nap Rucker BKN 333

1909 AL

	W	L	PCT	GB	R	OR	BA	FA	ERA
DETROIT	98	54	.645	—	666	493	.267	.959	2.26
PHILADELPHIA	95	58	.621	3.5	605	408	.257	.961	1.92
BOSTON	88	63	.583	9.5	597	550	.263	.955	2.60
CHICAGO	78	74	.513	20	492	463	.221	.964	2.04
NEW YORK	74	77	.490	23.5	590	587	.248	.948	2.68
CLEVELAND	71	82	.464	27.5	493	532	.241	.957	2.39
ST. LOUIS	61	89	.407	36	441	575	.232	.958	2.88
WASHINGTON	42	110	.276	56	380	656	.223	.957	3.04
					4264	4264	.244	.957	2.47

BATTING AVERAGE
Ty Cobb DET .... .377
Eddie Collins PHI .... .346
Nap Lajoie CLE .... .324

HITS
Ty Cobb DET 216
Eddie Collins PHI 198
Sam Crawford DET 185

DOUBLES
Sam Crawford DET 35
Nap Lajoie CLE 33
Ty Cobb DET 33

TRIPLES
Frank Baker PHI 19
Danny Murphy PHI 14
Sam Crawford DET 14

HOME RUNS
Ty Cobb DET 9
Tris Speaker BOS 7
two tied at 6

RUNS BATTED IN
Ty Cobb DET 107
Sam Crawford DET 97
Frank Baker PHI 85

SLUGGING AVERAGE
Ty Cobb DET .... .517
Sam Crawford DET.... .452
Eddie Collins PHI .... .449

STOLEN BASES
Ty Cobb DET 76
Eddie Collins PHI 67
Donie Bush DET 53

RUNS SCORED
Ty Cobb DET 116
Donie Bush DET 114
Eddie Collins PHI 104

WINS
George Mullin DET 29
Frank Smith CHI 25
Ed Willett DET 21

WINNING PERCENTAGE
George Mullin DET .... .784
Harry Krause PHI .... .692
Chief Bender PHI .... .692

EARNED RUN AVERAGE
Harry Krause PHI 1.39
Ed Walsh CHI 1.41
Chief Bender PHI 1.66

STRIKEOUTS
Frank Smith CHI 177
W. Johnson WAS........ 164
Heinie Berger CLE 162

SAVES
Frank Arellanes BOS...... 8
Jack Warhop NY 4
two tied at 3

COMPLETE GAMES
Frank Smith CHI 37
Cy Young CLE 30
George Mullin DET 29

SHUTOUTS
Ed Walsh CHI 8
Harry Krause PHI............. 7
Frank Smith CHI 7

GAMES PITCHED
Frank Smith CHI 51
Frank Arellanes BOS 45
Bob Groom WAS 44

INNINGS PITCHED
Frank Smith CHI 365
George Mullin DET 304
W. Johnson WAS........ 297

1909 NL

	W	L	PCT	GB	R	OR	BA	FA	ERA
★ PITTSBURGH	110	42	.724	—	699	447	.260	.964	2.07
CHICAGO	104	49	.680	6.5	635	390	.245	.961	1.75
NEW YORK	92	61	.601	18.5	623	546	.255	.954	2.27
CINCINNATI	77	76	.503	33.5	606	599	.250	.952	2.52
PHILADELPHIA	74	79	.484	36.5	516	518	.244	.961	2.44
BROOKLYN	55	98	.359	55.5	444	627	.229	.954	3.10
ST. LOUIS	54	98	.355	56	583	731	.243	.950	3.41
BOSTON	45	108	.294	65.5	435	683	.223	.947	3.20
					4541	4541	.244	.955	2.59

BATTING AVERAGE
Honus Wagner PIT .... .339
Mike Mitchell CIN .... .310
Dick Hoblitzell CIN ..... .308

HITS
Larry Doyle NY 172
Eddie Grant PHI.......... 170
Honus Wagner PIT 168

DOUBLES
Honus Wagner PIT 39
Sherry Magee PHI 33
Dots Miller PIT 31

TRIPLES
Mike Mitchell CIN.......... 17
Sherry Magee PHI 14
Ed Konetchy STL........... 14

HOME RUNS
Red Murray NY 7
three tied at.................... 6

RUNS BATTED IN
Honus Wagner PIT 100
Red Murray NY 91
Dots Miller PIT 87

SLUGGING AVERAGE
Honus Wagner PIT .... .489
Mike Mitchell CIN .... .430
Larry Doyle NY .... .419

STOLEN BASES
Bob Bescher CIN 54
Red Murray NY 48
Dick Egan CIN 39

RUNS SCORED
Tommy Leach PIT 126
Fred Clarke PIT 97
two tied at 92

WINS
T. Brown CHI 27
Howie Camnitz PIT 25
C. Mathewson NY 25

WINNING PERCENTAGE
C. Mathewson NY ..... .806
Howie Camnitz PIT ..... .806
T. Brown CHI .... .750

EARNED RUN AVERAGE
C. Mathewson NY...... 1.14
T. Brown CHI 1.31
Orval Overall CHI....... 1.42

STRIKEOUTS
Orval Overall CHI........ 205
Nap Rucker BKN 201
Earl Moore PHI 173

SAVES
T. Brown CHI 7
Doc Crandall NY 4
four tied at...................... 3

COMPLETE GAMES
T. Brown CHI 32
George Bell BKN 29
Nap Rucker BKN 28

SHUTOUTS
Orval Overall CHI........... 9
C. Mathewson NY 8
T. Brown CHI 8

GAMES PITCHED
T. Brown CHI 50
Al Mattern BOS............. 47
two tied at 44

INNINGS PITCHED
T. Brown CHI 343
Al Mattern BOS........... 316
Nap Rucker BKN 309

1910 AL

	W	L	PCT	GB	R	OR	BA	FA	ERA
★PHILADELPHIA	102	48	.680	—	673	441	.266	.965	1.79
NEW YORK	88	63	.583	14.5	626	557	.248	.956	2.59
DETROIT	86	68	.558	18	679	582	.261	.956	3.00
BOSTON	81	72	.529	22.5	638	564	.259	.954	2.46
CLEVELAND	71	81	.467	32	548	657	.244	.964	2.89
CHICAGO	68	85	.444	35.5	457	479	.211	.954	2.01
WASHINGTON	66	85	.437	36.5	501	550	.236	.959	2.46
ST. LOUIS	47	107	.305	57	451	743	.220	.944	3.09
					4573	4573	.243	.956	2.53

BATTING AVERAGE
Ty Cobb DET .... .385
Nap Lajoie CLE.......... .384
Tris Speaker BOS...... .340

HITS
Nap Lajoie CLE.......... 227
Ty Cobb DET 196
Eddie Collins PHI........ 188

DOUBLES
Nap Lajoie CLE.............. 51
Ty Cobb DET 36
Duffy Lewis BOS........... 29

TRIPLES
Sam Crawford DET....... 19
Danny Murphy PHI 18
Bris Lord CLE, PHI 18

HOME RUNS
Jake Stahl BOS 10
Ty Cobb DET 8
Duffy Lewis BOS............. 8

RUNS BATTED IN
Sam Crawford DET....... 120
Ty Cobb DET 91
Eddie Collins PHI.......... 81

SLUGGING AVERAGE
Ty Cobb DET .... .554
Nap Lajoie CLE.......... .514
Tris Speaker BOS...... .468

STOLEN BASES
Eddie Collins PHI.......... 81
Ty Cobb DET 65
two tied at 49

RUNS SCORED
Ty Cobb DET 106
Nap Lajoie CLE............. 92
Tris Speaker BOS......... 92

WINS
Jack Coombs PHI 31
Russ Ford NY 26
Walter Johnson WAS.... 25

WINNING PERCENTAGE
Chief Bender PHI........ .821
Russ Ford NY .... .813
Jack Coombs PHI ...... .775

EARNED RUN AVERAGE
Ed Walsh CHI 1.27
Jack Coombs PHI 1.30
W. Johnson WAS........ 1.35

STRIKEOUTS
W. Johnson WAS........ 313
Ed Walsh CHI 258
Jack Coombs PHI 224

SAVES
Ed Walsh CHI 5
Charley Hall BOS............. 5
Frank Browning DET 3

COMPLETE GAMES
Walter Johnson WAS..... 38
Jack Coombs PHI 35
Ed Walsh CHI 33

SHUTOUTS
Jack Coombs PHI 13
Russ Ford NY 8
Walter Johnson WAS...... 8

GAMES PITCHED
Walter Johnson WAS.... 45
Ed Walsh CHI 45
Jack Coombs PHI 45

INNINGS PITCHED
W. Johnson WAS......... 373
Ed Walsh CHI 370
Jack Coombs PHI 353

1910 NL

	W	L	PCT	GB	R	OR	BA	FA	ERA
CHICAGO	104	50	.675	—	712	499	.268	.963	2.51
NEW YORK	91	63	.591	13	715	567	.275	.955	2.68
PITTSBURGH	86	67	.562	17.5	655	576	.266	.961	2.83
PHILADELPHIA	78	75	.510	25.5	674	639	.255	.960	3.05
CINCINNATI	75	79	.487	29	620	684	.259	.955	3.08
BROOKLYN	64	90	.416	40	497	623	.229	.964	3.07
ST. LOUIS	63	90	.412	40.5	639	718	.248	.959	3.78
BOSTON	53	100	.346	50.5	495	701	.246	.954	3.22
					5007	5007	.256	.959	3.02

BATTING AVERAGE
Sherry Magee PHI ..... .331
Vin Campbell PIT .... .326
Solly Hofman CHI ...... .325

HITS
Bobby Byrne PIT 178
Honus Wagner PIT 178
two tied at 172

DOUBLES
Bobby Byrne PIT 43
Sherry Magee PHI 39
Zack Wheat BKN 36

TRIPLES
Mike Mitchell CIN 18
Sherry Magee PHI 17
two tied at 16

HOME RUNS
Fred Beck BOS 10
Wildfire Schulte CHI 10
two tied at 8

RUNS BATTED IN
Sherry Magee PHI 123
Mike Mitchell CIN 88
Red Murray NY 87

SLUGGING AVERAGE
Sherry Magee PHI ..... .507
Solly Hofman CHI ...... .461
Wildfire Schulte CHI... .460

STOLEN BASES
Bob Bescher CIN 70
Red Murray NY 57
Dode Paskert CIN 51

RUNS SCORED
Sherry Magee PHI 110
Miller Huggins STL 101
Bobby Byrne PIT 101

WINS
C. Mathewson NY 27
T. Brown CHI 25
two tied at 20

WINNING PERCENTAGE
King Cole CHI .... .833
Doc Crandall NY .... .810
C. Mathewson NY ...... .750

EARNED RUN AVERAGE
G. McQuillan PHI 1.60
King Cole CHI 1.80
T. Brown CHI 1.86

STRIKEOUTS
Earl Moore PHI 185
C. Mathewson NY 184
S. Frock PIT, BOS ... 171

SAVES
T. Brown CHI 7
Harry Gaspar CIN 5
two tied at 4

COMPLETE GAMES
T. Brown CHI 27
C. Mathewson NY 27
Nap Rucker BKN 27

SHUTOUTS
T. Brown CHI 7
three tied at 6

GAMES PITCHED
Al Mattern BOS 51
Harry Gaspar CIN 48
two tied at 46

INNINGS PITCHED
Nap Rucker BKN 320
C. Mathewson NY 318
George Bell BKN 310

1911 AL

	W	L	PCT	GB	R	OR	BA	FA	ERA
★PHILADELPHIA	101	50	.669	—	861	601	.296	.965	3.01
DETROIT	89	65	.578	13.5	831	776	.292	.951	3.73
CLEVELAND	80	73	.523	22	691	712	.282	.954	3.37
CHICAGO	77	74	.510	24	719	624	.269	.961	3.01
BOSTON	78	75	.510	24	680	643	.274	.949	2.73
NEW YORK	76	76	.500	25.5	684	724	.272	.949	3.54
WASHINGTON	64	90	.416	38.5	625	766	.258	.953	3.52
ST. LOUIS	45	107	.296	56.5	567	812	.239	.945	3.83
					5658	5658	.273	.953	3.34

BATTING AVERAGE
Ty Cobb DET .... .420
Joe Jackson CLE .... .408
Sam Crawford DET .... .378

HITS
Ty Cobb DET 248
Joe Jackson CLE 233
Sam Crawford DET 217

DOUBLES
Ty Cobb DET 47
Joe Jackson CLE 45
Frank Baker PHI 40

TRIPLES
Ty Cobb DET 24
Birdie Cree NY 22
Joe Jackson CLE 19

HOME RUNS
Frank Baker PHI 11
Ty Cobb DET 8
Tris Speaker BOS 8

RUNS BATTED IN
Ty Cobb DET 144
Frank Baker PHI 115
Sam Crawford DET 115

SLUGGING AVERAGE
Ty Cobb DET .... .621
Joe Jackson CLE .... .590
Sam Crawford DET .... .526

STOLEN BASES
Ty Cobb DET 83
Clyde Milan WAS 58
Birdie Cree NY 48

RUNS SCORED
Ty Cobb DET 147
Joe Jackson CLE 126
Donie Bush DET 126

WINS
Jack Coombs PHI 28
Ed Walsh CHI 27
Walter Johnson WAS.... 25

WINNING PERCENTAGE
Chief Bender PHI .... .773
Vean Gregg CLE .... .767
Eddie Plank PHI .. .742

EARNED RUN AVERAGE
Vean Gregg CLE 1.81
W. Johnson WAS 1.89
Joe Wood BOS 2.02

STRIKEOUTS
Ed Walsh CHI 255
Joe Wood BOS 231
W. Johnson WAS........ 207

SAVES
Eddie Plank PHI 5
Charley Hall BOS 4
Ed Walsh CHI 4

COMPLETE GAMES
Walter Johnson WAS.... 36
Ed Walsh CHI 33
two tied at 26

SHUTOUTS
Eddie Plank PHI.............. 6
Walter Johnson WAS..... 6
two tied at 5

GAMES PITCHED
Ed Walsh CHI 56
Jack Coombs PHI 47
Joe Wood BOS 44

INNINGS PITCHED
Ed Walsh CHI 369
Jack Coombs PHI 337
W. Johnson WAS........ 323

1911 NL

	W	L	PCT	GB	R	OR	BA	FA	ERA
NEW YORK	99	54	.647	—	756	542	.279	.959	2.69
CHICAGO	92	62	.597	7.5	757	607	.260	.960	2.90
PITTSBURGH	85	69	.552	14.5	744	557	.262	.963	2.84
PHILADELPHIA	79	73	.520	19.5	658	669	.259	.963	3.30
ST. LOUIS	75	74	.503	22	671	745	.252	.960	3.68
CINCINNATI	70	83	.458	29	682	706	.261	.955	3.26
BROOKLYN	64	86	.427	33.5	539	659	.237	.962	3.39
BOSTON	44	107	.291	54	699	1021	.267	.947	5.08
					5506	5506	.260	.958	3.39

BATTING AVERAGE
Honus Wagner PIT .... .334
Dots Miller BOS .... .333
Chief Meyers NY........ .332

HITS
Dots Miller BOS 192
Dick Hoblitzell CIN 180
Jake Daubert BKN 176

DOUBLES
Ed Konetchy STL........ 38
Dots Miller BOS 36
Owen Wilson PIT 34

TRIPLES
Larry Doyle NY 25
Mike Mitchell CIN 22
Wildfire Schulte CHI...... 21

HOME RUNS
Wildfire Schulte CHI...... 21
Fred Luderus PHI 16
Sherry Magee PHI 15

RUNS BATTED IN
Wildfire Schulte CHI.... 121
Owen Wilson PIT 107
Fred Luderus PHI 99

SLUGGING AVERAGE
Wildfire Schulte CHI... .534
Larry Doyle NY .... .527
Honus Wagner PIT .... .507

STOLEN BASES
Bob Bescher CIN 81
Josh Devore NY............ 61
Fred Snodgrass NY 51

RUNS SCORED
J. Sheckard CHI.......... 121
Miller Huggins STL 106
Bob Bescher CIN 106

WINS
Grover Alexander PHI... 28
C. Mathewson NY......... 26
Rube Marquard NY....... 24

WINNING PERCENTAGE
Rube Marquard NY .... .781
Doc Crandall NY .... .750
King Cole CHI .... .720

EARNED RUN AVERAGE
C. Mathewson NY....... 1.99
Lew Richie CHI 2.31
Babe Adams PIT........ 2.33

STRIKEOUTS
Rube Marquard NY 237
G. Alexander PHI........ 227
Nap Rucker BKN 190

SAVES
T. Brown CHI 13
Doc Crandall NY 5
four tied at...................... 4

COMPLETE GAMES
Grover Alexander PHI... 31
C. Mathewson NY......... 29
Bob Harmon STL 28

SHUTOUTS
Grover Alexander PHI.... 7
Babe Adams PIT............ 7
two tied at 5

GAMES PITCHED
T. Brown CHI 53
Bob Harmon STL 51
two tied at 48

INNINGS PITCHED
G. Alexander PHI........ 367
Bob Harmon STL 348
Lefty Leifield PIT 318

1912 AL

	W	L	PCT	GB	R	OR	BA	FA	ERA
★BOSTON	105	47	.691	—	799	544	.277	.957	2.76
WASHINGTON	91	61	.599	14	698	581	.256	.954	2.69
PHILADELPHIA	90	62	.592	15	779	658	.282	.959	3.32
CHICAGO	78	76	.506	28	638	646	.255	.956	3.06
CLEVELAND	75	78	.490	30.5	676	680	.273	.954	3.30
DETROIT	69	84	.451	36.5	720	777	.267	.950	3.78
ST. LOUIS	53	101	.344	53	552	764	.249	.947	3.71
NEW YORK	50	102	.329	55	630	842	.259	.940	4.13
					5492	5492	.265	.952	3.34

BATTING AVERAGE
Ty Cobb DET .... .410
Joe Jackson CLE .... .395
Tris Speaker BOS ...... .383

HITS
Ty Cobb DET 227
Joe Jackson CLE 226
Tris Speaker BOS 222

DOUBLES
Tris Speaker BOS 53
Joe Jackson CLE 44
Frank Baker PHI 40

TRIPLES
Joe Jackson CLE 26
Ty Cobb DET 23
two tied at 21

HOME RUNS
Frank Baker PHI 10
Tris Speaker BOS 10
Ty Cobb DET 7

RUNS BATTED IN
Frank Baker PHI 133
Duffy Lewis BOS 109
Sam Crawford DET 109

SLUGGING AVERAGE
Ty Cobb DET .... .586
Joe Jackson CLE .... .579
Tris Speaker BOS ..... .567

STOLEN BASES
Claude Milan WAS 88
Eddie Collins PHI 63
Ty Cobb DET 61

RUNS SCORED
Eddie Collins PHI 137
Tris Speaker BOS 136
Joe Jackson CLE 121

WINS
Joe Wood BOS 34
Walter Johnson WAS.... 32
Ed Walsh CHI 27

WINNING PERCENTAGE
Joe Wood BOS .... .872
Eddie Plank PHI......... .813
W. Johnson WAS....... .727

EARNED RUN AVERAGE
W. Johnson WAS....... 1.39
Joe Wood BOS 1.91
Ed Walsh CHI 2.15

STRIKEOUTS
W. Johnson WAS........ 303
Joe Wood BOS 258
Ed Walsh CHI 254

SAVES
Ed Walsh CHI 10
three tied at..................... 3

COMPLETE GAMES
Joe Wood BOS 35
Walter Johnson WAS.... 34
two tied at 32

SHUTOUTS
Joe Wood BOS 10
Walter Johnson WAS...... 7
Ed Walsh CHI 6

GAMES PITCHED
Ed Walsh CHI 62
Walter Johnson WAS.... 50
two tied at 43

INNINGS PITCHED
Ed Walsh CHI 393
W. Johnson WAS........ 368
Joe Wood BOS 344

1912 NL

	W	L	PCT	GB	R	OR	BA	FA	ERA
NEW YORK	103	48	.682	—	823	571	.286	.956	2.58
PITTSBURGH	93	58	.616	10	751	565	.284	.972	2.85
CHICAGO	91	59	.607	11.5	756	668	.277	.960	3.42
CINCINNATI	75	78	.490	29	656	722	.256	.960	3.42
PHILADELPHIA	73	79	.480	30.5	670	688	.267	.963	3.25
ST. LOUIS	63	90	.412	41	659	830	.268	.957	3.85
BROOKLYN	58	95	.379	46	651	754	.268	.959	3.64
BOSTON	52	101	.340	52	693	861	.273	.954	4.17
					5659	5659	.272	.960	3.40

BATTING AVERAGE
H. Zimmerman CHI .... .372
Chief Meyers NY .... .358
Bill Sweeney BOS ...... .344

HITS
H. Zimmerman CHI 207
Bill Sweeney BOS 204
Vin Campbell BOS 185

DOUBLES
H. Zimmerman CHI 41
Dode Paskert PHI 37
Honus Wagner PIT 35

TRIPLES
Owen Wilson PIT 36
Honus Wagner PIT 20
Red Murray NY 20

HOME RUNS
H. Zimmerman CHI 14
Wildfire Schulte CHI 13
three tied at 11

RUNS BATTED IN
H. Zimmerman CHI 103
Honus Wagner PIT 102
Bill Sweeney BOS 100

SLUGGING AVERAGE
H. Zimmerman CHI .... .571
Owen Wilson PIT .... .513
Honus Wagner PIT .... .496

STOLEN BASES
Bob Bescher CIN 67
Max Carey PIT 45
Fred Snodgrass NY 43

RUNS SCORED
Bob Bescher CIN 120
Max Carey PIT 114
two tied at 102

WINS
Larry Cheney CHI 26
Rube Marquard NY 26
Claude Hendrix PIT 24

WINNING PERCENTAGE
Claude Hendrix PIT ... .727
Larry Cheney CHI ...... .722
Jeff Tesreau NY .... .708

EARNED RUN AVERAGE
Jeff Tesreau NY 1.96
C. Mathewson NY 2.12
Nap Rucker BKN 2.21

STRIKEOUTS
G. Alexander PHI 195
Claude Hendrix PIT 176
Rube Marquard NY 175

SAVES
Slim Sallee STL 6
Nap Rucker BKN 4
Christy Mathewson NY ... 4

COMPLETE GAMES
Larry Cheney CHI 28
C. Mathewson NY 27
Grover Alexander PHI... 26

SHUTOUTS
Nap Rucker BKN 6
Marty O'Toole PIT........... 6
George Suggs CIN 5

GAMES PITCHED
Rube Benton CIN.......... 50
Slim Sallee STL 48
Grover Alexander PHI... 46

INNINGS PITCHED
G. Alexander PHI........ 310
C. Mathewson NY....... 310
two tied at 303

1913 AL

	W	L	PCT	GB	R	OR	BA	FA	ERA
★ PHILADELPHIA	96	57	.627	—	794	592	.280	.966	3.19
WASHINGTON	90	64	.584	6.5	596	561	.252	.960	2.72
CLEVELAND	86	66	.566	9.5	633	536	.268	.962	2.52
BOSTON	79	71	.527	15.5	631	610	.269	.961	2.93
CHICAGO	78	74	.513	17.5	488	498	.236	.960	2.33
DETROIT	66	87	.431	30	624	716	.265	.954	3.41
NEW YORK	57	94	.377	38	529	668	.237	.954	3.27
ST. LOUIS	57	96	.373	39	528	642	.237	.954	3.06
					4823	4823	.256	.959	2.93

BATTING AVERAGE
Ty Cobb DET .... .390
Joe Jackson CLE .... .373
Tris Speaker BOS ...... .365

HITS
Joe Jackson CLE 197
Sam Crawford DET 193
Frank Baker PHI 190

DOUBLES
Joe Jackson CLE 39
Tris Speaker BOS 35
Frank Baker PHI 34

TRIPLES
Sam Crawford DET 23
Tris Speaker BOS 22
Joe Jackson CLE 17

HOME RUNS
Frank Baker PHI 12
Sam Crawford DET 9
Ping Bodie CHI 8

RUNS BATTED IN
Frank Baker PHI 126
Duffy Lewis BOS 90
Stuffy McInnis PHI 90

SLUGGING AVERAGE
Joe Jackson CLE .... .551
Ty Cobb DET .... .535
Tris Speaker BOS ...... .535

STOLEN BASES
Clyde Milan WAS 75
Danny Moeller WAS 62
Eddie Collins PHI 55

RUNS SCORED
Eddie Collins PHI 125
Frank Baker PHI 116
Joe Jackson CLE 109

WINS
Walter Johnson WAS 36
Cy Falkenberg CLE 23
Reb Russell CHI 22

WINNING PERCENTAGE
W. Johnson WAS .... .837
Ray Collins BOS .... .714
Joe Boehling WAS ..... .708

EARNED RUN AVERAGE
W. Johnson WAS 1.09
Eddie Cicotte CHI 1.58
Willie Mitchell CLE 1.74

STRIKEOUTS
W. Johnson WAS 243
Vean Gregg CLE 166
Cy Falkenberg CLE 166

SAVES
Chief Bender PHI 12
Tom Hughes WAS 6
Hugh Bedient BOS 5

COMPLETE GAMES
W. Johnson WAS 29
Reb Russell CHI 26
Jim Scott CHI 25

SHUTOUTS
Walter Johnson WAS 11
Reb Russell CHI 8
Eddie Plank PHI.............. 7

GAMES PITCHED
Reb Russell CHI 51
Jim Scott CHI 48
Chief Bender PHI 48

INNINGS PITCHED
W. Johnson WAS 346
Reb Russell CHI 316
Jim Scott CHI 312

1913 NL

	W	L	PCT	GB	R	OR	BA	FA	ERA
NEW YORK	101	51	.664	—	684	515	.273	.961	2.43
PHILADELPHIA	88	63	.583	12.5	693	636	.265	.968	3.15
CHICAGO	88	65	.575	13.5	720	625	.257	.959	3.13
PITTSBURGH	78	71	.523	21.5	673	585	.263	.964	2.90
BOSTON	69	82	.457	31.5	641	690	.256	.957	3.19
BROOKLYN	65	84	.436	34.5	595	613	.270	.961	3.13
CINCINNATI	64	89	.418	37.5	607	717	.261	.961	3.46
ST. LOUIS	51	99	.340	49	523	755	.247	.965	4.24
					5136	5136	.262	.962	3.20

BATTING AVERAGE
Jake Daubert BKN ..... .350
Gavvy Cravath PHI .... .341
two tied at .... .317

HITS
Gavvy Cravath PHI 179
Jake Daubert BKN 178
George Burns NY 173

DOUBLES
Red Smith BKN............ 40
George Burns NY 37
Sherry Magee PHI 36

TRIPLES
Vic Saier CHI 21
Dots Miller PIT 20
Ed Konetchy STL.......... 17

HOME RUNS
Gavvy Cravath PHI 19
Fred Luderus PHI 18
Vic Saier CHI 14

RUNS BATTED IN
Gavvy Cravath PHI 128
H. Zimmerman CHI....... 95
Vic Saier CHI 92

SLUGGING AVERAGE
Gavvy Cravath PHI .... .568
B. Becker CIN, PHI.... .502
H. Zimmerman CHI .... .490

STOLEN BASES
Max Carey PIT.............. 61
Hy Myers BOS 57
Hans Lobert PHI 41

RUNS SCORED
Max Carey PIT.............. 99
Tommy Leach CHI........ 99
Hans Lobert PHI 98

WINS
Tom Seaton PHI 27
C. Mathewson NY......... 25
Rube Marquard NY....... 23

WINNING PERCENTAGE
Bert Humphries CHI.... .800
G. Alexander PHI .... .733
Rube Marquard NY..... .697

EARNED RUN AVERAGE
C. Mathewson NY........ 2.06
Babe Adams PIT........ 2.15
Jeff Tesreau NY.......... 2.17

STRIKEOUTS
Tom Seaton PHI 168
Jeff Tesreau NY.......... 167
G. Alexander PHI........ 159

SAVES
Larry Cheney CHI 11
T. Brown CIN 6
Doc Crandall NY 6

COMPLETE GAMES
Lefty Tyler BOS 28
C. Mathewson NY......... 25
Larry Cheney CHI 25

SHUTOUTS
Grover Alexander PHI..... 9
Tom Seaton PHI 6

GAMES PITCHED
Larry Cheney CHI 54
Tom Seaton PHI 52
Slim Sallee STL 49

INNINGS PITCHED
Tom Seaton PHI 322
Babe Adams PIT......... 314
two tied at 306

1914 AL

	W	L	PCT	GB	R	OR	BA	FA	ERA
PHILADELPHIA	99	53	.651	—	749	529	.272	.966	2.78
BOSTON	91	62	.595	8.5	588	511	.250	.963	2.35
WASHINGTON	81	73	.526	19	572	519	.244	.961	2.54
DETROIT	80	73	.523	19.5	615	618	.258	.958	2.86
ST. LOUIS	71	82	.464	28.5	523	614	.243	.952	2.85
CHICAGO	70	84	.455	30	487	560	.239	.955	2.48
NEW YORK	70	84	.455	30	538	550	.229	.963	2.81
CLEVELAND	51	102	.333	48.5	538	709	.245	.953	3.21
					4610	4610	.248	.959	2.73

BATTING AVERAGE
Ty Cobb DET .... .368
Eddie Collins PHI .... .344
two tied at .... .338

HITS
Tris Speaker BOS 193
Sam Crawford DET 183
Frank Baker PHI 182

DOUBLES
Tris Speaker BOS 46
Duffy Lewis BOS 37
two tied at 34

TRIPLES
Sam Crawford DET 26
Larry Gardner BOS 19
Tris Speaker BOS 18

HOME RUNS
Frank Baker PHI 9
Sam Crawford DET 8
two tied at 6

RUNS BATTED IN
Sam Crawford DET 104
Frank Baker PHI 97
Stuffy McInnis PHI 95

SLUGGING AVERAGE
Ty Cobb DET .... .513
Tris Speaker BOS ...... .503
Sam Crawford DET .... .483

STOLEN BASES
Fritz Maisel NY 74
Eddie Collins PHI 58
Tris Speaker BOS 42

RUNS SCORED
Eddie Collins PHI 122
Eddie Murphy PHI 101
Tris Speaker BOS 100

WINS
Walter Johnson WAS.... 28
Harry Coveleski DET 22
Ray Collins BOS 20

WINNING PERCENTAGE
Chief Bender PHI .... .850
Dutch Leonard BOS.... .783
Eddie Plank PHI......... .682

EARNED RUN AVERAGE
Dutch Leonard BOS... 1.01
Rube Foster BOS 1.65
W. Johnson WAS....... 1.72

STRIKEOUTS
W. Johnson WAS........ 225
Willie Mitchell CLE 179
Dutch Leonard BOS.... 174

SAVES
six tied at.......................... 4

COMPLETE GAMES
W. Johnson WAS.......... 33
Harry Coveleski DET ... 23
two tied at 22

SHUTOUTS
Walter Johnson WAS...... 9
Chief Bender PHI............ 7
Dutch Leonard BOS........ 7

GAMES PITCHED
Walter Johnson WAS.... 51
Doc Ayers WAS............. 49
two tied at 48

INNINGS PITCHED
W. Johnson WAS........ 372
H. Coveleski DET 303
two tied at 302

1914 NL

	W	L	PCT	GB	R	OR	BA	FA	ERA
★BOSTON	94	59	.614	—	657	548	.251	.963	2.74
NEW YORK	84	70	.545	10.5	672	576	.265	.961	2.94
ST. LOUIS	81	72	.529	13	558	540	.248	.964	2.38
CHICAGO	78	76	.506	16.5	605	638	.243	.951	2.71
BROOKLYN	75	79	.487	19.5	622	618	.269	.961	2.82
PHILADELPHIA	74	80	.481	20.5	651	687	.263	.950	3.06
PITTSBURGH	69	85	.448	25.5	503	540	.233	.966	2.70
CINCINNATI	60	94	.390	34.5	530	651	.236	.952	2.94
					4798	4798	.251	.958	2.78

BATTING AVERAGE
Jake Daubert BKN ..... .329
Beals Becker PHI....... .325
two tied at .... .319

HITS
Sherry Magee PHI 171
George Burns NY 170
Zack Wheat BKN 170

DOUBLES
Sherry Magee PHI 39
H. Zimmerman CHI....... 36
George Burns NY 35

TRIPLES
Max Carey PIT.............. 17
three tied at.................. 12

HOME RUNS
Gavvy Cravath PHI....... 19
Vic Saier CHI 18
Sherry Magee PHI 15

RUNS BATTED IN
Sherry Magee PHI 103
Gavvy Cravath PHI..... 100
Zack Wheat BKN 89

SLUGGING AVERAGE
Sherry Magee PHI ..... .509
Gavvy Cravath PHI .... .499
Joe Connolly BOS ..... .494

STOLEN BASES
George Burns NY 62
Buck Herzog CIN 46
Cozy Dolan STL............ 42

RUNS SCORED
George Burns NY 100
Sherry Magee PHI 96
Jake Daubert BKN 89

WINS
Dick Rudolph BOS........ 27
Grover Alexander PHI... 27
two tied at 26

WINNING PERCENTAGE
Bill James BOS........... .788
Bill Doak STL.............. .769
Dick Rudolph BOS..... .730

EARNED RUN AVERAGE
Bill Doak STL.............. 1.72
Bill James BOS........... 1.90
Jeff Pfeffer BKN 1.97

STRIKEOUTS
G. Alexander PHI........ 214
Jeff Tesreau NY.......... 189
Hippo Vaughn CHI...... 165

SAVES
Red Ames CIN................ 6
Slim Sallee STL 6
Larry Cheney CHI 5

COMPLETE GAMES
Grover Alexander PHI... 32
Dick Rudolph BOS........ 31
Bill James BOS............. 30

SHUTOUTS
Jeff Tesreau NY.............. 8
Bill Doak STL 7
two tied at 6

GAMES PITCHED
Larry Cheney CHI 50
Erskine Mayer PHI........ 48
Red Ames CIN.............. 47

INNINGS PITCHED
G. Alexander PHI........ 355
Dick Rudolph BOS...... 336
Bill James BOS........... 332

1915 AL

	W	L	PCT	GB	R	OR	BA	FA	ERA
★BOSTON	101	50	.669	—	668	499	.260	.964	2.39
DETROIT	100	54	.649	2.5	778	597	.268	.961	2.86
CHICAGO	93	61	.604	9.5	717	509	.258	.965	2.43
WASHINGTON	85	68	.556	17	569	491	.244	.964	2.31
NEW YORK	69	83	.454	32.5	584	588	.233	.966	3.09
ST. LOUIS	63	91	.409	39.5	521	679	.246	.949	3.07
CLEVELAND	57	95	.375	44.5	539	670	.241	.957	3.13
PHILADELPHIA	43	109	.283	58.5	545	888	.237	.947	4.33
					4921	4921	.248	.959	2.94

BATTING AVERAGE
Ty Cobb DET .... .369
Eddie Collins CHI .... .332
two tied at .... .322

HITS
Ty Cobb DET 208
Sam Crawford DET 183
Bobby Veach DET 178

DOUBLES
Bobby Veach DET 40
three tied at 31

TRIPLES
Sam Crawford DET 19
Jack Fournier CHI 18
two tied at 17

HOME RUNS
Braggo Roth CHI, CLE ... 7
Rube Oldring PHI 6

RUNS BATTED IN
Bobby Veach DET 112
Sam Crawford DET 112
Ty Cobb DET 99

SLUGGING AVERAGE
Jack Fournier CHI ...... .491
Ty Cobb DET .... .487
M. Kavanagh DET ..... .452

STOLEN BASES
Ty Cobb DET 96
Fritz Maisel NY 51
Eddie Collins CHI 46

RUNS SCORED
Ty Cobb DET 144
Eddie Collins CHI 118
Ossie Vitt DET 116

WINS
Walter Johnson WAS 28
three tied at 24

WINNING PERCENTAGE
Joe Wood BOS 750
Rube Foster BOS .... .704
two tied at .... .692

EARNED RUN AVERAGE
Joe Wood BOS 1.49
W. Johnson WAS 1.55
Ernie Shore BOS 1.64

STRIKEOUTS
W. Johnson WAS 203
Red Faber CHI 182
John Wyckoff PHI 157

SAVES
Carl Mays BOS 5
four tied at 4

COMPLETE GAMES
W. Johnson WAS 35
Ray Caldwell NY 31
Hooks Dauss DET 27

SHUTOUTS
Walter Johnson WAS 7
Jim Scott CHI 7
Guy Morton CLE 6

GAMES PITCHED
Harry Coveleski DET 50
Red Faber CHI 50
two tied at 48

INNINGS PITCHED
W. Johnson WAS 337
H. Coveleski DET 313
Hooks Dauss DET 310

1915 NL

	W	L	PCT	GB	R	OR	BA	FA	ERA
PHILADELPHIA	90	62	.592	—	589	463	.247	.966	2.17
BOSTON	83	69	.546	7	582	545	.240	.966	2.57
BROOKLYN	80	72	.526	10	536	560	.248	.963	2.66
CHICAGO	73	80	.477	17.5	570	620	.244	.958	3.11
PITTSBURGH	73	81	.474	18	557	520	.246	.966	2.60
ST. LOUIS	72	81	.471	18.5	590	601	.254	.964	2.89
CINCINNATI	71	83	.461	20	516	585	.253	.966	2.84
NEW YORK	69	83	.454	21	582	628	.251	.960	3.11
					4522	4522	.248	.964	2.75

BATTING AVERAGE
Larry Doyle NY .... .320
Fred Luderus PHI ...... .315
two tied at .... .307

HITS
Larry Doyle NY 189
Tommy Griffith CIN 179
Bill Hinchman PIT 177

DOUBLES
Larry Doyle NY 40
Fred Luderus PHI 36
Vic Saier CHI 35

TRIPLES
Tommy Long STL 25
Honus Wagner PIT 17
Tommy Griffith CIN 16

HOME RUNS
Gavvy Cravath PHI 24
Cy Williams CHI............. 13
Wildfire Schulte CHI...... 12

RUNS BATTED IN
Gavvy Cravath PHI..... 115
Sherry Magee BOS....... 87
Tommy Griffith CIN 85

SLUGGING AVERAGE
Gavvy Cravath PHI .... .510
Fred Luderus PHI ...... .457
Tommy Long STL ...... .446

STOLEN BASES
Max Carey PIT.............. 36
Buck Herzog CIN 35
two tied at 29

RUNS SCORED
Gavvy Cravath PHI....... 89
Larry Doyle NY 86
Dave Bancroft PHI........ 85

WINS
G. Alexander PHI.......... 31
Dick Rudolph BOS........ 22
two tied at 21

WINNING PERCENTAGE
G. Alexander PHI .... .756
Al Mamaux PIT .... .724
Fred Toney CIN .... .714

EARNED RUN AVERAGE
G. Alexander PHI....... 1.22
Fred Toney CIN 1.58
Al Mamaux PIT 2.04

STRIKEOUTS
G. Alexander PHI........ 241
Jeff Tesreau NY 176
Tom Hughes BOS....... 171

SAVES
Rube Benton CIN, NY..... 5
Tom Hughes BOS............ 5
Wilbur Cooper PIT 4

COMPLETE GAMES
Grover Alexander PHI... 36
Dick Rudloph BOS........ 30
Jeff Pfeffer BKN 26

SHUTOUTS
Grover Alexander PHI... 12
Al Mamaux PIT 8
Jeff Tesreau NY.............. 8

GAMES PITCHED
Tom Hughes BOS......... 50
Grover Alexander PHI... 49
Gene Dale CIN 49

INNINGS PITCHED
G. Alexander PHI......... 376
Dick Rudolph BOS...... 341
Jeff Tesreau NY.......... 306

1916 AL

	W	L	PCT	GB	R	OR	BA	FA	ERA
★BOSTON	91	63	.591	—	550	480	.248	.972	2.48
CHICAGO	89	65	.578	2	601	497	.251	.968	2.36
DETROIT	87	67	.565	4	670	595	.264	.968	2.97
NEW YORK	80	74	.519	11	577	561	.246	.967	2.77
ST. LOUIS	79	75	.513	12	588	545	.245	.963	2.58
CLEVELAND	77	77	.500	14	630	602	.250	.965	2.89
WASHINGTON	76	77	.497	14.5	536	543	.242	.964	2.66
PHILADELPHIA	36	117	.235	54.5	447	776	.242	.951	3.84
					4599	4599	.248	.965	2.81

BATTING AVERAGE
Tris Speaker CLE ...... .386
Ty Cobb DET .... .371
Joe Jackson CHI........ .341

HITS
Tris Speaker CLE 211
Joe Jackson CHI........ 202
Ty Cobb DET 201

DOUBLES
Jack Graney CLE.......... 41
Tris Speaker CLE 41
Joe Jackson CHI........... 40

TRIPLES
Joe Jackson CHI........... 21
Eddie Collins CHI........ 17
two tied at 15

HOME RUNS
Wally Pipp NY............... 12
Frank Baker NY 10
two tied at 7

RUNS BATTED IN
Del Pratt STL 103
Wally Pipp NY............... 93
Bobby Veach DET 91

SLUGGING AVERAGE
Tris Speaker CLE ...... .502
Joe Jackson CHI........ .495
Ty Cobb DET .... .493

STOLEN BASES
Ty Cobb DET 68
A. Marsans STL 46
Burt Shotton STL 41

RUNS SCORED
Ty Cobb DET 113
Jack Graney CLE........ 106
Tris Speaker CLE 102

WINS
Walter Johnson WAS.... 25
Bob Shawkey NY.......... 24
Babe Ruth BOS 23

WINNING PERCENTAGE
Eddie Cicotte CHI ...... .682
Babe Ruth BOS .... .657
H. Coveleski DET ...... .656

EARNED RUN AVERAGE
Babe Ruth BOS 1.75
Eddie Cicotte CHI 1.78
W. Johnson WAS....... 1.89

STRIKEOUTS
W. Johnson WAS........ 228
Elmer Myers PHI......... 182
Babe Ruth BOS 170

SAVES
Bob Shawkey NY............. 8
Allan Russell NY 6
three tied at..................... 5

COMPLETE GAMES
W. Johnson WAS.......... 36
Elmer Myers PHI........... 31
Joe Bush PHI................ 25

SHUTOUTS
Babe Ruth BOS 9
Joe Bush PHI.................. 8
Dutch Leonard BOS........ 6

GAMES PITCHED
Dave Davenport STL 59
Reb Russell CHI 56
Bob Shawkey NY.......... 53

INNINGS PITCHED
W. Johnson WAS........ 371
H. Coveleski DET 324
Babe Ruth BOS 324

1916 NL

	W	L	PCT	GB	R	OR	BA	FA	ERA
BROOKLYN	94	60	.610	—	585	471	.261	.965	2.12
PHILADELPHIA	91	62	.595	2.5	581	489	.250	.963	2.36
BOSTON	89	63	.586	4	542	453	.233	.967	2.19
NEW YORK	86	66	.566	7	597	504	.253	.966	2.60
CHICAGO	67	86	.438	26.5	520	541	.239	.957	2.65
PITTSBURGH	65	89	.422	29	484	586	.240	.959	2.76
CINCINNATI	60	93	.392	33.5	505	617	.254	.965	3.10
ST. LOUIS	60	93	.392	33.5	476	629	.243	.957	3.14
					4290	4290	.247	.963	2.61

BATTING AVERAGE
Hal Chase CIN .... .339
Jake Daubert BKN ...... .316
Bill Hinchman PIT ...... .315

HITS
Hal Chase CIN 184
Dave Robertson NY 180
Zack Wheat BKN 177

DOUBLES
Bert Niehoff PHI 42
Zack Wheat BKN 32
Dode Paskert PHI 30

TRIPLES
Bill Hinchman PIT 16
three tied at 15

HOME RUNS
Dave Robertson NY 12
Cy Williams CHI 12
Gavvy Cravath PHI 11

RUNS BATTED IN
H. Zimmerman CHI, NY 83
Hal Chase CIN 82
Bill Hinchman PIT 76

SLUGGING AVERAGE
Zack Wheat BKN .... .461
Hal Chase CIN .... .459
Cy Williams CHI .... .459

STOLEN BASES
Max Carey PIT 63
Benny Kauff NY 40
Bob Bescher STL 39

RUNS SCORED
George Burns NY 105
Max Carey PIT 90
Dave Robertson NY 88

WINS
Grover Alexander PHI... 33
Jeff Pfeffer BKN 25
Eppa Rixey PHI 22

WINNING PERCENTAGE
Tom Hughes BOS ...... .842
G. Alexander PHI .... .733
Jeff Pfeffer BKN .... .694

EARNED RUN AVERAGE
G. Alexander PHI 1.55
R. Marquard BKN 1.58
Eppa Rixey PHI 1.85

STRIKEOUTS
G. Alexander PHI 167
Larry Cheney BKN 166
Al Mamaux PIT 163

SAVES
Red Ames STL 7
three tied at 5

COMPLETE GAMES
G. Alexander PHI 38
Jeff Pfeffer BKN 30
Dick Rudolph BOS 27

SHUTOUTS
Grover Alexander PHI... 16
Lefty Tyler BOS 6
Jeff Pfeffer BKN 6

GAMES PITCHED
Lee Meadows STL 51
G. Alexander PHI 48
two tied at 45

INNINGS PITCHED
G. Alexander PHI 389
Jeff Pfeffer BKN 329
Dick Rudolph BOS 312

1917 AL

	W	L	PCT	GB	R	OR	BA	FA	ERA
★CHICAGO	100	54	.649	—	656	464	.253	.967	2.16
BOSTON	90	62	.592	9	555	454	.246	.972	2.20
CLEVELAND	88	66	.571	12	584	543	.245	.964	2.52
DETROIT	78	75	.510	21.5	639	577	.259	.964	2.56
WASHINGTON	74	79	.484	25.5	543	566	.241	.961	2.77
NEW YORK	71	82	.464	28.5	524	558	.239	.965	2.66
ST. LOUIS	57	97	.370	43	510	687	.245	.957	3.20
PHILADELPHIA	55	98	.359	44.5	529	691	.254	.961	3.27
					4540	4540	.248	.964	2.66

BATTING AVERAGE
Ty Cobb DET .... .383
George Sisler STL ..... .353
Tris Speaker CLE .... .352

HITS
Ty Cobb DET 225
George Sisler STL 190
Tris Speaker CLE 184

DOUBLES
Ty Cobb DET 44
Tris Speaker CLE 42
Bobby Veach DET 31

TRIPLES
Ty Cobb DET 23
Joe Jackson CHI........... 17
Joe Judge WAS 15

HOME RUNS
Wally Pipp NY 9
Bobby Veach DET 8
two tied at 7

RUNS BATTED IN
Bobby Veach DET 103
Ty Cobb DET 102
Happy Felsch CHI....... 102

SLUGGING AVERAGE
Ty Cobb DET .... .571
Tris Speaker CLE ...... .486
Bobby Veach DET ..... .457

STOLEN BASES
Ty Cobb DET 55
Eddie Collins CHI........... 53
Ray Chapman CLE....... 52

RUNS SCORED
Donie Bush DET 112
Ty Cobb DET 107
Ray Chapman CLE....... 98

WINS
Eddie Cicotte CHI 28
Babe Ruth BOS 24
two tied at 23

WINNING PERCENTAGE
Reb Russell CHI .... .750
Dave Danforth CHI .... .714
Carl Mays BOS .... .710

EARNED RUN AVERAGE
Eddie Cicotte CHI 1.53
Carl Mays BOS 1.74
Stan Coveleski CLE... 1.81

STRIKEOUTS
W. Johnson WAS........ 188
Eddie Cicotte CHI 150
Dutch Leonard BOS.... 144

SAVES
Dave Danforth CHI 9
Jim Bagby CLE................ 7
Bernie Boland DET......... 6

COMPLETE GAMES
Babe Ruth BOS 35
Walter Johnson WAS.... 30
Eddie Cicotte CHI 29

SHUTOUTS
Stan Coveleski CLE........ 9
Walter Johnson WAS..... 8
Jim Bagby CLE................ 8

GAMES PITCHED
Dave Danforth CHI 50
Jim Bagby CLE............. 49
Eddie Cicotte CHI 49

INNINGS PITCHED
Eddie Cicotte CHI 347
W. Johnson WAS........ 328
Babe Ruth BOS 326

1917 NL

	W	L	PCT	GB	R	OR	BA	FA	ERA
NEW YORK	98	56	.636	—	635	457	.261	.968	2.27
PHILADELPHIA	87	65	.572	10	578	500	.248	.967	2.46
ST. LOUIS	82	70	.539	15	531	567	.250	.967	3.03
CINCINNATI	78	76	.506	20	601	611	.264	.962	2.66
CHICAGO	74	80	.481	24	552	567	.239	.959	2.62
BOSTON	72	81	.471	25.5	536	552	.246	.966	2.77
BROOKLYN	70	81	.464	26.5	511	559	.247	.962	2.78
PITTSBURGH	51	103	.331	47	464	595	.238	.961	3.01
					4408	4408	.249	.964	2.70

BATTING AVERAGE
Edd Roush CIN .... .341
R. Hornsby STL .... .327
Zack Wheat BKN .... .312

HITS
Heinie Groh CIN 182
George Burns NY 180
Edd Roush CIN 178

DOUBLES
Heinie Groh CIN 39
F. Merkle BKN, CHI 31
Red Smith BOS 31

TRIPLES
Rogers Hornsby STL 17
Gavvy Cravath PHI 16
Hal Chase CIN 15

HOME RUNS
Dave Robertson NY 12
Gavvy Cravath PHI 12
Rogers Hornsby STL 8

RUNS BATTED IN
H. Zimmerman NY 102
Hal Chase CIN 86
Gavvy Cravath PHI 83

SLUGGING AVERAGE
R. Hornsby STL .... .484
Gavvy Cravath PHI .... .473
Edd Roush CIN .... .454

STOLEN BASES
Max Carey PIT 46
George Burns NY 40
Benny Kauff NY 30

RUNS SCORED
George Burns NY 103
Heinie Groh CIN 91
Benny Kauff NY 89

WINS
Grover Alexander PHI... 30
Fred Toney CIN 24
Hippo Vaughn CHI 23

WINNING PERCENTAGE
Ferdie Schupp NY ..... .750
Slim Sallee NY .... .720
Pol Perritt NY .... .708

EARNED RUN AVERAGE
G. Alexander PHI 1.86
Pol Perritt NY 1.88
Ferdie Schupp NY 1.95

STRIKEOUTS
G. Alexander PHI 201
Hippo Vaughn CHI 195
Phil Douglas CHI 151

SAVES
Slim Sallee NY 4
five tied at 3

COMPLETE GAMES
Grover Alexander PHI... 35
Fred Toney CIN 31
two tied at 27

SHUTOUTS
Grover Alexander PHI..... 8
Wilbur Cooper PIT 7
Fred Toney CIN 7

GAMES PITCHED
Phil Douglas CHI 51
Jesse Barnes BOS 50
Pete Schneider CIN 46

INNINGS PITCHED
G. Alexander PHI 388
Pete Schneider CIN 342
Fred Toney CIN 340

1918 AL

	W	L	PCT	GB	R	OR	BA	FA	ERA
★BOSTON	75	51	.595	—	474	380	.249	.971	2.31
CLEVELAND	73	54	.575	2.5	504	447	.260	.962	2.63
WASHINGTON	72	56	.563	4	461	412	.256	.960	2.14
NEW YORK	60	63	.488	13.5	493	475	.257	.970	3.03
ST. LOUIS	58	64	.475	15	426	448	.259	.963	2.75
CHICAGO	57	67	.460	17	457	446	.256	.967	2.69
DETROIT	55	71	.437	20	476	557	.249	.960	3.40
PHILADELPHIA	52	76	.406	24	412	538	.243	.959	3.22
					3703	3703	.254	.964	2.77

BATTING AVERAGE
Ty Cobb DET .... .382
George Burns PHI ..... .352
George Sisler STL ...... .341

HITS
George Burns PHI 178
Ty Cobb DET 161
two tied at 154

DOUBLES
Tris Speaker CLE 33
Harry Hooper BOS........ 26
Babe Ruth BOS 26

TRIPLES
Ty Cobb DET 14
Harry Hooper BOS........ 13
Bobby Veach DET 13

HOME RUNS
Tilly Walker PHI 11
Babe Ruth BOS 11
two tied at 6

RUNS BATTED IN
Bobby Veach DET 78
George Burns PHI 70
Frank Baker NY 68

SLUGGING AVERAGE
Babe Ruth BOS .... .555
Ty Cobb DET .... .515
George Burns PHI ..... .467

STOLEN BASES
George Sisler STL 45
Braggo Roth CLE.......... 35
Ty Cobb DET 34

RUNS SCORED
Ray Chapman CLE....... 84
Ty Cobb DET 83
Harry Hooper BOS........ 81

WINS
Walter Johnson WAS.... 23
Stan Coveleski CLE 22
two tied at 21

WINNING PERCENTAGE
Sam Jones BOS .... .762
W. Johnson WAS......... .639
Stan Coveleski CLE... .629

EARNED RUN AVERAGE
W. Johnson WAS........ 1.27
Stan Coveleski CLE... 1.82
Allen Sothoron STL.... 1.94

STRIKEOUTS
W. Johnson WAS........ 162
Jim Shaw WAS............ 129
Joe Bush BOS 125

SAVES
George Mogridge NY 7
Jim Bagby CLE 6
two tied at 4

COMPLETE GAMES
Carl Mays BOS 30
Scott Perry PHI 30
Walter Johnson WAS.... 29

SHUTOUTS
Carl Mays BOS 8
Walter Johnson WAS...... 8
Joe Bush BOS 7

GAMES PITCHED
Jim Bagby CLE 45
George Mogridge NY.... 45
Scott Perry PHI 44

INNINGS PITCHED
Scott Perry PHI 332
W. Johnson WAS........ 325
Stan Coveleski CLE.... 311

1918 NL

	W	L	PCT	GB	R	OR	BA	FA	ERA
CHICAGO	84	45	.651	—	538	393	.265	.966	2.18
NEW YORK	71	53	.573	10.5	480	415	.260	.970	2.64
CINCINNATI	68	60	.531	15.5	530	496	.278	.964	3.00
PITTSBURGH	65	60	.520	17	466	412	.248	.966	2.48
BROOKLYN	57	69	.452	25.5	360	463	.250	.963	2.81
PHILADELPHIA	55	68	.447	26	430	507	.244	.961	3.15
BOSTON	53	71	.427	28.5	424	469	.244	.965	2.90
ST. LOUIS	51	78	.395	33	454	527	.244	.962	2.96
					3682	3682	.254	.965	2.76

BATTING AVERAGE
Zack Wheat BKN .... .335
Edd Roush CIN .... .333
Heinie Groh CIN .... .320

HITS
C. Hollocher CHI.......... 161
Heinie Groh CIN 158
Edd Roush CIN........... 145

DOUBLES
Heinie Groh CIN 28
Les Mann CHI............... 27
Gavvy Cravath PHI 27

TRIPLES
Jake Daubert BKN........ 15
three tied at................... 13

HOME RUNS
Gavvy Cravath PHI 8
Walt Cruise STL.............. 6
Cy Williams PHI 6

RUNS BATTED IN
Sherry Magee CIN 76
George Cutshaw PIT 68
Fred Luderus PHI 67

SLUGGING AVERAGE
Edd Roush CIN........... .455
Jake Daubert BKN ..... .429
R. Hornsby STL .... .416

STOLEN BASES
Max Carey PIT.............. 58
George Burns NY 40
Charlie Hollocher CHI ... 26

RUNS SCORED
Heinie Groh CIN 88
George Burns NY 80
Max Flack CHI 74

WINS
Hippo Vaughn CHI........ 22
four tied at.................... 19

WINNING PERCENTAGE
Claude Hendrix CHI.... .731
E. Mayer PHI, PIT...... .696
Hippo Vaughn CHI...... .688

EARNED RUN AVERAGE
Hippo Vaughn CHI...... 1.74
Lefty Tyler CHI........... 2.00
Wilbur Cooper PIT 2.11

STRIKEOUTS
Hippo Vaughn CHI....... 148
Wilbur Cooper PIT 117
B. Grimes BKN 113

SAVES
four tied at....................... 3

COMPLETE GAMES
Art Nehf BOS 28
Hippo Vaughn CHI........ 27
Wilbur Cooper PIT 26

SHUTOUTS
Hippo Vaughn CHI.......... 8
Lefty Tyler CHI................ 8
Burleigh Grimes BKN...... 7

GAMES PITCHED
Burleigh Grimes BKN.... 40
Wilbur Cooper PIT 38
Hod Eller CIN................ 37

INNINGS PITCHED
Hippo Vaughn CHI...... 290
Art Nehf BOS.............. 284
Wilbur Cooper PIT 273

1919 AL

	W	L	PCT	GB	R	OR	BA	FA	ERA
CHICAGO	88	52	.629	—	667	534	.287	.969	3.04
CLEVELAND	84	55	.604	3.5	636	537	.278	.965	2.92
NEW YORK	80	59	.576	7.5	578	506	.267	.968	2.78
DETROIT	80	60	.571	8	618	578	.283	.964	3.30
ST. LOUIS	67	72	.482	20.5	533	567	.264	.963	3.13
BOSTON	66	71	.482	20.5	564	552	.261	.975	3.30
WASHINGTON	56	84	.400	32	533	570	.260	.960	3.01
PHILADELPHIA	36	104	.257	52	457	742	.244	.956	4.26
					4586	4586	.268	.965	3.21

BATTING AVERAGE
Ty Cobb DET .... .384
Bobby Veach DET ..... .355
George Sisler STL ...... .352

HITS
Bobby Veach DET 191
Ty Cobb DET 191
Joe Jackson CHI 181

DOUBLES
Bobby Veach DET 45
Tris Speaker CLE 38
Ty Cobb DET 36

TRIPLES
Bobby Veach DET 17
George Sisler STL 15
Harry Heilmann DET..... 15

HOME RUNS
Babe Ruth BOS 29
three tied at.................. 10

RUNS BATTED IN
Babe Ruth BOS 114
Bobby Veach DET 101
Joe Jackson CHI........... 96

SLUGGING AVERAGE
Babe Ruth BOS .... .657
George Sisler STL ..... .530
Bobby Veach DET ..... .519

STOLEN BASES
Eddie Collins CHI........... 33
George Sisler STL 28
Ty Cobb DET 28

RUNS SCORED
Babe Ruth BOS 103
George Sisler STL 96
Ty Cobb DET 92

WINS
Eddie Cicotte CHI 29
Stan Coveleski CLE...... 24
Lefty Williams CHI 23

WINNING PERCENTAGE
Eddie Cicotte CHI ...... .806
Hooks Dauss DET ..... .700
Lefty Williams CHI ..... .676

EARNED RUN AVERAGE
W. Johnson WAS....... 1.49
Eddie Cicotte CHI 1.82
Carl Weilman STL....... 2.07

STRIKEOUTS
W. Johnson WAS........ 147
Jim Shaw WAS 128
Lefty Williams CHI 125

SAVES
Allan Russell NY, BOS ... 5
three tied at..................... 4

COMPLETE GAMES
Eddie Cicotte CHI 30
Walter Johnson WAS.... 27
Lefty Williams CHI 27

SHUTOUTS
Walter Johnson WAS...... 7
three tied at..................... 5

GAMES PITCHED
Jim Shaw WAS.............. 45
A. Russell NY, BOS 44
two tied at 43

INNINGS PITCHED
Eddie Cicotte CHI 307
Jim Shaw WAS 307
Lefty Williams CHI 297

1919 NL

	W	L	PCT	GB	R	OR	BA	FA	ERA
★CINCINNATI	96	44	.686	—	577	401	.263	.974	2.23
NEW YORK	87	53	.621	9	605	470	.269	.964	2.70
CHICAGO	75	65	.536	21	454	407	.256	.969	2.21
PITTSBURGH	71	68	.511	24.5	472	466	.249	.970	2.88
BROOKLYN	69	71	.493	27	525	513	.263	.972	2.73
BOSTON	57	82	.410	38.5	465	563	.253	.966	3.17
ST. LOUIS	54	83	.394	40.5	463	552	.256	.963	3.23
PHILADELPHIA	47	90	.343	47.5	510	699	.251	.963	4.17
					4071	4071	.258	.968	2.91

BATTING AVERAGE
Edd Roush CIN .... .321
R. Hornsby STL .... .318
Ross Youngs NY .... .311

HITS
Ivy Olsen BKN 164
R. Hornsby STL 163
two tied at 162

DOUBLES
Ross Youngs NY 31
George Burns NY 30
Fred Luderus PHI 30

TRIPLES
Billy Southworth PIT 14
Hy Myers BKN 14
Edd Roush CIN 13

HOME RUNS
Gavvy Cravath PHI 12
Benny Kauff NY 10
Cy Williams PHI 9

RUNS BATTED IN
Hy Myers BKN 73
Edd Roush CIN 71
Rogers Hornsby STL 71

SLUGGING AVERAGE
Hy Myers BKN .... .436
Larry Doyle NY .... .433
two tied at .... .431

STOLEN BASES
George Burns NY 40
George Cutshaw PIT 36
Carson Bigbee PIT 31

RUNS SCORED
George Burns NY 86
Jake Daubert CIN 79
Heinie Groh CIN 79

WINS
Jesse Barnes NY 25
Slim Sallee CIN 21
Hippo Vaughn CHI 21

WINNING PERCENTAGE
Dutch Ruether CIN .... .760
Slim Sallee CIN .... .750
Jesse Barnes NY .... .735

EARNED RUN AVERAGE
G. Alexander CHI 1.72
Hippo Vaughn CHI 1.79
Dutch Ruether CIN 1.82

STRIKEOUTS
Hippo Vaughn CHI 141
Hod Eller CIN 137
G. Alexander CHI 121

SAVES
Oscar Tuero STL 4
five tied at 3

COMPLETE GAMES
Wilbur Cooper PIT 27
Jeff Pfeffer BKN 26
Hippo Vaughn CHI 25

SHUTOUTS
Grover Alexander CHI 9
Babe Adams PIT............. 7
Hod Eller CIN 7

GAMES PITCHED
Oscar Tuero STL 45
Meadows PHI, STL.... 40
two tied at 38

INNINGS PITCHED
Hippo Vaughn CHI 307
Jesse Barnes NY 296
Wilbur Cooper PIT 287

1920 AL

	W	L	PCT	GB	R	OR	BA	FA	ERA
★CLEVELAND	98	56	.636	—	857	642	.303	.971	3.41
CHICAGO	96	58	.623	2	794	665	.295	.968	3.59
NEW YORK	95	59	.617	3	838	629	.280	.970	3.31
ST. LOUIS	76	77	.497	21.5	797	766	.308	.963	4.03
BOSTON	72	81	.471	25.5	650	698	.269	.972	3.82
WASHINGTON	68	84	.447	29	723	802	.290	.963	4.17
DETROIT	61	93	.396	37	652	833	.270	.965	4.04
PHILADELPHIA	48	106	.312	50	558	834	.252	.959	3.93
					5869	5869	.283	.966	3.79

BATTING AVERAGE
George Sisler STL ...... .407
Tris Speaker CLE .... .388
Joe Jackson CHI .... .382

HITS
George Sisler STL 257
Eddie Collins CHI........ 222
Joe Jackson CHI......... 218

DOUBLES
Tris Speaker CLE 50
George Sisler STL 49
Joe Jackson CHI........... 42

TRIPLES
Joe Jackson CHI........... 20
George Sisler STL 18
Harry Hooper BOS........ 17

HOME RUNS
Babe Ruth NY 54
George Sisler STL 19
Tilly Walker PHI 17

RUNS BATTED IN
Babe Ruth NY 137
B. Jacobson STL 122
George Sisler STL 122

SLUGGING AVERAGE
Babe Ruth NY .... .847
George Sisler STL ..... .632
Joe Jackson CHI........ .589

STOLEN BASES
Sam Rice WAS 63
George Sisler STL 42
Braggo Roth WAS 24

RUNS SCORED
Babe Ruth NY 158
George Sisler STL 137
Tris Speaker CLE 137

WINS
Jim Bagby CLE 31
Carl Mays NY................ 26
Stan Coveleski CLE...... 24

WINNING PERCENTAGE
Jim Bagby CLE .... .721
Carl Mays NY............. .703
Dickie Kerr CHI .... .700

EARNED RUN AVERAGE
Bob Shawkey NY....... 2.45
Stan Coveleski CLE ... 2.49
Urban Shocker STL ... 2.71

STRIKEOUTS
Stan Coveleski CLE.... 133
Lefty Williams CHI 128
Bob Shawkey NY 126

SAVES
Dickie Kerr CHI 5
Urban Shocker STL 5
Bill Burwell STL............... 4

COMPLETE GAMES
Jim Bagby CLE 30
Red Faber CHI.............. 28
Eddie Cicotte CHI 28

SHUTOUTS
Carl Mays NY.................. 6
Urban Shocker STL 5
Bob Shawkey NY............ 5

GAMES PITCHED
Jim Bagby CLE 48
Doc Ayers DET 46
two tied at 45

INNINGS PITCHED
Jim Bagby CLE 340
Red Faber CHI............. 319
Stan Coveleski CLE.... 315

1920 NL

	W	L	PCT	GB	R	OR	BA	FA	ERA
BROOKLYN	93	61	.604	—	660	528	.277	.966	2.62
NEW YORK	86	68	.558	7	682	543	.269	.969	2.80
CINCINNATI	82	71	.536	10.5	639	569	.277	.968	2.84
PITTSBURGH	79	75	.513	14	530	552	.257	.971	2.89
CHICAGO	75	79	.487	18	619	635	.264	.965	3.27
ST. LOUIS	75	79	.487	18	675	682	.289	.961	3.43
BOSTON	62	90	.408	30	523	670	.260	.964	3.54
PHILADELPHIA	62	91	.405	30.5	565	714	.263	.964	3.63
					4893	4893	.270	.966	3.13

BATTING AVERAGE
R. Hornsby STL .... .370
Ross Youngs NY .... .351
Edd Roush CIN .... .339

HITS
R. Hornsby STL 218
Milt Stock STL............. 204
Ross Youngs NY 204

DOUBLES
Rogers Hornsby STL 44
three tied at.................. 36

TRIPLES
Hy Myers BKN 22
Rogers Hornsby STL 20
Edd Roush CIN............. 16

HOME RUNS
Cy Williams PHI 15
Irish Meusel PHI 14
George Kelly NY 11

RUNS BATTED IN
George Kelly NY 94
Rogers Hornsby STL 94
Edd Roush CIN............. 90

SLUGGING AVERAGE
R. Hornsby STL .... .559
Cy Williams PHI.......... .497
Ross Youngs NY. .... .477

STOLEN BASES
Max Carey PIT 52
Edd Roush CIN............. 36
Frankie Frisch NY 34

RUNS SCORED
George Burns NY 115
Bancroft PHI, NY 102
Jake Daubert CIN 97

WINS
G. Alexander CHI.......... 27
Wilbur Cooper PIT 24
Burleigh Grimes BKN.... 23

WINNING PERCENTAGE
B. Grimes BKN .... .676
G. Alexander CHI........ .659
Fred Toney NY .... .656

EARNED RUN AVERAGE
G. Alexander CHI....... 1.91
Babe Adams PIT........ 2.16
B. Grimes BKN 2.22

STRIKEOUTS
G. Alexander CHI........ 173
Hippo Vaughn CHI...... 131
B. Grimes BKN 131

SAVES
Bill Sherdel STL 6
Grover Alexander CHI 5
Hugh McQuillan BOS...... 5

COMPLETE GAMES
G. Alexander CHI.......... 33
Wilbur Cooper PIT 28
two tied at 25

SHUTOUTS
Babe Adams PIT............. 8
G. Alexander CHI............ 7

GAMES PITCHED
Jesse Haines STL......... 47
G. Alexander CHI.......... 46
Phil Douglas NY............. 46

INNINGS PITCHED
G. Alexander CHI........ 363
Wilbur Cooper PIT 327
B. Grimes BKN 304

1921 AL

	W	L	PCT	GB	R	OR	BA	FA	ERA
NEW YORK	98	55	.641	—	948	708	.300	.965	3.79
CLEVELAND	94	60	.610	4.5	925	712	.308	.967	3.90
ST. LOUIS	81	73	.526	17.5	835	845	.304	.964	4.62
WASHINGTON	80	73	.523	18	704	738	.277	.963	3.97
BOSTON	75	79	.487	23.5	668	696	.277	.975	3.98
DETROIT	71	82	.464	27	883	852	.316	.963	4.40
CHICAGO	62	92	.403	36.5	683	858	.283	.969	4.94
PHILADELPHIA	53	100	.346	45	657	894	.274	.958	4.60
					6303	6303	.292	.965	4.28

BATTING AVERAGE
Harry Heilmann DET.. .394
Ty Cobb DET .... .389
Babe Ruth NY .... .378

HITS
Harry Heilmann DET .. 237
Jack Tobin STL 236
George Sisler STL 216

DOUBLES
Tris Speaker CLE 52
Babe Ruth NY 44
two tied at 43

TRIPLES
Howard Shanks WAS ... 19
Jack Tobin STL 18
George Sisler STL 18

HOME RUNS
Babe Ruth NY 59
Ken Williams STL 24
Bob Meusel NY 24

RUNS BATTED IN
Babe Ruth NY 171
Harry Heilmann DET... 139
Bob Meusel NY 135

SLUGGING AVERAGE
Babe Ruth NY .... .846
Harry Heilmann DET .. .606
Ty Cobb DET .... .596

STOLEN BASES
George Sisler STL 35
Bucky Harris WAS 29
Sam Rice WAS 25

RUNS SCORED
Babe Ruth NY 177
Jack Tobin STL 132
R. Peckinpaugh NY 128

WINS
Carl Mays NY 27
Urban Shocker STL 27
Red Faber CHI 25

WINNING PERCENTAGE
Carl Mays NY .... .750
Urban Shocker STL ... .692
Joe Bush BOS .... .640

EARNED RUN AVERAGE
Red Faber CHI 2.48
G. Mogridge WAS 3.00
Carl Mays NY 3.05

STRIKEOUTS
W. Johnson WAS 143
Urban Shocker STL ... 132
Bob Shawkey NY 126

SAVES
Jim Middleton DET 7
Carl Mays NY 7
four tied at 4

COMPLETE GAMES
Red Faber CHI 32
Urban Shocker STL 31
Carl Mays NY 30

SHUTOUTS
Sad Sam Jones BOS 5
three tied at 4

GAMES PITCHED
Carl Mays NY 49
Urban Shocker STL 47
Bill Bayne STL 47

INNINGS PITCHED
Carl Mays NY 337
Red Faber CHI 331
Urban Shocker STL 327

1921 NL

	W	L	PCT	GB	R	OR	BA	FA	ERA
★NEW YORK	94	59	.614	—	840	637	.298	.971	3.55
PITTSBURGH	90	63	.588	4	692	595	.285	.973	3.17
ST. LOUIS	87	66	.569	7	809	681	.308	.965	3.62
BOSTON	79	74	.516	15	721	697	.290	.969	3.90
BROOKLYN	77	75	.507	16.5	667	681	.280	.964	3.70
CINCINNATI	70	83	.458	24	618	649	.278	.969	3.46
CHICAGO	64	89	.418	30	668	773	.292	.974	4.39
PHILADELPHIA	51	103	.331	43.5	617	919	.284	.955	4.48
					5632	5632	.289	.967	3.78

BATTING AVERAGE
R. Hornsby STL .... .397
Edd Roush CIN.......... .352
Austin McHenry STL.. .350

HITS
R. Hornsby STL 235
Frankie Frisch NY 211
Carson Bigbee PIT 204

DOUBLES
Rogers Hornsby STL 44
George Kelly NY 42
Jimmy Johnston BKN ... 41

TRIPLES
Rogers Hornsby STL 18
Ray Powell BOS 18
two tied at 17

HOME RUNS
George Kelly NY 23
Rogers Hornsby STL ... 21
Cy Williams PHI............ 18

RUNS BATTED IN
R. Hornsby STL 126
George Kelly NY 122
two tied at 102

SLUGGING AVERAGE
R. Hornsby STL .... .639
Austin McHenry STL.. .531
George Kelly NY .... .528

STOLEN BASES
Frankie Frisch NY 49
Max Carey PIT.............. 37
Jimmy Johnston BKN ... 28

RUNS SCORED
R. Hornsby STL 131
Frankie Frisch NY 121
Dave Bancroft NY....... 121

WINS
Burleigh Grimes BKN.... 22
Wilbur Cooper PIT 22
two tied at 20

WINNING PERCENTAGE
Bill Doak STL.............. .714
Art Nehf NY................. .667
B. Grimes BKN .... .629

EARNED RUN AVERAGE
Bill Doak STL.............. 2.59
Babe Adams PIT........ 2.64
Whitey Glazner PIT.... 2.77

STRIKEOUTS
B. Grimes BKN 136
Wilbur Cooper PIT 134
Dolf Luque CIN 102

SAVES
Lou North STL 7
Jesse Barnes NY 6
Hugh McQuillan BOS...... 5

COMPLETE GAMES
Burleigh Grimes BKN.... 30
Wilbur Cooper PIT 29
Dolf Luque CIN 25

SHUTOUTS
seven tied at 3

GAMES PITCHED
Jim Scott BOS 47
Joe Oeschger BOS........ 46
Hugh McQuillan BOS.... 45

INNINGS PITCHED
Wilbur Cooper PIT 327
Dolf Luque CIN 304
B. Grimes BKN 302

1922 AL

	W	L	PCT	GB	R	OR	BA	FA	ERA
NEW YORK	94	60	.610	—	758	618	.287	.975	3.39
ST. LOUIS	93	61	.604	1	867	643	.313	.968	3.38
DETROIT	79	75	.513	15	828	791	.305	.970	4.27
CLEVELAND	78	76	.506	16	768	817	.292	.968	4.60
CHICAGO	77	77	.500	17	691	691	.278	.975	3.93
WASHINGTON	69	85	.448	25	650	706	.268	.969	3.81
PHILADELPHIA	65	89	.422	29	705	830	.269	.966	4.59
BOSTON	61	93	.396	33	598	769	.260	.965	4.30
					5865	5865	.284	.969	4.03

BATTING AVERAGE
George Sisler STL ..... .420
Ty Cobb DET .... .401
Tris Speaker CLE .... .378

HITS
George Sisler STL 246
Ty Cobb DET 211
Jack Tobin STL............ 207

DOUBLES
Tris Speaker CLE 48
Del Pratt BOS 44
two tied at 42

TRIPLES
George Sisler STL 18
Ty Cobb DET 16
B. Jacobson STL 16

HOME RUNS
Ken Williams STL 39
Tilly Walker PHI 37
Babe Ruth NY 35

RUNS BATTED IN
Ken Williams STL 155
Bobby Veach DET 126
Marty McManus STL... 109

SLUGGING AVERAGE
Babe Ruth NY .... .672
Ken Williams STL ...... .627
Tris Speaker CLE ...... .606

STOLEN BASES
George Sisler STL 51
Ken Williams STL 37
Bucky Harris WAS 25

RUNS SCORED
George Sisler STL 134
Lu Blue DET 131
Ken Williams STL 128

WINS
Eddie Rommel PHI 27
Joe Bush NY 26
Urban Shocker STL 24

WINNING PERCENTAGE
Joe Bush NY .... .788
Eddie Rommel PHI .... .675
Bob Shawkey NY .... .625

EARNED RUN AVERAGE
Red Faber CHI............ 2.80
H. Pillette DET 2.85
Bob Shawkey NY 2.91

STRIKEOUTS
Urban Shocker STL 149
Red Faber CHI............ 148
Bob Shawkey NY 130

SAVES
Sad Sam Jones NY 8
Hub Pruett STL 7
Rasty Wright STL............. 5

COMPLETE GAMES
Red Faber CHI.............. 31
Urban Shocker STL 29
two tied at 23

SHUTOUTS
George Uhle CLE 5
three tied at..................... 4

GAMES PITCHED
Eddie Rommel PHI 51
George Uhle CLE 50
Urban Shocker STL 48

INNINGS PITCHED
Red Faber CHI............. 353
Urban Shocker STL ... 348
Bob Shawkey NY 300

1922 NL

	W	L	PCT	GB	R	OR	BA	FA	ERA
★NEW YORK	93	61	.604	—	852	658	.305	.970	3.45
CINCINNATI	86	68	.558	7	766	677	.296	.968	3.53
PITTSBURGH	85	69	.552	8	865	736	.308	.970	3.98
ST. LOUIS	85	69	.552	8	863	819	.301	.961	4.44
CHICAGO	80	74	.519	13	771	808	.293	.968	4.34
BROOKLYN	76	78	.494	17	743	754	.290	.967	4.05
PHILADELPHIA	57	96	.373	35.5	738	920	.282	.965	4.64
BOSTON	53	100	.346	39.5	596	822	.263	.965	4.37
					6194	6194	.292	.967	4.10

BATTING AVERAGE
R. Hornsby STL .... .401
Ray Grimes CHI......... .354
Hack Miller CHI.......... .352

HITS
R. Hornsby STL 250
Carson Bigbee PIT 215
Dave Bancroft NY 209

DOUBLES
Rogers Hornsby STL ... 46
Ray Grimes CHI........... 45
Pat Duncan CIN........... 44

TRIPLES
Jake Daubert CIN 22
Irish Meusel NY 17
two tied at 15

HOME RUNS
Rogers Hornsby STL 42
Cy Williams PHI............ 26
two tied at 17

RUNS BATTED IN
Rogers Hornsby STL .. 152
Irish Meusel NY 132
Zack Wheat BKN 112

SLUGGING AVERAGE
R. Hornsby STL .... .722
Ray Grimes CHI......... .572
Cliff Lee PHI............... .540

STOLEN BASES
Max Carey PIT.............. 51
Frankie Frisch NY 31
George Burns CIN 30

RUNS SCORED
R. Hornsby STL 141
Max Carey PIT............ 140
two tied at 117

WINS
Eppa Rixey CIN 25
Wilbur Cooper PIT 23
Dutch Ruether BKN 21

WINNING PERCENTAGE
Pete Donohue CIN..... .667
Eppa Rixey CIN .... .658
Johnny Couch CIN..... .640

EARNED RUN AVERAGE
Rosy Ryan NY 3.01
Pete Donohue CIN..... 3.12
Wilbur Cooper PIT 3.18

STRIKEOUTS
Dazzy Vance BKN 134
Wilbur Cooper PIT 129
Jimmy Ring PHI 116

SAVES
Claude Jonnard NY 5
Lou North STL 4
four tied at...................... 3

COMPLETE GAMES
Wilbur Cooper PIT 27
Dutch Ruether BKN 26
Eppa Rixey CIN 26

SHUTOUTS
Dazzy Vance BKN 5
Johnny Morrison PIT....... 5
two tied at 4

GAMES PITCHED
Lou North STL 53
Bill Sherdel STL 47
two tied at 46

INNINGS PITCHED
Eppa Rixey CIN 313
Wilbur Cooper PIT 295
Johnny Morrison PIT... 286

1923 AL

	W	L	PCT	GB	R	OR	BA	FA	ERA
★NEW YORK	98	54	.645	—	823	622	.291	.977	3.66
DETROIT	83	71	.539	16	831	741	.300	.968	4.09
CLEVELAND	82	71	.536	16.5	888	746	.301	.964	3.91
WASHINGTON	75	78	.490	23.5	720	747	.274	.966	3.99
ST. LOUIS	74	78	.487	24	688	720	.281	.971	3.93
PHILADELPHIA	69	83	.454	29	661	761	.271	.965	4.08
CHICAGO	69	85	.448	30	692	741	.279	.971	4.03
BOSTON	61	91	.401	37	584	809	.261	.963	4.20
					5887	5887	.282	.968	3.99

BATTING AVERAGE
Harry Heilmann DET.. .403
Babe Ruth NY............. .393
Tris Speaker CLE .... .380

HITS
C. Jamieson CLE 222
Tris Speaker CLE 218
Harry Heilmann DET... 211

DOUBLES
Tris Speaker CLE 59
George Burns BOS....... 47
Babe Ruth NY.............. 45

TRIPLES
Goose Goslin WAS....... 18
Sam Rice WAS............. 18
two tied at 15

HOME RUNS
Babe Ruth NY.............. 41
Ken Williams STL 29
Harry Heilmann DET..... 18

RUNS BATTED IN
Babe Ruth NY.............. 130
Tris Speaker CLE 130
Harry Heilmann DET... 115

SLUGGING AVERAGE
Babe Ruth NY............. .764
Harry Heilmann DET.. .632
Ken Williams STL .... .623

STOLEN BASES
Eddie Collins CHI.......... 47
Johnny Mostil CHI........ 41
Bucky Harris WAS 23

RUNS SCORED
Babe Ruth NY............. 151
Tris Speaker CLE 133
C. Jamieson CLE........ 130

WINS
George Uhle CLE 26
Sad Sam Jones NY 21
Hooks Dauss DET 21

WINNING PERCENTAGE
Herb Pennock NY .... .760
Sad Sam Jones NY ..... .724
Waite Hoyt NY .... .654

EARNED RUN AVERAGE
Stan Coveleski CLE... 2.76
Waite Hoyt NY 3.02
Elam Vangilder STL... 3.06

STRIKEOUTS
W. Johnson WAS........ 130
Joe Bush NY 125
Bob Shawkey NY 125

SAVES
Allan Russell WAS........... 9
Jack Quinn BOS 7
Slim Harriss PHI 6

COMPLETE GAMES
George Uhle CLE 29
Howard Ehmke BOS..... 28
Urban Shocker STL 24

SHUTOUTS
Stan Coveleski CLE........ 5
three tied at..................... 4

GAMES PITCHED
Eddie Rommel PHI 56
George Uhle CLE 54
Allan Russell WAS........ 52

INNINGS PITCHED
George Uhle CLE 358
Howard Ehmke BOS... 317
Hooks Dauss DET 316

1923 NL

	W	L	PCT	GB	R	OR	BA	FA	ERA
NEW YORK	95	58	.621	—	854	679	.295	.972	3.90
CINCINNATI	91	63	.591	4.5	708	629	.285	.969	3.21
PITTSBURGH	87	67	.565	8.5	786	696	.295	.971	3.87
CHICAGO	83	71	.539	12.5	756	704	.288	.967	3.82
ST. LOUIS	79	74	.516	16	746	732	.286	.963	3.87
BROOKLYN	76	78	.494	19.5	753	741	.285	.955	3.73
BOSTON	54	100	.351	41.5	636	798	.273	.964	4.22
PHILADELPHIA	50	104	.325	45.5	748	1008	.278	.966	5.30
					5987	5987	.286	.966	3.99

BATTING AVERAGE
R. Hornsby STL .... .384
Jim Bottomley STL...... .371
two tied at .... .351

HITS
Frankie Frisch NY 223
Jigger Statz CHI.......... 209
Pie Traynor PIT........... 208

DOUBLES
Edd Roush CIN............. 41
G. Grantham CHI.......... 36
C. Tierney PIT, PHI....... 36

TRIPLES
Pie Traynor PIT............. 19
Max Carey PIT.............. 19
Edd Roush CIN............. 18

HOME RUNS
Cy Williams PHI 41
Jack Fournier BKN........ 22
Hack Miller CHI............. 20

RUNS BATTED IN
Irish Meusel NY 125
Cy Williams PHI 114
Frankie Frisch NY 111

SLUGGING AVERAGE
R. Hornsby STL .... .627
Jack Fournier BKN..... .588
Cy Williams PHI .... .576

STOLEN BASES
Max Carey PIT.............. 51
G. Grantham CHI.......... 43
two tied at 32

RUNS SCORED
Ross Youngs NY 121
Max Carey PIT............ 120
Frankie Frisch NY 116

WINS
Dolf Luque CIN 27
Johnny Morrison PIT..... 25
G. Alexander CHI.......... 22

WINNING PERCENTAGE
Dolf Luque CIN .... .771
Rosy Ryan NY .... .762
Jack Scott NY .... .696

EARNED RUN AVERAGE
Dolf Luque CIN 1.93
Eppa Rixey CIN 2.80
Vic Keen CHI 3.00

STRIKEOUTS
Dazzy Vance BKN 197
Dolf Luque CIN 151
B. Grimes BKN 119

SAVES
Claude Jonnard NY 5
Rosy Ryan NY 4
five tied at 3

COMPLETE GAMES
Burleigh Grimes BKN.... 33
Dolf Luque CIN 28
Johnny Morrison PIT..... 27

SHUTOUTS
Dolf Luque CIN 6
J. Barnes NY, BOS......... 5
Hugh McQuillan NY 5

GAMES PITCHED
Rosy Ryan NY 45
Claude Jonnard NY 45
Joe Oeschger BOS....... 44

INNINGS PITCHED
B. Grimes BKN 327
Dolf Luque CIN 322
Jimmy Ring PHI........... 313

1924 AL

	W	L	PCT	GB	R	OR	BA	FA	ERA
★WASHINGTON	92	62	.597	—	755	613	.294	.972	3.35
NEW YORK	89	63	.586	2	798	667	.289	.974	3.86
DETROIT	86	68	.558	6	849	796	.298	.971	4.19
ST. LOUIS	74	78	.487	17	764	797	.294	.969	4.55
PHILADELPHIA	71	81	.467	20	685	778	.281	.971	4.39
CLEVELAND	67	86	.438	24.5	755	814	.296	.967	4.40
BOSTON	67	87	.435	25	725	801	.277	.967	4.36
CHICAGO	66	87	.431	25.5	793	858	.288	.963	4.75
					6124	6124	.290	.969	4.23

BATTING AVERAGE
Babe Ruth NY .... .378
C. Jamieson CLE .... .359
Bibb Falk CHI .... .352

HITS
Sam Rice WAS 216
C. Jamieson CLE 213
Ty Cobb DET 211

DOUBLES
Harry Heilmann DET 45
Joe Sewell CLE 45
two tied at 41

TRIPLES
Wally Pipp NY 19
Goose Goslin WAS 17
Harry Heilmann DET 16

HOME RUNS
Babe Ruth NY 46
Joe Hauser PHI 27
B. Jacobson STL 19

RUNS BATTED IN
Goose Goslin WAS 129
Babe Ruth NY 121
Bob Meusel NY 120

SLUGGING AVERAGE
Babe Ruth NY .... .739
H. Heilmann DET .... .533
Ken Williams STL .... .533

STOLEN BASES
Eddie Collins CHI 42
Bob Meusel NY 26
Sam Rice WAS 24

RUNS SCORED
Babe Ruth NY 143
Ty Cobb DET 115
Eddie Collins CHI 108

WINS
Walter Johnson WAS.... 23
Herb Pennock NY 21
two tied at 20

WINNING PERCENTAGE
W. Johnson WAS .... .767
Herb Pennock NY .... .700
Earl Whitehill DET ...... .654

EARNED RUN AVERAGE
W. Johnson WAS 2.72
Tom Zachary WAS 2.75
Herb Pennock NY 2.83

STRIKEOUTS
W. Johnson WAS........ 158
Howard Ehmke BOS... 119
Bob Shawkey NY 114

SAVES
Firpo Marberry WAS 15
Allan Russell WAS 8
Jack Quinn BOS 7

COMPLETE GAMES
Sloppy Thurston CHI 28
Howard Ehmke BOS..... 26
Herb Pennock NY 25

SHUTOUTS
Walter Johnson WAS...... 6
Dixie Davis STL 5
two tied at 4

GAMES PITCHED
Firpo Marberry WAS 50
Ken Holloway DET........ 49
two tied at 46

INNINGS PITCHED
Howard Ehmke BOS... 315
S. Thurston CHI 291
Herb Pennock NY 286

1924 NL

	W	L	PCT	GB	R	OR	BA	FA	ERA
NEW YORK	93	60	.608	—	857	641	.300	.971	3.62
BROOKLYN	92	62	.597	1.5	717	675	.287	.968	3.64
PITTSBURGH	90	63	.588	3	724	588	.287	.971	3.27
CINCINNATI	83	70	.542	10	649	579	.290	.966	3.12
CHICAGO	81	72	.529	12	698	699	.276	.966	3.83
ST. LOUIS	65	89	.422	28.5	740	750	.290	.969	4.15
PHILADELPHIA	55	96	.364	37	676	849	.275	.972	4.87
BOSTON	53	100	.346	40	520	800	.256	.973	4.46
					5581	5581	.283	.970	3.87

BATTING AVERAGE
R. Hornsby STL .... .424
Zack Wheat BKN .... .375
Ross Youngs NY .... .356

HITS
R. Hornsby STL 227
Zack Wheat BKN 212
Frankie Frisch NY 198

DOUBLES
R. Hornsby STL 43
Zack Wheat BKN 41
George Kelly NY 37

TRIPLES
Edd Roush CIN 21
Rabbit Maranville PIT ... 20
Glenn Wright PIT 18

HOME RUNS
Jack Fournier BKN........ 27
Rogers Hornsby STL 25
Cy Williams PHI 24

RUNS BATTED IN
George Kelly NY 136
Jack Fournier BKN...... 116
two tied at 111

SLUGGING AVERAGE
R. Hornsby STL .... .696
Cy Williams PHI .... .552
Zack Wheat BKN .... .549

STOLEN BASES
Max Carey PIT 49
Kiki Cuyler PIT 32
Cliff Heathcote CHI 26

RUNS SCORED
Frankie Frisch NY 121
R. Hornsby STL 121
Max Carey PIT............ 113

WINS
Dazzy Vance BKN 28
Burleigh Grimes BKN.... 22
two tied at 20

WINNING PERCENTAGE
Emil Yde PIT .... .842
Dazzy Vance BKN ...... .824
Jack Bentley NY .... .762

EARNED RUN AVERAGE
Dazzy Vance BKN 2.16
Hugh McQuillan NY ... 2.69
Eppa Rixey CIN 2.76

STRIKEOUTS
Dazzy Vance BKN 262
B. Grimes BKN 135
Dolf Luque CIN 86

SAVES
Jackie May CIN............... 6
Rosy Ryan NY 5
Claude Jonnard NY 5

COMPLETE GAMES
Dazzy Vance BKN 30
Burleigh Grimes BKN.... 30
Wilbur Cooper PIT 25

SHUTOUTS
five tied at 4

GAMES PITCHED
Ray Kremer PIT 41
Johnny Morrison PIT..... 41
Vic Keen CHI 40

INNINGS PITCHED
Burleigh Grimes BKN.. 311
Dazzy Vance BKN 309
Wilbur Cooper PIT 269

1925 AL

	W	L	PCT	GB	R	OR	BA	FA	ERA
WASHINGTON	96	55	.636	—	829	669	.303	.972	3.67
PHILADELPHIA	88	64	.579	8.5	830	714	.307	.966	3.89
ST. LOUIS	82	71	.536	15	897	909	.298	.964	4.85
DETROIT	81	73	.526	16.5	903	829	.302	.972	4.61
CHICAGO	79	75	.513	18.5	811	771	.284	.968	4.34
CLEVELAND	70	84	.455	27.5	782	810	.297	.967	4.49
NEW YORK	69	85	.448	28.5	706	774	.275	.974	4.33
BOSTON	47	105	.309	49.5	639	921	.266	.957	4.97
					6397	6397	.292	.968	4.39

BATTING AVERAGE
H. Heilmann DET....... .393
Tris Speaker CLE ...... .389
Al Simmons PHI......... .384

SLUGGING AVERAGE
Ken Williams STL .... .613
Ty Cobb DET.............. .598
Al Simmons PHI......... .596

STRIKEOUTS
Lefty Grove PHI 116
W. Johnson WAS........ 108
two tied at 95

HITS
Al Simmons PHI........... 253
Sam Rice WAS 227
Harry Heilmann DET... 225

STOLEN BASES
Johnny Mostil CHI......... 43
Sam Rice WAS 26
Goose Goslin WAS....... 26

SAVES
Firpo Marberry WAS..... 15
Jess Doyle DET.............. 8
Sarge Connally CHI....... 8

DOUBLES
Marty McManus STL..... 44
Earl Sheely CHI 43
Al Simmons PHI............ 43

RUNS SCORED
Johnny Mostil CHI....... 135
Al Simmons PHI........... 122
Earle Combs NY 117

COMPLETE GAMES
Sherry Smith CLE 22
Howard Ehmke BOS..... 22
Herb Pennock NY 21

TRIPLES
Goose Goslin WAS....... 20
Johnny Mostil CHI......... 16
George Sisler STL 15

WINS
Eddie Rommel PHI 21
Ted Lyons CHI.............. 21
two tied at 20

SHUTOUTS
Ted Lyons CHI................ 5
Joe Giard STL................. 4
Sam Gray PHI................. 4

HOME RUNS
Bob Meusel NY.............. 33
Ken Williams STL 25
Babe Ruth NY................ 25

WINNING PERCENTAGE
Stan Coveleski WAS.. .800
W. Johnson WAS....... .741
D. Ruether WAS .... .720

GAMES PITCHED
Firpo Marberry WAS..... 55
Rube Walberg PHI........ 53
two tied at 52

RUNS BATTED IN
Bob Meusel NY........... 138
Harry Heilmann DET... 133
Al Simmons PHI........... 129

EARNED RUN AVERAGE
S. Coveleski WAS....... 2.84
Herb Pennock NY 2.96
W. Johnson WAS....... 3.07

INNINGS PITCHED
Herb Pennock NY 277
Ted Lyons CHI............. 263
Eddie Rommel PHI 261

1925 NL

	W	L	PCT	GB	R	OR	BA	FA	ERA
★PITTSBURGH	95	58	.621	—	912	715	.307	.964	3.87
NEW YORK	86	66	.566	8.5	736	702	.283	.968	3.94
CINCINNATI	80	73	.523	15	690	643	.285	.968	3.38
ST. LOUIS	77	76	.503	18	828	764	.299	.966	4.36
BOSTON	70	83	.458	25	708	802	.292	.964	4.39
BROOKLYN	68	85	.444	27	786	866	.296	.966	4.77
PHILADELPHIA	68	85	.444	27	812	930	.295	.966	5.02
CHICAGO	68	86	.442	27.5	723	773	.275	.969	4.41
					6195	6195	.292	.966	4.27

BATTING AVERAGE
R. Hornsby STL .... .403
Jim Bottomley STL..... .367
Zack Wheat BKN .... .359

HITS
Jim Bottomley STL...... 227
Zack Wheat BKN 221
Kiki Cuyler PIT 220

DOUBLES
Jim Bottomley STL........ 44
Kiki Cuyler PIT 43
Zack Wheat BKN 42

TRIPLES
Kiki Cuyler PIT 26
three tied at................... 16

HOME RUNS
Rogers Hornsby STL 39
Gabby Hartnett CHI 24
Jack Fournier BKN........ 22

RUNS BATTED IN
R. Hornsby STL 143
Jack Fournier BKN...... 130
Jim Bottomley STL...... 128

SLUGGING AVERAGE
R. Hornsby STL .... .756
Kiki Cuyler PIT .... .593
Jim Bottomley STL..... .578

STOLEN BASES
Max Carey PIT.............. 46
Kiki Cuyler PIT 41
Sparky Adams CHI 26

RUNS SCORED
Kiki Cuyler PIT 144
R. Hornsby STL 133
Zack Wheat BKN 125

WINS
Dazzy Vance BKN 22
Eppa Rixey CIN 21
Pete Donohue CIN........ 21

WINNING PERCENTAGE
Bill Sherdel STL .... .714
Dazzy Vance BKN .... .710
Vic Aldridge PIT .... .682

EARNED RUN AVERAGE
Dolf Luque CIN 2.63
Eppa Rixey CIN 2.88
Art Reinhart STL 3.05

STRIKEOUTS
Dazzy Vance BKN 221
Dolf Luque CIN 140
two tied at 93

SAVES
Johnny Morrison PIT....... 4
Guy Bush CHI.................. 4
four tied at........................ 3

COMPLETE GAMES
Pete Donohue CIN........ 27
Dazzy Vance BKN 26
two tied at 22

SHUTOUTS
Dolf Luque CIN 4
Dazzy Vance BKN 4
Hal Carlson PHI.............. 4

GAMES PITCHED
Johnny Morrison PIT.... 44
Pete Donohue CIN........ 42
Guy Bush CHI............... 42

INNINGS PITCHED
Pete Donohue CIN...... 301
Dolf Luque CIN 291
Eppa Rixey CIN 287

1926 AL

	W	L	PCT	GB	R	OR	BA	FA	ERA
NEW YORK	91	63	.591	—	847	713	.289	.966	3.86
CLEVELAND	88	66	.571	3	738	612	.289	.972	3.40
PHILADELPHIA	83	67	.553	6	677	570	.269	.972	3.00
WASHINGTON	81	69	.540	8	802	761	.292	.969	4.34
CHICAGO	81	72	.529	9.5	730	665	.289	.973	3.74
DETROIT	79	75	.513	12	793	830	.291	.969	4.41
ST. LOUIS	62	92	.403	29	682	845	.276	.963	4.66
BOSTON	46	107	.301	44.5	562	835	.256	.970	4.72
					5831	5831	.281	.969	4.02

BATTING AVERAGE
Heinie Manush DET... .378
Babe Ruth NY............ .372
two tied at .... .367

HITS
Sam Rice WAS 216
George Burns CLE 216
Goose Goslin WAS..... 201

DOUBLES
George Burns CLE 64
Al Simmons PHI............ 53
Tris Speaker CLE 52

TRIPLES
Lou Gehrig NY 20
C. Gehringer DET 17
two tied at 15

HOME RUNS
Babe Ruth NY................ 47
Al Simmons PHI............ 19
Tony Lazzeri NY 18

RUNS BATTED IN
Babe Ruth NY............... 145
George Burns CLE 114
Tony Lazzeri NY 114

SLUGGING AVERAGE
Babe Ruth NY .... .737
Al Simmons PHI......... .566
Heinie Manush DET... .564

STOLEN BASES
Johnny Mostil CHI........ 35
Sam Rice WAS 25
Bill Hunnefield CHI........ 24

RUNS SCORED
Babe Ruth NY.............. 139
Lou Gehrig NY 135
Johnny Mostil CHI....... 120

WINS
George Uhle CLE 27
Herb Pennock NY 23
Urban Shocker NY........ 19

WINNING PERCENTAGE
George Uhle CLE ...... .711
Herb Pennock NY ...... .676
Red Faber CHI............ .652

EARNED RUN AVERAGE
Lefty Grove PHI 2.51
George Uhle CLE 2.83
Ted Lyons CHI........... 3.01

STRIKEOUTS
Lefty Grove PHI 194
George Uhle CLE 159
Tommy Thomas CHI.... 127

SAVES
Firpo Marberry WAS..... 22
Hooks Dauss DET 9
two tied at 6

COMPLETE GAMES
George Uhle CLE 32
Ted Lyons CHI.............. 24
Walter Johnson WAS.... 22

SHUTOUTS
Ed Wells DET 4

GAMES PITCHED
Firpo Marberry WAS..... 64
Joe Pate PHI................. 47
Lefty Grove PHI 45

INNINGS PITCHED
George Uhle CLE 318
Ted Lyons CHI............. 284
Herb Pennock NY 266

1926 NL

	W	L	PCT	GB	R	OR	BA	FA	ERA
★ST. LOUIS	89	65	.578	—	817	678	.286	.969	3.67
CINCINNATI	87	67	.565	2	747	651	.290	.972	3.42
PITTSBURGH	84	69	.549	4.5	769	689	.285	.965	3.67
CHICAGO	82	72	.532	7	682	602	.278	.974	3.26
NEW YORK	74	77	.490	13.5	682	668	.278	.970	3.77
BROOKLYN	71	82	.464	17.5	623	705	.263	.963	3.82
BOSTON	66	86	.434	22	624	719	.277	.967	4.03
PHILADELPHIA	58	93	.384	29.5	687	900	.281	.964	5.19
					5612	5612	.280	.968	3.84

BATTING AVERAGE
B. Hargrave CIN .... .353
Christenson CIN .... .350
Earl Smith PIT............ .346

HITS
Eddie Brown BOS....... 201
Kiki Cuyler PIT 197
Sparky Adams CHI 193

DOUBLES
Jim Bottomley STL........ 40
Edd Roush CIN............. 37
Hack Wilson CHI........... 36

TRIPLES
Paul Waner PIT 22
Curt Walker CIN............ 20
Pie Traynor PIT............ 17

HOME RUNS
Hack Wilson CHI........... 21
Jim Bottomley STL........ 19
Cy Williams PHI 18

RUNS BATTED IN
Jim Bottomley STL....... 120
Hack Wilson CHI........... 109
Les Bell STL 100

SLUGGING AVERAGE
Cy Williams PHI .... .568
Hack Wilson CHI........ .539
Paul Waner PIT .... .528

STOLEN BASES
Kiki Cuyler PIT.............. 35
Sparky Adams CHI 27
two tied at 23

RUNS SCORED
Kiki Cuyler PIT 113
Paul Waner PIT 101
two tied at 99

WINS
four tied at..................... 20

WINNING PERCENTAGE
Ray Kremer PIT .... .769
Flint Rhem STL........... .741
Lee Meadows PIT...... .690

EARNED RUN AVERAGE
Ray Kremer PIT 2.61
Charlie Root CHI........ 2.82
Jesse Petty BKN........ 2.84

STRIKEOUTS
Dazzy Vance BKN 140
Charlie Root CHI......... 127
two tied at 103

SAVES
Chick Davies NY............. 6
Ray Kremer PIT 5
Jack Scott NY 5

COMPLETE GAMES
Carl Mays CIN 24
Jesse Petty BKN........... 23
Charlie Root CHI........... 21

SHUTOUTS
Pete Donohue CIN.......... 5
Sheriff Blake CHI 4
Bob Smith BOS............... 4

GAMES PITCHED
Jack Scott NY 50
C. Willoughby PHI......... 47
Pete Donohue CIN........ 47

INNINGS PITCHED
Pete Donohue CIN...... 286
Carl Mays CIN 281
Jesse Petty BKN.......... 276

1927 AL

	W	L	PCT	GB	R	OR	BA	FA	ERA
★NEW YORK	110	44	.714	—	975	599	.307	.969	3.20
PHILADELPHIA	91	63	.591	19	841	726	.303	.970	3.95
WASHINGTON	85	69	.552	25	782	730	.287	.969	3.95
DETROIT	82	71	.536	27.5	845	805	.289	.968	4.12
CHICAGO	70	83	.458	39.5	662	708	.278	.971	3.91
CLEVELAND	66	87	.431	43.5	668	766	.283	.968	4.27
ST. LOUIS	59	94	.386	50.5	724	904	.276	.960	4.95
BOSTON	51	103	.331	59	597	856	.259	.964	4.68
					6094	6094	.285	.967	4.12

BATTING AVERAGE
Harry Heilmann DET.. .398
Al Simmons PHI......... .392
Lou Gehrig NY .... .373

HITS
Earle Combs NY 231
Lou Gehrig NY 218
two tied at 201

DOUBLES
Lou Gehrig NY 52
George Burns CLE 51
Harry Heilmann DET..... 50

TRIPLES
Earle Combs NY 23
Heinie Manush DET...... 18
Lou Gehrig NY 18

HOME RUNS
Babe Ruth NY............... 60
Lou Gehrig NY 47
Tony Lazzeri NY 18

RUNS BATTED IN
Lou Gehrig NY 175
Babe Ruth NY............. 164
two tied at 120

SLUGGING AVERAGE
Babe Ruth NY............. .772
Lou Gehrig NY .... .765
Al Simmons PHI......... .645

STOLEN BASES
George Sisler STL 27
Bob Meusel NY 24
three tied at................... 22

RUNS SCORED
Babe Ruth NY 158
Lou Gehrig NY 149
Earle Combs NY 137

WINS
Waite Hoyt NY 22
Ted Lyons CHI.............. 22
Lefty Grove PHI 20

WINNING PERCENTAGE
Waite Hoyt NY .... .759
Urban Shocker NY...... .750
Wilcy Moore NY .... .731

EARNED RUN AVERAGE
Waite Hoyt NY 2.63
Urban Shocker NY..... 2.84
Ted Lyons CHI........... 2.84

STRIKEOUTS
Lefty Grove PHI 174
Rube Walberg PHI...... 136
Tommy Thomas CHI... 107

SAVES
G. Braxton WAS 13
Wilcy Moore NY 13
two tied at 9

COMPLETE GAMES
Ted Lyons CHI.............. 30
Tommy Thomas CHI..... 24
Waite Hoyt NY 23

SHUTOUTS
Hod Lisenbee WAS 4

GAMES PITCHED
G. Braxton WAS 58
Firpo Marberry WAS..... 56
Lefty Grove PHI 51

INNINGS PITCHED
Tommy Thomas CHI... 308
Ted Lyons CHI............. 308
Willis Hudlin CLE 265

1927 NL

	W	L	PCT	GB	R	OR	BA	FA	ERA
PITTSBURGH	94	60	.610	—	817	659	.305	.969	3.66
ST. LOUIS	92	61	.601	1.5	754	665	.278	.966	3.57
NEW YORK	92	62	.597	2	817	720	.297	.969	3.97
CHICAGO	85	68	.556	8.5	750	661	.284	.971	3.65
CINCINNATI	75	78	.490	18.5	643	653	.278	.973	3.54
BROOKLYN	65	88	.425	28.5	541	619	.253	.963	3.36
BOSTON	60	94	.390	34	651	771	.279	.963	4.22
PHILADELPHIA	51	103	.331	43	678	903	.280	.972	5.35
					5651	5651	.282	.969	3.91

BATTING AVERAGE
Paul Waner PIT .... .380
Rogers Hornsby NY ... .361
Lloyd Waner PIT .... .355

HITS
Paul Waner PIT 237
Lloyd Waner PIT 223
Frankie Frisch STL 208

DOUBLES
R. Stephenson CHI....... 46
Paul Waner PIT 40
two tied at 36

TRIPLES
Paul Waner PIT 17
Jim Bottomley STL....... 15
F. Thompson PHI.......... 14

HOME RUNS
Hack Wilson CHI........... 30
Cy Williams PHI 30
Rogers Hornsby NY...... 26

RUNS BATTED IN
Paul Waner PIT 131
Hack Wilson CHI......... 129
Rogers Hornsby NY.... 125

SLUGGING AVERAGE
Chick Hafey STL......... .590
Rogers Hornsby NY.... .586
Hack Wilson CHI......... .579

STOLEN BASES
Frankie Frisch STL 48
Max Carey BKN 32
Harvey Hendrick BKN... 29

RUNS SCORED
Lloyd Waner PIT 133
Rogers Hornsby NY.... 133
Hack Wilson CHI......... 119

WINS
Charlie Root CHI........... 26
Jesse Haines STL......... 24
Carmen Hill PIT 22

WINNING PERCENTAGE
Benton BOS, NY......... .708
Jesse Haines STL....... .706
two tied at .... .704

EARNED RUN AVERAGE
Ray Kremer PIT 2.47
G. Alexander STL 2.52
Dazzy Vance BKN 2.70

STRIKEOUTS
Dazzy Vance BKN 184
Charlie Root CHI......... 145
Jackie May CIN........... 121

SAVES
Bill Sherdel STL 6
George Mogridge BOS ... 5
Art Nehf CIN, CHI 5

COMPLETE GAMES
Dazzy Vance BKN 25
Jesse Haines STL......... 25
Lee Meadows PIT......... 25

SHUTOUTS
Jesse Haines STL............ 6
Red Lucas CIN 4
Charlie Root CHI............. 4

GAMES PITCHED
Charlie Root CHI......... 48
Jack Scott NY 48
Rube Ehrhardt BKN 46

INNINGS PITCHED
Charlie Root CHI......... 309
Jesse Haines STL....... 301
Lee Meadows PIT....... 299

1928 AL

	W	L	PCT	GB	R	OR	BA	FA	ERA
★NEW YORK	101	53	.656	—	894	685	.296	.968	3.74
PHILADELPHIA	98	55	.641	2.5	829	615	.295	.970	3.36
ST. LOUIS	82	72	.532	19	772	742	.274	.969	4.17
WASHINGTON	75	79	.487	26	718	705	.284	.972	3.88
CHICAGO	72	82	.468	29	656	725	.270	.970	3.98
DETROIT	68	86	.442	33	744	804	.279	.965	4.32
CLEVELAND	62	92	.403	39	674	830	.285	.965	4.47
BOSTON	57	96	.373	43.5	589	770	.264	.971	4.39
					5876	5876	.281	.969	4.04

BATTING AVERAGE
Goose Goslin WAS.... .379
Heinie Manush STL ... .378
Lou Gehrig NY .... .374

HITS
Heinie Manush STL ... 241
Lou Gehrig NY 210
Sam Rice WAS 202

DOUBLES
Lou Gehrig NY 47
Heinie Manush STL 47
Bob Meusel NY 45

TRIPLES
Earle Combs NY 21
Heinie Manush STL 20
C. Gehringer DET 16

HOME RUNS
Babe Ruth NY 54
Lou Gehrig NY 27
Goose Goslin WAS 17

RUNS BATTED IN
Lou Gehrig NY 142
Babe Ruth NY 142
Bob Meusel NY 113

SLUGGING AVERAGE
Babe Ruth NY .... .709
Lou Gehrig NY .... .648
Goose Goslin WAS.... .614

STOLEN BASES
Buddy Myer BOS 30
Johnny Mostil CHI......... 23
Harry Rice DET............. 20

RUNS SCORED
Babe Ruth NY 163
Lou Gehrig NY 139
Earle Combs NY 118

WINS
Lefty Grove PHI 24
George Pipgras NY....... 24
Waite Hoyt NY 23

WINNING PERCENTAGE
G. Crowder STL.......... .808
Waite Hoyt NY .... .767
Lefty Grove PHI .... .750

EARNED RUN AVERAGE
G. Braxton WAS 2.51
Herb Pennock NY 2.56
Lefty Grove PHI 2.58

STRIKEOUTS
Lefty Grove PHI 183
George Pipgras NY..... 139
Tommy Thomas CHI... 129

SAVES
Waite Hoyt NY 8
Willis Hudlin CLE 7
two tied at 6

COMPLETE GAMES
Red Ruffing BOS 25
Lefty Grove PHI 24
Tommy Thomas CHI..... 24

SHUTOUTS
Herb Pennock NY 5
three tied at..................... 4

GAMES PITCHED
Firpo Marberry WAS..... 48
Ed Morris BOS.............. 47
George Pipgras NY....... 46

INNINGS PITCHED
George Pipgras NY..... 301
Red Ruffing BOS 289
Tommy Thomas CHI... 283

1928 NL

	W	L	PCT	GB	R	OR	BA	FA	ERA
ST. LOUIS	95	59	.617	—	807	636	.281	.974	3.38
NEW YORK	93	61	.604	2	807	653	.293	.972	3.67
CHICAGO	91	63	.591	4	714	615	.278	.975	3.40
PITTSBURGH	85	67	.559	9	837	704	.309	.967	3.95
CINCINNATI	78	74	.513	16	648	686	.280	.974	3.94
BROOKLYN	77	76	.503	17.5	665	640	.266	.965	3.25
BOSTON	50	103	.327	44.5	631	878	.275	.969	4.83
PHILADELPHIA	43	109	.283	51	660	957	.267	.971	5.52
					5769	5769	.281	.971	3.98

BATTING AVERAGE
R. Hornsby BOS .... .387
Paul Waner PIT .... .370
Freddie Lindstrom NY .358

HITS
F. Lindstrom NY 231
Paul Waner PIT 223
Lloyd Waner PIT 221

DOUBLES
Paul Waner PIT 50
Chick Hafey STL........... 46
two tied at 42

TRIPLES
Jim Bottomley STL........ 20
Paul Waner PIT 19
Lloyd Waner PIT 14

HOME RUNS
Hack Wilson CHI........... 31
Jim Bottomley STL........ 31
Chick Hafey STL........... 27

RUNS BATTED IN
Jim Bottomley STL........ 136
Pie Traynor PIT............ 124
Hack Wilson CHI......... 120

SLUGGING AVERAGE
R. Hornsby BOS .... .632
Jim Bottomley STL...... .628
Chick Hafey STL........ .604

STOLEN BASES
Kiki Cuyler CHI 37
Frankie Frisch STL 29
two tied at 19

RUNS SCORED
Paul Waner PIT 142
Jim Bottomley STL...... 123
Lloyd Waner PIT 121

WINS
Larry Benton NY 25
Burleigh Grimes PIT 25
Dazzy Vance BKN 22

WINNING PERCENTAGE
Larry Benton NY .... .735
Jesse Haines STL........ .714
Guy Bush CHI............. .714

EARNED RUN AVERAGE
Dazzy Vance BKN 2.09
Sheriff Blake CHI 2.47
Art Nehf CHI 2.65

STRIKEOUTS
Dazzy Vance BKN 200
Pat Malone CHI 155
Charlie Root CHI........ 122

SAVES
Bill Sherdel STL.............. 5
Hal Haid STL 5
two tied at 4

COMPLETE GAMES
Burleigh Grimes PIT 28
Larry Benton NY 28
Dazzy Vance BKN 24

SHUTOUTS
five tied at 4

GAMES PITCHED
Burleigh Grimes PIT 48
Ray Kolp CIN 44
Eppa Rixey CIN 43

INNINGS PITCHED
Burleigh Grimes PIT ... 331
Larry Benton NY 310
Eppa Rixey CIN 291

1929 AL

	W	L	PCT	GB	R	OR	BA	FA	ERA
★PHILADELPHIA	104	46	.693	—	901	615	.296	.975	3.44
NEW YORK	88	66	.571	18	899	775	.295	.971	4.17
CLEVELAND	81	71	.533	24	717	736	.294	.968	4.05
ST. LOUIS	79	73	.520	26	733	713	.276	.975	4.08
WASHINGTON	71	81	.467	34	730	776	.276	.968	4.34
DETROIT	70	84	.455	36	926	928	.299	.961	4.96
CHICAGO	59	93	.388	46	627	792	.268	.970	4.41
BOSTON	58	96	.377	48	605	803	.267	.965	4.43
					6138	6138	.284	.969	4.24

BATTING AVERAGE
Lew Fonseca CLE ...... .369
Al Simmons PHI......... .365
Heinie Manush STL ... .355

HITS
Dale Alexander DET ... 215
C. Gehringer DET 215
Al Simmons PHI.......... 212

DOUBLES
Roy Johnson DET......... 45
C. Gehringer DET 45
Heinie Manush STL 45

TRIPLES
C. Gehringer DET 19
Russ Scarritt BOS......... 17
Bing Miller PHI 16

HOME RUNS
Babe Ruth NY................ 46
Lou Gehrig NY 35
Al Simmons PHI............. 34

RUNS BATTED IN
Al Simmons PHI........... 157
Babe Ruth NY............... 154
Dale Alexander DET ... 137

SLUGGING AVERAGE
Babe Ruth NY............. .697
Al Simmons PHI......... .642
Jimmie Foxx PHI......... .625

STOLEN BASES
C. Gehringer DET 28
Bill Cissell CHI 26
Bing Miller PHI 24

RUNS SCORED
C. Gehringer DET 131
Roy Johnson DET........ 128
Lou Gehrig NY 127

WINS
G. Earnshaw PHI 24
Wes Ferrell CLE 21
Lefty Grove PHI 20

WINNING PERCENTAGE
Lefty Grove PHI .... .769
G. Earnshaw PHI .... .750
Wes Ferrell CLE .... .677

EARNED RUN AVERAGE
Lefty Grove PHI 2.81
F. Marberry WAS......... 3.06
T. Thomas CHI 3.19

STRIKEOUTS
Lefty Grove PHI 170
G. Earnshaw PHI 149
George Pipgras NY..... 125

SAVES
Firpo Marberry WAS 11
Wilcy Moore NY 8
Bill Shores PHI 7

COMPLETE GAMES
Tommy Thomas CHI...... 24
George Uhle DET 23
Sam Gray STL 23

SHUTOUTS
four tied at...................... 4

GAMES PITCHED
Firpo Marberry WAS..... 49
G. Earnshaw PHI 44
two tied at 43

INNINGS PITCHED
Sam Gray STL 305
Willis Hudlin CLE 280
Lefty Grove PHI 275

1929 NL

	W	L	PCT	GB	R	OR	BA	FA	ERA
CHICAGO	98	54	.645	—	982	758	.303	.975	4.16
PITTSBURGH	88	65	.575	10.5	904	780	.303	.970	4.36
NEW YORK	84	67	.556	13.5	897	709	.296	.975	3.97
ST. LOUIS	78	74	.513	20	831	806	.293	.971	4.66
PHILADELPHIA	71	82	.464	27.5	897	1032	.309	.969	6.13
BROOKLYN	70	83	.458	28.5	755	888	.291	.968	4.92
CINCINNATI	66	88	.429	33	686	760	.281	.974	4.41
BOSTON	56	98	.364	43	657	876	.280	.967	5.12
					6609	6609	.294	.971	4.71

BATTING AVERAGE
Lefty O'Doul PHI .... .398
Babe Herman BKN .... .381
R. Hornsby CHI.......... .380

HITS
Lefty O'Doul PHI 254
Lloyd Waner PIT 234
Rogers Hornsby CHI... 229

DOUBLES
J. Frederick BKN........... 52
Rogers Hornsby CHI..... 47
Chick Hafey STL........... 47

TRIPLES
Lloyd Waner PIT 20
Curt Walker CIN............ 15
Paul Waner PIT 15

HOME RUNS
Chuck Klein PHI............ 43
Mel Ott NY 42
two tied at 39

RUNS BATTED IN
Hack Wilson CHI......... 159
Mel Ott NY 151
Rogers Hornsby CHI... 149

SLUGGING AVERAGE
R. Hornsby CHI.......... .679
Chuck Klein PHI......... .657
Mel Ott NY .... .635

STOLEN BASES
Kiki Cuyler CHI 43
Evar Swanson CIN 33
Frankie Frisch STL 24

RUNS SCORED
Rogers Hornsby CHI... 156
Lefty O'Doul PHI 152
Mel Ott NY 138

WINS
Pat Malone CHI 22
Red Lucas CIN 19
Charlie Root CHI........... 19

WINNING PERCENTAGE
Charlie Root CHI........ .760
Guy Bush CHI............ .720
B. Grimes PIT .... .708

EARNED RUN AVERAGE
Bill Walker NY 3.09
B. Grimes PIT 3.13
Charlie Root CHI........ 3.47

STRIKEOUTS
Pat Malone CHI 166
Watty Clark BKN......... 140
Dazzy Vance BKN 126

SAVES
Johnny Morrison BKN..... 8
Guy Bush CHI................ 8
Lou Koupal BKN, PHI 6

COMPLETE GAMES
Red Lucas CIN 28

SHUTOUTS
Pat Malone CHI 5
F. Fitzimmons NY 4
Charlie Root CHI............. 4

GAMES PITCHED
Guy Bush CHI............... 50
C. Willoughby PHI......... 49
two tied at 43

INNINGS PITCHED
Watty Clark BKN......... 279
Charlie Root CHI......... 272
Guy Bush CHI............. 271

1930 AL

	W	L	PCT	GB	R	OR	BA	FA	ERA
PHILADELPHIA	102	52	.662	—	951	751	.294	.975	4.28
WASHINGTON	94	60	.610	8	892	689	.302	.974	3.96
NEW YORK	86	68	.558	16	1062	898	.309	.965	4.88
CLEVELAND	81	73	.526	21	890	915	.304	.962	4.88
DETROIT	75	79	.487	27	783	833	.284	.967	4.70
ST. LOUIS	64	90	.416	38	751	886	.268	.970	5.07
CHICAGO	62	92	.403	40	729	884	.276	.962	4.71
BOSTON	52	102	.338	50	612	814	.264	.968	4.70
					6670	6670	.288	.968	4.65

BATTING AVERAGE
Al Simmons PHI........ .381
Lou Gehrig NY .... .379
two tied at .... .359

HITS
Johnny Hodapp CLE... 225
Lou Gehrig NY 220
Al Simmons PHI......... 211

DOUBLES
Johnny Hodapp CLE..... 51
Manush STL, WAS 49
two tied at 47

TRIPLES
Earle Combs NY 22
Carl Reynolds CHI 18
Lou Gehrig NY 17

HOME RUNS
Babe Ruth NY 49
Lou Gehrig NY 41
two tied at 37

RUNS BATTED IN
Lou Gehrig NY 174
Al Simmons PHI.......... 165
Jimmie Foxx PHI......... 156

SLUGGING AVERAGE
Babe Ruth NY .... .732
Lou Gehrig NY .... .721
Al Simmons PHI......... .708

STOLEN BASES
Marty McManus DET 23
C. Gehringer DET 19
three tied at.................. 17

RUNS SCORED
Al Simmons PHI.......... 152
Babe Ruth NY 150
C. Gehringer DET 144

WINS
Lefty Grove PHI 28
Wes Ferrell CLE 25
two tied at 22

WINNING PERCENTAGE
Lefty Grove PHI .... .848
F. Marberry WAS .... .750
Sam Jones WAS........ .682

EARNED RUN AVERAGE
Lefty Grove PHI 2.54
Wes Ferrell CLE 3.31
Lefty Stewart STL 3.45

STRIKEOUTS
Lefty Grove PHI 209
G. Earnshaw PHI 193
Bump Hadley WAS 162

SAVES
Lefty Grove PHI 9
G. Braxton CHI, WAS 6
Jack Quinn PHI............... 6

COMPLETE GAMES
Ted Lyons CHI............... 29
Crowder STL, WAS 25
Wes Ferrell CLE 25

SHUTOUTS
George Pipgras NY......... 3
George Earnshaw PHI.... 3

GAMES PITCHED
Lefty Grove PHI 50
G. Earnshaw PHI 49
two tied at 44

INNINGS PITCHED
Ted Lyons CHI............. 298
Wes Ferrell CLE 297
G. Earnshaw PHI........ 296

1930 NL

	W	L	PCT	GB	R	OR	BA	FA	ERA
ST. LOUIS	92	62	.597	—	1004	784	.314	.970	4.40
CHICAGO	90	64	.584	2	998	870	.309	.973	4.80
NEW YORK	87	67	.565	5	959	814	.319	.974	4.59
BROOKLYN	86	68	.558	6	871	738	.304	.972	4.03
PITTSBURGH	80	74	.519	12	891	928	.303	.965	5.24
BOSTON	70	84	.455	22	693	835	.281	.971	4.91
CINCINNATI	59	95	.383	33	665	857	.281	.973	5.08
PHILADELPHIA	52	102	.338	40	944	1199	.315	.962	6.71
					7025	7025	.303	.970	4.97

BATTING AVERAGE
Bill Terry NY .... .401
Babe Herman BKN .... .393
Chuck Klein PHI .... .386

HITS
Bill Terry NY 254
Chuck Klein PHI 250
Babe Herman BKN 241

DOUBLES
Chuck Klein PHI 59
Kiki Cuyler CHI 50
Babe Herman BKN 48

TRIPLES
Adam Comorosky PIT ... 23
Paul Waner PIT 18
two tied at 17

HOME RUNS
Hack Wilson CHI 56
Chuck Klein PHI 40
Wally Berger BOS 38

RUNS BATTED IN
Hack Wilson CHI 190
Chuck Klein PHI 170
Kiki Cuyler CHI 134

SLUGGING AVERAGE
Hack Wilson CHI .... .723
Chuck Klein PHI .... .687
Babe Herman BKN .... .678

STOLEN BASES
Kiki Cuyler CHI 37
Babe Herman BKN 18
Paul Waner PIT 18

RUNS SCORED
Chuck Klein PHI 158
Kiki Cuyler CHI 155
Woody English CHI 152

WINS
Ray Kremer PIT 20
Pat Malone CHI 20
Fitzsimmons NY 19

WINNING PERCENTAGE
Fitzsimmons NY .... .731
Pat Malone CHI .... .690
Erv Brame PIT .... .680

EARNED RUN AVERAGE
Dazzy Vance BKN 2.61
Carl Hubbell NY 3.76
Bill Walker NY 3.93

STRIKEOUTS
Bill Hallahan STL 177
Dazzy Vance BKN 173
Pat Malone CHI 142

SAVES
Hi Bell STL 8
Joe Heving NY 6
Watty Clark BKN 6

COMPLETE GAMES
Erv Brame PIT 22
Pat Malone CHI 22
Larry French PIT 21

SHUTOUTS
Charlie Root CHI 4
Dazzy Vance BKN 4
two tied at 3

GAMES PITCHED
Hal Elliot PHI 48
Phil Collins PHI 47
Guy Bush CHI 46

INNINGS PITCHED
Ray Kremer PIT 276
Larry French PIT 275
Pat Malone CHI 272

1931 AL

	W	L	PCT	GB	R	OR	BA	FA	ERA
PHILADELPHIA	107	45	.704	—	858	626	.287	.976	3.47
NEW YORK	94	59	.614	13.5	1067	760	.297	.972	4.20
WASHINGTON	92	62	.597	16	843	691	.285	.976	3.76
CLEVELAND	78	76	.506	30	885	833	.296	.963	4.63
ST. LOUIS	63	91	.409	45	772	870	.271	.963	4.76
BOSTON	62	90	.408	45	625	800	.262	.970	4.60
DETROIT	61	93	.396	47	651	836	.268	.964	4.56
CHICAGO	56	97	.366	51.5	704	939	.260	.961	5.05
					6355	6355	.278	.968	4.38

BATTING AVERAGE
Al Simmons PHI......... .390
Babe Ruth NY............. .373
Ed Morgan CLE .... .351

HITS
Lou Gehrig NY 211
Earl Averill CLE........... 209
Al Simmons PHI.......... 200

DOUBLES
Earl Webb BOS 67
Dale Alexander DET 47
Red Kress STL 46

TRIPLES
Roy Johnson DET......... 19
Lou Gehrig NY 15
Lu Blue CHI 15

HOME RUNS
Lou Gehrig NY 46
Babe Ruth NY.............. 46
Earl Averill CLE............ 32

RUNS BATTED IN
Lou Gehrig NY 184
Babe Ruth NY............. 163
Earl Averill CLE........... 143

SLUGGING AVERAGE
Babe Ruth NY............. .700
Lou Gehrig NY .... .662
Al Simmons PHI.......... .641

STOLEN BASES
Ben Chapman NY......... 61
Roy Johnson DET........ 33
Jack Burns STL 19

RUNS SCORED
Lou Gehrig NY 163
Babe Ruth NY............. 149
Earl Averill CLE........... 140

WINS
Lefty Grove PHI 31
Wes Ferrell CLE 22
two tied at 21

WINNING PERCENTAGE
Lefty Grove PHI .... .886
F. Marberry WAS .... .800
Roy Mahaffey PHI...... .789

EARNED RUN AVERAGE
Lefty Grove PHI 2.06
Lefty Gomez NY 2.63
Lloyd Brown WAS...... 3.20

STRIKEOUTS
Lefty Grove PHI 175
G. Earnshaw PHI 152
Lefty Gomez NY 150

SAVES
Wilcy Moore BOS 10
Bump Hadley WAS........ 8
two tied at 7

COMPLETE GAMES
Lefty Grove PHI 27
Wes Ferrell CLE 27
G. Earnshaw PHI.......... 23

SHUTOUTS
Lefty Grove PHI 4
G. Earnshaw PHI............ 3

GAMES PITCHED
Bump Hadley WAS..... 55
Wilcy Moore BOS 53
Pat Caraway CHI 51

INNINGS PITCHED
Rube Walberg PHI...... 291
Lefty Grove PHI 289
G. Earnshaw PHI 282

1931 NL

	W	L	PCT	GB	R	OR	BA	FA	ERA
★ST. LOUIS	101	53	.656	—	815	614	.286	.974	3.45
NEW YORK	87	65	.572	13	768	599	.289	.974	3.30
CHICAGO	84	70	.545	17	828	710	.289	.973	3.97
BROOKLYN	79	73	.520	21	681	673	.276	.969	3.84
PITTSBURGH	75	79	.487	26	636	691	.266	.968	3.66
PHILADELPHIA	66	88	.429	35	684	828	.279	.966	4.58
BOSTON	64	90	.416	37	533	680	.258	.973	3.90
CINCINNATI	58	96	.377	43	592	742	.269	.973	4.22
					5537	5537	.277	.971	3.86

BATTING AVERAGE
Chick Hafey STL........ .349
Bill Terry NY............... .349
Jim Bottomley STL..... .348

HITS
Lloyd Waner PIT 214
Bill Terry NY 213
two tied at 202

DOUBLES
Sparky Adams STL....... 46
Wally Berger BOS......... 44
two tied at 43

TRIPLES
Bill Terry NY................. 20
Babe Herman BKN 16
Pie Traynor PIT............. 15

HOME RUNS
Chuck Klein PHI............ 31
Mel Ott NY 29
Wally Berger BOS......... 19

RUNS BATTED IN
Chuck Klein PHI.......... 121
Mel Ott NY 115
Bill Terry NY................ 112

SLUGGING AVERAGE
Chuck Klein PHI.......... .584
R. Hornsby CHI........... .574
Chick Hafey STL......... .569

STOLEN BASES
Frankie Frisch STL 28
Babe Herman BKN 17
two tied at 16

RUNS SCORED
Chuck Klein PHI........... 121
Bill Terry NY................ 121
Woody English CHI..... 117

WINS
Bill Hallahan STL 19
Heinie Meine PIT 19
Jumbo Elliott PHI 19

WINNING PERCENTAGE
Paul Derringer STL...... .692
Bill Hallahan STL .... .679
Guy Bush CHI............. .667

EARNED RUN AVERAGE
Bill Walker NY............. 2.26
Carl Hubbell NY 2.66
Ed Brandt BOS 2.92

STRIKEOUTS
Bill Hallahan STL 159
Carl Hubbell NY 156
Dazzy Vance BKN 150

SAVES
Jack Quinn BKN 15
Jim Lindsey STL 7
Jumbo Elliott PHI 5

COMPLETE GAMES
Red Lucas CIN 24
Ed Brandt BOS 23
Heinie Meine PIT 22

SHUTOUTS
Bill Walker NY 6
three tied at..................... 4

GAMES PITCHED
Jumbo Elliot PHI 52
Syl Johnson CIN 42
Phil Collins PHI 42

INNINGS PITCHED
Heinie Meine PIT 284
Larry French PIT........ 276
Syl Johnson CIN 262

1932 AL

	W	L	PCT	GB	R	OR	BA	FA	ERA
★NEW YORK	107	47	.695	—	1002	724	.286	.969	3.98
PHILADELPHIA	94	60	.610	13	981	752	.290	.979	4.45
WASHINGTON	93	61	.604	14	840	716	.284	.979	4.16
CLEVELAND	87	65	.572	19	845	747	.285	.969	4.12
DETROIT	76	75	.503	29.5	799	787	.273	.969	4.30
ST. LOUIS	63	91	.409	44	736	898	.276	.969	5.01
CHICAGO	49	102	.325	56.5	667	897	.267	.958	4.82
BOSTON	43	111	.279	64	566	915	.251	.963	5.02
					6436	6436	.277	.969	4.48

BATTING AVERAGE
Alexander DET, BOS. .367
Jimmie Foxx PHI........ .364
Lou Gehrig NY .... .349

HITS
Al Simmons PHI.......... 216
Heinie Manush WAS... 214
Jimmie Foxx PHI........ 213

DOUBLES
Eric McNair PHI........... 47
C. Gehringer DET......... 44
Joe Cronin WAS 43

TRIPLES
Joe Cronin WAS 18
Tony Lazzeri NY 16
Buddy Myer WAS 16

HOME RUNS
Jimmie Foxx PHI.......... 58
Babe Ruth NY............... 41
Al Simmons PHI............ 35

RUNS BATTED IN
Jimmie Foxx PHI.......... 169
Lou Gehrig NY 151
Al Simmons PHI........... 151

SLUGGING AVERAGE
Jimmie Foxx PHI.......... .749
Babe Ruth NY............. .661
Lou Gehrig NY .... .621

STOLEN BASES
Ben Chapman NY......... 38
Gee Walker DET........... 30
Johnson BOS, DET 20

RUNS SCORED
Jimmie Foxx PHI......... 151
Al Simmons PHI........... 144
Earle Combs NY 143

WINS
G. Crowder WAS 26
Lefty Grove PHI 25
Lefty Gomez NY 24

WINNING PERCENTAGE
Johnny Allen NY .... .810
Lefty Gomez NY .... .774
Red Ruffing NY.......... .720

EARNED RUN AVERAGE
Lefty Grove PHI 2.84
Red Ruffing NY.......... 3.09
Ted Lyons CHI........... 3.28

STRIKEOUTS
Red Ruffing NY........... 190
Lefty Grove PHI 188
Lefty Gomez NY 176

SAVES
Firpo Marberry WAS..... 13
Wilcy Moore BOS, NY 8
two tied at 7

COMPLETE GAMES
Lefty Grove PHI 27
Wes Ferrell CLE 26
Red Ruffing NY 22

SHUTOUTS
Tommy Bridges DET 4
Lefty Grove PHI 4

GAMES PITCHED
Firpo Marberry WAS..... 54
Sam Gray STL.............. 52
G. Crowder WAS 50

INNINGS PITCHED
G. Crowder WAS 327
Lefty Grove PHI 292
Wes Ferrell CLE 288

1932 NL

	W	L	PCT	GB	R	OR	BA	FA	ERA
CHICAGO	90	64	.584	—	720	633	.278	.973	3.44
PITTSBURGH	86	68	.558	4	701	711	.285	.969	3.75
BROOKLYN	81	73	.526	9	752	747	.283	.971	4.28
PHILADELPHIA	78	76	.506	12	844	796	.292	.968	4.47
BOSTON	77	77	.500	13	649	655	.265	.976	3.53
NEW YORK	72	82	.468	18	755	706	.276	.969	3.83
ST. LOUIS	72	82	.468	18	684	717	.269	.971	3.97
CINCINNATI	60	94	.390	30	575	715	.263	.971	3.79
					5680	5680	.276	.971	3.88

BATTING AVERAGE
Lefty O'Doul BKN....... .368
Bill Terry NY............... .350
Chuck Klein PHI....... .348

HITS
Chuck Klein PHI.......... 226
Bill Terry NY................ 225
Lefty O'Doul BKN....... 219

DOUBLES
Paul Waner PIT 62
Chuck Klein PHI........... 50
R. Stephenson CHI....... 49

TRIPLES
Babe Herman CIN 19
Gus Suhr PIT 16
Chuck Klein PHI........... 15

HOME RUNS
Chuck Klein PHI........... 38
Mel Ott NY 38
Bill Terry NY................. 28

RUNS BATTED IN
Don Hurst PHI............. 143
Chuck Klein PHI.......... 137
Pinky Whitney PHI...... 124

SLUGGING AVERAGE
Chuck Klein PHI......... .646
Mel Ott NY .... .601
Bill Terry NY............... .580

STOLEN BASES
Chuck Klein PHI............. 20
Tony Piet PIT 19
two tied at 18

RUNS SCORED
Chuck Klein PHI......... 152
Bill Terry NY................ 124
Lefty O'Doul BKN....... 120

WINS
Lon Warneke CHI 22
Watty Clark BKN.......... 20
Guy Bush CHI............... 19

WINNING PERCENTAGE
Lon Warneke CHI ...... .786
Guy Bush CHI............. .633
two tied at .... .625

EARNED RUN AVERAGE
Lon Warneke CHI 2.37
Carl Hubbell NY 2.50
Huck Betts BOS......... 2.80

STRIKEOUTS
Dizzy Dean STL.......... 191
Carl Hubbell NY 137
Pat Malone CHI 120

SAVES
Jack Quinn BKN 8
Ray Benge PHI 6
two tied at 5

COMPLETE GAMES
Red Lucas CIN 28
Lon Warneke CHI 25
Carl Hubbell NY 22

SHUTOUTS
Dizzy Dean STL.............. 4
Steve Swetonic PIT 4
Lon Warneke CHI 4

GAMES PITCHED
Larry French PIT........... 47
Dizzy Dean STL............ 46
Tex Carleton STL.......... 44

INNINGS PITCHED
Dizzy Dean STL.......... 286
Carl Hubbell NY 284
Lon Warneke CHI 277

1933 AL

	W	L	PCT	GB	R	OR	BA	FA	ERA
WASHINGTON	99	53	.651	—	850	665	.287	.979	3.82
NEW YORK	91	59	.607	7	927	768	.283	.972	4.36
PHILADELPHIA	79	72	.523	19.5	875	853	.285	.966	4.81
CLEVELAND	75	76	.497	23.5	654	669	.261	.974	3.71
DETROIT	75	79	.487	25	722	733	.269	.971	3.96
CHICAGO	67	83	.447	31	683	814	.272	.970	4.45
BOSTON	63	86	.423	34.5	700	758	.271	.966	4.35
ST. LOUIS	55	96	.364	43.5	669	820	.253	.976	4.82
					6080	6080	.273	.972	4.28

BATTING AVERAGE
Jimmie Foxx PHI......... .356
H. Manush WAS .... .336
Lou Gehrig NY .... .334

HITS
Heinie Manush WAS... 221
C. Gehringer DET 204
Jimmie Foxx PHI......... 204

DOUBLES
Joe Cronin WAS 45
Bob Johnson PHI........... 44
Jack Burns STL 43

TRIPLES
Heinie Manush WAS..... 17
Earl Averill CLE............. 16
Earle Combs NY 16

HOME RUNS
Jimmie Foxx PHI........... 48
Babe Ruth NY 34
Lou Gehrig NY 32

RUNS BATTED IN
Jimmie Foxx PHI......... 163
Lou Gehrig NY 139
Al Simmons CHI 119

SLUGGING AVERAGE
Jimmie Foxx PHI........ .703
Lou Gehrig NY .... .605
Babe Ruth NY .... .582

STOLEN BASES
Ben Chapman NY......... 27
Gee Walker DET........... 26
Evar Swanson CHI 19

RUNS SCORED
Lou Gehrig NY 138
Jimmie Foxx PHI......... 125
Heinie Manush WAS... 115

WINS
Lefty Grove PHI 24
G. Crowder WAS 24
Earl Whitehill WAS........ 22

WINNING PERCENTAGE
Lefty Grove PHI .... .750
Earl Whitehill WAS...... .733
Lefty Stewart WAS...... .714

EARNED RUN AVERAGE
Monte Pearson CLE .. 2.33
Mel Harder CLE 2.95
T. Bridges DET 3.09

STRIKEOUTS
Lefty Gomez NY 163
Bump Hadley STL....... 149
Red Ruffing NY............ 122

SAVES
Jack Russell WAS 13
Chief Hogsett DET 9
Wilcy Moore NY 8

COMPLETE GAMES
Lefty Grove PHI 21
Bump Hadley STL......... 19
Earl Whitehill WAS........ 19

SHUTOUTS
Oral Hildebrand CLE....... 6
Lefty Gomez NY 4
G. Blaeholder STL 3

GAMES PITCHED
G. Crowder WAS 52
Jack Russell WAS 50
Johnny Welch BOS....... 47

INNINGS PITCHED
Bump Hadley STL....... 317
G. Crowder WAS 299
Lefty Grove PHI 275

1933 NL

	W	L	PCT	GB	R	OR	BA	FA	ERA
★NEW YORK	91	61	.599	—	636	515	.263	.973	2.71
PITTSBURGH	87	67	.565	5	667	619	.285	.972	3.27
CHICAGO	86	68	.558	6	646	536	.271	.973	2.93
BOSTON	83	71	.539	9	552	531	.252	.978	2.96
ST. LOUIS	82	71	.536	9.5	687	609	.276	.973	3.37
BROOKLYN	65	88	.425	26.5	617	695	.263	.971	3.73
PHILADELPHIA	60	92	.395	31	607	760	.274	.970	4.34
CINCINNATI	58	94	.382	33	496	643	.246	.971	3.42
					4908	4908	.266	.973	3.34

BATTING AVERAGE
Chuck Klein PHI......... .368
Spud Davis PHI .... .349
Tony Piet PIT .... .323

HITS
Chuck Klein PHI........... 223
Chick Fullis PHI 200
Paul Waner PIT 191

DOUBLES
Chuck Klein PHI............. 44
Joe Medwick STL 40
F. Lindstrom PIT 39

TRIPLES
Arky Vaughan PIT......... 19
Paul Waner PIT 16
two tied at 12

HOME RUNS
Chuck Klein PHI............. 28
Wally Berger BOS......... 27
Mel Ott NY 23

RUNS BATTED IN
Chuck Klein PHI............ 120
Wally Berger BOS........ 106
Mel Ott NY 103

SLUGGING AVERAGE
Chuck Klein PHI.......... .602
Wally Berger BOS....... .566
Babe Herman CHI ..... .502

STOLEN BASES
Pepper Martin STL........ 26
Chick Fullis PHI 18
Frankie Frisch STL 18

RUNS SCORED
Pepper Martin STL...... 122
Chuck Klein PHI.......... 101
Paul Waner PIT 101

WINS
Carl Hubbell NY 23
three tied at................... 20

WINNING PERCENTAGE
Ben Cantwell BOS ..... .667
Carl Hubbell NY .... .657
Heinie Meine PIT .... .652

EARNED RUN AVERAGE
Carl Hubbell NY 1.66
Lon Warneke CHI 2.00
H. Schumacher NY 2.16

STRIKEOUTS
Dizzy Dean STL........... 199
Carl Hubbell NY 156
Tex Carlton STL........... 147

SAVES
Phil Collins PHI 6
three tied at...................... 5

COMPLETE GAMES
Dizzy Dean STL............. 26
Lon Warneke CHI 26
Ed Brandt BOS 23

SHUTOUTS
Carl Hubbell NY 10
Hal Schumacher NY 7
Larry French PIT............. 5

GAMES PITCHED
Dizzy Dean STL............. 48
Larry French PIT............ 47
two tied at 45

INNINGS PITCHED
Carl Hubbell NY 309
Dizzy Dean STL........... 293
Larry French PIT......... 291

1934 AL

	W	L	PCT	GB	R	OR	BA	FA	ERA
DETROIT	101	53	.656	—	958	708	.300	.974	4.06
NEW YORK	94	60	.610	7	842	669	.278	.973	3.76
CLEVELAND	85	69	.552	16	814	763	.287	.972	4.28
BOSTON	76	76	.500	24	820	775	.274	.969	4.32
PHILADELPHIA	68	82	.453	31	764	838	.280	.967	5.01
ST. LOUIS	67	85	.441	33	674	800	.268	.969	4.49
WASHINGTON	66	86	.434	34	729	806	.278	.974	4.68
CHICAGO	53	99	.349	47	704	946	.263	.966	5.41
					6305	6305	.279	.970	4.50

BATTING AVERAGE
Lou Gehrig NY .... .363
C. Gehringer DET .... .356
H. Manush WAS .... .349

HITS
C. Gehringer DET 214
Lou Gehrig NY 210
Hal Trosky CLE 206

DOUBLES
Hank Greenberg DET ... 63
C. Gehringer DET 50
Earl Averill CLE 48

TRIPLES
Ben Chapman NY 13
Heinie Manush WAS 11

HOME RUNS
Lou Gehrig NY 49
Jimmie Foxx PHI 44
Hal Trosky CLE 35

RUNS BATTED IN
Lou Gehrig NY 165
Hal Trosky CLE 142
H. Greenberg DET 139

SLUGGING AVERAGE
Lou Gehrig NY ..... .706
Jimmie Foxx PHI .... .653
H. Greenberg DET .... .600

STOLEN BASES
Bill Werber BOS 40
Jo-Jo White DET 28
Ben Chapman NY 26

RUNS SCORED
C. Gehringer DET 134
Bill Werber BOS 129
two tied at 128

WINS
Lefty Gomez NY 26
S. Rowe DET 24
Tommy Bridges DET 22

WINNING PERCENTAGE
Lefty Gomez NY .... .839
S. Rowe DET .... .750
Firpo Marberry DET ... .750

EARNED RUN AVERAGE
Lefty Gomez NY 2.33
Mel Harder CLE 2.61
Johnny Murphy NY 3.12

STRIKEOUTS
Lefty Gomez NY 158
T. Bridges DET 151
two tied at 149

SAVES
Jack Russell WAS 7
Lloyd Brown CLE 6
Bobo Newsom STL 5

COMPLETE GAMES
Lefty Gomez NY 25
Tommy Bridges DET 23
Ted Lyons CHI 21

SHUTOUTS
Mel Harder CLE 6
Lefty Gomez NY 6
Red Ruffing NY 5

GAMES PITCHED
Jack Russell WAS 54
Bobo Newsom STL 47
two tied at 45

INNINGS PITCHED
Lefty Gomez NY 282
T. Bridges DET 275
S. Rowe DET 266

1934 NL

	W	L	PCT	GB	R	OR	BA	FA	ERA
★ST. LOUIS	95	58	.621	—	799	656	.288	.972	3.69
NEW YORK	93	60	.608	2	760	583	.275	.972	3.19
CHICAGO	86	65	.570	8	705	639	.279	.977	3.76
BOSTON	78	73	.517	16	683	714	.272	.972	4.11
PITTSBURGH	74	76	.493	19.5	735	713	.287	.975	4.20
BROOKLYN	71	81	.467	23.5	748	795	.281	.970	4.48
PHILADELPHIA	56	93	.376	37	675	794	.284	.966	4.76
CINCINNATI	52	99	.344	42	590	801	.266	.970	4.37
					5695	5695	.279	.972	4.06

BATTING AVERAGE
Paul Waner PIT .... .362
Bill Terry NY................ .354
Kiki Cuyler CHI .... .338

HITS
Paul Waner PIT 217
Bill Terry NY................ 213
Ripper Collins STL...... 200

DOUBLES
Kiki Cuyler CHI 42
Ethan Allen PHI 42
Arky Vaughan PIT......... 41

TRIPLES
Joe Medwick STL 18
Paul Waner PIT 16
Gus Suhr PIT 13

HOME RUNS
Mel Ott NY 35
Ripper Collins STL........ 35
Wally Berger BOS......... 34

RUNS BATTED IN
Mel Ott NY 135
Ripper Collins STL....... 128
Wally Berger BOS....... 121

SLUGGING AVERAGE
Ripper Collins STL..... .615
Mel Ott NY .... .591
Wally Berger BOS..... .546

STOLEN BASES
Pepper Martin STL 23
Kiki Cuyler CHI 15
Dick Bartell PHI............ 13

RUNS SCORED
Paul Waner PIT 122
Mel Ott NY 119
Ripper Collins STL...... 116

WINS
Dizzy Dean STL............ 30
Hal Schumacher NY 23
Lon Warneke CHI 22

WINNING PERCENTAGE
Dizzy Dean STL.......... .811
Waite Hoyt PIT........... .714
H. Schumacher NY .... .697

EARNED RUN AVERAGE
Carl Hubbell NY 2.30
Dizzy Dean STL......... 2.66
Curt Davis PHI 2.95

STRIKEOUTS
Dizzy Dean STL.......... 195
Van Mungo BKN 184
Paul Dean STL 150

SAVES
Carl Hubbell NY 8
Dizzy Dean STL.............. 7
Dolf Luque NY 7

COMPLETE GAMES
Dizzy Dean STL............ 24
Carl Hubbell NY 23
Lon Warneke CHI 23

SHUTOUTS
Dizzy Dean STL.............. 7
Carl Hubbell NY 5
Paul Dean STL 5

GAMES PITCHED
Curt Davis PHI 51
Dizzy Dean STL............ 50
Snipe Hansen PHI 50

INNINGS PITCHED
Van Mungo BKN 315
Carl Hubbell NY 313
Dizzy Dean STL........... 312

1935 AL

	W	L	PCT	GB	R	OR	BA	FA	ERA
★DETROIT	93	58	.616	—	919	665	.290	.978	3.82
NEW YORK	89	60	.597	3	818	632	.280	.974	3.60
CLEVELAND	82	71	.536	12	776	739	.284	.972	4.15
BOSTON	78	75	.510	16	718	732	.276	.969	4.05
CHICAGO	74	78	.487	19.5	738	750	.275	.976	4.38
WASHINGTON	67	86	.438	27	823	903	.285	.972	5.25
ST. LOUIS	65	87	.428	28.5	718	930	.270	.970	5.26
PHILADELPHIA	58	91	.389	34	710	869	.279	.968	5.12
					6220	6220	.280	.972	4.45

BATTING AVERAGE
Buddy Myer WAS ...... .349
Joe Vosmik CLE .... .348
Jimmie Foxx PHI .... .346

HITS
Joe Vosmik CLE 216
Buddy Myer WAS 215
Doc Cramer PHI 214

DOUBLES
Joe Vosmik CLE 47
Hank Greenberg DET ... 46
Solters BOS, STL 45

TRIPLES
Joe Vosmik CLE 20
John Stone WAS 18
Hank Greenberg DET ... 16

HOME RUNS
Hank Greenberg DET ... 36
Jimmie Foxx PHI........... 36
Lou Gehrig NY 30

RUNS BATTED IN
H. Greenberg DET...... 170
Lou Gehrig NY 119
Jimmie Foxx PHI........ 115

SLUGGING AVERAGE
Jimmie Foxx PHI......... .636
H. Greenberg DET..... .628
Lou Gehrig NY .... .583

STOLEN BASES
Bill Werber BOS............ 29
Lyn Lary WAS, STL 28
Mel Almada BOS 20

RUNS SCORED
Lou Gehrig NY 125
C. Gehringer DET 123
H. Greenberg DET...... 121

WINS
Wes Ferrell BOS........... 25
Mel Harder CLE............ 22
T. Bridges DET 21

WINNING PERCENTAGE
Eldon Auker DET .... .720
Johnny Broaca NY..... .682
T. Bridges DET .... .677

EARNED RUN AVERAGE
Lefty Grove BOS........ 2.70
Ted Lyons CHI............ 3.02
Red Ruffing NY.......... 3.12

STRIKEOUTS
T. Bridges DET 163
S. Rowe DET............... 140
Lefty Gomez NY 138

SAVES
Jack Knott STL 7
five tied at 5

COMPLETE GAMES
Wes Ferrell BOS........... 31
Lefty Grove BOS........... 23
Tommy Bridges DET 23

SHUTOUTS
Schoolboy Rowe DET..... 6
Tommy Bridges DET 4
Mel Harder CLE.............. 4

GAMES PITCHED
R. Van Atta NY, STL..... 58
Jim Walkup STL............. 55
Ivy Andrews STL............ 50

INNINGS PITCHED
Wes Ferrell BOS.......... 322
Mel Harder CLE 287
Earl Whitehill WAS...... 279

1935 NL

	W	L	PCT	GB	R	OR	BA	FA	ERA
CHICAGO	100	54	.649	—	847	597	.288	.970	3.26
ST. LOUIS	96	58	.623	4	829	625	.284	.972	3.54
NEW YORK	91	62	.595	8.5	770	675	.286	.972	3.78
PITTSBURGH	86	67	.562	13.5	743	647	.285	.968	3.42
BROOKLYN	70	83	.458	29.5	711	767	.277	.969	4.22
CINCINNATI	68	85	.444	31.5	646	772	.265	.966	4.30
PHILADELPHIA	64	89	.418	35.5	685	871	.269	.963	4.76
BOSTON	38	115	.248	61.5	575	852	.263	.967	4.93
					5806	5806	.277	.968	4.02

BATTING AVERAGE
Arky Vaughan PIT...... .385
Joe Medwick STL ...... .353
Gabby Hartnett CHI ... .344

HITS
Billy Herman CHI........ 227
Joe Medwick STL 224
two tied at 203

DOUBLES
Billy Herman CHI.......... 57
Ethan Allen PHI 46
Joe Medwick STL 46

TRIPLES
Ival Goodman CIN 18
Lloyd Waner PIT 14
Joe Medwick STL 13

HOME RUNS
Wally Berger BOS......... 34
Mel Ott NY 31
Dolf Camilli PHI............. 25

RUNS BATTED IN
Wally Berger BOS....... 130
Joe Medwick STL 126
Ripper Collins STL...... 122

SLUGGING AVERAGE
Arky Vaughan PIT...... .607
Joe Medwick STL ...... .576
Mel Ott NY .... .555

STOLEN BASES
Augie Galan CHI........... 22
Pepper Martin STL....... 20
Bordagaray BKN.......... 18

RUNS SCORED
Augie Galan CHI......... 133
Joe Medwick STL 132
Pepper Martin STL..... 121

WINS
Dizzy Dean STL............ 28
Carl Hubbell NY 23
Paul Derringer CIN 22

WINNING PERCENTAGE
Bill Lee CHI................ .769
Slick Castleman NY .. .714
Dizzy Dean STL......... .700

EARNED RUN AVERAGE
Cy Blanton PIT............ 2.58
Bill Swift PIT............... 2.70
H. Schumacher NY 2.89

STRIKEOUTS
Dizzy Dean STL.......... 182
Carl Hubbell NY 150
two tied at 143

SAVES
Dutch Leonard BKN........ 8
Waite Hoyt PIT............... 6
Syl Johnson PHI 6

COMPLETE GAMES
Dizzy Dean STL............ 29
Carl Hubbell NY 24
Cy Blanton PIT.............. 23

SHUTOUTS
five tied at 4

GAMES PITCHED
Orville Jorgens PHI....... 53
Dizzy Dean STL............ 50
Jim Biven PHI 47

INNINGS PITCHED
Dizzy Dean STL.......... 324
Carl Hubbell NY 303
Paul Derringer CIN 277

1936 AL

	W	L	PCT	GB	R	OR	BA	FA	ERA
★NEW YORK	102	51	.667	—	1065	731	.300	.973	4.17
DETROIT	83	71	.539	19.5	921	871	.300	.975	5.00
CHICAGO	81	70	.536	20	920	873	.292	.973	5.06
WASHINGTON	82	71	.536	20	889	799	.295	.970	4.58
CLEVELAND	80	74	.519	22.5	921	862	.304	.971	4.83
BOSTON	74	80	.481	28.5	775	764	.276	.972	4.39
ST. LOUIS	57	95	.375	44.5	804	1064	.279	.969	6.24
PHILADELPHIA	53	100	.346	49	714	1045	.269	.965	6.08
					7009	7009	.289	.971	5.04

BATTING AVERAGE
Luke Appling CHI .... .388
Earl Averill CLE.......... .378
Bill Dickey NY .... .362

HITS
Earl Averill CLE........... 232
C. Gehringer DET 227
Hal Trosky CLE........... 216

DOUBLES
C. Gehringer DET 60
Gee Walker DET........... 55
two tied at 50

TRIPLES
Earl Averill CLE............ 15
Red Rolfe NY 15
Joe DiMaggio NY.......... 15

HOME RUNS
Lou Gehrig NY 49
Hal Trosky CLE............ 42
Jimmie Foxx BOS 41

RUNS BATTED IN
Hal Trosky CLE............ 162
Lou Gehrig NY 152
Jimmie Foxx BOS 143

SLUGGING AVERAGE
Lou Gehrig NY .... .696
Hal Trosky CLE........... .644
Jimmie Foxx BOS ...... .631

STOLEN BASES
Lyn Lary STL 37
J. Powell WAS, NY 26
Bill Werber BOS............ 23

RUNS SCORED
Lou Gehrig NY 167
Harlond Clift STL........ 145
C. Gehringer DET 144

WINS
Tommy Bridges DET 23
Vern Kennedy CHI........ 21
three tied at................... 20

WINNING PERCENTAGE
Monte Pearson NY .... .731
Vern Kennedy CHI..... .700
T. Bridges DET .... .676

EARNED RUN AVERAGE
Lefty Grove BOS........ 2.81
Johnny Allen CLE 3.44
Pete Appleton WAS ... 3.53

STRIKEOUTS
T. Bridges DET 175
Johnny Allen CLE 165
Bobo Newsom WAS ... 156

SAVES
Pat Malone NY.............. 9
Jack Knott STL 6
two tied at 5

COMPLETE GAMES
Wes Ferrell BOS........... 28
Tommy Bridges DET 26
Red Ruffing NY............. 25

SHUTOUTS
Lefty Grove BOS............. 6
Tommy Bridges DET 5
two tied at 4

GAMES PITCHED
Russ Van Atta STL 52
Jack Knott STL 47
two tied at 43

INNINGS PITCHED
Wes Ferrell BOS......... 301
T. Bridges DET 295
Bobo Newsom WAS ... 286

1936 NL

	W	L	PCT	GB	R	OR	BA	FA	ERA
NEW YORK	92	62	.597	—	742	621	.281	.974	3.46
CHICAGO	87	67	.565	5	755	603	.286	.976	3.53
ST. LOUIS	87	67	.565	5	795	794	.281	.974	4.48
PITTSBURGH	84	70	.545	8	804	718	.286	.967	3.89
CINCINNATI	74	80	.481	18	722	760	.274	.969	4.22
BOSTON	71	83	.461	21	631	715	.265	.971	3.94
BROOKLYN	67	87	.435	25	662	752	.272	.966	3.98
PHILADELPHIA	54	100	.351	38	726	874	.281	.959	4.64
					5837	5837	.278	.969	4.02

BATTING AVERAGE
Paul Waner PIT .... .373
Babe Phelps BKN ...... .367
Joe Medwick STL .... .351

HITS
Joe Medwick STL 223
Paul Waner PIT 218
Frank Demaree CHI.... 212

DOUBLES
Joe Medwick STL 64
Billy Herman CHI 57
Paul Waner PIT 53

TRIPLES
Ival Goodman CIN 14
Dolf Camilli PHI............. 13
Joe Medwick STL 13

HOME RUNS
Mel Ott NY 33
Dolf Camilli PHI............. 28
two tied at 25

RUNS BATTED IN
Joe Medwick STL 138
Mel Ott NY 135
Gus Suhr PIT 118

SLUGGING AVERAGE
Mel Ott NY .... .588
three tied at................ .577

STOLEN BASES
Pepper Martin STL........ 23
three tied at................... 17

RUNS SCORED
Arky Vaughan PIT....... 122
Pepper Martin STL...... 121
Mel Ott NY 120

WINS
Carl Hubbell NY 26
Dizzy Dean STL............ 24
Paul Derringer CIN 19

WINNING PERCENTAGE
Carl Hubbell NY .... .813
Red Lucas PIT .... .789
Larry French CHI .... .667

EARNED RUN AVERAGE
Carl Hubbell NY 2.31
D. MacFayden BOS... 2.87
Dizzy Dean STL.......... 3.17

STRIKEOUTS
Van Mungo BKN 238
Dizzy Dean STL.......... 195
Cy Blanton PIT............ 127

SAVES
Dizzy Dean STL............ 11
Don Brennan CIN 9
Bob Smith BOS............... 8

COMPLETE GAMES
Dizzy Dean STL............ 28
Carl Hubbell NY 25
Van Mungo BKN 22

SHUTOUTS
seven tied at 4

GAMES PITCHED
Dizzy Dean STL............ 51
Paul Derringer CIN 51
Claude Passeau PHI 49

INNINGS PITCHED
Dizzy Dean STL.......... 315
Van Mungo BKN 312
Carl Hubbell NY 304

1937 AL

	W	L	PCT	GB	R	OR	BA	FA	ERA
★NEW YORK	102	52	.662	—	979	671	.283	.972	3.65
DETROIT	89	65	.578	13	935	841	.292	.976	4.87
CHICAGO	86	68	.558	16	780	730	.280	.971	4.17
CLEVELAND	83	71	.539	19	817	768	.280	.974	4.39
BOSTON	80	72	.526	21	821	775	.281	.970	4.48
WASHINGTON	73	80	.477	28.5	757	841	.279	.972	4.58
PHILADELPHIA	54	97	.358	46.5	699	854	.267	.967	4.85
ST. LOUIS	46	108	.299	56	715	1023	.285	.972	6.00
					6503	6503	.281	.972	4.62

BATTING AVERAGE
C. Gehringer DET ...... .371
Lou Gehrig NY .... .351
Joe DiMaggio NY .... .346

HITS
Beau Bell STL 218
Joe DiMaggio NY 215
Gee Walker DET 213

DOUBLES
Beau Bell STL 51
Hank Greenberg DET ... 49
Wally Moses PHI 48

TRIPLES
Dixie Walker CHI 16
Mike Kreevich CHI 16
two tied at 15

HOME RUNS
Joe DiMaggio NY 46
Hank Greenberg DET ... 40
Lou Gehrig NY 37

RUNS BATTED IN
H. Greenberg DET 183
Joe DiMaggio NY 167
Lou Gehrig NY 159

SLUGGING AVERAGE
Joe DiMaggio NY .... .673
H. Greenberg DET ..... .668
Rudy York DET .... .651

STOLEN BASES
Chapman WAS, BOS ... 35
Bill Werber PHI 35
Gee Walker DET 23

RUNS SCORED
Joe DiMaggio NY 151
Red Rolfe NY 143
Lou Gehrig NY 138

WINS
Lefty Gomez NY 21
Red Ruffing NY 20
Roxie Lawson DET 18

WINNING PERCENTAGE
Johnny Allen CLE .... .938
Monty Stratton CHI .... .750
Red Ruffing NY .... .741

EARNED RUN AVERAGE
Lefty Gomez NY 2.33
Monty Stratton CHI 2.40
Johnny Allen CLE 2.55

STRIKEOUTS
Lefty Gomez NY 194
Newsom WAS, BOS ... 166
Lefty Grove BOS 153

SAVES
Clint Brown CHI 18
Johnny Murphy NY 10
Jack Wilson BOS 7

COMPLETE GAMES
W. Ferrell BOS, WAS ... 26
Lefty Gomez NY 25
Red Ruffing NY 22

SHUTOUTS
Lefty Gomez NY 6
Monty Stratton CHI 5
two tied at 4

GAMES PITCHED
Clint Brown CHI 53
Jack Wilson BOS 51
two tied at 41

INNINGS PITCHED
Ferrell BOS, WAS 281
Lefty Gomez NY 278
Newsom WAS, BOS ... 275

1937 NL

	W	L	PCT	GB	R	OR	BA	FA	ERA
NEW YORK	95	57	.625	—	732	602	.278	.974	3.43
CHICAGO	93	61	.604	3	811	682	.287	.975	3.97
PITTSBURGH	86	68	.558	10	704	646	.285	.970	3.56
ST. LOUIS	81	73	.526	15	789	733	.282	.973	3.95
BOSTON	79	73	.520	16	579	556	.247	.975	3.22
BROOKLYN	62	91	.405	33.5	616	772	.265	.964	4.13
PHILADELPHIA	61	92	.399	34.5	724	869	.273	.970	5.06
CINCINNATI	56	98	.364	40	612	707	.254	.966	3.94
					5567	5567	.272	.971	3.91

BATTING AVERAGE
Joe Medwick STL .... .374
Johnny Mize STL .... .364
two tied at .... .354

HITS
Joe Medwick STL 237
Paul Waner PIT 219
Johnny Mize STL 204

DOUBLES
Joe Medwick STL 56
Johnny Mize STL 40
Dick Bartell NY.............. 38

TRIPLES
Arky Vaughan PIT......... 17
Gus Suhr PIT 14
two tied at 12

HOME RUNS
Joe Medwick STL 31
Mel Ott NY 31
Dolf Camilli PHI.............. 27

RUNS BATTED IN
Joe Medwick STL 154
Frank Demaree CHI.... 115
Johnny Mize STL 113

SLUGGING AVERAGE
Joe Medwick STL .... .641
Johnny Mize STL........ .595
Dolf Camilli PHI........... .587

STOLEN BASES
Augie Galan CHI........... 23
Stan Hack CHI 16
four tied at..................... 13

RUNS SCORED
Joe Medwick STL 111
Stan Hack CHI 106
Billy Herman CHI 106

WINS
Carl Hubbell NY 22
three tied at.................. 20

WINNING PERCENTAGE
Carl Hubbell NY .... .733
Cliff Melton NY .... .690
two tied at .... .667

EARNED RUN AVERAGE
Jim Turner BOS 2.38
Cliff Melton NY 2.61
Dizzy Dean STL.......... 2.69

STRIKEOUTS
Carl Hubbell NY 159
Lee Grissom CIN 149
Cy Blanton PIT............ 143

SAVES
Mace Brown PIT 7
Cliff Melton NY............... 7
Lee Grissom CIN 6

COMPLETE GAMES
Jim Turner BOS 24
Lou Fette BOS 23
Bob Weiland STL.......... 21

SHUTOUTS
Jim Turner BOS 5
Lou Fette BOS 5
Lee Grissom CIN 5

GAMES PITCHED
Hugh Mulcahy PHI........ 56
Orville Jorgens PHI....... 52
two tied at 50

INNINGS PITCHED
C. Passeau PHI 292
Bill Lee CHI................. 272
Bob Weiland STL........ 264

1938 AL

	W	L	PCT	GB	R	OR	BA	FA	ERA
★NEW YORK	99	53	.651	—	966	710	.274	.973	3.91
BOSTON	88	61	.591	9.5	902	751	.299	.968	4.46
CLEVELAND	86	66	.566	13	847	782	.281	.974	4.60
DETROIT	84	70	.545	16	862	795	.272	.976	4.79
WASHINGTON	75	76	.497	23.5	814	873	.293	.970	4.94
CHICAGO	65	83	.439	32	709	752	.277	.967	4.36
ST. LOUIS	55	97	.362	44	755	962	.281	.975	5.80
PHILADELPHIA	53	99	.349	46	726	956	.270	.965	5.48
					6581	6581	.281	.971	4.79

BATTING AVERAGE
Jimmie Foxx BOS ...... .349
Jeff Heath CLE .... .343
Ben Chapman BOS ... .340

HITS
Joe Vosmik BOS......... 201
Doc Cramer BOS........ 198
two tied at 197

DOUBLES
Joe Cronin BOS............ 51
George McQuinn STL... 42
two tied at 40

TRIPLES
Jeff Heath CLE 18
Earl Averill CLE............. 15
Joe DiMaggio NY.......... 13

HOME RUNS
Hank Greenberg DET ... 58
Jimmie Foxx BOS 50
Harlond Clift STL 34

RUNS BATTED IN
Jimmie Foxx BOS 175
H. Greenberg DET...... 146
Joe DiMaggio NY........ 140

SLUGGING AVERAGE
Jimmie Foxx BOS ...... .704
H. Greenberg DET...... .683
Jeff Heath CLE .... .602

STOLEN BASES
Frank Crosetti NY 27
Lyn Lary CLE 23
Bill Werber PHI 19

RUNS SCORED
H. Greenberg DET...... 144
Jimmie Foxx BOS 139
C. Gehringer DET 133

WINS
Red Ruffing NY............. 21
Bobo Newsom STL....... 20
Lefty Gomez NY 18

WINNING PERCENTAGE
Red Ruffing NY.......... .750
Monty Pearson NY...... .696
Mel Harder CLE .... .630

EARNED RUN AVERAGE
Lefty Grove BOS........ 3.08
Red Ruffing NY 3.31
Lefty Gomez NY 3.35

STRIKEOUTS
Bob Feller CLE 240
Bobo Newsom STL..... 226
Lefty Mills STL 134

SAVES
Johnny Murphy NY 11
Archie McKain BOS 6
John Humphries CLE...... 6

COMPLETE GAMES
Bobo Newsom STL....... 31
Red Ruffing NY 22
three tied at.................. 20

SHUTOUTS
Red Ruffing NY 4
Lefty Gomez NY 4
two tied at 3

GAMES PITCHED
John Humphries CLE.... 45
Bobo Newsom STL....... 44
two tied at 43

INNINGS PITCHED
Bobo Newsom STL..... 330
George Caster PHI 280
Bob Feller CLE 278

1938 NL

	W	L	PCT	GB	R	OR	BA	FA	ERA
CHICAGO	89	63	.586	—	713	598	.269	.978	3.37
PITTSBURGH	86	64	.573	2	707	630	.279	.974	3.46
NEW YORK	83	67	.553	5	705	637	.271	.973	3.62
CINCINNATI	82	68	.547	6	723	634	.277	.971	3.62
BOSTON	77	75	.507	12	561	618	.250	.972	3.40
ST. LOUIS	71	80	.470	17.5	725	721	.279	.967	3.84
BROOKLYN	69	80	.463	18.5	704	710	.257	.973	4.07
PHILADELPHIA	45	105	.300	43	550	840	.254	.966	4.93
					5388	5388	.267	.972	3.78

BATTING AVERAGE
Ernie Lombardi CIN ... .342
Johnny Mize STL .... .337
F. McCormick CIN ..... .327

HITS
F. McCormick CIN 209
Stan Hack CHI 195
Lloyd Waner PIT 194

DOUBLES
Joe Medwick STL 47
F. McCormick CIN 40
two tied at 36

TRIPLES
Johnny Mize STL 16
Don Gutteridge STL...... 15
Gus Suhr PIT 14

HOME RUNS
Mel Ott NY 36
Ival Goodman CIN 30
Johnny Mize STL 27

RUNS BATTED IN
Joe Medwick STL 122
Mel Ott NY 116
Johnny Rizzo PIT........ 111

SLUGGING AVERAGE
Johnny Mize STL........ .614
Mel Ott NY .... .583
Joe Medwick STL .... .536

STOLEN BASES
Stan Hack CHI.............. 16
Ernie Koy BKN.............. 15
C. Lavagetto BKN 15

RUNS SCORED
Mel Ott NY 116
Stan Hack CHI............ 109
Dolf Camilli BKN 106

WINS
Bill Lee CHI.................. 22
Paul Derringer CIN 21
Clay Bryant CHI 19

WINNING PERCENTAGE
Bill Lee CHI................. .710
Clay Bryant CHI .... .633
Mace Brown PIT .... .625

EARNED RUN AVERAGE
Bill Lee CHI................. 2.66
Paul Derringer CIN 2.93
MacFayden BOS 2.95

STRIKEOUTS
Clay Bryant CHI.......... 135
Paul Derringer CIN 132
Vander Meer CIN......... 125

SAVES
Dick Coffman NY 12
Charlie Root CHI............ 8
two tied at 6

COMPLETE GAMES
Paul Derringer CIN 26
Jim Turner BOS............ 22
B. Walters PHI, CIN...... 20

SHUTOUTS
Bill Lee CHI.................... 9
D. MacFayden BOS........ 5
two tied at 4

GAMES PITCHED
Dick Coffman NY 51
Mace Brown PIT 51
Bill McGee STL............. 47

INNINGS PITCHED
Paul Derringer CIN 307
Bill Lee CHI................. 291
Clay Bryant CHI 270

1939 AL

	W	L	PCT	GB	R	OR	BA	FA	ERA
★NEW YORK	106	45	.702	—	967	556	.287	.978	3.31
BOSTON	89	62	.589	17	890	795	.291	.970	4.56
CLEVELAND	87	67	.565	20.5	797	700	.280	.970	4.08
CHICAGO	85	69	.552	22.5	755	737	.275	.972	4.31
DETROIT	81	73	.526	26.5	849	762	.279	.967	4.29
WASHINGTON	65	87	.428	41.5	702	797	.278	.966	4.60
PHILADELPHIA	55	97	.362	51.5	711	1022	.271	.964	5.79
ST. LOUIS	43	111	.279	64.5	733	1035	.268	.968	6.01
					6404	6404	.279	.969	4.62

BATTING AVERAGE
Joe DiMaggio NY .... .381
Jimmie Foxx BOS ...... .360
Bob Johnson PHI .... .338

HITS
Red Rolfe NY 213
G. McQuinn STL 195
Ken Keltner CLE 191

DOUBLES
Red Rolfe NY 46
Ted Williams BOS 44
Hank Greenberg DET ... 42

TRIPLES
Buddy Lewis WAS 16
B. McCosky DET 14
two tied at 13

HOME RUNS
Jimmie Foxx BOS 35
Hank Greenberg DET ... 33
Ted Williams BOS 31

RUNS BATTED IN
Ted Williams BOS 145
Joe DiMaggio NY 126
Bob Johnson PHI 114

SLUGGING AVERAGE
Jimmie Foxx BOS .... .694
Joe DiMaggio NY .... .671
H. Greenberg DET ..... .622

STOLEN BASES
George Case WAS 51
Mike Kreevich CHI 23
Pete Fox DET 23

RUNS SCORED
Red Rolfe NY 139
Ted Williams BOS 131
Jimmie Foxx BOS 130

WINS
Bob Feller CLE 24
Red Ruffing NY 21
two tied at 20

WINNING PERCENTAGE
Lefty Grove BOS .... .789
Red Ruffing NY .... .750
Bob Feller CLE .... .727

EARNED RUN AVERAGE
Lefty Grove BOS 2.54
Ted Lyons CHI 2.76
Bob Feller CLE 2.85

STRIKEOUTS
Bob Feller CLE 246
Newsom STL, DET 192
T. Bridges DET 129

SAVES
Johnny Murphy NY 19
Clint Brown CHI 18
two tied at 7

COMPLETE GAMES
Newsom STL, DET 24
Bob Feller CLE 24
Red Ruffing NY 22

SHUTOUTS
Red Ruffing NY 5
Bob Feller CLE 4

GAMES PITCHED
Clint Brown CHI 61
Chubby Dean PHI 54
E. Dickman BOS 48

INNINGS PITCHED
Bob Feller CLE 297
Newsom STL, DET 292
Dutch Leonard WAS ... 269

1939 NL

	W	L	PCT	GB	R	OR	BA	FA	ERA
CINCINNATI	97	57	.630	—	767	595	.278	.974	3.27
ST. LOUIS	92	61	.601	4.5	779	633	.294	.971	3.59
BROOKLYN	84	69	.549	12.5	708	645	.265	.972	3.64
CHICAGO	84	70	.545	13	724	678	.266	.970	3.80
NEW YORK	77	74	.510	18.5	703	685	.272	.975	4.07
PITTSBURGH	68	85	.444	28.5	666	721	.276	.972	4.15
BOSTON	63	88	.417	32.5	572	659	.264	.971	3.71
PHILADELPHIA	45	106	.298	50.5	553	856	.261	.970	5.17
					5472	5472	.272	.972	3.92

BATTING AVERAGE
Johnny Mize STL .... .349
F. McCormick CIN ..... .332
Joe Medwick STL ...... .332

HITS
F. McCormick CIN 209
Joe Medwick STL 201
Johnny Mize STL 197

DOUBLES
Enos Slaughter STL...... 52
Joe Medwick STL 48
Johnny Mize STL.......... 44

TRIPLES
Billy Herman CHI 18
Ival Goodman CIN 16
Johnny Mize STL.......... 14

HOME RUNS
Johnny Mize STL.......... 28
Mel Ott NY 27
Dolf Camilli BKN 26

RUNS BATTED IN
F. McCormick CIN 128
Joe Medwick STL 117
Johnny Mize STL........ 108

SLUGGING AVERAGE
Johnny Mize STL .... .626
Mel Ott NY .... .581
Hank Leiber CHI .... .556

STOLEN BASES
Lee Handley PIT 17
Stan Hack CHI 17
Bill Werber CIN 15

RUNS SCORED
Bill Werber CIN 115
Stan Hack CHI 112
Billy Herman CHI 111

WINS
Bucky Walters CIN........ 27
Paul Derringer CIN 25
Curt Davis STL 22

WINNING PERCENTAGE
Paul Derringer CIN .... .781
Bucky Walkers CIN..... .711
Larry French CHI .... .652

EARNED RUN AVERAGE
Bucky Walters CIN...... 2.29
Carl Hubbell NY 2.75
two tied at 2.93

STRIKEOUTS
Passeau PHI, CHI....... 137
Bucky Walters CIN...... 137
Mort Cooper STL 130

SAVES
Bob Bowman STL............ 9
Clyde Shoun STL............ 9
three tied at.................... 7

COMPLETE GAMES
Bucky Walters CIN........ 31
Paul Derringer CIN 28
Bill Lee CHI................... 20

SHUTOUTS
Lou Fette BOS 6
Bill Posedal BOS 5
Paul Derringer CIN 5

GAMES PITCHED
Clyde Shoun STL.......... 53
Rip Sewell PIT 52
Bob Bowman STL......... 51

INNINGS PITCHED
Bucky Walters CIN...... 319
Paul Derringer CIN 301
Bill Lee CHI.................. 282

1940 AL

	W	L	PCT	GB	R	OR	BA	FA	ERA
DETROIT	90	64	.584	—	888	717	.286	.968	4.01
CLEVELAND	89	65	.578	1	710	637	.265	.975	3.63
NEW YORK	88	66	.571	2	817	671	.259	.975	3.89
BOSTON	82	72	.532	8	872	825	.286	.972	4.89
CHICAGO	82	72	.532	8	735	672	.278	.969	3.74
ST. LOUIS	67	87	.435	23	757	882	.263	.974	5.12
WASHINGTON	64	90	.416	26	665	811	.271	.968	4.59
PHILADELPHIA	54	100	.351	36	703	932	.262	.960	5.22
					6147	6147	.271	.970	4.38

BATTING AVERAGE
Joe DiMaggio NY .... .352
Luke Appling CHI .... .348
Ted Williams BOS ...... .344

HITS
Rip Radcliff STL 200
Doc Cramer BOS 200
B. McCoskey DET 200

DOUBLES
Hank Greenberg DET ... 50
Lou Boudreau CLE 46
Rudy York DET 46

TRIPLES
B. McCoskey DET 19
Lou Finney BOS 15
Charlie Keller NY 15

HOME RUNS
Hank Greenberg DET ... 41
Jimmie Foxx BOS 36
Rudy York DET 33

RUNS BATTED IN
H. Greenberg DET...... 150
Rudy York DET 134
Joe DiMaggio NY 133

SLUGGING AVERAGE
H. Greenberg DET ..... .670
Joe DiMaggio NY .... .626
Ted Williams BOS ...... .594

STOLEN BASES
George Case WAS 35
Gee Walker WAS 21
Joe Gordon NY 18

RUNS SCORED
Ted Williams BOS 134
H. Greenberg DET 129
B. McCosky DET 123

WINS
Bob Feller CLE 27
Bobo Newsom DET 21
Al Milnar CLE 18

WINNING PERCENTAGE
S. Rowe DET .... .842
Bobo Newsom DET ... .808
Bob Feller CLE .... .711

EARNED RUN AVERAGE
Ernie Bonham NY 1.90
Bob Feller CLE 2.61
Bobo Newsom DET ... 2.83

STRIKEOUTS
Bob Feller CLE 261
Bobo Newsom DET 164
Johnny Rigney CHI..... 141

SAVES
Al Benton DET 17
Clint Brown CHI 10
Johnny Murphy NY 9

COMPLETE GAMES
Bob Feller CLE 31
Thorton Lee CHI 24
Dutch Leonard WAS 23

SHUTOUTS
Bob Feller CLE 4
Ted Lyons CHI................ 4
Al Milnar CLE................. 4

GAMES PITCHED
Bob Feller CLE 43
Al Benton DET.............. 42
two tied at 41

INNINGS PITCHED
Bob Feller CLE 320
Dutch Leonard WAS ... 289
Johnny Rigney CHI..... 281

1940 NL

	W	L	PCT	GB	R	OR	BA	FA	ERA
★CINCINNATI	100	53	.654	—	707	528	.266	.981	3.05
BROOKLYN	88	65	.575	12	697	621	.260	.970	3.50
ST. LOUIS	84	69	.549	16	747	699	.275	.971	3.83
PITTSBURGH	78	76	.506	22.5	809	783	.276	.966	4.36
CHICAGO	75	79	.487	25.5	681	636	.267	.968	3.54
NEW YORK	72	80	.474	27.5	663	659	.267	.977	3.79
BOSTON	65	87	.428	34.5	623	745	.256	.970	4.36
PHILADELPHIA	50	103	.327	50	494	750	.238	.970	4.40
					5421	5421	.264	.972	3.85

BATTING AVERAGE
Debs Garms PIT .... .355
Ernie Lombardi CIN ... .319
J. Cooney BOS .... .318

HITS
F. McCormick CIN 191
Stan Hack CHI 191
Johnny Mize STL 182

DOUBLES
F. McCormick CIN 44
Arky Vaughan PIT........ 40
Jim Gleeson CHI........... 39

TRIPLES
Arky Vaughan PIT......... 15
Chet Ross BOS 14
two tied at 13

HOME RUNS
Johnny Mize STL 43
Bill Nicholson CHI 25
Rizzo PIT, CIN, PHI 24

RUNS BATTED IN
Johnny Mize STL 137
F. McCormick CIN 127
M. Van Robays PIT..... 116

SLUGGING AVERAGE
Johnny Mize STL ...... .636
Bill Nicholson CHI ...... .534
Dolf Camilli BKN .... .529

STOLEN BASES
Lonny Frey CIN............. 22
Stan Hack CHI 21
Terry Moore STL........... 18

RUNS SCORED
Arky Vaughan PIT....... 113
Johnny Mize STL 111
Bill Werber CIN 105

WINS
Bucky Walters CIN........ 22
Paul Derringer CIN 20
Claude Passeau CHI 20

WINNING PERCENTAGE
Fitzsimmons BKN .... .889
Rip Sewell PIT .... .762
Bucky Walters CIN...... .688

EARNED RUN AVERAGE
Bucky Walters CIN..... 2.48
C. Passeau CHI 2.50
Rip Sewell PIT 2.80

STRIKEOUTS
Kirby Higbe PHI 137
Whit Wyatt BKN 124
C. Passeau CHI 124

SAVES
Jumbo Brown NY............. 7
Joe Beggs CIN................ 7
Mace Brown PIT 7

COMPLETE GAMES
Bucky Walters CIN........ 29
Paul Derringer CIN 26
Hugh Mulcahy PHI........ 21

SHUTOUTS
Manny Salvo BOS 5
Bill Lohrman NY.............. 5
Whit Wyatt BKN.............. 5

GAMES PITCHED
Clyde Shoun STL.......... 54
Mace Brown PIT 48
Claude Passeau CHI 46

INNINGS PITCHED
Bucky Walters CIN...... 305
Paul Derringer CIN 297
Kirby Higbe PHI 283

1941 AL

	W	L	PCT	GB	R	OR	BA	FA	ERA
★NEW YORK	101	53	.656	—	830	631	.269	.973	3.53
BOSTON	84	70	.545	17	865	750	.283	.972	4.19
CHICAGO	77	77	.500	24	638	649	.255	.971	3.52
CLEVELAND	75	79	.487	26	677	668	.256	.976	3.90
DETROIT	75	79	.487	26	686	743	.263	.969	4.18
ST. LOUIS	70	84	.455	31	765	823	.266	.975	4.72
WASHINGTON	70	84	.455	31	728	798	.272	.969	4.35
PHILADELPHIA	64	90	.416	37	713	840	.268	.967	4.83
					5902	5902	.266	.972	4.15

BATTING AVERAGE
Ted Williams BOS...... .406
Cecil Travis WAS...... .359
Joe DiMaggio NY .357

HITS
Cecil Travis WAS........ 218
Jeff Heath CLE 199
Joe DiMaggio NY........ 193

DOUBLES
Lou Boudreau CLE 45
Joe DiMaggio NY.......... 43
Walt Judnich STL.......... 40

TRIPLES
Jeff Heath CLE 20
Cecil Travis WAS 19
Ken Keltner CLE 13

HOME RUNS
Ted Williams BOS......... 37
Charlie Keller NY 33
Tommy Henrich NY 31

RUNS BATTED IN
Joe DiMaggio NY 125
Jeff Heath CLE 123
Charlie Keller NY 122

SLUGGING AVERAGE
Ted Williams BOS...... .735
Joe DiMaggio NY....... .643
Jeff Heath CLE .... .586

STOLEN BASES
George Case WAS 33
Joe Kuhel CHI 20
Jeff Heath CLE 18

RUNS SCORED
Ted Williams BOS...... 135
Joe DiMaggio NY........ 122
Dom DiMaggio BOS ... 117

WINS
Bob Feller CLE 25
Thorton Lee CHI 22
Dick Newsome BOS 19

WINNING PERCENTAGE
Lefty Gomez NY .... .750
Al Benton DET .... .714
Red Ruffing NY........... .714

EARNED RUN AVERAGE
Thorton Lee CHI 2.37
C. Wagner BOS 3.07
Marius Russo NY....... 3.09

STRIKEOUTS
Bob Feller CLE 260
Bobo Newsom DET 175
Thorton Lee CHI 130

SAVES
Johnny Murphy NY 15
Tom Ferrick PHI............. 7
Al Benton DET 7

COMPLETE GAMES
Thornton Lee CHI 30
Bob Feller CLE 28
Eddie Smith CHI 21

SHUTOUTS
Bob Feller CLE 6
three tied at.................... 4

GAMES PITCHED
Bob Feller CLE 44
Bobo Newsom DET 43
Clint Brown CLE 41

INNINGS PITCHED
Bob Feller CLE 343
Thorton Lee CHI 300
Eddie Smith CHI 263

1941 NL

	W	L	PCT	GB	R	OR	BA	FA	ERA
BROOKLYN	100	54	.649	—	800	581	.272	.974	3.14
ST. LOUIS	97	56	.634	2.5	734	589	.272	.973	3.19
CINCINNATI	88	66	.571	12	616	564	.247	.975	3.17
PITTSBURGH	81	73	.526	19	690	643	.268	.968	3.48
NEW YORK	74	79	.484	25.5	667	706	.260	.974	3.94
CHICAGO	70	84	.455	30	666	670	.253	.970	3.72
BOSTON	62	92	.403	38	592	720	.251	.969	3.95
PHILADELPHIA	43	111	.279	57	501	793	.244	.969	4.50
					5266	5266	.258	.972	3.63

BATTING AVERAGE
Pete Reiser BKN......... .343
J. Cooney BOS........... .319
Joe Medwick BKN...... .318

SLUGGING AVERAGE
Pete Reiser BKN......... .558
Dolf Camilli BKN .... .556
Johnny Mize STL........ .535

STRIKEOUTS
J. Vander Meer CIN 202
Whit Wyatt BKN 176
Bucky Walters CIN...... 129

HITS
Stan Hack CHI............. 186
Pete Reiser BKN......... 184
Danny Litwhiler PHI 180

STOLEN BASES
Danny Murtaugh PHI 18
Stan Benjamin PHI 17
two tied at 16

SAVES
Jumbo Brown NY............ 8
Hugh Casey BKN............ 7
Bill Crouch PHI, STL....... 7

DOUBLES
Pete Reiser BKN........... 39
Johnny Mize STL.......... 39
Johnny Rucker NY 38

RUNS SCORED
Pete Reiser BKN......... 117
Stan Hack CHI............. 111
Joe Medwick BKN....... 100

COMPLETE GAMES
Bucky Walters CIN........ 27
Whit Wyatt BKN 23
two tied at 20

TRIPLES
Pete Reiser BKN........... 17
Elbie Fletcher PIT 13
Johnny Hopp STL 11

WINS
Kirby Higbe BKN........... 22
Whit Wyatt BKN 22
two tied at 19

SHUTOUTS
Whit Wyatt BKN 7
J. Vander Meer CIN 6
two tied at 5

HOME RUNS
Dolf Camilli BKN 34
Mel Ott NY 27
Bill Nicholson CHI 26

WINNING PERCENTAGE
Elmer Riddle CIN .... .826
Kirby Higbe BKN......... .710
Ernie White STL.......... .708

GAMES PITCHED
Kirby Higbe BKN........... 48
Ike Pearson PHI............ 46
Hugh Casey BKN........... 45

RUNS BATTED IN
Dolf Camilli BKN 120
Bobby Young NY 104
two tied at 100

EARNED RUN AVERAGE
Elmer Riddle CIN 2.24
Whit Wyatt BKN 2.34
Ernie White STL......... 2.40

INNINGS PITCHED
Bucky Walters CIN...... 302
Kirby Higbe BKN.......... 298
Whit Wyatt BKN 288

1942 AL

	W	L	PCT	GB	R	OR	BA	FA	ERA
NEW YORK	103	51	.669	—	801	507	.269	.976	2.91
BOSTON	93	59	.612	9	761	594	.276	.974	3.44
ST. LOUIS	82	69	.543	19.5	730	637	.259	.972	3.59
CLEVELAND	75	79	.487	28	590	659	.253	.974	3.59
DETROIT	73	81	.474	30	589	587	.246	.969	3.13
CHICAGO	66	82	.446	34	538	609	.246	.970	3.58
WASHINGTON	62	89	.411	39.5	653	817	.258	.962	4.58
PHILADELPHIA	55	99	.357	48	549	801	.249	.969	4.48
					5211	5211	.257	.971	3.66

BATTING AVERAGE
Ted Williams BOS...... .356
Johnny Pesky BOS.... .331
Stan Spence WAS .... .323

HITS
Johnny Pesky BOS..... 205
Stan Spence WAS 203
two tied at 186

DOUBLES
Don Kolloway CHI.......... 40
Harlond Clift STL 39
Jeff Heath CLE 37

TRIPLES
Stan Spence WAS........ 15
Jeff Heath CLE 13
Joe DiMaggio NY.......... 13

HOME RUNS
Ted Williams BOS.......... 36
Chet Laabs STL............. 27
Charlie Keller NY 26

RUNS BATTED IN
Ted Williams BOS....... 137
Joe DiMaggio NY....... 114
Charlie Keller NY 108

SLUGGING AVERAGE
Ted Williams BOS...... .648
Charlie Keller NY .... .513
Walt Judnich STL........ .499

STOLEN BASES
George Case WAS 44
Mickey Vernon WAS..... 25
two tied at 22

RUNS SCORED
Ted Williams BOS....... 141
Joe DiMaggio NY........ 123
Dom DiMaggio BOS ... 110

WINS
Tex Hughson BOS........ 22
Ernie Bonham NY 21
two tied at 17

WINNING PERCENTAGE
Ernie Bonham NY ...... .808
Hank Borowy NY .... .789
Tex Hughson BOS..... .786

EARNED RUN AVERAGE
Ted Lyons CHI.......... 2.10
Ernie Bonham NY 2.27
Spud Chandler NY..... 2.38

STRIKEOUTS
Bobo Newsom WAS ... 113
Tex Hughson BOS...... 113
two tied at 110

SAVES
Johnny Murphy NY 11
Mace Brown BOS 6
Joe Haynes CHI.............. 6

COMPLETE GAMES
Ernie Bonham NY 22
Tex Hughson BOS........ 22
Ted Lyons CHI.............. 20

SHUTOUTS
Ernie Bonham NY 6

GAMES PITCHED
Joe Haynes CHI............. 40
George Castor STL....... 39
two tied at 38

INNINGS PITCHED
Tex Hughson BOS...... 281
Jim Bagby CLE 271
Eldon Auker STL......... 249

1942 NL

	W	L	PCT	GB	R	OR	BA	FA	ERA
★ST. LOUIS	106	48	.688	—	755	482	.268	.972	2.55
BROOKLYN	104	50	.675	2	742	510	.265	.977	2.84
NEW YORK	85	67	.559	20	675	600	.254	.977	3.31
CINCINNATI	76	76	.500	29	527	545	.231	.971	2.82
PITTSBURGH	66	81	.449	36.5	585	631	.245	.969	3.58
CHICAGO	68	86	.442	38	591	665	.254	.973	3.60
BOSTON	59	89	.399	44	515	645	.240	.976	3.76
PHILADELPHIA	42	109	.278	62.5	394	706	.232	.968	4.12
					4784	4784	.249	.973	3.31

BATTING AVERAGE
Ernie Lombardi BOS.. .330
Enos Slaughter STL... .318
Stan Musial STL .... .315

HITS
Enos Slaughter STL.... 188
Bill Nicholson CHI 173
two tied at 166

DOUBLES
Marty Marion STL 38
Joe Medwick BKN......... 37
Stan Hack CHI.............. 36

TRIPLES
Enos Slaughter STL...... 17
Bill Nicholson CHI 11
Stan Musial STL 10

HOME RUNS
Mel Ott NY 30
Johnny Mize NY............ 26
Dolf Camilli BKN 26

RUNS BATTED IN
Johnny Mize NY.......... 110
Dolf Camilli BKN 109
Enos Slaughter STL...... 98

SLUGGING AVERAGE
Johnny Mize NY.......... .521
Mel Ott NY .... .497
Enos Slaughter STL... .494

STOLEN BASES
Pete Reiser BKN........... 20
N. Fernandez BOS 15
Pee Wee Reese BKN ... 15

RUNS SCORED
Mel Ott NY 118
Enos Slaughter STL.... 100
Johnny Mize NY............ 97

WINS
Mort Cooper STL 22
Johnny Beazley STL..... 21
two tied at 19

WINNING PERCENTAGE
Larry French BKN ...... .789
J. Beazley STL............ .778
Mort Cooper STL .... .759

EARNED RUN AVERAGE
Mort Cooper STL 1.78
J. Beazley STL............ 2.13
Curt Davis BKN.......... 2.36

STRIKEOUTS
J. Vander Meer CIN 186
Mort Cooper STL 152
Kirby Higbe BKN......... 115

SAVES
Hugh Casey BKN.......... 13
Ace Adams NY 11
Joe Beggs CIN................ 8

COMPLETE GAMES
Jim Tobin BOS.............. 28
Claude Passeau CHI 24
Mort Cooper STL 22

SHUTOUTS
Mort Cooper STL 10
three tied at...................... 5

GAMES PITCHED
Ace Adams NY 61
Hugh Casey BKN.......... 50
two tied at 43

INNINGS PITCHED
Jim Tobin BOS............ 228
Mort Cooper STL 279
C. Passeau CHI 278

1943 AL

	W	L	PCT	GB	R	OR	BA	FA	ERA
★NEW YORK	98	56	.636	—	669	542	.256	.974	2.93
WASHINGTON	84	69	.549	13.5	666	595	.254	.971	3.18
CLEVELAND	82	71	.536	15.5	600	577	.255	.975	3.15
CHICAGO	82	72	.532	16	573	594	.247	.973	3.20
DETROIT	78	76	.506	20	632	560	.261	.971	3.00
ST. LOUIS	72	80	.474	25	596	604	.245	.975	3.41
BOSTON	68	84	.447	29	563	607	.244	.976	3.45
PHILADELPHIA	49	105	.318	49	497	717	.232	.973	4.05
					4796	4796	.249	.973	3.30

BATTING AVERAGE
Luke Appling CHI .... .328
Dick Wakefield DET ... .316
Ralph Hodgin CHI ...... .314

HITS
Dick Wakefield DET 200
Luke Appling CHI 192
Doc Cramer DET 182

DOUBLES
Dick Wakefield DET 38
George Case WAS 36
two tied at 35

TRIPLES
Johnny Lindell NY 12
Wally Moses CHI 12
two tied at 11

HOME RUNS
Rudy York DET 34
Charlie Keller NY 31
Vern Stephens STL 22

RUNS BATTED IN
Rudy York DET 118
Nick Etten NY 107
Billy Johnson NY 94

SLUGGING AVERAGE
Rudy York DET .... .527
Charlie Keller NY .... .525
Vern Stephens STL ... .482

STOLEN BASES
George Case WAS 61
Wally Moses CHI 56
Thurman Tucker CHI.... 29

RUNS SCORED
George Case WAS 102
Charlie Keller NY 97
Dick Wakefield DET 91

WINS
Spud Chandler NY 20
Dizzy Trout DET 20
Early Wynn WAS 18

WINNING PERCENTAGE
Spud Chandler NY ..... .833
Al Smith CLE .... .708
Ernie Bonham NY ...... .652

EARNED RUN AVERAGE
Spud Chandler NY 1.64
Ernie Bonham NY 2.27
T. Bridges DET 2.39

STRIKEOUTS
Allie Reynolds CLE 151
Hal Newhouser DET ... 144
Spud Chandler NY 134

SAVES
G. Maltzberger CHI....... 14
Mace Brown BOS 9
Joe Heving CLE.............. 9

COMPLETE GAMES
Spud Chandler NY 20
Tex Hughson BOS........ 20
three tied at................... 18

SHUTOUTS
Spud Chandler NY 5
Dizzy Trout DET 5
two tied at 4

GAMES PITCHED
Mace Brown BOS 49
Dizzy Trout DET 44
Roger Wolff PHI............. 41

INNINGS PITCHED
Jim Bagby CLE 273
Tex Hughson BOS...... 266
Early Wynn WAS 257

1943 NL

	W	L	PCT	GB	R	OR	BA	FA	ERA
ST. LOUIS	105	49	.682	—	679	475	.279	.976	2.57
CINCINNATI	87	67	.565	18	608	543	.256	.980	3.13
BROOKLYN	81	72	.529	23.5	716	674	.272	.972	3.88
PITTSBURGH	80	74	.519	25	669	605	.262	.973	3.06
CHICAGO	74	79	.484	30.5	632	600	.261	.973	3.24
BOSTON	68	85	.444	36.5	465	612	.233	.972	3.25
PHILADELPHIA	64	90	.416	41	571	676	.249	.969	3.79
NEW YORK	55	98	.359	49.5	558	713	.247	.973	4.08
					4898	4898	.258	.974	3.37

BATTING AVERAGE
Stan Musial STL .... .357
Billy Herman BKN ...... .330
Walker Cooper STL ... .318

HITS
Stan Musial STL 220
Mickey Witek NY......... 195
Billy Herman BKN 193

DOUBLES
Stan Musial STL 48
Vince DiMaggio PIT 41
Billy Herman BKN 41

TRIPLES
Stan Musial STL 20
Lou Klein STL 14
two tied at 12

HOME RUNS
Bill Nicholson CHI 29
Mel Ott NY 18
Ron Northey PHI........... 16

RUNS BATTED IN
Bill Nicholson CHI....... 128
Bob Elliott PIT.............. 101
Billy Herman BKN 100

SLUGGING AVERAGE
Stan Musial STL .... .562
Bill Nicholson CHI ...... .531
Walker Cooper STL ... .463

STOLEN BASES
Arky Vaughan BKN....... 20
Peanuts Lowrey CHI..... 13
three tied at................... 12

RUNS SCORED
Arky Vaughan BKN..... 112
Stan Musial STL 108
Bill Nicholson CHI 95

WINS
Elmer Riddle CIN 21
Mort Cooper STL 21
Rip Sewell PIT 21

WINNING PERCENTAGE
Mort Cooper STL 724
Rip Sewell PIT .... .700
Max Lanier STL .... .682

EARNED RUN AVERAGE
Howie Pollet STL 1.75
Max Lanier STL 1.90
Mort Cooper STL 2.30

STRIKEOUTS
J. Vander Meer CIN 174
Mort Cooper STL 141
Al Javery BOS 134

SAVES
Les Webber BKN 10
Ace Adams NY 9
Clyde Shoun CIN 7

COMPLETE GAMES
Rip Sewell PIT 25
Jim Tobin BOS............... 24
Mort Cooper STL 24

SHUTOUTS
Hi Bithorn CHI................. 7
Mort Cooper STL 6
two tied at 5

GAMES PITCHED
Ace Adams NY 70
Les Webber BKN 54
Ed Head BKN 47

INNINGS PITCHED
Al Javery BOS 303
J. Vander Meer CIN 289
Nate Andrews BOS..... 284

1944 AL

	W	L	PCT	GB	R	OR	BA	FA	ERA
ST. LOUIS	89	65	.578	—	684	587	.252	.972	3.17
DETROIT	88	66	.571	1	658	581	.263	.970	3.09
NEW YORK	83	71	.539	6	674	617	.264	.974	3.39
BOSTON	77	77	.500	12	739	676	.270	.972	3.82
CLEVELAND	72	82	.468	17	643	677	.266	.974	3.65
PHILADELPHIA	72	82	.468	17	525	594	.257	.971	3.26
CHICAGO	71	83	.461	18	543	662	.247	.970	3.58
WASHINGTON	64	90	.416	25	592	664	.261	.964	3.49
					5058	5058	.260	.971	3.43

BATTING AVERAGE
Lou Boudreau CLE .... .327
Bobby Doerr BOS ...... .325
Bob Johnson BOS ..... .324

HITS
S. Stirnweiss NY 205
Lou Boudreau CLE 191
Stan Spence WAS 187

DOUBLES
Lou Boudreau CLE 45
Ken Keltner CLE 41
Bob Johnson BOS 40

TRIPLES
Johnny Lindell NY 16
Snuffy Stirnweiss NY 16
Don Gutteridge STL 11

HOME RUNS
Nick Etten NY 22
Vern Stephens STL 20
three tied at 18

RUNS BATTED IN
Vern Stephens STL 109
Bob Johnson BOS 106
Johnny Lindell NY 103

SLUGGING AVERAGE
Bobby Doerr BOS ...... .528
Bob Johnson BOS ..... .528
Johnny Lindell NY ...... .500

STOLEN BASES
Snuffy Stirnweiss NY 55
George Case WAS 49
Glenn Myatt WAS 26

RUNS SCORED
S. Stirnweiss NY 125
Bob Johnson BOS 106
Roy Cullenbine CLE 98

WINS
Hal Newhouser DET 29
Dizzy Trout DET 27
Nels Potter STL 19

WINNING PERCENTAGE
Tex Hughson BOS ..... .783
H. Newhouser DET ..... .763
Nels Potter STL .... .731

EARNED RUN AVERAGE
Dizzy Trout DET 2.12
H. Newhouser DET 2.22
Tex Hughson BOS 2.26

STRIKEOUTS
Hal Newhouser DET ... 187
Dizzy Trout DET 144
Bobo Newsom PHI 142

SAVES
Joe Berry PHI 12
G. Maltzberger CHI....... 12
George Caster STL....... 12

COMPLETE GAMES
Dizzy Trout DET 33
Hal Newhouser DET 25
four tied at 19

SHUTOUTS
Dizzy Trout DET 7
Hal Newhouser DET 6
two tied at 4

GAMES PITCHED
Joe Heving CLE............. 63
Joe Berry PHI 53
Dizzy Trout DET 49

INNINGS PITCHED
Dizzy Trout DET 352
Hal Newhouser DET ... 312
Bobo Newsom PHI 265

1944 NL

	W	L	PCT	GB	R	OR	BA	FA	ERA
★ST. LOUIS	105	49	.682	—	772	490	.275	.982	2.67
PITTSBURGH	90	63	.588	14.5	744	662	.265	.970	3.44
CINCINNATI	89	65	.578	16	573	537	.254	.978	2.97
CHICAGO	75	79	.487	30	702	669	.261	.970	3.59
NEW YORK	67	87	.435	38	682	773	.263	.971	4.29
BOSTON	65	89	.422	40	593	674	.246	.971	3.67
BROOKLYN	63	91	.409	42	690	832	.269	.966	4.68
PHILADELPHIA	61	92	.399	43.5	539	658	.251	.972	3.64
					5295	5295	.261	.972	3.61

BATTING AVERAGE
Dixie Walker BKN ...... .357
Stan Musial STL .... .347
Joe Medwick NY .... .337

HITS
Phil Cavarretta CHI..... 197
Stan Musial STL 197
T. Holmes BOS........... 195

DOUBLES
Stan Musial STL 51
Augie Galan BKN.......... 43
T. Holmes BOS.............. 42

TRIPLES
Johnny Barrett PIT........ 19
Bob Elliott PIT 16
Phil Cavarretta CHI....... 15

HOME RUNS
Bill Nicholson CHI 33
Mel Ott NY 26
Ron Northey PHI........... 22

RUNS BATTED IN
Bill Nicholson CHI 122
Bob Elliott PIT 108
Ron Northey PHI......... 104

SLUGGING AVERAGE
Stan Musial STL .... .549
Bill Nicholson CHI ...... .545
Mel Ott NY .... .544

STOLEN BASES
Johnny Barrett PIT...... 28
Tony Lupien PHI........... 18
Roy Hughes CHI........... 16

RUNS SCORED
Bill Nicholson CHI 116
Stan Musial STL 112
Jim Russell PIT........... 109

WINS
Bucky Walters CIN........ 23
Mort Cooper STL 22
two tied at 21

WINNING PERCENTAGE
Ted Wilks STL .... .810
H. Brecheen STL .... .762
Mort Cooper STL .... .759

EARNED RUN AVERAGE
Ed Heusser CIN...... 2.38
Bucky Walters CIN..... 2.40
Mort Cooper STL 2.46

STRIKEOUTS
Bill Voiselle NY 161
Max Lanier STL 141
Al Javery BOS 137

SAVES
Ace Adams NY 13
Xavier Rescigno PIT....... 5
Freddie Schmidt STL 5

COMPLETE GAMES
Jim Tobin BOS.............. 28
Bucky Walters CIN........ 27
Bill Voiselle NY 25

SHUTOUTS
Mort Cooper STL 7
Bucky Walters CIN.......... 6
two tied at 5

GAMES PITCHED
Ace Adams NY 65
Les Webber BKN 48
Xavier Rescigno PIT 48

INNINGS PITCHED
Bill Voiselle NY 313
Jim Tobin BOS............. 299
Rip Sewell PIT 286

1945 AL

	W	L	PCT	GB	R	OR	BA	FA	ERA
★DETROIT	88	65	.575	—	633	565	.256	.975	2.99
WASHINGTON	87	67	.565	1.5	622	562	.258	.970	2.92
ST. LOUIS	81	70	.536	6	597	548	.249	.976	3.14
NEW YORK	81	71	.533	6.5	676	606	.259	.971	3.45
CLEVELAND	73	72	.503	11	557	548	.255	.977	3.31
CHICAGO	71	78	.477	15	596	633	.262	.970	3.69
BOSTON	71	83	.461	17.5	599	674	.260	.973	3.80
PHILADELPHIA	52	98	.347	34.5	494	638	.245	.973	3.62
					4774	4774	.255	.973	3.36

BATTING AVERAGE
S. Stirnweiss NY .... .309
T. Cuccinello CHI .... .308
J. Dickshot CHI .... .302

HITS
S. Stirnweiss NY 195
Wally Moses CHI 168
Vern Stephens STL 165

DOUBLES
Wally Moses CHI 35
Snuffy Stirnweiss NY 32
George Binks WAS 32

TRIPLES
Snuffy Stirnweiss NY 22
Wally Moses CHI 15
Joe Kuhel WAS 13

HOME RUNS
Vern Stephens STL 24
three tied at 18

RUNS BATTED IN
Nick Etten NY 111
Cullenbine CLE, DET 93
Vern Stephens STL 89

SLUGGING AVERAGE
S. Stirnweiss NY .... .476
Vern Stephens STL ... .473
Cullenbine CLE, DET. .444

STOLEN BASES
Snuffy Stirnweiss NY 33
George Case WAS 30
Glenn Myatt WAS 30

RUNS SCORED
S. Stirnweiss NY 107
Vern Stephens STL 90
Cullenbine CLE, DET.... 83

WINS
Hal Newhouser DET 25
Boo Ferriss BOS 21
Roger Wolff WAS 20

WINNING PERCENTAGE
H. Newhouser DET .... .735
D. Leonard WAS .... .708
Steve Gromek CLE .... .679

EARNED RUN AVERAGE
H. Newhouser DET ... 1.81
Al Benton DET 2.02
Roger Wolff WAS 2.12

STRIKEOUTS
Hal Newhouser DET ... 212
Nels Potter STL 129
Bobo Newsom PHI 127

SAVES
Jim Turner NY 10
Joe Berry PHI 5

COMPLETE GAMES
Hal Newhouser DET 29
Boo Ferriss BOS 26
three tied at 21

SHUTOUTS
Hal Newhouser DET 8
Boo Ferriss BOS 5
Al Benton DET 5

GAMES PITCHED
Joe Berry PHI 52
Allie Reynolds CLE 44
Marino Pieretti WAS 44

INNINGS PITCHED
Hal Newhouser DET ... 313
Boo Ferriss BOS 265
Bobo Newsom PHI 257

1945 NL

	W	L	PCT	GB	R	OR	BA	FA	ERA
CHICAGO	98	56	.636	—	735	532	.277	.980	2.98
ST. LOUIS	95	59	.617	3	756	583	.273	.977	3.24
BROOKLYN	87	67	.565	11	795	724	.271	.962	3.70
PITTSBURGH	82	72	.532	16	753	686	.267	.971	3.76
NEW YORK	78	74	.513	19	668	700	.269	.973	4.06
BOSTON	67	85	.441	30	721	728	.267	.969	4.04
CINCINNATI	61	93	.396	37	536	694	.249	.976	4.00
PHILADELPHIA	46	108	.299	52	548	865	.246	.962	4.64
					5512	5512	.265	.971	3.80

BATTING AVERAGE
Phil Cavarretta CHI.... .355
T. Holmes BOS........... .352
Goody Rosen BKN .... .325

HITS
T. Holmes BOS........... 224
Goody Rosen BKN 197
Stan Hack CHI............ 193

DOUBLES
Tommy Holmes BOS.... 47
Dixie Walker BKN 42
two tied at 36

TRIPLES
Luis Olmo BKN 13
Andy Pafko CHI 12
two tied at 11

HOME RUNS
Tommy Holmes BOS.... 28
Chuck Workman BOS... 25
B. Adams PHI, STL....... 22

RUNS BATTED IN
Dixie Walker BKN 124
T. Holmes BOS........... 117
two tied at 110

SLUGGING AVERAGE
T. Holmes BOS........... .577
W. Kurowski STL .... .511
Phil Cavarretta CHI.... .500

STOLEN BASES
R. Schoendienst STL.... 26
Johnny Barrett PIT........ 25
Dain Clay CIN 19

RUNS SCORED
Eddie Stanky BKN 128
Goody Rosen BKN 126
T. Holmes BOS........... 125

WINS
R. Barrett BOS, STL 23
Hank Wyse CHI 22
Ken Burkhart STL 19

WINNING PERCENTAGE
Ken Burkhart STL ...... .704
Hank Wyse CHI .... .688
Barrett BOS, STL....... .657

EARNED RUN AVERAGE
Hank Borowy CHI.... 2.13
C. Passeau CHI......... 2.46
H. Brecheen STL 2.52

STRIKEOUTS
Preacher Roe PIT....... 148
Hal Gregg BKN 139
Bill Voiselle NY 115

SAVES
Ace Adams NY 15
Andy Karl PHI 15
Xavier Rescigno PIT....... 9

COMPLETE GAMES
R. Barrett BOS, STL 24
Hank Wyse CHI 23
Claude Passeau CHI 19

SHUTOUTS
Claude Passeau CHI 5
three tied at..................... 4

GAMES PITCHED
Andy Karl PHI............... 67
Ace Adams NY 65
J. Hutchings BOS 57

INNINGS PITCHED
R. Barrett BOS, STL ... 285
Hank Wyse CHI 278
Hal Gregg BKN 254

1946 AL

	W	L	PCT	GB	R	OR	BA	FA	ERA
BOSTON	104	50	.675	—	792	594	.271	.977	3.38
DETROIT	92	62	.597	12	704	567	.258	.974	3.22
NEW YORK	87	67	.565	17	684	547	.248	.975	3.13
WASHINGTON	76	78	.494	28	608	706	.260	.966	3.74
CHICAGO	74	80	.481	30	562	595	.257	.972	3.10
CLEVELAND	68	86	.442	36	537	637	.245	.975	3.62
ST. LOUIS	66	88	.429	38	621	711	.251	.974	3.95
PHILADELPHIA	49	105	.318	55	529	680	.253	.971	3.90
					5037	5037	.256	.973	3.50

BATTING AVERAGE
M. Vernon WAS......... .353
Ted Williams BOS...... .342
Johnny Pesky BOS .... .335

HITS
Johnny Pesky BOS..... 208
Mickey Vernon WAS... 207
Luke Appling CHI........ 180

DOUBLES
Mickey Vernon WAS..... 51
Stan Spence WAS........ 50
Johnny Pesky BOS....... 43

TRIPLES
Hank Edwards CLE 16
Buddy Lewis WAS 13
two tied at 10

HOME RUNS
Hank Greenberg DET ... 44
Ted Williams BOS......... 38
Charlie Keller NY 30

RUNS BATTED IN
H. Greenberg DET...... 127
Ted Williams BOS....... 123
Rudy York BOS 119

SLUGGING AVERAGE
Ted Williams BOS...... .667
H. Greenberg DET..... .604
Charlie Keller NY .... .533

STOLEN BASES
George Case CLE 28
Snuffy Stirnweiss NY 18
Eddie Lake DET 15

RUNS SCORED
Ted Williams BOS....... 142
Johnny Pesky BOS..... 115
Eddie Lake DET 105

WINS
Hal Newhouser DET 26
Bob Feller CLE 26
Boo Ferriss BOS........... 25

WINNING PERCENTAGE
Boo Ferriss BOS........ .806
H. Newhouser DET.... .743
Spud Chandler NY..... .714

EARNED RUN AVERAGE
H. Newhouser DET.... 1.94
Spud Chandler NY..... 2.10
Bob Feller CLE 2.18

STRIKEOUTS
Bob Feller CLE 348
Hal Newhouser DET ... 275
Tex Hughson BOS...... 172

SAVES
Bob Klinger BOS............. 9
Earl Caldwell CHI........... 8
Johnny Murphy NY 7

COMPLETE GAMES
Bob Feller CLE 36
Hal Newhouser DET 29
Boo Ferriss BOS........... 26

SHUTOUTS
Bob Feller CLE 10
three tied at..................... 6

GAMES PITCHED
Bob Feller CLE 48
Boo Ferriss BOS........... 40
Bob Savage PHI 40

INNINGS PITCHED
Bob Feller CLE 371
Hal Newhouser DET ... 292
Tex Hughson BOS...... 278

1946 NL

	W	L	PCT	GB	R	OR	BA	FA	ERA
★ST. LOUIS*	98	58	.628	—	712	545	.265	.980	3.01
BROOKLYN	96	60	.615	2	701	570	.260	.972	3.05
CHICAGO	82	71	.536	14.5	626	581	.254	.976	3.24
BOSTON	81	72	.529	15.5	630	592	.264	.972	3.37
PHILADELPHIA	69	85	.448	28	560	705	.258	.975	3.99
CINCINNATI	67	87	.435	30	523	570	.239	.975	3.07
PITTSBURGH	63	91	.409	34	552	668	.250	.970	3.72
NEW YORK	61	93	.396	36	612	685	.255	.973	3.92
					4916	4916	.256	.974	3.42

*Defeated Brooklyn in a playoff 2 games to 0

BATTING AVERAGE
Stan Musial STL .... .365
Johnny Hopp BOS ..... .333
Dixie Walker BKN .... .319

HITS
Stan Musial STL 228
Dixie Walker BKN 184
Enos Slaughter STL.... 183

DOUBLES
Stan Musial STL 50
Tommy Holmes BOS 35
Whitey Kurowski STL.... 32

TRIPLES
Stan Musial STL 20
Phil Cavarretta CHI....... 10
Pee Wee Reese BKN ... 10

HOME RUNS
Ralph Kiner PIT 23
Johnny Mize NY............. 22
Enos Slaughter STL...... 18

RUNS BATTED IN
Enos Slaughter STL.... 130
Dixie Walker BKN 116
Stan Musial STL 103

SLUGGING AVERAGE
Stan Musial STL .... .587
Del Ennis PHI .... .485
Enos Slaughter STL... .465

STOLEN BASES
Pete Reiser BKN........... 34
Bert Haas CIN............... 22
Johnny Hopp BOS........ 21

RUNS SCORED
Stan Musial STL 124
Enos Slaughter STL.... 100
Eddie Stanky BKN 98

WINS
Howie Pollet STL 21
Johnny Sain BOS 20
Kirby Higbe BKN........... 17

WINNING PERCENTAGE
Murry Dickson STL .... .714
Kirby Higbe BKN.......... .680
Howie Pollet STL .... .677

EARNED RUN AVERAGE
Howie Pollet STL 2.10
Johnny Sain BOS 2.21
Joe Beggs CIN........... 2.32

STRIKEOUTS
Johnny Schmitz CHI ... 135
Kirby Higbe BKN.......... 134
Johnny Sain BOS 129

SAVES
Ken Raffensberger PHI... 6
four tied at....................... 5

COMPLETE GAMES
Johnny Sain BOS 24
Howie Pollet STL 22
Dave Koslo NY 17

SHUTOUTS
Ewell Blackwell CIN........ 6
Harry Brecheen STL....... 5
J. Vander Meer CIN 5

GAMES PITCHED
Ken Trinkle NY.............. 48
Murry Dickson STL 47
Hank Behrman BKN 47

INNINGS PITCHED
Howie Pollet STL 266
Dave Koslo NY 265
Johnny Sain BOS 265

1947 AL

	W	L	PCT	GB	R	OR	BA	FA	ERA
★NEW YORK	97	57	.630	—	794	568	.271	.981	3.39
DETROIT	85	69	.552	12	714	642	.258	.975	3.57
BOSTON	83	71	.539	14	720	669	.265	.977	3.81
CLEVELAND	80	74	.519	17	687	588	.259	.983	3.44
PHILADELPHIA	78	76	.506	19	633	614	.252	.976	3.51
CHICAGO	70	84	.455	27	553	661	.256	.975	3.64
WASHINGTON	64	90	.416	33	496	675	.241	.976	3.97
ST. LOUIS	59	95	.383	38	564	744	.241	.977	4.33
					5161	5161	.256	.977	3.71

BATTING AVERAGE
Ted Williams BOS....... .343
B. McCosky PHI......... .328
two tied at .... .324

HITS
Johnny Pesky BOS..... 207
George Kell DET......... 188
Ted Williams BOS....... 181

DOUBLES
Lou Boudreau CLE 45
Ted Williams BOS......... 40
Tommy Henrich NY 35

TRIPLES
Tommy Henrich NY 13
Mickey Vernon WAS.... 12
Dave Philley CHI........... 11

HOME RUNS
Ted Williams BOS......... 32
Joe Gordon CLE 29
Jeff Heath STL.............. 27

RUNS BATTED IN
Ted Williams BOS....... 114
Tommy Henrich NY 98
Joe DiMaggio NY 97

SLUGGING AVERAGE
Ted Williams BOS....... .634
Joe DiMaggio NY .... .522
Joe Gordon CLE .... .496

STOLEN BASES
Bob Dillinger STL........... 34
Dave Philley CHI........... 21
two tied at 12

RUNS SCORED
Ted Williams BOS....... 125
Tommy Henrich NY 109
Johnny Pesky BOS..... 106

WINS
Bob Feller CLE 20
Allie Reynolds NY 19
Phil Marchildon PHI 19

WINNING PERCENTAGE
Allie Reynolds NY .... .704
Joe Dobson BOS .... .692
Phil Marchildon PHI .... .679

EARNED RUN AVERAGE
Spud Chandler NY 2.46
Bob Feller CLE 2.68
two tied at 2.81

STRIKEOUTS
Bob Feller CLE 196
Hal Newhouser DET ... 176
W. Masterson WAS 135

SAVES
Joe Page NY................. 17
Eddie Klieman CLE....... 17
Russ Christopher PHI ... 12

COMPLETE GAMES
Hal Newhouser DET 24
Early Wynn WAS 22
Eddie Lopat CHI 22

SHUTOUTS
Bob Feller CLE 5
three tied at..................... 4

GAMES PITCHED
Eddie Klieman CLE....... 58
Joe Page NY................. 56
Earl Johnson BOS 45

INNINGS PITCHED
Bob Feller CLE 299
Hal Newhouser DET ... 285
Phil Marchildon PHI 277

1947 NL

	W	L	PCT	GB	R	OR	BA	FA	ERA
BROOKLYN	94	60	.610	—	774	668	.272	.978	3.82
ST. LOUIS	89	65	.578	5	780	634	.270	.979	3.53
BOSTON	86	68	.558	8	701	622	.275	.974	3.62
NEW YORK	81	73	.526	13	830	761	.271	.974	4.44
CINCINNATI	73	81	.474	21	681	755	.259	.977	4.41
CHICAGO	69	85	.448	25	567	722	.259	.975	4.10
PHILADELPHIA	62	92	.403	32	589	687	.258	.974	3.96
PITTSBURGH	62	92	.403	32	744	817	.261	.975	4.68
					5666	5666	.265	.976	4.07

BATTING AVERAGE
H. Walker STL, PHI ... .363
Bob Elliott BOS .... .317
Phil Cavarretta CHI .... .314

HITS
T. Holmes BOS 191
H. Walker STL, PHI 186
two tied at 183

DOUBLES
Eddie Miller CIN 38
Bob Elliott BOS 35
two tied at 33

TRIPLES
H. Walker STL, PHI 16
Stan Musial STL 13
Enos Slaughter STL 13

HOME RUNS
Ralph Kiner PIT 51
Johnny Mize NY 51
Willard Marshall NY 36

RUNS BATTED IN
Johnny Mize NY 138
Ralph Kiner PIT 127
Walker Cooper NY 122

SLUGGING AVERAGE
Ralph Kiner PIT .... .639
Johnny Mize NY .... .614
Walker Cooper NY ..... .586

STOLEN BASES
Jackie Robinson BKN ... 29
Pete Reiser BKN 14
two tied at 13

RUNS SCORED
Johnny Mize NY 137
J. Robinson BKN 125
Ralph Kiner PIT 118

WINS
Ewell Blackwell CIN 22
four tied at 21

WINNING PERCENTAGE
Larry Jansen NY .... .808
G. Munger STL .... .762
Ewell Blackwell CIN .... .733

EARNED RUN AVERAGE
Warren Spahn BOS ... 2.33
Ewell Blackwell CIN ... 2.47
Ralph Branca BKN 2.67

STRIKEOUTS
Ewell Blackwell CIN 193
Ralph Branca BKN 148
Johnny Sain BOS 132

SAVES
Hugh Casey BKN 18
Harry Gumbert CIN 10
Ken Trinkle NY 10

COMPLETE GAMES
Ewell Blackwell CIN 23
Johnny Sain BOS 22
Warren Spahn BOS 22

SHUTOUTS
Warren Spahn BOS 7
George Munger STL 6
Ewell Blackwell CIN 6

GAMES PITCHED
Ken Trinkle NY 62
Kirby Higbe BKN, PIT ... 50
H. Behrman PIT, BKN ... 50

INNINGS PITCHED
Warren Spahn BOS 290
Ralph Branca BKN 280
Ewell Blackwell CIN 273

1948 AL

	W	L	PCT	GB	R	OR	BA	FA	ERA
★CLEVELAND*	97	58	.626	—	840	568	.282	.982	3.22
BOSTON	96	59	.619	1	907	720	.274	.981	4.20
NEW YORK	94	60	.610	2.5	857	633	.278	.979	3.75
PHILADELPHIA	84	70	.545	12.5	729	735	.260	.981	4.43
DETROIT	78	76	.506	18.5	700	726	.267	.974	4.15
ST. LOUIS	59	94	.386	37	671	849	.271	.972	5.01
WASHINGTON	56	97	.366	40	578	796	.244	.974	4.65
CHICAGO	51	101	.336	44.5	559	814	.251	.974	4.89
					5841	5841	.266	.977	4.28

* Defeated Boston in a 1-game playoff

BATTING AVERAGE
Ted Williams BOS...... .369
Lou Boudreau CLE .... .355
Dale Mitchell CLE ...... .336

HITS
Bob Dillinger STL......... 207
Dale Mitchell CLE 204
Lou Boudreau CLE 199

DOUBLES
Ted Williams BOS......... 44
Tommy Henrich NY 42
Hank Majeski PHI 41

TRIPLES
Tommy Henrich NY 14
B. Stewart NY, WAS 13
two tied at 11

HOME RUNS
Joe DiMaggio NY.......... 39
Joe Gordon CLE 32
Ken Keltner CLE 31

RUNS BATTED IN
Joe DiMaggio NY... 155
Vern Stephens BOS ... 137
Ted Williams BOS....... 127

SLUGGING AVERAGE
Ted Williams BOS...... .615
Joe DiMaggio NY....... .598
Tommy Henrich NY ... .554

STOLEN BASES
Bob Dillinger STL.......... 28
Gill Coan WAS.............. 23
Mickey Vernon WAS..... 15

RUNS SCORED
Tommy Henrich NY 138
Dom DiMaggio BOS ... 127
two tied at 124

WINS
Hal Newhouser DET 21
Gene Bearden CLE 20
Bob Lemon CLE 20

WINNING PERCENTAGE
Jack Kramer BOS ...... .783
Gene Bearden CLE ... .741
Vic Raschi NY .... .704

EARNED RUN AVERAGE
Gene Bearden CLE ... 2.43
Bob Lemon CLE 2.82
H. Newhouser DET.... 3.01

STRIKEOUTS
Bob Feller CLE 164
Bob Lemon CLE 147
Hal Newhouser DET ... 143

SAVES
R. Christopher CLE....... 17
Joe Page NY................. 16
two tied at 10

COMPLETE GAMES
Bob Lemon CLE 20
Hal Newhouser DET 19
two tied at 18

SHUTOUTS
Bob Lemon CLE 10
Gene Bearden CLE 6
Vic Raschi NY................. 6

GAMES PITCHED
Joe Page NY................. 55
Al Widmar STL.............. 49
Frank Biscan STL 47

INNINGS PITCHED
Bob Lemon CLE 294
Bob Feller CLE 280
Hal Newhouser DET ... 272

1948 NL

	W	L	PCT	GB	R	OR	BA	FA	ERA
BOSTON	91	62	.595	—	739	584	.275	.976	3.38
ST. LOUIS	85	69	.552	6.5	742	646	.263	.980	3.91
BROOKLYN	84	70	.545	7.5	744	667	.261	.973	3.75
PITTSBURGH	83	71	.539	8.5	706	699	.263	.977	4.15
NEW YORK	78	76	.506	13.5	780	704	.256	.974	3.93
PHILADELPHIA	66	88	.429	25.5	591	729	.259	.964	4.08
CINCINNATI	64	89	.418	27	588	752	.247	.973	4.47
CHICAGO	64	90	.416	27.5	597	706	.262	.972	4.00
					5487	5487	.261	.974	3.95

BATTING AVERAGE
Stan Musial STL .... .376
Richie Ashburn PHI ... .333
T. Holmes BOS .... .325

HITS
Stan Musial STL 230
T. Holmes BOS 190
Stan Rojek PIT 186

DOUBLES
Stan Musial STL 46
Del Ennis PHI 40
Alvin Dark BOS 39

TRIPLES
Stan Musial STL 18
Johnny Hopp PIT 12
Enos Slaughter STL 11

HOME RUNS
Johnny Mize NY 40
Ralph Kiner PIT 40
Stan Musial STL 39

RUNS BATTED IN
Stan Musial STL 131
Johnny Mize NY 125
Ralph Kiner PIT 123

SLUGGING AVERAGE
Stan Musial STL .... .702
Johnny Mize NY .... .564
Sid Gordon NY .... .537

STOLEN BASES
Richie Ashburn PHI 32
Pee Wee Reese BKN ... 25
Stan Rojek PIT 24

RUNS SCORED
Stan Musial STL 135
Whitey Lockman NY ... 117
Johnny Mize NY 110

WINS
Johnny Sain BOS 24
Harry Brecheen STL 20
two tied at 18

WINNING PERCENTAGE
H. Brecheen STL .... .741
Sheldon Jones NY ...... .667
Johnny Sain BOS .... .615

EARNED RUN AVERAGE
H. Brecheen STL 2.24
Dutch Leonard PHI 2.51
Johnny Sain BOS 2.60

STRIKEOUTS
Harry Brecheen STL ... 149
Rex Barney BKN 138
Johnny Sain BOS 137

SAVES
Harry Gumbert CIN 17
Ted Wilks STL 13
Kirby Higbe PIT 10

COMPLETE GAMES
Johnny Sain BOS 28
Harry Brecheen STL 21
Johnny Schmitz CHI 18

SHUTOUTS
Harry Brecheen STL 7
three tied at 4

GAMES PITCHED
Harry Gumbert CIN 61
Ted Wilks STL 57
Kirby Higbe PIT 56

INNINGS PITCHED
Johnny Sain BOS 315
Larry Jansen NY 277
Warren Spahn BOS 257

1949 AL

	W	L	PCT	GB	R	OR	BA	FA	ERA
★NEW YORK	97	57	.630	—	829	637	.269	.977	3.69
BOSTON	96	58	.623	1	896	667	.282	.980	3.97
CLEVELAND	89	65	.578	8	675	574	.260	.983	3.36
DETROIT	87	67	.565	10	751	655	.267	.978	3.77
PHILADELPHIA	81	73	.526	16	726	725	.260	.976	4.23
CHICAGO	63	91	.409	34	648	737	.257	.977	4.30
ST. LOUIS	53	101	.344	44	667	913	.254	.971	5.21
WASHINGTON	50	104	.325	47	584	868	.254	.973	5.10
					5776	5776	.263	.977	4.20

BATTING AVERAGE
George Kell DET........ .343
Ted Williams BOS....... .343
Bob Dillinger STL........ .324

HITS
Dale Mitchell CLE 203
Ted Williams BOS....... 194
Dom DiMaggio BOS ... 186

DOUBLES
Ted Williams BOS......... 39
George Kell DET........... 38
Dom DiMaggio BOS 34

TRIPLES
Dale Mitchell CLE 23
Bob Dillinger STL.......... 13
Elmer Valo PHI 12

HOME RUNS
Ted Williams BOS......... 43
Vern Stephens BOS 39
four tied at..................... 24

RUNS BATTED IN
Vern Stephens BOS ... 159
Ted Williams BOS....... 159
Vic Wertz DET 133

SLUGGING AVERAGE
Ted Williams BOS...... .650
V. Stephens BOS........ .539
Tommy Henrich NY ... .526

STOLEN BASES
Bob Dillinger STL......... 20
Phil Rizzuto NY 18
Elmer Valo PHI 14

RUNS SCORED
Ted Williams BOS....... 150
Eddie Joost PHI 128
Dom DiMaggio BOS ... 126

WINS
Mel Parnell BOS 25
Ellis Kinder BOS 23
Bob Lemon CLE 22

WINNING PERCENTAGE
Ellis Kinder BOS .... .793
Mel Parnell BOS .... .781
Allie Reynolds NY .... .739

EARNED RUN AVERAGE
Mel Parnell BOS 2.77
Virgil Trucks DET........ 2.81
Bob Lemon CLE 2.99

STRIKEOUTS
Virgil Trucks DET........ 153
Hal Newhouser DET ... 144
two tied at 138

SAVES
Joe Page NY................. 27
Al Benton CLE 10
Tom Ferrick STL 6

COMPLETE GAMES
Mel Parnell BOS 27
Bob Lemon CLE 22
Hal Newhouser DET 22

SHUTOUTS
Ellis Kinder BOS 6
Virgil Trucks DET............ 6
Mike Garcia CLE............. 5

GAMES PITCHED
Joe Page NY................. 60
Dick Welteroth WAS 52
Tom Ferrick STL 50

INNINGS PITCHED
Mel Parnell BOS 295
Hal Newhouser DET ... 292
Bob Lemon CLE 280

1949 NL

	W	L	PCT	GB	R	OR	BA	FA	ERA
BROOKLYN	97	57	.630	—	879	651	.274	.980	3.80
ST. LOUIS	96	58	.623	1	766	616	.277	.976	3.45
PHILADELPHIA	81	73	.526	16	662	668	.254	.974	3.89
BOSTON	75	79	.487	22	706	719	.258	.976	3.99
NEW YORK	73	81	.474	24	736	693	.261	.973	3.82
PITTSBURGH	71	83	.461	26	681	760	.259	.978	4.57
CINCINNATI	62	92	.403	35	627	770	.260	.977	4.33
CHICAGO	61	93	.396	36	593	773	.256	.970	4.50
					5650	5650	.262	.975	4.04

BATTING AVERAGE
J. Robinson BKN .... .342
Stan Musial STL .... .338
Enos Slaughter STL... .336

HITS
Stan Musial STL 207
J. Robinson BKN 203
Bobby Thomson NY.... 198

DOUBLES
Stan Musial STL 41
Del Ennis PHI 39
two tied at 38

TRIPLES
Stan Musial STL 13
Enos Slaughter STL...... 13
Jackie Robinson BKN ... 12

HOME RUNS
Ralph Kiner PIT 54
Stan Musial STL 36
Hank Sauer CIN, CHI ... 31

RUNS BATTED IN
Ralph Kiner PIT 127
J. Robinson BKN 124
Stan Musial STL 123

SLUGGING AVERAGE
Ralph Kiner PIT .... .658
Stan Musial STL .... .624
J. Robinson BKN .... .528

STOLEN BASES
Jackie Robinson BKN ... 37
P. Reese BKN............... 26
four tied at.................... 12

RUNS SCORED
P. Reese BKN............. 132
Stan Musial STL 128
J. Robinson BKN 122

WINS
Warren Spahn BOS...... 21
Howie Pollet STL 20
K. Raffensberger CIN ... 18

WINNING PERCENTAGE
Preacher Roe BKN .... .714
Howie Pollet STL .... .690
two tied at .... .680

EARNED RUN AVERAGE
Dave Koslo NY 2.50
Howie Pollet STL 2.77
Preacher Roe BKN 2.79

STRIKEOUTS
Warren Spahn BOS 151
D. Newcombe BKN..... 149
Larry Jansen NY 113

SAVES
Ted Wilks STL 9
Jim Konstanty PHI 7
Nels Potter BOS 7

COMPLETE GAMES
Warren Spahn BOS...... 25
K. Raffensberger CIN ... 20
Don Newcombe BKN.... 19

SHUTOUTS
four tied at....................... 5

GAMES PITCHED
Ted Wilks STL 59
Jim Konstanty PHI 53
Erv Palica BKN 49

INNINGS PITCHED
Warren Spahn BOS.... 302
K. Raffensberger CIN . 284
Larry Jansen NY 260

1950 AL

	W	L	PCT	GB	R	OR	BA	FA	ERA
★NEW YORK	98	56	.636	—	914	691	.282	.980	4.15
DETROIT	95	59	.617	3	837	713	.282	.981	4.12
BOSTON	94	60	.610	4	1027	804	.302	.981	4.88
CLEVELAND	92	62	.597	6	806	654	.269	.978	3.74
WASHINGTON	67	87	.435	31	690	813	.260	.972	4.66
CHICAGO	60	94	.390	38	625	749	.260	.977	4.41
ST. LOUIS	58	96	.377	40	684	916	.246	.967	5.20
PHILADELPHIA	52	102	.338	46	670	913	.261	.974	5.49
					6253	6253	.271	.976	4.58

BATTING AVERAGE
Billy Goodman BOS ... .354
George Kell DET .... .340
Dom DiMaggio BOS .. .328

HITS
George Kell DET 218
Phil Rizzuto NY 200
Dom DiMaggio BOS ... 193

DOUBLES
George Kell DET........... 56
Vic Wertz DET 37
Phil Rizzuto NY............. 36

TRIPLES
Dom DiMaggio BOS 11
Bobby Doerr BOS 11
Hoot Evers DET............ 11

HOME RUNS
Al Rosen CLE 37
Walt Dropo BOS 34
Joe DiMaggio NY.......... 32

RUNS BATTED IN
Vern Stephens BOS ... 144
Walt Dropo BOS 144
Yogi Berra NY............. 124

SLUGGING AVERAGE
Joe DiMaggio NY........ .585
Walt Dropo BOS .... .583
Hoot Evers DET.......... .551

STOLEN BASES
Dom DiMaggio BOS 15
Elmer Valo PHI 12
Phil Rizzuto NY............. 12

RUNS SCORED
Dom DiMaggio BOS ... 131
Vern Stephens BOS ... 125
Phil Rizzuto NY........... 125

WINS
Bob Lemon CLE 23
Vic Raschi NY............... 21
Art Houtteman DET 19

WINNING PERCENTAGE
Vic Raschi NY............. .724
Eddie Lopat NY........... .692
Early Wynn CLE .... .692

EARNED RUN AVERAGE
Early Wynn CLE 3.20
Ned Garver STL......... 3.39
Bob Feller CLE 3.43

STRIKEOUTS
Bob Lemon CLE 170
Allie Reynolds NY 160
Vic Raschi NY............. 155

SAVES
Mickey Harris WAS....... 15
Joe Page NY................. 13
Tom Ferrick STL, NY 11

COMPLETE GAMES
Ned Garver STL............ 22
Bob Lemon CLE 22
two tied at 21

SHUTOUTS
Art Houtteman DET 4
three tied at..................... 3

GAMES PITCHED
Mickey Harris WAS....... 53
Ellis Kinder BOS 48
two tied at 46

INNINGS PITCHED
Bob Lemon CLE 288
Art Houtteman DET 275
Ned Garver STL.......... 260

1950 NL

	W	L	PCT	GB	R	OR	BA	FA	ERA
PHILADELPHIA	91	63	.591	—	722	624	.265	.975	3.50
BROOKLYN	89	65	.578	2	847	724	.272	.979	4.28
NEW YORK	86	68	.558	5	735	643	.258	.977	3.71
BOSTON	83	71	.539	8	785	736	.263	.970	4.14
ST. LOUIS	78	75	.510	12.5	693	670	.259	.978	3.97
CINCINNATI	66	87	.431	24.5	654	734	.260	.976	4.32
CHICAGO	64	89	.418	26.5	643	772	.248	.968	4.28
PITTSBURGH	57	96	.373	33.5	681	857	.264	.977	4.96
					5760	5760	.261	.975	4.14

BATTING AVERAGE
Stan Musial STL .... .346
J. Robinson BKN .... .328
Duke Snider BKN....... .321

HITS
Duke Snider BKN........ 199
Stan Musial STL 192
Carl Furillo BKN 189

DOUBLES
R. Schoendienst STL.... 43
Stan Musial STL 41
Jackie Robinson BKN ... 39

TRIPLES
Richie Ashburn PHI 14
Gus Bell PIT.................. 11
Duke Snider BKN.......... 10

HOME RUNS
Ralph Kiner PIT 47
Andy Pafko CHI 36
two tied at 32

RUNS BATTED IN
Del Ennis PHI 126
Ralph Kiner PIT 118
Gil Hodges BKN.......... 113

SLUGGING AVERAGE
Stan Musial STL .... .596
Andy Pafko CHI .... .591
Ralph Kiner PIT .... .590

STOLEN BASES
Sam Jethroe BOS.......... 35
Pee Wee Reese BKN ... 17
Duke Snider BKN.......... 16

RUNS SCORED
Earl Torgeson BOS..... 120
Eddie Stanky NY......... 115
Ralph Kiner PIT 112

WINS
Warren Spahn BOS 21
Robin Roberts PHI........ 20
Johnny Sain BOS 20

WINNING PERCENTAGE
Sal Maglie NY .... .818
Jim Konstanty PHI ...... .696
Curt Simmons PHI ..... .680

EARNED RUN AVERAGE
Jim Hearn STL, NY.... 2.49
Sal Maglie NY 2.71
Ewell Blackwell CIN ... 2.97

STRIKEOUTS
Warren Spahn BOS.... 191
Ewell Blackwell CIN 188
Larry Jansen NY 161

SAVES
Jim Konstanty PHI 22
Bill Werle PIT 8
two tied at 7

COMPLETE GAMES
Vern Bickford BOS........ 27
Warren Spahn BOS 25
Johnny Sain BOS 25

SHUTOUTS
four tied at....................... 5

GAMES PITCHED
Jim Konstanty PHI 74
Murry Dickson PIT 51
Bill Werle PIT 48

INNINGS PITCHED
Vern Bickford BOS...... 312
Robin Roberts PHI...... 304
Warren Spahn BOS 293

1951 AL

	W	L	PCT	GB	R	OR	BA	FA	ERA
★NEW YORK	98	56	.636	—	798	621	.269	.975	3.56
CLEVELAND	93	61	.604	5	696	594	.256	.978	3.38
BOSTON	87	67	.565	11	804	725	.266	.977	4.14
CHICAGO	81	73	.526	17	714	644	.270	.975	3.50
DETROIT	73	81	.474	25	685	741	.265	.973	4.29
PHILADELPHIA	70	84	.455	28	736	745	.262	.978	4.47
WASHINGTON	62	92	.403	36	672	764	.263	.973	4.49
ST. LOUIS	52	102	.338	46	611	882	.247	.971	5.17
					5716	5716	.262	.975	4.12

BATTING AVERAGE
Ferris Fain PHI............ .344
Minoso CLE, CHI........ .326
George Kell DET........ .319

HITS
George Kell DET.......... 191
Dom DiMaggio BOS ... 189
Nellie Fox CHI............. 189

DOUBLES
Sam Mele WAS 36
George Kell DET........... 36
Eddie Yost WAS 36

TRIPLES
Minoso CLE, CHI 14
Nellie Fox CHI............... 12
R. Coleman STL, CHI ... 12

HOME RUNS
Gus Zernial CHI, PHI 33
Ted Williams BOS......... 30
Eddie Robinson CHI 29

RUNS BATTED IN
G. Zernial CHI, PHI..... 129
Ted Williams BOS....... 126
Eddie Robinson CHI ... 117

SLUGGING AVERAGE
Ted Williams BOS...... .556
Larry Doby CLE .... .512
two tied at .... .511

STOLEN BASES
M. Minoso CLE, CHI 31
Jim Busby CHI 26
Phil Rizzuto NY............. 18

RUNS SCORED
Dom DiMaggio BOS ... 113
Minoso CLE, CHI 112
two tied at 109

WINS
Bob Feller CLE 22
Eddie Lopat NY............. 21
Vic Raschi NY............... 21

WINNING PERCENTAGE
Bob Feller CLE .... .733
Eddie Lopat NY........... .700
Allie Reynolds NY ...... .680

EARNED RUN AVERAGE
Rogovin DET, CHI 2.78
Eddie Lopat NY......... 2.91
Early Wynn CLE 3.02

STRIKEOUTS
Vic Raschi NY............. 164
Early Wynn CLE 133
Bob Lemon CLE 132

SAVES
Ellis Kinder BOS 14
Carl Scheib PHI 10
Lou Brissie PHI, CLE 9

COMPLETE GAMES
Ned Garver STL............. 24
Early Wynn CLE 21
Eddie Lopat NY............. 20

SHUTOUTS
Allie Reynolds NY 7
Eddie Lopat NY............... 5
two tied at 4

GAMES PITCHED
Ellis Kinder BOS 63
Lou Brissie PHI, CLE 56
Mike Garcia CLE........... 47

INNINGS PITCHED
Early Wynn CLE 274
Bob Lemon CLE 263
Vic Raschi NY............. 258

1951 NL

	W	L	PCT	GB	R	OR	BA	FA	ERA
NEW YORK*	98	59	.624	—	781	641	.260	.972	3.48
BROOKLYN	97	60	.618	1	855	672	.275	.979	3.88
ST. LOUIS	81	73	.526	15.5	683	671	.264	.980	3.95
BOSTON	76	78	.494	20.5	723	662	.262	.976	3.75
PHILADELPHIA	73	81	.474	23.5	648	644	.260	.977	3.81
CINCINNATI	68	86	.442	28.5	559	667	.248	.977	3.70
PITTSBURGH	64	90	.416	32.5	689	845	.258	.972	4.78
CHICAGO	62	92	.403	34.5	614	750	.250	.971	4.34
					5552	5552	.260	.975	3.96

*Defeated Brooklyn in a playoff 2 games to 1

BATTING AVERAGE
Stan Musial STL .... .355
Richie Ashburn PHI ... .344
J. Robinson BKN .... .338

HITS
Richie Ashburn PHI 221
Stan Musial STL 205
Carl Furillo BKN 197

DOUBLES
Alvin Dark NY 41
Ted Kluszewski CIN...... 35
two tied at 33

TRIPLES
Stan Musial STL 12
Gus Bell PIT.................. 12
Monte Irvin NY 11

HOME RUNS
Ralph Kiner PIT 42
Gil Hodges BKN............. 40
Roy Campanella BKN.... 33

RUNS BATTED IN
Monte Irvin NY 121
Sid Gordon BOS 109
Ralph Kiner PIT 109

SLUGGING AVERAGE
Ralph Kiner PIT .... .627
Stan Musial STL .... .614
R. Campanella BKN... .590

STOLEN BASES
Sam Jethroe BOS.......... 35
Richie Ashburn PHI 29
Jackie Robinson BKN ... 25

RUNS SCORED
Stan Musial STL 124
Ralph Kiner PIT 124
Gil Hodges BKN.......... 118

WINS
Sal Maglie NY 23
Larry Jansen NY 23
two tied at 22

WINNING PERCENTAGE
Preacher Roe BKN .... .880
Sal Maglie NY .... .793
D. Newcombe BKN.... .690

EARNED RUN AVERAGE
Chet Nichols BOS...... 2.88
Sal Maglie NY 2.93
Warren Spahn BOS ... 2.98

STRIKEOUTS
Warren Spahn BOS.... 164
D. Newcombe BKN..... 164
Sal Maglie NY 146

SAVES
Ted Wilks STL, PIT....... 13
Frank Smith CIN 11
Jim Konstanty PHI 9

COMPLETE GAMES
Warren Spahn BOS...... 26
Robin Roberts PHI........ 22
Sal Maglie NY 22

SHUTOUTS
Robin Roberts PHI.......... 6
K. Raffensberger CIN 5
two tied at 4

GAMES PITCHED
Ted Wilks STL, PIT..... 65
Bill Werle PIT................ 59
Jim Konstanty PHI 58

INNINGS PITCHED
Robin Roberts PHI...... 315
Warren Spahn BOS.... 311
Sal Maglie NY 298

1952 AL

	W	L	PCT	GB	R	OR	BA	FA	ERA
★NEW YORK	95	59	.617	—	727	557	.267	.979	3.14
CLEVELAND	93	61	.604	2	763	606	.262	.975	3.32
CHICAGO	81	73	.526	14	610	568	.252	.980	3.25
PHILADELPHIA	79	75	.513	16	664	723	.253	.977	4.15
WASHINGTON	78	76	.506	17	598	608	.239	.978	3.37
BOSTON	76	78	.494	19	668	658	.255	.976	3.80
ST. LOUIS	64	90	.416	31	604	733	.250	.974	4.12
DETROIT	50	104	.325	45	557	738	.243	.975	4.25
					5191	5191	.253	.977	3.67

BATTING AVERAGE
Ferris Fain PHI............ .327
Dale Mitchell CLE ...... .323
two tied at .... .311

HITS
Nellie Fox CHI............. 192
Bobby Avila CLE......... 179
two tied at 176

DOUBLES
Ferris Fain PHI............. 43
Mickey Mantle NY......... 37
two tied at 33

TRIPLES
Bobby Avila CLE........... 11
three tied at................... 10

HOME RUNS
Larry Doby CLE 32
Luke Easter CLE........... 31
Yogi Berra NY 30

RUNS BATTED IN
Al Rosen CLE 105
Eddie Robinson CHI ... 104
Larry Doby CLE 104

SLUGGING AVERAGE
Larry Doby CLE .... .541
Mickey Mantle NY...... .530
Al Rosen CLE .... .524

STOLEN BASES
Minnie Minoso CHI 22
Jim Rivera STL, CHI 21
J. Jensen NY, WAS 18

RUNS SCORED
Larry Doby CLE 104
Bobby Avila CLE......... 102
Al Rosen CLE 101

WINS
Bobby Shantz PHI 24
Early Wynn CLE 23
two tied at 22

WINNING PERCENTAGE
Bobby Shantz PHI ..... .774
Vic Raschi NY............. .727
Allie Reynolds NY ...... .714

EARNED RUN AVERAGE
Allie Reynolds NY 2.06
Mike Garcia CLE........ 2.37
Bobby Shantz PHI 2.48

STRIKEOUTS
Allie Reynolds NY 160
Early Wynn CLE 153
Bobby Shantz PHI 152

SAVES
Harry Dorish CHI 11
Satchel Paige STL........ 10
Johnny Sain NY 7

COMPLETE GAMES
Bob Lemon CLE 28
Bobby Shantz PHI 27
Allie Reynolds NY 24

SHUTOUTS
Allie Reynolds NY 6
Mike Garcia CLE............. 6
two tied at 5

GAMES PITCHED
Bill Kennedy CHI........... 47
Mike Garcia CLE........... 46
Satchel Paige STL......... 46

INNINGS PITCHED
Bob Lemon CLE 310
Mike Garcia CLE......... 292
Early Wynn CLE 286

1952 NL

	W	L	PCT	GB	R	OR	BA	FA	ERA
BROOKLYN	96	57	.627	—	775	603	.262	.982	3.53
NEW YORK	92	62	.597	4.5	722	639	.256	.974	3.59
ST. LOUIS	88	66	.571	8.5	677	630	.267	.977	3.66
PHILADELPHIA	87	67	.565	9.5	657	552	.260	.975	3.07
CHICAGO	77	77	.500	19.5	628	631	.264	.976	3.58
CINCINNATI	69	85	.448	27.5	615	659	.249	.982	4.01
BOSTON	64	89	.418	32	569	651	.233	.975	3.78
PITTSBURGH	42	112	.273	54.5	515	793	.231	.970	4.65
					5158	5158	.253	.976	3.73

BATTING AVERAGE
Stan Musial STL .... .336
F. Baumholtz CHI ...... .325
Ted Kluszewski CIN... .320

HITS
Stan Musial STL 194
Schoendienst STL 188
Bobby Adams CIN 180

DOUBLES
Stan Musial STL 42
Schoendienst STL 40
Roy McMillan CIN 32

TRIPLES
Bobby Thomson NY...... 14
Enos Slaughter STL...... 12
Ted Kluszewski CIN...... 11

HOME RUNS
Hank Sauer CHI............. 37
Ralph Kiner PIT 37
Gil Hodges BKN............. 32

RUNS BATTED IN
Hank Sauer CHI........... 121
Bobby Thomson NY.... 108
Del Ennis PHI 107

SLUGGING AVERAGE
Stan Musial STL .... .538
Hank Sauer CHI.......... .531
Ted Kluszewski CIN... .509

STOLEN BASES
Pee Wee Reese BKN ... 30
Sam Jethroe BOS......... 28
Jackie Robinson BKN... 24

RUNS SCORED
Stan Musial STL 105
Solly Hemus STL........ 105
J. Robinson BKN 104

WINS
Robin Roberts PHI........ 28
Sal Maglie NY 18
three tied at.................. 17

WINNING PERCENTAGE
Hoyt Wilhelm NY......... .833
Robin Roberts PHI..... .800
Joe Black BKN............ .789

EARNED RUN AVERAGE
Hoyt Wilhelm NY......... 2.43
Warren Hacker CHI ... 2.58
Robin Roberts PHI..... 2.59

STRIKEOUTS
Warren Spahn BOS 183
Bob Rush CHI............. 157
Robin Roberts PHI...... 148

SAVES
Al Brazle STL................ 16
Joe Black BKN.............. 15
two tied at 11

COMPLETE GAMES
Robin Roberts PHI........ 30
Murry Dickson PIT 21
Warren Spahn BOS 19

SHUTOUTS
Curt Simmons PHI 6
K. Raffensberger CIN 6
two tied at 5

GAMES PITCHED
Hoyt Wilhelm NY........... 71
Joe Black BKN............... 56
Eddie Yuhas STL........... 54

INNINGS PITCHED
Robin Roberts PHI...... 330
Warren Spahn BOS 290
Murry Dickson PIT 278

1953 AL

	W	L	PCT	GB	R	OR	BA	FA	ERA
★NEW YORK	99	52	.656	—	801	547	.273	.979	3.20
CLEVELAND	92	62	.597	8.5	770	627	.270	.979	3.64
CHICAGO	89	65	.578	11.5	716	592	.258	.980	3.41
BOSTON	84	69	.549	16	656	632	.264	.975	3.59
WASHINGTON	76	76	.500	23.5	687	614	.263	.979	3.66
DETROIT	60	94	.390	40.5	695	923	.266	.978	5.25
PHILADELPHIA	59	95	.383	41.5	632	799	.256	.977	4.67
ST. LOUIS	54	100	.351	46.5	555	778	.249	.974	4.48
					5512	5512	.262	.978	4.00

BATTING AVERAGE
M. Vernon WAS .... .337
Al Rosen CLE .... .336
two tied at .... .313

HITS
Harvey Kuenn DET 209
Mickey Vernon WAS ... 205
Al Rosen CLE 201

DOUBLES
Mickey Vernon WAS 43
George Kell BOS 41
Sammy White BOS 34

TRIPLES
Jim Rivera CHI 16
Mickey Vernon WAS 11
two tied at 9

HOME RUNS
Al Rosen CLE 43
Gus Zernial PHI 42
Larry Doby CLE 29

RUNS BATTED IN
Al Rosen CLE 145
Mickey Vernon WAS ... 115
Boone CLE, DET 114

SLUGGING AVERAGE
Al Rosen CLE .... .613
Gus Zernial PHI .... .559
Yogi Berra NY .... .523

STOLEN BASES
Minnie Minoso CHI 25
Jim Rivera CHI 22
Jackie Jensen WAS 18

RUNS SCORED
Al Rosen CLE 115
Eddie Yost WAS 107
Mickey Mantle NY 105

WINS
Bob Porterfield WAS 22
Bob Lemon CLE 21
Mel Parnell BOS 21

WINNING PERCENTAGE
Eddie Lopat NY .... .800
Whitey Ford NY .... .750
Mel Parnell BOS .... .724

EARNED RUN AVERAGE
Eddie Lopat NY 2.42
Billy Pierce CHI 2.72
Trucks STL, CHI 2.93

STRIKEOUTS
Billy Pierce CHI 186
V. Trucks STL, CHI 149
Early Wynn CLE 138

SAVES
Ellis Kinder BOS 27
Harry Dorish CHI 18
Allie Reynolds NY 13

COMPLETE GAMES
Bob Porterfield WAS 24
Bob Lemon CLE 23
Mike Garcia CLE 21

SHUTOUTS
Bob Porterfield WAS 9
Billy Pierce CHI 7
two tied at 5

GAMES PITCHED
Ellis Kinder BOS 69
Marlan Stuart STL 60
Morrie Martin PHI 58

INNINGS PITCHED
Bob Lemon CLE 287
Mike Garcia CLE 272
Billy Pierce CHI 271

1953 NL

	W	L	PCT	GB	R	OR	BA	FA	ERA
BROOKLYN	105	49	.682	—	955	689	.285	.980	4.10
MILWAUKEE	92	62	.597	13	738	589	.266	.976	3.30
PHILADELPHIA	83	71	.539	22	716	666	.265	.975	3.80
ST. LOUIS	83	71	.539	22	768	713	.273	.977	4.23
NEW YORK	70	84	.455	35	768	747	.271	.975	4.25
CINCINNATI	68	86	.442	37	714	788	.261	.978	4.64
CHICAGO	65	89	.422	40	633	835	.260	.967	4.79
PITTSBURGH	50	104	.325	55	622	887	.247	.973	5.22
					5914	5914	.266	.975	4.29

BATTING AVERAGE
Carl Furillo BKN .... .344
Schoendienst STL ...... .342
Stan Musial STL .... .337

HITS
Richie Ashburn PHI 205
Stan Musial STL 200
Duke Snider BKN........ 198

DOUBLES
Stan Musial STL 53
Alvin Dark NY 41
two tied at 38

TRIPLES
Jim Gilliam BKN............. 17
Bill Bruton MIL 14
two tied at 11

HOME RUNS
Eddie Mathews MIL 47
Duke Snider BKN.......... 42
Roy Campanella BKN... 41

RUNS BATTED IN
R. Campanella BKN.... 142
Eddie Mathews MIL ... 135
Duke Snider BKN........ 126

SLUGGING AVERAGE
Duke Snider BKN........ .627
Eddie Mathews MIL ... .627
R. Campanella BKN... .611

STOLEN BASES
Bill Bruton MIL 26
Pee Wee Reese BKN ... 22
Jim Gilliam BKN 21

RUNS SCORED
Duke Snider BKN........ 132
Stan Musial STL 127
Alvin Dark NY 126

WINS
Warren Spahn MIL........ 23
Robin Roberts PHI........ 23
two tied at 20

WINNING PERCENTAGE
Carl Erskine BKN........ .769
Warren Spahn MIL........ .767
two tied at .... .750

EARNED RUN AVERAGE
Warren Spahn MIL..... 2.10
Robin Roberts PHI..... 2.75
Bob Buhl MIL 2.97

STRIKEOUTS
Robin Roberts PHI...... 198
Carl Erskine BKN........ 187
Mizell STL................... 173

SAVES
Al Brazle STL................ 18
Hoyt Wilhelm NY........... 15
Jim Hughes BKN 9

COMPLETE GAMES
Robin Roberts PHI........ 33
Warren Spahn MIL........ 24
two tied at 19

SHUTOUTS
Harvey Haddix STL........ 6
Robin Roberts PHI.......... 5
Warren Spahn MIL......... 5

GAMES PITCHED
Hoyt Wilhelm NY........... 68
Al Brazle STL................ 60
Johnny Hetki PIT 54

INNINGS PITCHED
Robin Roberts PHI...... 347
Warren Spahn MIL...... 266
Harvey Haddix STL..... 253

1954 AL

	W	L	PCT	GB	R	OR	BA	FA	ERA
CLEVELAND	111	43	.721	—	746	504	.262	.979	2.78
NEW YORK	103	51	.669	8	805	563	.268	.979	3.26
CHICAGO	94	60	.610	17	711	521	.267	.982	3.05
BOSTON	69	85	.448	42	700	728	.266	.972	4.01
DETROIT	68	86	.442	43	584	664	.258	.978	3.81
WASHINGTON	66	88	.429	45	632	680	.246	.977	3.84
BALTIMORE	54	100	.351	57	483	668	.251	.975	3.88
PHILADELPHIA	51	103	.331	60	542	875	.236	.972	5.18
					5203	5203	.257	.977	3.72

BATTING AVERAGE
Bobby Avila CLE......... .341
Minnie Minoso CHI .... .320
two tied at .... .319

HITS
Nellie Fox CHI............. 201
Harvey Kuenn DET..... 201
Bobby Avila CLE......... 189

DOUBLES
Mickey Vernon WAS..... 33
Minnie Minoso CHI 29
Al Smith CLE 29

TRIPLES
Minnie Minoso CHI 18
Pete Runnels WAS....... 15
Mickey Vernon WAS..... 14

HOME RUNS
Larry Doby CLE 32
Ted Williams BOS......... 29
Mickey Mantle NY......... 27

RUNS BATTED IN
Larry Doby CLE 126
Yogi Berra NY.............. 125
Jackie Jensen BOS 117

SLUGGING AVERAGE
Ted Williams BOS...... .635
Minnie Minoso CHI .... .535
Mickey Mantle NY...... .525

STOLEN BASES
Jackie Jensen BOS 22
Jim Rivera CHI 18
Minnie Minoso CHI 18

RUNS SCORED
Mickey Mantle NY....... 129
Minnie Minoso CHI 119
Bobby Avila CLE......... 112

WINS
Bob Lemon CLE 23
Early Wynn CLE 23
Bob Grim NY................. 20

WINNING PERCENTAGE
S. Consuegra CHI...... .842
Bob Grim NY.............. .769
Bob Lemon CLE .... .767

EARNED RUN AVERAGE
Mike Garcia CLE........ 2.64
S. Consuegra CHI...... 2.69
Bob Lemon CLE 2.72

STRIKEOUTS
Bob Turley BAL............ 185
Early Wynn CLE 155
Virgil Trucks CHI......... 152

SAVES
Johnny Sain NY 22
Ellis Kinder BOS 15
Ray Narleski CLE 13

COMPLETE GAMES
Bob Porterfield WAS..... 21
Bob Lemon CLE 21
Early Wynn CLE 20

SHUTOUTS
Virgil Trucks CHI............. 5
Mike Garcia CLE............. 5

GAMES PITCHED
S. Dixon WAS, PHI....... 54
three tied at.................. 48

INNINGS PITCHED
Early Wynn CLE 271
Virgil Trucks CHI......... 265
Mike Garcia CLE......... 259

1954 NL

	W	L	PCT	GB	R	OR	BA	FA	ERA
★NEW YORK	97	57	.630	—	732	550	.264	.975	3.09
BROOKLYN	92	62	.597	5	778	740	.270	.978	4.31
MILWAUKEE	89	65	.578	8	670	556	.265	.981	3.19
PHILADELPHIA	75	79	.487	22	659	614	.267	.975	3.59
CINCINNATI	74	80	.481	23	729	763	.262	.977	4.50
ST. LOUIS	72	82	.468	25	799	790	.281	.976	4.50
CHICAGO	64	90	.416	33	700	766	.263	.974	4.51
PITTSBURGH	53	101	.344	44	557	845	.248	.971	4.92
					5624	5624	.265	.976	4.07

BATTING AVERAGE
Willie Mays NY............ .345
Don Mueller NY .... .342
Duke Snider BKN........ .341

HITS
Don Mueller NY 212
Duke Snider BKN........ 199
two tied at 195

DOUBLES
Stan Musial STL 41
three tied at.................. 39

TRIPLES
Willie Mays NY.............. 13
Granny Hamner PHI 11
Duke Snider BKN.......... 10

HOME RUNS
Ted Kluszewski CIN...... 49
Gil Hodges BKN............ 42
two tied at 41

RUNS BATTED IN
Ted Kluszewski CIN...... 141
Gil Hodges BKN........... 130
Duke Snider BKN........ 130

SLUGGING AVERAGE
Willie Mays NY............ .667
Duke Snider BKN........ .647
Ted Kluszewski CIN... .642

STOLEN BASES
Bill Bruton MIL 34
Johnny Temple CIN 21
Dee Fondy CHI............. 20

RUNS SCORED
Duke Snider BKN........ 120
Stan Musial STL 120
Willie Mays NY............ 119

WINS
Robin Roberts PHI........ 23
Johnny Antonelli NY 21
Warren Spahn MIL........ 21

WINNING PERCENTAGE
Johnny Antonelli NY ... .750
B. Lawrence STL .... .714
Ruben Gomez NY....... .654

EARNED RUN AVERAGE
J. Antonelli NY 2.30
Lew Burdette MIL........ 2.76
Curt Simmons PHI..... 2.81

STRIKEOUTS
Robin Roberts PHI...... 185
Harvey Haddix STL.... 184
Carl Erskine BKN........ 166

SAVES
Jim Hughes BKN 24
Frank Smith CIN 20
Marv Grissom NY 19

COMPLETE GAMES
Robin Roberts PHI........ 29
Warren Spahn MIL....... 23
Curt Simmons PHI 21

SHUTOUTS
Johnny Antonelli NY 6
three tied at...................... 4

GAMES PITCHED
Jim Hughes BKN 60
Al Brazle STL................ 58
Johnny Hetki PIT 58

INNINGS PITCHED
Robin Roberts PHI...... 337
Warren Spahn MIL...... 283
two tied at 260

1955 AL

	W	L	PCT	GB	R	OR	BA	FA	ERA
NEW YORK	96	58	.623	—	762	569	.260	.978	3.23
CLEVELAND	93	61	.604	3	698	601	.257	.981	3.39
CHICAGO	91	63	.591	5	725	557	.268	.981	3.37
BOSTON	84	70	.545	12	755	652	.264	.977	3.72
DETROIT	79	75	.513	17	775	658	.266	.976	3.79
KANSAS CITY	63	91	.409	33	638	911	.261	.976	5.35
BALTIMORE	57	97	.370	39	540	754	.240	.972	4.21
WASHINGTON	53	101	.344	43	598	789	.248	.974	4.62
					5491	5491	.258	.977	3.96

BATTING AVERAGE
Al Kaline DET .... .340
Vic Power KC .... .319
George Kell CHI .... .312

HITS
Al Kaline DET 200
Nellie Fox CHI 198
two tied at 190

DOUBLES
Harvey Kuenn DET 38
Vic Power KC 34
Billy Goodman BOS 31

TRIPLES
Andy Carey NY 11
Mickey Mantle NY 11
Vic Power KC 10

HOME RUNS
Mickey Mantle NY 37
Gus Zernial KC 30
Ted Williams BOS 28

RUNS BATTED IN
Ray Boone DET 116
Jackie Jensen BOS 116
Yogi Berra NY 108

SLUGGING AVERAGE
Mickey Mantle NY ...... .611
Al Kaline DET .... .546
Gus Zernial KC .... .508

STOLEN BASES
Jim Rivera CHI 25
Minnie Minoso CHI 19
Jackie Jensen BOS 16

RUNS SCORED
Al Smith CLE 123
Al Kaline DET 121
Mickey Mantle NY 121

WINS
Whitey Ford NY 18
Bob Lemon CLE 18
Frank Sullivan BOS 18

WINNING PERCENTAGE
Tommy Byrne NY .... .762
Whitey Ford NY .... .720
Billy Hoeft DET .... .696

EARNED RUN AVERAGE
Billy Pierce CHI 1.97
Whitey Ford NY 2.63
Early Wynn CLE 2.82

STRIKEOUTS
Herb Score CLE 245
Bob Turley NY 210
Billy Pierce CHI 157

SAVES
Ray Narleski CLE 19
Tom Gorman KC 18
Ellis Kinder BOS 18

COMPLETE GAMES
Whitey Ford NY 18
Billy Hoeft DET 17

SHUTOUTS
Billy Hoeft DET 7
three tied at 6

GAMES PITCHED
Ray Narleski CLE 60
Don Mossi CLE 57
Tom Gorman KC 57

INNINGS PITCHED
Frank Sullivan BOS 260
Whitey Ford NY 254
Bob Turley NY 247

1955 NL

	W	L	PCT	GB	R	OR	BA	FA	ERA
★BROOKLYN	98	55	.641	—	857	650	.271	.978	3.68
MILWAUKEE	85	69	.552	13.5	743	668	.261	.975	3.85
NEW YORK	80	74	.519	18.5	702	673	.260	.976	3.77
PHILADELPHIA	77	77	.500	21.5	675	666	.255	.981	3.93
CINCINNATI	75	79	.487	23.5	761	684	.270	.977	3.95
CHICAGO	72	81	.471	26	626	713	.247	.975	4.17
ST. LOUIS	68	86	.442	30.5	654	757	.261	.975	4.56
PITTSBURGH	60	94	.390	38.5	560	767	.244	.972	4.39
					5578	5578	.259	.976	4.04

BATTING AVERAGE
Richie Ashburn PHI ... .338
Willie Mays NY .... .319
Stan Musial STL .... .319

HITS
Ted Kluszewski CIN.... 192
Hank Aaron MIL 189
Gus Bell CIN 188

DOUBLES
Hank Aaron MIL............ 37
Johnny Logan MIL 37
Duke Snider BKN.......... 34

TRIPLES
Willie Mays NY.............. 13
Dale Long PIT............... 13
Bill Bruton MIL 12

HOME RUNS
Willie Mays NY.............. 51
Ted Kluszewski CIN...... 47
Ernie Banks CHI 44

RUNS BATTED IN
Duke Snider BKN........ 136
Willie Mays NY............ 127
Del Ennis PHI 120

SLUGGING AVERAGE
Willie Mays NY............ .659
Duke Snider BKN........ .628
Eddie Mathews MIL .... .601

STOLEN BASES
Bill Bruton MIL 25
Willie Mays NY.............. 24
Ken Boyer STL 22

RUNS SCORED
Duke Snider BKN........ 126
Willie Mays NY............ 123
two tied at 116

WINS
Robin Roberts PHI........ 23
Don Newcombe BKN.... 20
two tied at 17

WINNING PERCENTAGE
D. Newcombe BKN.... .800
Robin Roberts PHI..... .622
Joe Nuxhall CIN.......... .586

EARNED RUN AVERAGE
Bob Friend PIT........... 2.83
D. Newcombe BKN.... 3.20
Bob Buhl MIL 3.21

STRIKEOUTS
Sheldon Jones CHI..... 198
Robin Roberts PHI..... 160
Harvey Haddix STL..... 150

SAVES
Jack Meyer PHI 16
Ed Roebuck BKN.......... 12
two tied at 11

COMPLETE GAMES
Robin Roberts PHI....... 26
Don Newcombe BKN.... 17
Warren Spahn MIL........ 16

SHUTOUTS
Joe Nuxhall CIN.............. 5
Murry Dickson PHI.......... 4
Sheldon Jones CHI......... 4

GAMES PITCHED
Clem Labine BKN 60
Hoyt Wilhelm NY 59
Paul LaPalme STL........ 56

INNINGS PITCHED
Robin Roberts PHI...... 305
Joe Nuxhall CIN........... 257
Warren Spahn MIL...... 246

1956 AL

	W	L	PCT	GB	R	OR	BA	FA	ERA
★NEW YORK	97	57	.630	—	857	631	.270	.977	3.63
CLEVELAND	88	66	.571	9	712	581	.244	.978	3.32
CHICAGO	85	69	.552	12	776	634	.267	.979	3.73
BOSTON	84	70	.545	13	780	751	.275	.972	4.17
DETROIT	82	72	.532	15	789	699	.279	.976	4.06
BALTIMORE	69	85	.448	28	571	705	.244	.977	4.20
WASHINGTON	59	95	.383	38	652	924	.250	.972	5.33
KANSAS CITY	52	102	.338	45	619	831	.252	.973	4.86
					5756	5756	.260	.975	4.16

BATTING AVERAGE
Mickey Mantle NY ...... .353
Ted Williams BOS ...... .345
Harvey Kuenn DET .... .332

HITS
Harvey Kuenn DET 196
Al Kaline DET 194
Nellie Fox CHI 192

DOUBLES
Jimmy Piersall BOS 40
Al Kaline DET 32
Harvey Kuenn DET 32

TRIPLES
four tied at 11

HOME RUNS
Mickey Mantle NY 52
Vic Wertz CLE 32
Yogi Berra NY 30

RUNS BATTED IN
Mickey Mantle NY 130
Al Kaline DET 128
Vic Wertz CLE 106

SLUGGING AVERAGE
Mickey Mantle NY ...... .705
Ted Williams BOS ...... .605
two tied at .... .534

STOLEN BASES
Luis Aparicio CHI 21
Jim Rivera CHI 20
Bobby Avila CLE 17

RUNS SCORED
Mickey Mantle NY 132
Nellie Fox CHI 109
Minnie Minoso CHI 106

WINS
Frank Lary DET 21
five tied at 20

WINNING PERCENTAGE
Whitey Ford NY .... .760
three tied at .... .690

EARNED RUN AVERAGE
Whitey Ford NY 2.47
Herb Score CLE 2.53
Early Wynn CLE 2.72

STRIKEOUTS
Herb Score CLE 263
Billy Pierce CHI 192
Paul Foytack DET 184

SAVES
George Zuverink BAL ... 16
Tom Morgan NY 11
Don Mossi CLE 11

COMPLETE GAMES
Billy Pierce CHI 21
Bob Lemon CLE 21
Frank Lary DET 20

SHUTOUTS
Herb Score CLE 5
three tied at 4

GAMES PITCHED
George Zuverink BAL ... 62
Jack Crimian KC 54
Tom Gorman KC 52

INNINGS PITCHED
Frank Lary DET 294
Early Wynn CLE 278
Billy Pierce CHI 276

1956 NL

	W	L	PCT	GB	R	OR	BA	FA	ERA
BROOKLYN	93	61	.604	—	720	601	.258	.981	3.57
MILWAUKEE	92	62	.597	1	709	569	.259	.979	3.11
CINCINNATI	91	63	.591	2	775	658	.266	.981	3.85
ST. LOUIS	76	78	.494	17	678	698	.268	.978	3.97
PHILADELPHIA	71	83	.461	22	668	738	.252	.975	4.20
NEW YORK	67	87	.435	26	540	650	.244	.976	3.78
PITTSBURGH	66	88	.429	27	588	653	.257	.973	3.74
CHICAGO	60	94	.390	33	597	708	.244	.976	3.96
					5275	5275	.256	.977	3.77

BATTING AVERAGE
Hank Aaron MIL......... .328
Bill Virdon STL, PIT ... .319
R. Clemente PIT .... .311

HITS
Hank Aaron MIL.......... 200
Richie Ashburn PHI 190
Bill Virdon STL, PIT 185

DOUBLES
Hank Aaron MIL............ 34
three tied at.................. 33

TRIPLES
Bill Bruton MIL 15
Hank Aaron MIL............ 14
two tied at 11

HOME RUNS
Duke Snider BKN.......... 43
Frank Robinson CIN 38
Joe Adcock MIL 38

RUNS BATTED IN
Stan Musial STL 109
Joe Adcock MIL 103
Ted Kluszewski CIN.... 102

SLUGGING AVERAGE
Duke Snider BKN....... .598
Joe Adcock MIL .... .597
two tied at .... .558

STOLEN BASES
Willie Mays NY.............. 40
Jim Gilliam BKN............. 21
Bill White NY................. 15

RUNS SCORED
Frank Robinson CIN ... 122
Duke Snider BKN........ 112
Hank Aaron MIL.......... 106

WINS
Don Newcombe BKN.... 27
Warren Spahn MIL........ 20
Johnny Antonelli NY 20

WINNING PERCENTAGE
D. Newcombe BKN.... .794
Bob Buhl MIL............. .692
two tied at .... .655

EARNED RUN AVERAGE
Lew Burdette MIL....... 2.70
Warren Spahn MIL..... 2.78
J. Antonelli NY 2.86

STRIKEOUTS
Sheldon Jones CHI..... 176
Haddix STL, PHI 170
Bob Friend PIT............ 166

SAVES
Clem Labine BKN 19
Hersh Freeman CIN...... 18
Turk Lown CHI.............. 13

COMPLETE GAMES
Robin Roberts PHI........ 22
Warren Spahn MIL........ 20
Bob Friend PIT............. 19

SHUTOUTS
Johnny Antonelli NY 6
Lew Burdette MIL............ 6
Don Newcombe BKN....... 5

GAMES PITCHED
Roy Face PIT................. 68
Hersh Freeman CIN...... 64
Hoyt Wilhelm NY........... 64

INNINGS PITCHED
Bob Friend PIT............ 314
Robin Roberts PHI...... 297
Warren Spahn MIL...... 281

1957 AL

	W	L	PCT	GB	R	OR	BA	FA	ERA
NEW YORK	98	56	.636	—	723	534	.268	.980	3.00
CHICAGO	90	64	.584	8	707	566	.260	.982	3.35
BOSTON	82	72	.532	16	721	668	.262	.976	3.88
DETROIT	78	76	.506	20	614	614	.257	.980	3.56
BALTIMORE	76	76	.500	21	597	588	.252	.981	3.46
CLEVELAND	76	77	.497	21.5	682	722	.252	.974	4.05
KANSAS CITY	59	94	.386	38.5	563	710	.244	.979	4.19
WASHINGTON	55	99	.357	43	603	808	.244	.979	4.85
					5210	5210	.255	.979	3.79

BATTING AVERAGE
Ted Williams BOS...... .388
Mickey Mantle NY...... .365
G. Woodling CLE .... .321

HITS
Nellie Fox CHI............. 196
Frank Malzone BOS ... 185
Minnie Minoso CHI 176

DOUBLES
Billy Gardner BAL 36
Minnie Minoso CHI 36
Frank Malzone BOS 31

TRIPLES
Harry Simpson KC, NY ... 9
Gil McDougald NY 9
Hank Bauer NY 9

HOME RUNS
Roy Sievers WAS 42
Ted Williams BOS 38
Mickey Mantle NY 34

RUNS BATTED IN
Roy Sievers WAS 114
Vic Wertz CLE 105
three tied at.................. 103

SLUGGING AVERAGE
Ted Williams BOS....... .731
Mickey Mantle NY...... .665
Roy Sievers WAS ...... .579

STOLEN BASES
Luis Aparicio CHI 28
Minnie Minoso CHI 18
Jim Rivera CHI.............. 18

RUNS SCORED
Mickey Mantle NY....... 121
Nellie Fox CHI............. 110
Jimmy Piersall BOS 103

WINS
Jim Bunning DET.......... 20
Billy Pierce CHI............. 20
three tied at................... 16

WINNING PERCENTAGE
Dick Donovan CHI ..... .727
Tom Sturdivant NY .... .727
Jim Bunning DET .... .714

EARNED RUN AVERAGE
Bobby Shantz NY 2.45
Tom Sturdivant NY 2.54
Jim Bunning DET....... 2.69

STRIKEOUTS
Early Wynn CLE 184
Jim Bunning DET........ 182
C. Johnson BAL........... 177

SAVES
Bob Grim NY................. 19
Ray Narleski CLE 16
Ike Delock BOS 11

COMPLETE GAMES
Dick Donovan CHI 16
Billy Pierce CHI............. 16
Tom Brewer BOS.......... 15

SHUTOUTS
Jim Wilson CHI 5
Billy Pierce CHI 4
Bob Turley NY 4

GAMES PITCHED
George Zuverink BAL ... 56
Tex Clevenger WAS 52
Dick Hyde WAS 52

INNINGS PITCHED
Jim Bunning DET........ 267
Early Wynn CLE 263
Billy Pierce CHI........... 257

1957 NL

	W	L	PCT	GB	R	OR	BA	FA	ERA
★MILWAUKEE	95	59	.617	—	772	613	.269	.981	3.47
ST. LOUIS	87	67	.565	8	737	666	.274	.979	3.78
BROOKLYN	84	70	.545	11	690	591	.253	.979	3.35
CINCINNATI	80	74	.519	15	747	781	.269	.982	4.62
PHILADELPHIA	77	77	.500	18	623	656	.250	.976	3.80
NEW YORK	69	85	.448	26	643	701	.252	.974	4.01
CHICAGO	62	92	.403	33	628	722	.244	.975	4.13
PITTSBURGH	62	92	.403	33	586	696	.268	.972	3.88
					5426	5426	.260	.977	3.88

BATTING AVERAGE
Stan Musial STL .... .351
Willie Mays NY .... .333
two tied at .... .322

HITS
Schoendienst NY, MIL 200
Hank Aaron MIL 198
Frank Robinson CIN ... 197

DOUBLES
Don Hoak CIN 39
Stan Musial STL 38
Ed Bouchee PHI 35

TRIPLES
Willie Mays NY 20
Bill Virdon PIT 11
two tied at 9

HOME RUNS
Hank Aaron MIL 44
Ernie Banks CHI 43
Duke Snider BKN 40

RUNS BATTED IN
Hank Aaron MIL 132
Del Ennis STL 105
two tied at 102

SLUGGING AVERAGE
Willie Mays NY .... .626
Stan Musial STL .... .612
Hank Aaron MIL .... .600

STOLEN BASES
Willie Mays NY 38
Jim Gilliam BKN 26
Don Blasingame STL 21

RUNS SCORED
Hank Aaron MIL 118
Ernie Banks CHI 113
Willie Mays NY 112

WINS
Warren Spahn MIL 21
Jack Sanford PHI 19
Bob Buhl MIL 18

WINNING PERCENTAGE
Bob Buhl MIL .... .720
Jack Sanford PHI .... .704
Warren Spahn MIL ..... .656

EARNED RUN AVERAGE
J. Podres BKN 2.66
Don Drysdale BKN 2.69
Warren Spahn MIL 2.69

STRIKEOUTS
Jack Sanford PHI 188
Dick Drott CHI 170
Moe Drabowsky CHI ... 170

SAVES
Clem Labine BKN 17
Marv Grissom NY 14
Turk Lown CHI 12

COMPLETE GAMES
Warren Spahn MIL 18
Bob Friend PIT 17
Ruben Gomez NY 16

SHUTOUTS
Johnny Podres BKN 6
three tied at 4

GAMES PITCHED
Turk Lown CHI 67
Roy Face PIT 59
Clem Labine BKN 58

INNINGS PITCHED
Bob Friend PIT 277
Warren Spahn MIL 271
Lew Burdette MIL 257

1958 AL

	W	L	PCT	GB	R	OR	BA	FA	ERA
★NEW YORK	92	62	.597	—	759	577	.268	.978	3.22
CHICAGO	82	72	.532	10	634	615	.257	.981	3.61
BOSTON	79	75	.513	13	697	691	.256	.976	3.92
CLEVELAND	77	76	.503	14.5	694	635	.258	.974	3.73
DETROIT	77	77	.500	15	659	606	.266	.982	3.59
BALTIMORE	74	79	.484	17.5	521	575	.241	.980	3.40
KANSAS CITY	73	81	.474	19	642	713	.247	.979	4.15
WASHINGTON	61	93	.396	31	553	747	.240	.980	4.53
					5159	5159	.254	.979	3.77

BATTING AVERAGE
Ted Williams BOS...... .328
Pete Runnels BOS..... .322
Harvey Kuenn DET.... .319

HITS
Nellie Fox CHI............. 187
Frank Malzone BOS ... 185
Vic Power KC, CLE..... 184

DOUBLES
Harvey Kuenn DET....... 39
Vic Power KC, CLE....... 37
Al Kaline DET 34

TRIPLES
Vic Power KC, CLE....... 10
three tied at..................... 9

HOME RUNS
Mickey Mantle NY......... 42
Rocky Colavito CLE..... 41
Roy Sievers WAS 39

RUNS BATTED IN
Jackie Jensen BOS 122
Rocky Colavito CLE..... 113
Roy Seivers WAS 108

SLUGGING AVERAGE
Rocky Colavito CLE... .620
Bob Cerv KC.............. .592
Mickey Mantle NY ..... .592

STOLEN BASES
Luis Aparicio CHI 29
Jim Rivera CHI............... 21
Jim Landis CHI 19

RUNS SCORED
Mickey Mantle NY 127
Pete Runnels BOS...... 103
Vic Power KC, CLE....... 98

WINS
Bob Turley NY 21
Billy Pierce CHI............. 17
two tied at 16

WINNING PERCENTAGE
Bob Turley NY .... .750
Cal McLish CLE .... .667
Billy Pierce CHI.......... .607

EARNED RUN AVERAGE
Whitey Ford NY 2.01
Billy Pierce CHI......... 2.68
J. Harshman BAL....... 2.89

STRIKEOUTS
Early Wynn CHI 179
Jim Bunning DET........ 177
Bob Turley NY 168

SAVES
Ryne Duren NY............. 20
Dick Hyde WAS 18
Leo Kiely BOS 12

COMPLETE GAMES
Bob Turley NY 19
Billy Pierce CHI............. 19
Frank Lary DET 19

SHUTOUTS
Whitey Ford NY 7
Bob Turley NY 6
two tied at 4

GAMES PITCHED
Tex Clevenger WAS 55
D. Tomanek CLE, KC 54
Dick Hyde WAS 53

INNINGS PITCHED
Frank Lary DET 260
Pedro Ramos WAS..... 259
Dick Donovan CHI 248

1958 NL

	W	L	PCT	GB	R	OR	BA	FA	ERA
MILWAUKEE	92	62	.597	—	675	541	.266	.980	3.21
PITTSBURGH	84	70	.545	8	662	607	.264	.978	3.56
SAN FRANCISCO	80	74	.519	12	727	698	.263	.975	3.98
CINCINNATI	76	78	.494	16	695	621	.258	.983	3.73
CHICAGO	72	82	.468	20	709	725	.265	.975	4.22
ST. LOUIS	72	82	.468	20	619	704	.261	.974	4.12
LOS ANGELES	71	83	.461	21	668	761	.251	.975	4.47
PHILADELPHIA	69	85	.448	23	664	762	.266	.978	4.32
					5419	5419	.262	.977	3.95

BATTING AVERAGE
Richie Ashburn PHI ... .350
Willie Mays SF .... .347
Stan Musial STL .... .337

HITS
Richie Ashburn PHI 215
Willie Mays SF 208
Hank Aaron MIL........... 196

DOUBLES
Orlando Cepeda SF...... 38
Dick Groat PIT 36
Stan Musial STL 35

TRIPLES
Richie Ashburn PHI 13
three tied at................... 11

HOME RUNS
Ernie Banks CHI 47
Frank Thomas PIT 35
two tied at 31

RUNS BATTED IN
Ernie Banks CHI 129
Frank Thomas PIT 109
Harry Anderson PHI...... 97

SLUGGING AVERAGE
Ernie Banks CHI .... .614
Willie Mays SF .... .583
Hank Aaron MIL.......... .546

STOLEN BASES
Willie Mays SF 31
Richie Ashburn PHI 30
Tony Taylor CHI............. 21

RUNS SCORED
Willie Mays SF 121
Ernie Banks CHI 119
Hank Aaron MIL........... 109

WINS
Bob Friend PIT.............. 22
Warren Spahn MIL........ 22
Lew Burdette MIL.......... 20

WINNING PERCENTAGE
Warren Spahn MIL...... .667
Lew Burdette MIL........ .667
Bob Friend PIT........... .611

EARNED RUN AVERAGE
Stu Miller SF 2.47
Sam Jones STL 2.88
Lew Burdette MIL....... 2.91

STRIKEOUTS
Sam Jones STL 225
Warren Spahn MIL...... 150
two tied at 143

SAVES
Roy Face PIT................ 20
Clem Labine LA 14
Dick Farrell PHI............. 11

COMPLETE GAMES
Warren Spahn MIL........ 23
Robin Roberts PHI........ 21
Lew Burdette MIL.......... 19

SHUTOUTS
Carl Willey MIL............... 4
three tied at..................... 3

GAMES PITCHED
Don Elston CHI.............. 69
Klippstein CIN, LA......... 57
Roy Face PIT................. 57

INNINGS PITCHED
Warren Spahn MIL....... 290
Lew Burdette MIL........ 275
Bob Friend PIT............ 274

1959 AL

	W	L	PCT	GB	R	OR	BA	FA	ERA
CHICAGO	94	60	.610	—	669	588	.250	.979	3.29
CLEVELAND	89	65	.578	5	745	646	.263	.978	3.75
NEW YORK	79	75	.513	15	687	647	.260	.978	3.60
DETROIT	76	78	.494	18	713	732	.258	.978	4.20
BOSTON	75	79	.487	19	726	696	.256	.978	4.17
BALTIMORE	74	80	.481	20	551	621	.238	.976	3.56
KANSAS CITY	66	88	.429	28	681	760	.263	.973	4.35
WASHINGTON	63	91	.409	31	619	701	.237	.973	4.01
					5391	5391	.253	.977	3.86

BATTING AVERAGE
Harvey Kuenn DET.... .353
Al Kaline DET .... .327
Pete Runnels BOS..... .314

HITS
Harvey Kuenn DET..... 198
Nellie Fox CHI............ 191
Pete Runnels BOS...... 176

DOUBLES
Harvey Kuenn DET....... 42
Frank Malzone BOS 34
Nellie Fox CHI............... 34

TRIPLES
Bob Allison WAS............. 9
Gil McDougald NY 8
two tied at 7

HOME RUNS
Rocky Colavito CLE...... 42
H. Killebrew WAS 42
Jim Lemon WAS 33

RUNS BATTED IN
Jackie Jensen BOS 112
Rocky Colavito CLE.... 111
H. Killebrew WAS 105

SLUGGING AVERAGE
Al Kaline DET .... .530
H. Killebrew WAS ...... .516
Mickey Mantle NY...... .514

STOLEN BASES
Luis Aparicio CHI.......... 56
Mickey Mantle NY......... 21
two tied at 20

RUNS SCORED
Eddie Yost DET............ 115
Mickey Mantle NY...... 104
Vic Power CLE............. 102

WINS
Early Wynn CHI 22
Cal McLish CLE 19
Bob Shaw CHI 18

WINNING PERCENTAGE
Bob Shaw CHI .... .750
Cal McLish CLE .... .704
Early Wynn CHI .... .688

EARNED RUN AVERAGE
Hoyt Wilhelm BAL 2.19
C. Pascual WAS 2.64
Bob Shaw CHI 2.69

STRIKEOUTS
Jim Bunning DET........ 201
C. Pascual WAS 185
Early Wynn CHI 179

SAVES
Turk Lown CHI 15
three tied at................... 14

COMPLETE GAMES
Camilo Pascual WAS.... 17
Don Mossi DET............. 15
Milt Pappas BAL 15

SHUTOUTS
Camilo Pascual WAS...... 6
Early Wynn CHI 5
Milt Pappas BAL 4

GAMES PITCHED
George Staley CHI........ 67
Turk Lown CHI.............. 60
Tex Clevenger WAS 50

INNINGS PITCHED
Early Wynn CHI 256
Jim Bunning DET........ 250
Paul Foytack DET....... 240

1959 NL

	W	L	PCT	GB	R	OR	BA	FA	ERA
★LOS ANGELES*	88	68	.564	—	705	670	.257	.981	3.79
MILWAUKEE	86	70	.551	2	724	623	.265	.979	3.51
SAN FRANCISCO	83	71	.539	4	705	613	.261	.974	3.47
PITTSBURGH	78	76	.506	9	651	680	.263	.975	3.90
CHICAGO	74	80	.481	13	673	688	.249	.977	4.01
CINCINNATI	74	80	.481	13	764	738	.274	.978	4.31
ST. LOUIS	71	83	.461	16	641	725	.269	.975	4.34
PHILADELPHIA	64	90	.416	23	599	725	.242	.973	4.27
					5462	5462	.260	.977	3.95

* Defeated Milwaukee in a playoff 2 games to 0

BATTING AVERAGE
Hank Aaron MIL......... .355
J. Cunningham STL... .345
Orlando Cepeda SF... .317

HITS
Hank Aaron MIL.......... 223
Vada Pinson CIN 205
Orlando Cepeda SF.... 192

DOUBLES
Vada Pinson CIN 47
Hank Aaron MIL............. 46
Willie Mays SF 43

TRIPLES
Charlie Neal LA............. 11
Wally Moon LA.............. 11
two tied at 9

HOME RUNS
Eddie Mathews MIL....... 46
Ernie Banks CHI 45
Hank Aaron MIL............. 39

RUNS BATTED IN
Ernie Banks CHI 143
Frank Robinson CIN ... 125
Hank Aaron MIL........... 123

SLUGGING AVERAGE
Hank Aaron MIL......... .636
Ernie Banks CHI .... .596
Eddie Mathews MIL ... .593

STOLEN BASES
Willie Mays SF 27
three tied at.................... 23

RUNS SCORED
Vada Pinson CIN 131
Willie Mays SF 125
Eddie Mathews MIL 118

WINS
Lew Burdette MIL........... 21
Sam Jones SF 21
Warren Spahn MIL........ 21

WINNING PERCENTAGE
Roy Face PIT............. .947
Vern Law PIT .... .667
Johnny Antonelli SF... .655

EARNED RUN AVERAGE
Sam Jones SF 2.83
Stu Miller SF 2.84
Bill Buhl MIL................ 2.86

STRIKEOUTS
Don Drysdale LA......... 242
Sam Jones SF 209
Sandy Koufax LA 173

SAVES
Lindy McDaniel STL....... 15
Don McMahon MIL 15
Don Elston CHI.............. 13

COMPLETE GAMES
Warren Spahn MIL........ 21
Vern Law PIT 20
Lew Burdette MIL........... 20

SHUTOUTS
seven tied at 4

GAMES PITCHED
Bill Henry CHI 65
Don Elston CHI 65
Lindy McDaniel STL...... 62

INNINGS PITCHED
Warren Spahn MIL...... 292
Lew Burdette MIL........ 290
Johnny Antonelli SF.... 282

1960 AL

	W	L	PCT	GB	R	OR	BA	FA	ERA
NEW YORK	97	57	.630	—	746	627	.260	.979	3.52
BALTIMORE	89	65	.578	8	682	606	.253	.982	3.52
CHICAGO	87	67	.565	10	741	617	.270	.982	3.60
CLEVELAND	76	78	.494	21	667	693	.267	.978	3.95
WASHINGTON	73	81	.474	24	672	696	.244	.973	3.77
DETROIT	71	83	.461	26	633	644	.239	.977	3.64
BOSTON	65	89	.422	32	658	775	.261	.976	4.62
KANSAS CITY	58	96	.377	39	615	756	.249	.979	4.38
					5414	5414	.255	.978	3.87

BATTING AVERAGE
Pete Runnels BOS..... .320
Al Smith CHI .... .315
Minnie Minoso CHI ... .311

HITS
Minnie Minoso CHI 184
Nellie Fox CHI.............. 175
B. Robinson BAL 175

DOUBLES
Tito Francona CLE........ 36
Bill Skowron NY 34
two tied at 32

TRIPLES
Nellie Fox CHI............... 10
Brooks Robinson BAL..... 9

HOME RUNS
Mickey Mantle NY......... 40
Roger Maris NY 39
Jim Lemon WAS 38

RUNS BATTED IN
Roger Maris NY 112
Minnie Minoso CHI 105
Vic Wertz BOS............. 103

SLUGGING AVERAGE
Roger Maris NY .... .581
Mickey Mantle NY...... .558
two tied at .... .534

STOLEN BASES
Luis Aparicio CHI.......... 51
Jim Landis CHI 23
Lenny Green WAS........ 21

RUNS SCORED
Mickey Mantle NY....... 119
Roger Maris NY 98
two tied at 89

WINS
Jim Perry CLE............... 18
Chuck Estrada BAL 18
Buddy Daley KC 16

WINNING PERCENTAGE
Jim Perry CLE............. .643
Art Ditmar NY .... .625
Chuck Estrada BAL .... .621

EARNED RUN AVERAGE
F. Baumann CHI 2.67
Jim Bunning DET....... 2.79
two tied at 3.06

STRIKEOUTS
Jim Bunning DET......... 201
Pedro Ramos WAS..... 160
Early Wynn CHI 158

SAVES
Mike Fornieles BOS...... 14
J. Klippstein CLE 14
Ray Moore CHI, WAS... 13

COMPLETE GAMES
Frank Lary DET 15
Pedro Ramos WAS....... 14
Ray Herbert KC 14

SHUTOUTS
Jim Perry CLE................. 4
Whitey Ford NY 4
Early Wynn CHI 4

GAMES PITCHED
Mike Fornieles BOS...... 70
Gerry Staley CHI........... 64
Tex Clevenger WAS 53

INNINGS PITCHED
Frank Lary DET 274
Pedro Ramos WAS..... 274
Jim Perry CLE............. 261

1960 NL

	W	L	PCT	GB	R	OR	BA	FA	ERA
★PITTSBURGH	95	59	.617	—	734	593	.276	.979	3.49
MILWAUKEE	88	66	.571	7	724	658	.265	.976	3.76
ST. LOUIS	86	68	.558	9	639	616	.254	.976	3.64
LOS ANGELES	82	72	.532	13	662	593	.255	.979	3.40
SAN FRANCISCO	79	75	.513	16	671	631	.255	.972	3.44
CINCINNATI	67	87	.435	28	640	692	.250	.979	4.00
CHICAGO	60	94	.390	35	634	776	.243	.977	4.35
PHILADELPHIA	59	95	.383	36	546	691	.239	.974	4.01
					5250	5250	.255	.977	3.76

BATTING AVERAGE
Dick Groat PIT .... .325
Willie Mays SF .... .319
R. Clemente PIT .... .314

HITS
Willie Mays SF 190
Vada Pinson CIN 187
Dick Groat PIT 186

DOUBLES
Vada Pinson CIN 37
Orlando Cepeda SF 36
two tied at 33

TRIPLES
Bill Bruton MIL 13
Willie Mays SF 12
Vada Pinson CIN 12

HOME RUNS
Ernie Banks CHI 41
Hank Aaron MIL............ 40
Eddie Mathews MIL 39

RUNS BATTED IN
Hank Aaron MIL............ 126
Eddie Mathews MIL 124
Ernie Banks CHI 117

SLUGGING AVERAGE
F. Robinson CIN .... .595
Hank Aaron MIL.......... .566
Ken Boyer STL .... .562

STOLEN BASES
Maury Wills LA.............. 50
Vada Pinson CIN 32
Tony Taylor CHI, PHI.... 26

RUNS SCORED
Bill Bruton MIL 112
Eddie Mathews MIL 108
two tied at 107

WINS
Ernie Broglio STL.......... 21
Warren Spahn MIL........ 21
Vern Law PIT 20

WINNING PERCENTAGE
Ernie Broglio STL........ .700
Vern Law PIT .... .690
Warren Spahn MIL...... .677

EARNED RUN AVERAGE
Mike McCormick SF... 2.70
Ernie Broglio STL....... 2.74
Don Drysdale LA........ 2.84

STRIKEOUTS
Don Drysdale LA........ 246
Sandy Koufax LA 197
Sam Jones SF 190

SAVES
Lindy McDaniel STL...... 26
Roy Face PIT................ 24
Bill Henry CIN 17

COMPLETE GAMES
Warren Spahn MIL........ 18
Vern Law PIT 18
Lew Burdette MIL.......... 18

SHUTOUTS
Jack Sanford SF 6
Don Drysdale LA............. 5

GAMES PITCHED
Roy Face PIT................. 68
Lindy McDaniel STL...... 65
Don Elston CHI 60

INNINGS PITCHED
Larry Jackson STL...... 282
Lew Burdette MIL........ 276
Bob Friend PIT............ 276

1961 AL

	W	L	PCT	GB	R	OR	BA	FA	ERA
★NEW YORK	109	53	.673	—	827	612	.263	.980	3.46
DETROIT	101	61	.623	8	841	671	.266	.976	3.55
BALTIMORE	95	67	.586	14	691	588	.254	.980	3.22
CHICAGO	86	76	.531	23	765	726	.265	.980	4.06
CLEVELAND	78	83	.484	30.5	737	752	.266	.977	4.15
BOSTON	76	86	.469	33	729	792	.254	.977	4.29
MINNESOTA	70	90	.438	38	707	778	.250	.971	4.28
LOS ANGELES	70	91	.435	38.5	744	784	.245	.969	4.31
KANSAS CITY	61	100	.379	47.5	683	863	.247	.972	4.74
WASHINGTON	61	100	.379	47.5	618	776	.244	.975	4.23
					7342	7342	.256	.976	4.02

BATTING AVERAGE
Norm Cash DET .... .361
Al Kaline DET .... .324
Jimmy Piersall CLE.... .322

HITS
Norm Cash DET 193
B. Robinson BAL 192
Al Kaline DET 190

DOUBLES
Al Kaline DET 41
Tony Kubek NY............. 38
Brooks Robinson BAL... 38

TRIPLES
Jake Wood DET............. 14
Marty Keough WAS 9
Jerry Lumpe KC.............. 9

HOME RUNS
Roger Maris NY 61
Mickey Mantle NY 54
two tied at 46

RUNS BATTED IN
Roger Maris NY 142
Jim Gentile BAL 141
Rocky Colavito DET.... 140

SLUGGING AVERAGE
Mickey Mantle NY...... .687
Norm Cash DET .... .662
Jim Gentile BAL.......... .646

STOLEN BASES
Luis Aparicio CHI.......... 53
Dick Howser KC............ 37
Jake Wood DET............. 30

RUNS SCORED
Roger Maris NY 132
Mickey Mantle NY....... 132
Rocky Colavito DET.... 129

WINS
Whitey Ford NY 25
Frank Lary DET 23
Steve Barber BAL 18

WINNING PERCENTAGE
Whitey Ford NY .... .862
Ralph Terry NY .... .842
Luis Arroyo NY........... .750

EARNED RUN AVERAGE
Dick Donovan WAS ... 2.40
Bill Stafford NY 2.68
Don Mossi DET........... 2.96

STRIKEOUTS
Camilo Pascual MIN ... 221
Whitey Ford NY 209
Jim Bunning DET........ 194

SAVES
Luis Arroyo NY.............. 29
Hoyt Wilhelm BAL......... 18
Mike Fornieles BOS...... 15

COMPLETE GAMES
Frank Lary DET 22
Camilo Pascual MIN 15
Steve Barber BAL 14

SHUTOUTS
Camilo Pascual MIN 8
Steve Barber BAL 8
two tied at 4

GAMES PITCHED
Luis Arroyo NY.............. 65
Tom Morgan LA............ 59
Turk Lown CHI.............. 59

INNINGS PITCHED
Whitey Ford NY 283
Frank Lary DET 275
Jim Bunning DET........ 268

1961 NL

	W	L	PCT	GB	R	OR	BA	FA	ERA
CINCINNATI	93	61	.604	—	710	653	.270	.977	3.78
LOS ANGELES	89	65	.578	4	735	697	.262	.975	4.04
SAN FRANCISCO	85	69	.552	8	773	655	.264	.977	3.77
MILWAUKEE	83	71	.539	10	712	656	.258	.982	3.89
ST. LOUIS	80	74	.519	13	703	668	.271	.972	3.74
PITTSBURGH	75	79	.487	18	694	675	.273	.975	3.92
CHICAGO	64	90	.416	29	689	800	.255	.970	4.48
PHILADELPHIA	47	107	.305	46	584	796	.243	.976	4.61
					5600	5600	.262	.976	4.03

BATTING AVERAGE
R. Clemente PIT .... .351
Vada Pinson CIN .... .343
Ken Boyer STL .... .329

HITS
Vada Pinson CIN 208
R. Clemente PIT 201
Hank Aaron MIL.......... 197

DOUBLES
Hank Aaron MIL............ 39
Vada Pinson CIN 34
two tied at 32

TRIPLES
George Altman CHI 12
three tied at................... 11

HOME RUNS
Orlando Cepeda SF...... 46
Willie Mays SF 40
Frank Robinson CIN 37

RUNS BATTED IN
Orlando Cepeda SF.... 142
Frank Robinson CIN ... 124
Willie Mays SF 123

SLUGGING AVERAGE
F. Robinson CIN .... .611
Orlando Cepeda SF... .609
Hank Aaron MIL.......... .594

STOLEN BASES
Maury Wills LA.............. 35
Vada Pinson CIN 23
Frank Robinson CIN 22

RUNS SCORED
Willie Mays SF............ 129
Frank Robinson CIN ... 117
Hank Aaron MIL.......... 115

WINS
Joey Jay CIN 21
Warren Spahn MIL........ 21
Jim O'Toole CIN 19

WINNING PERCENTAGE
Johnny Podres LA ..... .783
Jim O'Toole CIN .... .679
Joey Jay CIN .... .677

EARNED RUN AVERAGE
Warren Spahn MIL...... 3.02
Jim O'Toole CIN 3.10
Curt Simmons STL 3.13

STRIKEOUTS
Sandy Koufax LA 269
Stan Williams LA......... 205
Don Drysdale LA......... 182

SAVES
Stu Miller SF 17
Roy Face PIT 17
two tied at 16

COMPLETE GAMES
Warren Spahn MIL........ 21
Sandy Koufax LA 15
two tied at 14

SHUTOUTS
Joey Jay CIN 4
Warren Spahn MIL........... 4

GAMES PITCHED
Jack Baldschun PHI...... 65
Stu Miller SF 63
Roy Face PIT................. 62

INNINGS PITCHED
Lew Burdette MIL......... 272
Warren Spahn MIL....... 263
Don Cardwell CHI 259

1962 AL

	W	L	PCT	GB	R	OR	BA	FA	ERA
★NEW YORK	96	66	.593	—	817	680	.267	.979	3.70
MINNESOTA	91	71	.562	5	798	713	.260	.979	3.89
LOS ANGELES	86	76	.531	10	718	706	.250	.972	3.70
DETROIT	85	76	.528	10.5	758	692	.248	.974	3.81
CHICAGO	85	77	.525	11	707	658	.257	.982	3.73
CLEVELAND	80	82	.494	16	682	745	.245	.977	4.14
BALTIMORE	77	85	.475	19	652	680	.248	.980	3.69
BOSTON	76	84	.475	19	707	756	.258	.979	4.22
KANSAS CITY	72	90	.444	24	745	837	.263	.979	4.79
WASHINGTON	60	101	.373	35.5	599	716	.250	.978	4.04
					7183	7183	.255	.978	3.97

BATTING AVERAGE
Pete Runnels BOS..... .326
Floyd Robinson CHI... .312
Chuck Hinton WAS.... .310

HITS
B. Richardson NY 209
Jerry Lumpe KC.......... 193
B. Robinson BAL 192

DOUBLES
Frank Robinson CHI 45
C. Yastrzemski BOS 43
Ed Bressoud BOS......... 40

TRIPLES
Gino Cimoli KC 15
three tied at.................. 10

HOME RUNS
H. Killebrew MIN........... 48
Norm Cash DET 39
two tied at 37

RUNS BATTED IN
H. Killebrew MIN 126
Norm Siebern KC........ 117
Rocky Colavito DET.... 112

SLUGGING AVERAGE
H. Killebrew MIN .... .545
Rocky Colavito DET.... .514
Norm Cash DET .... .513

STOLEN BASES
Luis Aparicio CHI 31
Chuck Hinton WAS....... 28
Jake Wood DET............ 24

RUNS SCORED
Albie Pearson LA 115
Norm Siebern KC........ 114
Bob Allison MIN 102

WINS
Ralph Terry NY 23
three tied at.................. 20

WINNING PERCENTAGE
Ray Herbert CHI .... .690
Whitey Ford NY .... .680
two tied at .... .667

EARNED RUN AVERAGE
Hank Aguirre DET...... 2.21
Robin Roberts BAL.... 2.78
Whitey Ford NY 2.90

STRIKEOUTS
Camilo Pascual MIN ... 206
Jim Bunning DET........ 184
Ralph Terry NY 176

SAVES
Dick Radatz BOS........... 24
Marshall Bridges NY 18
Terry Fox DET 16

COMPLETE GAMES
Camilo Pascual MIN 18
Jim Kaat MIN 16
Dick Donovan CLE 16

SHUTOUTS
Camilo Pascual MIN 5
Dick Donovan CLE 5
Jim Kaat MIN 5

GAMES PITCHED
Dick Radatz BOS.......... 62
John Wyatt KC.............. 59
two tied at 57

INNINGS PITCHED
Ralph Terry NY 299
Jim Kaat MIN 269
two tied at 258

1962 NL

	W	L	PCT	GB	R	OR	BA	FA	ERA
SAN FRANCISCO*103		62	.624	—	878	690	.278	.977	3.79
LOS ANGELES	102	63	.618	1	842	697	.268	.970	3.62
CINCINNATI	98	64	.605	3.5	802	685	.270	.977	3.75
PITTSBURGH	93	68	.578	8	706	626	.268	.976	3.37
MILWAUKEE	86	76	.531	15.5	730	665	.252	.980	3.68
ST. LOUIS	84	78	.519	17.5	774	664	.271	.979	3.55
PHILADELPHIA	81	80	.503	20	705	759	.260	.977	4.28
HOUSTON	64	96	.400	36.5	592	717	.246	.973	3.83
CHICAGO	59	103	.364	42.5	632	827	.253	.977	4.54
NEW YORK	40	120	.250	60.5	617	948	.240	.967	5.04
*Defeated Los Angeles in a playoff 2 games to 1					7278	7278	.261	.975	3.94

BATTING AVERAGE
Tommy Davis LA .... .346
F. Robinson CIN .... .342
Stan Musial STL .... .330

HITS
Tommy Davis LA 230
Frank Robinson CIN ... 208
Maury Wills LA............ 208

DOUBLES
Frank Robinson CIN 51
Willie Mays SF 36
Dick Groat PIT 34

TRIPLES
four tied at..................... 10

HOME RUNS
Willie Mays SF 49
Hank Aaron MIL............. 45
Frank Robinson CIN 39

RUNS BATTED IN
Tommy Davis LA 153
Willie Mays SF 141
Frank Robinson CIN ... 136

SLUGGING AVERAGE
F. Robinson CIN .... .624
Hank Aaron MIL .... .618
Willie Mays SF .... .615

STOLEN BASES
Maury Wills LA............ 104
Willie Davis LA.............. 32
two tied at 26

RUNS SCORED
Frank Robinson CIN ... 134
Maury Wills LA............ 130
Willie Mays SF 130

WINS
Don Drysdale LA............ 25
Jack Sanford SF 24
Bob Purkey CIN 23

WINNING PERCENTAGE
Bob Purkey CIN .... .821
Jack Sanford SF .... .774
Don Drysdale LA......... .735

EARNED RUN AVERAGE
Sandy Koufax LA 2.54
Bob Shaw MIL 2.80
Bob Purkey CIN 2.81

STRIKEOUTS
Don Drysdale LA......... 232
Sandy Koufax LA........ 216
Bob Gibson STL 208

SAVES
Roy Face PIT................ 28
Ron Perranoski LA........ 20
Stu Miller SF 19

COMPLETE GAMES
Warren Spahn MIL........ 22
Art Mahaffey PHI 20
Billy O'Dell SF 20

SHUTOUTS
Bob Gibson STL 5
Bob Friend PIT................ 5
two tied at 4

GAMES PITCHED
Ron Perranoski LA......... 70
Jack Baldshun PHI 67
Ed Roebuck LA............. 64

INNINGS PITCHED
Don Drysdale LA......... 314
Bob Purkey CIN 288
Billy O'Dell SF 281

1963 AL

	W	L	PCT	GB	R	OR	BA	FA	ERA
NEW YORK	104	57	.646	—	714	547	.252	.982	3.07
CHICAGO	94	68	.580	10.5	683	544	.250	.979	2.97
MINNESOTA	91	70	.565	13	767	602	.255	.976	3.28
BALTIMORE	86	76	.531	18.5	644	621	.249	.984	3.45
CLEVELAND	79	83	.488	25.5	635	702	.239	.977	3.79
DETROIT	79	83	.488	25.5	700	703	.252	.981	3.90
BOSTON	76	85	.472	28	666	704	.252	.978	3.97
KANSAS CITY	73	89	.451	31.5	615	704	.247	.980	3.92
LOS ANGELES	70	91	.435	34	597	660	.250	.974	3.52
WASHINGTON	56	106	.346	48.5	578	812	.227	.971	4.42
					6599	6599	.247	.978	3.63

BATTING AVERAGE
C. Yastrzemski BOS .. .321
Al Kaline DET .... .312
Rich Rollins MIN .... .307

HITS
C. Yastrzemski BOS ... 183
Pete Ward CHI............ 177
Albie Pearson LA 176

DOUBLES
C. Yastrzemski BOS 40
Pete Ward CHI.............. 34
two tied at 32

TRIPLES
Zoilo Versalles MIN 13
Jim Fregosi LA.............. 12
Chuck Hinton WAS 12

HOME RUNS
H. Killebrew MIN 45
Dick Stuart BOS............ 42
Bob Allison MIN 35

RUNS BATTED IN
Dick Stuart BOS........... 118
Al Kaline DET 101
H. Killebrew MIN 96

SLUGGING AVERAGE
H. Killebrew MIN .... .555
Bob Allison MIN .... .533
Elston Howard NY ..... .528

STOLEN BASES
Luis Aparicio BAL 40
Chuck Hinton WAS 25
two tied at 18

RUNS SCORED
Bob Allison MIN 99
Albie Pearson LA 92
two tied at 91

WINS
Whitey Ford NY 24
Jim Bouton NY 21
Camilo Pascual MIN 21

WINNING PERCENTAGE
Whitey Ford NY .... .774
Jim Bouton NY .... .750
Dick Radatz BOS .... .714

EARNED RUN AVERAGE
Gary Peters CHI 2.33
Juan Pizarro CHI 2.39
C. Pascual MIN 2.46

STRIKEOUTS
Camilo Pascual MIN ... 202
Jim Bunning DET........ 196
Dick Stigman MIN 193

SAVES
Stu Miller BAL.............. 27
Dick Radatz BOS.......... 25
three tied at.................. 21

COMPLETE GAMES
Ralph Terry NY 18
Camilo Pascual MIN 18
Dick Stigman MIN 15

SHUTOUTS
Ray Herbert CHI 7
Jim Bouton NY................ 6

GAMES PITCHED
Stu Miller BAL................ 71
Dick Radatz BOS........... 66
Bill Dailey MIN 66

INNINGS PITCHED
Whitey Ford NY 269
Ralph Terry NY 268
Monbouquette BOS 267

1963 NL

	W	L	PCT	GB	R	OR	BA	FA	ERA
★LOS ANGELES	99	63	.611	—	640	550	.251	.975	2.85
ST. LOUIS	93	69	.574	6	747	628	.271	.976	3.32
SAN FRANCISCO	88	74	.543	11	725	641	.258	.975	3.35
PHILADELPHIA	87	75	.537	12	642	578	.252	.978	3.09
CINCINNATI	86	76	.531	13	648	594	.246	.978	3.29
MILWAUKEE	84	78	.519	15	677	603	.244	.980	3.26
CHICAGO	82	80	.506	17	570	578	.238	.976	3.08
PITTSBURGH	74	88	.457	25	567	595	.250	.972	3.10
HOUSTON	66	96	.407	33	464	640	.220	.974	3.44
NEW YORK	51	111	.315	48	501	774	.219	.967	4.12
					6181	6181	.245	.975	3.29

BATTING AVERAGE
Tommy Davis LA .... .326
R. Clemente PIT .... .320
two tied at .... .319

HITS
Vada Pinson CIN 204
Hank Aaron MIL 201
Dick Groat STL 201

DOUBLES
Dick Groat STL 43
Vada Pinson CIN 37
two tied at 36

TRIPLES
Vada Pinson CIN 14
Tony Gonzalez PHI....... 12
two tied at 11

HOME RUNS
Willie McCovey SF........ 44
Hank Aaron MIL............ 44
Willie Mays SF 38

RUNS BATTED IN
Hank Aaron MIL.......... 130
Ken Boyer STL 111
Bill White STL 109

SLUGGING AVERAGE
Hank Aaron MIL.......... .586
Willie Mays SF .... .582
Willie McCovey SF..... .566

STOLEN BASES
Maury Wills LA.............. 40
Hank Aaron MIL............ 31
Vada Pinson CIN 27

RUNS SCORED
Hank Aaron MIL 121
Willie Mays SF 115
Curt Flood STL 112

WINS
Sandy Koufax LA 25
Juan Marichal SF.......... 25
two tied at 23

WINNING PERCENTAGE
Ron Perranoski LA..... .842
Sandy Koufax LA .... .833
two tied at .... .767

EARNED RUN AVERAGE
Sandy Koufax LA 1.88
Dick Ellsworth CHI..... 2.11
Bob Friend PIT........... 2.34

STRIKEOUTS
Sandy Koufax LA 306
Jim Maloney CIN 265
Don Drysdale LA......... 251

SAVES
Lindy McDaniel CHI...... 22
Ron Perranoski LA........ 21
two tied at 16

COMPLETE GAMES
Warren Spahn MIL........ 22
Sandy Koufax LA 20
Dick Ellsworth CHI........ 19

SHUTOUTS
Sandy Koufax LA 11
Warren Spahn MIL.......... 7
two tied at 6

GAMES PITCHED
Ron Perranoski LA........ 69
Jack Baldschun PHI...... 65
Larry Bearnarth NY....... 58

INNINGS PITCHED
Juan Marichal SF 321
Don Drysdale LA......... 315
Sandy Koufax LA 311

1964 AL

	W	L	PCT	GB	R	OR	BA	FA	ERA
NEW YORK	99	63	.611	—	730	577	.253	.983	3.15
CHICAGO	98	64	.605	1	642	501	.247	.981	2.72
BALTIMORE	97	65	.599	2	679	567	.248	.985	3.16
DETROIT	85	77	.525	14	699	678	.253	.982	3.84
LOS ANGELES	82	80	.506	17	544	551	.242	.978	2.91
CLEVELAND	79	83	.488	20	689	693	.247	.981	3.75
MINNESOTA	79	83	.488	20	737	678	.252	.977	3.57
BOSTON	72	90	.444	27	688	793	.258	.977	4.50
WASHINGTON	62	100	.383	37	578	733	.231	.979	3.98
KANSAS CITY	57	105	.352	42	621	836	.239	.974	4.71
					6607	6607	.247	.980	3.63

BATTING AVERAGE
Tony Oliva MIN .... .323
B. Robinson BAL .... .317
Elston Howard NY ..... .313

HITS
Tony Oliva MIN 217
B. Robinson BAL 194
B. Richardson NY 181

DOUBLES
Tony Oliva MIN 43
Ed Bressoud BOS......... 41
Brooks Robinson BAL... 35

TRIPLES
Rich Rollins MIN 10
Zoilo Versalles MIN....... 10
two tied at 9

HOME RUNS
H. Killebrew MIN 49
Boog Powell BAL 39
Mickey Mantle NY 35

RUNS BATTED IN
B. Robinson BAL 118
Dick Stuart BOS.......... 114
two tied at 111

SLUGGING AVERAGE
Boog Powell BAL........ .606
Mickey Mantle NY...... .591
Tony Oliva MIN .... .557

STOLEN BASES
Luis Aparicio BAL 57
Al Weis CHI 22
Vic Davalillo CLE 21

RUNS SCORED
Tony Oliva MIN 109
Dick Howser CLE 101
H. Killebrew MIN 95

WINS
Gary Peters CHI 20
Dean Chance LA 20
three tied at 19

WINNING PERCENTAGE
Wally Bunker BAL....... .792
Whitey Ford NY .... .739
Gary Peters CHI .... .714

EARNED RUN AVERAGE
Dean Chance LA 1.65
Joe Horlen CHI 1.88
Whitey Ford NY 2.13

STRIKEOUTS
Al Downing NY............ 217
Camilo Pascual MIN ... 213
Dean Chance LA 207

SAVES
Dick Radatz BOS.......... 29
Hoyt Wilhelm CHI 27
Stu Miller BAL 23

COMPLETE GAMES
Dean Chance LA 15
Camilo Pascual MIN 14
three tied at.................. 13

SHUTOUTS
Dean Chance LA 11
Whitey Ford NY 8
Milt Pappas BAL 7

GAMES PITCHED
John Wyatt KC.............. 81
Dick Radatz BOS.......... 79
Hoyt Wilhelm CHI 73

INNINGS PITCHED
Dean Chance LA 278
Gary Peters CHI 274
Jim Bouton NY 271

1964 NL

	W	L	PCT	GB	R	OR	BA	FA	ERA
★ST. LOUIS	93	69	.574	—	715	652	.272	.973	3.43
CINCINNATI	92	70	.568	1	660	566	.249	.979	3.07
PHILADELPHIA	92	70	.568	1	693	632	.258	.975	3.36
SAN FRANCISCO	90	72	.556	3	656	587	.246	.975	3.19
MILWAUKEE	88	74	.543	5	803	744	.272	.977	4.12
LOS ANGELES	80	82	.494	13	614	572	.250	.973	2.95
PITTSBURGH	80	82	.494	13	663	636	.264	.972	3.52
CHICAGO	76	86	.469	17	649	724	.251	.975	4.08
HOUSTON	66	96	.407	27	495	628	.229	.976	3.41
NEW YORK	53	109	.327	40	569	776	.246	.974	4.25
					6517	6517	.254	.975	3.54

BATTING AVERAGE
R. Clemente PIT .... .339
Hank Aaron MIL .... .328
Joe Torre MIL .... .321

HITS
Curt Flood STL 211
R. Clemente PIT 211
two tied at 201

DOUBLES
Lee Maye MIL 44
R. Clemente PIT 40
Billy Williams CHI.......... 39

TRIPLES
Dick Allen PHI.............. 13
Ron Santo CHI.............. 13
two tied at 11

HOME RUNS
Willie Mays SF 47
Billy Williams CHI........... 33
three tied at.................. 31

RUNS BATTED IN
Ken Boyer STL 119
Ron Santo CHI............ 114
Willie Mays SF 111

SLUGGING AVERAGE
Willie Mays SF .... .607
Ron Santo CHI............ .564
Dick Allen PHI............ .557

STOLEN BASES
Maury Wills LA.............. 53
Lou Brock CHI, STL....... 43
Willie Davis LA.............. 42

RUNS SCORED
Dick Allen PHI............. 125
Willie Mays SF 121
Lou Brock CHI, STL.... 111

WINS
Larry Jackson CHI 24
Juan Marichal SF.......... 21
Ray Sadecki STL.......... 20

WINNING PERCENTAGE
Sandy Koufax LA .... .792
Juan Marichal SF........ .724
Jim O'Toole CIN .... .708

EARNED RUN AVERAGE
Sandy Koufax LA 1.74
Don Drysdale LA........ 2.18
Chris Short PHI.......... 2.20

STRIKEOUTS
Bob Veale PIT............. 250
Bob Gibson STL 245
Don Drysdale LA......... 237

SAVES
Hal Woodeshick HOU ... 23
Al McBean PIT.............. 22
Jack Baldschun PHI...... 21

COMPLETE GAMES
Juan Marichal SF.......... 22
Don Drysdale LA........... 21
Larry Jackson CHI 19

SHUTOUTS
Sandy Koufax LA............. 7
three tied at..................... 5

GAMES PITCHED
Bob Miller LA 74
Ron Perranoski LA......... 72
Jack Baldschun PHI....... 71

INNINGS PITCHED
Don Drysdale LA......... 321
Larry Jackson CHI 298
Bob Gibson STL 287

1965 AL

	W	L	PCT	GB	R	OR	BA	FA	ERA
MINNESOTA	102	60	.630	—	774	600	.254	.973	3.14
CHICAGO	95	67	.586	7	647	555	.246	.980	2.99
BALTIMORE	94	68	.580	8	641	578	.238	.980	2.98
DETROIT	89	73	.549	13	680	602	.238	.981	3.35
CLEVELAND	87	75	.537	15	663	613	.250	.981	3.30
NEW YORK	77	85	.475	25	611	604	.235	.978	3.28
CALIFORNIA	75	87	.463	27	527	569	.239	.981	3.17
WASHINGTON	70	92	.432	32	591	721	.228	.976	3.93
BOSTON	62	100	.383	40	669	791	.251	.974	4.24
KANSAS CITY	59	103	.364	43	585	755	.240	.977	4.24
					6388	6388	.242	.978	3.46

BATTING AVERAGE
Tony Oliva MIN .... .321
C. Yastrzemski BOS .. .312
Vic Davalillo CLE .... .301

HITS
Tony Oliva MIN 185
Zoilo Versalles MIN..... 182
Rocky Colavito CLE.... 170

DOUBLES
C. Yastrzemski BOS 45
Zoilo Versalles MIN....... 45
Tony Oliva MIN 40

TRIPLES
Bert Campaneris KC.... 12
Zoilo Versalles MIN....... 12
Luis Aparicio BAL 10

HOME RUNS
Tony Conigliaro BOS.... 32
Norm Cash DET 30
Willie Horton DET 29

RUNS BATTED IN
Rocky Colavito CLE 108
Willie Horton DET 104
Tony Oliva MIN 98

SLUGGING AVERAGE
C. Yastrzemski BOS.. .536
T. Conigliaro BOS...... .512
Norm Cash DET .... .512

STOLEN BASES
Bert Campaneris KC..... 51
Jose Cardenal CAL....... 37
Zoilo Versalles MIN....... 27

RUNS SCORED
Zoilo Versalles MIN..... 126
Tony Oliva MIN 107
Tom Tresh NY 94

WINS
Mudcat Grant MIN 21
Mel Stottlemyre NY....... 20
Jim Kaat MIN 18

WINNING PERCENTAGE
Mudcat Grant MIN .... .750
Denny McLain DET..... .727
Mel Stottlemyre NY.... .690

EARNED RUN AVERAGE
Sam McDowell CLE.... 2.18
Eddie Fisher CHI 2.40
Sonny Siebert CLE 2.43

STRIKEOUTS
Sam McDowell CLE.... 325
Mickey Lolich DET 226
Denny McLain DET..... 192

SAVES
Ron Kline WAS............. 29
Eddie Fisher CHI 24
Stu Miller BAL............... 24

COMPLETE GAMES
Mel Stottlemyre NY....... 18
Mudcat Grant MIN 14
Sam McDowell CLE...... 14

SHUTOUTS
Mudcat Grant MIN 6
three tied at..................... 4

GAMES PITCHED
Eddie Fisher CHI 82
Ron Kline WAS.............. 74
Bob Lee CAL 69

INNINGS PITCHED
Mel Stottlemyre NY..... 291
Sam McDowell CLE.... 273
Mudcat Grant MIN 270

1965 NL

	W	L	PCT	GB	R	OR	BA	FA	ERA
★LOS ANGELES	97	65	.599	—	608	521	.245	.979	2.81
SAN FRANCISCO	95	67	.586	2	682	593	.252	.976	3.20
PITTSBURGH	90	72	.556	7	675	580	.265	.977	3.01
CINCINNATI	89	73	.549	8	825	704	.273	.981	3.88
MILWAUKEE	86	76	.531	11	708	633	.256	.978	3.52
PHILADELPHIA	85	76	.528	11.5	654	667	.250	.975	3.53
ST. LOUIS	80	81	.497	16.5	707	674	.254	.979	3.77
CHICAGO	72	90	.444	25	635	723	.238	.974	3.78
HOUSTON	65	97	.401	32	596	711	.237	.974	3.84
NEW YORK	50	112	.309	47	495	752	.221	.974	4.06
					6558	6558	.249	.977	3.54

BATTING AVERAGE
R. Clemente PIT .... .329
Hank Aaron MIL......... .318
Willie Mays SF .... .317

HITS
Pete Rose CIN............. 209
Vada Pinson CIN 204
Billy Williams CHI........ 203

DOUBLES
Hank Aaron MIL............ 40
Billy Williams CHI.......... 39
two tied at 35

TRIPLES
Johnny Callison PHI 16
three tied at................... 14

HOME RUNS
Willie Mays SF 52
Willie McCovey SF........ 39
Billy Williams CHI.......... 34

RUNS BATTED IN
Deron Johnson CIN 130
Frank Robinson CIN ... 113
Willie Mays SF 112

SLUGGING AVERAGE
Willie Mays SF .... .645
Hank Aaron MIL........... .560
Billy Williams CHI........ .552

STOLEN BASES
Maury Wills LA............... 94
Lou Brock STL............... 63
Jimmy Wynn HOU 43

RUNS SCORED
Tommy Harper CIN..... 126
Willie Mays SF 118
Pete Rose CIN............. 117

WINS
Sandy Koufax LA 26
Tony Cloninger MIL 24
Don Drysdale LA........... 23

WINNING PERCENTAGE
Sandy Koufax LA .... .765
Jim Maloney CIN .... .690
Sammy Ellis CIN......... .688

EARNED RUN AVERAGE
Sandy Koufax LA 2.04
Juan Marichal SF 2.13
Vern Law PIT 2.15

STRIKEOUTS
Sandy Koufax LA 382
Bob Veale PIT.............. 276
Bob Gibson STL 270

SAVES
Ted Abernathy CHI 31
Billy McCool CIN........... 21
Frank Linzy SF.............. 21

COMPLETE GAMES
Sandy Koufax LA 27
Juan Marichal SF 24
two tied at 20

SHUTOUTS
Juan Marichal SF.......... 10
Sandy Koufax LA 8
two tied at 7

GAMES PITCHED
Ted Abernathy CHI 84
Woodeshick HOU, STL.. 78
Lindy McDaniel CHI 71

INNINGS PITCHED
Sandy Koufax LA 336
Don Drysdale LA......... 308
Bob Gibson STL 299

1966 AL

	W	L	PCT	GB	R	OR	BA	FA	ERA
★BALTIMORE	97	63	.606	—	755	601	.258	.981	3.32
MINNESOTA	89	73	.549	9	663	581	.249	.977	3.13
DETROIT	88	74	.543	10	719	698	.251	.980	3.85
CHICAGO	83	79	.512	15	574	517	.231	.976	2.68
CLEVELAND	81	81	.500	17	574	586	.237	.977	3.23
CALIFORNIA	80	82	.494	18	604	643	.232	.979	3.56
KANSAS CITY	74	86	.463	23	564	648	.236	.977	3.55
WASHINGTON	71	88	.447	25.5	557	659	.234	.977	3.70
BOSTON	72	90	.444	26	655	731	.240	.975	3.92
NEW YORK	70	89	.440	26.5	611	612	.235	.977	3.42
					6276	6276	.240	.978	3.44

BATTING AVERAGE
F. Robinson BAL........ .316
Tony Oliva MIN .307
Al Kaline DET .... .288

HITS
Tony Oliva MIN 191
Frank Robinson BAL... 182
Luis Aparicio BAL 182

DOUBLES
C. Yastrzemski BOS 39
Brooks Robinson BAL... 35
Frank Robinson BAL..... 34

TRIPLES
Bobby Knoop CAL 11
Bert Campaneris KC..... 10
Ed Brinkman WAS 9

HOME RUNS
Frank Robinson BAL..... 49
H. Killebrew MIN 39
Boog Powell BAL 34

RUNS BATTED IN
Frank Robinson BAL... 122
H. Killebrew MIN 110
Boog Powell BAL 109

SLUGGING AVERAGE
F. Robinson BAL........ .637
H. Killebrew MIN .... .538
Al Kaline DET .... .534

STOLEN BASES
Bert Campaneris KC..... 52
Don Buford CHI 51
Tommy Agee CHI 44

RUNS SCORED
Frank Robinson BAL... 122
Tony Oliva MIN 99
two tied at 98

WINS
Jim Kaat MIN 25
Denny McLain DET....... 20
E. Wilson BOS, DET..... 18

WINNING PERCENTAGE
Sonny Siebert CLE .... .667
Jim Kaat MIN .... .658
E. Wilson BOS, DET... .621

EARNED RUN AVERAGE
Gary Peters CHI 1.98
Joe Horlen CHI 2.43
Steve Hargan CLE..... 2.48

STRIKEOUTS
Sam McDowell CLE.... 225
Jim Kaat MIN 205
E. Wilson BOS, DET ... 200

SAVES
Jack Aker KC................ 32
Ron Kline WAS............. 23
Larry Sherry DET.......... 20

COMPLETE GAMES
Jim Kaat MIN 19
Denny McLain DET....... 14
E. Wilson BOS, DET..... 13

SHUTOUTS
Luis Tiant CLE 5
Sam McDowell CLE....... 5
Tommy John CHI............. 5

GAMES PITCHED
E. Fisher CHI, BAL 67
Casey Cox WAS 66
Jack Aker KC................. 66

INNINGS PITCHED
Jim Kaat MIN 305
Denny McLain DET..... 264
E. Wilson BOS, DET ... 264

1966 NL

	W	L	PCT	GB	R	OR	BA	FA	ERA
LOS ANGELES	95	67	.586	—	606	490	.256	.979	2.62
SAN FRANCISCO	93	68	.578	1.5	675	626	.248	.974	3.24
PITTSBURGH	92	70	.568	3	759	641	.279	.978	3.52
PHILADELPHIA	87	75	.537	8	696	640	.258	.982	3.57
ATLANTA	85	77	.525	10	782	683	.263	.976	3.68
ST. LOUIS	83	79	.512	12	571	577	.251	.977	3.11
CINCINNATI	76	84	.475	18	692	702	.260	.980	4.08
HOUSTON	72	90	.444	23	612	695	.255	.972	3.76
NEW YORK	66	95	.410	28.5	587	761	.239	.975	4.17
CHICAGO	59	103	.364	36	644	809	.254	.974	4.33
					6624	6624	.256	.977	3.61

BATTING AVERAGE
Matty Alou PIT .... .342
Felipe Alou ATL .... .327
Rico Carty ATL .... .326

HITS
Felipe Alou ATL 218
Pete Rose CIN 205
R. Clemente PIT 202

DOUBLES
Johnny Callison PHI 40
Pete Rose CIN 38
Vada Pinson CIN 35

TRIPLES
Tim McCarver STL 13
Lou Brock STL 12
R. Clemente PIT 11

HOME RUNS
Hank Aaron ATL 44
Dick Allen PHI 40
Willie Mays SF 37

RUNS BATTED IN
Hank Aaron ATL 127
R. Clemente PIT 119
Dick Allen PHI 110

SLUGGING AVERAGE
Dick Allen PHI .... .632
Willie McCovey SF ..... .586
Willie Stargell PIT ...... .581

STOLEN BASES
Lou Brock STL 74
Sonny Jackson HOU 49
Maury Wills LA 38

RUNS SCORED
Felipe Alou ATL 122
Hank Aaron ATL 117
Dick Allen PHI 112

WINS
Sandy Koufax LA 27
Juan Marichal SF 25
two tied at 21

WINNING PERCENTAGE
Juan Marichal SF .... .806
Sandy Koufax LA .... .750
Gaylord Perry SF .... .724

EARNED RUN AVERAGE
Sandy Koufax LA 1.73
Mike Cuellar HOU 2.22
Juan Marichal SF 2.23

STRIKEOUTS
Sandy Koufax LA 317
Jim Bunning PHI 252
Bob Veale PIT 229

SAVES
Phil Regan LA 21
Billy McCool CIN 18
Roy Face PIT 18

COMPLETE GAMES
Sandy Koufax LA 27
Juan Marichal SF 25
Bob Gibson STL 20

SHUTOUTS
five tied at 5

GAMES PITCHED
Clay Carroll ATL 73
Pete Mikkelsen PIT 71
Darold Knowles PHI...... 69

INNINGS PITCHED
Sandy Koufax LA 323
Jim Bunning PHI 314
Juan Marichal SF 307

1967 AL

	W	L	PCT	GB	R	OR	BA	FA	ERA
BOSTON	92	70	.568	—	722	614	.255	.977	3.36
DETROIT	91	71	.562	1	683	587	.243	.979	3.32
MINNESOTA	91	71	.562	1	671	590	.240	.978	3.14
CHICAGO	89	73	.549	3	531	491	.225	.979	2.45
CALIFORNIA	84	77	.522	7.5	567	587	.238	.982	3.19
BALTIMORE	76	85	.472	15.5	654	592	.240	.980	3.32
WASHINGTON	76	85	.472	15.5	550	637	.223	.978	3.38
CLEVELAND	75	87	.463	17	559	613	.235	.981	3.25
NEW YORK	72	90	.444	20	522	621	.225	.976	3.24
KANSAS CITY	62	99	.385	29.5	533	660	.233	.978	3.68
					5992	5992	.236	.979	3.23

BATTING AVERAGE
C. Yastrzemski BOS .. .326
F. Robinson BAL........ .311
Al Kaline DET .... .308

HITS
C. Yastrzemski BOS ... 189
Cesar Tovar MIN 173
two tied at 171

DOUBLES
Tony Oliva MIN 34
Cesar Tovar MIN 32
C. Yastrzemski BOS 31

TRIPLES
Paul Blair BAL............... 12
Don Buford CHI 9

HOME RUNS
H. Killebrew MIN 44
C. Yastrzemski BOS 44
Frank Howard WAS 36

RUNS BATTED IN
C. Yastrzemski BOS ... 121
H. Killebrew MIN 113
Frank Robinson BAL..... 94

SLUGGING AVERAGE
C. Yastrzemski BOS .. .622
F. Robinson BAL........ .576
H. Killebrew MIL.......... .558

STOLEN BASES
Bert Campaneris KC..... 55
Don Buford CHI 34
Tommy Agee CHI 28

RUNS SCORED
C. Yastrzemski BOS ... 112
H. Killebrew MIN 105
Cesar Tovar MIN 98

WINS
Jim Lonborg BOS 22
Earl Wilson DET 22
Dean Chance MIN 20

WINNING PERCENTAGE
Joe Horlen CHI .... .731
Jim Lonborg BOS ...... .710
Earl Wilson DET .... .667

EARNED RUN AVERAGE
Joe Horlen CHI 2.06
Gary Peters CHI 2.28
Sonny Siebert CLE 2.38

STRIKEOUTS
Jim Lonborg BOS 246
Sam McDowell CLE.... 236
Dean Chance MIN 220

SAVES
Minnie Rojas CAL......... 27
John Wyatt BOS 20
Bob Locker CHI 20

COMPLETE GAMES
Dean Chance MIN 18
Jim Lonborg BOS 15
Steve Hargan CLE........ 15

SHUTOUTS
four tied at........................ 6

GAMES PITCHED
Bob Locker CHI 77
Minnie Rojas CAL......... 72
Bill Kelso CAL............... 69

INNINGS PITCHED
Dean Chance MIN 284
Jim Lonborg BOS 273
Earl Wilson DET 264

1967 NL

	W	L	PCT	GB	R	OR	BA	FA	ERA
★ST. LOUIS	101	60	.627	—	695	557	.263	.978	3.05
SAN FRANCISCO	91	71	.562	10.5	652	551	.245	.979	2.92
CHICAGO	87	74	.540	14	702	624	.251	.981	3.48
CINCINNATI	87	75	.537	14.5	604	563	.248	.980	3.05
PHILADELPHIA	82	80	.506	19.5	612	581	.242	.978	3.10
PITTSBURGH	81	81	.500	20.5	679	693	.277	.978	3.74
ATLANTA	77	85	.475	24.5	631	640	.240	.978	3.47
LOS ANGELES	73	89	.451	28.5	519	595	.236	.975	3.21
HOUSTON	69	93	.426	32.5	626	742	.249	.974	4.03
NEW YORK	61	101	.377	40.5	498	672	.238	.975	3.73
					6218	6218	.249	.978	3.38

BATTING AVERAGE
R. Clemente PIT .... .357
Tony Gonzalez PHI.... .339
Matty Alou PIT .... .338

HITS
R. Clemente PIT 209
Lou Brock STL 206
Vada Pinson CIN 187

DOUBLES
Rusty Staub HOU 44
Orlando Cepeda STL.... 37
Hank Aaron ATL 37

TRIPLES
Vada Pinson CIN 13
Lou Brock STL 12
Billy Williams CHI.......... 12

HOME RUNS
Hank Aaron ATL 39
Jimmy Wynn HOU 37
two tied at 31

RUNS BATTED IN
O. Cepeda STL............. 111
R. Clemente PIT 110
Hank Aaron ATL 109

SLUGGING AVERAGE
Hank Aaron ATL .... .573
Dick Allen PHI............. .566
R. Clemente PIT .... .554

STOLEN BASES
Lou Brock STL 52
Maury Wills PIT............. 29
Joe Morgan HOU 29

RUNS SCORED
Lou Brock STL 113
Hank Aaron ATL 113
Ron Santo CHI............. 107

WINS
Mike McCormick SF...... 22
F. Jenkins CHI 20
two tied at 17

WINNING PERCENTAGE
Dick Hughes STL........ .727
Mike McCormick SF... .688
Bob Veale PIT............. .667

EARNED RUN AVERAGE
Phil Niekro ATL.......... 1.87
Jim Bunning PHI........ 2.29
Chris Short PHI.......... 2.39

STRIKEOUTS
Jim Bunning PHI 253
F. Jenkins CHI 236
Gaylord Perry SF 230

SAVES
Ted Abernathy CIN 28
Frank Linzy SF 17
Roy Face PIT................. 17

COMPLETE GAMES
F. Jenkins CHI 20
three tied at.................... 18

SHUTOUTS
Jim Bunning PHI 6
three tied at...................... 5

GAMES PITCHED
Ron Perranoski LA........ 70
Ted Abernathy CIN 70
Ron Willis STL 65

INNINGS PITCHED
Jim Bunning PHI 302
Gaylord Perry SF 293
F. Jenkins CHI 289

1968 AL

	W	L	PCT	GB	R	OR	BA	FA	ERA
★DETROIT	103	59	.636	—	671	492	.235	.983	2.71
BALTIMORE	91	71	.562	12	579	497	.225	.981	2.66
CLEVELAND	86	75	.534	16.5	516	504	.234	.979	2.66
BOSTON	86	76	.531	17	614	611	.236	.979	3.33
NEW YORK	83	79	.512	20	536	531	.214	.979	2.79
OAKLAND	82	80	.506	21	569	544	.240	.976	2.94
MINNESOTA	79	83	.488	24	562	546	.237	.973	2.89
CALIFORNIA	67	95	.414	36	498	615	.227	.977	3.43
CHICAGO	67	95	.414	36	463	527	.228	.977	2.75
WASHINGTON	65	96	.404	37.5	524	665	.224	.976	3.64
					5532	5532	.230	.978	2.98

BATTING AVERAGE
C. Yastrzemski BOS .. .301
Danny Cater OAK ...... .290
Tony Oliva MIN .... .289

HITS
B. Campaneris OAK ... 177
Cesar Tovar MIN 167
two tied at 164

DOUBLES
Reggie Smith BOS........ 37
Brooks Robinson BAL... 36
C. Yastrzemski BOS 32

TRIPLES
Jim Fregosi CAL 13
Tom McCraw CHI 12
two tied at 10

HOME RUNS
Frank Howard WAS 44
Willie Horton DET 36
Ken Harrelson BOS 35

RUNS BATTED IN
Ken Harrelson BOS 109
Frank Howard WAS 106
Jim Northrup DET 90

SLUGGING AVERAGE
Frank Howard WAS ... .552
Willie Horton DET ...... .543
Ken Harrelson BOS ... .518

STOLEN BASES
B. Campaneris OAK 62
Jose Cardenal CLE....... 40
Cesar Tovar MIN 35

RUNS SCORED
Dick McAuliffe DET....... 95
C. Yastrzemski BOS 90
two tied at 89

WINS
Denny McLain DET....... 31
Dave McNally BAL........ 22
two tied at 21

WINNING PERCENTAGE
Denny McLain DET.... .838
Ray Culp BOS .... .727
Luis Tiant CLE .... .700

EARNED RUN AVERAGE
Luis Tiant CLE 1.60
Sam McDowell CLE... 1.81
Dave McNally BAL..... 1.95

STRIKEOUTS
Sam McDowell CLE.... 283
Denny McLain DET..... 280
Luis Tiant CLE 264

SAVES
Al Worthington MIN....... 18
Wilbur Wood CHI 16
Dennis Higgins WAS 13

COMPLETE GAMES
Denny McLain DET....... 28
Luis Tiant CLE 19
Mel Stottlemyre NY....... 19

SHUTOUTS
Luis Tiant CLE 9
three tied at..................... 6

GAMES PITCHED
Wilbur Wood CHI 88
Hoyt Wilhelm CHI 72
Bob Locker CHI 70

INNINGS PITCHED
Denny McLain DET.... 336
Dean Chance MIN 292
Mel Stottlemyre NY..... 279

1968 NL

	W	L	PCT	GB	R	OR	BA	FA	ERA
ST. LOUIS	97	65	.599	—	583	472	.249	.978	2.49
SAN FRANCISCO	88	74	.543	9	599	529	.239	.975	2.71
CHICAGO	84	78	.519	13	612	611	.242	.981	3.41
CINCINNATI	83	79	.512	14	690	673	.273	.978	3.56
ATLANTA	81	81	.500	16	514	549	.252	.980	2.92
PITTSBURGH	80	82	.494	17	583	532	.252	.979	2.74
LOS ANGELES	76	86	.469	21	470	509	.230	.977	2.69
PHILADELPHIA	76	86	.469	21	543	615	.233	.980	3.36
NEW YORK	73	89	.451	24	473	499	.228	.979	2.72
HOUSTON	72	90	.444	25	510	588	.231	.975	3.26
					5577	5577	.243	.978	2.99

BATTING AVERAGE
Pete Rose CIN........... .335
Matty Alou PIT........... .332
Felipe Alou ATL .... .317

HITS
Pete Rose CIN........... 210
Felipe Alou ATL 210
Glenn Beckert CHI...... 189

DOUBLES
Lou Brock STL.............. 46
Pete Rose CIN.............. 42
Johnny Bench CIN........ 40

TRIPLES
Lou Brock STL.............. 14
R. Clemente PIT 12
Willie Davis LA.............. 10

HOME RUNS
Willie McCovey SF........ 36
Dick Allen PHI.............. 33
Ernie Banks CHI 32

RUNS BATTED IN
Willie McCovey SF...... 105
Billy Williams CHI.......... 98
Ron Santo CHI.............. 98

SLUGGING AVERAGE
Willie McCovey SF..... .545
Dick Allen PHI............. .520
Billy Williams CHI....... .500

STOLEN BASES
Lou Brock STL.............. 62
Maury Wills PIT............ 52
Willie Davis LA.............. 36

RUNS SCORED
Glenn Beckert CHI...... 98
Pete Rose CIN.............. 94
Tony Perez CIN 93

WINS
Juan Marichal SF.......... 26
Bob Gibson STL 22
F. Jenkins CHI 20

WINNING PERCENTAGE
Steve Blass PIT .... .750
Juan Marichal SF....... .743
Bob Gibson STL .... .710

EARNED RUN AVERAGE
Bob Gibson STL 1.12
Bobby Bolin SF 1.99
Bob Veale PIT............. 2.05

STRIKEOUTS
Bob Gibson STL 268
F. Jenkins CHI 260
Bill Singer LA 227

SAVES
Phil Regan LA, CHI....... 25
Joe Hoerner STL 17
Clay Carroll ATL, CIN ... 17

COMPLETE GAMES
Juan Marichal SF.......... 30
Bob Gibson STL 28
F. Jenkins CHI 20

SHUTOUTS
Bob Gibson STL 13
Don Drysdale LA............. 8
two tied at 7

GAMES PITCHED
Ted Abernathy CIN 78
Phil Regan LA, CHI....... 73
Clay Carroll ATL, CIN ... 68

INNINGS PITCHED
Juan Marichal SF........ 326
F. Jenkins CHI 308
Bob Gibson STL 305

1969 AL

EAST	W	L	PCT	GB	R	OR	BA	FA	ERA
●BALTIMORE	109	53	.673	—	779	517	.265	.984	2.83
DETROIT	90	72	.556	19	701	601	.242	.979	3.32
BOSTON	87	75	.537	22	743	736	.251	.975	3.93
WASHINGTON	86	76	.531	23	694	644	.251	.978	3.49
NEW YORK	80	81	.497	28.5	562	587	.235	.979	3.23
CLEVELAND	62	99	.385	46.5	573	717	.237	.976	3.94

WEST	W	L	PCT	GB	R	OR	BA	FA	ERA
MINNESOTA	97	65	.599	—	790	618	.268	.977	3.25
OAKLAND	88	74	.543	9	740	678	.249	.978	3.71
CALIFORNIA	71	91	.438	26	528	652	.230	.978	3.55
KANSAS CITY	69	93	.426	28	586	688	.240	.975	3.72
CHICAGO	68	94	.420	29	625	723	.247	.981	4.21
SEATTLE	64	98	.395	33	639	799	.234	.974	4.35
					7960	7960	.246	.978	3.63

BATTING AVERAGE
Rod Carew MIN................ .332
Reggie Smith BOS .... .309
Tony Oliva MIN .... .309

HITS
Tony Oliva MIN 197
Horace Clarke NY 183
Paul Blair BAL 178

DOUBLES
Tony Oliva MIN 39
Reggie Jackson OAK.......... 36
Davey Johnson BAL........... 34

TRIPLES
Del Unser WAS 8
Horace Clarke NY 7
Reggie Smith BOS 7

HOME RUNS
Harmon Killebrew MIN 49
Frank Howard WAS 48
Reggie Jackson OAK 47

RUNS BATTED IN
Harmon Killebrew MIN 140
Boog Powell BAL 121
Reggie Jackson OAK 118

SLUGGING AVERAGE
Reggie Jackson OAK ...... .608
Rico Petrocelli BOS......... .589
Harmon Killebrew MIN .... .584

STOLEN BASES
Tommy Harper SEA 73
Bert Campaneris OAK........ 62
Cesar Tovar MIN................ 45

RUNS SCORED
Reggie Jackson OAK ... 123
Frank Howard WAS 111
Frank Robinson BAL 111

WINS
Denny McLain DET 24
Mike Cuellar BAL 23
four tied at 20

WINNING PERCENTAGE
Jim Palmer BAL .... .800
Jim Perry MIN .... .769
Dave McNally BAL .... .741

EARNED RUN AVERAGE
Dick Bosman WAS.......... 2.19
Jim Palmer BAL 2.34
Mike Cuellar BAL 2.38

STRIKEOUTS
Sam McDowell CLE 279
Micky Lolich DET 271
Andy Messersmith CAL.... 211

SAVES
Ron Perranoski MIN........... 31
Ken Tatum CAL.................. 22
Sparky Lyle BOS................ 17

COMPLETE GAMES
Mel Stottlemyre NY 24
Denny McLain DET 23
two tied at............................ 18

SHUTOUTS
Denny McLain DET 9
Jim Palmer BAL 6
Mike Cuellar BAL 5

GAMES PITCHED
Wilbur Wood CHI 76
Ron Perranoski MIN........... 75
Sparky Lyle BOS................ 71

INNINGS PITCHED
Denny McLain DET 325
Mel Stottlemyre NY 303
Mike Cuellar BAL 291

1969 NL

EAST	W	L	PCT	GB	R	OR	BA	FA	ERA
★NEW YORK	100	62	.617	—	632	541	.242	.980	2.99
CHICAGO	92	70	.568	8	720	611	.253	.979	3.34
PITTSBURGH	88	74	.543	12	725	652	.277	.975	3.61
ST. LOUIS	87	75	.537	13	595	540	.253	.978	2.94
PHILADELPHIA	63	99	.389	37	645	745	.241	.978	4.17
MONTREAL	52	110	.321	48	582	791	.240	.971	4.33

WEST	W	L	PCT	GB	R	OR	BA	FA	ERA
ATLANTA	93	69	.574	—	691	631	.258	.981	3.53
SAN FRANCISCO	90	72	.556	3	713	636	.242	.974	3.25
CINCINNATI	89	73	.549	4	798	768	.277	.973	4.13
LOS ANGELES	85	77	.525	8	645	561	.254	.980	3.09
HOUSTON	81	81	.500	12	676	668	.240	.975	3.60
SAN DIEGO	52	110	.321	41	468	746	.225	.975	4.24
					7890	7890	.250	.977	3.60

BATTING AVERAGE
Pete Rose CIN .... .348
Roberto Clemente PIT .... .345
Cleon Jones NY .... .340

HITS
Matty Alou PIT.................. 231
Pete Rose CIN 218
Lou Brock STL 195

DOUBLES
Matty Alou PIT.................. 41
Don Kessinger CHI 38
two tied at............................ 33

TRIPLES
Roberto Clemente PIT 12
Pete Rose CIN 11
two tied at............................ 10

HOME RUNS
Willie McCovey SF 45
Hank Aaron ATL................. 44
Lee May CIN 38

RUNS BATTED IN
Willie McCovey SF 126
Ron Santo CHI 123
Tony Perez CIN................. 122

SLUGGING AVERAGE
Willie McCovey SF .... .656
Hank Aaron ATL.............. .607
Dick Allen PHI .... .573

STOLEN BASES
Lou Brock STL 53
Joe Morgan HOU 49
Bobby Bonds SF 45

RUNS SCORED
Pete Rose CIN 120
Bobby Bonds SF 120
Jimmy Wynn HOU............ 113

WINS
Tom Seaver NY.................. 25
Phil Niekro ATL 23
two tied at............................ 21

WINNING PERCENTAGE
Tom Seaver NY............... .781
Juan Marichal SF .... .656
two tied at........................ .654

EARNED RUN AVERAGE
Juan Marichal SF 2.10
Steve Carlton STL........... 2.17
Bob Gibson STL.............. 2.18

STRIKEOUTS
Ferguson Jenkins CHI...... 273
Bob Gibson STL............... 269
Bill Singer LA................... 247

SAVES
Fred Gladding HOU 29
Wayne Granger CIN........... 27
Cecil Upshaw ATL.............. 27

COMPLETE GAMES
Bob Gibson STL................. 28
Juan Marichal SF 27
Gaylord Perry SF 26

SHUTOUTS
Juan Marichal SF 8
Ferguson Jenkins CHI......... 7
Claude Osteen LA................ 7

GAMES PITCHED
Wayne Granger CIN........... 90
Dan McGinn MON.............. 74
two tied at............................ 71

INNINGS PITCHED
Gaylord Perry SF 325
Claude Osteen LA............. 321
Bill Singer LA.................... 316

1970 AL

EAST	W	L	PCT	GB	R	OR	BA	FA	ERA
★BALTIMORE	108	54	.667	—	792	574	.257	.981	3.15
NEW YORK	93	69	.574	15	680	612	.251	.980	3.25
BOSTON	87	75	.537	21	786	722	.262	.974	3.90
DETROIT	79	83	.488	29	666	731	.238	.978	4.09
CLEVELAND	76	86	.469	32	649	675	.249	.979	3.91
WASHINGTON	70	92	.432	38	626	689	.238	.982	3.80

WEST	W	L	PCT	GB	R	OR	BA	FA	ERA
MINNESOTA	98	64	.605	—	744	605	.262	.980	3.23
OAKLAND	89	73	.549	9	678	593	.249	.977	3.30
CALIFORNIA	86	76	.531	12	631	630	.251	.980	3.48
KANSAS CITY	65	97	.401	33	611	705	.244	.976	3.78
MILWAUKEE	65	97	.401	33	613	751	.242	.978	4.20
CHICAGO	56	106	.346	42	633	822	.253	.975	4.54
					8109	8109	.250	.978	3.72

BATTING AVERAGE
Alex Johnson CAL............ .329
Carl Yastrzemski BOS .... .329
Tony Oliva MIN .... .325

HITS
Tony Oliva MIN 204
Alex Johnson CAL............ 202
Cesar Tovar MIN.............. 195

DOUBLES
Cesar Tovar MIN 36
Tony Oliva MIN 36
Amos Otis KC 36

TRIPLES
Cesar Tovar MIN 13
Mickey Stanley DET 11
Amos Otis KC..................... 9

HOME RUNS
Frank Howard WAS 44
Harmon Killebrew MIN 41
Carl Yastrzemski BOS 40

RUNS BATTED IN
Frank Howard WAS 126
Tony Conigliaro BOS 116
Boog Powell BAL 114

SLUGGING AVERAGE
Carl Yastrzemski BOS .... .592
Boog Powell BAL .... .549
Harmon Killebrew MIN ... .546

STOLEN BASES
Bert Campaneris OAK........ 42
Tommy Harper MIL 38
Sandy Alomar CAL 35

RUNS SCORED
Carl Yastrzemski BOS 125
Cesar Tovar MIN 120
two tied at........................ 109

WINS
Dave McNally BAL 24
Jim Perry MIN 24
Mike Cuellar BAL 24

WINNING PERCENTAGE
Mike Cuellar BAL .... .750
Dave McNally BAL .... .727
two tied at........................ .667

EARNED RUN AVERAGE
Diego Segui OAK 2.56
Jim Palmer BAL 2.71
Clyde Wright CAL 2.83

STRIKEOUTS
Sam McDowell CLE 304
Mickey Lolich DET 230
Bob Johnson KC 206

SAVES
Ron Perranoski MIN.......... 34
Lindy McDaniel NY............ 29
two tied at......................... 27

COMPLETE GAMES
Mike Cuellar BAL 21
Sam McDowell CLE 19
Jim Palmer BAL 17

SHUTOUTS
Jim Palmer BAL 5
Chuck Dobson OAK............. 5
two tied at............................ 4

GAMES PITCHED
Wilbur Wood CHI 77
Mudcat Grant OAK............. 72
Darold Knowles WAS......... 71

INNINGS PITCHED
Sam McDowell CLE 305
Jim Palmer BAL 305
Mike Cuellar BAL 298

1970 NL

EAST	W	L	PCT	GB	R	OR	BA	FA	ERA
PITTSBURGH	89	73	.549	—	729	664	.270	.979	3.70
CHICAGO	84	78	.519	5	806	679	.259	.978	3.76
NEW YORK	83	79	.512	6	695	630	.249	.979	3.46
ST. LOUIS	76	86	.469	13	744	747	.263	.977	4.05
PHILADELPHIA	73	88	.453	15.5	594	730	.238	.981	4.17
MONTREAL	73	89	.451	16	687	807	.237	.977	4.50

WEST	W	L	PCT	GB	R	OR	BA	FA	ERA
●CINCINNATI	102	60	.630	—	775	681	.270	.976	3.71
LOS ANGELES	87	74	.540	14.5	749	684	.270	.978	3.82
SAN FRANCISCO	86	76	.531	16	831	826	.262	.973	4.50
HOUSTON	79	83	.488	23	744	763	.259	.978	4.23
ATLANTA	76	86	.469	26	736	772	.270	.977	4.35
SAN DIEGO	63	99	.389	39	681	788	.246	.975	4.38
					8771	8771	.258	.977	4.05

BATTING AVERAGE
Rico Carty ATL .... .366
Joe Torre STL .... .325
Manny Sanguillen PIT ..... .325

HITS
Billy Williams CHI 205
Pete Rose CIN 205
Joe Torre STL 203

DOUBLES
Wes Parker LA 47
Willie McCovey SF 39
Pete Rose CIN 37

TRIPLES
Willie Davis LA 16
Don Kessinger CHI 14
two tied at 10

HOME RUNS
Johnny Bench CIN 45
Billy Williams CHI 42
Tony Perez CIN 40

RUNS BATTED IN
Johnny Bench CIN 148
Billy Williams CHI 129
Tony Perez CIN 129

SLUGGING AVERAGE
Willie McCovey SF .... .612
Tony Perez CIN .... .589
Johnny Bench CIN .... .587

STOLEN BASES
Bobby Tolan CIN 57
Lou Brock STL 51
Bobby Bonds SF 48

RUNS SCORED
Billy Williams CHI 137
Bobby Bonds SF 134
Pete Rose CIN 120

WINS
Gaylord Perry SF 23
Bob Gibson STL 23
Ferguson Jenkins CHI 22

WINNING PERCENTAGE
Bob Gibson STL .... .767
Gary Nolan CIN .... .720
Luke Walker PIT .... .714

EARNED RUN AVERAGE
Tom Seaver NY 2.81
Wayne Simpson CIN 3.02
Luke Walker PIT 3.04

STRIKEOUTS
Tom Seaver NY 283
Bob Gibson STL 274
Ferguson Jenkins CHI 274

SAVES
Wayne Granger CIN 35
Dave Giusti PIT 26
Jim Brewer LA 24

COMPLETE GAMES
Ferguson Jenkins CHI 24
Gaylord Perry SF 23
Bob Gibson STL 23

SHUTOUTS
Gaylord Perry SF 5
three tied at 4

GAMES PITCHED
Ron Herbel SD, NY 76
Dick Selma PHI 73
two tied at 67

INNINGS PITCHED
Gaylord Perry SF 329
Ferguson Jenkins CHI 313
Bob Gibson STL 294

1971 AL

EAST	W	L	PCT	GB	R	OR	BA	FA	ERA
● BALTIMORE	101	57	.639	—	742	530	.261	.981	3.00
DETROIT	91	71	.562	12	701	645	.254	.983	3.64
BOSTON	85	77	.525	18	691	667	.252	.981	3.83
NEW YORK	82	80	.506	21	648	641	.254	.981	3.45
WASHINGTON	63	96	.396	38.5	537	660	.230	.977	3.70
CLEVELAND	60	102	.370	43	543	747	.238	.981	4.28

WEST	W	L	PCT	GB	R	OR	BA	FA	ERA
OAKLAND	101	60	.627	—	691	564	.252	.981	3.06
KANSAS CITY	85	76	.528	16	603	566	.250	.978	3.25
CHICAGO	79	83	.488	22.5	617	597	.250	.975	3.13
CALIFORNIA	76	86	.469	25.5	511	576	.231	.980	3.10
MINNESOTA	74	86	.463	26.5	654	670	.260	.980	3.82
MILWAUKEE	69	92	.429	32	534	609	.229	.977	3.38
					7472	7472	.247	.980	3.47

BATTING AVERAGE
Tony Oliva MIN .... .337
Bobby Murcer NY .... .331
Merv Rettenmund BAL .... .318

HITS
Cesar Tovar MIN 204
Sandy Alomar CAL 179
Rod Carew MIN 177

DOUBLES
Reggie Smith BOS 33
Paul Schaal KC 31
two tied at 30

TRIPLES
Freddie Patek KC 11
Rod Carew MIN 10
Paul Blair BAL 8

HOME RUNS
Bill Melton CHI 33
Norm Cash DET 32
Reggie Jackson OAK 32

RUNS BATTED IN
Harmon Killebrew MIN 119
Frank Robinson BAL 99
Reggie Smith BOS 96

SLUGGING AVERAGE
Tony Oliva MIN .... .546
Bobby Murcer NY .... .543
Norm Cash DET .... .531

STOLEN BASES
Amos Otis KC 52
Freddie Patek KC 49
Sandy Alomar CAL 39

RUNS SCORED
Don Buford BAL 99
Bobby Murcer NY 94
Cesar Tovar MIN 94

WINS
Mickey Lolich DET 25
Vida Blue OAK 24
Wilbur Wood CHI 22

WINNING PERCENTAGE
Dave McNally BAL .... .808
Vida Blue OAK .... .750
Chuck Dobson OAK .... .750

EARNED RUN AVERAGE
Vida Blue OAK 1.82
Wilbur Wood CHI 1.91
Jim Palmer BAL 2.68

STRIKEOUTS
Mickey Lolich DET 308
Vida Blue OAK 301
Joe Coleman DET 236

SAVES
Ken Sanders MIL 31
Ted Abernathy KC 23
Fred Scherman DET 20

COMPLETE GAMES
Mickey Lolich DET 29
Vida Blue OAK 24
Wilbur Wood CHI 22

SHUTOUTS
Vida Blue OAK 8
Mel Stottlemyre NY 7
Wilbur Wood CHI 7

GAMES PITCHED
Ken Sanders MIL 83
Fred Scherman DET 69
Tom Burgmeier KC 67

INNINGS PITCHED
Mickey Lolich DET 376
Wilbur Wood CHI 334
Vida Blue OAK 312

1971 NL

EAST	W	L	PCT	GB	R	OR	BA	FA	ERA
★PITTSBURGH	97	65	.599	—	788	599	.274	.979	3.31
ST. LOUIS	90	72	.556	7	739	699	.275	.978	3.87
CHICAGO	83	79	.512	14	637	648	.258	.980	3.61
NEW YORK	83	79	.512	14	588	550	.249	.981	3.00
MONTREAL	71	90	.441	25.5	622	729	.246	.976	4.12
PHILADELPHIA	67	95	.414	30	558	688	.233	.981	3.71

WEST	W	L	PCT	GB	R	OR	BA	FA	ERA
SAN FRANCISCO	90	72	.556	—	706	644	.247	.972	3.33
LOS ANGELES	89	73	.549	1	663	587	.266	.979	3.23
ATLANTA	82	80	.506	8	643	699	.257	.977	3.75
CINCINNATI	79	83	.488	11	586	581	.241	.984	3.35
HOUSTON	79	83	.488	11	585	567	.240	.983	3.13
SAN DIEGO	61	100	.379	28.5	486	610	.233	.974	3.23
					7601	7601	.252	.979	3.47

BATTING AVERAGE
Joe Torre STL .... .363
Ralph Garr ATL .... .343
Glenn Beckert CHI .... .342

HITS
Joe Torre STL 230
Ralph Garr ATL 219
Lou Brock STL 200

DOUBLES
Cesar Cedeno HOU 40
Lou Brock STL 37
two tied at............................ 34

TRIPLES
Joe Morgan HOU 11
Roger Metzger HOU 11
Willie Davis LA 10

HOME RUNS
Willie Stargell PIT 48
Hank Aaron ATL................. 47
Lee May CIN 39

RUNS BATTED IN
Joe Torre STL 137
Willie Stargell PIT 125
Hank Aaron ATL 118

SLUGGING AVERAGE
Hank Aaron ATL................. .669
Willie Stargell PIT .... .628
Joe Torre STL .... .555

STOLEN BASES
Lou Brock STL 64
Joe Morgan HOU 40
Ralph Garr ATL................. 30

RUNS SCORED
Lou Brock STL 126
Bobby Bonds SF 110
Willie Stargell PIT 104

WINS
Ferguson Jenkins CHI........ 24
three tied at 20

WINNING PERCENTAGE
Don Gullett CIN .... .727
Steve Carlton STL............ .690
Al Downing LA................. .690

EARNED RUN AVERAGE
Tom Seaver NY................ 1.76
Dave Roberts SD 2.10
Don Wilson HOU 2.45

STRIKEOUTS
Tom Seaver NY................ 289
Ferguson Jenkins CHI...... 263
Bill Stoneman MON.......... 251

SAVES
Dave Giusti PIT 30
Mike Marshall MON........... 23
Jim Brewer LA.................... 22

COMPLETE GAMES
Ferguson Jenkins CHI........ 30
Tom Seaver NY................ 21
two tied at............................ 20

SHUTOUTS
four tied at 5

GAMES PITCHED
Wayne Granger CIN........... 70
Jerry Johnson SF............... 67

INNINGS PITCHED
Ferguson Jenkins CHI...... 325
Bill Stoneman MON.......... 295
Tom Seaver NY................ 286

1972 AL

EAST	W	L	PCT	GB	R	OR	BA	FA	ERA
DETROIT	86	70	.551	—	558	514	.237	.984	2.96
BOSTON	85	70	.548	.5	640	620	.248	.978	3.47
BALTIMORE	80	74	.519	5	519	430	.229	.983	2.54
NEW YORK	79	76	.510	6.5	557	527	.249	.978	3.05
CLEVELAND	72	84	.462	14	472	519	.234	.981	2.97
MILWAUKEE	65	91	.417	21	493	595	.235	.977	3.45

WEST	W	L	PCT	GB	R	OR	BA	FA	ERA
★OAKLAND	93	62	.600	—	604	457	.240	.979	2.58
CHICAGO	87	67	.565	5.5	566	538	.238	.977	3.12
MINNESOTA	77	77	.500	15.5	537	535	.244	.974	2.86
KANSAS CITY	76	78	.494	16.5	580	545	.255	.980	3.24
CALIFORNIA	75	80	.484	18	454	533	.242	.981	3.06
TEXAS	54	100	.351	38.5	461	628	.217	.972	3.53
					6441	6441	.239	.979	3.07

BATTING AVERAGE
Rod Carew MIN .318
Lou Piniella KC .312
two tied at .308

HITS
Joe Rudi OAK 181
Lou Piniella KC 179
Bobby Murcer NY 171

DOUBLES
Lou Piniella KC 33
Joe Rudi OAK 32
Bobby Murcer NY 30

TRIPLES
Joe Rudi OAK 9
Carlton Fisk BOS 9
Paul Blair BAL 8

HOME RUNS
Dick Allen CHI 37
Bobby Murcer NY 33
two tied at 26

RUNS BATTED IN
Dick Allen CHI 113
John Mayberry KC 100
Bobby Murcer NY 96

SLUGGING AVERAGE
Dick Allen CHI .603
Carlton Fisk BOS .538
Bobby Murcer NY .537

STOLEN BASES
Bert Campaneris OAK 52
Dave Nelson TEX 51
Freddie Patek KC 33

RUNS SCORED
Bobby Murcer NY 102
Joe Rudi OAK 94
Tommy Harper BOS 92

WINS
Wilbur Wood CHI 24
Gaylord Perry CLE 24
Mickey Lolich DET 22

WINNING PERCENTAGE
Catfish Hunter OAK .750
Blue Moon Odom OAK .714
Luis Tiant BOS .714

EARNED RUN AVERAGE
Luis Tiant BOS 1.91
Gaylord Perry CLE 1.92
Catfish Hunter OAK 2.04

STRIKEOUTS
Nolan Ryan CAL 329
Mickey Lolich DET 250
Gaylord Perry CLE 234

SAVES
Sparky Lyle NY 35
Terry Forster CHI 29
Rollie Fingers OAK 21

COMPLETE GAMES
Gaylord Perry CLE 29
Mickey Lolich DET 23
two tied at 20

SHUTOUTS
Nolan Ryan CAL 9
Wilbur Wood CHI 8
Mel Stottlemyre NY 7

GAMES PITCHED
Paul Lindblad TEX 66
Rollie Fingers OAK 65
Wayne Granger MIN 63

INNINGS PITCHED
Wilbur Wood CHI 377
Gaylord Perry CLE 343
Mickey Lolich DET 327

1972 NL

EAST	W	L	PCT	GB	R	OR	BA	FA	ERA
PITTSBURGH	96	59	.619	—	691	512	.274	.978	2.81
CHICAGO	85	70	.548	11	685	567	.257	.979	3.22
NEW YORK	83	73	.532	13.5	528	578	.225	.980	3.27
ST. LOUIS	75	81	.481	21.5	568	600	.260	.977	3.42
MONTREAL	70	86	.449	26.5	513	609	.234	.978	3.60
PHILADELPHIA	59	97	.378	37.5	503	635	.236	.981	3.67

WEST	W	L	PCT	GB	R	OR	BA	FA	ERA
●CINCINNATI	95	59	.617	—	707	557	.251	.982	3.21
HOUSTON	84	69	.549	10.5	708	636	.258	.980	3.77
LOS ANGELES	85	70	.548	10.5	584	527	.256	.974	2.78
ATLANTA	70	84	.455	25	628	730	.258	.974	4.27
SAN FRANCISCO	69	86	.445	26.5	662	649	.244	.974	3.70
SAN DIEGO	58	95	.379	36.5	488	665	.227	.976	3.78
					7265	7265	.248	.978	3.46

BATTING AVERAGE
Billy Williams CHI .333
Ralph Garr ATL .325
Cesar Cedeno HOU .320

HITS
Pete Rose CIN 198
Lou Brock STL 193
Billy Williams CHI 191

DOUBLES
Cesar Cedeno HOU 39
Willie Montanez PHI 39
Ted Simmons STL 36

TRIPLES
Larry Bowa PHI 13
Pete Rose CIN 11
two tied at 8

HOME RUNS
Johnny Bench CIN 40
Nate Colbert SD 38
Billy Williams CHI 37

RUNS BATTED IN
Johnny Bench CIN 125
Billy Williams CHI 122
Willie Stargell PIT 112

SLUGGING AVERAGE
Billy Williams CHI .606
Willie Stargell PIT .558
Johnny Bench CIN .541

STOLEN BASES
Lou Brock STL 63
Joe Morgan CIN 58
Cesar Cedeno HOU 55

RUNS SCORED
Joe Morgan CIN 122
Bobby Bonds SF 118
Jimmy Wynn HOU 117

WINS
Steve Carlton PHI 27
Tom Seaver NY 21
two tied at 20

WINNING PERCENTAGE
Gary Nolan CIN .750
Steve Carlton PHI .730
Milt Pappas CHI .708

EARNED RUN AVERAGE
Steve Carlton PHI 1.97
Gary Nolan CIN 1.99
Don Sutton LA 2.08

STRIKEOUTS
Steve Carlton PHI 310
Tom Seaver NY 249
Bob Gibson STL 208

SAVES
Clay Carroll CIN 37
Tug McGraw NY 27
Dave Giusti PIT 22

COMPLETE GAMES
Steve Carlton PHI 30
Ferguson Jenkins CHI 23
Bob Gibson STL 23

SHUTOUTS
Don Sutton LA 9
Steve Carlton PHI 8
Fred Norman SD 6

GAMES PITCHED
Mike Marshall MON 65
Clay Carroll CIN 65
Pedro Borbon CIN 62

INNINGS PITCHED
Steve Carlton PHI 346
Ferguson Jenkins CHI 289
Phil Niekro ATL 282

1973 AL

EAST	W	L	PCT	GB	R	OR	BA	FA	ERA
BALTIMORE	97	65	.599	—	754	561	.266	.981	3.07
BOSTON	89	73	.549	8	738	647	.267	.979	3.65
DETROIT	85	77	.525	12	642	674	.254	.982	3.90
NEW YORK	80	82	.494	17	641	610	.261	.976	3.34
MILWAUKEE	74	88	.457	23	708	731	.253	.977	3.98
CLEVELAND	71	91	.438	26	680	826	.256	.978	4.58

WEST	W	L	PCT	GB	R	OR	BA	FA	ERA
★OAKLAND	94	68	.580	—	758	615	.260	.978	3.29
KANSAS CITY	88	74	.543	6	755	752	.261	.974	4.21
MINNESOTA	81	81	.500	13	738	692	.270	.978	3.77
CALIFORNIA	79	83	.488	15	629	657	.253	.975	3.57
CHICAGO	77	85	.475	17	652	705	.256	.977	3.86
TEXAS	57	105	.352	37	619	844	.255	.974	4.64
					8314	8314	.259	.977	3.82

BATTING AVERAGE
Rod Carew MIN .350
George Scott MIL .306
Tommy Davis BAL .306

HITS
Rod Carew MIN 203
Dave May MIL 189
Bobby Murcer NY 187

DOUBLES
Sal Bando OAK 32
Pedro Garcia MIL 32
two tied at 30

TRIPLES
Rod Carew MIN 11
Al Bumbry BAL 11
Jorge Orta CHI 10

HOME RUNS
Reggie Jackson OAK 32
Frank Robinson CAL 30
Jeff Burroughs TEX 30

RUNS BATTED IN
Reggie Jackson OAK 117
George Scott MIL 107
John Mayberry KC 100

SLUGGING AVERAGE
Reggie Jackson OAK .531
Sal Bando OAK .498
Frank Robinson CAL .489

STOLEN BASES
Tommy Harper BOS 54
Billy North OAK 53
Dave Nelson TEX 43

RUNS SCORED
Reggie Jackson OAK 99
three tied at 98

WINS
Wilbur Wood CHI 24
Joe Coleman DET 23
Jim Palmer BAL 22

WINNING PERCENTAGE
Catfish Hunter OAK .808
Jim Palmer BAL .710
Vida Blue OAK .690

EARNED RUN AVERAGE
Jim Palmer BAL 2.40
Bert Blyleven MIN 2.52
Bill Lee BOS 2.74

STRIKEOUTS
Nolan Ryan CAL 383
Bert Blyleven MIN 258
Bill Singer CAL 241

SAVES
John Hiller DET 38
Sparky Lyle NY 27
Rollie Fingers OAK 22

COMPLETE GAMES
Gaylord Perry CLE 29
Nolan Ryan CAL 26
Bert Blyleven MIN 25

SHUTOUTS
Bert Blyleven MIN 9
Gaylord Perry CLE 7
Jim Palmer BAL 6

GAMES PITCHED
John Hiller DET 65
Rollie Fingers OAK 62
Doug Bird KC 54

INNINGS PITCHED
Wilbur Wood CHI 359
Gaylord Perry CLE 344
Nolan Ryan CAL 326

1973 NL

EAST	W	L	PCT	GB	R	OR	BA	FA	ERA
● NEW YORK	82	79	.509	—	608	588	.246	.980	3.27
ST. LOUIS	81	81	.500	1.5	643	603	.259	.975	3.25
PITTSBURGH	80	82	.494	2.5	704	693	.261	.976	3.74
MONTREAL	79	83	.488	3.5	668	702	.251	.974	3.73
CHICAGO	77	84	.478	5	614	655	.247	.975	3.66
PHILADELPHIA	71	91	.438	11.5	642	717	.249	.979	4.00

WEST	W	L	PCT	GB	R	OR	BA	FA	ERA
CINCINNATI	99	63	.611	—	741	621	.254	.982	3.43
LOS ANGELES	95	66	.590	3.5	675	565	.263	.981	3.00
SAN FRANCISCO	88	74	.543	11	739	702	.262	.974	3.79
HOUSTON	82	80	.506	17	681	672	.251	.981	3.78
ATLANTA	76	85	.472	22.5	799	774	.266	.974	4.25
SAN DIEGO	60	102	.370	39	548	770	.244	.973	4.16
					8062	8062	.254	.977	3.67

BATTING AVERAGE
Pete Rose CIN .... .338
Cesar Cedeno HOU .... .320
Garry Maddox SF .... .319

HITS
Pete Rose CIN 230
Ralph Garr ATL 200
Lou Brock STL 193

DOUBLES
Willie Stargell PIT 43
Al Oliver PIT 38
two tied at 36

TRIPLES
Roger Metzger HOU 14
Garry Maddox SF 10
Gary Matthews SF 10

HOME RUNS
Willie Stargell PIT 44
Davey Johnson ATL 43
Darrell Evans ATL 41

RUNS BATTED IN
Willie Stargell PIT 119
Lee May HOU 105
two tied at 104

SLUGGING AVERAGE
Willie Stargell PIT .... .646
Darrell Evans ATL .... .556
Davey Johnson ATL .... .546

STOLEN BASES
Lou Brock STL 70
Joe Morgan CIN 67
Cesar Cedeno HOU 56

RUNS SCORED
Bobby Bonds SF 131
Joe Morgan CIN 116
Pete Rose CIN 115

WINS
Ron Bryant SF 24
Tom Seaver NY 19
Jack Billingham CIN 19

WINNING PERCENTAGE
Tommy John LA .... .696
Don Gullett CIN .... .692
Ron Bryant SF .... .667

EARNED RUN AVERAGE
Tom Seaver NY 2.08
Wayne Twitchell PHI 2.50
Mike Marshall MON 2.66

STRIKEOUTS
Tom Seaver NY 251
Steve Carlton PHI 223
John Matlack NY 205

SAVES
Mike Marshall MON 31
Tug McGraw NY 25
two tied at 20

COMPLETE GAMES
Tom Seaver NY 18
Steve Carlton PHI 18
Jack Billingham CIN 16

SHUTOUTS
Jack Billingham CIN 7
Dave Roberts HOU 6
two tied at 5

GAMES PITCHED
Mike Marshall MON 92
Pedro Borbon CIN 80
Elias Sosa SF 71

INNINGS PITCHED
Steve Carlton PHI 293
Jack Billingham CIN 293
Tom Seaver NY 290

1974 AL

EAST	W	L	PCT	GB	R	OR	BA	FA	ERA
BALTIMORE	91	71	.562	—	659	612	.256	.980	3.27
NEW YORK	89	73	.549	2	671	623	.263	.977	3.32
BOSTON	84	78	.519	7	696	661	.264	.977	3.72
CLEVELAND	77	85	.475	14	662	694	.255	.977	3.80
MILWAUKEE	76	86	.469	15	647	660	.244	.980	3.77
DETROIT	72	90	.444	19	620	768	.247	.975	4.17

WEST	W	L	PCT	GB	R	OR	BA	FA	ERA
★OAKLAND	90	72	.556	—	689	551	.247	.977	2.95
TEXAS	84	76	.525	5	690	698	.272	.974	3.82
MINNESOTA	82	80	.506	8	673	669	.272	.976	3.64
CHICAGO	80	80	.500	9	684	721	.268	.977	3.94
KANSAS CITY	77	85	.475	13	667	662	.259	.976	3.51
CALIFORNIA	68	94	.420	22	618	657	.254	.977	3.52
					7976	7976	.258	.977	3.62

BATTING AVERAGE
Rod Carew MIN .... .364
Jorge Orta CHI .... .316
Hal McRae KC .... .310

HITS
Rod Carew MIN 218
Tommy Davis BAL 181
Don Money MIL 178

DOUBLES
Joe Rudi OAK 39
George Scott MIL 36
Hal McRae KC 36

TRIPLES
Mickey Rivers CAL 11
Amos Otis KC 9
two tied at 8

HOME RUNS
Dick Allen CHI 32
Reggie Jackson OAK 29
Gene Tenace OAK 26

RUNS BATTED IN
Jeff Burroughs TEX 118
Sal Bando OAK 103
Joe Rudi OAK 99

SLUGGING AVERAGE
Dick Allen CHI .... .563
Reggie Jackson OAK .... .514
Jeff Burroughs TEX .... .504

STOLEN BASES
Billy North OAK 54
Rod Carew MIN 38
John Lowenstein CLE 36

RUNS SCORED
Carl Yastrzemski BOS 93
Bobby Grich BAL 92
Reggie Jackson OAK 90

WINS
Catfish Hunter OAK 25
Ferguson Jenkins TEX 25
four tied at 22

WINNING PERCENTAGE
Mike Cuellar BAL .... .688
Catfish Hunter OAK .... .676
Ferguson Jenkins TEX ..... .676

EARNED RUN AVERAGE
Catfish Hunter OAK 2.49
Gaylord Perry CLE 2.52
Andy Hassler CAL 2.61

STRIKEOUTS
Nolan Ryan CAL 367
Bert Blyleven MIN 249
Ferguson Jenkins TEX 225

SAVES
Terry Forster CHI 24
Tom Murphy MIL 20
Bill Campbell MIN 19

COMPLETE GAMES
Ferguson Jenkins TEX 29
Gaylord Perry CLE 28
Mickey Lolich DET 27

SHUTOUTS
Luis Tiant BOS 7
Catfish Hunter OAK 6
Ferguson Jenkins TEX 6

GAMES PITCHED
Rollie Fingers OAK 76
Tom Murphy MIL 70
Steve Foucault TEX 69

INNINGS PITCHED
Nolan Ryan CAL 333
Ferguson Jenkins TEX 328
Gaylord Perry CLE 322

1974 NL

EAST	W	L	PCT	GB	R	OR	BA	FA	ERA
PITTSBURGH	88	74	.543	—	751	657	.274	.975	3.49
ST. LOUIS	86	75	.534	1.5	677	643	.265	.977	3.48
PHILADELPHIA	80	82	.494	8	676	701	.261	.976	3.92
MONTREAL	79	82	.491	8.5	662	657	.254	.976	3.60
NEW YORK	71	91	.438	17	572	646	.235	.975	3.42
CHICAGO	66	96	.407	22	669	826	.251	.969	4.28

WEST	W	L	PCT	GB	R	OR	BA	FA	ERA
●LOS ANGELES	102	60	.630	—	798	561	.272	.975	2.97
CINCINNATI	98	64	.605	4	776	631	.260	.979	3.42
ATLANTA	88	74	.543	14	661	563	.249	.979	3.05
HOUSTON	81	81	.500	21	653	632	.263	.982	3.48
SAN FRANCISCO	72	90	.444	30	634	723	.252	.972	3.80
SAN DIEGO	60	102	.370	42	541	830	.229	.973	4.61
					8070	8070	.255	.976	3.62

BATTING AVERAGE
Ralph Garr ATL .... .353
Al Oliver PIT .... .321
two tied at .... .314

HITS
Ralph Garr ATL 214
Dave Cash PHI 206
Steve Garvey LA 200

DOUBLES
Pete Rose CIN 45
Al Oliver PIT 38
Johnny Bench CIN 38

TRIPLES
Ralph Garr ATL 17
Al Oliver PIT 12
Dave Cash PHI 11

HOME RUNS
Mike Schmidt PHI................ 36
Johnny Bench CIN 33
Jimmy Wynn LA 32

RUNS BATTED IN
Johnny Bench CIN 129
Mike Schmidt PHI.............. 116
Steve Garvey LA 111

SLUGGING AVERAGE
Mike Schmidt PHI............. .546
Willie Stargell PIT .... .537
Reggie Smith STL .... .528

STOLEN BASES
Lou Brock STL 118
Davey Lopes LA................. 59
Joe Morgan CIN 58

RUNS SCORED
Pete Rose CIN 110
Mike Schmidt PHI.............. 108
Johnny Bench CIN 108

WINS
Phil Niekro ATL 20
Andy Messersmith LA 20
two tied at............................ 19

WINNING PERCENTAGE
Andy Messersmith LA ..... .769
Don Sutton LA.................. .679
Buzz Capra ATL............... .667

EARNED RUN AVERAGE
Buzz Capra ATL.............. 2.28
Phil Niekro ATL 2.38
John Matlack NY 2.41

STRIKEOUTS
Steve Carlton PHI 240
Andy Messersmith LA 221
Tom Seaver NY................ 201

SAVES
Mike Marshall LA................ 21
Randy Moffitt SF 15
Pedro Borbon CIN 14

COMPLETE GAMES
Phil Niekro ATL 18
Steve Carlton PHI 17
Jim Lonborg PHI 16

SHUTOUTS
John Matlack NY 7
Phil Niekro ATL 6
two tied at.............................. 5

GAMES PITCHED
Mike Marshall LA.............. 106
Larry Hardy SD 76
Pedro Borbon CIN.............. 73

INNINGS PITCHED
Phil Niekro ATL 302
Andy Messersmith LA 292
Steve Carlton PHI 291

1975 AL

EAST	W	L	PCT	GB	R	OR	BA	FA	ERA
• BOSTON	95	65	.594	—	796	709	.275	.977	3.99
BALTIMORE	90	69	.566	4.5	682	553	.252	.983	3.17
NEW YORK	83	77	.519	12	681	588	.264	.978	3.29
CLEVELAND	79	80	.497	15.5	688	703	.261	.978	3.84
MILWAUKEE	68	94	.420	28	675	793	.250	.971	4.34
DETROIT	57	102	.358	37.5	570	786	.249	.972	4.29

WEST	W	L	PCT	GB	R	OR	BA	FA	ERA
OAKLAND	98	64	.605	—	758	606	.254	.977	3.29
KANSAS CITY	91	71	.562	7	710	649	.261	.976	3.49
TEXAS	79	83	.488	19	714	733	.256	.971	3.90
MINNESOTA	76	83	.478	20.5	724	736	.271	.973	4.05
CHICAGO	75	86	.466	22.5	655	707	.255	.978	3.93
CALIFORNIA	72	89	.447	25.5	628	723	.246	.971	3.89
					8281	8281	.258	.975	3.79

BATTING AVERAGE
Rod Carew MIN .... .359
Fred Lynn BOS .... .331
Thurman Munson NY .... .318

HITS
George Brett KC 195
Rod Carew MIN 192
Thurman Munson NY 190

DOUBLES
Fred Lynn BOS 47
Reggie Jackson OAK 39
two tied at 38

TRIPLES
Mickey Rivers CAL 13
George Brett KC 13
Jorge Orta CHI 10

HOME RUNS
George Scott MIL 36
Reggie Jackson OAK 36
John Mayberry KC 34

RUNS BATTED IN
George Scott MIL 109
John Mayberry KC 106
Fred Lynn BOS 105

SLUGGING AVERAGE
Fred Lynn BOS .... .566
John Mayberry KC .... .547
George Scott MIL .... .515

STOLEN BASES
Mickey Rivers CAL 70
C. Washington OAK 40
Amos Otis KC 39

RUNS SCORED
Fred Lynn BOS 103
John Mayberry KC 95
Bobby Bonds NY 93

WINS
Jim Palmer BAL 23
Catfish Hunter NY 23
Vida Blue OAK 22

WINNING PERCENTAGE
Mike Torrez BAL .... .690
Dennis Leonard KC .... .682
Jim Palmer BAL .... .676

EARNED RUN AVERAGE
Jim Palmer BAL 2.09
Catfish Hunter NY 2.58
Dennis Eckersley CLE 2.60

STRIKEOUTS
Frank Tanana CAL 269
Bert Blyleven MIN 233
G. Perry CLE, TEX 233

SAVES
Goose Gossage CHI ... 26
Rollie Fingers OAK 24
Tom Murphy MIL 20

COMPLETE GAMES
Catfish Hunter NY 30
Jim Palmer BAL 25
Gaylord Perry CLE, TEX 25

SHUTOUTS
Jim Palmer BAL 10
Catfish Hunter NY 7
two tied at 5

GAMES PITCHED
Rollie Fingers OAK 75
Paul Lindblad OAK 68
Goose Gossage CHI 62

INNINGS PITCHED
Catfish Hunter NY 328
Jim Palmer BAL 323
G. Perry CLE, TEX 306

1975 NL

EAST	W	L	PCT	GB	R	OR	BA	FA	ERA
PITTSBURGH	92	69	.571	—	712	565	.263	.976	3.02
PHILADELPHIA	86	76	.531	6.5	735	694	.269	.976	3.82
NEW YORK	82	80	.506	10.5	646	625	.256	.976	3.39
ST. LOUIS	82	80	.506	10.5	662	689	.273	.973	3.58
CHICAGO	75	87	.463	17.5	712	827	.259	.972	4.57
MONTREAL	75	87	.463	17.5	601	690	.244	.973	3.73

WEST	W	L	PCT	GB	R	OR	BA	FA	ERA
★CINCINNATI	108	54	.667	—	840	586	.271	.984	3.37
LOS ANGELES	88	74	.543	20	648	534	.248	.979	2.92
SAN FRANCISCO	80	81	.497	27.5	659	671	.259	.976	3.74
SAN DIEGO	71	91	.438	37	552	683	.244	.971	3.51
ATLANTA	67	94	.416	40.5	583	739	.244	.972	3.93
HOUSTON	64	97	.398	43.5	664	711	.254	.979	4.05
					8014	8014	.257	.976	3.63

BATTING AVERAGE
Bill Madlock CHI .... .354
Ted Simmons STL .... .332
Manny Sanguillen PIT ..... .328

HITS
Dave Cash PHI 213
Steve Garvey LA 210
Pete Rose CIN 210

DOUBLES
Pete Rose CIN 47
Dave Cash PHI 40
two tied at 39

TRIPLES
Ralph Garr ATL 11
three tied at 10

HOME RUNS
Mike Schmidt PHI 38
Dave Kingman NY 36
Greg Luzinski PHI 34

RUNS BATTED IN
Greg Luzinski PHI 120
Johnny Bench CIN 110
Tony Perez CIN 109

SLUGGING AVERAGE
Dave Parker PIT .... .541
Greg Luzinski PHI .... .540
Mike Schmidt PHI .... .523

STOLEN BASES
Davey Lopes LA 77
Joe Morgan CIN 67
Lou Brock STL 56

RUNS SCORED
Pete Rose CIN 112
Dave Cash PHI 111
Davey Lopes LA 108

WINS
Tom Seaver NY 22
Randy Jones SD 20
Andy Messersmith LA 19

WINNING PERCENTAGE
Tom Seaver NY .... .710
Burt Hooton CHI, LA .... .667
four tied at .... .625

EARNED RUN AVERAGE
Randy Jones SD 2.24
Andy Messersmith LA 2.29
Tom Seaver NY 2.38

STRIKEOUTS
Tom Seaver NY 243
John Montefusco SF 215
Andy Messersmith LA 213

SAVES
Rawley Eastwick CIN 22
Al Hrabosky STL 22
Dave Giusti PIT 17

COMPLETE GAMES
Andy Messersmith LA 19
Randy Jones SD 18
two tied at 15

SHUTOUTS
Andy Messersmith LA 7
Randy Jones SD 6
Jerry Reuss PIT 6

GAMES PITCHED
Gene Garber PHI 71
Will McEnaney CIN 70
two tied at 67

INNINGS PITCHED
Andy Messersmith LA 322
Randy Jones SD 285
Tom Seaver NY 280

1976 AL

EAST	W	L	PCT	GB	R	OR	BA	FA	ERA
●NEW YORK	97	62	.610	—	730	575	.269	.980	3.19
BALTIMORE	88	74	.543	10.5	619	598	.243	.982	3.31
BOSTON	83	79	.512	15.5	716	660	.263	.978	3.52
CLEVELAND	81	78	.509	16	615	615	.263	.980	3.48
DETROIT	74	87	.460	24	609	709	.257	.974	3.87
MILWAUKEE	66	95	.410	32	570	655	.246	.975	3.64

WEST	W	L	PCT	GB	R	OR	BA	FA	ERA
KANSAS CITY	90	72	.556	—	713	611	.269	.978	3.21
OAKLAND	87	74	.540	2.5	686	598	.246	.977	3.26
MINNESOTA	85	77	.525	5	743	704	.274	.973	3.72
CALIFORNIA	76	86	.469	14	550	631	.235	.977	3.36
TEXAS	76	86	.469	14	616	652	.250	.976	3.47
CHICAGO	64	97	.398	25.5	586	745	.255	.979	4.25
					7753	7753	.256	.977	3.52

BATTING AVERAGE
George Brett KC .333
Hal McRae KC .332
Rod Carew MIN .331

HITS
George Brett KC 215
Rod Carew MIN 200
Chris Chambliss NY 188

DOUBLES
Amos Otis KC 40
three tied at 34

TRIPLES
George Brett KC 14
Phil Garner OAK 12
Rod Carew MIN 12

HOME RUNS
Graig Nettles NY 32
Sal Bando OAK 27
Reggie Jackson BAL 27

RUNS BATTED IN
Lee May BAL 109
Thurman Munson NY 105
Carl Yastrzemski BOS 102

SLUGGING AVERAGE
Reggie Jackson BAL .502
Jim Rice BOS .482
Graig Nettles NY .475

STOLEN BASES
Billy North OAK 75
Ron LeFlore DET 58
Bert Campaneris OAK 54

RUNS SCORED
Roy White NY 104
Rod Carew MIN 97
Mickey Rivers NY 95

WINS
Jim Palmer BAL 22
Luis Tiant BOS 21
Wayne Garland BAL 20

WINNING PERCENTAGE
Bill Campbell MIN .773
Wayne Garland BAL .741
Doc Ellis NY .680

EARNED RUN AVERAGE
Mark Fidrych DET 2.34
Vida Blue OAK 2.36
Frank Tanana CAL 2.44

STRIKEOUTS
Nolan Ryan CAL 327
Frank Tanana CAL 261
B. Blyleven MIN, TEX 219

SAVES
Sparky Lyle NY 23
Dave LaRoche CLE 21
two tied at 20

COMPLETE GAMES
Mark Fidrych DET 24
Frank Tanana CAL 23
Jim Palmer BAL 23

SHUTOUTS
Nolan Ryan CAL 7
three tied at 6

GAMES PITCHED
Bill Campbell MIN 78
Rollie Fingers OAK 70
Paul Lindblad OAK 65

INNINGS PITCHED
Jim Palmer BAL 315
Catfish Hunter NY 299
Vida Blue OAK 298

1976 NL

EAST	W	L	PCT	GB	R	OR	BA	FA	ERA
PHILADELPHIA	101	61	.623	—	770	557	.272	.981	3.10
PITTSBURGH	92	70	.568	9	708	630	.267	.975	3.37
NEW YORK	86	76	.531	15	615	538	.246	.979	2.94
CHICAGO	75	87	.463	26	611	728	.251	.978	3.93
ST. LOUIS	72	90	.444	29	629	671	.260	.973	3.61
MONTREAL	55	107	.340	46	531	734	.235	.976	3.99

WEST	W	L	PCT	GB	R	OR	BA	FA	ERA
★CINCINNATI	102	60	.630	—	857	633	.280	.984	3.51
LOS ANGELES	92	70	.568	10	608	543	.251	.980	3.02
HOUSTON	80	82	.494	22	625	657	.256	.978	3.55
SAN FRANCISCO	74	88	.457	28	595	686	.246	.971	3.53
SAN DIEGO	73	89	.451	29	570	662	.247	.978	3.65
ATLANTA	70	92	.432	32	620	700	.245	.973	3.87
					7739	7739	.255	.977	3.50

BATTING AVERAGE
Bill Madlock CHI .... .339
Ken Griffey CIN .... .336
Garry Maddox PHI .... .330

HITS
Pete Rose CIN 215
W. Montanez SF, ATL 206
Steve Garvey LA 200

DOUBLES
Pete Rose CIN 42
Jay Johnstone PHI 38
two tied at 37

TRIPLES
Dave Cash PHI 12
Cesar Geronimo CIN 11
two tied at 10

HOME RUNS
Mike Schmidt PHI 38
Dave Kingman NY 37
Rick Monday CHI 32

RUNS BATTED IN
George Foster CIN 121
Joe Morgan CIN 111
Mike Schmidt PHI 107

SLUGGING AVERAGE
Joe Morgan CIN .... .576
George Foster CIN .... .530
Mike Schmidt PHI .... .524

STOLEN BASES
Davey Lopes LA 63
Joe Morgan CIN 60
two tied at 58

RUNS SCORED
Pete Rose CIN 130
Joe Morgan CIN 113
Mike Schmidt PHI 112

WINS
Randy Jones SD 22
Jerry Koosman NY 21
Don Sutton LA 21

WINNING PERCENTAGE
Steve Carlton PHI .... .741
John Candelaria PIT .... .696
two tied at .... .677

EARNED RUN AVERAGE
John Denny STL 2.52
Doug Rau LA 2.57
Tom Seaver NY 2.59

STRIKEOUTS
Tom Seaver NY 235
J.R. Richard HOU 214
Jerry Koosman NY 200

SAVES
Rawley Eastwick CIN 26
Skip Lockwood NY 19
Ken Forsch HOU 19

COMPLETE GAMES
Randy Jones SD 25
Jerry Koosman NY 17
John Matlack NY 16

SHUTOUTS
John Matlack NY 6
John Montefusco SF 6
two tied at 5

GAMES PITCHED
Dale Murray MON 81
Charlie Hough LA 77
Butch Metzger SD 77

INNINGS PITCHED
Randy Jones SD 315
J.R. Richard HOU 291
two tied at 271

1977 AL

EAST	W	L	PCT	GB	R	OR	BA	FA	ERA
★NEW YORK	100	62	.617	—	831	651	.281	.979	3.61
BALTIMORE	97	64	.602	2.5	719	653	.261	.983	3.74
BOSTON	97	64	.602	2.5	859	712	.281	.978	4.16
DETROIT	74	88	.457	26	714	751	.264	.978	4.13
CLEVELAND	71	90	.441	28.5	676	739	.269	.979	4.10
MILWAUKEE	67	95	.414	33	639	765	.258	.978	4.32
TORONTO	54	107	.335	45.5	605	882	.252	.974	4.57

WEST	W	L	PCT	GB	R	OR	BA	FA	ERA
KANSAS CITY	102	60	.630	—	822	651	.277	.978	3.52
TEXAS	94	68	.580	8	767	657	.270	.982	3.56
CHICAGO	90	72	.556	12	844	771	.278	.974	4.25
MINNESOTA	84	77	.522	17.5	867	776	.282	.978	4.38
CALIFORNIA	74	88	.457	28	675	695	.255	.976	3.76
SEATTLE	64	98	.395	38	624	855	.256	.976	4.83
OAKLAND	63	98	.391	38.5	605	749	.240	.970	4.05
					10247	10247	.266	.977	4.07

BATTING AVERAGE
Rod Carew MIN .388
Lyman Bostock MIN .336
Ken Singleton BAL .328

HITS
Rod Carew MIN 239
Ron LeFlore DET 212
Jim Rice BOS 206

DOUBLES
Hal McRae KC 54
Reggie Jackson NY 39
two tied at 38

TRIPLES
Rod Carew MIN 16
Jim Rice BOS 15
Al Cowens KC 14

HOME RUNS
Jim Rice BOS 39
Graig Nettles NY 37
Bobby Bonds CAL 37

RUNS BATTED IN
Larry Hisle MIN 119
Bobby Bonds CAL 115
Jim Rice BOS 114

SLUGGING AVERAGE
Jim Rice BOS .593
Rod Carew MIN .570
Reggie Jackson NY .550

STOLEN BASES
Freddie Patek KC 53
Mike Page OAK 42
two tied at 41

RUNS SCORED
Rod Carew MIN 128
Carlton Fisk BOS 106
George Brett KC 105

WINS
Jim Palmer BAL 20
Dave Goltz MIN 20
Dennis Leonard KC 20

WINNING PERCENTAGE
Paul Splittorff KC .727
Ron Guidry NY .696
Dave Rozema DET .682

EARNED RUN AVERAGE
Frank Tanana CAL 2.54
Bert Blyleven TEX 2.72
Nolan Ryan CAL 2.77

STRIKEOUTS
Nolan Ryan CAL 341
Dennis Leonard KC 244
Frank Tanana CAL 205

SAVES
Bill Campbell BOS 31
Sparky Lyle NY 26
Lerrin LaGrow CHI 25

COMPLETE GAMES
Jim Palmer BAL 22
Nolan Ryan CAL 22
two tied at 21

SHUTOUTS
Frank Tanana CAL 7
three tied at 5

GAMES PITCHED
Sparky Lyle NY 72
Tom Johnson MIN 71
Bill Campbell BOS 69

INNINGS PITCHED
Jim Palmer BAL 319
Dave Goltz MIN 303
Nolan Ryan CAL 299

1977 NL

EAST	W	L	PCT	GB	R	OR	BA	FA	ERA
PHILADELPHIA	101	61	.623	—	847	668	.279	.981	3.71
PITTSBURGH	96	66	.593	5	734	665	.274	.977	3.61
ST. LOUIS	83	79	.512	18	737	688	.270	.978	3.81
CHICAGO	81	81	.500	20	692	739	.266	.977	4.01
MONTREAL	75	87	.463	26	665	736	.260	.980	4.01
NEW YORK	64	98	.395	37	587	663	.244	.978	3.77

WEST	W	L	PCT	GB	R	OR	BA	FA	ERA
● LOS ANGELES	98	64	.605	—	769	582	.266	.981	3.22
CINCINNATI	88	74	.543	10	802	725	.274	.984	4.22
HOUSTON	81	81	.500	17	680	650	.254	.978	3.54
SAN FRANCISCO	75	87	.463	23	673	711	.253	.972	3.75
SAN DIEGO	69	93	.426	29	692	834	.249	.971	4.43
ATLANTA	61	101	.377	37	678	895	.254	.972	4.85
					8556	8556	.262	.977	3.91

BATTING AVERAGE
Dave Parker PIT 338
Garry Templeton STL...... .322
George Foster CIN.......... .320

HITS
Dave Parker PIT............... 215
Pete Rose CIN 204
Garry Templeton STL........ 200

DOUBLES
Dave Parker PIT............... 44
Dave Cash MON 42
two tied at............................ 41

TRIPLES
Garry Templeton STL........ 18
three tied at 11

HOME RUNS
George Foster CIN............. 52
Jeff Burroughs ATL 41
Greg Luzinski PHI 39

RUNS BATTED IN
George Foster CIN............. 149
Greg Luzinski PHI 130
Steve Garvey LA 115

SLUGGING AVERAGE
George Foster CIN.......... .631
Greg Luzinski PHI .... .594
Reggie Smith LA .... .576

STOLEN BASES
Frank Taveras PIT 70
Cesar Cedeno HOU 61
Gene Richards SD 56

RUNS SCORED
George Foster CIN........... 124
Ken Griffey CIN 117
Mike Schmidt PHI............. 114

WINS
Steve Carlton PHI 23
Tom Seaver NY, CIN 21
four tied at 20

WINNING PERCENTAGE
John Candelaria PIT .... .800
Tom Seaver NY, CIN 778
Larry Christenson PHI..... .760

EARNED RUN AVERAGE
John Candelaria PIT 2.34
Tom Seaver NY, CIN 2.58
Burt Hooton LA................ 2.62

STRIKEOUTS
Phil Niekro ATL 262
J.R. Richard HOU 214
Steve Rogers MON 206

SAVES
Rollie Fingers SD 35
Bruce Sutter CHI 31
Goose Gossage PIT........... 26

COMPLETE GAMES
Phil Niekro ATL 20
Tom Seaver NY, CIN 19
two tied at............................ 17

SHUTOUTS
Tom Seaver NY, CIN 7
Rick Reuschel CHI 4
Steve Rogers MON.............. 4

GAMES PITCHED
Rollie Fingers SD 78
Dan Spillner SD.................. 76
Dave Tomlin SD.................. 76

INNINGS PITCHED
Phil Niekro ATL 330
Steve Rogers MON 302
Steve Carlton PHI 283

1978 AL

EAST	W	L	PCT	GB	R	OR	BA	FA	ERA
★NEW YORK*	100	63	.613	—	735	582	.267	.982	3.18
BOSTON	99	64	.607	1	796	657	.267	.977	3.54
MILWAUKEE	93	69	.574	6.5	804	650	.276	.977	3.65
BALTIMORE	90	71	.559	9	659	633	.258	.982	3.56
DETROIT	86	76	.531	13.5	714	653	.271	.981	3.64
CLEVELAND	69	90	.434	29	639	694	.261	.980	3.97
TORONTO	59	102	.366	40	590	775	.250	.979	4.55

WEST	W	L	PCT	GB	R	OR	BA	FA	ERA
KANSAS CITY	92	70	.568	—	743	634	.268	.976	3.44
CALIFORNIA	87	75	.537	5	691	666	.259	.978	3.65
TEXAS	87	75	.537	5	692	632	.253	.976	3.42
MINNESOTA	73	89	.451	19	666	678	.267	.977	3.69
CHICAGO	71	90	.441	20.5	634	731	.264	.977	4.22
OAKLAND	69	93	.426	23	532	690	.245	.971	3.62
SEATTLE	56	104	.350	35	614	834	.248	.978	4.72
* Defeated Boston in a 1-game playoff					9509	9509	.261	.978	3.77

BATTING AVERAGE
Rod Carew MIN .... .333
Al Oliver TEX .... .324
Jim Rice BOS .... .315

HITS
Jim Rice BOS 213
Ron LeFlore DET 198
Rod Carew MIN 188

DOUBLES
George Brett KC 45
Carlton Fisk BOS 39
Hal McRae KC 39

TRIPLES
Jim Rice BOS 15
Rod Carew MIN 10
Dan Ford MIN 10

HOME RUNS
Jim Rice BOS 46
Larry Hisle MIL 34
Don Baylor CAL 34

RUNS BATTED IN
Jim Rice BOS 139
Rusty Staub DET 121
Larry Hisle MIL 115

SLUGGING AVERAGE
Jim Rice BOS .... .600
Larry Hisle MIL .... .533
Doug DeCinces BAL .... .526

STOLEN BASES
Ron LeFlore DET 68
Julio Cruz SEA 59
Bump Wills TEX 52

RUNS SCORED
Ron LeFlore DET 126
Jim Rice BOS 121
Don Baylor CAL 103

WINS
Ron Guidry NY 25
Mike Caldwell MIL 22
two tied at 21

WINNING PERCENTAGE
Ron Guidry NY .... .893
Bob Stanley BOS .... .882
Larry Gura KC .... .800

EARNED RUN AVERAGE
Ron Guidry NY 1.74
John Matlack TEX 2.27
Mike Caldwell MIL 2.36

STRIKEOUTS
Nolan Ryan CAL 260
Ron Guidry NY 248
Dennis Leonard KC 183

SAVES
Goose Gossage NY 27
Dave LaRoche CAL 25
Don Stanhouse BAL 24

COMPLETE GAMES
Mike Caldwell MIL 23
Dennis Leonard KC 20
Jim Palmer BAL 19

SHUTOUTS
Ron Guidry NY 9
Mike Caldwell MIL 6
Jim Palmer BAL 6

GAMES PITCHED
Bob Lacey OAK 74
Dave Heaverlo OAK 69
Elias Sosa OAK 68

INNINGS PITCHED
Jim Palmer BAL 296
Dennis Leonard KC 295
Mike Caldwell MIL 293

1978 NL

EAST	W	L	PCT	GB	R	OR	BA	FA	ERA
PHILADELPHIA	90	72	.556	—	708	586	.258	.983	3.33
PITTSBURGH	88	73	.547	1.5	684	637	.257	.973	3.41
CHICAGO	79	83	.488	11	664	724	.264	.978	4.05
MONTREAL	76	86	.469	14	633	611	.254	.979	3.42
ST. LOUIS	69	93	.426	21	600	657	.249	.978	3.58
NEW YORK	66	96	.407	24	607	690	.245	.979	3.87

WEST	W	L	PCT	GB	R	OR	BA	FA	ERA
● LOS ANGELES	95	67	.586	—	727	573	.264	.978	3.12
CINCINNATI	92	69	.571	2.5	710	688	.256	.978	3.81
SAN FRANCISCO	89	73	.549	6	613	594	.248	.977	3.30
SAN DIEGO	84	78	.519	11	591	598	.252	.975	3.28
HOUSTON	74	88	.457	21	605	634	.258	.978	3.63
ATLANTA	69	93	.426	26	600	750	.244	.975	4.08
					7742	7742	.254	.978	3.58

BATTING AVERAGE
Dave Parker PIT .334
Steve Garvey LA .316
Jose Cruz HOU .315

HITS
Steve Garvey LA 202
Pete Rose CIN 198
Enos Cabell HOU 195

DOUBLES
Pete Rose CIN 51
Jack Clark SF 46
Ted Simmons STL 40

TRIPLES
Garry Templeton STL 13
Dave Parker PIT 12
Gene Richards SD 12

HOME RUNS
George Foster CIN 40
Greg Luzinski PHI 35
Dave Parker PIT 30

RUNS BATTED IN
George Foster CIN 120
Dave Parker PIT 117
Steve Garvey LA 113

SLUGGING AVERAGE
Dave Parker PIT .585
Reggie Smith LA .559
George Foster CIN .546

STOLEN BASES
Omar Moreno PIT 71
Frank Taveras PIT 46
Davey Lopes LA 45

RUNS SCORED
Ivan DeJesus CHI 104
Pete Rose CIN 103
Dave Parker PIT 102

WINS
Gaylord Perry SD 21
Ross Grimsley MON 20
two tied at 19

WINNING PERCENTAGE
Gaylord Perry SD .778
Don Robinson PIT .700
Burt Hooton LA .655

EARNED RUN AVERAGE
Craig Swan NY 2.43
Steve Rogers MON 2.47
Pete Vuckovich STL 2.55

STRIKEOUTS
J.R. Richard HOU 303
Phil Niekro ATL 248
Tom Seaver CIN 226

SAVES
Rollie Fingers SD 37
Kent Tekulve PIT 31
Doug Bair CIN 28

COMPLETE GAMES
Phil Niekro ATL 22
Ross Grimsley MON 19
two tied at 16

SHUTOUTS
Bob Knepper SF 6
three tied at 4

GAMES PITCHED
Kent Tekulve PIT 91
Mark Littell STL 72
Donnie Moore CHI 71

INNINGS PITCHED
Phil Niekro ATL 334
J.R. Richard HOU 275
Ross Grimsley MON 263

1979 AL

EAST	W	L	PCT	GB	R	OR	BA	FA	ERA
●BALTIMORE	102	57	.642	—	757	582	.261	.980	3.26
MILWAUKEE	95	66	.590	8	807	722	.280	.980	4.03
BOSTON	91	69	.569	11.5	841	711	.283	.977	4.03
NEW YORK	89	71	.556	13.5	734	672	.266	.981	3.83
DETROIT	85	76	.528	18	770	738	.269	.981	4.28
CLEVELAND	81	80	.503	22	760	805	.258	.978	4.57
TORONTO	53	109	.327	50.5	613	862	.251	.975	4.82

WEST	W	L	PCT	GB	R	OR	BA	FA	ERA
CALIFORNIA	88	74	.543	—	866	768	.282	.978	4.34
KANSAS CITY	85	77	.525	3	851	816	.282	.977	4.45
TEXAS	83	79	.512	5	750	698	.278	.979	3.86
MINNESOTA	82	80	.506	6	764	725	.278	.979	4.13
CHICAGO	73	87	.456	14	730	748	.275	.972	4.10
SEATTLE	67	95	.414	21	711	820	.269	.978	4.58
OAKLAND	54	108	.333	34	573	860	.239	.972	4.75
					10527	10527	.270	.978	4.22

BATTING AVERAGE
Fred Lynn BOS .... .333
George Brett KC .... .329
Brian Downing CAL .... .326

HITS
George Brett KC 212
Jim Rice BOS 201
Buddy Bell TEX 200

DOUBLES
Cecil Cooper MIL 44
Chet Lemon CHI 44
two tied at 42

TRIPLES
George Brett KC 20
Paul Molitor MIL 16
two tied at 13

HOME RUNS
Gorman Thomas MIL 45
Fred Lynn BOS 39
Jim Rice BOS 39

RUNS BATTED IN
Don Baylor CAL 139
Jim Rice BOS 130
Gorman Thomas MIL 123

SLUGGING AVERAGE
Fred Lynn BOS .... .637
Jim Rice BOS .... .596
Sixto Lezcano MIL .... .573

STOLEN BASES
Willie Wilson KC 83
Ron LeFlore DET 78
Julio Cruz SEA 49

RUNS SCORED
Don Baylor CAL 120
George Brett KC 119
Jim Rice BOS 117

WINS
Mike Flanagan BOS 23
Tommy John NY 21
Jerry Koosman MIN 20

WINNING PERCENTAGE
Mike Caldwell MIL .... .727
Mike Flanagan BAL .... .719
Jack Morris DET .... .708

EARNED RUN AVERAGE
Ron Guidry NY 2.78
Tommy John NY 2.97
Dennis Eckersley BOS 2.99

STRIKEOUTS
Nolan Ryan CAL 223
Ron Guidry NY 201
Mike Flanagan BAL 190

SAVES
Mike Marshall MIN 32
Jim Kern TEX 29
two tied at 21

COMPLETE GAMES
Dennis Martinez BAL 18
three tied at 17

SHUTOUTS
Dennis Leonard KC 5
Mike Flanagan BAL 5
Nolan Ryan CAL 5

GAMES PITCHED
Mike Marshall MIN 90
Sid Monge CLE 76
Jim Kern TEX 71

INNINGS PITCHED
Dennis Martinez BAL 292
Tommy John NY 276
Mike Flanagan BAL 266

1979 NL

EAST	W	L	PCT	GB	R	OR	BA	FA	ERA
★PITTSBURGH	98	64	.605	—	775	643	.272	.979	3.41
MONTREAL	95	65	.594	2	701	581	.264	.979	3.14
ST. LOUIS	86	76	.531	12	731	693	.278	.980	3.72
PHILADELPHIA	84	78	.519	14	683	718	.266	.983	4.16
CHICAGO	80	82	.494	18	706	707	.269	.975	3.88
NEW YORK	63	99	.389	35	593	706	.250	.978	3.84

WEST	W	L	PCT	GB	R	OR	BA	FA	ERA
CINCINNATI	90	71	.559	—	731	644	.264	.980	3.58
HOUSTON	89	73	.549	1.5	583	582	.256	.978	3.19
LOS ANGELES	79	83	.488	11.5	739	717	.263	.981	3.83
SAN FRANCISCO	71	91	.438	19.5	672	751	.246	.974	4.16
SAN DIEGO	68	93	.422	22	603	681	.242	.978	3.69
ATLANTA	66	94	.413	23.5	669	763	.256	.970	4.18
					8186	8186	.261	.978	3.73

BATTING AVERAGE
Keith Hernandez STL....... .344
Pete Rose PHI .... .331
Ray Knight CIN .... .318

HITS
Garry Templeton STL....... 211
Keith Hernandez STL....... 210
Pete Rose PHI 208

DOUBLES
Keith Hernandez STL....... 48
Warren Cromartie MON 46
Dave Parker PIT................ 45

TRIPLES
Garry Templeton STL........ 19
three tied at 12

HOME RUNS
Dave Kingman CHI 48
Mike Schmidt PHI.............. 45
Dave Winfield SD 34

RUNS BATTED IN
Dave Winfield SD 118
Dave Kingman CHI 115
Mike Schmidt PHI............. 114

SLUGGING AVERAGE
Dave Kingman CHI .... .613
Mike Schmidt PHI............ .564
Dave Winfield SD .... .558

STOLEN BASES
Omar Moreno PIT 77
Billy North SF 58
two tied at.......................... 44

RUNS SCORED
Keith Hernandez STL....... 116
Omar Moreno PIT 110
two tied at.......................... 109

WINS
Phil Niekro ATL 21
Joe Niekro HOU 21
three tied at........................ 18

WINNING PERCENTAGE
Tom Seaver CIN .... .727
Joe Niekro HOU .... .656
Silvio Martinez STL .... .652

EARNED RUN AVERAGE
J.R. Richard HOU 2.71
Tom Hume CIN 2.76
Dan Schatzeder MON 2.83

STRIKEOUTS
J.R. Richard HOU 313
Steve Carlton PHI 213
Phil Niekro ATL 208

SAVES
Bruce Sutter CHI 37
Kent Tekulve PIT................ 31
Gene Garber ATL............... 25

COMPLETE GAMES
Phil Niekro ATL 23
J.R. Richard HOU 19
two tied at.......................... 13

SHUTOUTS
Tom Seaver CIN 5
Steve Rogers MON 5
Joe Niekro HOU 5

GAMES PITCHED
Kent Tekulve PIT................ 94
Enrique Romo PIT.............. 84
Grant Jackson PIT 72

INNINGS PITCHED
Phil Niekro ATL 342
J.R. Richard HOU 292
Joe Niekro HOU 264

1980 AL

EAST	W	L	PCT	GB	R	OR	BA	FA	ERA
NEW YORK	103	59	.636	—	820	662	.267	.978	3.58
BALTIMORE	100	62	.617	3	805	640	.273	.985	3.64
MILWAUKEE	86	76	.531	17	811	682	.275	.977	3.71
BOSTON	83	77	.519	19	757	767	.283	.977	4.38
DETROIT	84	78	.519	19	830	757	.273	.979	4.25
CLEVELAND	79	81	.494	23	738	807	.277	.983	4.68
TORONTO	67	95	.414	36	624	762	.251	.979	4.19

WEST	W	L	PCT	GB	R	OR	BA	FA	ERA
●KANSAS CITY	97	65	.599	—	809	694	.286	.978	3.83
OAKLAND	83	79	.512	14	686	642	.259	.979	3.46
MINNESOTA	77	84	.478	19.5	670	724	.265	.977	3.93
TEXAS	76	85	.472	20.5	756	752	.284	.977	4.02
CHICAGO	70	90	.438	26	587	722	.259	.973	3.92
CALIFORNIA	65	95	.406	31	698	797	.265	.978	4.52
SEATTLE	59	103	.364	38	610	793	.248	.977	4.38
					10201	10201	.269	.978	4.03

BATTING AVERAGE
George Brett KC.............. .390
Cecil Cooper MIL .... .352
Miguel Dilone CLE .... .341

HITS
Willie Wilson KC 230
Cecil Cooper MIL 219
Mickey Rivers TEX........... 210

DOUBLES
Robin Yount MIL 49
Al Oliver TEX...................... 43
Jim Morrison CHI 40

TRIPLES
Willie Wilson KC 15
Alfredo Griffin TOR............. 15
two tied at............................ 11

HOME RUNS
Reggie Jackson NY............ 41
Ben Oglivie MIL................. 41
Gorman Thomas MIL 38

RUNS BATTED IN
Cecil Cooper MIL 122
George Brett KC............... 118
Ben Oglivie MIL................ 118

SLUGGING AVERAGE
George Brett KC.............. .664
Reggie Jackson NY......... .597
Ben Oglivie MIL................ .563

STOLEN BASES
R. Henderson OAK 100
Willie Wilson KC................. 79
Miguel Dilone CLE 61

RUNS SCORED
Willie Wilson KC 133
Robin Yount MIL 121
Al Bumbry BAL 118

WINS
Steve Stone BAL................ 25
Tommy John NY 22
Mike Norris OAK 22

WINNING PERCENTAGE
Steve Stone BAL.............. .781
Rudy May NY .... .750
Scott McGregor BAL .... .714

EARNED RUN AVERAGE
Rudy May NY 2.47
Mike Norris OAK 2.54
Britt Burns CHI 2.84

STRIKEOUTS
Len Barker CLE................ 187
Mike Norris OAK 180
Ron Guidry NY 166

SAVES
Dan Quisenberry KC.......... 33
Goose Gossage NY 33
Ed Farmer CHI 30

COMPLETE GAMES
Rick Langford OAK 28
Mike Norris OAK 24
Matt Keough OAK 20

SHUTOUTS
Tommy John NY 6
Geoff Zahn MIN.................... 5
two tied at............................. 4

GAMES PITCHED
Dan Quisenberry KC........... 75
Doug Corbett MIN 73
two tied at............................ 67

INNINGS PITCHED
Rick Langford OAK 290
Mike Norris OAK 284
Larry Gura KC 283

1980 NL

EAST	W	L	PCT	GB	R	OR	BA	FA	ERA
★ PHILADELPHIA	91	71	.562	—	728	639	.270	.979	3.43
MONTREAL	90	72	.556	1	694	629	.257	.977	3.48
PITTSBURGH	83	79	.512	8	666	646	.266	.978	3.58
ST. LOUIS	74	88	.457	17	738	710	.275	.981	3.93
NEW YORK	67	95	.414	24	611	702	.257	.975	3.85
CHICAGO	64	98	.395	27	614	728	.251	.974	3.89

WEST	W	L	PCT	GB	R	OR	BA	FA	ERA
HOUSTON*	93	70	.571	—	637	589	.261	.978	3.10
LOS ANGELES	92	71	.564	1	663	591	.263	.981	3.24
CINCINNATI	89	73	.549	3.5	707	670	.262	.983	3.85
ATLANTA	81	80	.503	11	630	660	.250	.975	3.77
SAN FRANCISCO	75	86	.466	17	573	634	.244	.975	3.46
SAN DIEGO	73	89	.451	19.5	591	654	.255	.980	3.65
					7852	7852	.259	.978	3.60

*Defeated Los Angeles in a 1-game playoff

BATTING AVERAGE
Bill Buckner CHI .... .324
Keith Hernandez STL .... .321
Garry Templeton STL .... .319

HITS
Steve Garvey LA 200
Gene Richards SD 193
Keith Hernandez STL 191

DOUBLES
Pete Rose PHI 42
Bill Buckner CHI 41
Andre Dawson MON 41

TRIPLES
Rodney Scott MON 13
Omar Moreno PIT 13
two tied at 11

HOME RUNS
Mike Schmidt PHI 48
Bob Horner ATL 35
Dale Murphy ATL 33

RUNS BATTED IN
Mike Schmidt PHI 121
George Hendrick STL 109
Steve Garvey LA 106

SLUGGING AVERAGE
Mike Schmidt PHI .... .624
Jack Clark SF .... .517
Dale Murphy ATL .... .510

STOLEN BASES
Ron LeFlore MON 97
Omar Moreno PIT 96
Dave Collins CIN 79

RUNS SCORED
Keith Hernandez STL 111
Mike Schmidt PHI 104
Dale Murphy ATL 98

WINS
Steve Carlton PHI 24
Joe Niekro HOU 20
Jim Bibby PIT 19

WINNING PERCENTAGE
Jim Bibby PIT .... .760
Jerry Reuss LA .... .750
Steve Carlton PHI .... .727

EARNED RUN AVERAGE
Don Sutton LA 2.21
Steve Carlton PHI 2.34
Jerry Reuss LA 2.52

STRIKEOUTS
Steve Carlton PHI 286
Nolan Ryan HOU 200
Mario Soto CIN 182

SAVES
Bruce Sutter CHI 28
Tom Hume CIN 25
Rollie Fingers SD 23

COMPLETE GAMES
Steve Rogers MON 14
Steve Carlton PHI 13
two tied at 11

SHUTOUTS
Jerry Reuss LA 6
J.R. Richard HOU 4
Steve Rogers MON 4

GAMES PITCHED
Dick Tidrow CHI 84
Tom Hume CIN 78
Kent Tekulve PIT 78

INNINGS PITCHED
Steve Carlton PHI 304
Steve Rogers MON 281
Phil Niekro ATL 275

1981 AL

EAST	W	L	PCT	GB	R	OR	BA	FA	ERA
MILWAUKEE**	62	47	.569	—	493	459	.257	.982	3.91
BALTIMORE	59	46	.562	1	429	437	.251	.983	3.70
●NEW YORK*†	59	48	.551	2	421	343	.252	.982	2.90
DETROIT	60	49	.550	2	427	404	.256	.984	3.53
BOSTON	59	49	.546	2.5	519	481	.275	.979	3.81
CLEVELAND	52	51	.505	7	431	442	.263	.978	3.88
TORONTO	37	69	.349	23.5	329	466	.226	.975	3.82

WEST	W	L	PCT	GB	R	OR	BA	FA	ERA
OAKLAND*†	64	45	.587	—	458	403	.247	.980	3.30
TEXAS	57	48	.543	5	452	389	.270	.984	3.40
CHICAGO	54	52	.509	8.5	476	423	.272	.979	3.47
KANSAS CITY**	50	53	.485	11	397	405	.267	.982	3.56
CALIFORNIA	51	59	.464	13.5	476	453	.256	.977	3.70
SEATTLE	44	65	.404	20	426	521	.251	.979	4.23
MINNESOTA	41	68	.376	23	378	486	.240	.978	3.98
					6112	6112	.256	.980	3.66

BATTING AVERAGE
Carney Lansford BOS ..... .336
Tom Paciorek SEA .... .326
Cecil Cooper MIL .... .320

HITS
R. Henderson OAK 135
Carney Lansford BOS 134
two tied at 133

DOUBLES
Cecil Cooper MIL 35
Al Oliver TEX 29
Tom Paciorek SEA 28

TRIPLES
John Castino MIN 9
three tied at 7

HOME RUNS
four tied at 22

RUNS BATTED IN
Eddie Murray BAL 78
Tony Armas OAK 76
Ben Oglivie MIL 72

SLUGGING AVERAGE
Bobby Grich CAL .... .543
Eddie Murray BAL .... .534
Dwight Evans BOS .... .522

STOLEN BASES
Rickey Henderson OAK 56
Julio Cruz SEA 43
Ron LeFlore CHI 36

RUNS SCORED
Rickey Henderson OAK 89
Dwight Evans BOS 84
Cecil Cooper MIL 70

WINS
four tied at 14

WINNING PERCENTAGE
Pete Vuckovich MIL .... .778
Mike Torrez BOS .... .769
Dennis Martinez BAL ...... .737

EARNED RUN AVERAGE
Steve McCatty OAK 2.32
Sammy Stewart BAL 2.33
Dennis Lamp CHI 2.41

STRIKEOUTS
Len Barker CLE 127
Britt Burns CHI 108
two tied at 107

SAVES
Rollie Fingers MIL 28
Goose Gossage NY 20
Dan Quisenberry KC 18

COMPLETE GAMES
Rick Langford OAK 18
Steve McCatty OAK 16
Jack Morris DET 15

SHUTOUTS
four tied at 4

GAMES PITCHED
Doug Corbett MIN 54
Rollie Fingers MIL 47
Shane Rawley SEA 46

INNINGS PITCHED
Dennis Leonard KC 202
Jack Morris DET 198
Rick Langford OAK 195

1981 NL

EAST	W	L	PCT	GB	R	OR	BA	FA	ERA
ST. LOUIS	59	43	.578	—	464	417	.265	.981	3.63
MONTREAL**†	60	48	.556	2	443	394	.246	.980	3.30
PHILADELPHIA*	59	48	.551	2.5	491	472	.273	.980	4.05
PITTSBURGH	46	56	.451	13	407	425	.257	.979	3.56
NEW YORK	41	62	.398	18.5	348	432	.248	.968	3.55
CHICAGO	38	65	.369	21.5	370	483	.236	.974	4.01

WEST	W	L	PCT	GB	R	OR	BA	FA	ERA
CINCINNATI	66	42	.611	—	464	440	.267	.981	3.73
★LOS ANGELES*†	63	47	.573	4	450	356	.262	.980	3.01
HOUSTON**	61	49	.555	6	394	331	.257	.980	2.66
SAN FRANCISCO	56	55	.505	11.5	427	414	.250	.977	3.28
ATLANTA	50	56	.472	15	395	416	.243	.976	3.45
SAN DIEGO	41	69	.373	26	382	455	.256	.977	3.72
					5035	5035	.255	.978	3.49

*Winner of first half **Winner of second half †Winner of playoff

BATTING AVERAGE
Bill Madlock PIT .... .341
Pete Rose PHI .... .325
Dusty Baker LA .... .320

HITS
Pete Rose PHI 140
Bill Buckner CHI 131
Dave Concepcion CIN 129

DOUBLES
Bill Buckner CHI 35
Ruppert Jones SD 34
Dave Concepcion CIN 28

TRIPLES
Craig Reynolds HOU.......... 12
Gene Richards SD 12
Tommy Herr STL................. 9

HOME RUNS
Mike Schmidt PHI................ 31
Andre Dawson MON 24
two tied at.......................... 22

RUNS BATTED IN
Mike Schmidt PHI................ 91
George Foster CIN............. 90
Bill Buckner 75

SLUGGING AVERAGE
Mike Schmidt PHI............. .664
Andre Dawson MON .... .553
George Foster CIN........... .519

STOLEN BASES
Tim Raines MON................ 71
Omar Moreno PIT 39
Rodney Scott MON 30

RUNS SCORED
Mike Schmidt PHI............... 78
Pete Rose PHI 73
Andre Dawson MON 71

WINS
Tom Seaver CIN 14
Steve Carlton PHI 13
F. Valenzuela LA................ 13

WINNING PERCENTAGE
Tom Seaver CIN .... .875
Steve Carlton PHI .... .765
Jerry Reuss LA................ .714

EARNED RUN AVERAGE
Nolan Ryan HOU 1.69
Bob Knepper HOU 2.18
Burt Hooton LA................ 2.28

STRIKEOUTS
F. Valenzuela LA.............. 180
Steve Carlton PHI 179
Mario Soto CIN................. 151

SAVES
Bruce Sutter STL.............. 25
Greg Minton SF 21
Neil Allen NY 18

COMPLETE GAMES
F. Valenzuela LA............... 11
Mario Soto CIN.................. 10
Steve Carlton PHI 10

SHUTOUTS
Fernando Valenzuela LA...... 8
Bob Knepper HOU 5
Burt Hooton LA.................... 4

GAMES PITCHED
Gary Lucas SD.................. 57
Greg Minton SF................. 55
two tied at.......................... 51

INNINGS PITCHED
F. Valenzuela LA............... 192
Steve Carlton PHI 190
Mario Soto CIN................. 175

1982 AL

EAST	W	L	PCT	GB	R	OR	BA	FA	ERA
●MILWAUKEE	95	67	.586	—	891	717	.279	.980	3.98
BALTIMORE	94	68	.580	1	774	687	.266	.984	3.99
BOSTON	89	73	.549	6	753	713	.274	.981	4.03
DETROIT	83	79	.512	12	729	685	.266	.981	3.80
NEW YORK	79	83	.488	16	709	716	.256	.979	3.99
CLEVELAND	78	84	.481	17	683	748	.262	.980	4.11
TORONTO	78	84	.481	17	651	701	.262	.978	3.95

WEST	W	L	PCT	GB	R	OR	BA	FA	ERA
CALIFORNIA	93	69	.574	—	814	670	.274	.983	3.82
KANSAS CITY	90	72	.556	3	784	717	.285	.979	4.08
CHICAGO	87	75	.537	6	786	710	.273	.976	3.87
SEATTLE	76	86	.469	17	651	712	.254	.978	3.88
OAKLAND	68	94	.420	25	691	819	.236	.974	4.54
TEXAS	64	98	.395	29	590	749	.249	.981	4.28
MINNESOTA	60	102	.370	33	657	819	.257	.982	4.72
					10163	10163	.264	.980	4.07

BATTING AVERAGE
Willie Wilson KC .... .332
Robin Yount MIL .... .331
Rod Carew CAL .... .319

HITS
Robin Yount MIL 210
Cecil Cooper MIL 205
Paul Molitor MIL 201

DOUBLES
Robin Yount MIL 46
Hal McRae KC 46
Frank White KC 45

TRIPLES
Willie Wilson KC 15
Larry Herndon DET 13
Robin Yount MIL 12

HOME RUNS
Reggie Jackson CAL 39
Gorman Thomas MIL 39
Dave Winfield NY 37

RUNS BATTED IN
Hal McRae KC 133
Cecil Cooper MIL 121
Andre Thornton CLE 116

SLUGGING AVERAGE
Robin Yount MIL .... .578
Dave Winfield NY .... .560
Eddie Murry BAL .... .549

STOLEN BASES
R. Henderson OAK 130
Damaso Garcia TOR....... 54
Julio Cruz SEA 46

RUNS SCORED
Paul Molitor MIL 136
Robin Yount MIL 129
Dwight Evans BOS 122

WINS
LaMarr Hoyt CHI 19
three tied at 18

WINNING PERCENTAGE
Pete Vuckovich MIL .... .750
Jim Palmer BAL .... .750
Britt Burns CHI .... .722

EARNED RUN AVERAGE
Rick Sutcliffe CLE 2.96
Bob Stanley BOS 3.10
Jim Palmer BAL 3.13

STRIKEOUTS
Floyd Bannister SEA......... 209
Len Barker CLE................. 187
Dave Righetti NY............... 163

SAVES
Dan Quisenberry KC 35
Goose Gossage NY 30
Rollie Fingers MIL 29

COMPLETE GAMES
Dave Stieb TOR 19
Jack Morris DET................. 17
Rick Langford OAK 15

SHUTOUTS
Dave Stieb TOR 5
Geoff Zahn CAL 4
Ken Forsch CAL.................... 4

GAMES PITCHED
Ed Vande Berg SEA............ 78
Tippy Martinez BAL............ 76
Dan Quisenberry KC 72

INNINGS PITCHED
Dave Stieb TOR 288
Jim Clancy TOR 267
Jack Morris DET............... 266

1982 NL

EAST	W	L	PCT	GB	R	OR	BA	FA	ERA
★ST. LOUIS	92	70	.568	—	685	609	.264	.981	3.37
PHILADELPHIA	89	73	.549	3	664	654	.260	.981	3.61
MONTREAL	86	76	.531	6	697	616	.262	.980	3.31
PITTSBURGH	84	78	.519	8	724	696	.273	.977	3.81
CHICAGO	73	89	.451	19	676	709	.260	.979	3.92
NEW YORK	65	97	.401	27	609	723	.247	.972	3.88

WEST	W	L	PCT	GB	R	OR	BA	FA	ERA
ATLANTA	89	73	.549	—	739	702	.256	.979	3.82
LOS ANGELES	88	74	.543	1	691	612	.264	.979	3.26
SAN FRANCISCO	87	75	.537	2	673	687	.253	.973	3.64
SAN DIEGO	81	81	.500	8	675	658	.257	.976	3.52
HOUSTON	77	85	.475	12	569	620	.247	.978	3.41
CINCINNATI	61	101	.377	28	545	661	.251	.980	3.66
					7947	7947	.258	.978	3.60

BATTING AVERAGE
Al Oliver MON .... .331
Bill Madlock PIT .... .319
Leon Durham CHI .... .312

HITS
Al Oliver MON 204
Bill Buckner CHI 201
Andre Dawson MON 183

DOUBLES
Al Oliver MON 43
Terry Kennedy SD............. 42
Andre Dawson MON 37

TRIPLES
Dickie Thon HOU 10
three tied at 9

HOME RUNS
Dave Kingman NY............... 37
Dale Murphy ATL 36
Mike Schmidt PHI............... 35

RUNS BATTED IN
Dale Murphy ATL 109
Al Oliver MON 109
Bill Buckner CHI 105

SLUGGING AVERAGE
Mike Schmidt PHI............. .547
Pedro Guerrero LA............ .536
Leon Durham CHI .... .521

STOLEN BASES
Tim Raines MON................. 78
Lonnie Smith STL............... 68
Omar Moreno PIT 60

RUNS SCORED
Lonnie Smith STL............. 120
Dale Murphy ATL............. 113
Mike Schmidt PHI............. 108

WINS
Steve Carlton PHI 23
Steve Rogers MON 19
F. Valenzuela LA 19

WINNING PERCENTAGE
Phil Niekro ATL .... .810
Steve Rogers MON .... .704
Manny Sarmiento PIT ..... .692

EARNED RUN AVERAGE
Steve Rogers MON 2.40
Joe Niekro HOU 2.47
Joaquin Andujar STL........ 2.47

STRIKEOUTS
Steve Carlton PHI 286
Mario Soto CIN................. 274
Nolan Ryan HOU 245

SAVES
Bruce Sutter STL................ 36
Greg Minton SF................... 30
Gene Garber ATL................ 30

COMPLETE GAMES
Steve Carlton PHI 19
F. Valenzuela LA 18
Joe Niekro HOU 16

SHUTOUTS
Steve Carlton PHI 6
Joaquin Andujar STL........... 5
Joe Niekro HOU 5

GAMES PITCHED
Kent Tekulve PIT................. 85
Greg Minton SF................... 78
Rod Scurry PIT.................... 76

INNINGS PITCHED
Steve Carlton PHI 296
F. Valenzuela LA............... 285
Steve Rogers MON 277

1983 AL

EAST	W	L	PCT	GB	R	OR	BA	FA	ERA
★ BALTIMORE	98	64	.605	—	799	652	.269	.981	3.63
DETROIT	92	70	.568	6	789	679	.274	.980	3.80
NEW YORK	91	71	.562	7	770	703	.273	.978	3.85
TORONTO	89	73	.549	9	795	726	.277	.981	4.12
MILWAUKEE	87	75	.537	11	764	708	.277	.982	4.02
BOSTON	78	84	.481	20	724	775	.270	.979	4.34
CLEVELAND	70	92	.432	28	704	785	.265	.980	4.43

WEST	W	L	PCT	GB	R	OR	BA	FA	ERA
CHICAGO	99	63	.611	—	800	650	.262	.981	3.67
KANSAS CITY	79	83	.488	20	696	767	.271	.974	4.25
TEXAS	77	85	.475	22	639	609	.255	.982	3.31
OAKLAND	74	88	.457	25	708	782	.262	.974	4.35
CALIFORNIA	70	92	.432	29	722	779	.260	.977	4.31
MINNESOTA	70	92	.432	29	709	822	.261	.980	4.67
SEATTLE	60	102	.370	39	558	740	.240	.978	4.12
					10177	10177	.266	.979	4.06

BATTING AVERAGE
Wade Boggs BOS .... .361
Rod Carew CAL .... .339
Lou Whitaker DET .... .320

HITS
Cal Ripken BAL 211
Wade Boggs BOS 210
Lou Whitaker DET 206

DOUBLES
Cal Ripken BAL 47
Wade Boggs BOS 44
two tied at 42

TRIPLES
Robin Yount MIL 10
three tied at 9

HOME RUNS
Jim Rice BOS 39
Tony Armas BOS 36
Ron Kittle CHI 35

RUNS BATTED IN
Cecil Cooper MIL 126
Jim Rice BOS 126
Dave Winfield NY 116

SLUGGING AVERAGE
George Brett KC .... .563
Jim Rice BOS .... .550
Eddie Murray BAL .... .538

STOLEN BASES
R. Henderson OAK 108
Rudy Law CHI 77
Willie Wilson KC 59

RUNS SCORED
Cal Ripken BAL 121
Eddie Murray BAL 115
Cecil Cooper MIL 106

WINS
LaMarr Hoyt CHI 24
Rich Dotson CHI 22
Ron Guidry NY 21

WINNING PERCENTAGE
Moose Haas MIL .... .813
Rich Dotson CHI .... .759
Scott McGregor BAL .... .720

EARNED RUN AVERAGE
Rick Honeycutt TEX 2.42
Mike Boddicker BAL 2.77
Dave Stieb TOR 3.04

STRIKEOUTS
Jack Morris DET 232
Floyd Bannister CHI 193
Dave Stieb TOR 187

SAVES
Dan Quisenberry KC 45
Bob Stanley BOS 33
Ron Davis MIN 30

COMPLETE GAMES
Ron Guidry NY 21
Jack Morris DET 20
Dave Stieb TOR 14

SHUTOUTS
Mike Boddicker BAL 5
Britt Burns CHI 4
Dave Stieb TOR 4

GAMES PITCHED
Dan Quisenberry KC 69
Ed Vande Berg SEA 68
Ron Davis MIN 66

INNINGS PITCHED
Jack Morris DET 294
Dave Stieb TOR 278
Dan Petry DET 266

1983 NL

EAST

EAST	W	L	PCT	GB	R	OR	BA	FA	ERA
● PHILADELPHIA	90	72	.556	—	696	635	.249	.976	3.34
PITTSBURGH	84	78	.519	6	659	648	.264	.982	3.55
MONTREAL	82	80	.506	8	677	646	.264	.981	3.58
ST. LOUIS	79	83	.488	11	679	710	.270	.976	3.79
CHICAGO	71	91	.438	19	701	719	.261	.982	4.07
NEW YORK	68	94	.420	22	575	680	.241	.976	3.68

WEST	W	L	PCT	GB	R	OR	BA	FA	ERA
LOS ANGELES	91	71	.562	—	654	609	.250	.974	3.10
ATLANTA	88	74	.543	3	746	640	.272	.978	3.67
HOUSTON	85	77	.525	6	643	646	.257	.977	3.45
SAN DIEGO	81	81	.500	10	653	653	.250	.979	3.62
SAN FRANCISCO	79	83	.488	12	687	697	.247	.973	3.70
CINCINNATI	74	88	.457	17	623	710	.239	.981	3.98
					7993	7993	.255	.978	3.63

BATTING AVERAGE
Bill Madlock PIT .... .323
Lonnie Smith STL .... .321
two tied at .... .318

HITS
Jose Cruz HOU 189
Andre Dawson MON 189
Rafael Ramirez ATL 185

DOUBLES
Al Oliver MON 38
Johnny Ray PIT 38
Bill Buckner CHI 38

TRIPLES
Brett Butler ATL 13
Omar Moreno HOU 11
two tied at 10

HOME RUNS
Mike Schmidt PHI 40
Dale Murphy ATL 36
two tied at 32

RUNS BATTED IN
Dale Murphy ATL 121
Andre Dawson MON 113
Mike Schmidt PHI 109

SLUGGING AVERAGE
Dale Murphy ATL .... .540
Andre Dawson MON .... .539
Pedro Guerrero LA .... .531

STOLEN BASES
Tim Raines MON 90
Alan Wiggins SD 66
Steve Sax LA 56

RUNS SCORED
Tim Raines MON 133
Dale Murphy ATL 131
two tied at 104

WINS
John Denny PHI 19
three tied at 17

WINNING PERCENTAGE
John Denny PHI .... .760
three tied at .... .652

EARNED RUN AVERAGE
Atlee Hammaker SF 2.25
John Denny PHI 2.37
Bob Welch LA 2.65

STRIKEOUTS
Steve Carlton PHI 275
Mario Soto CIN 242
Larry McWilliams PIT 199

SAVES
Lee Smith CHI 29
Al Holland PHI 25
Greg Minton SF 22

COMPLETE GAMES
Mario Soto CIN 18
Steve Rogers MON 13
Bill Gullickson MON 10

SHUTOUTS
Steve Rogers MON 5
three tied at 4

GAMES PITCHED
Bill Campbell CHI 82
Kent Tekulve PIT 76
G. Hernandez CHI, PHI 74

INNINGS PITCHED
Steve Carlton PHI 284
Mario Soto CIN 274
Steve Rogers MON 273

1984 AL

EAST	W	L	PCT	GB	R	OR	BA	FA	ERA
★DETROIT	104	58	.642	—	829	643	.271	.979	3.49
TORONTO	89	73	.549	15	750	696	.273	.980	3.86
NEW YORK	87	75	.537	17	758	679	.276	.977	3.78
BOSTON	86	76	.531	18	810	764	.283	.977	4.18
BALTIMORE	85	77	.525	19	681	667	.252	.981	3.72
CLEVELAND	75	87	.463	29	761	766	.265	.977	4.25
MILWAUKEE	67	94	.416	36.5	641	734	.262	.978	4.06

WEST	W	L	PCT	GB	R	OR	BA	FA	ERA
KANSAS CITY	84	78	.519	—	673	686	.268	.979	3.91
CALIFORNIA	81	81	.500	3	696	697	.249	.980	3.96
MINNESOTA	81	81	.500	3	673	675	.265	.980	3.86
OAKLAND	77	85	.475	7	738	796	.259	.975	4.49
CHICAGO	74	88	.457	10	679	736	.247	.981	4.13
SEATTLE	74	88	.457	10	682	774	.258	.979	4.31
TEXAS	69	92	.429	14.5	656	714	.261	.977	3.91
					10027	10027	.264	.979	3.99

BATTING AVERAGE
Don Mattingly NY .... .343
Dave Winfield NY .... .340
Wade Boggs BOS .... .325

HITS
Don Mattingly NY 207
Wade Boggs BOS 203
Cal Ripken BAL 195

DOUBLES
Don Mattingly NY 44
Larry Parrish TEX 42
George Bell TOR 39

TRIPLES
Dave Collins TOR 15
Lloyd Moseby TOR 15
two tied at 10

HOME RUNS
Tony Armas BOS 43
Dave Kingman OAK 35
three tied at 33

RUNS BATTED IN
Tony Armas BOS 123
Jim Rice BOS 122
Dave Kingman OAK 118

SLUGGING AVERAGE
Harold Baines CHI .... .541
Don Mattingly NY .... .537
Dwight Evans BOS .... .532

STOLEN BASES
Rickey Henderson OAK 66
Dave Collins TOR 60
Brett Butler CLE 52

RUNS SCORED
Dwight Evans BOS 121
R. Henderson OAK 113
Wade Boggs BOS 109

WINS
Mike Boddicker BAL........... 20
Bert Blyleven CLE 19
Jack Morris DET 19

WINNING PERCENTAGE
Doyle Alexander TOR ..... .739
Bert Blyleven CLE............ .731
Dan Petry DET .... .692

EARNED RUN AVERAGE
Mike Boddicker BAL.......... 2.79
Dave Stieb TOR 2.83
Bert Blyleven CLE 2.87

STRIKEOUTS
Mark Langston SEA 204
Dave Stieb TOR 198
Mike Witt CAL 196

SAVES
Dan Quisenberry KC........... 44
Bill Caudill OAK................ 36
G. Hernandez DET............ 32

COMPLETE GAMES
Charlie Hough TEX 17
Mike Boddicker BAL........... 16
Rich Dotson CHI 14

SHUTOUTS
Geoff Zahn CAL 5
Bob Ojeda BOS.................. 5
two tied at........................... 4

GAMES PITCHED
G. Hernandez DET............. 80
Dan Quisenberry KC 72
Aurelio Lopez DET 71

INNINGS PITCHED
Dave Stieb TOR 267
Charlie Hough TEX 266
Doyle Alexander TOR 262

1984 NL

EAST	W	L	PCT	GB	R	OR	BA	FA	ERA
CHICAGO	96	65	.596	—	762	658	.260	.981	3.75
NEW YORK	90	72	.556	6.5	652	676	.257	.979	3.60
ST. LOUIS	84	78	.519	12.5	652	645	.252	.982	3.58
PHILADELPHIA	81	81	.500	15.5	720	690	.266	.975	3.62
MONTREAL	78	83	.484	18	593	585	.251	.978	3.31
PITTSBURGH	75	87	.463	21.5	615	567	.255	.980	3.11

WEST	W	L	PCT	GB	R	OR	BA	FA	ERA
● SAN DIEGO	92	70	.568	—	686	634	.259	.978	3.48
ATLANTA	80	82	.494	12	632	655	.247	.978	3.57
HOUSTON	80	82	.494	12	693	630	.264	.979	3.32
LOS ANGELES	79	83	.488	13	580	600	.244	.975	3.17
CINCINNATI	70	92	.432	22	627	747	.244	.977	4.16
SAN FRANCISCO	66	96	.407	26	682	807	.265	.973	4.39
					7894	7894	.255	.978	3.59

BATTING AVERAGE
Tony Gwynn SD .... .351
Lee Lacy PIT .... .321
Chili Davis SF .... .315

HITS
Tony Gwynn SD 213
Ryne Sandberg CHI 200
Tim Raines MON 192

DOUBLES
Johnny Ray PIT 38
Tim Raines MON 38
two tied at 36

TRIPLES
Juan Samuel PHI 19
Ryne Sandberg CHI 19
Jose Cruz HOU 13

HOME RUNS
Dale Murphy ATL 36
Mike Schmidt PHI 36
Gary Carter MON 27

RUNS BATTED IN
Gary Carter MON 106
Mike Schmidt PHI 106
Dale Murphy ATL 100

SLUGGING AVERAGE
Dale Murphy ATL .... .547
Mike Schmidt PHI .... .536
Ryne Sandberg CHI .... .520

STOLEN BASES
Tim Raines MON 75
Juan Samuel PHI 72
Alan Wiggins SD 70

RUNS SCORED
Ryne Sandberg CHI 114
Tim Raines MON 106
Alan Wiggins SD 106

WINS
Joaquin Andujar STL 20
Mario Soto CIN 18
Dwight Gooden NY 17

WINNING PERCENTAGE
Mario Soto CIN .... .720
Alejandro Pena LA .... .667
Dwight Gooden NY .... .654

EARNED RUN AVERAGE
Alejandro Pena LA 2.48
Dwight Gooden NY 2.60
Orel Hershiser LA 2.66

STRIKEOUTS
Dwight Gooden NY 276
F. Valenzuela LA 240
Nolan Ryan HOU 197

SAVES
Bruce Sutter STL 45
Lee Smith CHI 33
Jesse Orosco NY 31

COMPLETE GAMES
Mario Soto CIN 13
F. Valenzuela LA 12
Joaquin Andujar STL 12

SHUTOUTS
Alejandro Pena LA 4
Joaquin Andujar STL 4
Orel Hershiser LA 4

GAMES PITCHED
Ted Power CIN 78
Gary Lavelle SF 77
Greg Minton SF 74

INNINGS PITCHED
Joaquin Andujar STL 261
F. Valenzuela LA 261
Joe Niekro HOU 248

1985 AL

EAST	W	L	PCT	GB	R	OR	BA	FA	ERA
TORONTO	99	62	.615	—	759	588	.269	.980	3.31
NEW YORK	97	64	.602	2	839	660	.267	.979	3.69
DETROIT	84	77	.522	15	729	688	.253	.977	3.78
BALTIMORE	83	78	.516	16	818	764	.263	.979	4.38
BOSTON	81	81	.500	18.5	800	720	.282	.977	4.06
MILWAUKEE	71	90	.441	28	690	802	.263	.977	4.39
CLEVELAND	60	102	.370	39.5	729	861	.265	.977	4.91

WEST	W	L	PCT	GB	R	OR	BA	FA	ERA
★KANSAS CITY	91	71	.562	—	687	639	.252	.980	3.49
CALIFORNIA	90	72	.556	1	732	703	.251	.982	3.91
CHICAGO	85	77	.525	6	736	720	.253	.982	4.07
MINNESOTA	77	85	.475	14	705	782	.264	.980	4.48
OAKLAND	77	85	.475	14	757	787	.264	.977	4.41
SEATTLE	74	88	.457	17	719	818	.255	.980	4.68
TEXAS	62	99	.385	28.5	617	785	.253	.980	4.56
					10317	10317	.261	.979	4.15

BATTING AVERAGE
Wade Boggs BOS .... .368
George Brett KC .... .335
Don Mattingly NY .... .324

HITS
Wade Boggs BOS 240
Don Mattingly NY 211
Bill Buckner BOS 201

DOUBLES
Don Mattingly NY 48
Bill Buckner BOS 46
Wade Boggs BOS 42

TRIPLES
Willie Wilson KC 21
Brett Butler CLE 14
Kirby Puckett MIN 13

HOME RUNS
Darrell Evans DET 40
Carlton Fisk CHI 37
Steve Balboni KC 36

RUNS BATTED IN
Don Mattingly NY 145
Eddie Murray BAL 124
Dave Winfield NY 114

SLUGGING AVERAGE
George Brett KC .... .585
Don Mattingly NY .... .567
Jesse Barfield TOR .... .536

STOLEN BASES
Rickey Henderson NY 80
Gary Pettis CAL 56
Brett Butler CLE 47

RUNS SCORED
Rickey Henderson NY 146
Cal Ripken BAL 116
Eddie Murray BAL 111

WINS
Ron Guidry NY 22
Bret Saberhagen KC 20
two tied at 18

WINNING PERCENTAGE
Ron Guidry NY .... .786
Bret Saberhagen KC .... .769
Jimmy Key TOR .... .700

EARNED RUN AVERAGE
Dave Stieb TOR 2.48
Charlie Leibrandt KC 2.69
Bret Saberhagen KC 2.87

STRIKEOUTS
B. Blyleven CLE, MIN 206
Floyd Bannister CHI 198
Jack Morris DET 191

SAVES
Dan Quisenberry KC 37
Bob James CHI 32
two tied at 31

COMPLETE GAMES
Bert Blyleven CLE, MIN 24
Charlie Hough TEX 14
Mike Moore SEA 14

SHUTOUTS
Bert Blyleven CLE, MIN 5
Jack Morris DET 4
Britt Burns CHI 4

GAMES PITCHED
Dan Quisenberry KC 84
Ed Vande Berg SEA 76
two tied at 74

INNINGS PITCHED
B. Blyleven CLE, MIN 294
Oil Can Boyd BOS 272
Dave Stieb TOR 265

1985 NL

EAST	W	L	PCT	GB	R	OR	BA	FA	ERA
●ST. LOUIS	101	61	.623	—	747	572	.264	.983	3.10
NEW YORK	98	64	.605	3	695	568	.257	.982	3.11
MONTREAL	84	77	.522	16.5	633	636	.247	.981	3.55
CHICAGO	77	84	.478	23.5	686	729	.254	.979	4.16
PHILADELPHIA	75	87	.463	26	667	673	.245	.978	3.68
PITTSBURGH	57	104	.354	43.5	568	708	.247	.979	3.97

WEST	W	L	PCT	GB	R	OR	BA	FA	ERA
LOS ANGELES	95	67	.586	—	682	579	.261	.974	2.96
CINCINNATI	89	72	.553	5.5	677	666	.255	.980	3.71
HOUSTON	83	79	.512	12	706	691	.261	.976	3.66
SAN DIEGO	83	79	.512	12	650	622	.255	.980	3.41
ATLANTA	66	96	.407	29	632	781	.246	.976	4.19
SAN FRANCISCO	62	100	.383	33	556	674	.233	.976	3.61
					7899	7899	.252	.979	3.59

BATTING AVERAGE
Willie McGee STL .... .353
Pedro Guerrero LA .... .320
Tim Raines MON .... .320

HITS
Willie McGee STL 216
Dave Parker CIN 198
Tony Gwynn SD 197

DOUBLES
Dave Parker CIN 42
Glenn Wilson PHI 39
Tommy Herr STL 38

TRIPLES
Willie McGee STL 18
Juan Samuel PHI 13
Tim Raines MON 13

HOME RUNS
Dale Murphy ATL 37
Dave Parker CIN 34
two tied at 33

RUNS BATTED IN
Dave Parker CIN 125
Dale Murphy ATL 111
Tommy Herr STL 110

SLUGGING AVERAGE
Pedro Guerrero LA .... .577
Dave Parker CIN .... .551
Dale Murphy ATL .... .539

STOLEN BASES
Vince Coleman STL 110
Tim Raines MON 70
Willie McGee STL 56

RUNS SCORED
Dale Murphy ATL 118
Tim Raines MON 115
Willie McGee STL 114

WINS
Dwight Gooden NY 24
John Tudor STL 21
Joaquin Andujar STL 21

WINNING PERCENTAGE
Orel Hershiser LA .... .864
Dwight Gooden NY .... .857
Bryn Smith MON .... .783

EARNED RUN AVERAGE
Dwight Gooden NY 1.53
John Tudor STL 1.93
Orel Heshiser LA 2.03

STRIKEOUTS
Dwight Gooden NY 268
Mario Soto CIN 214
Nolan Ryan HOU 209

SAVES
Jeff Reardon MON 41
Lee Smith CHI 33
two tied at 27

COMPLETE GAMES
Dwight Gooden NY 16
F. Valenzuela LA 14
John Tudor STL 14

SHUTOUTS
John Tudor STL 10
Dwight Gooden NY 8
two tied at 5

GAMES PITCHED
Tim Burke MON 78
Mark Davis SF 77
Scott Garrelts SF 74

INNINGS PITCHED
Dwight Gooden NY 277
John Tudor STL 275
F. Valenzuela LA 272

1986 AL

EAST	W	L	PCT	GB	R	OR	BA	FA	ERA
● BOSTON	95	66	.590	—	794	696	.271	.979	3.93
NEW YORK	90	72	.556	5.5	797	738	.271	.979	4.11
DETROIT	87	75	.537	8.5	798	714	.263	.982	4.02
TORONTO	86	76	.531	9.5	809	733	.269	.984	4.08
CLEVELAND	84	78	.519	11.5	831	841	.284	.975	4.57
MILWAUKEE	77	84	.478	18	667	734	.255	.976	4.01
BALTIMORE	73	89	.451	22.5	708	760	.258	.978	4.30

WEST	W	L	PCT	GB	R	OR	BA	FA	ERA
CALIFORNIA	92	70	.568	—	786	684	.255	.983	3.84
TEXAS	87	75	.537	5	711	743	.267	.980	4.11
KANSAS CITY	76	86	.469	16	654	673	.252	.980	3.82
OAKLAND	76	86	.469	16	731	760	.252	.978	4.31
CHICAGO	72	90	.444	20	644	699	.247	.981	3.93
MINNESOTA	71	91	.438	21	741	839	.261	.980	4.77
SEATTLE	67	95	.414	25	718	835	.253	.975	4.65
					10449	10449	.262	.979	4.18

BATTING AVERAGE
Wade Boggs BOS .... .357
Don Mattingly NY .... .352
Kirby Puckett MIN .... .328

HITS
Don Mattingly NY 238
Kirby Pucket MIN 223
Tony Fernandez TOR 213

DOUBLES
Don Mattingly NY 53
Wade Boggs BOS 47
two tied at 39

TRIPLES
Brett Butler CLE 14
Ruben Sierra TEX 10
two tied at 9

HOME RUNS
Jesse Barfield TOR 40
Dave Kingman OAK 35
Gary Gaetti MIN 34

RUNS BATTED IN
Joe Carter CLE 121
Jose Canseco OAK 117
Don Mattingly NY 113

SLUGGING AVERAGE
Don Mattingly NY .... .573
Jesse Barfield TOR .... .559
Kirby Puckett MIN .... .537

STOLEN BASES
Rickey Henderson NY 87
Gary Pettis CAL 50
John Cangelosi CHI 50

RUNS SCORED
Rickey Henderson NY 130
Kirby Puckett MIN 119
Don Mattingly NY 117

WINS
Roger Clemens BOS 24
Jack Morris DET 21
Ted Higuera MIL 20

WINNING PERCENTAGE
Roger Clemens BOS .... .857
Dennis Rasmussen NY ... .750
Jack Morris DET .... .724

EARNED RUN AVERAGE
Roger Clemens BOS 2.48
Ted Higuera MIL 2.79
Mike Witt CAL 2.84

STRIKEOUTS
Mark Langston SEA 245
Roger Clemens BOS 238
Jack Morris DET 223

SAVES
Dave Righetti NY 46
Don Aase BAL 34
Tom Henke TOR 27

COMPLETE GAMES
Tom Candiotti CLE 17
Bert Blyleven MIN 16
two tied at 15

SHUTOUTS
Jack Morris DET 6
Bruce Hurst BOS 4
Ted Higuera MIL 4

GAMES PITCHED
Mitch Williams TEX 80
Dave Righetti NY 74
Greg Harris TEX................. 73

INNINGS PITCHED
Bert Blyleven MIN 272
Mike Witt CAL 269
Jack Morris DET............... 267

1986 NL

EAST	W	L	PCT	GB	R	OR	BA	FA	ERA
★NEW YORK	108	54	.667	—	783	578	.263	.978	3.11
PHILADELPHIA	86	75	.534	21.5	739	713	.253	.978	3.85
ST. LOUIS	79	82	.491	28.5	601	611	.236	.981	3.37
MONTREAL	78	83	.484	29.5	637	688	.254	.979	3.78
CHICAGO	70	90	.438	37	680	781	.256	.980	4.49
PITTSBURGH	64	98	.395	44	663	700	.250	.978	3.90

WEST	W	L	PCT	GB	R	OR	BA	FA	ERA
HOUSTON	96	66	.593	—	654	569	.255	.979	3.15
CINCINNATI	86	76	.531	10	732	717	.254	.978	3.91
SAN FRANCISCO	83	79	.512	13	698	618	.253	.977	3.33
SAN DIEGO	74	88	.457	22	656	723	.261	.978	3.99
LOS ANGELES	73	89	.451	23	638	679	.251	.971	3.76
ATLANTA	72	89	.447	23.5	615	719	.250	.978	3.97
					8096	8096	.253	.978	3.72

BATTING AVERAGE
Tim Raines MON............ .334
Steve Sax LA .... .332
Tony Gwynn SD .... .329

HITS
Tony Gwynn SD 211
Steve Sax LA 210
Tim Raines MON.............. 194

DOUBLES
Von Hayes PHI.................. 46
Steve Sax LA 43
Sid Bream PIT 37

TRIPLES
Mitch Webster MON........... 13
Juan Samuel PHI 12
Tim Raines MON................ 10

HOME RUNS
Mike Schmidt PHI............... 37
Glenn Davis HOU.............. 31
Dave Parker CIN 31

RUNS BATTED IN
Mike Schmidt PHI............. 119
Dave Parker CIN 116
Gary Carter NY 105

SLUGGING AVERAGE
Mike Schmidt PHI............. .547
Darryl Strawberry NY ...... .507
Kevin McReynolds SD .... .504

STOLEN BASES
Vince Coleman STL 107
Eric Davis CIN.................... 80
Tim Raines MON................ 70

RUNS SCORED
Tony Gwynn SD 107
Von Hayes PHI................. 107
two tied at............................ 97

WINS
F. Valenzuela LA................ 21
Mike Krukow SF 20
two tied at.......................... 18

WINNING PERCENTAGE
Bob Ojeda NY .... .783
Dwight Gooden NY .... .739
Sid Fernandez NY .... .727

EARNED RUN AVERAGE
Mike Scott HOU 2.22
Bob Ojeda NY 2.57
Ron Darling NY 2.81

STRIKEOUTS
Mike Scott HOU 306
F. Valenzuela LA.............. 242
Floyd Youmans MON....... 202

SAVES
Todd Worrell STL.............. 36
Jeff Reardon MON 35
Dave Smith HOU.............. 33

COMPLETE GAMES
F. Valenzuela LA............... 20
Rick Rhoden PIT 12
Dwight Gooden NY 12

SHUTOUTS
Mike Scott HOU 5
Bob Knepper HOU 5
two tied at............................. 3

GAMES PITCHED
Craig Lefferts SD............... 83
Roger McDowell NY.......... 75
two tied at.......................... 74

INNINGS PITCHED
Mike Scott HOU 275
F. Valenzuela LA.............. 269
Bob Knepper HOU 258

1987 AL

EAST	W	L	PCT	GB	R	OR	BA	FA	ERA
DETROIT	98	64	.605	—	896	735	.272	.980	4.02
TORONTO	96	66	.593	2	845	655	.269	.982	3.74
MILWAUKEE	91	71	.562	7	862	817	.276	.976	4.62
NEW YORK	89	73	.549	9	788	758	.262	.983	4.36
BOSTON	78	84	.481	20	842	825	.278	.982	4.77
BALTIMORE	67	95	.414	31	729	880	.258	.982	5.01
CLEVELAND	61	101	.377	37	742	957	.263	.975	5.28

WEST	W	L	PCT	GB	R	OR	BA	FA	ERA
★MINNESOTA	85	77	.525	—	786	806	.261	.984	4.63
KANSAS CITY	83	79	.512	2	715	691	.262	.979	3.86
OAKLAND	81	81	.500	4	806	789	.260	.977	4.32
SEATTLE	78	84	.481	7	760	801	.272	.980	4.48
CHICAGO	77	85	.475	8	748	746	.258	.981	4.29
CALIFORNIA	75	87	.463	10	770	803	.252	.981	4.38
TEXAS	75	87	.463	10	823	849	.266	.976	4.63
					11112	11112	.265	.980	4.46

BATTING AVERAGE
Wade Boggs BOS .... .363
Paul Molitor MIL .... .353
Alan Trammell DET .... .343

HITS
Kevin Seitzer KC 207
Kirby Puckett MIN 207
Alan Trammell DET 205

DOUBLES
Paul Molitor MIL 41
Wade Boggs BOS 40
two tied at 38

TRIPLES
Willie Wilson KC 15
Luis Polonia OAK 10
Phil Bradley SEA 10

HOME RUNS
Mark McGwire OAK 49
George Bell TOR 47
four tied at 34

RUNS BATTED IN
George Bell TOR 134
Dwight Evans BOS 123
Mark McGwire OAK 118

SLUGGING AVERAGE
Mark McGwire OAK .... .618
George Bell TOR .... .605
Wade Boggs BOS .... .588

STOLEN BASES
Harold Reynolds SEA 60
Willie Wilson KC 59
Gary Redus CHI 52

RUNS SCORED
Paul Molitor MIL 114
George Bell TOR 111
two tied at 110

WINS
Roger Clemens BOS 20
Dave Stewart OAK 20
Mark Langston SEA 19

WINNING PERCENTAGE
Roger Clemens BOS .... .690
Tommy John NY .... .684
Jimmy Key TOR .... .680

EARNED RUN AVERAGE
Jimmy Key TOR 2.76
Frank Viola MIN 2.90
Roger Clemens BOS 2.97

STRIKEOUTS
Mark Langston SEA 262
Roger Clemens BOS 256
Ted Higuera MIL 240

SAVES
Tom Henke TOR 34
Jeff Reardon MIN 31
Dave Righetti NY 31

COMPLETE GAMES
Roger Clemens BOS 18
Bruce Hurst BOS 15
Bret Saberhagen KC 15

SHUTOUTS
Roger Clemens BOS 7
Bret Saberhagen KC 4

GAMES PITCHED
Mark Eichhorn TOR 89
Mitch Williams TEX 85
Dale Mohorcic TEX 74

INNINGS PITCHED
Charlie Hough TEX 285
Roger Clemens BOS 282
Mark Langston SEA 272

1987 NL

EAST	W	L	PCT	GB	R	OR	BA	FA	ERA
● ST. LOUIS	95	67	.586	—	798	693	.263	.982	3.91
NEW YORK	92	70	.568	3	823	698	.268	.978	3.84
MONTREAL	91	71	.562	4	741	720	.265	.976	3.92
PHILADELPHIA	80	82	.494	15	702	749	.254	.980	4.18
PITTSBURGH	80	82	.494	15	723	744	.264	.980	4.20
CHICAGO	76	85	.472	18.5	720	801	.264	.979	4.55

WEST	W	L	PCT	GB	R	OR	BA	FA	ERA
SAN FRANCISCO	90	72	.556	—	783	669	.260	.980	3.68
CINCINNATI	84	78	.519	6	783	752	.266	.979	4.25
HOUSTON	76	86	.469	14	648	678	.253	.981	3.84
LOS ANGELES	73	89	.451	17	635	675	.252	.975	3.72
ATLANTA	69	92	.429	20.5	747	829	.258	.982	4.63
SAN DIEGO	65	97	.401	25	668	763	.260	.976	4.27
					8771	8771	.261	.979	4.08

BATTING AVERAGE
Tony Gwynn SD .... .370
Pedro Guerrero LA .... .338
Tim Raines MON .... .330

HITS
Tony Gwynn SD 218
Pedro Guerrero LA 184
Ozzie Smith STL 182

DOUBLES
Tim Wallach MON 42
Ozzie Smith STL 40
Andres Galarraga MON 40

TRIPLES
Juan Samuel PHI 15
Tony Gwynn SD 13
two tied at 11

HOME RUNS
Andre Dawson CHI 49
Dale Murphy ATL 44
Darryl Strawberry NY 39

RUNS BATTED IN
Andre Dawson CHI 137
Tim Wallach MON 123
Mike Schmidt PHI............. 113

SLUGGING AVERAGE
Jack Clark STL................. .597
Eric Davis CIN................. .593
Darryl Strawberry NY ...... .583

STOLEN BASES
Vince Coleman STL 109
Tony Gwynn SD 56
Billy Hatcher HOU 53

RUNS SCORED
Tim Raines MON............... 123
Vince Coleman STL 121
Eric Davis CIN................... 120

WINS
Rick Sutcliffe CHI 18
Shane Rawley PHI 17
two tied at............................ 16

WINNING PERCENTAGE
Mike Dunne PIT .... .684
Dwight Gooden NY .... .682
Rick Sutcliffe CHI .... .643

EARNED RUN AVERAGE
Nolan Ryan HOU 2.76
Mike Dunne PIT 3.03
Orel Hershiser LA............. 3.06

STRIKEOUTS
Nolan Ryan HOU 270
Mike Scott HOU 233
Bob Welch LA 196

SAVES
Steve Bedrosian PHI.......... 40
Lee Smith CHI.................... 36
Todd Worrell STL............... 33

COMPLETE GAMES
Rick Reuschel PIT, SF 12
F. Valenzuela LA................ 12
Orel Hershiser LA............... 10

SHUTOUTS
Rick Reuschel PIT, SF 4
Bob Welch LA 4

GAMES PITCHED
Kent Tekulve PIT 90
Rob Murphy CIN 87
Frank Williams CIN 85

INNINGS PITCHED
Orel Hershiser LA.............. 265
Bob Welch LA 252
F. Valenzuela LA............... 251

1988 AL

EAST	W	L	PCT	GB	R	OR	BA	FA	ERA
BOSTON	89	73	.549	—	813	689	.283	.984	3.97
DETROIT	88	74	.543	1	703	658	.250	.982	3.71
MILWAUKEE	87	75	.537	2	682	616	.257	.981	3.45
TORONTO	87	75	.537	2	763	680	.268	.982	3.80
NEW YORK	85	76	.528	3.5	772	748	.263	.978	4.26
CLEVELAND	78	84	.481	11	666	731	.261	.980	4.16
BALTIMORE	54	107	.335	34.5	550	789	.238	.980	4.54

WEST	W	L	PCT	GB	R	OR	BA	FA	ERA
●OAKLAND	104	58	.642	—	800	620	.263	.983	3.44
MINNESOTA	91	71	.562	13	759	672	.274	.986	3.93
KANSAS CITY	84	77	.522	19.5	704	648	.259	.980	3.66
CALIFORNIA	75	87	.463	29	714	771	.261	.979	4.31
CHICAGO	71	90	.441	32.5	631	757	.244	.976	4.12
TEXAS	70	91	.435	33.5	637	735	.252	.979	4.05
SEATTLE	68	93	.422	35.5	664	744	.257	.980	4.15
					9858	9858	.259	.981	3.97

BATTING AVERAGE
Wade Boggs BOS .... .366
Kirby Puckett MIN .... .356
Mike Greenwell BOS .... .325

HITS
Kirby Puckett MIN 234
Wade Boggs BOS 214
Mike Greenwell BOS 192

DOUBLES
Wade Boggs BOS 45
three tied at 42

TRIPLES
Willie Wilson KC 11
Harold Reynolds SEA 11
Robin Yount MIL 11

HOME RUNS
Jose Canseco OAK 42
Fred McGriff TOR 34
Mark McGwire OAK 32

RUNS BATTED IN
Jose Canseco OAK 124
Kirby Puckett MIN 121
Mike Greenwell BOS 119

SLUGGING AVERAGE
Jose Canseco OAK .... .569
Fred McGriff TOR .... .552
Gary Gaetti MIN .... .551

STOLEN BASES
Rickey Henderson NY 93
Gary Pettis DET 44
Paul Molitor MIL 41

RUNS SCORED
Wade Boggs BOS 128
Jose Canseco OAK 120
Rickey Henderson NY 118

WINS
Frank Viola MIN 24
Dave Stewart OAK 21
Mark Gubicza KC 20

WINNING PERCENTAGE
Frank Viola MIN .... .774
Bruce Hurst BOS .... .750
Mark Gubicza KC .... .714

EARNED RUN AVERAGE
Allan Anderson MIN 2.45
Ted Higuera MIL 2.45
Frank Viola MIN 2.64

STRIKEOUTS
Roger Clemens BOS 291
Mark Langston SEA 235
Frank Viola MIN 193

SAVES
Dennis Eckersley OAK 45
Jeff Reardon MIN 42
Doug Jones CLE 37

COMPLETE GAMES
Roger Clemens BOS 14
Dave Stewart OAK 14
Bobby Witt TEX 13

SHUTOUTS
Roger Clemens BOS 8
three tied at 4

GAMES PITCHED
Chuck Crim MIL 70
Bobby Thigpen CHI 68
Mitch Williams TEX 67

INNINGS PITCHED
Dave Stewart OAK 276
Mark Gubicza KC 270
Roger Clemens BOS 264

1988 NL

EAST	W	L	PCT	GB	R	OR	BA	FA	ERA
NEW YORK	100	60	.625	—	703	532	.256	.981	2.91
PITTSBURGH	85	75	.531	15	651	616	.247	.980	3.47
MONTREAL	81	81	.500	20	628	592	.251	.978	3.08
CHICAGO	77	85	.475	24	660	694	.261	.980	3.84
ST. LOUIS	76	86	.469	25	578	633	.249	.981	3.47
PHILADELPHIA	65	96	.404	35.5	597	734	.239	.976	4.14

WEST	W	L	PCT	GB	R	OR	BA	FA	ERA
★LOS ANGELES	94	67	.584	—	628	544	.248	.977	2.97
CINCINNATI	87	74	.540	7	641	596	.246	.980	3.35
SAN DIEGO	83	78	.516	11	594	583	.247	.981	3.28
SAN FRANCISCO	83	79	.512	11.5	670	626	.248	.980	3.39
HOUSTON	82	80	.506	12.5	617	631	.244	.978	3.40
ATLANTA	54	106	.338	39.5	555	741	.242	.976	4.09
					7522	7522	.248	.979	3.45

BATTING AVERAGE
Tony Gwynn SD .... .313
Rafael Palmeiro CHI .... .307
Andre Dawson CHI .... .303

HITS
A. Galarraga MON 184
Andre Dawson CHI 179
Rafael Palmeiro CHI 178

DOUBLES
Andres Galarraga MON 42
Rafael Palmeiro CHI 41
Chris Sabo CIN 40

TRIPLES
Andy Van Slyke PIT 15
Vince Coleman STL 10
two tied at 9

HOME RUNS
Darryl Strawberry NY 39
Glenn Davis HOU.............. 30
two tied at 29

RUNS BATTED IN
Will Clark SF 109
Darryl Strawberry NY 101
two tied at......................... 100

SLUGGING AVERAGE
Darryl Strawberry NY ...... .545
A. Galarraga MON .... .540
Will Clark SF .... .508

STOLEN BASES
Vince Coleman STL 81
Gerald Young HOU............ 65
Ozzie Smith STL 57

RUNS SCORED
Brett Butler SF 109
Kirk Gibson LA 106
Will Clark SF 102

WINS
Orel Hershiser LA.............. 23
Danny Jackson CIN 23
David Cone NY 20

WINNING PERCENTAGE
David Cone NY .... .870
Tom Browning CIN........... .783
two tied at........................ .742

EARNED RUN AVERAGE
Joe Magrane STL............. 2.18
David Cone NY 2.22
Orel Hershiser LA............. 2.26

STRIKEOUTS
Nolan Ryan HOU 228
David Cone NY 213
Jose DeLeon STL 208

SAVES
John Franco CIN 39
Jim Gott PIT 34
Todd Worrell STL 32

COMPLETE GAMES
Orel Hershiser LA.............. 15
Danny Jackson CIN 15
Eric Show SD 13

SHUTOUTS
Orel Hershiser LA................. 8
Tim Leary LA....................... 6
Danny Jackson CIN 6

GAMES PITCHED
Rob Murphy CIN 76
Jeff Robinson PIT................ 75
Juan Agosto HOU 75

INNINGS PITCHED
Orel Hershiser LA.............. 267
Danny Jackson CIN 261
Tom Browning CIN........... 251

1989 AL

EAST	W	L	PCT	GB	R	OR	BA	FA	ERA
TORONTO	89	73	.549	—	731	651	.260	.980	3.58
BALTIMORE	87	75	.537	2	708	686	.252	.986	4.00
BOSTON	83	79	.512	6	774	735	.277	.980	4.01
MILWAUKEE	81	81	.500	8	707	679	.259	.975	3.80
NEW YORK	74	87	.460	14.5	698	792	.269	.980	4.50
CLEVELAND	73	89	.451	16	604	654	.245	.981	3.65
DETROIT	59	103	.364	30	617	816	.242	.979	4.53

WEST	W	L	PCT	GB	R	OR	BA	FA	ERA
★OAKLAND	99	63	.611	—	712	576	.261	.979	3.09
KANSAS CITY	92	70	.568	7	690	635	.261	.982	3.55
CALIFORNIA	91	71	.562	8	669	578	.256	.985	3.28
TEXAS	83	79	.512	16	695	714	.263	.978	3.91
MINNESOTA	80	82	.494	19	740	738	.276	.982	4.28
SEATTLE	73	89	.451	26	694	728	.257	.977	4.00
CHICAGO	69	92	.429	29.5	693	750	.271	.975	4.23
					9732	9732	.261	.980	3.88

BATTING AVERAGE
Kirby Puckett MIN .... .339
Carney Lansford OAK ..... .336
Wade Boggs BOS .... .330

HITS
Kirby Puckett MIN 215
Wade Boggs BOS 205
Steve Sax NY 205

DOUBLES
Wade Boggs BOS 51
Kirby Puckett MIN 45
Jody Reed BOS 42

TRIPLES
Ruben Sierra TEX.............. 14
Devon White CAL 13
Phil Bradley BAL 10

HOME RUNS
Fred McGriff TOR............... 36
Joe Carter CLE 35
Mark McGwire OAK 33

RUNS BATTED IN
Ruben Sierra TEX............. 119
Don Mattingly NY 113
Nick Esasky BOS 108

SLUGGING AVERAGE
Ruben Sierra TEX........... .543
Fred McGriff TOR............. .525
Robin Yount MIL .... .511

STOLEN BASES
R. Henderson NY, OAK 77
Cecil Espy TEX 45
Devon White CAL.............. 44

RUNS SCORED
R. Henderson NY, OAK ... 113
Wade Boggs BOS 113
two tied at......................... 101

WINS
Bret Saberhagen KC 23
Dave Stewart OAK 21
two tied at........................... 19

WINNING PERCENTAGE
Bret Saberhagen KC .... .793
Bert Blyleven CAL .... .773
Storm Davis OAK .... .731

EARNED RUN AVERAGE
Bret Saberhagen KC........ 2.16
Chuck Finley CAL 2.57
Mike Moore OAK.............. 2.61

STRIKEOUTS
Nolan Ryan TEX 301
Roger Clemens BOS........ 230
Bret Saberhagen KC 193

SAVES
Jeff Russell TEX................. 38
Bobby Thigpen CHI........... 34
three tied at 33

COMPLETE GAMES
Bret Saberhagen KC 12
Jack Morris DET 10
Chuck Finley CAL 9

SHUTOUTS
Bert Blyleven CAL 5
Kirk McCaskill CAL.............. 4
Bret Saberhagen KC........... 4

GAMES PITCHED
Chuck Crim MIL 76
Rob Murphy BOS............... 74
Kenny Rogers TEX 73

INNINGS PITCHED
Bret Saberhagen KC 262
Dave Stewart OAK 258
Mark Gubicza KC 255

1989 NL

EAST	W	L	PCT	GB	R	OR	BA	FA	ERA
CHICAGO	93	69	.574	—	702	623	.261	.980	3.43
NEW YORK	87	75	.537	6	683	595	.246	.976	3.29
ST. LOUIS	86	76	.531	7	632	608	.258	.982	3.36
MONTREAL	81	81	.500	12	632	630	.247	.979	3.48
PITTSBURGH	74	88	.457	19	637	680	.241	.975	3.64
PHILADELPHIA	67	95	.414	26	629	735	.243	.979	4.04

WEST	W	L	PCT	GB	R	OR	BA	FA	ERA
●SAN FRANCISCO	92	70	.568	—	699	600	.250	.982	3.30
SAN DIEGO	89	73	.549	3	642	626	.251	.976	3.38
HOUSTON	86	76	.531	6	647	669	.239	.977	3.65
LOS ANGELES	77	83	.481	14	554	536	.240	.981	2.95
CINCINNATI	75	87	.463	17	632	691	.247	.980	3.73
ATLANTA	63	97	.394	28	584	680	.234	.976	3.70
					7673	7673	.246	.978	3.50

BATTING AVERAGE
Tony Gwynn SD .... .336
Will Clark SF .... .333
Lonnie Smith ATL............ .315

HITS
Tony Gwynn SD 203
Will Clark SF 196
Roberto Alomar SD 184

DOUBLES
Pedro Guerrero STL........... 42
Tim Wallach MON 42
Howard Johnson NY 41

TRIPLES
Robby Thompson SF 11
Bobby Bonilla PIT.............. 10
two tied at............................. 9

HOME RUNS
Kevin Mitchell SF 47
Howard Johnson NY 36
two tied at........................... 34

RUNS BATTED IN
Kevin Mitchell SF 125
Pedro Guerrero STL......... 117
Will Clark SF 111

SLUGGING AVERAGE
Kevin Mitchell SF .... .635
Howard Johnson NY .... .559
Will Clark SF .... .546

STOLEN BASES
Vince Coleman STL 65
Juan Samuel PHI, NY 42
Roberto Alomar SD 42

RUNS SCORED
Howard Johnson NY 104
Will Clark SF 104
Ryne Sandberg CHI 104

WINS
Mike Scott HOU 20
Greg Maddux CHI 19
two tied at......................... 18

WINNING PERCENTAGE
Scott Garrelts SF............. .737
Sid Fernandez NY .... .737
Mike Bielecki CHI .... .720

EARNED RUN AVERAGE
Scott Garrelts SF............. 2.28
Orel Hershiser LA............ 2.31
Mark Langston MON 2.39

STRIKEOUTS
Jose DeLeon STL 201
Tim Belcher LA................. 200
Sid Fernandez NY............ 198

SAVES
Mark Davis SD 44
Mitch Williams CHI 36
John Franco CIN 32

COMPLETE GAMES
Tim Belcher LA................... 10
Bruce Hurst SD 10
three tied at 9

SHUTOUTS
Tim Belcher LA.................... 8
Doug Drabek PIT 5
two tied at............................ 4

GAMES PITCHED
Mitch Williams CHI 76
Rob Dibble CIN 74
Jeff Parrett PHI.................. 72

INNINGS PITCHED
Orel Hershiser LA............. 257
Tom Browning CIN............ 250
two tied at......................... 245

1990 AL

EAST	W	L	PCT	GB	R	OR	BA	FA	ERA
BOSTON	88	74	.543	—	699	664	.272	.980	3.72
TORONTO	86	76	.531	2	767	661	.265	.986	3.84
DETROIT	79	83	.488	9	750	754	.259	.979	4.39
CLEVELAND	77	85	.475	11	732	737	.267	.981	4.26
BALTIMORE	76	85	.472	11.5	669	698	.245	.985	4.04
MILWAUKEE	74	88	.457	14	732	760	.256	.976	4.08
NEW YORK	67	95	.414	21	603	749	.241	.980	4.21

WEST	W	L	PCT	GB	R	OR	BA	FA	ERA
● OAKLAND	103	59	.636	—	733	570	.254	.986	3.18
CHICAGO	94	68	.580	9	682	633	.258	.980	3.61
TEXAS	83	79	.512	20	676	696	.259	.979	3.83
CALIFORNIA	80	82	.494	23	690	706	.260	.978	3.79
SEATTLE	77	85	.475	26	640	680	.259	.979	3.69
KANSAS CITY	75	86	.466	27.5	707	709	.267	.980	3.93
MINNESOTA	74	88	.457	29	666	729	.265	.983	4.12
					9746	9746	.259	.981	3.91

BATTING AVERAGE
George Brett KC .... .329
R. Henderson OAK .... .325
Rafael Palmeiro TEX .... .319

HITS
Rafael Palmeiro TEX 191
Wade Boggs BOS 187
Roberto Kelly NY 183

DOUBLES
George Brett KC 45
Jody Reed BOS 45
two tied at 44

TRIPLES
Tony Fernandez TOR 17
Sammy Sosa CHI 10
three tied at 9

HOME RUNS
Cecil Fielder DET 51
Mark McGwire OAK 39
Jose Canseco OAK 37

RUNS BATTED IN
Cecil Fielder DET 132
Kelly Gruber TOR 118
Mark McGwire OAK 108

SLUGGING AVERAGE
Cecil Fielder DET .... .592
R. Henderson OAK .... .577
Jose Canseco OAK .... .543

STOLEN BASES
R. Henderson OAK 65
Steve Sax NY 43
Roberto Kelly NY 42

RUNS SCORED
Rickey Henderson OAK ... 119
Cecil Fielder DET 104
Harold Reynolds SEA 100

WINS
Bob Welch OAK 27
Dave Stewart OAK 22
Roger Clemens BOS 21

WINNING PERCENTAGE
Bob Welch OAK .... .818
Roger Clemens BOS .... .778
two tied at .... .750

EARNED RUN AVERAGE
Roger Clemens BOS 1.93
Chuck Finley CAL 2.40
Dave Stewart OAK 2.56

STRIKEOUTS
Nolan Ryan TEX 232
Bobby Witt TEX 221
Erik Hanson SEA 211

SAVES
Bobby Thigpen CHI 57
Dennis Eckersley OAK 48
Doug Jones CLE 43

COMPLETE GAMES
Jack Morris DET 11
Dave Stewart OAK 11
five tied at 7

SHUTOUTS
Roger Clemens BOS 4
Dave Stewart OAK 4
three tied at 3

GAMES PITCHED
Bobby Thigpen CHI 77
Jeff Montgomery KC 73
Duane Ward TOR 73

INNINGS PITCHED
Dave Stewart OAK 267
Jack Morris DET 250
Bob Welch OAK 238

1990 NL

EAST	W	L	PCT	GB	R	OR	BA	FA	ERA
PITTSBURGH	95	67	.586	—	733	619	.259	.979	3.40
NEW YORK	91	71	.562	4	775	613	.256	.978	3.43
MONTREAL	85	77	.525	10	662	598	.250	.982	3.37
CHICAGO	77	85	.475	18	690	774	.263	.980	4.34
PHILADELPHIA	77	85	.475	18	646	729	.255	.981	4.07
ST. LOUIS	70	92	.432	25	599	698	.256	.979	3.87

WEST	W	L	PCT	GB	R	OR	BA	FA	ERA
★CINCINNATI	91	71	.562	—	693	597	.265	.983	3.39
LOS ANGELES	86	76	.531	5	728	685	.262	.979	3.72
SAN FRANCISCO	85	77	.525	6	719	710	.262	.983	4.08
HOUSTON	75	87	.463	16	573	656	.242	.978	3.61
SAN DIEGO	75	87	.463	16	673	673	.257	.977	3.68
ATLANTA	65	97	.401	26	682	821	.250	.974	4.58
					8173	8173	.256	.980	3.79

BATTING AVERAGE
Willie McGee STL .... .335
Eddie Murray LA .... .330
Dave Magadan NY .... .328

HITS
Brett Butler SF 192
Lenny Dykstra PHI 192
Ryne Sandberg CHI 188

DOUBLES
Gregg Jefferies NY 40
Bobby Bonilla PIT 39
Chris Sabo CIN 38

TRIPLES
Mariano Duncan CIN 11
Tony Gwynn SD 10
three tied at 9

HOME RUNS
Ryne Sandberg CHI 40
Darryl Strawberry NY 37
Kevin Mitchell SF 35

RUNS BATTED IN
Matt Williams SF 122
Bobby Bonilla PIT 120
Joe Carter SD 115

SLUGGING AVERAGE
Barry Bonds PIT .... .565
Ryne Sandberg CHI .... .559
Kevin Mitchell SF .... .544

STOLEN BASES
Vince Coleman STL 77
Eric Yelding HOU 64
Barry Bonds PIT 52

RUNS SCORED
Ryne Sandberg CHI 116
Bobby Bonilla PIT 112
Brett Butler SF 108

WINS
Doug Drabek PIT 22
Ramon Martinez LA 20
Frank Viola NY 20

WINNING PERCENTAGE
Doug Drabek PIT .... .786
Ramon Martinez LA .... .769
John Tudor STL .... .750

EARNED RUN AVERAGE
Danny Darwin HOU 2.21
Zane Smith MON, PIT 2.55
Ed Whitson SD 2.60

STRIKEOUTS
David Cone NY 233
Dwight Gooden NY 223
Ramon Martinez LA 223

SAVES
John Franco NY 33
Randy Myers CIN 31
Lee Smith STL 27

COMPLETE GAMES
Ramon Martinez LA 12
Doug Drabek PIT 9
Bruce Hurst SD 9

SHUTOUTS
Mike Morgan LA 4
Bruce Hurst SD 4
six tied at 3

GAMES PITCHED
Juan Agosto HOU 82
Paul Assenmacher CHI 74
Greg Harris SD 73

INNINGS PITCHED
Frank Viola NY 250
Greg Maddux CHI 237
Ramon Martinez LA 234

1991 AL

EAST	W	L	PCT	GB	R	OR	BA	FA	ERA
TORONTO	91	71	.562	—	684	622	.257	.980	3.50
BOSTON	84	78	.519	7	731	712	.269	.981	4.01
DETROIT	84	78	.519	7	817	794	.247	.983	4.51
MILWAUKEE	83	79	.512	8	799	744	.271	.981	4.14
NEW YORK	71	91	.438	20	674	777	.256	.979	4.42
BALTIMORE	67	95	.414	24	686	796	.254	.985	4.59
CLEVELAND	57	105	.352	34	576	759	.254	.976	4.23

WEST	W	L	PCT	GB	R	OR	BA	FA	ERA
★MINNESOTA	95	67	.586	—	776	652	.280	.985	3.69
CHICAGO	87	75	.534	8	758	681	.262	.982	3.79
TEXAS	85	77	.525	10	829	814	.270	.979	4.47
OAKLAND	84	78	.519	11	760	776	.248	.982	4.57
SEATTLE	83	79	.512	12	702	674	.255	.983	3.79
KANSAS CITY	82	80	.506	13	727	722	.264	.980	3.92
CALIFORNIA	81	81	.500	14	653	649	.255	.984	3.69
					10172	10172	.260	.981	4.09

BATTING AVERAGE
Julio Franco TEX............ .341
Wade Boggs BOS .... .332
Ken Griffey Jr. SEA .... .327

HITS
Paul Molitor MIL 216
Cal Ripken BAL................. 210
two tied at........................ 203

DOUBLES
Rafael Palmeiro TEX......... 49
Cal Ripken BAL................. 46
Ruben Sierra TEX 44

TRIPLES
Lance Johnson CHI........... 13
Paul Molitor MIL 13
Roberto Alomar TOR 11

HOME RUNS
Cecil Fielder DET 44
Jose Canseco OAK............ 44
Cal Ripken BAL................. 34

RUNS BATTED IN
Cecil Fielder DET 133
Jose Canseco OAK 122
Ruben Sierra TEX 116

SLUGGING AVERAGE
Danny Tartabull KC .... .593
Cal Ripken BAL................ .566
Jose Canseco OAK .... .556

STOLEN BASES
Rickey Henderson OAK 58
Roberto Alomar TOR 53
Tim Raines CHI................. 51

RUNS SCORED
Paul Molitor MIL 133
Jose Canseco OAK 115
Rafael Palmeiro TEX........ 115

WINS
Scott Erickson MIN............. 20
Bill Gullickson DET............ 20
Mark Langston CAL 19

WINNING PERCENTAGE
Scott Erickson MIN.......... .714
Mark Langston CAL .... .704
Bill Gullickson DET.......... .690

EARNED RUN AVERAGE
Roger Clemens BOS....... 2.62
T. Candiotti CLE,TOR 2.65
Bill Wegman MIL............. 2.84

STRIKEOUTS
Roger Clemens BOS........ 241
Randy Johnson SEA 228
Nolan Ryan TEX 203

SAVES
Bryan Harvey CAL 46
Dennis Eckersley OAK 43
Rick Aguilera MIN 42

COMPLETE GAMES
Jack McDowell CHI 15
Roger Clemens BOS 13
two tied at........................... 10

SHUTOUTS
Roger Clemens BOS............. 4
four tied at 3

GAMES PITCHED
Duane Ward TOR 81
Mike Jackson SEA 72
Gregg Olson BAL............... 72

INNINGS PITCHED
Roger Clemens BOS........ 271
Jack McDowell CHI 254
Jack Morris MIN 247

1991 NL

EAST	W	L	PCT	GB	R	OR	BA	FA	ERA
PITTSBURGH	98	64	.605	—	768	632	.263	.981	3.44
ST. LOUIS	84	78	.519	14	651	648	.255	.982	3.69
PHILADELPHIA	78	84	.481	20	629	680	.241	.981	3.86
CHICAGO	77	83	.481	20	695	734	.253	.982	4.03
NEW YORK	77	84	.478	20.5	640	646	.244	.977	3.56
MONTREAL	71	90	.441	26.5	579	655	.246	.979	3.64

WEST	W	L	PCT	GB	R	OR	BA	FA	ERA
● ATLANTA	94	68	.580	—	749	644	.258	.978	3.49
LOS ANGELES	93	69	.574	1	665	565	.253	.980	3.06
SAN DIEGO	84	78	.519	10	636	646	.244	.982	3.57
SAN FRANCISCO	75	87	.463	19	649	697	.246	.982	4.03
CINCINNATI	74	88	.457	20	689	691	.258	.979	3.83
HOUSTON	65	97	.401	29	605	717	.244	.974	4.00
					7975	7975	.250	.980	3.68

BATTING AVERAGE
Terry Pendleton ATL .... .319
Hal Morris CIN................ .318
Tony Gwynn SD .... .317

HITS
Terry Pendleton ATL 187
Brett Butler LA................. 182
Chris Sabo CIN 175

DOUBLES
Bobby Bonilla PIT.............. 44
Felix Jose STL 40
two tied at........................... 36

TRIPLES
Ray Lankford STL 15
Tony Gwynn SD 11
Steve Finley HOU 10

HOME RUNS
Howard Johnson NY 38
Matt Williams SF 34
Ron Gant ATL 32

RUNS BATTED IN
Howard Johnson NY 117
Barry Bonds PIT............... 116
Will Clark SF 116

SLUGGING AVERAGE
Will Clark SF .... .536
Howard Johnson NY .... .535
Terry Pendleton ATL .... .517

STOLEN BASES
Marquis Grissom MON....... 76
Otis Nixon ATL 72
Delino DeShields MON 56

RUNS SCORED
Brett Butler LA................. 112
Howard Johnson NY 108
Ryne Sandberg CHI 104

WINS
John Smiley PIT 20
Tom Glavine ATL 20
Steve Avery ATL 18

WINNING PERCENTAGE
Jose Rijo CIN .... .714
John Smiley PIT .... .714
Steve Avery ATL .... .692

EARNED RUN AVERAGE
Dennis Martinez MON..... 2.39
Jose Rijo CIN 2.51
Tom Glavine ATL 2.55

STRIKEOUTS
David Cone NY 241
Greg Maddux CHI 198
Tom Glavine ATL 192

SAVES
Lee Smith STL 47
Rob Dibble CIN 31
two tied at.......................... 30

COMPLETE GAMES
Tom Glavine ATL 9
Dennis Martinez 9
Terry Mulholland PHI 8

SHUTOUTS
Dennis Martinez MON.......... 5
Ramon Martinez LA 4
three tied at 3

GAMES PITCHED
Barry Jones MON.............. 77
Paul Assenmacher CHI...... 75
Mike Stanton ATL.............. 74

INNINGS PITCHED
Greg Maddux CHI 263
Tom Glavine ATL 247
Mike Morgan LA 236

1992 AL

EAST	W	L	PCT	GB	R	OR	BA	FA	ERA
★TORONTO	96	66	.593	—	780	682	.263	.984	3.91
MILWAUKEE	92	70	.568	4	740	604	.268	.986	3.43
BALTIMORE	89	73	.549	7	705	656	.259	.985	3.79
CLEVELAND	76	86	.469	20	674	746	.266	.978	4.11
NEW YORK	76	86	.469	20	733	746	.261	.982	4.21
DETROIT	75	87	.463	21	791	794	.256	.981	4.60
BOSTON	73	89	.451	23	599	669	.246	.978	3.58

WEST	W	L	PCT	GB	R	OR	BA	FA	ERA
OAKLAND	96	66	.593	—	745	672	.258	.979	3.73
MINNESOTA	90	72	.556	6	747	653	.277	.985	3.70
CHICAGO	86	76	.531	10	738	690	.261	.979	3.82
TEXAS	77	85	.475	19	682	753	.250	.975	4.09
CALIFORNIA	72	90	.444	24	579	671	.243	.979	3.84
KANSAS CITY	72	90	.444	24	610	667	.256	.980	3.81
SEATTLE	64	98	.395	32	679	799	.263	.982	4.55
					9802	9802	.259	.981	3.95

BATTING AVERAGE
Edgar Martinez SEA........ .343
Kirby Puckett MIN .... .329
Frank Thomas CHI.......... .323

HITS
Kirby Puckett MIN 210
Carlos Baerga CLE 205
Paul Molitor MIL 195

DOUBLES
Edgar Martinez SEA........... 46
Frank Thomas CHI............. 46
two tied at 40

TRIPLES
Lance Johnson CHI............ 12
Mike Devereaux BAL 11
Brady Anderson BAL......... 10

HOME RUNS
Juan Gonzalez TEX 43
Mark McGwire OAK 42
Cecil Fielder DET 35

RUNS BATTED IN
Cecil Fielder DET 124
Joe Carter TOR 119
Frank Thomas CHI........... 115

SLUGGING AVERAGE
Mark McGwire OAK .... .585
Edgar Martinez SEA......... .544
Frank Thomas CHI.......... .536

STOLEN BASES
Kenny Lofton CLE.............. 66
Pat Listach MIL 54
Brady Anderson BAL......... 53

RUNS SCORED
Tony Phillips DET............. 114
Frank Thomas CHI........... 108
Roberto Alomar TOR 105

WINS
Kevin Brown TEX 21
Jack Morris TOR 21
Jack McDowell CHI 20

WINNING PERCENTAGE
Jack Morris TOR .... .777
Juan Guzman TOR .... .762
Mike Mussina BAL .... .762

EARNED RUN AVERAGE
Roger Clemens BOS........ 2.41
Kevin Appier KC 2.46
Mike Mussina BAL 2.54

STRIKEOUTS
Randy Johnson SEA 241
Melido Perez NY 218
Roger Clemens BOS........ 208

SAVES
Dennis Eckersley OAK....... 51
Rick Aguilera MIN 41
Jeff Montgomery KC 39

COMPLETE GAMES
Jack McDowell CHI 13
Roger Clemens BOS.......... 11
Kevin Brown TEX 11

SHUTOUTS
Roger Clemens BOS............ 5
Mike Mussina BAL 4
Dave Fleming SEA.............. 4

GAMES PITCHED
Kevin Rogers TEX.............. 81
Duane Ward TOR 79
Steve Olin CLE 72

INNINGS PITCHED
Kevin Brown TEX 266
Bill Wegman MIL 262
Jack McDowell CHI.......... 261

1992 NL

EAST	W	L	PCT	GB	R	OR	BA	FA	ERA
PITTSBURGH	96	66	.593	—	693	595	.255	.984	3.35
MONTREAL	87	75	.537	9	648	581	.252	.980	3.25
ST. LOUIS	83	79	.512	13	631	604	.262	.985	3.38
CHICAGO	78	84	.481	18	593	624	.254	.982	3.39
NEW YORK	72	90	.444	24	599	653	.235	.981	3.66
PHILADELPHIA	70	92	.432	26	686	717	.253	.978	4.11

WEST	W	L	PCT	GB	R	OR	BA	FA	ERA
●ATLANTA	98	64	.605	—	682	569	.254	.982	3.14
CINCINNATI	90	72	.556	8	660	609	.260	.984	3.46
SAN DIEGO	82	80	.506	16	617	636	.255	.981	3.56
HOUSTON	81	81	.500	17	608	668	.246	.981	3.72
SAN FRANCISCO	72	90	.444	26	574	647	.244	.982	3.61
LOS ANGELES	63	99	.389	35	548	636	.248	.972	3.41
					7539	7539	.252	.981	3.50

BATTING AVERAGE
Gary Sheffield SD .... .330
Andy Van Slyke PIT .... .324
John Kruk PHI .... .323

HITS
Terry Pendleton ATL 199
Andy Van Slyke PIT 199
Ryne Sandberg CHI 186

DOUBLES
Andy Van Slyke PIT 45
three tied at 40

TRIPLES
Deion Sanders ATL............ 14
Steve Finley HOU 12
Andy Van Slyke PIT 12

HOME RUNS
Fred McGriff SD 35
Barry Bonds PIT 34
Gary Sheffield SD 33

RUNS BATTED IN
Darren Daulton PHI.......... 109
Terry Pendleton ATL 105
Fred McGriff SD 104

SLUGGING AVERAGE
Barry Bonds PIT.............. .624
Gary Sheffield SD .... .580
Fred McGriff SD .... .556

STOLEN BASES
Marquis Grissom MON....... 78
Delino DeShields MON 46
two tied at............................ 44

RUNS SCORED
Barry Bonds PIT.............. 109
Dave Hollins PHI 104
Andy Van Slyke PIT 103

WINS
Greg Maddux CHI 20
Tom Glavine ATL 20
four tied at 16

WINNING PERCENTAGE
Bob Tewksbury STL......... .762
Tom Glavine ATL .... .714
Bill Swift SF .... .714

EARNED RUN AVERAGE
Bill Swift SF 2.08
Bob Tewksbury STL........ 2.16
Greg Maddux CHI 2.18

STRIKEOUTS
John Smoltz ATL 215
David Cone NY 214
Greg Maddux CHI 199

SAVES
Lee Smith STL 43
Randy Myers SD 38
John Wetteland MON......... 37

COMPLETE GAMES
Terry Mulholland PHI 12
Doug Drabek PIT 10
Curt Shilling PHI................ 10

SHUTOUTS
David Cone NY 5
Tom Glavine ATL 5
five tied at 4

GAMES PITCHED
Joe Boever HOU 81
Doug Jones HOU 80
two tied at............................ 77

INNINGS PITCHED
Greg Maddux CHI 268
Doug Drabek PIT 257
John Smoltz ATL............... 247

AL MOST VALUABLE PLAYER VOTING

Player	1st	2nd	3rd	Tot
Dennis Eckersley OAK	18	5	1	306
Kirby Puckett MIN	3	4	8	209
Joe Carter TOR	4	6	3	201
Mark McGwire OAK	1	0	5	155
Dave Winfield TOR	2	5	2	141
Roberto Alomar TOR	3	4	1	118
Mike Devereaux BAL	0	1	3	109
Frank Thomas CHI	0	0	1	108
Cecil Fielder DET	0	2	1	83
Paul Molitor MIL	0	0	1	63
Carlos Baerga CLE	0	0	0	31
Edgar Martinez SEA	0	0	0	29
Jack Morris TOR	0	0	0	18
Roger Clemens BOS	0	0	1	17
Brady Anderson BAL	0	0	0	16
Juan Gonzalez TEX	0	1	0	15
Ken Griffey Jr. SEA	0	0	1	13
Pat Listach MIL	0	0	0	8
Jack McDowell CHI	0	0	0	5
George Bell CHI	0	0	0	3
Mike Bordick OAK	0	0	0	2
Mike Mussina BAL	0	0	0	2
Albert Belle CLE	0	0	0	1

AL CY YOUNG AWARD VOTING

PLAYER	1st	2nd	3rd	Tot
Dennis Eckersley OAK	19	3	3	107
Jack McDowell CHI	2	12	5	51
Roger Clemens BOS	4	7	7	48
Mike Mussina BAL	2	4	4	26
Jack Morris TOR	1	1	2	10
Kevin Brown TEX	0	1	6	9
Charles Nagy CLE	0	0	1	1

AL ROOKIE OF THE YEAR VOTING

Player	1st	2nd	3rd	Tot
Pat Listach MIL	20	7	1	122
Kenny Lofton CLE	7	15	5	85
Dave Fleming SEA	0	3	14	23
Cal Eldred MIL	1	3	8	22

NL MOST VALUABLE PLAYER VOTING

Player	1st	2nd	3rd	Tot
Barry Bonds PIT	18	16	2	304
Terry Pendleton ATL	4	16	4	232
Gary Sheffield SD	2	3	17	204
Andy Van Slyke PIT	0	1	0	145
Larry Walker MON	0	0	0	111
Darren Daulton PHI	0	0	0	100
Fred McGriff SD	0	0	0	100
Bip Roberts CIN	0	0	0	64
Marquis Grissom MON	0	0	0	54
Tom Glavine ATL	0	0	0	18
Greg Maddux CHI	0	0	0	14
Ryne Sandberg CHI	0	0	0	12
Barry Larkin CIN	0	0	0	12
Doug Jones HOU	0	0	0	8
John Kruk PHI	0	0	0	8
Mark Grace CHI	0	0	0	6
Delino DeShields MON	0	0	0	6
Ray Lankford STL	0	0	0	5
Jeff Bagwell HOU	0	0	0	4
Dave Hollins PHI	0	0	0	3
Brett Butler LA	0	0	0	2
Ozzie Smith STL	0	0	0	2
Otis Nixon ATL	0	0	0	1
John Wetteland MON	0	0	0	1

NL CY YOUNG AWARD VOTING

PLAYER	1st	2nd	3rd	Tot
Greg Maddux CHI	20	4	0	112
Tom Glavine ATL	4	19	1	78
Bob Tewksbury STL	0	1	19	22
Lonnie Smith STL	0	0	3	22
Doug Drabek PIT	0	0	1	1

NL ROOKIE OF THE YEAR VOTING

Player	1st	2nd	3rd	Tot
Eric Karros LA	22	2	0	116
Moises Alou MON	2	8	6	40
Reggie Sanders CIN	0	7	2	23
Tim Wakefield PIT	0	4	7	19
Donovan Osborne STL	0	3	3	12
Mike Perry STL	0	0	2	2
Ben Rivera PHI	0	0	1	1
Frank Seminara SD	0	0	1	1
Brian Williams HOU	0	0	1	1
Mark Wohlers ATL	0	0	1	1